AN

EGYPTIAN HIEROGLYPHIC DICTIONARY.

WITH AN INDEX OF ENGLISH WORDS, KING LIST AND GEOGRAPHICAL LIST WITH INDEXES, LIST OF HIEROGLYPHIC CHARACTERS, COPTIC AND SEMITIC ALPHABETS, ETC.

IN TWO VOLUMES
VOL. II

BY SIR E. A. WALLIS BUDGE, KNT., F.S.A.,

M.A. AND LITT.D., CAMBRIDGE; M.A. AND D.LITT., OXFORD; D.LIT., DURHAM;
SOMETIME SCHOLAR OF CHRIST'S COLLEGE, CAMBRIDGE, AND TYRWHITT HEBREW SCHOLAR;
KEEPER OF THE EGYPTIAN AND ASSYRIAN ANTIQUITIES, BRITISH MUSEUM.

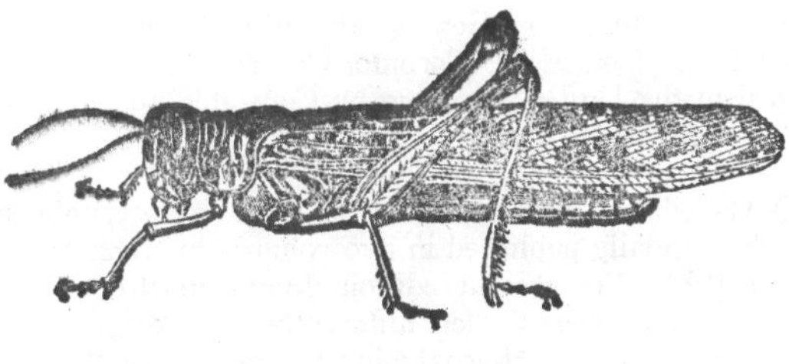

DOVER PUBLICATIONS, INC.
NEW YORK

Published in Canada by General Publishing Company, Ltd., 30 Lesmill Road, Don Mills, Toronto, Ontario.

Published in the United Kingdom by Constable and Company, Ltd., 10 Orange Street, London WC2H 7EG.

This Dover edition, first published in 1978, is a republication of the work originally published in two volumes by John Murray, London, in 1920. The present edition differs in the following ways: the volumes are divided differently; the originally appended List of Egyptian Hieroglyphic Characters in the Fount of Messrs. Harrison and Sons (a printer's catalogue) is here omitted; the dedication page is reproduced in black and white rather than in color; and a specially prepared new text, "On the Arrangement of Words in This Dictionary," has been added.

International Standard Book Number: 0-486-23616-1
Library of Congress Catalog Card Number: 77-90344

Manufactured in the United States of America
Dover Publications, Inc.
180 Varick Street
New York, N.Y. 10014

kheri ḥeb tep , , the chief reader of the divine books.

kheriu kefāu , Mar. Karn. 52, 12, a class of soldiers.

Kheriu-autu , B.D. 168, the gods who are provided with offerings.

Kheriu-ȧakhu , Ṭuat XI, the gods who are provided with disks of light.

Kheriu-āmu, etc. , Ṭuat XII, the gods who have food when the heads appear from the windings of a serpent-god.

Kher-āḥa , the god of Kher-āḥa.

Kheriu-āḥāu-em-Ȧment , Ṭuat V, the gods who are masters of time in the Ṭuat.

Kheri-beq-f , B.D. 17, 100, one of the seven spirits who guarded Osiris.

Kheriu-m'nen , Ṭuat VII, the gods who are masters of the rope with which Qān is tied.

Kheriu-metaḥu , Ṭuat VII, the gods who attacked Māmu, , and slit open his body.

Kheriu-nuḥ-em-Ṭuat , Ṭuat V, the land-measuring gods who allot estates to the righteous.

Kheriu-Nutchi , Ṭuat V, nine gods who hold fast the serpent Nutchi.

Kheri-ermen-Saḥ , one of the 36 Dekans.

Kheriu-ḥeteput , B.D. 168, the gods who possess sepulchral meals.

kheri-khepti , , , one of the 36 Dekans.

Kheri-khepti-Serit , , , Tomb Seti I, Denderah II, 10, one of the 36 Dekans; var. .

Kheriu-khepti-Kenemut , , , Tombs Seti I, Ram. II, Ram. IV, Denderah II, 10, one of the 36 Dekans; Gr. χαρχνουμις.

Kherit-Khenti-Sekhem , P. 567, a god who protected the chin.

Kheriu-sebu , Ṭuat XI, the gods of the stars who sing at sunrise.

Kheri-she (?) , N. 773......

Kheri-Kenem , Zod. Dend., one of the 36 Dekans.

Kherit-teka , Mar. Aby. I, 45, a fire-goddess.

Kheri-ṭesu (?) , Mar. Aby. I, 45, the god of .

kherit , , a holder, vase, box.

kheri-ā , , , scribe's box, packet, étui, case.

kheri-ā , I, 39, colour, ochre (?)

kheri-ā , Rec. 30, 68, a rope of the magical boat.

kheri-merḥ , salve box, unguent case.

kheri-khenf , N. 518A, a basket or bowl of khenfu cakes.

kheri-set, Nástasen Stele 49, brazier; , Ḥerusȧtef Stele 50, candlestick; , a bronze candlestick.

kheri-gen, a pot of grease, or a grease pot.

kher, evil, wickedness.

khera, Rev. 11, 168, a garment.

kheribesh, Rec. 30, 95, , Rev. 11, 122, 12, 34, 54, armour; Copt. ϧⲉⲗⲗⲓⲃⲱϣ.

kherp, P. 339, to rule, to direct, to present, to offer; var. .

khersa, Peasant 326 . . . .

kherses, Rev. 13, 94 = Copt. ϩⲁⲣⲟⲥ.

khersheri, Rev. 11, 123, young manservant; Copt. ϧⲉⲗϣⲏⲣⲓ.

Kheritȧ, P. 493 . . . . . .

kherti, , , mason, artificer; plur. , , L.D. III, 140B.

kherti neter, , , , , , , , a funerary mason or workman; plur. , .

S

s . This sign was used indifferently with at a very early period, and its original sound, which seems to have been somewhat like the Heb. ז or ס, was forgotten. The Coptic equivalent for both and is c.

s , a causative prefix; var. .

s, si , , personal and absolute pronoun, 3rd fem.; var. or .

s , = .

s ; see **àsi** , an interrogative particle.

s[a] , , , , , a male human being, man, person; Copt. ca, Amharic ሰው:; , IV, 1118, , the two parties in a lawsuit.

s[a]-t , T. 58, , M. 217, N. 589, , woman, any woman; plur. , Amharic ሴት:

s[a]-t ḥemt , Pap. 3024, 98, , , Ḥerusàtef Stele 90; plur. ; Copt. cϩιμє.

s[a] , a native of Elephantine (Syene); , a wise man; , Rec. 29, 165, a well-known man; , a native of the Delta; , Love Songs 1, 3, a slave of his belly; , a man of eternity, *i.e.*, a dead man; , IV, 966, millions of men; , Rec. 6, 8, sailor folk; , Mar. Karn. 53, 23, a crying person.

s[a] neb , , everybody, all folk.

s = , to know.

sa-t , , , , , , , , Mar. Aby. I, 6, 37, , bar, bolt, beam, pillar, mast, pole; , pillar of the earth; dual , IV, 498, 1220, the two bolts of a door or gate; plur. , , , Rec. 27, 232, , IV, 707, , Mar. Karn. 42, 11, bolts, beams, masts, flagstaffs; Copt. coι.

s-t , , , , , , , seat, throne, place; see **às-t** .

s-t , U. 132A, N. 440A, , P. 440, M. 544, N. 1125, a kind of goose.

s-t , Rec. 29, 148, geese.

s-t , sheep; see ; Copt. єcaγ, єcooγ.

sa-t , , a kind of goose.

sa-āsh , a kind of goose (?)

sa , P. 162, U. 573, M. 624, , , , , son; Copt. ϣє (?); , N. 947, , divine son; , wicked son, accursed offspring; , limb, member; , IV, 1078, son who is heir; , son of the heart, *i.e.*, beloved

son; , Rec. 16, 110 = ;

, son, opener of the belly, *i.e.*, firstborn son;

, son's son, *i.e.*, grandson;

,

eldest son; , first son, *i.e.*, eldest son;

, male child;

,

B.M. 138, 4, son to son, heir to heir.

saiu , Siut 15, people, men.

sa-t , P. 393, M. 561, N. 1168,

, U. 575, , , ,

, daughter; , Shipwreck 129, little girl.

Sa-ti , U. 598, ,

U. 217, M. 529, N. 964, 1108, ,

P. 466, , , the two divine daughters Isis and Nephthys;

, , , Rec. 27, 225, the two daughters of Nut;

, U. 218, the two daughters of Tem;

, A.Z. 1900, 20, two daughters of the Nile-god.

Sa-ti båt , P. 79, , M. 109,

, M. 334, 707, the two daughters of the king of the North.

Saåmer-f , P. 320,

, M. 627, , , "his beloved son"—title of a funerary priest, title of the high-priest of Ḥeru-shefit.

sa nesu , king's son, prince.

sa-t nesu , king's daughter, princess.

Sa Rā , , , ,

son of Rā, a title first adopted by kings under the Vth dynasty; , I, 54.

Sa Repāt , Rec. 33, 33, son of a chief.

sa ḥur , A.Z. 1899, 73, son of begging, *i.e.*, beggar.

sa ḥemm , ,

, son of fever, *i.e.*, a fever patient.

sa-ḥer-shef , A.Z. 1908, 20, the name of an amulet.

sa s[a] , A.Z. 1899, 73, , Leyd. Pap. 2, 14, , ibid. 4, 1,

, Metternich Stele 52, son of a gentleman as opposed to , a beggar;

, Peasant 1116, B. 61.

sa-ta , Rec. 10, 114, cerastes; Copt. ⲤⲒⲦ.

sa ta (?) , creatures that live in the earth.

Sait , Ṭuat XI, a group of desert goddesses.

saiu , A.Z. 1908, 117,

, stars; Copt. ⲤⲒⲞⲨ.

Sa-tt-åakhuit , Ombos II, 133, a goddess.

Sa-t-Åmenti (?) , U. 575,

, N. 965, a goddess, regent of Peter

.

Sa-pa-nemmå

, B.D. 164, 9, a god (?)

Sa-maāt , Ṭuat VII, a hawk-god; reading perhaps Ba-maāt.

Sa-t Ḥe-t-Ḥer , Denderah III, 9, 28, 29, IV, 63, a serpent-goddess of Denderah.

Sa-sȧ-t = see.

Sa-ti-Sȧ-t, Tomb Ram. IV; see.

Sa-s-pa, Ombos I, 45, a ram-god.

Sa-Se[m]t, Ṭuat I, the Serpent-warder of the 1st Gate.

Sa-semu, one of the 36 Dekans; Gr. Σεσμε.

Sa-ser-t, Denderah II, 10, Zod. Dend., one of the 36 Dekans; var.; Gr. Σισρω.

Sa-ti-Ser-t, Tomb Seti I, Annales I, 86, one of the 36 Dekans; Gr. Ισρω.

Sa-seshem, one of the 36 Dekans; Gr. Σισεσμε.

Sa-qeṭ, Denderah II, 10, one of the 36 Dekans; Gr. Σικετ.

Sa-ti-qeṭ, Ramesseum, one of the 36 Dekans.

Sa-ta, T. 317, B.D. 87, 3, Denderah III, 14, Ṭuat V, a long-lived serpent-goddess.

Sa-ta, Rec. 31, 170, a mythological serpent.

Sa-ta, the name of a constellation.

Sa-Tathenen, Ṭuat VII, a hawk-god in the Ṭuat.

saut, intestines, entrails, the lower back part of the body.

sa, mosaic pavement.

sa-t, earth, ground, soil, pavement; Copt. ⲉⲥⲏⲧ.

sa-ti, threshold.

sait (?), ground.

sa-t aḥ, field, arura (Gr. ἀρούρα = 10,000 sq. cubits); see; Copt. ⲥϯⲟϩⲉ, ⲥϯⲱϩⲉ, ⲥⲉⲧⲉⲓⲱϩⲉ.

sa, sa-t, a land measure = $\frac{1}{8}$th of a schoinios or arura (ἀρούρα), *i.e.*, 1250 square cubits.

sat (?), a measure of land, arura.

sa, Edict 25, IV, 995, a corps of soldiers, an order of priests, a gang or company of workmen, a class of officials; Rec. 33, 123, five orders of priests; phylarch; overseer of the order.

sau, sorcerer, enchanter, reciter of spells.

sa, P. 666, Rec. 12, 68, Rec. 4, 22, Rec. 27, 227, B.D. 15, 7, protection, an object that gives or bring protection, amulet, talisman, phylactery; Peasant 186, he who is in charge of someone, servant; Rec. 4, 22, 5, 96, the 14 amulets.

Sa en ānkh, Rec. 16, 56, Culte 90, the magical fluid of life; see U. 562.

Sau (?) Thes. 133, a name of the Dekans.

Sa, Berg. I, 20, a god who gave praise, , to Rā; , Denderah IV, 79, an ape-god, a foe of Āapep.

Saiu, Ṭuat IX, a group of gods who cast spells by tying knots in a rope.

Sait, the consorts of the same.

Sa-ur, U. 422, , T. 242, a god.

sa Ḥeru, dawn, morning; compare Heb. שַׁחֲרִים.

sa-ta, , , , , homage, praise; , to do homage.

Sa-ta, P. 370, , U. 218, N. 1147, a god, director of spirit-souls.

Sait-ta, Ombos II, 133, a goddess.

sa, , A.Z. 1907, 77, a mat.

sa, a kind of wood (?)

sa ur, , , , , "great SA"—a kind of seed or fruit used in medicine.

sa en Ȧst, a plant used in medicine.

sa, P. 623, , N. 946, , , U. 4, 208, M. 63, , P. 44, , P. 44 = , M. 63, N. 31, , N. 116, , N. 31, , Rec. 31, 21, , ibid. 31, 30, , Mar. Karn. 52, 16, , , , , Rec. 27, 228, to guard, to protect, to beware of, to take heed, to protect oneself, to watch, to take care of.

sa-t, guard, protection.

sa-t, IV, 967, duties, charges, responsibilities.

saiu, , , , , , , , warder, watchman, shepherd, drover, herd, keeper, guardian; plur. , Rec. 30, 192, , , , P. 437, M. 622, , N. 1226, , , , , , , , , , , , , L.D. III, 140B, , Israel Stele 24; , donkey-herd; , gazelle-herd.

Saiu —, L.D. III, 140D, "good shepherd"—a title of Seti I; , Rev. 6, 25, keeper of the book, librarian (?)

saiti, Treaty 31, , , , , , , , , , watchman, guardian; plur. , , divine custodians.

sa, imprisonment, restraint.

saiu-t, cords, fetters, restraint of any kind, bonds.

Saiu Set, B.D. 23, 3, "fetters of Set," *i.e.*, the name of certain bandages placed over the mouth.

Sa, B.D. 142, 71, "Shepherd"—a title of Osiris.

Sai, a mythological crocodile.

Sa, Nesi-Åmsu 32, 41, a form of Āapep.

Sa em Geb, the gate of the 9th Division of the Ṭuat.

sa, Koller 13, 5, ram, sheep; plur. ; Heb. שֶׂה, Assyr. , Arab. شاة.

sa-t, Rec. 27, 191, , tomb, grave, shelter, wall; plur. , Rec. 30, 188.

sau, I, 78, places where cattle are bred or housed.

sau, U. 394, , to cut off (nose or ears as punishment), to break, to destroy.

saiu, breakers, broken, destroyers.

sa, to be weak or feeble.

sa-ā, Åmen. 4, 5, weak, feeble man; plur.

sa, Peasant B. 122, 128, , Rec. 36, 214, , Rec. 26, 234, , ibid. 29, 144; var. , to yield, to give way, to go away, to depart, to wander away, to desert, to fall away; varr. , U. 534, , P. 231.

sai, deserter, one who fails to do something.

sa-t, desertion, failing.

sa ta, Rec. 31, 166, to run away.

sa, to cut, to carve.

sa, U. 510, , T. 323, to know.

sa, to be full, satisfied; see .

sai, Rec. 33, 6, coast region.

s-au, to call, to cry out; var. .

s-auu, B.D. 127B, 16, , B.D. 64, 32, enlargers.

Sau, the city-god of Saïs; , the god of Lower Saïs; , the god of Upper Saïs.

saub (?), to teach, to admonish, to instruct; Copt. ϲⲃⲟ.

sauṭ, fear, anguish, quaking.

sab, to play the flute.

sab, P. 711, N. 1358, , P. 372, , , N. 692, 1148, wolf, jackal; plur. , P. 245, , M. 468, , N. 809, 1057; , U. 566, , T. 356, P. 477, , N. 801, A.Z. 1907, 19, , IV, 617, jackal of the South; Heb. זְאֵב, Syr. ܕܐܒܐ, Arab. ذِئْب.

Sab, P. 617, the Wolf-god or Jackal-god; , T. 169, M. 178, , N. 689.

Sabu, N. 950, the wolf or jackal guides of the Ṭuat.

Sab-res, T. 356, , N. 176, Ȧnpu (Anubis).

Sab-khenti-Seshesh, IV, 958, Anubis of the sistrum city.

sab, judge, chief, master; , IV, 1118, judge of the king's house; , judge belonging to Nekhen; , master scribe; , master policeman; , Rec. 6, 136, a title of the finance minister.

sab taiti, , chief judge.

Sab-ur, Rec. 29, 157, Great Judge, the name of a god.

sabut, T. 319, , U. 500, wisdom.

sab = , time, period.

s-ab, to show graciousness or affection; caus. of .

sab, Rev. 5, 92, door, pylon.

sab, Rev. 12, 119, place of correction.

sabu, a kind of goose.

Sapathar, the name of a Hittite chief.

sam, to burn, to consume; caus. of ; var. .

sam-t, , , a burning, fire, conflagration.

sannār, , , a vegetable substance (?)

sanḥem, , , locust, grasshopper; plur. , Thes. 1206, Mar. Karn. 55, 74, , ; Heb. סָלְעָם, Leviticus xi, 22.

Sanḥem, Sinsin I, grasshopper-city in Sekhet-ḥetepet.

Sanes, , Rev. 2, 170, , , Rev. 8, 172, , a group of gods who occupy the same shrine; Gr. σύνναοι.

Sar, , , , , , , Osiris.

Sar , , Ṭuat VI: (1) a jackal-headed stake of torture; (2) a sceptre surmounted by (Ṭuat XI).

sar-t , flax (?); Copt. ⲥⲟⲗ (?)

Sarma , Bibl. Eg. V, 215, a Semitic proper name.

saḥ penu , a plant, ratsbane (?)

saḥetemti , Hh. 314; see **sanḥem.**

sash , T. 341, P. 140, M. 169, N. 655, to open (the ears), to prick up the ears; var. , P. 204.

sash , , to grind, to rub down.

sasha , an animal (?)

saq , crocodile (?)

saq , Rev. 5, 95, vegetables (?)

saker , Rev. 13, 49, to journey, to sail; Copt. ϣϭⲏⲣ.

Sag , Ros. Mon. 23, a fabulous hawk-headed animal, with the fore legs of a lion, the hind legs of a horse, a tail like a lily, seven paps, a ruff round the neck and striped sides.

sat , , , leg.

sat , to pour out water, to water.

sati , Rec. 3, 118, flood.

satt , , quaking, trembling, terror, fear; Copt. ⲥⲧⲱⲧ.

Sati (?) , Ṭuat V, a god who guarded the river of fire.

Satit (?) , T.S.B.A. III, 424, a goddess of .

sath , U. 350, , , to pour out a libation.

saṭṭ , Rec. 32, 177, to tremble, to shake.

saṭu , terror, quaking.

saṭ-t , P. 662, M. 773, rag, something torn; , Åmen. 21, 1.

Så , U. 368, a black bull-god; var. , N. 719 + 17.

Så-t , U. 368, a black cow-goddess; var. , N. 719 + 17.

Så-t-Baq-t , U. 369, goddess of the olive tree.

Så-kam , U. 368, a god, son of Så-t-kamt; var. , N. 719.

Så-t-kamt , U. 368, a goddess; var. , N. 719.

så , Rev , flame, fire.

Såamiu , a class of devils; see .

s-åakhu , , , to glorify, to make bright or shining, to praise, to recite formulae for the benefit of someone, to perform rites, to do good to.

s-åakhu-t , laudation, praise, a formula of praise.

s-åakhu , , commemorative formulae of praise of the dead.

Såatiu , B.D. (Saïte) 90, 2, a group of gods.

s-åu , Rev. 16, 109; caus. of .

s-åur, Rec. 27, 86, to make pregnant.

såf, U. 135, N. 443, a cake for offering.

såam, P.S.B. 11, 265, to feed, to give to eat.

såmå, incense (?)

sån, N. 1120, , T. 7, P. 234, M. 516, , , Rec. 32, 78, , Peasant 309, , to rub, to rub dry, to wipe, to wipe away.

sån, , Metternich Stele 73, 217, , to hasten the steps.

sån, fire-stick, fire-drill, wood for kindling a fire.

sån, a kind of boat.

Sån, Düm. Temp. Insch. 25, a god of learning and letters, one of the seven sons of Meḥurit.

s-åri, to make, to cause to make or be made; caus. of .

såshå, T. 393, M. 406, to shine (?) like a star, .

s-åthi, to carry off, to seize; caus. of **åthi**,

Såthasiu åmiu Ṭuat, Ṭuat X, a group of drowned beings in the Ṭuat.

sā, Rec. 35, 57, , a beam, plank of a ship; plur. , .

sāa, Nåstasen Stele 14, to, up to; Copt. ϢⲀ.

s-āa, Rec. 11, 56, , IV, 750, 1011, to magnify, to make great; caus. of ; , Merenptaḥ I.

Sāaba, B.D.G. 348, father of Harpokrates.

sāam, to slay.

sāamu, a plant (parasitic ?).

sāi, Thes. 1206, to squat, to bow down.

sāb, Rec. 17, 146, 147, a kind of bread.

sāb, , IV, 657, to deck, to decorate, to adorn; see .

s-ām, Rec. 16, 57, , , , , , , , , to swallow, to absorb; caus. of , .

sāmiu, , , , , devourers.

Sām-em-snef, a serpent-fiend.

Sām-em-qesu, a serpent-fiend.

Sām-ta, Berg. I, 25, a crocodile-god.

sāmu, , , a plant.

sām, , , to inlay, to cover over, to plate, to decorate; , IV, 669, inlaid.

sām, inlayings, stones for inlay

sān, IV, 839; see and .

s-ānkh, Metternich Stele 88, , to vivify.

s-ānṭ, , , to destroy, to blot out, to wipe out; see **āntch.**

s-ār, Rec. 32, 80, , to bring, to bring up; see .

sāriu, porters, bearers, carriers.

Sārȧut, Berg. I, 35, Edfû I, 13A, a god who assisted the dead.

Sārit-neb-s, Berg. II, 8, , D.E. 20, Thes. 28, Denderah III, 24, , the goddess of the 2nd hour of the night.

s-ārq, , , to make an end of, to finish; see .

sāḥ, , , to be free-born, to possess high rank and nobility; , ennobled.

sāḥ, , , a free-born man (?) gentleman, high rank, nobility, honour; , IV, 1072, the king's second noble.

sāḥ, , , , , A.Z. 1900, 30, , Nav. Lit. 68, , , , noble, free, a name given to the mummy; , Rec. 36, 78, the dead.

Sāḥ, , , , the divine mummy of Osiris.

Sāḥ, Ṭuat VII, a god in the Ṭuat.

Sāḥ ȧb (ḥat), Ṭuat III, a god in the Ṭuat.

sāḥ, sāḥu, , , a garment.

s-āḥā, , , to set upright, to erect; caus. of .

s-āḥā Ṭeṭ, Rec. 3, 51, 4, 30, to set up the Ṭeṭ, or backbone of Osiris.

sāḥā Ṭeṭ, the festival of setting up the Ṭeṭ.

s-āsha, A.Z. 1900, 129 = , to make many, to multiply; caus. of .

s-āqa, Israel Stele 16, , Rec. 29, 155, , ibid. 30, 201, , to make to enter; caus. of .

s-āk, to defend, to protect; caus. of .

Sāks, Rev., a god; Gr. Σαξ (?)

s-āṭ, IV, 894, to cut, to destroy, to slay; caus. of .

s-ātcha, Thes. 1199, to spoil, to do evil, to commit a crime; caus. of .

si, U. 549, 604, T. 303, P. 204 + 6, M. 307 (var. , N. 1002), an interrogative particle.

Si, B.D. 31, 2, a crocodile-god; see .

sif, , = , , , child, babe.

sir, giraffe.

su, B.M. 138, 4, they.

su, protector, shepherd.

su, suȧ, P. 411, , P. 432 = , to drink; Copt. ce.

su-t, P. 433, drink.

suu (?), ground, region.

Susu, P. 265, a lake in the Ṭuat.

Susu, M. 477, N. 1244, the god of Lake Susu.

su-t, wheat, corn, grain; Copt. coⲩo.

sua, to pass, to pass on, to pass away.

sua; U. 401, , Rec. 26, 225, , to cut; , to cut into, to cut the throat of an animal, to stab.

s-uash, to worship, to praise, to adore; caus. of ; Copt. ⲱϣ.

Suatcheb, P.S.B. 13, 513, a form of Geb.

suȧs, B.D. 42, 3, decay, corruption.

s-uāb, to purify; caus. of .

sui, darkness, night.

s-uba, to make an entrance, to force open, to pierce, to penetrate; caus. of .

s-ubub, to present, to offer, to thrust forward; see **uba**.

s-un, to make an opening, to force open; caus. of ; Copt. oⲩⲱn.

Sun-ḥa-t; see .

sun, A.Z. 49, 59, a fish; , Verbum I, 196, arrow.

sunu, Rev. 14, 6, the divine hunter.

sun, P. 170, , to suffer pain, to be ill.

sun-t, the art of the physician; , P.S.B. 11, 304, medical matters, the science of medicine.

sunu, Rec. 17, 21, , Love Songs 2, 11, physician, doctor, , I, 38, chief physician; plur. , I, 42; Copt. caein, cнini.

sun, to destroy.

sun, pool, lake, tank.

sunȧ-t, B.D. (Saïte) 145, IV, 16, an unguent.

suni, wine of Syene (Aswân).

sunf ḥat (?), to make glad, to gratify.

s-unem, to make to eat, to feed; caus. of = .

Sunth, P. 352, , P. 467, , M. 531, , N. 1068, 1245, , N. 1110, a god who traversed heaven nine times in a night; var. , P. 265.

sur, M. 588, , T. 345, , U. 191, to drink; Copt. ce.

surȧ (suȧ), , , to drink, drinker, toper, drunkard.

surȧu, P. 692, , P. 94, drinkers.

sur-t, T. 71, , U. 191, , M. 225, , N. 603, , drink; , IV, 1115, water supply.

sur-t, bead, oval ball; var. ; mother-of-pearl beads.

suru-t (?), a bird.

s-ursh, to make to be green or fertile; caus. of **ursh.**

suh, , , to utter words as the result of some great or sudden emotion, to speak in an ecstasy, to prophesy.

suḥ, , air, wind.

suḥ-t, Pap. 3024, 79, , Metternich Stele 62, egg; Copt. coore.

suḥ, balls of incense.

Suḥit (?), Denderah III, 12, a goddess of Denderah.

s-ukha, Peasant 282, to stupefy, to make silly; caus. of **ukha.**

s-user, to strengthen; caus. of .

s-usekh, to walk with long strides; caus. of **usekh.**

s-ush, , to praise, to worship, to adore; caus. of **uash.**

S-ush Ḥeriu, title of the high-priest of the 10th Nome of Upper Egypt.

sush, to break (?)

sush-t, tie, fetter, cord.

sut, var. , White Crown.

sutut, IV, 520, to walk, to travel.

s-utekh, to treat a body with drugs, to embalm; caus. of ; var. . A title of Anubis is , "the embalmer."

s-uthet, , , to cook, to roast, to bake.

s-uthet, to fatten birds.

s-uṭekh, to embalm; var. .

s-utcha, , to strengthen, to heal, to save; caus. of .

s-utcha, , to go, to go forward; caus. of .

seb, N. 692, 1148, jackal; see .

seb, U. 460 . . . . .

seb, , see **ȧsi** , an interrogative particle.

sebi, , , , , , Peasant 322, to lead, to conduct, to guide, to traverse, to pass through, to march in front; , guide of the words of the gods.

sebbi 〔hieroglyphs〕, to lead, etc.; 〔hieroglyphs〕, I, 50, a dead man; 〔hieroglyphs〕, decay of the body; 〔hieroglyphs〕, he lived 59 years.

sebseb 〔hieroglyphs〕, to lead, to guide.

sebi-t 〔hieroglyphs〕, conductor, guide; 〔hieroglyphs〕, traverser of eternity —a title of Rā and of Osiris; 〔hieroglyphs〕, this book of traversing eternity.

sebbi 〔hieroglyphs〕, V, 1112, a general envoy.

sebi-t, sebiu-t 〔hieroglyphs〕, Shipwreck 161, 〔hieroglyphs〕, freight, cargo of a boat or ship, load of a camel or ass; 〔hieroglyphs〕, a loader of ships.

sebb 〔hieroglyphs〕, Berl. 6910, to load.

Sebit 〔hieroglyphs〕, Rec. 20, 42, a serpent-goddess.

seb 〔hieroglyphs〕, evil, wickedness; 〔hieroglyphs〕, decay, waste.

sebit 〔hieroglyphs〕, fish offal, a poor kind of fish.

seb 〔hieroglyphs〕, Shipwreck 56, an offering by fire.

seb-t 〔hieroglyphs〕, louse; plur. 〔hieroglyphs〕; Copt. ⲥⲓⲃ (?)

seb-t 〔hieroglyphs〕, tress, lock of hair, hair clippings.

sebi 〔hieroglyphs〕, a period of time, anniversary, annual festival (?)

seb 〔hieroglyphs〕, to play a flute.

sba 〔hieroglyphs〕, flute; Copt. ⲥⲏⲃⲉ.

sba 〔hieroglyphs〕, doors; Copt. ⲥⲃⲉ.

Sba-Rā 〔hieroglyphs〕, Edfû I, 81, a title of the Nile-god.

sbau 〔hieroglyphs〕, star-gods.

sbau 〔hieroglyphs〕, punishment, correction; Copt. ⲥⲃⲱ.

sebakh (sebkh) 〔hieroglyphs〕, to shut in, to preserve.

s-baq (sebq) 〔hieroglyphs〕, to make to shine; caus. of 〔hieroglyphs〕.

sebaq (sebq) 〔hieroglyphs〕, leg, thigh; see 〔hieroglyphs〕.

s-baq (sebq) 〔hieroglyphs〕, to make pregnant; caus. of 〔hieroglyphs〕.

s-bagi 〔hieroglyphs〕, to make weak or helpless; caus. of 〔hieroglyphs〕.

sebȧ 〔hieroglyphs〕, a mythological serpent-fiend.

sebȧth 〔hieroglyphs〕, Canopus Stele 10, provisions.

sebit 〔hieroglyphs〕, Rec. 4, 21, 〔hieroglyphs〕, a plant, flag, rush.

Sebu 〔hieroglyphs〕, Rec. 31, 21, a group of gods.

seben 〔hieroglyphs〕, U. 304, 532, 551, P. 605, 〔hieroglyphs〕, Rec. 30, 187, to retreat, to wriggle away (of a serpent); 〔hieroglyphs〕, to roll away the hours.

seben-t 〔hieroglyphs〕, U. 611, retreat, withdrawal.

sebnen 〔hieroglyphs〕, Rec. 31, 168, to retreat; see **seben**.

sebenben 〔hieroglyphs〕, M. 280, 〔hieroglyphs〕, Rec. 31, 168, to retreat, to collapse; 〔hieroglyphs〕, P. 180.

sebennu, U. 540, T. 296, , P. 230, crowns.

sebeḥ , , , to cry, cry.

Sebkhas , one of the 36 Dekans; Gr. Σουχωs.

Sebeshsen , Annales I, 84, one of the 36 Dekans; Gr. Σουχώs.

sebeq (?) , Israel Stele 22, , happy, fortunate.

sebq-t , bone chamber.

sebt-t , crown of flowers, wreath.

sebt , wall, fort; Copt. ⲥⲟⲃⲧ.

sebti , a royal title.

sebth , P. 349, 1065, , N. 766, P. 708, , Rec. 30, 186, to inhale, to smell.

sep , a sign of multiplication; , Rec. 2, 111, to multiply; = 10 × 10.

sep , , , , , , , time, season, fate, luck, occasion, opportunity, hap, accident, condition, case, situation, kind, sort, mode, means, manner, habit, way, behaviour, action, characteristic, aim, object, purpose, subject, case at law, trial, affair, act, like, equal, expedient; Copt. ⲥⲡ; , , ill-luck, calamity, fault, failure; , one at a time, one by one; , every particular; , L.D. III, 140B, another good example; , Israel Stele 8, every one on his land; , Åmen. 15, 18, moreover, another case; , IV, 1078, happiness; , IV, 944, calamity, disaster; , on every occasion; , time of trouble; , A.Z. 1880, 49; , a bad turn; , a bold act; , , twice, repetition; , duplicity; , , second time; , , never again; , T. 283, , , at once, forthwith; Copt. ⲛ̄ⲥⲟⲡ; , gold twice refined; , gold thrice refined; plur. , U. 88, , N. 1110, , , , IV, 351, , ; , frequently; , , Rec. 16, 110 [say] four times (a rubrical direction); , good times, Rec. 20, 40; , millions of times; , righteousness; , unique in abilities; , A.Z. 1905, 26, unmatched for abilities; , IV, 410, 1082.

sep , , the case in court, a legal decision; , a criminal offence; , it is a case for punishment; , IV, 752, cases of trespass; , just cases; , the case of evil-doers; , IV, 1109, their case comes on again.

sep, Rev. = , , Rev. 13, 23, time of judgement.

sep tepi, , , , primeval time; , lands of primeval time.

sepi, Rev. 13, 23, to supplicate.

sepsep, Stele of Ptolemy I, 18, , Rec. 15, 18, , Rec. 13, 22, to ask for, to supplicate, petition; Copt. ⲥⲉⲡⲥⲱⲡ.

sepi, Peasant 199, , , to remain over; , Shipwreck 38, not one was left; , L.D. III, 140c, there remains no trace; see ; Copt. ⲥⲉⲉⲡⲉ.

sepp, to remain over; Copt. ⲥⲉⲉⲡⲉ.

sepit, U. 549, T. 303, , Rechnungen 49, , P.S.B. 19, 263, , , , , , , remainder, remains, gleanings.

sep-t, pots for storing corn.

Sep Rā, Palermo Stele, the name of a sun-temple.

sep, worm, serpent.

Sep-ḥer, Sallier IV, 13, 9, a god (?)

sep, Rec. 16, 136, to dip; Copt. ⲥⲉⲡ, ⲥⲟⲡ.

sep, Rec. 26, 64, tackle of a boat.

sep, Thes. 1124, couch, dîwân.

sep-t, , stairs, steps.

sep, , , to cut, to slay, to destroy, to smite.

sep Rev. 12, 21 = , Copt. ⲥⲉⲉⲡⲉ.

sep, Rev. 13, 37, Nomes; see .

sep-ti (?), Lit. 22, = , two plumes.

Sep, Rec. 3, 49, a god.

Sepit, Berg. I, 19, , a wailing-goddess, a form of Hathor (?)

sepa, to benefit, to thrive, to prosper.

Sepa, U. 537, , U. 538, , T. 305, , , , B.D. 17, 87, , , Rec. 30, 187, B.D. 69, 7: (1) a reptile-god (?); (2) the chief of the seven spirits who guarded Osiris.

Sepa-ur, T. 304, a god (?)

Sepa-Ḥeru, U. 329, , T. 300, the Sepa of Horus.

Sepa-ḥer, P. 270, , M. 485, , N. 1251, , Rec. 30, 199, the god with a [hideous] face like Sepa.

Sepa-shā-t, , Ṭuat III, a god of slaughter.

sepi, Rec. 3, 56, trough, basin.

sepi, Rec. 3, 50, crusts of bread.

sepi, Rec. 3, 45, rag, shred, strip of cloth.

sepi, Rev. 11, 167, thread; Copt. ⲥⲉⲡⲡⲓ.

Sepi, Rec. 3, 44, a god.

sepin (?), IV, 670, a kind of wood.

Sepen (?), Ombos I, 186–188, one of the 14 kau of Rā.

sper, Rec. 26, 229, , , to come forth, to set out.

s-per[r], to make to come forth; caus. of .

sper, to ask, to pray, to entreat.

sepeḥ, IV, 1075, , , Ȧmen. 7, 19, 11, 17, to lasso, to take captive.

sepḥu, order, command (?)

s-pekhar, , , to write, to inscribe, to register.

Sepkh-kenmem, the name of one of the 36 Dekans.

seps, Hh. 564, to shake down the hair (?)

Sepsu, Rec. 31, 14, , Mission 13, 117 gods with dishevelled hair.

seps, to overthrow, to slay.

seps, A.Z. 1906, 107, 109, to skip, to jump, to dance; var. .

seps, to build.

sept-ti, , the two lips; see .

sept ḥeri, upper lip.

sept kheri, lower lip.

sept, IV, 655, bank, shore; , Pap. 3024, 67, the bank of the stream.

sept, , a plant, hyoscyamus (?); Copt. ⲥⲁϥϯ.

sepṭ, leg, thigh, foreleg.

Sepṭ-masti-ent-Ruruti, B.D. 153A, 9, part of the hunting net of the Akeru-gods.

sepṭ, , to be ready, prepared; , his soul is prepared; , provided with a watchful, intelligent face.

Sepṭ-metu, the name of the 6th Gate in the Ṭuat.

s-peṭ, to make to stretch, to extend; caus. of .

sef, N. 429, , , , , Shipwreck 144, , to cut, to slay, to kill.

sef, , knife; plur. ; Copt. ⲥⲏϥⲉ, Arab. سيف, Eth. ሰይፍ:, Syr. ܣܝܦܐ, Gr. ξίφος.

sef, Mar. Karn. 55, 67, , Rec. 16, 141, to melt by fire, to boil, to cook, to steep, to macerate.

sefsef, to melt by fire, to liquefy.

sefsef, , to pour out, to overflow.

sef-t, , a kind of sacred oil.

sef, Peasant 316, Pap. 3024, 107, , , to be gracious, mild, gentle, pitiful, compassionate; , Rec. 13, 12, a soft answer.

sef, babe, child, boy; varr. , .

Sef-ti , , the two children, *i.e.*, Shu and Tefnut.

Sefi-peri-em-Ḥesher, etc. , B.D. 164, 8, a title of the Sun-god.

sfa , to strain, to purify; see **sefi.**

sfa-t , , annoyance, pitiful, clement.

Sfȧ , Ṭuat I, a serpent-god.

sfi , , Rec. 5, 95, , Rec. 5, 96, , Rec. 5, 93, , to mix, to mingle, to strain, to clarify, to purify.

sfen , IV, 971, , Peasant 150, to be patient, long-suffering, mild, gentle.

sfenu , exile (?) orphan (?); plur. , IV, 1076.

sfenṭi , A.Z. 1900, 30, a kind of plant.

sefrit , Hh. 452 . . . .

s-fekh , , Rec. 29, 155, , , to loose, to open; caus. of ; see ; , unwrapped.

s-fekhfekh , to put off clothes, to undress, to loose; see .

Sefekh , Wört. 1212 . . . . . .

sefek , to cut, to slay, to cleave.

sefkek , , to pour out, to be poured out, exhausted.

sefth , to slay, to kill.

sem , form, image, kind, manner.

sem , to collect, to heap together.

sem , to bless; Copt. ⲥⲙⲟⲩ.

semsem , , to bless, to pray.

sem (?) , a kind of metal; see **tchām.**

sem , , , , , , , , , herbs, vegetables; Copt. ⲥⲓⲙ.

sem, semati , , , , = : (1) a priestly official; (2) title of the high-priest of Coptos and Panopolis.

semi-t , U. 557, , , , , (see **khaskh-t**), , , desert, hill country, hill cemetery; , P. 82, M. 112, N. 86, hills; , IV, 1015, hill of truth, *i.e.*, the grave; , IV, 430, hill of the spirit-bodies; , hill of the east; , hill of the west.

Set Ȧmentt (Semi-t Ȧmentt) , B.D.G. 85, the mountain necropolis on the west bank of the Nile.

Set (Semit) , Ṭuat I; B.D.G. 81, 83, a god.

Semti , , , , , , , the nesu bȧti name of King ; = sem-t, Rec. 28, 170.

semsem , , horse; plur. .

smai, U. 418, T. 238, 339, P. 611, N. 627, to unite, to join oneself to someone or something, to copulate; joining heaven to earth.

sma, cemetery (?); var.

sma en ta the transport of a dead body over the river to the tomb.

smai-ta, Rec. 31, 19, Rec. 34, 177, Hh. 548, Amherst I, to bury, burial, "union with the earth"; Copt. ⲧⲱⲙⲥ.

sma ta, Peasant 44, side of a field or road, border or edge of a road; border of a field; A.Z. 1900, 27, the two sides of a road.

sma-t, gut, intestine, rectum, bowel; Rec. 26, 80; plur., U. 518, T. 328.

sma, phallus.

sma-ti, testicles.

smaiu, male relatives, kinsmen, cousins, connections.

smai hru nefer, a man who assists at a festival, addicted to revelry.

smai, spouse, consort, wife, concubine.

smait, female relatives, connections, cousins.

smaiut, IV, 1081, Peasant 191, (var. Rec. 34, 179, Rec. 33, 291), Rec. 16, 110, gang, company, band, troop, evil allies, associates, confederates, fiends, devils; allies of Set.

smait, Rec. 24, 166, Rec. 17, 113, a royal title.

smai (?), IV, 200, part of the double crown.

sma ta, Methen, a title, governor (?); var.

smai taui, Palermo Stele, , , , uniter of the Two Lands, *i.e.*, of Upper and Lower Egypt—a royal title or name.

smait taui (?), throne room (?)

smaiui (?), Rec. 27, 84, twin mountains (Gebelên ?)

Smai, , Rec. 31, 12, the title of a god.

Smai, , , , a name of Set.

Smait, the title of a god or devil.

Smati, , , , , B.D. 145, 146, VI, 23, the doorkeeper of the 6th Pylon.

Smaiu, , , , , B.D. 17, 138, 18A, 2, H. 1, 19, 5, Nesi-Âmsu 22, 11, fiends.

Smaiut, Rec. 31, 168, a group or company of gods; , P.S.B. 13, 569.

Smaiti, B.D. 64, 14, the two goddesses Isis and Nephthys.

Smati-uati, B.D. 169, 15, a divine title.

Smatt-Bast, B.D. 125, see **Basti.**

Smai-Nu, , Mission 13, 50, , Edfû I, 79, a title of the Nile-god.

Smai-ta, Tomb of Seti I, one of the 75 forms of Rā (No. 70).

Smai-taui, , D.R.G. 60, , IV, 82: (1) a serpent-god; (2) a moon-god; (3) a Horus-god of ; (4) a title of Set.

Smai-taui, B.D.G. 348, a title of Harpokrates son of Hathor.

smait, assembly, reunion, gathering.

smai-t, , enclosure, a shut-in place; plur.

smai-t, IV, 1121, bolt (?) fastening.

sma, , Rec. 16, 142, , , to mix; , Koller 1, 7, a mixture of six parts.

sma kh-t, , Metternich Stele 20, , to eat.

sma[i]u keku, thick darkness, utter darkness, outer darkness, gloom, obscurity; varr. , , , .

smai, , , , , Rev. 6, 147, temple, lock, tress, hair; Copt. ⲥⲙⲙⲁⲩ.

sma, tree with thick foliage.

sma, a plant; plur. , A.Z. 1908, 120, , , , , leaves, foliage, twigs, branches, vegetables.

smait, , , , , , , Rec. 8, 171, couch, bed, bier, mat, platform, part of a boat.

sma, to render clear or visible.

s-ma, to make to see; caus. of .

sma, Metternich Stele 41, , ibid. 157, , to cut up, to slay.

sma, IV, 614, a beast slain as an offering.

Smaur-Bekha , Ombos II, 139, the bull-gods Smamur and Bachis.

Sma-kheftiu-f , Ṭuat III, a ram-god.

smasma, to pray, to recite; var. .

smaȧ , , to feed; Copt. ⲦⲀⲀⲞ (?).

s-maȧr, IV, 1199, , to make miserable, to oppress; caus. of .

s-maā, to make true, to justify, to prove true or innocent, to correct, to pay what is due or obligatory, to discharge a duty or debt, to dedicate; caus. of .

s-maā kheru , Rec. 29, 147, , , , , , , , , , to make true the word, *i.e.*, to prove innocent, to procure the acquittal of someone.

smai, M. 785, to equip a boat, to rig a boat.

s-mau, , to repair, to renew, to rebuild; caus. of .

s-mau, Mission 13, 58 . . . . . .; caus. of .

smam, , , , to slay, to kill.

smamu, slaughterer.

smam, , , , B.D. 62, 5, a bull-god.

Smamit, Ombos II, 233, a cow-goddess of offerings.

Smamur, Denderah IV, 79, a bull-god or goddess.

smam, IV, 809, to crush; , to crush foreign lands.

smam (s-am), to kindle, to set fire to; caus. of .

smam-t (s-am-t), Pap. 3024, 13, blaze, a kindling.

smam, dense (of darkness).

smasu, Rec. 27, 84, eldest, first-born; see **smesu.**

smasu-t (smesu-t), eldest (fem.)

smȧ, herald, reporter, announcer; Copt. ⲤⲘⲘⲈ.

smȧn, , U. 14, a kind of incense.

smā (?), to kill, to slay.

s-mār, Rec. 32, 79, to please, to make happy, to adorn, to decorate caus. of .

s-mār-t, adornment, decoration, rich or festal apparel.

smi-t, shadow, protection.

smiu, devourers, avenging gods and fiends.

smu, U. 506, T. 321, flesh, members.

smun (or **s-m-un**), Peasant 44, assuredly, really and truly, verily.

smep, slaughter, death.

smen, P. 124, M. 93, N. 100, incense.

s-men, P. 635, M. 510, N. 1092, P. 636, 637, M. 512, 514, N. 1095, 1097, Rec. 30, 187, to stablish, to fix firmly in position, to establish oneself; caus. of ; Copt. ⲥⲙⲓⲛⲉ, ⲥⲉⲙⲛⲓ.

smen-smen, T. 398, M. 400, to establish, be established.

smen, order, foundation.

smen, bronze.

smen, Metternich Stele 62, a kind of goose; Copt. ⲥⲙⲟⲩⲛⲉ.

Smen, B.D. 17, 37, a goose-god, a dweller in , Mar. Aby. I, 44.

smenu, image, figure.

Smennu, T. 24, a god.

smenu, Rec. 15, 179, to rage, to shake.

s-menmen IV, 1111, to unsettle, to make to move; caus. of .

s-menkh, to set in good order, to adorn, to beautify, to endow richly; caus. of .

s-menkh-t, adornment.

Smenkhit, Rec. 3, 54, a goddess.

Smen-ti (?), a lioness-goddess.

smeri, emery; var.

s-meh-t, Rec. 26, 79, to make to forget; caus. of .

s-meḥ, to flood, to submerge, to fill full.

smeḥit, flooding.

smeḥ, a kind of boat or ship.

smeḥ, to pray, to beseech.

smeḥ, Rec. 15, 152, garlands.

smeḥi, the left hand, the left side; Gr. 'Ασμαχ; see Herodotus II, 30.

s-mes, to deliver a woman; caus. of ; Copt. ⲑⲙⲉⲥⲓⲟ.

smesmes = **negesges**, to overflow.

smesu, Metternich Stele 222, eldest, firstborn.

smesit, Mission 13, 51, firstborn (fem.).

smesu, title of the high-priest of Metelis.

smesun, pot, vessel.

smeseru (?), Rev. 11, 90 . . . . . .

Smet; see **Mestȧ,** one of the four sons of Horus.

Smet, Berg. I, 17, a crocodile-god.

smet, smetsmet, B.D. 125, Neg. Con. 15 . . . .

smet . . . ., Famine Stele 17 . . . .

s-met.

Smet[r]-āqa, B.D. 58, 5, the rudder in the magical boat.

smeti, Rec. 5, 95, to paint the eyes.

Smetti, B.D. 144, the Watcher of the 1st Ārit.

s-metr, Rec. 17, 44; caus. of .

semthek, part of the name of Psammetichus; with fem. art. , A.Z. 1881, 68.

Smeṭ, one of the 36 Dekans; Gr. Σματ.

smeṭ, eye paint (?)

smeṭ, servants, subordinates, underlings; see .

sen, Rec. 4, 30, they, them, their; see .

sen-nu, second, fellow.

sen, to bow, to pay homage, to entreat.

senu, suppliant.

senn-ti, worshipper, adorer.

sennit, B.D. 168A, 22, acclamations.

sen, senȧ, to smell, to kiss, to do homage, adoration.

senu, IV, 1220, homage.

senn-t, kiss, embrace.

sen ta, IV, 1028, IV, 910, IV, 908, to smell the earth, to kiss the earth, to do homage by bowing with the face to the ground.

senn ta, Mar. Aby. II, 36, to kiss the ground, *i.e.*, pay homage.

sennti ta, Ȧmen. 14, 16, payer of homage.

senȧ ta, adorer, worshipper.

sen ṭ, Rec. 16, 56, to smell (*i.e.*, kiss) the hand.

sensen, to praise, to acclaim; Copt. ⲥⲉⲗⲥⲱⲗ.

sensen, to breathe, to snuff the air.

sensen-ti, a breathing.

sen, to cut, to cut off, to split.

sen-t, a slit, a cutting, wound.

senȧ, slayer; fem. .

senn, T. 353, Mission 13, 117, to slit, to cut open, to overthrow; those who cut.

sen, ploughshare; Copt. CINE.

sen-t, U. 431 . . . . ; var., T. 247.

sensen-t, T. 247 . . . . ; var., U. 431.

Sensen-t, N. 706, a mythological locality.

sen (not **sensh**), to open; see .

sen, seni, U. 235, , , IV, 1220, , , , , , , , , Koller Pap. 5, 1, , Metternich Stele 240, , to open, to expand, to throw open a door, to pass over or away from, to pass on in front; late forms are: , , Rev. 11, 174; Copt. CINE.

senn, senni, , , , , , A.Z. 1907, 125, Rec. 36, 201, to pass over, to go beyond, to pass in front, to pass away from, to flutter away (of a bird); , way, road; Copt. CNAEIN, CNHINI.

senni, , , , officer, leader, chief, fighter in the van of an army; plur. , Anastasi I, 23, 6, Mar. Karn. 53, 38, , , Rev. 11, 144, 173, , P. 41, M. 62, , N. 29.

seni, , , sufferer, a wretched, needy, or miserable man.

seni meni, Tutānkh. 8, , , P. 1116B, 38, 54, in a state of flux and ruin, topsy-turvy.

sen-t, P. 365, N. 1078, lie, false statement.

sennȧ, , , , sufferer, sorrower; plur. .

sen-t, decay, a passing away.

sen, Rev. 14, 34, clay.

sen, , , Thes. 1297, , to copy, to make a likeness or transcript of anything.

senit, P. 424, M. 607, N. 1212, , Thes. 1286, , Rev. 14, 68, model, copy, likeness, archetype (of a book); , IV, 1150, in likeness of.

senn, Rev. 6, 29, , , , Rec. 19, 93, , Thes. 1122, copy, duplicate, transcript, list, notes of a case, report.

Sen-ṭ-Rā, B.D. 115, 7, the "similitude of Rā."

senn, IV, 1032, to make a copy or likeness.

sennu, , , , , , (*sic*), likeness, image, copy, figure, statue.

Senen, Denderah II, 11, , one of the 36 Dekans.

sen-t, senȧt, , , , , , , , draughtboard and draughts; , to play at draughts.

sen-t, case, box.

senni (?), a counter in a game.

sen-t (?), Peasant 23, a kind of stone; compare, ruby (?)

sen-t; see.

senn; see, foundation.

senn, Rec. 4, 22, a precious stone, ruby (?)

senȧ (?), winds, breaths.

senȧ, sennȧ, to pass; see sen.

senȧnȧ, Åmen. 7, 1, pass quickly.

Senȧn (?), Berg. I, 13, a god, a defender of the dead.

senȧh, B.D. 145, IX, 34, injury, damage.

senȧs, A.Z. 1906, 103; see.

senā, to turn back, to repulse.

s-nāā, with, to reduce to the consistence of paste (of drugs used in medicine), to knead; caus. of; , B.D. 125, III, 20.

seni-t, case, chamber, cabin, box; Copt. ⲥⲉⲛⲏ.

senu, Rev. 12, 99, bread, bread cakes; , IV, 768, Annales III, 110.

Senu, Ṭuat VII, a company of gods who fed Rā.

senu, N. 62, T. 268, pot, vase, vessel, jar.

senu, I, 3, 4, wine of Pelusium; Gr. Σαϊν.

senu, Methen, assessor of taxes.

senu, physician (?); Copt. ⲥⲁⲉⲓⲛ.

senu, to see, to weep (?)

senu (?), B.D. 64, 14, district (?)

senu; see.

sennu, privilege, right.

senu, Nāstasen Stele 65 . . . .

senui, Nāstasen Stele 68, ; see.

s-nukh, L.D. III, 140c, to burn up, to scorch, to shrivel.

senut (senupet ?), a plant.

senb, P. 453, wall, fortification.

senb-t, U. 438, T. 250, wall, fortification; plur. P. 306, P. 352, N. 1067, N. 741, N. 742, N. 164, Rec. 27, 59, Rec. 30, 194.

senb, a cool, wholesome wind or breeze.

senb-t, P. 392, N. 1166, A.Z. 1880, 49, beaker, jar, libation vessel; plur. ; see.

senb, Rec. 5, 96, Rec. 5, 92, 95, to bind, to tie, to tear into strips, strip of cloth or linen, bandage.

s-nebi, Hymn Darius 23, to make to swim.

senb, Rec. 16, 57, 31, 18, Peasant 115, to be overthrown (?) to be evilly entreated (?)

senbå-t, jar, vase, vessel, pot.

senp, to cut, to slay.

senpu, slaughterers, slaughterings.

senf, blood; Copt. ⲥⲛⲟϥ.

senfu, a flux of blood.

senf, bloody-eyed.

Senfiu, gods of blood, or gods of blood colour.

senf, knife (?)

senf, garment, raiment, dress.

senf, last year; var. ; Copt. ⲥⲛⲟⲩϥ.

s-nef, Peasant 279, to unload a boat, to give relief to.

s-nefi, to produce air, to fan.

s-nefekhfekh, to loosen, to untie, to undo mummy bandages; caus. of.

s-nem (s-unem), IV, 352, A.Z. 1880, 49, Love Songs 8, 5, to feed, to supply with food, to enjoy food, to eat ravenously; caus. of **unem**.

s-nemm (s-unem), Rec. 36, 81, to feed, to satisfy with food, to devour; caus. of **unem**.

snem, Peasant 282, greediness, voracity.

snem, abundance, plenty.

snem, IV, 1184, food.

snem-t, IV, 1054, 1055, IV, 753, IV, 1158, food supply, provisions, offerings in abundance.

snem, snemm, A.Z. 1873, 151, spawn of fish.

snem, to grieve, to mourn, grief, sorrow.

snem åb (ḥat), grief of heart, sorrow.

snemm, A.Z. 1906, 113, to tear out the hair in grief; Mission 13, 229.

s-nem, IV, 911, Rec. 30, 193, to pray, to supplicate, to beg; see ; caus. of .

snem , , IV, 386, , , , Tombos 8, , flood, storm, tempest, thunder rain.

Snem, Snemmti , , , Hh. 441, a title of Set.

Snemti , B.D. 99, 14, a god.

s-nemȧ , to step, to walk; caus. of .

Snemf ; see ; , Rec. 5, 92, the god of the preceding year.

s-nemeḥ , , , , to humble oneself, to abase oneself, to beg, to pray, to supplicate; caus. of .

s-nemmeḥ , Rec. 35, 125, , to humble oneself, to beg, to pray; caus. of .

snemeḥu , , , , A.Z. 1905, 28, prayer, petition, entreaty, supplication, begging.

Snemkhef , Ṭuat XII, a serpent-god in the Ṭuat.

s-nems , to feed, to nourish, to fill, to provide with.

s-neh , , Rev. 3, 38, to enslave, to reduce to subjection, to regulate; see **s-nehi.**

s-nehi , IV, 130, 1006, , Rec. 4, 131, , , , , to muster soldiers, to place soldiers in their positions for fighting, to marshal forces, to register, to make an inventory; , IV, 1006, to register a district.

Sneh Rā , the name of a festival.

s-nehas , A.Z. 1900, 20, to make watchful or vigilant, to keep awake; caus. of or .

Snehaqarha (?) , B.D. 162, 2, a mythological locality; var. .

snehu , B.D. (Saïte) 75, 3, part of a building (?)

s-nehep , , , , to marshal troops, to set in motion (of the stars); caus. of .

s-nehemhem , Sphinx 14, 206, to make a noise; caus. of .

sneḥ , , , , , , , , , , , , to tie, to bind, to fetter; Copt. ⲥⲱⲛϩ.

sneḥneḥ , to tie, to bind, to fetter; Copt. ⲥⲱⲛϩ.

sneḥ-t , band, fillet, tie.

sneḥu , binding, bandage, tie, fetter.

sneḥu , wings (?) feathers (?)

s-neḥa , to destroy, to make a ruin of; caus. of .

s-neḥem, to rescue, to deliver; caus. of ; Copt. ⲛⲟϩⲉⲙ.

sneḥem, M. 328, N. 159, 860, , , Rec. 15, 161, grasshopper, locust; plur. ; Copt. ⲥⲁⲛⲛⲉϩ, Heb. סָלְעָם.

snekha-t, droppings from the nose.

s-nekht, IV, 657, , IV, 1154, to strengthen; caus. of .

s-nekhtu Ebers Pap. 80, 1, rigor (?)

sens, to smell; see .

sens, IV, 1063, , , A.Z. 1906, 108, , , , , , , to praise, to acclaim, to adore.

sens, , , A.Z. 35, 16, praises, hymns.

Sens-åab-t, Ṭuat XII, a singing-god of Sinaitic origin (?)

sensh (?), , , , , B.D. 149, XIV, 7, , , , to open, to unbolt a door; see **sesh** .

senshu, B.D. 75, 3, , Rec. 16, 130, chambers.

Senshit, Ṭuat I, the serpent-goddesses who open the gates to Åfu-Rā.

s-neshemshem, Sphinx 14, 209, to sharpen, to file; caus. of .

s-neshen, to pierce, to open; caus.

S-neshni, , , , storm, bad weather, the storm-fiend.

senshen, B.D. 38A, 8, *i.e.*, , lily, lotus; Heb. שׁוּשַׁן, שׁוֹשָׁן, Syr. ܫܘܫܢܐ, Aram. שׁוֹשַׁנְתָּא, Arab. سُوسَن, Gr. σοῦσον.

Senshen , B.D. 38A, 8, lily of feldspar (associated with).

s-neq, IV, 920, , , , , to suckle; , , IV, 920; caus. (?) compare Heb. יָנַק, Copt. ⲥⲱⲛⲕ.

Senq, , title of the high-priestess of Apis, and of the high-priestess of Libya Mareotis.

senk, Gol. 14, 131, greediness.

senki, Åmen. 7, 14, 18, 8, greedy man (?)

senk-ḥat, B.D. 174, 19, strong-willed.

senk, , , A.Z. 1900, 27, 1906, 110, , night, evening, darkness.

senk, sight.

senk, senk-ti, , , = **stu-t**, rays of light.

Senk = , B.D. 168, a light-god, a title of Rā.

Senki, Tomb of Seti I, one of the 75 forms of Rā (No. 9).

Senkit, Ṭuat VIII, a goddess in the Circle Ḥapseshmus.

Senk-ḥer, Tomb of Seti I, , a light-god, one of the 75 forms of Rā (No. 62); read **Sti-ḥer** , .

senk, senk-ti , = **sti** , to light a fire.

senk-ti = **sti** , to pour out.

senkti , Rec. 16, 57, , = , , to emit seed, to beget.

Senktiu = **Stiu** , Asiatic and Nubian desert dwellers.

Senktett , Hh. 339; see **Sektett.**

sent , Rec. 13, 58, custom, use, wont; Copt. ⲥⲱⲛⲧ.

sent , Jour. As. 1908, 289, creatures, created things; Copt. ⲥⲱⲛⲧ.

senti , IV, 1085, , Rec. 3, 46, statue, figure, likeness; , , Sphinx Stele 2, 7.

senti , to found, to establish; see .

sent , something founded or established, ground, the solid earth.

senti , , , , foundation; Copt. ⲥⲛ̄ⲧⲉ.

senti , , the bottom of anything.

sennti , , foundation; Copt. ⲥⲛ̄ⲧⲉ.

senti ta , , to lay a foundation, the earth's foundation; , Rec. 21, 90.

sent, senti , , = and , fear; Copt. ⲥⲛⲁⲧ.

sentu (stut) , , fire, flames.

senti (sti) = , to beget.

sentit , Rec. 6, 147, matter of the body, bodily members; var. .

Senti = **Stiu,** desert dwellers.

sent , , to cry, to grieve.

s-neter , to cense, to purify, to smoke; see **s-nether** and **nether.**

senter , the substance used in censing or smoking, incense.

Senthes , Ṭuat X, a light-goddess.

sentegsi , Rec. 13, 53 = Gr. σύνταξις.

senth , to found, to establish.

senth-t , establishment, provision, endowment.

senth-t , = , fear.

Senthit , , Rec. 6, 148: (1) the bodily members; (2) the name of a goddess; var. .

senṭ , , Rec. 30, 187, to fear; see .

senṭ-t , , fear; Copt. ⲥⲛⲁⲧ.

senṭu , timid man.

senṭ , foundation; Copt. ⲥⲛ̄ⲧⲉ.

Senṭ , Ṭuat VI, a warder-god.

s-netchem, to make happy or pleasant; caus. of .

s-netchem, to rest, to sit, to be at ease, to seat someone.

s-netchem sti, to produce a sweet smell.

s-netchemnetchem, , to be at rest, at ease.

snetchemnetchemu, men who can be kept quiet, or bribed to be silent.

s-netcher, to restrain, to grip; caus. of .

ser, prince, noble; , IV, 1158, nobles of the courtiers.

ser er neḥeḥ . everlasting prince, a title of Osiris.

Ser āa, Tomb Seti I, one of the 75 forms of Rā (No. 27).

ser, M. 726, N. 1329, , Rec. 11, 180, , ram; fem. , ; varr. , ; compare [ ] , N. 719.

Ser-t, Serȧ-t, , , , , , , Tombs Seti I, Ram. II, Ram. IV, Denderah II, 10, Zodiac Dend., one of the 36 Dekans; Gr. Σρω.

ser, serȧ, M. 726, , N. 1329 . . . .

ser, Rec. 30, 192, to arrange, to order.

ser, Shipwreck 31, to predict; , , to proclaim, to announce, to publish, to pronounce, to order, to direct troops; Copt. ⲥⲱⲣ.

ser, Nȧstasen Stele 52, advice, order.

serser, Nȧstasen Stele 10, Ḥerusȧtef Stele 72, 109, to comfort, to console; Copt. ⲥⲟⲗⲥⲗ̄.

ser meṭut, to arrange words in order, to compose a work.

Ser-kheru, B.D. 125, III, , one of the 42 assessors of Osiris.

seriu, giraffes.

ser, serr, , , to write, to engrave, to trace, to draw.

serr, A.Z. 1873, 60 . . . .

ser, , , , a kind of goose; fem. , , Rev. 14, 34 (glossed by ΧΗΝΑΓΡΙΟΥ); plur. .

ser, wool; Copt. ⲥⲟⲣⲧ.

ser, , drum, tambourine.

ser, skin, a kind of disease.

ser, , = , arrow.

Ser-t, , , B.D. 58, 5, a part of the boat of the deceased.

ser-t, IV, 998, fan; see .

ser, U. 28A, , N. 255A, cheese (?) butter (?); , butter of the South; , butter of the North.

ser, , grain, barley; see , compare Heb. שְׂעִיר.

serser , to fight, to do battle.

Serser , , , , , a fiery region in the Ṭuat; ; the lake of boiling water in the same place.

serȧ , , grain, barley.

serȧ , , a kind of goose; plur. .

serȧ , ram; varr. , , Rec. 3, 56, , .

Serȧt-beqt , B.D. 177, 6, a cow-goddess.

Seri , Ṭuat XII, a god in the Ṭuat.

seri-t , , IV, 998, , IV, 998, fan.

serit , , , , , sickness, nausea.

seru , scorpion; Copt. ⲥⲗⲏ.

Seru , Berg. I, 17, a bird-god (goose-god?)

s-rukh (?) , Mission 13, 223 = (?)

s-rut , Rev. 15, 162; see .

s-ruṭ , , , ; see .

s-ruṭ-tȧ , planted; see .

serpet , nettle (?) mustard; compare Heb. סִרְפָּד, Isaiah lv, 13.

serpeṭ , mustard.

seref , Sphinx Stele 6, , , rest, repose, leisure, refreshment; Copt. ⲥⲣ̄ϥⲉ, ⲥⲣⲟϥⲧ.

seref , to be hot, warm, warmth, heat, flame, fire, the vigour produced by heat; , Wild Cattle scarab; compare Heb. שָׂרַף.

seref , , , water flood, inundation.

Seref , Edfû I, 80, a title of the Nile-god.

s-rem , to make to weep; caus. of ; Copt. ⲣⲓⲙⲉ.

s-rerem , to make to weep.

serem , water flood, torrent.

Serem , B.D. 39, 9, a foe of Āapep.

Serem-taui , Nesi-Ȧmsu 32, 27, a form of Āapep.

serem-t , , , , , , , yeast, barm, sediment, dregs, lees; see ; Copt. ⲥⲟⲣⲉⲙ (?)

seremre[m ?] , fermented liquor.

s-renp , , to rejuvenate; caus. of .

serḥu , to fetter, to overthrow.

s-rekh, to make to know; , Nâstasen Stele 14; caus. of .

serekhi, Peasant 255, the accused, the defendant.

Serekhi, , B.D. 125, II, one of the 42 assessors of Osiris.

serekh, Mission 13, 131, throne; varr. , , .

s-rekhsha, Nâstasen Stele 61, fighter (?); caus. (?)

s-res, , , , to wake up, to keep awake, to be vigilant.

Seres-ḥer, B.D. 147, 4, the warder of the 3rd Ārit.

Seres-tepu, the warder of the 4th Ārit.

Seresh-en-mau, Denderah IV, 67, a funerary coffer at Denderah.

serq, , , , to open [the windpipe], to breathe; see ,

Serqit, Ṭuat VII, , a goddess who strangled Neḥa-ḥer.

Serq[it], Ṭuat X, the scorpion-goddess of the Ṭuat.

Serqit, U. 599, N. 964, , , , Berg. I, 19, Cairo Pap. III, 4, the scorpion-goddess; , Mar. Aby. I, 44.

Serq, Ṭuat X, a serpent-god.

serq, Nâstasen Stele 43, an edible plant (?)

Serqi, Tomb Seti I, one of the 75 forms of Rā (No. 36).

serqu, , food, provisions, sustenance, nourishment.

serqu, stream, flood.

serk, scorpion.

serk, to breathe, to snuff the wind; see .

Serṭiu, B.D. 125, II, one of the 42 assessors of Osiris.

seh-t (?), Rec. 31, 22, a portion of the body.

s-hai, , , to turn aside, to turn down, to make to descend; caus. of .

seha, , , to crush, to beat (of the winds), opposition.

seha, destruction, overthrow.

sehi, a kind of seed or grain.

sehi, Rec. 36, 173, to flee, to escape, to hasten.

s-hebi, to put to shame, to disgrace; see , shame, disgrace, ignominy.

seheb-t, shame, disgrace, ignominy.

sehem, to heat, to melt.

seher, seherr, Rec. 4, 21, , , a precious stone, carnelian (?)

s-heri ḥat, to give content to the heart, to pacify; caus. of .

seherri, Peasant 249, one who quiets; , he who keeps Egypt quiet.

sehrȧ, Rev. 13, 43, bark, boat.

s-herp , Rec. 27, 86, to plunge into water; caus. of ; Copt. ϩⲟⲣⲡ.

s-hett , Rec. 17, 44, subjugation; see .

seḥ , to discuss, to talk over a thing, to take counsel; , Dream Stele 27, took counsel with his heart; , Thes. 1295.

seḥu , , wise man, sage, skilled, trained.

seḥ , , Rec. 29, 152, 31, 30, , , hall, chamber, council hall or chamber; plur. .

seḥ menu , U. 605, hall of the shrine.

seḥ-t en unem , dining room.

seḥ en utchā maā , court of justice.

seḥ en menkhut , clothes chamber, wardrobe.

seḥ neter , the name of a tool or instrument.

seḥ neter , , the holy chamber in which Anubis mummified Osiris; plur. , U. 15, , N. 238.

Seḥu , a title of Osiris.

seḥ , U. 193, N. 605, , T. 72, M. 226, , to draw in a net, to pull the cord of a net, to strain, to stretch, to unyoke.

seḥ (?), Bubastis 51, a kind of vessel.

seḥ , to rub, to pound, to crush.

seḥseḥ , to rub away, to pound; see .

seḥseḥ , U. 493, N. 945, a bird.

seḥa , to array, to deck out, to dress.

seḥā (?) , to mummify.

s-ḥāā , to make to rejoice; caus. of .

seḥu , Israel Stele 19, , , B.D. 113, 2, to collect, to gather together; Copt. ⲥⲱⲟⲩϩ.

s-ḥur , to revile, to curse; caus.; Copt. ⲥϩⲟⲩⲉⲣ, ⲥϩⲟⲩⲣ.

s-ḥebi , , , to celebrate a festival, to rejoice, to make glad; caus.

Seḥpu , P. 685, a god (?)

seḥem , , to destroy, to break up, to pound, to chop; varr. , .

s-ḥemi , to turn back, to drive away; caus. of .

s ḥem-t , , , = s-t ḥem-t , , woman; Copt. ⲥϩⲓⲙⲉ.

seḥen , Rev. 12, 34, command; Copt. ⲥⲁϩⲛⲉ.

seḥenti , those who give orders, officers, commanders.

s-ḥeri , Rec. 16, 109, , , , to drive away; caus. of .

Seḥer-t-baiu-s, Ṭuat VIII, a Circle in the Ṭuat.

Seḥerit-ṭu, D.E. 20, Thes. 28, , Berg. II, 8, , , Denderah III, 24, IV, 84, , the goddess of the 3rd hour of the night.

s-ḥes, to turn back (?), to advance against; caus. of .

s-ḥeqa, to make to rule; caus. of .

s-ḥeqr, , to keep hungry, to let hunger, to starve; caus. of ; Copt. ϩⲟⲕⲉⲣ.

s-ḥetep, , , to make to be at peace, to pacify, to appease, to propitiate, to unite with; caus. of .

Seḥetepit [nether], a goddess.

seḥetepi, censer; for the four-fold censer see Bubastis, 51.

seḥetput, propitiatory offerings.

s-ḥetep ḥem (?)-t-s, the title of the prophet of Hathor of Denderah.

s-ḥetch, , to illumine, to light up; caus. of .

sekh, U. 437, N. 760, , Rec. 30, 69, , M. 340, to hold, to grasp; , T. 308; Copt. ⲥⲱϣ, ϣⲱϣ.

sekh, , , to strike, to beat, to strike (the lyre), to play a harp; , beating, bastinado; Copt. ⲥⲁϣ.

sekh-t, , Rec. 35, 126, blow, stripe, beating, punishment.

sekh, to reap; Copt. ⲱⲥϩ, ⲱⲥϧ.

sekh-t, , field; , Rev. 6, 7, garden lands; Copt. ⲥⲱϣⲉ.

Sekhti, Ṭuat I, a field-god in the Ṭuat.

Sekh-t-ḥer, Berg. I, 18, a bird-god.

sekh = = , event, incident.

sekh, to run; **sekhs** ; **sekhsekh** .

sekh, A.Z. 1900, 128, Peasant 188, to be deaf; varr. , , ; Copt. ⲥⲱϩ.

skhi, deaf man.

skhu, deaf.

sekhekh, A.Z. 70, 171, , , , , to weigh, to balance, a measure of length; , Thes. 102, balance of the earth; , Rev. 3, 12; Copt. ϣⲏϣ.

skha, , , to remember, to think out, to commemorate.

skhau, memorial, memorandum, remembrance.

skha, hall.

Skhait-Ḥeru, , , a cow-goddess, a form of Isis or Hathor.

skhai, A.Z. 1866, 103, , IV, 1079, , to be deaf; , IV, 1180, to pay no heed to, to turn away from advice; , IV, 1033, to turn a deaf ear to; , A.Z. 1912, 55, to ignore; Copt. ⲥⲱϩ.

skhai-t, IV, 409, deafness.

skha-t, a kind of plant used in funerary offerings.

skha-t pet, the name of a star or part of the sky near Orion.

skha-t ....., Rec. 30, 185 .....

skhaā, to cut, sword, knife.

skhai, Åmen. 14, 8, to wound; var. , cut, stroke, blow.

Skhaut, B.D. 169, 19, a cow-goddess.

skhab, , A.Z. 1905, 37, , , to lick up, to swallow, to chew up.

skhabiu, devourers.

skhab, to travel.

Skhabes, Zod. Dend., one of the 36 Dekans; Gr. Σουχως.

Skhabsenfunen, Ṭuat III, a warder-god.

skhap, a kind of land.

skham, A.Z. 1879, 62, , to be strong.

skhamu, Peasant 211, to reject, one rejected.

skhar, , , , , to milk; , IV, 743, to milk.

skhar, a kind of tree, log.

skharu, planks.

skharu, IV, 742, 1148, garments made of a kind of linen.

s-kharṭ, , Sphinx 4, 64, to rejuvenate; caus. of .

skhas, to hasten, to run.

s-khaker, , , to ornament, to decorate; caus. of .

skhakeru, decorations.

skhati, Rev. 11, 168, plaited thing; Copt. ⲥⲏϩ.

s-khāi, , , to make to rise up or appear, to celebrate a festival, to crown a king; caus. of .

skhāi-t, IV, 209, rising, appearance, coronation.

Skhāit-baiu-s, a name of Hathor.

s-khār, Rec. 16, 108, to inflame, to stir up to wrath; caus. of .

Skhi, Ṭuat I, Rec. 3, 116, a god in the Ṭuat.

Skhit, Ṭuat I, a gatekeeper-goddess.

skhu, Rec. 30, 192, , = , width, breadth.

skhu-t = , hall, chamber.

skhun, , , to curse, to revile, to ill-wish, wrathful, angry, furious, passionate, irascibility.

skhunnu, angry man.

Skhuni, B.D. 125; see **Serekhi.**

s-khus, A.Z. 1908, 129, to form, to fashion, to build; caus. of .

skheb, , to swallow, to drink; var. .

s-khep = , to make to become; caus. of .

Skhep-kenmem, one of the 36 Dekans.

Skhepti-ser-t, one of the 36 Dekans.

s-khepi, to make to run, to bring, to lead; caus. of ; , a successful advance.

skhep-[t], a kind of grain.

s-kheper, Peasant 199, 289, , to make to be or exist, to fashion, to form, to create, to produce; caus. of .

s-kheperu, , , those who make or create.

s-khemi, to be unmindful of, to forget; caus. of .

skhem, , (*sic*) , , , , , shrine, holy of holies; plur. , , , , , Rec. 29, 166.

skhem, , sistrum.

skhem, Canopus Stele, statue, figure.

skhem ; see .

Skhemi[t], Rec. 12, 13, a goddess.

sekhmekh, IV, 918, to amuse oneself, to rejoice, pleasure.

skhen, P. 176, N. 212, , P. 702, , N. 1204, , U. 51, , , , , to fold in the arms, to embrace, to contain, to hold; , to fold the wings.

skhenn, N. 960.

skhen-t, embrace, she who embraces, *i.e.*, nurse.

skhenu, suckling, babe, any child in arms.

skhenu, T. 196, P. 459, , , embraces.

skhen, , , , , U. 51A, N. 282A, breast offering.

skhen, the name of a festival.

skhen-t, P. 710 ....

skhenui (?), , P. 177, 392, P.S.B. 17, 260, the two horizons.

Skhenit, Berg. I, 24, a form of Sekhmit.

Skhenȧ, Berg. I, 17, an ibis-god.

Skheni, , , Litanie 38, 94, "Embracer"—a title of Rā.

Skhenu, , Ṭuat XI and XII: (1) a singing-god; (2) a bearer of the serpent Meḥen; each god was reborn daily.

Skhen-ur, U. 281, , N. 719, , A.Z. 1910, 128, , B.D.

146, X, 43, , the god who acted as guardian of the 10th Pylon.

Skhen-ba , Tomb of Seti I, one of the 75 forms of Rā (No. 38).

Skhen-Nefer , "Beautiful embracer"—a name of Shu.

Skhen-rekhtt , Berg. II, 13, a name of the Other World.

Skhen-khaibut , Ṭuat VIII, one of the nine gods of the bodyguard of Åfu-Rā.

Skhen-ṭuatiu , Ṭuat XI, the gate of the 11th Division of the Ṭuat.

skhen , , , , to happen, a happening, event, occurrence; , at the happening of the event; , Rosetta Stone, Rec. 6, 11, with good fortune; Copt. ϣⲁϣⲛⲓ, ϣⲥ̄ⲛⲉ, ϣⲥ̄ⲛⲏ.

skhen , Rec. 6, 10, journey, transit.

skhen , , abscess, skin disease.

s-kheni , , , , , to alight, to stand still, to come to rest; caus. of .

skhen-t , , pillar, support; plur. .

skhenut IV , Hh. 365, , Thes. 1218, the four pillars which support the sky.

skhenut , Rec. 3, 48, the four legs of a vessel.

skhen-t , , the double crown of Upper and Lower Egypt; with , the article = Gr. ψχεντ.

skhenu (?) , IV, 1142, cakes (?)

s-khenn , to strike a blow, to smite; caus.

s-khenn , , to overthrow, to dig down a wall; caus.

s-khensh , to make to stink; caus. of ; Copt. ϣⲛⲟϣ.

skher ; plur. , . For the various meanings of the word see .

skher reth , mankind, the ways of men.

skher kha-t , Peasant 209, what is planned in the inmost mind.

skherui , the two jaws.

skheru , chambers.

Skheriu , one of the 42 assessors of Osiris.

Skheriu , , , , , B.D. 125; see **Serekhi.**

Skher-shetau-ur-ā , Ṭuat II, a title of Åfu-Rā.

s-kher , , , , , , to overthrow; caus. of .

Skheru , B.M. 32, 34, the overthrown, the damned, the defeated.

Skher-ānṭ-f , , , B.D. 149, VI, the serpent-god of the 6th Åat; Saïte var. .

Skher-reremu , B.D. (Saïte) 149, the god of the 6th Åat.

skheru , Shipwreck 64, plated (?) scale-work (?)

s-khert, to rejuvenate; caus. of .

skhes, U. 157, T. 14, , P. 708, M. 251, 378, , Metternich Stele 59, to run, to hasten; var. .

skhesu, Israel Stele 5, swift runners, hasty fugitives.

skhes, A.Z. 1908, 129, to provide, to supply, to make.

s-khesef, to make to go back, to repulse; caus. of .

skhet, , Peasant 207, , to snare birds in a net.

skhet, , net.

skhet, Pap. 3024, 139, fowler, hunter, snarer.

s-kheṭ, , to be turned upside down, to stand on the head; caus. of .

skheṭiu, , , men and women immersed in fire head downwards.

skheṭiu, fiends, the damned.

Skheṭui, the two ape-gods of the 7th day of the month.

s-kheṭkheṭ, Rec. 29, 151, to overturn, to be thrown down; see and .

ses, U. 247, 249, , , Rec. 31, 30, , to strengthen, to raise up.

ses, IV, 1141, treasure, stuff.

ses, , = **s-sen**, , , to breathe, to smell; caus. of .

ses (?), trouble, want.

ses, , door bolt; plur. , , , , .

ses, horse; Heb. סוּס.

ses, Shipwreck 72, hot ashes; = ; see .

ses, a garment of some kind.

ses, Canopus Stele 21 . . . .

ses-ti (?), the two ankles.

Sesa, Berg. I, 13, a god who told his fellows the name of the deceased.

sesi = , P. 293, , T. 259, , U. 447, to move, to walk, to pass.

Sesi, Ṭuat IX, an enchanted serpent.

sesu, Rec. 30, 72 . . . .

sesun, , to destroy.

sesunṭ, Hymn to Rā (Ani 20, 10) . . . .

s-suteni, to make to reign; caus. of .

Sesba, Denderah IV, 59, a ram-god.

s-sepṭ, Peasant 286, to prepare, to sharpen weapons.

sesef, , fire, hot ashes, tinder (?)

sesef-t, disgust, indignation.

sesem-t, , horse, mare (?); plur. ; Heb. סוּסִים.

sesen-t, IV, 918, breathing, breath, smell.

s-sen , P. 457, , Rec. 31, 175, , Rec. 31, 174, to make to open.

s-sens , to acclaim, to congratulate; caus. of .

s-sent = , to terrify, to make afraid; caus. of .

Sesent-ȧakhut , , a lioness-goddess in the Ṭuat.

sesḥa , a kind of weapon or neck-stick for prisoners or slaves (?)

sesḥen (?) , to destroy.

s-setchem (*sic*), B.D. 169, 21, to make to hear; caus. of .

sesh , P. 169, 287, , Düm. Hist. In. II, 18, , , Rechnungen 4, 70, , , , Methen 8, to write, to draw, to make a design; , to do into writing; , Tombos 8, , IV, 692, chased work in metal, figured (bronze); Copt. ⲥϩⲁⲓ, ⲥϧⲁⲓ.

sesh , P. 695, , , , writing, inscription, written roll of papyrus, book, copy of a document, handwriting; plur. , , , , , , , , , , , IV, 337, writings, letters, books, documents, archives, decrees, handwriting, the columns of a book, papers, title-deeds, registers, literature; , established in writing; , Rec. 21, 91, fine papyrus rolls; Copt. ⲥϩⲁⲓ.

seshit , L.D. III, 140B, Rec. 19, 19, wall-paintings, mural designs with descriptive texts.

sesh Uinen , the writings of the Greeks, *i.e.*, the Greek language and letters.

sesh meṭut neter , Rosetta Stone, sacred writing, hieroglyphs.

sesh shaȧ , the writing of books, *i.e.*, demotic.

seshu en ȧsut , IV, 1120, old registers.

seshu nu per ānkh , hieroglyphic writing; , Rev. 12, 112, copyists of hieroglyphic texts.

seshu en rā , Amherst Pap. 20, books of practical magic.

sesh en Ḥa-nebu (nebu Meḥt) , Greek writing.

sesh nu ḥetch nub , , register of silver and gold.

sesh en shātt , demotic writing.

seshu ḥebsu , IV, 1110, closed books.

sesh , , , , writer, designer, scribe; plur. , , ; , Rec. 31, 10, a divine scribe; , P. 185, , M. 300, , N. 399, the two divine scribes Thoth and Sesheta.

sesh-t sḥem-t , a female scribe.

sesh aḥ-t , scribe or registrar of fields or estates; plur. , IV, 1120.

sesh āa 〔hiero〕, IV, 1026, 〔hiero〕, chief scribe.

sesh menfit 〔hiero〕, scribe of the militia.

sesh meṭut neter 〔hiero〕, 〔hiero〕 〔hiero〕, Rec. 31, 174, scribe of the words of the god, *i.e.*, a scribe who copied hieroglyphic texts.

sesh metcha-t 〔hiero〕, 〔hiero〕, writer of books, a copyist of hieratic texts.

sesh metcha-t en Ḥeru ka nekht, 〔hiero〕, scribe of the book of Horus, the mighty Bull.

sesh metcha-t neter 〔hiero〕 〔hiero〕 Rec. 33, 3, scribe of books of the god, *i.e.*, theological scribe.

sesh en neter ḥe-t 〔hiero〕, scribe of the temple.

sesh en setem 〔hiero〕, "scribe of hearing," *i.e.*, a scribe who wrote from dictation; 〔hiero〕, great deputy scribe.

sesh ḥeri tchatcha 〔hiero〕, chief scribe.

sesh ḥesb ḥeq-t 〔hiero〕, IV, 1045, scribe of the reckoning of the grain.

sesh ḥetep neter 〔hiero〕, scribe of the offerings made to the god, *i.e.*, registrar of ecclesiastical revenues; 〔hiero〕, scribe of the revenues of all the gods.

sesh khau-t 〔hiero〕, 〔hiero〕, scribe of the altar.

sesh kheri khetem-t 〔hiero〕, Décrets 23, scribe of the things under seal.

sesh kheri tchatcha 〔hiero〕, deputy scribe.

sesh khetem-t (?) neter 〔hiero〕, IV, 1165, scribe of the sealing of the god.

seshu sunu 〔hiero〕, scribe of the wages list.

sesh spekhar per en Pteḥ 〔hiero〕 〔hiero〕, scribe and designer of the house of Ptaḥ.

sesh seḥu 〔hiero〕, scribe of the collectings.

sesh shāit 〔hiero〕, Rec. 21, 96, letter scribe, secretary, clerk.

sesh shā-t en Āa-perti 〔hiero〕 〔hiero〕 scribe of the rolls of Pharaoh, a royal secretary.

sesh ..... 〔hiero〕, scribe to the magistrate.

sesh qeṭut 〔hiero〕, 〔hiero〕, 〔hiero〕, Rec. 34, 48, 〔hiero〕, IV, 1056, 〔hiero〕, 〔hiero〕, drawer of pictures, limner; 〔hiero〕, limner of the house of gold; 〔hiero〕, limner of the temple of Ptaḥ; 〔hiero〕, limner of Āmen.

Sesh 〔hiero〕, P. 185, 〔hiero〕, M. 300, 〔hiero〕, N. 899, 〔hiero〕, B.D. (Saïte) 70, 1, divine scribe, *i.e.*, Thoth; dual, Thoth and Sesheta (?)

Seshit 〔hiero〕, B.D.G. 1125, a consort of Thoth; var. 〔hiero〕.

Sesh netch (?) 〔hiero〕, the god of the 12th day of the month.

seshu 〔hiero〕, 〔hiero〕, IV, 731, ink, materials for ink; 〔hiero〕, IV, 706, coloured ochres used by scribes; 〔hiero〕, to rub down colour for ink.

seshu 〔hiero〕, Rec. 30, 183 = 〔hiero〕 = 〔hiero〕, dribblings.

sesh 〔hiero〕, to sprinkle, to spread; Copt. ϣⲱϣ.

sesh 〔hiero〕, 〔hiero〕, 〔hiero〕, 〔hiero〕, 〔hiero〕, 〔hiero〕, 〔hiero〕, 〔hiero〕, 〔hiero〕, 〔hiero〕, 〔hiero〕, 〔hiero〕, 〔hiero〕, to draw the bolts of a door, to open, to pass through, to

make a passage, passage, opening, to spread out a skin (IV, 1104); [hieroglyphs], to inaugurate an altar; [hieroglyphs], M. 170, to cut or pare the nails. [hieroglyphs] is a mistake for [hieroglyphs], just as [hieroglyphs] is for [hieroglyphs].

sesh-t [hieroglyphs], passage, open way.

sesh [hieroglyphs], courses, openings (?); [hieroglyphs], free, unfettered.

seshu [hieroglyphs], Rev. 10, 136, ancestors.

sesh [hieroglyphs], [hieroglyphs], [hieroglyphs], to beat out, to spread out.

sesh [hieroglyphs], B.M. 569, product, material, substance.

seshut [hieroglyphs], divisions (?)

sesh [hieroglyphs], [hieroglyphs], room, chamber.

seshsh [hieroglyphs] = [hieroglyphs].

seshsh [hieroglyphs], U. 492, N. 945, to water.

sesh-t [hieroglyphs], U. 551, A.Z. 49, 58, urine.

sesh-t [hieroglyphs], outflow, overflow.

seshsesh [hieroglyphs], a kind of drink.

sesh [hieroglyphs] (?), P. 242, to decay; var. [hieroglyphs] (?) [hieroglyphs], P. 241.

sesh [hieroglyphs], to scorn, to despise, scorn, contempt; [hieroglyphs], Rev. 13, 13; Copt. ⲥⲱϣ.

sesh [hieroglyphs], [hieroglyphs], devil, a devilish man.

sesh-tȧ [hieroglyphs], a man with devilish qualities.

sesh [hieroglyphs], N. 404, [hieroglyphs], IV, 157, [hieroglyphs], Hymn Darius 29, [hieroglyphs], [hieroglyphs], [hieroglyphs], [hieroglyphs], [hieroglyphs], [hieroglyphs], swamp, home of waterfowl, nest; plur. [hieroglyphs], Pap. 3024, 95, [hieroglyphs], [hieroglyphs]; [hieroglyphs], the young king; [hieroglyphs], IV, 564; [hieroglyphs], the two great nests, B.D. 17; [hieroglyphs], the two pools of sport.

Sesh [hieroglyphs], the name of a god and of a city.

sesh [hieroglyphs], hair, tress, lock.

sesh [hieroglyphs], IV, 391, to shine, to give out light.

sesh [hieroglyphs], night, evening, darkness; see [hieroglyphs].

sesh [hieroglyphs], [hieroglyphs], [hieroglyphs], able, skilful, knowledge, learned man.

Seshit-m'k-t-neb-s [hieroglyphs], Ṭuat I and II, one of the pilot-goddesses of Åf.

sesh [hieroglyphs], a kind of cake or bread used for offerings.

sesh-t [hieroglyphs], [hieroglyphs], a kind of grain (?) used in offerings.

seshsh [hieroglyphs], a kind of grain or fruit.

sesh [hieroglyphs], P. 241, 242, sistrum.

seshshit [hieroglyphs], [hieroglyphs], [hieroglyphs]; [hieroglyphs], sistrum; plur. [hieroglyphs], [hieroglyphs], Rec. 15, 47, [hieroglyphs], IV, 1059, [hieroglyphs]; [hieroglyphs], "sing ye to sistra"; [hieroglyphs], IV, 917, [hieroglyphs], statues with sistra; [hieroglyphs], Canopus Stele 6, 29, 31, 34.

seshsh [hieroglyphs], to rattle a sistrum.

seshshit [hieroglyphs], A.Z. 1908, 16, a kind of amulet.

seshsesh, U. 392, lotus (?); see .

seshesh = , lotus flower, lily.

seshsh, to weigh, to balance; see .

sesha, to be wise, skilled, trained; , Rec. 29, 164, , Shipwreck, 139, to make to know, to inform.

s-shai, IV, 943; see .

seshau, riches, what is advantageous; **em sesha** , Shipwreck 129, with luck or good fortune.

Seshshȧ, Ṭuat X, a god who announced to the stars the birth of Rā daily.

seshȧ = , to pass; Copt. ⲥⲓⲛⲉ.

seshȧu sau, skilled, able, wise.

s-shāṭ, to destroy; caus. of ; Copt. ϣⲱⲧ.

seshi, N. 1339 . . . .

seshit, , A.Z. 1900, 23, night, evening, darkness.

seshu, IV, 722, , , , IV, 935, ring, ring-money.

seshu, T. 377, to be loose, untied.

seshu (read sekher) A.Z. 1900, 129, concern, business.

seshu, writings, documents.

s-shu, free from, vacant, empty; caus. of .

Seshu, Nebqed 12, 19, a form of Set.

seshua = , to praise, to honour.

s-shebṭ, to exhaust, to render helpless; caus. of .

seshep = , Rec. 27, 222, 34, 176, 182, to receive. For words beginning with the sign see also under **shesep.**

seshep, P. 624, M. 607, N. 1211, , to polish.

seshep, , , , , , , , , light, radiance, day, daytime, the solar disk.

Seshpi, , , the Light-god.

seshep, white apparel, bandlet.

seshef, Rev. 14, 22, to abominate, to despise.

seshem, , , , , , to guide, to lead, to direct, to administer, to govern.

seshem-t, , guidance, administration.

seshmi-t, guide (fem.)

seshmu, , , guides, leaders.

seshem, , image or statue of a god.

Seshmi, Ṭuat X, a winged-serpent.

Seshmi-uat-ḥeḥ, Guide of the path of eternity—a title of Rā.

Seshmi-pet, Guide of heaven—a title of Rā.

Seshmi-en-uat-ṭeser-t, Ṭuat IV, a god of Restau.

Seshem-en-Tem, Ṭuat VIII and XI, a form of Tem which sprang from the serpent Ānkhfemkhaibit, a form of Tem in the Circle Sesheta.

Seshem-neteru, leader of the gods.

Seshem-netherit, Tomb Seti I, one of the 75 forms of Rā (No. 37).

Seshmit-ḥeri-ȧb-t uȧa-t-s, the goddess of the 5th hour of the night.

Seshemseshem (?), Ṭuat XI, one of the 12 bearers of Meḥen into the eastern sky.

Seshmu-Ṭuat, the guides of the Other World.

Seshmu, one of the 36 Dekans; varr.

s-shem, to make warm or hot, to heat; caus. of

s-shemm, Peasant 245, to warm, to heat; caus. of

s-shemsi, to make to follow; caus. of

seshem shen (?), Rev. 14, 33, mighty formula, strong spell.

seshen, to open, to make a way through; var. of and

seshen, seshni, to weave.

Seshen-ur, Rec. 30, 187, a god; see **Sekhnur**.

seshen-t, web in a hand loom, cloth.

seshenn, a kind of head cloth, fillet.

seshen, U. 501, Metternich Stele 63, to grieve.

s-shen, to alight, to hover over; caus. of

seshen, Rev. 11, 185, lotus, lily; plur. Rec. 29, 148, Pap. 3024, 135, IV, 918, 1165; IV, 1165, summer lily; Heb. שׁוּשַׁן, Syr. ܫܘܫܢܐ, Arab. سوسن. Copt. ϣⲱϣⲉⲛ, Gr. σοῦσον.

seshshen, U. 395, A.Z. 45, 135, lily, lotus; see

seshshen, an offering.

seshen, IV, 629, cup in the form of a lily.

seshen-t [ ], Rec. 36, 210, a place where the deceased purified himself; var.

Seshnit, Rec. 32, 84, the name of a water-goddess.

Seshnnit, , , Lib. Fun. II, 89, the name of a funerary goddess and of a city.

Seshen-uāb, B.D. 81A, "Holy lily"—a title of Rā.

Seshenu en Nefer-Temu B.D. 81B, the lily of Nefer-Temu.

seshnai, Tutānkhāmen 9, to pray.

seshnu, Rec. 28, 169, a fish; plur.

s-sher = , Rec. 16, 108, to fall down, to overthrow; caus. of = .

sesher, Jour. As. 1908, 263, devil.

s-sherr, Peasant 251, to make less, to belittle; caus. of .

sesher, Mission 223, a garment or stuff.

sesheru, , , = , plans, etc.; see .

sesher-t, IV, 1159, , bread cake, food.

sesher-t, dung, excrement.

Seshrui urui, , Ombos I, 143, the two sacred arrows of Ombos.

sesher, L.D. III, 140D, blocked up, stopped.

s-shes, to open, to unbolt; caus. of .

seshes (?), a kind of wood or precious stone.

seshsa (shesa), Precepts of Åmenemḥat 1, 12, , Åmen. 27, 26, , Anastasi IV, 2, 7, , , , , , , , to be skilled, able, clever, , IV, 1152, skilful.

seshsa-t (shesa-t), , skill, ability.

seshsa, Rec. 21, 84, to go.

seshsa (sesha), night, evening, darkness.

seshsait (seshait), , a seed used in medicine.

seshsau (seshau), Anastasi IV, 2, 6, , Koller 2, 4, antelope, deer, goat, roe.

Seshesp-taui, Ombos I, 108, a lioness fire-goddess.

sesht, to weave; var. .

sesht, Rev. 12, 71, a strip of blue linen.

sesht, Rec. 13, 30, figure, form.

s-sheta, IV, 671, , to hide, to keep secret, to conceal; caus. of ; Copt. ϣⲱϣⲧ.

seshetat, , , , , , Rev. 11, 186, , secret, mystery; plur. , , , , , ,

, it is a very real mystery; , mysteries of the god of the horizon.

Seshta , Ṭuat VIII, a circle in the Ṭuat.

Seshtai , , "He who is secret"—a divine title.

Seshtai , Tomb of Seti I, one of the 75 forms of Rā (No. 44).

Seshtait , Thes. 31, , the goddess of the 4th hour of the day.

Seshtait åru , goddess of the 10th hour of the day.

Seshtau åru , beings with invisible forms.

Seshta Åsår , B.D. 168, VII, 1, a bull-god.

Seshta baiu , Ṭuat VIII, one of the nine guards of Rā.

Seshta ren , "Hidden name"—a title of God.

seshta , bandlet, tiara.

seshtu , crocodiles, secret powers of evil.

seshṭ , , , , bandlet, cord of a book, girdle, etc.; see .

seshṭ , lock of hair.

seshṭ-t , , window, balcony (?); plur. , , Rec. 27, 222; Copt. ϣⲟⲩϣⲧ.

seshṭer (?) , Rec. 11, 64, a light-shooting star, .

seq , , , , , to gather together, to collect.

Seq uarf , Ombos I, 61, a hunting-god.

seq , , a kind of pulse (?) leaf; plur. , Rec. 4, 27; , Annales IX, 156.

s-qa , , to exalt, to prolong life; caus. of .

Sqaiu , , the gods who exalt men and prolong their lives; compare the following name:—

Seqa-nu-baiu-peter-ḥeḥ , Thes. 31, the goddess of the 3rd hour of the day.

sqa — , IV, 809; see **seqrȧ ānkh** .

s-qebb , Rec. 30, 189, , , to cool, to refresh; caus. of .

Seqbeb , the doorkeeper of the 3rd Pylon; compare the following:—

Seqbit , B.D. 142, 5, 25, a goddess.

seqer , , , , to strike, to beat (a drum), to break open a door.

seqrȧ ānkh , IV, 612, a combatant captured alive; compare the following:—

Seqrȧ-tchatchau , Ṭuat VII, a star-god.

s-qeṭi , Metternich Stele 224, , , to travel, to sail; caus. of .

s-qeṭṭ , to travel, to sail.

Seqṭ-t , B.D. (Saïte) I, 18, a boat of Orion, .

seqeṭiu, wandering stars; compare the two following names:—

Seqeṭ-ḥati, etc., Ombos II, 134, a mythological being.

S-qeṭi-ḥer, B.D. 144, the watcher of the 2nd Ārit.

sek = .

seki, U. 426, , T. 244, , to dig out a lake.

seki, to constrain, to contend against, to fight.

seki, to destroy, to bring to an end.

Seki, Ṭuat XII, one of the gods who towed the boat of Åf through Ānkh-neteru; he was reborn daily.

seksek, U. 530, , IV, 812, to crush, to destroy.

Seksek, B.D. 35, 3, a serpent-god who attacked the dead; var. .

Seksekit, B.D. 75, 4, a goddess; var. .

sek = .

s-kek, to make dark, to darken, to cover over; caus. of .

skek, IV, 1057 ......

ska, to plough; Copt. ϹΚⲀⲒ.

ska, Rec. 3, 53, with ....

s-kami, , , to bring to an end, to make complete, to finish; caus. of ; , perfect of tongue, *i.e.*, skilled in speech, eloquent.

skam, to be old and grey-haired.

skami, , , old man, grey-headed man; plur. , the aged; Copt. ϹΚⲒⲘ.

s-kamkam, Thes. 1199; caus. of .

s-kep, to flood, to inundate; caus. of .

skep, , to strike, to overthrow, to roll away.

skem, Rec. 5, 90 ....

Skemu nen-t, , B.D. 78, 44, a group of gods.

sken, to eat or drink in a gluttonous manner.

sken-tȧ, habitual glutton or drunkard.

skennu, oil, unguent, salve, pomatum.

Skenu, Ṭuat X, a light-god.

s-ker = , to put to silence.

seker, a place shut in, the coffin.

Seker, Sekri, U. 326, 556, 557, , T. 270, , N. 953, , , , , originally the god of the Ṭuat of Memphis, later the Death-god par excellence.

Sekri, a form of Seker in the Ṭuat.

Seker [ ], , Seker, personification of his domain.

Seker, Denderah IV, 84, , Berg. II, 8, , warder of the 6th Pylon.

Seker, Berg. I, 16, a god who filled the deceased with Truth.

Seker em shetait, a form of Osiris.

Sekri ḥeri shā-f, Ṭuat IV, a form of Seker.

Seker khenti Petchu, P. 607.

Seker, , the festival of Seker.

Seksen, P. 650, , P. 726, , M. 751, a messenger, , of Rā.

Sekt, Denderah II, 48, 49, a name given to several of the sacred boats at Denderah.

Sekti, Sekt-t, , , the boat of the setting sun which bore Åfu-Rā through the Ṭuat; see .

Sekt-t, the god of the Sekt-t boat.

Sekktiāks, Leemans Mon. 3, 210–213 = Gr. Σιαξ.

Seg, a mythological animal; see **Sega.**

seg ...., Pap. 3024, 26........

Sega, a mythological animal with a hawk's head.

sega, Rev. 11, 124, to covet, to seize (?)

segab, Israel Stele 24, , A.Z. 34, 8, to shout, to raise a cry.

s-gāa, Rec. 27, 88, to destroy, to let perish; caus. (?)

Segi, Ṭuat I, a singing-god.

segeb, Metternich Stele 7, to cry out.

s-gemḥ, Peasant 213, to make to see; caus. of .

s-genn, to make weak or helpless; caus. of .

s-genn, , , , to anoint; caus. of ; ⲥⲟϭⲛ.

seger, to strike, to fight; see .

s-ger, Rec. 26, 65, , , , to make silent, to still, silence, rest; caus. of .

sgergu, parts of a ship.

set, absolute pron. 3rd sing., common.

set, later form of .

Set (Setesh = Sutekh, , , , , , the god of evil.

Set, B.D. 42, protector of the backbone of Osiris.

Set, Ṭuat V, a bull-god who destroyed the dead.

Set, Edfû I, 9 fgh, a god of and and .

Set nehsi, Ṭuat X, a Set-headed sceptre which was revivified at dawn daily.

set, Jour. As. 1908, 277 = , earth, ground; Copt. ⲥⲏⲧ.

set, , , , Jour. As. 1908, 290, ground, earth, soil; see .

sti, , , , smell, scent, or odour; Copt. ⲥϯ.

sti-ḥeb, festival scent or perfume.

Sti-ḥer, Tomb. Ram. IX, 10, a serpent-god.

set (sti), Nav. Lit. 71, , Rec. 12, 48, , to light a fire, to burn.

set-t, , , Hymn Darius 15, fire, flame; , divine fire; Copt. ⲥⲁⲧⲉ.

stu ḥeb, the name of the 25th day of the month.

Set em år-t-f, Ṭuat III and IV, a fiery serpent-god of the 5th Gate.

Set em ḥer-f, Ṭuat III, a serpent-god in the boat Herer.

Set ḥeḥ, Ṭuat XI, "Everlasting fire," a fiery serpent that destroyed all who tried to escape from the pits of fire.

set, sti, , Rec. 32, 67, to eject seed, to beget, to sow seed.

sti, U. 157, , to sow seed; Copt. ⲥⲓϯ.

Sti, title of the priest of Elephantine.

set, thread, string, cord.

set, hairy tail; varr. , .

sti, the festival of the tail; see .

sett, , , ; , to quake, to tremble; see ; Copt. ⲥⲧⲱⲧ.

sett, U. 491, N. 915, trembling, quaking.

setti, A.Z. 1905, 19, the leaping of fish.

sta, , to pull, to haul, to drag, to draw, to tow; see .

staiu, , those who bring along, towers of a boat.

Sta, Mar. Aby. I, 45, a god of .

stan-t, draughtboard (?); var. .

staḥ, Rev. 14, 46, to reject, to cast aside.

staḥ-t, Rev. 14, 46, refuse, waste.

s-taḥen, to make bright or shining, to clarify; caus. of or .

stå, P. 265, , M. 476, N. 1244, , , the White Crown.

S-t-ån, Thes. 818, Rec. 16, 106, a goose-god.

sti...., Åmen. 10, 8 ....

Stu, Ṭuat X, a light-god.

s-tut, to collect, to gather together; caus. of .

s-tut, IV, 973, , , Hymn Darius 43, to observe some custom, to do something that is usually done, to make a copy or image, to fashion, to typify, to symbolize; , Thes. 1483, to compare in words; caus. of .

steb, , to enjoy, to relish; var. .

step, , to select, to choose; Copt. ⲥⲱⲧⲡ.

step, to cut, to cut off.

step = .

stef, Rec. 27, 83, , , foam, froth (of beer).

stef, , , to cut, to slay for sacrifice.

stem, to hear; Copt. ⲥⲱⲧⲙ; see **setchem**.

Stennu, Edfû I, 77, a title of the Nile-god.

s-ten; IV, 350, , to distinguish, to make a difference between, to exalt; , making a difference between the languages of all countries; caus. of .

Sten taui, A.Z. 1872, 109, B.D. (Saïte) 125, 62, a title of Thoth.

sten, to slay, to kill.

stenu, the White Crown.

s-tenem, B.D. 151, V, 3, to lead astray, to mislead; caus. of .

steḥ, , , to split, to open.

s-teḥen, to sparkle, to twinkle (of stars), to scintillate, to make light; caus. of or .

Setekh = = = Set, the god of evil.

Setesh; var. of and , the later , the god of evil.

s-teken, to make to approach, to bring near; caus. of .

stekniu, , porters, those who bring in offerings, invaders.

steg, , to hide oneself, to take refuge.

seth, , , , , , , to asperge, to pour out a libation; see .

seth-t, , libation basin; plur. .

seth, smell, odour, scent; , the smell of flesh; Copt. ⲥϯ.

seth, hair, tail.

setha, , to tow, to drag, to pull, to lead.

sethaiut, those who tow the boat of Rā.

sethau, , corridors or passages through which boats are towed.

s-tham, , , to dress, to clothe, dress, apparel, garment; caus.

s-tham, Rec. 27, 86, to fecundate.

sthar, Rec. 5, 96 = , , to lie down.

Sethasiu, Ṭuat. X, a class of beings on the waters of the Ṭuat.

Sethu, Ṭuat VIII, a serpent-god.

sethuit, cords, strings.

sethep, to slay, to kill.

sethepu, the slain in the Ṭuat.

s-them, to wrap up in cloth, to bandage; var. .

sethen, draughtboard (?); var.

sethen, conspicuous, prominent; varr.

s-then, Ebers Pap. 94, 9, , to distinguish, to make a difference; caus. of .

sethen ḥer, of distinguished appearance.

sethenu, distinctions, distinguishing qualities or attributes.

Sethenu, Denderah IV, 67, a sacred coffer at Denderah.

Sethenu, Edfû I, 21, an ape-god—an associate of Thoth; var. .

Sethenit, Ṭuat XI, a group of four goddesses—servants of Maāt.

Sethen-ḥat, Ṭuat IV, a god of the South.

Sethen-ḥath, Ṭuat IV, the name of a god in the Ṭuat.

Sethenu-tep (?), Ṭuat XI, a group of southern god-kings.

s-thenem, to turn back, to turn aside or away, to lead astray; caus. of .

sether, to be shaken, disturbed.

sether-t, Rec. 30, 72, eyelids, eyelashes (?); , Hh. 209.

s-theḥen, to sparkle, to scintillate, to coruscate; caus. of .

s-thes, (*sic*), B.D. 140, 13, , to exalt, to lift up; , to raise a song of praise; caus. of .

sethesu, those who raise songs of praise or recite words of power.

sethes, what is supported or exalted, the sky, heaven.

sethes Shu, what supports Shu ( ).

sethesu Shu, B.D. 110, 13, , B.D. 18, 9, the four supports of Shu.

sethes, Rev. 11, 119, a carrying pole, staff.

s-thes, to unravel, to untie, to solve a difficulty; caus. of .

s-theken, to penetrate; , to copulate; caus.

sethtȧ, P. 265, , N. 1244, the White Crown of Upper Egypt.

sethetch, to burn; Copt. ⲥⲁⲧⲉ.

seṭ, stone, flint (?)

seṭ, Pap. 3024, 79, , Edict 28, to break, to smash, to break open, to cut, to pierce.

seṭ-t, breach, break.

Seṭ-qesu, B.D. 125, II, a god of Ḥensu, one of the 42 assessors of Osiris; varr.

seṭ, tail, rump; , A.Z. 35, 17, 11, the tail in the mouth; Copt. ⲥⲁⲧ.

seṭ, hair, fur, foliage of trees.

seṭ-t, flame, fire; see .

seṭ, to sow seed; see .

seṭ, a strong smell, odour, scent, perfume; see .

seṭ, to dress, to array in fine apparel.

seṭṭ, Thes. 1204, to quake, to tremble; Copt. ϲⲧⲱⲧ.

sṭa, Rec. 34, 177, IV, 614, to tremble, to quake.

sṭaṭa = ; Copt. ϲⲧⲱⲧ.

sṭau, palsy, quaking paralysis.

Sṭa-ta, Ṭuat IV, god of earthquakes.

s-ṭa, to lay, to place; caus. of .

seṭ aḥ, Temp. Inschr. 79, 28 = , a parcel of land.

sṭit, bandlet, headcloth, kafîyyah, pagari.

sṭu, to chew.

sṭu, B.D. 64, 35 (Nebseni), oars (?)

s-ṭu, to make bad, to defame, to decry, to vilify; caus.

sṭukh, to embalm, to mummify.

sṭeb, Amherst Pap. 1, Peasant 50, B.D. 71, 3, bandlet, belt, girdle, hangings of a shrine, part of a square cloth, fringe.

sṭeb, to chew food, to eat, to drink.

sṭeb, misery, trouble, disaster; plur. .

s-ṭebeḥ, to provide, to equip, to supply; caus. of .

sṭef, to cut, to slay.

Sṭefit, Ṭuat X, a mythological axe, from which proceed Netheth and Kenȧt.

Sṭefiu, Ṭuat X, a group of gods of slaughter who fetter Āapep.

sṭefu, fetters, ropes of torture.

sṭef, to purify, to clarify.

Sṭef, Edfû I, 81, a title of the Nile-god.

sṭemu, B.D. 99, 11, edicts for slaughter (?)

sṭeni[t], property, wealth.

sṭer, A.Z. 35, 17, to clear a way.

sṭeḥ, A.Z. 45, 130, IV, 968, Thes. 1480, Pap. 3024, 18, to humble, to abase, to push aside.

sṭeḥ, to push open a door.

s-ṭeḥen, to lighten, lightning, storm; caus. of .

sṭekh, to treat with drugs, to mummify.

s-ṭeka, to hide; caus. of .

s-ṭega, Metternich Stele 169, IV, 84, to hide, to hide oneself.

Sṭega-khatt , Berg. II, 11, a form of Åment, as hider of the dead.

Seṭti , Ṭuat XI, the name of a god in the Ṭuat.

s-ṭeṭi , to make permanent or durable; caus. of .

setch , A.Z. 1906, 112, child, babe.

Setchti , Nav. Lit. 61, , Rev. 11, 91, the two children, *i.e.*, Shu and Tefnut.

setchetch , form, image.

s-tcha = , to go, to depart, to die; caus. of .

setchai-t , IV, 1161, a laughing matter, jest, joke.

setchai-t , Book of Gates 128 . . . .

setcham-t , hoe, hatchet.

setchaḥui , the two shin bones of Osiris.

setchit , B.D. 99, 21, a kind of seed.

setcheb , , Rec. 32, 80, 81, disaster, misfortune, calamity.

setchef , to kill, to slay; see .

s-tchefa , , to feed, to provision, to supply, to provide for; caus. of .

setchefa , , food, provisions, supplies.

Setchfit , Ombos I, 47, a hippopotamus-goddess.

setcher , Rec. 26, 229, , B.D. 89, 3, 166, 1, to pass the night, to lie down, to sleep.

setchru , B.D. 99, 22, the dead.

Setcheri-ur , T. 380, a son of Nut.

setcher , Famine Stele 32, strong one, creator.

setcher , to support, to bear up.

setcher , IV, 259, dwelling, strong building.

setcheḥ-t , , shin bone; dual , Metternich Stele 28, , Metternich Stele 158.

Setcheḥ , U. 542, T. 297, P. 236, a serpent-fiend.

s-tcheser , , IV, 217, to beautify, to sanctify; caus. of .

Setchet-t , fire, flame.

Setch-ti , Tomb of Seti I, , Ṭuat II, one of the 75 forms of Rā (No. 71).

s-tcheṭ-t , something published; see , published; , Israel Stele 1, things proclaimed abroad; , Israel Stele 9, 10, to make a proverb of someone; Copt. ϩⲓⲱⲓϣ.

setcheṭ-t , Rec. 2, 111, tales, stories, sayings, speeches, addresses; Copt. ϣⲁϫⲉ.

s-tcheṭef , to wound, to snare; caus. of .

s-tcheṭem , Pap. 3024, 44 . . . .

S

s = Heb. שׁ and שׂ.

s a causative prefix; var.

s = , health, in the formula .

s = **su** , III, 142, absolute pron. 3rd sing. masc.; compare Heb. הוּא.

s, si , , pers. and absolute pron. 3rd fem.; varr. , ; compare Heb. הִיא.

s , = .

s[a] , a man, person, body.

s[a]neb , everybody.

S, St (?) , = **Ȧst,** or **Ȧs-t** , Isis; Copt. ⲏⲥⲉ.

s, sȧ , , , to go, to go away, to depart; , to go up; , to go down.

sa-t , a kind of goose; plur. .

sa-ta , homage, praise.

sa-t , N. 288A, a kind of bird.

sa-t , , attack, overthrow,

sa , U. 615, N. 162, , A.Z. 1899, 45, , A.Z. 1900, 20, to break, to destroy, to constrain.

sasa , , , , , Rec. 9, 38, Jour. E. A. III, 104, to run against, to attack, to charge, to overthrow.

sa , back, hinder parts (later , ,); Copt. ⲥⲟⲓ; , , IV, 968, , high-backed, haughty, proud; with or prefixed, after, in the following of (, , , Ȧmen. 9, 10); , at the back of; , as the result of; , towards, to the back of.

sa , back, , , , , to turn the back in flight, to flee; , .

sa , A.Z. 1906, 130, a shrine or sanctuary in which a god or goddess was housed.

sa, saut , Rec. 33, 69, , , , , , , , , , IV, 840, , IV, 684, , M. 379, , N. 656; plur. , , , , Rec. 30, 186, a wall, walled building, fort, castle, fortified gateway.

sa, sȧa , , , , , , , , varr. , , to know; , unknown, unheeded, disregarded.

sau, IV, 969, Rev. 8, 73, , , sage, wise man, one who is educated.

saȧu, U. 487, N. 938, the wise, wise ones.

sa-t, N. 1135, , wisdom, knowledge, learning.

Sa, Sȧa, N. 657, , M. 387, , Rec. 31, 29, , IV, 498, , , , , , wisdom or knowledge deified.

Sau , , the god of the 3rd hour of the day.

Sa-ur, U. 396, , , B.D. 174, 16, a god in the Ṭuat.

sa, U. 562, the magical strength of the god .

sa neter, the god's protection; , U. 562, "Governor of the god's protection."

sa-Ḥeru, , , dawn, morning; compare Heb. שַׁחֲרִים.

sa Ḥer-t, A.Z. 1908, 17, an amulet.

sa, T. 338, , N. 625 . . . .

sa, sai, Rec. 27, 57, , Rec. 15, 39, , , , , , , , , , , , , , to be full, filled full, satisfied; , U. 518, , T. 328, full, glutted; , Rec. 32, 79; Copt. ⲥⲉⲓ.

sai, Jour. As. 1908, 274, , Rev. 13, 7, satiety; Copt. ⲥⲉⲓ.

sau, Peasant 242, , , Ȧmen. 23, 15, , , Rec. 31, 147, satiety, fullness, drunkenness; , Ȧmen. 25, 8, drunken men.

sa-t, IV, 1182, satiety.

sa-t, offerings of food.

sa-t, , , , , , , , evil, scorn (of a god), moral weakness or evil; var. .

sait, weakness.

sau, corruption, decay.

sai-ā, P. 1116B, 54, , Ȧmen. 21, 4, to be weak or helpless.

sai-ā, IV, 1078, 1079, , , weak-armed, a useless man.

Sa (?), a mythological crocodile.

sa, Rec. 16, 131, tress, hair; plur., P. 1116B, 42.

sa, , , , the name of the 14th and 17th days of the moon.

sa-t (?) ..., Sphinx 6........

sa , B.D. (Saïte), 17, 37, to burn.

Sa-ba , the name of a fiend.

Sa-t , one of the 36 Dekans; Gr. Σρω.

sa-t, sȧa , , , , , , , , , , bandlet, tunic, garment, cloth, mummy swathings, apparel.

sait , , a plant or seed used in medicine.

saut , N. 813........

Saȧ , U. 381, the name of a god made by Geb.

saȧ-t , , dirt, filth.

Saȧpȧ , Rev. 11, 181 ....

saȧr , something bad or evil; , Peasant 136, lack of water.

saȧru , , extortioner, oppressor.

s-ȧakhu , M. 101, , P. 176, , , to glorify, to make bright or shining, to praise, to recite formulae of praise, to do good to, to perform rites; , P. 66, M. 195, N. 34, , good things or qualities.

s-ȧakhut , , glorifications, songs of praise, formulae recited for the benefit of the spirit-souls of the dead.

sȧaṭ , to make weak, to reduce; var. .

saȧsi , speech (?) speaker (?

saābu , Gol. 6, 11, loaf, cake.

Saār , Harris 76, 9, name of a tribe or people; compare Heb. שֵׂעִיר.

saār , , Anastasi III, 6, 9, vegetable growth, underwood, a kind of plant (?)

saārtȧ , , hair of an animal, goat's hair; Copt. ⲤⲞⲢⲦ; Heb. שְׂעָרָה.

saārisa , Rec. 11, 180, soldier's pike; Gr. σάρισα, hat, sarīsa(-issa).

sai , Rec. 4, 26, a kind of crown.

sau , sixty; see the pun in A.Z. 1905, 27; Copt. ⲤⲈ.

s-au , Peasant 272, , IV, 618, caus. of , to extend, to make wide or broad, to rejoice.

s-au ȧb (ḥat) , to make glad the heart, to rejoice.

s-au , P. 465, , N. 1107, to masturbate.

sau , Thes. 1296, to watch, to guard.

sau , beam of wood, pillar, post, pole; see .

sau, sau-t , Treaty 17, , , , A.Z. 1905, 26, 27, 1913, 14, absolute pron. 3rd sing.

sau , , , gold.

sau , Rechnungen 67, vessel, a moist substance (?)

sauababa , Anastasi I, 23, 4, to withdraw, to shrink back, to return; compare Heb. תּוּב, Syr. ܬܳܒ, Arab. ثاب.

sauṭ, to quake, to fear, to be afraid.

sab, jackal; plur.; var.

Sabu àmiu she en ānkh, Ṭuat IV, the jackal-gods of the Lake of life.

sab, Rec. 29, 157, to melt away, to drip away (of the body in the earth).

sabu, Hh. 269 . . . .

sab-t, Rev. 12, 117, hill, mountain.

saba, enemy, wicked man.

sabar, Anastasi III, 12, 2, Harris I, 37A, 7, bush, thicket, vine, berries: compare Heb. שִׁבֹּלֶת, the supposed singular of שִׁבֳּלִים.

sabar, Anastasi IV, 13, 1, P.S.B. 13, 412, a liquid made from the same (?)

sabi, Rev. 13, 3, to smile, to laugh; Copt. ⲥⲱⲃⲓ.

sabiu, foes, enemies.

sabi-t, Rev. 13, 23, reed; plur.; Copt. ⲥⲏⲃⲓ.

sabmer, Àmen. 27, 17, friend, companion; Copt. ϣⲃⲉⲣ, ϣⲫⲏⲣ. A mistake for **smer**.

Sabs, B.D. 144, the herald of the 2nd Ārit; varr.

sap-t, Rec. 30, 68, a plant.

Sapt-khenti, (*sic*), Tombs Seti I, Ram. II, one of the 36 Dekans; Gr. Σπτχνε;

Saparar, L.D. III, 146, 14, a Hittite king; in cuneiform Shu-ub-bi-lu-li-u-ma.

Sapathar, Mar. Aby. II, Text 5, 10, a Hittite chief.

sapā, Khnemuḥetep 206; read, P.S.B. 12, 88.

Sapertargessu, Gol. 4, 9, 10, a Hittite country.

safit, Rev. 14, 21, sword.

s-am, to seize, to grasp; caus. of.

sam, wild bull; fem.

Sam-ur, T. 273, T. 359; see **Smaur**.

s-am, Hh. 521, to kindle, to burn; caus. of.

Sam-ba, "Fiery soul"—the name of a fiend or devil.

samut, hair, locks, tresses.

samāna, a disease.

Samārtasa, L.D. III, 165 (read , Alt. K. 782), a rebel chief or king.

samāktȧ, Rechnungen 59, A.Z. 1909, 86, P.S.B. 19, 263, , prop, support, balk of timber.

samis ; see **sems.**

saninis, A.Z. 51, 70, kinsman; Gr. *συγγενής*.

sanre, Harris 37A, 2, , Hearst Pap. 11, 9, a plant.

sanrȧa ....

sanrua, Koller 4, 5 ....

sar, to go (?)

sar-t, wall (?); see .

sar, Rec. 26, 231, , to act wisely or honourably, honour, good disposition (?) right-mindedness (?); plur. , II, 129; , Ḥeruemḥeb 3, irrational.

sar-t, IV, 1183, , , IV, 67, , IV, 160, Thes. 1282, , IV, 481, , honour, understanding (?); , Ḥeruemḥeb 11, a reasoning intelligence.

sar, Pap. 3024, 28, , to do wrong, to act with perversity.

saru, a perverse man; plur. , , oppressors or oppressed, perverse men, sinners.

Sariu, B.D. 64, 17, a group of gods.

sar-t, N. 612, cake, loaf (?); varr. , U. 205, (?), T. 80, (?), M. 233.

sar-t, , a water plant; Copt. ⲥⲟⲗ (?), Gr. *σαρί*.

sar-t, IV, 548, grain.

sarsar, Love Songs 2, 5, twigs, branches.

sar, a kind of drink.

sarpatȧ, Love Songs 2, 8, a plant; compare Heb. סִרְפַּד, thorn plant, Isaiah lv, 13.

sarem, sediment, dregs, lees.

sarem, , , torrent, water flood.

Sarem, , ; var. , Edfû I, 78, a title of the Nile-god.

sarkh, Rec. 32, 181, to destroy, to waste.

Sarqit, Tomb Seti I, a star-goddess in the northern sky.

sarqu, Alt. K. 801, snow; Heb. שֶׁלֶג, Syr. ܬܠܓܐ, Arab. ثلج.

sartit, , Rev. 6, 26, to cut and gather wheat; Copt. ⲥⲣⲏⲧ.

sarṭ ; see .

sarṭiuṭs, Copt. Cat. = Gr. στρατιώτης, commander-in-chief, general.

sahu, Peasant 20, a plant.

s-ahh, to disgust, to cause loathing; caus. of .

saḥ, , , toe, finger (?); plur. , Rec. 29, 150, , , , ; , feet, legs (?)

saḥ, T. 349, , N. 902, Rec. 31, 170, , Pap. 3024, 152, , , , Shipwreck 34, , ibid. 178, , , , to approach, to draw near to, to succeed in acquiring, to reach land, to land from a boat, to acquire, to possess.

saḥsaḥ, to approach.

saḥ ta, , Peasant 326, to reach the shore, to land.

saḥ-t, IV, 1111, , , Anastasi I, 24, 1, , , , holding, possession, landed property, estate, allotment, site of a temple, homestead, vicinity, environs, neighbourhood; plur. , T. 18, , P. 573.

saḥu, Rec. 20, 42, , property.

saḥ, title deeds (?)

saḥu-ta (?), Love Songs 2, 10, , , , neighbours, the people on a farm or homestead.

saḥ, a wooden object, paddle (?) pole (?)

Saḥ, U. 221, 516, , T. 349, P. 77, 648, , M. 704, , T. 328, , N. 20, , M. 746, N. 917, 1156, , P. 719, , Rec. 26, 229, 27, 221, 32, 84, , , , , , , , , , Thes. 82, Orion, one of the 36 Dekans.

Saḥit, T. 328, , , , , B.D. 23, 5, , Rec. 31, 174, the goddess of Orion.

Saḥit, Ṭuat III, a goddess in the Ṭuat with her face turned behind her.

Saḥu, , , Nesi-Åmsu 27, 21, the star-gods in the constellation of Orion.

Saḥu XII, B.D. 64, 22, the 12 stars of Orion.

Saḥ, the boat of Osiris.

Saḥ-t-ni (?), Rec. 31, 171 ....

Saḥ-en-Mut-f, B.D. 125, III, 30, the door fastening of the Hall of Maāti.

s-akhakh , , P. 427, M. 611, N. 1216, to blow (of flowers), to burst into flower; caus. of .

sakhit , Rev. 14, 16, impudence, arrogance; Copt. ϲⲱϣ.

Sakhiu = , B.D. 64, 8.

s-akhefkhef , Rec. 31, 14, to burn up, to consume; caus. of .

Sakhmit-urr-peḥ (?) , a wind-goddess.

sakhniu , supports, legs of a chair or throne, the four pillars of heaven.

sasnȧ , to anoint.

saskut , Peasant 21, a seed used in medicine (?)

s-ash , IV, 420, to praise; caus.

sash-t (shas-t) , Rec. 31, 27 = (?).

sasher-t , , U. 205, , U. 185, , N. 624, a fire offering of meat and bread.

saq , T. 370, 377, P. 683, , T. 287, , N. 126, 1258, , M. 447, , N. 885, , , Rec. 31, 18, , , , , , , to collect, to gather together, to assemble.

saq-t , P. 204, assembly, gathering.

saq ḥat , to collect the wits or senses.

Saq baiu , , B.D. 58, 4, 122, 2, a title of the divine ferryman Ḥerfḥaf.

Saq ḥā , "Gatherer of members"—a title of Osiris.

saq , , , , , to act with severity or violence, to be strict, to be severe, to behave haughtily.

saqi , a violent man.

saqaiqa-t , Love Songs 4, 3, claw-sheath.

saqu , Rec. 19, 92, to burn, to scorch.

saquti , sculptor; plur. .

Saqnaqait , B.D. 164, 5, a fire-goddess, a Sûdânî form of Sekhmit-Bast-Rā.

s-aqeḥ , P. 707, , to produce, to hew, to carve; caus. of **aqeḥ** , .

sakaȧ , a man given to quarrelling.

sak-t , , fight, strife, a fighting man.

saki , warrior, soldier; plur. , , ; see also .

sakaȧ , an official.

sakamā (?) , a kind of bird.

sakut , young asses; Copt. ⲥⲏϫ.

saker, soldier (?) warrior, fighter.

sag, Rec. I, 46, foolish man (?); Copt. ⲥⲟϭ.

saga, Anastasi I, 23, 2, to march, to walk, to wander.

saga, Anastasi I, 25, 6, hair-cloth; Copt. ⲥⲟⲕ, ⲥⲱⲕ.

sagabin (?), Anastasi III, 3, 7, pool (?) lake (?)

sagartha, wooden weapons, spears (?)

sat, to weaken, to be weak; caus. (?)

Satȧ, U. 534, T. 298, P. 231, a serpent-fiend in the Ṭuat.

Satȧrna, A.Z. 1880, 82, a king of Mitanni and a father-in-law of Ȧmen-ḥetep III; Tell al-Amarna, Shut-[tar-na], Berl. V.A. Th. 271, obv. 18.

satekhta (?), Alt-K. 823, an article of furniture.

sath, to bring, to carry.

sath, barge for stone, lighter.

Sathtȧ, P. 204 + 4, N. 851, P. 80, M. 109, N. 23, the god of Sebut, the "jackal of the South."

saṭ, to tremble, to quake, to be terrified, terror.

saṭṭ, Rec. 34, 177, to quiver, to be weak; Copt. ⲥⲧⲱⲧ.

saṭ, the name of a monthly festival; var.

saṭem, Rev. 15, 19 = , to grow.

saṭertȧ, Alt-K. 827, colonnade, storey of a house (?); compare Heb. שְׂדֵרָה, 1 Kings vi, 9.

s-atch, T. 331, U. 624, T. 337, P. 818, to make to be green = , M. 244, N. 622, M. 245; caus. of

satch, a monthly festival; plur.

sȧ, pers. pron. 3rd sing. fem.

sȧ, man, person = ; , Metternich Stele 18, everyone.

Sȧ, B.D. 142, III, 36, a town of Osiris.

sȧ, to go; var.

sȧi, III, 143, to come.

sȧsȧ, Rec. 29, 150, A.Z. 1900, 36, to hasten.

sȧi, to diminish, to decay.

sȧ-t, (var.), the "Ram"—one of the 36 Dekans.

sȧ-t, ; var. , beads.

sȧa, P. 82, M. 112, to know.

sȧa-t, N. 803, wisdom, knowledge; var.

sȧa ḥat, IV, 971, Thes. 1481, knowing of heart, *i.e.*, wise.

Sȧa, a form of Thoth.

Sȧa ⸻, U. 439, T. 250, M. 12, ⸻, P. 9, ⸻, N. 114, ⸻, Nesi-Ȧmsu 32, 1, B.D. 17, 63, 116, 6, 136B, 12, 169, 19, the god of knowledge and intelligence.

Sȧa ⸻, Ombos I, 186–188, one of the 14 Kau of Rā.

Sȧa-ȧbu (?)-tchār-khatut ⸻, B.D. 125, III, 36, the doorkeeper of the hall of Maāti.

Sȧa-Ȧmenti ⸻, U. 396.

Sȧa-Ȧmenti-Rā ⸻, U. 396, ⸻, B.D. 174, 15, a god; var. ⸻

Sȧa-Ḥeru-.... ⸻, Ombos I, 143, a form of Horus.

sȧa-t ⸻, serpent.

sȧaa ⸻, Ȧmen. 3, 2, 23, 2 = ⸻, to know.

sȧat-t (?) ⸻, Ebers Pap. 38, 1, to be oblique-eyed, to squint (?)

sȧa ⸻, weakness, badness, evil; var. ⸻.

sȧa-t ⸻, N. 954, ⸻, cloth, stuff, loincloth; var. ⸻

sȧa-t ⸻, B.D. 110, 36, a garment of Rā.

sȧa ⸻, a seed or fruit used in medicine; ⸻, sȧa of the South; ⸻, sȧa of the North.

Sȧa ⸻, B.D. 99, 19, the city and city-god of Siut.

Sȧait ⸻, the form of Hathor worshipped at Lycopolis.

sȧai ⸻, ⸻, ⸻, to know by sight, to recognize.

sȧau reṭ ⸻, Ḥeru-sātef Stele 115, a class of infantry.

sȧab ⸻, ⸻, ⸻, ⸻, ⸻, mistakes for ⸻ = ⸻; compare Heb. זְאֵב.

Sȧabȧu ⸻, the Jackal-god.

sȧab ⸻, a castrated animal for sacrifice; plur. ⸻, B.D. 69, 13; Copt. ⲥⲃ̄ⲃⲉ.

sȧab ⸻, reeds, marsh plants.

Sȧamiu ⸻, a class of hairy fiends.

s-ȧakhu ⸻; caus. of ⸻. For other examples see p. 635, A.

sȧati ⸻, ⸻, ⸻, ⸻, ⸻, cheater, deceiver, trickster, swindler, impostor.

Sȧatiu ⸻, ⸻, B.D. 90, 3, 9, a group of gods.

Sȧater (?) ⸻, Ombos I, 73, a god of agricultural produce.

s-ȧath ⸻, Rec. 31, 175, to destroy.

s-ȧaṭ ⸻, ⸻, to paralyse, to cripple.

sȧṭṭi ⸻, destroyer, waster.

Sȧaṭṭ ta ⸻, Nesi-Ȧmsu 32, 23, "Earth-destroyer"—a form of Āapep.

s-ȧā ⸻, U. 213, ⸻, U. 565, ⸻, P. 601, ⸻, P. 694, ⸻, P. 381, ⸻, to make to enter, to store up, to advance on a road.

s-ȧȧā, T. 268, to introduce; var. , M. 427.

s-ȧȧār-t, Hh. 385, a sailing, an advance by boat.

sȧu, P. 42, , N. 29, to lead; var. , M. 62.

s-ȧu, , T. 191, N. 1288, , I, 78, , Rec. 27, 219, , , to proclaim, to cry out, to complain, to curse, to vilify, to calumniate; var. , P. 676.

Sȧu, Rec. 27, 219, a group of gods in the Ṭuat.

sȧu, , , , to drink; see .

sȧu, P. 613, pool, lake, drinking trough.

sȧu, , sheep; Copt. ⲉⲥⲟⲟⲩ.

Sȧu, T. 315, , Metternich Stele, a mythological serpent.

sȧunu, wages, hire, price; Copt. ⲥⲟⲩⲉⲛⲧ, ⲥⲟⲩⲛ̄; see .

s-ȧur, M. 587 (var. , P. 410), , , to make pregnant; caus. of ; Copt. ⲱ̄, ⲱⲱ.

sȧur, , , Ȧmen. 12, 11, to drink.

s-ȧuḥ, , Edict 26, to submerge, to plunge.

s-ȧb, Rec. 26, 28, to thirst; caus. of ; Copt. ⲉⲓⲃⲉ.

sȧb, fiend, enemy.

sȧb-t, , , strife, enmity (?)

s-ȧbki, B.D. 145, VII, 46, to make to weep, to grieve.

s-ȧp, Rec. 21, 14, , , , , , to revise, to inspect, to check accounts, to examine or enquire into, to make a scrutiny, to audit, to test, to visit in order to inspect, to commit to the care of; caus. of .

sȧpi, , , inspector.

sȧpi kebenti, inspector of the fleet.

sȧpti, , , inspector.

sȧp-t, , , , , inspection, revision, investigation, visitation (of a temple), enquiry, list, copy.

Sȧp-t ur-t, the great examination, *i.e.*, the Last Judgement.

Sȧp, , , Berg. 49, Examiner, Inspector—a name of Osiris;

sȧp-t, , , his judgment hall.

sȧpu, , , the divine examiners, inspectors or judges.

Sȧpit, B.D.G. 1323, consort of Rā of Saïs, .

sȧpi, , , , , to build, to set in order.

sȧf, to pollute; Copt. ⲥⲟⲟϥ, ⲥⲱⲱϥ.

sȧfi, , , the name of the moon on its 10th day.

sȧfu, sword; Syr. ܣܝܦܐ, Arab. سَيْف.

sȧm, darkness (?) rain-storm.

s-ȧm , IV, 345, , , to make oneself pleasant, to ingratiate, to show oneself gracious, to heal; caus. of .

sȧmȧi , Rev. 13, 30, demand, protest, objection, opposition.

sȧms , club, cudgel.

s-ȧn , T. 512, P. 204, 700, ; U. 371, M. 213, N. 684, , P. 688, , Rec. 29, 145, , ibid., 30, 194, , , Sphinx Stele 11, , , , to advance quickly, to run, to hasten; , to hasten the steps.

s-ȧnn , Rec. 15, 179, , , to run, to hasten.

sȧnu , Methen, , N. 29, 659, 788, , P. 700, , runners, bearers, porters.

sȧn-t , a light swift boat; plur. , Rec. 4, 27.

sȧn en Uatch-ur , Salt Pap. 825, the dolphin or sea-bull of the Mediterranean.

sȧn , Thes. 1206, , , , , , , , , , , to rub, to rub in an unguent or medicament, to apply an unguent, to smear, to anoint, to salve, to rub down, to crush grain.

sȧnsȧn , P. 777; var. of , , P. 661, M. 772.

sȧn ȧb , to anoint the heart, *i.e.*, to flatter (?)

sȧn , IV, 1207, , oint-ments, unguents.

sȧn-t , Rec. 31, 29, , , , , , , , , earth used in sealing, clay.

sȧnȧ , , Jour. As. 1908 passim, knowledge; Copt. ⲥⲟⲟⲩⲛ.

Sȧnu-t , the name of a serpent on the royal crown.

sȧnu , , , price; see .

sȧn-nu , M. 480, two; var. of , P. 267, , N. 1248.

s-ȧnti , Rec. 24, 164, to fetter.

sȧr ȧb , U. 172, to sadden (?)

sȧrit , fan, umbrella.

sȧhem , to block the way, to detain.

sȧḥ , nobleman.

sȧkhi , Rhind Pap. 58, proof, test, trial.

sȧs (?), su (?) , , six; , , sixth; , , , festival of the 6th day; plur. ; , house of the greatest of six; Copt. ⲥⲟⲟⲩ, ⲥⲉⲩ.

sȧs , , Rec. 27, 226, six-threaded stuff.

s-ȧst , P. 67, N. 35, to occupy a seat.

sȧsh , N. 754, offering (?)

sȧsh-t, N. 646 = , M. 124, offering (?)

Sȧshesa, N. 975, a god who made the ladder that reached from earth to heaven.

sȧq, , , to carve, to model.

sȧqti, sculptor.

s-ȧq, Peasant 295, to destroy; caus. of or .

s-ȧqer, , , L.D. III, 140B, , Rev. 6, 23, to make perfect; caus. of .

sȧka, B.D. 17, 34 (Ani) . . . . . .

sȧken, to destroy, to ruin.

s-ȧgeb, to flood, to deluge; caus. of .

sȧt, something foul (?)

sȧti, , , , , slaughterer, executioner; plur. , , gods who slay.

s-ȧti, to prove, to show; caus.

s-ȧth; caus. of **ȧthi** .

sȧṭ, , running of the ear (?)

sȧṭ, a kind of bread offering (?); , a kind of bread-offering (?)

s-ȧṭ, s-ȧaṭ, , , , to make weak, to reduce.

sȧṭi, headsman, executioner.

s-ȧṭṭi, to rebuke, to punish, overthrow.

s-ȧṭen, to transfer; caus. of **ȧṭen** .

sȧtchti, A.Z. 1900, 20, child.

s-āai, IV, 612, , , , A.Z. 1900, 20, , Rec. 11, 165, to magnify; caus. of ; , Rec. 20, 40, large; , Love Songs 7, 7, , magnified.

sāauiȧ, a man of years and dignity, a notable; plur. , .

sāau, Hh. 783, , Rec. 30, 66, planks or beams of a ship.

sāabut, P. 297, a set of four jars for libations or purifications.

sāam, , , Love Songs 7, 7, Rechnungen 78, a plant which has grown on a tree.

sāi, , , , fatigue, evil, misery.

s-āb (for s-uāb), P. 297, 612, , P. 112, , N. 80, , N. 343, , P. 373, , U. 566, , , , , , to purify, to cleanse; caus. of **uāb** .

s-āb, to beautify, to decorate; caus.

sābu, Festschrift 117, 11, beauties, decorations, ornaments, jewellery.

sāb, a kind of fancy bread.

sāb, to castrate; Copt. ⲥⲃ̄ⲃⲉ.

sāb, ox; Copt. ⲥⲉⲃⲓ.

sābi, A.Z. 17, 57, to be ready or prepared (to fight).

s-āp, to make to advance, to fly (?); caus. of or .

s-ām, to make to eat, to feed; caus. of , to swallow.

s-ām, , to swallow, to absorb, a swallowing or bolting of food.

sāmiu, , swallowers, devourers.

sām, a plant or flower.

sām, IV, 711, inlaid: , with lapis lazuli; , with gold; , with leather (?)

s-āma, to make to swallow; caus. of .

s-ān, to turn back; caus. of .

s-ān, to beautify; caus. of .

sānn, to bind, to tie, to twist.

s-ānkh, Hymn Darius 42, , , , , Nâstasen Stele 40, to feed, to nourish, to support, to bring up, to nurture; Copt. ⲥⲁⲁⲛϣ, ϣⲁⲛⲉϣ.

s-ānkh ȧb, to vivify the heart, to inspire courage.

sānkhu, Peasant 221, sustainer, vivifier.

Sānkhiu, Rev. 14, 59, the gods who sustain life.

s-ānkh, , , , , to carve a life-like image or statue, to commemorate the dead by making a statue.

sānkhi, sculptor, engraver, portrait painter.

Sānkhi-khaibitu, Berg. 23, a bird-god who revivified dead human shadows.

s-ānṭ, to make strong; caus. of .

s-ānṭu, , IV, 269, to destroy; caus.

s-āri, IV, 753, Rec. 34, 182, Sphinx Stele 3, , Rec. 32, 80, IV, 897, , Rev. 12, 62 (var.), , IV, 966, , , to bring, to bring up; , Thes. 1479, to present petitions.

sāri-t, approach.

sāriu, , bringers, porters, carriers.

Sārit maāt, IV, 423, the name of a building.

Sārit, IV, 270, the name of a goddess.

Sār-neb-s, the name of the 2nd hour of the night.

s-ār, to make a fire to burn, to make an offering.

sār, Rev. 12, 91, a plant; Gr. σάρι, Lat. sarī (Pliny, N.H. 13, 23, 45).

sār, A.Z. 1899, 15 . . . .

sāri, IV, 635, a pitcher and stand; compare Arab. زير.

s-ārq, Dream Stele 36, , Rec. 10, 61, to make an end of, to finish.

sāḥ, U. 644, to pay honour to, to receive honour.

sāḥ, royal rank and dignity.

sāḥ, M. 634, , to be noble, to play the king or nobleman; , P. 331.

sāḥ, , , freeman, nobleman, gentleman; plur. ; an aged noble; Copt. ⲥⲁϩ, ⲥⲁϩ.

sāḥ-t, a kind of garment worn by a nobleman.

sāḥ, U. 298, the form of a man that exists in heaven, the spirit-body; plur. , T. 143, , N. 113, 539, , U. 516, , T. 327, , P. 6, , M. 8. Later forms are:— , , , ; plur. , , ; , a sāḥ with his soul; , perfect spirit-bodies.

Sāḥ, Ṭuat VII, the divine spirit-body, the god of all spirit-bodies.

Sāḥ, Thes. 82, the spirit-body of Orion .

Sāḥ-ȧb, Ṭuat III, a god.

Sāḥ-ḥeq, Rec. 4, 28, a god.

s-āḥā, Palermo Stele, , P. 387, , , to erect, to set up straight; late form ; , , to set up the Ṭeṭ, *i.e.*, to reconstitute the backbone of Osiris; Copt. ⲥⲟⲟϩⲉ.

s-āḥā, to stablish time or life; , U. 430, , T. 246.

sāḥā-t = , climbing pole.

sāḥā, Jour. As. 1908, 249, , , , Rev. 13, 42, to curse; Copt. ⲥⲟϩⲉ.

s-ākh, , , to raise up, to lift up on high; caus. of .

sāsh-t, a kind of disease.

s-āsha, , , to multiply; caus. of .

s-āsha-t, Coronation Stele (relief at top), to multiply.

s-āsha, to utter many cries.

sāshatȧ, manifold, numerous.

sāshat, , , , , to ward off, to restrain, to obstruct, to remove; Copt. ⲥⲱϣⲧ.

sāshat, , , chief officer, inspector; plur. , .

s-āq, , , , , T. 386, M. 402, to make to enter, to introduce; caus. of .

sāqi, , , , introducer.

sāq neter, Annales III, 109, the festival of the introduction of the god.

sāq-t, Rec. 31, 20, IV, 658, Peasant 198, IV, 1145, entrance, introduction.

sāq, Rev. 11, 167, sack, bag; Heb. שַׂק, Syr. ܣܩܐ, Chald. סַקָּא, Assyr. shakku, Eth. ሠቅ፡, Copt. ⲥⲁⲕ.

s-āq, Rec. 27, 127, to cut, to destroy.

s-āqa, Koller I, 8, A.Z. 1900, 35, Mar. Aby. I, 6, 37, (*sic*), to make right, to test a bow, to set in strict order.

sāg, to capsize, to overthrow.

sāti-t, Rev. 14, 67, arrow; Copt. ⲥⲱⲧⲉ.

s-ātcha, Åmen. 16, 4, 17, 18, L.D. III, 140c, to do wrong, to commit a crime, to falsify weights, to rob.

s-ātcha meṭut, Åmen. 14, 2, 20, 9, to deceive by speech.

si, III, 142, Nåstasen Stele 39, Anastasi I, 28, 5 = , to come, to go.

si, A.Z. 1878, 48, fullness, satiety; Copt. ⲥⲓ.

si-t, infant, child (fem.) =

si, L.D. III, 194, 12, waterfowl.

siu, star; plur. Rev. 14, 7; Copt. ⲥⲓⲟⲩ; double star.

siu siti, Rev. 14, 20, a shooting star.

Siu uāti, the planet Venus as a morning star.

siu-t, Rec. 33, 119, door.

sif, Thes. 1198, child, son, boy, babe.

sif, Rev. 2, 77, pitch, bitumen =

simu, Rev. 13, 15, field or garden produce, herbs, vegetables; Copt. ⲥⲓⲙ, ⲥⲓⲙⲓⲁⲙ.

sirȧ, siri, A.Z. 1880, 96, umbrella, parasol.

siri, the badge of a regiment, flag, fan, umbrella.

siriu, fan-bearers, umbrella-bearers

sir-patȧ, Harris 500, 2, 8, fan, fly-whisk.

sir-putȧ, Rec. 21, 92, a kind of fan or umbrella made of leather (?)

sir-ḥattȧ, Rec. 16, 99, palm-leaf mat; = Gr. σειρά (?)

Sirsa (?), Thes. 129, a star-god; var.

sir-ṭima, Åmen. 6, 3 . . . .

siḥ, to come, to arrive.

siḥ, Rec. 3, 39, pavilion, port, landing-stage.

siḥ, Rev., to mummify.

siḥ, Rec. 21, 94, to be hypnotized, to be in a state of religious ecstasy, to be mad; compare Copt. ⲥⲓϩⲉ.

siḥu, Pap. Mag. 170, spell, charm, bewitchment, hypnotism (in the

phrase ; var. , Amherst Pap. 20).

siḥsiḥ , to punish; var. ; Copt. ⲥⲉϩⲥⲱϩ.

siḥ-t , Rev. 13, 26, punishment; Copt. ⲥⲟϩⲉ.

siḥsiḥ , lamentation, grief, punishment.

sikh , , Rev. 12, 28, cry, signal.

sikh-t , Rec. 33, 122, mastery.

sikh-t , loss, injury.

sikha-t , Jour. As. 1908, 249, folly, madness; Copt. ⲥⲓϩⲉ.

sish åḥ-ti , Rev. 14, 65, a yoke of oxen.

siki , Rev. 14, 15, destruction.

sit , smell, odour; see , Copt. ⲥϯ.

sit , Rev. 11, 180 = , begetter.

sit , to set on fire.

siti , the shooting of a star; see .

sitcheṭu (?) , storytellers, talkers, chatterers; see ; caus. of .

su, sut , , , , , pers. pron. 3rd sing. masc.; also used as a particle.

sut , U. 180, 227, a particle.

su , IV, 1076, captive, prisoner.

su-t , N. 379, , U. 100, , P. 225, a joint of meat, a meat offering; , P. 705.

su-t (nesu-t?) , Kahun 3, 2, , A.Z. 49, 20, , A.Z. 1908, 121, , Hh. 437, , A.Z. 49, 19, the plant of the South, the byssus plant.

su-t , Rechnungen 70, plant used in making boats.

sut (?) , B.D. 64, 14, hair (?)

sut (?) ...... , IV, 506 ....

su (for **sesu**) , a period of time, day, with the number of the day of the month; Copt. ⲥⲟⲩ—.

susu , Rev. 14, 13, a period of time; Copt. ⲥⲟⲩⲥⲟⲩ.

su (?) [ ], Rev. 14, 12, evening.

su , , a measure of length = $\frac{1}{16}$th of a schoinios, or 625 square cubits; in superficial measure su = $\frac{1}{6}$th of a square schoinios.

su = , guard, protector.

su , Rev. 13, 22 = , to drink, drink; Copt. ⲥⲱ.

su = , to saw; Copt. ⲃⲓⲥⲉ.

suu (?) , to cut = .

suu (?) = , Shipwreck 55, to cut down trees.

su-t , wind, breeze.

su-t , , IV, 1132, , , , , , Rev. 30, 217, , , Rev. 14, 46, corn, grain, wheat; Copt. ⲥⲟⲩⲟ, ⲥⲟⲩ.

su-t, a kind of disease.

suu (?), region, territory, province.

suu (?), B.D. 163, 18, evil, wickedness.

suu (?), T. 265, 283, P. 51, M. 31, N. 64, to pray (?); late form (?)

sua, Ḥerusȧtef Stele 88, sheep, ovis platyura; Heb. שֶׂה, Arab. شَاه, Copt. ⲉⲥⲁⲩ, ⲉⲥⲟⲟⲩ, ⲉⲥⲱⲟⲩ.

s-ua, T. 241, T. 348, N. 965, P. 605, N. 940, to pass, to pass away, to continue on a journey; caus.

Suau, U. 418, T. 238, a group of gods (?)

sua, store, place of safe storage.

s-uaa = , to adore; caus. of .

sua, night, evening, darkness; see ; Copt. ⲉⲩϣⲏ.

suasua-t, Rec. 16, 131, flame, fire, heat.

suan (sun), to know, to recognize; Copt. ⲥⲟⲟⲩⲛ.

suan, Rec. 33, 119, price; Copt. ⲥⲟⲩⲉⲛ.

suar, Anastasi IV, 17, 1, Alt. K. 769, garments, tunics (?); compare Heb. שׁוּל in שׁוּלָיו, Isaiah vi, 1, etc.

s-uarekh, to make green or fertile; var. ; caus.

s-uaḥ, L.D. III, 140c, , to establish, to make to continue, to develop; caus. of .

s-uaḥ ȧb, to pay attention.

suaḥ, , egg; Copt. ⲥⲟⲟⲩϩⲉ.

s-uash, , , , to praise, to adore; caus. of ; Copt. ⲱϣ.

suashu, praises.

suag, foolish, lewd.

suaga, , to curse, to ban.

suatȧ, carriage, transport.

s-uatch, U. 624, N. 701, , , to make to flourish; , the transmittal of property; caus. of ; var. , T. 337.

Suatchi, "maker to flourish"—a title of the god Shu.

S-uatch ȧr-ti, Rec. 31, 30, "green-eyed."

Suatchit ȧṭebiu pet, Ṭuat XII, a fire-goddess who guided Rā.

suȧ-t , , pill, globule, pastille, bead; plur. ; varr. , .

suuȧn .... , Mar. Karn. 52, 17 ....

s-uāb , Rec. 20, 40, Annales III, 109, to plate, to cover with metal; to cover a floor with plates of silver.

sui , to adore.

Sui , B.D. 31, 2, , a crocodile-god; var. .

S-uba , , to open up a way, to force an entrance, to pierce, to penetrate; caus. of ; , IV, 422 = , opening the face.

s-ubak , to make to conceive; caus. of (?)

suma , Rev., obstinate, head-strong; Copt. ϭⲟⲟⲙⲉ (?)

s-umet , IV, 890, to strengthen; caus.

s-un , Dream Stele 38, , to make to be; caus. of .

s-un , , to make an opening, to force open; caus. of ;

s-un-ḥer , to reveal; Copt. ⲟⲩⲱⲛ.

sun, sunnu , Anastasi I, 25, 6, , to sell; Copt. ⲥⲟⲩⲛ̅.

sun-t , P. 87, , N. 46, , , , A.Z. 1906, 28, , Rec. 33, 5, , , , , , , , Festschrift 3, , Rev. 14, 41, price, hire, wages, salary; Copt. ⲥⲟⲩⲛⲧ̅.

sun-t , trade, business, buying and selling.

sunu , wages; **ur sunu** , paymaster.

sun-t , U. 429, , T. 246 ......

sun , to suffer pain, distress, suffering, destruction.

sunit , sickness, malady.

sun , to straighten.

sun , , , Rev. 11, 148, , Rev. 14, 15, , Rev. 12, 31, , Rev. 13, 90, to know; , Rev. 12, 53, wise or learned men; Copt. ⲥⲟⲟⲩⲛ.

sunu , Mar. Aby. I, 8, 86, , pool, lake, tank, canal, aqueduct.

sunu , T. 345, , P. 282; varr. , M. 525, , N. 1106, , wall, fortress, seat, throne.

Sunu , a god and a town.

sunun , , to flatter, to wheedle, to cajole, to use blandishments, to persuade, to talk someone over.

sununu , Anastasi I, 23, 8, flattery, cajolery, entreaty.

sunsun , , Ȧmen. 14, 15, to entreat, to petition, to supplicate, to converse.

suntȧ , Rev., resin, balsam; Copt. ⲥⲟⲛⲧⲉ.

Sunth, P. 352, , N. 1068, , P. 467, N. 854, , M. 531, , N. 1110, , P. 265, , N. 1245, , M. 336, a god.

s-ur, to increase, to magnify; caus. of .

s-ur; caus. of , to be pregnant.

sur, drink; Copt. ⲥⲱ.

surȧ (suȧ), , , , to drink; Copt. ⲥⲱ; , drinkers.

surȧ, toper, tippler, drunkard, swiller; plur. ; , drinking companions.

surȧ ḥeq-t, beerhouse, tavern.

surȧ, a kind of fish.

surȧ-t, white bead.

s-urkh, to make to be green or fertile; varr. , ; caus.

s-urṭ, , , , to make to grow; caus. of .

s-urṭ, Shipwreck 20, 21, to make motionless; caus. of .

suh, IV, 751, , A.Z. 1905, 38, , Thes. 1318, , Leyd. Pap. 7, 13, L.D. III, 140B, , IV, 973, Thes. 1483, , Anastasi I, 27, 8, to brag, to boast, to exaggerate.

suhaiu, boaster.

suh, Rougé I.H. II, 126, P.S.B. 23, 252, , , , , L.D. III, 65A, 6, , Leyd. Pap. 2, 11, to overthrow, to be terrified, to be confused, dazed.

s-uhen, IV, 780, Mar. Karn. 17A, to overthrow; caus. of .

suḥ, , , , wind, air, breath.

suḥ-t, N. 757, 758, , , , Rev. 14, 1, egg; plur. , IV, 949, , Jour. As. 1908, 292; , ostrich-eggs; , fish spawn; , Rec. 32, 80, created germ; , Hymn Darius 23, hidden germ; Copt. ⲥⲟⲟⲩϩⲉ.

suḥit, A.Z. 1878, 48, testicle; dual , ; Copt. ⲥⲱⲟⲩϩⲓ.

suḥ, Rev. 13, 37, , Rev. 5, 93, to cover over, to wrap up, to envelop.

suḥ, T. 25, Rec. 30, 192, , P. 742, , T. 355,

, N. 175, , Åmen. 18, 10, , , a kind of cloth, garment, vestment, a short coat, loin-cloth; plur. , P. 635, , M. 509, , N. 1092.

suḥ-t , A.Z. 45, 135, bowl, vessel.

suḥ , Rev., , Jour. As. 1908, 307, , to curse; Copt. ⲥⲁϩⲟⲩ; var. (Copt. ⲥϩⲟⲩⲣ).

suḥ ikh , Rev. 12, 61, , Rev. 14, 32, reunion of spirits; Copt. ⲥⲟⲟⲩϩ ⲓϧ.

sukha , remembrance; see .

sukha , B.D. 90, 1, etc., evil remembrance, bad dream (?)

sukha , IV, 848, ruin, destruction.

sukhu (?) , to darken, to obscure; , Åmen. 16, 9.

sukheṭ , B.D. 190, 4, to embalm; caus. of .

Sukhṭu , Rec. 27, 220, the gods who preside over embalmment.

s-us-t , ruin, destruction; caus.

s-usekh , , Rec. 17, 94, , , , , to make wide or broad, to enlarge, to extend; caus. of ; , , , , , to lengthen the stride, to walk with long strides.

susekhtȧ , , Rec. 20, 40, spacious.

Susek ; see .

s-ush , to micturate; caus. of .

sush-t , , Ebers 74, 17, urine.

sush , to measure.

sush , , , chain, cord, measuring cord.

sush-t , drought, dryness.

s-usha , , to praise, to worship, to adore; caus.

suq , Rev. 12, 73, bailiff (?)

suqa , an incense-burner, censer.

suk , Rev. 14, 13, to play the fool; Copt. ⲥⲟϭ.

sug , a piece of flesh, an offering.

sug , , babe, sucking child.

sug , , A.Z. 1907, 123, , , Anastasi I, 9, 6, , Rec. 21, 88, to be helpless, foolish, half-witted, wretched, miserable.

sug , Jour. As. 1908, 294, silly, foolish; Copt. ⲥⲟϭ.

s-uga , , Hymn to Nile 2, 15, to make to vomit; caus.

sugait , rebuke (?) correction (?)

Sugaṭi , B.D. (Saïte) 165, 14, a Nubian god.

sut , Rev. 12, 70, strip of linen, rag; Copt. ⲥⲁϯ, ⲥⲏⲧⲉ.

sut, ties, bonds.

sut-t, cake, ball.

Sut (for **Sutesh** (?)), , Berg. I, 6, , Set, the god of evil.

suti, fire, flame.

Suti, , , , , B.D. 9, 4, 17, 115, 28, 8, 42, 8, 99, 19, 108, 7, , Set, the god of evil.

sutiu (?), needy man.

sutut, , , Sphinx Stele 5, , , , , , Love Songs V, 7, , IV, 1193, , to go for a walk, to walk about a place, to pass, to journey, to march, to travel; varr. , IV, 1064, , , , , Rev. 12, 44.

sutut, Sphinx Stele 8, journey.

sutut, , , , , , traveller.

sutsut, , , to take a walk, to travel.

suten, king. The equation provided by P. 92, M. 112, N. 700, = = , shows that in the Early Empire the reading of was **nesu**; compare also the equation = , Rec. 26, 235, and see A.Z. 49, 22. See **nesu**.

suteni, P. 602, , , , to be king, to rule.

sutenit, IV, 572, , , , , , , , , , , , , , , , IV, 575, , , the state of being king, kingdom, kingship, sovereignty, royalty, rule; , royal, kingship.

suten (shes nesu), IV, 742, , , , , , , , royal linen, *i.e.*, byssus; Copt ϣєнс.

sutenu (?), crown of the South.

suten, , , , , to kill.

suteniu, , , butchers, slaughterers.

suten, lake, flood, inundation.

sutenu, for , to walk with long steps.

s-uter, to purify, to cleanse; caus. of .

Suter = Σωτηρ, the "Saviour-god."

s-utekh, to treat a body with drugs, to embalm; caus.

Sutekh, , , the Hittite form of the Egyptian name of the god Set.

sutek (?) (?) Rhind Math. Pap. 203 . . . . . .

s-uṭ, to detain, to make tarry; caus.

s-uṭen, to make straight; caus.; Copt. ⲥⲟⲟⲩⲧⲛ̄.

s-uṭekh , , to embalm; caus.

s-utch , IV, 1032, , IV, 1035, , , , to bequeath, to settle one in an inheritance; caus. of .

s-utcha , , , Koller 5, 4, , , to make strong, to refresh, to protect, to make healthy, to heal, to save; caus. of .

sutcha-ȧb , , Peasant 36, "Make glad the heart!"—a greeting at the beginning of a letter.

s-utcha , , to go, to go forward; , Leyd. Pap. 16, 1, to die.

s-utchā , to pass a decree of judgement; caus.

seb , , block, brick (of iron), an offering.

seb, sebȧ , , flute; Copt. ⲥⲏⲃⲉ.

seb-t , , reed, tube, flute; Copt. ⲥⲏⲃⲉ.

seb , reed, marsh flower; plur. , ; , sweet reed.

seb, seb-t , , , , , , cedar; plur. , U. 565; Copt. ⲥⲏⲃⲉ, ⲥⲓⲃⲉ.

seb , N. 950 = **s-uben** .

seb (sebesh?) , U. 567, N. 750, to endow (?) to give (?)

seb , , = , to pass through.

seb , , Rec. 17, 145, ox, castrated beast; see ; Copt. ⲥⲉⲃⲓ.

Seb , Thes. 65, the planet Mercury.

Sebit , Rec. 3, 116, the name of a goddess.

seb-t , U. 588, M. 819, a kind of grain.

sebseb , , , girdle, bandlet.

Sebsebā-Menu , B.D. (Saïte) 49, 60; see **Besu-Menu**.

sba , P. 74, 470, , M. 104, 711, , N. 16, Rec. 33, 119; , Rev. 14, 40, , Rev. 13, 30, , Rev. 13, 34, door; plur. , P. 296, , Rec. 31, 17, great door of heaven; , Love Songs 5, 9, outer door; ,

, palace gates; , hell's gates; , gates of the horizon; , folding doors; Copt. ⲥⲃⲉ.

Sbatt , , Berg. II, 11, a form of Ȧment.

sba-t , part of a chariot.

Sbai, Sbi , , , Litanie 14, , Ṭuat X, a serpent-warder of the 11th Gate.

Sba en sethesu Shu , B.D. 17, 56, *i.e.*, Sba-tcheser.

Sbau shetau neteru , B.D. 141, 57, the gods of the mystic doors in the Ṭuat.

Sbau Ṭuatiu , B.D. 141, 54, the doors of the Ṭuat; .

Sba tcheser , B.D. 17, 56, the door of sunrise, the last door in the Ṭuat.

sba , Rec. 2, 109, , Anastasi I, 28, 1, , , , , , , Rev. 11, 124, to teach, to bring up, to educate, to instruct, to train, to learn, to levy a tax; , Peasant 260, instructed; , U. 213; Copt. ⲥⲃⲱ.

sba-t , , , Ikhernefer 6, , , pupil, teaching, training, instruction, education; plur. .

sbait , Ȧmenemḥat I, 1, , , , Ȧmen. 27, 8, , , , , , , , IV, 1090, , , , , IV, 968, teaching, instruction, training, education, learning, wisdom, lore of books, doctrine, punishment, correction, tax, impost; , great death penalty; Copt. ⲥⲃⲱ.

sbati , L.D. III, 194, , Ȧmen. 27, 15, instruction.

sbai , Rec. 2, 111, , , wise man, teacher, instructor.

sbait , teacher, instructor; , assistant teacher.

sbau , , , learning, instruction, teachers.

sbau (?) , , , place of instruction, schoolroom.

sba ur , an instrument used in performing the ceremony of "opening the mouth."

sba , Shipwreck 129, , , star; plur. , U. 496, , T. 319, P. 308, N. 94, , P. 694, , , , , , , ; Copt. ⲥⲓⲟⲩ.

Sba , , , a star-god; plur. , , , , Rec. 20, 41.

Sbait, Thes. 91, Ṭuat I, the Star-goddess Sothis, regent of the 11th hour of the night.

Sbaiut, star-goddesses in general.

Sba àabti tcha pet, Thes. 67, the planet Mars, the planet that moved onwards and retreated; he is also called the Red Horus.

Sba àmenti tcha pet, Thes. 65, the planet Saturn; called also Horus, bull of heaven.

Sba uāti, Thes. 13, Thes. 73, 76, Rec. 32, 79, ibid. 30, 67, Ḥeru-beḥṭ as a morning and evening star.

Sbaiu meḥu, Tomb Ram. IV, one of the 36 Dekans.

Sbaiu en Àsàr, the star-gods of Osiris.

sbaiu nu mu, stars of the water.

Sba en khau, A.Z. 1899, 15, star of thousands.

Sbait neb-t uàa, Ṭuat XI, the star-goddess of the boat of Àf.

Sbaiu Rā, B.D. 168, the warders of the gates of Rā.

sbaiu shepsu, Thes. 133, the Dekans.

Sba shemā, Thes. 65–67, the planet Jupiter; called also "travelling star," and.

Sba-ṭua, N. 948, the morning star.

Sba-tcha, Thes. 65–67, the planet Venus; other names are.

sba, Nàstasen Stele 38, cut, castrated; Copt. ⲥⲃⲃⲉ.

Sba, a name of Āapep; the Enemy Āapep.

Sba-ent-Sba, Nesi-Àmsu 32, 32, a form of Āapep.

sbai, to laugh; see; Copt. ⲥⲱⲃⲉ.

sbaḥ, Jour. As. 1908, 172, propitiation (?) = Copt. ⲥⲉⲥⲃⲟϩ (?)

sbakh, to keep, to guard, to protect.

Sbakh senu, Rec. 4, 28, a god.

Sbasit, T.S.B.A. III, 424, a goddess of and.

sbashi, Rev. 11, 140, 12, 17, Rev. 12, 25, Rev. 12, 34 = Copt. ⲥⲃϣⲉ (?)

s-baq, to make pregnant; caus. of.

s-baq (sebq), U. 566, Rec. 31, 14, to anoint; , the shining eye of the Moon; caus. of .

sbak , Rev. 11, 141, little, small; Copt. cßok.

Sbak, Sebakȧu , the planet Mercury.

sbȧ , sword, scimitar.

sebȧ , Rec. 27, 218, A.Z. 1905, 37, to be inimical, hostile, unfriendly, to act as an enemy.

sebȧ , enemy, foe, demon, devil, wicked man; plur.

sebȧ-t , Rec. 31, 10, enmity, hostility, rebellion, hateful things.

Sebȧ , a serpent-god of evil, arch-enemy of Rā; plur. , the associates of Sbȧ.

Sebȧ, Sebȧu , the "Enemy" par excellence, *i.e.*, the Devil, , Sebȧu, worker of evil.

Sbȧ[t] , Pap. Qenna 4, consort of Sbȧ.

sbȧ , A.Z. 1905, 29, violent wind, an unfavourable or head wind.

sbȧu , Hh. 448, parts of a boat.

sbȧ , Ȧmen. 24, 9, Rec. 31, 174, Rev. 12, 108, 13, 39, to laugh; Copt. cωße.

sbȧ-t , laugh, jest, mockery, jibe.

Sbȧk , the Crocodile-god; Gr. Σουχις.

sbi-t , Nȧstasen Stele 50, hostile country; plur. , ibid. 63.

sbit , shadows.

sbith , Jour. As. 1908, 255, scoffing, jest, mockery.

sbu , U. 123, N. 432, a kind of offering.

Sbut , P. 80, M. 109, N. 23, a city of the god .

sben , Peasant 126, ibid. 221, , Peasant 163, L.D. III, 140c, Rec. 16, 57, , to run aground (of a ship), to turn back, to retreat, to yaw about (of a boat).

s-benben , Rec. 35, 127, to be overthrown, to collapse; caus.

sben-t, T. 843, P. 222, cattle for sacrifice.

Sben-ḥesq-khaibiut, Ṭuat II, a warrior-god.

sben, cord, fillet.

sben, U. 517, T. 328, a part of a crown (?)

sben-t, Peasant B2, 120, a pregnant woman.

sben, hay, grass.

s-bner, I, 53, to make pleasant, to please, to treat affectionately.

sbaner (sebner), to make pleasant or pleased; caus of .

Sbenqa, B.D. 146, the doorkeeper of the 3rd Pylon.

s-beha, I, 135, to chase, to put to flight; caus. of .

sbeḥ, P. 611, N. 760, M. 396, N. 949, M. 826, P. 204, Rec. 16, 110, Åmen. 4, 18, Jour. As. 1908, 31, to cry out, to call, cry, outcry, lamentation; Copt. ⲥⲱⲃϩ.

sbeḥ, Rev. 21, 208 = ⲥⲃⲟϩ in ϯⲥⲉⲥⲃⲟϩ = .

sbeḥ, cry, prayer, entreaty, wail, petition, imprecation; plur. wail of a tom-cat; cry of a whole nest of young birds.

sebḥit, cry, supplication; cry of woe.

sebḥut, Love Songs 4, 6, cry, cry of goose, wail.

s-beḥ = .

Sebḥuf, Ṭuat XII, one of 12 gods who towed the boat of Åf through the serpent Ānkh-neteru, and who were re-born daily.

sbekh, T. 178, P. 521, M. 160, N. 651, to protect, to act as a wall to someone.

sbekhbekh, B.D. 17 (Ani), 137 . . . .

sbekh-t, gate, gate-tower; plur. IV, 174, ; var. , doors.

Sbekh-t, the pylon deified; plur. .

Sbekh-ti, Ṭuat XI, a doorkeeper-god.

sbekh-t åakhu-t, "gate of the horizon"—a temple in the Heroopolite Nome.

Sbekh-t Åger-t, Ṭuat XI, the 11th Pylon.

sbekh-t ur-t, "the Great Gate."

sbekhut shetaut, the "hidden doors" of the Ṭuat.

sbekh-t ta pen, "gate of this land"—a title of the king.

Sbekhut Ṭuat, B.D. 141, 55, the Pylons of the Ṭuat.

sbekh-t, IV, 629, a stand for some object.

sbekh-t, a kind of plant.

sbekh-t, a kind of measure.

Sbekhas, Thes. 113, Zodiac Dend.: (1) one of the 36 Dekans; (2) one of the seven stars of Orion; var. ; Gr. *σουχως*.

Sbekhekhth, Thes. 113, one of the seven stars of Orion.

Sbesanka; see **Besu-Menu.**

s-besh, U. 567, , to eject from the body, to vomit; caus.

sbeshu, U. 519, , T. 329, what is ejected from the body, vomit.

sbesh-t, gate, door, pylon; plur.

sbeshi, Rec. 30, 95, shield; Copt. ⲥⲃϣⲉ.

Sbeshes, Thes. 113 = : (1) the 9th Dekan; (2) one of the seven stars of Orion.

Sbeshes mer, Denderah II, 10, one of the 36 Dekans.

Sbeshta, , , Thes. 113, one of the seven stars of Orion.

sbeq, , few, little, small; Copt. ⲥⲟⲃⲕ̄.

sbeq, , Rec. 4, 119, to be wise (?) learned (?)

sbeq-t, IV, 887, something advantageous or profitable.

sbeq, a complete body (?)

sbeq, , to collect, to gather together.

Sbeq ḥer, Ṭuat VIII, a crocodile-god in the Circle Ḥetemit-khemiu.

Sbeq, , Berg. II, 2, a protector of the dead.

Sbeqit, , Champ. Mon. 139, Berg. II, 1: (1) a lioness-goddess; (2) a goddess in mummy-form.

sbeq, to be short or contracted; compare Copt. ⲧⲥⲃⲕⲟ.

sbeq, , , , , to travel, to journey.

sbeqåu, U. 487, P. 640, , M. 671, N. 938, traveller (?)

sbeq, U. 622, N. 755, , , leg, thigh; dual , P. 572, ; Heb. שׁוֹק, Arab. ساق.

Sbeq en Shesmu, B.D. 153A, 8, a part of the hunting net of the Akeru-gods.

Sbeq en Tem, B.D. 153B, 5, a part of the hunting net of the Akeru-gods.

sbeq-t, , , , a name of the left eye of Horus, *i.e.*, the moon.

s-beq , , , , , , to anoint, to possess pleasing qualities or attributes, graceful; caus. of ; **s-beqa** , to anoint; caus. of .

sbeqit , an oiled or scented woman.

s-beq , to make pregnant; caus. of = .

Sbek , N. 965, 1359, , U. 600, , IV, 574, , , Rec. 26, 65, , , the Crocodile-god; Gr. Σουχος. Other forms are:— , U. 565, , P. 711, , N. 1360, , B.D. 171, the Crocodile-god par excellence. See Herod. II, 68, 69; Ammianus Marcellinus XXII, 15; Diodorus I, 35; Aelian, de Nat. An. X, 21; Plutarch, De Iside 75, etc.

Sbek , Ombos I, 185, Ṭuat XI, a god in the boat of Rā who destroyed Āapep.

Sbek-neb-peḥu , B.D. (Saïte) 113, 3, Sebek, god of the swamp.

Sbek-neb-meḥt-geb (?) , Ombos I, 42, a crocodile-god of Ombos.

Sbek sheṭ-ti , , Hymnen 22, , a form of the Crocodile-god worshipped in Middle Egypt.

Sbek , , , Thes. 65–67, the planet Mercury. Its god was .

sbek , to cut, to carve, to destroy.

sbek , A.Z. 1878, 48, little, small; Copt. ⲥⲟⲃⲕ̄.

Sbeg , , , Thes. 65–67, D.E. 20, the planet Mercury in the form of a bull-headed hawk.

Sbeg, Sbega , , , B.D. 136A, a god, son of Geb and Nut.

sebt , , Rev. 12, 34, , Rev. 11, 122, wall, citadel, gate; , Rec. 36, 211 = ; Copt. ⲥⲟⲃⲧ.

sebti , , , wall, fort, blockhouse; plur. ; , IV, 832; varr. , , , Copt. ⲥⲟⲃⲧ.

sebt , Leyd. Pap. 3, 13, Shipwreck 149, to laugh, to smile, laughter; , P. 1116B, 41, the laughter of pain; Copt. ⲥⲱⲃⲉ.

sebtȧ , Rev. 13, 43, equipment; var. ; Copt. ⲥⲟⲃⲧⲉ.

sebti , Rev. 11, 131, 145, , Rev. 13, 63, preparation, preparedness; Copt. ⲥⲟⲃϯ.

sbeth , to laugh; Copt. ⲥⲱⲃⲉ.

sbeth , IV, 219, to inhale, to smell.

sbeth-ti , Rec. 36, 211; var. , , fort, citadel.

sebṭ , , to prepare, to equip; Copt. ⲥⲟⲃⲧⲉ.

sebṭi , , Rev. 13, 63, wall; plur. , Ḥerusȧtef Stele 130; Copt. ⲥⲟⲃⲧ.

Sebṭi , a name of Alexandria.

s-beṭesh , to make weak or feeble; caus. of .

sep , the rest, remainder; Copt. ⲥⲉⲉⲡⲉ.

sep .

sep-t , Rec. 30, 4, list, writing, document, ordinance.

sep , P. 418, M. 599, N. 1204, , , Rec. 26, 64, to equip a boat with tackle, to work the tackle.

sep-t , , , Rec. 26, 64, , Décrets 29, 107, tackle of a boat; , equipment of a keben-t boat (*i.e.*, a boat of Byblos).

sep , flax; Copt. ⲥⲉⲡⲡⲓ.

sep-t , T. 376, linen (?)

sep , to fight, to slay.

sep-t , a kind of instrument.

Sep , B.D.G. 41, 693, 1064, Berg. 49, Metternich Stele 129, , , a Heliopolitan form of Osiris; , Piānkhi Stele 101, the road of Sep; , Hymn of Darius 32, the gods of the company of Osiris.

Sepit , a goddess.

Sepi ḥeb , the festival of Sepi.

sep-t , , , , nome, country; plur. , , , T. 146, P. 188, 668, M. 778, , N. 904, , P. 696, ; , P. 304, the two divine nomes; , Rec. 33, 3, wooded land.

Sep-t en tchet-tt , Berg. II, 12, a name of the necropolis.

sep-t , Rec. 16, 72, estate.

sep , to pass the time (?)

Spa , a god.

s-pa , U. 568, , N. 751, 759, , , N. 758, to make to fly; caus. of .

Sepi , a worm-like fish (?)

sepu (?) , Peasant 155 . . . .

sepu , a dose of medicine.

s-penā , to overturn, to capsize; caus. of .

s-perr , Rec. 34, 177, , IV, 968, Thes. 1480, to make to come forth, to act with strength; caus. of ; Copt. ⲡ̄ⲣⲣⲉ.

sper , P. 400, , N. 1179, , , , , Ȧmen. 20, 16, , , , , to arrive at a place, to come.

Sper-t neter-s , Ṭuat XII: (1) a wind-goddess of dawn; (2) one of the 12 goddesses who towed the boat of Ȧf into the eastern sky.

sper, to ask, to beseech, to implore, to make a complaint.

sper-t, IV, 970, prayer, petition, request.

speru, Hh. 439, IV, 971, petitions, prayers.

speṙu, petitioner, plaintiff.

sper-ti, IV, 1111, plaintiff, petitioner.

sper, U. 123, rib; plur., Rec. 30, 67; Copt. ⲥⲡⲓⲣ.

sper, a metal vessel or object.

sper-t, a mineral substance.

speḥ, N. 424, 509, T. 263, 323, to lasso, to fetter, to bind.

speḥ-t, lasso, tie, fetter.

Speḥ, Rec. 31, 31, the name of a god.

Speḥ-[t]-ur-t, N. 976, a goddess who tied the legs of animals for sacrifice.

speḥ-t, U. 312, parts of the body, a joint from the lower part of the back of some animal.

s-peḥ, Rec. 26, 13, to make to arrive; caus. of .

s-pekha, to divide, to separate, to open the bowels; caus. of .

s-pekhar, to write, to engrave, to draw designs, to enroll, to register; , designer of the temple of Ptaḥ.

s-pekhar, Rec. 31, 31, to make to go round, to surround, to brandish [weapons]; caus. of .

spes, to overthrow, to slay.

spes, A.Z. 1906, 107, 109, to skip, to jump, to dance.

spes, to build.

Spes, B.D. 137, 50, 179, 3, the name of a god.

sept; see .

septi, T. 61, N. 594, M. 219, Peasant 167, Rev. 13, 27, the two lips; Rec. 26, 233; = שְׂפַת הַיְאֹר, Gen. xli, 3; on my lip; Copt. ⲥⲡⲟⲧⲟⲩ, Heb. שְׂפָתַיִם, Arab. شَفَة.

sept, rim of a vessel, edge, margin of a lake; the water's edge; , shore of the Mediterranean.

sept, plinths, bases (?)

Sept, the name of a god = (?)

Sept-ti (?), Litanie 22, two plumes of Rā.

Septi-khenu

, Denderah II, 10, one of the 36 Dekans; Gr. Σπτχνε.

Septi-ṭenb , B.D. 36, 2, a title of Āpshait.

Sept , , to be ready, prepared; see .

sept , preparation, arrangement.

sept , ready for the road; , , with strong sharp horns ready to attack; , provided with a mouth, *i.e.*, able to speak skilfully and boldly.

Septit , , a form of Hathor.

sepṭ , , , , , , , , IV, 975, to be prepared, ready; , T. 271, ready; , ready for an opportunity; , U. 94, IV, 372, with ready eye; , IV, 1084, , with ready, skilful tongue; , with ready mouth; , , IV, 388, , , IV, 1014, ready with watchful intelligent face; , IV, 1152, provided with skilled fingers; Copt. cⲂⲧⲉ.

sepṭeṭ , , , A.Z. 45, 124, , to be ready, prepared; Copt. cⲂⲧⲱⲧ.

sepṭit , U. 260, T. 277, a woman or goddess with child.

sepṭu , , people who are provided with goods, *i.e.*, the well-to-do, the wealthy.

sepṭi[t] , , , rations, provisions, daily food, stores of food.

Sepṭu , Berg. I, 14, a crocodile-god.

Sepṭu , Ombos I, 186–188, one of the 14 kau of Rā.

Sepṭ-āb , Berg. I, 16, an ibis-god, a protector of the dead.

Sepṭ-ȧbehu , U. 282, N. 719 + 10, , N. 719, , A.Z. 1910, 128, , a god.

Sepṭ-ābui , B.D. 110, 40, , IV, 616, , , , Rev. 11, 72, a title of several bull-gods.

Sepṭ-t-uauau , Ṭuat II, the 2nd Gate of the Ṭuat.

Sepṭu-meṭut , the 6th Gate of the Ṭuat.

Sepṭu-ḥennu-ti , B.D. 78, 42, , Rec. 28, 166, a title of Rā and of Ȧmen.

Sepṭu-ḥer , Berg. I, 16, : (1) a lion fire-god; (2) an ibis-god, the god of the 18th day of the month.

Sepṭu-kheri-neḥait , , B.D. 125, III, 21, a mystic title of the deceased.

Sepṭu-kesu, etc. , etc., B.D. 145A, the doorkeeper of the 16th Pylon.

Sepṭu , P. 701, , N. 719, , U. 281, , , U. 219, P. 200, 669, M. 779, , , Rec. 27, 222, , , , a god of the Eastern Delta.

Sepṭu , Ṭuat XI, the zodiacal light (?)

Sepṭit, U. 221, P. 309, 603, 643, N. 52, , N. 1056, , N. 1242, , M. 680, , Hh. 393, , , , , , , B.D. 101, 13, 110, 33, 149, 11, Thes. 86 ff., the Dog-star; , N. 168; , the rising of Sothis which marked the beginning of the Egyptian year; Gr. Σωθις.

Sepṭit, Tomb Seti I, Sothis, the queen of the 36 Dekans.

Sepṭiu, B.D. (Saïte) 17, 57, 32, 5, 130, 7, the Sothic deities.

Sepṭu, , , Rec. 19, 18: (1) the followers of Sepṭ in the Eastern Delta; (2) allies of the Libyans.

Sepṭu, — titles of: — , , Goshen 2.

Sepṭu-Ḥeru-ȧab-t, the god Sepṭ + the Eastern Horus.

Sepṭu-Shu, Goshen 2, Sepṭ-Shu son of Rā.

Sepṭu-Gemḥes, U. 219, P. 200, 669, M. 779, 936, , , a form of Horus worshipped in the Eastern Delta.

Sepṭ, a mythological worm.

sepṭ, U. 94, 372, , U. 401, to cut, to slay.

sepṭ, B.D. 145, VI, 24, a kind of wood.

sepṭ-t, , , a triangular plot of ground.

sepṭ, , , , a kind of stone, stone scrapers (?)

Sepṭat-ānkh, Ṭuat VIII, the name of a goddess in the Ṭuat.

sepṭu, triangle.

s-peṭetch, N. 806, to collect, to gather together; caus.

septch, triangle.

sef, , , , U. 180, Hh. 88, yesterday, day before yesterday; Copt. ⲥⲁϥ.

Sef, B.D. 17, 15, a lion-god, symbol of "yesterday."

Sef-maa-ḥeḥ-en-renput, B.D. 42, 13, a title of Osiris.

sef, Rec. 16, 110, flame, fire, heat, blaze.

sefsef, to smelt, to liquefy, to cook; .

Sefsef, a god; see **Tchesef.**

sef, , , to rub down, to cut up, punishment.

sef, knife; see ; plur. , A.Z. 1900, 21, ; ; , to knap flint knives.

sefa, , , , to suffer or endure vexation, to feel disgusted or annoyed.

sef ḥer, to be long-suffering.

sef-t, , , annoyance.

sefu, , , mild or patient man, gracious; plur. , the meek.

sefa, to kill, to slay.

sefi, , , to be young, babe, child, a title of the rising sun.

sefit (?), Rec. 21, 82, patience (?)

s-fi, Rev. 14, 4, to make to rise; caus.

sefi , , unguent, scented oil, an anointed person.

sefsef , to pour out, to overflow; see .

sefi , , Rev. 12, 46, , Rev. 12, 25, , Rev. 12, 26, sword, knife; Copt. ⲥⲏϥⲉ.

sefi , Rev., sword, knife; Copt. ⲥⲏϥⲉ.

sefu , IV, 501, to kill, to slay.

sefsef , , , to sharpen.

s-fen , , Rec. 16, 56, , to be gracious, to suffer patiently, to endure, weary, annoyed, vexed; caus.

sefni , Israel Stele, 15, gracious.

sefnu , , , IV, 970, Thes. 1481, a kindly man, indolent, patient.

sefna , to slumber.

sefen , to split, to cleave.

sfenṭ , to slay, to stab, knife, sword, dagger; , a reed-cutter's knife.

sfenṭ àḥ , butcher, sacrificing official.

s-fenṭ , Hymn to Nile 1, 8, 9, to loathe, to be troubled or disgusted at something, to suffer, to endure; caus.

Sefer, Sefert , , U. 648, , Rev. 1, 158, 2, 19, Mon. Civ. 33, 5, a fabulous animal with the head of a hawk and a pair of wings.

sefekh , , , , , , Hh. 416, seven; varr. = 4 + 3, = 5 + 2; fem. , U. 630, , U. 631, , T. 305, 307, T. 306; Copt. ⲥⲁϣϥ, Heb. שֶׁבַע.

sefekh nu , , seventh.

sefkhu = , seventy; Copt. ϣϥⲉ.

Sefkhit , Rec. 3, 116, a goddess.

Sefkhit-ābut , IV, 339, , , , , A.Z. 1905, 75, , Rev. 11, 153, a goddess of letters, writing, numbers and painting and consort of Thoth.

s-fekh , U. 448, P. 125, M. 94, N. 100, , Rec. 31, 25, , , , Rec. 29, 155, to loosen, to untie, to unbind, to relax, to set free; caus. of ; , Rec. 31, 26, , undone, set free, unbolted (of a door); , to break or remove a seal; , to cut off, to cut away.

s-fekhekh , U. 3, T. 233, 281, , N. 218, to unloose, to untie; , P. 237, , N. 707; caus. of .

s-fekhu , P. 245, , M. 468, , N. 1057, , Rec. 27, 223, 31, 171, , to put off one's garments, to undress.

sefkhu , B.M. 448, of .

sefkhi[t], Rec. 17, 149, undressing chamber (?)

Sefekh[it] neb-s, a goddess.

sefekh, Hh. 162 . . . . . .

sefekh en nemtt, sandals (?)

s-fekk, , to pour out, to be poured out, exhausted; caus.

sefkek-t, destruction, exhaustion.

sefeg, P. 216, Rec. 30, 197 . . . .; , P. 216, , Rec. 31, 175.

seft, IV, 1022, to slay, to offer up sacrifice.

seft, Koller Pap. 1, 5, , , IV, 666, knife, sword; plur. ; , Anastasi I, 25, 7, belt knife, dagger; , a sword five cubits long; Copt. CHqe, Syr. ܣܦܣܦܐ, Arab. سَيْف, Eth. ሰይፍ : Gr. ξίφος.

seft, Thes. 1284, , animals to be slaughtered.

seftu, butcher, slaughterer.

seft, , , , , , pitch, a kind of holy oil; var.

seft, , B.D., Rec. 4, 87, 20, a kind of bird.

seft, a kind of ground or earth.

seftseft, to stride.

sefth, U. 58, , U. 38, N. 310, , , , , a kind of sacred oil.

seft, to slay, to kill.

sefṭi, slaughterer.

seft, , A.Z. 1880, 95, sword, dagger.

sem, , , Rec. 27, 230, , , a kind of priest, director; , overseer of the sem priests.

sem, E.T. 1, 53, confidant.

semu, , the deified priests of Ptaḥ and Apis at Memphis.

Sem, Palermo Stele, a god.

sem . . . ., M. 693 . . . . . .

semut (?), Rec. 31, 169 . . . .

Semu taui, Rec. 27, 222, "guide of the Two Lands"—a title of a god.

sem, semi, , , , , , , to bless; Copt. CMOY.

sem, , Rev., blessing; Copt. CMOY.

sem, , Rev. 14, 10, to resemble.

sem, Rec. 3, 48, picture.

sem, , , , , , L.D. III, 194, 30, , form, image, kind, manner, practice, custom.

sem-t (?), Rev. 11, 147, , Rev. 12, 87, form, likeness; Copt. CMOT.

sem, action, custom (?)

sem, Sphinx Stele 5, , , deed, undertaking.

sem, U. 625, U. 493, 578, N. 860, 1326, , M. 716, , N. 945, , , , , , , , , herb, grass, pasture, field, crop, herbage; plur. , , , , , Thes. 1288, , IV, 749, , Rec. 31, 175; Copt. ⲥⲓⲙ.

sem-t, T. 89, , M. 241, , N. 620, herbs, vegetables.

semit, herbs, field produce; , Love Songs 1, 10, flowers of speech.

sem, to pile offerings upon an altar.

sem, Rec. 6, 136, temple (of the head); see .

sem ; var ; see **tchām**.

sem-ui, U. 368, two bulls.

sem-t, a kind of animal, lizard (?)

semsem, Rec. 22, 2, , , , , , horse, a pair of horses (?); plur. ; compare Heb. סוּסִים.

sem-t, a night garment, apparel.

Sem-t, Semtt, , , Rec. 28, 169, , , the Theban necropolis.

semu, N. 936, lands, domains.

s-ma, Rev. 11, 173, to inform, to report news or intelligence; Copt. ⲧⲁⲙⲟ.

sma, , to unite, to join oneself to someone or something.

smai ta, Rec. 31, 19, union [with] earth, *i.e.*, burial.

sma, T. 11, P. 191, M. 193, N. 702, Rec. 31, 28, , T. 332, , Rec. 26, 78, , temple; , the two temples; , P. 423, M. 340, N. 760, hair, hairy temples.

smai, dresser of the body of the god ( ).

sma, , Rec. 1, 48, a bundle of cloth.

sma, , an amulet (?) a triangular object.

sma, Rev. 13, 3, to resemble.

sma, P. 183, , M. 289, , , Rec. 8, 124, 20, 42, ; varr. , , to slay, to kill.

sma-t, Rec. 27, 57, slaughter.

smau, slaughterer.

sma, U. 275, knife, sword.

Smạ, P. 568, the god of the vertebrae of Osiris.

sma, , U. 589, , M. 823, , , , a bull or cow slain as a sacrifice; fem. ; plur.

III, P. 669, , M. 779, , P.S.B. 15, 156.

Smati, U. 596, , P. 682, a bull-god.

Smait, U. 493, , N. 945, , B.D. 177, 7, a cow-goddess.

Sma-ur, U. 280, , T. 273, P. 25, M. 35, N. 124, a bull-god; fem. , T. 359, , N. 177.

Smait urit, P. 613, , P. 712, N. 802, 1363, , N. 945, , T. 359, a cow-goddess.

Sma . . . . tȧ, Rec. 31, 12, a goddess.

Sma, "Bull"—name of a boat of Ȧāḥmes I.

s-maȧr, see ; caus. of .

s-maā, Hh. 453, , Rec. 20, 42, , Rec. 33, 36, , Ȧmen. 10, 12, to make or prove true, to prove innocent, to justify, to correct, to discharge a duty or debt, to pay what is due or obligatory, to pay vows, to dedicate; caus. of ; , applied to the wind, a direct or favourable wind.

Smaā-ḥuti, Tomb of Seti I, one of the 75 forms of Rā (No. 74).

s-maā, , , III, 141, to ascribe righteousness or blessing to someone; Copt. ⲥⲙⲁⲙⲁⲁⲧ, ⲥⲙⲟⲩ.

s-maā, to appeal for justice, to pray to have a wrong righted.

s-maā-t, an appeal, petition; , righteous edicts.

s-maā kheru, , to make true the word, *i.e.*, to prove innocent, to justify a person.

s-maā kheru, Thes. 1482, justifier.

s-maā, to make straight or level the path of someone; , we make straight for thee the roads of Ȧgert.

s-maā, to cut, to dig.

smaāiu, slaughterers.

smaām, to make a noise, to terrify with noise.

smaāḥ, to entreat, to supplicate.

Smai (?) B.D. (Saïte) 110, a lake in Sekhet-Ȧaru.

s-maui, IV, 863, , , , , , to renew, to repair, to rebuild; caus. of .

Smam, M. 772, , , , , , , to slay, to kill, to slaughter.

smam-t, slaughter.

smamu, victim, sacrifice, the slain.

smamiu, butchers, slaughterers, the avenging gods.

smam, bull, wild bull; plur., Peasant 207.

Smamit, a cow-goddess.

Smam[it], B.D. 110, 43, a goddess of Sekhet-Åaru.

Smam-ur, B.D. 17, 114, a bull-god who was the soul of the Earth-god Geb.

Smamit urit, Rec. 30, 186, a cow-goddess.

smam ta, Peasant 309, burial.

Smam-ti, B.D. 145, VI, 25, the porter of the 6th Pylon.

s-mam, to please, to gratify; caus. of.

Smami, a name of Set.

smamu, foliage.

Smamu, cloud-gods (?)

Smant-urt, N. 177; see **Sma-ur.**

s-mar; varr., IV, 1089, to make miserable; caus. of.

smatchit, Rec. 30, 67, a part of a ship.

smȧ, IV, 973, Rev. 13, 30, to report, to inform, to make an announcement; Copt. ϲⲙⲙⲉ.

semmȧi, Rev. 11, 145, 150, to report, to inform against, to accuse; Copt. ϲⲙⲙⲉ.

smȧ, herald, reporter.

smȧ, smi, report, story, narrative, proclamation, declaration; Copt. ϲⲉⲙⲓ.

smȧ-t, utterance, speech, word, order.

semmȧi, Rev. 12, 22, report, accusation.

smȧ, B.D. 169, 23, whip; plur., Peasant 186;, B.D. 149, II, 8.

Smȧ, B.D. 169, 23, a sacred animal (?) in Abydos.

smȧ, unguent, salve, cream, butter.

smȧi nu neh-t, paste made from the fruit of the sycomore-fig tree.

smȧn, a kind of incense or perfume.

Smȧn, the Incense-god.

Smȧtit, Rec. 16, 109, a goddess.

smȧti, Mar. Aby. I, 6, 37, weigher (?)

smā, Rec. 29, 146, 30, 188, a pole used in working a boat; plur. , Rec. 30, 68; , P. 390, M. 556, N. 1163.

s-[a]mm' , to burn up, to consume; caus. of .

s-mār , Rec. 33, 3, , ibid. 32, 79, , , , to please, to make happy, to dress a god or a man in festal attire; var. , Rec. 16, 56; caus. of ; , festal raiment.

Smi , , "Slayer"—a name of Set; plur. , Nesi-Ȧmsu 14, 15, , the associates of Set.

smi-t , fight, combat, battle.

smun , , A.Z. 1896, 39, Ḥeruemḥeb 11, , , , , Metternich Stele 188, assuredly, really and truly, verily, to acclaim.

smuḥ , Rec. 36, 78, petition, supplication.

smut (?) , to report.

s-men , , , , , to stablish, to be established; caus. of ; Copt. ⲥⲙⲓⲛⲉ, ⲥⲉⲙⲛⲓ.

smen-tȧ , N. 1230, stablisher, stablished.

smenn , P. 672, M. 662, , , established; , IV, 204, done into writing effectively.

smen-t , U. 559, IV, 655, , , Coronation Stele, a stablishing, stability, a standing still, halt.

smen , order, foundation.

Smen user , A.Z. 1906, 133, the title of a priest.

smenti , IV, 344, porter, carrier.

smenti , a pair of members of the body.

Smenu , P. 742, a god.

Smentt , T. 355, , N. 175, , N. 811, a goddess.

Smen maāt em Uast , a title of Ȧmen-Rā.

smen , Stunden 44.........

smenu , , , image, form, statue; plur. .

smenut , Rec. 32, 64, monuments.

smenu , IV, 428, objects made of bronze.

smenu , N. 976, parts of a ladder, rungs (?)

smen , U. 571, T. 387, P. 699, M. 665, N. 1281, , , a kind of goose; Copt. ⲥⲙⲟⲩⲛⲉ.

smen-t , goose.

Smen , N. 953, a goose-god; var. .

s-menmen , , Rec. 31, 15, to make to move, to remove; caus.

smen-t , withdrawal, departure.

smen-t , P. 611, incense, perfume.

s-menkh , , IV, 1184, to complete, to make perfect, to set in good order, to beautify, to endow richly, to

embellish; , perfected, established; caus. of .

smenkh-t , adornment.

smer , , , , , , , , , a title of nobility; fem. ; plur. , , , IV, 1073, , IV, 898, 1094, , , Thes. 1285, ; , M. 391, , N. 658; , the chief smer; , the smeru of the Court.

smer uāti , , , , a title of nobility higher than smer, perhaps unique smer; plur. ; , smer, only one of love, a title of nobility.

smeriu , , a guild of priests; , leaders of the caravan (?)

Smer nesert , the goddess of the 8th hour of the night.

s-mer , to make to suffer, inflict pain; caus. of .

smer , Rev. 12, 65, the left hand; Heb. שְׂמֹאל, Assyr. , Arab. شمال, Syr. ܣܡܠܐ. The Egypt. , the ἀσμαχ of Herodotus II, 30, is probably a mistake for (?)

smer-t , B.D. 172, 15, eyelids.

smer , Rec. 6, 6, to dress, to array.

smer , ornamental raiment.

smer , Rev. 11, 167 ....

s-meh , , Rec. 26, 79, to make to forget; caus.

smeḥ , , to cry out, to beseech, to pray.

s-meḥ , , , Rev. 11, 125, to flood, to submerge, to fill full.

s-meḥ-åb , to satisfy.

smeḥ , P. 421, M. 603, N. 1208, , a boat. In the Pyramid Texts its length is 770 cubits, .

smeḥ , a kind of wine or beer (?); Copt. ⲥⲙⲁϩ (?)

smeḥi , Anastasi I, 23, 4, , Rougé I.H. II, 125, the left hand, left side; Gr. ἀσμάχ; see Herodotus II, 30, and .

s-mekh (s-khem) , Pap. 3024, 68, IV, 943, , IV, 965, 1161, to forget; , Hymn to Nile 16, 9; caus. of .

smekh (skhem) , Thes. 1207, image.

s-mekhṭ (?) , B.D. 169, 5, ...

s-mes , P. 243, to deliver a woman; , A.Z. 1873, 131; Copt. ⲑⲙⲉⲥⲓⲟ.

smesu , Mar. Aby. I, 8, 86, goslings just hatched.

smesit , IV, 225, midwife.

sems, to burn, to consume.

sems, stake, club, mallet, mace.

sems, to look; Copt. ⲥⲟⲙⲥ.

sems àa-t, T. 374, N. 695, M. 125, covering, a kind of garment.

semsu, U. 440, T. 251, P. 697, N. 968, Metternich Stele 245, eldest, firstborn; plur. T. 255, P. 215, T. 326, Rec. 32, 81; U. 516, older than the eldest.

Semsu h[ai]-t, eldest of a priest's college.

Semsu qeṭ-t en Ptaḥ, T. 87, M. 240, N. 618, the eldest-born of the workshop of Ptaḥ, a title of the high-priest of Ptaḥ.

sems utut, Rhind Pap. 24, a title of Thoth.

Sems neb àakhu, Denderah II, 11, one of the 36 Dekans.

Semsit set nekhenkhen-t (*sic*), Rec. 34, 191, one of the 12 Thoueris goddesses.

semsu, A.Z. 1906, 112, a priest's title.

semsun, pot, vessel.

Semseru, Rec. 36, 202, a god.

semkett, Palermo Stele, U. 220, M. 263, P. 177, the boat of the evening sun; var. M. 263, 657; see **Sektt.**

Smet, U. 219, M. 496; see **Mestà**, one of the four sons of Horus.

smet, Rev. 14, 37, eye-paint; Copt. ⲥⲧⲏⲙ.

smeti, the parts of the eyelids to which kohl was applied.

Smeti, Denderah II, 10, one of the 36 Dekans; Gr. ⲥⲙⲁⲧ.

smet, P. 402, M. 574, N. 1180, Àmen. 21, 12, to hear, to listen, to eavesdrop (?)

Smeti, Rec. 21, 78, enquirer, investigator.

Smet, Smetà, P. 618, N. 1299, N. 873, a god.

smett, Rec. 26, 75; var. Rec. 26, 75, a god (?) . . .

Smetu, B.D. 144, the watcher of the 1st Ārit.

smet, a kind of grain or seed used in medicine.

smetà, Rev. 12, 62, form; Copt. ⲥⲙⲟⲧ.

s-meter , , , , , , , , , , , , , to enquire into a matter, to make an investigation, to verify, to inspect, to examine; , IV, 1076; caus. of .

s-meṭ , to make to speak, to declare; caus. of .

smeṭ , , , kind, manner, copy, likeness, form, similitude; Copt. CMOT.

smeṭ-t , servant, serf, subordinate, slave born on an estate, underling; plur. , , IV, 97, , .

Smeṭ , a crocodile-god, the god of the 23rd day of the month.

smeṭ , , , Thes. 1323, to walk, to move, to carry.

Smeṭ-t , , , , , , , half month, the half-monthly festival; plur. , T. 12, M. 763; , , , the festival of the 15th day of the month.

Smeṭ , , , Tomb Seti I, one of the 36 Dekans; var. , Tomb Ram. IV; Gr. Σματ.

Smeṭ meḥ-t , Annales I, 88, Mercury.

Smeṭ res-t , Annales I, 88, Jupiter.

Smeṭ ser-t , Annales I, 85, one of the 36 Dekans.

Smeṭsmeṭ , B.M. 1075, a hippopotamus-goddess.

smeṭ , rows of inlaid stones, inlayings.

smeṭ-t , U. 65, N. 320, , , , , eye paint, kohl, antimony; Copt. CTHM.

smeṭ-t , Thes. 1207, , weapons, tools, implements.

smetchetchu , U. 1 = , abomination.

sen , , , , , pronom. suffix 3rd pers. plur., they, them, their; dual , N. 1238 = , M. 675; , M. 677, N. 1239 = , P. 642 = , Hh. 342; , P. 549, Rec. 30, 69.

senui , masc. two; fem. **senti** ; Copt. CNAY.

sen-nu , U. 151, , T. 122, , U. 317, 575, , P. 267, , N. 1248, , M. 480, , , , , , , , , , , , , second; fem. , , ; , Peasant 215, a man who says one thing and means another; , , , second time; , , A.Z. 45, 125, second of two.

sen-nu, Pap. 3024, 106, Shipwreck 42, , , , , , , , , A.Z. 45, 126, fellow, counterpart, companion, neighbour, colleague.

sen, U. 549, T. 304, , N. 33, , M. 487, , , , , , , brother; , kinsman; , Philadelphus; fem. ; , Adelphoi; dual , M. 169, , N. 655, , , , , Rec. 33, 30, , , , , Rec. 33, 30, , IV, 618, , , , two brothers, two brother-gods, *e.g.*, Horus and Set, or Set and Thoth; , P. 466, M. 529, , N. 1108, Shu and Tefnut; plur. , U. 23, , U. 557, , U. 299, , T. 137, , Rec. 29, 153, 31, 26, , ibid. 31, 26, , Rec. 29, 76, , , , , , brethren; , , Shipwreck 126, brothers and sisters: , Coronation Stele 18, the king's brothers; Copt. CON.

senȧ, brother; fem. .

Senȧ, P. 273, , M. 487, N. 1254, a god.

sen en ȧt, P. 434, M. 621, N. 1225, father's brother, uncle.

sen-t, T. 260, N. 887, , P. 488, , M. 488, , , , , , , sister; , sister-wife; , royal sister; dual , T. 172, N. 763, , M. 140, N. 647, , N. 740, , IV, 618, , , Rec. 29, 157, , , , IV, 860, , , , , , , ; plur. , Rec. 29, 153, , , .

Sen-tȧ, P. 273, , M. 488, N. 1254, a goddess (?)

sensen, T. 173, , N. 107, , P. 76, , N. 19, , T. 283, , M. 30, , , Treaty 7, , , , , , , , , , , , , Rec. 20, 41, to meet, to join, to associate with, to be friends, to unite, friendship.

senseni, friend; plur. , P. 486, , , .

sensen, Rec. 1, 38, Thes. 522, , Berg. I, 33, the festival of the two bulls, *i.e.*, of the conjunction of the sun and moon in the month of Epiphi.

sensenti, Åmen. 11, 13 . . . .

Sen-nefer, B.D. 78, 28, a title of a god.

sen, thief; Copt. CONI.

sen, needy, sufferer, sick (?) a failure (?)

senn , Metternich Stele 55, to be wretched, needy or miserable.

senn , to make a mistake in speaking, blunder, a false statement, lie (?); compare , P. 365, N. 1078, lie.

senu = , Ḥeru-sȧtef Stele 28, helpless, infirm; Copt. ϣⲱⲛⲉ.

sen , Leyd. Pap. 98 . . . .

sen , U. 181, I, 53, , P. 164, M. 328, , N. 859, , A.Z. 1910, 125, , to smell, to kiss; , Shipwreck 134, to kiss a wife; , I, 53, he kissed his foot; , he kissed the earth, *i.e.*, did homage.

senȧ er ta ; see **sen-ta.**

sen ta , Rec. 26, 234, , Hh. 307, , to smell the earth, to kiss the ground in homage; , P. 8, , U. 179.

sennut , P. 356, , N. 1070, acclamations, homage.

sensen , T. 376, , M. 333, , A.Z. 1908, 119, , to breathe.

sensen , to have a bad smell; , smell, odour.

sen-t , T. 343, , P. 222, a festival of the 6th day (?)

sennu , , Rec. 27, 225, , IV, 414, , Rec. 26, 224, an offering.

sen , T. 316, , P. 274, to bind (?)

sen, senȧ-t , , box, case, chamber, room.

senti , P. 48, Rec. 31, 163, , Palermo Stele, , T. 173, P. 119, M. 153, N. 107, , T. 283, , Rec. 27, 225, the two halves of Egypt, *i.e.*, Upper and Lower Egypt, a double shrine of Rā which was symbolic of all Egypt.

sen-t , pole, mast, flagstaff; plur. , Rec. 20, 40, 42; , ; , IV, 1105, the north pole of the palace.

senit , masts, flagstaffs.

sen-t (?) , ground, basis, foundation.

sen-t , IV, 1174, , Anastasi I, 15, 4, plinth, pedestal of an obelisk.

sen , , to copy, to make a likeness or transcript.

sen , to follow in the track of.

senn , IV, 412, to make a copy or likeness.

senn , copy, duplicate, transcript.

sennu , IV, 1034, , IV, 1036, , , , , , , likeness, image, copy, figure, statue; plur. , , .

senn , , , a kind of precious stone, ruby (?)

sna (?) , to walk docilely, to follow.

snā, fiends, foes, enemies.

s-nāā, to reduce to the consistence of paste (drugs used in medicine), to knead; caus. of ,

snib, Metternich Stele 65, 66, 69, health; see .

snif (?), blood; see .

snin, to pass; var. , Rev. 11, 141; Copt. ⲥⲓⲛⲉ.

snu, Methen, a class of men on an estate.

snu, , pot, jar, vessel, vase.

snu, wine of Pelusium (?) drink; compare , I, 3, 4 = Gr. Σαϊν.

snu, Ḥerusȧtef Stele 135, vineyard.

s-nu, to bind, to tie.

s-nukh, , , to warm, to heat, to cook, to burn up, to boil; caus.; Copt. ⲥⲉⲗϩⲟ.

snutt, Ebers 41, 15, a plant used in medicine.

s-nuṭ, B.D. 64, 35, carrier.

snutchem (?), Hh. 369, to bear (?) to carry (?)

senb, , , , , , to be sound or healthy, health, strength; , , enjoying good health; in = health. Perhaps = שָׁלוֹם.

senb, , , to protect.

senbi, Rev. 13, 80, vigour, health.

senb-t, Shipwreck 158, , health.

senb-t, P. 1116B, 34.......

senbeb, P. 429, M. 614, N. 1218, , IV, 559, to say "good health" to anyone.

Senbu, N. 1182, , N. 1182, the Health-god.

Senbit-ȧb, Ombos II, 132, a goddess.

Senb-Kheperu, the 11th hour of the day.

senb-t, , , , jar, vase, vessel, pot, libation vessel; plur. , , A.Z. 1880, 49; vessel of silver-gold.

s-neb, to kindle, to light a fire; caus. of **neb.**

s-nebb, to kindle, to light a fire; caus. of **nebb** for **nebneb.**

s-nebneb, to kindle, to light a fire; caus. of **nebneb.**

senb, to bind, to tie, girdle, belt.

senb, , , , , , to build a wall, to surround with walls, to hem in or surround (the enemy).

senb-t, , , , , a wall, a girdle wall; plur. , , P.S.B. 27, 110.

senb-t, , , all-embracing heaven.

senb, , , to overthrow, to drive back, to repel.

senb , , evil person or thing, a beast of a man.

senb , , chaplet or crown made of plants or flowers.

senb , a wall of shrubs, *i.e.*, green hedge, avenue (?)

senb , a kind of tree; plur. ; , the gum or fruit of the same.

senbu , Rec. 30, 67, parts of a ship or boat.

snef , , blood; Copt. ⲥⲛⲟϥ.

snef , Rev. 14, 19, sacrificial priest (?)

snef , , the year that is past, last year; Copt. ⲥⲛⲟⲩϥ.

s-nefer , , , A.Z. 1905, 25, , to beautify, to please, to make happy, to decorate a tomb with texts and drawings; caus. of ; , I, 52, to please the heart, to gratify.

s-nefekhfekh , N. 656, Hh. 195, , Rec. 31, 17, , , Sphinx 14, 204, to untie, to loosen.

s-nem , , , to grieve, to mourn, grief, pain, sorrow.

snem , , to make an offering of propitiation.

snemm , to feed, to satisfy with food.

snem , N. 637, , T. 335, , P. 809, food.

snem , food in abundance, plenty.

snem , Peasant 153, a kind of weed or plant.

s-nemeḥ, s-nemmeḥ , ; var. , to pray, to beg, to humble oneself; caus.

s-nerit , IV, 385, conquest, conqueror; from .

s-nehi , IV, 1174, , to muster soldiers, to place soldiers in their positions for fighting, to marshal forces; caus.

s-nehep , IV, 966, Thes. 1479, to muster levies of soldiers, to call up troops; caus.

s-neheṭ , U. 444, , T. 253, to subdue; caus.

sneḥi , Rev. 11, 165 = , to command; Copt. ⲟⲩⲉϩ-ⲥⲁϩⲛⲉ.

sneḥi , Décrets 107, copy (?)

s-nekh , U. 573, , N. 967, , N. 757, to bring up, to rear a child; caus. of .

s-nekhekh , , to prolong one's life, to become old; caus.

sennekh-t , , axe.

snekha , B.D. 35, 2, to unload (?) to disembark (?)

s-nekhakha , Sphinx 14, 208, to slay.

s-nekhebkheb , T. 161, N. 688, Sphinx 14, 208, , Hh. 148, A.Z. 1910, 129, to unbolt a door.

s-nekhen , IV, 579, to rejuvenate; caus.

s-nekht , I, 145, P. 447, N. 1121, to strengthen; caus.

sensu , to praise, to adore, to acclaim.

sensu , IV, 936, , praises.

sensen, A.Z. 1906, 107, to praise, to acclaim; Copt. ⲥⲉⲗⲥⲱⲗ.

sens, to smell; see .

sensh, M. 214, 728, N. 685, 978, to open the ears; read .

sensh, to open, to make a way into; read .

s-neq, U. 48, , U. 369, P. 606, N. 143, , P. 602, , N. 803, , Rec. 26, 224, , , Rec. 26, 233, to suckle; caus. (?) Copt. ⲥⲱⲛⲕ, ⲧⲥⲛ̄ⲕⲟ; compare Heb. יָנַק.

s-neqeb, Metternich Stele 5, to suffer pain; caus.

s-neqmi, , , to feed, to nourish; caus.

senk-àb, U. 399, strong-willed.

senk-t, Rec. 36, 214 = , darkness, evening.

s-nketket, Sphinx 14, 210, to agitate, to shake; caus.

sent, , , , , , , Rev. 11, 174, fear, timidity; Copt. ⲥⲛⲁⲧ.

senti, crier.

sent, , = , evil, enmity.

sentiu, enemies.

sent, senṭ-t, , , garment, bandlet.

senti = , to found, to establish.

senti[t], cabin, canopy.

sentit, Litanie 14, sight, seer; var. .

sneter, , IV, 718, , , , , , , ; late forms , , , incense; Copt. ⲥⲟⲛⲧⲉ.

Sneterba, Berg. I, 23, a bird-god.

senth, to cut down timber.

senth, T. 282, N. 132, to found, to establish, custom, habit.

senthi, P. 407, M. 583, N. 1189, founder.

Senthi-ur, Dream Stele 12, the title of a priest.

senthi, Ikhernefert 14, cabin, shrine of a sacred boat, canopy.

s-nether, , , U. 9, , , , , , to cense, to purify with natron.

snether, , , , , , , , , , , , , , incense; . , to offer incense; , fresh incense.

senṭ, Rec. 27, 228, , , , , , , , , to fear; , timid of heart; , IV, 658, faces of fear, terror-stricken faces; Copt. ⲥⲛⲁⲧ.

senṭ-t, , , Àmen. 23, 7, , , ,

, , , , , , Jour. As. 1908, 299, fear; Copt. **ⲥⲛⲁⲧ**.

senṭu , IV, 972, , timid man.

Senṭ , Berg. I, 11, , Rec. 4, 28, a lion-god; , B.D. 1B, 8, 17, 46, a name of the heart of Osiris.

Senṭ - nef - Àmentiu , Ṭuat V, a god who burned the dead.

senṭ , T. 292, sails of a boat.

senṭ-t , Ḥerusàtef Stele 28, acacia wood.

Senṭit , Rec. 24, 161, a Canopic jar-goddess; var. .

sneṭer , incense; see **snether**.

sentch , P. 684, U. 270, , N. 719 + 6, P. 20, 543, , M. 71, , Hh. 551, , , , to fear; Copt. **ⲥⲛⲁⲧ**.

sentch-t , fear.

s-netchem , IV, 219, , , , , , , , , , to rest, to sit down, to seat oneself; ; L.D. III, 140B, seated; caus.

s-netchem netchem , , to seat oneself, to be at ease; caus.

s-netchem , U. 61, , N. 315, , , Pap. 3024, 19, , to make pleasant, to heal, to make happy; caus.

snetchemu , those who are at ease.

s-netchem àb , I, 59, to make glad the heart.

s-netches , to belittle, to make little; caus.

ser , , , , , , , , , prince, chief, nobleman, elder; plur. , , , , , , , , , , , , ; , chief nobles; , chief inspectors.

ser-t , , governorship, magistracy.

Ser-pu-āa, etc. , B.D. 153B, 11, the fowler who worked the net of the Akeru-gods.

Ser-tchatcha-t , M. 700, , N. 1321, a title of Ànpu.

ser , , , P. 1116, B 26, , Rec. 31, 170, , , , Metternich Stele 78, , , Rev. 11, 147, , , , Jour. As. 1908, 309, to announce, to dispose, to arrange, to order, to direct, to decree, to challenge; , Rev. 13, 42, to struggle; Copt. **ⲥⲱⲣ**.

seru (?) , precept, speech, prophecy.

ser-t , , , order, disposal.

serut, IV, 500, praises, glorifications.

Ser-t-nehepu-em-āḥā-s, etc., etc., B.D. 145, 146, the 19th Pylon.

ser, drum, tambourine.

seru, Rev. 14, 12, tambourine players.

ser, Rec. 33, 27, L.D. III, 194, , to arrange, to order, to exalt.

Ser, Ṭuat XII, one of the 12 gods who towed the boat of Åf through the serpent Ānkh-neteru; he was reborn daily.

Ser, Mar. Aby. I, 45, a god of .

Seru, Berg. I, 13, a serpent-god.

s-rer, to make to go round, to revolve; caus.

ser, fire, flame; . the warm breath of life.

ser, wool; Copt. ⲥⲟⲣⲧ.

ser, P. 441, M. 544, N. 1125, U. 133, a kind of goose; plur. , Rec. 29, 148.

ser, little; , faint-hearted.

ser (?), to be fettered, restraint.

seru, leg-bands, anklets.

ser-t, , , thorn, goad, a pointed tool or instrument; Copt. ⲥⲟⲩⲣⲓ.

ser-t, B.D. 58, 4, the name of a part of a boat.

serr, , , , to write, to engrave.

serser, Rev. 12, 30, to decorate to ornament; Copt. ⲥⲉⲗⲥⲱⲗ.

sera-t (?), a kind of linen.

serat, Jour. As. 1908, 301, prosperity, prosperous condition.

serȧ, water-pot; var. .

Serȧu, T. 309, a serpent-fiend in the Ṭuat.

seri-t, kindness, gentleness.

seri-t, , , Westcar Pap. 7, 19, disease, sickness, nausea.

seri-t, , , fan; var. .

s-ru, , , , Décrets 18, 107, to divert, to turn away; caus. of .

s-ruȧ, to make to cease, to divert; caus.

s-rukh, Hh. 433 . . . . . . ; caus.

s-rukheṭ, a mistake for , to embalm.

s-rut, Rev. 13, 10 = , to flourish.

s-ruṭ, , , to make to grow or to flourish, to make strong or firm or hard, to make solid; caus.

s-ruṭu, Hh. 448, evil growth.

s-ruṭ mau, , Gol. Hamm. 11, 58, recruits (?)

s-rutch, T. 260, , P. 692, , M. 663, , N. 1278, , , IV, 879, to make to grow, to make strong or firm or hard, to make solid; caus. of

serp-t, Rev, 11, 185, flower of the lily.

seref, , , , Åmen. 23, 3, to rest, to refresh oneself, repose, leisure.

seref, , , P. 204, M. 338, N. 864, to be hot, to be angry, warm, warmth, heat, flame, fire; compare Heb. √שׂרף.

serfu, , B.M. 828, Sphinx 11, 135, Rev. 8, 73, Jour. As. 1908, 299, an angry man; , IV, 970, a man who blows hot and cold.

seref-åb, warm-hearted.

seref-t, heat, warmth.

seref, hot drink.

serfu-t, inflamed sores, carbuncles, boils.

Serref, Rev. 11, 180 = (?) a mythological creature.

seref, to submerge, to be submerged, water flood.

serfi, to pay heed to; , heed it not.

s-rem, to make to weep; caus. of .

s-rekhi, , , to make to know, to give information against; , IV, 1004; , U. 491, P. 192, M. 363, N. 914.

srekh-t, Peasant 42, Pap. 3024, 125, information.

serkhi, the accused, the defendant.

Serkhi, , a title of Set.

serekh, IV, 160, 896, Thes. 1283, , Piehl III, 16, 19, , Hymn Darius 6, blazon, cognizance, throne.

serekh-t, , , , throne, throne chamber.

seres = **sås**, a six-ply stuff.

s-res, , Hh. 426, , to arouse, to wake up, to keep awake, to be vigilant; caus.

serq, P. 361, , N. 1074, , , , , , , , , , to open [the windpipe], to breathe, to inhale, to expand the lungs, to be refreshed.

serqu, Rec. 27, 86, men and women, people.

Serqit, a goddess of the royal crown.

Serqit, U. 599, P. 216, , P. 508, , N. 1140, 1241, , , , the Scorpion-goddess; , , the double Scorpion-goddess.

Serqit ḥetu, , T. 309, , T. 207, , N. 1140, , Rec. 30, 192, , Metternich Stele 23, the Scorpion-goddess.

serṭ, to glean in a cornfield; Copt. ⲥⲣⲏⲧ, ⲥⲣⲓⲧ.

s-ruṭ, , , = , to plant.

s-erṭā (?), to make to give; caus. of .

serṭebu, injury.

sertchȧ, to polish.

seh-t, Rec. 31, 22, a portion of the body.

s-ha, M. 261, , Ȧmen. 14, 10, 15, 20, 17, 13, 20, 21, , IV, 658, to make to go down.

seha-t, P. 117, , Rec. 31, 170, , descent.

s-ha (?), to turn aside, to overthrow.

s-ha, , Peas. 1116B, 19, 40, , Leyd. Pap. 2, 11, , , , Gol. Hamm. 13, 106, to rout, to overturn, to throw into confusion, to repulse, to rebel, to cause tumult; , Rec. 16, 109.

sehau, , Rev. 13, 36, a quarrelsome or contentious man.

seha, confusion, rebellion, riot.

sehi (?), booth, pavilion.

sehu-t, = .

s-hebi, to put to shame, to disgrace; caus. of .

s-hep, maker of laws, lawgiver; caus.

s-heri, to give or cause content, to satisfy, to pacify; caus. of **heri**.

s-herr, IV, 926, 1030, , Rec. 31, 170, to quiet, to pacify; caus.

sehrit, IV, 971, , , Peas. 1116, B, 65, satisfaction, pacification.

seherrit, pleasure, satisfaction.

seher, a kind of precious stone, carnelian (?)

Sehrȧt, Ombos I, 46, a moon-goddess.

sehri[t], , boat, houseboat, dahabîyyah.

seḥ, Rev. 14, 66 = ⲥⲉϩ, ⲥⲱϩ (?)

seḥ = .

seḥ, hall, chamber; var. .

seḥ, counsel.

seḥi, , , trained, skilled, clever, cunning, instructed, wise man.

seḥ aṭu, IV, 945 .....

Seḥseḥ, , P. 178, M. 269, N. 888, the Lake of Seḥseḥ; , P. 303, , U. 493, N. 945, the Mountain of Seḥseḥ; , Rec. 31, 171.

seḥseḥi[t], Theban Ostraka C. 1, a kind of disease.

seḥa, to sit.

s-ḥa, , , , IV, 484, , Rec. 34, 177, to strip, to undress; caus.

s-ḥap, , , to hide, to clothe, to conceal; caus.

s-ḥā, , to make to rejoice, to gladden; var. ; caus.

Seḥā, Orion; varr. , , .

seḥi, to rise (of a flood).

seḥiḥ-t, a kind of insect or bird.

Seḥith …, Ṭuat VI, a goddess.

seḥu …, Rec. 22, 2, …, …, Rec. 33, 34, …, IV, 767, Annales III, 109, …, …, …, …, …, …, to collect, to gather together, to assemble, to sum up, to add up a total; Copt. ⲥⲱⲟⲩϩ.

seḥu …, …, …, L.D. III, 219E, 14, summary, abridgment, collection, edition, list (of troops), inventory, catalogue; …, IV, 945, gathered into the store.

seḥutut …, collections, groups of things.

seḥu …, …, III, 139, Ḥerusâtef Stele 6, 12, crown, tiara, diadem.

seḥu …, wind, air, gale (?)

seḥu-t …; see …, egg.

s-ḥui …, …, …, …, to stink, filth; caus. of ….

s-huā (?) …, to disarrange, to confuse; caus.

s-ḥur …, …, …, …, …, …, Åmen. 25, 17, 20, to curse; caus.; Copt. ⲥⲁϩⲟⲩ, ⲥϩⲟⲩⲱⲣ.

seḥuràu …, abuse, revilings, curses.

seḥuru …, the accursed.

Seḥur …, Love Songs 2, 3, the name of a district.

s-ḥebi …, IV, 943, …, IV, 753, …, …, …, …, to make glad, to keep the feast, to keep holiday; …, Rec. 20, 40, arrayed in festal attire.

seḥbu …, …, shouts of joy, festival cries.

seḥbu …, …, Sallier II, 6, 9, wind, air.

seḥbenben (?) …, U. 113, N. 422 . . . .

Seḥeptt …, B.D. 104, 5, the name of a boat or of a boat-god.

seḥef …, IV, 935 . . . .

s-ḥemi …, U. 86, …, N. 363, …, …, to turn back, to drive away; …, to avert ill luck; caus.

s-ḥem …, …, …, …, …, to pound, to crush, to break up, to grind.

s-ḥen …, …, to provide.

s-ḥeni …, …, …, …, …, …, …, Rev. 12, 18, …, Rec. 21, 85, …, …, to command, to be in command of something, to order, to direct, to rule, to administer, to entrust with a commission; Copt. ⲥⲁϩⲛⲉ.

seḥen-t …, …, …, L.D. III, 219, 18, authority, command, administration, list, summary; Copt. ⲥⲁϩⲛⲉ.

seḥenu …, …, Rechnungen 37, order, decree, delivery.

seḥenu …, …, …, …, …, …, housemaster, thief (?)

Seḥenti-requ, , B.D. 146, the door-keeper of the 5th Pylon.

s-ḥen, to make to go back; caus.

seḥenti, repulser.

s-ḥenḥen, to turn away; caus.

seḥnu, crown.

seḥentu, A.Z. 17, 57, a piece of armour.

s-ḥeri, T. 287, Hh. 370, , M. 50, , P. 170, , M. 128, , , , , , , , , , , , , , , , , , , to drive away, to repulse; caus. Copt. ϲⲁϩⲣ.

seḥer, Rec. 8, 139, fighter.

Seḥrit-ṭu, the 3rd hour of the night.

seḥer (?), N. 293, a kind of club.

s-ḥeri, , , , , to bear up, to exalt; caus.

s-ḥes, to make to advance, to attack; caus.

s-ḥeqa, , to make to rule; caus.

s-ḥeq, to cut, to hack in pieces; caus.

s-ḥeqer, to keep hungry, to let hunger, starve; caus.; Copt. ϩⲟⲕⲉⲣ.

seḥeqer-t, Rec. 26, 78, hunger.

Seḥtt, a city of Osiris

s-ḥetep, Rec. 31, 21, , , to make to be at peace, to pacify, to appease, to propitiate, to unite with; , pacifiers; , to pacify the heart; , to pacify the ka; caus.

seḥetput, , Åmen. 8, 11, propitiatory offerings.

Seḥetep neterui, the title of the priest of the 10th Nome (Uatchet) of Upper Egypt.

Seḥetep Sekhmit, , Rev. 15, 16, propitiatory addresses to Sekhmit.

Seḥetep taui, B.D. 124, 7, a god of offerings; (Saïte).

seḥetpi, , , , , Mar. Aby. I, 6, 28, , , , censer; plur. , .

s-ḥetem, , , IV, 969, , , , , , , , , to destroy; caus.

seḥetemu, Peasant 222, destroyer.

Seḥetem-t, etc., B.D. 99, 28, the banks of the stream sailed on by the magical boat.

seḥeṭu, U. 618, , M. 327, , P. 798, N. 857, , U. 469, , P. 169,

, T. 220, 356, , U. 560, P. 668, , N. 983, the sky of the Ṭuat, the nether heaven; plur. , P. 789, , N. 801, , M. 778.

Seḥeṭ , Rec. 26, 228, the god of the sky of the Ṭuat.

s-ḥetch , U. 37, T. 266, , , , , , to illumine, to light up, to throw light on, to clear up, to explain; caus.; Copt. ⲥⲁϩⲧⲉ.

seḥetchut , , light, rays, radiance.

s-ḥetch ta , dawn.

seḥetch , the name of a chamber in a temple.

seḥetch , a heaven of stars.

Seḥetch ur , , , , B.D. 53, 2, B.M. 32, 280, "Great illuminer"—a name of the Sun-god; , Rec. 30, 67.

Seḥetch renpu , , Rec. 33, 36, a title of Rā.

Seḥetch khatut , Tomb Seti I, one of the 75 forms of Rā (No. 10).

s-ḥetch , Hh. 494, to be troubled; caus. of .

seḥetch , , inspector, overseer, officer of a boat; , inspector of servants of the Ka.

seḥetch-t , a case at law.

seḥetch per , to transfer a house.

seḥetch-t , box, case.

s-ḥetchen ḥat (?) , to distract the mind.

seḥetcher-t , bleached cloth.

sekh , to make to be.

sekh , , , , width, breadth.

sekh-t , , , hall, chamber.

sekhu , Rec. 37, 69, slaughter-house.

sekh-t , a broad boat, barge, lighter.

sekh , to stretch out the sky.

sekh , IV, 1153, to tarry (?)

sekh , , to cut, to cut off, to reap; Copt. ⲱⲥϧ.

sekhi , U. 537, , Rec. 27, 86, , Rev. 11, 163, , Ebers Pap. 109, 12, , , , , to strike, to break, to defeat, to overthrow, to beat (a drum), to mark cattle, to knap flints, to strike a lyre (Leyd. Pap. 59); , to play a zither; , to aim blows with a stick; , Rec. 17, 144, to bastinado; , to strike a light, kindle a fire; Copt. ⲥⲁϣ.

sekhsekh , B.D. 64, 17, to beat to pieces.

sekh-t , , , Leyd. Pap. 5, 11, IV, 1076, , , , , beating, punishment, blow, stripe, stroke; , Edict 28, , 100 strokes with a stick; , Mar. Karn. 53, 35, the wounded; Copt. ⲥⲏϣⲉ.

sekh-ti, Rec. 14, 42, a man who has been bastinadoed.

sekh-ti, bitter (?); Copt. ϲιϣⲉ.

sekh-t, deafness.

sekhi, Anastasi IV, 2, 7, Koller 2, 4, deaf man.

sekh-t, T. 333, P. 825, M. 249, N. 703, Rec. 31, 31, field, meadow; plur. U. 419, U. 624; Copt. ⲥⲱϣⲉ.

sekh-ti, field labourer, peasant, countryman; plur.

sekh-t — ta sekh-t, IV, 1130, "field bread."

Sekhti, a field-god; plur.

Sekhti-Sekhti, Ṭuat I and IX, a god.

Sekhti-t, the Field-goddess.

Sekh-t åaru, T. 73, T. 227, T. 244, P. 100, M. 628, M. 280, N. 1337, IV, 499, "Field of Reeds"; plur. see also U. 475, 483, T. 263, 396, P. 171, 198, 200, 326, 327, 462, 603, 631, M. 110, 370, 502, 630, N. 605, 765, 871, 895, 903, 930, 942, 964, 1089 ff., 1337. Later forms are :—

Sekh-t åanru, the region in the Ṭuat where the souls of the blessed dead lived and served Osiris.

Sekh-t åarru, B.D. 149, the 2nd Åat.

Sekh-t åakhu, N. 167, the field of the spirit-souls in the Other World.

Sekhut åmiut Åasu, N. 628, T. 340, a mythological locality.

Sekh-t āa-t, B.D. 179, 9, "the Great Field"—a region in the Ṭuat.

Sekh-t ānkh, P. 393, M. 560, N. 1167, "the Field of Life"—a mythological locality.

Sekh-t uatchu, P. 204, N. 853, "green field"—a region in the Ṭuat; var. P. 608.

Sekhut uatch-t, T. 334, N. 704, P. 608, M. 249, "Emerald Fields," *i.e.*, the sky.

Sekh-t uatchit nefer-t, Ombos I, 175, the goddess of fertile cultivated land.

Sekh-t Paāt, P. 396, M. 565, N. 1172, a mythological locality.

Sekh-t mefkat 〔hieroglyphs〕
P. 180, M. 280, 〔hieroglyphs〕 N. 892,
"turquoise field," *i.e.*, the sky.

Sekh-t nebt ḥeteput 〔hieroglyphs〕
〔hieroglyphs〕 a district in the Ṭuat where offerings were abundant.

Sekh-t Nentȧ 〔hieroglyphs〕
〔hieroglyphs〕 P. 603, field of the day and night sky.

Sekh-t neḥeḥ 〔hieroglyphs〕,
B.D. 78, 30, field of eternity, *i.e.*, the Other World, or the necropolis.

Sekh-t en Serser-t 〔hieroglyphs〕
〔hieroglyphs〕, 〔hieroglyphs〕, Rec. 26, 226, a district in the Ṭuat containing the boiling lake Serser (or, Neserser-t).

Sekh-t neteru 〔hieroglyphs〕, P. 81,
M. 111, N. 25, B.D. 177, 8, 9, field of the gods.

Sekh-t Rā 〔hieroglyphs〕, B.D. 180,
32, field of Rā.

Sekh-t Rā 〔hieroglyphs〕, Palermo Stele:
(1) a sun-temple near Memphis; (2) 〔hieroglyphs〕,
a district of Memphis; (3) 〔hieroglyphs〕,
B.D. 180, 32, the part of heaven in which Rā lived; plur. 〔hieroglyphs〕, P. 68, 〔hieroglyphs〕
〔hieroglyphs〕, N. 36.

Sekh-t Ruruti 〔hieroglyphs〕, "field of the two Lion-gods"—the name of the place in the sky occupied by Rā at the 3rd hour of the day.

Sekh-t Ḥeru 〔hieroglyphs〕 "field of Horus."

Sekh-t ḥeteput 〔hieroglyphs〕, U. 193,
422, 〔hieroglyphs〕, T. 396, 〔hieroglyphs〕
〔hieroglyphs〕, T. 73, 〔hieroglyphs〕, P. 252,
〔hieroglyphs〕, 〔hieroglyphs〕,
〔hieroglyphs〕, 〔hieroglyphs〕,
〔hieroglyphs〕; dual (?), 〔hieroglyphs〕,

〔hieroglyphs〕, U. 427, 〔hieroglyphs〕
〔hieroglyphs〕, T. 244, "field of offerings," the region of offerings of the Kingdom of Osiris in the Ṭuat; plur. 〔hieroglyphs〕, N. 170, 〔hieroglyphs〕
〔hieroglyphs〕, U. 578.

Sekhut ḥetep-t 〔hieroglyphs〕
〔hieroglyphs〕, T. 333, 〔hieroglyphs〕,
P. 824, 〔hieroglyphs〕 N. 703, the god of the fields of offerings.

Sekhit ḥetep 〔hieroglyphs〕, Ombos I, 175:
(1) a goddess of life, health, and joy; (2) the field of offerings personified, 〔hieroglyphs〕
〔hieroglyphs〕.

Sekhut Khakha 〔hieroglyphs〕
〔hieroglyphs〕, N. 1159....

Sekh-t Kheprer 〔hieroglyphs〕
P. 174, 〔hieroglyphs〕, N. 942, the field of the Beetle-god.

Sekh-t khet-f 〔hieroglyphs〕, Rec.
30, 190, a region in the Ṭuat.

Sekh-t sanḥemu 〔hieroglyphs〕
〔hieroglyphs〕, 〔hieroglyphs〕,
B.D. 125, III, 19, Respirazione 5, "field of the grasshoppers"—a region in the Ṭuat.

Sekh-t Sȧsȧ 〔hieroglyphs〕,
B.D. 98, 7, a field of fire in the Ṭuat.

Sekh-t ka 〔hieroglyphs〕, T. 92,
the region of a royal KA in the Ṭuat.

Sekhti-ka 〔hieroglyphs〕, B.D. 110,
33, a section of the fields of offerings.

Sekh-t Tchatcha 〔hieroglyphs〕
〔hieroglyphs〕, Rec. 26, 226, "field of the Chief," *i.e.*, of Osiris.

Sekh-t Tcher 〔hieroglyphs〕, P. 572
....

Sekh-t Tcheser-t 〔hieroglyphs〕
Metternich Stele 167, the "holy field."

sekh-t (?), Rec. 30, 67, parts of a ship.

sekhsekh , , Ȧmen. 22, 17, to flee, to betake oneself to flight.

sekhu-t , a hastening.

sekh[se]khti , , courier, envoy.

s-khekh , to weigh, to balance; caus.; Copt. ϣнϣ.

sekhsekh = , to have pleasure.

skha , P. 186, , P. 697, , U. 220, , Rec. 31, 18, Pap. 3024, 56, , , , , , , to remember, to call to mind, to commemorate some person or thing, to think, to think out; var. .

skha-t , , , record, decree.

skhai , Rec. 6, 13, letters, writing; , Greek letters; Copt. ⲥϩⲁⲓ, ⲥϧⲓ.

skhai , , , , recorder, record, remembrancer, writer.

skhait , Peasant 189, something which ought to be remembered.

skhau , , , , , , memorandum, remembrance, memory, memorial, memorial service; , commemorative formulas; , an unpleasant recollection; , everlasting remembrance.

skhaut , Thes. 1285, memorial.

Skhait Ḥeru , P. 615, M. 782, N. 1149, , , B.D. 169, 19, , , , a cow-goddess, a form of Isis or Hathor.

skha , P. 351, , N. 1067, to enter among (?); caus. (?) of .

s-kha , Jour. E.A. 3, 105, to pass the night.

skhai = , IV, 1079, to be deaf; , Anastasi I, 36, 3, L.D. III, 140c, to turn a deaf ear to; Copt. ⲥⲱϩ.

skha-t , wound, sore, bruise; Copt. ⲥⲁϣ.

skha-t , , , , , a kind of fruit (?)

skhaā , to form, to fashion, something cast.

skhaā-t , A.Z. 1868, 107, hare.

s-kha , N. 1005, 1007; , Love Songs 2, 6, , to row, stroke of an oar; caus.

skhabu , devourers.

s-khap , , , , to swallow, to devour.

s-khap , to form, to fashion; caus.

skham , Jour. As. 1908, 275, to pluck out; Copt. ⲥⲱϧⲉⲙ.

skham , Jour. As. 9, 10, 506 . . . . ; Copt. ⲥⲁϧⲉⲙ.

s-khamm , to make hot; caus.

skhan, to hasten; suddenly.

skhan, Rev. = ⲥⲁϩⲛⲉ.

s-khann, to breach a wall, to overthrow; caus.

skhanit, ruins, overthrow.

s-khank, Leyd. Pap. 10, 1, to strain through a sieve; caus.

skhank-t, a vessel, a sieve.

s-khar, Rec. 26, 235, to smear, to overlay with a metal, to plate, to wash over, to milk, to provide or supply; caus.; Copt. ⲥⲁϩⲣ, ⲥⲁⲣϩ.

skhar-t, Harris I, 30, 5, covering.

skhar-t, Rechnungen 70, deck of a boat.

skhar-t, a kind of fruit or seed.

skharāa, Rougé I.H. II, 114; varr., to abuse, to curse, to ill-wish; Copt. ⲥϩⲟⲩⲉⲣ, ⲥϩⲟⲩⲣ.

s-khakh, to hurry, to hasten, to accelerate, to scatter (?)

s . . . khakha, I, 130 = (?), to be glad, to rejoice.

s-khak, to strain through a cloth, to squeeze.

s-khaker, Ikhernefert 15, to ornament, to decorate; caus. of ; , decorated.

s-khāi, to make to rise up or appear, to celebrate a festival, to crown a king; caus.

skhāi-t, coronation, one who is crowned.

skhāiu, celestial bodies that rise like the sun, selected things.

s-khār, Pap. 3024, 110, to infuriate, to make angry; caus.

s-khi, to ascend, to scale walls; caus. of .

s-khi, Rec. 12, 72, to remove, to thrust away.

skhi, skhu, Rev. 12, 66, gall; Love Songs 5, 2, gall of geese; Copt. ⲥⲓϣⲉ.

Skhui, B.D. 114, 18, a serpent-god.

Skhui, B.D. 64, 18, a pair of gods in the Ṭuat.

skhinasha, to stimulate, to stir up, to incite, to exasperate.

skhu, draftsman; Copt. ⲥϩⲁⲓ.

skhua, deaf.

skhun, skhunn, to curse, to revile, to ill-wish, wrathful, angry, furious, passionate, irascibility.

skhunnu, angry man.

skhun, slaughter house.

s-khus, Leyd. Pap. 13, 12, to form, to fashion, to build.

skhuṭ, IV, 60, , Thes. 1284, , to provide, to strengthen, to fortify, to fill; , IV, 1161.

skhuṭ-t, IV, 413, provision, filling.

s-kheb, to draw back the bolts of a door.

s-khebkheb, M. 175, to draw back the bolts of a door, to enter = , T. 161, N. 688; varr. , Thes. 1204, .

skhebut (?), Thes. 1289, prisons (?)

s-khepi, U. 482, , N. 976, Rec. 31, 161, to make to come, to bring, to lead, to set in motion, to make to run, to promulgate (of a decree); caus. of .

skhep-t, Décrets 25, event, occurrence.

Skhepti, the "runner"—a name of a god.

skhep-t, U. 143, , , a kind of grain, a sacrificial drink.

s-kheper, Peasant 289, , , , A.Z. 1905, 101, , Jour. As. 1908, 275, to make to be or exist, to fashion, to form, to create, to produce, to bring up children; caus.

Skheper khaut, Tomb Seti I, one of the 75 forms of Rā (No. 51).

skhef, seven; Copt. ⲥⲁϣϥ.

skhef, , , to write.

skhef, Rec. 36, 135, impurity.

skhefa, to rebel (?); Copt. ϣϥⲱ (?)

skhem, , U. 235, , P. 2, M. 2, N. 112, , , , , , , , , , , , , , , , , to be strong, to strengthen oneself, to prevail over, to gain the mastery, strong, strength, might, power; , P. 163, , Litanie 88; Copt. ϣϫⲟⲙ.

skhem, uncon-quered; , U. 524, , T. 331.

skhemu, , power, man of power, chief, ruler; plur. , IV, 973, , IV, 614, , , , ; , IV, 966, chief of chiefs.

skhemit, P. 63, , M. 84, N. 91, strong woman or goddess.

skhemtiu, mighty ones.

skhemit, Åmenemḥat 3, 6, a kind of priest.

skhem åb, , Thes. 1480, , ; , bold-hearted, courageous, violent, fem. ; plur. , , , .

Skhem årif, , , Mar. Aby. II, 23, 9, 11, 19, he who doeth mighty deeds, a potentate. Used as a title.

skhem em re, IV, 13, strong in the mouth, *i.e.*, of bold or insolent speech.

skhem ḥer, bold-faced, of threatening aspect.

Skhem, M. 252, N. 34, 978, 1328, "Power," the life power of a god or man personified, the name of a god; with, P. 13, with and, P. 112; divine power; see Rev. Crit. Nov. 26, 1900.

Skhem, U. 446, T. 255, U. 514, Power, Divine Power, a Power of Nature; T. 327, Power of Powers; plur. U. 515, B.D. passim.

Skhemu, U. 643, 645, U. 515, T. 327, N. 828, P. 553, 610, Rec. 31, 32, ibid. 26, 226, the divine Powers, the deified "powers" of men.

Skhemui, P. 73, M. 103, N. 14, M. 700, the two divine Powers.

Skhemui, Berg. I, 13, a god who befriended the dead.

Skhem, Berg. I, 12, a serpent-god of libations.

Skhemiu, Ṭuat IX, a company of gods who towed the boat of Rā.

Skhemit, U. 390, Rec. 30, 68, Rev. 15, 16, Rec. 31, 11, Rec. 26, 152, Ṭuat X, a lioness-headed goddess, the consort of Ptaḥ, sister of Bast, and mother of Nefer-Temu. For a list of her titles see P.S.B. 25, 218.

Skhemit, in various localities, *e.g.*, Mar. Aby. 1, 44, 45.

Skhemit, a fire-goddess (late forms).

Skhemit, the goddess of the 4th month; Copt. KOIAK.

Skhem åmi Abetch, P. 7, M. 10, N. 114, a title of Osiris.

Skhem årif, Rec. 34, 177, "Potentate," the name of a god.

Skhem āa, title of Osiris.

Skhem-ā-kheftiu, Ṭuat II, a god in the Ṭuat.

Skhemit Uast, Ṭuat II, a lioness-goddess.

Skhemit Uatchit, B.D. 23, a wind-goddess.

Skhem-ur, U. 393, P. 577, U. 514, 516, T. 326, U. 516, the "Great Power" of heaven.

Skhemit-Bast-Rā, B.D. 164, 1, a Nubian goddess (?)

Skhemef, N. 978, a god (?)

Skhemit em åakhu-s, Ṭuat XII, a fire-goddess.

Skhem em åb-f, B.D. 153A, 2, a god of the net of the Akeru-gods.

Skhemit em kheftiu-s, Ṭuat I, a gatekeeper-goddess.

Skhemit em ṭesu-sen, B.D. 144, the doorkeeper of the 7th Ārit.

Skhemit meṭu, Ṭuat IX, a singing-goddess.

Skhem en pet khenti utchat, Denderah IV, 61, a ram-god.

Skhem nefer, etc., B.D. 141, 24 and 148, the name of the Rudder of the northern sky.

Skhem neteru, the door of the 5th hour.

Skhemit ren-s em ḥemu-t, B.D. 141 and 148, one of the seven divine Cows.

Skhem ḥer, Ṭuat I, Nesi-Åmsu 32, 28: (1) a crocodile-god who praised Rā; (2) a form of Āapep.

Skhem ḥer, Tomb of Seti I, one of the 75 forms of Rā (No. 26).

skhem shu-t "strong pinioned"—a title of the Winged Disk.

Skhem taui, Hh. 487, a title of Anubis.

Skhemit ṭesu, etc. etc., B.D. 145 and 146, the 4th Pylon in Sekhet-Āaru.

skhem, P. 409, M. 586, N. 1191, sceptre, wooden symbol of power; P. 459.

skhemti, P. 617, P. 81, IV, 887, Tombos Stele 2, the crowns of the South and North united; Gr. ψχέντ.

Skhemti, P. 1116B, 60, the goddesses Nekhebit and Uatchit.

skhem, A.Z. 1906, 123, Westcar 10, 3, an instrument of music, sistrum (?); dual L.D. III, 194, 37; plur.

skhemi, to play a sistrum.

skhem, Peasant 58 =

s-khemi, to be unmindful of, to forget, to ignore; caus. of

skhem, Rev. 13, 27, little; Copt. ϣⲏⲙ.

skhem, to recite, to decree.

skhemu, Rec. 32, 183; var. decrees, edicts, addresses.

s-khemm, to make hot; caus. of

skhemekh, P. 401, M. 573, N. 1180, IV, 345, to amuse oneself, to rejoice,

to feel pleasure, , Love Songs 4, 1, , delight, pleasure, recreation, holiday, joke, sport, laughing-stock; caus. (?)

skhen-t , , pillar, support; plur. , Rec. 27, 226, , , L.D. III, 194, 16, legs of a chair or bed.

skhenut , IV, 612, , A.Z. 1900, 30, , , B.D. 172, 42, the four pillars of the sky.

skhen, skhenn , Rec. 33, 4, , , , , , , , , , to fold in the arms, to embrace, to contain, to hold.

skhen ȧs-t , B.D. 153B, 17, to embrace one's throne.

skhenu , spells, incantations.

Skhen ur , , B.D. 146, the doorkeeper of the 10th Pylon.

Skhen maāt , the name of a sacred boat.

s-khen, s-khenn , , , , , , , , to hover over, to come to rest, to stand still, to alight; , L.D. III, 140B, to halt on the way.

skheniu[t] , Rec. 8, 9, place of alighting.

skhennu , P. 430, M. 615, , N. 1220, , those who alight.

skhenu , repose, alighting; , , a moment of leisure.

skhen , share, portion.

skhen , bandlet, tiara (?), a special kind of cord.

skhen-t , Rev. 13, 119, , Rev. 13, 92, crown; Gr. ψχέντ.

skhen , abscess, skin disease.

skhenn , to rot away, to decay.

skhenuiu , dyers (?)

s-khenn , , , to make to fall, to overthrow, to breach a wall; caus.

skhennu , things that terrify or frighten.

skhenȧ-t , table, bank, support.

skhenȧ , Rev. = , fortune, hap, event; Copt. ϣⲁϣⲛⲓ.

skheni , Rev. 13, 75, event, fortune; plur. , Canopus Stele.

skhenu , , events, conditions, circumstances.

s-khensh , Rec. 26, 65, , to make to stink; caus.

s-khenti , P. 176, M. 316, N. 917, , , , , , , Rec. 27, 222, , , , , , IV, 1031, , Hh. 393, to promote, to put in front, to make to advance, to make to sail to the south, or upstream; caus. of .

skhenṭ-t (?) , Maxims of Ani. . . . .

skher = , to inform.

skher , to plan, to design, plan, design, destiny, arrangement, intention, advice, opinion, character, affair, condition, dispensation, scheme, business, plot, kind, species, behaviour, manner, habit, wont, use, custom, device, mark, trace; plur. , , , ; , Sphinx Stele 11, condition, existence; , to direct, to lead; , P. 1116B, 67, useful plans; , under his directions; , celestial existence; , manner of life; , eternal plan; , manner of the innocent.

skhri , Peasant 191, 235, captain of a boat.

skhrit , , , report, writing, document, plan; var. .

skher , , B.D. 30B (Ani), to offend (?)

s-kher , U. 321, , , , , , , P.S.B. 10, 48, , , , to overthrow.

skher-t , defeat, overthrow.

skheru , bowls overfull.

Skher ..... , B.D. 149, 150, a god of the 6th Åat.

Skher-remu , B.D. 149, the god of the Åat Åmḥet.

s-kher , to cut, to pierce.

skher , Rec. 33, 5, , to present offerings (?)

s-kheri (?) , , to belittle, to underrate.

s-kherp , Sphinx Stele 3, to set at the head, to establish; caus.

s-kherṭ , to rejuvenate (?); caus.

skhes , , , Leyd. Pap. 8, 13, Mar. Karn. 53, 37, , Love Songs 3, 4, , , to run, to hasten = .

skhesu , runners.

s-khesef , Rec. 27, 219, , , to make to go back, to give evidence against; caus. of .

skheshen (?) , Rec. 26, 65; var. ....

s-kheti , T. 171, , P. 118, to turn back, to repulse; caus. of .

s-khetkhet , Love Songs 4, 8, , , to repulse, to drive back; caus. of .

s-khet = , to be upside down, head downwards; caus. of .

s-khet , Rev. 14, 2, to fall; caus.

Skhetiu , fiends, devils; fem. .

skhet , , , N. 989, , , , , , , , , , Rec. 27, 232, ,

, to twist, to tie, to peg out a snare, to lay a net, to erect a shelter made of leaves and branches, to build a booth, to weave; Åmen. 12, 9, to weave words; Copt. ⲥⲱϩⲉ.

skhet , Israel Stele 20, , , , , to snare, to catch birds in a net.

s-khetkhet , to snare in a net.

skheti , M. 772, , P. 661, , P. 777, , , hunter, fowler, snarer; plur. , , , , .

skhet , , U. 193, , , net.

Skhet , Edfû I, 77, , , , a name of the Nile-god and of the Inundation.

Skhetiut , B.D. 112, 2, the goddesses of the chase.

skhet , IV, 1153, , IV, 1175, , to mould bricks.

skhet , IV, 367, division; , without division (of an obelisk), *i.e.*, monolithic.

skhet , plants, bushes.

s-khetkhet , enquiry, investigation; Copt. ϣⲟⲧϣⲉⲧ, ϩⲟⲧϩⲉⲧ.

skheṭ , injury, harm.

s-kheṭ , U. 459, , , , to be turned upside down; , placed head downwards; caus.

s-kheṭkheṭ , P. 694, , N. 1039, , Rec. 30, 193, to overthrow, to upset; , N. 1155, a woman with pendent breasts; caus.

skheṭi , Rec. 32, 85, a person who is head downwards; plur. , men hung from a barge head downwards.

skheṭiu , fiends, the damned.

skheṭ , B.D. 189, 1 . . . . . .

skheṭu , a class of stars.

Skheṭ ḥer āsh-åru , B.D. 144, the doorkeeper of the 1st Ārit.

s-kheṭ , Rec. 19, 19, to make sail.

ses = , to roast, to burn.

ses-t = , the light of a fire, a bright fire.

ses = **s-sen** , to smell, to breathe; caus.

sesi = , to smell.

ses (?) , to drink.

ses , , horse; **ses-t** , filly, mare; Heb. סוּס.

Ses , L.D. III, 208E, a name or title of Rameses III.

ses , Rec. 29, 144, , , Mar. Karn. 53, 34, to walk, to flee; varr. , .

ses-t (?) , ankle-joint (?); dual ; plur. .

ses-t , Rec. 15, 152, a garment of some kind, bandlet; Heb. שֵׁשׁ.

sesut, IV, 692, inlayings of copper (?)

ses — ḥeb en ses, festival of the 6th day of the month.

ses, , , , , day; plur. , IV, 390, seasons, periods of time; Copt. ⲥⲟⲩ, ⲥⲏⲩ, ⲥⲟⲩⲥⲟⲩ.

sesu, , L.D. III, 65A, , Rec. 19, 15, time, seasons.

s-sa, P. 409, M. 585, N. 1191, to strip off clothes, to undress; caus.

s-sa, , to make to depart, to drive away, to expel; caus.

s-sa, I, 131, , Décrets 29, Shipwreck 53, , IV, 160, L.D. III, 140C, , , , to feed, to fill with food, to sate, to satisfy; caus.; Copt. ⲧⲥⲓⲟ.

sesa, Décrets 30, sufficiency, provision, ration.

sesaa, repletion (?) headache.

sesim (?), horses = Heb. סוּסִים (?) סוּסִים (?)

Sesu, Sesostris, *i.e.*, Usertsen III; Gr. Σεσοώσις.

Sesu, , , Anastasi I, 12, 3, 18, 8, 27, 3, 5 = Rameses II.

s-suash, B.M. 448, to praise; caus. (?)

s-sun, N. 446, , , , , , , , Rev. 11, 66, , L.D. III, 140B, to destroy by fire, to scorch, to blast; caus.

sesun-t, a withering, a scorching.

s-sun àb, to be sick, to feel nausea, mental or physical.

s-sur, to give to drink; caus.

s-sutut, Rec. 4, 136, to walk, to walk about; caus.

s-seb, to cut, to destroy; caus. Copt. ⲥⲃⲃⲉ, ⲥⲉⲃⲉ.

s-sebi (?), Pap. 3024, 111, to make to smile or laugh; caus.; Copt. ⲥⲱⲃⲉ, ⲥⲱⲃⲓ.

s-sebeq, , , to choose, to elect, to indicate by a sign; caus.

s-sepṭ, IV, 653, , IV, 707, , , Mar. Karn, 36, 28, to prepare, to sharpen weapons; caus.

sesef, , , Suppl. 1118........

sesfi, Thes. 1201, A.Z. 1905, 17, , Israel Stele 7, to smelt, to melt, to cook, fire, hot ashes, tinder; , to make a blaze of something.

sesem, a pair of horses; varr. , , ; Heb. סוּסִים (?)

sesem-t, , , , horse, mare (?); plur. , IV, 699, , IV, 659, , Love Songs 1, 8, ; Heb. סוּסִים.

sesmi, a kind of disease.

s-sen, M. 81; var. , N. 88 .....

s-sen, U. 565, , T. 31, , Hh. 346, , Rec. 29,

156, , , , to smell, to breathe; caus.

sesen-t , breathing, breath, smell.

s-seni = , to make open.

sesen-t , P. 169, an opening.

sesenu , Rec. 17, 94, ; see **khemenu.**

Sesenu , , the eight primeval gods; see **Khemenu.**

s-senb , IV, 914, , , A.Z. 1900, 128, to make sound or healthy, to heal; caus. of .

s-sentch , , Wört. 1307, to terrify, to make afraid; caus. of .

sesentchem , I, 139, , Leyd. Pap. 3, 4, , IV, 718, , , , , Ikhernefert 15, , Harris I, 71A, 7, , a sweet-smelling, costly kind of wood.

Seser , Rec. 31, 169; for .

s-serṭ , IV, 749, to plant, to cultivate; caus. of .

s-seḥu , destroy, destruction (?); caus.

s-sekh (s-usekh) , U. 425, T. 244, 333, P. 456, to enlarge, to make broad; caus.

s-skhem , to make strong or powerful; caus. of .

s-sqebḥ (?) , Rec. 4, 136, to refresh, to make cool; caus.

seska , B.D. 70, 3, A.Z. 49, 56, a part of the body (?)

seska , a kind of grain or seed.

sesh , for , arrow.

sesh , , to unbolt, to open; see **sen** .

sesh-kha-t , , "opener of the body"—a kind of medicine, aperient (?)

sesh , to pour out, to flow.

seshti , the two breasts.

sesh , to be white.

sesh , byssus.

seshu , IV, 666, ring money, rings.

sesh-t , , a kind of grain (?) used in making offerings; , U. 155, white sesh-t; , U. 156, green sesh-t.

sesh-t , , , drought, dryness.

Sesh-t ; see , and P.S.B. 17, 253.

sesha , a bird.

s-sha , , Gol. Ham. 14, 143, , Gol. Pap. 9, 30, , Koller Pap. 4, 5, to ordain, to decree, to authorize, to instruct, to commission; , B.D. 64 (Rubric, Nu 5).

sesha-t , IV, 271, order, decree (?)

sesha (?) , T. 339, N. 627, Verbum 387, guide (?) leader (?)

s-sha , M. 692, , N. 552 . . . .

Sesha-t (Seshait), T. 268, M. 426, Rec. 30, 194, 31, 28, A.Z. 1906, 124, IV, 1074, B.D. 57, 6, 152, 31, 169, 18, the goddess of learning, wisdom, architecture, etc.

Seshaȧ, U. 381, the learned one.

seshuȧ, able, wise, a wise man, skilful, cunning.

seshaut, N. 984 ....

Seshshȧ, Ṭuat X, the name of a god in the Ṭuat.

seshā-t, A.Z. 1908, 19, a kind of amulet.

s-shi, T. 264; var.

Seshu, Stele of Palermo, U. 539, T. 295, a god of learning, writing, and literature.

s-shu, U. 415, P. 274, M. 489, P. 334, 335, to lift up into heaven (?); caus. of

s-shui, to dry up, to make empty; caus.

s-shu, Rev., to repulse.

seshuit, Jour. As. 1908, 273, Rev. 12, 114, wound, stripe, blow, calamity, disaster, misfortune, weakness, emptiness; Copt. ⲥⲁϣ.

s-shua, to despoil, to impoverish; caus.

s-shui, Rev. = , to be strong.

seshumi, Jour. As. 1908, 304, to be weak; Copt. ⲥⲱϣⲙ.

s-shebsheb, to vomit.

seshp, Rec. 16, 133, to receive.

seshp-t, U. 488, P. 172, N. 939, a female who has conceived.

Seshpui, P. 391, M. 558, N. 1165, the two pillars of Rā.

seshp (shesp), Hh. 381, Rec. 31, 19, to shine.

seshp-t (shesp-t), N. 1365, light, rays.

seshp-t (shesp-t), T. 373, M. 125, N. 694, = = a white garment or fillet or bandlet, white apparel; Copt. ϣⲱⲡ.

seshpu, dried grapes (?)

seshpen (?), ulcer, boil, blain (?)

seshepsut, noble words.

seshem, form, similitude, likeness, copy, manner, behaviour, procedure, service, state, condition, action, conduct, design.

seshem reth, A.Z. 1908, 16, the name of an amulet.

Seshem, Rec. 4, 28, picture or statue of a god; plur.

; fem. , IV, 386, Rec. 3, 2, serpent image.

Seshmit , a title of the moon.

Seshmit , , goddess of the 2nd hour of the day.

Seshmit , , , Zod. Dend., Thes. 31, one of the 36 Dekans.

Seshem Åf (?) , the rejected body of the Night Sun-god Åf.

s-shem , U. 482, , , , , , , , , , to guide, to lead, to direct, to administer, to govern; caus.

s-shem åb , to direct the mind.

seshem , IV, 1113, , , administration.

seshem-t , , M. 355, , , , Thes. 1289, guide, guidance, direction; , Rec. 36, 155, the conducting of the festal service in the temple.

seshmi , , , guide, leader, director; plur. , , , , , Rec. 19, 19; , leader of peace, *i.e.*, peacemaker; , divine guides.

seshmu , P. 100, , P. 309, , Peasant 54, , , , Peasant 191, , U. 504, T. 321, , uraeus guide; , N. 951.

seshem ḥeb , A.Z. 1906, 131, director of ceremonies of the festival.

seshmu kh-t , director of the universe.

seshmu taui , director of the royal palace.

seshem , , , , a sacred boat, a portable shrine.

Seshmit , , divine guide, title of a goddess.

Seshem Åffi , Ṭuat VIII, a fish-god.

Seshem årānbfi , Ṭuat VIII, a dog-god.

Seshem Åst , Ṭuat VIII, a form of Isis.

Seshem Åsår , Ṭuat VIII, the form of Osiris in the Circle Ås-neteru.

Seshem ānkh , Ṭuat III, "Living Form"—a god.

Seshem ba neteru , Ṭuat VIII, a ram-god in the Circle Åakebi.

Seshem Nut , Ṭuat VIII, the form of Nut in the Circle Ṭuat.

Seshem Neb-t-ḥe-t , Ṭuat X, a form of darkness at the 2nd door of the dark road to Saïs.

Seshem nes-f , Ṭuat VII, a star-god.

Seshem neter , Cairo Pap. IV, 2, a god.

Seshem remu neteru, Ṭuat VIII, a ram-god in the Circle Åakebi.

Seshem Ḥeru, Ṭuat X, a god who destroyed the dead.

Seshem Ḥeru, Ṭuat VIII, form of Horus in the Circle Ås-neteru.

Seshmu Ḥeḥ, B.D. 17, 47, a title of Uatch-urȧ.

Seshem Khatri, Ṭuat VIII, an ichneumon-god.

Seshem Kheperȧ, Ṭuat VIII, the form of Kheperȧ in the Circle Sesheta.

Seshem shet (?), Ṭuat X, a serpent form of Horus.

Seshem Shu, Ṭuat XII, the form of the Sun-god at sunrise.

Seshem Shu, Ṭuat VIII, the form of Shu in the Circle Sesheta.

Seshem ka Åmenti, Ṭuat VIII, a bull-god in the Circle Åakebi.

Seshem Geb, Ṭuat VIII, the form of Geb in the Circle Ṭuat.

Seshmu taui, B.D. 148, 8, a solar-god.

Seshem Tathenn, Ṭuat VIII; see Tathenn.

Seshem Tefnut, Ṭuat VIII, the form of Tefnut in the Circle Ṭuat.

seshemu, IV, 373, the Syrian hills where cedars were felled.

s-shemm, to warm, heat; caus. of .

s-shen, B.D. 64, 50, to alight, to protect (?); caus. of = .

seshen, a mistake for , to open, to make a way through.

s-shen, s-shenn, P. 306, , , to overthrow, to breach or pull down a wall; caus. of = .

seshen, P. 420, M. 601, storm, hurricane.

seshen, a field of lilies.

seshen, lily knosps.

seshen, lily water, extract of lotus.

seshen-t, Rec. 36, 210, garden-house, booth.

seshen-tchet (?), a kind of reed basket.

seshshen, Z.D.M.G. 46, 117, Love Songs 2, 8, lily, iris, lotus; see , and compare Heb. שׁוּשַׁן; Gr. σοῦσον.

sesher = , to plan, to arrange.

sesheru = = , plans, etc.

sesher, U. 553, to draw out, to clean out, to sweep out, to milk; Copt. ⲥⲁϩⲣ, ⲥⲁⲣϩ.

sesher, I, 149, dung, excrement.

sesher, U. 276, , N. 719, , Rec. 31, 171, , to make to shine, to emit light, to bleach (?)

sesher-t, U. 68, , N. 328, , Rec. 31, 172, bleached linen; plur. , U. 394, , B.D. 174, 13, .

s-shes, to open, to unbolt; see .

s-shesp, Rec. 30, 196, to make to receive; caus.

s-sheser, see .

sesheser, , corn, grain.

sshek, Rec. 27, 224 (var.), to cover over, to protect (?)

s-sheker = , caus. of .

s-sheta, , , to hide, to make secret, to make a mystery of something, to make confidential; caus.; Copt. ϣωϣⲧ.

sesheta, mystery, secret; a secret of the royal harîm.

seshetṭ, A.Z. 1906, 130, to mount, to ascend, to roll up, to revolve.

seshetṭ, Mar. Karn. 35, 63, to make a horse prance about, to perform feats of horsemanship, to circuit like a star.

seshetṭ, the orbit of the sun, light-circle.

seshetṭ, IV, 615, , A.Z. 1905, 23, a planet (?) comet, or shooting star.

seshetṭ, to decorate, to put on a garland.

seshetṭ, U. 155, , P. 162, 685, N. 1040, , N. 520, , to tie, to bind, to tie round, to gird on.

seshetṭ, P. 346, 413, T. 43, , , , , bandage, bandlet, string, cord of a book, girdle, belt, turban, diadem, tiara; , a bandlet crown; , a crown with plumes; , IV, 1055, garlands on their heads.

seshetṭ, Kubbân Stele 8, crown, diadem.

seshetṭ, Palermo Stele, festival of the bandlet or crown.

seshetṭ, Rev. 6, 22, list, document, inventory.

seshetṭ, whip.

seshetṭ-t, Rec. 21, 82, , Thes. 1202, Mar. Karn. 54, 48, , Koller Pap. 5, 1, , , verandah, window, opening in a wall, balcony (?) porch (?); Copt. ϣⲟⲩϣⲧ.

seshetṭ, A.Z. 1870, 171, niche in a wall.

s-sheper (*sic*), Rev. 14, 21, = ...

seq, , , Rec. 27, 227, to gather together, to collect.

seq, P. 95, , P. 285, 331, 608, , P. 645, to smite, to strike; see .

seq, Rev. 11, 170, to destroy; Copt. ⲥⲱⲕ.

seq ḥer, Rev. = Copt. ⲥⲉⲕ ϩⲟ.

seq, sacking, haircloth; Heb. שַׂק; Gr. σάκκος; Copt. ⲥⲟⲕ, ⲥⲱⲕ.

seq, Sphinx Stele 12; see **s-āṛq**.

s-qai, , , , , , ,

, Rec. 31, 175; , Rhind Pap. note 112, , Ani V, to exalt, , A.Z. 1905, 28, to prolong life; caus.

S-qai-nu-baiu, etc. the name of the 3rd hour of the day.

sqar to sail; Copt.

sqaḥ , , to plaster, to smear.

s-qā , to vomit, to pour out; caus.

sqā ānkhiu , IV, 1147, , see .

sqān (?) , to be laid waste, destroyed.

squ , , fuel (?) fire (?)

sqeb , , Mar. Karn. 54, 57, captive, prisoner of war.

sqeb = .

sqeb , to see, to look at, the eye.

s-qeb , , to cool, to refresh.

s-qebb (*sic*), , , to cool, to refresh; caus.

sqebbu , bath-house, bath.

Sqeb , B.D. 142, V, 1 ( ), a god.

Sqeb = = , a god.

Seqbit , B.D. 142, V, 25, a goddess.

s-qeb , Metternich Stele 7, to cry out, to wail; caus.

s-qebḥ , P. 394, , M. 561, to cool, to refresh; caus.

sqef , to leave, what is left; Copt.

sqem , var. , to destroy, to annihilate.

s-qema , Rec. 36, 133, to consolidate; caus.

s-qen , , , to make bold, to encourage; caus.

s-qen, s-qenn , , Rev. 11, 93, to anoint oneself, to put on fat.

sqer , to sail; Copt.

sqer , Palermo Stele, , , P. 77, U. 403, , P. 68, , , , , , Rec. 26, 229, , ibid. 31, 172, , , , , , , , , to beat, to strike, to fight, to capture prisoners; , to break open a door; Copt. CIKE.

sqer-t , fight.

sqerȧ , , , , prisoner, captive.

sqeru , prisoner, captive, fettered; plur. , , .

sqerȧ ānkh , Palermo Stele, , IV, 1004, , IV, 617, , , a combatant captured alive; plur. , .

sqernu, fighter, conqueror.

Sqerit, Ombos II, 130, a goddess.

Sqer tchatchau, Ṭuat VII, the name of a star-god in the Ṭuat.

sqeḥ, , , to hew, to cut.

seqes (?), Anastasi I, 10, 9, some hard substance.

s-qeṭ (?), , , P.S.B. 16, 238, disposition, inclination, relationship, a mathematical term; caus.

s-qeṭ, Hh. 472; caus. of .

s-qeṭi, U. 192, , U. 478, , P. 382, , , , , , , to sail, to travel about in a boat; caus.

s-qeṭṭ, N. 954, , N. 138, , , , , (*sic*), Gol. Hamm. 14, 134, , to sail, to travel about in a boat.

sqeṭut, Pap. 3024, 71, , , IV, 697, , , , a journey by boat, a sailing, a boat procession, a course on the river.

sqeṭu, Shipwreck 27, , sailor, paddler; plur. , , (?), Pap. 3024, 62, , .

Sqeṭi, Hh. 371, a god.

Sqeṭi-ḥer, the warder of the 2nd Ārit.

sek = .

sek, to cover, to dress.

sek re, U. 253, , T. 273, , P. 26, , M. 36, , to purify the mouth.

Sek re, Ṭuat I, a serpent-god in the Ṭuat.

Sek re, the god of the 6th hour of the night.

Sek ḥer, B.D. 136B, 3, a god of the lake of Fire.

sek, , , , , , , to pull, to draw, to draw away, to carry off, to make an end of, to destroy.

seki, Peasant 205, , , , , , , , , P. 64, N. 498, to perish, to come to an end, to make cease, to diminish, to be destroyed; , N. 938.

sek, , , the end, death, the finish of a matter.

seki-t, pain, anguish, despair; failure of courage.

sekk, to bring to an end (years).

seksek, , , Peasant 317, , IV, 685, Mar. Karn. 53, 27, , IV, 716, , , , , to crush, to destroy, to subdue, to cut down, to overthrow.

seksek-t, destruction, overthrow.

seka , , , , , , , , fighter, warrior, athlete; plur. , , , , , , Peasant 303, , , IV, 653, 659, , Thes. 1203, warriors, athletes, fighters, guards, soldiers, armed servants, strong men, rebels, murderers.

seki-t , struggle, fight, battle, slaughter.

seki-t , Rec. 17, 116, slaughter-house (?)

Sek , the name of a god (, P. 219).

seku , ; see .

sek āḥā , , A.Z. 1872, 41, , "Time divider"—a title of Thoth.

seki , , to grind grain, to pound grain into flour.

sekit , , , , , meal, flour.

sek , , to plough; Copt. ⲥⲕⲁⲓ.

sek , to transport by boat, to ferry over.

sekut , IV, 707, ships of a certain kind.

sek , T. 275, , P. 28, M. 39, lake, sea (?)

ska , T. 342, P. 221, then, at that time.

ska , P. 621, Rec. 31, 173, , N. 119, 824, , , , , , Åmen. 8, 17, , , to plough; Copt. ⲥⲕⲁⲓ, ⲥϫⲁⲓ.

skaiu , ploughmen.

skaut , , IV, 499, ploughed land, tillage.

skau , , oxen for ploughing.

ska , an animal for the plough (?)

ska , Nåstasen Stele 31, throne.

s-kami , Åmen. 4, 14, , Mar. Karn. 52, 19, , , Décrets 108, , to make to endure for a long time, to bring life to a close, to finish, to complete; caus.

skami , , to be grey-haired, white-haired, greyness; , oil for grey hair; Copt. ⲥⲕⲓⲙ, ⲥϫⲓⲙ; , Rec. 27, 219, the grey-haired god.

s-kamm , to blacken, to defile; caus.

s-kamkam , to destroy, to overthrow, to annihilate.

skar , Ḥerusåtef Stele 44, a kind of sacrificial vessel; , the same in silver.

skå , an object like a short javelin, (Lacau).

skȧ-t, ski-t, M. 125, N. 695, , T. 374 . . . . . .

sku, U. 427, T. 245, then, at that time.

skep, , Rev. 12, 41, a cry (?)

Skem, Rec. 30, 199; var. , ibid. 27, 219, the grey-haired god.

sken, to cleave, to split.

sken, Peasant 178, , a beast of a man, glutton, drunkard.

sken, , unguent, oil; Copt. ⲥⲟϭⲛ.

sker, to cut, to smite.

sker, Rev. 11, 131, 12, 52, , Rev. 11, 134, to sail.

sekhem, Koller 1, 5, a metal weapon.

Sekkes, Rec. 31, 31, a god.

Seksen, P. 650, , P. 726, , M. 751, a god, a messenger of Rā.

Sektit, Rec. 30, 187, , , , , , , Rev. 13, 2, the boat of the setting sun. The old form is ; see U. 470, T. 221, 222, etc.

Sektit, the sacred boat of the Nome Prosopites.

seg, deaf; and see .

seg, opposition.

seg-t, the foal of an ass; Copt. ⲥⲏϭ.

sga, to attack (?)

sga, A.Z. 1905, 31, , Rev., to be struck dumb with astonishment, dumb; , Anastasi I, 17, 1.

sgai, Rev. 14, 12, quack of a goose.

s-gab, , to utter cries, to call out.

s-gab, Rec. 10, 6, to make to bow, to force.

s-gap, Rec. 21, 86, to cry out, cry, lamentation; see ; Copt. ϣⲕⲁⲛ.

sgar, , Anastasi V, 19, 7, fort, fortress, castle, tower.

sgā (?), to carry (?)

sgi, to remove.

s-geb (?), , Rec. 14, 97, , Metternich Stele 44, 47, Ḥeruemḥeb 21, , Ḳubbân Stele 25, to utter a cry; Copt. ϣⲕⲁⲛ, ϣϭⲁⲛ.

sgeb, captive, prisoner.

Sgeb, L.D. III, 206, a god of the torture chamber.

Sgeb-ȧm, etc., B.D. 145A, the door-keeper of the 14th Pylon.

s-gebgeb, to constrain, to compel submission.

s-gep, , Rev. 13, 30, wailing, lamentation.

segmu (?), perfume (?); Copt. ⲥⲟϭⲛ (?)

s-gemḥ, to make to see; caus.

s-genn, Rev. 6, 26, , to anoint, perfumed oil, A.Z. 1884, 88, to prepare anointing oil; caus.; Copt. ⲥⲟϭⲛ̄.

sgen, Rev. , Rev. 11, 132, perfume, anointing oil; Copt. ⲥⲟϭⲛ̄.

sgenn, , Koller 2, 1, , , oil, ointment, balsam from Sinai; Copt. ⲥⲟϭⲛ̄.

s-genn, , to make weak or helpless; caus.

sgenniu, the inert, helpless ones.

sger, to beat (a drum); see .

sger, fort, fortress, a strong enclosed place.

s-ger, , Rec. 26, 65, , IV, 967, , , to make silent, to still, to hush, to silence; caus. of ; , the tomb; , the dead.

sgeru, the silent ones.

sger-t, silence, stillness.

Sger-t, the city of silence, *i.e.*, the grave.

Sger, Berg. 33, *i.e.*, .

sgeri, Rec. 3, 35, drachm.

s-gerḥ, , , , , Rec. 13, 48, , , Rev., to be at peace, to quiet, to pacify, to subdue; caus.; Copt. ⲥϭⲣⲁϩⲧ̄.

Sgerḥit, P.S.B. 25, 221, "Tranquilliser"—a title of Skhemit.

sgergu, , , parts of a ship.

Seges, M. 826, , N. 1318, a town and a town-god.

Segt, Rev. 14, 40 = .

set, absolute pron. 3rd com.

sett, U. 197, P. 100, absolute pron. 3rd fem. she.

set, later form of .

set, , they, them.

set, M. 459, throne, seat; plur. , M. 174, P. 607.

set, to break = .

set, , to break, to cut, to bite.

set, tail; , tail in the mouth, *i.e.*, encircled.

set, , tail of an animal; , an animal that carries its tail high.

set, babe; var. .

set, a stone; varr. , .

Set (Setesh), U. 5, 72, 351, , N. 333, Hh. 333 , , , , , , , , Rec. 27, 228, , M. 63, P. 174, , , the god of evil; , B.M. 46631; , the

children of Set, *i.e.*, fiends and devils, , N. 951, the Set-gods, heavenly and earthly; , IV, 808.

setȧ-t , T. 192, P. 677, , N. 1289, appertaining to Set.

Set na shenu , Rec. 16, 119, Set of the acacias.

Set , the star of Set, *i.e.*, Mercury.

Set (Setekh?) , Edfû I, 91, god of .

Set-......... , the god of the 5th day of the month.

set , to sow seed; Copt. ϲιϯ.

set , N. 796.

set , B.D. 179, 2 . . . . . .

set-t (?) , Love Songs V, 5, summer-house (?)

set-t = , wall.

sta-t (sthit) , Palermo Stele, , II, 7, , , , , , , a measure of land, the arura; plur. , .

stai-t (sthit) , , thread, cord, string, measuring cord.

sta (sthiu?) , repurchase; plur. , Rev. 14, 46.

stai (sthi) , to measure land.

sta , Rec. 21, 15, , Ȧmen. 22, 3, to hold a possession legally.

set, sta , IV, 1102, , , , , Ȧmen. 20, 1, , , , Jour. As. 1908, 269, , , , , , , , , , , to bring, to conduct, to lead, to tow, to draw or drag along, to withdraw, to unbolt a door, to place alongside, to compare; Copt. ⲧⲁⲥⲑⲉ.

stas (stasta?) , Pap. 3024, 12, to lead.

stasta , to press, to urge on, to drive.

sta (sthi) , IV, 966, leader, guide; , Rev. 14, 49, dealer in vegetables.

staiu , , , , , , , , haulers, towers of a boat, bringers, leaders.

Staiu Rā , Ṭuat VIII, those who tow the boat of Rā.

Staiu (Sthiu) , Ṭuat II, the blasphemers of Rā who were condemned to destruction.

stastau , rebels, opponents.

Sta , B.D. 168, IV, a bull-god—a form of Osiris.

Stait , Ṭuat XII, a wind-goddess who was reborn daily.

Sta en Ȧsȧr, etc. , etc., B.D. 145, 146, the 13th Pylon.

sta , , receptacle, an object in which to carry things.

sta , water-course, canal; , IV, 944.

sta , Anastasi I, 14, 8, ramp; inclined way up to walls of a besieged city.

Statt (sthitt) , , , , , , the funeral moun-

tain, cemetery, the grave; , the Theban necropolis.

sta (stha) , Hh. 544, , , filth, offal, anything beastly or abominable.

sta , fiends, devils, a term of abuse applied to the enemy.

sta-t (sthi-t) , IV, 53, 426, a plate or sheet of metal; , made of a single sheet.

sta, sti , Rec. 16, 132, , Ȧmen. 6, 6, to light a fire, to make to burn, to make fire; , to cast utchats; Copt. ⲥⲁⲧⲉ.

stai , fire.

sta , forge, furnace, oven, kiln.

sta , Rec. 3, 4, light, radiance.

staib , to stop, to shut up, to close; Copt. ϣⲧⲁⲙ, ϣⲧⲉⲙ.

stȧr , Rev. 11, 182, splendour; Copt. ⲥⲧⲏⲗ, ⲥϯⲉⲗⲗⲓ.

sti , A.Z. 1905, 19, , Hymn Darius 27, to eject seed, to beget, to sow seed; Copt. ⲥⲓⲧⲉ.

sti , Rec. 3, 49, , Rec. 3, 48, to pour out water, to pour out a libation, to make water, to drip, to overflow, a flowing out, effusion; , sprinkled, watered, poured out.

stit , seed, moisture, outpouring.

stiu , vases, water vessels.

stiut , IV, 615, Rec. 20, 40, , rays, light, splendour, radiance; , sunshine; , light-emitter.

Sti reh pet , one of the 36 Dekans.

sti – ḥeb sti , the name of the 11th day of the month.

sti , Palermo Stele, , T. 206, , Anastasi I, 23, 3, , to shoot arrows, to eject something from a case, to throw, to harpoon; , jeter la vendange; , IV, 1203; , Peasant 228, to spear fish; , IV, 1062, to shoot game in the desert.

sti , to shoot a glance of the eye;

em sti , in the sight of, opposite to.

sti , , , , Peasant 239, bowman, archer, shooter; plur. , , , Israel Stele 5; , a lascivious man.

Sti , , B.D. (Saïte) 24, 4, 46f., 149, 14, a title of Set.

Stit , , , , B.D. 125, 1, 10, , , , , a goddess of the First Cataract, consort of Khnemu.

Sti åru , Thes. 31, , Denderah III, 24, the goddess of the 10th hour of the day.

Sti ṭesui (?) , , B.D. 149, Denderah IV, 80, a serpent-god, 70 cubits long, who lived in the 4th Åat.

Stiu , , , , , , , , Asiatics and Nubians.

sti-t , an Asiatic woman; plur. , Rec. 31, 13.

sti-t , Leyd. Pap. 14, 4, ground, grave (?)

sti-t , , Rec. 36, 216, the name of a chamber in a temple.

sti , , , , , , to light a fire, to kindle, flame, fire; , T. 206, , , , to kindle sacred or ceremonial fire.

sti-t , , , , Rec. 27, 229, , fire, flame.

Sti , , Ṭuat III, a fire-spitting serpent-god, the protector of the holy gods.

Set (Sti) em år-t-f , , "Fire in his eye"—the god of the 6th Pylon.

Set (Sti) ḥer , Ṭuat VIII, a serpent-warder of the 7th Gate.

sti-t , , , , , boil, blain, ulcer, carbuncle, swelling.

sti , , , , , , , , , bad smell, scent or odour; Copt. ⲥϯ.

sti neter , , IV, 219, the scent of the god.

sti ḥeb , , , , , , incense burnt at a festival.

sti akh-t (?) , , , Harris I, 40, 9 . . . . . .

sti , , drink offering, measure of wine.

sti (?) , leg, knee (?)

Sti , Tomb Ram. VI, 50, a god.

sti , to weave; Copt. ⲥⲱⲧⲉ.

sti , Rev. 13, 15, 28, smell, odour; Copt. ⲥϯ.

stia (?) , Hh. 433 . . . . . .

stim , fodder, vegetables, garden stuff; see , Copt. ⲥⲓⲙ.

sti-t , Rev. 15, 17 = , grass, verdure.

stu (?) , to provide (?)

s-tua, to give thanks, to glorify; caus.

stur, to work, to prepare.

s-tur, to cleanse, to purify; caus.

stuha, to turn aside, to set free, to disturb.

stukh, , , , to treat with drugs, to embalm a dead body.

s-tut, , Peasant 249, , , to observe some custom, to do something usually done, to make a copy or image, to fashion, to typify, to symbolize, counterpart, image; , Rec. 20, 40.

s-tut, , to collect, to gather together; caus. of .

steb-t, Mission 13, 50, decree, edict.

steb (?), Rev. 14, 46, farming tools.

stebaf, Rev. 11, 145, , ibid. 11, 150, a tool or weapon; Copt. ⲥⲟⲧⲃⲉϥ (?)

stebu, , , to drink with enjoyment; var. .

s-tebḥ, to provide with food, to provision; caus. of ; see .

step, L.D. III, 194, 35, to advance.

step, T. 287, P. 39, M. 49, , , , to cut, to cut off, to slay.

step-t, M. 203, , N. 683, , , a piece of meat specially selected and cut off for an offering; plur. , P. 540, , N. 680, , , , , , , Rec. 20, 43.

step, , , , to select, to choose; Copt. ⲥⲱⲧⲡ̄.

stepu, , , , a chosen person or thing; , picked words; , selections from a book; , choice bread; , the pick of the stable; , a bag of fine linen garments; , Shipwreck 94, the choicest of Egypt; , IV, 390, selected in olden time.

stepep, P. 204, , M. 203, N. 683 = .

steppu, a chosen person.

step sa, P. 184, 193, M. 292, , P. 651, 730, M. 753, , , , to perform magical ceremonies with the view of obtaining life and the protection of the god; , P. 695, , P. 593, , IV, 1016.

step sa, protected by an amulet.

step sa, , , , , , , a chamber in the sanctuary wherein the transfer of the divine power from the god to the king took place; compare , "He gave him life, strength, health, and joy of heart in the step sa chamber," IV, 1013. Step sa is also used as a title for the palace and the king himself, *e.g.*, IV, 194.

step, the name of the 20th day of the month.

step, a garment made of a special kind of stuff.

step, a kind of plant.

stef, to cut, to hack, to slay for sacrifice; varr.

stefu, Rec. 19, 92, butcher.

stef, to turn aside or away.

stef, to be pure, to be refined; clear, pure, refined (of copper, IV, 708).

stef-t, a disease of the belly, purge (?)

Stef, Edfû I, 81, a title of the Nile-god.

stef (?) ....

s-tem, P. 189, to make an end of; caus. of . The variant passages M. 357 and N. 908 give .

s-tem = , to turn back.

stem, fodder, field or garden produce; see ; Copt. CIⲙ.

stem, an assistant priest; see .

s-ten, to mark out, to distinguish, to make a difference between, to exalt; caus. of for ; , to distinguish between winter and summer; , De Hymnis 47, [thou] distinguisher who hast distinguished.

stennu, a noble or distinguished man.

stenit (sic), B.D. 125, II, 39, (var. in Nu), distinctions.

s-tenn, to swell (of a boil).

sten, M. 678, N. 1240, P. 642, a kind of garment.

sten, to slay, to kill.

Stenit, the name of a serpent on the royal crown.

Stenu, Rev. 13, 120, , Coronation Stele, 8, 9, the White Crown.

s-tenem, s-tenemm, Osiris 34, to lead astray, to mislead, to lose the way; caus. of .

stenemu, he who leads astray, he who makes a mistake.

ster, worked, chased (of metal).

ster, B.D. 169, 25, wooden tablet (?)

ster, a kind of plant.

ster-t, purification, pure thing.

sterit, P. 1116B, 21, to make prayer or supplication.

steh, a wooden instrument used in grinding.

steh, Rev. 11, 60, revolt.

steḥ, Rev. 14, 46, rubbish, waste.

s-teḥen, Rec. 15, 178, , to sparkle; caus. of = .

Stekh, IV, 1085 = or, Set.

stekhi, malign magic.

stekhu, to treat a body, living or dead, with drugs, to mummify; see ; var.

setkhekh, to treat a body with drugs; see and.

Setesh, = , Set; varr. , .

setshu, Gol. Hamm. 12, 93 . . . .

s-teka, to light a lamp; caus. (?)

s-teken, to make to approach, to bring near; caus.

stekniu, , porters, those who bring offerings, invaders.

steg, to hide oneself, to take refuge; see.

s-tega, Hymn Darius 32, to see; caus.

steter, , Rev. 14, 68, stater; Gr. στατήρ; Copt. ⲥⲁⲧⲉⲉⲣⲉ.

seth, lo! behold!

seth, P. 338, M. 640, to reach out (a hand).

s-th (s-thes), to bear up; see.

seth (sthi), seed; Copt. ⲥⲓϯ.

seth (sthi), U. 422, , T. 242, , , to eject seed, to beget, to sow seed.

seth (sthi), Rec. 30, 187, to light a fire.

sthu-t, light, radiance, splendour.

seth (sthi), to spear fish.

Sthiu, IV, 661, , Asiatics and Nubians.

seth (sthi-t), , Stele of Ptolemy I, 14, land, estate, pasture land.

seth-t (sthi-t), , , , , , , , Rec. 32, 79, garment, apparel, festal raiment; , Rec. 27, 219, , Rec. 31, 174.

seth-t, , libation vessel.

seth-t, , Rec. 36, 216, chamber.

sthi-t, a tiring woman.

Sthit, Sthåit, , P. 297, , Anc. Eg. III, 239, , a goddess of the First Cataract, consort of Khnemu.

Seth (Sthi)-ḥer, Litanie 62, a form of Rā.

Sthit-s-mm-Nu, Rec. 34, 190, one of the 12 Thoueris goddesses, she presided over the month.

seth-t, Rec. 27, 225, , to frighten, to terrify.

seth (sti), U. 9, P. 293, , , , smell, odour, scent, perfume; plur. , T. 282, 332, P. 294; , T. 347, foul stink; Copt. ⲥϯ.

seth ḥeb, U. 56, , , , ointment used on festal occasions.

stha, U. 331, 553, T. 317, , P. 226, , Rec. 31, 27, , , Rec. 27, 225, to tow, to drag, to pull, to lead; see .

sthaut, N. 971, towings of boats.

sthaiu, those who-tow boats; , unseen haulers of boats.

stha, , a jar, a vessel.

s-tham, , to clothe, to wrap up in cloth, to bandage.

Seth-àb, Ṭuat VII, a goddess.

Sthethi, Hh. 343, a god.

Sthu, Ṭuat IX, a monster serpent-warder of the 9th Gate.

sthep, U. 548, T. 303, , , , to cut in pieces, to slay.

sthep, , P. 681, to select, to choose.

stheput, portions of meat selected for offerings; , cattle chosen for offerings.

sthepu, , Rec. 36, 216 . . . .

sthep, T. 185, P. 183, 196, 674, N. 1282, M. 291, , U. 491, P. 579, , Hh. 425, to remove, to carry away, to transport.

s-then; caus. of .

sthenà, , a distinguished person or statue, eminent, prominent, notable.

sthen, to journey, to retreat.

sthensthen, to travel, to journey, to conduct a party.

sthenà, Anastasi I, 28, 2, , P. 1116B, 43, to compare.

sthenà-t, a thing compared with something else.

s-thenem, , , to turn back, to turn aside or away, to lead astray; caus. of .

sther-t, eyelid, eyelashes.

sther = **senther**, natron, incense.

s-thes, , , , , to exalt, to lift up, to exalt oneself, to be exalted; caus. Copt. ϫⲓⲥⲉ.

sthesu, , , those who lift up or exult; , those who lift up praises or who raise the song of praise.

sthesu Shu, , , the four supports of Shu.

s-thes, , , IV, 659, , to lie at full length, laid out, stretched out, to lie prone, dead body; , , the dead.

Seṭ, Palermo Stele = , Set—the god of evil.

seṭ, to cut, to pierce.

seṭ, , Israel Stele 4, Tombos Stele 11, Rec. 30, 220, , , , , , , to break, to smash, to cleave, to breach a wall.

seṭ-t, , breach, break, opening.

seṭ ⟨hieroglyphs⟩, a kind of canal, a branch of the Nile.

Sṭit-qesu ⟨hieroglyphs⟩, "Breaker of bones," one of the 42 assessors of Osiris.

seṭ ⟨hieroglyphs⟩, to loathe, to be disgusted.

seṭ ⟨hieroglyphs⟩, impurity, dross.

seṭ ⟨hieroglyphs⟩, to dress, to clothe, to array in fine apparel.

sṭiu ⟨hieroglyphs⟩, dressers.

sṭit ⟨hieroglyphs⟩, bandlet, headcloth, garment; varr. ⟨hieroglyphs⟩.

seṭ ⟨hieroglyphs⟩, T. 38, 310, P. 564, ⟨hieroglyphs⟩, Âmen. 13, 4, ⟨hieroglyphs⟩, ⟨hieroglyphs⟩, tail, rump; plur. ⟨hieroglyphs⟩, Shipwreck 163; ⟨hieroglyphs⟩ ⟨hieroglyphs⟩, P.S.B. 13, 412, tail in the air; Copt. ⲥⲁⲧ.

Seṭ ⟨hieroglyphs⟩, Palermo Stele, ⟨hieroglyphs⟩, ⟨hieroglyphs⟩, ⟨hieroglyphs⟩, "festival of the tail"; plur. ⟨hieroglyphs⟩, IV, 569, 1095. A festival which the king celebrated every 30 years, or after great events, however frequent, or whenever he wished to obtain a renewal of his life from the gods.

seṭ ent pet ⟨hieroglyphs⟩, ⟨hieroglyphs⟩, the name of the 27th or 28th day of the month.

seṭ-t ⟨hieroglyphs⟩, Anastasi I, 6, 1, section of a book, page, column of a papyrus.

sṭet ⟨hieroglyphs⟩; see ⟨hieroglyphs⟩.

seṭ pennu ⟨hieroglyphs⟩, rat's-tail, a herb used in medicine.

seṭu nu māmā (?) ⟨hieroglyphs⟩, a plant or herb used in medicine.

seṭ su ⟨hieroglyphs⟩, a kind of plant.

seṭ sheps-t (?) ⟨hieroglyphs⟩, A.Z. 1880, 95, a part of a chariot.

seṭ-t (sṭit) ⟨hieroglyphs⟩, Rev. 12, 66, ⟨hieroglyphs⟩, Rev. 14, 20, fire; Copt. ⲥⲁⲧⲉ.

sṭa ⟨hieroglyphs⟩, T. 27, ⟨hieroglyphs⟩, N. 198, P. 611, 707, Rec. 27, 217, 34, 177, ⟨hieroglyphs⟩, U. 215, ⟨hieroglyphs⟩, ⟨hieroglyphs⟩, to quake, to tremble.

sṭeṭiu ⟨hieroglyphs⟩, those who shake, old men.

sṭaṭa (seṭṭ) ⟨hieroglyphs⟩, to quake, to tremble; Copt. ⲥⲧⲱⲧ.

sṭau ⟨hieroglyphs⟩, palsy, quaking paralysis, the shaking sickness.

sṭa ⟨hieroglyphs⟩, a kind of marsh bird, bittern (?)

Sṭa ur ⟨hieroglyphs⟩, U. 187, ⟨hieroglyphs⟩, T. 66, ⟨hieroglyphs⟩, M. 221, ⟨hieroglyphs⟩, N. 598, ⟨hieroglyphs⟩, ⟨hieroglyphs⟩, Rec. 29, 153, ⟨hieroglyphs⟩, "Great quaker," god of the thunder and earthquakes.

Sṭa meṭsu ⟨hieroglyphs⟩, U. 419, ⟨hieroglyphs⟩, T. 240, the ancient storm-gods.

Sṭa-ta ⟨hieroglyphs⟩, P. 304, "Earth-shaker"—the name of a god.

sṭa-t ⟨hieroglyphs⟩, a kind of prickly shrub used as a protection for encampments, "thorn scrub" or "thorn bush."

sṭaf (sṭef) ⟨hieroglyphs⟩, Rev. 12, 62, pure; Copt. ⲥⲟⲧϥ.

s-ṭu , , , to defame, to run down, to decry, to vilify; caus.

sṭu [ ], to run aground (of a ship).

s-ṭua , to pass the morning; caus. of ṭua .

sṭukh , , , , to treat a body with drugs, to embalm a dead body.

sṭeb , , Peasant 50, bandlet, belt, girdle, hangings of a shrine, a part of a square cloth.

sṭeb , , , , stake, instrument of torture, misery, disaster, calamity; plur. , .

sṭebȧ , a wretched man.

sṭebu , Rev. 12. 22, a tool or weapon.

s-ṭeb , , , to chew, to ruminate; Copt. ⲥⲁⲧⲃⲉ.

sṭebȧ . . . .

s-ṭebḥ , , , , to arrange, to provide, to equip, to supply; caus.

sṭebḥut , , provision, equipment, tools, implements, furniture; plur. , , Tanis Pap. 19.

sṭeput , portions of an animal selected for sacrifice.

sṭef , , L.D. III, 140c, to make ready, to prepare.

sṭef , to cut in pieces, to slay.

sṭem , U. 65, N. 320, , N. 323, , N. 324, , U. 421, , T. 241, to paint the eyelids with stibium.

sṭem-t , eye-paint.

sṭem-t , stibium, antimony, eye-paint; Copt. ⲥⲧⲏⲙ, Gr. στίμμις.

sṭem , Hh. 336, Rec. 27, 58, to hear; Copt. ⲥⲱⲧⲙ.

sṭem , Rec. 2, 30, assistant priest.

s-ṭem (?) , to bring to an end.

s-ṭemȧ , T. 264, M. 417, to join, to unite; caus.; Copt. ⲧⲱⲙⲓ.

sṭen , , Coronation Stele 22, crown.

sṭenu , wearer of a crown, prince.

sṭenit , rule, dominion, sovereignty.

sṭenȧ , to dam a river.

sṭenu , swift courier.

s-ṭenem ; see .

sṭer , a kind of plant.

sṭekh , P. 61, M. 82, N. 89, , N. 72, to defend, to protect.

sṭekh , Hh. 5. . . . . .

sṭekhi , , Israel Stele 14, to overthrow, to defeat; see .

s-ṭesher T. 281, , N. 131, , to redden; caus.

sṭeshru , red things, bloody wounds.

s-ṭeku, , to hide; caus.

s-ṭega, , , , Metternich Stele 49, , IV, 385, to hide, to run away and hide; caus.

Sṭeg, B.D. 168, a bull-god.

Sṭeg, a proper name (?); , IV, 1071.

s-ṭega, Hymn Darius, 7, to look, to examine; caus.

sṭegaut, B.D. 108, 6, watchers (?)

seṭṭ-t, trembling, quaking, shaking.

s-ṭeṭ, L.D. III, 140B, to stablish; caus.

setch, M. 194, to sprinkle, to scatter, to sow.

setch, P. 397, M. 566, N. 1173, seed.

setch, Rec. 27, 58, , to break, to break open.

setch, P. 185, to strike a balance, to make a reckoning.

setch (?), Mar. Karn. 52, 8, to lay waste, to be wasted.

setchu åbu (?), Stele Usertsen III, "broken hearts" (used to describe the timid broken-spirited peoples of the Northern Sûdân).

setchu, P. 424, M. 607, , N. 1212, archers.

Setchtiu, , , Rec. 32, 79, archers (?)

setch-t, U. 184, 322, 513, T. 88, N. 619, , Rec. 30, 198, 31, 170, , , , , flame, fire; Copt. ϲⲁⲧⲉ.

Setchti, Ṭuat II, a fire-god in the Ṭuat.

Setchit-usrit, Nesi-Åmsu 27, 16, a title of Sekhmit.

setch, Rec. 30, 188, tail, hair, bristles.

setch = , the festival of the tail; see **seṭ**.

setch, A.Z. 1906, 112, child, babe, infant; fem. , , , , .

setchti, IV, 1072, young.

setch, , form, image.

setchetch, form, image.

setch, pot, vessel.

setch (?), M. 826, a kind of wood.

s-tcha, P. 636, , P. 163, to go, to depart = ; , to depart in peace, *i.e.*, to die.

setcha-t, departure.

Setcha, Ros. Mon. 23, Champ. Mon. 378, a fabulous animal with the head of a serpent and the legs and tail of a lion.

setcha, Jour. As. 9, sér. 10, 506 . . . .

s-tchai, U. 642, , , , , = , to be well, happy, amused, to enjoy oneself; , Love Songs 7, 9.

setchasetcha, Rev., mockery, jest; Copt. ⲥⲱϫ.

s-tchai ḥer, A.Z. 1908, 70, , A.Z. 1905, 28, , , Anastasi I, 8, 7, , Ȧmen. 27, 8, , , Sphinx Stele 5, , Jour. As. 1908, 282, to laugh, to joke, to jest, to have pleasure in something.

s-tchai, A.Z. 1878, 48, , , , Rev. 12, 16, , Rev. 11, 123, 12, 66, 14, 36, , Rev. 11, 139, to say, to recite, to narrate; Copt. ϣⲁϫⲉ, ⲥⲁϫⲓ.

setchait, Rec. 27, 8, word, speech; plur. , Rev. 13, 11; Copt. ϣⲁϫⲉ, ⲥⲁϫⲓ.

setchain, Rev., counsel; Copt. ⲥⲟϭⲛⲓ.

setchaiḥ, , Jour. As. 1908, 267, , Rev. 12, 47, , Rev. 14, 16, rejoicing, jest, joke, amusement.

setchaut, seal.

s-tcham, to wrap up, to envelop; var. , .

setcham, to beget, to act the part of a male.

setchami, , , protector.

setchamāut, Rec. 4, 127, virtues, virility (?)

setchamut, , , A.Z. 1872, 37, hoe, hatchet.

setchaḥui, , , , shin bones; var. .

setchakhmu, A.Z. 1864, 107, bat; Copt. ϭⲉⲛϭⲉⲗⲟ.

s-tchām, to plate with gold or silver, plating metal; caus.

setcheb, a measure of land = 100 cubits.

ṡetcheb, U. 240, P. 102, M. 90, N. 97, to subsist, to exist, a synonym of , to live.

setchbu (?), Wört. 763, 1389, men, mankind in general.

setcheb, U. 4, 376, 451, M. 396, , Rec. 32, 80, 81, , disaster, calamity, misfortune; plur. , U. 448, , , .

s-tchefa, , , , , Ȧmen. 21, 11, , , , to feed, to provision, to provide for, to supply; caus.

setchef, Annales III, 110, bread, food in general.

setchef, to kill, to slay.

setchem, U. 40, P. 187, , P. 401, 835, M. 573, N. 1180, , , , , , , , , III, 143, , to hear, to hear a case, to hearken, to obey; , to obey the dictates of the belly.

setchemsetchem , , , , , Rec. 33, 35, to listen carefully.

setchem-t , U. 631, , , , , a hearing.

setchemu , , hearer, listener; plur. , .

setchemu , a kind of tradesman.

setchem , judge of the māb-t court.

setchemiu , , , , IV, 1109, , Edict 22, officers or judges who hear cases.

setchem āsh , attendant in the Place of truth; , IV, 619, , Rec. 8, 134, subordinate officers, chief servants (?)

Setchemi , B.D.G. 776, Anc. Eg. III, 226, a bull-god, the god of hearing; , B.D.G. 699, a form of Isis of Mendes.

Setchem ȧnsi , B.D. 115, 7, a kind of garment (?)

Setchem (?) em snef , Ombos II, 134, a mythological being.

setchem meṭu-f , , , the name of the 19th day of the month.

setchem ḥeri , B.D. 125, I, 21, the upper leaf of the door of the hall of Osiris.

setchem kheri , B.D. 125, I, 21, the lower leaf of the door of the hall of Osiris.

setchem , to paint the eyelids with stibium; see , .

setchen , Rec. 3, 3, to overthrow.

setcher , , III, 141, , to be strong, to make strong.

setcher , , fort, strong place; plur. .

setcher , T. 338, P. 820, N. 702, Hh. 453, , , IV, 659, , , , , , III, 143, , , , , to pass the night, to lie down to sleep or in death, to sleep, the opposite of , to pass the day; , A.Z. 1900, 27, the sleepless One, *i.e.*, God.

setcheri , , , , , , he who is lying down asleep or dead; plur. , , , .

setcheriu , P. 204, N. 847, sleepers, *i.e.*, the blessed dead.

setcherit , sexual intercourse.

setcherit , a night camping ground.

setcherit , T. 333, P. 824, N. 703 . . . . . .

setcher (?) , B.D. 1B, 19, bier (?)

setcherit, sickness, prostration; , II, 5.

Setcherit, , the rest festival.

setcherit, , , sleeping draught, drugged beer.

Setchriu, A.Z. 1900, 21, the sleeping gods.

Setcherur, T. 380, a god.

setcheḥ, , the shin bone; dual , .

setcheḥ, U. 542, T. 297, P. 226, a mythological serpent.

s-tcheser, , , IV, 834, , to beautify, to make grand or splendid, to promote to high rank; caus.

setcheseru, splendid or magnificent things.

s-tcheser s-tcheser, to complete, to beautify.

s-tcheṭ, , , Åmen. 11, 14, , to tell, to narrate, to describe, to speak; caus.; Copt. ϣⲁϫⲉ.

setcheṭi, narrator, story teller.

setcheṭu, , , , Anastasi I, 26, 3, speech, stories, narratives, tales, descriptions, precepts, sayings.

setcheṭ-t, , , Åmen. 14, 14, narrative, story.

setcheṭ, hall, chamber.

setcheṭha, Rev., to jest; see .

sh = Heb. שׁ, Copt. ϣ.

sha, she, A.Z. 45, 129, estate, field.

sha, lake, pool, cistern, tank, ornamental water in a garden, trough, laver; plur., P. 830, N. 773; Copt. ϣⲏⲓ.

sha āa, IV, 1047, a large water garden.

Sha-t Åsår, lake of Osiris, a name of the Fayyûm.

Sha en Åsår, B.D. 122, 6, lake of Osiris (the Fayyûm).

Sha uāb: (1) basin of purification; (2), a name of the lake of the temple of Denderah; (3), a name of Lake Moeris.

Sha-t ur-t, a part of the Fayyûm.

sha-t pet, a kind of incense.

Shatt pet, T. 175, 279, M. 28, 65, 156, P. 60, N. 86, 110, a title of Nut.

sha qāḥ, P. 1116B, 30, tanks in which fish were kept ready for eating.

Sha ṭesui (?), a lake in the Oasis of Khârgah (?)

Sha Asbiu, B.D. 63B, 2, the lake of Fire in the Ṭuat.

Sha Ageb, B.D. 189, 11, the lake of Ageb, *i.e.*, the celestial sea.

Sha Åaru, P. 637, N. 1379, M. 515, the lake of Reeds in the Other World.

Sha åqer, B.D. 172, 40, lake of Perfection, a lake wherein the righteous bathed.

Sha ur, B.D. 117, 3, a large lake in the Ṭuat; Rhind Pap. note 42, the great lake of Khensu.

Sha Maāti, B.D. 17, 51, lake of Truth, a lake in the Ṭuat.

Sha em māfk-t, B.D. 39, 19, the lakes of Turquoise in the Ṭuat.

Sha en Amu, B.D. 98, 6, lake of Fire in the Ṭuat.

Sha en ānkh, N. 762, Ṭuat IV, lake of Life, a lake in the Ṭuat.

Sha en maāt, Peasant 54, "lake of Truth."

Sha en maātiu, B.D. 168, lake of the Speakers of the truth.

Sha en māāt, Berg. II, 395, B.D. 17, 46, a lake in the Ṭuat.

Sha en Ḥeru, the lake of Horus in the Ṭuat.

Sha en ḥesmen, the lake of Natron in the Ṭuat.

Sha ent ḥetche-t, B.D. 145, 36, lake of Light in the Ṭuat.

Sha en Kha, Rec. 27, 223, the name of a lake in the Ṭuat; see , N. 966, , U. 576.

Sha en khebentiu, B.D. 130, 10, lake of the Wicked.

Sha en Sab, Rec. 26, 233, the lake of the Jackal in the Ṭuat.

Sha sab, Rec. 26, 233, , the lake of the Jackal in the Ṭuat.

Sha en s-ḥetep, B.D. 96–97, 7, lake of Propitiation.

Sha en setchet, B.D. (Nebseni) 17, 41, a lake of Fire in the Ṭuat.

Sha en qebḥ, N. 762, the lake of Cold Water in the Ṭuat.

Sha Nu, , the Celestial ocean.

Sha Nesȧsȧ (Sha en Sȧsȧ ?), , a lake of Fire in the Ṭuat; varr. , .

Sha Neserser, B.D. 71, 18, a lake of Fire in the Ṭuat; varr. , .

Sha neter, B.D. 172, 42, the pool of the God in the Ṭuat.

Sha Ḥi, T. 378, , N. 625, a lake in the Ṭuat.

Sha ḥeru, the lake of the Celestial beings.

Sha ḥeḥ, B.D. 131, 10, the lake of a million years.

Sha Ḥetep, B.D. 110, 6, the lake of the god Ḥetep.

Sha kharu, B.D. 149, II, 6, the lake where the kharu geese lived in the Ṭuat.

Sha Sharu (?), a lake in the Ṭuat.

Sha Ṭat-tȧ, U. 481, , N. 144, a lake in the Ṭuat.

Sha Tcheser-t, the lakes of the goddess Tchesert in the Ṭuat.

sha (?), phallus (?)

sha (?), B.D. 98, 8, lacuna (?)

sha-t, , , , things.

sha-t (?) [ ], hundred; usually written ; Copt. ϣⲉ, ϣⲟⲧ. The reading shent has been proposed (A.Z. 1898, 138); , two hundred; Copt. ϣⲏⲧ; , U. 516, T. 327, hundreds.

sha-t (?), 100-thread stuff.

sha, P. 440, , M. 656, , garden, meadow, estate, plain.

sha (?), , grove, orchard.

sha, shaut, , , , , , , , , P.S.B. 13, 411, flowering shrub, flower, a vine

in blossom; plur. [hieroglyphs], IV, 1167, [hieroglyphs], Anastasi I, 25, 3, IV, 772; [hieroglyphs], [hieroglyphs], flowers in general, the plants in a garden, garden; Copt. ϣⲱϣⲛⲟⲩ.

shau [hieroglyphs], Rec. 3, 12, 110, melon plant.

sha [hieroglyphs], Hh. 437, reeds.

sha-t [hieroglyphs], [hieroglyphs], [hieroglyphs], wine, drink.

Sha [hieroglyphs], a fabulous animal like a greyhound with a straight tail in the form of an axe.

Sha-t [hieroglyphs], Metternich Stele 86, a mythological animal, parent of Menu.

sha [hieroglyphs], [hieroglyphs], a kind of dog; plur. [hieroglyphs].

sha-t [hieroglyphs], bitch.

sha, shaȧ [hieroglyphs], [hieroglyphs], [hieroglyphs], [hieroglyphs], [hieroglyphs], pig; plur. [hieroglyphs]; Copt. ⲉϣⲱ.

shau [hieroglyphs], Peasant B 2, 138, pig; [hieroglyphs], Metternich Stele 86, white sow.

Shaȧ [hieroglyphs], B.D. 36, [hieroglyphs], B.D. 112, 5, the black pig of Set speared by Horus.

sha-t [hieroglyphs], [hieroglyphs], claw of a bird, talon, a measure; [hieroglyphs], great span = 3½ palms (14 fingers); [hieroglyphs], little span = 3 palms (12 fingers).

sha-ti [hieroglyphs] = [hieroglyphs], Sphinx I, 257.

sha-t [hieroglyphs], part of the body of an animal; [hieroglyphs], skin (?) of a dog.

sha-t [hieroglyphs], U. 582, body; [hieroglyphs], N. 70 = [hieroglyphs], T. 48, [hieroglyphs], M. 59, [hieroglyphs], P. 89.

sha-t [hieroglyphs], P. 477, N. 1265, emissions of the body.

sha pet [hieroglyphs], U. 609, storm, tempest.

sha [hieroglyphs] = [hieroglyphs], to read, to proclaim; Copt. ⲱϣ.

shaa [hieroglyphs], to steer, to sail a boat.

sha, shai [hieroglyphs], [hieroglyphs], Thes. 1285, [hieroglyphs], [hieroglyphs], to fix, to appoint, to decide, to determine, to destine, to predestinate, to allot, to design, to decree, to ordain, to commission, to authorize.

sha-t [hieroglyphs], [hieroglyphs], Amherst Pap. 26, [hieroglyphs], [hieroglyphs], [hieroglyphs], A.Z. 45, 125, something decreed or ordained by God, what is ordained by man or fixed by custom, what is seemly or fitting, dues, revenue, taxes, impost.

shau [hieroglyphs], A.Z. 1874, 87, [hieroglyphs], IV, 1116, [hieroglyphs], what is decreed or ordered or ordained, fate, destiny.

sha-t [hieroglyphs], [hieroglyphs], profit, benefit.

shai [hieroglyphs], Rev., use, utility, worth; Copt. ϣⲁⲩ-.

shait [hieroglyphs], Rec. 3, 44, [hieroglyphs], A.Z. 1905, 28, 39, [hieroglyphs], IV, 530, [hieroglyphs], tax, impost, produce of a country.

shaiu [hieroglyphs], P.S.B. 10, 42, dues, revenues, treasures.

sha [hieroglyphs], a kind of bread, loaves, food in general.

shaȧ [hieroglyphs], Rev. 13, 107, book, writing, document.

shaȧ, Westcar Pap. 12, 17, estate, garden, orchard, grove.

shaȧu, wine, drink.

shaȧu, A.Z. 1900, 37, beads (?)

shaȧs, , , , to go, to travel, to journey.

shaȧsiu, goings, goers.

shaȧs, wicket-gate (?)

shaā (sha), Rev. 11, 125, , Rec. 21, 77, , , , up to, as far as, until; IV, 647, , as far as; Copt. ϣⲁ.

shaā-t, Jour. As. 1908, 979, until; Copt. ϣⲁⲧ.

shaāut (sha-t) (?), until; Copt. ϣⲁⲧⲉ.

shaā, Rev. 13, 8 = ϣⲁ, of use and wont, *e.g.*, ϣⲁϥⲥⲱⲧⲙ̄.

shaā, shaȧā (shā), , , , , , to begin; , Rev. 15, 38, the source of life.

Shaāit, the goddess of primeval matter—a form of Hathor.

shaāȧ-mes, Rev. 14, 7, firstborn; Copt. ϣⲁⲙⲓⲥⲉ.

shaā, shaā-t, Supp. 1223, , Rec. 33, 32, warehouse, storehouse, granary.

shaā (shā), , , , Rev. 12, 79, sand; Copt. ϣⲱ.

shaā, to smite, to conquer.

shaāi, slaughter, slayer.

shaāit (shāiti), , blow, stroke, ill luck (?)

shaā, Mar. Karn. 55, 75, beggar.

shaāi, Rev. 11, 149, something written.

Shaāi, , , Rev. 11, 183; see **Shai.**

shaāim, Rev. 13, 20, stable.

shaāikh, Rev. 14, 17, dust; Copt. ϣⲟⲉⲓϣ.

shaāber (?), Rev. 11, 133, outside; Copt. ϣⲁⲃⲟⲗ.

shaām, Rev. 11, 182, to desire; var. ; Copt. ϣⲉⲙⲙⲉⲓ.

shaāmtuf, Rev. 12, 14, 13, 21 = Copt. ϣⲁⲛⲧⲉϥ.

shaār, tooth; Copt. ϣⲁⲗ (?)

shaār, Jour. As. 1908, 255, to bargain, to haggle; Copt. ⲉⲣϣⲁⲁⲣ.

shaār, Mar. Karn. 54, 42, , , , , to vow, to promise, to boast.

shaār, Amherst Pap. 28, , door, gate, prison; Heb. שַׁעַר.

shaārki, Rev. 12, 118, drought; compare Arab. شرق.

shaās, Shipwreck 163, a product of the enchanted island.

shaāsha, Rev. 12, 17, rail, railing; Copt. ϣⲱϣ.

shaāsha, Rec. 33, 120, reverence, respect.

shaāshaā, Rec. 33, 120, 138, Rev. 13, 29, boast, glory, fame, renown; Copt. ϣⲟⲩϣⲟⲩ.

shaāshaā, Rev., to winnow; Copt. ϣⲱϣ ⲉ ⲃⲟⲗ.

shaāshaā, Rec. 3, 38, terrace, walk with trees planted by the side.

shai, Israel Stele 8, Rec. 21, 95, a man's fate, his fortune and allotted span of life.

shai bȧn, Israel Stele 8, ill luck.

shai nefer, good luck.

shait, Treaty 10, ill luck, evil destiny, a blow of fate.

Shai, Ȧmen. 21, 16, A.Z. 1873, 138, Todt. (Leps.), pl. 50, Pap. Ani 3, B.M. 32, 411, Jour. As. Sér. X, 9, 434, 460, 473, 491, 508, 552, Berg. 73, the god Luck or Fate or Destiny who reckons the days ( ) of men.

Shait, Ȧmen. 9, 11, Hh. 330, the goddess Fate.

Shai, Litanie 37, a dog-god.

Shai, Tomb of Seti I, one of the 75 forms of Rā (No. 37).

Shai, a benevolent serpent-god.

Shai, Lanzone 129, a crocodile-god who ate the hearts of the dead.

shai, Rec. 12, 98, a kind of seed.

shaii, well, fountain, tank, cistern; Copt. ϣⲏⲓ.

shau, P. 38, M. 48 = , T. 286, to injure (?)

shau, in the name P. 498, P. 510.

shau, to be hot, to burn, fire.

shau, Rev. 13, 25, Rev. 12, 118, dry, parched; Copt. ϣⲟⲟⲩⲉ

shaut, Rev. 14, 12, dryness.

Shau, B.D. 141–142, 121, 142, III, 15, a city with the special cult of Osiris.

shau, Rev. 13, 6, Rec. 16, 69, Jour. As. 1908, 283, to glorify oneself, to boast oneself over someone or something; Copt. ϣⲟⲩ, ϣⲟⲩϣⲟⲩ.

shau, Ȧmen. 12, 4, to be of value, property, stuff, possessions, goods, something which is of worth or value, something useful, advantage, benefit; , Theban Ostraka No. 2; , most valuable of all.

Shau, Rec. 36, 53, P.S.B. 15, 35, = , the god of prosperity and of good luck and good fortune.

shau (?), abode, dwelling.

shau-t, P. 414, M. 593, N. 1198, garden, park.

shau, excrement.

sha, a disease of the eye.

shauti (shuti), Rev. 11, 174, the two plumes of a crown.

shau, Rec. 30, 66, parts of the magical boat.

shauaȧ, leather whip, stick.

shauaȧ, slab of stone for a statue.

shauabu, Rec. 15, 18, the melon plant; plur. , Love Songs 3, 13, ; Copt. ϣοοϐε.

shauab-t, melons (?) the figs of the persea tree (?)

shauabti, , a figure made of stone, wood, faïence, etc., which was placed in the tomb to perform the work of a slave on behalf of the deceased; var. ; see .

shauabti, IV, 733, A.Z. 34, 166, , pot, vessel, vase, jar.

shauar, Rec. 19, 96, part of a shrine.

shauā, writing, document, letter, book; see .

shaubu, flame, fire; compare Heb. שָׁבִיב, Job xviii, 5.

shab-t, A.Z. 1905, 5, daily service, obligation.

Shab (?), Ḥerusȧtef Stele 15, tribe; compare Eth. ሰብእ:

shab-t, P. 373, N. 1149, B.D. ed. Nav. 172, 28, , Rec. 31, 25, , water melon (?); plur. , P. 367, , B.D. 172, 28, , IV, 1194, ; Copt. ϣωϐε.

shab-t, dried melon plants, hay.

shabarth, stream, flow of water; Heb. שִׁבֹּלֶת.

shabu, IV, 481, , food.

shabu, altars laden with food offerings.

shabu, to shorten sail, to furl a sail.

shabu, to strike, to smite, to hew stones.

shabu, a worked stone, masonry.

shabu, , a funereal figure; varr. .

Shabu, a fire-god; see **Ashbu**.

shabn, Rev. 12, 87, , junction, union, accord, unison; Copt. ϣωπϐ.

shabt, Jour. As. 1908, 255, staff, stick; see .

shabti, , , see .

shabṭ-t, Rec. 1, 48, Love Songs 2, 3, , staff, stick, rod, bâton, walking-stick; plur. , , , , Åmen. 15, 1, , Sallier I, 6, 5, 6; Heb. שֵׁבֶט, Copt. ϣⲃⲱⲧ, Syr. ܫܒܛܐ.

shapu, Anastasi IV, 12, 3, to dance.

Shapu-neter-år-t-ka, B.D. 163, 11, name of one of the two Utchats of Rā.

shapsh, Rev. 11, 171, fore-arm; Copt. ϣⲱⲡϣ.

shaf, to burn up; Copt. ϣⲱϥ.

shafi, to be angry, to act as an enemy, to swell (of a boil), swelling; Copt. ϣⲁϥⲉ.

shafit, Jour. As. 1908, 294, , , wickedness, sin, want; Copt. ϣⲁϥⲧ; Amhar. ስፍት.

sham, B.D. 130, 10, to be foul or dirty.

sham' to wash out clothes (?)

sham', , Anastasi IV, 11, 8, V, 6, 1, Sallier I, 9, to desire (?)

sham'-t a wooden bar or tool.

shamāit (?), a kind of seed used in medicine; , an infusion of the same.

Sham' bār, Anastasi III, Rev. 6, 7, a proper name; according to Alt K. 850 = שמבעל.

shamit, fulling, cleansing; var. .

shamu, Peasant 279, dirty clothes to be washed.

shamu, Thes. 1203, to traverse.

shamu, a kind of drink.

shames-t, an ear of corn; plur. , , , ; var. ; Copt. ϩⲙⲥ, ϭⲉⲙⲥ.

shamsh, Rev. 13, 30 = , to serve.

shanash, Rec. 3, 33 = , to stink.

shansh, , , foul or stinking matter; Copt. ϣⲛⲟϣ.

shanu, Gen. Epist. 64 .....

shanr, to rub off, to rub away.

shanr, A.Z. 1871, 133, bristle, wool (?)

shanrefi, Anastasi I, 24, 1, the bristling of the hair through fright.

sharr, Rev. 13, 30, , Jour. As. 1908, 250, , , , to pray, prayer; Copt. ϣⲗⲏⲗ.

sharram, , Rev. 14, 10, inflammation of the eyes.

sharri, Rev. 12, 114, lamentation.

sharitȧ-t, Anastasi I, 23, 3, 24, 3, gulf, precipice, chasm.

sharrur, Rev. 14, 15, joy; Copt. ϣⲗⲟⲩⲗⲁⲓ.

sharef, Rev. 11, 134, 140, to injure; Copt. ϣⲗⲟϥ.

sharfi (?), Anastasi I, 10, 3, ruffled, dishevelled.

sharm, III, 8, to be unused (of weapons).

sharm', Harris I, 78, 11, to be peaceful, to be unoccupied, idle, to be free to do what one pleases.

sharm', Thes. 1204, Rougé I.H. II, 125, Harris I, 42, 7, to greet, to salute, to offer salutations, to salaam, to sue for mercy; compare the meanings of the Heb. √שלם.

sharmā, Israel Stele 26, peace, content; Heb. שְׁלוֹם, Arab. سَلَمَات.

sharm'tȧ, Anastasi I, 17, 5, a meal of reconciliation.

sharmātȧ, tribute; Heb. שִׁלְמָה.

sharḥu, Rev. 14, 51, irrigation channels.

sharsh, to be swift, to hasten; varr.

sharsha, Rev. 12, 48, to dispute, to contend; Copt. ϣⲉⲣϣⲓ.

Sharshar (?), B.D. 163, 8, the name of an Utchat.

Sharsharkhet, B.D. 163, 11, a name of one of the two Utchats of Rā.

Sharshatȧkatȧ, B.D. 165, 9, a name of Ȧmen.

Sharṭana, Sharṭenu, Mar. Karn. 52, 1; **Sharṭina**, a Mediterranean people, Sardinians (?)

Sharṭshaq, Rec. 35, 57, the name of a fiend.

Shahab, Berg. I, 35, god of the south wind. He has a lion's head, horns, and two pairs of wings.

shaḥqarȧ, Anastasi I, 10, 3, a term of abuse.

shakha, Rev., the approach (of death).

shakhent (?), I, 13, a plant.

shas, to cut, to kill.

shasi, U. 554, T. 303, U. 459, Rec. 36 210,

N. 657, [hieroglyphs], [hieroglyphs], [hieroglyphs], B.D. 180, 32, Metternich Stele 58, [hieroglyphs], B.D. 63B, 4, [hieroglyphs], [hieroglyphs], U. 223, P. 515, [hieroglyphs], Rev. 11, 186, to go, to travel, to advance, to travel about in general.

shasiu [hieroglyphs], B.D. 152, 6, travellers.

shass [hieroglyphs], N. 172, [hieroglyphs], T. 348, to go, to travel, to advance.

Shasu [hieroglyphs], [hieroglyphs], [hieroglyphs], [hieroglyphs], the country of the nomad Semites.

Shasu [hieroglyphs], [hieroglyphs], [hieroglyphs], [hieroglyphs], [hieroglyphs], [hieroglyphs], nomad Semites; Copt. ϣⲱⲥ.

shasu [hieroglyphs] = [hieroglyphs], ears of corn.

Shasi [hieroglyphs], Rec. 6, 156, a god of the dead.

shasha [hieroglyphs], [hieroglyphs], [hieroglyphs], to build.

shasha [hieroglyphs], [hieroglyphs], [hieroglyphs], to tread down, to trample under foot.

shasha-t [hieroglyphs], a treading down.

shasha [hieroglyphs], [hieroglyphs], [hieroglyphs], Rec. 1, 46, ignominious, vile.

shasha [hieroglyphs], [hieroglyphs], Jour. As. 1908, 275, vase; Copt. ϣⲁϣⲟⲩ.

shasha [hieroglyphs], [hieroglyphs], [hieroglyphs], [hieroglyphs], [hieroglyphs], [hieroglyphs], [hieroglyphs], a plant, the seed from the same, beads.

shasha-t [hieroglyphs] [hieroglyphs], Rec. 14, 15, things sown, seed.

shashait [hieroglyphs], IV, 1127, [hieroglyphs], IV, 1123, necklace.

shashaut [hieroglyphs], [hieroglyphs], ornaments for the neck or head.

shashait [hieroglyphs], [hieroglyphs], [hieroglyphs], [hieroglyphs], throat; see [hieroglyphs].

Shashaqa [hieroglyphs], Rec. 21, 13 = Shishak.

shashatâ-t [hieroglyphs], [hieroglyphs], [hieroglyphs], [hieroglyphs], Rev. 14, 40, [hieroglyphs], Rev. 2, 43, [hieroglyphs], Jour. As. 1908, 312, window; Copt. ϣⲟⲩϣⲧ.

shashaṭ-t [hieroglyphs], Rec. 33, 137, window; Copt. ϣⲟⲩϣⲧ.

shaqa [hieroglyphs], P.S.B. 24, 45 ......

shaqar [hieroglyphs], a wooden tool or instrument.

shaqarqabi [hieroglyphs], Koller 4, 21, a kind of Sûdânî fruit (?)

shaqiu [hieroglyphs], rings, earrings.

shaqiq [hieroglyphs], to delight in; var. [hieroglyphs].

shaqu [hieroglyphs], Rechnungen 49, a weight = 22 ṭeben and 5 qet; plur. [hieroglyphs].

shaqu [hieroglyphs], [hieroglyphs], a wooden decoration in circular form of a pillar, chaplet.

shaqu [hieroglyphs], a leather object; [hieroglyphs], IV, 692, leather bands, quivers or cases made of leather.

shak [hieroglyphs], P. 369, to bandage = [hieroglyphs], N. 1145.

Shaka-Åmen-Shakanasa, B.D. 163, 11, a Nubian god (?)

shakaika, Rev. 13, 26, passion (?)

Shakanasa, B.D. 163, 11, a form of Åmen (?)

shakarāa (?), Inscr. Hier. 28, some strong-smelling object (?)

Shakarshau, L.D. III, 211, 4, a Mediterranean people.

shakiki, Rev., to delight in.

shaknen, Rev. 11, 152, to fight, to contend; var., Rev. 14, 15; Copt. ϣϭⲡⲏⲛ.

shaker, Rev. 13, 49, 14, 64, Rec. 30, 115, money, tax, hire, wages; Copt. ϣϭⲏⲣ.

shaker, IV, 715, IV, 775, a kind of precious stone, rings, ring money (?); Copt. ϣϭⲟⲩⲣ, ϭϣⲟⲩⲣ (?)

Shakershau, Mar. Karn. 52, 14, a Mediterranean people.

shagar, Gol. 1, 10, ditch, conduit, grave (?)

shagar, Mar. Aby. III, 54, 4, cage, wicker hamper; compare Heb. סְגוֹר.

shagig, Rev. 12, 113, to delight in, to desire.

shagnen, to quarrel, to fight; Copt. ϣϭⲡⲏⲛ.

shager, rings, ring money (?) tax; Copt. ϣϭⲟⲩⲣ.

shataȧ, a part of a ship.

shatȧb, to gag, to muzzle, to shut up; Copt. ϣⲧⲟⲃ (?)

shatȧbutȧ, leather gags (?)

shatirtȧ-t, gulf, precipice.

Shatbaka, one of the 36 Dekans.

shaṭ, L.D. III, 140B, IV, 814, Rec. 31, 24, IV, 387, Siuṭ 15, A.Z. 1905, 8, to dig, to quarry.

shaṭ, whip; compare Heb. שׁוֹט, Eth. ሰውጥ:

shaṭa, to steal, to pillage.

shaṭi, Rev. 14, 60, payment, rent.

shaṭirtȧ-t, Anastasi I, 23, 1, ibid. 24, 3, gulf, precipice.

shaṭḥi, Rev. 11, 132, to pour out a libation.

shȧ (?), Rev. 14, 35, nose.

shȧu, U. 553, P. 282, shade, shadow; see.

shȧs, to run.

shȧku, U. 29, a kind of cake symbolic of the teats of Isis (?); var., N. 257A.

shā, shāi, U. 136, T. 107, N. 444, , P. 599, , , , , , , Rev. 12, 40, to cut, to slay, to cut down trees, to hollow out a boat.

shāā, Annales X, 192, to cut, to cut off, to slay.

shāi-t , , IV, 761, , a cutting up, section, carnage, massacre, slaughter; see .

shāiut, A.Z. 1900, 38, , Mission 13, 117, , pieces of meat cooked or uncooked.

shā-t (shāt?), U. 380, , U. 272, , N. 315, 719, 874, , T. 50, P. 667, 684, N. 995, , , , , , , , knife, butcher's knife, wound, gash; plur. , Rec. 31, 17, 31, , , , ; see .

shā, to seek, to ask, to beg.

shā-t, Rec. 29, 146, , a kind of scented wood.

shā, to form, to fashion, to build.

shā , , barren ground, sandy soil (?)

shā, N. 707, , , , , , , , , , sand; , a sand offering; , Rec. 4, 29, the bed of Osiris; , those who are on their sand, *i.e.*, dwellers in the desert; Copt. ϣω.

Shāu, Thes. 1296, sand-men, *i.e.*, dwellers in the desert.

shā-t, shāi-t, U. 136, , IV, 1157, , , , IV, 1137, , , , , bread, bread-cake, sacrificial bread, a mess of boiled grain, food; plur. , , , , Rec. 3, 44, , ibid., , ; , , IV, 501; see the following:—

shā-t, bull cakes; , goose cakes; , obelisk cakes; , IV, 956, white cake.

shāi-t, cake, loaf; , , a kind of cake; , , Love Songs V, 1, sweet cakes, date cakes.

shā-t, shāi-t, U. 585, , T. 309, , T. 351, , Koller 3, 5, , , , , , , , , , letter, writing; plur. , , , , Anastasi I, 13, 4, , , Rec. 21, 83, letters, literature; for see **metcha-t**; , B.D. 141, 1.

Shāi-t en sensen, , , , , "Book of breathings"—the title of a funerary work greatly esteemed in the Graeco-Roman Period.

Shāi-t ent Teḥuti, Book of Thoth.

shāaut, Sphinx III, 132, human sacrifices.

shā . . . . . (?), Åmen. 9, 1 . . . . . .; plur. (?), Åmen. 8, 6.

shāi-t, Rec. 35, 204, sanctuary.

shāi, to gnaw, to nibble.

shāiṭ, slaughter; see .

shāutȧ, vase, pot, vessel.

shāfu, Rec. 8, 134, Verbum I, 196, to attack, to fight, to surround.

shāmu, B.D. 162, 12, decorated (?)

shāmrekh-t (?), Nåstasen Stele 67 . . . . . .

Shār-ur, Denderah III, 9, 28, a serpent-god.

shāsh, to split, be opened.

shāsh-t, U. 62 = , N. 316, knife.

shāsh-t, Rev. 14, 137, dust; Copt. ϣοειϣ.

shāq, P. 643, M. 680, , to shave; var. ; Copt. ϩωωκε.

shāti, P.S.B. 13, 438, a measure (?)

shāṭ, Methen 17, , Anastasi, IV 2, 11, , , , , , , to cut, to cut off, to slay; Copt. ϣωωт.

shāṭ, , , , , , slaughter, carnage, wounds (?) slaughterers.

shāṭu, Mar. Karn. 52, 20, slayers, slaughterers.

Shāṭ, B.D. 95, 2, the gods of slaughter.

shāṭ, canal; Copt. ϣεт.

shi, infant, child.

shi, , , Rec. 27, 88, fiend, demon, Shai (?)

shi, Rev. 11, 146, basin, lake; Copt. ϣηι.

ship, Rev., shame, disgrace; Copt. ϣιπε.

shim-t, , place, house, shrine, building.

shu (shemm ?), fire, heat.

shu, , , , , , , , , , , light, the sun, daylight.

shuti, Rec. 27, 84, light.

Shu, U. 241, , U. 185, , U. 415, T. 243, N. 1067, 1381, , U. 425, , , Rec. 30, 69, , , , , , , , , , , , Rec. 27, 87, , Rev. 13, 5, the Air-god, the Sun-god; , P. 606, Shu and Tefnut; Gr. Σωσις.

Shu, Mar. Aby. I, 44, 45, , .

Shu-t, , , the consort of Shu.

Shu-ti, Ombos I, 96 = Shu and Tefnut.

Shu, Ṭuat VI, a spirit who destroyed the dead.

Shu, Denderah III, 78, a child-god.

Shu, Ṭuat VI, a jackal-headed standard.

Shu, Tomb of Seti I, one of the 75 forms of Rā (No. 13).

Shu, Berg. I, 18, a god who assisted the dead.

Shutt (?), B.D. 112, 2, a group of goddesses of Mendes.

Shu em ḥerit urit (?), Berg. I, 14, a form of Shu.

Shu neb maāt, the god of the 1st hour of the day.

Shu enti em Åten, a title of Rā-Harmakhis.

shu, U. 181, , Rec. 31, 12, , Rec. 27, 84, air, wind; , wind of the body, flatulence.

shui, , , , , , to be dry, arid, hot; Copt. ϣοουε, ϣουωου, τϣουιο.

shuiu, dry, arid; , U. 461, parched fields.

shuu, dry, hot; Copt. ϣουιε.

shuȧ, drought, heat.

shu-t, , , , , , , , , , , A.Z. 35, 18, , , , , B.D. 112, 2, waste or desert land, untilled or unfruitful ground, a dry place; Copt. ϣοουε.

shuit, Anastasi I, 26, 2, parched soil.

shuu, grains of dry incense.

Shu, A.Z. 1865, 28, a desert tribe.

shut (?), IV, 945, , , a class of servants (?)

shu, U. 558, P. 282, , P. 615, 683, M. 525, 783, N. 1142, , , Sphinx Stele 8, shade, shadow; plur. , P. 683; , IV, 655, the shadow had turned; var. .

shui, T. 367, P. 201, 658, 713, M. 765, 788, N. 182, , , , , to be lacking, wanting, empty; , A.Z. 1902, 93, , empty; , P. 694, he of the empty hand; plur. , helpless, indigent.

shu-t, T. 199, 200, P. 311, N. 747, , U. 477, , , , empty, needy; , without; , Metternich Stele 57, faultless; , guileless, lacking evil; plur. , , IV, 620, wants, needs.

shuu, a man lacking sense, needy man; plur. , N. 937, , , ; , a heartless or stupid man.

shui-t, P. 713, , M. 788, , , a vain or empty thing; , empty years, *i.e.*, years of famine; Copt. ϣουειτ.

shu , IV, 1132, , blank papyrus; , , Anastasi I, 1, 6, , , A.Z. 1900, 31, , uninscribed rolls of papyri.

shu, shui , P. 565, , P. 463, , P. 464, , , , , Jour. As. 1908, 259, 300, to rise up, to lift up; Copt. ϣⲱⲓ.

shuȧu , M. 541, , P. 463, U. 486, , those who lift up.

shushu , , to exalt, to extol.

shu-t , heaven, sky.

shu , Rec. 21, 85, to unload a ship.

shu , Rec. 21, 89, to haggle, to trade as a merchant.

shui-t , business, commerce.

shuit, shuiti , Rechnungen 61, , , merchant; plur. , Mar. Aby. I, 8, 84, , ; , to do business, to "make bazaar."

shuti , , merchant, trafficker.

shu-t , T. 44, P. 89, M. 52, N. 37, , U. 621, , P. 712, , Dream Stele 9, , , , , , , , feather, hair, foliage, wing; plur. , P. 173, 710, N. 1353, , N. 940.

shuti , , , the two feathers or temples of Osiris.

shuti , T. 359, , M. 214, N. 685, 1363, , N. 759, , , Rec. 27, 222, , , , , , , , , , , , , , , , , a crown ornament consisting of a pair of feathers; , , pinions, feathers.

shut ent apṭu , goose feathers.

shut ent bȧk , hawk's feathers.

Shut-ent-bȧk , B.D. 153B, 9, part of the hunting net of the Akeru-gods.

shu-t resti , , "south feather"—a kind of plant.

shu-t Teḥuti , "Thoth's feather"—a kind of plant.

shui-t , , , , , Koller 2, 9, , , reeds, herbage in general.

shu , she-ass.

shu , , U. 31A, N. 259A, an offering, whey (?)

shu , well, lake, cistern, tank.

shua , U. 583, N. 1233, , Rec. 26, 67, , , , Mar. Karn. 37B, 7, , to be weak, miserable, wretched, poor, helpless, to beg.

shuau , , , ,

, poor man, beggar, one destitute; plur. , P. 1116B, 56, , Rec. 16, 59; Copt. ϣⲟⲟⲩⲉ (?)

shuaut , U. 431, , T. 246, vile ones.

shuab , Rec. 2, 107, IV, 73, a kind of tree, persea; Copt. ϣⲃⲉ, ϣⲟⲩⲉ.

shuā (shā) , to begin.

shuā (shā) , Jour. As. 1908, 275 = , to kill.

shuām (shām) , , little; Copt. ϣⲏⲙ.

shuār (shār) , , = , to smite, to strike, to be smitten; Copt. ϣⲱⲣ.

shuārt (shārut) , blows, stripes.

shui , to illumine.

shui-t , Peasant 223, , , , , shade, shadow; plur. .

Shui , B.D. (Saïte) 31, 1, a crocodile-god.

shuib-t , Ḳubbân Stele 2, shade, shadow.

shuim-t (shim-t) , place, house, building, shrine.

shuiḥ , Sphinx Stele 11 = , to travel, to journey.

shub , , , cake, loaves, bread, food.

shub , Rev. 12, 107, course.

shubu, shubi-t (qubu, qubi-t,?) , , , , Thes. 1206, , shade, shadow.

shubti , A.Z. 1908, 117, shade, shadow.

shubbi , shade, shadow.

shum , Jour. As. 1908, 277, little; Copt. ϣⲏⲙ.

shum kharshere , Rev. 12, 111, little child; Copt. ϣⲏⲙ ϩⲣϣⲏⲣⲉ.

shur , Rev., to gather the grape harvest; Copt. ϫⲱⲱⲗⲉ.

shurp , Rev., first; Copt. ϣⲱⲣⲡ, = ⲡ̄ⲣϣⲱⲣⲡ.

shursh , Jour. As. 1908, 248, to contend, to struggle; Copt. ϣⲉⲣϣⲓ.

shushu = , to leap, to dance.

sheb , , collar, necklace, pectoral.

shebi , IV, 893, , IV, 892, , beaded collar, necklace, beads.

sheb, shebu , U. 429, N. 376, , T. 245, , U. 98A, , U. 98, , P. 78, , M. 108, , M. 705, N. 21, , Rec. 26, 224, , , , Rec. 33, 29, , Metternich Stele 239, , IV, 1045, , IV, 1155, , , , , , food offerings, food.

shebb-t, Anastasi I, 26, 2, food, provisions.

sheb-t, A.Z. 1864, 107, food-offering; N. 46, a joint of meat; M. 184, a bundle of vegetables (?)

sheb-t, a kind of incense; Copt. ϣⲟⲟⲩ (?)

sheb, throat; Copt. ϣⲟⲩⲱⲃⲉ.

shebb-t, throat; Copt. ϣⲃⲱⲃⲉ.

Shebb-en-Mesti, B.D. 99, 17, a post in the magical boat.

sheb, to mix, to prepare drink, to brew; var.

shebb, to brew beer, to mix drink.

shebsheb, Mythe 1, 5, to mix, to prepare drink, to brew beer; U. 98, N. 377.

sheb-t, a kind of drink.

shebb-t, a kind of drink.

sheb, IV, 1078, to change, to exchange; Copt. ϣⲓⲃⲉ.

sheb-t, exchange; IV, 685, changes, rebellions; Copt. ϣⲉⲃⲓⲱ.

shebsheb, IV, 1074, to calculate times and seasons.

sheb-t (?), clepsydra.

shebb-t ent gerḥ, change of the night (?)

shebut, Åmen. 20, 10, speech, answer.

shebti; see .

Shebtiu, the gods who assisted in building temples.

sheb, to cut, to slay.

sheb, A.Z. 1900, 20, to wound.

shebsheb, fighting.

shebut, IV, 685, rebellious, rebels; see .

sheb, Rec. 16, 141, a tree or plant.

shebb-t, a kind of reed.

sheb-t, P. 660, 772, M. 769, the tie of the Green crown, .

sheb-t, a measure for dates.

sheba, U. 295, P. 87, T. 372, N. 672, 732, 1348, a meat offering; plur. , pieces of meat.

shebu, to shorten sail, to furl a sail.

sheben, , Anastasi I, 3, 3, , , , to mix together, to be mixed, to alloy; Copt. ϣⲟⲛⲃ, ϣⲟⲛϥ.

shebenu, IV, 665, , Rev. 6, 26, various, divers, mixed, miscellaneous; , disordered apparel.

sheben, sacrificial cakes of various kinds.

sheben, , an aromatic substance.

shebnu, a kind of berry or seed; Copt. ϣⲃⲓⲛ.

shep = = , a measure, the palm of the hand = four fingers; see **shesp** .

shep, to become; Copt. ϣⲱⲡⲉ.

shep, , to flow, to run out.

sheput, the flow of the poison.

shepi-t, , wound with a discharge, fistula (?)

shepi, , , , , Rev. 11, 135, , to be ashamed; , Israel Stele 8, ashamed; Copt. ϣⲓⲡⲉ.

shep, shepȧ, Rev. 13, 48, , Rec. 12, 109, , Rev. 13, 41, gift, present, dowry.

shepp, Thes. 943, rich, wealthy.

shep, basket, a prize of victory.

shep-t, , Rev., reward; Copt. ϣⲁⲡ.

shep, Rev. 11, 183, light.

shepu, light, radiance, splendour.

shep-t, a bright object.

shep-t, blindness, glaucoma.

shep, U. 319, 608, , P. 498, 510, , Rec. 26, 67, 31, 27, Metternich Stele 43, , A.Z. 1900, 27, , , to be blind, to make blind; , I have blinded his eyes.

shepu, the blind, the unseeing.

Shep-ḥer, Rec. 31, 30, , a crocodile-god.

Shepit, a form of the goddess Ȧpit .

shep-t Khensu, A.Z. 1908, 19, the name of an amulet.

shepa, U. 171; var. . . . .

shepash, , Rev. 2, 4 = , forearm, thigh.

Shepi, Ṭuat VI, a warder of the 5th Gate.

shepen-t, , a scabby eruption of the skin; Copt. ϣϥⲱⲛⲓ.

shepen-t, IV, 821, , , a beer measure.

shepen, , a plant used in medicine; , , , V, 3, the seed of the same.

shepen-t, P. 610, a tree.

shepsi, IV, 1182, to be noble, venerable, holy, honoured; , august.

shepses, to be honourable or splendid, to make splendid.

sheps, , noble, honourable, venerable, magnificent, glorious, stately, splendid, grand, admirable, august, majestic, sumptuous, gorgeous.

shepsu, P. 630, nobility, majesty.

shepsu, shepsesu, , P. 1116B, 10, nobleman, gentleman, man of wealth and position; plur. , U. 501, , T. 320, , P. 94, , Rec. 31, 164, , Rec. 13, 30; , IV, 1014, the august one in Khemenu (Hermopolis).

shepsit, M. 272, N. 889, , Metternich Stele 53, , Rec. 17, 145, , honourable lady, gentlewoman, woman of wealth and position, goddess; plur.

shepses, , A.Z. 45, 124, honours, high positions, wealth, treasures; , men of wealth; , Leyd. Pap. 3, 2, dainty food.

shepsu (?), N. 817, august thrones; , P. 178, a noble throne.

shepsi, a holy vessel; , A.Z. 1868, 86, a sacred vase; .

sheps, funerary monument or statue.

shepses, Verbum I, 407, to work in stone.

Sheps, Ombos I, 186–188, one of the 14 kau of Rā.

Shepsi, Rec. 17, 119, a ram-headed form of Thoth.

Shepsu, Ombos I, 85, gods of offerings.

Sheps, Ṭuat VII, a god with a boomerang.

shepesh, forearm = ; plur. ; Copt. ϣⲱⲡϣ.

shepesh, scimitar; see ; , Rev. 12, 49, the scimitar shepesh.

Shepesh, the name of a god.

Shepsh-t, A.Z. 1906, 125, , Rev. 14, 22, a goddess.

shept (?), a kind of fish.

shep-t, , shame, disgrace, ignominy; , B.D. 14, 10, 183, 12, shame, ill-will, ill-temper, a disease; , IV, 370; , words of shame.

Shept in , P. 348, , M. 649, the two gods who eat (?)

shepti (?), , to go, to depart (?)

shepṭ, shame, disgrace; Copt. ϣⲡⲓⲧ.

shef, Rec. 20, 42, ram.

shef, shefȧt, L.D. III, 65A, , strength, might, power, valour, vigour, energy, force.

shefshef-t, P. 267, , M. 480, , IV, 701, , power, might; , whose power is beneficent.

shefit, , IV, 967, , Rev. 11, 180, strength, might.

shefshefiu, , A.Z. 46, 130, valiant men, courageous.

Shefi, Ṭuat III, a form of Osiris.

Shefiti, , Rec. 32, 176, , he of divine strength.

Shefut, , Ṭuat I, a warder of the gates of the Earth.

Shefshefit, P. 267, , M. 480, N. 1247, a god.

Shefit-ḥa-t, the four-headed ram-god Khnemu.

shef, shefā, , Rev. 11, 68, to grasp, to seize; var. ; Copt. ⲕⲱⲱϣⲉ (?)

shefā, to attack.

shefshef = , to bring in.

shef, , to swell; Copt. ϣⲁϥⲉ, ϣⲁϥⲓⲱⲟⲩ.

shefu-t, , swelling, pustule, tumour.

Shef-ḥer, Ṭuat VI, a god; fem. , B.D. (Saïte) 145, 38.

shefu, , foam, froth.

shefu, a herb.

shefshef-t, a seed used in medicine.

Shef[t] beṭ-t, IV, 44, , the god of the month Tybi (Copt. ⲧⲱⲃⲓ).

shef-t, , district; varr. .

shefa, Rev. 11, 138, awe.

shefen (?), Rec. 29, 150......

shefen, Alex. Stele 1, 5, a small bird; plur. .

sheft = , before.

shefti, , Rev. 14, 21, , Rev. 14, 10, 21, enemy; var. ; Copt. ϣⲁϥⲧⲉ.

sheft, , writing, document, book, list; plur. .

shefṭi, enemy = ; Copt. ϣⲁϥⲧⲉ.

shefṭ, , Rec. 25, 195, to seize, to grasp.

Shefṭ beṭ-t, the god of the month Tybi (Copt. ⲧⲱⲃⲉ).

shefṭi-t, Rev. 11, 132, , , , Leyd. Pap. 7, 2, bier, funeral bed.

shefṭu, Peasant 305, , , , L.D. III, 65A, 15, , Åmen. 27, 9, book, writing, roll, volume, list, magistrate's charge sheet (IV, 1109); plur. , , Rec. 26, 13.

shem, , relative, kin, father-in-law; Copt. ϣⲟⲙ.

shemi-t, fem. of preceding; Copt. ϣⲱⲙⲉ.

shemu, Rev. 13, 1, little ones; , Rev. 14, 13, young folk; Copt. ϣⲏⲙ.

shem-t (?), Rev. 14, 13, boon companions.

shem, Rougé I.H. II, 117 = , a wise man, a skilled tradesman, knowing.

shemu, Leyd. Pap. 6, 6, spells, incantations.

shem, , , , Rec. 27, 88, , , to go, to march, to travel; , , , Ḥerusåtef Stele 81, , Åmen. 13, 1, going, goer; Copt. ϣⲉ, ϣⲉⲓ.

shemm, to go, to travel.

shemu, , , traveller; plur. , , , , advancing hosts; , , .

shem-t, , , N. 659, , P. 606, , journey, a going; plur. , U. 390, .

shemm-t, P. 402, M. 574, N. 1180, ways, journeys.

shem ra, , , to set the mouth in motion against someone, to speak evil, to slander.

shem ra, IV, 971, Thes. 1482, slanderer, backbiter.

shem ḥer mu, Thes. 1251, to be a confederate or ally of someone, to owe allegiance to someone.

shem ta, to act as pilot or guide.

shem-t āanra, Gol. 6, 14, Alt K. 848, a kind of bread, cake.

shem ra khet, a kind of incense.

Shem Rā (Ḥe-t Shem-Rā), Palermo Stele, a building.

shem reth, , , the name of a serpent amulet.

shemu, P. 204, , N. 1160, 1161 . . . . . .

shemut (?), IV, 839. . . . .

shemi-t, a wooden object, tool (?)

Shemshem, Ṭuat III, a god in the Ṭuat.

Shemti, Tomb of Seti I, one of the 75 forms of Rā (No. 72).

Shemti, , , Ṭuat IX, a serpent with four heads at each end of his body and eight pairs of legs.

shem, , , A.Z. 1906, 29, , to be hot; varr. and .

shemm , , , Ȧmen. 4, 17, 5, 15, 6, 1, 11, 13, , to be or become hot, hot; Copt. ϩⲙⲟⲙ, Heb. חָמַם, Syr. ܫܚܡ, Arab. حمّ.

shemm-t , , A.Z. 1906, 122, heat, fire, flame, fever; plur. .

shemm-t , , , some hot, strong-smelling substance.

shemshem-t , U. 640, , , , sesame seed; Copt. ⲥⲉⲙⲥⲏⲙ, Arab. سمسم.

shemshem , hot wind, sirocco.

shem , demon, foe.

shemm , to inundate, the summer inundation.

shem, shemu , , L.D. III, 140B, , , Rec. 30, 183, , , , A.Z. 1906, 128, , Jour. As. 1908, 290, the season of summer; , Pap. 3024, 86, days of summer; Copt. ϣⲱⲙ. It began soon after July 19 and ended about November 15; its four months were:

1. = Pachons. 3. = Epiphi.
2. = Payni. 4. = Mesore.

Shemu , Ombos I, 90, the god of Summer; Copt. ϣⲱⲙ.

shemu , Israel Stele 25, Rev. 6, 26, 12, 217, , Rechnungen 74, , , , Pap. 3024, 69, , , , , IV, 499, P. 1116B, 19, , Ȧmen. 6, 9, , Ȧmen. 19, 4, , Rev. 14, 51, , Rev. 14, 46, the harvest; Copt. ϣⲱⲙ.

shem-t , , , house, shrine.

shemm-t , Rev. 13, 20, , stable, stud farm; plur. ; , Rev. 6, 26, chief of the stud farm.

shemshem , Amherst Pap. 48, room (?) chamber (?)

shma , M. 216, N. 586, to pray, to make a vow.

shma , T. 55, to go.

shma , , , foreigner, stranger; plur. **shmau** , used in a bad sense, devils, demons; Copt. ϣⲙ̀ⲙⲟ.

shmai , enemy, demon, destroyer.

shma , , , , demon, evil spirit; plur. , Rec. 31, 30.

Shma (shmai) , "fighter"—a title of Horus.

Shma , the god of the 25th day of the month.

Shmait-ȧakhu , Ṭuat IX, a singing-goddess.

Shmaȧu-mer , Ombos II, 134, a mythological being.

shmau (?) , Rec. 30, 67......

shmam = , to be hot.

shmamu , , Rec. 3, 2, stranger, foreigner, demon; plur. , , IV, 39, , Rec. 15, 178, nomad ruffians, barbarians; Copt. ϣⲙⲙⲟ.

shmam , Ebers 92, 3, to vow, to offer up, to pray.

shmam , , , , , a plant.

shmā , to go, to travel = , Copt. ⲙⲟⲟϣⲉ.

shmā (= , A.Z. 1907, 9, Champollion, Notices I, 649), , , , , , , , , , , , , , , the South, the country of the South, *i.e.*, Upper Egypt; , , , South and North, *i.e.*, Upper and Lower Egypt.

Shmāit , Ani 20, 10, one of the uraei on the brow of Rā.

Shmāit , the goddess of the South.

Shmāu , A.Z. 1910, 128, gods of the South.

shmā , B.D. 169, 9, , grain of the South.

shmā , stone of the South, emerald.

shmā-t , bandlet made of a special kind of linen; , A.Z. 1907, 20, .

shmā-t , a plant.

shmāit , Rev. 14, 9, , Rev. 15, 17, books of the South.

shmā-s , , , , Sphinx Stele 10, , , , , Sphinx Stele 10, the crown of the South.

shmāi , , , , to sing, to play a musical instrument, singer, player; , musician; , musicians.

shmāi-t , Rec. 16, 70, , , , , , singing woman; plur. , , , , Rec. 29, 166, singers male and female, choir.

shmā , , Jour. As. 1908, 263, 266, , Rev. 14, 15, to destroy, to ruin, to overthrow, to undo, corrupt, perverse; Copt. ϭⲟⲟⲙⲉ.

Shmentheth , Ṭuat IV, a goddess in the Ṭuat.

shemer , Rev. = ϣⲙⲙⲟ (?) stranger, foreigner.

shemer-t , , Rougé, I.H. II, 115, bow; plur. , ; , "bow of heaven" (Ṭuat X) on which Set and Horus stand; Copt. ϫⲉⲃⲉⲗ (?)

Shemer-t , Ombos I, 143, the divine bow which destroyed the king's foes.

Shemer-thi , , Ṭuat X, a bow-god and bow-goddess.

shems , T. 270, , M. 433, , Rec. 14, 21, , , , B.M. 49343, , Rec. 11, 172, , , , , T. 209, P. 160, , Rec. 15, 47, to follow in the train of some one, to be a member of a bodyguard, an adherent, an associate, a follower; Copt. ϣⲙϣⲉ, Heb. שַׁמֵּשׁ.

shems , service, following.

shems-t , U. 313 (*bis*), service (?)

shemsi åb , to follow one's desire or inclination; , the name of a room in the palace.

shemsi ānti , performance of a ceremony in which myrrh was offered.

shemsi utcha , to follow regularly and systematically.

shemsi menkh-t , a festival in which a bandlet played a prominent part.

shemsi Ḥeru , Palermo Stele, celebration of a festival of Horus.

shemsi khenu-t , Rec. 6, 11, to celebrate the cult of a statue.

shemsi sekh-t , Rev. 14, 65, to perform field service.

Shems Seker , a festival of Seker in which the god went round the walls.

shemsu , M. 394, , , , , , , , servant, attendant, ministrant, follower; plur. , , , , , , IV, 992, , Rec. 20, 42, , , , Rec. 36, 216, train, retinue, bodyguard.

shems-t āa-t , a lady of high birth, a descendant of an old family.

shems nesu , IV, 1001, , IV, 1026, a royal envoy to foreign lands.

Shemsu , Rec. 2, 126, , Hymn Darius 31, follower of the god, a member of the divine bodyguard; plur. , P. 6, , M. 8, , Rec. 30, 191, , ibid. 33, 35, , , , .

Shemsu , , Ṭuat XII, a god in the Ṭuat.

Shemsu , Thes. 131, a group of stars in the Thigh (Great Bear).

Shemsi Åsår , Methen 34, follower of Osiris; plur. , N. 487, 698, , M. 408, ; , chief followers of Osiris.

Shemså en Meḥi , B.D., a follower of Meḥi.

Shemsu en Nebertcher , B.D., the followers of Nebertcher.

Shemsi en Teḥuti , B.D. 183, 4, follower of Thoth.

Shemsu neteru , B.D., the followers of the gods.

Shemsu neter āa , followers of the Great God.

Shemsu Rā, T. 236, P. 699, U. 495, M. 253, N. 1162, N. 157, the followers of Rā; followers of Rā in the train of Osiris.

Shemsu Ḥāp, Nesi-Ȧmsu 12, 6, the followers of the Nile-god.

Shemsu Ḥeru, P. 166, M. 319, N. 832, P. 462, M. 518, N. 1099 (see also P. 175, N. 947), the followers, *i.e.*, successors of Horus (the kings of the Predynastic Period).

Shemsut Ḥe-t-Ḥer, B.D., Rec. 27, 223, the followers of Hathor.

shemsi, Rec. 11, 170 = .

shemes, ear of corn; plur. ; see ; Copt. ϩⲙⲥ̄, ϧⲉⲙⲥ̄.

shemt = , yeast.

Shemtt, a goddess.

shen = , to hover over, to alight.

Shen-t-ȧmm (?), Ṭuat IX, a fiery, blood-drinking serpent-god.

shenu, U. 213, P. 453, P. 689, to go round, to encircle, to surround, to enclose, to shut up in the hand, to beleaguer a city, to obstruct a road.

shenu, circuit, circle, periphery, circumference, orbit, revolution; , the two circuits, , Thes. 165.

shenn, T. 82, 304, A.Z. 1908, 117, circle, circuit.

shenn-t, circle.

shen-t, T. 275, U. 234, Tombos Stele 2, a circuiting, a going round, revolution.

shen ȧten, IV, 808, the circuit of the solar disk.

Shen ur, T. 275, P. 28, Tombos Stele 16, N. 67, M. 38, A.Z. 1905, 15, the Great Circle; IV, 617, the circuit of the Great Circle; the islands of Shen-ur.

shenu ent pet, the circuit of heaven.

shenu en ta, the circuit of the earth.

sheni-t, circle, circuit.

shenu, endless time, eternity; = 10,000,000 years.

sheni-t, , , a chamber in a temple.

Sheniut, B.D. 17, 32, the chamber of punishment of Osiris.

shenu-t, Leyd. Pap. 10, 13, , courtyard, court (?)

shenu, , , , court official, court nobleman; plur. **shenut**, Rec. 30, 187, 31, 18, , , ibid. 26, 234, 31, 170, , Peasant 140, , , , , , , , the court of a king or god.

shenit, , , , , , , , the nobles at Court; , the four sons of Horus.

Shenit, B.D. 30B, 4, the divine court of Osiris.

Shenu, , the honourable or beatified dead.

Shennu, Ṭuat III, the gods who avenged Rā.

Shen-ur, Ombos I, 319, a god of offerings.

Shenit-urit, Denderah II, 54, a form of Hathor.

shenu, , , lake, the Nile-flood.

shenu, Koller 4, 3, vases, vessels.

shenu, archetype of a manuscript.

shen, U. 555, , Hh. 328, to rage, to wrangle, to fight, to dispute; Copt. ϣⲓⲛⲉ.

shenȧu, N. 1000, , U. 602, N. 995, 999, wrangler, striver.

shenn, Rev. 12, 119, to dispute; , Ȧmen. 14, 3, litigious man.

shenn-t, dispute.

sheni ȧb, Peasant 270, to be wroth, to be angry, to quarrel.

shen, Peasant 130, , Pap. 3024, 74, , , dis-quietude, enmity (?) danger (?)

shen, , hateful, hostile, inimical.

shennu, Ȧmen. 9, 8, 16, 14, fighters, enmity, strife.

shnu, , , , , , soldiers, warriors, fighters.

sheni, , , , Nȧstasen Stele 10, , to be sick, to be helpless, depressed, cast down; Copt. ϣⲱⲛⲉ.

shenn, Rec. 32, 84, to be ill, sick,

shenn, Rev. 14, 12, , Rev. 13, 3, mental sickness, disgust.

shenn-t, oppression, weariness.

shen-t, , , , sickness, illness; Copt ϣⲱⲛⲉ.

shnu, , , evils, evil beings or things.

shnu, , , a sick man.

shenn ⟨hieroglyphs⟩ = ⟨hieroglyphs⟩, trouble, nausea.

shen, shnu ⟨hieroglyphs⟩, to speak, to proclaim, to tell, to relate, to ask, to enquire into, to cast a spell, to recite incantations, to adjure, to conjure, to curse, to blaspheme, to work magic; Copt. ϣⲓⲛⲉ.

shni ⟨hieroglyphs⟩, invoker, pleader, entreater.

shni-t ⟨hieroglyphs⟩, IV, 694, ⟨hieroglyphs⟩, adjuration, incantation, spell, ban, curse, order for allotment; Copt. ϣⲓⲛⲉ.

shnu ⟨hieroglyphs⟩, magical formulae, spells, incantations.

shnu ⟨hieroglyphs⟩, IV, 1114, litigant, disputant, party in a law case, the plaintiff (?)

shenn ⟨hieroglyphs⟩ Rev. 14, 14, to demand; Copt. ϣⲓⲛⲉ.

shenn ⟨hieroglyphs⟩, to cry out, to invoke, to entreat.

shenn-t ⟨hieroglyphs⟩, ⟨hieroglyphs⟩, appeal, a seeking, enquiry, petition.

shen-t ⟨hieroglyphs⟩, I, 13, ⟨hieroglyphs⟩, IV, 1081, 1115, a case at law, a judicial inquiry; **shen-t khe-t** ⟨hieroglyphs⟩, to have a case at law.

shenit ⟨hieroglyphs⟩, Rec. 17, 47, ⟨hieroglyphs⟩, Rev. 14, 74, a legal interrogation, a case for trial by law.

shenit ⟨hieroglyphs⟩, a seeking out, quest.

shnu ⟨hieroglyphs⟩, views, opinions, speculations (?)

shen, shni ⟨hieroglyphs⟩, to tie up, to tie together, to load.

shen-t ⟨hieroglyphs⟩, ⟨hieroglyphs⟩, a tie, binding.

shnà-t ⟨hieroglyphs⟩, cord, tie, rope.

shnu ⟨hieroglyphs⟩, Pap. 3024, net; plur. ⟨hieroglyphs⟩, Love Songs 4, 8; ⟨hieroglyphs⟩, Rec. 16, 110, fishing net; Copt. ϣⲛⲉ.

shen ⟨hieroglyphs⟩, P. 281, ⟨hieroglyphs⟩, M. 525, N. 1106, ⟨hieroglyphs⟩, P. 302, ⟨hieroglyphs⟩, ⟨hieroglyphs⟩, hair, foliage of a plant or tree; ⟨hieroglyphs⟩, berries of a tree, fruit.

shennu ⟨hieroglyphs⟩, wig.

shen-ti ⟨hieroglyphs⟩, hairy.

shen, shenn ⟨hieroglyphs⟩, Rev. 14, 23, ⟨hieroglyphs⟩, a tree; plur. ⟨hieroglyphs⟩, A.Z. 1905, 19, ⟨hieroglyphs⟩, groves gardens; Copt. ϣⲏⲛ.

shen benrà ⟨hieroglyphs⟩, palm fibre (?); Copt. ϣⲟⲩⲃⲉⲛⲉ.

shen ta ⟨hieroglyphs⟩, Peasant 33, ⟨hieroglyphs⟩, Rec. 27, 87, ⟨hieroglyphs⟩, ⟨hieroglyphs⟩, grass, herbage; ⟨hieroglyphs⟩, a kind of tree: Copt. ϣⲱϣⲏⲛ (?)

Shen ⟨hieroglyphs⟩, B.D. 17, 70 ff., a storm cloud that covered the right eye of Rā.

Shenit (?), P. 815, M. 244, , Denderah I, 6, , Berg. I, 19, a serpent-goddess.

shen-t, B.D. 137, 16, flesh, member, limb.

shen-ti, , a kind of bird, heron (?)

shenshen, a kind of bird, heron (?) (Perhaps a verb.)

shnȧ, , fish spawn, stinking fish.

shnȧu = , small, little.

shenȧ-t, Rec. 30, 67, the circuit of heaven.

shnȧ-t, N. 1066, , P. 350, , , , storm, hurricane, tempest; plur. , U. 470.

shni-t, rainstorm, tempest.

shnȧ-t, U. 609, T. 223, hailstones.

Shnȧt, a goddess of Busiris.

Shnȧ-t-pet-uthes-t-neter, B.D. 141 and 148, one of the seven divine Cows.

Shnȧt-neteru (?), one of the seven divine Cows.

shnā, A.Z. 47, 112, , , IV, 498, , , , , Rec. 34, 179, , , , , A.Z. 30, 127, , , , , , , to repulse, to drive back, to turn away; Copt. ϣⲱⲛ, ϣⲱⲛϩ.

shnāu, Thes. 1251, , A.Z. 35, 17, men who kept the road clear for processions.

shnā-t, IV, 1193, repulse; , , repulsings, stoppages; , hesitating, timid (of fish).

shnā, repulsive (a man's character).

shnā, warder, guard, guardian.

shnā ȧb, to resist, to oppose, to be obstinate.

shnā, , , , , , , , storm, tempest, hurricane; variants:—

shnār, , , Ȧmen. 13, 1, 14, 7, storm, tempest.

shnā, the side of a road.

shnā, Rec. 24, 96, , , , granary, barn; plur. , , Décrets 29.

shnāu, P. 422, , M. 605, , Peasant 64, cabin of a boat, shrine.

shnā-ti ....

shnā, shnār, , , , , , , a plant used in medicine.

shnā, shnār, , , a seed or fruit used in medicine.

shnā, lion.

shnā-t, shenrā-t, , , breast.

shnār , , , , , , , , , to turn back, to drive back, to keep off.

shnāriu , Rougé I.H. 256, a class of officials.

shnār , , a disease, stoppage of bowels (?)

Shnār , B.D.G. 785, a god of Shnār in the Delta.

Shnār , , a sacred serpent.

Shnār[it] , B.D.G. 263, a goddess of .

shni , , Rev. 11, 162 = Copt. ϣⲓⲛⲉ, to seek after.

Shnit , Ṭuat I, a light-goddess.

shnu , musician.

Shnu , B.D. 142, III, 12, a city of Osiris.

shnu , food, produce.

shnu , , , fruit, grain.

shnu , B.D. 125, I, 16 . . .

shnu-t , P. 395, M. 563, N. 1170, , , , , , , , , , granary; plur. , , , , , , , IV, 1026; Copt. ϣⲉⲩⲛⲉ.

shneb , a horn weapon or tool.

shneb-t , U. 169, P. 204 , Ikhernefert 15, , IV, 612, , , , , , , , , Rec. 4, 22, , , , , , , , , skin, hide; Copt. ϣⲛ̄ϥⲉ.

shnebi-t , skin, hide.

shnep , to sniff the air, to smell, nostrils.

shnep , a fine cloth.

shnep , , , , IV, 1104, a reed mat (?); var. .

shnep , to seize, to carry off, to draw off.

Shnep , , , a title of the Nile-flood.

shneptiu , a class of workmen or labourers.

shnef-t , , , a substance used in medicine; , a salve made of the same.

shnem , P. 110, 112, , M. 75, , N. 77, , A.Z. 1908, 115, , Metternich Stele 249, , , to join to, to unite with, to attain to, to be protected; see ; , U. 558.

shnem-t , nurse.

Shnemit urit , P. 112, "Great Protectress"—a name of the Sky-goddess; varr. , M. 78, , N. 80.

shnem , to smell; Copt. ϣⲱⲗⲙ.

shnem , smell, odour

shnem = **khnem** .

shenrā, to turn back, to repulse, to keep away.

shenrā; see **shenār**.

Shenḥer, a god.

shens, U. 110, N. 377A, IV, 498, a kind of cake or bread.

shens peri ḥer khaut, shewbread.

shens, skin, animal (?)

shensu, Rev. 13, 32, Rev. 13, 32 = **shes nesu**, apparel of the king, *i.e.*, byssus; Copt. ϣⲛ̄ⲥ.

shensetch-t, tunic.

shensh, Hh. 472, to open.

shent, Rev. 14, 34, Rev. 12, 63, Rev. 12, 64, Rechnungen 77, tunic, cloth; Copt. ϣⲉⲛⲧⲱ.

shent, Rec. 33, 120, seal, sealer.

shent, shenn-t, acacia, Spina acacia Nilotica; Rec. 15, 141, black acacia; Copt. ϣⲟⲛⲧⲉ, Heb. שִׁטָּה, Arab. سنط.

shenti (?) a hairy plant (?); Copt. ϣⲟⲛϯ.

shent, Metternich Stele 244, brushwood, "bush," thicket, thorny growth; Copt. ϣⲟⲛϯ.

Sheni-t, P. 815, M. 244, a cow-goddess.

Shentit, Berg. I, 10, Rec. 3, 44, ibid. 3, 47, ibid. 3, 49, a form of the goddess Isis.

Shent-ti, a title of Isis and Nephthys.

Shentit, B.D. 131, the sanctuary of the goddess Shentit.

shent to revile, to abuse, to curse; Copt. ϣⲱⲛⲉ.

shent-t, revilings, curses, abominable persons and things.

shenti, accursed.

shenti, enemy, foe, grief, distress, sickness, trouble; plur., A.Z. 1900, 128; Copt. ϣⲱⲛⲧ (?)

shentiu, IV, 968, men of violence.

shenti, a title of Set.

shentiu, court nobles, ministers.

shentiu, IV, 613, companies, assemblies (of rebels).

Shentait, a cow-goddess—a form of Hathor.

Shentthit, Mission 13, 127; see

shenth, to revile, to abuse.

Shenth, U. 555, T. 303, a serpent-fiend in the Ṭuat.

Shenthet, P. 662, M. 773, a proper name (?)

shentheth, U. 602, M. 303, N. 1000, hostility.

shenṭ, acacia; dual, P.S.B. 25, 220; plur., IV, 387; Heb. שִׁטָּה, Arab. سنط, Copt. ϣⲟⲛⲧⲉ.

shenṭit, tunic; plur., IV, 1071. Late forms; Copt. ϣⲉⲛⲧⲱ.

Shenṭi, a name of Set.

shenṭesh (?), orchard, large garden, wood; plur.; see.

Shentch, an acacia sacred to Isis.

shentch, acacia; see.

shentchetch-t, herbs, vegetables.

shentchu-t, U. 478, T. 43, tunic, short drawers; inspector of all tunics; Copt. ϣⲉⲛⲧⲱ.

shentch-ti, keeper of the tunics or robes.

sher.

sher m', compound preposition.

sher, Rec. 16, 109, to fall down; see.

sher, sherr, N. 156, Rec. 30, 72, U. 495, T. 236, to be small, to become small, to be diminished; Copt. ϣⲓⲣⲉ.

sher, a little.

sher-t, IV, 691, Åmen. 25, 20, little, small, insignificant, a small thing, a thing of little value.

sherȧ ȧb, to lack courage, to be unwilling, to have no mind to do a thing.

sherr, Metternich Stele 40 ....

sher, III, 142, Metternich Stele 56, little boy, child; Copt. ϣⲏⲣⲉ.

sher, a young god.

sher, sherȧ, IV, 691, III, 143, boy, son; plur.; Copt. ϣⲏⲣⲉ.

sherȧ en sherȧ, son's son, grandson.

sherr, boy, youth, little man; plur., U. 512, P. 86, U. 171, N. 45; Copt. ϣⲏⲣⲉ.

sherȧ-t, Israel Stele 12,

, Westcar 5, 19, 6, 3, little girl, daughter, maiden; plur. .

Sherriu , U. 512, , T. 325, , B.D. 123, 3, the lesser gods.

sher , small canal.

sher, sherȧ , , , IV, 385, , , to stop up, to block, to wall up, to close, to obstruct the passage.

sherȧ-t , obstruction, bar.

sher-t , Rec. 31, 13, obstacle.

sher-t , , bond, tie, fetter.

sher-t , U. 393, T. 341, M. 214, N. 685, , Rec. 30, 190, , Ȧmen. 17, 7, , , , , (*sic*), , nose; Copt. ϣⲁⲓ.

sherti, sherȧti , , , , , , , , , the two nostrils.

sher-t , P. 169, 786, the bow of a boat.

Sherit , Ombos II, 132, a goddess.

shersher , , Gersher Pap. I, 21, , Sphinx I, 111, air, wind, sniffings of air; see .

sher-t , Rec. 3, 53, earth taken from a holy place and used as an amulet.

sher-t , a kind of cake, loaf.

sher-t, sherȧ-t , , , , Anastasi IV, 2, 10, Koller 2, 8, , , Rec. 26, 78, , , , grain, flour.

sheri-t , , , , a kind of land, salty land (?)

sherit , a dwelling place.

sherp-t , , , , seed for early crops.

sherp , incense = .

sherp-t , cord, part of the tackle of a ship.

Sherm , B.D. 168, a god who helped the dead.

sherḥ , , water channel; Copt. ϣⲗⲉϩ (?)

sherḥ , a kind of myrrh, or myrrh-producing tree.

shersek , to destroy.

shersh , , IV, 697, to hasten, to flee.

shersh , to plunder, to carry off.

sheheb , to be hot, burnt up, parched; Copt. ϣⲱϩⲉⲃ.

sheheb , , , , the hot south wind.

Shehbi , , the god of the south wind.

shes , U. 110 = , cake, loaf, bread.

shest , Rec. 27, 57 = **ȧshest** , an interrogative particle.

shes , ; see = .

shes , P. 592, , , , , , , a band or garment made of linen; , P. 592, festal

band; ⟨hieroglyphs⟩, Rev. 11, 167 = ⟨hieroglyphs⟩ (?);
Heb. שֵׁשׁ, Gen. xli, 42.

shes åkeb ⟨hieroglyphs⟩, apparel
of mourning.

shes nesu ⟨hieroglyphs⟩, royal linen, byssus; Copt.
ϣⲉⲛⲥ.

shes tepi ⟨hieroglyphs⟩, linen of the finest
quality.

shes ⟨hieroglyphs⟩, white
stone, alabaster; plur. ⟨hieroglyphs⟩; Heb.
שֵׁשׁ.

shes ⟨hieroglyphs⟩, IV, 743, ⟨hieroglyphs⟩, white
grain, winnowed grain.

shesit ⟨hieroglyphs⟩,
Rec. 22, 103, ashes, white dust or powder.

shes ⟨hieroglyphs⟩, A.Z. 1864, 107, ⟨hieroglyphs⟩,
antelope = ⟨hieroglyphs⟩.

shes ⟨hieroglyphs⟩, cord, string,
rope; plur. ⟨hieroglyphs⟩.

shes maā (maāt) ⟨hieroglyphs⟩, "cord
of rule," in the phrase ⟨hieroglyphs⟩, to perform ceremonies in regular and fitting continuity
for ever, ⟨hieroglyphs⟩ (or ⟨hieroglyphs⟩, millions of
times); Demot. ⟨hieroglyphs⟩ = Gr. ἐπὶ πλεον.

shes ⟨hieroglyphs⟩, Ebers Pap. 99, 18, ⟨hieroglyphs⟩,
B.D. 160, 2, ⟨hieroglyphs⟩, blow, stripe, injury,
wound.

shesshes-t ⟨hieroglyphs⟩, evil, misfortune.

shesshes ⟨hieroglyphs⟩, Ebers Pap. 41, 12, ⟨hieroglyphs⟩,
A.Z. 1900, 128, to hide (?)

shesshes ⟨hieroglyphs⟩, Koller 5, 2, ⟨hieroglyphs⟩,
⟨hieroglyphs⟩, B.D. (Nu) 64, 19, to see.

shesshes-t ⟨hieroglyphs⟩, Rec. 29, 159........

shesu (gersheru?) ⟨hieroglyphs⟩, soldier; plur.
⟨hieroglyphs⟩, Thes. 1251, ⟨hieroglyphs⟩.

shes ⟨hieroglyphs⟩, U. 538, P. 229, vase,
vessel.

shesshes ⟨hieroglyphs⟩, U. 182, a kind
of drink (?)

Shesshes ⟨hieroglyphs⟩, Ṭuat IX, a
crocodile-god with a tail terminating in a serpent.

shesa ⟨hieroglyphs⟩, U. 188, ⟨hieroglyphs⟩,
⟨hieroglyphs⟩, T. 67, ⟨hieroglyphs⟩, N. 599, ⟨hieroglyphs⟩,
Décrets 108, IV, 1017, ⟨hieroglyphs⟩, Rec.
31, 170, ⟨hieroglyphs⟩, IV, 1073, ⟨hieroglyphs⟩,
IV, 749, ⟨hieroglyphs⟩, Pap. 3024, 84,
⟨hieroglyphs⟩, to be cunning,
wise, skilled, learned, able; see ⟨hieroglyphs⟩
⟨hieroglyphs⟩.

shesa ḥer ⟨hieroglyphs⟩, IV, 1152, skilful.

shesa-t ⟨hieroglyphs⟩, knowledge, skill,
ability.

shesa-t ⟨hieroglyphs⟩, Rec. 30,
191, wise woman.

shesau ⟨hieroglyphs⟩, B.D.
188, 3, ⟨hieroglyphs⟩, IV, 1184, intellectual abilities.

shesau ⟨hieroglyphs⟩, ⟨hieroglyphs⟩,
⟨hieroglyphs⟩, ⟨hieroglyphs⟩,
⟨hieroglyphs⟩, Litanie 71, the "wise"
member, i.e., the tongue.

shesa ⟨hieroglyphs⟩, P. 589, ⟨hieroglyphs⟩,
⟨hieroglyphs⟩, N. 1038, to plough.

Shesa ⟨hieroglyphs⟩,
P. 589, a skilled ploughing-god of Shnā.

shesa-t ⟨hieroglyphs⟩, T. 101,
⟨hieroglyphs⟩, P. 815, ⟨hieroglyphs⟩,
⟨hieroglyphs⟩, N. 141, ⟨hieroglyphs⟩, ⟨hieroglyphs⟩,
⟨hieroglyphs⟩, U. 645, night, darkness.

Shesa-t māk-t neb-s ⟨hieroglyphs⟩
⟨hieroglyphs⟩, ⟨hieroglyphs⟩

Ṭuat II, a goddess in the Ṭuat.

shesau , , antelope; Copt. ϣⲟϣ, ϣⲟϣⲟⲩ (?)

shesa-t , a plant or herb.

shesait , Koller 4, 2, , , white earth, powder (?)

shesait , IV, 875, a kind of precious stone?

Shesau , L.D. III, 55A, IV 194 = **Shasu** , nomads of the desert.

Shesatheth , Ṭuat X, a goddess.

shesp (shep) , P. 161, 163, , , , , , , , , Peasant 192, , , . , Rhind Pap. 32, , , P. 251, , to take, to acquire, to accept, to receive, to receive seed, *i.e.*, to conceive ( ); , acceptable; Copt. ϣⲱⲡ.

shespep , P. 603, 604 = **shesp.**

shesp àur , to conceive.

shesp àb , to be pleased, heart's desire.

shesp ā , to greet.

shesp āḥa , to fight; , to set out on a journey.

shesp tep , to make a beginning.

shespiu , , Rec. 6, 7, those who receive, those who are taken, *i.e.*, prisoners.

Shesp Àmen uthes t nefer-f , Rec. 20, 40, a shrine of Àmen.

shesp-t àtru , , , , the festival of receiving water.

shesp āa-t , the name of a festival.

shesp ḥetch , Rec. 21, 101, the earliest dawn of day.

Shespi (Shepi) , Tomb of Seti I, one of the 75 forms of Rā (No. 42).

Shespiu , B.D. 168, 9, a group of gods who assisted the dead.

Shespiu , Ṭuat XI, the gods who carried Methen into the eastern sky.

Shespit , Thes. 112, , one of the seven stars of Orion. Its god was .

Shespit , Rec. 6, 156, a goddess of the dead.

Shespit enth khemiu ḥepu , Berg. II, 13, lodge of the never-moving (?) stars—a title of Nut.

shesp (shep) , , , , , Peasant 43, , , statue, image, figure, the Sphinx; plur. , , , Rec. 36, 202, sphinxes; **ḥena-nà shesp** , so help me, God!

sheshput , figures of women with tambourines.

shesp (shep) , IV, 84, , , a measure = a handbreadth, width of the palm, span = 0·075 m.; Copt. ϣⲟⲡ, Heb. טֶפַח, Assyr. .

shespit (shepit) , Love Songs 3, 11, , hand.

shesp-t, De Hymnis 27, chamber, hut, shed, lodge, arbour, booth in a garden, summer house.

shesp (shep), Jour. As. 1908, 282, moment; Copt. ϫⲡ.

shesp, light, radiance, splendour.

shesp (shep) = , to vomit, to cast up.

shesp-t (shep-t), something round or polished, a berry, a fruit; Copt. ϣⲟⲡ, ϣⲱⲡⲉ, ϣⲟⲟϥⲉ.

shesp-t, Shipwreck 50, an edible plant or root.

shesp (shep), a seed used in medicine.

shesp, Rec. 30, 66, parts of a ship; , Rec. 30, 66.

shesem, to be weary, exhausted (?)

shesm-t, dimness of sight, an eye disease (?)

shesm, A.Z. 1877, 32, 1880, 13, earth used in making faïence.

shesm, IV, 1104, P.S.B. 13, 147, skin of an animal, a leather roll.

Shesm, the "bull of the gods" with seven necks and uraei.

shesm-t, P. 814, M. 243, , T. 99, , IV, 1099, a mineral substance.

Shesemtt, U. 390, B.D. 174, 8, , Hh. 413, 414, , Hh. 178, a lioness-headed goddess.

Shesmit, Rec. 29, 151, , Hh. 414, the name of a goddess.

Shesmā (?), T. 305, a mythological serpent.

shesmu, Rev. 13, 37, judge, assessor.

Shesmu, U. 511, 541, , T. 41, , T. 324, Berg. 56, B.D. 17, 27, 153, 8, 170, 6, the executioner of Osiris who dwelt in , Mar. Aby. I, 44. He is identified with , B.D. 17, 27.

Shesmu, Berg. I, 11, a lion-god.

Shesmu àmi nuṭ-f, Rec. 37, 67, a god.

Shesmu, T. 41, a star-god; var. (?)

Shesmu, Tombs Seti I, Ram. II, Ram. IV, one of the 36 Dekans; Gr. Σεσμε.

shesmuti, Rec. 31, 13, a class of women.

sheser, to walk, to march against, to attack.

sheser, to measure with a cord.

sheser, a cord for measuring.

sheser, Rec. 16, 56, to propose, to purpose, to design, to govern.

shesru, Ḥeruemḥeb 8, designs, purposes, decisions.

sheser-t, canon, ordinance.

sheser , , , , utterance, speech, decree; , IV, 1109, A.Z. 1906, 124, song; , a proving, testing, examining.

sheser , P. 704, , , to shoot.

sheser-t , U. 514, , T. 326, a shooting.

sheser , P. 704, , N. 661, Rec. 26, 235, , , Hymn Darius 11, , , A.Z. 1905, 16, , arrow, spear, dart; plur. , , A.Z. 1900, 20, .

sheseru (?)-Rā , Ṭuat VIII, three arrows or shuttles (?)

sheser , an animal for sacrifice.

shesru , IV, 1143, bags of spices or unguent.

Shesrȧ , Ṭuat X, a light-god.

shesesh (shesh) nesu , IV, 821; var. ; Copt. ϣⲉⲛⲥ, Heb. שֵׁשׁ.

Shest (Shesmt) , U. 561, , U. 565, , M. 499, , M. 122, N. 646, 962, , N. 170, , P. 632, , Hh. 128, a place sacred to Horus.

Shestȧ , T. 225, , ; see **Ḥeru-Shestȧ**.

Shest (Shesm-t)-tcha (?) , I, 119, a title.

Shest-tȧ, Shestt , U. 390, B.D. 174, 8, , T. 225, , N. 1081, a goddess who is mentioned with Sekhmit; see **Shesmtt**.

Shest-sett (sti) , Pyr. 2209B, a goddess (?)

shesta , Rec. 26, 231; , Rec. 26, 230 . . . .

shesti , a bull-god (?)

shesteb = , lapis lazuli; see .

shesh , vessel, pot; Copt. ϣⲁϣⲟⲩ, ϣⲟϣⲟⲓ.

shesh = , throat.

shesh , Rec. 31, 21, nest, home.

shesh , sistrum; plur. , IV, 98.

shesh , , to move rapidly, to hasten; , P. 414, M. 593, N. 1198, very rapidly, quickly.

shesh , antelope; see ; Copt. ϣⲟϣ.

shesh , white hair.

shesh-t , a precious stone of white colour.

sheshti , king.

sheshtȧ-t , wanting, diffident.

sheq , razor (?); see , to shave; Copt. ϩⲱⲱⲕⲉ.

sheku , N. 257A, a kind of cake; var. , U. 29.

sheku , , a funerary offering.

sheku ȧb, A.Z. 1900, 128 = , rebels.

sheken, A.Z. 1908, 18, an amulet.

sheker, M. 517, N. 1098, 1242, , to decorate, be decorated = ; Copt. ϩⲱⲱⲕⲉ, ϭⲱⲕ.

Shekershau, Mar. Karn. 52, 1, a Mediterranean people.

shet, Love Songs 2, 3, to divide.

shet, Rec. 3, 49, 5, 92, to take out, to withdraw.

shet, works in a quarry, hewings of stone.

shetshet, Rev. 12, 22, to rend, to tear; Copt. ϣⲉⲧϣⲱⲧ.

shet, , A.Z. 1906, 113, grief, sorrow.

sh[ta]-t, Gol. Ham. 10, 48, office.

shetut (?) , writings, documents, books.

Shetshet; see **Teshtesh**.

shet, , , , , , , turtle, tortoise (?)

Shet, Nesi-Åmsu 32, 26, 1, a form of Āapep, a foe of Rā (B.D. 83, 4, 161).

Sheta, , , , the constellation of the Tortoise, one of the 36 Dekans; Gr. Σιτ.

shet-t, shta, , , , , , Rec. 3, 50, , covering, shroud, garment, bandlet.

shta-t Ḥeru, a kind of garment.

shta, forest, plantation, orchard; plur. , Rec. 21, 14; Copt. ϣⲧⲁ.

shta, , , arable land, the land covered by the Nile; var. .

shta, , , , , , , , , to be difficult, hard to pass over or through, to be hidden or secret, hard to understand, mysterious.

Shta, a god incomprehensible.

shta-t, , , mystery, difficult thing, something hidden, something rare, curious; plur. , , , , , , , IV, 345, 900, mysteries, difficulties; , Rec. 15, 179, impassable valleys; , U. 207, secret; , N. 1042; , mysteries of the two horizons; , hidden of forms; , P. 167, , T. 289, , Rec. 31, 25, those whose seats are hidden; , those whose arms are hidden; , the god of the hidden soul; , Rec. 26, 231, , Litanie 37, , a title of Rā; , , , , a title of Åmen; , of invisible body; , secret properties; , , invisible form.

Shtai, , , hidden one, mysterious being, secret one.

shta-t , , , , , , , , , , , , , , , hidden place, shrine, sanctuary, secret chamber, coffin, sarcophagus, grave, tomb, cemetery; A.Z. 1906, 9.

shtai-t , IV, 992, , , shrine, coffin, sarcophagus; var. .

shta-t , , vulture.

Shta , B.D. 168, a god in mummied form.

Shtat , a title of Āapep.

Shtait , , , Metternich Stele 199, , , , the vulture-goddess—a title of the goddess Nekhebit.

Shtait , , Berg. II, 13, , B.D. 168, a form of Nut.

Shta , B.D.G. 699, a Bubastite form of Isis.

Shta-t , , B.D. 147, the name of the 4th Āat.

Shta-ti , Tomb of Seti I, one of the 75 forms of Rā (No. 31).

shta-ti , Litanie 31, the two hidden countries.

Shtai , Ṭuat IV, a sailor of the boat of Rā.

Shta ȧb , Ṭuat V, , Tomb Ram. VI, 50, a warder-god.

Shtau ȧsut , T. 289, M. 66, N. 128, gods whose abodes are invisible.

Shtau āu , , B.D. 168, the gods of hidden arms.

Shta-t besu , Ṭuat X, the name of the 10th Gate.

Shta Mesutt , Berg. II, 11, a form of the goddess of Ȧment.

Shtait em Ṭuat , Cairo Pap. I, 3, a being whose head was a pot of fire.

Shta ḥer , Mar. Aby. I, 45, B.D. 136A, 18, a god of .

Shtau ḥeru saiu uatu , B.D. 141, 59, the unseen gods who guard the ways.

shta , Rev. 11, 149 = , to proclaim.

shtau , Pap. 3024, 3, 11, wooden objects.

shta āa ur , Rec. 30, 68, part of a ship's tackle.

shta , the number 200; Copt. ϢΗΤ.

shtamuti , the name of a bandlet.

shtar , a betrothed virgin, bride.

shti , , he who is hidden, *i.e.*, one who is in his coffin, *i.e.*, dead; plur. , , the dead.

shti-t , A.Z. 1906, 30, a kind of cloth.

shti (sheṭti) , Rev. 13, 36, pit, hole, excavation.

shti , Jour. As. 1908, 275, to demand, to take away.

shtut , Hearst Pap. XI, 15....

shteb , IV, 648, , , IV, 271, , to revolt, to tread in grain.

shteb , to kill = .

shteb, cage, basket.

shtem = Copt. ϣⲑⲉⲙⲙⲣⲱ, Rev., to be silent.

shtem, , Ptaḥ-ḥetep XI, 13, , Gol. Ham. 14, 147, to fight, to revile, to curse, to swear; compare Heb. שָׁטַם, Arab. شتم.

shtem-t, Åmen. 22, 20, revilings, abuse (?)

shtem, Rev. 14, 14, bolt (?); Copt. ϣⲧⲉⲙ.

sheth, P. 256, 690, , M. 780, to be covered, dressed, arrayed.

sheth, P. 539, Rec. 30, 192, , P. 614, M. 780, N. 1136, garment, raiment; , P. 708.

sheth-t, Rec. 27, 218, , coffin, sarcophagus.

shethi-t, , coffin, sarcophagus.

Shethu, Thes. 112: (1) a crocodile-headed lion; (2) one of the seven stars of Orion; var. .

shethu, Rec. 30, 193, a kind of fish.

sheṭ, A.Z. 1873, 17, a weight = five ṭeben.

sheṭ, Rec. 5, 93, to pound drugs, *e.g.*, myrrh.

sheṭ-t, , , , , , , mortar, grinder, rubbing-stone.

sheṭ, shṭi, U. 154, 284, 432, 470, 510, T. 22, P. 670, , P. 93, , , , N. 1146, , T. 247, , , , , Koller 5, 4, , , , Love Songs 7, 8, , IV, 1108, , Rechnungen 52, to take, to seize, to snatch, to carry or drag away, to withdraw, to transport, to drag out, to disembowel a beast, to save, to deliver, to remove, to dig out a well, to work out, to levy taxes. On the derivatives of , see Rec. 11, 117 ff.; Copt. ϣⲓⲧⲉ.

shṭiu, deliverers.

shṭi, Rec. 16, 72, title of an official.

shṭi, , to go deeply into a subject, to study profoundly, to search magical books, to penetrate mysteries.

sheṭ, to tread out corn.

sheṭṭ, , Rec. 19, 16, to dig, to excavate.

sheṭ-ti, digger, excavator.

sheṭ, slaughter, a killing.

sheṭsheṭ, Rev. 13, 4, to kill, to overthrow; Copt. ϣⲉⲧϣⲱⲧ.

Sheṭ-ba, Berg. I, 18, a ram-god.

shṭit, mast of a ship (?); plur. , Décrets 29, , Leyd. Pap. 4, 10, ; Copt. ϣⲧⲉ.

sheṭsheṭ-tȧ, Love Songs V, 9, the working of oars.

sheṭ, I, 51, , , , , P. 289, , , , IV, 920, , to suckle, to nurse, to rear a child, to train, to educate; , suckler of the gods; , guardian, tutor, trustee.

sheṭ unem, to fatten.

sheṭ-t, Kubbân Stele 11, , Israel Stele 7, , IV, 1104, , water skin; plur. , , B.D, 99, 18.

sheṭ-t, , , , vulva, vagina.

sheṭsheṭ, T. 31, 32, N. 201, 204, , P. 75, M. 105, N. 17, the vulva of the sky ().

sheṭ, Pap. 3024, 67, IV, 499, , farm, plot of ground, estate, ditch, dyke, an earthwork, pool, fish-pond; plur. , IV, 1111, , , , , A.Z. 1905, 9,

shṭi-t, , IV, 660, irrigated land; plur. , Rec. 14, 107, IV, 835.

shṭi-t, Ebers Pap. 65, 15, , , , , , , tank, lake, canal, water-course, cistern.

shṭi, vase, vessel, pot.

Shṭit-shemā-t, B.D. 125, III, 18, a lake in Sekhet-Åaru.

sheṭ, , , , to read, to recite, to pray, to mutter an incantation, to pronounce letters, to declaim poetry, to strike up a tune.

sheṭ-t, IV, 966, , , A.Z. 1908, 70, reading, recitation, incantation, spell, liturgy; plur. .

sheṭi re, IV, 1114, a deposition.

Sheṭ-kheru, B.D. 125, III: (1) one of the 42 assessors of Osiris; (2) the god of the 13th day of the month.

sheṭṭ, , to read, to recite.

sheṭṭ-t, recitation.

sheṭ, to tie up in linen, to swathe a mummy.

sheṭ, , , cord, bandlet, bandage; plur. , B.M. 448.

sheṭ-t, mummy.

sheṭ, IV, 756, a kind of bird.

sheṭ, IV, 745, fat (of geese).

sheṭ, Litanie 78, , Mission I, 229, crocodile, large reptile; plur. , Hh. 438.

Sheṭu, Ṭuat XII: (1) the eight morning stars; (2) the constellation of the Tortoise; (3) , A.Z. 49, 125, a "great god."

sheṭ-t, P.S.B. 19, 263, , Rechnungen 43, a bread offering, ferment, yeast.

shṭa (sheṭṭa), Rev. 14, 16, cultivated lands.

shṭa, shṭȧ-t, , , , crypt.

Sheṭau, Ṭuat X, a warder of the 10th Gate.

shṭaqit, , , prison; Copt. ϣⲧⲉⲕⲟ.

shṭȧ, Rev. 6, 26, 11, 129 . . . .

shṭi, Rev., rejected, cast down; Copt. ϣⲧⲏⲟⲩⲧ.

shṭi-t, A.Z. 1878, 49, , pit; Copt. ϣⲱⲧⲉ, ϣⲱϯ.

shṭi, reward, remuneration; Copt. ϣⲓⲧⲉ.

Shṭu, Ṭuat XI, a god, one of the 12 bearers of Meḥen.

Shṭu, a god, a form of Horus.

shṭep (?), B.D. 151, 6, a chamber in a temple.

shṭefi (?), V, 1083, ...

shṭen (?), B.D. 26, 5, bound, tied up; perhaps to be read **sheṭ nett.**

sheṭḥu, Rec. 2, 127, Love Songs 5, 2, , Rec. 5, 95, L.D. III, 219, 21, Anastasi IV, 12, 1, a kind of drink, new wine, must; Gr. ζύθος.

sheṭḥu, Rec. 31, 27, a kind of land, dyke, bank.

sheṭḥ-t, canal.

shetch-t, a digging; , festival of strewing sand.

shetch-t, a kind of offering.

Q

q = Heb. ק; Copt. ⲕ and ϭ.

qa, qai , , , , , , , , , , , , to be high, to be exalted, to be long (opposed to); , , to exalt, to be exalted; , U. 298, N. 1233, long (of nails or claws); , long-bearded P. 609.

qaȧ , P. 158, exalted one.

qa ȧb , haughty, arrogant.

qaqa ȧb , Inscription of Ḥenu 6, haughty, arrogant.

qa āḥā , Metternich Stele 88, a long life; , a very, very long life.

qa pet , , , , IV, 1077, the height of heaven.

qa remen , IV, 1031, high of shoulder, *i.e.*, stiff-necked.

Qa khā , A.Z., 1897, 98, "high crown," a title of Tirhakah.

qa kheru , IV, 988, , loud-voiced; fem. , , B.M. 138.

qa sa , IV, 968, high-backed, *i.e.*, stiff-necked, obstinate.

qa qa (qaui) in , B.D. 149, IV, 1, two very high mountains.

Qa , exalted one, a god.

Qaȧ , , , B.D. 150, a god.

Qa-ȧb-nti-menȧu , Ombos II, 134, a mythological being.

Qa-ā , the god of the high (long) arm.

Qa-t-ā , , Ṭuat I, one of the 12 goddesses who opened the Gates of the Earth to Rā.

Qa-āau , Denderah IV, 62, a bull-god with a loud voice.

Qa-ba , , Tomb Seti I, one of the 75 forms of Rā (No. 59).

Qa-t-em-ȧakhu-s , Ṭuat I, one of the 12 goddesses of the Gates of the Earth; var. .

Qa-[t]-em-sepu-s , Ṭuat XII, a fire-goddess.

Qa-t-em-sekhem-s , Ṭuat I, a goddess in the Ṭuat.

Qa-meri-mut-f , Thes. 120, one of the 36 Dekans.

Qa-mertu-neb , Denderah II, 10, a god.

Qa-neb-m'ka-ba-f, Berg. I, 23, a bird-god.

Qa-ha-ḥetep, B.D. 149, the god of the 8th Åat.

Qa-ḥer-åat-f, B.D. 125, III, 15, a title of Osiris.

Qa-ḥer-f, B.D. 182, 25, a god.

Qa-t-kheru, etc., etc., B.D. 145 and 146, the 10th Pylon.

Qaserpit, Ombos II, 133, a goddess.

Qa-shuti, Hymn Darius, 37, the god of the high plumes (Åmen-Rā).

Qa-shefshef, Ṭuat XII, , a sailor-god who attacked Āapep with his paddle.

Qa-ṭem-t, Ṭuat IX, a chamber in Åment.

qaa, , , N. 663, , Rec. 30, 189, , ibid. 31, 28, , Pap. 3024, 59, , , , hill, high ground, high place.

qaqa, B.D. 17, 9, , hill, high place.

qa-t, U. 229, , IV, 974, , , , P. 174, M. 440, N. 941 = , P. 174, N. 941, U. 494, T. 235 = , high land, *i.e.*, the Nile banks above the river; plur. , ; Copt. ⲔⲀⲈⲒⲈ.

qa-t, high, fine building.

qa-t, height (in the sense of length).

qai-t, , IV, 364, , , Love Songs 2, 4, , , Hymn Darius 23, the land high above the surface of the Nile; Copt. ⲔⲀⲒⲈ, ⲔⲞⲒ.

qai-t, , a high place; and see .

qai en ānkh, "hill of life"—a name of the territory of the temple of Denderah.

Qa, N. 767, a title of Temu.

Qau, , the god of Creation.

Qa, Qait, , , , B.D. 1, the high place on which the god of creation stood.

Qaqa, , , , B.D. 17, 9, a hill in Khemenu on which the heavens rested.

qaqa = , night, darkness, obscurity.

qa, form, manner; var. .

qaå, , , , , , state, condition, form, image, manner, aspect, phase, style; varr. , , .

qa unemi, food; Copt. ϬⲒⲚⲞⲨⲰⲘ; **qa surå**, drink; Copt. ϬⲒⲚⲤⲰ.

qaå en ret, Rev. 13, 119, , growth; Copt. ϬⲒⲚⲢⲰⲦ.

qaȧ ḥenuti, the condition of working men.

qai en menmen, Rev. 11, 141, condition of quaking (of the earth).

qai en qenqen, Rev. 11, 141, combat.

qa-t, Rev., food.

qai, Ȧmen. 23, 17, plate, vessel of food.

qaqa = or = **unem** to eat.

qa, qaa, Metternich Stele 215, Hymn Darius 22, B.D. 64 (Nebseni), 40, B.D. 64 (Nu), 15, to be putrid, foul, corruption, to vomit; compare Heb. קִיא.

qaut (?), IV, 876, foes, enemies, filthy folk.

qa, goat; Copt. ϭⲓⲉ.

qaa, Rec. 29, 155, pergola, shrubbery.

qait, a seed or fruit used in medicine.

qaqa, a seed or fruit.

qaqa, Hearst Pap. 1, 17, a medicinal decoction made from.

qa-t, qaa-t, T. 200, N. 791, bolt; plur., T. 162, M. 176, N. 688, Rec. 27, 55, 31, 174, Hh. 148, U. 494, T. 235; U. 269; see; Copt. ⲕⲗⲗⲉ.

qaqa, boat, barge; see; state barge; Arab. ذَهَبِيَّة.

qaqa, B.D. (Saïte) 64, 25, to peep, to look at, to pry into.

qaȧ, Rec. 21, 14, 79, 92, A.Z. 1899, 145, by, near.

qaȧs, to bind, to fetter; see.

Qaȧsu, the gods who fetter.

qaā, to vomit; see; Heb. קִיא (?); Arab. قَاءَ; Eth. ቀየአ:

qaāu, spittings, vomitings, U. 333–5.

Qai, B.D. 145, 45: (1) a fire-god; (2) a god of, Mar. Aby. I, 45.

Qaiqashau, Harris I, 77, 3, name of a tribe or people.

qau, P. 184, T. 221, N. 897, Rec. 26, 65, Rec. 26, 65, IV, 424, U. 469; height of the ridges of the land above the river; see.

qauath, A.Z. 1899, 36, a title of a craftsman.

qaur (qar), boat, barge; plur. Mar. Aby. I, 8, 85.

qaur, transport man, carrier; plur. , L.D. III, 140B, carriers by boat, gold-carriers.

qaus, to bind, to fetter; see .

qautȧ-t, Koller 1, 5, , weapon (?), part of the equipment of a chariot.

qab, , to double, to multiply, to be bowed (of the legs); Copt. κωϐ.

qabu, , crushed, overwhelmed, doubled over oneself.

qab, , B.D. 146, XV, 39, the middle of anything; **em qab** , within; compare Heb. בְּקֶרֶב.

qab, , , intestines, interior of the body; Heb. קֶרֶב.

qabu, P. 345, M. 646, , Rec. 26, 79, , the folds of a serpent, windings, coils.

Qab, N. 961, the windings of the lake of Kha .

Qabi, , a mythological serpent.

qab en Ȧmentt, the innermost part of the Other World.

qab-t, , breast, breasts of a woman, nipple; Copt. εκιϐε, κιϥι.

Qab-t-ent-Shu, etc., , B.D. 125, III, 31, the doorkeeper of the hall of Maāti.

qab, pot, vessel.

qafi, A.Z. 1908, 132, Anastasi I, 11, 4, to be choked, suffocated.

qamȧi, , , , an unguent.

Qambasuṭnt (?), Stele of Nȧstasen, Cambyses; Pers. Kabujiya, Gr. Καμβύσης, Bab. . Recently doubts have been cast upon this identification.

qamṭet (?), to weep, to mourn, to lament.

qamṭet, A.Z. 96, 41, , mourners.

qan-t, Rechnungen XVII, 2, 3, , bolt; plur. , U. 269, A.Z. 1910, 129; see , , ; Copt. κλλε, κελλι.

qanr, qanr-t, , Leyd. Pap. 44, , , , ground, earth, dust, dirt; Copt. χιπιρι (?)

qanrai (?), bolts; Copt. κλλε.

qar, hole, hollow.

qar-t, B.D. 180, 11, a pit in the Ṭuat wherein souls lived.

qarr, A.Z. 1874, 65, cellar, chamber.

qar, boat, barge.

qarr, , boat, barge, flat for transport.

qaru, , , carriers, metal carriers; plur. , L.D. III, 140c, , , Ḳubbân Stele 10.

qar, T. 84, , N. 615, , Rec. 30, 185, basket, bundle.

qar, Anastasi I, 7, 5, the last word of a book.

qar-t, P.S.B. 13, 412, bolt; plur. , .

qarr, Rec. 15, 67, frog; Copt. ⲕⲣⲟⲩⲣ.

Qarr, "Frog man"—a proper name; Copt. ⲕⲣⲟⲩⲣ.

qarr, burnt offerings; Copt. ϭⲗⲓⲗ.

qarr, collar; Copt. ⲕⲗⲁⲗ.

qarr, to be light, swift, weak; compare Heb. √קָלַל.

qarȧu, , light, weak, delicate; **qerȧ**; **qerr**.

qarmātȧ, Mar. Karn. 55, 62, foreskins.

qarnatȧ, Mar. Karn. 54, 54, , ibid. 54, 55, , ibid. 54, 50, 51, P.S.B. 10, 150, Rec. 22, 70, Thes. 1201, , Rougé I.H. 143, 37, foreskins; ; compare Heb. עָרְלָה.

qarḥutȧ, a metal pot; Heb. קַלַּחַת, Copt. ϭⲁⲗⲁϩⲧ.

qars-t = , burial.

qarret, ground, earth, street (?); var. .

qartȧ, city, town; compare Heb. קֶרֶת.

qartȧ, , ring, seal ring.

qarrtȧ, ring, seal ring.

qartchan, A.Z. 1905, 103, , , IV, 669, , axe; Heb. גַּרְזֶן, Deut. xix, 5, Isaiah x, 15.

Qahaqu, Harris I, 76, 6, 78, 10, Anastasi I, 17, 4, name of a tribe or people.

qaḥ, , , cut stones, masonry; var. .

qaḥa, , , Rec. 37, 21, to break, to tame lions, to fetter; see ; Copt. ⲕⲱϩ.

qaḥa, fetters, shackles, instruments of imprisonment.

qaḥa, , light, fire (?); Copt. ⲕⲱϩⲧ.

qaḥa, parched, dried.

qaḥau-t, windows (?) openings for light or heat.

qaḥaq, to break, to break in, to fetter.

qaḥi-t, B.D. 146, 50, fire; Copt. ⲕⲱϩⲧ.

Qaḥu, B.D. 149, a god in the 10th Áat.

qas, , to heave up, to vomit; see .

qas, U. 510, P. 204, N. 761, , T. 179, , , , , , , , ; var. , to tie, to bind, to fetter.

qass-t, , fetter, bond, tie; plur. .

qasu, T. 310, P. 550, 609, N. 806, , T. 234, P. 610, , Rec. 30, 66, 31, 15, , , , bonds, fetters, ties, bindings.

qas; see .

qas, a rope ladder (?)

qas = and , bone.

qasau, the planks of a boat (?)

Qaq, N. 767, a proper name (a pun on).

Qatȧ, P. 282, , M. 525, N. 1106, a god.

qatartȧ, incense; Heb. קְטֹרֶת, Assyr. ḳu-ta-ru .

qat ḥaur, , , Piehl, Sphinx 2, 7, the whole, altogether; Gr. καθ' ὅλου.

qathre-t, village, small town; Heb. קִרְיָת,

qaṭ-t, T. 35, N. 133, , M. 116, , grass, stubble; plur. ; Arab. قَتّة.

Qaṭ, Litanie 80, a form of the Sun-god.

qaṭ, heat, fire.

qaṭit, a kind of animal (?).

qatcha, , Amherst 1, , Anastasi I, 24, 3, thorns, scrub, stubble, "bush"; Heb. קוֹץ.

qatcha, , A.Z. 1905, 103, mud, rubble.

qatchatcha, a kind of cake, loaf.

qatchatcha, to hew; Heb. קָצַץ.

qatchauar, oil, unguent.

qatchamār (?), , , a kind of stuff for clothing.

Qatcharṭi, Anastasi Pap. I, 23, 6, a chief of Asher.

qatchaḥ, Rougé I.H. II, 125, to smash, to break, to scatter.

qȧ, , , , Pap. 3024, 50, Peasant 41, , form, manner, state, condition; plur. , A.Z. 1905, 24, divine forms; Copt. ϭⲓⲛ-.

qȧ, Jour. E.A. III, 103, with , all at once.

qȧ n semt, Ḳubbân Stele 12, the manner of the country.

qȧu, to wake up (?)

qȧḥ, to stretch out the hands in prayer.

qȧs, to tie, to bind, to fetter; see ; , under the ban.

qȧs, , to vomit, to overflow, efflux.

Qȧṭmus, Rec. 6, 6, the name Cadmus.

qā, A.Z. 1900, 30, , , to vomit.

qā, vomit, sickness.

qā, B.D. 145, 84 . . . .

qā, , , a kind of precious stone; see and .

qā-ḥat, Rec. 23, 201, well-pleased, content, agreeable (?); Copt. ⲁⲕϩⲏⲧ.

qāf, side.

Qān, Ṭuat VII, a god fettered by the Hour-gods.

qār, , , driver (?); plur. , , Rev. 6, 81; see .

qār, Rev. 14, 20, a fiend (?)

qāḥ, P. 173, , N. 940, 1312, P. 646, , , , Ebers Pap. 38, 5, to thrust with a horn, to stretch out the hand and arm; , I, 124.

qāḥ, , , , , , , , , arm, shoulder; dual , ; plur. , , , Ḥerusȧtef Stele 132, , ; Copt. ⲕⲉϩ in ⲕⲉⲗⲉⲛⲕⲉϩ, ⲕⲉⲗⲉⲧ ⲕⲉϩ.

qāḥ, U. 577, the tip [of a horn].

Qāḥ-ȧabti, B.D. 1, 21, the left shoulder of Osiris.

qāḥu, the margin of a book.

qāḥ, IV, 659, , A.Z. 35, 18, L.D. III, 229c, , , elbow, bend of a river, angle, corner, coign; , Ḥerusȧtef Stele 13, , Nȧstasen Stele 17, the four quarters of the country or of the world; Copt. ⲕⲟⲟϩ.

qāḥu, Ḳubbân Stele 30, P. 1116B, 30, applied to tanks in which fish are kept.

qāḥ, Rec. 13, 19, 14, 14, earth, ground; Copt. ⲕⲁϩ.

qāq, Rev. 12, 49, to cry out, cry; Copt. ⲕⲁⲕ.

qi, Rev. 11, 139, with , state, condition, mode, manner; Copt. ϭⲁ, ϭⲓⲛ.

Qi, a title or name of a god.

qi en ȧri menkh-t, Canopus Stele = τὸν στολισμόν.

qi en Ȧst, Rev. 2, 351, ceremony in honour of Isis.

qi en ānkh, Rev., living; Copt. ϭⲓⲛⲱⲛϩ.

qi en berā ... , Rev. 2, 351, "la mise en livre."

qi tekh ..., celebration of the drink festival.

qi ..., a kind of mineral unguent or incense.

qi ..., ..., ...

qi ..., ..., Rev. 12, 91, ..., ..., Rec. 27, 190, field, estate; Copt. ⲔⲀⲒⲈ.

qi ..., to be high, exalted.

qim ..., Rev. 12, 61, to move, to shake.

Qitaui ..., a mythological serpent.

qu ..., IV, 1130, a kind of bread, loaf.

ququ ..., Rec. 15, 102, a kind of fruit, palm nuts (?); Gr. κουκίοφορον.

qu-t ..., farm, grange.

qu ..., Thes. 1481, to attack (?)

qu ..., B.D. 161, 5, parts of the body of the infernal Tortoise.

quȧa ..., Gardiner, Theban Ostraka 70, a fish.

qui ..., Rev. 11, 184, little one; Copt. ⲔⲞⲨⲒ.

ququp-t ..., Rev. 12, 71, the hoopoe.

qunek ..., ..., ..., bread, food.

qur ..., boats, barges.

quru ..., porters, boatmen.

qur-t ..., ..., a fruit.

qus-t ..., ..., Rec. 14, 46, a measure; Gr. χοῦς, Copt. ϪⲎⲤ.

qeb, qebb ..., ..., U. 11, 33, 79, 344, ..., ..., ..., ..., ..., U. 222, ..., ..., ..., P. 1116B, 36, Israel Stele 23, to be cool, to refresh oneself, the opposite of ...; ... ..., a cool place; Copt. ⲔⲂⲀ, ϫⲂⲞⲂ, ⲔⲎⲂ.

qeb ḥat ..., cool of heart, not inflamed with wrath.

qeb seref ..., IV, 970, Thes. 1481, a man who blows hot and cold alternately.

qebb-t ..., ..., Rec. 29, 147, something cool, quiet speech.

qebu, qebbu ..., ..., Love Songs 7, 8, cool water.

qebb ..., a tank of cool water, the Nile.

qebbu ..., dykes.

qeb, qebb ..., ..., cool breeze, a refreshing, a cooling.

qeb meḥ ..., the cool north wind.

qebui ..., Rec. 18, 165, ..., ..., the north wind, icy winds.

Qeb ..., Berg. I, 35, ..., ..., the god of the North Wind.

qeb ..., ..., ..., a tree or plant from which oil is extracted; plur. ..., Rec. 2, 107.

qeb āa ..., "great cooler"—a kind of ointment.

qeb ..., IV, 1162, oil, jars of oil.

qeb ..., ..., Theban Ostraka B, 6, pot, jar, vase.

qeb ..., ..., ..., the innermost part; Heb. קֶרֶב.

qeb-t ..., Sphinx 2, 80, intestines, bowels, the viscera.

qebu, the internal coils of a serpent.

Qeb, the name of a many-coiled mythological serpent.

qeb, , Åmen. 6, 9, to double, to increase; Copt. κωϐ.

qeb, circuit, company, group, order, series; , IV, 39, the circuit of the Delta; , IV, 926, the circle of the smeru; , , the great assembly.

qebu, group of people, company, multitude; , Coronation Stele 3, companies of soldiers.

Qeb-Åmentt, B.D. 1B, 8, 17, 46, the abode of the heart of Osiris.

qeb renput, Rec. 32, 179, doubler or multiplier of years, a divine title.

qeb-t, Metternich Stele 144, , , , , arm, shoulder, breast, teat, nipple, throat, gullet.

qeb-t, , a mineral earth.

qeba, Rev. 12, 50, , Rev. 12, 46, to take vengeance.

Qebak, Thes. 818, Rec. 16, 106, a goose-god.

qebȧ-t, , garment, shirt; Copt. κοϐι.

qebi, , wild honey; Copt. κεϐι.

qebi, , Åmen. 8, 2, , Jour. As. 1908, 256, to vex, to tease; Copt. κωωϐε.

qebqebi-t, Åmen. 24, 10, , , to overthrow, to defeat, to massacre; Copt. ϭιϐϭιϐ.

qebni, A.Z. 1908, 8, , , a ship of Byblos.

Qebr, Rev. 2, 13 = الكبير (?) the Great One.

qebḥ, , , , to cool, to be cool, to refresh oneself.

qebḥ, coolness, refreshing.

qebḥ-t, Rec. 6, 12, , , Rec. 31, 32, place of coolness, bath, sanctuary; , bath-master.

qebḥu, libationer.

qebḥ-tȧ, T. 292, libationer (?)

Qebḥit, P. 604, the goddess of libations.

Qebḥit, the goddess on the royal crown who brought cooling.

qebḥi-t, , , , libation vase.

qebḥu, , , , , , , , , , Rec. 27, 222, cool water, libation, the watery mass of heaven, the celestial abyss; , the cool water of Elephantine.

qebḥu, , , , , , , the Cataract region, the lands flooded by the Nile, the great deep of heaven.

qebḥ, pond or lake with waterfowl.

qebḥu, Rec. 29, 148, A.Z. 1910, 133, , , waterfowl.

qebeḥ-ti, fowler, marsh-man.

Qebḥu, U. 483, M. 393, N. 147, , P. 154, , N. 784, 1169, , Hh. 325, , A.Z. 1906, 130, the sky, heaven.

Qebḥit, , , , the Sky-goddess.

Qebḥut, P. 392, , M. 561, , N. 1163, , M. 795, 825, N. 1317, a goddess, the daughter of Anubis.

Qebḥit-urit, Berg. II, 13, a form of Nut.

Qebḥ-neteru-Ḥe-t, Palermo Stele, the name of a temple.

Qebḥ-senu-f, U. 219, T. 60, M. 218, , N. 593, , P. 262, , M. 483, 495, , T. 197, , N. 1294, , , , a son of Horus, god of the western heaven and earth and protector of the liver and gall-bladder.

Qebḥ-senui-f: (1) the god of the 4th hour of the night; (2) , , the god of the 7th day of the month.

Qebḥ-senuf, B.D. 99, 22, a bolt-peg in the magical boat.

Qebḥ, the name of the pyramid tomb of Shepseskaf.

qebes, Rougé I.H. II, 126, , to subdue, to tie, to fetter, to conquer; Heb. כָּבַשׁ.

qebes, , , a tree.

qebta, Rec. 2, 109, to be stopped up, choked.

qebti, IV, 1126 = , the title of an official; see **qenbet.**

qepag, to dance, dance.

qef, , , to uncover, to reveal.

qef-t, an unveiling.

qefqef, Rec. 24, 163 . . . . . .

qef, qefau, , , , Rec. 35, 58, , , Metternich Stele 122, , , , , , IV, 385, power, strength, confidence, magical power.

qefa-t, Love Songs 2, 12, wooden bolts or bars (?)

qefå, Jour. As. 1908, 256, to rob, to assault; Copt. ⲕⲱⲱϥⲉ.

qefen, U. 569, , P. 426, M. 610, N. 1214, to clasp, to enclose.

qefen, to build a house, to set up a wall.

qefen-t, P. 204, M. 342, N. 869, vulva, vagina.

qefen, , , , Rechnungen 37, to be hot, to bake.

qefen, , , Rec. 3, 56, , sacred cake or bread.

Qefnu, B.D. 142, II, 10, a city of Osiris.

Qeftenu, an ape-god, sacred monkey.

qefṭen, , , , a sacred monkey; plur.

Qefṭenu, B.D. 42, 28, 153B, 9, an ape-god who worked the net of the Akeru-gods.

qem =, to bring to an end, to complete.

qem , , , =, to find; Copt. ϭιne.

Qem-baiu-s, the name of a festival.

Qem-baiu set, a title or name of Hathor; var. .

qem, Rev. 13, 9, to behave or act in a seemly manner.

qem, , , Rev. 13, 15, , reed; plur. , A.Z. 1908, 121, , Rec. 3, 50; var. , papyrus nilotica; Heb. גֹּמֶא, Eth. ገሚዕ:

qema, , , Rev. 13, 94, reed, coarse grass; plur. , Rec. 3, 49; Heb. גֹּמֶא.

qemama, reed.

qema, Nåstasen Stele 35, meadow, garden; Copt. ϭωμ, ϭωμε, ϣωμ (?)

qema, U. 361, , A.Z. 1910, 133, , , , B.D. (Todt., N.) 2, 325, , , to throw, to hurl, to cast away, to throw a boomerang; var. .

qemau, U. 461, boomerang, weapon.

qema, to overturn, to overthrow.

qema, to work in metal.

qemau =, woodcutters (?) miners (?)

qema, U. 382, , IV, 967, , , , , , , , , , , , to make, to fashion, to form, to create, to beget; , B.D. 113, 2, created by a word.

qema-t, , , , IV, 1044, , product, natural product, natural disposition.

qemaiu, created beings or things, creation.

qemau, creator, god of creation.

Qemau ur, Great Creator; plur. , Rec. 31, 27.

qemai-t, corn, grain.

qema, qemam, , B.D. 142, VI, 18, Metternich Stele 2, , , , , , , , , , , , , , statue, form, image.

qema-ti, statue, image, form.

qemam, , , , , to form, to fashion, to create.

qemamu (?), , Love Songs 4, 2,

, , , created things and beings.

qemam-t , Rec. 16, 57, mother, parent.

Qemamu , B.D. 179, 2, the Creator.

qemamu , something wrought, worked (of metal).

qemamu , , Rec. 33, 7, workers in wood or metal.

qemam , A.Z. 1907, 123, to move; Copt. ⲔⲒⲘ.

qemamtiu , wailings, wailers, those who lament; see **qemtiu** .

qemat , to lament, to moan, to groan; varr. , .

qemȧ , IV, 63 . . . .

qemȧit , , , Koller 4, 2, , A.Z. 1905, 15, , , Love Songs 1, 7, , an Arabian gum or resin; Copt. ⲔⲞⲘⲘⲎ, Gr. κόμμι (gummi), Herodotus II, 86, 96; , the finest qemȧi.

qemȧi , , a liquid preparation of qemȧi; var. .

qemȧi-t ent ānti , IV, 329, the gum of the myrrh tree.

qemȧit khentiu , Rec. 22, 103, a drug.

qemȧ-t , cut, wound, hole, slit.

qemȧ-ti , statue, image, form.

qemā , to sing or play an instrument; see **shemā**.

qemā , IV, 61, , , B.D. (Saïte) 163, 8, empty, helpless (?); var. .

qemi = , a kind of unguent, gum.

Qemi , Rev. 14, 16, the land of the South—Upper Egypt.

qemḥ , , , A.Z. 1908, 121, to see, to look, to perceive.

qemḥu , , leaves, leaf-work.

qemḥu , T. 57, M. 217, N. 588, , , , , , , bread made of fine flour; compare Heb. קֶמַח, Arab. قمح, Syr. ܩܡܚܐ Eth. ቀምሕ:

qemḥi-t , Rec. 31, 167, fine wheaten flour.

qemḥu , crown of the head.

Qemḥes , , "He who sees"—a title of Horus and Rā.

qemqemut , Rev. 14, 11, tambourines; Copt. ⲔⲈⲘⲔⲈⲘ.

qemt , image, statue; var. .

qemtiu , wailings, wailers, those who lament or groan; var. .

qemtu (?) , inert, helpless, weak or feeble men; var. .

qemṭ , Rec. 34, 178, , A.Z. 1870, 171, , , , to weep, to wail, to lament.

qemtch, to lament, to weep, to wail.

qen, qenu, much, many; very great many.

qen, qeni, Rec. 33, 6, to be strong, to make strong, to fortify, to have power over, to overcome, to conquer, to be master of, to possess, to lord it over someone, to vanquish, to beat, to strike, to thresh.

qenȧ-t, P. 662, 780, M. 773, wounded, stricken, beaten.

qenu, strong, bold, brave, mighty, fight, battle, victory, the prize of victory.

qen-t, might, power, strength, valour.

qen, warrior, soldier, man of war; plur. IV, 975, cavalry.

qeni, a strong man, something strong.

qeni-t, troops, braves, forces.

Qen-ȧb-f, B.D. 39, 15, a storm-god.

Qen-Ȧmen, the name of a horse of Seti I.

qenn, Peasant 46, ; see .

qenqen, Rec. 21, 97, Nȧstasen Stele 46, , Ȧmen. 12, 5, , Ȧmen. 14, 16, , Koller 2, 4, , Love Songs 2, 3, to beat, to strike, to fight, beating, fight, battle.

qenqenu (?), IV, 668, broken pieces, fragments.

qenqennu, Ḥeru-sȧtef Stele 78, 82, fight, battle.

qenqeni-t, a wooden tool used for beating.

qenqeniu, tools or instruments used in beating, mallets.

qenqen-[t], Hh. 559, a place of beating, torture ground.

Qenqentiu, Hh. 366, a group of gods.

qen, Nȧstasen Stele 33 . . . . . .

qen, to suffer injury or calamity.

qen-t, injury, wrong, misfortune.

qenu, IV, 1109, defeat, weakness, misfortune, injury, damage, famine, calamity, offence, violence, murder (?)

qenu, IV, 968, violent men, wrongdoers.

qen, qeni, to be fat; Copt. ⲕⲉⲛⲓ.

qenn, L.D. III, 194, 35, to be fat; Copt. ⲕⲉⲛⲛⲉ, ⲕⲛ̄ⲛⲉ.

qenqen, Rhind Pap. 34, to eat, to feed.

qen, waterflood.

Qenqentt, B.D. 110, 38, a goddess in Sekhet-Ȧaru.

Qenqen-t (?), B.D. 110, a lake in Sekhet-Âaru.

qen, Rec. 8, 134, Leyd. Pap. 14, 11, , , , , to make perfect, to finish, to make an end of, to complete, refined (of metal); Copt. ⲔⲎⲚ.

qen-t = , estate, landed property.

qen-tiu, , Pap. 3024, 97, ends of the earth, boundaries.

Qenti (?), IV, 655, remote land (?)

qenti, IV, 383 = **semti**, two hill lands or deserts.

qennui, twisters of yarn (?) weavers (?)

qen, Leyd. Pap. 10, 5, , IV, 1104, , Rev. 11, 169, mat, carpet, rug, sack; , Rec. 5, 90, a palm-leaf mat; Copt. ϬⲞⲞⲨⲚⲈ.

qen, qenu, , , , , seat, chair of state, throne, couch, litter.

qennuiu, throne bearers (?)

qen-ti, body, belly.

qen-ti (?), , a plant or seed used in medicine, reed (?)

qenn, qennȧ, IV, 1146, reed; varr. , ; Heb. קָנֶה.

qenȧ, IV, 1024, to bewail, to lament; compare Heb. קִינָה.

qenȧ, Shipwreck 44, , , Treaty 36, , to embrace, to hug (a shadow,).

qenȧ, U. 645, , Shipwreck 133, , IV, 1163, , Festschrift 117, 9, , Anastasi I, 25, 5, , Love Songs 3, 13, , Rec. 31, 170, , , , P. 1116B, 13, embrace, hug, breast-bone, bosom, breast, body, belly; Copt. ⲔⲞⲨⲚ.

qenȧ, IV, 705, , IV, 666, , , , , Amherst 26, , Ikhernefert 11, , , , Rec. 1, 49, , , Rec. 19, 96, bearing-pole, litter, palanquin, chair, portable shrine or naos; , L.D. III, 194.

qenȧ, N. 954, , , a garment, cape (?) coarse cloth; Copt. ϬⲞⲞⲨⲚⲈ.

qenȧ, Rec. 31, 20, a leather garment.

qenȧ-t, P. 204 + 11, garment, cape (?)

qenȧ, , Thes. 1201, , sheaf, bundle of grain.

qenȧ-t, , , a kind of ochre (?) coloured earth.

qenȧ, qennȧ, , a kind of drink.

qenȧu; see , , and .

qenȧu, , well-fed, fattened.

qeni, B.D. 149, 1, a kind of cloth, sacking (?)

qenu, breast; Copt. ⲔⲞⲨⲚ.

qenu, a strong bull, a powerful animal.

qenu, , a fine strong horse, stallion (?)

qenu, heat, fire, burn.

qenu, incense (?) ochre (?)

qenb, , , Rec. 5, 86, corner of a building, angle, nook; dual , opposite corners.

qenbiu, A.Z. 1900, 30, corners (of the earth).

qenb-t, rectangular chamber.

qenb-t, A.Z. 45, 125, , a court official; plur. , IV, 966, , , , , , , , the upper classes; , Rec. 14, 75, tribunals.

qenebtiu nu u, IV, 1120, , , peoples on the land.

qenb-t, Rec. 33, 121, , document; plur. , .

qenb, IV, 1075, to tie, to bind.

qenb, part of a dowry.

qenfi, , to knead dough, to prepare bread.

qenr-t, Dublin Pap. 4, B.D. 15 . . . .

qenḥ, A.Z. 1878, 49, to tie, to fetter; Copt. ϭωnϩ.

qenḥ, to be moved or incited by ill-feeling or envy.

qenḥit, shrine, chapel; plur. , Rev. 13, 23, , Rev. 13, 8; Gr. κόγχη, κόγχος, Copt. κnϩє.

qenuḥi (qenḥit?), shrine, chapel.

qenḥ, , the name of the 24th day of the moon.

qenekht, strong = **qen** + **nekht.**

qens (?), IV, 160, given (?)

qens, IV, 1197 = .

qens, decay, corruption; Copt. κnooc.

qenns, violence, wrong; Copt. ϭonc̄.

qent, to be angry; Copt. ϭωnт̄.

qenṭ, IV, 1082, , IV, 269, , , , to be wroth, to rage, to be furious; Copt. ϭωnт̄.

qenṭ-t, P.S.B. 24, 44, , , , wrath, rage, anger, fury; , , Love Songs 2, 12, 13, angry; , Rec. 21, 99, the raging of the sea.

qentchau, some object given as a dowry.

qer, inhabitant, dweller.

qer, Rec. 31, 31, to be master of.

qerr, light, weak, delicate; var. ; compare Heb. קלל.

qer-t, hollow, cavern, cave, source of the Nile, circle; plur. , , the 12 circles in the Ṭuat.

qerut-shetaut, the hidden circles.

qeri-t, cave, cavern, natural hole in the ground.

qerr-t, Rec. 3, 46, hole, cavern, grotto, circle in the Ṭuat, hole in a vessel, spout; Heb. קִיר; plur., Rec. 31, 172.

qer-ti-t, Hymn Darius 15, , Rev. 13, 13, cavern, hole, cave, den.

Qer-ti, Qerr-ti, Berg. I, 15, the two caverns in the First Cataract out of which the Nile was believed to rise; , the bodies of the Qerti; , L.D. III, 140B.

Qerr-t, the 5th Division of the Ṭuat.

Qerti, B.D. 125, II, the god of the Qerti, one of the 42 assessors of Osiris.

Qerr-ti, Tomb Seti I, one of the 75 forms of Rā (No. 28).

Qertiu, the gods of the Nile caverns.

Qerr-t Sar, Ṭuat VII, the Circle of Osiris.

qer-t, qerȧ-t, door bolt; dual, Dream Stele 22; plur.; Copt. κηλλι.

qer, qerr, U. 388, , U. 420, , wind, sky.

qerr, to make an offering by fire; compare Copt. ϭλιλ, ϣλιλ.

qerr, an offering by fire; compare Copt. ϭλιλ.

qerr, to bake pottery; compare Copt. ϭλιλ.

qerr-t, U. 522, T. 320, fire, flame.

qerr, Annales V, 112, oven, furnace.

qerr, Sphinx 14, 167, frog; Copt. κρουρ.

qerr, drinking pot, water pot; Copt. κελωλ, Arab. قُلَّة.

Qerr, Qerrȧ, N. 1133, , P. 445, M. 552, a serpent-fiend in the Ṭuat.

qerai-t, Rev. 12, 10, victory, conquest; Copt. ϭρο.

qer, qerȧ, Israel Stele 16, to return.

qerȧ, Ḥeruemḥeb 3, weak; see .

qerȧ, Rec. 25, 192, abode, habitation.

Qerȧ, , B.D. 17, 142, (1) a storm-god; (2) the name of the block on which the enemies of Osiris were slain daily.

qerȧ, Shipwreck 57, , rainstorm, tempest, hurricane, thunderstorm.

qerȧu, door bolt; plur. ; var.

qerȧs, to wrap up a

body in linen and prepare it for burial, winding sheet, sepulture; see ⟨hieroglyphs⟩; ⟨hieroglyphs⟩, a happy burial; Copt. ⲔⲀⲓⲤⲉ.

Qerȧstt ⟨hieroglyphs⟩, the place of burial in the hills, cemetery.

Qerȧstt ⟨hieroglyphs⟩, Berg. II, 12, a form of the goddess Ȧment.

qerā ⟨hieroglyphs⟩, Jour. As. 1908, 251, lie; Copt. ϭⲟⲗ.

qerā ⟨hieroglyphs⟩, ⟨hieroglyphs⟩, Rev. 12, 45, shield, buckler; plur. ⟨hieroglyphs⟩, Mar. Karn. 53, 27; Copt. ϭⲗ̄.

qeri-ā (?) ⟨hieroglyphs⟩, ⟨hieroglyphs⟩, Rec. 15, 87, ⟨hieroglyphs⟩, porter (?); var. ⟨hieroglyphs⟩; plur. ⟨hieroglyphs⟩.

qeru ⟨hieroglyphs⟩, Hymn Darius 18 . . . .

qeru ⟨hieroglyphs⟩, Rec. 8, 137, leader; plur. ⟨hieroglyphs⟩.

qeruḥ ⟨hieroglyphs⟩, to make drunk; Copt. ϭⲗⲁϩ.

qerbaiu ⟨hieroglyphs⟩, Rev. 12, 113, pots of drink.

Qerpiais ⟨hieroglyphs⟩, Rec. 33, 3, a Greek month.

qerps ⟨hieroglyphs⟩, to beat, to strike.

qerf ⟨hieroglyphs⟩, ⟨hieroglyphs⟩, ⟨hieroglyphs⟩, ⟨hieroglyphs⟩, B.D. 26, 6, ⟨hieroglyphs⟩, B.D. 169, 3, to be wrapped up, swathed, tied, fastened together.

qerf-t ⟨hieroglyphs⟩, ⟨hieroglyphs⟩, ⟨hieroglyphs⟩, ⟨hieroglyphs⟩, a headdress, headcloth, tiara, bandlet, head decoration, garment, shawl, a kind of garment; Copt. ϭⲟⲗⲃⲓ (?)

qerf ⟨hieroglyphs⟩, ⟨hieroglyphs⟩, a kind of cloth, sail.

qerf ⟨hieroglyphs⟩, a mass of dough (?) bread.

qerf-t ⟨hieroglyphs⟩, Ebers Pap. 87, 6, a swelling of the glands, ulcer (?)

qerf ⟨hieroglyphs⟩, ⟨hieroglyphs⟩, Rev. 13, 15, guile, deceit; Copt. ⲕⲣⲟϥ.

qerrm ⟨hieroglyphs⟩, Rev. 14, 45, pleasure (?) delight (?)

qermȧ ⟨hieroglyphs⟩, Rec. 13, 126, festal attire (?)

qernatȧ ⟨hieroglyphs⟩, Mar. Karn. 54, 54, ⟨hieroglyphs⟩, ibid. 54, 46, prepuces; according to some leather coverings for the tips of phalli, ⟨hieroglyphs⟩.

Qerner ⟨hieroglyphs⟩, Nesi-Ȧmsu 32, 19, a form of Ȧapep.

qerḥ-t ⟨hieroglyphs⟩, ⟨hieroglyphs⟩, Metternich Stele 119, Rec. 3, 45, 53, 4, 21, ⟨hieroglyphs⟩, vase, vessel, the mould from which the model of Osiris was made; Heb. קְלָחַת; plur. ⟨hieroglyphs⟩, IV, 1150, Annales III, 109, Ḥeruemḥeb 24; ⟨hieroglyphs⟩ Harris Pap. I, 19в; Copt. ϭⲗⲁϩⲧ.

qerḥ ⟨hieroglyphs⟩, a kind of serpent.

Qerḥit ⟨hieroglyphs⟩, ⟨hieroglyphs⟩, ⟨hieroglyphs⟩, ⟨hieroglyphs⟩, ⟨hieroglyphs⟩, ⟨hieroglyphs⟩, IV, 386, ⟨hieroglyphs⟩, Leyd. Pap. 7, 5, 56, a divine spirit.

Qerḥit ⟨hieroglyphs⟩, B.D.G. 859, a goddess of ⟨hieroglyphs⟩ (Succoth).

qerḥu ⟨hieroglyphs⟩, night, darkness; Copt. ⲭⲱⲣϩ.

Qerḥep ⟨hieroglyphs⟩, Ombos I, 1, 8, a god of Ombos.

qeres ⟨hieroglyphs⟩, ⟨hieroglyphs⟩, ⟨hieroglyphs⟩, ⟨hieroglyphs⟩, ⟨hieroglyphs⟩, ⟨hieroglyphs⟩, ⟨hieroglyphs⟩, ⟨hieroglyphs⟩, to wrap a dead body in cloth and make it ready for burial; ⟨hieroglyphs⟩, I, 15, two who

are buried, a double burial; , IV, 965, , buried; Copt. ⲕⲱⲱⲥ.

qeres , Hh. 548, , Pap. 3024, 54, , U. 582, , N. 963, , Rec. 30, 70, , Rec. 31, 19, , Pap. 3024, 43, , , , , coffin, mummy equipment, bier, burial, sepulture.

qeres-t , , , Shipwreck 169, , Peasant 308, , , , , , , funeral, burial, sepulture, funeral bier; , a happy burial; Copt. ⲕⲁⲉⲓⲥⲉ.

qersu , , , , coffin, sarcophagus; plur. .

qeres , the sarcophagus chamber, the mummy chamber.

Qersu , T. 268, M. 427, a name of the Sky-god Nu.

Qersu-t , T. 268, , N. 719 + 26, a name of the goddess Nut; var. , M. 426.

qersh , Rev. 13, 6, fraud, guile, deceit; Copt. ⲕⲱⲣϣ.

qerq-t , U. 530, seed-land (?)

qerq-ut , , seed; Copt. ϭⲣⲟϭ, ϫⲣⲟϫ.

qerqer , P. 174, N. 941, , , , to move, to roll; var. .

Qerqer , P. 267, , M. 479, , N. 1246; , Rec. 31, 11, the god who was the scribe or secretary of Osiris.

qerqer-t , beating.

Qertnetchenau (?) , IV, 781, 11A, , IV, 781, 11C, name of a country.

qeheb , to butt with the horns; var. .

Qeheq , Harris Pap. 76, 6, 78, 10, a people alien and hostile to Egypt.

qeḥ , naos, shrine.

qeḥ , wooden cramp, peg, bolt.

qeḥ , , , , Rev. 13, 95, angle, corner; Copt. ⲕⲟⲟϩ.

qeḥ , a kind of stone, flint; , A.Z. 1879, 53.

qeḥqeḥ , , to cut stone, to hammer out, to carve, to engrave; Copt. ⲕⲁϩⲕϩ. . .

qeḥqeḥu , artificers, artisans.

qeḥḥ-ut (sic), B.D. (Nebseni) 172, 20, castrated cattle, oxen.

qeḥȧit (?) , Rev. 14, 18, spreading (?)

qeḥes , gazelle; fem. ; var. ; Copt. ϭϩⲟⲥ.

qeḥsher , Stele C. 100 (Louvre) = Copt. ⲕⲁϣⲟⲩⲗⲓ (?)

qeḥeq, qeḥqeḥ , , to be old, weak, broken; Copt. ⲕⲉϩⲕⲉϩ, ϫⲉϩϫϩ.

qes , to spit out, to spew, to vomit; see and .

qes , to build, to found.

qes , a walled enclosure.

qesu , B.D. 125, I, 15, preserves of birds, goose-pens.

qes , Jour. As. 1908, 262 = , violence; Copt. ϭⲟⲛⲥ.

qes-ti , Famine Stele 14, curse, misery.

qes , Rec. 33, 6, lack, want; , Rec. 33, 6, troubles (?)

qes , , , , time, period; , every time, always; , times of the ancestors.

qes , N. 1234, , U. 320, , , , , , , Rev., bone, body, skeleton; plur. , U. 290, T. 158, N. 688, , M. 175, , U. 448, T. 178, 756, , , ; Copt. ⲕⲁⲥ.

qes , P. 435, M. 608, N. 1213, shaft of a spear, spear.

qes , , , , , , Rec. 5, 92, , , , Rev. 11, 186, to wrap a body in linen and prepare it for burial; see , etc.; Copt. ⲕⲱⲱⲥ.

qes , to tie, to fetter, to bind.

qes ānkh , , Rec. 4, 22, a kind of stone.

qesqes , to grumble, to complain; Copt. ⲕⲁⲥⲕⲉⲥ.

qesqesu , Rec. 5, 86, reeds.

qesȧu , , burial; Copt. ⲕⲁⲓⲥⲉ.

qesȧs , , , a mummified body, burial; , happy burial.

qesen , T. 217, , U. 607, , , , , , to be bad, evil, unpleasant, detestable, baleful, injurious, grievous, grief.

qesnu , evil beings or things.

qesen-t , , evil, calamity, plur. , P. 1116B, 32, , Pap. 3024, 10, , , injurious, violent; , lean years; , Ḳubbân Stele 9, lacking water; , Anastasi I, 21, 2, the height of misery.

qesṭ-t , Rechnungen 69, a market (?) = קְשִׁיטָה (?)

qesh , reed; Copt. ⲕⲁϣ.

qeq-t , , a small boat.

qeq (unem) , , to eat; see **unem** .

Qeq-ḥa (Unem-ḥa) , , Berg. I, 34, a turtle-god; see **Unemḥa.**

Qeq-snef (Unem-snef) ; see **Unem-snef.**

qeq-t , darkness, night; var ; Copt. ⲕⲁⲕⲉ.

qeqȧ = ; Copt. ⲔⲀⲔⲈ.

qek , to strike, to beat (?)

qet , Leyd. Pap. 4, 9, fine linen.

Qetqet , B.D. 110, a lake in Sekhet-Åaru.

Qettbu (?) , B.D. 110, 13, a god of Sekhet-Åaru.

qeṭ , III, 141, , IV, 161, Thes. 1283, , Mar. Aby. I, 6, 21, , Rev. 13, 2, to build, to fashion, to form, to mould, to construct; , self-builder; , constructor of his own body; Copt. ⲔⲰⲦ.

qeṭu , Åmen. 21, 19, 24, 14, builder, mason; plur. , Pap. 3024, 60; , Décrets 9, .

qeṭu , P. 397, , N. 1173, , P. 407, , N. 617, , IV, 223, , modeller, moulder, potter, the divine potter; plur. , B.D. (Saïte) 124, 7.

Qeṭ-t ṭen-t , Ṭuat V, a goddess in the Ṭuat.

qeṭ , to design, to make a picture or likeness of anything, to copy, to outline something.

qeṭ, qeṭ-t , T. 172, P. 119, N. 107, , M. 152, , IV, 434, , T. 249, , N. 769, , Israel Stele 13, , form, image, likeness, similitude, like, manner, kind, similarity, circle; , unanimously; , like; Copt. ⲔⲞⲦ.

qeṭi , Rosetta Stone, with = ⲔⲀⲐⲀⲠⲈⲢ.

qeṭi with = ⲠⲔⲰⲦⲈ.

qeṭ — mȧ qeṭ , M. 166, , altogether, in a body, collectively, in entirety, whole, totality.

qeṭ, qeṭṭ , IV, 350, , Rec. 32, 79, , ibid. 37, 78, , Gol. Hamm. 13, 124, , IV, 1083, , IV, 1082, , characters, dispositions, qualities, abilities, virtues; , Rec. 36, 210, , Rec. 32, 78, 33, 28; , a good character; , IV, 971, A.Z. 39, 47, thoughts; , a man of great ability or character; , a man of virtues or ability; , his character was unique.

qeṭ , design, drawing, plan, the draughtsman's craft; plur. , T. 334, , N. 704.

qeṭut , outline drawing.

qeṭu, designers, draughtsmen.

qeṭ-t, T. 87, , a draughtsman's office, a sculptor's workshop.

qeṭ-t Rev. 13, 62, town; Copt. ⲔⲰⲦ.

qeṭ, , , circle, orbit.

qeṭi, , , Anastasi I, 26, 4, , , , , , , , , , , , Rev. 14, 8, to go round, to turn round; Copt. ⲔⲰⲦⲈ. , IV, 85, that stream is turned round, and one goes down stream in sailing to the south, *i.e.*, that river flows southwards instead of northwards like the Nile; , throughout.

qeṭ-t, Rec. 5, 96, circuit.

qeṭi, revolution; Copt. ⲔⲰⲦⲈ.

qeṭi, , , , sailor, oarsman; plur. , P. 649, , P. 723, , M. 749, , , , , , Thes. 1296, , , in , T. 340, , M. 167, , N. 654; , sailors in general, ordinary crews; , , , divine sailors; , Egyptian sailors; , Rec. 21, 84, Syrian sailors.

Qeṭu, , , IV, 649, , , IV, 613, Asien 240 ff., the natives of Qeṭi, , the "Circle," *i.e.*, the North Syrian coast about the Gulf of Issus and the deserts between the Euphrates and the Mediterranean.

Qeṭi, Rec. 6, 152, a god of the abyss.

Qeṭ, , , Tomb Seti I, Zod. Dend., Annales I, 86, one of the 36 Dekans.

Qeṭqeṭ, Annales I, 85, one of the 36 Dekans.

Qeṭkha, one of the 36 Dekans; Gr. Κατκουατ.

Qeṭ-ka, Qeṭṭ-ka, Rec. 4, 28, , , the god of the 10th hour of the day.

Qeṭṭ-ka, Berg. I, 3, one of the watchers of the body of Osiris.

qeṭi, , , , , Åmen. 23, 5, , Metternich Stele 98, , , , , , Rev. 14, 35, , , Rev. 12, 32, to sleep.

qeṭ-t, sleep, slumber.

qeṭṭi, U. 387, 689, , T. 346, , , , to sleep; Copt. ⲔⲞⲦ in ⲀⲚⲔⲞⲦ (?) or ⲚⲔⲞⲦ.

qeṭu, qeṭṭu, , , , Rec. 32, 80, , ibid. 32, 86, , sleepers.

qeṭṭ-t, , , Rev., to turn, to return.

qeṭ-t , , , Rec. 7, 112, , , Mar. Karn. 42, 11, , , , , , Rev. 13, 41, cassia; var. ; , Rec. 4, 21, cassia bark; Gr. κιττώ, Heb. קְדָּה.

qeṭ-t , a kind of grain.

qeṭ-t , , , IV, 666, , , a weight = $\frac{1}{10}$th of an uṭen, drachma, didrachma, the half of a stater, obolus; plur. , Åmen. 17, 18, , Åmen. 18, 4; Copt. ⲔⲒⲦⲈ, ⲔⲒϮ.

qeṭ, qeṭṭ , , craft, cunning, astuteness.

Qeṭ , , , , , Nesi-Åmsu 22, 4, 29, 21, 32, 18, a mythological serpent of evil, devil; plur. .

qeṭbit , L.D. III, 229c, district, estate (?)

qeṭem , , , , N. 759, fine gold; Heb. כֶּתֶם.

Qeṭshu , , the "nude" or Syrian goddess.

K

k = Heb. כ, Copt. ⲕ and sometimes ϭ.

k = pronoun, 1st pers. sing.; 2nd pers. sing. masc., thou, thee, thy.

k = , moreover; = , another, also.

ka , U. 438, T. 169, 237, P. 717, M. 745, thou, thee; , P. 431, M. 617, N. 1221; , Rev. 14, 165 (dual), ye two.

ka , , a particle meaning something like O then! verily, certainly, now behold!

ka-t , A.Z. 46, 140, a particle, verily, assuredly; and see .

ka , Rev. 11, 151, 12, 24, another.

kai, ki , , , , another; fem. .

kaiu, kiu , A.Z. 1884, 89, , Rec. 33, 6, Israel Stele 24, Leyd. Pap. 4, 1, , , , , , , Mar. Aby. I, 6, 45, , , , Åmen. 11, 1, 13, 20, 20, 13; **kaut, kauit** , , , ; plur. of ka and ki (another), strangers, foreigners, aliens, men of foreign speech.

Kaiu , B.D. 143, 7, a group of gods who destroyed souls.

ka , contracted, tight, narrow; Copt ϭⲱⲟⲩ.

kai , , , P. 1116B, 62, to think, to think out, to devise, to meditate, to speak, to repeat, to say, cry out, call out, tell out, to sing; varr. , , , B.D. 144, 3, , A.Z. 1906, 125.

ka-t , IV, 365, , , , , thought, meditation; , A.Z. 1901, 45, , , thought of the heart.

Kaa , B.D. 98, 8, a god, bringer of offerings.

ka , , , , P. 607, N. 619, , T. 88, , image, genius, person, double, character, disposition, the vital strength of the Ba-soul (, B.D. 30B, 4, the ka residing in the body); plur. , , , T. 258, 307, , . The word has some of the meanings of the Coptic ⲕⲱ, the Greek εἴδωλον, and the Latin genius. Sometimes seems to mean "name," , Rhind Pap. 24. Late forms, and , Rev.

kau , , Hymn Darius 24, the kau of the living in the Other World, living human beings in this world.

ka, associated with the Ba-soul and the Sekhem or vital strength, , P. 112.

ka — **ḥem ka**, minister of the ka, the priest of the ka; **ḥe-t ka**, , , III, 139, , B.M. 138, 1, the house or chapel of the ka; plur. .

ka, phantom (?) , Shipwreck 114, A.Z. 1908, 65, "this ghost (or phantom) island."

Ka, T. 39, a proper name (?) "the blossom proceeding from Ka."

Ka, Mission 13, 123, "the father of the fathers of the gods," *i.e.*, , and see **Khemenu.**

Kait, Mission 13, 123, consort of , and one of the four elemental goddesses = ; she was the grandmother, , of the gods.

kau, T. 88, , N. 618, the kau of ; , B.D. (Saïte) 110, 3.

Kaau, Rec. 31, 169, a group of gods (?)

Ka, Ombos I, 85, a god of offerings.

Kau, Ombos I, 186, one of the 14 kau of Rā.

kau, L.D. III, 194, 13, the 14 kau of Rā = , word of power; , light; , strength; , power; , vigour; , abundance; , majesty; , burial; , preparedness; , stability; , sight; , hearing; , feeling, perception; , taste. The Ombos list (I, 186–188) is as follows:— (1) ; (2) ; (3) ; (4) ; (5) ; (6) ; (7) ; (8) ; (9) ; (10) ; (11) ; (12) ; (13) ; (14) .

Ka-em-ānkh-neteru, Ṭuat XII, a serpent-god; see **Ānkh-neteru.**

Kaḥerka, IV, 44, , A.Z. 1901, 129, the goddess of the 4th month; Copt. ϫⲟⲓⲁϩⲕ, ϫⲟⲓⲁⲕ.

Kaḥerka, , , the ϫⲟⲓⲁϩⲕ festival; plur. .

kaḥerka, , a pot or vessel used at the Khoiak festival.

Kaḥetep, T. 176, , M. 158, N. 65, , N. 112, , T. 284, , P. 54, , M. 32, B.D. 128, 6, a god of offerings, a form of Osiris.

Kaḥetep, the name of a festival.

Ka Shu, Ṭuat I, a pilot of the boat of Rā.

kau, U. 220, P. 404, M. 577, N. 1183, , food, provisions, sustenance, supplies; , my daily food (or bread).

Kau-urit, Ombos II, 131, a goddess.

ka = , to be high.

ka-t, place (?) district (?)

ka-t, M. 202, N. 681, Pap. 3024, 62, work, labour, toil; plur. ; see Suppl. 1231; , in process of building.

kau-ti, A.Z. 1899, 37, , A.Z. 1902, 114, , A.Z. 1899, 37, , workman, labourer, artisan, craftsman; plur. , L.D. III, 140B, A.Z. 1899, 37, .

ka-t Ṭeḥuti, "works of Thoth," *i.e.*, writing, sculpture, painting.

ka-t shu-t, a herb used in medicine.

ka, P. 77, 646, , N. 1039, , Rev. 12, 11, , Rev. 13, 5, bull; plur. , Rec. 29, 148, , T. 389, , M. 404, , T. 334, , N. 704, , Thes. 1288; , bull for sacrifice; , Palermo Stele, white bull; , red bull; , IV, 195, 695, bull of the herd.

ka àtcher, young bull, calf; Copt. ⲕⲧⲏⲣ.

Ka nekht, "mighty bull"—a title of kings.

ka req, a "cut" bull; Copt. ⲕⲁⲗⲟⲩⲕⲓ.

Ka, Düm. Temp. Inschr. 25, a god of letters and learning, one of the seven sons of Meḥurit.

Ka, U. 635, the bull with a light in his eye.

Ka, Berg. I, 18, a calf-god.

Kauarsh, Cyrus; Heb. כּוֹרֶשׁ.

Kai (?), Rec. 16, 106, one of the watchers of Osiris.

Kaui, U. 538, T. 317, , the double Bull-god.

Kaui, Ṭuat III, the two bull-gods who form the ends of the boat of the Earth.

Kau, Rec. 27, 218, 31, 14, , Rec. 26, 226, bull-gods.

Ka àakhu, Mythe 4, , Denderah IV, 84, , Berg. II, 8, a bull-god, warder of the 1st Pylon.

Ka Àmentt, Ṭuat X, the bull of the Ṭuat, *i.e.*, Osiris.

Ka Ànu, Denderah III, 19, the Bull-god of Denderah.

Ka àru, Ṭuat III, a god.

Ka Àsàr, B.D.G. 102, a form of Osiris.

Ka ānkh, Lanzone 1212, a bull-god of .

Ka āshemu, N. 165, Bull of the gods—a title of the "Great God."

Ka ur, B.D. 178, 7, "Great Bull"—a title of the God of heaven.

Ka ur ḥu Kens, U. 178, the Bull-god of Nubia.

Ka pesṭ neteru, "Bull of the nine gods."

Kamut-f, Rec. 29, 164, , Hymn Darius 27, , Metternich Stele 154, , A.Z. 1905, 30, "bull of his mother," the name of several self-begotten gods; Gr. Καμῆφις.

Ka meshru, N. 165 . . . .

Ka Nut, U. 452, a title of Geb.

Ka n-erṭa-nef nebȧ-f, one of the guardians of the body of Osiris.

Ka Nekhen, U. 416, , T. 237, a title of Horus.

Ka neteru, Ṭuat I, a singing-god.

Ka neteru, T. 307, a title of .

Ka Rā, U. 577 a four-horned mythological bull; var. , N. 966.

Ka renp, bull that reneweth his youth—a title of the Sun-god.

Ka hemhem-t, Ṭuat VI, a roaring lion-god.

Ka ḥenti, B.D. 53, 1, a bull-god.

Ka khepreri, B.D. 163, 9, a title of Ȧmen.

ka shesp-t, Rec. 30, 67, the name of a part of the tackle of a boat.

Ka Kam ur, U. 306, the Bull-god of Kamur.

Ka taui, Denderah IV, 84, , Mythe 3, , Berg. II, 8, the god of the 2nd hour of the night.

Ka thai Kauit, B.D. 141, 23, the Bull of the seven divine Cows.

Ka Ṭuat, Ṭuat I, a singing-god.

Ka ṭer, Hh. 101, one of seven spirits who guarded the body of Osiris.

ka-t, Ebers Pap. 94, 17, , Rec. 27, 88, , vulva, vagina, mother; , concubines, women in general.

ka-ti, the gravid uterus.

Kat Tefnut, N. 970, the vagina of Tefnut.

kai-t, , cow; plur. , Rec. 27, 58.

ka-t, A.Z. 1905, 36, , Rec. 33, 5, cow, a female animal; plur. , B.D. 142, III, 25, ; , the two cows Isis and Nephthys.

Kauit VII ( ), B.D. 148, the seven divine Cows and their Bull.

ka-t (?), a plant.

kau (?), a fruit or seed.

kau, Shipwreck 48, radishes (?)

kaa, IV, 1096, brown stone objects.

kaȧ, boat, cattle boat.

kaȧri, goat; plur. ; var. A reading suggested for was "kamali," *i.e.*, camel.

Kaȧrik, B.D. 165, 3, a Nubian (?) name of Ȧmen.

kai, , Ȧmen. 24, 7, though, even though, assuredly.

kai, IV, 695, gum (?) oil-seed (?)

kai-t, , dung, filth, excrement; var. .

kait, B.D (Saïte) 64, 18, ape; plur. , Shipwreck 165; var. .

ka, A.Z. 1900, 37 . . . .

kau, , , , , , to be high.

kauati, A.Z. 1899, 36, workman (?) workman's title (?); var. , , .

kaushana, Anastasi I, 24, 5, part of the harness of a horse.

Kab, the name of a god = (?)

kabi, to weep, to lament, to mourn.

kabi-t, B.D. 18, D, 4, mourning, lamentation.

kabu, , , a measure for liquids.

kaḥusa, , footstool; Heb. כֶּבֶשׁ, 2 Chron. ix, 18.

kap, P. 79, M. 109, N. 22, , , Rec. 27, 222, 30, 194, , Leyd. Pap. 11, 1, , , , , , Dream Stele 21, , , to perfume, to cense.

kap, M. 706, censings.

kap-t, , , , incense; Gr. κῦφι.

kapu, Rec. 22, 103, vase for incense

kap, Shipwreck 43, , P.S.B. 14, 205 shelter, place of concealment.

kap-t, U. 513, , IV, 901, , , furnace, oven, bakery; plur. , T. 325.

kapkaput, a kind of bread or cake.

kap, kapu, , , hollow of the hand, sole of the foot; plur. , Mar. Karn. 54, 55, ; compare Heb. כַּף, Arab. كَفّ, Syr. ܟܰܦܳܐ, Copt. ϭⲟⲡ.

kap-t, A.Z. 1908, 17, a kind of amulet.

kap, U. 258, N. 718, , ,

, Rec. 2, 116, to hide, to conceal, to cover with clothes, to dress; Copt. кнп.

Kap, Berg. II, 13, a title of the goddess Nut.

Kapu, the name of the 9th day of the month.

kapu, Rechnungen 35, hunter, snarer, lier-in-wait; plur.

kapu, Nile 5, 1–4 . . . . . .

Kap, the crocodile of Set.

kapi = .

kap, to be dirty, dark, foul.

Kapu, a title of Set as fiend, enemy, lier-in-wait, lurker.

Kapur, Rougé I.H. 125, 26, a Libyan foe of Rameses III.

kapus, to oppress, to suppress; Heb. כָּבַשׁ.

kapnut, A.Z. 1908, 8, IV, 707, boats of Byblos in Syria.

Kapni, a man of Byblos.

kaf = , to drive off, to chase away, to dispel, to disperse.

kafr, village, hamlet; Heb. כָּפָר, Arab. كفر, Syr. ܟܦܪܐ, Assyr. (Rawl. C.I. II, 32, 3, 10).

kam, Peasant 182, IV, 895, to end, to bring to an end, to finish, to complete; Thes. 1483; , endless; to end years; , A.Z. 1905, 25, the end of a moment; , A.Z. 1900, 130; , A.Z. 1900, 132, for ever.

kam-t, Shipwreck 118, the end, end of a period, completion, a finish; Åmen. 6, 3, Åmen. 9, 3, 20, 2.

kami[t], finished products.

kam, Pap. 3024, 9, 8 . . . . . .

kamkam, Thes. 1199, to vanish, to pass away, to disappear, to decay.

kam, kami, to be black; Copt. кⲁⲙⲉ.

kamm, Rev. 13, 15, 14, 10, to be black; Copt. кⲙⲟⲙ, кⲙⲉⲙ.

kam-t, T. 26, N. 208, a black thing, black; , strong black, *i.e.*, jet black; , black and white; Copt. кⲁⲙⲉ.

Kammåu, with , Jour. As. 1908, 285, Egyptians.

kami-t, books of the black land, *i.e.*, Egyptian literature.

kami-t, Rev. 14, 65, black cow; , black cattle.

Kam-ur, Rec. 27, 190, the Red Sea.

Kamȧmut, M. 772 (bis) = , P. 661, , P. 776, a black animal-goddess (?)

Kam-ā, Denderah IV, 61, B.D.G. 720, a hawk-god of .

Kam-ur, P. 605, a bull-god; , Rougé I.H. 158, the divine Kamur bulls.

Kam-ur, N. 648, , T. 274, a fort or town (?)

Kam-ur, Ombos I, 319, the god of the lake of Kamur.

Kam-ur, B.D. 64, 13, a lake in the Ṭuat.

Kamit-urit, T. 274, P. 27, M. 38, , N. 67, , M. 141, a goddess.

Kam-neb-mesen-t (?), Denderah I, 30, a lion-god.

Kam-ḥer, Rec. 31, 29, "Black face"—a title of the crocodile Rerek.

kam , , buckler, shield.

kam , , black wood.

kam-t , , , , black stone or black powder.

kam-ti , , image, statue.

kamt-t (var.), grain plant; plur. , .

kamu , , seeds or fruit of the kam plant.

kam , , , , , , , Rev. 4, 76, , , , garden; plur. , , , Rec. 21, 15, , Anastasi I, 25, 4, ; Heb. כֶּרֶם, Copt. ϭⲱⲙ.

kamut , Hh. 457, , , wheat, grain; Heb. קֶמַח (?); , , wheaten bread.

kam , vine; Copt. ϭⲙⲉ.

kamu en ȧrp , vineyard.

kami , , , gardener; plur. , A.Z. 1900, 36; , ; Copt. ϭⲙⲉ.

kamā (?) , Anastasi I, 23, 5, A.Z. XV, 36, Alt-K. 32; compare Heb. כְּמוֹ, as, like.

kam'ȧar, kamȧl , , , A.Z. 1906, 21, camel; plur. , P.S.B. 12, 83; Heb. גָּמָל, Syr. ܓܡܠܐ, Arab. جَمَل, Eth. ገመል:, Copt. ϭⲁⲙⲟⲩⲗ, ϫⲁⲙⲟⲩⲗ. The word , has also been regarded as a plural of kam'ȧar, and read kamaliu.

Kam'itha, L.D. III, 160, 165, a Hittite proper name.

kam'r, Gol. 3, 13, to skip, to dance, dancer.

kam'råa, Alt-K. 983, tooth.

kam'ḥu-t, , , Anastasi I, 17, 6, IV, 14, 2, 17, 6, bread made of fine wheaten flour; var. ; Heb. קֶמַח, Arab. قَمْح, Eth. ቀምሕ:

kam's, Düm. H.I. I, 24, 25, 39, 40 . . . .

kamen, A.Z. 1873, 17, , , Åmen. 24, 9, , dark, cloudy, misty, gloomy, lowering, black, blind; compare Heb. כָּמַן, Arab. كَمَن, Syr. ܟܡܢ.

kamtcharna, Mar. Karn. 55, 61, armour.

kani (kami), Peasant 263, gardener.

kanu (kamu), , (here = mu), vineyard, garden; Heb. כֶּרֶם.

kanu, reed; Heb. קָנֶה.

kanḥi, shrine; plur. ; Copt. ⲕⲛ̄ϩⲉ, Gr. κόγχε.

kanka, Rec. 16, 152, Auswahl 12, 34, a log of wood, beam, balk.

kanektu, IV, 672, a log of wood, beam, balk.

kar, frog; Copt. ⲕⲣⲟⲩⲣ.

kare, Ḥerusâtef Stele 48, a sanctuary vessel.

karr, Ḥerusâtef Stele 55, , , Nåstasen Stele 35, a vessel or measure for incense; Copt. ⲕⲉⲗⲱⲗ (?)

kar, object, thing, instrument, tool, utensil, apparatus, furniture, goods.

karkar, IV, 667, anything round, staff, stick, roll, cylinder; Heb. כִּכָּר.

karkar, , A.Z. 1880, 95, stone boulders; compare Heb. גַּל and גִּלְגַּל and כִּכָּר.

kar, karå, N. 160, , Rec. 27, 227, 31, 17, , , , , , , , , Rec. 19, 96, shrine, sanctuary, chapel; plur. , , , , gods of the same sanctuary.

Karåut, B.D. 84, 4, the gods of a shrine.

kar, kari, , , , Åmen. 10, 11, boat, fishing boat, skiff; plur. , Koller Pap. 3, 7; Heb. כְּלִי, Isaiah xviii, 2.

kari, Thes. 1254, , gardener; plur. , .

karå-t, place of restraint, prison; Heb. כֶּלֶא.

Karåmemti (?), Nesi-Åmsu 32, 30, a form of Āapep.

Karȧstt, B.D.G. 1079, a goddess of Panopolis with the attributes of Rāit and Tefnut.

kari[t], B.D. 64, 7, shrine, sanctuary; and see **kar**.

kari, Rec. 30, 217 .....

kari, Rec. 19, 92 ......

karistātes = εὐλογιστής, A.Z. 51, 93.

karuai, a call, outcry; Heb. √קָרָא.

Karpus, Bibl. Ég. V, 211, a proper name; compare Heb. כַּרְפַּס.

karf, Rev. = , guile, fraud; Copt. ⲕⲣⲟϥ.

karm, Rev. 13, 102, crown; Copt. ⲕⲗⲟⲙ.

karm, , Rev. = Copt. ϭⲱⲣⲙ.

karm'tȧu, Koller 4, 6, a kind of stone used in inlaying bracelets, etc.

kareḥtȧ, , , (?), a measure (?) pannier, basket.

karsa, , , cordage, sacking, rope-work.

karsha, Jour. As. 1908, 310, fraud, deceit, guile; Copt. ⲕⲱⲣϣ.

karshatȧ, cake, loaf, bread; Gr. κυλλάστις.

karkartȧ, lamb; Heb. כַּר.

karkartȧbuȧa, Koller 4, 5, objects made of leather (?)

kartha, , , cord, lace, thong of a whip.

kartha, Love Songs 2, 1, a kind of goose.

kaha, Rec. 10, 64; see .

Kaharsa, etc., B.D. 164, 4, a title (or name) of Sekhmit-Bast-Rā.

kahi[t], terror, awe.

kaheb, Ḳubbân Stele 5, to smite, to strike; var. .

kaheb-ḥetch-t, a kind of incense.

kahem, Ḳubbân 4, to smite, to strike.

kahes, grief, sorrow.

kahes, Peasant 213, to cry out.

kas, Nȧstasen Stele 37, a sanctuary pot or vessel.

kasab, Rec. 15, 141, reed-work, mat (?)

Kasika, B.D. 165, 3, a name of Ȧmen.

kash, IV, 335, a product of Punt, the pearl oyster (?); compare Copt. ⲕⲁϣ- in ⲕⲁϣⲁⲃⲏⲗ.

Kashi, Nubian, a Sûdânî man; Copt. ⲉϭⲱϣ, ⲉⲑⲱϣ.

Kashit, Nubian woman; Copt. ⲉϭⲟⲟϣⲉ, ⲉⲑⲟϣⲓ.

kak in , Hh. 201.

kaka , Leyd. Pap. 13, 2, , Rec. 10, 62, plant with a bitter taste; compare Gr. *κίκι* (Herodotus II, 94), *κίκινον*. The Heb. קִיקָיוֹן, has also been compared with **kaka**.

kaka-t , boil, blain, pustule, carbuncle; Copt. ⲕⲱⲕ.

kaka , Nâstasen Stele 40........

kaka , darkness, night; Copt. ⲕⲁⲕⲉ; var. .

Kaka , Berg. I, 17, a god.

kakai (kaki) , Jour. As. 1908, 289, darkness.

kaka , worm, serpent.

kakmen-t , Rec. 21, 91, a vessel.

katȧ , runner, driver, charioteer (?)

katu (?) , caldron, boiling pot, kettle; Copt. ⲕⲁϫⲓ (?)

katem, katem-t , fine gold; var. , Ȧmen. 18, 12; Heb. כֶּתֶם.

kath , IV, 973 = **ka-t** .

kath , pot, vessel, a kind of dye (?); plur. .

katha , Edict 22, , Tutānkhȧmen 7, a plant from which a dye was made; Copt. ϭⲟⲩϭ, ϫⲟⲩϫ, Lat. carthamus tinctorius (?)

katha , the seed of the above plant.

katha , an instrument or tool of bronze.

katha , charioteer, driver.

kathab , pot, vessel, vase.

kathan , Rec. 17, 145, L.D. III, 219E, 14, , driver, charioteer, caravan leader.

kathatȧ , a cloth made of linen or wool or hair, covering, garment; Heb. כְּסוּת.

katch ; see .

katcha , Nâstasen Stele 36, a vessel, pot.

katchai ; see and .

katchen , charioteer, leader of the baggage waggons of an army or of a caravan; , chief overseer of waggons.

kȧ , Hh. 385 = .

kȧ , U. 69 = , N. 328, to bow.

kȧ = , another (masc.).

kȧ-t = = , Jour. As. 1908, 249, another (fem.)

kȧa , P. 439 = , M. 655.

kȧa , boat.

kȧu , U. 211, , U. 273, to acclaim, greet (?)

kȧu , P. 109 = , M. 75, etc., to move (?)

kȧu uā , Rev., another; Copt. ⲕⲉ ⲟⲩⲁ.

kȧri, A.Z. 1906, 21, P.S.B. 13, 32, goat (?) mule (Rec. 8, 85); , Wört. Suppl. 1277; var. .

kā, a precious stone used in inlaying; var. .

kā, Rev. 12, 116, to leave.

kāf, Rev. 11, 88, to overthrow.

kāmȧ, Rev. 12, 119, injury, violence.

kāmi, Rev. 12, 117, to injure.

kārti-t, Rev. 13, 26, butcher's knife, goad.

ki, B.D. 163, 6, Thes. 1204, a particle of asseveration, also, moreover.

ki, , , masc. other, another; , one to another; , one embraces the other; , Nȧstasen Stele 61, another place; , another chapter; , another person; , once again, another time; , , another, *i.e.*, a variant, reading; , Ȧmen. 17, 3, once again; Copt. ⲕⲉ.

keti, B.D. 153, 11, , , , fem., another, the other; ..... , B.D. 153, 11, one .... the other; , other matters; , others.

kiu, kui, IV, 330, , IV, 85, , , , , others; , other kings; Copt. ⲕⲟⲟⲩⲉ.

Ki, Thes. 818, a hawk-headed bull-god.

ki-t, Rec. 32, 82; var. ....

kiariu, L.D. III, 140c, carriers of gold.

kiu, Shipwreck 165, apes.

kimi, , hen; Copt. ϭⲁⲓⲙⲉ.

kināmu bundle; Heb. כִּנְעָה.

kirshu-t, cakes, loaves; var. .

Kirgipa, A.Z. 1880, 82, a princess of Mitani. Tall al-'Amârnah Tablets Gi-lu-khi-pa.

kish, to smelt (?); Copt. ϭⲱϣ.

kith, to perish, be destroyed.

ku, U. 96, 291, 534, T. 179, P. 93, 647, M. 129, Rec. 14, 165, 34, 178, pers. pron. 2nd sing. masc.; with nouns in dual .

ku, , others.

ku, P. 104, M. 71; var. , N. 73, to move.

ku-t (?), Rec. 32, 82; var. ......

kunut, fig tree; Copt. ⲕⲛ̄ⲧⲉ.

kuȧ, , , , , , pers. pron. 1st sing.

kufi (kef), Rev. 13, 4, 26, ape (?) = ; compare Heb. קוֹפִים, 1 Kings x, 22, 2 Chron. ix, 21.

kureshtȧ-t , A.Z. 1869, 147, bread, cake; Gr. κυλλάστις.

kuqȧuf , Rev. 12, 66, fir-cones; Copt. ⲕⲟⲩⲕⲟⲩⲡⲁⲣⲓⲁ.

kuth (?) a kind of bread.

keb , arm, shoulder; , the two shoulders.

kebb , U. 325, 534, to coil up (of a serpent).

keb-t , the arch of the sky, vault of heaven.

Kebit , Rev. 14, 7, goddess of heaven.

Kebatchaȧ , A.Z. 1849, 78, Cambyses; Pers. , Bab. , Gr. Καμβύσης.

kebu ; see , sandals.

kebu , B.D. (Saïte) 36, 1, to open.

keben-t , , , A.Z. 1908, 8, , a large sea-going boat, a ship of Byblos; plur. , A.Z. 1908, 8, , , Rec. 6, 8, , Rec. 22, 2.

kebes , , cypress.

kep , , , hollow of the hand or foot; Heb. כַּף, Copt. ϭⲟⲡ.

keput , Thes. 1201, , P.S.B. 10, 15, Mar. Karn. 54, 46, hands cut off from slain enemies; , Mar. Karn. 54, 54.

kepi , Rev. 12, 37, cloud; Copt. ϭⲏⲡⲉ.

kep , hiding place, refuge.

Kep-ḥer , B.D. 151, a god.

kep , Rev. 13, 56, to seize; Copt. ϭⲱⲡ.

kepu, keput , , , hunters, snarers.

kepri , Rev. 14, 40 = = Copt. ⲕⲏⲡⲉ, chamber, furnace.

kef , Rec. 31, 20, knife.

Kef-pesesh , N. 252A, , an instrument used in performing the ceremony of opening the mouth; var. , .

kefa , , to spit out, to pour out, to flow.

keff , to pour out, to vomit, to escape (of a fluid).

kefau , vomit.

kefa , U. 568, Rec. 31, 163, Shipwreck 60, Peasant 56, , Ebers Pap. 94, 11, , , , , , , , , , , , , , , to lay bare, to denude, to unclothe, to divest, to strip, to deprive, to spoil, to dismantle, to unveil, to uncover, to unfold, to pull off (wigs); , none at all.

kefa ȧb , , loyal, devoted; plur. , IV, 1116; , Leyd. Pap. 2, 9.

kefa, hinder part, backside, rump, tail; plur. , , Hearst Pap. 5, 13, 8, 16; , backs (of the leaves of a tree); Copt. ϫⲁϥ (?)

kefai, kefi , , to be naked, uncovered, despoiled.

Kefaiu , B.D. 145, 79, a group of gods.

keft .... , Peasant 321 ....

kefa , Israel Stele 2, , , , , , to drive away, to put an end to (a storm).

kef-t , IV, 1139, , Rec. 1, 50, a seizure; , Pap. 3024, 139, .

kefā , IV, 663, 893, , IV, 711, , Edict 22, to seize, to grasp, to capture, to collect taxes, to plunder; see .

Kefāu , IV, 35, "capturer"—a title; plur. , Mar. Karn. 54, 45, troops, soldiers.

Kefi , Ṭuat X, a warder-god.

keftu , a ship of Keft, *i.e.*, Phoenicia; plur. , IV, 707, .

Keftenu , Berg. I, 20, an ape-god; var. .

kem , Rev., total = .

kem , Rev. 13, 9, to behave correctly.

kemu , L.D. III, 219E, 9 = .

kem-t , Rev. 12, 49, lamentation.

Kem , Ombos I, 186, one of the 14 kau of Rā.

Kemkem , B.D. 75, 4, a god.

kemkem , Rev. 13, 26, to be strong, to prevail; Copt. ϭⲙϭⲟⲙ.

kema-t , a weeping woman.

Kembåthet , A.Z. 1849, 78, Cambyses.

Kemnu , Annales I, 85, one of the 36 Dekans; Gr. ΚΟΝΙΜΕ.

kemḥ = **gemḥ** , to see.

kemes = , ear of corn.

ken , , , , , , to be angry, to feel indignation, to revile, to curse; , to blaspheme the name of God; compare Heb. קָנָא.

kenå-t , , wrath, anger, reviling, curse, abuse; compare Heb. קִנְאָה.

kenåu , , cursings, hatred.

Kenit , B.M. 191, a Syrian goddess, a form of Qeṭshit, who appears as a naked woman.

kenn, moisture, liquid.

kenn, reed; Heb. קָנֶה.

kenken, P.S.B. 12, 83, to sing to a beaten drum, to clap the hands rhythmically.

kenken, A.Z. 1905, 25, to lash with the tail.

kennarut, musical instruments, harps; Heb. כִּנֹּרוֹת, 1 Kings x, 21.

Kenȧt, Ṭuat X, a goddess, consort of Seṭfit (?)

kenȧnȧur, harp; Heb. כִּנּוֹר, Syr. ܟܢܵܪܵܐ, Gr. κινύρα, Copt. ϭⲓⲛⲏⲣⲁ, Arab. كِنَّار.

kenu, Rev. 12, 39, ear of corn; Copt. ⲕⲛⲁⲁⲩ.

kennu, fatted bird.

Knufi, L.D. V, 39, a late form of; Gr. Χνέφ, Κνήφ, Κνοῦφις, Copt. ⲭⲛⲟⲩⲙⲓⲥ, ⲭⲛⲟⲩⲫⲓⲥ, ⲭⲛⲟⲩⲃⲓⲥ.

Kenbutcha, Cambyses; Heb. כַּנְבּוּזִי.

kenfā, to nip, to squeeze, to crush.

Kenmet, Berg. I, 20, an ape-god, the associate of Thoth.

Kenem-ti, Edfû I, 21, one of three holy apes.

kenem-t, B.D. 125, II, 29, A.Z. 1900, 20, darkness.

Kenem-ti, B.D. 125, II, one of the 42 assessors of Osiris.

Kenkenemmti, an ape-god, the associate of Thoth.

Kenemm-ti, Nesi-Ȧmsu 32, 25, a form of Āapep.

Kenem, Kenmem, Denderah II, 10, Zod. Dend., Tomb Seti I, Ram. II, one of the 36 Dekans; Gr. ΚΟΝΙΜΕ, ΧΝΟΥΜΙΣ.

Kenemtiu, IV, 896, the people of the Great Oasis (Khârgah).

kenem (*sic*), to break forth.

kenem-t (?), a kind of precious earth or stone.

kenemu, P. 408, M. 584, N. 1189, a sacred skin (?)

kenmut, P. 443, M. 547, a bird.

kenmut, P. 776, N. 1128, P. 661, P.S.B.A. 16, 136, ape, monkey.

Kenmut, one of the 36 Dekans; Gr. ΧΝΟΥΜΙΣ.

kenḥ, B.D. 172, 25, night, gloom, obscurity, darkness; var.

kenḥ, a name of the 24th day of the month; var.

kens (?), force, violence; Copt. ϭⲟⲛⲥ.

kens, Hearst Pap. VII, 10, Pap. 3027, 4, 7, the placenta, the "after-birth."

kensa, perinaeum.

kens, bow; Arab. قَوس (?)

Kensu, Nubians.

kenku-t, Stat. Tab. 34, IV, 707, logs of a special kind of wood.

kent, Rev. 14, 8, wrath; Copt. ϭⲱⲛⲧ.

Ker, B.D. 39, 13 = (?) an earth-god.

Kerit, Denderah I, 51, a goddess of Punt.

ker-ti, the two horns.

kerr, burnt offering; Copt. ϭⲗⲓⲗ.

kerȧ-t, shrine, chapel, coffer, coffin, chest; plur.

Kerāsher, Kalasirian; see Herodotus IV, 116.

keri-t, habitation, abode.

keriu, mules (?) goats.

kerp, Rev. 11, 188, to declare, to make clear; Copt. ϭⲱⲗⲡ.

kerf, to seize, to carry off, to pluck away; Copt. ϭⲱⲣϥ.

Ke[r]ent, Denderah IV, 79, a god.

kerḥ, A.Z. 1906, 147, Rec. 18, 182, Rev. 14, 11, night; Copt. ϭⲱⲣϩ.

kerḥ ur, the great night festival.

kerḥ netches, the little night festival.

keresh-t, Koller I, 3, Rec. 16, 72, cake, bread, loaf; Gr. κυλλάστις.

kerreshttȧ, A.Z. 1868, 146 = κυλλάστις.

Kerrshrā, Kalasirian; see Herodotus IV, 116; var.

kerk, Rev. 11, 173, 12, 11, to be equipped, equipment; Copt. ϭⲟⲣϭ.

kerek, Hearst Pap. IV, 11, a seed or fruit used in medicine.

kerker, to circle, to mark out a circle with a stick.

kerker, Rev. 14, 43, talent; Heb. כִּכָּר, Copt. ϭⲓⲛϭⲱⲣ.

keh, Thes. 1206, to smite, to strike, to throw.

keha, rebellion.

Kehai, a title of Set.

kehau, U. 606 . . . .

keheb, kehab, A.Z. 1907, ii, 15, to smite, to strike, to attack, to pillage, to overthrow.

Kehab, a title of Set.

kehes, disgust, chagrin.

kehet, Rec. 2, 147, a kind of tree

keḥ, to act gently or slowly.

keḥa, N. 506, a cake offering.

Keḥau, U. 509, T. 323, in the proper name

Keḥau, Litanie 60 . . . .

keḥu, Ebers Pap. 39, 4 . . . . . .

keḥen, cup, vessel.

keḥna (?), A.Z. 1905, 108, night, darkness.

keḥsi, Demot. Cat. 18 . . . .

keḥek, Rec. 4, 134, to be old, aged, senility.

keḥkeḥ, Mar. Aby. II, 36, Rec. 16, 57, Anastasi I, 2, 1, to be old.

keḥkeḥi, old man, old age.

Keḥkeḥ, the "aged one"—a title of Thoth.

keḥkeḥ-t, Westcar 7, 19, age, aged.

Keḥkeḥit, B.D. 75, 4, a goddess; see **Seksekit**.

K-khert (?), a star in the Ṭuat, Ṭuat VII.

kes, P. 204, (?) Rec. 27, 59, Rev. 11, 137, to bow, to do homage; to force a woman.

kesu, bowings.

kesȧu, P. 9, 703, P. 341, bowings, homage.

kesu, N. 1361, Rec. 27, 217; var. homage.

kes, kesȧ, N. 328, 648, M. 143, U. 68, T. 393, M. 407, to bow, to do homage, to submit.

kess, U. 442, T. 29, to bow, to do homage.

keskes, P. 605, to do homage.

keskes, A.Z. 1906, 123, to dance, dancing.

keskes, to rub down unguent.

keskesu, A.Z. 1905, 101, to take short flights, to flap the wings.

Kes, Tomb Ram. III, 58, a god; varr. Cairo Pap. 4, 2.

kes, Rec. 36, 162, to lie, to deceive.

keskes, Rev. 14, 13, to chatter foolishly, to jest; Copt. ⲕⲁⲥⲕⲉⲥ.

ksantha, Rev. 11, 180, yellow; Gr. ξανθα.

kesb-t; plur. P. 200, N. 936, P. 669, M. 779, Anastasi IV, 2, 11, a kind of fruit tree, sycamore-fig tree (?)

kesb-t, the fruit of the above tree.

kesfen, a mineral.

kesem, IV, 1075, to turn aside, to lose the way, wandering, error.

kesem, Rev. 14, 10, stormy; Copt. ϭⲱⲥⲙ.

Kesmiu nen-t, B.D. 78, 44, a group of gods in the Ṭuat.

Kesem heh Ȧmentt, Ombos II, 134, a mythological being.

kesh , to sprinkle, to moisten.

keshu , , a seed or fruit used in medicine.

Keshtt , Ombos I, 84, a deity who presided over the products of Cush.

Kesh-t ..... , Ombos II, 246, a god (?)

keshp , Rev. 13, 26, 14, 19, to be hot, dry (?)

kek , to praise, to applaud.

kek = .

kek , Thes. 1201 ......

kek , heat, flame, fire.

Kektiu ..... , a class of stars.

kek, kekȧ , U. 50, 533, , , , , , , , , , , , , Rev. 11, 183, darkness, gloom, obscurity; Copt. ⲔⲀⲔⲈ.

keku reruti , the outside darkness.

keku smau , , , , deepest gloom or darkness, absolute blackness.

Keki , , , darkness personified, one of the four elemental gods; see **Khemenu.**

Keku , Ṭuat VIII, a god in the Circle Seḥert-baiu-s.

Kekit , , , , darkness personified—one of the four elemental goddesses.

kek , the dark water.

Kek , , Edfû I, 80, a title of the Nile-god.

kek , Thes. 1201, a plant; plur. .

kek neḥes , Rec. 4, 21, Nubian bark; Copt. ⲔⲞⲨⲔⲈ.

kek-t , a gnawing animal or insect, weevil (?) shrewmouse (?); compare Copt. ⲔⲈⲔ.

keki , Rev. 14, 10, a gloomy-faced man.

kekit , Rev. 14, 22, darkness.

Kekr , B.D. 39, 13, a god who judged Āapep.

kekrer (?) , , A.Z. 1872, 107 ....

kekes , A.Z. 1873, 15, , to dance; see .

ket , , to be small or little, tiny, helpless, abject; , small; Copt. ⲔⲞⲨⲒ.

ketit , , , , , babe, child, girl, boy, small, little; plur. **kettiu** , Leyd. Pap. 4, 2, , Ḥeruemḥeb 3, ; , not small ones.

ket ȧb , Rec. 3, 3, IV, 390, 932, modesty, timidity, thought, design.

ket , , , another; , another; , another (fem.).

ket , Nȧstasen Stele 60, other things, property of others.

ket-akh (kh-t) , , , , , IV, 1089, , other things, other people's things.

ket-kha-t , Rev. 13, 59, other; plur. , ; , Rec. 21, 78, the other chiefs; Copt. ⲕⲉⲭⲱⲟⲩⲡⲓ, with ⲡ and ⲡⲓ.

ket kha-t , shaft of a pillar; var.

ket , , , baldness.

ketȧ-t , cooking pot; plur. , U. 51; see .

ketu , Nȧstasen Stele 4, 6, also; Copt. ⲕⲉ.

ketu-t , cooking pot; plur. , T. 323.

ketu-t , B.D. 17, 33, , ibid. 31, weapons of slaughter, gods of the divine cooking pots.

ketui-t , , B.D. 167, 26, cooking pot; plur. , Litanie 65.

Ketui-ti , Tomb of Seti I, one of the 75 forms of Rā (No. 65).

Ketuitt ṭent ba , Ṭuat II, a lioness-goddess.

ketfi = , serpent, reptile.

ketn , Rev. 11, 168, tunic; Gr. χιτών.

keteshtȧ , bread, loaf.

ketket , to stammer, to stutter.

ketket , to beat, to shake; Copt. ϭⲉⲧϭⲱⲧ.

ketket , A.Z. 1900, 31, 1905, 25, 37, to walk with short quick steps, to quake.

ketket , Nȧstasen Stele 49, , ibid. 43, pectorals, neckbands.

ketket , a kind of herb or plant.

keṭ , Ȧmen. 25, 2 = .

ketchaketcha , to kill, to throw down; Copt. ϭⲉϫϭⲟϫ.

G

g = Heb. ק and ג and Copt. ϭ.

g[a] , IV, 767, Annales III, 109, , IV, 613, , Metternich Stele 58, , A.Z. 1900, 28, , Rec. 29, 155, , , , to be in distress, to suffer want, to lack air, to be choked, suffocated; , , a constricted windpipe; , a narrow way or path; , exhausted (?)

g[a] , , Metternich Stele 170, 171, a suffocated child.

ga, gau , T. 277, , T. 181, , P. 903, , , , P. 1116B, 26, , , , , , , , to be in sore straits, to be in great need, to suffer want, to be obstructed, shut in, blockaded, deprived of something, to be empty of; Copt. ϭωογ, ϭηγ, χηογ.

gau — en gau , Pap. 3024, 64, without.

ga-t , , , , , want, need, poverty.

gau-t , Greene II, 24, , Thes. 1209, want, need.

gai , , , needy one.

Ga àsut , B.D. 142, 4, 14, a title of Osiris.

ga , B.D. 102, 2, strain (?) contraction (?)

ga-t , , Rec. 4, 30, , , , , , , , , , coffer, chest, coffin, shrine, receptacle, basket, cradle; , IV, 334, baskets.

Ga nu sa Àst , "cradle of the son of Isis"—a name of Apollinopolis Magna.

ga , unguent or unguent pot.

ga , throw-stick, boomerang.

gaa , T. 293, , to overturn (pun on the name).

ga , , , a kind of bull; , Koller 3, 6, young ga bulls.

ga-t , , B.D. 164, 13, claw (of a lion).

ga , , to sing, to sing to a musical instrument.

gaga , , , to cry (of a bird), to cackle; var. .

Gaga ur , B.D. 56, 2, 59, 2, "Great Cackler"—a title of Geb.

gaut , , B.D. 28, 4, 99, 23, thoughts (?)

ga , , Thes. 1202, , Annales IX, 155, to see, to look; varr. , .

gaga , Love Songs 5, 11, to ogle, to "make eyes at."

Gagait (?) , Ombos II, 130, a goddess.

gaȧ-t , shrine, chapel.

Gaȧubekh .... , Canopus Stele 32 = τὰ Κικήλλια.

Gaā .... , Ombos II, 132, a goddess.

Gai , Ṭuat VI, a god.

gai[t] , Rechnungen 66, bottle, wine-pot; , P.S.B. 13, 411, to work the bottle, *i.e.*, to get drunk.

gai , , , Ȧmen. 17, 6, to smear, to bedaub.

gai-t , A.Z. 1906, 30, , Love Songs 2, 9, a strong-smelling unguent made from the cyperus (?); varr. , ; .

gai-t , , , , Annales IX, 156, , , , , cyperus; var. , the seed or berries of the same; Copt. ⲕⲓⲱⲟⲩ.

Gait , , , B.D. 263, a lake full of scented flowers in the Ṭuat.

gai , Rev. 13, 22 = Copt. ϭⲓ in ⲟⲩⲉⲗⲗϭⲓ.

gai , kind, manner, style of.

Gaisers , Καισαρος, Caesar.

gau-t , Anastasi I, 23, 7, , defile, a mountain pass.

gaua , N. 628, , Ȧmen. 21, 4, , to blockade, to besiege; see , T. 340, .

gaua , to sing, to praise; var. .

gaua , , a kind of horse, stallion (?)

gauana , Israel Stele 6, sacks, bags to hold clothes; Copt. ϭⲟⲟⲩⲛⲉ.

gauasha , Rec. 14, 11, , , , Thes. 1200, , to break, to smash.

gauasha , Mission I, 607, , , to turn away, to expel, to pluck out, to cut down (of trees); , A.Z. 1880, 95.

gauaten , Anastasi I, 24, 6, IV, 3, 1, , Koller 3, 2, to tie, to bind, to tie together, to repair.

gauf-t , a seed used in medicine (?)

gaum (?), Berg. I, 30, to be weak, fatigue, weakness, helplessness.

gab, Love Songs 1, 11, 5, 3, arm; dual , Thes. 1201, , Festschrift 117, ; varr. , ; Copt. ϭⲃⲟⲓ, ϫⲫⲟⲓ.

gab, place of rest.

gab, B.D. 149, 7, 4, to look with evil design, malign glance.

gab, L.D. III, 229C, , to be weak, to be sick, feeble, to fail in health, defective (in quality), short (in weight), exhausted, tired, adversity, misery; Copt. ϭⲃⲃⲉ, ϫⲉⲃⲓ, ϭⲟⲟⲃ, ϭⲱⲃ, ϫⲱⲃ, ϫⲉⲃⲓⲱⲟⲩ; Sphinx 14, 221, a bad year; , Love Songs 4, 5.

gabu, Rec. 21, 90, a thing of no value.

gabi, to be wretched, miserable, weak, helpless.

gabgab, to be broken or overthrown, to be dashed in pieces; see and ; Copt. ϭⲃⲃⲉ.

gabga[b]iu, Rev. 6, 111, the slain, those overthrown in battle = and .

gab-t, A.Z. 1907, 125, , A.Z. 1905, 19, , leaf, leaves, foliage; Copt. ϭⲱⲃⲉ.

gab-ti, B.D. 172, 15, hair, tress, foliage.

gabun, tired, wearied.

gabesbes, Sallier Pap. II, 13, 15 . . . .

gabgu, a kind of goose.

gap, Anastasi 4, 2, 10, Koller 2, 1, 8, to catch (?) to seize (?)

gafi, IV, 949, , Koller 4, 3, , a long-tailed monkey, the pratas monkey, ape (cercopithecus); plur. , Shipwreck 165, , B.D. 136A, 5, , Litanie 64; see ; compare Heb. plur. קֹפִים, 1 Kings x, 22 = קוֹפִים, 2 Chron. ix, 21, Gr. *κῆβος*, *κῆπος*, *κεῖπος*.

Gaf, the Ape-god—a form of Rā.

gaf, to knead dough, to force, to compel; , Åmen. 12, 17.

gafgaf, a kind of bread or cake.

gamai, an oily plant.

gami-t, hen (?); Copt. ϭⲁⲓⲗⲉ (?)

gamḥ, to see, to look upon, to perceive; see .

gan ⟨hieroglyphs⟩, ⟨hieroglyphs⟩, weak, helpless, soft, fluid (of unguent).

gann ⟨hieroglyphs⟩, ⟨hieroglyphs⟩ ⟨hieroglyphs⟩, Anastasi I, 23, 5, Koller 5, 3, to faint, to drop with fatigue, to be helpless, weak; see ⟨hieroglyphs⟩; Copt. ϭⲛⲟⲛ, ϭⲏⲛ, ϫⲏⲛ, ϭⲛⲟ.

gann ⟨hieroglyphs⟩, tongue (?)

gann ⟨hieroglyphs⟩, B.M. 5639A, 16, lamp-stand (?)

ganu ⟨hieroglyphs⟩, ⟨hieroglyphs⟩ ⟨hieroglyphs⟩, reed, marsh flower; see ⟨hieroglyphs⟩; Heb. קָנֶה.

ganuiu ⟨hieroglyphs⟩, A.Z. 1900, 33, water plants.

ganraga ⟨hieroglyphs⟩, Mélanges 3, 2, 153, but read **gantga** ⟨hieroglyphs⟩ ⟨hieroglyphs⟩ = ⟨hieroglyphs⟩ ⟨hieroglyphs⟩, to transfer, to translate, to render; compare Heb. עָתַק.

gansa ⟨hieroglyphs⟩, Åmen. 8, 20, 13, 11, 18, 17 . . . .

gangar ⟨hieroglyphs⟩, ⟨hieroglyphs⟩, to sing; Copt. ϭⲛϭⲛ, ϫⲉⲛϫⲉⲛ.

gar ⟨hieroglyphs⟩, purse, bag, wallet.

gar ⟨hieroglyphs⟩, Rev. 12, 9, lie, false-hood; Copt. ϭⲟⲗ.

gara (?) ⟨hieroglyphs⟩, Anastasi IV, 14, 5, fire, furnace (?)

garagantesi ⟨hieroglyphs⟩, Rev. 12, 67, gourd, pumpkin; Gr. κολόκυνθος. Glossed by Copt. ⲕⲁⲗⲁⲕⲁⲛⲑⲓ.

garbu, garpu ⟨hieroglyphs⟩, Koller 2, 1, ⟨hieroglyphs⟩, Alt-K. 1059, ⟨hieroglyphs⟩, Anastasi I, 26, 5, ⟨hieroglyphs⟩, to hammer, to rework, to bolt together; compare Heb. כָּלַף.

garp-t ⟨hieroglyphs⟩, dove, a kind of pigeon; Copt. ϭⲣⲟⲙⲡⲉ.

garḥ ⟨hieroglyphs⟩, night, darkness; Copt. ϫⲱⲣϩ.

garsetep (?) ⟨hieroglyphs⟩, a kind of medicinal unguent.

garta ⟨hieroglyphs⟩, ⟨hieroglyphs⟩, ⟨hieroglyphs⟩, ⟨hieroglyphs⟩, a medicinal plant and the unguent made from it; Copt. ϭⲁⲣⲁⲧⲉ.

gartchana ⟨hieroglyphs⟩, a pronged instrument; Heb. קִלְּשׁוֹן, 1 Sam. xiii, 21.

gaḥ ⟨hieroglyphs⟩, ⟨hieroglyphs⟩, ⟨hieroglyphs⟩, ⟨hieroglyphs⟩, to rest, to be weary.

gaḥes ⟨hieroglyphs⟩, ⟨hieroglyphs⟩, gazelle, antelope; fem. ⟨hieroglyphs⟩; plur. ⟨hieroglyphs⟩, Koller 3, 6, ⟨hieroglyphs⟩; Copt. ϭⲁϩⲟⲥ.

gas ⟨hieroglyphs⟩, ⟨hieroglyphs⟩, ⟨hieroglyphs⟩, ⟨hieroglyphs⟩, ⟨hieroglyphs⟩, to smear, to anoint; Copt. ⲟϭⲥ.

gasu ⟨hieroglyphs⟩, anointings.

gas ⟨hieroglyphs⟩, Berg. I, 56, embalming chamber; var. ⟨hieroglyphs⟩.

Gasut ⟨hieroglyphs⟩, N. 975, the Bull-god of heaven.

gas ⟨hieroglyphs⟩, ⟨hieroglyphs⟩, Love Songs 7, 6, grief, mourning, stiff, stiff-necked; var. ⟨hieroglyphs⟩

gas ⟨hieroglyphs⟩, Peasant 162, to go out of repair, to fall away; var. ⟨hieroglyphs⟩.

gasar, ring, signet; plur. , Copt. ⲕⲥⲟⲩⲣ, ϣϭⲟⲩⲣ.

gasf-t, a seed or fruit used in medicine.

gash, A.Z. 1868, 9, , to spill, to pour out, to sprinkle, to bedew, a pouring out, inundation.

gash, to flatter, to wheedle; Copt. ⲕⲱⲣϣ.

gash, , reed; plur. , A.Z. 1900, 30, , ; var. ; Copt. ⲕⲁϣ.

gashu, Rec. 21, 96, a bird.

Gaqit (?), Ombos II, 132, a goddess.

gatȧ-t, , a kind of cake or bread.

gatȧ, , salve, ointment, unguent; var.

gatha, Ȧmen. 13, 5, to smite, to strike, to be violent (?)

Gaṭa, B.D. (Saïte) 78, 19, a god.

gȧ-t (?), Décrets 29, a kind of bread.

gȧu, , cyperus; Copt. ⲕⲓⲱⲟⲩ.

gȧu, a sculptor's wallet.

gȧf, ape, monkey; plur. in Heb. קֹפִים or קוֹפִים.

gȧḥi[t], Mission 13, 7, a kind of plant.

gā, gāi, , a kind of precious stone.

gā, Jour. As. 1908, 255, to wait; Copt. ϭⲱ.

gāa, censer; Copt. ϫⲏ.

gāi en ānkh, Rec. 13, 36, the act of living; Copt. ϭⲓⲛⲱⲛϩ.

gārāb, Rev. 12, 68, the sea cray-fish or spiny lobster, the Palinurus (?), perhaps also the stag-beetle; Gr. *κάραβος*, glossed by *καραβ*.

gāḥ, to reach out, to stretch out, to extend.

gāḥ, chapel, shrine.

Gāsantrā, Rev. 11, 180, Cassandra; Gr. *Κασαντρα*.

gāgā (gaga), Rev. 12, 39 = ⲕⲁⲕ in ⲁϣⲕⲁⲕ.

gi, Rev. 13, 58 = *τὸ προσήκον*.

gi, form, like, manner, character.

gi unema, Rev., the act of eating; Copt. ϭⲓⲛⲟⲩⲱⲙ.

gi en ȧu, the act of coming; Copt. ϭⲓⲛⲉⲓ.

gi en ānkh, Jour. As. 1908, 271, the act of living; Copt. ϭⲓⲛⲱⲛϩ.

gi en uben, Rev. 13, 40, rising.

gi en reg, Rev., running away.

gi en sef, Rev. 12, 108, the manner of yesterday.

gi en tchara, Rev. 13, 103 . . . .; Copt. ϭⲓⲛϭⲁⲗⲟ (?)

gi su, Rev. 12, 115, drinking; Copt. ϭⲓⲛⲥⲱ.

gi segerḥ, Rev., condition of peace.

gi, throne, steps, high place, terrace.

gi, to be corrupt, to perish.

gi-t, Rec. 4, 21, a plant or herb;

gi, mason, artisan.

gir, Jour. As. 1908, 268, seat, throne; Copt. ⲕⲟⲗⲗⲉ (?)

giti, Rev. 12, 26 . . . . . . ; Copt. ϭⲏⲟⲩ.

gitcha (?), hand (?); Copt. ϭⲓϫ (?)

gu, a kind of cattle.

gu, sack, bag, basket; plur., L.D. III, 16A, baskets [of tribute].

gui-t, coffer, chest.

gu-t (?), a kind of workman; plur., Gol. Hamm. 11, 76.

gu, cyperus of various kinds: of, of, of, of, of, and of the Oasis; cyperus berries; Copt. ⲕⲓⲱⲟⲩ.

gu, Rev. 11, 174, Rev. 12, 49, Jour. As. 1908, 248, to be choked, to be blocked up, to be restrained or constrained; Copt. ϭⲱⲟⲩ, ϭⲏⲟⲩ.

gua, to besiege, to shut up, to shut in, to blockade, to put under restraint; var.

gua, Hh. 487, tightness or twisting of the chest, a disease.

gua-t, box, a place of restraint.

gui, altar.

gui, honour, praise.

gug, to abuse (?); IV, 1104, each cursed the other.

geb, A.Z. 1906, 147, Love Songs 4, 6, a kind of goose.

Geb, U. 210, N. 936, Rec. 32, 87, an Earth-god, the son of Shu and Tefnut, the husband of Nut, and the father of Osiris, Isis, Set, Nephthys, Horus. As the creator of the Cosmic Egg he is called the "Great Cackler,"; Gr. Κήβ. Later forms are: Rec. 17, 94, A.Z. 1906, 147–149.

Gebb, U. 382, A.Z. 1906, 148, the Earth-god.

Geb, Rec. 27, 87 = or = or; see note in Rec. 17, 94.

Geb, Ṭuat X, a god who came out of the chain that fetters Set, and who fettered Uamemti.

Geb, Tomb of Seti I, one of the 75 forms of Rā (No. 15).

Geb, Ṭuat VI, a jackal-headed stake of torture.

Geb, Denderah IV, 80, Quelques Pap. 93, an ithyphallic god akin to Menu.

Gebai, *i.e.*, Menu of Coptos.

Geb in, in, in, Mar. Aby. I, 44.

Geb ur, Ṭuat XII, a form of Horus of the East.

Geb khenti khat pesṭ-t, Hh. 242, Geb, chief of the nine gods.

Geb qenbti, Ṭuat II, a god with a knife-shaped phallus.

Geb, B.D. 99, 7, god of the celestial ocean.

geb (for), the celestial ocean or Nile.

Gebit, Berg. II, 13, the goddess whose bowed body forms the sky.

geb, geba, arm; a piece of ground; dual; Copt. ϭⲃⲟⲓ, ϫⲫⲟⲓ.

gebb, A.Z. 1906, 149, earth, ground.

geb, T. 388, M. 404, a bundle of spice.

geb, IV, 367, 372, sacks of grain.

geb-t, leaf, leaves, buds; Copt. ϭⲱⲃⲉ.

geb, to fail, to collapse, to be helpless; Copt. ϭⲃⲃⲉ.

gebi, Demot. Cat., to be weak, to collapse; var., Jour. As. 1908, 300; Copt. ⲕⲱⲱⲃⲉ, ϭⲃⲃⲉ.

gebiu, Rev., helpless folk.

gebgeb, T. 310, M. 126, Rec. 30, 192, Rec. 8, 136, Stat. Tab. 39, to overthrow, to slay; the overthrown, slain; Copt. ϭⲓⲃϭⲓⲃ.

gebgebi, IV, 658, a defeated and overthrown enemy.

gebgebit, dead bodies.

gebgeb, deformed, lame (?) a disease of the leg.

gebgebi, ant (?); Copt. ϭⲁϫⲓⲃ.

geba = .

geba, B.D. 149, VII, 4, to cast evil or threatening glances.

geba, B.D. 144, 12, tree, foliage, booth (?)

gebir, Rev. 12, 57, great man; compare Arab. كبير.

gebir, Rev. 11, 168, web, tissue.

gebga, Hh. 472, Rec. 26, 225, ibid. 26, 228; varr., a kind of goose.

gebt, throne, throne chamber.

gebṭ, two arms; see .

gep, U. 496, P. 164, M. 328, N. 859, to rain, to flood.

gep , , , flood, storm, inundation; , a flood of water.

gep , nausea, sickness, a fit of vomiting.

gepȧut Rev. 11, 181, feet; Copt. ϭⲟⲡ.

gepu , Sphinx Stele 12, an evil glance (?)

gepes , Suppl. 1297 . . . .

gef , Rev. 13, 84, vengeance, avenger; Copt. ⲕⲃⲁ.

gef , IV, 1120, , , , , U. 423, ape, monkey; plur. , T. 242, , , Litanie 64; compare Heb. plur. קוֹפִים, קֹפִים.

Gefut , U. 423, , T. 242, the ape-gods of heaven.

gefen , IV, 1139, A.Z. 1908, 132, to revile (?) to abuse (?)

gem, gemi , , , , , , , , , , , , U. 515, , to find, to discover; , U. 200, T. 78, M. 231, N. 610, , ; to find a mouth, *i.e.*, to speak; Copt. ϭⲓⲛ, ϭⲓⲛⲉ, ϫⲉⲙ, ϫⲓⲙⲓ.

gemi-t , , , Pap. 3024, 155, something found; plur. .

gemm , , P. 360, N. 1073, to find; , to find a way or means, *i.e.*, to effect something.

gemgem , Mar. Karn. 52, 16, , Anastasi I, 28, 3, , B.D. 113, 2.

gemgem , Verbum I, 336, 2, to search out, to investigate, to reckon up.

gem usher , Ebers Pap. 18, 1, 89, 1, "found illegible or destroyed,"—a scribe's note indicating a lacuna in the text.

Gemi , Berg. I, 13, a god who found places for the dead.

Gemut , , Rec. 29, 147, a group of gods (?)

Gem ḥusu , B.D. 177, 3; see .

Gemu ḥeru , B.D. 58, 3, a group of gods.

Gem ḥesu , U. 363, , B.D. 177, 3, , A.Z. 1900, 27, , IV, 943, , , , , a name or title of Rā.

gemi , , , to be sorrowful, in despair.

gemgem , , to pant, to breathe with difficulty.

gemut , , , , , mourning, grief, mourners (?)

gem , , Rev. 12, 11, strength, power, might; Copt. ϭⲟⲙ.

gemgem , , N. 877, , Rec. 26, 227, 228, , , P. 342, , Shipwreck 59, , Leyd. Pap. 3, 4, , A.Z. 1905, 37,

, Love Songs 1, 2, 7, 12, , , to break, to smash, to crush, to seize, to touch, to handle, to try by the taste or touch.

gem-t , a bird; plur. .

gemi , , a herb, garden plants.

gemi , Hh. 9 . . . .

gemu , Koller Pap. 3, 8, a kind of precious stone.

gemaḥ , to weigh, to grasp, to enclose, to bind.

Gematcha , Demot. Cat. III, 247, 4, Cambyses.

gemȧ , Rev. 14, 100, garden.

gemā , Rev. 13, 64, evil; Copt. ϭⲟⲟⲙⲉ.

gemuḥ , , to see, to perceive, to scrutinize; see **gemḥ**.

gemnen , Rev. 15, 102, cumin; Heb. כַּמֹּן, Gr. κύμινον, Arab. كَمّان.

gemr , Rev. 11, 169, , Rev. 11, 174, camel; Copt. ϭⲁⲙⲟⲩⲗ.

gemḥ , , , , , , , to see, to look, to perceive; var. .

gemḥ-t , sight, glance, look.

gemḥ-t , , wick of a lamp; plur. , .

gemḥ , , A.Z. 1867, 107, to weep, to mourn.

gemḥ-t , , , , weeping woman, wailing woman, widow.

gemḥ-t , , IV, 200, the hair over the temples or by the sides of the head; , B.D. 146, 15, 1, hair, foliage; , crown of the head.

gemḥ , A.Z. 1908, 120, leaves of trees, foliage.

gemḥu , P.S.B. 13, 317, I, 99, part of a shrine; , two stones for doors of a tomb.

gemsh , hair, lock, tress.

gen , P. 562, , U. 491, bull; var. , N. 915; plur. , B.D. 69, 13.

gen-t , N. 979, , , P. 364, N. 1078, , , , , L.D. III, 194, 27, memorial, record, archive, memorandum; plur. , Rec. 31, 25, , A.Z. 1880, 49, , IV, 500, , , , Tombos Stele 15, , , IV, 1183, , Mar. Karn. 52, 20, , Thes. 1285, annals.

gengenu , Rougé I.H. 256, records, archives, annals.

gen , , reed, plant; plur. , Leyd. Pap. 4, 14, , water plants; var. ; Heb. קָנֶה.

gengen-t, Peasant 32, , a seed or plant used in medicine.

Genur , N. 979, , B.D. 14, 4, a god who presided over offerings; varr. , .

Gengen ur , B.D. 54, 2, , the Goose-god who laid the Cosmic Egg; var. (Saïte) .

Gen urit , a goddess of offerings.

Gen ḥesu , P. 204; see .

gen , A.Z. 1899, 95, a copper object.

genu , metal pots or vases.

gen , , to cry out, to beg, to beseech; , petitioner; Copt. ϭⲛⲟⲩ.

genn , Jour. As. 1908, 259, to be gentle or gracious; Copt. ϭⲛⲟⲛ.

gen , , to be weak, helpless, limp.

genn , , , , , , to be weak or helpless, to be paralysed or spellbound; Copt. ϭⲛⲟⲛ, ϭⲏⲛ, ϫⲏⲛ, ϭⲛⲟ.

genn , , Rec. 33, 6, weaknesses, defects, troubles.

genu , IV, 502, helpless man, weak; plur. , weak beings or things.

gen-t , Jour. As. 1908, 276, heap, abundance; Copt. ϭⲛⲱⲟⲩ.

gennu , L.D. III, 65A, 14, lamp-stands, candlesticks, stands for offerings.

genu , , a kind of bird, crane (?)

genbut , , a man with woolly hair (?); plur. , IV, 695, , , , a people of Punt.

genf , A.Z. 45, 132, to revile, to abuse.

genmȧ , Jour. As. 1908, 293, = , friend, fosterer.

genmu , U. 498, , T. 319, servants, vassals.

genkha , Westcar Pap. 7, 3, to work (?)

genkha , IV, 86, to be subject to, to toil under orders (?)

genkha , Tombos Stele 16, , star, luminary; plur. , , Rec. 27, 225, A.Z. 1908, 131, 29, 52, 53.

genkha pe-t , dove, pigeon; Copt. ϭⲣⲟⲙⲡⲉ.

gensh , wing; see .

gent , B.D. 38A, 6, slit, wound.

gent , , to be wroth, angry; var. ; Copt. ϭⲱⲛⲧ̄.

ger , , , Rec. 21, 86, P.S.B. 31, 13, also, further, moreover, but; is often written wrongly for , *e.g.*, Nâstasen Stele 30.

ger-t , Rec. 31, 173, 33, 29, , B.D. 64, 22, but; Copt. ϭⲉ.

gert (?) , a kind of rat, mole (?); Heb. חֹלֶד, Gr. ἄλλος (?)

ger , , , to furnish, to found, etc.; see .

ger (gerg) , , possessor, owner, master; var. .

Ger teka , , a god of .

Ger ṭes , , a god of .

ger , , , to lie, falsehood; see .

ger , Åmen. 7, 7, 9, Rec. 31, 165, , Love Songs 3, 4, to be still, silent; Copt. ϭω.

ger re , silent-mouthed.

geru , Peasant 211, , the silent man, *i.e.*, a poor man.

geru (gergu) , Rev. 8, 141, subjects.

gerr , U. 498, T. 319, to run away, to flee in terror.

geru , hunters.

gerger , to destroy, to demolish.

ger , balsam plant or tree; , Décrets 108, incense.

gerut , scented unguent.

ger , Rev. 12, 26, buckler, shield; Copt. ϭλ.

geri , Rev. 13, 34, bolt; Copt. κηλ, κελι.

gerr , , Rev. 13, 76, burnt sacrifice, offering; Copt. ϭλιλ.

gerā , Rev. 13, 33, strip of cloth, rag (?)

gerā , to drive away, to reject; Copt. ϫωωρε.

gerā-t , a kind of wooden weapon or tool.

geri , Rev., pilgrim; Copt. ϭοιλε, Heb. גֵּר.

geriu , Love Songs 4, 9, a kind of bird.

geri , wig, headdress.

grugus , Rev. 12, 69, crocus, saffron; Gr. *κρόκος*.

Gerbatus , L.D. III, 160, the name of a Hittite.

gerp , Rev. 13, 29, to be wrapped up.

gerp , Jour. As. 1908, 302, to reveal; , to reveal a matter; Copt. ϭωλπ.

gerem , garland, crown; Copt. κλομ.

germi , a kind of wild plant used in medicine, wild parsley; Copt. κρⲁⲙ (carthamus silvestris).

germpi , dove, pigeon; Copt. ϭρομπι.

grenbeṭ , P.S.B. 1888, 373 = .

gerḥ , A.Z. 1905, 29, , Leyd. Pap. 5, 13, Rechnungen 43, , to cease, to come to rest, to die down (of the wind), finished.

gerḥ , , , , , , , , , , , , , , , Rev. 11, 126, , , , , night, darkness; plur. , T. 339, N. 626,

, P. 537, , , A.Z. 1905, 22; , a whole night; Copt. ϭⲱⲣϩ. For the 12 hours of the night see Thes. 28.

Gerḥ , Ṭuat V, Night, a black vaulted figure in the kingdom of Seker.

Gerḥ , one of the four elemental gods; see **Khemenu.**

Gerḥ , the Night-god, night personified.

Gerḥit , one of the four elemental goddesses, consort of Gerḥ, a personification of night.

Gerḥ en åp-t renput , B.D. 25, 3, the "night of counting years," night of judgement.

Gerḥ en årit såp-t, etc. , B.D. 18F, the "night of counting up the dead," night of judgement.

Gerḥ en āḥa-ā , B.D. 18, 3, night of the battle between Horus and Set.

Gerḥ en utchā meṭut , B.D. 19, 10, night of weighing words and deeds.

Gerḥ en Haker , B.D. 18E, 3, night of Haker.

Gerḥ en ḥati , L.D. IV, 67, night wherein a tear of Isis dropped into the Nile and caused the Inundation; Arab. Lêlet an-Nukṭah. The modern festival of the "Night of the Drop" was celebrated on the 11th day of Paoni (June 17).

Gerḥ en khet khau , B.D. 18, 3, night of fights.

Gerḥ en kheb ta , B.D. 18F, night of the ceremony of ploughing up the earth after it had been soaked in blood.

Gerḥ en sāḥā sennu en Ḥeru , B.D. 18C, 4, night of erecting the pavilion of Horus.

Gerḥ en sāḥā Ṭeṭ em Ṭeṭu , B.D. 18A, 4, night of setting up the Ṭeṭ pillar.

Gerḥ en setcher Åst resut , B.D. 18D, 4, watch-night of Isis.

Gerḥ en shesp Ḥeru meskhen neteru , B.D. 19, 10, night of the resurrection of Horus.

Gerḥ en sheta åru , B.D. 18H, night of the secret ceremonies (of Osiris).

Gerḥit , the name of a mythological serpent.

Gersi , B.D. 144, the doorkeeper of the 18th Pylon.

gersh , a plant used in medicine.

gershtå , a weapon (?)

gersheri , "young man," "Kalasirian" (Herodotus IV, 116); Copt. ϩⲡ̄ϣⲓⲣⲉ (?)

gerg , to occupy, to take over something; Copt. ϭⲱⲗ.

gerg , P. 833, , N. 775, , T. 345, P. 609, N. 148, , Thes. 120, , Rec. 20, 40, , , , , , , , , Barsha 2, XXI, , A.Z. 45, 125, to found, to establish, to settle a country or district, to make ready or habitable, to equip, to furnish, to prepare; , well founded; Copt. ϭⲱⲣϭ, ϭⲣⲏϭⲉ.

gerg per, to found a house, to marry; , IV, 97, to found or set up a statue; , L.D. III, 140B, to found a town; , L.D. III, 140B, to stablish heaven and earth; , Mar. Aby. I, 7, 68, towns colonized by Egypt.

gerg-t, , , , , possessions, equipment, furniture, furnishing, mastery of a house; plur. , house furniture; , Ḳubbân Stele 12.

gergi, , , possessor, landlord, overlord; , founder of this earth; , landlord of the Two Lands, *i.e.*, of all Egypt.

gergut, kinsfolk, posterity.

gergut, P. 162, M. 252, (?), Hh. 465, , Hh. 563, Rev. 6, 29, homesteads, settlements.

gergu, parts of a ship.

gerg-t, I, 78, fishpond, ornamental water.

gerg, , , , , to lie; varr. , ; Copt. ϭⲟⲗ.

gerg-t, , , , , , lie, falsehood, untruth; plur. , , , IV, 970, ; , A.Z. 1879, 51, highly coloured lies; Copt. ϭⲟⲗ.

gergi, Thes. 1482, , IV, 971, liar; plur. , L.D. III, 140E, IV, 1078, , , Rec. 35, 126, ; , IV, 971, speakers of lies.

gert, Rev., sword; Copt. ϭⲟⲣⲧⲉ.

gertȧ, , , Rev. 13, 104, finger ring.

geḥ, Rev. 13, 89, , Rev. 13, 39 = , chapel, shrine; Copt. ⲕⲛ̄ϩⲉ.

geḥ, , , Rec. 31, 27, to be weak, helpless.

geḥu, helpless ones.

geḥ, a disease of the feet.

geḥes, , , A.Z. 1866, 99, , Rec. 29, 148, , , , , IV, 171, gazelle; fem. , , Rev. 11, 150; var. , Copt. ϭⲁϩⲥⲓ, ϭⲟϩⲥⲓ, ϭϩⲟⲥ, ϭϫⲟⲥ, ϣϫⲟⲥ.

Geḥsit, a gazelle-goddess.

geḥes, Leyd. Pap. 8, 5, , Westcar 2, 1, , Westcar 12, 5, toilet-case, box, chest.

ges, , , Palermo Stele, one half; , one year and a half; Copt. ϭⲟⲥ, ϫⲟⲥ, ϭⲓⲥ, ϫⲉⲥ.

ges, , , U. 209, 490, P. 97, 191, M. 362, N. 914, 1142, , T. 208, the side; , east, *i.e.*, left side; , west, *i.e.*, right side;

, the south; U. 580, one on this side, one on that side; dual , P. 182, , P. 667, 776, , N. 891, , , the two sides; , the two sides of a house; , both sides of a boat; , all sides; plur. , N. 976.

ges — en ges for ,

er ges , , , by, near; **er gesui** , U. 585, on both sides; **ṭat ḥer ges** , IV, 971, 1090, , Thes. 1482, to set oneself on one side, *i.e.*, to show favour or partiality.

ges , IV, 362, , the upper part of an obelisk, *i.e.*, the pyramidion.

gesi , he who is at the side, bystander.

ges , , fold, resting-place of a flock; , shepherds' pens; , IV, 1114, town enclosures.

gesu , , men employed in government storehouses.

gesi , , , to stride, to run; Copt. ϭⲟϫⲓ.

ges-t , P. 376, N. 1151, , A.Z. 1908, 118, course, stride; plur. ; , lord of running, the jackal.

gesges , , , , , , to increase, to overflow, to fill to overflowing.

gesges , A.Z. 1873, 131, gifts (?)

ges , Rev. = , to tie, to bind.

ges , Ebers Pap. 106, 4, , , , , , , , , , to smear with oil or unguent, to anoint; , IV, 688, rubbed with oil.

gesu , unguent, oil.

gesges , , to mix ointment.

gesges , , , , , to measure.

gesa , to measure with cord.

gesa , Peasant 312, , , , to fall (?) to waver, to be untrue (of scales), falsehood.

gesa , Rev. 11, 148, to be troubled.

gesa , a kind of stone.

Gesi , Cairo Pap. IV, 2, a god.

gesu , , , flatulence, a disease (?); Copt. ϭⲱⲥ.

gesu , hide, skin.

Geseptiu (?) , Thes. 59, the gods of the 7th day of the month.

gespekh , a kind of bread or cake.

gesfen , Ebers Pap. 48, 13, 60, 7, , ibid. 65, 3, a seed used in medicine.

gesem, Rev., windstorm; Copt. ϭⲟⲥⲙ.

gesem, rainstorm, flood; Copt. ϭⲱⲥⲙ, ϭⲟⲥⲙ.

gesr, Rec. 1, 52, , Rev. 17, 146, bunch, bundle, measure.

gesḥu (?), U. 324 . . . .

gestȧ, IV, 503, , , Peasant 305, , , Rec. 6, 127, , , scribe's writing palette; , ebony palette.

Gestȧ, , , one of the four sons of Horus; see **Ȧmest, Mestȧ.**

gestir, Rec. 4, 121, unguent (?)

gestep, to protect (?)

gesth, to run, to stride; Copt. ϭⲟϫⲓ.

gesṭ, , to run, to stride; Copt. ϭⲟϫⲓ.

gesṭeb; var. (?) . . . .

gesh, , to pour out, to sprinkle, to bedew; Copt. ϫⲱϣ.

gesh-t, a pool, lake.

geshȧ, reed, rush; varr. , , ; Copt. ⲕⲁϣ.

Geshi, a form of the Sun-god.

geshp, Rev. 13, 29, to recite magic prayers; compare Heb. כָּשַׁף.

geg, the bark of a tree; Copt. ⲕⲟⲩⲕⲉ.

geg, the cry of the goose or of the "divine hawk" ( ); see .

geg = = , to eat.

geg, , , , , , B.D. (Nu) 64, 19, to peep, to pry into, to look with curiosity, to wink the eyes.

get, , fish-pool; Copt. ϭⲱⲧ.

get, an unguent.

Getȧ, Ṭuat VI, a god in the Ṭuat.

geti, a fruit.

geten, heap, pile (?); Copt. ϫⲁⲧ-ⲙⲉ (?)

geteg, Rev. 12, 66, to move rapidly.

getcham, Rev. 12, 26, a handful; Copt. ϭⲁϫⲙⲏ.

T

t = Heb. ת and Copt. ⲧ.

t , , , , thou, thee.

t = , bread, loaf, cake.

t , IV, 890, while, whilst, when, as, because, since, during.

t = , to give.

t , staff, support; var. .

t (?) , Gen. Epist. 63, misery, wretchedness.

ta , , demon. pron. "this," later the fem. article; Copt. ⲧⲁⲓ, ⲧⲏ.

ta , Rev., this; Copt. ⲧⲏ.

ta , , moment, time; see **at** .

ta , Rev. 13, 75, time; Copt. ⲧⲏ.

ta-t , part, portion (in arithmetic).

ta , T. 392, , M. 406, , , , , , , , , Rev. 11, 181, , ground, land, earth, world, soil, dust; Copt. ⲧⲟ, ⲑⲟ.

ta-t , Nâstasen Stele 10, land, country.

taui , , , , , , , , , , , , , , A.Z. 97, 73, 74, the Two Lands, *i.e.*, South-land and North-land, or Upper and Lower Egypt, the former being the realm of Horus, , and the latter that of Set, , Rec. 15, 150.

taiu , , , , , , , Jour. As. 1908, 291, lands, the world; , U. 573, N. 967, the four quarters of the world.

ta with **ḥetch** , , "earth lightening," *i.e.*, dawn, daybreak.

ta with **sma** , B.D. 1B, 2, , B.D. 17, 47, 49 = , to bury in the earth.

tau , P. 829, landsmen, people of a country, men, folk.

Tauiu (?) , , people of the Two Lands, *i.e.*, Egyptians.

Ta-merȧu , the people of the land of the Nile-flood, *i.e.*, the Egyptians.

ta-temu(?), tamu (?) , , IV, 1076, , Ḥeruemḥeb 5, , , Ȧmen. 22, 11, all the men and women inhabiting a country, population.

Ta Ȧabetch , T. 274, "land of the head-box of Osiris"—a royal title.

Ta ȧakhu , land of the Spirits, a part of the Central or Southern Sûdân.

Ta ur , the east, the right side of a ship, starboard.

ta ber , , , unenclosed or waste land, foreign land.

Ta meḥ, , the land of he North, the Delta, Lower Egypt.

Ta neḥeḥ, , , "Land of Eternity," *i.e.*, the grave.

Ta neter, "Land of the God," the southern part of the Eastern Desert and Arabia.

Taiu nu neteru, B.D., "Lands of the Gods," *i.e.*, Arabia and other countries to the east of Egypt.

Taui Rekhti, B.D. I, 16, 18D, 3, etc., the countries of Isis and Nephthys; var. , , .

Ta kharu (or **Åa**) , B.D., land (or, island) of the kharu birds.

ta sebek, a kind of earth, clay.

ta shu, Rev. 14, 51, uncultivated land.

Ta shemā, the land of the South, the South, Upper Egypt.

Ta , , the primeval Earth-god, husband of the Sky-goddess .

Tatiu, B.D. 49, 19, Earth-gods as opposed to sky-gods .

Ta, Ṭuat III: (1) the Earth-god; (2) , a district god, Ṭuat VIII; (3) , the god of a Circle.

Ta åakhut, Ṭuat VI, the abode of Osiris in the Ṭuat.

Taui Åger, Pap. Ani 2, 9, the districts of the Ṭuat of Memphis and Heliopolis.

Ta ānkhtt, land of Life, *i.e.*, the Ṭuat, the cemetery, the grave.

Ta uāb, the Pure Land, *i.e.*, the Ṭuat.

Ta ur, B.D. 40, 5, Great Land, a part of the Ṭuat.

Ta mes tchet, B.D. 140, 7, a title of the Ṭuat.

Ta en maāt, 163, 12, "land of Truth"—a name of the kingdom of Osiris.

Ta en maā kheru, Ani 1, 27, "land of Truth-speaking," a name of the kingdom of Osiris. For , "land," , "island" may perhaps be read.

Ta nefer, B.D. 140, 5, "beautiful Land," a title of the Ṭuat.

Ta ḥe-t ānkh, Ṭuat VI, the abode of Osiris in the Ṭuat.

Ta ḥer-sta-nef, Pap. Ani 2, 5, a title of Osiris.

Ta Sekri, Ṭuat V, the domain of Seker.

Ta shet, Ombos I, 319, "Land of the Lake," *i.e.*, the Fayyûm.

Ta sheta, B.D. 22, 3, "the hidden Land," *i.e.*, the Other World.

Ta qebb, B.D. 61, 8, "Land of Refreshing," *i.e.*, the Ṭuat.

Ta tubå (Tautbå ?), a god of food.

Ta tebu, B.D. 85, 15, a district in the Ṭuat; var. .

Ta Ṭuat, the land of the Other World.

Ta Ṭeser, , the "holy Land"; see **Ta Tcheser**.

Ta tcheser, T. 175, , P. 121, , M. 157, , N. 110, B.D. 182, 12, "the holy Land," *i.e.*, the Ṭuat.

Ta tchet, "Land of Eternity," *i.e.*, the Ṭuat.

ta, , , fluid of some kind, drink (?)

ta, Rev. = = = , to journey.

ta, U. 97, N. 375, , T. 335, , , , , , , , , , , , , , , , bread, loaf, cake, a cake made of fruit, *e.g.*, , V, 161, mulberry bread; , B.D. 169, 21, 22, the four cakes of Sekhem and Āqenu; , B.D. 189, 20, the seven cakes; , T. 344, the three meals of heaven; , the two meals of earth.

tata, , , sacrificial bread.

ta asher, , , a kind of toasted bread presented as an offering.

Ta ȧkhem khesetch, T. 288, M. 65, N. 126, the bread incorruptible eaten by the blessed.

ta āa āa, a kind of cake.

ta uāb, holy bread (made by the god Ptaḥ).

ta Menu (?), Berg. I, 14, cakes of Menu.

ta en ȧāh, IV, 1131, bread of the moon, *i.e.*, of the month.

tau en unem, Rec. 17, 145, "eating bread"—a kind of bread.

ta en sekh-t, a "field-bread"—a kind of bread.

Ta en tchet, "everlasting bread" eaten by the blessed.

tau nefer, bread made of fine flour.

tau nefer āḥā (?), Rec. 17, 145, a kind of bread.

tau re, , Anastasi III, 2, 5.

tau ḥeru, bread of the celestials, *i.e.*, bread of angels.

ta ḥetch, a pyramid loaf of white bread.

ta sȧf, , a kind of bread.

ta ṭua, T. 63, the morning bread.

ta, , Bubastis 51, slab of stone, stone, altar slab.

Ta (?), Rec. 26, 224, , the god Thoth.

ta, , , , , Pap. 3024, 88, , , , Pap. 3024, 47, , Metternich Stele 80, to glow, to be red-hot, to burn, to be ardent, to be angry, hot, burning, to be hot, to boil (of water), fiery.

tau, taȧu, , , hot, heated, fire, flame.

tau, a fiery man, one of ardent disposition.

ta ȧb, , a man who is naturally irascible.

ta kha-t, a fiery man, ardent, irascible.

Ta re, "Fiery mouth"—the name of a mythological serpent.

ta re, enemy, foe.

Tau reṭui, B.D. 125, II, one of the 42 assessors of Osiris.

ta-t, Rougé I.H. 256, , Ȧmen. 20, 8, 21, company, assembly, crowd, mob, tribunal; , great council; , great council of the city; , council of the land; taken into court (of a case at law); Copt. ⲑⲟ.

ta, boundary.

ta, a plant.

ta, Rev. 11, 178, to defile, to pollute, to be impure.

tata, to masturbate, to pollute; var.

tataȧ-t, copulation, masturbation, sexual pollution.

Ta-t, Rev. 11, 186, the Ṭuat or Other World; see **Ṭuat.**

taȧ, demonst. pron. fem. this; see

taȧ, Rev. 11, 131 = , to adore.

Taȧtt, P. 1, N. 326, , P. 326, , N. 326, 985, , U. 66, 67, , U. 67, , T. 380, , a goddess who wove apparel for the deceased in the Other World; var. , U. 66; and see **Tai.**

taȧr, to bind, to fetter; var.

taȧt, Rev. = Copt. ⲧⲉⲧ.

taān-t, Jour. As. 1908, 238, completion.

Ta-āa-t-pa-khent, Mar. Karn. 42, 21, title of a goddess.

tai, conjunctive particle; Copt. ⲧⲉ.

tai, belonging to; **tai-ȧ**, my, mine; **tai-k**, **tai-t**, thy, thine; **tai-f**, his; **tai-s**, her, hers; **tai-n**, our, ours; **tai-ten**, your, yours; **tai-sen**, **tai-u**, their, theirs. Demotic forms are: ⲧⲁ, my, mine (Rev. 11, 124); , Rev. 11, 168, , Rev. 13, 2, his; Copt. ⲧⲱ in ⲧⲱⲓ, ⲧⲱⲕ, ⲧⲱϥ, ⲧⲱⲛ, etc.

tai, A.Z. 1905, 25, , Rec. 31, 197, to withstand, to resist; Copt. ⲧⲁⲓⲟ.

tai, Rec. 32, 84, , to clothe, to dress, to array in apparel.

tai-t, Rec. 32, 84, , a sheet of cloth or linen, sail, awning, garment, clothing, apparel; , mummy swathings.

Tai, Tai-ti, "bandaged one"—a title of Osiris.

Tait, T. 376, Rec. 27, 232, 31, 172, Rec. 32, 67, Ṭuat VII, B.D. 82, 8, Leyd. Pap. 10, 1, the goddess of weaving; varr., T. 380, N. 326.

Tait, Ṭuat VII, a star-goddess (?)

tai-t, door, gate, portal, threshold; Copt. ⲧⲟⲩⲁ.

Taitt, the "Gate," par excellence, *i.e.*, the tomb.

Taitt, Berg. II, 12, a form of Ȧment.

tai, scorpion.

taiu (?) ∩∩∩∩∩, B.D. 108, 3, fifty; Copt. ⲧⲁⲓⲟⲩ, ⲧⲁⲓⲟ.

tai-f, belonging to him, his; Copt. ⲧⲱϥ, ⲧⲉϥ.

tair, fiend, enemy; see

tai-set, belonging to her, hers; see

Tau, T. 6, P. 368, a god of apparel.

tauai, Rev. 12, 38, morning; Copt. ⲧⲟⲟⲩⲓ.

tauf, to be hot, burning, fiery.

tauf, furnace, kiln, oven.

Taurit, a hippopotamus-goddess.

tauḥ (?), Love Songs 4, 10, to sink down.

taush-t, borders, boundaries; see

tab-t, brick, tile, slab; var.; Copt. ⲧⲱⲃⲉ, ⲧⲱⲱⲃⲉ, ⲧⲱⲃⲓ.

taf, Hearst Pap. 9, 18, furnace, oven.

tamam, sack, bag, skin; var.

tamȧ, Rev. 13, 76, what is fitting, seemly; Copt. ⲧⲟⲟⲙⲉ.

tami, Rev. 14, 19, to be silent; Copt. ⲧⲱⲙ.

tamit, Rev. 13, 92, the midst of; Copt. ⲧⲙⲏⲧⲉ.

tamu, Peasant 131, some disgusting thing or quality; var.

tamen-t, Rev. = Copt. ⲧⲙⲓⲛⲉ, this manner.

Tanen, Rev. 6, 96, a very ancient earth-god; the "great Tanen."

Tanen-t, consort of Tanen, an earth-goddess.

Tanen-t, B.D. 17, 122: (1) a mythological locality; (2) an important sanctuary of Seker; (3) the burial-place of Osiris.

Ta neb-t ȧur, Ombos I, 193, a goddess of offerings.

Ta nett em khen uåa 〔hieroglyphs〕, Denderah III, 10, a title of Hathor.

Ta nett em tcheser (?) 〔hieroglyphs〕 Denderah II, 50, a name of the solar disk.

Tar 〔hieroglyphs〕, B.D. 164, 16, 〔hieroglyphs〕 Åmen. 5, 10, 12, 16, a fiend in the Ṭuat.

taru 〔hieroglyphs〕, fiends, demons, devils, enemies.

tarara 〔hieroglyphs〕, Rev. 14, 13, to rejoice; Copt. ⲧⲉⲗⲏⲗ.

Taráush 〔hieroglyphs〕, Darius; Pers. 𒁹𒈨𒌋𒁹 𒀭𒈨 𒁹, Da-a-ra-ya-va-u-sh, Bab. 𒁹𒈨𒌋𒁹 𒀭𒈨, Da-ri-ya-mush, Gr. Δαρεῖος.

Tariush 〔hieroglyphs〕, 〔hieroglyphs〕, Darius.

Tarush 〔hieroglyphs〕, Darius; var. 〔hieroglyphs〕.

Tar-Tiseb 〔hieroglyphs〕, L.D. III, 146, 5, 〔hieroglyphs〕 L.D. III, 146, 3, the name of a Hittite envoy to Rameses II.

tahan 〔hieroglyphs〕 forehead; varr. 〔hieroglyphs〕, 〔hieroglyphs〕, 〔hieroglyphs〕; Copt. ⲧⲉϩⲛⲉ.

taḥ 〔hieroglyphs〕, B.D. 110, 37, 〔hieroglyphs〕, 〔hieroglyphs〕, 〔hieroglyphs〕, to dip in water, to submerge, to plunge into water, to sink.

taḥ-t 〔hieroglyphs〕, Rec. 31, 30, submersion.

taḥ-t 〔hieroglyphs〕, 〔hieroglyphs〕, 〔hieroglyphs〕, Metternich Stele 54, 57, a Delta woman; 〔hieroglyphs〕, dwellers in the Delta marshes.

taḥ-t 〔hieroglyphs〕, Leyd. Pap. 7, 10, 〔hieroglyphs〕, 〔hieroglyphs〕, scoriae, sediment (?) scum, froth (?)

taḥua 〔hieroglyphs〕, dross, lees, dregs, sediment (?)

taḥen 〔hieroglyphs〕, 〔hieroglyphs〕, to be bright, to shine, to glitter, to sparkle; see 〔hieroglyphs〕, 〔hieroglyphs〕, etc.

takheb 〔hieroglyphs〕, sweat, any exudation or emission of the body; var. 〔hieroglyphs〕.

takhbustá 〔hieroglyphs〕, 〔hieroglyphs〕, Harris 500, 2, 4, 12, sack.

takhen 〔hieroglyphs〕, P. 229.......; var. 〔hieroglyphs〕, U. 538.

tas 〔hieroglyphs〕, Rev., harshness, abruptness; 〔hieroglyphs〕, Rev.; Copt. ⲧⲱⲥ.

Tasakhrit (?) 〔hieroglyphs〕, Treaty 29, a goddess.

Ta-sen-t-nefer-t 〔hieroglyphs〕, Ombos II, 156, 181, Tefnut, the consort of Ḥeru-ur of Ombos.

tash 〔hieroglyphs〕, P. 73, M. 103, N. 13, 〔hieroglyphs〕, 〔hieroglyphs〕, 〔hieroglyphs〕, boundary, frontier; plur. 〔hieroglyphs〕, P. 338, M. 640, 〔hieroglyphs〕, 〔hieroglyphs〕, IV, 647, 〔hieroglyphs〕, 〔hieroglyphs〕; Copt. ⲧⲟϣ.

tagaru 〔hieroglyphs〕, Ḥerusâtef Stele 33, a mineral.

tat (?) 〔hieroglyphs〕, to nurse, to suckle; var. 〔hieroglyphs〕.

Tatt 〔hieroglyphs〕; see **Taått**, U. 66.

tatutu, B.D. (Saïte) 145, 16, a kind of wood.

Tatunen, B.D. 84, 13, 180, 13, ; var. **Tatuinen**, B.D. 64, 10, 11.

Tatenen, Budge, Gods of Egypt 509 ff., an ancient Earth-god, one of the creators of the world; varr. **Tatunen, Tathunen.**

tatha, Mar. Aby. 1, 7, 57 . . . .

Tathunen, ; see **Tatenen.**

Tathenen, Ṭuat VIII, an elemental god (see) with four forms , , , .

Tathenen, Ṭuat VIII, the territory of the above-mentioned god.

Taṭara, L.D. III, 164, the name of a Hittite; var. , L.D. III, 165.

tȧ, a mark of the dual, later .

tȧ, Tombos Stele 3, on the one hand.

tȧ, Tombos Stele 3, IV, 83, staff, support.

tȧ, to beat, to break, to smash.

tȧ-t, U. 104, N. 413, a crushing, a beating.

tȧtȧ, , IV, 613, L.D. III, 65A, , IV, 621, , , , Rec. 4, 35, to break, to smash, to smite, to trample upon, to crush underfoot, to stamp upon.

tȧtȧ, Rev. 12, 95, an assembly (?)

tȧ, Rev. 13, 73, time; Copt. ⲦⲎ.

Tȧ[t], Rec. 16, 129, a goddess.

tȧ-t, A.Z. 1900, 128, , , IV, 1074, , , , , , , , Tombos Stele, 10, emanation, part, portion; plur. , IV, 53; Copt. ⲦⲞ, ⲦⲞⲒ.

tȧ, form, counterpart; , forms, images, likenesses.

tȧa, divine emanation, essence of a god; var. .

tȧ akh-t, Rhind Pap. 26, share, lot, portion.

tȧti, Khnemuḥetep 116, the two sides of a door.

tȧ-t, Jour. As. 1908, 264, part payment, share, portion; Copt. ⲦⲞ.

Tȧ, Mar. M.D. I, 20, a god (?)

Tȧ-t-sheta, Ombos I, 143, a form of Khensu.

tȧ-t, tȧi-t, , room, chamber.

tȧ, tȧ-tȧ, , , variegated; Copt. ⲦⲞⲈⲦⲞⲈ.

tȧu (?), , Rec. 4, 22, colour, paint, stones of different colours.

tȧ, tȧa, Metternich Stele, 170, , ibid. 203, , to cry out, to weep, to lament.

tȧa-t, cry, lamentation.

tȧa, Rec. 16, 57, weeper.

tȧ, , , barley; Copt. ⲈⲒⲰⲦ, ⲒⲞⲦ.

tȧui, , P.S.B. 24, 44, pair of sandals; see **tui**, .

tȧui, tu, tut , varr. , , , , A.Z. 1913, 144, abso. pron. 2nd sing.

tȧurȧn , walking sticks.

tȧp , a kind of cattle; var. .

Tȧnasasa , B.D. 165, 9, the name of a foreign god (?)

tȧr , to destroy, to make an end of.

tȧrer , bread oven; ; Copt. ⲧⲣⲓⲣ, ⲑⲣⲓⲣ.

tȧrȧa , , D'Orbiney 16, 10, door; varr. , , U. 325 (?) compare Syr. [Syriac], Ch. תְּרַע.

Tȧrimāus (?) , Rec. 33, 3, a proper name—Telemachus.

Tȧrsha , see , Mar. Karn. 52, 1.

Tȧrgannasa , L.D. III, 165, a Hittite name; var. .

tȧhamu = **tehem** , the deep, abyss.

tȧkhr , Anastasi IV, 16, 9, military leather tunic; compare Chald. תַּחְרָא (?)

tȧs , to sit, to seat oneself.

tȧsa , P.S.B. 15, 475, , to set, to insert, to inlay.

tȧsa , a kind of cake or loaf.

tȧshes , to cook, to bake.

Tȧkȧ-taḥa-meru , U. 533 . . . .

Tȧkamāit (Tȧkmit) , Harris 501, a goddess (?)

tȧkr , eunuch; compare Copt. ⲥⲕⲟⲩⲣ, ϭⲓⲟⲩⲣ, ⲥⲓⲟⲩⲣ.

ṭā , Rev. 11, 182, glory, praise.

tāam , , , , a vegetable, garlic (?); compare Heb. שׁוּמִים (sing. שׁוּם), Arab. ثُوم, Syr. [Syriac], Assyr. , Rawl. C.I.W.A. II, 7, 43 (col. 2).

tām-t , Rev. 13, 4, food, bread.

tāt (tat) , Rev. 11, 185 = .

ti [ ], Rec. 20, 91, wind; Copt. ⲧⲏⲩ, ⲧⲏⲟⲩ, ⲑⲏⲟⲩ.

ti-t (?) , B.D. 83, 13 . . . .

tit , , , pus, dirt, foetid matter; , Rec. 15, 67, excrement of crocodiles; compare Heb. טִיט, Assyr. , Rawl. C.I.W.A., V, 32, 26 (col. 3).

ti-ti , , together, altogether.

titi , to chatter, to babble.

Titiu , , the name of a constellation (?)

tini , B.D. 153B, 3, 5, 6, 7, 8, 9, 10 = , ye, you.

tinu (tin) , Rev., to break; Copt. ⲧⲛ̄ⲛⲟ.

tir , Rev. 11, 55 = , strength, might, power.

tiråa (tråa) , , door, the two leaves of a door; Syr. ܬܪܥܐ, Chald. תְּרַע.

tir (tra)-ushebti , Rec. 2, 15, a kind of magical figure; see .

tirka (traka) , , Gol. 7, 4, a kind of bread or beer (?)

Tirku , Koller 4, 5, a foreign people or tribe.

tiḥu , Rec. 36, 81, mob, crowd.

tika , Rev. 11, 179, fire, spark, torch; Copt. ⲧⲓⲕ.

titth , Rev. = (?)

Tiṭur (Tatar) , L.D. III, 165, a Hittite proper name; var. , L.D. III, 164B.

tu , T. 333, P. 824, N. 703, a demonstrative particle, a mark of the passive.

tu ; see .

tu = , demons. pron. 1st sing.

tu , , , , A.Z. 1913, 144, abso. pron. 2nd sing.

tu , , one, *i.e.*, the king; , "one (the king) gave me."

tutu , , Åmen. 8, 11, one, anyone.

tu , Leyd. Pap. 6, 12, Mar. Aby. 11, 28, 4, to say yes, a particle of assent.

tu , , to speak.

tutu , Rev. 13, 22, to reject.

tu = , mountain; plur. , Rev. 13, 19; Copt. ⲧⲁⲩ, ⲧⲟⲟⲩ, ⲧⲟⲩ, ⲧⲱⲟⲩ.

tu, tua , Hh. 344, , wind, air, breath; , Rougé I.H. II, 116; Copt. ⲧⲏⲩ.

tui , , , , , , Rec. 30, 155, sandals; Copt. ⲧⲟⲟⲩⲉ, ⲑⲱⲟⲩⲓ.

tut unshå , Anastasi I, 24, 3, "wolf's feet"—a kind of herb.

tu-t , U. 88A, N. 365A, a sacrificial cake, bread of offering.

tu-t , IV, 389, walls, defences.

tua , T. 361, P. 642, , T. 361, P. 359, 642, , M. 677, N. 1239, , P. 694, , P. 698, , T. 243, , , , A.Z. 1872, 100, 1897, 98, to bear up, to support, to lift oneself up; , P. 94, , N. 56, , those who are lifted up.

tua , a supporter, adherent; plur. , IV, 1115, servants, retinue, household staff.

tua , pillar, support; see .

tuau , , Rec. 29, 151, staff, support.

Tuait , Denderah II, 55, a goddess, the support of the northern sky.

Tuait , Rec. 27, 190, a goddess.

tua, , Peasant 299, , Metternich Stele 101, , , , , , to pray to, to praise, to address, to make a report, to honour; Copt. ⲦⲀⲒⲞ.

tuau, praises, honourings, glorifyings.

tuau, , petitioner, dependant, client, subject; , , beggar, a boastful man (?); plur. .

tua, petition.

tua, air, wind, breath; varr. , ; Copt. ⲦⲎⲨ.

tuau, wicked men, evil beings; see .

tua, Ȧmen. 14, 5, 7, 19, disease (?)

tuau, pustules, swellings, warts; Copt. ⲐⲞⲒ, ⲦⲞⲈ.

tuaut, U. 60, , N. 312, , , , , , a kind of scented oil or pomade; varr. , .

Tuam-t (?), U. 210 ....

tuan, you, your; see .

tuaha, Ȧmen. 5, 16, to turn back, to repulse.

tuaka (taka), Rev., to destroy; Copt. ⲦⲀⲔⲞ.

tuȧ, Thes. 1297, Love Songs 2, 1, , IV, 897, , IV, 209, , Rec. 20, 42, , I, I being.

tuȧ, Rec. 6, 117 = , thee.

tuȧ, Jour. As. 1908, 268, morning; Copt. ⲦⲞⲞⲨⲒ, Amhar. ጧት:

tui, vile, abominable.

Tui, Ṭuat III, a goose-god.

tui, Rev. 13, 4, = = , , , this; Copt. ⲦⲀⲒ.

tui, B.D. (Saïte) 162, 3 ....

tuia (?), B.D. 39, 10 ....

tuis, lo, behold!

Tuba, Litanie 5, a form of the Sun-god; var. .

tuben, grease, fat; see .

tuf, B.D. 1, 29, his.

tup, a kind of cattle.

tu-n, , , L.D. III, 140, belonging to us, our; Copt. ⲦⲰⲚ.

tun, , , , , , , Rev., , Rec. 16, 108, to rise up, to mount on the back of an animal for sacrifice; var. ; Copt. ⲦⲰⲞⲨⲚ.

tun, to fly into the air.

tun, Jour. As. 1908, 283, resurrection; Copt. ⲦⲰⲞⲨⲚ.

tun, , , , rising flood, inundation.

Tun âḥ (?) , Edfû I, 81, a title of the Nile-god.

Tun ābui (ḥenti) , , the god of the 27th day of the month or the festival of that day.

Tun ḥat , Berg. I, 15, a ram-god.

tun , U. 639 (with), , T. 84, , M. 238, , N. 615, , , , fig tree (?); var. ; compare Heb. תְּאֵנָה, Arab. تين, Syr. ܬܐܬܐ, Chald. תְּינְתָא.

tun , , , figs.

tun , Rev. 12, 53, = ⲉ ⲧⲏⲛⲉ (?) to the limit of.

tuni , B.D. 189, 25; and see , B.D. 164, 4.

tunit , , Jour. As. 1908, 252, products, plants, vegetables.

tunnu , babe, child.

tunnu , Rhind Math. Pap., "the difference"—a term used in making calculations; ibid., the "middle difference."

tunuḥ , , Jour. As. 1908, 265, the rising of evil; Copt. ⲧⲱⲟⲩⲛϩⲱⲟⲩ.

tur, turi (later **tui**) , B.D. 145, IV, 16, , , Hymn Darius 4, , , IV, 752, , , , , , to be clean, to cleanse, to purify, to celebrate a ceremony of purification, purified; , pure; , to pray with a pure heart; , clean-handed.

tur , M. 717, , N. 1327, , P. 83, M. 113, N. 27, a holy sacrificial cake.

tur , , , , , willow, reed; varr. , ; Copt. ⲧⲱⲣⲉ.

turȧ-t , A.Z. 1907, III, 22, , staff, willow stick, wand.

tur , IV, 671, part of a waggon or chariot ( ).

tur , , , paint, colour; var. **tru** .

tur , T. 344, , N. 600, to reject, to turn from, to loathe.

tur-t , defilement, impurity.

Turaush , Darius.

turā , Rev. 11, 184, to go bail for.

Turimkus , Rec. 6, 5, Telemachus.

turpu , , a kind of goose; varr. , .

Turper (?) , Nesi-Ȧmsu 32, 37, a form of Āapep.

Turshau , , , , Mar. Karn. 52, 1, 14, 53, 3, 56, L.D. III, 209B, a Mediterranean people.

turt , Rev. 11, 185 = (?); glossed by ⲧⲟⲩⲗⲧ.

tuher , , , ,

, L.D. III, 160, 164, 165, Rougé I.H. 145, 52, a term of abuse (?) applied to Hittite soldiers.

tuḥu , Anastasi I, 16, 8 . . . .

tuk , , thou.

tug , B.D. 169, 24, to be clothed, dressed.

tut , , , , , , , , to beget, to procreate; , Rec. 3, 55, "begetter of the self-begetter"; see under **utt** .

tut , , , , , , Rev. 14, 75, , , , to collect, to gather together, to assemble; caus. ; , the assembled gods; , IV, 1160, all of them; Copt. ⲧⲟⲩⲱⲧ, ⲑⲟⲩⲱⲧ.

tut àb , to collect the heart, *i.e.*, to gather one's wits together, to collect oneself.

tut ma (?) , to collect the eyes, *i.e.*, to gaze intensely, to fix the eyes on something.

tut , , , , , , , Peasant 261, to be like someone or something, to resemble, like, alike, just as, even as; , what is usual; [to do things] which are usually done [under the circumstances]; , B.D. 136B, 12; , B.D. 127A, 11, , B.D. 127B, 17, , B.D. 133, 6.

tut , Palermo Stele, , , , , Nåstasen Stele 36, Ḥerusàtef Stele 33, , , , , , , , , , , Rev. 11, 174, image, likeness, similitude, statue; dual , P. 590 ( ), ; plur. , P. 319, , M. 626, , , , A.Z. 1899, 95; , B.M. 569, 16, sandstone statues; , royal statue; Copt. ⲧⲟⲩⲱⲧ, ⲑⲱⲟⲩⲧ.

tut , Image One, *i.e.*, First Image, God; , "Image, producer of all the gods, Image, father of all things"; , "Image of Åmen, Image of Åtem, Image of Kheperà"; , "he hath no like"; , every person is the image of his brother.

tut , U. 276, N. 719 + 8, a goddess, statue of a goddess; plur. .

Tut-en-àrit-Rā , B.D. 17, 79, a title of Meḥurit.

tut , to weep; Copt. ⲧⲟⲩⲉⲓⲧ.

Tutu , , B.D.G. 722, a lion-god, son of Neith; var. .

tuten , P.S.B. 31, 9, you; Copt. ⲧⲏⲩⲧⲛ̄.

tuth , U. 559, to collect, to gather together.

tuthen , you; Copt. ⲧⲏⲩⲧⲛ̄.

teb, teb-t , , sandal, shoe, sole of the foot; dual **tebti, tebit**

, A.Z. 1900, 30, , IV, 390, , IV, 612, , IV, 545, , thy two sandals; varr. .

tebtebti , sandals, soles of the feet.

tebi , Koller 2, 1, , to be covered with leather, to be shod or provided with sandals, to shoe.

tebteb , B.D. (Nebseni) 64, 35, , to walk, to come.

tebteb , Rhind Pap. 30, to move about quickly.

teb , Palermo Stele, , hippopotamus; var. .

teb , to beat, to strike.

tebteb , , to beat, to strike with a knife, to stab.

tebtebit , Rec. 8, 139, the slain.

tebteb , IV 658, , to pull, to draw, to drag, to haul, to tug, to draw the sword (?), to wind, to pull up, to lift up.

tebteb , Rec. 8, 166, depth (of a river).

Tebteb , Hh. 343, a god.

teb , something beaten, drum; Heb. תֹּף.

teb , cycle of time (?); var. .

teb , spelt; Copt. ⲃⲱϯ.

tebteb , U. 182, a kind of grain.

teb-t , IV, 198, brick, plaque; , B.D. 137, the four glazed faïence plaques; var. ; Copt. ⲧⲱⲃⲉ.

Teb, Tebȧ , T. 245, , U. 428, a god with a fierce eye.

teba , panther.

teba-t , Rev. 14, 34, brick; Copt. ⲧⲱⲃⲉ.

tebati (?) , bricks of metal, ingots.

tebȧ , M. 696, a fruit (?)

tebȧ , Rev. 11, 184, requiter; Copt. ⲧⲃⲉⲟⲩ (?)

tebȧ , box, chest, coffer; Copt. ⲧⲏⲃⲉ.

tebiu (?) , Peasant 30, a plant used in medicine; var. .

tebu , a measure.

tebu , vessels for beer or wine.

teben , Hh. 355, quick, swift.

teben , to revolve, circuit, cycle, circle, drum, tambourine; see .

teben , the rounded top of the head, skull.

teben , lock of hair over the temple, side-lock; varr. .

teben , Rec. 30, 154, helmet, head-covering.

teben, grease, fat.

teben , a weight; see **ṭeben** .

tebni , Rev. 2, 351 = περίπλους(?); see **ṭeben.**

Tebha , Nesi-Âmsu 2, 10, , a serpent-fiend, god of storm; Gr. Τυφῶν.

tebeḥ the , Rec. 4, 23; 5, 89, seven objects used in the Osiris mysteries.

tebeḥ , slaughtering weapons ( ).

Tebsu , , Rec. 31, 13, a god or devil.

tebsu , , Peasant 31, a plant used in medicine.

tep , , , , , , Rec. 14, 37, the head, the top of anything, point, tip (of the nose), head of fruit, the beginning (of a journey); plur. , , ; , T. 277, P. 30, M. 41, , the heads or principal points or sections of a book; **uaḥ tep** , to bow the head; , IV, 430, a head awake, *i.e.*, a keen watcher; , to give the head, *i.e.*, to attack; , Rec. 4, 31, from head to foot; , to add up the total.

tep , high ground; plur. , high banks (?)

Tep , the name of a lake at Thebes.

tepit , Anastasi IV, 2, 8; Koller 2, 6, , , part of a boat.

tepiu , Rec. 21, 87, tops of the masts.

tepi — , , Rec. 21, 91, the foremost point of the bows of a ship, the hindmost part of the stern.

tep , , person, man or woman, individual; plur. , Shipwreck 178; , as one man; , the person of every man; , of the Āamu four heads, *i.e.*, persons.

tep , on, upon, in, at, about, by; , upon; , before.

tepti , P. 204, 303, , P. 473, , N. 852, upon; , Koller 3, 7, at hand.

tepi , N. 911, , , , , , , , , , , he who is on, over, or above someone or something, he who is or that which is pre-eminent, foremost, first, best, leader, chief, captain, officer, governor; , first, or eldest son; , the very best spells; fem. **tepi-t** , N. 174 = , T. 351; , N. 798, U. 493, = , T. 251; , U. 391; plur. , , , , P. 337.

tepȧ , P. 69, 204, 614, the one on, he who is on (earth).

tepi ta , dweller on the earth, *i.e.*, a living man; plur. , as opposed to , "dweller on the mountain," *i.e*, a dead man.

tepi ṭu , a cemetery official, a mountain dweller.

Tepi ṭu-f , , , "he who is on his hill"—a title of the god Anubis.

Tepi-ṭu-s , , Mar. Aby. I, 45, consort of Anubis.

tepi , principal, capital; , principal and interest.

tepi ra , the principal, a sum of money on which interest is reckoned.

tepi renput , first day of each year (?)

tepi , the first day of a period of time:—

tepi renp-t , , , New Year's Day, the New Year festival; plur. , P. 399, M. 570, N. 1176,

tepi åbṭet , P. 70, the first day of the month; plur. , N. 45, 959, , T. 290, , T. 289.

tepi smat-f , the first day of the half month; plur. , N. 959, , N. 45, , T. 289, 290; , the first day of the ten-day period; plur. ; , P. 223, , beginnings of seasons.

tepi Per-t , the first [day] of the season Pert.

tepi m'sheru , the earliest twilight.

tepi en shemu , first-fruits of the summer.

tepi hru , , the name of the 8th day of the month.

tepi trå , the first [part] of a period of time, the beginning of a season; , , , IV, 1034.

tepi ṭuai-t , IV, 938, , , , , the earliest dawn, first appearance of day.

tepi-t , Love Songs 7, 7, the first lady; , Love Songs 5, 8, the first or best of the maidens.

tepi , Åmen. 20, 18, chief (?); plur. , , captive chiefs.

tepiu , P. 70, M. 100, N. 5, , , the best, choicest offerings; , the best (metal); , the finest grain; , N. 362, the best tchām metal in all the world; , the choicest oblations; , every-thing of the very best; , , Rec. 31, 27, the best families, the aris-tocracy.

tepi-t , , , , , unguent of the first quality.

tepiu , P. 239, the finest apparel ( ).

tepiu (?) , the finest geese.

tepi åau , Ḥerusåtef Stele 99, the finest cattle.

tepi åaut Uatchit , T. 336, P. 812, M. 254, N. 640, chief of the dignities of Uatchit.

Tepi åtru , IV, 421, "first on the river," a name of the sacred barge of Åmen.

Tepi ānkhiu , P. 169, chief of the living.

tepi ut , chief in command.

tepi metr, possessing the faculty of administering justice in the highest degree.

tepi en ȧḥ, the finest (horses) of the stud farm.

tepi-t nui, B.D. 149, XIV, 7, the head of the celestial waters.

Tepi nebu kau, P. 169, chief of the lords of doubles.

tepi nefer, the greatest good or happiness; the best possible way.

Tepi ḥe-t, Palermo Stele, the name of a sanctuary of Rā.

tepi ḥesb, Peasant 274, of the greatest eminence as a correct accountant.

tepi ḥesb meṭ-t nefer-t, the finest language imaginable.

Tepi shemsu Rā, U. 495, chief of the followers of Rā.

tep ā, the beginning of things and time, of old, primeval time, straightway, immediately; Shipwreck 34, before (we could land); his former condition; Berg. 58.

tep āui, remote antiquity, primeval time, olden time, past age, the earliest period, the Predynastic Period.

Tepi ā, a man or god of olden time, forbear, ancestor, progenitor, predecessor; plur. **tepi āui**, U. 187, T. 66, M. 221, N. 598, U. 199, T. 77, N. 609, T. 316, T. 365, N. 71, Rec. 26, 230, IV, 1084, ancestral nobility; ancestral documents; ancestral house; B.D. 124, 12, ancestors of the year; B.D. 124, 14, ancestors of Rā.

Tepiu-āui, U. 199, T. 77, N. 609, M. 230, ancestor-gods.

Tepiu-āui-Akhabiu, B.D. 153A, 11, a title of the Akeru-gods.

Tepi-ā-ȧakhu, Denderah II, 10, one of the 36 Dekans; Gr. *Τπηχυ*.

Tepiu-āui-ȧakhu, B.D. 124, 15, the ancestors of the Light-god.

Tepiu-āui-Ȧn-sebu, U. 419, T. 239, the ancestors of Ȧn-sebu (?)

Tepi-āui-Un, P. 461, M. 517, N. 1098, ancestor of Un.

Tepi-ā-baiu, one of the 36 Dekans; Gr. *Τπηβιου, Τπιβιου*.

Tepiu-āui-Rā, U. 399, B.D. 124, 14, the ancestors of Rā.

Tepiu-āui-renp-t, B.D. 124, 12, the ancestors of the year.

Tepi-āui-khent, , , Tombs Seti I and Ram. II, one of the 36 Dekans; Gr. Τπηχοντι.

Tepi-āui-Septit, Denderah II, 10, one of the 36 Dekans.

Tepi-āui-Smet̥, Tombs Seti I and Ram. II, , , Denderah II, 10, one of the 36 Dekans.

Tepi-āui-qerr-en-pet, U. 420, : (1) the ancestor-gods of the circle (or wind) of the sky; (2) a title of the , .

Tepi-āui-Kenmet, one of the 36 Dekans.

Tepiu-āui-Geb, B.D. 153A, 23, ancestors of Geb the Earth-god.

tepi-mas-t, , grief (?) sorrow (?)

tep ra, P. 643, M. 680, N. 1241, , , , , mouth; , IV, 974, mouth of the god, *i.e.*, divine oracle; Copt. ⲧⲁⲡⲣⲁ, ⲧⲁⲡⲣⲟ.

tep-t ra, , , , , , utterance, speech; plur. , U. 553, , B.D. 182, 11, , , , , ; Copt. ⲧⲁⲡⲣⲟ.

tep ra, the base of a triangle (?)

tep ra Sebek, , , *i.e.*, "crocodile's mouth"—a disease of the eye.

tep res, Annales III, 109, the South.

tep ret̥, M. 777, , U. 374, P. 667, N. 994, B.D. 172, 36, , , , , , , formula, precept, instruction, rule, decree, law, ordinance, an ancient copy or custom, prescription; plur. , N. 74, , P. 106, , , , .

tep ret̥ hepu, the course of the law.

Tepi, , Ṭuat IX, a serpent with four human heads at each end of his body, and eight pairs of legs.

Tepi-t, IV, 614, , B.D. 32, 10, a serpent crown or a serpent in a crown.

Tepui (Tchatchaui (?), Ṭuat XI, a two-headed god: one head faces to the right and the other to the left.

Tepu (Tchatchaiu), Ṭuat II, a corn-god.

Tepit-besses, , , Ṭuat III, a goddess.

Tepit-netchemu-seth, P. 695, chief of the sweet-smelling gods.

Tepi-khu-f, L.D. V, 39, a jackal-god.

Tepui (Tchatchaui)-sa-then, Ṭuat IV, a man-headed serpent with two pairs of human legs.

Tepi-sekh-t-f, T. 333, , P. 825, M. 249, N. 703, a god.

Tepiu-shetau, B.D. 168, , Ṭuat VII, the gods of mysteries.

Tepi-thrȧ, Ṭuat X, a light-god.

tep, boat; , the boat of the god [Rā]; see **ṭep** .

tep, box, chest, coffer, coffin.

tep, hippopotamus.

tep, to burn, fire, flame.

tep, Rec. 20, 40, a kind of plant.

tep, , to taste; see ; Copt. ⲧⲱⲡ.

tepai-t (?), A.Z. 1900, 37, , , , , , , food, fare, victuals, nourishment, drink.

tepau, B.D. 145, 14, a kind of cattle; see .

tepȧ, , , , IV, 669, , , a kind of cattle; see and .

tepȧ, , IV, 758, to sniff, to snuff the air, to breathe; var. .

tepi, Rec. 4, 27, bark, boat.

tepȧ, Rev. = , bark, boat; Copt. ⲧⲟⲡ.

tepiu, a kind of voracious fish.

tepen, Rev. 13, 12, = , circuit.

tepenn, , cumin; Copt. ⲧⲁⲡⲛ̄, ⲧⲁⲡⲉⲛ, ⲑⲁⲡⲉⲛ, Lat. cuminum.

tepḥ, Rec. 20, 91 = .

tepḥit, , , , , , IV, 919, , Rec. 13, 15, cave, cavern, den, hollow, gulf; plur. ; var. .

Tepḥi[t]-neb-s, etc., B.D. 145, 146, the 20th Pylon.

Tepḥut Ḥāp, B.D. 100, 3, the sources of the Nile.

Tepḥit shetait, , the 7th Division of the Ṭuat.

Tepḥit-tcha-t, , , Rec. 27, 189, the coffin of Seker the Death-god.

tepḥit, Mission V, 518, a funerary garment.

tepḥu, , apples (?); compare Heb. תַּפּוּחַ.

Teptiu (?), Nȧstasen Stele 46, ibid. 17, the army of the Nine Tribes of Nubia who fought with bows and arrows.

tepṭi-t, Nȧstasen Stele 63, bow.

Tepṭ, Denderah IV, 59, god of bows and arrows.

tef, , , Pap. 3024, 77, , B.D. 86, 2, , this; , IV, 966, these words.

tef, IV, 765, , , , , , father; plur. , , T. 319 = , U. 499, , P. 711 = , N. 1356, , M. 545 = , P. 442, N. 1126, , , IV, 864; , Hh. 379, my mother and father.

Tefu, T. 319 = of U. 499, the father-gods of the Ṭuat.

teftef, IV, 1054, father of father, grandfather.

Tef-f.... = Eupator.

Tef-f-meri, , = Philopator.

tef, bread, cake, food in general.

tef, a seed or fruit (?)

teftef, shrubs, bushes.

tef, U. 326, , U. 532, Rec. 27, 191, , , to spit, to eject anything from the body.

teftef, to pour out; var. .

Teftef-Nu, Denderah IV, 62, a warrior-god.

tefi, Anastasi IV, 2, 5, Koller 2, 3, Thes. 1202, , Festschrift 117, 6, , Rec. 21, 14, , , to hop, to skip, to spring into the air, to bubble up (of water), to palpitate.

teftef, Koller 4, 5, , A.Z. 1873, 63, to spring up, to lift the feet in trespass, to step over.

tef-t, De Hymnis 39, the leap of a fish.

tefi-t, Pap. 3024, 34, hoppings, jumpings, leapings, skippings.

tefå, , , saw.

tefå, Åmen. 7, 13, to cultivate or tend a tree (?)

teftefa, Rev. 11, 167, to work gems into a stone, to inlay, to embroider.

tefen, Thes. 1482, IV, 972, Rec. 17, 5, helpless one, orphan (?) destitute person.

tefen, , , , , to rejoice, to be glad, to enjoy, to praise.

tefen, to rise up, to spring up, to hop.

tefnuit, the "hopper"—a kind of bird.

tefen, to spit, to pour out.

Tefen, Metternich Stele 51, one of the seven scorpions which accompanied Isis in her wanderings in the Delta; var. .

Tefnit, ibid. 58, consort of the preceding.

Tefen, U. 453, a judge of the dead.

Tefnit, U. 425, 453, P. 62, 198, M. 83, , T. 243, , N. 599, consort of the preceding.

Tefnit, Tomb Seti I, one of the 75 forms of Rā (No. 14).

Tefnut, U. 242, N. 1108, , N. 933, 970, , , , , , , B.D. 169, 8, Shu and Tefnut were produced by the masturbation of Temu, or by Åusāusit, the shadow of Tem.

Tefnut, Ṭuat I, Denderah III, 78: (1) a singing-goddess; (2) a deity touching the lips with the tip of a finger.

tefnu, Rec. 3, 46, a kind of cake.

tefrer, resin (?); compare Copt. τεϐλε.

tefḥā, P. 441, , M. 545, a kind of bird, crane (?); var. , N. 1126.

tem, U. 378, T. 184, , Koller 2, 1, , , , , , , to make an end of,

to finish, to complete, to come to an end, to finish one's course; , A.Z. 1905, 33, to shut; , Peasant 286, to shut the mouth; Copt. ⲧⲱⲙ.

temm , U. 313, , IV, 752, , , Ḥeru-emḥeb 16, to finish, to complete, to make an end of; compare Heb. תָּמַם, Arab. تَمَّ, Syr. ܬܡ.

temi , , , all, the whole, the entire thing, complete.

temȧu , , all, complete.

temu, temmu , P. 439, , M. 655, , IV, 967, , IV, 895, , IV, 470, , , , , , , , , all peoples, mankind, mortals, men and women.

temui , N. 774, , P. 833, N. 768, full (dual, of the two hands).

tem-tȧ, temm-tȧ , N. 339, , P. 457, , , , completely, entirely, wholly.

temm-tu , all, complete.

Tem, Temu , U. 207, , N. 624, , , , the great god of Ȧn (Heliopolis) and the first living Man-god; the creator of heaven and earth, for he fashioned the phallus of Shu and the womb of Tefnut , N. 969, 970, his first consort was Ȧusāusit (Σαῶσις), and his last Temit .

Tem , Ṭuat III, an aged god who punishes the wicked.

Tem , Ṭuat VI, one of nine spirits who destroyed the dead.

Tem , Ṭuat VI, a jackal-headed stake to which the damned were fettered.

Tem , Ṭuat XI, a staff surmounted by a human head wearing a disk.

Tem , a form of Rā during the last three hours of the day.

Tem , Tomb of Seti I, one of the 75 forms of Rā (No. 11).

Tem , Denderah IV, 80, an ape-god, and god of bows and arrows.

Tem , Berg. II, 2, a god who re-joined the members of the dead.

Tem , one of the 36 Dekans; varr. , **Temati** ; Gr. Τωμ.

Temit , , the consort of Tem.

Temit , Berg. II, 2, a goddess who re-joined the members of the dead.

Tem-Ȧsȧr , a member of the triad of Heroopolis.

Tem-Rā , , the Sun-god by night and day.

Temu-Ḥeru-ȧakhuti , , Tem + Harmakhis.

Tem-Khepᵣer , N. 663, Tem + the Beetle-god—a form of Rā.

Tem-Kheperȧ , , Rā in the late evening and early morning.

Tem-sa-åru (?), L.D. III, 28, B.D.G. 856, a god of .

Tem-sep , B.D. 125, II, one of the 42 assessors of Osiris.

Temu-sma-Khebit , B.D. 38, 1, a form of Tem.

Tem-Teḥuti , B.D. 175, 6, Tem + Thoth.

tem, tem-t , U. 608, T. 332, , no, not, none, not at all, by no means, nothing, nought, not any, nothingness, without; , P. 665, those without; **tem unn** , non-existent; , the dead; , clawless; , unknown; , unsatisfied; Copt. ⲦⲘ.

temi-t , so that not.

tem erṭa , not to permit, not to allow, not to cause.

tem pesiu per ṭe-t khaiu , Excommunication Stele 5, the name or description of a class of people (secret society?) who were expelled from Napata.

tem, temm , to die, to perish, the end, death.

tem , with **ḥa-t** , stubborn, obdurate; Copt. ⲦⲰⲘ ⲠϨⲎⲦ.

temiu , the dead, the damned.

temiutiu , Litanie 8, the dead, the damned.

tem in the title , A.Z. 1902, 96.

temui , A.Z. 1902, 96, lands, estates.

temm , Ebers Pap. 70, 18, 19 . . . .

tem, temi , to sing, to declaim, to praise.

temiu , choristers, singers, choir.

tem , Rev. 13, 29, mat; Copt. ⲦⲘⲎ.

tem , Rev. 13, 32, to be arrayed or dressed.

tem-t , Rec. 5, 92, , Rec. 4, 22, , Rec. 5, 96, bandage, bandlet, covering, attachment, sack, bag, pouch; Copt. ⲦⲰⲘⲈ.

tem-t , Rec. 4, 29, sledge of a shrine, framework, crate, wicker box; Copt. ⲦⲘⲎ.

temmu , B.D. 153A, 23, parts of a net.

Temm reu ubenu, etc. , B.D. 153A, 18, the pole of the hunting net of the Akeru-gods.

tem-t , Rec. 17, 147, , a kind of fish.

temi, tem-t , , , , to join together (?)

temm , , to compress, to squeeze together.

temu , , , , some hard, compact substance.

tem, temi , , , , , , , to cut, to engrave, to inscribe; varr. , .

temtem , Verbum I, 336, 3, , , , Rev. 14, 11, , , , , A.Z. 35, 16, to cut, to carve, to scrape, to scratch, to engrave; Copt. ⲧⲙⲧⲙ.

temmut , IV, 1082, writings, documents, inscriptions.

tema , Rev. 14, 11, to strike a lyre, to play the harp.

tema , a kind of sacred tree, nut tree (?); plur. .

tema , , to bind together; var. .

tema , , , Rec. 27, 222, sack, mat; Copt. ⲧⲙⲏ.

tema-t , , , apparel.

Tema, Temam, Temamti , , , Denderah II, 10, one of the 36 Dekans; var. ; Gr. Τωμ.

Tema-t ḥer-t , one of the 36 Dekans; var. .

tema-ti, temam-ti , , , , pair of wings; varr. , .

temaȧs (?) , Rev. 11, 65, sand-bank, mud-flat.

temā , roll, book, document, writing.

temāu , wind, breeze; , a fair wind.

temai-t , case, box, chest.

temam , Rec. 27, 222, Gol. Ḥamm. 9, 33, , IV, 1113, , , Leyd. Pap. 3, 10, sack, mat; plur. , B.D. 1B, 15, 181, 1, , A.Z. 1900, 20; Copt. ⲧⲙⲏ.

temam-t , , , , , , apparel made of wool or hair; Copt. ⲧⲟⲙⲓ.

temamu , the dead.

Temam , Rec. 29, 151, a serpent-god.

temȧi , , to bind, to join together; var. .

temi , inundation, Nile-flood.

temi , a kind of close hard stone.

temi-t , , a kind of disease, hard boils (?)

temi , Rev. 11, 144, town townsman; Copt. ϯⲙⲉ.

temi, Rec. 13, 76, what is fitting or seemly; Copt. ⲧⲟⲟⲙⲉ.

ṭemum-t, a damned person or thing.

temr, to mix together, to compound.

temr, a kind of small fish.

temeḥ, , , A.Z. 1900, 37, , , A.Z. 1906, 116, , Rec. 4, 22, a kind of precious stone or earth, a kind of ochre (?)

Temḥu, , Libyans; , Libyan women.

Temḥi-[t], a goddess of the Red Land, , or desert.

tems, Thes. 1481, IV, 971, to turn towards, to direct a course.

tems, , to be striped or variegated.

temsu, IV, 1082, , brightly coloured paintings (?)

tems, , , , Mission 13, 51, , a charge against someone, indictment, decree of doom; plur. , , , B.D. 125, III, 16; var. .

Tems khentt, , one of the 36 Dekans; var. .

tems, Anastasi I, 26, 2, , , , to hide, to cover over, to bury; Copt. ⲧⲱⲙⲥ, ⲑⲱⲙⲥ.

temsu, B.D. 41, 9, wooden objects.

ten, pron. 2nd sing. fem. thou; older .

ten, , , , , , pron. 2nd plur. you, your; Copt. ⲧⲏⲛⲟⲩ.

ten, , , demonst. pron. this.

ten, at the rate of.

ten, Rev., hole of a serpent.

teni (?), , , to cut, to divide; var. .

ten, teni, B.D. 52, 4, , , , , , where?; , Dream Stele 31, "where are they?"; Copt. ⲧⲱⲛ.

tennu, whence? Copt. ⲧⲱⲛ.

ten, teni, , , , , , Ḥeruemḥeb 23, , , , , , , , to raise, to elevate, to exalt, to distinguish, to promote to high rank, to increase; , to enlarge the land; , to increase births; varr. , .

teni, , , to possess honour or fame, to be honourable; var. .

tennu, L.D. III, 194, 14, magnificent (statues).

ten, tennu , each, every; , IV, 1045, every hour; , every time he riseth; , Koller 4, 7, of every sort and kind.

teni , Thes. 1204, to count, to reckon, to estimate.

tennu , impost, tax, rent, census.

tennu-t , Rev. 11, 149, men who pay rent or taxes, tenants.

tennu-t , number, quantity, amount, extent; , great number; , very many; , IV, 968, to calculate numbers.

tenn , Rev. 12, 45, ground, earth; Copt. ⲉⲓⲧⲛ̀.

Tennu , a god, the "father of the Gods."

Tenn , a primitive earth-god; see **Tatenen.**

Tennit , the female counterpart of **Tennu.**

Tennit Ȧnit sheta-t ȧru , Edfû I, 25, a goddess.

tena , basket.

Tenait , B.D. 79, 5, a district in the Ṭuat.

tenȧ , Israel Stele 11, basket (?)

teni (?) , to divide, to separate.

tenȧ-[t] , piece, portion; , rations, allowance.

tenȧ-t , the name of the 7th and 23rd days of the month; var. .

tenȧ , Rougé I.H. II, 114, , to be aged, to grow old, old, old age, maturity, aged man, a title of respect; var. .

tenȧ , Rev. 12, 11, brave, distinguished.

tenȧ , Jour. As. 1908, 288, whence; Copt. ⲧⲱⲛ.

tenȧ , Rev. 14, 8, to pray, to cry out, to invoke; and see .

tenȧu , circular vessel, pot or tray.

tenȧi (?) , Jour. As. 1908, 256 = (?)

tenȧs , heavy, ponderous.

tenit , B.D. (Saïte) 145, 36, outcry, cry, clamour.

tenu , A.Z. 1908, 17, dyke (?) piece, portion; see , and **ṭena** .

tenu , eclipse (?); compare Copt. ⲑⲉⲛⲓⲱ.

tennut , Rev. 14, 11, women players of tambourines.

tennu , the "old" canal; var. .

tennu , weakness, failure.

Tennu , a foreign tribe or nation.

tennu, L.D. III, 194, 15, birds.

tenbekh, B.M. 5645, 12, , , , Peasant 161, , to shrink from, to hesitate, to waver, to fail, to deceive.

tenbekh-t, fright, shrinking.

tenfiu, Rev. 14, 11, harpers.

tenem, Peasant B 2, 98, , B.D. 169, 23, IV, 363, , , , , to wander, to err, to go astray, to lose the way, to turn aside from.

tenemm, see .

tenemu, Peasant 18, a plant used in medicine (?)

Tenemi, , B.D. 125, II, one of the 42 assessors of Osiris.

Tenemi-t, B.D. 169, 8, , Ombos I, 61, a goddess who gave drink to the dead.

tener, , , , , , , to be strong, strength, brave, valiant; compare Copt. ϫⲱⲱⲣⲉ.

tenreku, , , Anastasi IV, 12, 1, carob wine.

tenher, box, chest, coffer.

tenḥ, , , a pair of wings; plur. , Rev. 14, 4; Copt. ⲧⲛϩ.

tenkhenui, N. 1165, P. 391, , a pair of obelisks.

tens, , , to be heavy, to be weighty, ponderous; see .

tens, A.Z. 1871, 111, hippopotamus, symbol of Typhon, or Set.

tent, belonging to.

tent āmu, a kind of disease.

tent ḥetrȧ, belonging to the horse, horse-soldier, cavalry.

tenta (?), Rev. 12, 93, scorpion.

tentȧ, a kind of grain, seed, or fruit.

Ten-ti, Lit. 47, a form of the Sun-god.

tentem, a kind of grain, seed, or fruit.

tenten, , , to be strong, to attack, aggressive; var. .

tenth, a plant (?)

tentha-t, , , throne pavilion, throne; varr. , , .

Tenṭen, the name of a serpent deity.

tenntchai, Rev. 11, 188, shrine, sanctuary.

ter, , , , a particle.

ter, terȧ, Gol. Ḥamm. 13, 112, , , , Rec. 32, 16, Thes. 1481, IV, 970, ,

, Rec. 16, 57, , to pay honour, to revere, to applaud, to have a regard for; , Åmen. 25, 7, , ibid. 21, 11.

terr , IV, 1182, to revere; Copt. ⲧⲣ̄ⲣⲉ.

ter , to be weak.

ter = = ⲧⲏ, time.

ter = , time, season.

ter , Rev. 13, 19, to produce.

ter-t , Rec. 2, 107, , , willow tree; plur. , Pap. 3024, 92, , Rec. 2, 62, , Metternich Stele 77, ; varr. , ; Copt. ⲧⲱⲣⲉ (ⲃⲱ ⲛ̄ ⲧⲱⲣⲉ), ⲑⲱⲣ.

ter , , stuff, cloth, bandlet, garment; , Rec. 6, 8, a byssus cloth; varr. , .

ter , , to destroy, to wipe out, to efface, to obliterate; , Jour. As. 1908, 308, destruction of sensuality.

terit , , destruction.

ter , to guide.

terter , Rev. 12, 27, strong place, fort; Copt. ϫⲁⲗϫⲉⲗ.

terr , oven, furnace; Assyr. , Rawl. C.I.W.A., V, Obv. I, l. 27, Heb. תַּנּוּר, Syr. ܬܢܘܪܐ Arab. تَنُّور.

ter-ti , the two eyeballs of Rā.

ter-ti = , the two birds, *i.e.*, Isis and Nephthys.

ter-ti = .

ter, trå, tri , Rec. 33, 6, , , , , , , time, season; fem. ; plur. , , , IV, 766; , , festivals; , at all times, always; , time of dawn; , time of evening; , Sphinx Stele 8, Rec. 17, 147, midday; , Rec. 17, 130, the night season; Copt. ⲧⲏ.

trå-ui , IV, 1045, , IV, 430, , , , the two times, *i.e.*, morning and evening.

trå-t, teri-t , , toe, claw, talon.

terri , Jour. As. 1908, 312, to destroy.

teri , Rev. 13, 38 = , to revere, to worship.

tru = , stream, river.

tru , , Ḳubbân Stele 3, , colour, paint.

terp , to give, to administer, to provide offerings.

terp , to bind, to tie together.

terp , a kind of goose; plur. .

terf, to write, to copy, writing, document.

tert, Rev. 12, 78, stairs; Copt. ⲧⲱⲣⲧ.

Tertiu (?), the dwellers in deserts and mountains.

teh, heat, flame.

tehi, Treaty 13, to cross over, to transgress, to infringe, to violate a frontier, to break into, to trespass, to invade, to attack; IV, 1021, to transgress a law; to go off the road, to err; to wander (of the mind); Israel Stele 13, to invade a nation.

tehu, Peasant 237, Ȧmen. 5, 12, 17, 6, transgressor, marauder, invader, attacker.

tehi-t, Peasant 281, Pap. 3024, 11, attack, invasion.

teha, Jour. As. 1908, 277, trouble.

tehab, to beat, to strike.

tehab, a kind of wood, wooden instrument; plur. ; var.

teham, III, 143, to muster an army, to collect by force.

tehan, to appoint to an office, to promote; var.

tehani, to greet, to salute, to pay homage by touching the ground with the forehead.

tehar, oven, furnace.

tehȧ, Rev. 13, 27, trouble; Copt. ⲧⲱϩ.

tehār, Rev. 11, 182, brave, distinguished.

tehāra, Rev. 11, 182, the blooming one (?); Gr. θάλεια (?)

tehur, IV, 686, a "brave," a soldier; see

teheb, a kind of wood.

tehem, B.M. 138, to cry out; Copt. ⲧⲉϩⲉⲙ (?)

tehem, Thes. 1205, to muster an army, to round up men, to drive cattle, to attack; var.

tehem, to water.

tehem, to cook, to boil.

tehen-t, forehead; Copt. ⲧⲉϩⲛⲉ.

tehenn, to adore, to touch the earth with the forehead in homage.

tehennu, Ebers Pap. 85, 14, paroxysm (?)

tehni, to appoint to some rank or dignity, to promote, to dedicate; var.

teher, Thes. 1204, brave man, soldier.

tehteh, Rev., lead; Copt. ⲧⲁϩⲧ.

teḥt, lead; var. ; Copt. ⲧⲁϩⲧ.

teḥȧsṭ, a kind of metal, brass (?); var.

teḥia, Rev., to wallow, to sprawl about; Copt. ⲧⲱϩ.

teḥut, a plant, and the seed or fruit of the same used in medicine (Ebers Pap.)

teḥen, to sparkle, to coruscate, to scintillate, the lightning flash; var. ; Culte Divin, 157.

teḥen-t, P.S.B. 15, 444, Ȧmen. 6, 8, Hymn Darius 38, sparkle-stone, crystal, faïence, blue porcelain.

Teḥen-t (Theḥen-t), a name of the sacred boat of Heroopolites.

Teḥentiu, A.Z. 1900, 20, the sparkling gods, stellar luminaries (?)

Teḥnu, Libyans; see also **Theḥnu**.

teḥnu, Hh. 364, flint knives (?) obsidian knives (?)

teḥer, Rev. 12, 39, to be jealous; Copt. ⲧⲱϩⲣ̄.

teḥes-t, (sic), a kind of metal, copper (?); var.

teḥsu, Festschrift (Leemans) 3, shoemaker.

teḥs, to beat, to break, to hammer.

tekh, plummet, the little weight which served as the tongue of the scales; Ḳubbân 13, just weight; Rev. 3, 12, the regulation of justice.

tekhȧ, A.Z. 1900, 33, weigher, the pointer of the scales.

tekhi, ibis, crane; Copt. ϯϭⲓ (?)

Tekhi, a title of Thoth as regulator of times and seasons.

Tekhi, the god of the 1st month (Thoth).

Tekhi[t], goddess of the 1st month.

Tekh-en-bu-maāt, B.D. 125, III, 28, name of the door-bolt of the hall of Maāti.

tekhit, Rec. 16, 141, violet (?); var. ; water or essence of violets.

tekh-t, Nȧstasen Stele, a wine cup or bowl; Ebers 66, 19, wineskin (?)

tekh, a mixture of bread and wine or bread and beer.

tekhi, IV, 688, to drink, to be or to become drunk; Copt. ϯϩⲉ, ⲑⲓϭⲓ.

tekhu, Love Songs 2, 2, drink.

tekhȧu, drunkard; plur.

tekhu, butler.

tekhtȧ, habitual drunkard.

Tekhu, N. 618, , T. 87, M. 240, the cupbearer of Horus.

tekh, the "drunken" festival.

tekhait (tekhit), Rev. 14, 15, , drunkenness; Copt. ⲑⲁϩⲓ.

tekhab (tekheb), Rev. 13, 15, , Rev. 14, 12, flooded or irrigated land.

tekhan (tekhen), Rev. 13, 19, to hide, to protect.

tekhanu, Rev. 12, 117, a hiding place.

tekhanu (tekhnu), Rec. 15, 16, a kind of stone.

tekhar, Rev. 14, 10, to be troubled.

tekhi[t], Rev. 12, 36, massacre, slaughter.

tekheb, , , , , , , , , , Rec. 5, 86, , , A.Z. 1900, 37, , , to dip in water, to steep in water, to plunge into water, to flood, to wet, to moisten, to anoint.

tekheb, , any foetid moisture from the body, sweat, etc.; var.

tekhbustȧ, Harris 500, rev. 2, 4, sack, sacking; var.

tekhbekh, , Leyd. Pap. 67 (=), to shrink back from, to hesitate, to waver.

tekhen, , Rev. 13, 19, , , , Nȧstasen Stele 40, , Rev. 13, 19, to hide, to cover over, to protect; Copt. ⲧⲁⲛϩⲟ (?)

tekhen, , Ebers 60, 10, , to have running or rheumy eyes (?)

tekhnen, Verbum II, § 123, to have diseased eyes (?)

tekhen, , A.Z. 1906, 123, , , to beat a drum or tambourine, to play an instrument of music.

tekhenu, , musician, player; var.

tekhen, , , , obelisk; plur. ; IV, 756, ; , IV, 747, great obelisks; , IV, 642, very large obelisks; , P. 391, , M. 558, , , , a pair of obelisks; , , IV, 397, , IV, 56, , a pair of large obelisks 108 cubits (162 feet) high.

Tekhnui, , P. 391; var. , N. 1165, the two obelisks of Rā.

Tekhnu IV, Rec. 4, 30, the four obelisks used in a ceremony of Osiris.

tekhen , T. 317, Rec. 27, 192, ibis (?)

tekhes , , = , , to slay, to kill.

tekhtekh , U. 495, T. 236, N. 157, , Anastasi I, 28, 6, , Rec. 16, 129, , Love Songs 1, 10, , , , Rev. 13, 69, to be disarranged, in wrong order, topsy-turvy, involved, confused, muddle, disorder; , , Anastasi I, 28, 3, confused speech, meaningless chatter; , B.D. 17, 135, disarranged hair; Copt. ⲧⲉϩ-ⲧⲱϩ, ⲧⲁϩⲧϩ, ⲑⲁϩⲑⲉϩ.

tekhtekhut , Rec. 26, 225, confusion, disorder.

Tekhtekh , N. 1135, , M. 549, an abusive epithet applied to Āapep.

tes , , a stone or metal knife; var. , and .

tes ḥetch-t , Rec. 4, 21, a white precious stone.

tes theḥen , a sparkling stone.

tes-t , I, 117, a feminine title (?)

tesȧf = , bread, cake, dough.

tesitesi , Rev. 11, 188, judges (?) Glossed by ⲇⲓⲇⲓⲟⲩ.

t su , see A.Z. 30, 81, P.S.B. 15, 471 (is a prefix).

tsu , staff, support.

tesef , , bread, cake, dough.

tesh , ordinance, law, regulation; plur. , , Copt. ⲑⲱϣ.

tesh , to rub down, to crush.

tesh , Amherst Pap. 28, , , Peasant 179, , IV, 892, , , , to depart from, to leave, to be separated from, to separate, to crush, to cleave; , Rec. 27, 88, inseparable.

teshtesh , Ebers 69, 12, , , to separate, to divide, to pound, to triturate.

Teshtesh , A.Z. 1869, 139, , Rec. 4, 31, a model of Osiris used in the performance of resurrection ceremonies.

tesh , I, 140, , Rec. 33, 118, frontier, boundary region; plur. , , , Ȧmen. 7, 12, 15.

tesh-t , Copt. Cat. 406, nome; Copt. ⲧⲟϣ, ⲧⲱϣ.

teshu , Rev. 11, 125, dwellers in a nome.

Tesh , Ombos I, 84, a city-god.

tesh , Rev. 11, 167 . . . . . .

tesha , , to split, to cleave, to divide, to crush.

teshi , a kind of stone.

teshi , Rev. 11, 169, band, bundle (?)

teshb (?) , to break, to split.

t-sheps , , Rec. 16, 136, , , ,

IV, 329, , Shipwreck 163, , Rec. 32, 66, the cinnamon tree, cinnamon; , Festschrift (Leemans) 117, 13, , cinnamon oil or pomade.

teshen-t , a metal tool or weapon.

tesher , red, redness; see ; Copt. ⲧⲣⲟϣ.

teshri , a red cow.

teq , to cut, to slay, to strike.

teq , spark, fire, lamp, torch; Copt. ϯⲕ.

teqem , Rev. 12, 49, to unsheath a sword; Copt. ⲧⲟⲕⲙ.

teqen , to rule, to govern.

teqer , to be strong, mighty; var. .

teqer , Nâstasen Stele, 45 ....

Teqer , Mar. M.D. 49, Sphinx I, 90, Rec. 21, 136, the name of a Libyan dog owned by Antef-āa; in Egyptian .

teqes , , A.Z. 1908, 35, 131, to pierce, to penetrate, to cut, to stab; Copt. ⲧⲱⲕⲥ.

tek , Pap. 3024, 15, , to enter, to invade.

tek , to disturb, to break the peace.

tekk , A.Z. 1905, 25, Gol. Ḥamm. 110, , , Rec. 8, 141, , Rec. 12, 70, , , to thwart, to attack, to rob, to invade.

tekku , robber, marauder, invader; plur. , IV, 614, , IV, 647.

tektek , Mission 13, 58, B.D. 113, 3, , Rev. 11, 62, 12, 8, 70, to invade, to attack; var. , .

teki (?) , to kindle a fire, light a lamp.

teku , flame, lamp; plur. .

tekk-t a kind of insect, weevil (?)

teka , to see; var. .

teka , Rec. 3, 57 grain, fruit.

teka , T. 206, , , , , , spark, fire, flame, lamp, torch; , Rec. 3, 49, many lamps; Copt. ϯⲕ.

Tekait , U. 335, Rec. 30, 187, a fire-goddess.

Tekait , Ṭuat IX, a fiery, blood-drinking serpent.

Tekait , the consort of Maa-ḥes .

Tekau IV , B.D. 137A, the four holy torches or lamps.

Tekaharsapusaremkakarmit , B.D. (Saïte) 164, 4, a magical name.

Teka-ḥer , , Ṭuat III, (1) a serpent in the boat Penā; (2) the serpent-warder of the 4th Gate.

tekan, Jour. As. 1908, 307, to drive away, to reject; Copt. ⲧⲱϭⲡ (?)

tekas, A.Z. 1908, 131, to pierce, to cut into; varr. ; Copt. ⲧⲱⲕⲥ̄, ⲑⲱⲕⲥ̄.

tekȧu, Rev. 11, 174, part of a ship.

teku, bread, loaf, cake.

tekem, B.D. 78, 3, to approach.

tekem, Rev. 14, 49, a kind of oil.

tekmu, drawers of swords; Copt. ⲧⲉⲕⲙ̄ⲙ̄, ⲧⲟⲕⲙ̄ⲙ̄.

Tekem, B.D. (Saïte 42) 72, 7, a god; varr. , Nav. Todt. II, 111.

Tekmi, Ṭuat V, a jackal-god.

teken, U. 543, , Peasant 145, Pap. 3024, 71, , IV, 1016, , U. 543, to approach, to draw near, to enter; Copt. ⲧⲟϫ, ⲧⲟϭ.

teknu, he who enters; plur. .

tekennu, Rec. 20, 41, to pierce the sky (of high towers or buildings).

teknu, tekennu, Sphinx, 3, 151, human victim, a substitute in a death ceremony.

Teken-en-Rā, the god of the 13th day of the month.

teken-t, U. 544, , T. 299 ....

Tekneru, Mar. M.D. 49, Rec. 11, 80, the name of one of the hunting dogs of Ȧntef-āa.

teker, Rev., to come, to approach; var. .

teks, A.Z. 1908, 131, to pierce, to penetrate; var. ; Copt. ⲧⲱⲕⲥ̄.

teksa, Rev. 11, 168, the flat part of the back.

teksa, Rec. 35, 84, a broad, flat knife.

teksa-t, Rev. 11, 188, , Rev. 14, 33, table.

tektek, a kind of plant; plur. .

teg, tega, to see, to look at, to examine, var. .

teg, Rev. 13, 48 ....

teg, Rev. 14, 67, plant; Copt. ⲧⲱϭⲉ.

teg, plants, seeds.

tega, see .

tega (?), to bandage; as in for .

tegas, B.D. 39, 22, to remove, to carry on.

tegen = , to approach, to draw near.

teges, Berg. I, 56, slaughter-house (?)

teges, Rec. 35, 84, a metal (?)

tegteg, Rev. 12, 70, , to attack, to destroy.

tet, , to collect; var. ; Copt. ϴωογτ.

tet, , form, likeness, image; var. .

Tetui, P. 590, the two statues, .

Tet-ti åb (ḥat), U. 598, a double goddess, the two daughters of the four gods of the Great House, , N. 964.

tet, Rev. 12, 33, , Rev. 11, 146 = , pylon.

tet-ti (?), basement of a temple.

tet, , , Hh. 445, skin, hide.

tet, pot, cauldron; var. .

tet, to turn, to withdraw.

tet, an amulet symbolic of the uterus of Isis.

Tetå, Rec. 30, 2, a god.

Tetåān, the name of a foe of Amasis I.

teti (?), stick, pole; plur. .

teti, see .

tetbu (?), B.D. 137, 40, to smear, to daub.

tetef, Ḥerusåtef Stele, 59, his, its.

tettet, B.D. 164, 3, to subdue, to do away.

teth, nurse, attendant.

teṭme-t, a kind of seed (?)

TH

th = sometimes Heb. ט; Copt. ϫ or ϭ.

th, = , thee, thou.

th[a], soldier, bowman; plur.

th-t, writing, book, document, list, warrant.

th-t, sages, learned men; , "the sages of the House of Life," *i.e.*, the learned men of the College attached to the temple.

th-t, a gathering of people.

th-t, a kind of goose.

tha, thai, P. 777, M. 772, , man, male, masculine; plur. , T. 197, P. 678, N. 1293, , Rec. 31, 25, , Nåstasen Stele 44, , Hymn Darius 32, ; , men and women, males and females; , the male genital organs; , seed; , a man child; , a virile young man; , ganders; Copt. ϭo, ϫo.

tha-t, the governor-in-chief, the headman of a town or village; , B.D. (Saïte) 145, 23, the Arab Mudîr or Wazîr.

tha-t, governor and judge of the Two Lands.

tha-t meḥ, governor of the North, *i.e.*, of Lower Egypt.

tha-t mer nu-t nu Tamerȧ, governor-general of Egypt.

tha-t en sa, governor of a grade of priests in the temple.

tha-t resu (shemā?), governor of the South, *i.e.*, of Upper Egypt.

tha, the "male"—a title of Geb the Earth-god.

Thaui, , Bubastis 51, , B.D. (Saïte) 164, 11, twin gods or goddesses, Shu and Tefnut, Isis and Nephthys, etc.

Thau uru, P. 319, M. 626, a class of divine males mentioned in connection with .

Tha nefer, "Beautiful boy"—the name of a star.

thau (?), T. 316, the solid parts of a body as opposed to the liquid, .

thau (?), B.D. 153A, 30, birds, fowls.

tha, , to be angry, inflamed.

tha àb (ḥat), Thes. 1481, IV, 970, to be wroth, to fly into a rage.

tha, to wrap up, to envelop, to clothe.

tha, bandlet; see

thau, IV, 1089, roll, writing, document, order, edict.

tha, to bear, to carry, bearer, carrier.

thai meḥ-t, B.D. 164, 1, fan-bearer, fan-bearer on the right hand of the king.

thai metcha-t, carrier of the book, *i.e.*, accountant, agent.

thai seri-t, banner-bearer of an army.

thai seḥetpit, Rec. 16, 56, thurifer.

thai shebt, Rec. 7, 190, wand-bearer, staff-bearer.

thai, Thes. 1200, Hh. 550, to seize, to take, to carry off, to grasp, to lay violent hands on, to ravish, to steal; Copt. ϫⲓ, ϭⲓ, ϫⲏⲩ, ϫⲓⲟⲩⲉ.

tha-t, thau-t, plunder, theft.

thai, seizer, thief.

thai, Treaty 17, offence, injury.

thait, theft.

thau, thief, robber.

thau, "robbers"—the name given to some of the pieces used in playing a game on a draughtboard; A.Z. 1866, 99.

thai, to work on some hard substance, to model, to be worked or engraved (of metal); Koller 1, 7, Rec. 34, 48, graven with a chisel.

thaiu Anastasi I, 21, 7, graven objects.

thau, U. 429, T. 246, P. 334, P. 707, wind, air, respiration, breath; plur. P. 156, N. 786, M. 215, N. 686, Rec. 33, 36; Copt. ⲧⲏⲩ.

thau, date palm (?) olive (?)

tha, A.Z. 1906, 118, grain, drop, pellet, bead, necklace.

tha; var. to shave, to frizz the hair; see

tha, B.M. 5645, a kind of animal (?)

tha en unsh (?), Love Songs 2, 2, "wolf's paw," *i.e.*, mandragora, "love apple," and compare the following.

thaui (?) —, Åmen. 12, 18, , Åmen. 13, 4.

tha-ti, L.D. III, 194, 17, the double throne or chair of state on which the king was crowned.

thaår, IV, 896, , Sphinx 1, 22, to restrain, to coerce.

thaårtu (=), Nåstasen Stele 11; 12, to cross over; Copt. ϫιοορ.

thaås, A.Z. 1913, 128, to give an order.

thaåtå, Love Songs 7, 11, a kind of plant, olive (?); compare Heb. זַיִת (?)

thai, , a measure (?) fire-drill (?)

thaiu, the accursed spawn of Āapep.

thai-t, sadness (?) sorrow (?)

thaua, to dress the hair, to cut the hair, to shave (?)

Thauathasasa, L.D. III, 164B, a Hittite proper name.

Thatmār (Tham'r), Thes. 1203, a Libyan proper name.

that-ṭå (?), Rechnungen 35, ferryman (?)

thab, IV, 770, Annales III, 110, , , jar, cup, pot, vessel; plur., IV, 636.

thab-t, , , , grain, corn.

Thabu, a god of wine and beer.

thab-t, , stick, staff.

thabsha, to work stone, stonemason.

thapr, vessel, pot.

thapr (?), P. 635, M. 510, N. 1093 . . . .

thapga, Anastasi III, 5, 4 =, of Anastasi IV, 9, 5, barracks.

Thafui, , , B.D. 17, 112, the double form of Horus containing the souls of Osiris and Rā.

tham, Rec. 31, 12, male, masculine, to act a man's part.

thami, IV, 1081, Shipwreck 19, , Rec. 31, 171, , , , , , , , , to cover over, to clothe, to dress, to wrap up in, to enclose, to wind round, to bind.

tham-t, B.D. 125, III, 17, coverings, face-cloths.

Thamaā, the god of Western Thebes; var. ; Copt. ϫⲏⲙⲉ (?)

Thamākana, Alt-K. 1153, a devil who caused sickness; var.

thamr, lion.

thames, P.S.B. 20, 198, to devour, to consume.

than or, chief officer.

thanreḥ, Anastasi I, 9, 7, to forget; Heb. סָלַח.

thant, throne, chair of state; var.; see

thanti-t, throne, chair of state; see

thanṭ, poles, timbers, bearing-poles.

thar, Tombos Stele 9, IV, 84, IV, 1078, to embrace, to enclose, to surround.

thar, Mission 13, 117, to be strong, to be protected, fortified, strong; Copt. ϫⲟⲣ, ϫⲟⲟⲣ, ϫⲟⲟⲣⲉ.

tharei, whole, sound, strong, protected.

thar-t, strength, a strong thing, a protected thing.

thar-t, Jour. E.A. 3, 104, an enclosed and strong place, a walled enclosure, fortress.

tharit, safe or protected thing.

tharr, a kind of cake; plur.

tharȧa, a kind of cake.

tharān (?) — sā, Nȧstasen Stele 40, from — to.

tharin, Alt-K. 1162, buckler; var. P.S.B. 10, 472; Heb. שִׁרְיוֹן.

tharb, pot, vessel.

tharḥ, to invade, to transgress.

tharstȧ-t, some part or parts of the body.

thartȧ, a kind of boat.

thartȧ, Rec. 17, 146, bread made of fine flour; Heb. סֹלֶת, Chald. סוּלְתָּא, Arab. سُلت (Dozy I, 671), Assyr. sil-la-tu

thaḥab, Anastasi IV, 2, 5, Koller 2, 3, a place where horses are exercised.

thaḥr, to ill-treat, to beat.

thasȧs, chief, master.

tha serit, IV, 998, IV, 998, flag bearer, colour bearer of an army; see

thash, boundary, frontier; see : Copt. ⲧⲟϣ.

thak, Rougé I.H. 2, 125 . . . . .

thakar, strong building, an enclosed and fortified place, tower.

Thakaru, Thes. 1208, , Rec. 21, 916, , , , Alt-K. 1171, a Mediterranean people.

Thakar-Bāra, Rec. 21, 78, , the name of a Syrian governor; Heb. זכר-בעל.

Thakaretha, Harris Pap. Mag., a magical name.

thakatȧ, covering, bandlet.

thakrau, Harris I, 57, 13, shutters, lattices.

thaga, Koller 1, 5, 2, 1, , IV, 701, , , IV, 732, a kind of tree, the wood of the same.

thagapu, Anastasi IV, 9, 5, barracks; see .

thaten-t, throne; see .

thatha (?), a metal pot, vessel, or bowl.

Thathait, Litanie 15, 47, a form of the Sun-god.

Thath-neteru, Ṭuat VI, a god.

thȧ-t, Thes. 1281, IV, 157, emanation, exudation.

Thȧt, a goddess of Ṭeṭ-t, , Busiris.

thȧaiu, a class of officials, clerks (?)

thȧfthȧf, T. 305 . . . .

Thȧref, T. 317, the name of a magical serpent.

thȧthȧ, Rev. 6, 26, to stamp with the feet, to gallop.

thȧthȧ, B.D. 169, 2, dances, skippings.

thā (?), to run (?)

th-āmit, Rev. 13, 27 = ϫⲓⲛⲉⲓⲙⲉ, in the state of knowing.

thi, scribe, learned man; plur. ; , Rec. 33, 4, copyists attached to the college, sages.

thi-t, , band, tie.

thinen, Berg. I, 9 . . . .

thithi, Love Songs 5, 6, , Rec. 21, 97, , Rec. 1, 46, , ibid. 1, 52, to wrangle, to dispute, to chatter, to gossip.

thetthet, , chatter, gossip.

thu, thut, T. 211, N. 335, , pron. 2nd sing. masc., thou.

thu (?), to mount up.

thua, to lift up, to bear, to carry.

thua, IV, 278, to bind on a crown.

thua, N. 979, defects (?) offences (?)

thuȧt, T. 284, crown; see and .

thui, that.

thub, sole, sandal; see ; Copt. ⲑⲱⲟⲩⲧ, ⲧⲟⲟⲩⲧ.

thupar, horn, trumpet; , trumpet bearer, trumpeter; compare Heb. שֹׁפָר.

thupar, Anastasi I, 17, 7, scribe, copyist, secretary; Heb. סוֹפֵר, Aram. סַפְרָא, Syr. ܣܦܪܐ.

thuprath, Mar. Aby. I, Text 11, a Hittite chariot.

thuf, , , , Rev. 6, 26, papyrus; var. ; Copt. ϫⲟⲟⲩϥ, Heb. סוּף.

thumāqana, Alt-K. 1153, a devil of sickness; var. .

thun, , to bear, to carry, to rise up; Copt. ⲧⲱⲟⲩⲛ.

thurn, Rec. 1, 48, buckler, breast cover of leather; var. ; Heb. שִׁרְיוֹן.

thurḥ, to sin, to trespass.

thurtȧ, , fine flour; Heb. סֹלֶת.

thut, U. 574, N. 968, , a particle; , T. 271, P. 22, M. 33, N. 123, , U. 581, N. 962, , B.D. 180, 37, , B.D. 180, 27.

thut, U. 220, to be collected.

thut, U. 559, form, image.

thut, T. 266, , M. 43, 421, crown.

thutȧ, P. 34, crown.

thutha, , , , the piping of a bird, the cry of the hawk, twitterings.

Thuthu, Rec. 6, 151, 31, 18, the name of a god.

thuth ken, Ebers 63, 9, a seed.

thebit, N. 942, , T. 312, P. 174, , U. 554, T. 173, M. 154, , N. 970, , T. 32, 301, U. 553, Rec. 27, 60, , sandal; dual , P. 573, ; plur. , P. 408, M. 584, N. 813, 1190, , P. 612, ; , sandals white and black; see also ; Copt. ⲧⲟⲟⲩⲉ.

thebit, Rec. 4, 119, the sole of the foot.

thebu, , , , sandal-maker, worker in leather; plur. , Anastasi I, 26, 4, , , ; , sandal-maker to the king.

Thebti …, Metternich Stele 53, a pair of goddesses.

thebu-t … . Rec. 30, 68, a part of a ship.

theb …, …, …, Rev. 14, 73, calf, cow; compare Copt. ⲧⲃ in ⲧⲃⲛⲏ.

theb (tcheb) …, bird-cage; see also **tcheb** …, … .

theb-t …, sistrum.

theb …, copper coins, obolus, assarium; var. … .

thebeb …, T. 312, to break in, to smash.

Theba …, Rec. 26, 229, a god (?)

thebu …, …, Mar. Karn. 55, 61, Rec. 21, 77, Theban Ostraka B, 6, vase, pot, vessel; plur. …, IV, 666.

thebu …, …, Rec. 17, 145, a weight for meat, a measure; var. … .

thebn …, a lock of hair, curl; var. …, … .

Thebeh …, Typhon; var. … .

thebhen …, De Hymnis 36, to hop, to skip, to frisk (of animals).

thebtheb …, …, to tie up to (with …, IV, 658), to suspend, to tie (dead bodies to a wall).

thebtheb …, to dance, the belly-dance.

thebtheb-t …, dispute, argument.

thep …, a kind of goose.

thepȧ …, Rec. 30, 192, …, to breathe, to snuff the air.

theput …, the dead (?)

theph̨-t …, T. 303, …, P. 86, …, N. 44, …, N. 662, hole in the ground, cavern, cave; plur. …, P. 236, …, N. 656, …, Rec. 29, 154; …, the vault of the sky.

Theph̨ut petriu …, N. 656, …, M. 381, a group of shrines (?) in the Ṭuat.

Theph̨-t sheta-t …, Ṭuat VII, the 7th division of the Ṭuat.

thef …, to move about, to shake (?)

thefthef …, to dance, to wag (the head).

thefthef …, …, to spit, to pour out water; var. … .

thef …, papyrus plant; var. …; Copt. ϫⲟⲟⲩϥ, Heb. סוּף.

thefȧ …, U. 541, T. 297 = …, T. 305 . . . . . .

Thefnut …, …, consort of Shu; see …, …, P. 62, M. 83.

Thefnut …, Berg. I, 14, a lioness-goddess; see **Tefnut.**

theften …, P. 707 . . . .

theftenn …, Ȧmen. 11, 20, envoy, messenger (?)

them, them-t …, …, P. 62, M. 84, N. 91, P.S.B. 15, 37, Rec. 21, 197 = …, pron. 2nd fem. sing.

them, bandlet, tiara, apparel.

them, Åmen. 22, 6, 23, 9, to see (?)

thema, bold, brave, strong.

thema-ā, , IV, 657, , hero, warrior.

Thema, Ṭuat III, a god.

Thema-re, Ṭuat XII, a singing-god.

Themȧt-ḥer-t, Tomb Seti I, one of the 36 Dekans; var. , , Tomb Ram. IV; Gr. ΤΩΜ.

Themat-kher-t, , Tombs Seti I and Ram. II, one of the 36 Dekans.

thema-t A.Z. 1908, 16, the vulture amulet; var. .

thema, Hh. 377, seat, throne; , B.M. 828, Sphinx, 2, 132, scribe of the throne.

thema-t, mat (?) Copt. ⲧⲙⲏ.

thema, IV, 1110, lands, estates.

Themath, Ṭuat X, a lioness-goddess.

Themȧ-taui, P. 266, , M. 479, N. 1246, a god.

Themmit, Tomb Ram. IX, 10, god of the serpent .

themu, , for , writing, plan, drawing.

Themeḥ, , Libyan; plur. , , , , Mar. Karn. 53, 26.

Themḥu, Ṭuat V, the Libyans in the Ṭuat.

Themḥu, Rec. 30, 63, the "Libyan" god.

themes, Rec. 32, 80, to write, to make marks, to paint coloured pictures, to be of various colours, to be striped; var. .

themes, P. 604, striped, coloured (of the rump of an animal).

themes, Dream Stele 20, writing board, inscribed tablet.

themes-t, P. 172, N. 939, a writing, list, register; plur. , P. 346, , M. 646, , ; see .

themes, a condemned person.

themess-t, P. 681, 773, M. 770, design, writing, picture, document.

Themes-en-khentt, Tomb Seti I, , Denderah II, 10, one of the 36 Dekans.

thmes-t, midwife; Copt. ϴⲙⲉⲥⲓⲟ.

themth, Hh. 337 . . . . . .

themthem, a dry measure.

then = , abso. pron. 2nd fem. sing.

then , , , later , , pron. 2nd plur. ye, your; , N. 1385 (dual); Copt. ϴⲏⲛⲟⲩ.

then = , this.

then , , P. 307, 312, , where? ; var. ; Copt. ⲧⲱⲛ.

then , , IV, 222, , , , , , , , Rec. 30, 185, to lift up, to raise, to promote, to distinguish.

then-t something great or distinguished; plur. .

Then-àru , Tomb of Seti I, one of the 75 forms of Rā (No. 54).

Then-neteru , Ṭuat XII, the gate of the 12th division of the Ṭuat.

Then-reṭ , B.D. 125, II, the name of one of the 42 judges of Osiris.

then , B.D. 178, 23, a kind of tree; var. .

then , course, throughout.

then-t, thenn-t , U. 234, , Rec. 26, 66, , ibid. 26, 74, , , ibid. 31, 16, place, abode, sanctuary of Seker; plur. .

Thenen , Tomb of Seti I, one of the 75 forms of Rā (No. 3).

Thennit , B.D.G. 42, 699, 1352, , consort of Menthu and a form of Hathor.

thenà , T. 307, P. 173, 260, M. 493, where? ; see , ; Copt. ⲧⲱⲛ.

thenà , , to be old, old age, aged.

Thenà , Ṭuat XII, one of the 12 gods who towed the boat of Àf through the serpent Ānkh-neteru; he was re-born daily.

thenà, theniu , IV, 639, , pitcher, bowl, dish; plur. , L.D. III, 65A, 15.

thenà , Åmen. 14, 11 . . . . .

thenà-ti , Åmen. 15, 17, , Åmen. 20, 19, , Åmen. 25, 10 . . . .

thenàa , boomerang, camel stick.

theni , N. 940, where? ; see , , ; Copt. ⲧⲱⲛ.

thenu , pron. 2nd plur.; Copt. ⲑⲏⲛⲟⲩ.

thenu , IV, 700, , IV, 1141, , , , each, every.

thenu , U. 253, T. 196, P. 288, 678, N. 1293, M. 726, to count, to reckon.

thenut , A.Z. 1904, 89, , , Rec. 31, 11, , , IV, 1143, number, reckoning, computation, census (of cattle), calculations.

thenut , weight, quantity.

Thenu-t , the name of a festival.

thennu , Rechnungen 63, a plank or log of wood.

Thennui (?) , T. 302, a magical name (?) mentioned with .

thenpu IV, 930 . . . .

thenf , , , , , to dance, to play an instrument or sing to a dance.

thenf , Rec. 20, 216, drink.

thenf-t , vessel or pot of drink.

thenfit , Edict 4, sail.

thenem , N. 514A, an offering, milk (?)

thenem , the first milk in the breasts after childbirth; var. ; Copt. ϫⲉⲗⲙⲓ.

Thenem , T.S.B.A. III, 424, a nurse-goddess.

thenem , to weep, to make to weep.

thenemu , , Hh. 556, dens, caves.

thenem , , to turn away from, to turn back, to reject; var. .

Thenemi , B.D. 125, II, one of the 42 assessors of Osiris; see .

thenr , strong, bold, brave.

thenḥ-ti , Åmen. 16, 20 . . . .

thenḥer , Peasant 175, a bird.

thentut , Meir 8, a breed of cows.

thenti , , Tombos Stele 3, throne, chair of state.

thenta-t , , Rec. 27, 222, throne, chair of state, throne-chamber.

Thenti , Tomb Seti I, one of the 75 forms of Rā (No. 47).

thentenr , Rec. 8, 139, braves, soldiers.

thentha-t , IV, 565, , B.D. 180, 7, , L.D. III, 16A, throne, throne room, chair of state; , IV, 573; , throne mounted on a boat.

thenthen , Anastasi I, 24, 8, to run, to run away, to flee.

Thenthen-neteru , the name of the 12th Gate of the Ṭuat.

ther , I, 133, number.

ther , , stuff, apparel.

ther-t , U. 563, willow tree; var. ; Copt. ⲧⲱⲣⲉ.

Therit , Rec. 27, 53, the goddess of the willow tree.

therut , an offering.

therȧ , time, season, year; plur. ; varr. , .

therȧ , U. 538, T. 295, P. 229 . . . . .

theri , to sprinkle, to moisten.

therit , Rec. 31, 29, reverence, adoration, prayer, entreaty.

therri-t , III, 17, , Dream Stele 27, mound raised up against a besieged city; compare Heb. סֹלְלָה, and see **therther**.

theru , to paint, painting, writing (?)

theru , U. 562, colour, paint.

Therut, U. 220, T. 323, , U. 510, a god or goddess (?)

theru, Berg. II, 399, to diminish, to reduce.

therut, bandlet, fetter.

therru, U. 563, to cleanse, to purify; var. (?)

therp, T. 390, M. 404, , U. 131A, a kind of goose; plur. , , Rec. 1, 48, 29, 148.

therp, , to waddle (like a goose), to dandle a child.

therf, , , Peasant 294, to dance.

threm, thremm, , to weep, to cause to weep; , to weep in their hearts.

therḥeḥ, to rejoice (?)

Thertȧ, Rec. 27, 53, a god.

therther, to overcome, to destroy.

therther, Rev. 12, 78, , earthwork, mounds thrown up around a besieged city; Copt. ⲧⲱⲣⲧⲣ̄.

thertcher, Thes. 1322, walls.

theh, to attack, to transgress, to invade; varr. , , .

thehtheh, Amherst Pap. 42, raider, invader.

theh, a kind of plant used in medicine.

theheb, A.Z. 1905, 19, to frisk, to gambol (of young of animals).

thehem, , A.Z. 1906, 126, to shout for joy, to praise.

theḥ, IV, 840, to approach, to invade.

theḥ-t, approach.

theḥu, IV, 502, , , to rejoice, to make merry.

theḥeḥ, Rec. 22, 2, , , , , , , , , to rejoice.

theḥḥu, , , joy, gladness.

theḥḥut, IV, 894, , Rec. 29, 166, rejoicings; var. .

Theḥḥut, gods who rejoice, or divine rejoicings.

Theḥbith, Ṭuat VI, a goddess.

theḥef-ti, a plant.

theḥen, Mar. Karn. 53, 28, Jour. E.A. III, 98, IV, 656, 710, Love Songs 5, 5, , to advance, to meet, to touch, to twitch (of the nerves or muscles, P.S.B. 13, 412); Copt. ϫⲱϩ, ϭⲱϩ.

theḥen, T. 334, , P. 826, , M. 249, , , to sparkle, to scintillate, to glitter, to shine.

theḥenḥen, , U. 563, to sparkle.

theḥen-t, U. 563, , U. 626, , lightning-stone, crystal, any bright or sparkling substance, blue-glazed faïence, etc.

Theḥen, Ombos I, 186, one of the 14 kau of Rā.

Theḥen-åṭebu, etc., T. 334, P. 826, M. 249, N. 704, one of the four bulls of Tem.

Theḥnit-tepå-khat, Rec. 34, 190, one of the 12 Thoueris goddesses.

Theḥnu, U. 564, M. 766, the Libyans; var.

Theḥen, IV, 840 . . . .

theḥenu, U. 64, N. 318, Libyan unguent.

theḥnen-t, T. 89, N. 619 . . . . . .

theḥes, skin of a beast, hide; compare Heb. תַּחַשׁ, Assyr., takh-shu.

thekh, a drinking festival; var.

thekhthekh, to mix a drink; varr.; Copt. ⲧⲉϩ, ⲑⲱϩ, ⲧⲱϩ.

thes, T. 336, M. 254, N. 640; see.

Thesi-en-khentt, one of the 36 Dekans; var.

thes, thess, T. 159, M. 175, 688, U. 482, Åmen. 19, 7, 25, 1, Peasant 257, to knot, to tie, to tie together, to tie on something (a crown or a garment), to bind corn, to coil, to twine, to plait, to weave; M. 785, M. 782; Copt. ϭⲱⲥ.

thes meḥu, A.Z. 1906, 123, B.M. 828, to weave a crown, to tie on a crown.

thes metcheḥ, Sphinx 3, 132, to tie on a girdle.

thes qebsu (beqsu), U. 310, to tie together the entrails (?)

thes qesu, P. 612, to tie together the bones, to reconstitute the body.

thes-t, Koller 4, 6, thread.

thes-t, Rec. 31, 171, tie, band, knot (?)

thesthes, B.D. 145, 24, fillet, band, tie.

thes, thes-t, P. 568, knot, tie, ligature, backbone, vertebrae, spine; plur., U. 517, T. 328, T. 183.

thess-t, tie, knot.

thesut VII, the seven magical knots that protected a man.

thes-t, frame, framework with bars (?) bearing pole, carrying-pole of a litter.

Thesu, Ṭuat X, an archer-god.

Thesu VII, B.D. 71, 16, seven gods who assisted at the judgment and condemnation of the wicked.

Thes-ām, Berg. I, 25, a bull-god.

Thes-ārq, Denderah II, 10, 11, one of the 36 Dekans; Gr. ΘΕΣΟΑΚ.

Thes-t-up-t, Ṭuat IV, a horned goddess.

Thes-usfu, P. 708, a fiend or devil (?)

Thes-ḥeru, Ṭuat X, a serpent-god, son of Sekri. He has a head at each end of his body, moves on four human legs, and Ḥeru-Khenti is perched on his back.

Thesi-Ṭesher-t, B.D. (Saïte) 149, the god of the 3rd Åat.

thes, chamber, room.

thes-t, sarcophagus, funerary coffer.

thest-tå, burial, funeral.

thes, A.Z. 1905, 22,: (1) to arrange times and seasons; (2) to wear an amulet.

thes, to command, to arrange, to direct, to levy, to raise taxes.

thesu, Gol. Ḥamm. 14, 135, captain, commandant, chief officer, general, master, commander; , Coronation Stele 3, trusted officers; Copt. ϫⲟⲉⲓⲥ.

thesu, captain:— captain of bowmen; , captain of soldiers; , IV, 1120, captain of a fortress; , captains of ferrymen; Copt. ϫⲟⲉⲓⲥ.

thess, captain, general; plur., Coronation Stele 15.

thess, master, chief; varr.; Copt. ϫⲟⲉⲓⲥ.

thesit, lady, chieftainess, a title of the goddess Nekhebit; Copt. ϫⲟⲉⲓⲥ.

thes-t, A.Z. 1879, 29, levies from districts, troops, bodies of soldiers, regiments.

thes-t, the working folk on an estate, peasants.

thes, to compose a connected statement, to arrange words in logical sequence.

thes, I, 116, IV, 221, IV, 1090, proverb, saying, formula, charm, spell, incantation, declaration, statement, what a man wants to say, accusation of a plaintiff, speech or defence of a defendant, sentence, aphorism, apophthegm, "word," precept; IV, 1082, speech of a petitioner; IV, 430, a statement which is a tissue of lies.

thesu, speeches, proverbs, precepts, statements, charms, spells, orders, commands.

thes-t, thess-t, plot, plan, crafty design; , an abominable plot.

thesu, law-makers, arrangers, disposers, managers.

thes maā, N. 163, speech of law.

thes pekhar (?) , , a rubrical direction meaning to transpose conversely, *e.g.*, "The strength of Horus is my strength": **thes pekhar,** *i.e.*, "My strength is as the strength of Horus."

thesi , T. 271, P. 22, 97, 604, M. 32, N. 122, , Ḳubbân Stele 11, , , , , , , , , , Koller 1, 8, , , , , , , , , Metternich Stele 59, , to lift up, to raise, to rise, to raise oneself, to ascend a hill, to lift away, to bear up, to support, to be high (of price), to lift up an offering to a god, to set aside, high (of bows); Copt. ⲭⲓⲥⲉ, ⲭⲟⲥⲉ, ϭⲓⲥⲓ, ϭⲟⲥⲓ.

thess , T. 29, , , Hh. 564, to lift up, to raise, to rise, to mount, to be exalted; Copt. ⲭⲓⲥⲉ.

thesi , ascent, ascender.

thesu bȧti , Tombos Stele 13, wearers of the double crown.

thesi semsem , mounted soldier, knight; var. .

thesi-t , , Rec. 27, 228, a rising, revolt, insurrection.

thes-ut , , supports, props, pillars; , , , , the four pillars of heaven; plur. .

Thesu-urut , U. 434, , T. 248, a group of gods who raised the dead.

Thesu ur , T. 285, , P. 35, M. 44, , N. 65, , B.D. 127B, 7, a god.

Thesi-khā-netrui (?) , a title of Khensu Nefer-ḥetep.

Thesi-tchatcha (?) , U. 423, , T. 243, the "head-raising" god.

Thesi-tchatchau-neteru , Ṭuat XII, a singing dawn-god of Sinaitic origin (?)

thesi-t , Hh. 343, , , , , , , , a ridge of ground, high ground, bank of a river; Copt. ϭⲓⲥ, ⲭⲓⲥⲉ.

thes , dyke (?); plur. .

thes-ta , estate, domain, field; the of Neḥa-ḥer in the Ṭuat was 450 cubits long.

thesi , , , Rev. 11, 179, to speak haughtily or proudly.

thesi , pride, arrogance.

thesi ḥat , , B.D. 178, 3, high of heart or courage, bold, proud, haughty; compare Copt. ⲭⲁⲥⲓ ϩⲏⲧ.

thesi , , what rises to the surface of a liquid, scum, to skim.

thesut , Peasant 299, troubles, difficulties.

thes-ti , , jaws (?) the beak of a bird.

thesut , , teeth.

thess (?) , U. 168, downcast, dejected.

thesȧu , , ; see .

thesȧu , an excitable man, a man prone to anger

thesȧu, to command, to direct; see .

thesȧu taiu, director of lands"—a royal title.

thesȧs, chief, lord, master; varr. ; Copt. ϫⲟⲉⲓⲥ.

thesȧsiu, words, speeches, formulae; see .

thesi[t], a kind of fancy bread used as an offering.

thesi, to lie on the back, dead (?)

th-su; see .

Thesbu, T. 292, the god of circumcision (?)

thesf-ti, a kind of collar or necklace.

thesem, tower on a wall, bastion; plur. , Israel Stele 23.

thesem, Hh. 355, , greyhound; plur. , IV, 809, .

thesm-t, bitch.

thesemu-tchatcha (?), B.D. 145, 40, dog-headed.

Thesmu Ḥeru, B.D. 13, 1, the greyhounds of Horus.

Th-senȧ-t nefer-t, "the beautiful sister"—a title of Tefnut.

thesten (?), Rec. 31, 170, 172, girdle (?)

thesthes, a kind of unguent.

thek, thee, thou.

thek = ⲙⲉⲧⲛⲓⲑⲓⲟⲥ, A.Z. 1868, 55, P.S.B. 13, 38, magnet; compare ⲧⲉϭ, to stick, to adhere.

thek-t, loaf, cake; Copt. ϭⲁϭⲉ (?)

Thekem, B.D. 99, 13, a god of offerings; var. , B.D. (Saïte) 72, 4.

theknu, watchman, spy, human victim; plur. , A.Z. 34, 8, var. , Israel Stele 24.

thektan, , A.Z. 34, 22, Sphinx 3, 151, spies, human victims, Libyan soldiers (?)

thet, Koller I, 6, ; Metternich Stele, 3, 5, to separate, to release, to set free, to be destroyed.

thet, , Rec. 24, 76, 85, table, altar, thick staff, cudgel (?)

thet en renp-t, an aromatic substance used in making kyphi; var. .

Thett, Metternich Stele 51, one of the seven scorpion-goddesses of Isis.

theta, to send back, to reverse.

thetef, , to hop, to skip, to scatter (?)

thetef, , , , , , to pour out, to sprinkle, to pour out by drops.

thetef, Metternich Stele 170, fountain (?)

thetef, a measure.

thetthet, Åmen. 12, 10, 13, 1, 22, 20, to gossip, to chatter.

theth, Hh. 386, to alight.

theth re, Åmen. 5, 10, babbler.

theth-t, T. 308, tie, binding.

thethi, Décrets 108, inscription.

Thethu, U. 549, T. 304, a serpent-fiend in the Ṭuat.

thether, Rev. 13, 6 = ; Copt. ⲧⲱⲣⲉ.

thethḥeḥut (theḥtheḥut), rejoicings; var.

theṭef, to spread, to scatter; var. .

theṭef, to distil, to sprinkle; see .

Ṭ

ṭ, = Heb. ד and ט; Copt. ϯ.

ṭ, U. 373, P. 434, to give, to set, to place; , U. 61, N. 314; , P. 176, 364; , P. 176, M. 316, N. 383, Rec. 31, 167; to lay oneself flat on the belly in homage.

ṭu (?), sandals; Copt. ⲧⲟⲟⲩⲉ.

ṭe-t (?), , , the hand; perhaps to be read **ṭer-t** for ; dual , P. 630, , N. 1371, Hh. 439, , N. 1043, , A.Z. 1908, 116, , , ; plur. , P. 204, T. 385, , Metternich Stele 24, 25, , , , ; **ṭe-t àab-t**, Nåstasen Stele 9, the left hand.

ṭeṭ-t-k àb-k, P. 83, M. 113, thy heart's desire; var. , N. 27.

ṭe-t, IV, 659, the hands cut off from slain enemies.

ṭe-ut, , , , , Rec. 26, 66, a gang of five labourers or slaves; var. .

Ṭe-t Åmen, Ṭuat X, the colossal right hand that grasps the chain whereby Āapep is fettered.

Ṭe-t ent Åst, etc., B.D. 99, 21, 153A, 8: (1) the opening in the net of the Akeru-gods; (2) the of the net, B.D. 153A, 21; (3) a part of the magical boat.

ṭe-t setem, Rec. 17, 146, servant.

ṭe-t (?), hand, *i.e.*, the trunk of an elephant.

ṭe-t, IV, 1121, [ ], calf, young ox.

ṭe-ti, yearling.

ṭe-t, Anastasi I, 24, 5, part of a chariot, pole (?)

ṭe-t ḥau (?), pole (?) of a chariot.

ṭa, the article "the" (fem.); Copt. ϯ.

ṭa, U. 403, to smite; , I, 32, "smiter of all lands."

ṭa, B.D. 45, 2, to flee, to escape, to pass away.

ṭa, a wild animal.

ṭa, flame, fire.

ṭa, , , , to tremble, to shake, to quake.

ṭa-t, trembling, quaking.

ṭa, B.D. 39, 11, emission of seed; see also , .

ṭaṭa, Love Songs, 2, 2; , B.D. 125, II, to produce an emission of seed irregularly; varr. , .

ṭa, garment, vestment; var.

ṭåa ; see **ṭaå** .

Ṭa-t, P. 77, P. 162, M. 107, N. 20, , M. 413, a very ancient name for the Other World; see **Ṭuat**; , N. 765, a lake in the Other World.

Ṭait, , U. 445, a god, the Ṭuat personified.

Ṭatiu, T. 254, , P. 185, M. 298, N. 899, , U. 445, the gods of the Ṭuat.

ṭa (ṭi?), Hh. 558, , M. 785, , , , , to give, to set, to place, to cause, to allow; see **erṭi** , , ; , T. 236, U. 495, , N. 156, "give!"; , P. 204, , B.D. 65, 7; , , I will not permit; , , give thyself, *i.e.*, show thyself.

ṭaṭa (ṭiṭi?), T. 87, 209, N. 618, I, 36, , , , , to give, to set, to place.

ṭa-t (ṭi-t), , , gift, present, tribute.

ṭaṭa-t (ṭiṭi-t), , T. 85, gift; , IV, 938, gifts.

ṭaṭa, , , giver; plur. , P. 148, , P. 435, M. 622, N. 1227, , , , , .

ṭaṭa ȧb, , , , what the heart gives, *i.e.*, will, pleasure, desire; , to go with pleasure.

ṭa aq-t, Rev., to destroy; Copt. ⲧⲁⲕⲟ, ϯⲁⲕⲱ.

ṭa aka, Rev., to destroy; Copt. ⲧⲁⲕⲟ, ϯⲁⲕⲱ.

ṭaȧ ta, , , to put on the earth, *i.e.*, to give birth to; , A.Z. 1907, pl. 1, 3, to land at a place.

ṭa ȧm-t, Rec. 27, 6, to inform; Copt. ⲧⲁⲙⲙⲟ.

ṭa ȧri, to cause to do, to make to be done.

ṭa ȧthi, Rev. 11, 141, to carry off; Copt. ϯϫⲓ.

ṭa ā, , , to give the hand, to help, to assist; Copt. ϯⲧⲟⲟⲧ.

ṭa ānkh, Rec. 27, 8, to rear, to keep alive; Copt. ⲧⲁⲛϩⲟ.

ṭa ānkh, one to whom life hath been given; , "dowered with life, stability, serenity, health, and all joy of heart like Rā."

Ṭa-ānkhit, Lanzone 112, a divine midwife, .

ṭa ās, Rev., to fine, to mulct; Copt. ϯⲟⲥⲉ.

ṭa āq, Rev. 12, 41, , Rev. 11, 165, to destroy; Copt. ⲧⲁⲕⲟ.

ṭa uai, Rec. 27, 7, to set on the way; Copt. ⲧⲁⲟⲩⲟ.

ṭa uāb-t, Rec. 27, 6, to purify; Copt. ⲧⲃⲃⲟ.

ṭa un, to cause to be.

ṭa peḥui (?), Rec. 37, 21, to decay, to die off; Copt. ϯ ⲉⲫⲁϩⲟⲩ.

ṭa em àb, to put in the heart, *i.e.*, to bear in mind.

ṭa em ḥer en, to put in the face of, *i.e.*, to put before; , to lay a charge on one.

ṭa meḥ, Rev., to kindle a fire; Copt. ϯⲙⲟϩ.

ṭa mesha, Rev. 11, 184, to walk; Copt. ϯⲙⲟⲟϣⲉ.

ṭa metr, to correct.

ṭa nia, Jour. As. 1908, 252, to appoint; Copt. ϯⲛⲉⲓ.

Ṭa nubit, Lanzone 112, a divine midwife.

ṭaṭa re, appellant, plaintiff, petitioner.

ṭa er às-t, to put in [its] place, *i.e.*, to restore.

ṭa er ber, Rev. 12, 87, to sell; Copt. ϯ ⲉⲃⲟⲗ.

ṭa rekh, to make to know, *i.e.*, to inform.

ṭa (ṭi) res-tep, IV, 1153, to set a watchman.

ṭa reṭui, Ḥerusàtef Stele 118, to direct the feet towards someone or something.

ṭa ḥa, Mar. Karn. 53, 21, to exercise care.

ṭa ḥep, Rev. 14, 15, to hide; Copt. ϯϩⲱⲡ.

ṭa ḥem-t, Rev. 12, 107, to marry.

ṭa ḥems, Rec. 27, 7, to dwell, to make inhabited; Copt. ⲧϩⲉⲙⲥⲟ.

ṭa ḥer, to turn the face towards someone.

ṭa ḥer ges, to set aside, to push out of the way, to yield, to become partial; , impartial.

ṭa ḥer ta, to put on the ground, to depose, to throw into the street.

ṭa khamm, Rev. 11, 141, to inflame; Copt. ϯϧⲙⲟⲙ.

ṭa kheper, , , Rev. 11, 142, to make to be, to beget; , IV, 1106, to cause to be done into writing; Copt. ϯϣⲱⲡⲉ.

ṭa sa, Annales III, 109, to give the back, *i.e.*, to turn the back in flight, to visit.

ṭa siàu, Rec. 27, 7, Rev. 11, 140, to give to drink; Copt. ⲧⲥⲓⲟ, ϯⲥⲉⲓ.

Ṭa-sma-ba-er-kha-t, Berg. I, 23, a bird-god who rejoined the soul to the body.

ṭa senṭ, to terrify, to frighten.

ṭa thau, to give breath to someone, *i.e.*, to spare the life of.

ṭa ṭe-t (?), to give the hand, *i.e.*, to help.

ṭa tchatcha, , Ḥerusàtef Stele 118, to give the head, *i.e.*, to show oneself.

ṭa tchatcha er ta, to lay the head on the ground, *i.e.*, to die.

ṭau, rations, provisions.

ṭa ḥetch, white bread.

ṭaṭau, , , Ebers Pap., rev. 11, 1ff., Koller 4, 2, , , , , , fuller's earth; Copt. ϯϯ in ⲡⲉϥϯϯ.

ṭa-ti (?), bundles (?)

ṭaà, Rec. 31, 14, a sheet of cloth or linen.

ṭaȧa, Peasant 46, garment, sheet of cloth.

ṭaȧu, B.D. 82, 8, , A.Z. 1906, 28, garment, sheet of cloth, cordage; , A.Z. 49, 108 = ; Copt. ⲑⲱϯ.

ṭauȧ shennu, coverings made of hair.

ṭaȧu, loaf of bread or cake.

Ṭaȧnȧuna, L.D. III, 211, 4, , Harris I, 76, 7, , Alt-K. 1188, a Mediterranean people. The mātu Danuna (B.M. 88–10–13, 56) of the Tall al-'Amârnah tablets.

ṭaȧr (ṭar), Peasant 210, , to use force (usually in a bad sense), to oppress, to constrain, to use the corvée, to ill-treat.

ṭaȧr-t, oppression, restraint.

ṭauar, a measure of some kind.

ṭaus (ṭius), P.S.B. 15, 475, to cut into, to engrave; Copt. ⲧⲱⲥ.

ṭab, P. 292, T. 117A, , Hh. 220, fig; plur. , Shipwreck 47, ; , fig trees; var. , P. 94, M. 118, N. 57; plur. ; , P. 692, a string of figs.

ṭabu (?), oboli, assarii; var.

ṭap, U. 146, T. 117, N. 454 ....

ṭaṭaf (ṭiṭif), to sprinkle.

Ṭafnut (Ṭifnut), a goddess—the female counterpart of Shu.

ṭamam, , sack, mat; var. ; see **tema, temam.**

ṭamer-t (ṭimer-t), , heaven, sky.

Ṭamṭ, Tomb Seti I, one of the 75 forms of Rā (No. 1).

ṭang, P. 401, , M. 572, (*sic*), N. 1179, dwarf; Amharic ድንክ :

ṭar, Rec. 31, 14, to oppress; see .

Ṭarṭeniu, , Rougé I.H. 206, 240, a Mediterranean people.

ṭarina (m'rina ?), Annales IV, 132, lords, nobles.

ṭas, an object painted on early coffins (Lacau), knife (?)

ṭas, , to slit, to cut up, to make gashes.

ṭakr (ṭikr), Rev. 11, 178; see , to set away, to carry off (?)

ṭag, IV, 1208, to plant = ; Copt. ⲧⲱϭⲉ.

Ṭag, N. 1179; see , the dwarf-god.

ṭagi, A.Z. 1864, 107, bat.

Ṭaṭemtch (?), Tomb Seti I, one of the 75 forms of Rā (No. 1).

Ṭatenen-t (Ṭitenen-t), a primitive earth-goddess.

ṭȧa, emission of seed; see , , .

ṭȧa , , , Rev. 6, 22, garment, vestment, cordage; var. ; Copt. ⲑⲱϯ.

ṭȧabiu (ṭabiu), wolves, jackals, hyenas; Assyr. (Rawl. C.I.W.A. II, 6, 4, 1), Heb. זְאֵב, Arab. ذِئْب, Syr. ܕܐܒܐ, Chald. דֵּיבָה, Eth. ዝእብ፡.

ṭȧar-t ; var. , oppression, constraint, restraint.

ṭȧb, Rec. 27, 223, wolf; Heb. זְאֵב.

ṭȧs, to sit.

ṭȧṭȧ, Hymn Darius 34, to trample upon, to beat down.

ṭāb-t, purification, a purifying.

ṭi, A.Z. 1912, 99, , A.Z. 1893, 108, , here, there; Copt. ⲧⲁⲓ, ⲧⲏ.

ṭi, Nȧstasen Stele 68, , Dream Stele 31, , to wait, to stand still, to remain; , Rec. 21, 86.

ṭi-t, pleading, defence (?)

ṭi-t, B.D. 102, 6, produce, gifts.

Ṭius , , *i.e.*, Δῖος, the 1st month of the Macedonian year = part of October and part of November.

ṭibnu , , Nȧstasen Stele 40, 47, beasts, cattle; Copt. ⲧⲃⲛⲟⲟⲩⲉ.

Ṭifnu-t, the female counterpart of the god Shu.

ṭimȧi-t, Ḥerusȧtef Stele 143, towns.

ṭirga, dwarf; see .

Ṭiṭi , , Mar. Karn. 52, 13, Thes. 1203, a Libyan king.

ṭiṭi, B.M. 5633, 9, pot, vessel, measure.

ṭiṭi-t, Love Songs, 3, 12, wine cellar (?)

Ṭith, Ṭuat VII, a goddess in the Ṭuat.

ṭu (?) , T. 229, , , , five; , , , the festival of the five epagomenal days; Copt. ϯⲏ.

ṭu-nu , **ṭu-nut**, fifth.

Ṭu-uti, Ṭuat III, two goose-gods in the Ṭuat.

ṭu, to give; , , givers.

ṭu er ta , , IV, 322, 329, to land at a place.

ṭu (tchu) , U. 1, T. 347, , , , , , , , , to be bad, or evil, or stinking; , Rec. 31, 18; , T. 347, be not thou bad of smell; **bu ṭu** , , badness, wickedness.

ṭu-t, P. 643, M. 679, N. 1241, , , , , Jour. As. 1908, 285, , bad thing, evil, wickedness; plur. , , , Peasant 288, , Rec. 16, 132.

ṭutȧ, evil man, wicked person.

ṭu qeṭu, IV, 1078, evilly disposed men, men naturally bad.

Ṭu-t, B.D. 15 (Ani, sheet 20), 44, god of evil in the form of a serpent.

Ṭuti, B.D.G. 1356, , the god of evil, *i.e.*, Set.

Ṭuṭu (Ṭui), Nesi-Ȧmsu 32, 15, , Ṭuat X, god of evil, *i.e.*, Āapep, or Set.

Ṭuṭu, , , , one of the 42 judges in the hall of Osiris, a devil in the 7th Pylon of the Ṭuat, a title of Āapep.

Ṭuṭu-f, , , , , , B.D. 125, II, one of the 42 assessors of Osiris.

Ṭuṭu-ḥer, Tomb Ram. IX, 10, a serpent-god.

Ṭu-ḥetep, a name or title of a god.

Ṭuṭu-s (?), B.D. 122, 3, the name of a rudder.

Ṭu-qeṭu, a title of Set.

ṭu, A.Z. 1878, 49, , , , , , , hill, mountain; plur. , IV, 1062, , IV, 889, , IV, 955, , , , Rec. 13, 15, ; , Rev. 11, 68; Copt. ⲦⲞⲞⲨ.

ṭutiu, L.D. III, 140, mountaineers.

Ṭui (?), N. 969, , the two mountains, *i.e.*, of sunrise and sunset (Bakha and Manu?).

Ṭui, N. 969, the two mountains between which the deceased emerges (?)

Ṭuit, Rec. 16, 109, a mountain-goddess (?)

Ṭu ȧmi Khert-neter, the mountain in the Other World.

Ṭu Ȧmenu, "hill of the west"—a name of the cemetery.

Ṭu uāb, , , "holy mountain," the modern Gebel Barkal at the foot of the Fourth Cataract.

ṭu bȧa-t, B.D.G. 3, 183, a hill of metal, or a hill containing mines.

Ṭu-f, U. 570, , B.D. 31, 4, read **Tepi ṭu-f,** "he who is on his hill," *i.e.*, Anubis; fem. , P. 608.

Ṭu menkh (?) Rerek, B.D. 149, a mountain in the 7th Ȧat; var. (Saïte) .

Ṭu en Āmau, Rec. 16, 51 . . . . . .

Ṭu en Bakha, mount of Sunrise; see **Bakha.**

Ṭu en Bekhan, , mount of Sunrise.

Ṭu en Maātiu, the hill of the righteous, the holy hill of the beatified.

Ṭu en Khent, the hill country south and east of Egypt.

Ṭu en Khert-neter, B.D. 149, a mountain in the 4th Āat.

Ṭu en Kenmut, the mountain ridge between Egypt and the Oasis of Khârgah.

Ṭu en Kesh, the Nubian hills.

Ṭu Ḥeru-nub, mount of the Golden Horus.

Ṭu semi, U. 493, N. 945, the mountain of .

Ṭu Seḥseḥ, U. 493, N. 945, the mountain of .

Ṭui qaui āaui, B.D. 149, a high double mountain on which lived a serpent 70 cubits long.

Ṭu ṭesh[er], the Red Mountain (near Cairo).

ṭu, N. 679 . . . .

ṭu-t, a bird.

ṭu, Bubastis 51, a kind of altar vessel.

ṭu-ā (?), Hearst Pap. XI, 16, , knife, scalpel, knife used in circumcision (?)

Ṭu-ā, T. 292; var. , god of circumcision (?)

ṭu, , bandlet, garment.

ṭu, lion.

ṭuṭu, lion; var. .

Ṭuṭu, a son of the goddess Neith.

ṭua, to do something in the morning.

ṭua, , , , , , , , , , the morning, to-morrow morning; Copt. ⲧⲟⲟⲩⲓ, ϩⲧⲟⲟⲩⲉ, Amharic ጡት, ṭuwat.

ṭuait, U. 512, T. 325, , , Rec. 29, 147, , , , , , , , the dawn, the early morning.

ṭuai, III, 143, , matutinal, belonging to the dawn.

Ṭuai [ ], Rec. 32, 85, god of the dawn.

Ṭuau, B.D. 17, 16, a lion-god, symbol of "To-day."

Ṭuau, P. 671, , M. 660, , N. 1275, , P. 178, , P. 356, , N. 1070; , N. 68, the star of the morning.

Ṭua-t, P. 244, M. 446, N. 1056, the planet Venus as a morning star.

Ṭuai-ti, , , god of the morning; , Ṭuai is his father and mother.

Ṭua ur, P. 589, , P. 643, M. 680, , N. 953, 1242, the "great star of the morning."

Ṭua-t neter, title of the high-priestess of Āmen.

ṭua neter, U. 199, N. 24, 888, P. 80, 172, M. 110, P. 178, M. 268, M. 688, T. 276, P. 29, M. 40, N. 68, B.D. 109, 10, the star of the god. Later forms are:—

ṭua, U. 47, P. 677, U. 226, T. 192, N. 1289, IV, 1081, to praise, to adore, to honour.

ṭua-t, praise, a hymn of praise; plur.

ṭuau, Thes. 1286, praises, praisers, written hymns of praise.

ṭua neter, to thank God, to offer thanksgiving.

ṭua sa (?), Ḥerusȧtef Stele 67 . . . .

Ṭuai, Ṭuat I, a singing-god.

Ṭuati, Mar. Aby. I, 45, a double god whose shrines were in and .

Ṭuaiu, Ṭuat X and XI, a group of singing-gods.

Ṭuaānu, M. 484, a god; varr. N. 1251, P. 269.

Ṭua-ti m'ketit en neb-s, Ṭuat IX, the Hour-goddess in the 9th Division of the Ṭuat.

Ṭua-mut-f, U. 219, M. 663, M. 495, N. 592, 1279, Berg. I, 7, one of the four sons of Horus and god of the eastern quarter of the heavens. He protected the lungs and heart of the deceased.

Ṭua-mut-f, the god of the 3rd hour of the night.

Ṭua-mut-f, the god and festival of the 6th day of the month.

Ṭua-mut-f, goddess of the 14th day of the month.

Ṭua-mut-f, B.D. 99, 22, a bolt-peg in the magical boat.

Ṭua-qebḥ-f . . . ., Denderah III, 9, 29, a serpent-god.

Ṭua-t, U. 381, B.M. 708, Rec. 32, 176, a very ancient name for the land of the dead,

and of the Other World; , Rec. 26, 225; , the everlasting Ṭuat; , the hidden Ṭuat.

Ṭuat , Ṭuat VIII, a circle in the Ṭuat.

Ṭua-ti , , , , , , , the god of the Ṭuat; varr. , , , B.D. 172, 25.

Ṭuati , , Ṭuat XII: (1) a god with a paddle; (2) one of the 75 forms of Rā (No. 41), Tomb Seti I; (3) a star-god in the Ṭuat (VII); (4) a singing-god (Ṭuat I).

Ṭuatiu , P. 245, , N. 1057, , , , , the gods and other beings of the Ṭuat; , Horus of the Ṭuat (XI), a form of Åf the dead Sun-god.

ṭuai-t , , Rev. 12, 116, death, destruction.

ṭuaut , hollows, abysses, empty places.

ṭua-t , a plant; plur. .

ṭua-ut (?) , , out-cry, roar; plur. , , , .

ṭua , , to bear, to carry, to support.

ṭua-taui , Palermo Stele, "Ṭua-taui" ships of 100 cubits (in length).

ṭua-t , pillar, one of the four supports of the sky; var. **tua** .

Ṭuaȧu , Denderah IV, 63, a serpent-warder of a coffer.

ṭuau-t (?) , , , holy oil or unguent.

ṭuaut , , P. 647, , , P. 716, , , M. 744 . . . . .

Ṭuatheth , Ṭuat VII, a star-goddess.

ṭuȧ , vineyard.

ṭuȧ , U. 96, , , M. 201, N. 374, , , , to call, to cry out.

ṭuȧ-t , , Rec. 29, 146, , a bird.

ṭuȧ , mountain, hill.

ṭuȧu , P. 398, , N. 1175, , , pot, vase, vessel, kind of drink (?)

ṭuȧu , a drink offering, libation (?)

ṭui , to cry out, to call; , crier; plur. .

Ṭui , Ṭuat VIII, a god.

Ṭuit , Ṭuat X, a group of four goddesses who acclaim Rā.

ṭuma (ṭmau?) , bodies of singing-men or singing-women, choirs.

ṭun , T. 308, , Rec. 30, 192, to string a bow.

ṭun , Rec. 21, 8, 27, 226, , Anastasi I, 25, 9, , , Ḥerusȧtef Stele 104,

, ibid. 108, , , Rec. 16, 109, , , A.Z. 1908, 118, , Rev. 12, 114, , to stretch out, to reach out, to extend, to stretch the legs in walking, to lift up, to rise up, to raise, to bear; Copt. ⲧⲱⲟⲩⲛ; see also and .

ṭun , A.Z. 1872, 121, , to draw and quarter (?)

ṭun , to get on the back of a bull tied and bound for sacrifice in order to stab him.

Ṭuniā , , the name of one of the instruments used in performing the ceremony of Opening the Mouth.

Ṭun-peḥti , the name of the doorkeeper of the 2nd Ȧrit.

Ṭunn-Maāu , , Ṭuat IV, one of the haulers of the boat of Ȧf.

Ṭun-ḥat , the god of the 10th day of the month.

Ṭun-ḥati , B.D. 144, the doorkeeper of the 2nd Ȧrit.

Ṭunānu , N. 1251; var. , P. 269, a god.

ṭunu , a plant or shrub.

ṭun ; var. , Rev., a green substance.

ṭunu , Annales 9, 155 . . . .

ṭur , , , to clean, to purify; var. , , B.D. 99, 31.

ṭeb , , Hh. 396, sandal, sole of the foot; Copt. ⲧⲟⲟⲩⲉ.

ṭeb-ti , , Ḥerusȧtef Stele 15, , Nȧstasen Stele 64, sandals, soles of the feet, footsteps.

ṭeb , , Rec. 27, 223, , , , , , hippopotamus, pig; var. ; plur. , Peasant 206, , Ȧmen. 7, 3.

ṭeb , , horn; dual **ṭebui** , ; , horn of the South, , horn of the North; Copt. ⲧⲁⲡ.

ṭeb , IV, 657, , IV, 651, horn, *i.e.*, wing, of an army.

ṭeb , Koller 1, 8, horns (of a bow).

ṭebi-t , ; see .

ṭeb , to decorate, to adorn; see **tcheba** .

ṭeb , to wall up, to stop up, to block a passage.

ṭebb , Peasant 234, to stifle, to suffocate, to have the nose stopped.

ṭebb , a little bag, scrotum (?); Copt. ⲑⲉⲃⲓ.

ṭeb-t , Metternich Stele 53, , settlement, inhabited district.

ṭeb-t , , box, coffer, coffin, sarcophagus, shrine; Copt. ⲑⲉⲃⲓ.

Ṭebutiu (Tchebutiu) , Berg. 72, , ,

Rec. 31, 163, , Rec. 30, 190, the gods in their shrines or coffins.

ṭeb-t , , , , , Rev. 14, 36, brick, tile, block, the tile on which a woman sits to bring forth (Rec. 2, 109); , Rev. 14, 14, the four faïence bricks or tiles in Heliopolis; Copt. ⲧⲱⲃⲉ.

ṭeb-t , T. 13, 14 . . . . . .

ṭeb, ṭeba , Methen 7, , U. 146A, N. 454, , P. 94, M. 118, N. 57, , , fig; plur. , , , , , , ; var. ; Copt. ⲃⲏⲧ.

ṭeb , fig wine.

ṭebi-t , , a fruit-bearing shrub or tree.

ṭebit , the fruit of the same.

ṭebi-t , , jars of fig wine.

ṭeba , , to lack strength, be helpless; , I, 42, "his condition is hopeless" (of a sick man).

ṭeba , Peasant 48, , to requite, to restore something, to pay back, to reward, to indemnify, to exchange, to barter, to pay; Copt. ⲧⲱⲱⲃⲉ.

ṭebau , Peasant 318, reward, answer, reply, payment, restitution; **er ṭebu** , in return for, because of; Copt. ⲉ ⲧⲃⲉ.

ṭeba-t , a table of offerings.

ṭeba , , to shut up, to close up, to cover over; see .

ṭeba-t , , , funerary chest or coffer, coffin, sarcophagus, tomb; , shroud (?)

ṭeba , Rev. 13, 86 = , vestment; Copt. ⲑⲃⲓⲱ.

Ṭeba , , Ṭuat III and IX, a goddess who swathed Osiris.

Ṭebai , Ṭuat XII, a sailor-god who attacked Āapep daily.

Ṭebait , Ṭuat VIII, a goddess in the Circle Ḥep-seshemu-s.

Ṭeba-t-neteru-s , Ṭuat VIII, the 8th Division of the Ṭuat.

Ṭeba-ṭemṭ , Lit. 40, 97, one of the 75 forms of Rā.

ṭeban , enmity, deceit.

ṭebar , Rec. 19, 95 = , shrine, inner chamber; compare Heb. דְּבִיר, 1 Kings vi, 5, 16, etc.

Ṭebati , , Tomb Seti I, one of the 75 forms of Rā (No. 35).

ṭebȧ , finger; see .

ṭebȧ-t , Rev. 13, 41, box.

ṭebȧ , reward, restitution.

ṭebi , Rev. 14, 68, payment, discharge of a debt.

Ṭebi, Ṭuat III, a dog-headed ape-god.

ṭebi-t, part of a chariot; plur., Anastasi I, 26, 6, , .

ṭebi-t, plinth, pedestal, brick base (?); , , Rev. 13, 11.

ṭebu, Love Songs 4, 3, cage, prison.

ṭebu, a period of time; var. .

Ṭebu, B.D. (Saïte) 85, 8, a god (?)

Ṭebmesthumut (?), Hh. 233, a god (?)

ṭeben, P. 122, M. 91, , U. 194, 514, M. 336, Rec. 31, 20, , , , , , , , A.Z. 1908, 117, , , Nåstasen Stele 36, to revolve, to go about, to wander round a place, to make the circuit of a place.

ṭebnen, Rec. 31, 27, to wander round.

ṭebenben, L.D. III, 140B, to wander, to circle; see .

ṭeben-ṭeben, to revolve, to wander; see .

ṭeben, , , ; , T. 275, , P. 28, M. 38, , N. 68, circle, circuit, circumference, a circular surface; , around, roundabout.

Ṭeben pekhar Meḥ (?)-nebu T. 275, , P. 28, , M. 38, , N. 68, , N. 98, the complete circuit of the northern coast of the Mediterranean and of the Greek Islands.

Ṭeben-ur, Ombos I, 83, a god of marsh produce and sea produce.

Ṭeben-semu (seshmu)-taui, B.D. 141 and 148, the rudder of the western heaven.

ṭeben, tambourine, flat drum.

ṭeben-t, Ḳubbân Stele 16, , the lock of hair that grew over the right temple; var. .

ṭeben en tchatcha (?), IV, 712, helmet.

ṭeben, Ebers Pap. 93, 19, a kind of garment.

ṭeben, U. 258, P. 265, M. 477, N. 718, 1245; var. , coffer, sarcophagus.

ṭeben, Peasant 166, , , IV, 1124, , , a weight = 10 qeṭ-t , or about 91 grammes.

ṭeben, , clay (?)

ṭeben, Rev. 13, 41, weight of silver (?)

Ṭebha (Tchebha), a form of Āapep, or Set; Gr. Τύφων.

ṭebḥ, U. 219, , P. 315, N. 162, IV, 1007, , Pap. 3024, 80, ,

, , to pray, to beseech, to entreat, to supplicate; Copt. ⲧⲱⲃϩ.

ṭebḥu , beggar, suppliant, petitioner.

ṭebḥe-t , N. 380, , Rec. 31, 170, , , , entreaty, prayer, supplication.

ṭebḥu , , , Ȧmen. 17, 19, 20, , Rec. 27, 231, , , , propitiatory offerings.

ṭebeḥ-t or **ṭebeḥ-t ḥetep** , , IV, 770, , , Eg. Texts 1, 53, , Rec. 26, 211, , IV, 872, , offerings and offering table.

ṭebḥ , , , , something that is required or is necessary, necessary equipment, furniture, tools, implements; plur. , .

ṭebḥ , , , , , , , , a grain measure.

ṭebḥ , , IV, 635, pot, vessel, vase; plur. .

ṭebḥ (?) , Stele of Ptolemy I. . . . . . .

Ṭeb-ḥer (Tcheb-ḥer) , Berg. 16, a jackal-god with two serpent-rods (?)

Ṭeb-ḥerk , god of the 8th day of the month.

Ṭeb-ḥer-keha-at , B.D. 144, the herald of the 5th Ȧrit; varr. , , B.D. 147.

Ṭebḥes , N. 154, a god of funerary offerings.

ṭebkhu , IV, 781, slaughter, Heb. טָבַח, compare Arab. طَبَخَ, Syr. ܛܒܚ.

ṭebṭeb , , , , , Ȧmen. 5, 11, to stab, to slay, to kill.

ṭebṭeb , Ebers Pap. 42, 10, to beat (of the heart).

ṭep , , to spit, spittle, exudation.

ṭep , to shine upon, to illumine.

ṭep , bandlet, tiara, fillet for the head.

ṭep , box, chest, coffer; plur. , .

ṭep , , , , , , to taste; , A.Z. 1905, 38, , ibid. 37, , U. 49; Copt. ⲧⲱⲡ.

ṭep-t , U. 15, , , , , , taste; Copt. ϯⲡⲉ.

ṭep-t re , something pleasant to the smell or taste.

ṭep-t , U. 108, , , U. 49, N. 280, , , a kind of cake or bread, dainty pastry.

ṭep , fruit, pomegranates (?).

Ṭepit, the town-god of Ṭepa—a division of the town Pe-Ṭep.

ṭep-t, Ȧmen. 25, 15, , , , , Peasant 221, a boat or barge; , Palermo Stele, the royal barge.

Ṭepu - neteru ; see .

Ṭep-ta, Ṭuat III, the tunnel, with a bull at each end, through which Åf was towed in his boat. Called also .

ṭep , , to row, to paddle.

ṭepu, Hh. 392, , N. 1005, 1007, paddle, oar; dual , , M. 826, N. 1318, a pair of paddles; Compare Heb. דַּף, Arab. دَفَّة.

ṭepi , , paddler, rower, boatman in general.

ṭepa, to overstep, to transgress.

Ṭepait, the goddess of Ṭep.

ṭepȧ, to sniff, to snuff the air.

Ṭepȧn, Ṭuat V, a serpent-god, servant of Seker.

Ṭepi, Ṭuat IX, a singing-god.

ṭepi, Rev. 11, 65, hippopotamus.

ṭepi, Tombos Stele 9, IV, 84, 616, , Israel Stele 20, "devourer"—an epithet of the crocodile.

ṭepit, taste; Copt. ⲧⲟⲡ, ϯⲡⲉ.

Ṭepit, a title of Hathor.

ṭepu, vase, vessel, pot.

ṭepḥ, apple; plur. , ; Copt. ϫⲉⲡⲏϩ, Heb. תַּפּוּחַ, Arab. تُفَّاح.

ṭepḥ-t, a kind of seed or grain.

ṭepḥ-t, Rec. 5, 92, , , , cave, cavern, hole in the ground; see .

ṭepṭ-t (?), Nȧstasen Stele 24, bow.

ṭeptch, Ebers Pap. 102, 9, to taste (?)

ṭef, pot, urn, large vessel.

ṭefa, abundance of food; see .

Ṭef-mat-er-nenu-f, Edfû I, 80, a title of the Nile-god.

ṭefen, to hasten; var. .

ṭefen, to rejoice; var. .

Ṭefen, Metternich Stele, one of the seven scorpions of Isis.

ṭefṭef , , to spit, to exude moisture; var. .

ṭefṭef-t, Rougé I.H. II, 115, spittle, moisture.

ṭem, Rec. 30, 197, , B.D. 172, 17, , , , , , Rec. 15, 158, to name, to bestow a title, to proclaim a name or title, to pronounce, to cry out in shrill tones, to have a piercing voice; , named, spoken; , something recited.

ṭem, Rec. 4, 135, IV, 896, to sharpen, to whet, to cut an inscription, to cut through, to pierce, to be stung or bitten by a reptile; , his crown pierced the sky; Copt. ⲧⲱⲙ.

ṭemṭem, to whet, to sharpen, to cut.

ṭem-t, slaughter.

ṭem, ṭema-t, M. 111, N. 24, P. 81, knife, sword, the act of cutting, killing, slaying, the edge of a sword; plur. , M. 335, M. 447, N. 1258, B.D. 148, 13; B.D. (Ani), 15, 45.

ṭem-ā, Berg. II, 407, to hack.

Ṭemur (?), B.D. 142, 99, a form of Osiris.

ṭem ra (?), etc., B.D. 136A, 15 . . . . . .

Ṭem-[ṭe]si, etc., etc., B.D. 145 and 146, name of the 21st Pylon.

ṭem, worm, serpent; plur. ; worm-eaten.

Ṭem, "Worm"—a title or name of Āapep.

ṭem, Amen. 5, 6, to shut the eyes.

ṭemm, U. 494, T. 235, T. 200, N. 791, to unite with.

ṭem, L.D. III, 219E, 21, enclosure (?) cage (?)

ṭema, III, 138, IV, 612, Rec. 15, 178, to bind, to tie together, to gather together, to collect.

ṭemau, bodies of men, companies, choirs.

ṭema, Ebers Pap. 101, 8, conflux, confluence.

Ṭema-t sti-t, a serpent on the royal crown.

ṭema, M. 718, the front portion of a skirt or tunic.

ṭema, sacking, mat; plur. .

ṭema-t, IV, 617, wing, pinion; dual , pair of wings.

ṭema, vessel, bowl of drink; , a vessel made of tchām metal.

ṭema, Shipwreck 137, to grovel on the belly.

ṭemaā, Hymn Darius 24 . . . .

ṭemaā, M. 207, N. 668, fortress.

Ṭemaā ȧt, N. 668, M. 207, "Fortress of the Father"—a name of Horus.

Ṭemau, Ṭuat X, a god in the Ṭuat.

ṭemam, to complete, to finish; see .

ṭemam, to tie, to bind together.

ṭemam-ti, B.D. 78, 23, a pair of tresses or wings.

ṭemam, company, assembly, choir of singers ( ).

ṭemam, sacking, mat; varr.

ṭemam-t, the front part of a tunic, garment.

Ṭemamm, Denderah II, 10, one of the 36 Dekans; Gr. ΤΩΜ.

ṭemam, IV, 809, to kneel, to bow in homage; see .

Ṭemathth, Tomb Ram. IX, 10, a god (?)

ṭemȧ, P. 117, M. 98, N. 104, 972, Rec. 32, 78, Peasant 154, Shipwreck 137, Åmen. 4, 15, 13, 5, 15, 1, Rougé I.H. II, 125, to touch, to approach, to come near to, to join, to be united to, to bring together, to grovel on the ground; Copt. ⲧⲱⲙⲉ, ⲧⲱⲙⲓ, ⲧⲱⲱⲙⲉ, ⲧⲟⲟⲙⲉ.

ṭemȧ-t, Shipwreck 79, touch.

ṭemȧ, Pap. 3024, 150, to be united with (the earth), *i.e.*, be dead.

ṭemȧ, Rec. 26, 15, union (?)

ṭemȧ, ṭemȧ-t, Rec. 31, 27, town, village; Copt. ϯⲙⲉ.

ṭemȧiu, Rec. 29, 153, villagers, townsmen; Israel Stele, the inhabitants of his town.

ṭemȧi-t, Rec. 13, 12, Ḥerusȧtef Stele 82, town, village, hamlet; plur. IV, 676, 1004, Rec. 4, 130, 20, 40, the inhabited part of the whole country.

ṭemȧ, P. 413 = M. 591, N. 1197, a kind of stuff of a green or yellow colour.

ṭemȧi, a kind of stuff; see .

ṭemi; var. Rec. 13, 12, village, town; Copt. ϯⲙⲓ.

ṭemi, stick, staff, wooden instrument.

ṭemseb, Canopus Stele 34, choir (?)

ṭemgi, a stone.

ṭemṭ, Hh. 189, Rec. 29, 158,

Rec. 6, 152, Litanie 19, , to unite with; , Rec. 26, 226, to add figures together, to do addition; Copt. ⲦⲰⲘⲚⲦ.

ṭemṭ , Nâstasen Stele 36, , Rec. 4, 21, the whole number, the result of addition, the total, in all.

ṭemṭ sma , IV, 337, to reckon up a total; , A.Z. 1907, 3, 21, "united with and bound up in life and serenity."

ṭemṭ-tȧ , all, entire; , all Egypt; , all eternity.

ṭemṭiu (?) , all (plur.), people, folk, multitude, everybody.

Ṭemṭiu , B.D. 23, 6, the entire company of the gods.

Ṭemṭu , Ṭuat IX, a god who swathed Osiris.

Ṭemṭit , the name of a serpent on the royal crown; var. .

Ṭemṭit , Ṭuat VIII, a goddess of the Circle Ḥep-seshemu-s.

Ṭemṭit , Ṭuat VII, a goddess.

Ṭemiṭ-mut-set , Ombos II, 133, a goddess.

Ṭemṭ-ḥā-t , Tomb Seti I, one of the 75 forms of Rā (No. 43).

ṭemṭ-t , a collection of sayings, compilation, book.

ṭemṭi-t , IV, 384, a stated time, a time reckoned upon.

ṭemṭ-t , Rec. 27, 86, pellet, globule.

ṭemṭ-t , ring (?) ornament.

ṭemṭ-t , A.Z. 1908, 16, , an amulet in the form of a vulture.

ṭemṭ , A.Z. 1908, 16, vulture amulet; and see .

ṭemṭ-t , Rec. 16, 110, scaffold, slaughter-house.

ṭemṭi[t] , a kind of ground or land, mud of a stream (?)

Ṭemṭria-t , Rec. 6, 5, 33, 3, the name Demetria.

ṭemtchi , Hh. 357, , U. 493, , U. 181, T. 238, 272, P. 23, M. 34, N. 107, 405, , T. 172, N. 123, , P. 119, 130, , M. 778, N. 73, , P. 668, , U. 418, M. 152, , N. 945, to unite with; Copt. ⲦⲰⲘⲚⲦ.

ṭemtch-t , Hh. 435, Rec. 26, 226, in all, altogether, total, summation.

ṭemtchiu , Rec. 30, 70, the whole company of the gods.

ṭen = or .

ṭen = , this.

ṭen , Hymn Darius 5, , to raise up, raised, high, distinguished; see .

ṭen, Rec. 30, 186, 31, 30, , , , , to cut, to cut off, to cut to pieces, to cleave, to split, to wound (of a reptile).

ṭenn, Rec. 6, 19, to cut, to split.

ṭen-t, , a cutting, division.

Ṭenn, Rec. 31, 31, a name or title of a god.

Ṭenit, , Ṭuat VII, a goddess.

Ṭent-baiu, Ṭuat III, an hour-goddess.

ṭenṭen, P. 610, N. 803, 988, , , Anastasi I, 11, 7, , , , , to attack, to do violence, violent wrath, the violence of the wind.

ṭenṭen, to wander through a district, to invade (?)

ṭenṭenu, P. 473, M. 539, , assaulter, attack, attacker; , N. 1118, attacked.

Ṭenṭen, U. 280, a name or title of a god.

Ṭenṭen, a title of Āapep.

Ṭenṭenȧ, B.D. 145A, the doorkeeper of the 8th Pylon.

Ṭenṭenit, , the name of a serpent on the royal crown.

Ṭenṭenit, Ṭuat I, , one of the 12 guides of Rā.

Ṭenṭenit-uḥesq-t-khak-ȧb, , , the Hour-goddess of the 10th Division of the Ṭuat.

ṭen, , to dig a canal (?)

ṭen-t, a plot of ground, field.

ṭen-t, B.D. 42, 15, chamber, abode.

ṭennu-t, Rec. 6, 7, office, a government building.

ṭennu, Rec. 13, 65, border, boundary; Copt. ⲧⲏⲛⲉ.

ṭen, Anastasi I, 13, 2, Israel Stele 17 . . . .

ṭen, vase, vessel, bucket; plur. , .

ṭenȧ, T. 229, old age (?)

ṭenȧ, Rec. 32, 177, venerable man.

ṭenȧ, , to cut, to divide, to separate, to distribute.

ṭenȧ-t, , , , , part, portion, lot, share.

ṭenȧu, lot, part, share, division.

ṭenȧ-t, , , , , , , the quarter of a month, the festival that ended each quarter.

ṭenȧ tep, the 1st quarter of the moon.

Ṭenȧ, B.D. 64, 17, the god of the quarters of the moon.

ṭenȧ-t, Ȧmen. 6, 14, divisions (?) shares (?)

ṭenȧ, , to embank, to build the sides of a canal or dyke.

ṭenȧ-t, Peasant 237, B.D. 125, II, , P.S.B. 34, 308, embankment, dyke, barrage, dam; plur. , Anastasi I, 15, 5; , IV, 312, a stone dyke.

ṭenȧu, , fields; Copt. ⲧⲏⲛⲉ.

ṭenȧ-t, IV, 770, , A.Z. 70, 171, , , , a measure = $\frac{1}{2}$ of a sa and $\frac{1}{8}$th of a tama; plur. .

ṭenȧ, , , , basket; plur. , , metal baskets; Heb. טֶנֶא, Deut. xxviii, 5.

ṭenȧ, B.D. (Hunefer, 1, 16), a special kind of chamber.

ṭenȧ, Rev. 13, 4, to question, to interrogate; Copt. ϫⲛⲟ.

ṭenȧs, see , heavy, burdensome.

Ṭenȧs, a title of the hippopotamus of Set; var. .

Ṭenānu, P. 269, the name or title of a god; varr. , M. 484, , N. 1251.

Ṭeni, "the Aged," a name or title of Rā.

ṭeni-t, , A.Z. 1905, 27, Rec. 21, 14, writings, documents, registry, list, inventory.

ṭennuit, , list, inventory.

ṭennu = Copt. ⲉⲧⲟⲩⲛ.

ṭennu, Nåstasen Stele 10, where; see , .

ṭennu, each, every, many; see .

ṭennu, Dream Stele 23, number, many; see , .

ṭennut, Thes. 1296, time expired soldiers.

ṭennu, , old age, old man.

ṭennu, an old canal; var. .

ṭennu, canal, stream.

ṭennut, , the land lying near a canal, field, area; plur. .

ṭennu, IV, 367, , Rec. 33, 4, share, part, division.

ṭenu, Rev. 13, 50, rent, royalty, due, tax.

ṭenut, Thes. 1205, , outcries, the roars of a lion.

ṭennu, loaf, cake.

ṭenb, B.D. 36, 2, to gnaw.

Ṭenpu, B.D. 34 = , gods of the year (?)

ṭenem, milk (?); var. .

Ṭenem, "worm"—a title of Āapep; , B.D. 163 (title), worms, serpents.

ṭenemm, to turn back or aside, to go out of the way.

ṭenemu, wanderer, one who has lost his way.

ṭenemmu (?), Åmen. 7, 16, retreatings (?)

ṭenemm, foul, dirty, unclean.

ṭenmi, to turn aside, to go out of the way.

Ṭenmi; see .

ṭenr, Rev. 13, 56, strength; Copt. ϫⲣⲟ.

ṭenrega-t, Anastasi I, 2, 4, Koller 2, 3, deaf.

ṭenrega-t, a kind of plant shaped like an ear (?); var. .

ṭenḥ, Thes. 1201, to bind, to tie, to fetter, to truss (a bird); Copt. ϭⲛⲁϩ.

ṭenḥṭenḥ, to tie, to fetter, to bind.

ṭenḥ-t, (?), tie, fetter.

ṭenḥ, wing; plur. , A.Z. 1905, 25, Thes. 1205, ; Copt. ⲧⲛ̄ϩ.

Ṭenḥ-uā, Ombos I, 47, the son of Urt-en-kerua.

ṭenḥes-t (?), knife.

ṭenkhnekh, Lib. Fun. 2, 39, to be joined to, united.

ṭens, Åmen. 13, 20, to be loaded heavily, weight, load, burden, heavy; , Åmen. 20, 3, loaded.

ṭensu (?), B.D. 153A, 5, the weights of a net; , ibid. 28, the lower weights.

ṭens, Rec. 20, 216, as applied to food (), indigestible (?)

ṭens ḥat, Peasant 209, A.Z. 1905, 37, , to have the mind seriously occupied with some difficult problem, to be weighed down with care.

ṭens, IV, 614, to cut down.

Ṭens-sma-keku, Ṭuat VIII, the name of a door of a Circle.

ṭensmen = + .

ṭensmen, A.Z. 1907, 125, to be heavy, weighty.

ṭensmen, Rec. 21, 79, dignity, honour, grave demeanour.

ṭeng, dwarf, pygmy; , a dancing dwarf; compare Amharic ድንክ ፡

ṭeng, a property or defect (?) possessed by certain ears; see .

Ṭenti (?), Litanie 68, a form of the Sun-god Rā.

Ṭenten, Berg. I, 34, a serpent-god with bloody eyes, .

ṭentha, steps, throne.

ṭentha-t, Annales V, 95, litter, couch.

ṭenṭ, to slaughter, to kill.

Ṭenṭ, Ṭuat XI, a ram-god who provided offerings.

Ṭenṭ baiu, B.D. (Nebseni) 17, 27, the name of the slaughter block of Osiris.

ṭentch, N. 69, var. of, T. 276, P. 30, M. 40, U. 456, to attack, to rage.

Ṭentchen, A.Z. 1910, 128, a title or name of a god.

ṭeru, P. 664, vases, pots.

Ṭer-t, a bird-(goose?) god.

ṭer, IV, 1150, B.M. 447, to drive out, to expel, to blot out, to erase, to expunge, to destroy, to overcome, to subdue, to conquer, to overthrow; destroyers; to tramp the earth; IV, 1164, to found; to destroy a god in his shrine.

ṭer in, T. 249; var. in Unȧs.

ṭer neken, a kind of flowering plant; plur.

Ṭer, Ṭuat V, a two-headed serpent.

Ṭerit nesh[nu]t, Ṭuat IX, a fiery blood-drinking serpent.

Ṭeri kheftiu, B.D. (Saïte) 125, a title of Ām-mit.

Ṭer ṭu, Berg. I, 18, a jackal-god.

ṭer, Prisse Pap. 7, 5, to reap (a harvest).

ṭer, a kind of cloth, linen; Rec. 6, 9, byssus cloth.

ṭerȧ-t, Rec. 5, 96, linen bandlet.

ṭerȧ, time, season; Copt. ⲦⲎ; see.

Ṭeri, Ṭuat VII, a god.

Ṭeriush, Darius; Pers. [cuneiform], Heb. דָּרְיָוֶשׁ.

Ṭeru, Ṭuat X, a light-god.

ṭeru, Mar. Karn. 35, 65 . . . .

ṭerp, Rec. 4, 126, IV, 1026, to make an offering, to pour out a libation; Berg. II, 395 . . . . .

ṭerpt, IV, 1115, a gift, an offering, supply, provision.

ṭerpu, IV, 499, Israel Stele 7, Ȧmen. 17, 12, Ȧmen. 11, 3, supplies, food, sustenance.

ṭerp, a kind of goose; varr.

ṭerf, Thes. 1285, IV, 969, Thes. 1481, to write, to inlay inscriptions; to make writing speak.

ṭerf, Ebers Pap. 1, 8, writing, inscription, document.

ṭerfu, Rec. 4, 117, writings, books, literature.

ṭergi-t, bat; Heb. עֲטַלֵּף, Copt. ϫⲉⲗϫⲟⲩ; compare ἀττέλαβος, Herod. 4, 172.

ṭerta = , to put oneself on the earth, *i.e.*, to land from a boat.

ṭert, stairway, terrace; Copt. ⲧⲱⲣⲧ.

Ṭerṭeniu, , , Rec. 8, 140, the name of a Mediterranean people.

ṭeh, , Rec. 33, 6, to attack, to invade; see .

ṭehan, , to thrust forward, to promote, to appoint to a higher rank or dignity.

ṭehan, see , .

ṭehani (ta), , see , to do homage.

ṭehmu-t (?), chamber (?), entrance (?)

ṭehen, , , , IV, 663, Rec. 35, 125, to thrust forward, to promote, to appoint to a higher rank or dignity, *e.g.*, to make a man captain of a boat; , A.Z. 1905, 38, to run the head against something, to oppose; , Festschrift (Leemans) 117, to rush (into water); var. .

ṭehen, , , , to bow down and touch the earth with the forehead in homage, to make obeisance, to prostrate oneself, to salute.

ṭehnu, IV, 1086, 1114, , one who has been appointed head.

ṭehen ta, A.Z. 35, 16, , , var. .

ṭehen-t, , , forehead; , , B.D. 163, 9; Copt. ⲧⲉϩⲛⲉ.

ṭehen-t, A.Z. 1908, 2, B.D. 168, III, 2, a mountain peak, prominent hill.

Ṭehni Åmentt, Rec. 2, 109, the Peak of the West.

ṭehni, to dedicate something by deed, to appoint something to a certain purpose, to allocate, to endow; var. .

ṭeher-t, furnace, oven (?)

ṭeḥ, A.Z. 1908, 130, , IV, 64, 968, , , low, lowly.

ṭeḥṭeḥ, P. 302, to hang down (?) pendent (?) of the breasts of a woman, .

Ṭeḥṭeḥ, Ṭuat I, an ape-god in the Ṭuat.

ṭeḥu, A.Z. 1899, 73, equipment, what is necessary.

ṭeḥṭeḥ (ṭeḥuṭeḥu), the mixed food given to geese.

ṭeḥu, , , grain, food for geese (?)

ṭeḥa, , , to be low, abased, lowly.

ṭeḥaåu, abasement, indignity.

ṭeḥa, straw; plur. , Ȧmen. 24, 13, , Ȧmen. 15, 15, 25, 12, , Rev. 6, 110, , Rev. 6, 110; Copt. ⲧⲱϩ.

ṭeḥamut, Koller Pap. 1, 2, straw; Copt. ⲧⲱϩ.

ṭeḥat, lead; see .

ṭeḥaṭiu, Ȧmen. 18, 13, leaden objects.

ṭeḥȧ = , cringing one.

ṭeḥȧ, a member of the body.

ṭeḥāāut, , , , IV, 480, a kind of plant.

Ṭeḥi, the god Thoth; Copt. ⲑⲟⲟⲩⲧ.

ṭeḥu, Ḳubbân Stele 23, declarations.

ṭeḥu, lead.

Ṭeḥuti (Tcheḥuti), U. 2, P. 615, M. 783, N. 1142, , A.Z. 1900, 35, , Ani 15, 47, , , , , , the ibis-god, the scribe of the gods; Copt. ⲑⲟⲟⲩⲧ, ⲑⲱⲑ.

Ṭeḥuti, chief titles of: , Pap. Ani 3, dweller in Khemenu; , P. 615; , B.D. (Saïte), 58, 15, judge of the gods; , Nesi-Ȧmsu 33, 17, master of words of power; , B.D. 58, 14, bull of Maāt; , Thoth the ibis; , Thoth the Great; , , Thoth the Twice Great; , Thoth, great one of spells; , Thoth, lord of the divine Word, just scribe of the Company of the Gods; , Thoth, Bull in Ṭeṭ-t.

Ṭeḥuti, , , , Mar. Aby. I, 44, 45.

Ṭeḥuti, god of the 13th day of the month.

Ṭeḥuti, the god of the 1st day of the month; the name of a festival on the 19th day of the month of Thoth.

Ṭeḥuti ȧn ȧrit, etc., Goshen 2, Thoth as bringer of the eye of Rā.

Ṭeḥuti em atri (var.), the god of the 6th hour of the day.

Ṭeḥuti, B.D. (Saïte) 23, 2, Thoth the magician.

Ṭeḥuti, Edfû I, 12, 16, Thoth of Edfû.

Ṭeḥuti Ḥāpi, B.D. 62, 3, Thoth and the Nile-god.

Ṭeḥuti khenti neb Ṭuat, Ṭuat VI, an ape-god—a form of Thoth.

Ṭeḥuti ḥeri khenṭ-f, Ṭuat II, an ibis-god with a knife-shaped phallus.

Ṭeḥuti sa Ȧner, B.D. 134, 6, a form of Thoth.

Ṭeḥuti seḥetep nesrit, Ombos I, 185, Thoth in the boat of Rā.

Ṭeḥuti sheps, Ombos I, 143, the holy Thoth.

Ṭeḥutit, N. 999, the great festival of Thoth.

ṭeḥen, to shine (applied to the brightness of grain).

ṭeḥen, some bright coloured substance, blue faïence.

ṭeḥer-t, IV, 662, Culte Divin, 42, 44, hairy hide, the hide of an animal, skin, leather; plur., Edict 25; Rec. 21, 91, ox-hides; A.Z. 1900, 27, plumage of a bird.

ṭeḥrȧ, Rechnungen 69, dressed hide; Theban Ost. B. 14, water-skins made of the hide of a donkey.

ṭeḥer-t, Rev. 11, 128, any sad or evil condition of mind or body, fear, anguish, anxiety, shame, sickness, jealousy, and the like; plur., IV, 1077; Copt. ⲧⲱϩⲣ̄.

ṭeḥer, an afflicted man.

ṭeḥerȧ-t, sickness, terror, bitter (in mind).

ṭeḥerr-t, a kind of plant.

ṭeḥt-t, lead; varr.; Copt. ⲧⲁ ◌,ⲧ.

ṭeḥtiu, IV, 686, leaden objects; var.

ṭekh, to drink, to drink oneself drunk; see; drunk; Copt. ϯϩⲉ.

ṭekh, vine.

ṭekh (?), U. 568, N. 751, to hide (?)

ṭekh (?), Rev. 1, 59, Thes. 1205, to beat, to strike, to overthrow.

ṭekhṭekh, Rev. 13, 59, revolution, convulsion, disturbed times.

ṭekhut, Anastasi I, 23, 3, boulders on a road, a rough stony road.

ṭekhar, Rev. 13, 27, terrible, frightening.

ṭekhȧ, Ȧmen. 18, 1, the weight or pointer of a balance.

ṭekhen, Metternich Stele, 187, to cover over, to hide.

ṭekhen, Lib. Fun. 2, 39, to strike, to play an instrument of music, to strike the harp, to beat the drum.

ṭekhen-t, the playing of music.

ṭekhenit, a tambourine player; tambourine women.

ṭekhenu, obelisk; var.

ṭekhṭekh, the mixed food given to geese; var.

ṭes, Hh. 321, self = or; himself.

ṭes, to sit, to be seated.

ṭes, Rec. 17, 145, , , , pot, vase, vessel, jug.

Ṭesi-ruṭu-en-neter, B.D. 153B, 14, collector of prey in the net of the Akeru-gods.

ṭes, , a kind of plant.

ṭes, , , to knife, to cut, to hack in pieces, to divide.

ṭes, U. 401, , P. 188, M. 352, N. 904, Rec. 31, 20, , a knife of flint or metal; , a ready knife; , a knife of fire, *i.e.*, a red-hot knife; plur. , , , , , ; varr. , , .

ṭes, a kind of stone, flint, , Rec. 4, 21, , black flint, white flint.

Ṭes (?), B.D. 110 (Saïte), a lake in Sekhet-Åaru.

Ṭes-am-miti-em-sheta-f, Ṭuat VIII, a door in the Ṭuat.

Ṭes-åakhu, Ṭuat XII, a singing-god.

Ṭes-åakhu, Ṭuat VIII, a door of the Circle Åat-Setkau.

Ṭes-āḥā-ser (?)-Tathenen, Ṭuat VIII, a door of the Circle Ṭuat.

Ṭes-ākhem-baiu, Ṭuat VIII, a door of the Circle Åsneteru.

Ṭes-t-baiu, Ṭuat I, one of the 12 guides of Rā.

Ṭesu-em-årit-f, Ṭuat VIII, a star-god.

Ṭesu-em-nes-f, Ṭuat VII, a star-god.

Ṭes-em-ḥer-f, Ṭuat III, the steersman of the boat Herer.

Ṭes-neb-terer . . . ., Ṭuat VIII, a door of the Circle Sesheta.

Ṭes-Rā-kheftiu-f, Ṭuat VIII, a door of the Circle Ḥetemit-Khemiu.

Ṭes-t-ermen-ta, Ṭuat VIII, a door of the Circle Ḥetepet-neb-per-s.

Ṭes-khaibitut-ṭuatiu, Ṭuat VIII, a door of the Circle Åakebi.

Ṭes-sepṭ-nesut, Ṭuat VIII, a door of the Circle Seḥert-baiu-s.

Ṭes-sma-keku, Ṭuat VIII, a door of the Circle Åakebi.

Ṭes-sekhem-åru, Ṭuat VIII, a door of the Circle Ḥep-seshemu-s.

Ṭes-sheta-theḥen-neteru, Ṭuat VIII, a door of the Circle Åakebi.

ṭeser-t, something splendid or holy, see ; , splendid or beautiful things; , B.M. 797, holy places.

ṭeser åri, to act in a lordly manner.

ṭeseru, , , , large stones (?)

Ṭeser-åab-t, Ṭuat XII, a wind-goddess, one of the 12 bearers of the boat of Åf into the upper sky.

Ṭeser-t-ȧn-t, Ṭuat IX, a singing-goddess.

Ṭeser-ȧri, Ṭuat IX, a god with a serpent-staff.

Ṭeser-ā, Ṭuat VII, a star-god.

Ṭeser-t-baiu, Ṭuat XI, the last Gate in the Ṭuat.

Ṭeser-t-baiu, Ṭuat IV, a district in the Ṭuat.

Ṭeser-t tep, B.D. 168, XIII, 1, B.D. 168, XIV, 1, a goddess in the Ṭuat.

ṭeser-t, , , a drink made from red grain.

ṭ-sekhen, to cause to be embraced (?)

ṭesh, to drink, to drink oneself drunk; see .

ṭesh, the drinking festival; var. .

ṭesh, , to pierce, to stab, to gore, to thrust.

Ṭesh, , Rec. 15, 18, a district.

Ṭeshesh, a figure of Osiris; see **Teshtesh.**

ṭesh, to yield, to give way; var. .

ṭeshṭesh = , to run back or away, to give ground.

Ṭeshṭesh, Rec. 4, 31, a figure of Osiris; see .

ṭesh; see .

ṭeshṭesh, to flow out, to overspread (of water).

ṭesh (ṭesher), P.S.B. 13, 412, to be red in colour, russet, reddish, carroty.

ṭesh (ṭesher), , red grain plants.

ṭesh, red grain.

ṭesh-t (ṭesher-t), , the red land (?) something appertaining to red, horrible.

Ṭesh-t (Ṭesher-t), the red land, *i.e.*, the desert.

ṭeshu (ṭesheru), the "red" fiends, associates of Set.

Ṭeshut (Ṭeshrut), Metternich Stele 11, note 2, the fish that piloted the boat of Rā.

ṭesh, Rec. 13, 100, to assign; Copt. ⲧⲱϣ.

ṭesher, , , to be red, to become red; Copt. ⲧⲣⲟϣ, ⲑⲣⲟϣ, ⲑⲱⲣϣ.

ṭesher, to terrify; , B.D. 179, 4.

ṭesher-ti, horrible, terrible.

ṭesher, U. 431, M. 774, , T. 246, , P. 662, , P. 781, , , , blood, gore.

ṭesher-t, B.D. 32, 5, red thing, red flame; , B.D. (Nebseni) 17, 44, , B.D. 179, 6, lord of blood (?), *i.e.*, slayer; , B.D. 179, 7.

ṭeshrut, , "red" devils.

ṭesheru, B.D. 182, 20, , , , , the "red ones," *i.e.*, the wicked gods who were associated with Set

Ṭesheru, B.D. 96, 2, Nesi-Ȧmsu 5, 3, red devils symbolized by red clouds.

ṭesher-t, T. 336, , U. 518, , P. 173, , N. 840, 939, , M. 254, , Rec. 16, 131, 31, 11, , , the "Red" Crown, which symbolized the sovereignty of Lower Egypt, or the North; plur. , P. 427, M. 611, N. 1216; , B.D. 149, III, 4.

Ṭeshrit, the goddess of the Red Crown.

ṭesher—ḥeb ṭesher, Palermo Stele, the "Red" Festival.

ṭesher, red; , B.D. 99, 16, red wing; , B.D. 145, 40, red pomade, like the modern cam-wood unguent used in the Sûdân; , B.D. 145, 51, red hair.

Ṭesher, B.D. 142, III, 6, a city sacred to Osiris.

Ṭesher ȧr-ui, Berg. I, 3, one of the eight gods who guarded Osiris and who dwelt in Ḥe-t Ȧnes , B.D. 17, 104; , Edfû I, 10 f.

Ṭesher mestcher, P. 604, "red ear," a title of Babȧu .

Ṭesheru ḥeru-sen, B.D. 42, 21, "those whose faces are red"—a class of beings in the Ṭuat.

ṭesher-t, a vase or pot made of "red" material used in funerary ceremonies; plur. , , , , a pair of red vases; , a set of four red pots.

ṭesher, a kind of **ānti**, or myrrh; Heb. דְּ.

ṭesher, , , , the myrrh tree (?)

ṭesher, , red grain, sand (?)

Ṭesher-t, , , , , , the "red" land, *i.e.*, the Desert.

ṭesher-t, , , , , a red fish.

ṭesher-t, , a red calf.

ṭeshes, Rec. 16, 110, to cut, to divide.

ṭeq, IV, 754, a kind of grain.

ṭeq, IV, 171, , , , fruit; var. .

Ṭeqq, N. 1047, the name or title of a god.

ṭeqer, Ebers Pap. 109, 4, , , ...; , I, 13, a writing of ....

ṭeqer, , , , fruit, fruit-bearing plants.

ṭeqer ta (?), ground produce, vegetables (?)

ṭeqeru (?), Rec. 27, 220, ...

teka, , to look, to see; varr. , .

Ṭekait, Ombos II, 133, a goddess.

ṭeken, to approach, to draw near to someone, to touch.

ṭeker, see .

Ṭekṭek-ba-en-Ḥeru, Denderah IV, 62, a serpent-god, warder of a coffer.

ṭeg, , , , , , to hide oneself, to be hidden.

ṭegai-t, Leyd. Pap. 4, 5, something hidden, hidden.

ṭeg, , , Israel Stele 6, to fail, to give way (of the legs).

ṭeg, Rec. 4, 126, to come, to walk, to march.

ṭegṭeg, ṭegṭegi, , , to march, to invade (?)

ṭegga, Rec. 12, 70, to run quickly (?)

ṭeg, Peasant, B. 2, 106, , , , , , , A.Z. 1900, 27, 1905, 19, , B.D. 18, II, 4, , U. 541, T. 297, , to look at, to see.

Ṭegaȧ, "Seer"—title of a god (?)

ṭegait, Mar. Karn. 35, 70, sight, view.

ṭega-t, B.D. 112, 5; Ebers Pap. 51, 21, , look, sight, glance.

ṭegg, U. 316, to see, to look at carefully, to examine, to scrutinize.

ṭegg-t, IV, 617, sight, appearance; , Rev. 11, 92, glances.

ṭegaṭegai, to look very carefully at something.

ṭega, Amherst Pap. 24, IV, 1174, , Ḥerusȧtef Stele 134, , , , to plant, to inlay metal, to plate.

ṭegaṭega, to inlay metal, to plant.

ṭega, , , , , Ȧmen. 6, 11, , , , Mission 1, 611, plants, seeds (?) carobs.

ṭegas, Israël Stele 5, , , , , A.Z. 1900, 24, , , to tread, to walk upon, to follow a road, to tread in the footsteps of another; Copt. ⲧⲁϭⲥⲉ.

ṭegasut, Rev. 6, 29, footsteps.

Ṭegas; see **Ȧnqers.**

ṭegi, Rec. 13, 53, gardens = Gr. παράδεισων, Copt. ⲧⲱϭⲉ.

ṭegi-t (ṭergi-t), , Rec. 31, 138, , plover, bat; Copt. ϫⲁⲗⲭⲟⲩ.

ṭegem, Metternich Stele 202, to be weak, smitten.

ṭegem, , A.Z. 1884, 88, , , , , castor oil plant.

ṭeges, to walk, to follow in the footsteps of another, a journey, travel; var. .

ṭegsa-t, boat, skiff.

ṭetri-t (?), B.D. 99, 12 . . . . . .

ṭet-khaiu (?), Excommunication Stele 5 . . . . . .

ṭeṭ, , Anastasi III, 2, 5, a kind of fruit tree; Copt. ϫⲓϫⲓ (?)

ṭeṭ-t, , IV, 629, , bowl, dish, pot, vessel, shell; plur. , IV, 665, , Koller 3, 8; varr. , .

Ṭeṭ, , Rec. 26, 80, the name of a god (?)

ṭeṭ (?), to touch = (?)

ṭeṭa, , to masturbate; see .

Ṭeṭun, P. 78, 200, , N. 21, 1323, P. 669, , N. 936, , N. 852, , M. 705, , M. 779, , Rec. 30, 71, IV, 986, , IV, 575, an ancient Sûdânî god with the title , N. 936, , P. 200, , Coronation Stele 2, "chief of Ta-Sti."

ṭeṭem-t, , ; , a kind of plant, seedlings (?)

TCH

tch = Heb. צ, Copt. ϫ.

Tcha (?), N. 955, a serpent that came forth from Rā.

tche-t, A.Z. 1908, 16, serpent amulet.

Tchit (?), T. 703, a serpent-goddess.

tche-t, P. 19, M. 21, , N. 120, , body, person, bodily form; , divine body, *i.e.*, a god; , a dead body; , my own body or person.

tche-ti, Litanie 61, the "two children," *i.e.*, Shu and Tefnut.

tche = or , pupil of the eye.

tche-t, , Hh. 23, , , the people who belong to the land, serfs, peasants, dependants.

tche-t, , , , , , Rec. 31, 11, eternity, everlastingness; , U. 521, , U. 521, , T. 330, , ever-lasting for ever; , T. 152, , N. 502, P. 21, , M. 23, , , , for ever; , all eternity; , unending eternity.

Tche-t, Berg. 26, eternity personified.

tche-t, , , , , , place, house, abode; , divine abode, the Ṭuat; see **metch-t** ; = **metch-t** , abyss.

tche-t, , Peasant 265, funerary property.

tche-t, Palermo Stele, the name of a sailing (?) festival; , the first tche-t festival.

tche-t, A.Z. 1907, 14, papyrus.

tcha, , to be sound, healthy; see ; , U. 118, N. 427, sound, healthy (of white teeth).

tchau-t, U. 65, N. 320, , U. 561 = , N. 345, , N. 346, , IV, 752, well-being, health, soundness; , IV, 1143, health of heart, heart's wish; , Jour. As. 1908, 281, good direction of heart.

tchau ȧb, P. 410, M. 587, N. 1192, sound of heart; , P. 409 = , M. 586, N. 1191, and , P. 409 = , M. 585, N. 1191.

Tchau-ȧb, Hh. 469, a god, brother of Seker.

tcha-t, , sound, firm, well, healthy.

tcha-t, safe, strong (of a building).

tcha, Rev. 14, 45 = , scribe of the record office.

tchau (?), title of an official.

tcha-t, M. 683, palm of the hand, hollow of the hand; plur., M. 242; , T. 91, handfuls of water; see ; var. .

tcha, to stretch, to extend, to draw out, to reach out towards, to strike down, to fell, to oppose, to resist; , immovable; , IV, 1107, to correct a fault.

tcha-t, a putting forth, extension, spacious, resistance, opposition.

tchaȧu, opponent, he who resists, enemy.

tchaȧu-t, a spreading out, resistance, wrong; , wrongfully.

tcha-ā, Leyd. Pap. 12, 2, , to reach out the hand in protection, or with hostility; .

tcha re, IV, 62, 64, 1031, to speak scornfully of sacred things or of offerings.

tcha-t, the rest, the remainder, residue, balance; varr. , L.D. III, 65A, 6.

tcha, A.Z. 1908, 85, , fire-stick, a wooden tool or instrument.

tcha-t (?), a cutting tool, a sharp-edged instrument.

Tcha aqru (?), B.D. 125, II; see **Qerrti.**

Tcha ati, B.D. 125, II; see **Qerrti.**

tcha, to set out on a journey, to make a passage, to travel.

tchaa-t, T. 194, P. 677, N. 1291, passage, journey.

tcha-t, Rec. 31, 29, , a kind of cake.

tchau-t, U. 38A, bread for the journey, viaticum.

tcha = ϫι in ϫιnιoop.

tcha, tchai, U. 451, T. 259, , M. 375, 590, N. 944, 1195, Rec. 31, 17, , U. 190, M. 224, N. 601, , T. 70, , to cross a river in a boat, to make a passage by boat, to slip (of the foot), U. 451; , borne, carried; , U. 475, , T. 228, sail, sailings; , A.Z. 1905, 22, how well thou sailest!

tcha-t, P. 188, , N. 905, , N. 914, , passage by boat, passage, transport, boat, ferry-boat, barge.

tchaȧui, Rev. 11, 174, ship, ferry-boat; Copt. ϫοι.

Tchaȧui, P. 400, , M. 570, , N. 1177, the ferryman of truth, the Egyptian Charon.

tchai , Rev. 12, 35, ship, boat; plur. ; Copt. ϫⲟⲓ.

tchaau , T. 187, P. 675, N. 1284, , Rec. 29, 154, those who sail, sailors, ferrymen.

tchai āa , Rec. 24, 161, a priestly title.

tcha āa-t , B.D. 133, 19, the great sailing, the Great Boat (?)

Tcha-t neter , , the "passage of the god" festival.

Tchat , Zod. Dend., one of the 36 Dekans.

Tcha unnut , Ṭuat I, a star-god who acted as guide of Åf.

Tcha benu Åsår , "travelling benu of Osiris"—a title of the star Venus.

Tcha-t Ṭuat , , Ṭuat I, IX, the name of a sailor-god in the Ṭuat.

tcha , the west wind.

tcha , Jour. As. 1908, 264, impurity.

tcha , Jour. As. 1908, 266, dishonour, blemish (physical or moral); Copt. ϭⲁⲉⲓⲟ, ϫⲁⲓⲱⲟⲩ.

tcha-t , Jour. As. 1908, 269, humiliation, shame.

tcha, tchau , , , , fiend, devil, demon, enemy; fem. , , , .

tcha-t , Thes. 1251, a term of abuse.

tchai , Jour. As. 1908, 254, to steal, theft; Copt. ϫⲓⲟⲩⲉ.

tchai , , , devil, fiend, foe, enemy; fem. , ; plur. , , .

Tchai , B.D. 15, 3, an enemy of Rā; plur. (masc.) and (fem.) B.M. 32, 144.

tchai , Rev., impure man.

tchai , wrong, evil; compare Copt. ϫⲁⲓ.

tchai-t , pain, discomfort.

tchai-t , iniquity.

tcha-t , , A.Z. 1905, 58, sin, guilt, reprehensible thing, offence.

tchau-t , hostilities, enmity.

tchatcha , , , , foe, enemy; Copt. ϫⲁϫⲓ.

tcha-t , , B.D. 178, 12, a measure (?) vessel.

tchatchaåu , A.Z. 1905, 103, , pot, vase, vessel, bowl; Copt. ϫⲱ, ϫⲱⲓ.

tcha-t , Rec. 3, 53, , Rec. 27, 226, , , bag, sack, stuff, garment, apparel.

tcha-t , Rec. 27, 226, , , , , , a bird, crane (?)

tchaȧ , P.S.B. 13, 37, an amulet.

ṭchaåu , cloth, stuff, garment.

tchaȧ-t , cloth, stuff, garment.

tchaȧ, Jour. As. 1908, 255, injustice; Copt. ϭⲟⲓ.

tchaȧu (?), crane (?)

tchaȧuṭ, Thes. 1124, throne-chamber, throne.

tchaȧs, to command troops, to be lord and master, captain.

tchaȧs, Dream Stele 33, , to know, to possess knowledge, to direct, to command.

tchaȧs, , knowledge, wisdom, speech of wisdom (?); , fore-knowledge, primeval wisdom, the wisdom of ancient times.

tchaȧsu, sage, wise man.

Tchaȧs, the god of Knowledge; , the seven wise gods who presided over painting and writing; , master (?) commander.

Tchaȧsu VII, Düm. Temp. Inschr. 45, the Seven Divine Masters of Wisdom who helped Thoth to plan the universe. Their names were: Neferḥat, Neferpeḥui, Nebṭesheru, Ka, Bȧk, Khekh, and Sȧn.

tchaȧs, , a kind of plant used in medicine.

tchaȧsu, the seed of the same.

tchaā, Rec. 15, 16 = , to lament, lamentation.

tchaāu, a kind of seed or grain.

tchaāiu, a kind of plant.

tchaāb, Metternich Stele 193, to be hot, to glow, to roast, to cook.

tchaāb-t, var. , hot, glowing embers.

tchaām, A.Z. 1878, 48, strength.

tchaām, Rev. 14, 19, quietness, rest; Copt. ϭⲁⲗⲏ.

tchaāmi, Rev. 14, 12, to devour.

tchaāmi, Rec. 15, 17, book; Copt. ϫⲱⲱⲙⲉ.

tchaār, Rev. 12, 84, bolt; Copt. ϭⲗⲟ.

tchaāri, Rev. 11, 139, to drive away, to repulse.

tchaāq, Rougé I.H. II, 125, to cry out; compare Heb. צָעַק, Arab. صعق.

tchaāqtȧ, cry, outcry; compare Heb. צְעָקָה.

tchaāṭiṭ, stick, staff.

tchaātchai (tchātchi), Rev. 12, 33, to run; Copt. ϭⲟϫⲓ.

tchai; see , to reach out towards.

tchai-t, , cloth, stuff, garment; see the following:

tchai-ut, whole garments as opposed to rags.

tchai, Rev. 11, 141, valley, lake (?)

tchaiu (?), Anastasi I, 16, 8, a kind of ground or land (?)

tchai, wall; Copt. ϫⲟ, ϫⲟⲓ.

tchaiua, Ḥerusȧtef Stele 19, an inner chamber in a temple.

tchait, Rev. 14, 33, olives, olive trees; Copt. ϫⲟⲉⲓⲧ.

tchaau, Siut 15, B.D. 70, 2, hair, foliage.

tchau, evening, darkness, night.

tchau, IV, 1127, cloth, stuff, garment.

tchau-t, T. 379, a garment made by Horus for Osiris.

Tchau, Ṭuat VII, a rectangular lake or pool measuring 440 cubits × 440 cubits.

tchau, L.D. 229c, domain.

tchau-t, Nȧstasen Stele 30, a chamber or hall of a temple.

tchau, an amulet.

tchaut, Rec. 12, 118, young animals.

tchauatȧ, Anastasi IV, 12, 9, P.S.B. 13, 411, a kind of flying insect (?) bird (?) crane (?)

tchauf, Rec. 15, 16, papyrus; Copt. ϫⲟⲟⲩϥ.

tchaut, twenty; Rec. 5, 95 = 23; Copt. ϫⲟⲩⲱⲧ.

tchaut nu-t, twentieth.

Tchauti, Ṭuat I, a hawk-god.

tchab, want, need, weakness, impotence, starvation; see ; Copt. ϭⲱⲃ.

tchab, a plant, a vegetable; Copt. ϭⲱⲃⲉ.

tchaba, Anastasi I, 23, 9, Thes. 1206, soldiers, host, army; Heb. צָבָא, plur. צְבָאִים; צְבָאָה, plur. צְבָאוֹת, Assyr. ṣa-a-bu (Brünnow, List, 8137), in plur. , Eth. ፀብእ፡

tchabaȧ-t, Rev. 14, 34, very hot embers, fire.

tchabagi, to dip, to immerse, to submerge; var. ; Heb. צָבַע, Syr. ܨܒܥ, Arab. صبغ; compare Assyr. , "dyed stuff" (Rawl. C.I.W.A. V, 15, 6, 13).

tchabagaiu, drowned men.

tchabḥu, Peasant 229, a fisherman who catches fish by a particular kind of means or instrument.

tchabgatchaqa, to be upside down.

Tchapr, a proper name; compare Heb. צִפּוֹר.

tchapurm', an animal, goat (?); compare Heb. צָפִיר, Syr. ܨܦܝܪܐ.

tchapurtȧ, round things, rings, cakes; compare Heb. צְפִירָה.

tchapqa, dancer, acrobat.

tchafi, Israel Stele 7, Rev. 12, 48, Rev. 13, 27, to be hot, to burn, to be angry; Copt. ϫⲟϥ.

tchaff, to be hot, to burn, to be angry, to roast.

tchafu, B.D. 146, 32, flames, fire.

tchaf, roasted food.

tcham, T. 385, P. 611, M. 402, to throw up the arms or hands in gladness.

tcham, sceptre; see

tcham, to copulate, to beget.

tcham, youth, young man; plur. IV, 924, 1006, L.D. III, 140B, Rev. 12, 17, young men, young soldiers, recruits, young folk in general, descendants, posterity; Copt. ϫⲱⲙ.

tchamu nu thau, A.Z. 35, 17, the generations of men, the human race.

Tchamaā, the god of Western Thebes; Copt. ϫⲏⲙⲉ.

tchamaā, Rev. 14, 36, papyrus, a roll of papyrus, a sheet of calculations, book, volume, document; Copt. ϫⲱⲱⲙⲉ, ϫⲱⲙ.

tchamā, dry land, parched ground; compare Heb. צִמָּאוֹן, Eth. ጸምአ:, Arab. ظَمِئَ, to be thirsty.

tchamā, Rev., calm (of the weather); Copt. ϫⲁⲙⲏ.

tchamā (?), chair of state, throne.

tchames, P.S.B. 20, 198, to devour, to consume.

tchan, Rev., soft, easy-going, feeble; Copt. ϫⲁⲛⲉ.

tchani-t, Jour. As. 1908, 273, feebleness, idleness, supineness; Copt. ϫⲏⲛ, ϫⲛⲁⲁⲩ.

Tchan-t, the sacred boat of the Nome of Gynaecopolites.

tchanna, Anastasi I, 24, 1, to shake, to shiver through fear, to become gooseflesh, tribulation, fear.

tchanariu (?); see **tchanri**.

tchanaḥu, Rechnungen 69, rudder handle.

tchaniḥ, arm; Copt. ϭⲛⲁϩ.

Tchanu, P. 418, M. 598, N. 1203, the four long-haired gods who stand in the east of the sky.

tchanf, Rev. 13, 37, to offer, chance; Copt. ϫⲱⲛϥ.

tchanr, B.M. 138, 3, to recompense, to requite, to reward.

tchanr, branch of a tree, staff, bar; Copt. ϫⲁⲗ.

tchanri (?), a disease of the skin.

tchanrri, scorpion; fem. ; plur. .

tchant, Rev., to experience, to try.

tchar, , to spy, to scrutinize; Copt. ϫⲉⲣ.

tchar, , spy, guide (?)

tchar, , , , Rec. 16, 137, to burn, to dissolve, to boil away; Copt. ϫⲉⲣ, ϫⲱⲣ, ϫⲱⲗ.

tchar, Rec. 16, 57, Åmen. 11, 19, 25, 4, , something unpleasant or hateful (?); plur. , Åmen. 10, 2.

tchar, enemy, rebel.

tchar, Rev. 12, 207, (for), , , to weigh out, to measure, to compute; , Gol. Ḥamm. 13, 121.

tchar-t, registration office.

tchar, Rev. 11, 186, Jour. As. 1908, 248, to be strong, to act violently, to overcome; Copt. ϫⲣⲟ, ϫⲱⲱⲣⲉ.

tchar ḥer, Rev., bold; Copt. ϫⲁⲣⲃⲁⲗ.

Tchar-t, Metternich Stele 73, a mythological scorpion.

tchara, , Rev. 12, 52, to overcome; Copt. ϫⲣⲟ.

tchara, to be bound, tied.

tchara, Rev. 12, 40, to cover; Copt. ϭⲱⲗ, ϫⲱⲗ.

tchara, Rev. 13, 103, strong.

tcharȧ, strong, mighty; Copt. ϫⲱⲣⲉ, ϫⲱⲣⲓ, ϫⲱⲱⲣⲉ.

tcharāa, , Thes. 1198, to strike, to cast down, to smite to the earth; Heb. צָרַע.

tcharā, Dem. Cat....

tchari, Rev. 13, 106, hard (of stone).

tchari-t, Rev. 13, 14, , Rev. 14, 51, area; Copt. ϫⲏⲣⲉ.

tcharu, Peasant 281, excuse, apology.

tchar-ut (?), Ȧnastasi I, 12, 4 ....

tcharm, Rev. 11, 172, to make a sign; Copt. ϫⲱⲣⲙ.

tcharm, Rev. 13, 15, , , Rec. 4, 21, a plant; Copt. ϭⲗⲏⲓⲙⲓ, Arab. الرشاد, Raphanus lyratus (Loret).

tcharm, the seed or fruit of the same, a perfume.

tcharna, see .

tchareḥ, A.Z. 1878, 48, , , Rev. 11, 166, , poor, wretched, miserable; Copt. ϭⲣⲱϩ, ϫⲟⲗϩ.

tcharkha, Rev. 11, 168, ...

tchar-khams, Rev. 11, 169 ....; Copt. ϫⲟⲟⲗⲉ ϩⲙⲥ (?)

tchart, , , , , ,

Rec. 15, 125, a kind of fruit, carob; Copt. ϭⲁⲣⲁⲧⲉ.

tcharṭ, skiff, boat, ship; plur. ; var. .

Tchahar, a name or title of a god of sickness.

tchaḥ, Rev. 12, 61, to touch.

tchaḥ, Thes. 1206, to crush; , Rev.; Copt. ϫⲁϩ, ϫⲟϩ (?)

tchaḥ, to anoint, to smear; Copt. ϫⲱϩ.

tchaḥeḥ, , to rejoice; var. .

tchas, to order, to arrange, to command.

tchasȧ, a wise or learned man; see **tchaȧs** .

tchas, plants, flowers, vegetables; var. .

tchasu, a kind of vessel (?)

tchasfa, , , to inaugurate a house or establishment.

tchasfait, Jour. As. 1908, 307, an establishment; Copt. ϫⲁⲥϥⲉ.

tchasha-t, a kind of cake offering.

tchaqi, Rev. 12, 47, to effect; Copt. ϫⲱⲕ.

tchaka, Rev., to be perfect; Copt. ϫⲱⲕ (ⲉ ⲃⲟⲗ).

tchakitcha .... , Rev. 13, 4, gnat, midge; Copt. ϫⲉⲕϫⲓⲕ.

tchat, storehouse, warehouse, magazine.

tchati (?), Rec. 3, 56, throne, throne-chamber, seat.

Tchat Ṭuat: (1) a crocodile-god; (2) a singing-god who gave water to the dead.

tchatt, N. 727 ....

tchatȧḥ, to confine, to shut up.

tchatu (?), to burn, fire.

tchat-tu (?), Hh. 479, wand, rod, stick.

tchaṭ, U. 510, , T. 323, to stick an animal, to cut the throat of a beast.

tchaṭi-t, urine.

Tchaṭiu, Ṭuat X, a group of gods in the Ṭuat.

tchaṭu, I, 38, , IV, 349, , , , hall of a building, hall with pillars, audience chamber.

tchaṭfȧu, Rev. 13, 40, reptiles.

tchatcha-t (?), , , estate, domain, landed property; plur. , , , .

Tchatcha-t ent ȧakhu, the domain of the spirit-souls.

Tchatcha t (?) Ȧmentt, the domain of Ȧmenti, *i.e.*, the cemetery.

Tchatcha-t ent ḥeḥ, the domain of eternity, *i.e.*, the tomb.

Tchatcha-t tcheser-t, the holy domain, the cemetery, the Other World.

tchatchau, heads, *i.e.*, people, the crowd.

tchatcha, Rec. 5, 97, head; Copt. ϫⲱϫ; Methen 6, upon; Copt. ϩⲓϫⲛ̄.

tchatcha-t, U. 449, T. 257, N. 162, 1321, M. 700, a high official, chief of a company of priests, member of council or of a college, judge, etc.

Tchatcha-ti, IV, 1192, the two Chiefs or Judges.

tchatcha-t, Hh. 354, B.M. 447, Rec. 31, 28, 171, Rec. 36, 135, Rec. 30, 193, Rec. 31, 173, court of judges, council of statesmen, board of guardians, college, board of overseers, the task masters of the Other World, chiefs, foremen. Later forms are: IV, 267, the double council.

Tchatcha-t ur-t, IV, 1114, the Great Council, the Chief Council of a city or town.

tchatcha-t nesu (?), A.Z. 1900, 35, Royal College (?), Royal Council (?)

tchatcha-t nesu (?) āa-t, B.D. 18 and 20, the great council of judges.

Tchatcha-t Abṭu, B.D. 18F, Osiris, Isis, Upuatu, and Ṭeṭ.

Tchatcha-t Ȧnu, B.D. 18A, Tem, Shu, Tefnut, Osiris, Thoth.

Ṭchatcha-t Ȧsȧr, the court of judges of Osiris.

Tchatcha-t up mitu, B.D. 18G, Thoth, Osiris, Anubis, Ȧsṭenu, the council of the judgement of the dead.

Tchatcha-t ur-t em Ȧnu, P. 577, the Great Council of gods in Heliopolis.

Tchatcha-t Pe-Ṭep, B.D. 18D, Horus, Isis, Mestȧ, and Ḥepi.

Tchatcha-t Naȧrruṭf, var., B.D. 18, I and 20, Rā, Osiris, Shu, Bebi.

Tchatcha-t Rekhti, B.D. 18E, Horus, Isis, Anubis, Mestȧ, Thoth.

Tchatcha-t Restau, B.D. 18J, Horus, Osiris, Isis, and another god.

Tchatcha-t khebs-ta, B.D. 18H, three unnamed gods.

Tchatcha-t khesef-t Āapepi, Ṭuat III, the divine judges who condemned Āapep.

Tchatcha-t Sekhem, B.D. 18C, Osiris and Ḥeru-khenti-n-ȧriti.

Tchatcha-t ṭaṭa-t, etc., Ṭuat VIII, the gods who distributed rations to the dead.

Tchatcha-t Ṭuat, the Council of the Other World, the judges in the Ṭuat.

Tchatcha-t Ṭuat, Ṭuat V, the judges of Time in the Ṭuat.

Tchatcha-t Ṭeṭu (Tcheṭu), B.D. 18B, Osiris, Isis, Nephthys, Horus.

tchatcha, Thes. 1323, , , , Banishment Stele 9, throne, throne-chamber, seat.

tchatcha, walled places, government offices.

tchatcha, B.D. 99, 16, a part of a boat.

tchatcha-t, Leyd. Pap. 7, 13, lyre (?)

tchatcha-t, Thes. 524, , harp, zither, lyre.

tchatcha-ti (?), harper.

tchatcha, , to fill with water, to water.

tchatchai, Jour. As. 1908, 297, to break; Copt. ϫⲏϫ.

tchȧ-t, Rec. 27, 226, 29, 150, a kind of bird (?)

tchā =, IV, 1157 ......

tchā, , desert; , Genre 45 .....; Copt. ϫⲁⲓⲉ.

tchā, A.Z. 72, 107, to roast meat (?)

tchā, , , , , storm, gale of wind, hurricane; plur. , , Åmen. 5, 14, , Åmen. 3, 15, , ; , storm of wind; , Peasant 244, violent storm; , the moist wind from the north; , Åmen. 3, 15.

Tchā, B.D. 39, 18, a storm-god.

tchā, Rec. 20, 40 ....

tchā, IV, 807, , , stick, staff, stalk.

tchā, , stalk, stem, straw, weed.

tchāā, , , , straw, weed.

tchātchā, IV, 36, to beat, to strike; , to knock at a door.

tchāā, to try, to test.

tchāu, a kind of fish.

tchāb, M. 689, seat, throne (?)

tchāb =, finger.

tchāb, to tally (?)

tchāb-t, , , Rec. 1, 51, 17, 146, varr. , , fuel, material for a fire; , B.D. 147, I, 12, Leyd. Pap. 3, 11, , animals' dung for fuel.

tchāb, Rec. 16, 141, a kind of seed used in making the incense Kyphi—aspalathus (?)

Tchābu (=), P. 282, , M. 528, N. 1106, gods with their hair () dressed (?)

tchām, T. 244, , Rec. 26, 229, , sceptre; plur. , U. 474, T. 233, P. 94, 619, N. 1306, , N. 944, , B.D. (Saite) 30, 3.

tchāāmȧu, U. 550, T. 304, sceptres; see .

Tchāmu, P. 645, 673, 692, M. 664, 767, N. 1279, 1311, the sceptres of the sons of Horus.

Tchāmu-ti, Ṭuat IX, a god with a serpent sceptre.

Tchām en Ȧnpu, B.D. 96, 3, the magical sceptre of Ȧnpu.

Tchām en ṭes, B.D. 125, III, 25, a magical sceptre called .

tchām, Palermo Stele , Koller 3, 8, , L.D. III, 194, , Rec. 6, 11, white-gold, a kind of precious metal; , IV, 367, the finest tchām; , IV, 849, real tchām; , tchām from the hill-top.

tchāmti (?), bowmen, fighting men.

Tchāmtiu, B.M. 32, 442, a class of fiends.

tchār, Mar. Karn. 35, 60, , Rec. 31, 10, , P. 1116 B. 6, , Rec. 26, 228, , Book of Breathings III, 13, , Koller 2, 6, , Anastasi IV, 28, , A.Z. 2, 14, , Rev. 7, 23, , Peasant 93, to test, to try, to seek, to pry into, to investigate, to explore, to look out for someone, to search into; Copt. ϫⲱⲣ, ϫⲏⲣ.

Tchār khat, B.D. 125, III, 37, "searcher of the reins"—a title of the god of the Judgement.

tchār, Rec. 16, 159, , to sift.

tchāru, , a sieve.

tchār-t, twig, branch; Copt. ϫⲁⲗ, ϫⲱⲱⲗⲉ (?)

tchārȧ, B.D. 178, 28, fort, fortress (?)

Tchārukha, Scarab Ȧmenḥetep III, a city, situation unknown.

tchāḥ, prison.

tchāt, olive oil; Copt. ϫⲟⲉⲓⲧ, compare Heb. זַיִת, Syr. ܙܝܬܐ, Arab. زَيْتُون, Eth. ዘይት:

Tchātt, a country in the Sûdân which produced silver.

tchāṭ (?), wind-storm, tempest.

tchātch, to keep watch, to observe.

tchitch, , blossom, flower; compare Heb. צִיץ.

tchuu, A.Z. 1900, 129, mountain; see **ṭu**; Copt ⲧⲟⲟⲩ.

tchua-t, the period of culmination of a star; var.

Tchuā, T. 292, the name or title of a god.

Tchun, Edfû I, 81, a title of the Nile-god.

tcheb, tcheba, U. 229, P. 25, 690, P. 785, U. 401, U. 405, T. 272, 273, 385, P. 169, 380, to supply, to furnish with, to equip, to provide, to decorate.

tcheba-t, P. 584, M. 401, equipment, decoration.

tcheb, Rec. 3, 46, food, provisions.

tcheb, tcheba, to give something in place of something, to restore, to replace, to indemnify, to supply, to pay for, to discharge a debt or obligation, to requite, to reward, to barter, to exchange; Copt. ⲧⲱⲱⲃⲉ.

tchebb, to pay, to requite, to reward.

tchebu, payment, reward, recompense, remuneration, price, bribe; Jour. As. 1908, 279, place of retribution.

tcheb = ⲧⲃⲉ in ⲉ ⲧⲃⲉ (Rev.).

tcheb — **er tcheb**, in return for, because of, instead of; later forms are A.Z. 33, 122, = ⲉ ⲧⲃⲏⲏⲧϥ, = ⲉ ⲧⲃⲏⲏⲧⲟⲩ; Rev. 13, 39, wherefore? because of what? Copt. ⲉ ⲧⲃⲉ.

tcheb, Rev. 12, 119, punishment, retribution in a bad sense.

tcheb, Rec. 5, 96, to clothe, to dress, to dress up, to deck (of the living), to bandage, to provide with grave-cloths, bandages, etc. (of the dead).

tcheb, a kind of stuff or garment; veils or bandlets.

tchebuit, funerary wrappings and other equipment.

tcheb-t, P. 614, M. 780, N. 1137, funerary box or coffer, coffin, sarcophagus, the coffin chamber; plur. ; Heb. תֵּבָה, Copt. ⲑⲉⲃⲓ; see

tcheb-ti, B.D. 189, 22, he who is coffined, *i.e.*, dead.

Tchebti, A.Z. 1905, 41, a god.

tcheb, IV, 814, Rec. 13, 203, A.Z. 1900, 28, Rec. 31, 147, Metternich Stele 41,

, to block up, to obstruct, to stop (a canal) to be blocked up.

tcheb , a kind of cage of wicker-work.

tchebu , lattice work (?) the woodwork of a fishing or hunting net.

tchebu , IV, 663, , Anastasi I, 267, part of a chariot; compare Heb. צָב.

tchebu , A.Z. 1907, 125, , Rec. 4, 126, , flowers, foliage, garden arbour; varr. , the flowers of Un-Nefer.

tchebȧu , raft made of reeds.

tcheb , to pierce, to stab; var. .

tchebtcheb , to pierce, to stab; varr. .

tcheb , javelin, spear, harpoon; plur. , A.Z. 1879, 21, the chain or rope attached to a harpoon.

tcheb-t , T. 163, , M. 176, brick, seal; dual , two bricks, double seal; plur. , IV, 765; , bricks, *i.e.*, ingots of gold; , Thes. 1287, ruined brickwork; Copt. ⲧⲱⲃⲉ.

Tcheb , Rec. 26, 132, a god.

Tcheb , Ṭuat III, a dog-headed god; see **Ṭebi**.

tcheb , timid, fearful (?)

tchebā , the number 10,000; plur. , Dream Stele 23, myriads, thousands, hundreds, tens; Copt. ⲧⲃⲁ.

tchebā , Åmen. 11, 13, , ibid. 17, 7, finger; dual , P. 196, 420, M. 602, N. 859, 1207, , U. 430; plur. , U. 480, T. 246, N. 1293, , T. 196, , P. 678, , N. 764, fingers of iron; Heb. אֶצְבַּע, Arab. أُصْبُع, Copt. ⲧⲏⲃⲉ, ⲧⲏⲏⲃⲉ, Syr. ܨܒܥܐ, Eth. አጽባዕት : plur. አጻብዕ :

tchebā Set , N. 302, the name of an offering.

Tchebā (?) , god of .

Tchebā ur en Sekri , B.D. 153A, 7, the pole of the net of the Akeru-gods.

Tchebāu en Ḥeru-semsu , B.D. 99, 20, the paddles of the magical boat.

Tchebā en Sekri , B.D. 153A, 17, the name of a part of the magical net.

Tchebā en Shesmu , B.D. 153B, 5, the name of a part of the magical net.

Tchebāui en tepu āa Rā , B.D. 153A, 19, the name of two parts of the net of the Akeru-gods.

Tchebāui netcherui, B.D. 153A, 19, "grasping fingers"—a name of two parts of the magical net.

tchebā, A.Z. 1905, 19, , to seal, to be sealed; Copt. ⲧⲱⲱⲃⲉ.

tchebā, seal; "great seal"; "little seal," U. 583, N. 963.

tchebāi-t, IV, 1072, IV, 1044, seal; plur. , A.Z. 45, 124, A.Z. 1899, 86, , IV, 209, seal rings, seals of office; Copt. ⲧⲃⲃⲉ, Heb. טַבַּעַת, Assyr. ti-im-bu-'-u (Winckler, El-Amarna, 24, 2, 20), and ṭim-bu-u-bi (Rawlinson, C.I.W.A. V, 26, 7, Obv. 4).

tchebātiu, IV, 1116, keeper of seals, treasurers.

Tchebā, Ṭuat I, god of the seal (?)

tchebā, trouble, misery; , Dream Stele 37, troubled; Copt. ϫⲱⲃ.

tchebā-t (?), Rev. 12, 10, instant; Copt. ϫⲉⲡ (?)

tchebā, a plant or wood used in making kyphi incense.

tchebā-t, roasted food.

tchebu, revenue, income.

tchebḥa, to tear out, to rip open.

tchepeḥ, apple; Heb. תַּפּוּחַ.

tchef, to spit, to eject moisture.

tchefu, drop of water.

tcheftchef, to drip, to sprinkle, to pour out, to drop tears; , Litanie 47.

tchef, the pupil of the eye.

tcheftchef-t, a disease of the eye, rheum of the eyes (?)

Tchef-en-utchat, a god.

tchefa, U. 202, , T. 79, 331, M. 232, , P. 102, M. 90, N. 620, 621, food, celestial food or offerings.

tchefu, to provide with food, to supply with offerings.

Tchef, Ombos I, 186, one of the 14 kau of Rā.

Tchef, the Food-god; fem. **Tchefit**

Tchef, Ombos I, 85, a god of offerings.

Tchefit, B.D. 110, 35, a goddess and a locality in Sekhet-Aaru.

tchef, a kind of tree.

tchef, wretchedness, misery, sadness; Copt. ϫⲱϥ, ϫⲓϥ.

tchefi, to be agitated, to tremble.

tcheftchef, to patter with the feet, to walk with quick short steps.

tchefi-t, a place of trembling in Ȧmenti.

tchefen, A.Z. 1906, 124, to rejoice; see **tefen**.

tchefen, to beget.

tchefen, child, offspring; , Rec. 15, 152, , Rec. 33, 3, 4.

tchefenti, a statue, figure of an ancestor.

tchefeṭ-t, pupil of the eye; see , B.D. 101, 4.

tchefetch, B.D. 101, 4, pupil of the eye; , Thes. 1200.

tchem = , sceptre.

tchem (?), a pair of wings.

tchems, a kind of bird.

tchemten = , a substance used in making incense.

Tchemtch-ḥātut, Tomb of Seti I, one of the 75 forms of Rā (No. 43).

tchen, round about, near (?)

tchen, to advance in a hurry.

tchen-t, A.Z. 1899, 95, a metal object, weapon or tool.

tchenn-t, top of the head, skull, the head and gills of a fish.

tchennu-t, Rev. 6, 26, , threshing floor; plur. , Ȧmen. 19, 8, , Rec. 31, 21; Copt. ϫⲛⲟⲟⲩ.

tchenȧ, U. 418, , T. 238, to cut through (?)

tchenȧ-t, U. 418, , T. 238, , Rec. 26, 79, , ibid. 27, 219, , ibid. 29, 156, dyke.

tchenȧ-t, P. 222, , a festival of the last quarter of the month; , Rec. 31, 32, 161.

tchenȧ-t, U. 546, vase, vessel (?)

tchenȧu, instruments, tools, weapons.

tchenu, U. 201, , T. 78, , N. 610, , T. 331, a kind of tree.

Tchennutt, U. 458, a serpent-fiend in the Ṭuat.

tchennuṭ (tchenṭ), attack, wrath, anger, angry; see , and ; Copt. ϫⲱⲛⲧ.

tchenben, IV, 1101, an article of tribute.

tchenp, to cut, to divide.

tchenp-t, Rec. 27, 219 . . . . . .

tchenf, Rosetta Stone 38, ceremonies performed in honour of someone.

Tchener-ti, a title of Isis and Nephthys.

tchenḥ, T. 187, M. 785, , U. 492, P. 192, , P. 615, M. 364, N. 916, wing, pinion; dual , U. 362; plur. , N. 1163, , P. 390, , U. 570, P. 452.

tchenḥ, to invade, to attack.

tchenḥ-t, beam, part of a ship; , B.D. 99, 29.

tchens, weight, heavy; see ṭens , .

Tchenti , , Litanie 68, a form of the Sun-god Rā.

Tchenti, Tomb Seti I, a two-headed god—one of the 75 forms of Rā.

tchentha, throne, throne-room; see and .

tchenṭ, U. 96, N. 374, 1377, , P. 631, 662, 689, M. 773, , T. 276, , Rec. 30, 194, 32, 85, Hh. 414, , Rec. 26, 230, , to attack with violence, to rage against.

Tchenṭru, T. 198, 276, N. 1294, , P. 679, , , M. 40, N. 68, a god (?)

Tchenṭtchenṭer, P. 301; see .

tchentch, wrath, anger, angry, fury, attack; see **tchentchen** and **tchenṭ**.

Tchentchen, B.D. 180, 11, a god.

tchentchen, Rec. 32, 85, , B.D. 39, 12, to attack with violence; see .

tchentchenu, the attackers, besiegers.

tchentchen-t, Rec. 31, 26, attack.

tcher-t, Coptos 8, 6, , bread, food, sustenance.

tcher-t, U. 3, 550, T. 29, 32, P. 613, M. 781, N. 179, 1138, palm of the hand; Copt. ⲦⲞⲞⲦ.

tcherȧ-t, Rec. 31, 30, hand.

Tcher-t, T. 308, the Great Hand in heaven; compare the hand , in Ṭuat X.

tcher , , , , when, since, whilst, as; , Rec. 14, 12, because; , Rev.

tcher enti, tcher entet , , , Rec. 4, 31, because.

tcher , , to be near the limit or boundary, by the side of something, near; , P. 431, M. 617, N. 1222.

tcher, tcheru , U. 520, T. 329, , U. 521, , T. 330, , M. 701 (bis), , , , border, boundary, limit; plur. , IV, 620, , , , , , , ; , limit of the earth; , limitless eternity; , IV, 426, limitless; , , unlimited; , T. 271, P. 22, M. 33, N. 123, without limit; , boundless; Copt. ⲦⲀⲢ, ⲦⲎⲢ.

tcher, a protecting door, a boundary door.

tcherȧ, boundary; Copt. ⲦⲎⲢ.

tcher , , , Rev. 11, 143, all, the whole; plur. ; , all the gods; Copt. ⲦⲎⲢ.

tcher — **er tcher**, to the limit of, all; , all of it; Copt. ⲧⲏⲣϥ; , U. 405, all of you; , all thy desire; , U. 131, N. 439; , U. 461.

tcher-ā , IV, 1074, , IV, 1143, before.

tcher baḥ , , , , from of old; , ancestors.

tcher ḥa-t , from the beginning.

tcher-ti , belonging to olden time, he who is of olden time.

tchertiu , Tombos Stele 15, IV, 344, , , ancestors, forbears, predecessors, beings, human or divine, of ancient time; , Rec. 16, 109, , Rec. 3, 116, ancestral gods.

tchertcheru , B.M. 5645, Rev. 2, ancestral gods.

tchertcheriu ; fem. ....

Tcher, Tcherȧ-t , , , "ancestress"—a title of Isis and of Nephthys both of whom were represented as women, cows or birds, *i.e.*, hawks, vultures, etc. Isis was the "Great Ancestress," , and Nephthys the "Little Ancestress," .

Tcher-ti , U. 313, 448, , T. 256, P. 473, M. 539, N. 1118, , , , , , , , , , , Nesi-Åmsu 1, 1, the two ancestresses Isis and Nephthys.

Tcher-ȧakhu , Ṭuat VIII, a god of the Circle Seḥert-baiu-s.

Tcher-ȧtf , B.M. 46631, a god.

Tcherit-pet (?) , Ombos II, 133, a goddess.

tcher-t , U. 572, P. 475, 673, N. 1262, , T. 381, hawk, falcon, vulture, kite, glede; plur. , T. 77; Copt. ⲧⲣⲉ.

tcher , Peasant 243, 280, Rec. 32, 78, , to bring to an end, *i.e.*, to finish, to fashion, to construct, to make an end of, *i.e.*, to destroy.

tcher , , Rec. 21, 39 to bandage, to tie up, to envelop; , M. 426, bandaged, swathed = , T. 268, buried; Copt. ϫⲱⲗ.

tcher-t , oppression, restraint.

tcheru-t , , coffin, chest, coffer.

Tcherut (?) , Rec. 31, 163, a group of gods.

tcheri-t , , , chamber, store, dwelling, private room, shrine.

tcheru , A.Z. 45, 133, B.D. 144, 24, , , , , , Osiris 27, rump, chine; , B.D. 18, I, 2, the divine rump of Osiris; Copt. ⲧⲱⲣⲓ.

tchertcherui , buttocks, rump.

tcher-ti, belonging to the back or rump.

tcheru, P. 565, skull.

tcheru, a circuit wall of a building.

tcherui (?), Rec. 3, 48, the two halves of a mould.

tchertcher, N. 690 = M. 172.

tcherui, ochre, coloured earths used in illuminating papyri.

tcherut, beads, pills, pellets, small balls.

tcheru, crocodiles.

Tcherȧ, Rec 30, 66, a god.

Tcherȧ-t, B.M. 46631, consort of .

tcherȧ-t, M. 665, N. 1281; var. T. 381, vulture, kite, glede; Copt. ⲧⲣⲉ.

tcherȧ, to work, to finish, to complete, to execute, to be complete or finished; L.D. III, 194, 32, finished, *i.e.*, hewn stones.

tcherȧ, A.Z. 1868, 112, to constrain, to use strength, to enclose or imprison, to fortify.

tcherȧ, IV, 660, strong one or thing; A.Z. 1905, 101, very, very.

tcherȧ, Thes. 1289, IV, 1087, wall, fort.

tcherȧ-t, wall, palisade, wooden palings for defence; plur. Leyd. Pap. 2, 10.

tcherȧ-t, IV, 1057, coffer, funerary chest.

tcherȧ-t, domicile.

tcherȧ-ti, L.D. III, 194, 32, part of a temple court.

tcherȧ, B.M. 5645, Rev. 3, stupid, arrogant.

tcherȧtcherȧ; var., to boast, to talk an alien speech.

tcherȧu, B.D. 145, 77, the lower part of the body.

tcheri-t; see **tcher-t**.

tcheritcheri, Ȧmen. 26, 11, to boast (?)

tcheru, B.D. 172, 17, vulture, kite, glede; Copt. ⲧⲣⲉ.

tcherp, see .

tchernit, a kind of seed or grain.

tcheres, B.D. 64, 19, chamber (?) room (?)

tchert, qualities, attributes.

tchertiu, musicians; Copt. ⲧⲱⲣⲉ.

tcherṭ (?), a powerful bird, vulture, hawk, eagle = (?)

tchertch , Rec. 15, 121 = .

tchertcher , Rec. 36, 202, , to be foreign or alien.

tchertcherȧ-t , P. 1116B, 29, strange or foreign speech.

tchertcheru , foreigner, alien, boaster.

tchertcheru , Pap. 3024, 117, , Rec. 36, 202, boasters, those who assume rank to which they are not entitled.

tchertcheru , leaves of trees, foliage.

tcheḥ , , I, 98, a kind of stuff, girdle; or (?) P. 303.

tcheḥ, tcheḥti , U. 600, , Décrets 48, , , , , lead; Copt. ⲦⲀϨⲦ.

Tcheḥtcheḥ , Ṭuat I, an ape-god; var. .

tcheḥā , an animal.

tcheḥāu , Hh. 437, leather straps (?)

tcheḥāua , P. 662, 782, M. 774 . . . . . .

Tcheḥuti , , , Rec. 33, 37, 34, 179, , ibid. 29, 144, , , the god Thoth; Copt. ⲐⲞⲞⲨⲦ.

tcheḥer , leather strap; plur. , Hh. 439.

Tcheḥer , a proper name; in Heb. צְחָא, Ungnad, Aram. Pap. 20.

Tcheḥes , B.D. 149, a serpent in Ȧat VII.

tches , , self; , , himself; , , herself; , U. 558, , , themselves; , , myself; , , thyself; , U. 319, , , IV, 346, thyself (fem.).

tches , seal; , royal seal.

tches , to cut, to divide.

tches , , knife; plur. ; var. ṭes .

tchestches , to knife, to hack in pieces, to chop up; , double knife (?)

tchestches , U. 458 . . . .

tches , pot, vase, water-jar; var. .

Tcheses , B.D. (Saïte) I, 45, 30, a goddess.

tchesȧu , N. 1317, to hail, to address.

tchesu , T. 355, P. 8, 70, M. 10, 101, N. 7, 114, 175, , M. 826, to hail, to greet, to address, to question; , P. 611.

tchesp , Suppl. 1385 . . . .

Tchesef , B.D. 146, the doorkeeper of the 9th Pylon.

tchesef , fire, heat.

tchesef , vase, vessel, pot.

tchesef, B.D. 63B, 4, , B.D. 153A, 2, 18, 25, 30, , B.D. 153A, 6, to tie, to bind (?)

tcheser, T. 29, P. 76, M. 106, , T. 175, , P. 121, M. 157, , Rec. 26, 228, , Metternich Stele 51, , , , , , , to be beautiful, to beautify, to hold in honour, to account holy; , to make a good road, to prepare a path.

tcheser, holy of hand; , holy of arm; , of holy creation; , a beautiful, *i.e.*, holy, place; , magnificent; , , Rec. 29, 153.

tcheser, IV, 357, splendour, magnificence, glory, splendid rank, exalted honour; plur. , IV, 967, , high honours, splendours (of the sun), holy things.

tcheser-t, holy things.

tcheseru, U. 474, , M. 767, , Rec. 31, 21, , Rec. 33, 38, , B.D. 30A, 5, holy things; , , Rec. 33, 28, a holy place or country.

tcheser, , Rec. 4, 137, the "splendid" hall of a house or temple, chapel.

Tcheser-tcheseru, IV, 381, , IV, 919, , IV, 422, "splendour of splendours" or "holy of holies"—the name of the temple built at Dêr al-Baḥarî by Ḥatshepset.

Tchesrit, Ṭuat IX, the gate to Ṭuat X.

Tcheseru, Rec. 33, 27, , the "holy country," *i.e.*, the Land of the Dead.

Tchesertt, , , the necropolis.

Tcheser-t, B.D. 81B, 5, a name of the Ṭuat.

tcheser-t, U. 90, , N. 367, , E.T. 1, 53, , , , a kind of sacrificial drink; , , vessels of "holy" or "exalted" drink.

tcheser-t, U. 47, , N. 277, a table of holy offerings.

Tcheserit, a name of the Eye of Horus.

Tcheserit, B.D. 110, 37, a goddess in Sekhet Åaru.

Tcheserå-åru (?), Denderah IV, 79, a bull-god.

Tcheser-ā, , a title of the god Åmen.

Tcheser-em-per-f, etc., Denderah IV, 61, a jackal-god.

Tcheserit-hent, Ombos II, 131, a goddess.

Tcheser-seshetait, Berg. II, 9, , Thes. 28, 31, D.E. 20, the goddess of the 9th hour of the day and of the 6th hour of the night; var. , Denderah III, 24.

Tcheser-tep, U. 510, 548, , T. 311, 323, , , B.D. 125, II, one of the 42 assessors of Osiris.

Tcheser-tep-f, Rec. 30, 194, one of the 42 Assessors of Osiris.

Tcheser-ṭeṭȧ, T. 309, son of .

tcheser-t, the name of a plant.

tcheser, a measure = 4 palms = 16 fingers.

tchet, , fat, unguent; see ; , an oil used in making kyphi.

tcheteb, to sting (of a scorpion).

tchetf-t, the holy worm.

Tchet-s, Ṭuat XI, a serpent-goddess who was reborn daily.

tcheṭ, mark of quotation; Copt. ϫⲉ.

tcheṭ, , , , to speak, to say, to declare, to tell, to narrate; Copt. ϫⲱ; , to make a speech; , , introduces a quotation; Copt. ϫⲉ; , T. 191, P. 676, N. 1288, to announce or declare a name; , to read a report, to tell news; , IV, 1031, to tell a lie; , otherwise said.

tcheṭṭ, to speak, to say.

tcheṭṭ-t, IV, 165, something spoken.

tcheṭ meṭu, P. 405, M. 578, N. 1184, , , to recite formulae; , N. 896, P. 183, , P. 467, 470, "recite the formula four times."

tcheṭ-t, word, speech, language; plur. , sayings, proverbs, aphorisms; , Sayings of the Fathers; , speech of Negroland, Sûdânî language.

tcheṭi-t, Ḳubbân Stele 16, , A.Z. 1905, 33, something spoken, word, saying.

tcheṭu, , speaker, spokesman.

Tcheṭ, U. 372, , U. 374, the Divine Word, speech deified.

Tcheṭ-t-ur-t, M. 487, N. 1254, , P. 273, 489, the "great word" personified, a form of Isis of Busiris (Berg. I, 35).

tcheṭ-t, star, the time of the culmination of a star.

tcheṭ-t, olive tree; plur. , ; Heb. זַיִת, Arab. زيت, Copt. ϫⲟⲉⲓⲧ.

tcheṭṭu, olives.

tcheṭ, P. 92, , M. 121, , N. 699, , , to be stable, to be permanent, abiding, established firmly, lasting, enduring; , U. 255.

tcheṭṭ, M. 252, lasting, enduring; , N. 699, , , P. 92, M. 121, N. 699, those who are permanent, lasting.

tcheṭ, , , stability, as in the group , "life, stability, serenity."

tcheṭ-tȧ, an enduring person or thing.

tcheṭtcheṭ, , Thes. 1285, , , , , to be permanent, stable, abiding, enduring; , enduring; ; varr. , , , , .

Tchetchi, the "stablished one," or he of the Tcheṭ pillar, *i.e.*, Osiris.

tchetchit, Rec. 4, 134, something established.

tcheṭ-t, grave, tomb, sepulchre.

tcheṭu (?), pillars or parts of pillars; , Rec. 30, 66.

tcheṭ, , , the sacred pillar or tree trunk which was worshipped in certain parts of the Delta in predynastic times, and with which the backbone of Osiris was subsequently identified.

tcheṭ, , an amulet that was supposed to endue the wearer with the permanence and stability of the backbone of Osiris; , the backbone of Osiris, the sacrum bone.

Tcheṭ, Ombos I, 186, one of the 14 kau of Rā.

Tcheṭṭi, , B.D. 1, 13, a title of Osiris.

Tcheṭit, a goddess, a form of Hathor.

Tcheṭut (?), Denderah III, 25, the two goddesses of Tcheṭ-t (Busiris).

Tcheṭu, M. 121, , P. 92, the "stable ones" in the Ṭuat; var. .

Tcheṭȧ-t, P. 189, M. 354, , N. 906, a lake in the Ṭuat.

Tcheṭ-ḥeft, Berg. I, 18, a dog-god.

Tcheṭit-ṭent, Ṭuat V, a goddess who lived on the blood of the dead.

tcheṭ, to shine, light, brilliance, radiance.

tcheṭ-tu, Anastasi I, 11, 4, blinded, dazzled.

tcheṭa, Ebers Pap. 76, 20, , , , Rec. 31, 16, , , , fat, firm, solid.

tcheṭau (?), fattened geese.

Tcheṭun, Mission 13, 51, a Sûdânî god; see .

tcheṭuḥ (?), produce, crops.

tcheṭeb-t, P. 218, a kind of building, store (?); plur. , P. 609.

tcheṭeb, Rec. 35, 58, , Metternich Stele 55, 73, , , , , , to stick with a knife or spear, to stab, to pierce, to wound, to sting, to bite (of a reptile); , stuck, pierced.

tcheṭeb, Anastasi I, 21, 3, sting of an insect.

Tcheṭbi, Ṭuat IV, , the serpent-guardian of the Gate Neb-t-setchfau.

tcheṭeb, a kind of fish.

tcheṭeb, to collect, to gather together.

Tcheṭ-pa-neter-ȧuf-ānkh, a theoretical name which is probably the equivalent of צָפְנַת פַּעְנֵחַ (Gen. xli, 45), the name given to Joseph by Pharaoh.

tcheṭpu, an iron tool or instrument.

tcheṭf-t, , , worm, serpent; plur. ; Copt. ϫⲁⲧϥⲉ.

tcheṭf-t, dagger, stilus, scraper.

Tcheṭf-t, B.D. 110, a boat in Sekhet-Åaru.

tcheṭem, a heap, a measure, a vessel full of something; , a mass of food or grain; , a vessel filled with something.

tcheṭem-t, bundles of vegetables, bunches of grapes, etc.

tcheṭem, Metternich Stele 189, to stab, to stick, to sting (of a scorpion).

Tcheṭmit, Ṭuat X, a light-goddess.

tcheṭen, to be hot, fire.

tcheṭna, a kind of cloth.

tcheṭnu, plots of cultivated ground.

tcheṭṭer, M. 149, , N. 650 . . . . . .

tcheṭeḥ, Israel Stele 16, , IV, 767, , Rec. 17, 147, , IV, 1076, , P.S.B. 10, 49, , Rev. 13, 52, , , to tie, to bind, to constrain, to shut in, to imprison; Copt. ϫⲱⲧϩ.

tcheṭḥu-t, Rec. 21, 96, , prison, place of restraint.

tcheṭeḥ (?), produce, food.

tcheṭek ḥat, A.Z. 1872, 33 . . . . . .

tcheṭku, a kind of lake.

tcheṭteh, Rev., prison, restraint; Copt. ⲧⲁⲧϩⲟ.

tchetch (?), B.D. 174, 18, a kind of standard (?)

II.

LIST OF EGYPTIAN KINGS.

PREDYNASTIC KINGS: KINGS OF LOWER EGYPT.

1. ....pu
2. Ska
3. Khaȧu (?)
4. Tȧu
5. Thesh
6. Neheb (?)
7. Uatch-nār (?)
8. Mekha
9. .....a

PREDYNASTIC KINGS: KINGS OF UPPER EGYPT.

10. Nār-mer

11. Tchar (?) the "Scorpion"

DYNASTY I.

12. Men, Ṁenȧ (Μήνης)

13. Ȧtet I (Ἄθωθις)

14. Ȧtet II (? Κενκένης)

15. Ȧta, or Ȧtati, or Ȧtet III (?) (Οὐενέφης ?)

16. Semti (Οὐσαφάιδος)

17. Merpeba (Μιεβὶς)

18. Smerkha (?) (? Σεμέμψης), Ḥu or Nekht

19. Qebḥu

HORUS NAMES OF KINGS OF DYNASTY I:—

20. Khent Tȧ

21. Tcheṭ Ȧt

22. Qa-ā. His name was Sen.

23. Ka

DYNASTY II.

24. **Baiu-neter** .

25. **Batchau** (Βοηθὸς) .

26. **Ka-kau** (Καιέχως) .

27. **Ba-n-neter** (Βίνωθρις) ; .

28. **Uatchnes** (Τλὰς) , .

29. **Sentá** (Σεθένης) , .

30. **Nefer-ka I,** or **Nefer-ka-Rā I** (Νεφερχέρης) , .

31. **Nefer-ka-Seker** , .

32. **Ḥutchfa** , .

33. **Tchatchai** or **Bebi** ; var. .

34. **Neb-ka I (Neb-ka-Rā I)** , .

HORUS NAMES OF KINGS OF DYNASTY II :—

35. **Ḥetep-sekhemui** .

36. **Rā-neb** .

37. **Sekhem-åb Per-en-maāt**

38. **Per-åb-sen** , .

39. **Khā-sekhem** .

40. **Khā-sekhemui** .

DYNASTY III.

41. **Neter khat Tcheser I** ; ; , .

42. **Tcheser II, Åtet IV** (?) , .

43. **Neb-ka II (Neb-ka-Rā II)** ; , .

44. **Setches** .

45. **Nefer-ka-Rā II** .

46. **Ḥu (Ḥuni)** , .

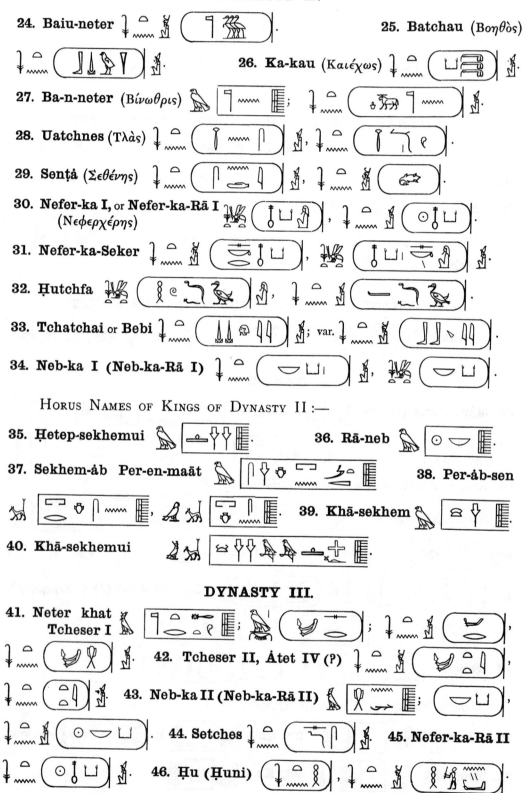

Horus Names of Kings of Dynasty III :—

47. Khā-ba  **48. Ka-Ḥeru (?)** 

49. To this dynasty, too, belongs the king whose name has been read 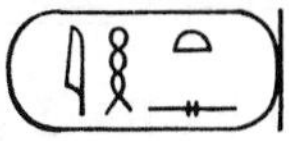 **Åḥtes,** 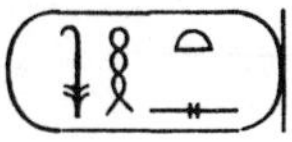 **Su-ḥetes,** and 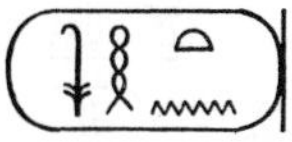 **Stnḥ.**

DYNASTY IV.

50. Seneferu 

51. Khufu (Χέοψ) 

52. Tcheṭ-f-Rā or **Ṭeṭ-f-Rā** 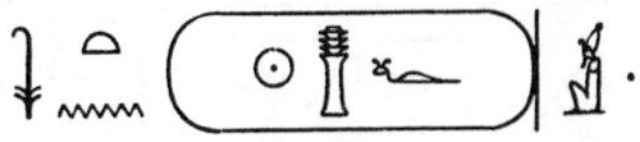

53. Khā-f-Rā (Χεφρῆν, Κεφρήν) 

54. Men-kau-Rā (Μενχέρης) 

55. Shepses-ka-f 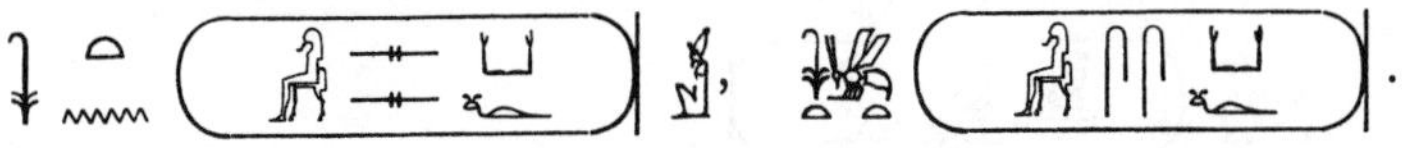

DYNASTY V.

56. User-ka-f (Οὐσερχέρης) 

57. Saḥu-Rā 

58. Nefer-åri-ka-Rā I  The Abydos List gives **Kakaå** 

59. Shepses-ka-Rā  ; his "son-of-Rā" name may have been **Åså** 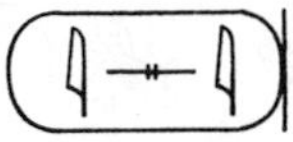 ; see A.Z. 50, 3.

60. Nefer-f-Rā  ; var. **Khā-nefer-Rā** 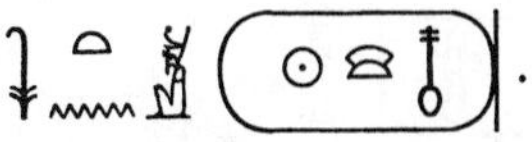

61. En-user-Rā Ån I 

62. **Men-kau-Ḥeru**  ; var. **Ȧkau-Ḥeru** .

63. **Ṭeṭ-ka-Rā I** (Ταγχέρης) **Ȧssȧ** 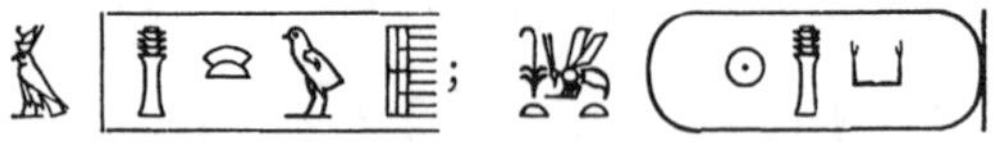 ; var. **Maāt-ka-Rā I** .

64. **Unȧs** (Ὄννος) .

DYNASTY VI.

65. **Tetȧ (Ȧtet V)** 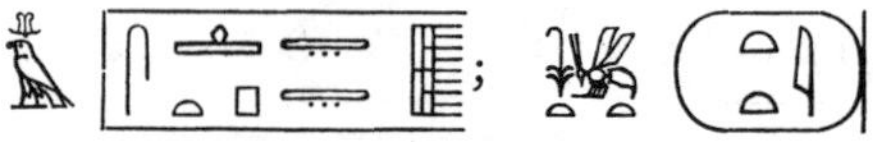.

66. **User-ka-Rā I Ȧti I** 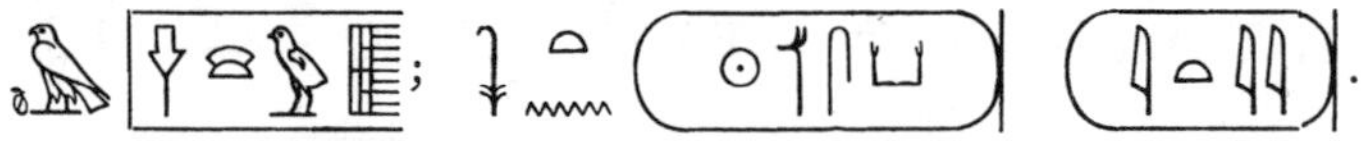.

67. **Meri-Rā Pepi I** .

68. **Mer-en-Rā I Meḥti-em-sa-f I** (Μεθουσουφίς) , .

69. **Nefer-ka-Rā III, Pepi II** 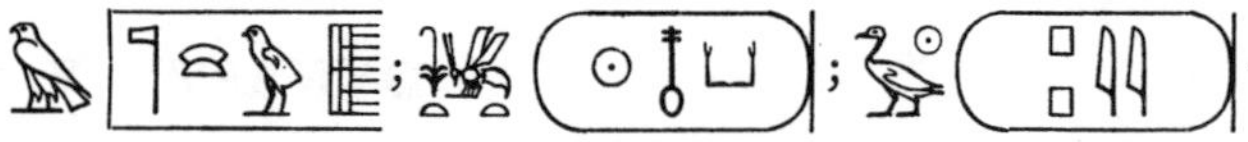.

70. **Mer-en-Rā II, Meḥti-em-sa-f II** .

71. **Neter-ka-Rā** 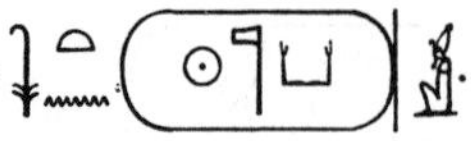. 72. **Net-ȧqerti** (Νίτωκρις) .

73. **Nefer-ka II** 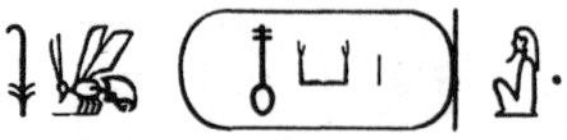.

DYNASTIES VII (?) AND VIII.

74. **Men-ka-Rā** 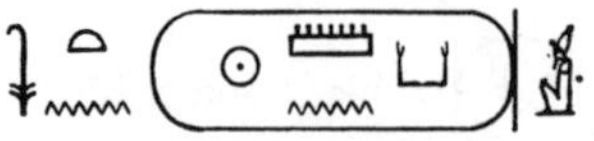. 75. **Nefer-ka-Rā IV** 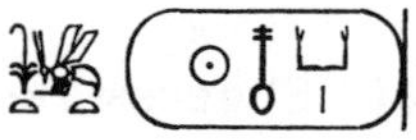.

76. **Nefres (?)** 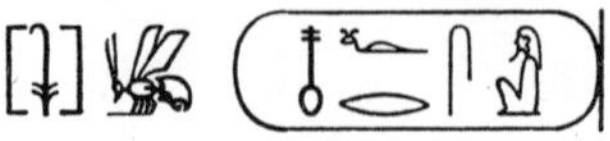. 77. **Ȧb (?)** .

78. **Nefer-ka-Rā V Nebi** 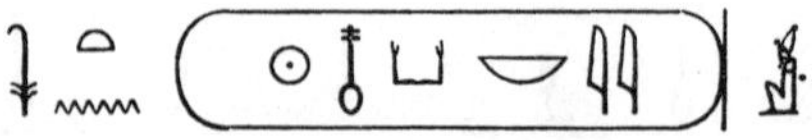

79. **Ṭeṭ-ka-Rā II Maā .....** 

80. **Nefer-ka-Rā VI Khenṭu** 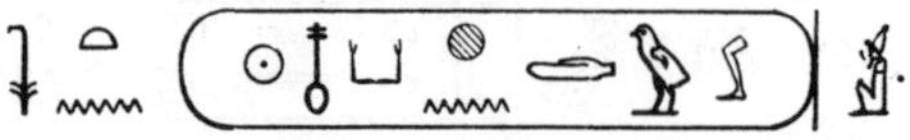.

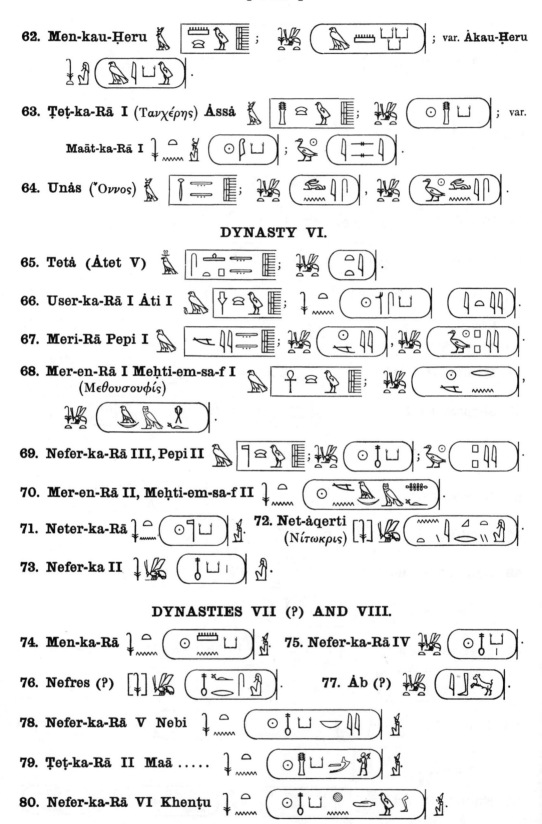

81. **Mer-en-Ḥer I** 

82. **Senefer-ka I Senefer-ka-Rā I** 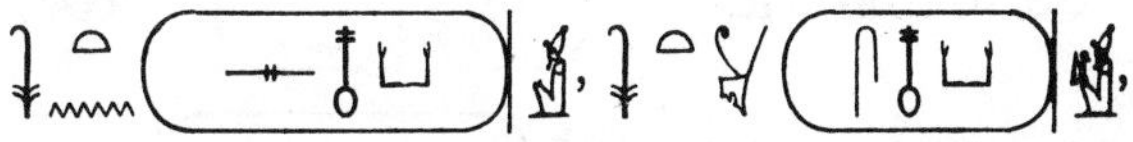
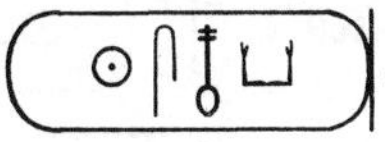.

83. **En-ka-Rā I** 

84. **Nefer-ka-Rā VII, Terrl (?)** 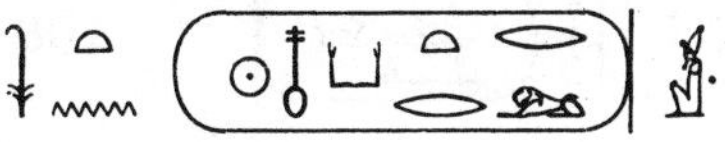

85. **Nefer-ka-Ḥeru** 

86. **Nefer-ka-Rā VIII, Pepi III Senb** 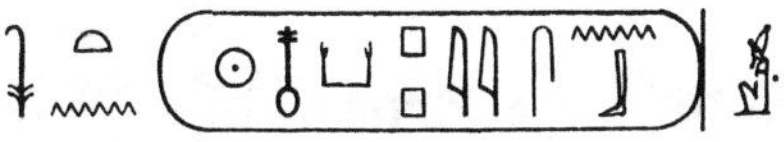

87. **Senefer-ka II Ānnu** 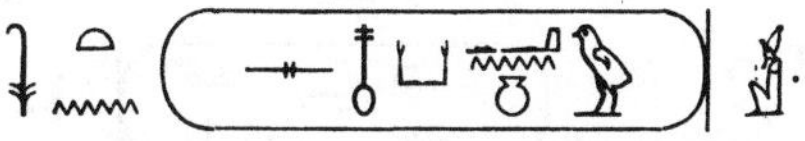

88. **Ȧn (?)-kau-Rā** 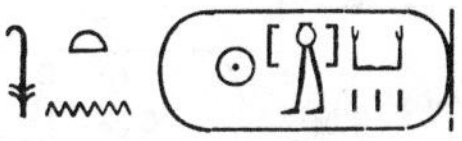.

89. **Nefer-kau-Rā** 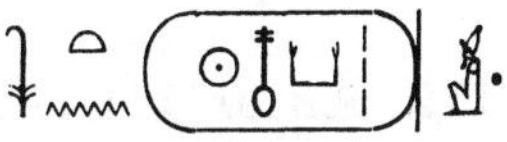

90. **Nefer-kau-Ḥeru** 

91. **Nefer-ȧri-ka-Rā II** 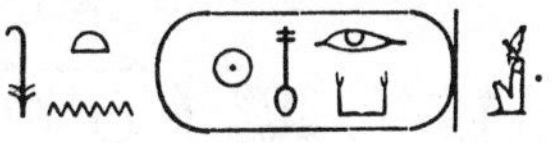

92. **Ȧti II (Othoes)** 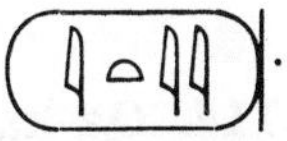

93. **Sekhem-ka-Rā I** 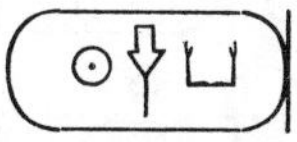.

94. **Ȧi-em-ḥetep** 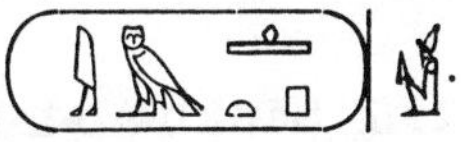

95. **Uatch-ka-Rā I** 

DYNASTIES IX AND X.

96. **Nefer-ka-Rā IX** 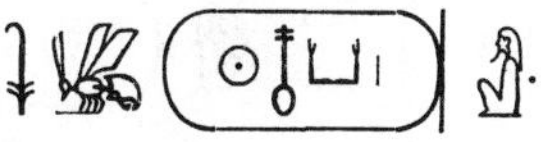

97. **Ȧb-meri-Rā (Meri-ka-Rā I?) Khati I** (**'Αχθώης**) 

[Names of five kings wanting here.]

98. **Meri-[Ȧāḥ?]** .

99. **Nefer-ka-Rā X** 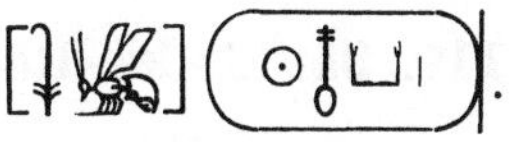

100. **Uaḥ-ka-Rā I Khati II** 

101. **Ka-meri-Rā II** 

102. **Neb-kau Khati III** 

To this period probably belong :—

103. Skhā-n-Rā .

104. Khā-user-Rā I .

105. Nub-taui-Rā .

106. Āa-ḥetep-Rā I .

107. Āa-khā-Rā I .

108. Maā-åb-Rā .

DYNASTY XI.

109. Åntef I the **Erpā** .

110. Menthu-ḥetep I tep ā

111. Åntef II (?) .

112. Åntef III (?) Uaḥ-ānkh ; .

113. Åntef IV (?) Nekht-neb-tep-nefer ; .

114. Qa-ka-Rā I Åntef V (?) ; .

115. Sānkh-åb-taui Menthu-ḥetep II ; .

116. Neb-ḥep (?)-Rā Menthu-ḥetep III ;

The 3rd and 4th signs in this cartouche probably represent , and if so, we should read **Neb-ḥep-Rā**, and so have the of the Abbott Papyrus.

117. Åntef VI (?) ; .

118. Neb-taui-Rā Menthu-ḥetep IV ; .

119. Sānkh-ka-Rā Menthu-ḥetep V ; .

To this period probably belongs :—

120. . . . . . åb-khent-Rā ; .

DYNASTY XII.

121. Seḥetep-àb-Rā I Àmen-em-ḥat I ('Αμμενέμης) 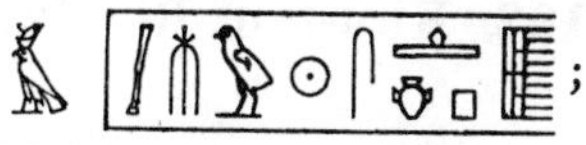

var. 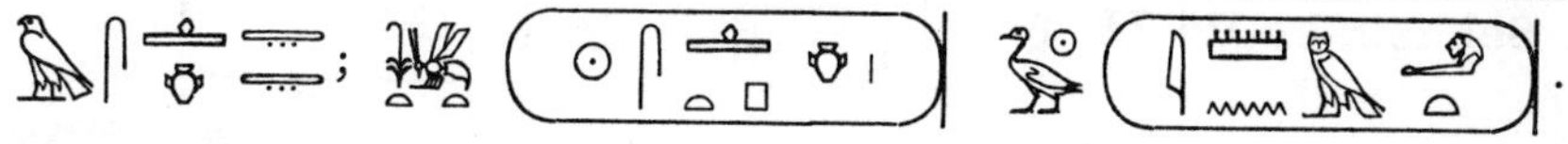

122. Kheper-ka-Rā I Usert-sen I (Sen-usert) (Σεσόγχωσις) 

123. Nub-kau-Rā Àmen-em-ḥat II ('Αμμενέμης) 

124. Kheper-khā-Rā I· Usert-sen II (Sen-usert) (Σέσωστρις) 

125. Khā-kau-Rā Usert-sen III (Sen-usert) (Λαχάρης) 

126. En-Maāt-Rā Àmen-em-ḥat III ('Αμερής) 

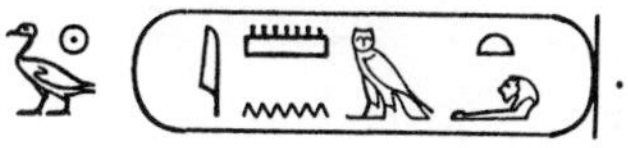

127. Au-àb-Rā I Ḥer 

var. 

128. Maā-kheru-Rā Àmen-em-ḥat IV ('Αμμενέμης) 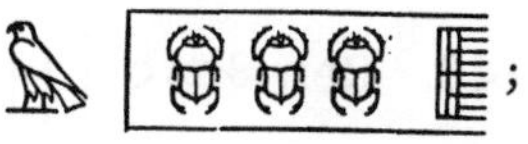

129. Sebek-neferu-Rā (Σκεμίοφρις) 

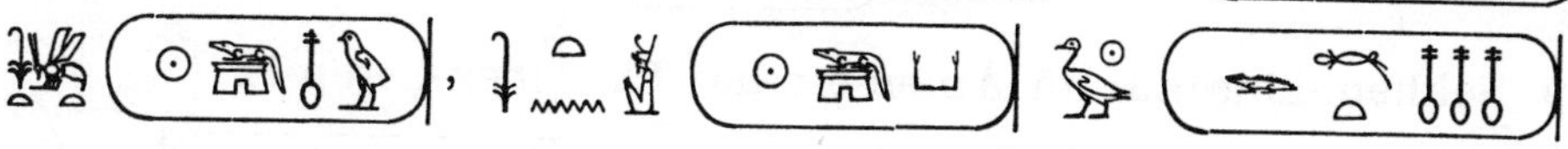

To this period probably belong :—

130. Àmen-em-ḥat V (?) 

131. Senefer-àb-Rā I Usert-sen IV (Sen-usert) 

DYNASTY XIII.

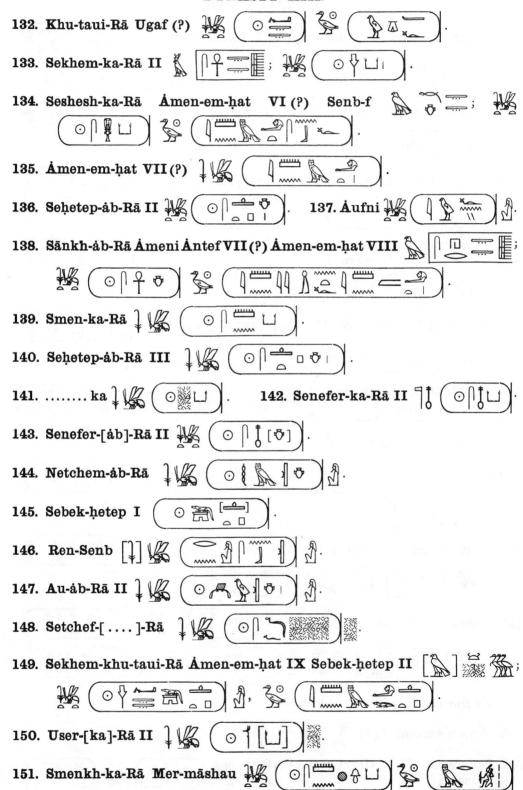

132. Khu-taui-Rā Ugaf (?) .

133. Sekhem-ka-Rā II .

134. Seshesh-ka-Rā Åmen-em-ḥat VI (?) Senb-f 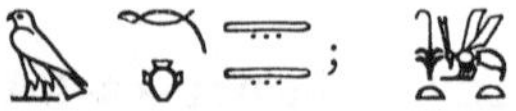
.

135. Åmen-em-ḥat VII (?) 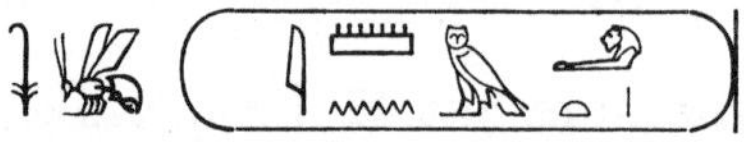.

136. Seḥetep-åb-Rā II 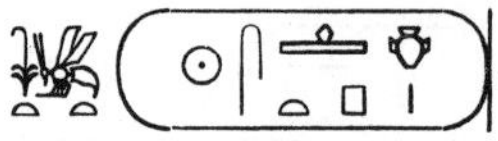. 137. Åufni .

138. Sānkh-åb-Rā Åmeni Åntef VII (?) Åmen-em-ḥat VIII 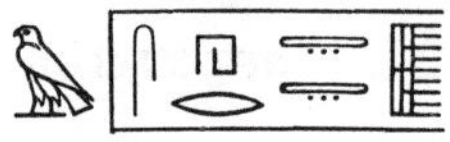
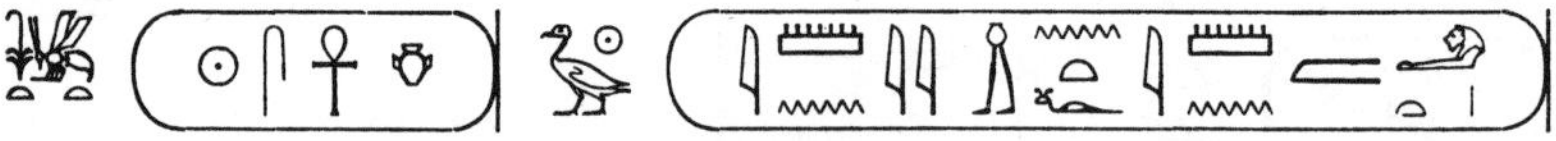.

139. Smen-ka-Rā 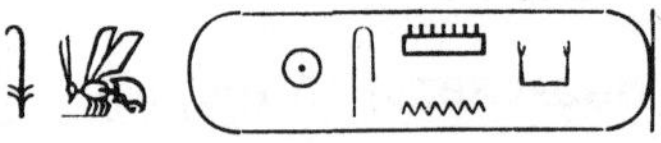.

140. Seḥetep-åb-Rā III 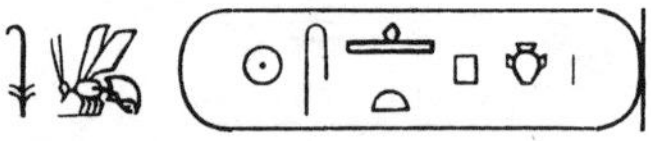.

141. .... ka 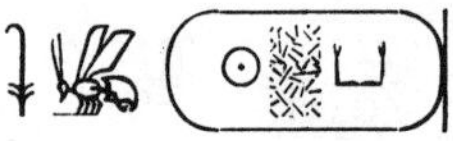. 142. Senefer-ka-Rā II .

143. Senefer-[åb]-Rā II 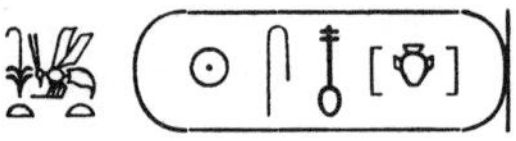.

144. Netchem-åb-Rā 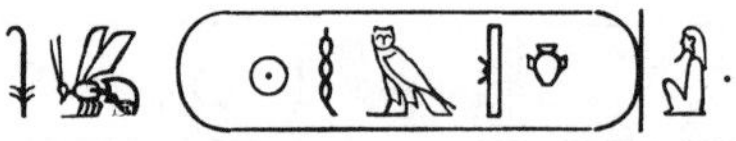.

145. Sebek-ḥetep I .

146. Ren-Senb .

147. Au-åb-Rā II .

148. Setchef-[. . . .]-Rā 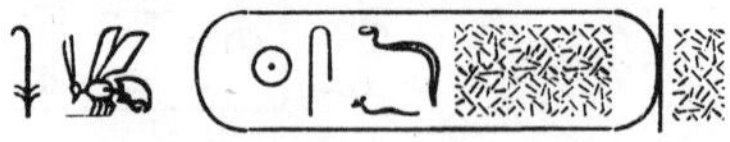.

149. Sekhem-khu-taui-Rā Åmen-em-ḥat IX Sebek-ḥetep II 
.

150. User-[ka]-Rā II 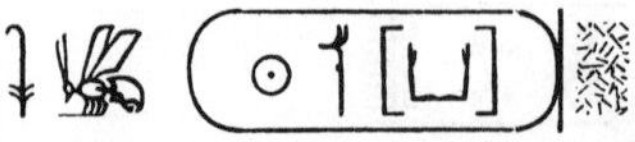.

151. Smenkh-ka-Rā Mer-māshau 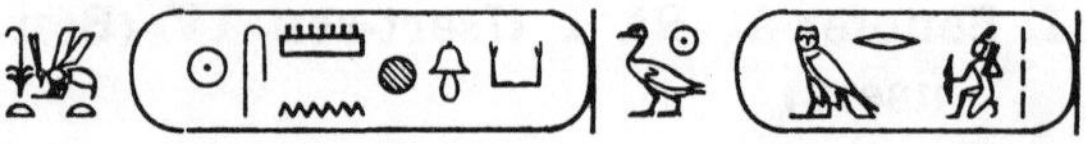

152. ..... -ka-[Rā] 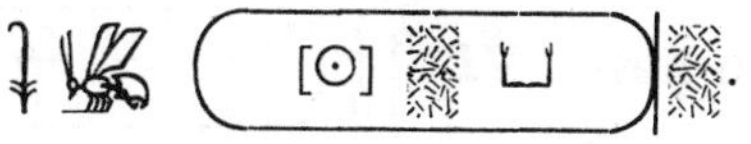

153. Ka-Set-[Rā] I 

154. Sekhem-suatch-taui-Rā Sebek-ḥetep III 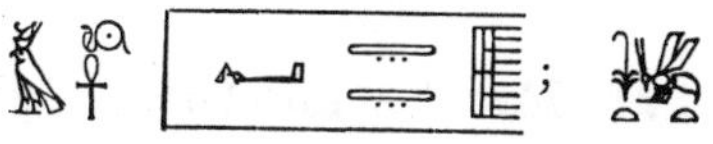

155. Khā-seshesh-Rā Nefer-ḥetep I 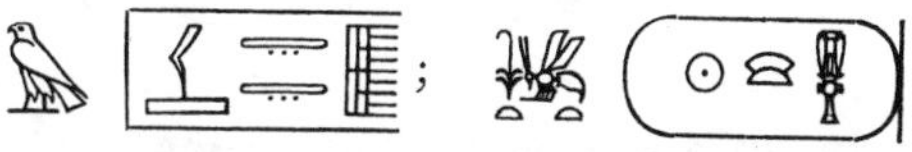

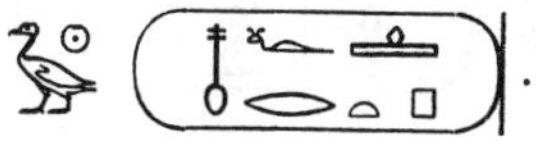

156. Sa-Ḥet-Ḥer (Sa-Hathor) 

157. Khā-nefer-Rā Sebek-ḥetep IV 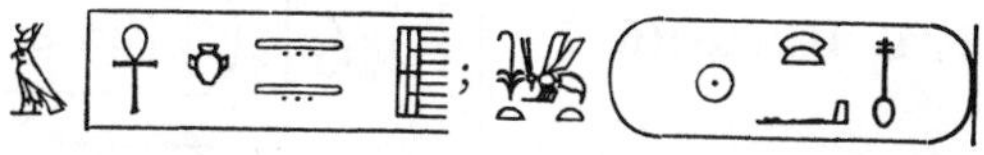

158. Khā-ka-Rā 

159. Khā-ānkh-Rā Sebek-ḥetep V 

160. Khā-ḥetep-Rā Sebek-ḥetep VI 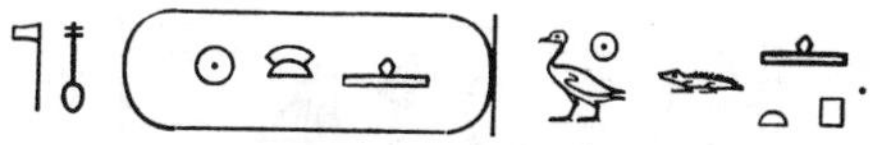

161. Uaḥ-ȧb-Rā I Āā-ȧb 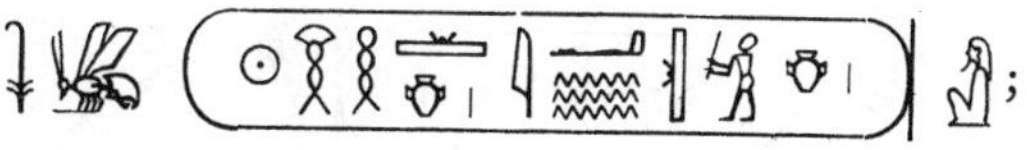 var. Āā-ȧb

162. Mer-nefer-Rā Ȧi I 

163. Mer-ḥetep-Rā I Ȧn or Ȧnȧ 

164. Mer-ḥetep-Rā II Sebek-ḥetep VII 

165. Sānkh-en-Rā Senb (?) 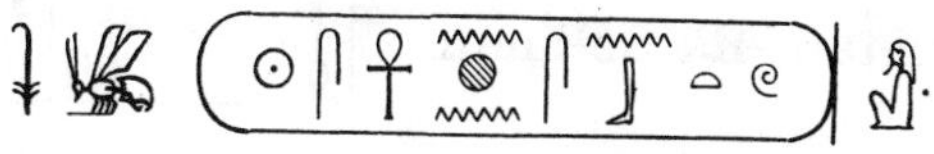

166. Mer-sekhem-Rā I Ȧn .... 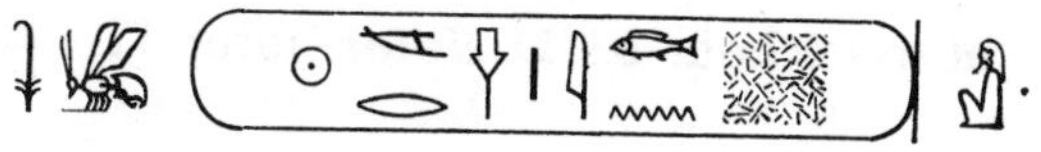

167. Suatch-ka-Rā Ḥeruȧ 

168. Mer-netchem-Rā 

169. Mer-ānkh-Rā Menthu-ḥetep VI 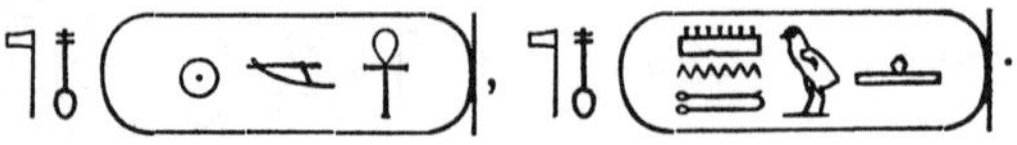

170. Mer-kheper-Rā 

171. Mer-ka(kau)-Rā Sebek-ḥetep VIII 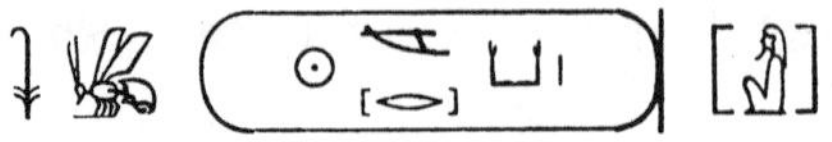;

var. 

172. Ṭeṭ-nefer-Rā Ṭaṭu-mes 

173. Neb-maāt-Rā I 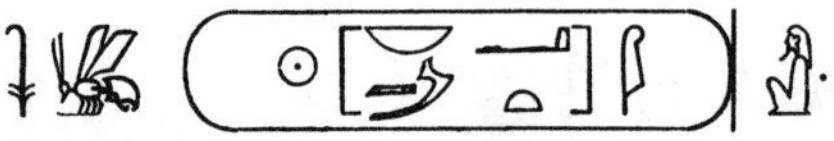

174. Uben-Rā I 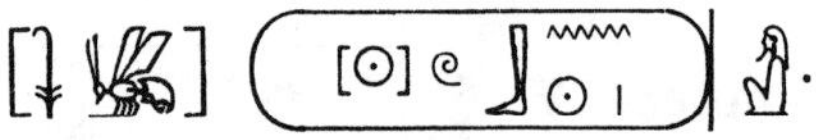

175. . . . . . ka-Rā 

176. Neb-maāt-Rā II 

177. Ṭeṭ-ānkh-Rā Mentu-em-sa-f 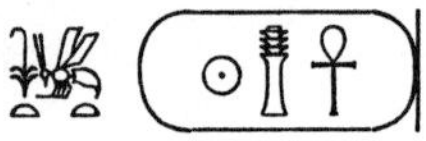 ; var. 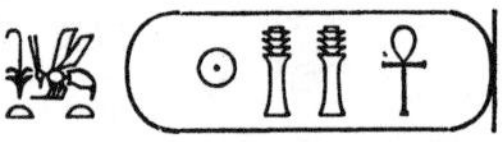,

178. Neḥsi 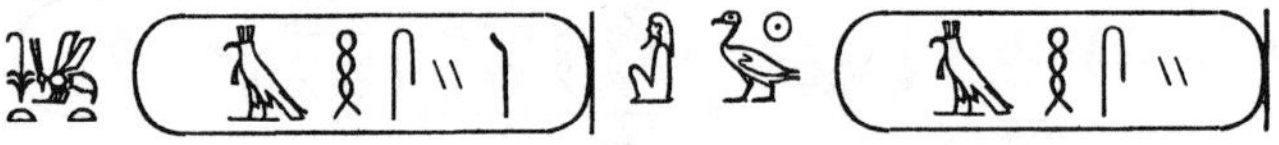

179. Khā-kheru-Rā 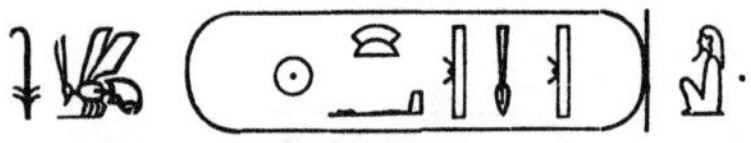

180. Neb-f-au-Rā 

The following kings probably belong to the XIIIth dynasty :—

181. Senefer-taui-Rā Sekhem 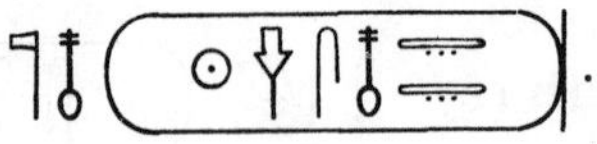

182. Mer-sekhem-Rā II Nefer-ḥetep II 

183. Ṭeṭ-ḥetep-Rā Ṭaṭa-mesu II (?) 

184. Suaḥ-en-Rā Senb-mȧ-ȧu 

DYNASTY XIV

(According to the Turin Papyrus).

185. **Seḥeb-Rā** 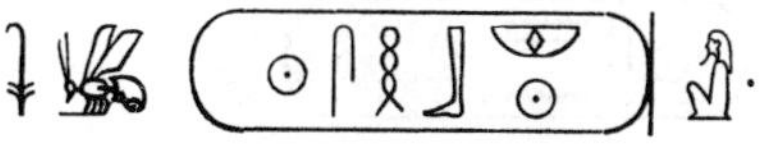

186. **Mer-tchefau-Rā** 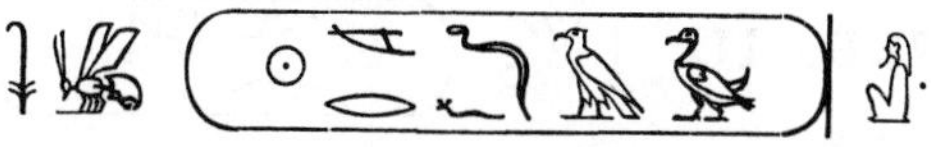

187. **Senb-ka-Rā** 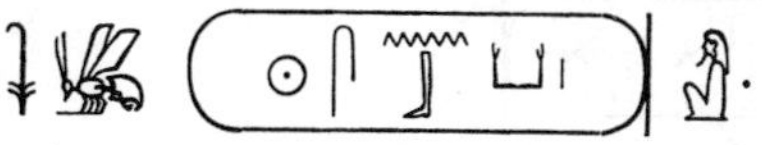

188. **Neb-tchefau-Rā I** 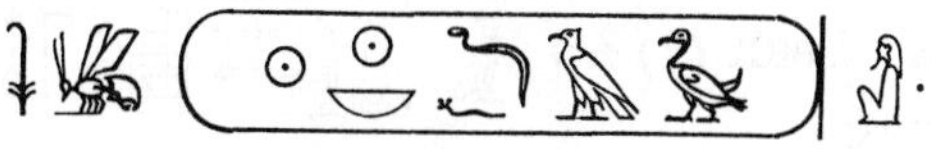

189. **Uben-Rā II** 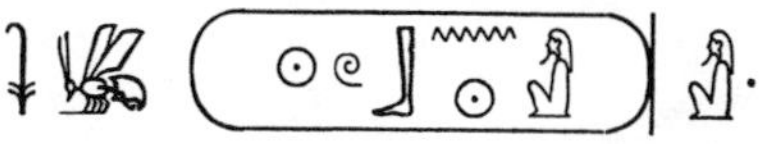

190. **[Neb ?]-tchefau-Rā II** 

191. **Uben-Rā III** 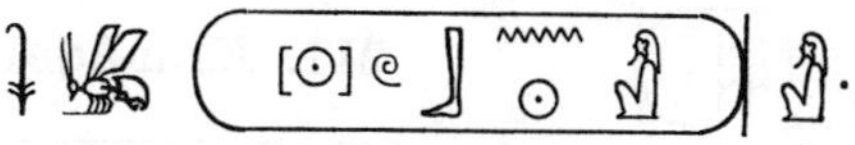

192. **Aut-åb-Rā III** 

193. **Her-åb-Rā** 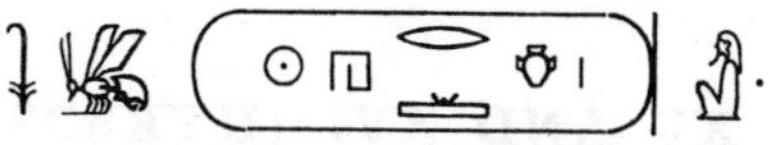

194. **Neb-sen-Rā** 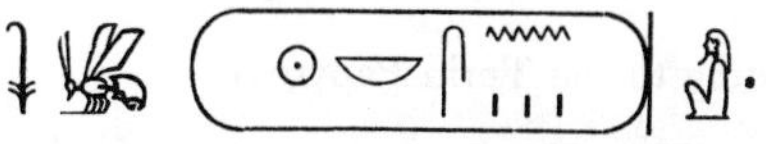

195. **. . . . . -Rā** 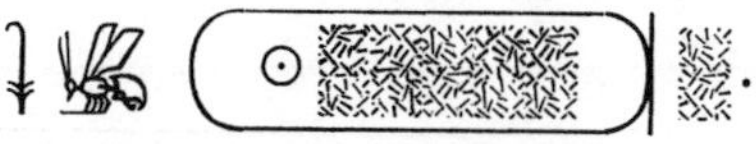

196. **Sekheper-en-Rā** 

197. **Ṭeṭ-kheru-Rā** 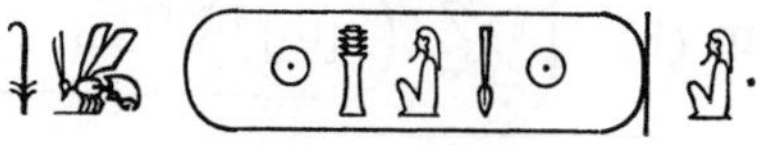

198. **Sānkh-ka-Rā II** 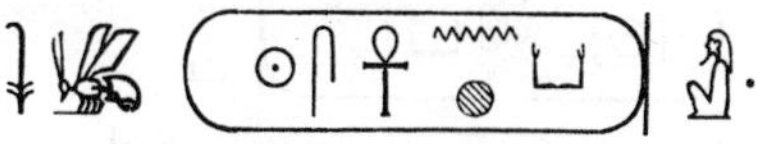

199. **Nefer-Tem- . . . . -Rā** 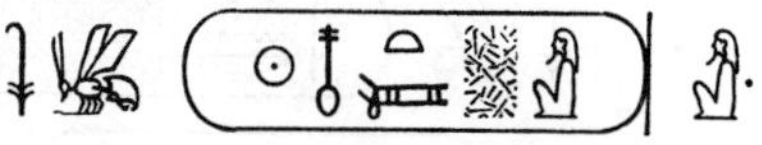

200. **Sekhem- . . . . -Rā I** 

201. **Ka- . . . . -Rā** 

202. **Nefer-åb-Rā I** 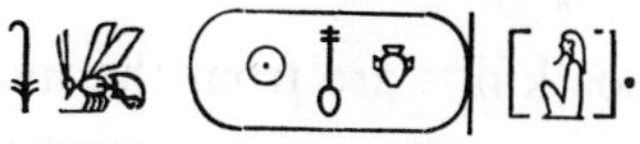

203. **Å- . . . . -Rā** 

204. **Khā- . . . . . -Rā** 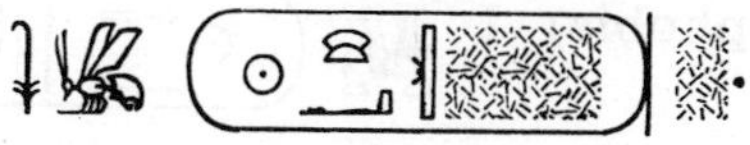

205. **Ānkh-ka-Rā I** 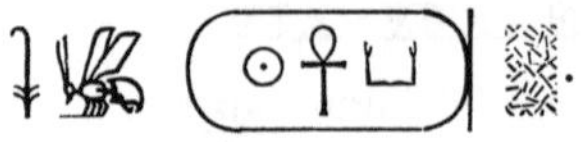

206. **Smen-.........-Rā** 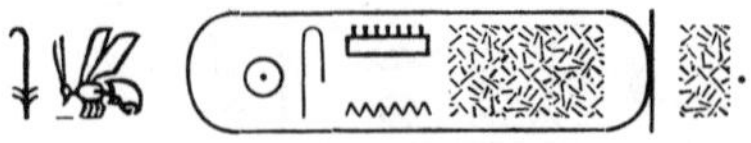

207. **Mer-sekhem (?)-Rā III** 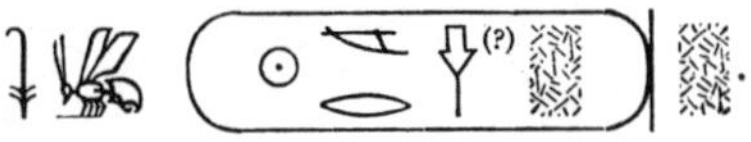

208. **Seba-....-Rā** 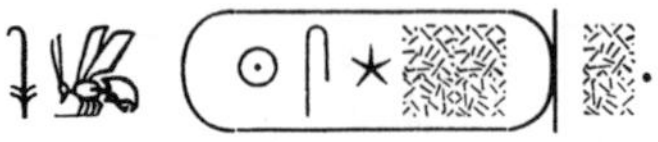

209. **Men-khāu-Rā Sesh (?)-ȧb** 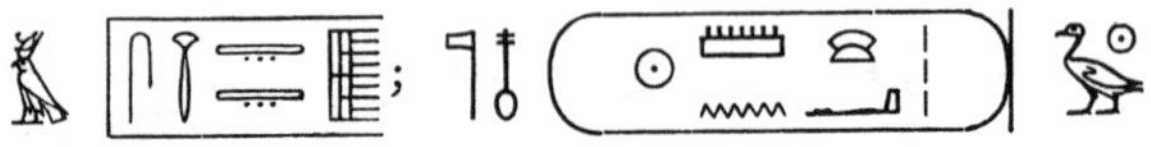
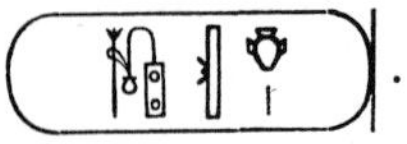

The following probably belong to the period of Dynasty XIV :—

210. **Sebkai** 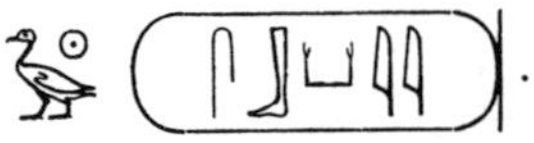 211. **Khu-ȧqer** 

212. **Sebek-ka-Rā** 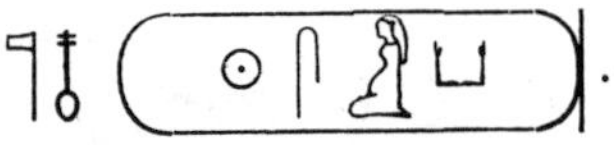

DYNASTIES XV AND XVI (HYKSOS)

(According to the Turin Papyrus).

213 to 215. [Names unknown.]

216. **.....-ka-[Rā] Āanatȧ** 

217. **....-ka-[Rā] Bebenem (?)** 

218. **....-ka-[Rā]** 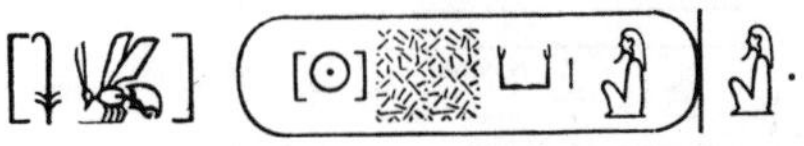

219. **Ȧn-nub (?)-........** 

220. **Ȧ.... (Aphobis)** 

221. **Ȧp......... (Aphobis)** 

The following names of Hyksos kings are from the monuments :—

222. **User-ka-Rā III Khentcher (Salitis ?)** 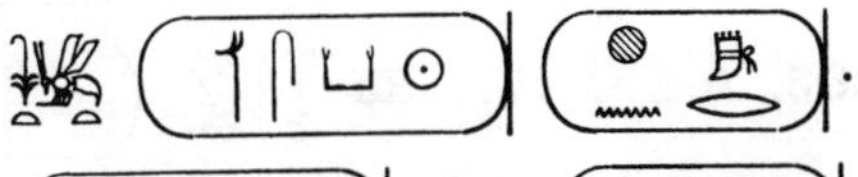

223. **Āa-user-Rā Ȧpepȧ (Aphobis) I** 
(Perhaps No. 220.)

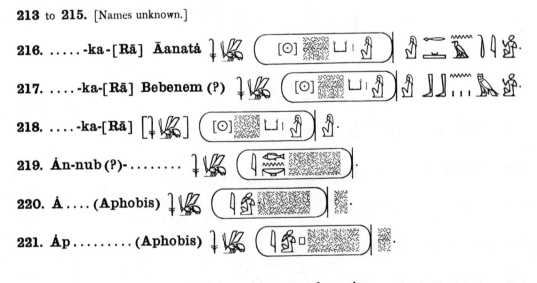

224. Suser-en-Rā Khian ('Ιάννας) ; .

225. Neb-khepesh-Rā Ȧpep II (Perhaps No. 221).

226. Āa-ārq-Rā .

227. Mer-user-Rā I-ābeq-her ; var. .

228. Āa-qenn-Rā Ȧpepȧ III ; .

The following kings probably reigned during the Hyksos Period :—

229. Āa-peḥti-Set Nubti ; var. , Brit. Mus. Scarab, No. 32368.

230. Āa-peḥ-Rā .

231. Āa-neter-Rā .

232. Āa-ḥetep-Rā II .

233. Āa-khā-Rā II .

234. Uatch-ka-Rā II .

235. Nub-ka-Rā .

236. Neb-ṭeṭ-Rā .

237. Nub- . . . . -Rā .

238. Ne-ka-Rā II .

239. Khā-user-Rā II .

240. Khā-mu (?)-Rā (?).

241. Ka-Set-Rā II Sekhenn- . . . . . .

242. . . . . . . -Set-Rā (?).

243. Semqen .

244. Ānt-her .

245. Āamu .

246. Iāpeq-her .

247. Iāmu .

248. Ipeq-Ḥeru .

249. Uatcheṭ .

250. Seket [hieroglyphs]   251. Sheshá [hieroglyphs]

252. Qar [hieroglyphs]

DYNASTY XVII

(According to the Turin Papyrus).

253. Sekhem-.....-Rā II [hieroglyphs]

254. Sekhem-.....-Rā III [hieroglyphs]

255. Sekhem-.....-Rā IV [hieroglyphs]

256. Ses-.....-Rā [hieroglyphs]

257. Neb-ári-au-Rā I [hieroglyphs]

258. Neb-ári-au-Rā II [hieroglyphs]

259. Smen-.....-Rā [hieroglyphs] ; var. (?) **Smen-taui-Rā**

[hieroglyphs]

260. Suser-.....-Rā [hieroglyphs]

261. Sekhem-.....-Rā V [hieroglyphs]

262. .....-.....-Rā [hieroglyphs]   263. Áu.......

[hieroglyphs]   264. Set...... [hieroglyphs]

265. Sunu...... [hieroglyphs]   266. Ḥeru......

[hieroglyphs]   267. Án-áb...... [hieroglyphs]

268. .... [hieroglyphs] ....   269. Penen-set... [hieroglyphs]

The following kings, whose names are taken from the monuments, also probably belong to Dynasty XVII.

270. **Khu-taui-sekhem-Rā**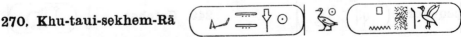

271. Ḥetep-àb-Rā Ḥeru-netch-tef 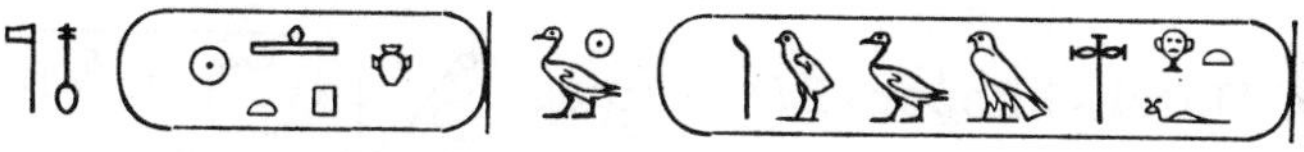.

272. Sekhem-uatch-khāu-Rā Sebek-em-sa-f I 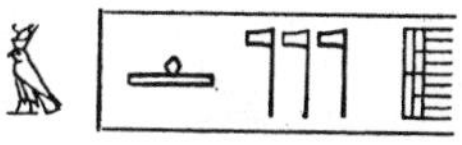 .

273. Sekhem-sheṭ-taui-Rā Sebek-em-sa-f II  .

274. Seshesh-Rā her-ḥer-maāt Àntef VIII Āa .

275. Seshesh-Rā upu-em-Maāt Àntef IX Āa ; .

276. Nub-kheper-Rā Àntef X Āa 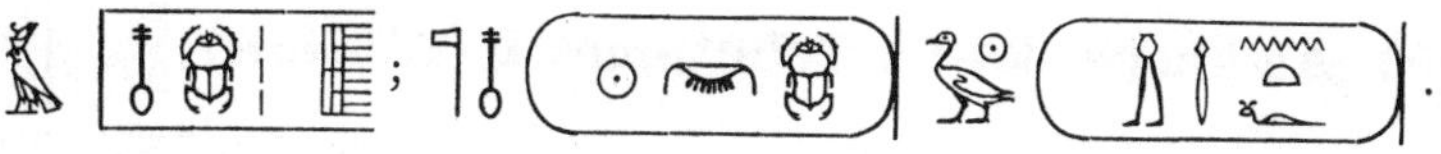.

277. Sekhem-nefer-khāu-Rā Up-uaut-em-sa-f .

278. Sekhem-uaḥ-khā-Rā Rā-ḥetep 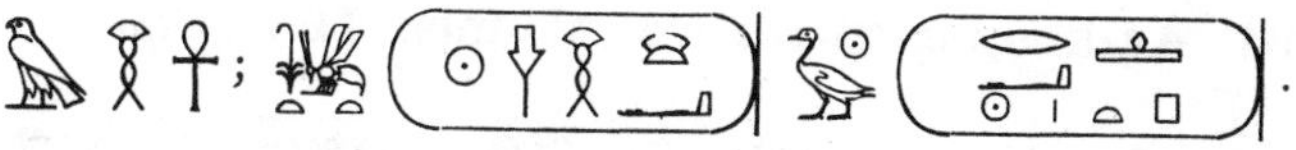.

279. Sekhem-smen-taui-Rā Teḥuti 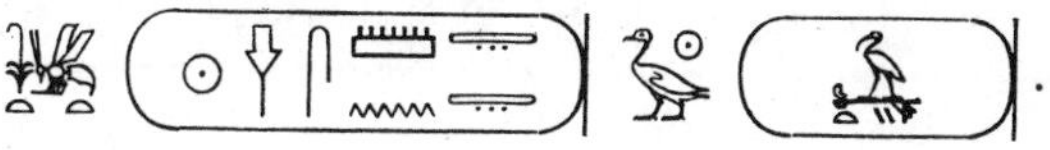.

280. Sekhem-Rā-sāa-taui 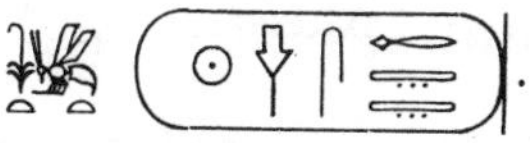.

281. Sekhem-Rā-ānkh-taui 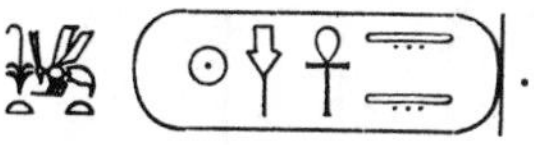.

282. Rā-mes-suser-taui 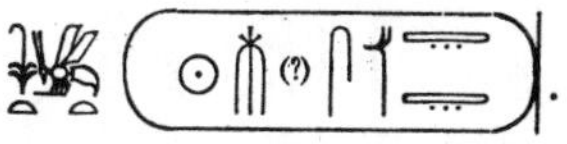.

283. Suatch-en-Rā I 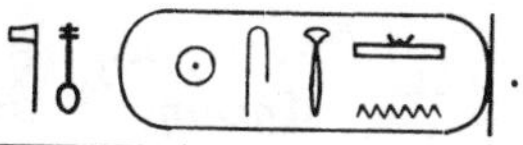.

284. Suatch-en-Rā II 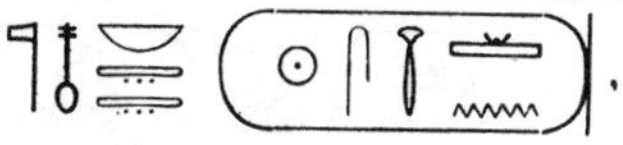.

285. Skhent-en-Rā 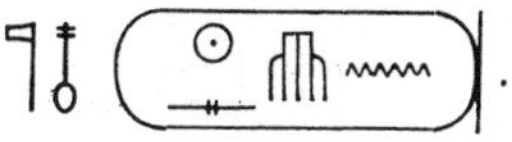.

286. Senekht-en-Rā 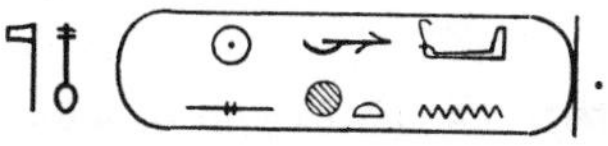.

287. Seqenen-Rā I Tau-āa ;

var. Seqen-en-Rā 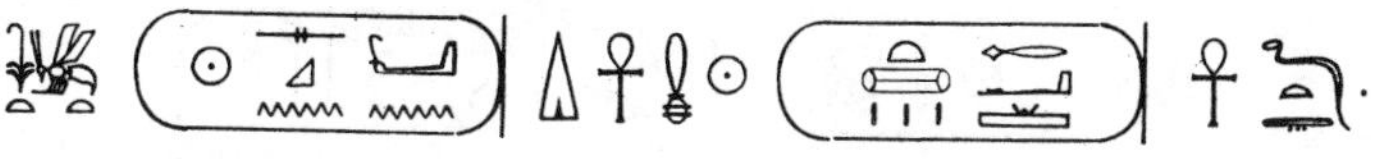.

288. Seqenen-Rā II Tau-āa Āa .

289. Seqenen-Rā III Tau-āa Qen .

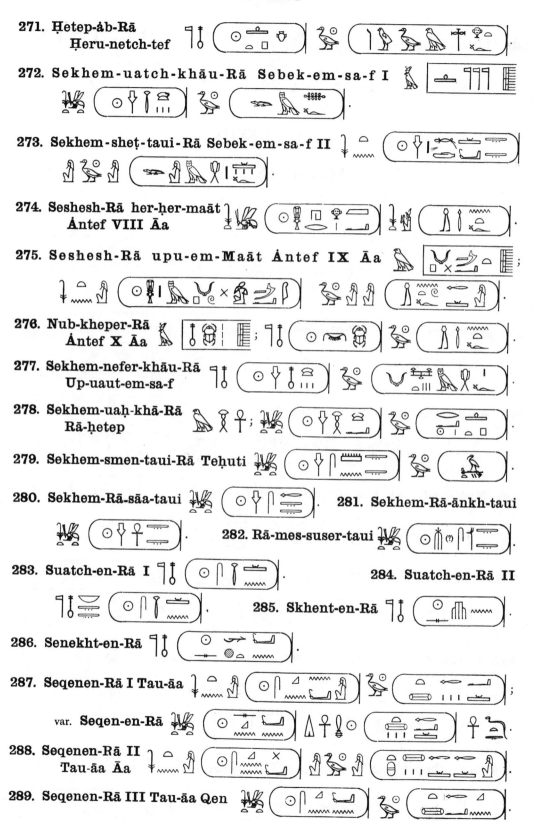

290. **Uatch-kheper-Rā Kames** 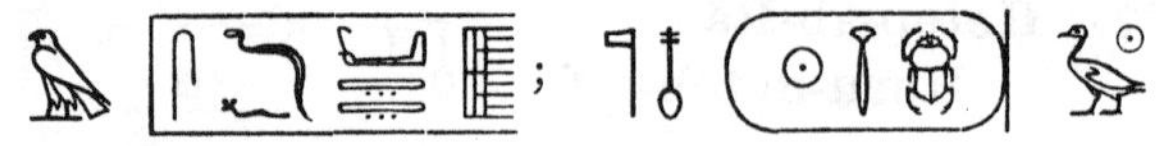
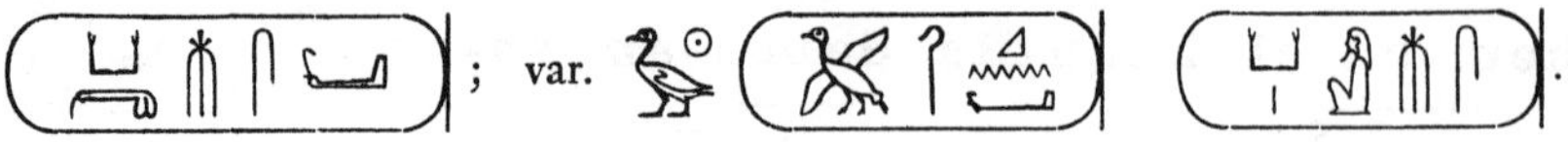

DYNASTY XVIII.

291. **Neb-peḥti-Rā Ȧāḥmes I** (Ἄμωσις) 

292. **Tcheser-ka-Rā Ȧmen-ḥetep I** (Ἀμενωφθὶς) 
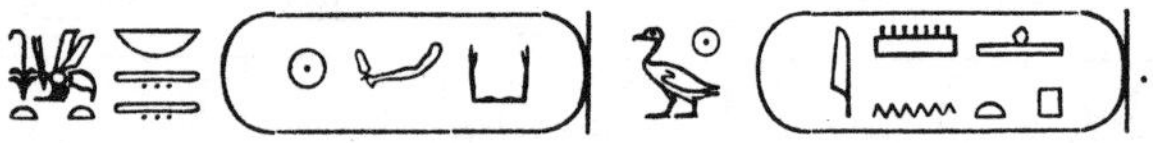

293. **Āa-kheper-ka-Rā Teḥuti-mes I** (Τέθμωσις) 

294. **Āa-kheper-en-Rā Teḥuti-mes II** (Χέβρων) 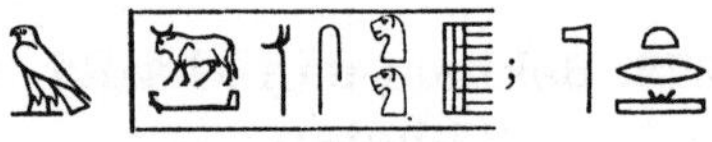
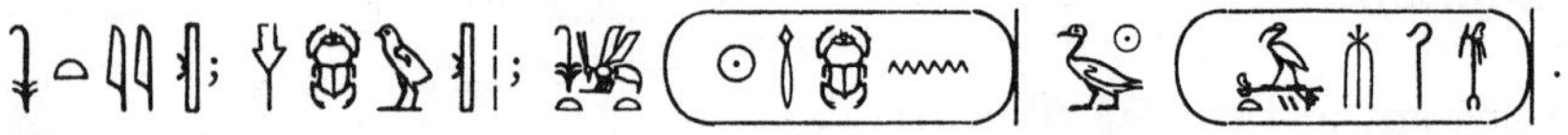

295. **Maāt-ka-Rā II Ḥat-shepsut** (Ἀμενσίς) 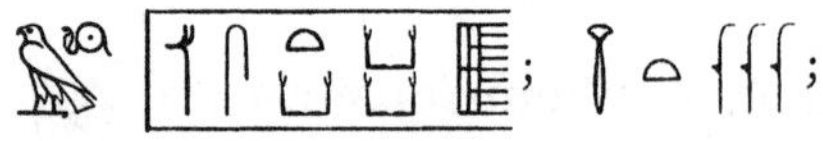

296. **Men-kheper-Rā I Teḥuti-mes III** (Μισάφρις, Μήφρης) 

297. **Āa-kheperu-Rā Ȧmen-ḥetep II** (Μισφραγμούθωσις) 
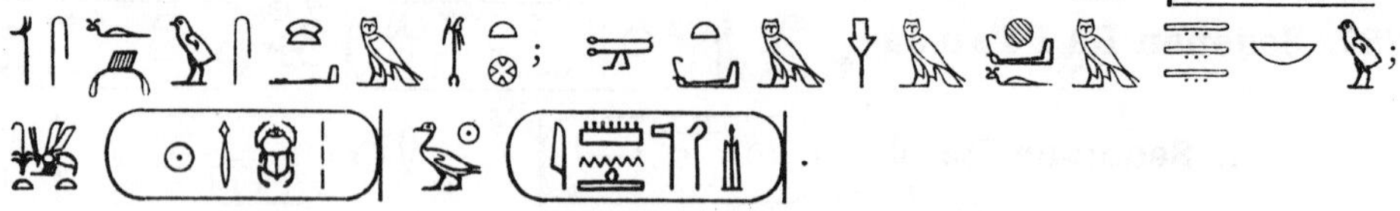

298. **Men-kheperu-Rā Teḥuti-mes IV** (Τούθμωσις) 
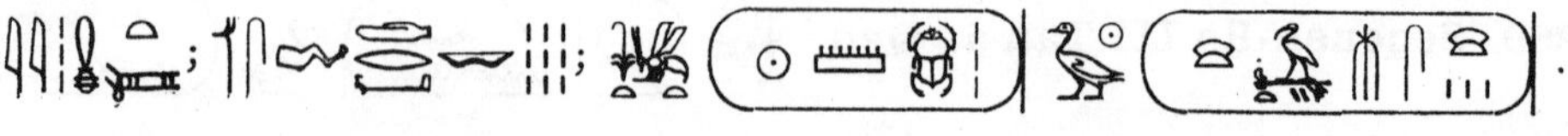

299. Neb-Maāt-Rā III Ȧmen-ḥetep III (Ἀμένωφις) ; ; ; . The Nesu-bȧt name is rendered in the Tall al-'Amârnah Tablets by Ni-ib-mu-a-ri-ya and Mi-im-mu-ri-ya .

Some of the Mesopotamian wives of Ȧmen-ḥetep III were :—

300. Tī (in cuneiform **Te-i-i**), . Her father's name was **Iuȧa** , and her mother's was **Thuȧu** .

301. Kilgipa (in cuneiform Gi-lu-khi-pa), , sister of Tushratta, king of Mitani.

302. Dadukhipa (Egyptian form not known).

303a. Nefer-kheperu-Rā Uā-en-Rā Ȧmen-ḥetep IV ; ; ; .

The commonest equivalents for the first part of his Nesu-bȧt name, Nefer-kheperu-Rā, are Na-ap-khu-ru-ri-a , Na-ap-khar-ri-ya , Ni-ip-khu-ur-ri-ri-ya , Na-ap-khu-ra-ri-ya .

303b. Nefer-kheperu-Rā Uā-en-Rā Ȧakhu-en-Ȧten ; ; ; .

304. Ānkh-kheperu-Rā Sāa-ka-Rā Tcheser-kheperu .

305. Kheperu-neb-Rā Tut-ānkh-Ȧmen ; ; ; .

306. Kheper-kheperu-Rā Ȧri-maāt Ȧi II ; ; ; .

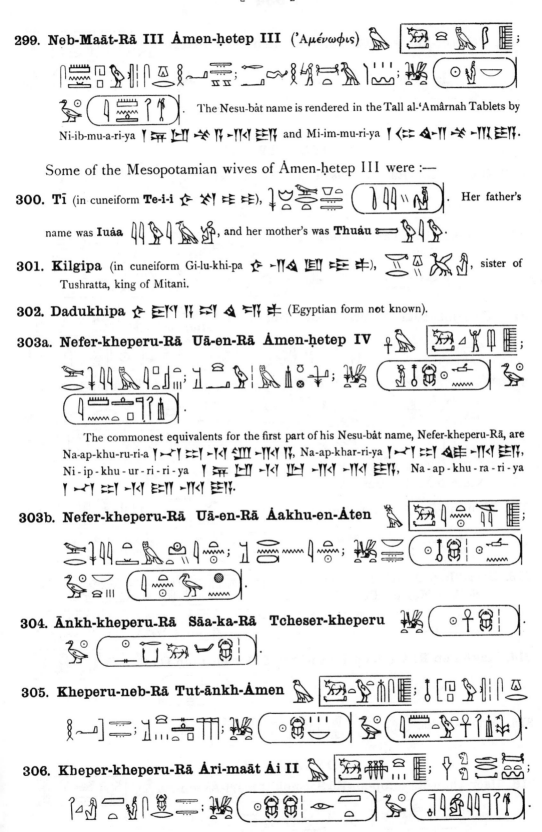

307. Tcheser-kheperu-Rā Åmen-em-ḥeb mer-en-Ḥeru 

DYNASTY XIX.

308. Men-peḥti-Rā Rāmessu I (Ῥαμέσσης) 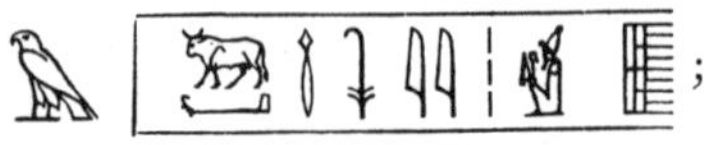

309. Men-maāt-Rā I Seti I meri-Ptaḥ (Σέθως, Σέθωσις) 

310. User-maāt-Rā I setep-en-Rā Rāmeses II (Ῥαμέσσης Μιαμοῦν) 

311. Ba-en-Rā I Mer-en-Ptaḥ I (Menephthah) (Ἀμενωφάθ) **ḥetep-ḥer-maāt**

312. Men-må-Rā Åmen-meses, king of Thebes, 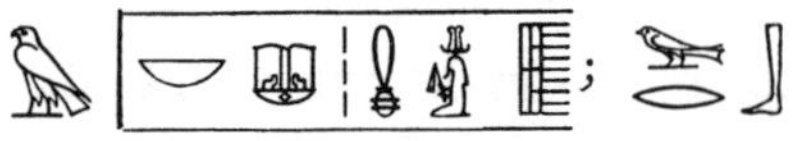
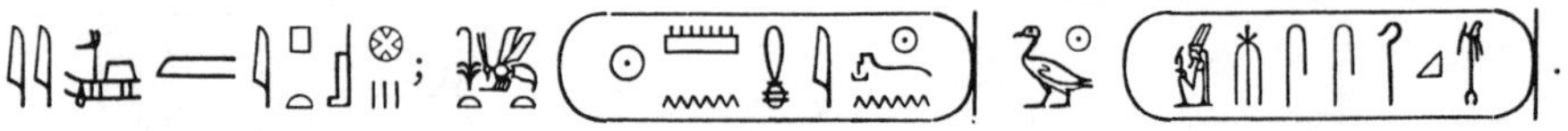

313. User-kheperu-Rā mer Åmen Seti II Mer-en-Ptaḥ II 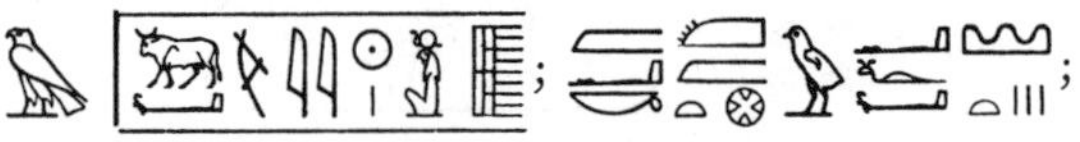
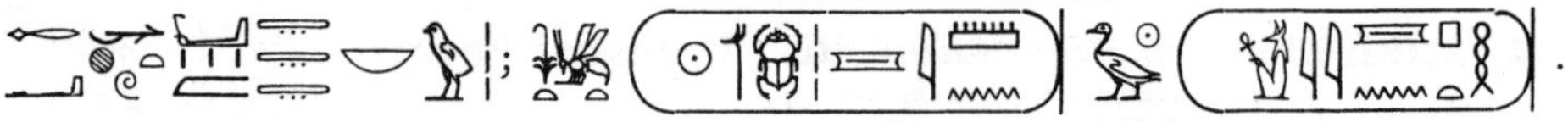

314. Åakhu-en-Rā setep-en-Rā Sa-Ptaḥ I Mer-en-Ptaḥ III 

315. Årsu, a Syrian, 

DYNASTY XX.

316. User-khāu-Rā setep-en-Rā Set-nekht meri-Åmen-Rā 

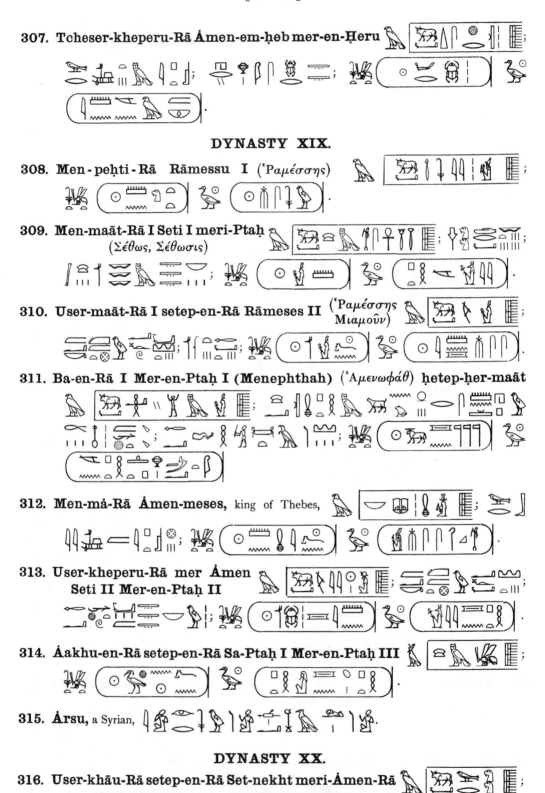

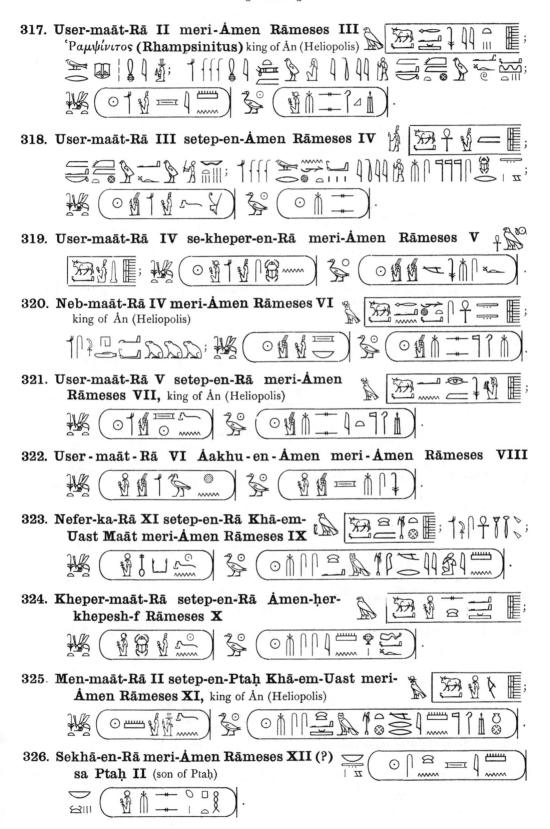

317. User-maāt-Rā II meri-Åmen Rāmeses III 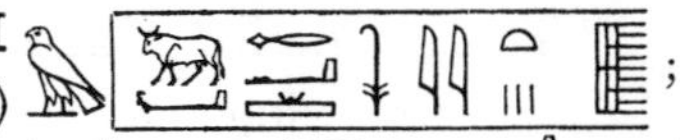
ʽΡαμψίνιτος (Rhampsinitus) king of Ån (Heliopolis)

318. User-maāt-Rā III setep-en-Åmen Rāmeses IV 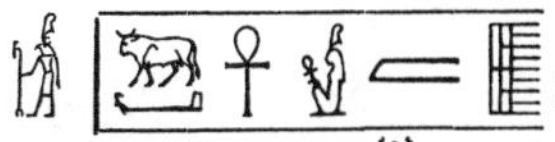

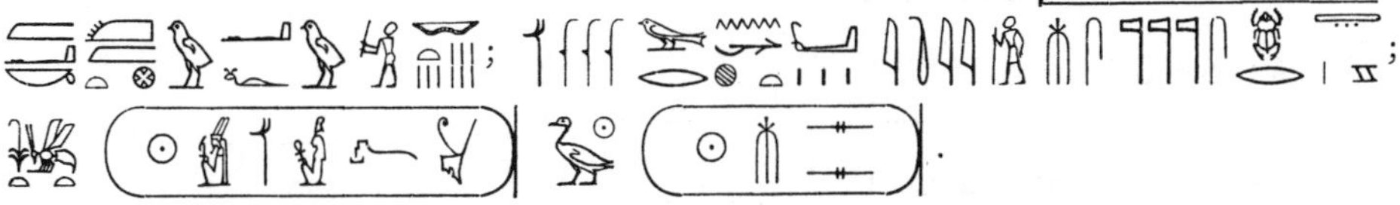

319. User-maāt-Rā IV se-kheper-en-Rā meri-Åmen Rāmeses V 

320. Neb-maāt-Rā IV meri-Åmen Rāmeses VI 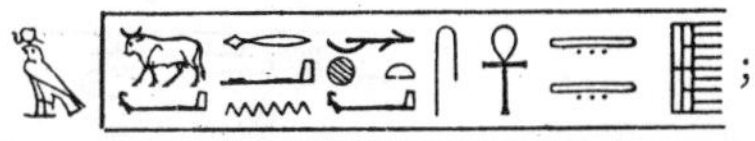
king of Ån (Heliopolis)

321. User-maāt-Rā V setep-en-Rā meri-Åmen Rāmeses VII, king of Ån (Heliopolis) 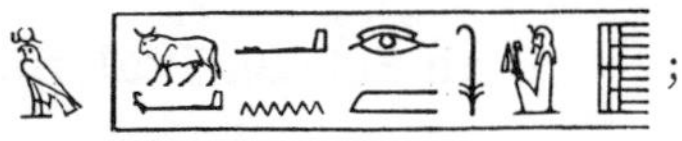

322. User-maāt-Rā VI Åakhu-en-Åmen meri-Åmen Rāmeses VIII

323. Nefer-ka-Rā XI setep-en-Rā Khā-em-Uast Maāt meri-Åmen Rāmeses IX 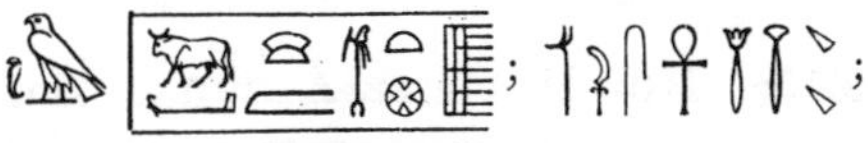

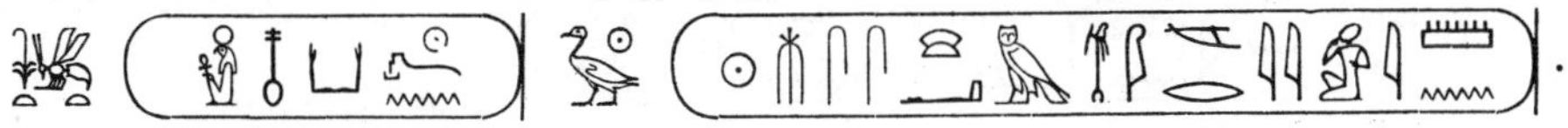

324. Kheper-maāt-Rā setep-en-Rā Åmen-ḥer-khepesh-f Rāmeses X 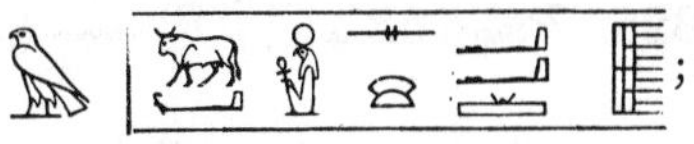

325. Men-maāt-Rā II setep-en-Ptaḥ Khā-em-Uast meri-Åmen Rāmeses XI, king of Ån (Heliopolis) 

326. Sekhā-en-Rā meri-Åmen Rāmeses XII (?) sa Ptaḥ II (son of Ptaḥ) 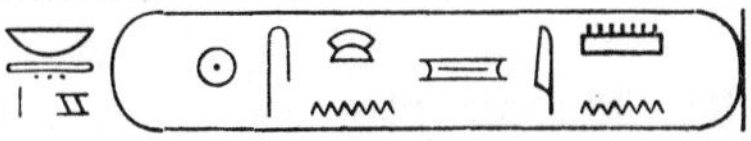

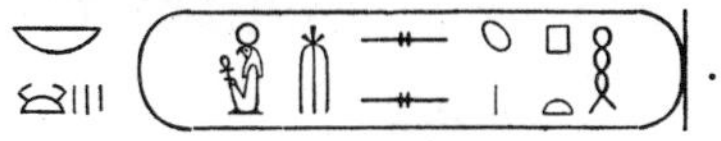

To this period Gauthier (Livre des Rois, Cairo, 1913, p. 225) assigns the following :—

User-maāt-Rā neb-khepesh 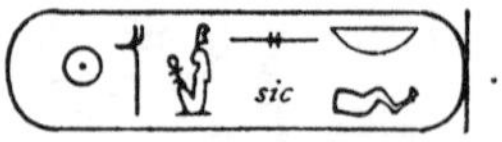.

Åmen-maāt (?) meri-Rā setep-en-Rā  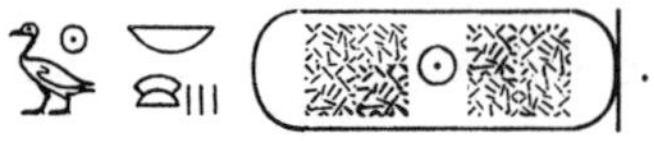.

Åmen-Rāmeses 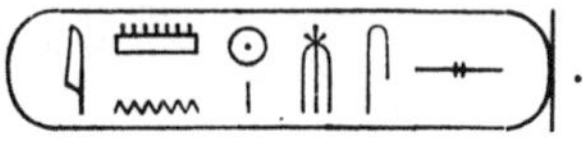.

Rāmeses meri-Åmen .

Smen-maāt-Rā Åmen-mes .

User-maāt-Rā ḥeq Uast Rāmeses merr-Åmen 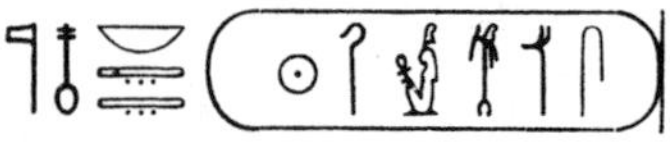 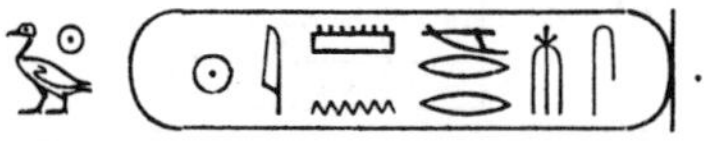.

User setep-en-Rā Mes ..... .

Ptaḥ Seti Sa-Ptaḥ meri .

DYNASTY XXI.

A. High-priests of Åmen at Thebes.

327A. Ḥer-Ḥeru as high-priest of Åmen-Rā, king of the gods:— 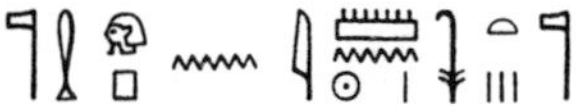 .

327B. Ḥer-Ḥeru sa-Åmen as king and son of Åmen:— ; .

328. Pai-ānkh , son of Ḥer-Ḥeru sa-Åmen.

329A. Pai-netchem I, son of Pai-ānkh, as high-priest of Åmen-Rā 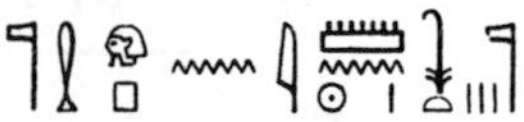 

329B. Pai-netchem I as king :—**Kheper-khā-Rā I setep-en-Åmen Pai-netchem meri-Åmen** .

330. Tchet-Khensu-åuf-ānkh 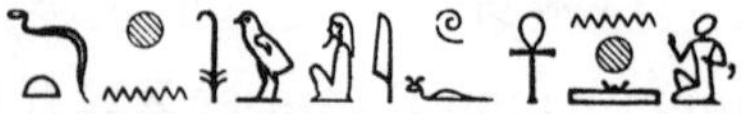, son of Pai-netchem I.

331. Masaherth, son of Pai-netchem I meri-Åmen  .

332A. Men-kheper-Rā II, son of Pai-netchem I, as high-priest of Åmen :— 
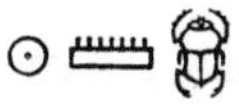 (without cartouche).

332B. Men-kheper-Rā II as king :— 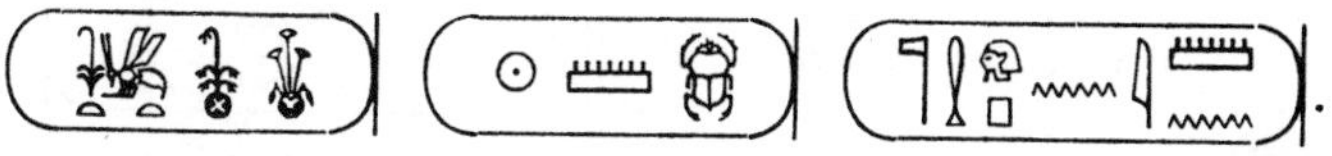

333A. Pai-netchem II, son of Men-kheper-Rā, as high-priest of Åmen-Rā :— 

333B. Pai-netchem II as king :— 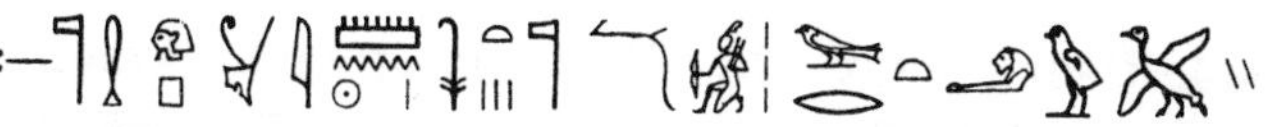

334. Taȧ-kheperu-Rā setep-en-Rā Pasebkhān 
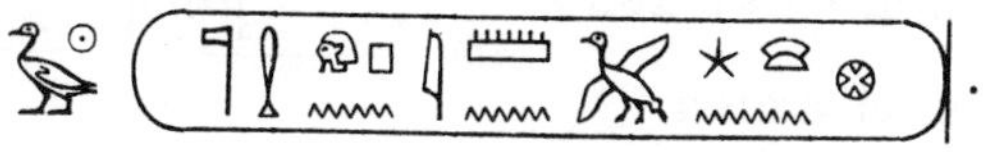

335. Åuapet, or **Åuuapet,** high-priest of Åmen-Rā and son of Shashanq I, 

DYNASTY XXI.

B. Kings of Tanis.

336. Ḥetch-kheper-Rā I setep-en-Rā Nes-ba-neb-Ṭeṭ (Σμένδης) meri-Åmen

337. Taȧ-kheperu-Rā setep-en-Rā Pasebkhān I meri-Åmen 
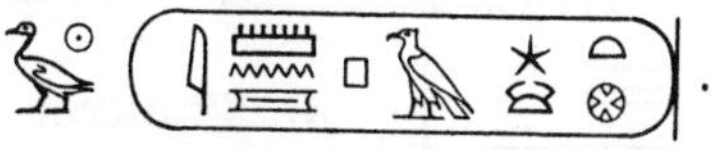

338. Kheper-khā-Rā II setep-en-Åmen Pasebkhān II meri-Åmen 

339. User-maāt-Rā VII setep-en-Åmen Åmen-em-Åpt meri-Åmen 

340. Neter-kheper-Rā setep-en-Åmen Sa-Åmen meri-Åmen 

341. Āa-kheper-Rā I setep-en-Åmen Pasebkhān III meri-Åmen

DYNASTY XXII.

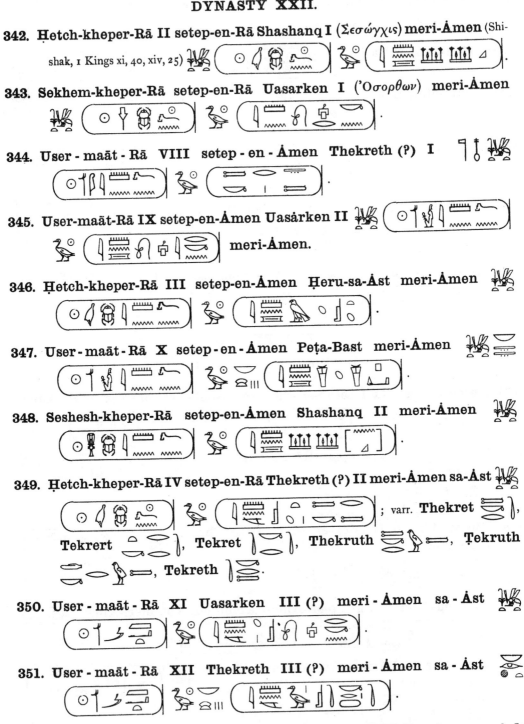

342. Ḥetch-kheper-Rā II setep-en-Rā Shashanq I (Σεσώγχις) meri-Åmen (Shishak, 1 Kings xi, 40, xiv, 25) .

343. Sekhem-kheper-Rā setep-en-Rā Uasarken I (Ὀσορθων) meri-Åmen .

344. User-maāt-Rā VIII setep-en-Åmen Thekreth (?) I  .

345. User-maāt-Rā IX setep-en-Åmen Uasårken II   meri-Åmen.

346. Ḥetch-kheper-Rā III setep-en-Åmen Ḥeru-sa-Åst meri-Åmen  .

347. User-maāt-Rā X setep-en-Åmen Peṭa-Bast meri-Åmen  .

348. Seshesh-kheper-Rā setep-en-Åmen Shashanq II meri-Åmen  .

349. Ḥetch-kheper-Rā IV setep-en-Rā Thekreth (?) II meri-Åmen sa-Åst  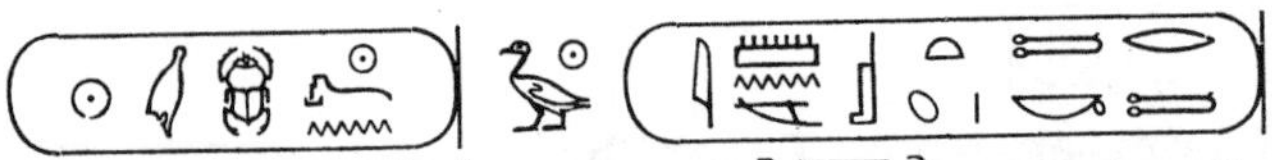; varr. Thekret , Tekrert , Tekret , Thekruth , Ṭekruth , Tekreth .

350. User-maāt-Rā XI Uasarken III (?) meri-Åmen sa-Åst  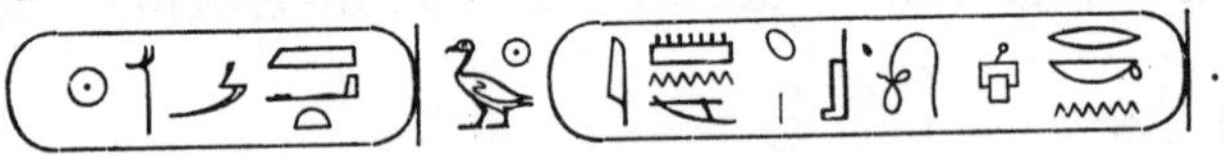.

351. User-maāt-Rā XII Thekreth III (?) meri-Åmen sa-Åst  .

352. User-maāt-Rā XIII setep-en-Rā Shashanq III meri-Åmen  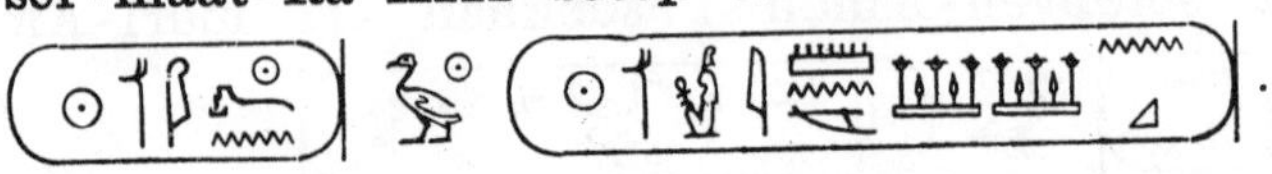.

353. User-maāt-Rā XIV setep-en-Åmen Pamåi meri-Åmen 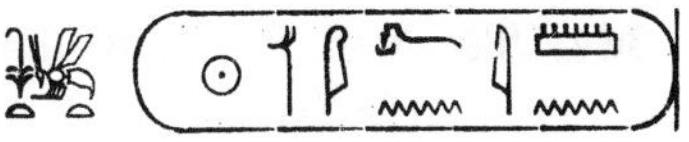

.

354. Āa-kheper-Rā II Shashanq IV meri-Åmen .

DYNASTY XXIII.

355. Seher-åb-Rā Peṭa-Bast sa Bast .

356. Āa-kheper-Rā III setep-en-Åmen Uasarkenå meri-Åmen-Rā

.

THE NUBIAN CONQUEROR OF EGYPT FROM NAPATA.

357. Piānkhi meri-Åmen 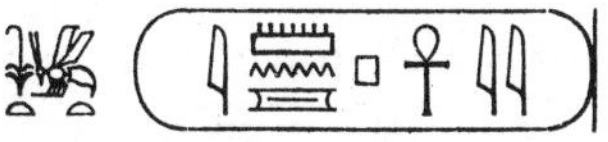.

The inscriptions also mention :—

358. User-maāt-Rā XV Piānkhi meri-Åmen Sa Bast 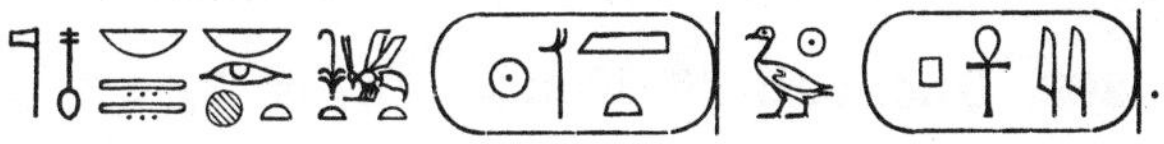.

and :—

359. Senefer-f-Rā Piānkhi 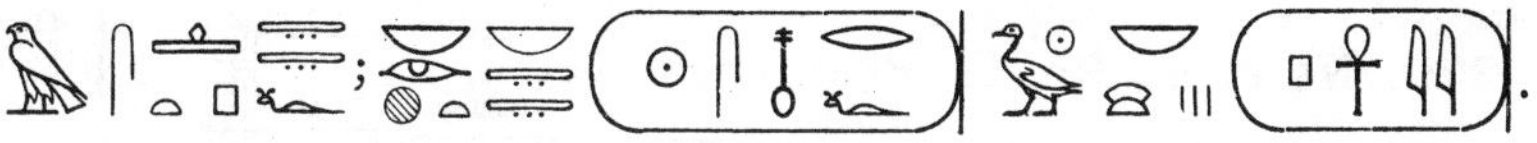.

Kashta .

DYNASTY XXIV.

360. Shepses-Rā Tafnekht I 

.

361. Uaḥ-ka-Rā II Bakenrenef (Βόκχορις) .

362. Uaḥ-åb-Rā II Tafnekht II .

DYNASTY XXV. (NUBIANS).

363. Nefer-ka-Rā XII Shabaka (Σαβάκων) 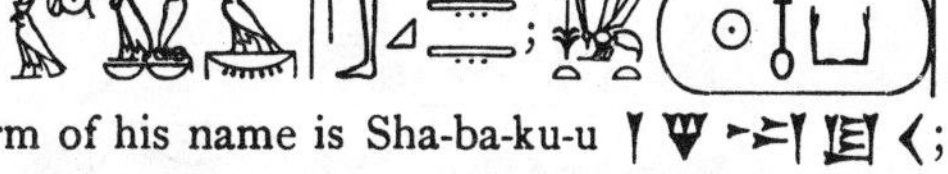

. The Assyrian form of his name is Sha-ba-ku-u 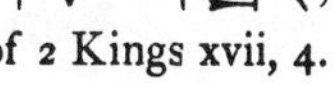; he must not be confounded with the סוא of 2 Kings xvii, 4.

364. Ṭeṭ-kau-Rā Shabataka (Σεβιχώς)

His son Piānkhi assumed royal titles thus :—

365. Men-kheper-Rā III Piānkhi

366. Nefer-Tem-[åa]khu-Rā Taharqa (the תִּרְהָקָה of Isa. xxxvii, 9) II; . The Assyrian form of his name is Tar-ḳu-u .

367. Ba-ka-Rā Tanuat-Åmen

The Assyrian form of his name is Tan-da-ma-ni-e .

DYNASTY XXVI.

368. Uaḥ-åb-Rā III Psemthek I (Ψαμμήτιχος)

369. Uhem-åb-Rā Nekau (נְכֹה or נְכוֹ, 2 Kings xxiii, 29; Jer. xlvi, 2; Νεχαώ, Νεκώς)

370. Nefer-åb-Rā II Psemthek II

371. Ḥāā-åb-Rā I Uaḥ-åb-Rā IV (חָפְרַע, Jer. xliv, 30, Οὔαφρις, Ἀπρίης)

372. Khnem-åb-Rā Åāḥmes II (Ἄμωσις) **sa Net**

373. Ānkh-ka-Rā II Psemthek III

DYNASTY XXVII. (Persians.)

374. Mesut-Rā Kambåthet, or Cambyses, (Pers. Ka[m]-b-u-j-i-ya, ; varr. **Kenbutcha** , **Kambasuṭent**

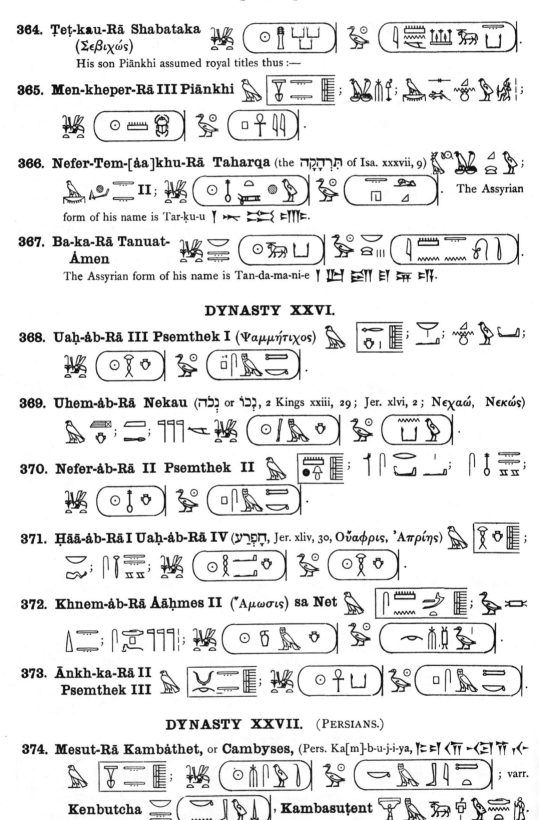

375. Setut-Rā Ȧntriusha I, or **Darius** (Pers. D-a-ra-ya-va-u-sh , Gr. Δαρεῖος), the son of Hystaspes, ; varr. 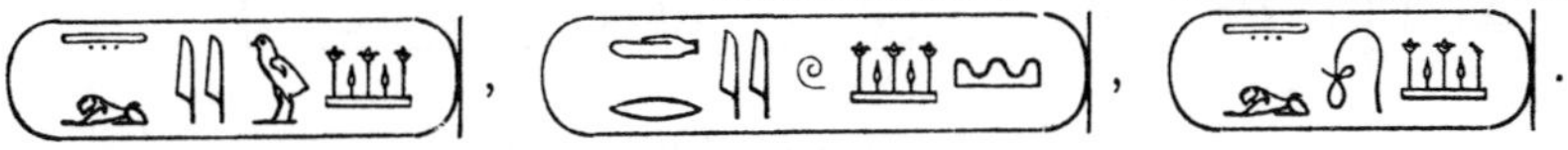.

376. Khshaiarsha, or **Xerxes** (Pers. Kh-sha-ya-a-r-sha-a , Gr. Ξέρξες ὁ μέγας), the great Pharaoh 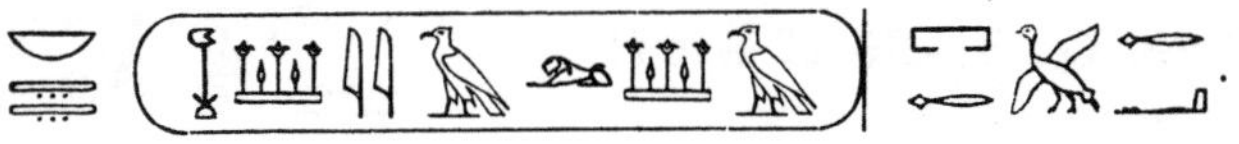.

377. In his reign revolted **Khabbasha** 

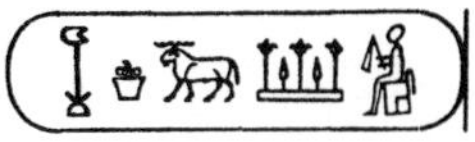; var. .

378. Artakhashassha, or **Artaxerxes** (Pers. A-r-ta-kh-sh-tr-a ), the Great Pharaoh 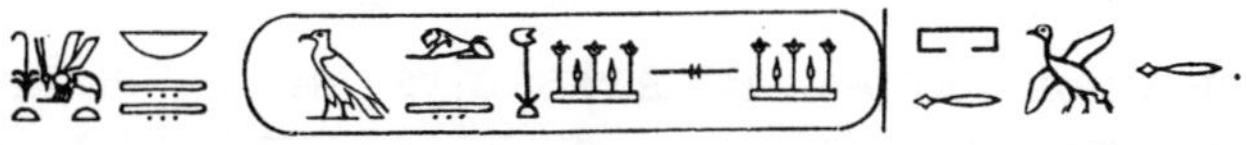.

379. Meri-Ȧmen-Rā-neb-Heb-user-khepesh Ȧntriusha II or **Darius Ochus** or **Nothus** .

DYNASTY XXVIII.

[*Wanting.*]

DYNASTY XXIX.

380. Ba-en-Rā II Naifāaurutˌ (Νεφερίτης) .

381. Khnem-maāt-Rā Hagr (Ἄχωρις) 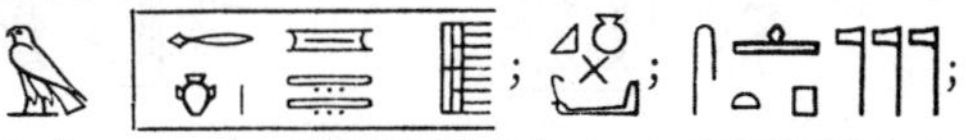;

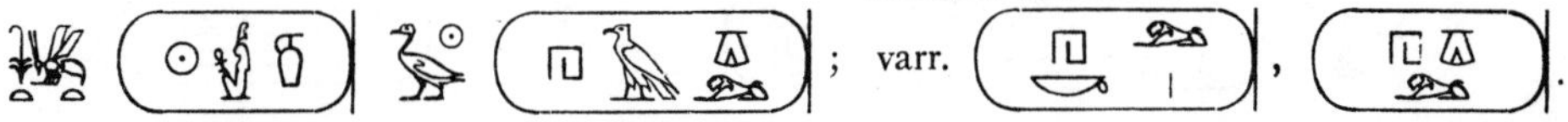.

382. Ptaḥ-user setep-en-Rā Psa-Mut (Ψάμμουθις) 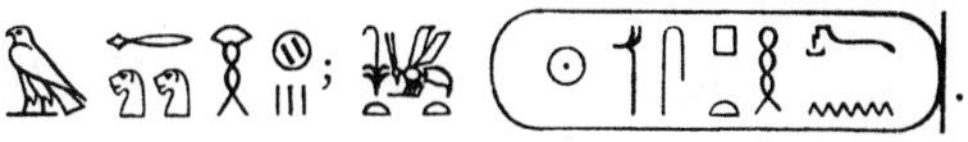.

.

DYNASTY XXX.

383. Senetchem-ȧb-Rā setep-en-Ȧmen Nekht-Ḥeru-ḥeb (Νεκτανέβης) **meri-Ȧmen** 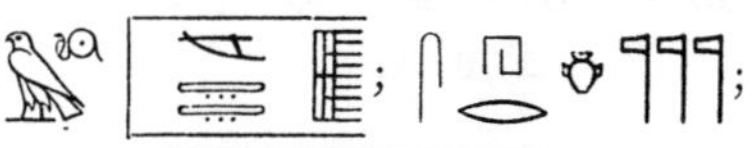;

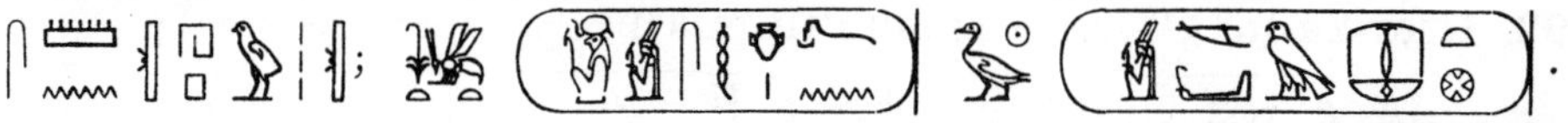.

384. Ȧri-maāt-en-Rā Tche-ḥer (Τέως) **setep-en-Ȧn-ḥer** ;

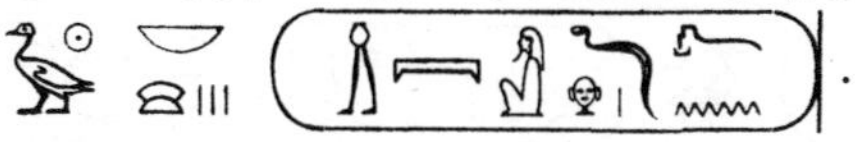.

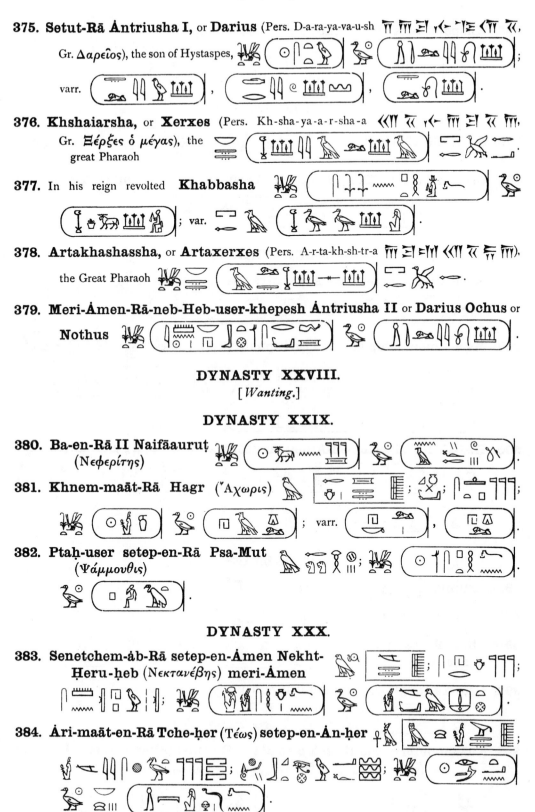

385. Kheper-ka-Rā II Nekht-neb-f (Νεκτανεβὸς) 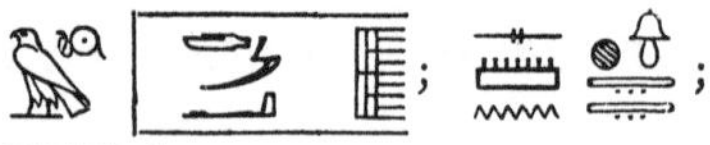

POSITION DOUBTFUL.

386. Qa-ka-Rā II Ȧn II 

387. User-maāt-Rā XVI Setep-en-Ȧmen Ȧmen-ruṭ meri-Ȧmen 

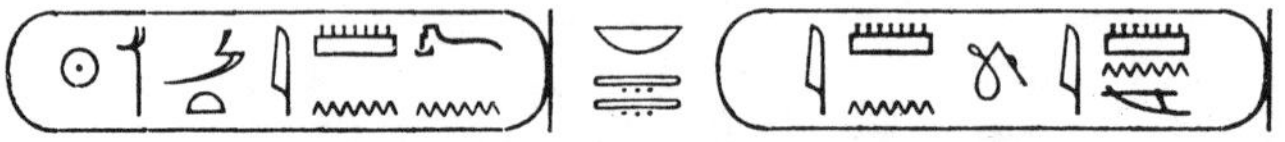

MACEDONIANS.

388. Meri-Ȧmen setep-en-Rā Arksȧnṭrs (Alexander the Great) 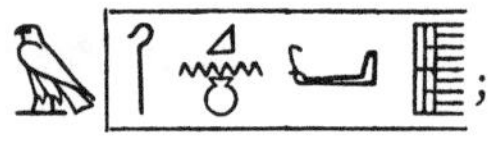

389. Meri-Ȧmen setep-en-Rā Phiriupus (Philip Arrhidaeus) 

 ; varr.

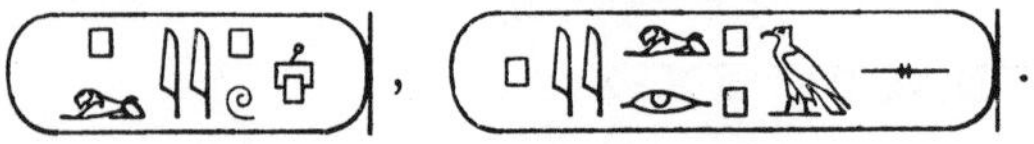

390. Ḥāā-ȧb-Rā II setep-en-Ȧmen Ȧrksenṭrs (Alexander II), **Per-āa** (Pharaoh),

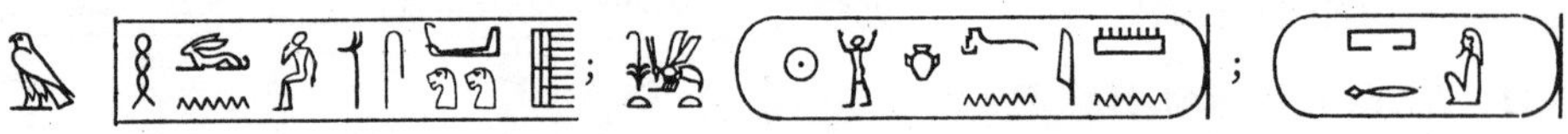

PTOLEMIES.

391A. Ptlmis  (Ptolemy I, Soter 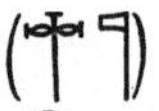 I).

391B. Pṭlmis, the Satrap, 

391C. Meri-Rā setep-en-Ȧmen Pṭulmis 

392. User-ka-Rā IV meri-Ȧmen Ptlumis (Ptolemy II, Philadelphus I) ,

393. Ȧuā-en-neterui-senui setep-en-Rā sekhem-ānkh-en-Ȧmen Ptulmis (Ptolemy III, Euergetes 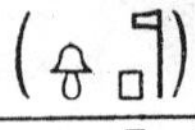 I), everliving, beloved of Ptaḥ,

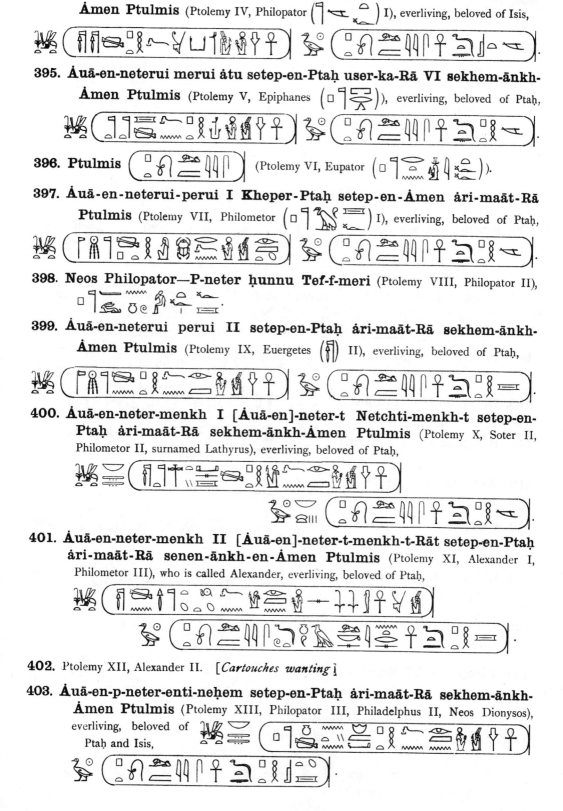

394. Åuā-en-neterui menkhui setep-en-Ptaḥ user-ka-Rā V sekhem-ānkh-Åmen Ptulmis (Ptolemy IV, Philopator 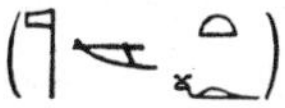 I), everliving, beloved of Isis,

395. Åuā-en-neterui merui åtu setep-en-Ptaḥ user-ka-Rā VI sekhem-ānkh-Åmen Ptulmis (Ptolemy V, Epiphanes ), everliving, beloved of Ptaḥ,

396. Ptulmis 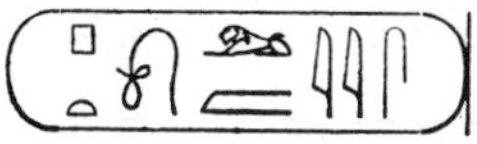 (Ptolemy VI, Eupator ).

397. Åuā-en-neterui-perui I Kheper-Ptaḥ setep-en-Åmen åri-maāt-Rā Ptulmis (Ptolemy VII, Philometor  I), everliving, beloved of Ptaḥ,

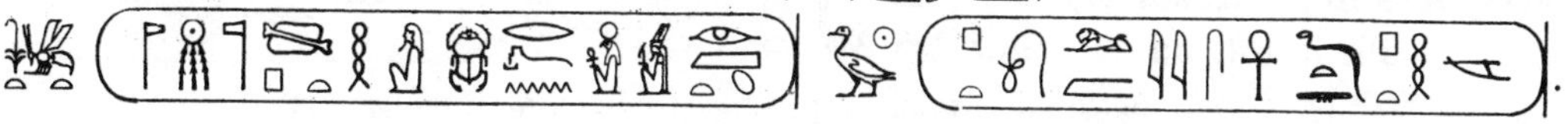

398. Neos Philopator—P-neter ḥunnu Tef-f-meri (Ptolemy VIII, Philopator II),

399. Åuā-en-neterui perui II setep-en-Ptaḥ åri-maāt-Rā sekhem-ānkh-Åmen Ptulmis (Ptolemy IX, Euergetes  II), everliving, beloved of Ptaḥ,

400. Åuā-en-neter-menkh I [Åuā-en]-neter-t Netchti-menkh-t setep-en-Ptaḥ åri-maāt-Rā sekhem-ānkh-Åmen Ptulmis (Ptolemy X, Soter II, Philometor II, surnamed Lathyrus), everliving, beloved of Ptaḥ,

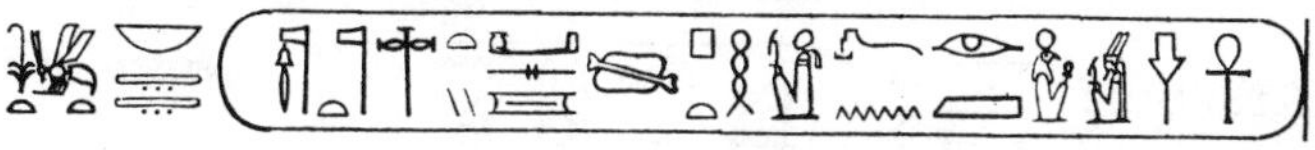

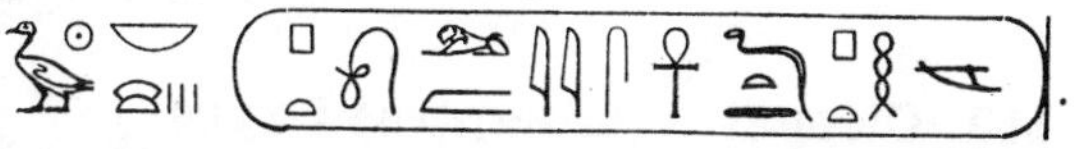

401. Åuā-en-neter-menkh II [Åuā-en]-neter-t-menkh-t-Rāt setep-en-Ptaḥ åri-maāt-Rā senen-ānkh-en-Åmen Ptulmis (Ptolemy XI, Alexander I, Philometor III), who is called Alexander, everliving, beloved of Ptaḥ,

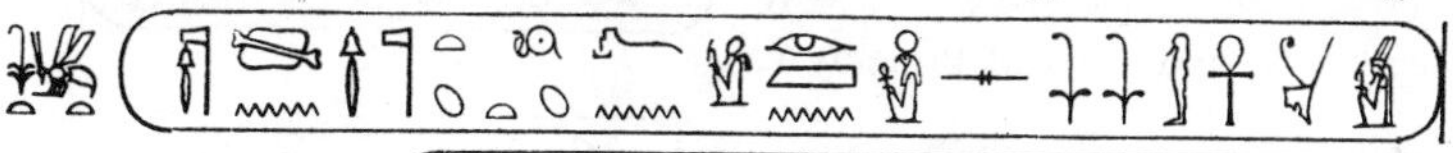

402. Ptolemy XII, Alexander II. [*Cartouches wanting*]

403. Åuā-en-p-neter-enti-neḥem setep-en-Ptaḥ åri-maāt-Rā sekhem-ānkh-Åmen Ptulmis (Ptolemy XIII, Philopator III, Philadelphus II, Neos Dionysos), everliving, beloved of Ptaḥ and Isis,

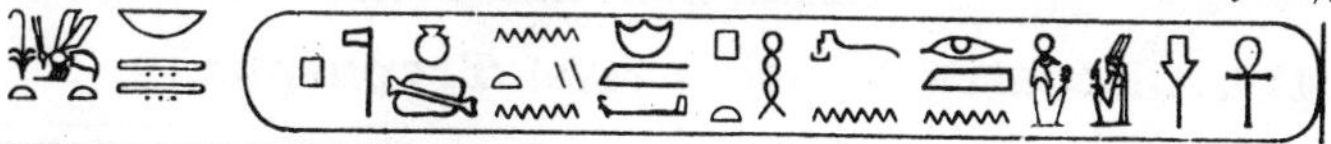

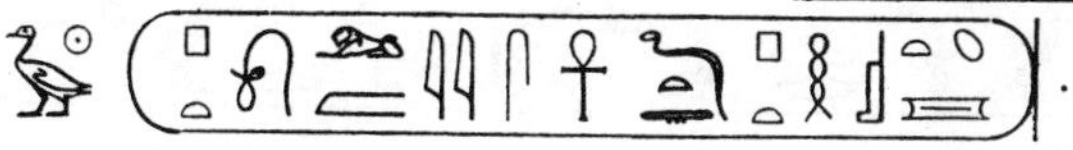

404. Ptolemy XIV. [*Cartouches wanting.*]

405. Ptolemy XV. [*Cartouches wanting.*]

406. Ptulmis (Ptolemy XVI, Philopator IV, Philometor IV, Caesarion), who is called **Caesar,** everliving, beloved of Ptaḥ and Isis, 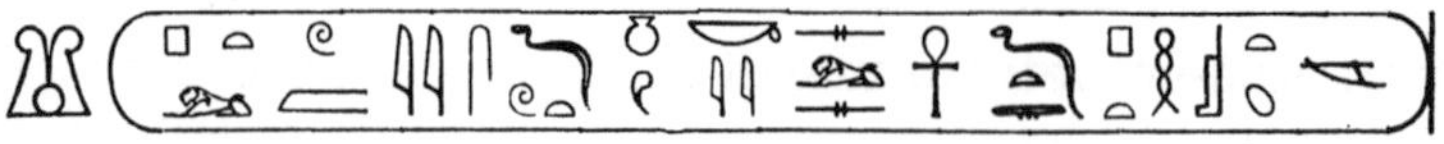, son of the sun, lord of crowns, **Caesar Philopator Philometor** 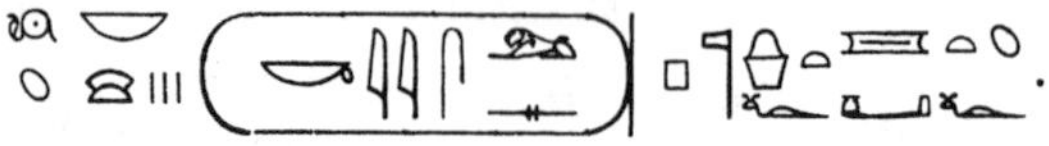.

PTOLEMAIC QUEENS AND PRINCESSES.

406a. Berenice I (Barnig[a]) , the fourth wife of Ptolemy I.

407. Arsinoë (Arsenai) Philadelpha 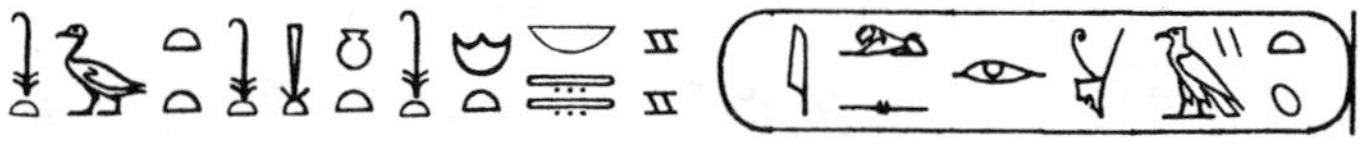 , daughter of Ptolemy I and sister and wife of Ptolemy II.

408. Arsinoë II Philadelpha Khnem-ȧb-en-Maāt meri-neteru Arsenaai (?) 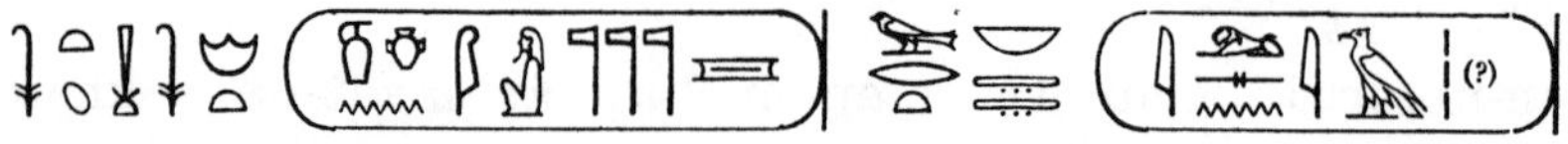.

409. Philotera (Pilutera), youngest daughter of Ptolemy I 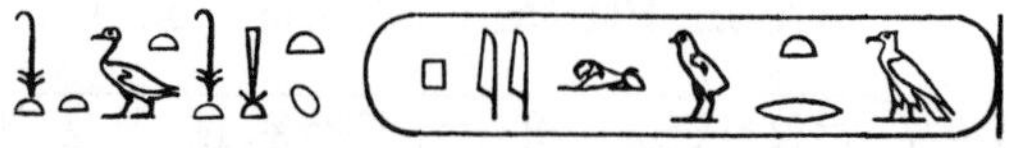.

410. Berenice II (Barniga) , wife of Ptolemy III.

411. Berenice III (Barniga) 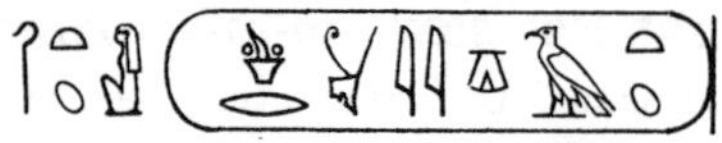, daughter of Ptolemy III and Berenice II.

412. Arsinoë III (Arsenai) , sister and wife of Ptolemy IV.

413. Cleopatra (Qlauptra) I Syra , daughter of Antiochus III and wife of Ptolemy V.

414. Cleopatra II Soteira 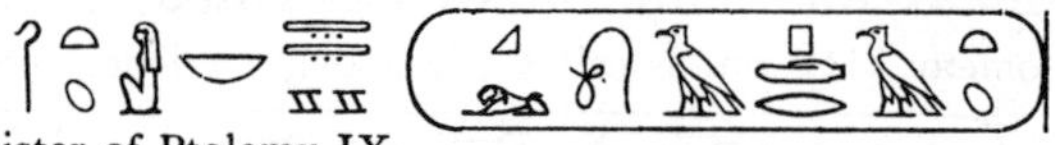, sister and wife of Ptolemy VII, and sister of Ptolemy IX.

415. Cleopatra III Kokke , niece and wife of Ptolemy IX.

416. Cleopatra IV Berenice IV 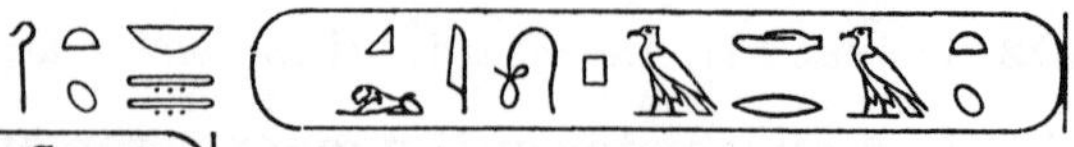; , wife of Ptolemy XI.

417. Cleopatra V, who is called **Tryphaena,** 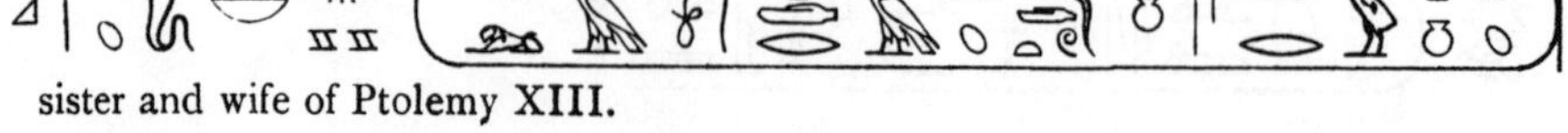, sister and wife of Ptolemy XIII.

She is the *'Aklâ'ûbaṭrâ* አክሉኡበጥራ፡ daughter of Baṭlîmôs, በጥሊሞስ፡ var. *'Abṭĕlmâwôs*, አብጥልማዎስ፡) of Abyssinian writers. (See Brit. Mus. MS. Orient. 661, fol. 80*b* 3, fol. 81*b* 1.)

418. Cleopatra VI and her son **Caesarion** 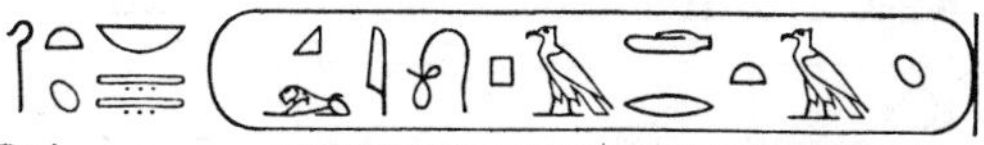

.

ROMAN EMPERORS.

419. Augustus (B.C. 30–A.D. 14) **Ḥeq ḥequ setep-en-Ptaḥ Autkrtr** (Αὐτοκράτωρ) **Kaisrs** (Καῖσαρος) 

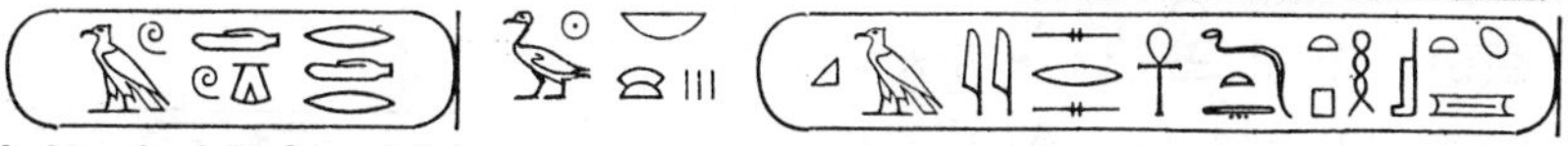, everliving, beloved of Ptaḥ and Isis.

420. Tiberius (A.D. 14–37) **Autkrtr Teberis Kisrs** 

, everliving, beloved of Ptaḥ and Isis.

421. Caius Caesar Germanicus Caligula (A.D. 37–41) **Ḥeq ḥequ Autkrtr meri Ptaḥ Åst Kais Kaisrs Germ[a]nikis** 

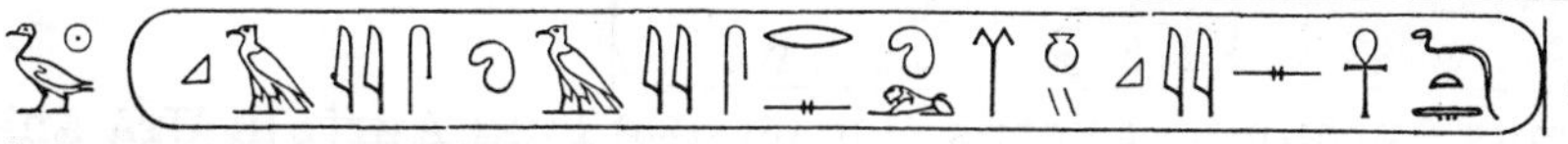, everliving, beloved of Ptaḥ and Isis.

422. Tiberius Claudius Germanicus (A.D. 41–54) **Ḥeq ḥequ Autkrtr Teber[i]s Klts Kaisrs Kermanikes** 

, everliving, beloved of Ptaḥ and Isis.

423. Nero Claudius Caesar Germanicus (A.D. 54–68) **Ḥeq ḥequ setep-en-Ptaḥ meri Åst Autkrtr Narani Kaisrs Karmniks** 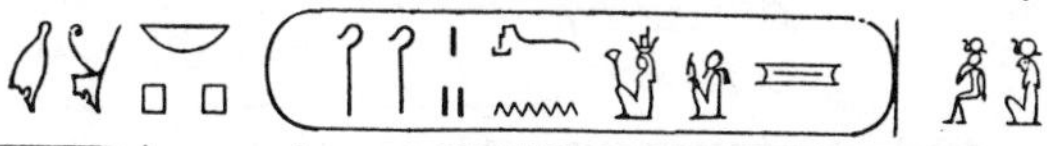

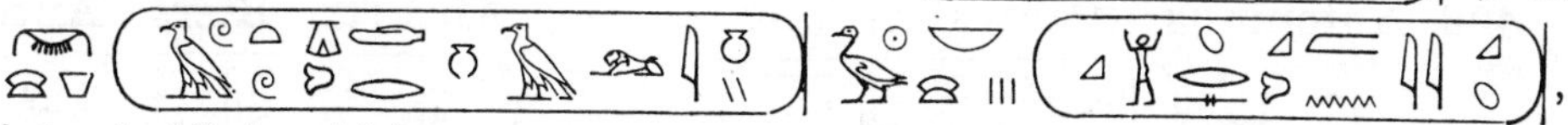, beloved of Ptaḥ and Isis.

424. Servius Galba Caesar (A.D. 68) **Saruu Glbs Autkrtr Kaisrs enti khu**

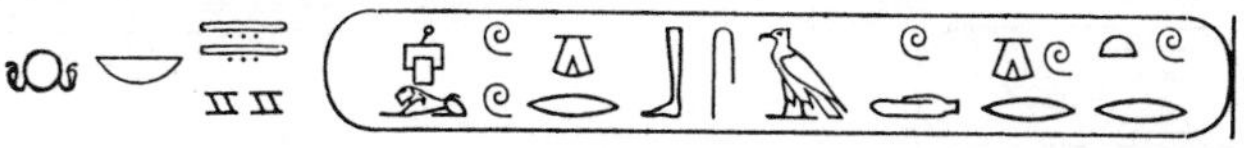, who is glorious.

425. Marcus Otho (A.D. 69) **Mrks Autuns Kisrs Autkrtr**

.

426. Vespasian (A.D. 69–79) **Autkrtr Kisrs Uspisins**

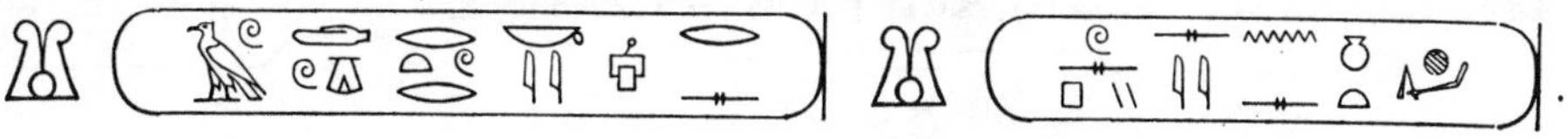.

427. Titus (A.D. 79–81) **Autkrtr Tatas Ksrs**

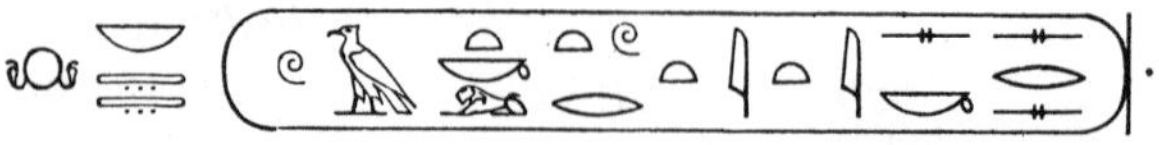

428. Domitianus (A.D. 81–96) **Autkrtr Kisrs T[u]mtin[u]s Germ[a]nik[u]s**

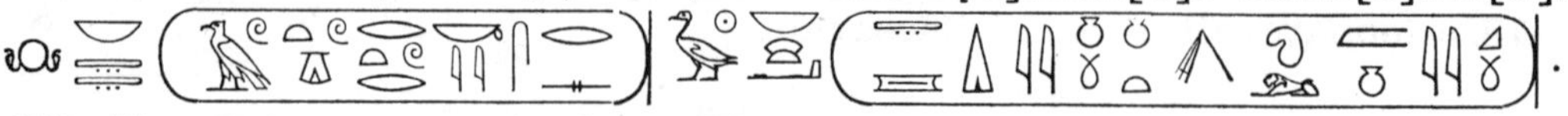

429. Nerva (A.D. 96–98) **Autkrtr Kisrs Nerrus (?)**

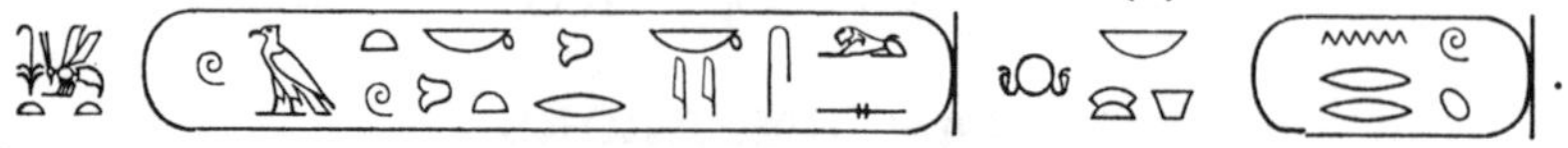

430. Trajan (A.D. 98–117) **Autkrtr Kisrs Neru Trin[u]s Sebastes ānkh tchet meri Åst**

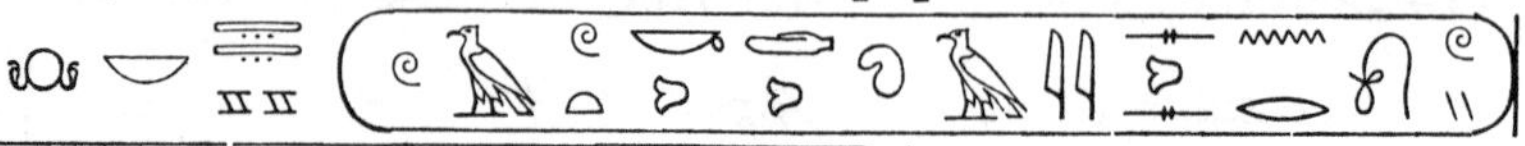

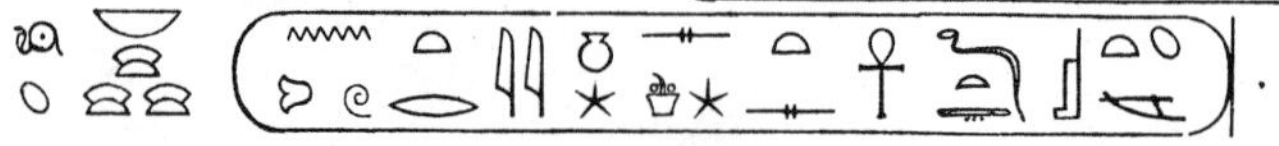

431. Hadrian (A.D. 117–138) **Autkrtr Kisrs Trainus Atrinus**

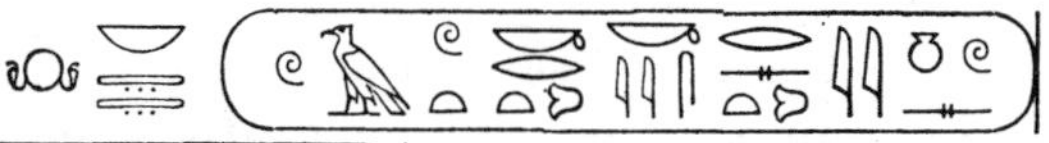

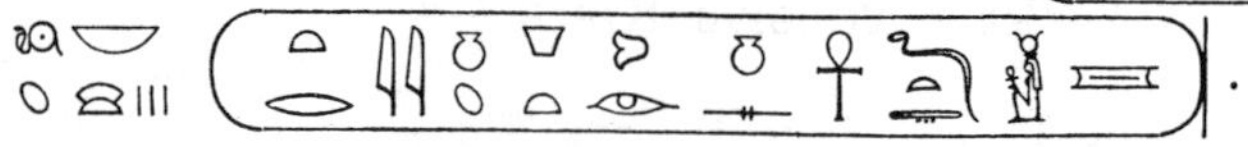

432. Antoninus Pius (Caesar Titus Aelius Hadrian) (A.D. 138–161) **Autkrtr Kisrs Tatas Alis Atrinus Antuninus Seb[a]sts Usbus**

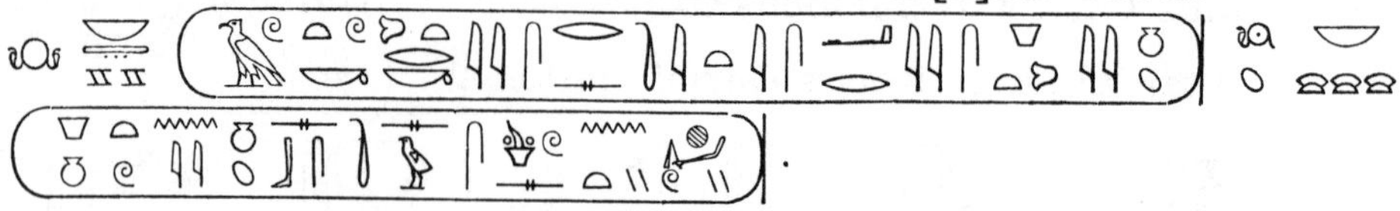

433. Lucius Aurelius and **Verus** (A.D. 161–180) **Luki Aur[e]li Urā ānkh tchet**

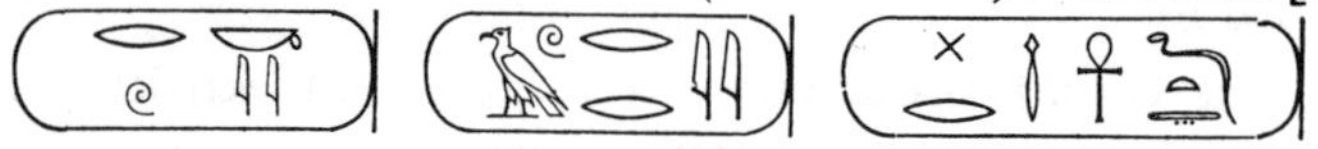

, everliving.

434. Commodus (A.D. 180–192) **Autkrtr Antaninus Kamatus**

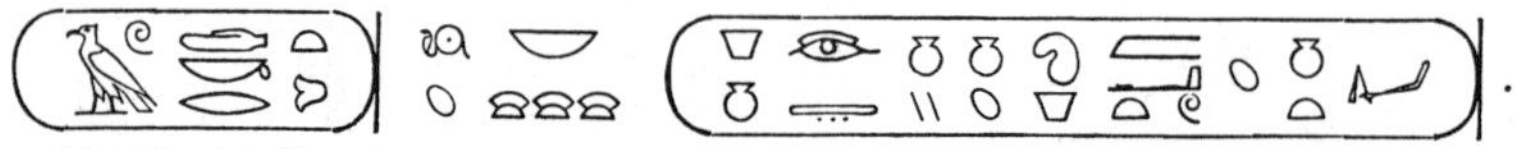

435. Septimius Severus (A.D. 193–211) **Autkrtr Kisrs Sauris**

436. Antoninus (Caracalla) (A.D. 211–217) **Autkrtr Kisrs Antun[i]nus**

437. Geta (A.D. 211–212) **Autkrtr Kis-ars Getas**

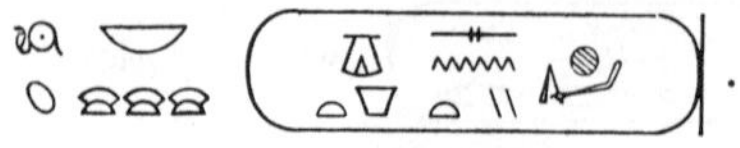

438. Philip (A.D. 244–249) **Autkrtr Kisrs Philipp[u]s**

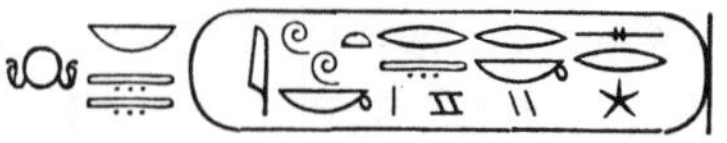

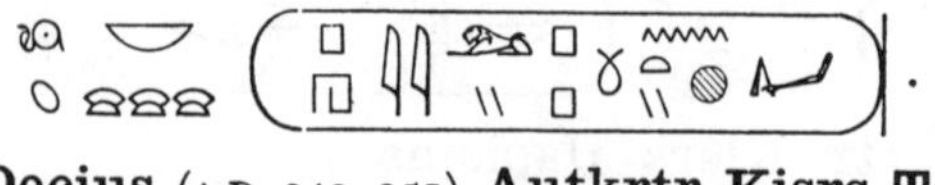

439. Decius (A.D. 249–251) **Autkrtr Kisrs Takis**

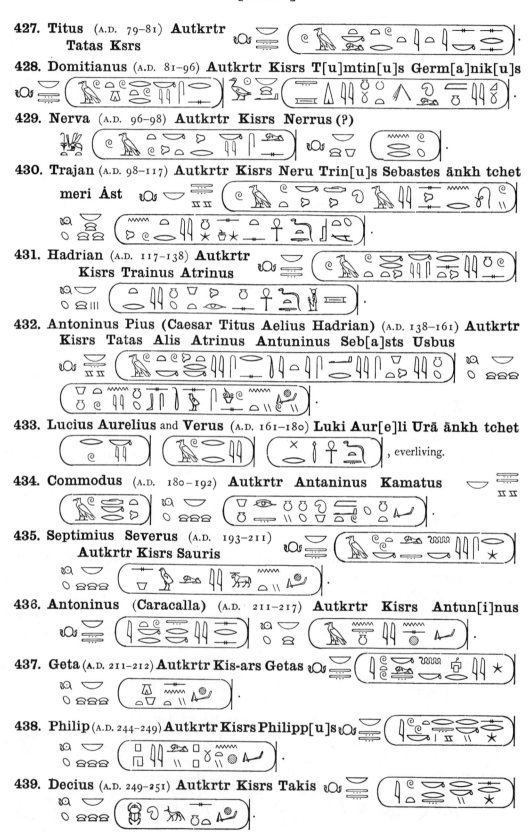

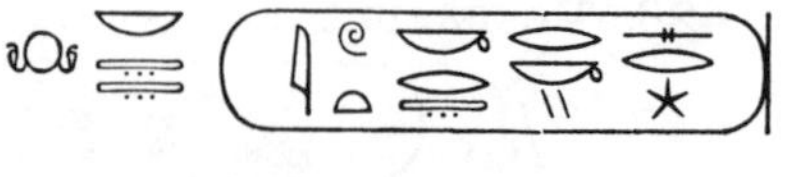

III.

NAMES OF COUNTRIES, DISTRICTS, LOCALITIES, CITIES, TOWNS, ETC.

Aare, L.D. 3, 88, a district in Syria; situation unknown.

Aȧsi, IV, 805 (Ram. III,), a Sûdânî country; situation unknown.

Aimenu, Rec. 20, 114, , IV, 806, a Sûdânî country; situation unknown.

Aisekna, Rec. 20, 115, a Sûdânî country; situation unknown.

Auaur (Aur), P. 260, a town; situation unknown.

Auȧb, a sanctuary in Ḥebenu.

Aumer (?) Aunem (?), IV, 805, , Rec. 20, 114, a Sûdânî country; situation unknown.

Auḥep, , the sanctuary of the god **Ȧḥi**, and of Denderah.

Auṭeni......, B.D.G. 8, a sanctuary (?) at Thebes or Memphis.

Abu, N. 719, , M. 180, . P. 298, , , , , , , , Dream Stele 10, , Elephantine, 'Ιηβ, the "place of ivory"; var. , , "Stone of Ȧabu," *i.e.*, granite; , "Abu of the South," *i.e.*, Semnah.

Abṭ, Abetch, , , , , , N. 701, , P. 71, 307 722, N. 7, , , , , , , , , , , , Hh. 302, , , Abydos, the district of Abydos, the capital of the 8th Nome of Upper Egypt and centre of the cult of Osiris in the South; Copt. ϵⲃⲱⲧ, Ἄβυδος; see .

Abṭu meḥtt, "Abydos of the North," a town in the Fayyûm, Abûṣîr al-Malik (?) A.Z. 1907, 28.

Abetch, IV, 988, P. 8, , Berlin 7272, , , the 8th Nome of Upper Egypt (Thinites).

Apeṭ, P.S.B.A. 218, a town in Egypt.

Amu, B.D. 98, 7, the Fire-city.

Amur-ta (?), Crocodilopolis (Gebelên).

Amsu [ ], IV, 798, a Sûdânî country; situation unknown.

Anuȧsherr, A.Z. 65, 28, a district in the Sûdân.

Arbin, Aribi, Rev. 12, 26, Arabia; Assyr.

Arp[a]kh, Ȧrrapakha, Rev. 24, 160, (Ptolemy VI, 1, 2); var. ; Assyr.

Arm'ina, A.Z. 49, 78, Armenia; Pers. Behis. 1, 15.

Arsa, IV, 791, a district in Syria; situation unknown.

Arek, IV, 796, a Sûdânî country; situation unknown.

Aḥ, Aḥu, B.D.G. 1027, Famine Stele III: (1) a Sûdânî country (?); (2) a name of Leontopolis.

Akh = , P. 427, M. 612, N. 707, 1216, a town in the Delta.

Akhamrur, IV, 791, a district in Syria; situation unknown.

Ast, Rec. 20, 115; see [ ].

Ashia, Rev. 24, 160, a country; situation unknown.

Asher, Ashru, the name of the district and lake at Thebes sacred to the goddess Mut; they lay between Karnak and Luxor.

Aker, a canal in the 3rd Nome of Lower Egypt (Libya-Mareotis).

Akthata, a district of Syria.

Agnȧ, IV, 802, a Sûdânî country; situation unknown.

Ati, Rev. 12, 20, the land of the .

Atef, B.D.G. 6, a name of: (1) Sma-Beḥt; (2) Diospolis in the Delta.

Atef ur, the name of a town near Memphis and of its god.

Atef-peḥ, the 14th Nome of Upper Egypt; , the capital of .

Atef-khent, the 13th Nome of Upper Egypt (Lycopolites); , the capital of the same, *i.e.*, , q.v.

Atekh, a name of .

Aṭ, see .

Ȧa, B.D.G. 8, a suburb of Memphis (?)

Ȧati, the two cemeteries; positions unknown.

Åa-t åakhu, a name of Edfû.

Åat åakhut en åakhu khenti netchemtchem ānkh-t, a name of Edfû.

Åa-t Åsår Nekhen, the tomb of Osiris at Nekhen.

Åa åtru (?), a town near Gebelên in Upper Egypt.

Åa-t āq-t ent Åmentt, B.D.G. 35, the site of the temple of Thothmes III at Madînat Habû.

Åa uāb, "holy island," a name of the Island of Philae.

Åa-t uāb, A.Z. 1904, 142, "holy sepulchre," *i.e.*, the tomb of Osiris at Philae; Gr. 'Αβατον.

Åa ur (Mer ur ?): (1) a town in the Delta; (2), a town in Upper Egypt (Arsinoë ?)

Åa-t ur, B.D. 142, III, 10, a town of Osiris.

Åa-t ur ent ḥeṭer Ḥeru, a name of Edfû.

Åa-t Utcha, B.D.G. 181: (1) a suburb of Alexandria; (2) a district of Letopolis.

Åa-t baiu, the necropolis of Mendes; Gr. Θμοῦϊς.

Åa-t bar (Åubar), L.D, III, 252, 122, , IV, 785, , the name of several places in Syria; compare Heb. אָבֵל (fertile land, meadow).

Åa-t Beḥetch, a quarter of Edfû.

Åa-t Pe (Pu ?), the necropolis of Pe-Ṭep, q.v.

Åapu, , Rec. 2, 31, , Panopolis. Perhaps another name for **Khemenu**; Copt. ϣⲙⲓⲛ, Arab. اخميم, Eth. አክሚም: አክምም:

Åa Pega, the temple of Osiris in the nome of Pharbaetites.

Åa-t Pegas; see **Åa-t Pega.**

Åa-t Pteḥ, a section of the Labyrinth.

Åa-t Maāt, , a name of Edfû.

Åa maāti, "Island of truth," the abode of Osiris in the Ṭuat.

Åa måtru, Åa m åtru, Rev. 14, 21, , Rec. 10, 133, , , a name of Gebelên.

Åamur, Rec. 33, 128, a name of Gebelên.

Åa-t Menuār, the temple of Osiris in Mareotis.

Åa-t menkhet, the sanctuary of the serpent god or goddess **Shenār**; var.

Åa-t Meri, the necropolis of Mareotis.

Åa meḥ, "Island of the north," an island near Pelusium.

Åa-t mesq, "Tomb of the bull's hide," a name of Abydos.

Åa nasha (Mer-nasha), Harris I, 61 B, 10, a town in Egypt.

Åa-en-åufras, "Island of Åufras," *i.e.*, Cyprus.

Åa en Åbui (Åbi?), Rech. 99, an island near Memphis.

Åa en Åsi, "Island of Åsi," *i.e.*, Cyprus. The correct spelling of **Åsi** is . The form is found on the Stele of Canopus; this is a corruption of , "Island of **Å**unt**å**nai."

Åa-t nebeḥ, the tomb of Osiris at Busiris.

Åaut en Beḥṭ, the holy tombs of Edfû.

Åa-t nebs, see .

Åa nefer, a town in Egypt.

Åa nefer en åṭ, a name of Edfû.

Åa-t nefer, Rec. 11, 80, a town in Lower Egypt.

Åa-t nem-t, a district of Denderah.

Åa-t ent mu, B.D 149, a district in the Ṭuat.

Åanreka (read), IV, 792, a district in Syria; situation unknown.

Åa-t Nekheb, a district in the Nome Diospolites.

Åa-t ent Kher-āḥa, B.D. 149, the 14th Åat in the Ṭuat.

Åa-t Neserneser (Åa-t en Serser?): (1) a district in the Nome Hermopolites; (2) a district in the Ṭuat.

Åa en serser, Hh. 356, ; see **Åa-t Neserneser.**

Åa en shau, an estate of King Khufu (Cheops).

Åa-t ent qāḥu, B.D. 149, a district in the Ṭuat.

Åa en Kam-ur, a name of Athribis.

Åa netrit, a town of Isis.

Åa-t netråt, Rec. 5, 88, a temple of Isis.

Åa-t netrit ent Rā, a district near Denderah where Horus overthrew Set.

Åaraṭs Rec. 33, 6, Aradus; Heb. אַרְוָד, Tall al-'Amârnah , Assyr. , Gr. Ἄραδος, Ὀρθωσια, Arab. ارواد, Syr. ܐܪܘܕ, the modern Ruwâd.

Åa-t Ruṭ, a town in the Nome Maḥetch, (Ḳôm 'al-Aḥmar?),

Åarma (Åalma), Leontopolis in the Athribite Nome.

Åarmaȧ, Gol. 4, 8, a district in Syria; situation unknown.

Åa rek (Åa-lek), the "Island of Philae," at the south end of the First Cataract; Copt. ⲡⲓⲗⲁⲕ, Arab. بلاق.

Åa-t Rek (Åa Lek), with the article, the temple town of Philae.

Åaretȧ, IV, 791, a district or town in Syria (Aradus ?); see **Åaraṭs**.

Åa-t heben, a town in Upper Egypt.

Åa-t Ḥerui (?), Lower Egypt; a cemetery of Horus and Set (?).

Åa-t Ḥeḥu, a sanctuary in Ḥensu (Herakleopolis).

Åa ḥetep, a name of Edfû.

Åa-t khet (?), Rec. 11, 80, a town in the Delta (?)

Åakhas, Eg. Res. 73, 109, a district in Syria; situation unknown.

Åakhatu, Rec. 20, 115, a district in Syria; situation unknown.

Åa-t khenu a district in the Nome Athribites.

Åa-t khnem, a district in the Nome Åm-peḥ.

Åai khnemu, a town in Egypt.

Åa-t sab-shu (?), a district of Horus of Nekhen.

Åa-t Sebek, Methen 11, a village in the Delta.

Åa sma, a name of Edfû.

Åa Seneferu, a town near Gîzah.

Åa-t Skhau, a town of Osiris; situation unknown.

Åastȧ, IV, 791, a district in Syria; situation unknown.

Åa-t shā-t, a name of Per-Reḥreḥ (?).

Åa-t shā, a sandy district; situation unknown.

Åa sher, Natron Island, the Wâdî Naṭrûn (?)

Åa-t qema ḥetchḥetchui, Khemenu (Hermopolis).

Åakatȧ, Rec. 20, 118, a district in Syria; situation unknown.

Åa-t kek, Rec. 33, 176, a town near al-Hîbah.

Åa-t Geb, a district near Edfû.

Åatuba, IV, 792, a district in Syria; situation unknown.

Åa-t Tefnut, a name of Denderah.

Åa-t Tenen, a sanctuary in the Nome Prosopites; Copt. ⲡⲁⲑⲁⲛⲟⲛ.

Åa-t Tha, a name of **Ånit**, the modern Asnâ (Latopolis).

Åa-t tha Per-ḥemut, the necropolis of the Nome Sebennytes. The name means something like Andropolis-Gynaecopolis; see Strabo XVII, 803.

Åa-t tham, Annales, 4, 179, Rhind Pap. 24, 56; var. the town and necropolis of Western Thebes; Copt. ϪⲎⲘⲈ.

Åathaker (*sic*), IV, 790, a district in Syria; situation unknown.

Åathn, IV, 792, a district in Syria: situation unknown.

Åa-t ṭa (?), the 6th Nome of Upper Egypt (Tentyrites).

Åa-t ṭa (?), the capital of the 6th Nome of Upper Egypt (Denderah).

Åaṭamm, Anastasi I, 22, 1, a country in Northern Syria; compare Heb. אֲדֻמִּים.

Åa-t Ṭeb, a town in the Nome Pharbaetites.

Åaṭmamt, L.D. 3, 252, 98, a district in Syria; situation unknown.

Åaṭråa, L.D. III, 252, 100, a district in Syria; situation unknown; see

Åa-t Tchefa, a district in the Ṭuat where food was stored.

Åa tchestches, a district in one of the Oases.

Åa-t Tcheṭmi, a village to the south-east of Thebes.

Åaa, IV, 799, a Sûdânî country; situation unknown.

Åa, Åau, IV, 800, a Sûdânî country; situation unknown.

Åaiuran (Åaiulan), L.D. III, 252, 26, Ajalon; compare Heb. אַיָּלוֹן, Josh. x, 12, Assyr.

Åau, Rec. 20, 114, IV, 806, a Sûdânî country; situation unknown.

Åaui, IV, 805, a Sûdânî country; situation unknown.

Åaur (?), IV, 805, a Sûdânî country; situation unknown.

Åabu, A.Z. 1908, 118, the capital of **Ta-set**, *i.e.*, Nubia, the 1st Nome of Upper Egypt (Elephantine); see **Abu**, Elephantine.

Åab kher, Rec. 32, 69, a place; situation unknown.

Åabtet, a name of **Ḥerur**, near Beni Ḥasan.

Åabṭu, Abydos; see, Aram. Pap. 20, אבוט.

Åam, the capital of the Nome Åment.

Åamu kehek, A.Z. 1883, 88, a nomad tribe conquered by Åmenḥetep I.

Åama, a country in the Egyptian Sûdân.

Åamȧ, IV, 797, a Sûdânî country; situation unknown.

Åantem, IV, 797, a Sûdânî country; situation unknown.

Åar, IV, 803, a Sûdânî country; situation unknown.

Åarakaraka, IV, 796, a Sûdânî country; situation unknown.

Åah, IV, 799, a Sûdânî country; situation unknown.

Åahetb, the 5th station on the Ḳanâ-Ḳuṣêr Road, near the Red Sea.

Åakhekh, a town in Egypt.

Åakhet, IV, 802, a Sûdânî country; situation unknown.

Åakh-t Åmen, the vine land of Libya-Mareotis; var. **Åakh-t Men**.

Åakh-t Menḥ, the vine land of Libya-Mareotis.

Åakhu-t, a name of the temple of Åmen-Rā at Thebes.

Åakhu-t, a funerary temple of Men-kau-Ḥeru.

Åakhu-t, the name of the pyramid of Khufu at Gîzah.

Åakhu Åsut, the name of the pyramid of Neb-ḥep-Rā (Menthuḥetep) at Thebes.

Åakhu ā-f user ȧsut nebt enti khet ta, a name of Denderah.

Åakhu mennu, Rec. 32, 64, a name of Karnak.

Åakhu-t ent Rā ḥeri neteru, a name of Thebes.

Åakhu Åment, var., a temple of Osiris in the Nome Åment.

Åakhut-en-Åten, a town built by Åmenḥetep IV near the modern village of Tall al-'Amârnah; called also **Pa Åtenher**.

Åakhu-t ent Åmen-ren-f, a name of Thebes.

Åakhu-t en Rā, a temple of Horus in Edfû.

Åakhu-t ḥeḥ, a name of the temples of Edfû and Denderah.

Åakhu-t sheta-t, "hidden horizon," a name of the tomb.

Åakhu-t taui, a name of Memphis.

Åasen, IV, 802, a Sûdânî country; situation unknown.

Åak, IV, 802, a Sûdânî country; situation unknown.

Åakaraka, a Sûdânî country; situation unknown.

Åaku, Åauk, a district near the modern Gebel Aḥmar.

Åag, B.D.G. 76, an estate of Åssȧ.

Åati, Mar. Karn. 52, 7, a canal in An (Heliopolis).

Åatuārt (?), IV, 801, a Sûdânî country; situation unknown.

Åatef, Åteftit, a Nubian town with quarries of , rubies (?)

Åaṭ, B.D. 149, 45, a town in the Ṭuat.

Åaṭ, a district in the Nome of Menu.

Åāatchem, IV, 798, [], a Sûdânî country; situation unknown.

Åāu, a town in Egypt.

Åār Åamu (Åāl Åamu), a town in Egypt.

Åārsa, IV, 789, a district in Syria; situation unknown.

Åāshu, Åāshȧa, IV, 806 (Ram. III), a Sûdânî country; situation unknown.

Åāthen, IV, 804, a Sûdânî country; situation unknown.

Åi, IV, 788, a district in Syria; situation unknown.

Åit, B.D.G. 9, a sanctuary at Latopolis.

Åibra, IV, 793, a district in Syria; situation unknown.

Åim'r, Rec. 20, 116, a district in Syria; situation unknown.

Åimers, Methen 11, a village or estate in the Delta.

Åinu (Åinnu), IV, 791, a district in Syria; situation unknown.

Åiranra (?), IV, 792, a district in Syria; situation unknown.

Åikhka (?), Nȧstasen Ṡtele 46, a Sûdânî country; situation unknown.

Åitua, IV, 790, a district in Syria; situation unknown.

Åuu, Rec. 3, 2, IV, 385, a district in Syria; situation unknown.

Åu-t, a name of Abu (Elephantine).

Åu-t n Net Åmenit (?), a name of Sni (Latopolis).

Åuaram . . ., Rec. 13, 3, a town in Egypt.

Åuȧnȧu, IV, 784, a district in Syria; situation unknown; Heb. אוֹנוֹ, 1 Chron. viii, 12. The modern Kafr 'Anâ (?)

Åuȧnȧuqu, IV, 789, a district in Syria; situation unknown.

Åuā (Åuāut?), a quarter of Memphis.

Åuāt, IV, 805, a Sûdânî country; situation unknown.

Åubar, IV, 784, a name of many districts in Syria; compare Heb. אָבֵל, "fertile land," "meadow."

Åubarrna, IV, 789, a district in Syria; situation unknown.

Åubatȧ, IV, 791, a district in Syria; situation unknown.

Åubir (?) , IV, 781, 785, a district in Syria; situation unknown.

Åupa , Anastasi I, 17, 1, 22, 6, Anastasi IV, 16, 11, a district in Syria; Tall al-'Amârnah .

Åum'i , IV, 793, a district in Syria; situation unknown.

Åun en Ån-nef (?) , a sanctuary of Khnemu-Rā at Latopolis.

Åuna , A.Z. 35, 18, a town in the district of Ḥensu.

Åunam' , IV, 788, a district in Syria; situation unknown.

Åunufr , IV, 789, a district in Syria; situation unknown.

Åuntånai , Cyprus; Assyrian *mat* **Ya-at-na-na** , *mat* **At-na-na** , Gr. Κύπρος.

Åur , Rec. 20, 114, a Sûdânî country; situation unknown.

Åurina , IV, 789, a district in Syria; situation unknown.

Åurm' , IV, 790, 793, a district in Syria; situation unknown.

Åurna , IV, 793, a district in Syria; situation unknown.

Åusāas , P. 423, , M. 605, N. 1210, the district of Ånu sacred to the goddess Åusāasit.

Åushå , , IV, 799, a Sûdânî country; situation unknown.

Åushen , IV, 801, a Sûdânî country; situation unknown.

Åukam' , IV, 793, a district in Syria; situation unknown.

Ȧugertt , the necropolis of Heliopolis; see **Ȧgertt** .

Åutir , IV, 790, a district in Syria; situation unknown.

Åutrāa , , IV, 785, a district in Syria; Heb. אֶדְרֶעִי, Numb. xxi, 33, LXX 'Εδραΐν, Eusebius 'Αδραά.

Åuthu , Anastasi I, 21, 1, , L.D. III, 131, a district near Tyre; Tall al-'Amârnah .

Åb , Famine Stele 15 = **Abu** , Elephantine.

Åb , a name of Khemenu (Hermopolis).

Åb , , IV, 799, a Sûdânî country; situation unknown.

Åbaråa , L.D. 3, 252, 40, the name of several places in Syria.

Åbarteth , IV, 790, a district in Syria; situation unknown.

Åbakhi , Rec. 20, 118, a district in Syria; situation unknown.

Åbatå , IV, 790, a district in Syria; situation unknown.

Åbua , IV, 805, a Sûdânî country; situation unknown.

Åbureth , Rec. 20, 116, a district in Syria; situation unknown.

Åbre , the name of several districts in Syria; compare Heb. אָבֵל, a meadow-like country.

Åbrannu , IV, 792, a district in Syria; situation unknown.

Åbhat , , B.M. 657, a country in the Northern Sûdân.

Åbsau, Rec. 20, 114, , IV, 806, a Sûdânî country; situation unknown.

Åbsaqaba, Åbsaqbu, , Anastasi I, 27, 6, a district (?) in Syria.

Åbsi, IV, 803, a Sûdânî country; situation unknown.

Åbskhen, Nåstasen Stele 53, a country in the Eastern or Southern Sûdân.

Åbshatna, IV, 794, a district in Syria; situation unknown.

Åbshek, , a town near the modern Abû Simbel in Nubia; Gr. Ἀβουγκίς, Ptolemy IV, 7, 16, Aboccis, Pliny VI, 29.

Åbt, Rev. 13, 37, , Jour. As. 1908, 314, Abydos; see Abetch.

Åbti, B.D.G. 18, a quarter of Saut (Lycopolis).

Åbti, B.D.G. 181, a sanctuary of Thoth in Khemenu (Hermopolis).

Åbthesȧ, IV, 800, a Sûdânî country; situation unknown.

Åbṭu, Abydos; see .

Åbṭu, a sanctuary of the Åbṭu fish (?); situation unknown.

Åp, Åpi, Åpu, , , , , , , , , , Panopolis, the capital of the nome (Panopolites) and the centre of the cult of Menu, or Khem, or Åmsu; perhaps another name for Khemenu ; Copt. ϣⲙⲓⲛ, Arab. اخميم, Eth. አክሚም : አክሞም :

Åp, Åpit, , , , , , , , , , , , , , , , , , Nåstasen Stele 37, , , , , , the temple of Åmen-Rā (Karnak) at Thebes.

Åp-t ur-t, the sanctuary of the goddess Åpit at Thebes.

Åput nub, Nåstasen Stele 14, the "golden temple" at Napata; see Diodorus III, 6.

Åp-t shemā, , the southern Åpt, *i.e.*, the temple of Luxor.

Åpamai, Rec. 33, 6, Apamea (Assyr. , B.M. S.P. 1, 176), on the river Ṣîlḥu; varr. , .

Åpaqȧ, Rec. 20, 118, probably one of the four cities called אֲפֵק, Josh. xix, 30, אֲפֵקָה, in Josh. xiii, 4, xv, 53, 1 Sam. xxix, 1, 1 Kings xx, 26; Assyr. .

Åpitcha, Rec. 20, 116, a district in Syria; compare Heb. אֶבֶץ, Josh. xix, 20.

Åpuqen, IV, 784, a district in Syria; situation unknown.

Åpthen, , IV, 784; var. , a district in Syria; situation unknown.

Åpṭu, Mission 13, 4, Abydos (?)

Åpptchu, IV, 798, a Ṣûdâni country; situation unknown.

Åfresh, a town in Egypt.

Åft, IV, 799; var., a Sûdânî country; situation unknown.

Åfttit, a town near Buhen (Wâdî Ḥalfah).

Åfth, IV, 799; see .

Åm-t, a part of the Nome **Seshesht**.

Åmm, capital of the Nome .

Åma Utch (?), a sanctuary of Osiris at Letopolis.

Åmam, Åmmaau, a country in the Sûdân.

Åmån, Rec. 20, 116, a district in Syria; situation unknown.

Åm'r, Anastasi III, 8, 7; compare Heb. אֱמֹרִי.

Åm'ur, Rec. 11, 67, the land of the Amorite; Tall al-'Amârnah .

Åm'ut (?), IV, 788, a district in Syria; situation unknown.

Åm'resk, IV, 789, a district in Syria; situation unknown.

Åm'rashak, Rec. 20, 117, a district in Syria; situation unknown.

Åm'hur, IV, 794, a district in Syria; situation unknown.

Åm'shana, var., IV, 782, a district in Syria; situation unknown.

Åm'kau, IV, 793, a district in Syria; situation unknown.

Åm'tå, Eg. Res. 71, 120, a district in Syria; compare Heb. אַמָּה, 2 Sam. viii, 1.

Åmit, Rec. 11, 146, B.D. 17, 90, 91, 93, Buto.

Åmu (?), IV, 802, a Sûdânî country; situation unknown.

Åmu āas, a town near Letopolis.

Åmubes (?), IV, 803, a Sûdânî country; situation unknown.

Åmurt, the necropolis of Thebes.

Åmpeḥ, the 19th Nome of Lower Egypt.

Åment, Rev. 13, 30; , Rev. 11, 186 = .

Åmen-t, Libya-Mareotis, the 3rd Nome of Lower Egypt.

Åmen-t Ånpu (?), U. 575, and N. 965, a district in Egypt or the Ṭuat.

Åmen heri åb, a town near Åbshek (Abû Simbel).

Åmen kheperu, B.D.G. 29, a sanctuary in the Nome Sept (Arabia).

Åmen sekher, B.D.G. 3, a cemetery at Thebes.

Åmen tehen , "Åmen of the hill," the district of Tehen at Thebes.

Åmenu-t Khufu , B.D.G. 32, an estate of Khufu.

Åmentȧ , Rec. 20, 119, a country conquered by Rameses III.

Åmḥet , , , , , the temple of Osiris and cemetery of Memphis (Ṣaḳḳârah); , the cemetery of Babylon of Egypt.

Åmmekhas , IV, 803, a Sûdânî country; situation unknown.

Åmkhent , the 18th Nome of Lower Egypt (Bubastites).

Åmestrek , Rec. 20, 115, a Sûdânî country; situation unknown.

Åmter , Crocodilopolis, near Gebelên.

Ån , , P. 220, , , Rec. 26, 75, 31, 162, , , , , , , , , A.Z. 1873, 105, Heliopolis, the capital of the Nome (Heliopolites); Heb. אוֹן, Assyr. , Copt. ⲱⲛ.

Ån Rā , the Ånu of Rā.

Ån , , Tentyra (Denderah).

Ån nut Tem , , , Hermonthis.

Ån en Pteḥ , , , Denderah.

Ån en Nut , Denderah.

Ån Menth , , "the Ån of Menthu," Hermonthis.

Ån meḥ , , "Ån of the North," Heliopolis; Heb. אוֹן, Copt. ⲱⲛ; , a town near Tanis; , P.S.B. 15, 444, Heliopolis and Hermonthis.

Ån Shemā , , , , , "Ån of the South," Hermonthis; Copt. ⲉⲣⲙⲟⲛⲧ, ⲉⲣⲙⲉⲛⲧ, the modern Armant.

Ånut , the towns of the Nome Nefer Åabti (Heroopolites).

Ån-t , a "valley" near Memphis.

Ån-ti , , , , , , Rec. 10, 133, , Gebelên, in Upper Egypt.

Ån-t , the valley of , near Beni Ḥasan.

Ån-t ḥesmen , , , , , , : (1) a region to the west of Cairo, *i.e.*, the "Natron Valley," Wâdî l-Naṭrûn; Arab. وادى النطرون, the "Natron Mountain" of the Copts, ⲡⲧⲟⲟⲩ ⲙⲡⲓϩⲟⲥⲉⲙ; (2) a district of Al-Ḳâb.

Ån-t ḥetch Nekhen (?) , , , capital of the Nome Ten (?)

Ånt Seneferu , an estate of Seneferu.

Åntt teḥen , "crystal valley," a district near Ḥensu (Herakleopolis).

Ån , B.D.G. 48, the Canopic arm of the Nile.

Ȧna, IV, 802, a Sûdânî country; situation unknown.

Ȧnȧ, a town in Upper Egypt.

Ȧnȧuben, IV, 790, a district in Syria; situation unknown.

Ȧnȧurepȧa, IV, 782, a district in Syria; situation unknown.

Ȧnȧugasa (Ȧngas), IV, 665, 704, 716, a district in Syria; var. , Alt-K. 595, Tall al-'Amârnah; Assyr.

Ȧnȧutena, IV, 791, a district in Syria; situation unknown.

Ȧnnasa, Rec. 8, 137, a district in Syria; situation unknown.

Ȧnnāui, IV, 793, a district in Syria; situation unknown.

Ȧni, Hh. 161, Rec. 10, 140, 27, 87, , IV, 1121, Sen, Sni (Asnâ).

Ȧnit, , a canal in the Nome of Sepṭ .

Ȧnini (?), Eg. Res. 84, 140, a district in Syria; situation unknown.

Ȧnnukherut, , IV, 283, a district in Syria; compare Heb. אֲנָחֲרַת, Josh. 19, 19.

Ȧneb, , , IV, 1089, , , , Memphis; , the eastern quarter of Memphis.

Ȧneb, , , : (1) a town near Pelusium; (2) , , Edfû; (3) , the capital of (Heroonpolites); Gr. Γέῤῥον, Heb. שׁוּר (?)

Ȧneb, a strong city in the Delta.

Ȧneb ḥetch-t, "White wall," Gr. Λευκὸν τεῖχος, the 1st Nome of Lower Egypt (Memphites); , the eastern quarter of Memphis, , the "White-walled City" (Memphis).

Ȧneb Sebek, a quarter of Memphis.

Ȧnbeth, , , IV, 797, a Sûdânî country; situation unknown.

Ȧnpu, , , the 17th Nome of Upper Egypt (Cynopolites).

Ȧnpu mer ānkh, B.D.G. 60, an estate of .

Ȧnpu sānkh, B.D.G. 60, a town in the Nome Ȧnpu.

Ȧnem, a town in the Theban Nome.

Ȧnm'im' (?), , L.D. 3, 156, a district in Syria; situation unknown.

Ȧnem'rȧ, L.D. III, 252, 67, a district in Syria; situation unknown.

Ȧnmua (?), IV, 797, a Sûdânî country, situation unknown.

[Ȧ]ner en Beḥuṭ, the sandstone quarry of Edfû.

Ȧner ruṭ, "Sandstone Town," a name of the necropolis.

Ȧnruar, Ḥerusȧṭef Stele 82, a town in the Sûdân.

Ånertha , IV, 789, a district in Syria; situation unknown; Tall al-'Amârnah .

Ånrethu , IV, 690, the district of Ullaza (?)

Ånkenna , IV, 797, a Sûdânî country; situation unknown.

Ån ta neter-t , , Denderah.

Åntebt , IV, 805, a Sûdânî country; situation unknown.

Ånttepus , IV, 802, a Sûdânî country; situation unknown.

Ån Thar , a district near Edfû.

Ånthaqeb , IV, 791, a district in Syria; situation unknown.

Ånthka , Rec. 20, 116, a district in Syria; situation unknown.

Ånṭḥu , ( ), Ḳubbân Stele 30, B.D.G. 1320, a swampy district in the Nome , Natho; Assyr. , Gr. Ναθώ, Νεουτ.

Åntches , B.D. 15 (Litany), a mythological locality.

Åra, Åla , IV, 788, a district in Syria; situation unknown.

Åra (Åla) , , a town on the Island of Meroë, 'Alwah; Arab. علوه.

Årit (Pårit) , , : (1) a district in the Nome of Set; (2) a district in the Nome Sma-Beḥuṭ.

Årara , Gol. 4, 3, a district; situation unknown.

Årâna , IV, 710, a district in Syria; situation unknown.

Åri , , a name of Sekhem (Letopolis).

Årpenkha , IV, 793, a district in Syria; situation unknown.

Åri sheps , Rec. 27, 4, a town in Egypt.

Åru , T. 351, the name of a country.

Åru , M. 181, the name of a town.

Åru , Rec. 23, 125, a name of Ḥebenu .

Åruna (read **Åuna**) , , Ionia and the Ionians, Greeks, etc.; Heb. יָוָן, Ezek. xxvii, 13, Isa. lxvi, 19, בְּנֵי הַיְּוָנִים, Joel iv. 6, Assyr. , , Copt. ОⲨⲈⲈⲒⲈⲚⲒⲚ, ОⲨⲈⲒⲚⲒⲚ.

Årapakha , Rec. 20, 116, , IV, 719; var. ; Assyr. , Gr. 'Αρραπαχῖτις.

Årp-ḥesp , , , , a name of Sunnu (Aswân).

Årapusnen , Rec. 20, 117, a district in Syria; situation unknown.

Årmåa (?) , IV, 796, a Sûdânî country; situation unknown.

Årm'then , L.D. 3, 252, 126, a district in Syria, situation unknown.

Årenna , , , Treaty 26, a district in Syria; situation unknown.

Ȧrnam', Rev. 2, 4, 92, a district in Syria; situation unknown.

Ȧrnir (?), IV, 789, a district in Syria; situation unknown.

Ȧrenth, Mar. Aby. II, 4, 15, , , Annales 4, 129, the Orontes; Assyr. .

Ȧr-t Rā , , "Eye of Rā"—a name of Thebes.

Ȧrherr (?), L.D. III, 252, 70, a district in Syria; situation unknown.

Ȧras, IV, 790, , Rec. 21, 98, , Rec. 10, 209, , , Rec. 32, 69, , a district in Syria; Tall al-'Amârnah .

Ȧrras, Nástasen Stele 53, a country in the Eastern or Southern Sûdân.

Ȧrsha . . . ., IV, 793, a district in Syria; situation unknown.

Ȧrka, Gol. 4, 8, a district; situation unknown.

Ȧrkan, Rec. 20, 116, a district in Syria; situation unknown.

Ȧrkara, Rec. 20, 116, , Ḥerusȧtef Stele 28, a city and country in the Sûdân.

Ȧrkarka, Mar. Aby. II, 2, a district; situation unknown.

Ȧrgaṭ, a district in Northern Syria; Tall al-'Amârnah .

Ȧrteti (?), , , a district in the Nome **Ka-Kam** (Athribites).

Ȧrtȧqana, Alt-K. 121; compare אֶלְתְּקֹן, Joshua xv, 50.

Ȧrtug, L.D. III, 131, a district in Syria; situation unknown.

Ȧrtut, IV, 687, a district in Syria; var. ; Tall al-'Amârnah .

Ȧrtnai (?), Ḥerusȧtef Stele 157, a country in the Sûdân.

Ȧrtenu, L.D. III, 131, a district in Syria; situation unknown.

Ȧrtgu, Rev. 19, 18; see **Ȧrtug**.

Ȧrth, Ȧrtheth, , , a country in the Sûdân.

Ȧrtha, Rec. 20, 118; see .

Ȧrthakna, IV, 788, a district in Syria; situation unknown.

Ȧrthu, Mar. Karn. 38, , , , Rev. 3, 159, , , IV, 689, , IV, 788, , , Gol. 4, 2, a district in Syria; Tall al-'Amârnah (?)

Ȧraṭ, Arvad; Heb. אַרְוַד, Tall al-'Amârnah (other forms are: , , , etc.), Gr. 'Ορθωσία, Arab. أرواد, the modern Ruwâd.

Ȧraṭana, Rec. 20, 118, a district in Syria; situation unknown.

Ȧhau (?), IV, 798, a Sûdânî country; situation unknown.

Ȧhat (?), IV, 805 (Ram. III,), a Sûdânî country; situation unknown.

Ȧhi en Bast, a quarter of Sheṭenu.

Ȧḥaa, IV, 798, a Sûdânî country; situation unknown.

Ȧḥautt, IV, 806, a Sûdânî country; situation unknown.

Ȧḥni (?), Rec. 15, 68, a town in Egypt.

Ȧkhnȧ, IV, 802, a Sûdânî country; situation unknown.

Ȧkhenu, Rec. 28, 23, Leontopolis.

Ȧs, Ȧss, B.D.G. 70, a town near Memphis (?)

Ȧsti, the two Egypts—Upper and Lower.

Ȧs en neteru neterit, a sanctuary in Heliopolis.

Ȧs-t au ȧb, Denderah.

Ȧs-t au ȧb enti neteru nebu, Denderah.

Ȧs-t ȧabi, B.D.G. 15, a district near Neruṭef.

Ȧs-t ȧab-s Ḥe-t-Ḥer, Denderah.

Ȧs-t ȧāḥ, B.D.G. 11, "Seat of the Moon," *i.e.*, the capital of the Oasis of Tchestchestt or (Dâkhlah).

Ȧs-t ȧb = **Per-bar-ȧs-t**, a town in the Western Delta; Arab Balbês بلبيس.

Ȧs-t ȧb Rā, Palermo Stele, B.D.G. 14, a sun-temple near Ṣaḳḳârah.

Ȧs-t ȧr menu en Ḥe-t-Ḥer er seḥetep neteru, Denderah.

Ȧs-t ȧr-t (?) Ḥeru, "Seat of the Eye of Horus," *i.e.*, a district in Sekhet-Ḥemam (Wâdî an-Naṭrûn).

Ȧs-t Ȧs-t emkhet ḥā-s, Denderah.

Ȧs-t ȧten em nub, a temple of Horus at Edfû.

Ȧs-t uāb, "Holy place," *i.e.*, Philae.

Ȧst Unep, a name of Edfû.

Ȧs-t ur-t en ḥem Ḥeru-Ȧakhuti, a common name of the shrine of Harmakhis.

Ȧs-t per Ḥet-Ḥer kher menu, Denderah.

Ȧs-t per seshem en Ḥet-Ḥer urth nebt taui ȧm, Denderah.

Ȧs-t pesȧs ta, a name of Denderah, "bake-house."

Ȧs-t pesh Nebti, "place of the division of the two Horus gods," *i.e.*, Denderah.

Ȧs-t m's menu ent Ḥet-Ḥer ȧms, Denderah.

Ȧs-t m' snef sa, Denderah.

Ȧs-t Menti, a place in the region of Mareotis.

Ȧs-t mer ȧb en Rā, the sanctuary of Hathor at Denderah.

Ȧs-t meskhen-t en Ȧsı, "birthplace of Isis"—a name of Denderah.

Ȧs-t nai, a village near Edfû.

Ȧs-t nefer-t, a temple of Horus in Ḥensu (Herakleopolis).

Ȧs-t nefer-t, the temple of Hathor at Denderah.

Ȧs-t nefer-t en neteru neterit, the temple of Denderah.

Ȧs-t enth mut Ḥeru, Denderah.

Ȧs-t en Rā, Edfû.

Ȧs-t ent Rā Ḥeru-ȧakhuti, Denderah.

Ȧs-t en Ḥur (?), a town near Sni (Asnâ).

Ȧs-t enth ḥem-t nesu, "Seat of the Queen," *i.e.*, Denderah.

Ȧs-t ent Ḥet-Ḥer nebt Ȧn, Denderah.

Ȧs-t n sek tchet, Denderah.

Ȧs-t en ta neterit em tchām, Denderah.

Ȧs-t neterui, Edfû.

Ȧs-t neteru, a sanctuary of Ȧmen-Rā in Pa khen Ȧment (Diospolis Parva).

Ȧs-t Rā, or **Rā ḥep-t**, a temple of Rā in Denderah.

Ȧs-t Rā, a temple of Horus in Edfû.

Ȧs-t hi, "Place of joy," *i.e.*, Denderah.

Ȧsut Ḥeru, "The Seats of Horus," *i.e.*, Denderah.

Ȧs-t ḥeḥ, "Seat of Eternity": (1) Denderah; (2), a sanctuary in Bekha; (3), a common name for the tomb.

Ȧs-t ḥeq, "Seat of the Governess," *i.e.*, Edfû.

Ȧs-t khaṭbut em āq en netert ten, Denderah.

Ȧs-t khnem ȧten, Edfû.

Ȧs-t sekhem ānkh en neter, Denderah.

Ȧs-t sekhenu en ākhemu, "Place where divine images alight," *i.e.*, the Theban Necropolis.

Ȧs-t sekhen en Ḥeru ȧakhuti, Edfû.

Ȧs-t sekhen en suatch ba, Sni (Asnâ).

Ȧs-t shātu menu en neb Ȧn ȧm-s, Denderah.

Ȧs-t shā meḥtt, the sandy region north of Lake Moeris.

Ȧs-t shā shemā, the sandy region south of Lake Moeris.

Ȧs-t Shu, Edfû.

Ȧs-t shepset ḥent neterit, Denderah.

Ȧs-t sheta-t, the temple of Edfû.

Ȧs-t qen Ḥeru em baḥ mut-f Ȧst, Denderah.

Ȧs-t Qerḥit, a sanctuary in Thek (Pithom).

Ȧs-t Tem, *i.e.*, Ȧn (On, Heliopolis).

Ȧs-t Tem = **Per-Ȧtem** = **Thek**, the Pithom of the Bible.

Ȧs-t tekh, "Seat of drunkenness," *i.e.*, Denderah.

Ȧs-t tettet, a district (?) in the Fayyûm.

Ȧs-t The, a sanctuary near Dakkah.

Ȧs-t ṭa kaut, a town or village near Memphis.

Ȧs-t Ṭemṭ, the sanctuary of Osiris at Saut (Lycopolis, Asyûṭ).

Ȧs-t ṭekh enth Ḥeru-ȧakhuti, "Seat of the drink (or drunkenness) of Rā Harmakhis," *i.e.*, Denderah.

Ȧs-t tcheser, Denderah.

Ȧsar, Anastasi I, 23, 6, Asher; compare Heb. אָשֵׁר, Josh. xvii, 7.

Ȧsȧr Nemur (Merur), the temple of Osiris-Mnevis.

Ȧsi, IV, 707, Mar. Aby. II, 2, Rec. 32, 69, Rec. 19, 18, Cyprus; Gr. Κύπρος. The form which is found on the Canopus Stele (l. 9) is a corruption of **Ȧuntȧnai.**

Ȧsi (?), Rec. 20, 116, a district in Syria; situation unknown.

Ȧsir, Gol. 4, 5, Asher; compare Heb. אָשֵׁר.

Ȧsur, Ȧssur, IV, 668, 726, Mar. Karn. 38, Assyria; Assyr. , Heb. אַשּׁוּר, Syr. ܐܬܘܪ, **Athûr.**

Ȧssur, with, the Assyrian.

Ȧsb-t, "the throne" par excellence, a name of Edfû; varr.

Ȧspau, IV, 798, Rec. 20, 114, a Sûdânî country; situation unknown.

Ȧser (?), Mar. Aby. II, 2, Asher (?)

Åserhebu, IV, 804, a Sûdânî country; situation unknown.

Åsḥemu, a town near Tanis.

Åsqarna, Åsqalna, Israel Stele 27, Ascalon; Heb. אַשְׁקְלוֹן, Tall al-'Amârnah. The modern 'Asqalân.

Åstses, IV, 803, a Sûdânî country; situation unknown.

Åsthen, IV, 802, a Sûdânî country; situation unknown.

Åsṭṭ, Ashdod; Heb. אַשְׁדּוֹד, Assyr.

Åsṭrs, III, 143, a city in the Southern Sûdân.

Åshamb, IV, 791, an Asiatic country; situation unknown.

Åshar (?), Syria.

Åshushkhen, IV, 783, a district in Syria; situation unknown; var. Alt-K. 153.

Åsher, IV, 1019, the quarter of Thebes that contained the temple of Mut.

Åsher, B.D.G. 102, a canal of Bubastis.

Åshseth, IV, 800, a Sûdânî country; situation unknown.

Åqa, Rec. 20, 116, a district in Syria; situation unknown.

Åqar, IV, 785, a district in Syria; situation unknown.

Åqen, a district near the Second Cataract.

Åqsu, IV, 805 (Ram. III,), a Sûdânî country; situation unknown.

Åqṭua, IV, 781, a district in Syria; situation unknown.

Åkaita, Ḳubbân Stele 9, Rec. 14, 97, a gold-producing district in Nubia.

Åkarkar, Nåstasen Stele 51, a country in the Sûdân.

Åkartå, L.D. III, 88A, a country in Syria; Tall al-'Amârnah.

Åkat, Mar. Aby. II, 2, a district in Syria (?)

Åkath, Annales IV, 130, a district in Syria; situation unknown.

Åku, a district in Upper Egypt (Gebel Aḥmar ?).

Åkes, Åkses (?), B.D. 149, a city in the 9th Åat.

Åksep, IV, 782, a district in Syria; Heb. אַכְשָׁף (Josh. xi, 1), Assyr.

Åkesh; see; Heb. כּוּשׁ, Assyr.

Åktames, IV, 786, a district in Syria; situation unknown.

Ågert, Ågertt, the necropolis of Ån (Heliopolis); varr.

Ågerbemren, Canopus Stele 25 = , the Herakleum; see .

Åtår, IV, 781, a district in Syria; situation unknown.

Åtåkar, IV, 791, a district in Syria; situation unknown.

Åti, , , B.D. (Saïte) 142, I, 20, the 9th Nome of Lower Egypt (Busirites).

Åtu, L.D. III, 209C, a district in Syria; situation unknown; , a canal in the Delta.

Åtur, IV, 791, a district in Syria; situation unknown.

Åtur, a town near Thebes.

Åtur āa, "great stream," *i.e.*, the canal of the 2nd Nome of Lower Egypt; , the Canopic arm of the Nile; varr. , ; , West stream, the Canopic arm of the Nile.

Åtur ent Ta-ṭesher (?) , a well at the 1st station on the Ḳanâ-Ḳuṣêr road.

Åtugenr, IV, 790, a district in Syria; situation unknown.

Åteb, B.D.G. 78, a town in the Thebaïd; , a district in the Nome (Apollinopolites).

Åtbana, IV, 791, a district in Syria; situation unknown.

Åtef peḥ, , ; see .

Åtef khent ; see .

Åteftit, B.D.G. 79, , Mission 13, 3, a town in Northern Nubia; Tasitia (?)

Åtmem (?), IV, 782, Alt-K. 178, a district in Syria; Heb. אֲדֻמִּים, Josh. xv, 7, xviii, 17.

Åtnep, IV, 801, a Sûdânî country; situation unknown.

Åtra, , IV, 796, a Sûdânî country; situation unknown.

Åter shemā, a name of Coptos.

Återti shemā, temple of Osiris at .

Åtremåāu, N. 796, a Sûdânî country; situation unknown.

Åtrennu, IV, 791, a district in Syria; situation unknown.

Åtrten, IV, 792, a district in Syria; situation unknown.

Åthabu, B.D. 163, 1, a Nubian city (?)

Åtga, IV, 805, a Sûdânî country; situation unknown.

Åttauma, IV, 792, a district in Syria; situation unknown.

Åthana, IV, 791, a district in Syria; situation unknown.

Åthar, Rec. 20, 118, , a district in Syria.

Åthimaā, Rev. 12, 86, Western Thebes; Copt. ϪΗⲘⲈ.

Âthitaui , a fortified town on the Nile between Memphis and Mer-tem.

Âtheniu , IV, 806, a district in the Sûdân.

Âthshet (?) B.D.G. 101, a town in Egypt.

Âṭah , the 4th station on the Ḳanâ-Ḳuṣêr road.

Âṭir (Âṭil) , L.D. III, 252, 28, , a district in Syria; situation unknown; Heb. אַדָּר, Josh. xvi, 5.

Âṭṭaqnâ , Alt-K. 204, a district in Syria; situation unknown.

Âṭurm' (Âṭulm') , a district in Syria; situation unknown.

Âṭurna , Anastasi I, 22, 5, a district in Northern Syria; Heb. אֲדוֹרַיִם, 2 Chron. xi, 9.

Âṭmâa , L.D. III, 252, 55, , a district in Syria; Heb. אָדָם, Josh. xix, 36.

Âṭm', Âṭum' , , Edom; Heb. אֱדוֹם, Gr. Ἰδουμαία, Assyr.

Âṭr, Âṭraua , , Mar. Aby. II, 2, a district in Syria (?)

Âṭremam , L.D. 3, 252, 19, Adoraim; Heb. אֲדוֹרַיִם, 2 Chron. xi, 9.

Âṭeḥ , , , , , , , , , B.D.G. 39, 1320, a swamp district in the 7th Nome in the Delta; **Nâṭḥ** = Natho.

Âtchai , Anastasi I, 22, 4, , Alt-K. 205, a district in Syria; situation unknown.

Âtchana , Rec. 20, 115, a district in Syria; situation unknown; Heb. אׇזֵן, 1 Chron. vii, 24.

Âtchannâuâ (?) , IV, 794, , Alt-K. 208, a district in Syria; situation unknown.

Âtchet , a town in the Fayyûm.

Âtchtem , Rec. 20, 115, a scribe's mistake for , IV, 798.

Ā Argsanṭres

"palace of Alexander," *i.e.*, Alexandria.

Ā meḥti , Lower Egypt.

Ā en Uatchit Sessu , Anastasi I, 27, 5, the country of Uatchit of Sessu.

Ā[ui?] en Ḥāp-t , the two doors of the Nile town (Elephantine?)

Āâatchmâa , Eg. Res. 81, 66, a district in Syria; situation unknown.

Āâru , B.D.G. 104, a temple of Osiris in Ḥe-t-ta-ḥer-âb (Athribis).

Āai-t en Beḥuṭ , Edfû.

Āaina , IV, 783, 785, a district in Syria; situation unknown; compare Heb. עִיּוֹן, 1 Kings xv, 20.

Āau, Āu, , IV, 800, a district in the Sûdân; situation unknown.

Āauah, Āauh, , IV, 798, a Sûdânî country; situation unknown.

Āauneh, Rec. 20, 114, a scribe's mistake for , IV, 798.

Āabs neb nebs, a town in the Nome Åm Khent (Bubastites).

Āam, a country of Western Asia, or Western Asia; see the following:

Āamtt, , Western Asia; var. .

Āa em ma ḥeru, , name of the site of the temple of Rameses II at Abû Simbel.

Āamqu, IV, 785, , a district in Syria; situation unknown; compare Heb. עֵמֶק.

Āamthen ....., , , , Ins. of Methen, a village in the Delta.

Āa-t enti āap, "temple of the Winged Disk," a name of Edfû.

Āarna, L.D. III, 252, 32, , IV, 1651, 782, , IV, 650, a district in Syria; situation unknown.

Āareṭåa, Eg. Res. 83, 110, a district in Syria; situation unknown; compare Heb. עֲרָד, Judges i, 16.

Āareṭåa Nebatbath, L.D. III, 252, 110 and 111, a district in Syria; situation unknown. Read , Nebata.

Āareṭåat Rebath, L.D. III, 252, 108 and 109, a district in Syria; situation unknown.

Āak, , IV, 783, , , Accho or Ptolemais; Heb. עַכּוֹ, Tall al-'Amârnah, Assyr., Phoen. עך, Arab. عكّا, Syr. ܥܟܘ, Gr. Ἄκη.

Āagana, a town near Gebelên; var. .

Āatåka, a district in Syria; situation unknown; compare Heb. עֲתָךְ, I Sam. xxx, 30.

Āaṭṭmåa, L.D. III, 252, 79, a district in Syria; situation unknown.

Āaṭ en sekhet (?), B.D.G. 136, the 2nd station on the Ḳanâ-Ḳuṣêr road.

Āatchaba, , B.D.G. 137, Mendes.

Āāa, Rec. 20, 114, a Sûdânî country; situation unknown.

Āāi (?), B.D.G. 104, a town in Egypt.

Ākhākhui (?), B.D.G. 132, a town on the site of Sararîyah.

Āina, perhaps the district of Moses' Wells; compare Heb. עַיִן.

Āinini (?), Anastasi I, 27, 6, a district in Syria; situation unknown.

Āunu-åb, a town in the Nome of Sep .

Āubur, IV, 798, a district in Syria; situation unknown.

Åutarā, IV, 785, a district in Syria; compare Heb. עֲדְרֶעִי.

Āb, B.D.G. 105, a town in Egypt.

Ābui neteru, a village near Memphis.

Āpu, a town near Thebes.

Āpur, Harris 500, a district; situation unknown; compare Heb. עֵפֶר.

Āper, a sanctuary of Osiris.

Āper: (1) a district of Memphis; (2) a town in the Delta.

Āper, B.D. 141, 142, 90, a town in the Ṭuat.

Āperåar, Alt-K. 254; compare Heb. עפר אל.

Āper ur, IV, 783 "Great Āper"—a district in Syria.

Āper sher, IV, 783, "Little Āper"—a district in Syria.

Āmau, Rec. 32, 69, a region in the Sûdân.

Āmau, Rec. 32, 66, , Rec. 19, 19, a Sûdânî country whence came gold.

Āmamu, Rec. 3, 2, , Sphinx 4, 121, , a country in the Sûdân; , the people of the same.

Āmu, IV, 329, a district in the land of Punt.

Ān, the Nome Heroopolites (the Arabian Nome) in the Eastern Delta.

Ān, , B.D.G. 117, , , the capital of the Nome (Heroopolites).

Ānu, , , , , , Piānkhi Stele 3, A.Z. 1900, 130, districts in the 3rd, 8th and 15th Nomes of Lower Egypt; varr. , .

Ān, the quarries of Ṭûrah opposite Memphis.

Ān, , IV, 785, a district in Syria; compare Heb. עֵין.

Ānu . . . . . n, Rec. 20, 115, a foreign country; situation unknown.

Ānep, P. 499, , , Rec. 27, 87, , , Hymn Darius 27, , , Thmuis in the Delta.

Ānnagar, Eg. Res. 70, 110, a district in Syria; situation unknown.

Ānnemgar, Ānnagar, Rec. 20, 118; see .

Ān ḥer, Denderah.

Ānkh, "The City of Life," *i.e.*, Thebes.

Ānkhtt, , "Land of Life," a name of the Necropolis.

Ānkhiu Khufu, B.D.G. 125, an estate of Khufu.

Ānkh shet, B.D.G. 127, the name of an estate of Khāfrā, and of Shepseskaf.

Ānkh taui, , , , , "Life of the Two Lands," *i.e.*, a district of Memphis.

Ānkh taui, the name of a necropolis.

Ānshau, IV, 781, a people or country of Northern Syria.

Ānqenāmu (?), IV, 786, a district in Syria; compare Heb. ענקנעם for עןיקנעם (Alt-K. 273).

Āntui, Āntchui (?), B.D.G. 122, a district in the 4th Nome of Lower Egypt (Prosopites), ; see Ä.Z. 47, 50; , , , , B.D.G. 133, the canal of the district; , , Dem. Cat. 425, Rec. 33, 123, Gebelên in Upper Egypt.

Āntennu (?), B.D. 169, 22, a mythological locality (?)

Āntch, a town in Egypt; = ; = , B.D. 125 (Neg. Confession).

Āntch, , , : (1) a district in the 2nd Nome of Lower Egypt; (2) a canal in Mendes.

Āntchem, IV, 802, a Sûdânî country; situation unknown.

Āntchemet, , , IV, 798, a Sûdânî country; situation unknown.

Āntchttȧ, T. 146, , T. 266, , M. 422, the god of Āntchet (?)

Ārit, , a town near Beni Ḥasan.

Ārutcha, , , a canal in the Nome Theb-neter (Sebennytus).

Ārm', Ārmȧ, Ä.Z. 1899, 73, 49, 78, , II, 158, Ārmȧ (Ālmȧ), Ārm'tt (Ālm'tt), Elam; Heb. עֵילָם, Babyl.

Ārqatu, IV, 729, a district in Syria; Tall al-'Amârnah

Ārq ḥeḥ, , , , , a name of the tomb of Osiris at Abydos.

Ārka, B.D.G. 131, a town in Egypt.

Ārti Ḥeru, , , , , , : (1) a part of the town of ; (2) the capital of the Nome Men.

Āhau, IV, 798, , Rec. 22, 114, a Sûdânî country; situation unknown.

Āhuur, IV, 804, a Sûdânî country; situation unknown.

Āḥ ȧakhu, a name of the tomb of an Apis bull.

Āḥ-t ur-t, , a sanctuary of Ȧmen-Rā in the Nome Sȧpi shemā.

Āḥā, a quarter of the town of Ḥensu (Herakleopolis).

Ākh, Ākhui (?), , B.D.G. 133, a town near Per Mātchet (Oxyrhynchus).

Āsterut, , IV, 782, a district in Syria; situation unknown; compare Heb. עַשְׁתָּרוֹת.

Āqett, a country which produced turquoises.

Āqen, Āken, Āgen-t, , , , , , a canal in Mendes.

Āqna-t, Ḥerusȧtef Stele 93, a city in the Sûdân; Gr. Ἀκίνη (?); see Pliny VI, 184.

Āka, L.D. III, 131, Akko; Heb. עַכּוֹ, Tall al-'Amârnah, Gr. Ἄκη, Arab. عَكَّا, Syr. ܥܟܘ.

Ākatem (?), a town in Egypt.

Āken, Rec. 10, 140 =.

Āken, Āgen, , , , B.D.G. 135, a town near Asnâ.

Ākna, Anastasi I, 21, 4; see **Āka**.

Āksapu, Anastasi I, 21, 4, a district in Syria; compare Heb. אַכְשָׁף (?)

Ākesh [], B.D. 142, 4, 9, a town famous for the cult of Osiris.

Āgni (?), , Rec. 10, 140, a town near the modern Mata'anah.

Ātchaḥuth, Eg. Res. 82, 85, a district in Syria; situation unknown.

Iāabar (Iāabal), Rec. 20, 118; see.

Iāan, Anastasi I, 22, 1, a district in Syria; situation unknown.

Iāqebȧar, Iāqebȧal, , (*sic*), IV, 785, , , a district in Syria; compare Heb. יַעֲקֹב אֵל.

Iua, , , IV, 798, , Rec. 20, 114, a Sûdânî country; situation unknown.

Ib, Elephantine; Heb. papyrus יב; see **Abu**.

Ib (Demotic) = , Elephantine.

Ium', the sea, a large lake, applied to Lake Moeris; Heb. יָם, Copt. ⲉⲓⲟⲙ; , *i.e.*, "the sea," whence the Arabic Al-Fayyûm الفَيّم.

Imār, Alt-K. 218, a foreign city; situation unknown.

Iurm', IV, 793; see **Urm**.

Iureḥum', L.D. 3, 252, 112, , Eg. Res. 85, 139, a district in Syria; situation unknown.

Iurṭen, Alt-K. 231, the Jordan district; Heb. יַרְדֵּן.

Iurtcha, Eg. Res. 84, 133, a district in Syria; varr. , IV, 783, , , IV, 783, Tall al-'Amârnah.

Iuḥamam, Eg. Res. 78, 35, a district in Syria; situation unknown.

Iuṭhmārk, L.D. 3, 252, 29, a country or district; site unknown. Its name means neither "kingdom of Judah," nor "hand of the king."

Ib, Rev. 11, 130, 153, 12, 53; see **Abu**, Hebrew papyrus יב.

Ibrāamu, Iblāamu, IV, 783, a district in Syria; compare Heb. יִבְלְעָם.

Ipu, , IV, 783, , Anastasi I, 25, 2, Joppa; Tall

al-'Amârnah, Heb. יָפוֹ, Gr. Ἰόππη, Arab. يافا, Syr. ܝܘܦܐ.

Im' ent Ḥau-nebu B.D.G. 180, the Ionian Sea.

Im en seqeṭ-t, the Red Sea.

Imḥ, a town in Egypt.

Inaȧuā, a town near Memphis.

Inuāmu, Rec. 20, 118, IV, 74, 665, 744, Israel Stele 27, a district in Syria; Tall al-'Amârnah.

Intchath, Rec. 20, 118, Alt-K. 226, a district in Syria; situation unknown.

Irut (Ilut), IV, 785, a district in Syria; situation unknown.

Irep, Rec. 20, 117, a district in Syria; situation unknown.

Irṭuna, Anastasi I, 23, 1, Jordan; read; Heb. יַרְדֵּן.

Irtcha, IV, 783, IV, 783, IV, 648, L.D. III, 252, 59, a district in Syria; situation unknown.

Ih, a suburb of Memphis.

Iha, Rec. 20, 118, a district in Syria; situation unknown.

Iḥm' (Iḥem), Iḥemm', IV, 784, IV, 649, a district in Syria; situation unknown.

Isantȧ, Rec. 20, 115, a district in Syria; Heb. יְשָׁנָה, 2 Chron. xiii, 19.

Ikama, a district in Syria; situation unknown.

Igaṭi, Anastasi I, 17, 8, a district in Syria; situation unknown.

Itȧkhab, IV, 789, a district in Syria; situation unknown.

Uatu Ḥeru [ ], Anastasi I, 27, 2, a fortress in the Eastern Delta.

Uaȧ, IV, 804, a Sûdânî country; situation unknown.

Uaāpekȧu (Demotic), the district of the Gap at Abydos.

Uainn (Demotic), Ionia, Greece, Greek.

Uauat, [ ], Rec. 2, 120, a province of Northern Nubia;, the Nile of Nubia.

Uauā[h], Rec. 20, 114, a scribe's mistake for **Ruṭuāhu** [ ], IV, 798.

Uabu-t, Rev. 4, 101, the 19th Nome of Lower Egypt (Oxyrhynchites).

Uaf, a town near Memphis.

Uanres, Famine Stele, a Sûdânî country whence came silver.

Uarshai, II, 158, Rec. 22, 137, Orchoë.

Uarth, IV, 685, a district in Syria; situation unknown.

Uahȧ, A.Z. 51, 71, Oasis, Khârgah (?)

Uahthuarkȧ...., Alt-K. 318, a district or town in Syria.

Uaḥ (?), A.Z. 51, 71, the Oasis par excellence, *i.e.*, Khârgah; Copt. ⲟⲩⲁϩⲉ, Arab. واح, واحة.

Uaḥ-t, near Ta ȧa-t ent Nenu, an oasis not identified.

Uaḥ, the country of the Oasis; Copt. ⲟⲩⲁϩⲉ.

Uaḥ ȧst (?), IV, 1134, a town in Egypt.

Uaḥ-t meḥ, Northern Oasis, Oasis Parva, *i.e.*, Baḥarîyah.

Uaḥ-t res, Southern Oasis, Oasis Magna, *i.e.*, Khârgah.

Uakh, the Oasis of Khârgah.

Uas, P. 702, the 4th Nome of Upper Egypt (Diospolites).

Uas, Thebes, the capital of the 4th Nome of Upper Egypt.

Uas-Meḥ, Thebes of the North, *i.e.*, Thebes in Lower Egypt (Diospolis Parva).

Uas Shemā, Thebes of the South, *i.e.*, Thebes in Upper Egypt (Diospolis Magna).

Uash baiu, a town in Egypt.

Uag, a station on the Ḳanâ-Ḳuṣêr road.

Uaten [ ], Sphinx 14, 158, a town in the Delta.

Uatch, the 10th Nome of Upper Egypt (Aphroditopolites); for the reading see Rec. 35, 1.

Uatch-t, the capital of the 10th Nome of Upper Egypt (Aphroditopolis); Rec. 18, 181, 27, 84, = the town on both sides of the river; Rec. 35, 12, the eastern part of the city.

Uatch ur, a canal in the 6th Nome of Upper Egypt.

Uatch ur, Rec. 27, 190, the "Great Green Water," *i.e.*, the Mediterranean Sea; compare Eth. ባሕር : ዐቢይ : Brit. Mus. 660, Or. 35, 2, 18.

Uatch urȧ āa Meḥu, the "Very Great Green Water of the North Land," *i.e.*, the Mediterranean Sea.

Uatch ur Ḥau nebtiu, B.D.G. 180, A.Z. 1900, 130, the Ionian Sea.

Uatch Mer, a town in Egypt.

Uatches, the town of Buto.

U-ȧmen (?), "hidden district."

Uȧtatchtȧm, IV, 805, a district in the Sûdân; situation unknown.

Uāb-t, Philae.

Uāb, , , , Silsilah.

Uāb-t, the shrine of Horus of Edfû.

Uābu, a district in the Sûdân; situation unknown.

Uāb ȧsut, the pyramid of Userkaf .

Uān, IV, 891, a country of Northern Syria.

Uāni (?), Rev. 14, 18, a town in Egypt (?)

Uār, , , , a name of Kher-āḥau (Babylon of Egypt); the two parts of the city were , .

Uār, , a district in Lower Egypt.

Uār-t, , , , a name of the Nile and of certain canals leading into Uār.

Uārkhata (?), B.D.G. 1011, a town in Egypt.

Uis, Rec. 6, 8, a town in Egypt.

Uu Benu, , a district in the Nome (Tanites).

Ubeḥ (?) [], IV, 800, a Sûdânî country; situation unknown.

Up neterui, , a quarter of the town of Mendes.

Ups (?), Nȧstasen Stele 45, a country in the Sûdân.

U Peq, , , , , , , , B.M. 448, , the district of the Gap, the name of a large "gap" in the mountains behind Abydos.

U Peqr, Ikhernefert 20; see ; varr. , .

Uu Pega, , , , variant of the preceding.

Upta (?), L.D. III, 16A, in , Ṭu en Up ta "Mountain of the Crown of the earth," *i.e.*, a district to the south of Egypt.

Up tesh, B.D.G. 22, the entrance to the Fayyûm.

Umess, Rec. 20, 114; see **Amessu** [], IV, 798.

Un, , , , the 15th Nome of Upper Egypt (Hermopolites).

Un, B.D. 149, , a city of the 12th Ȧat.

Unn, the "City of hours" (?)

U nai, IV, 789, a district in Syria; situation unknown.

Unȧs-t, a town; site unknown.

Uu en ānkh [], name of a part of Sni (Asnâ).

Unu Meḥ, , a town near the modern Damanhûr—Hermopolis Parva.

Unu Shemā, U. 311, , T. 259, , Rec. 31, 169, , , B.D. 28, 5, , Unu, the capital of the 15th Nome of Upper Egypt, Hermopolis; also called Unu of the South, .

Uu en uāb, a district in Egypt.

Ununȧt (?), name of a place (?)

Unp , , , B.D.G. 149 = , Edfû.

U en nesu Taui , a district near Memphis.

Uu en Rā nefer , , Piānkhi Stele, a town near Bubastis.

Unḥtchartȧ , a lake or canal near Tanis.

Unkh , a town in the Nome Tekh.

Unes , , , B.D. 125, II, , Hermopolis of Upper Egypt.

Unes , , , a canal in Upper Egypt.

Unshek , Bubastis 34A, a district in the Sûdân.

Un ta uat em nefer-t Men-kheperrā , IV, 814, Rec. 13, 203, name of the canal made by Thothmes III in the First Cataract.

Unth , B.D. 125, Neg. Con. (var.), a district in Egypt (?)

Uu en Thar , a district in the Eastern Delta.

Ur-t , , , B.D.G. 154, a canal near Edfû.

Ur , the Labyrinth.

Ur , Rec. 2, 112, a Theban cemetery = .

Ur ȧab-t Menkheperrā , Annales 3, 110, a temple of Thothmes III.

Ur ȧmakh , an estate of Ȧssȧ.

Ur manu , an estate of Khufu.

Ur Khāfrā , the pyramid of Khāfrā.

Ur kau , an estate of Khāfrā.

Ur ka Saḥurā , an estate of Saḥurā.

Uri, Urit , , B.D. 125, Neg. Con., a town in Egypt.

Urit , a canal or lake at Tanis.

U Ru (?) , , , Rec. 20, 116, 118, a district in Syria; situation unknown.

Urm' , IV, 793, a district in Syria; situation unknown.

Uhȧ , Rev. 12, 62, Oasis; Copt. ογαϩε.

Uheb , , the swamp land of the Nome (Busirites).

Uhem kheper , , Denderah.

Uḥ-t , IV, 676, a country conquered by Thothmes III.

Uḥat , the name of a country, the region of the Oases (?)

Uḥā ta , Rec. 27, 191, , , a suburb of Heliopolis.

Uḥut , , Stat. Taf. 31, a district; situation unknown.

Uu Ḥeru , , , "estate of Horus," a name of several districts in Egypt.

Uu Ḥeru-maati (?) , , , , a district in the Nome of Thes-Ḥeru.

Us , A.Z. 1877, 146 = , Thebes.

Uspenpet, Bubastis.

User, Unu (Hermopolis Magna).

User (Demotic), Thebes.

User, a mountain in Northern Syria.

User, Edfû.

User ḥat, B.D.G. 165, the house of the sacred boat Åmen-user-ḥati at Thebes.

User Kheper Rā, Sphinx 14, 163, a town in Egypt (?)

Usekh, Rec. 15, 88, a town in the Oasis of Khârgah.

Usekh-t Maāti, the temple of Osiris at Athribis.

Usesh sekhef res, etc., Denderah.

Us (?) seshmi, Rec. 11, 129, a town in Egypt.

Ustt, a portion of the 14th Nome of Upper Egypt.

Ukemtt, Famine Stele, a Sûdânî country whence came mother of emerald.

Ug, B.D.G. 173, a canal in the Delta.

Uga, B.D.G. 172 = , q.v.

Ugar, a canal in the 7th Nome of Upper Egypt.

Utåu, Uthåu, IV, 797, a district in the Sûdân; situation unknown.

Utuit ḥetch, B.D.G. 175, a frontier station of the 2nd Nome of Upper Egypt.

Utent, Uthent, IV, 798, B.D. 64, 19, a Sûdânî country; situation unknown; varr.

Utennutt, a Sûdânî country; situation unknown.

Utheth, a Sûdânî country; var.

Uthentiu, IV, 617, a Sûdânî people.

Uthes Ḥer, the 2nd Nome of Upper Egypt (Apollinopolites).

Uthes ḥeḥtt, the Necropolis of Abydos.

Uṭent, IV, 803, a Sûdânî country; situation unknown.

Utcha, a name of Egypt as the country of the Eye of Rā.

Utchārit, IV, 1027, a district in the Delta.

Utchā tchatchau (?), a town in the Fayyûm.

Uu tcheser sesheta, a district near Bubastis.

Ba, the pyramid tomb of Nefer-årikarā.

Baiu, the pyramid tomb of Åti.

Ba-t, the 3rd station on the Ḳanâ-Ḳuṣêr road.

Ba-ti, A.Z. 46, 69, the Two Lands (Egypt).

Ba neb Ṭeṭ (Tcheṭ), B.D.G. 185, or Per Ba neb Ṭeṭ, the capital of the Nome Ḥat meḥit, Mendes; Assyr.

Ba-tet, Rec. 11, 161, Mendes.

Baȧa, Rec. 20, 115; see **Baȧm**.

Baȧm, IV, 798, a Sûdânî country; situation unknown.

Baȧrut, IV, 782, 986, a district in Syria; compare Heb. בְּאֵרוֹת, Josh. ix, 17, 2 Sam. iv, 2.

Baȧrratcha, L.D. III, 252, 123, a district in Syria; situation unknown.

Baitȧ Āntȧ, L.D. III, 156, a district in Syria; Heb. בֵּית־עֲנוֹת, Josh. xv, 59.

Baitȧ Shaȧr, Anastasi I, 22, 8, a district in Syria; situation unknown.

Baitȧ Ṭaquna, Alt-K. 331, a district in Syria; compare Heb. בֵּית־דָּגוֹן, Josh. xv, 41, xix, 27.

Baitȧ Ṭuquna, Rec. 20, 117; see.

Bau, IV, 797, a Sûdânî country; situation unknown.

Bauȧ, L.D. III, 187, a country in Syria; situation unknown.

Bau-Kem, Bau-Qem, Bau-Gem, B.D.G. 211, a Sûdânî country whence the worship of Hathor, Shu, Tefnut, and other Sûdânî gods was introduced into Egypt.

Batu (Baut), a Sûdânî country; situation unknown.

Babar (Babal), Rev. 11, 167, Babylon; Heb. בָּבֶל; var., Babyl., Pers.

Bar, Bur, IV, 783, Eg. Res. 71, 112, a district in Syria; situation unknown.

Barbar, Rec. 20, 115, a Sûdânî country; situation unknown.

Barȧst, B.D.G. 197, a city in the Delta near the Libyan frontier.

Barua, Nȧstasen Stele 18, the capital of the Island of Meroë, the ruins of which lie near the modern village of Bagrawîr, about 40 miles south of the Atbarâ; Gr. Μερόη, Μεροαῖος.

Barbatu, Eg. 73, 106, a district in Syria; situation unknown.

Barmam, L.D. III, 252, 33, a district in Syria; compare Heb. בִּלְעָם, 1 Chron. vi, 70, in Manasseh (Brugsch).

Barhaȧ, Gol. 4, 9, a foreign country; situation unknown.

Barg, L.D. III, 131, a district in Syria; situation unknown, Tall al-'Amârnah.

Bartȧ , Anastasi I, 20, 8, a district in Syria, Bêrût; Tall al-'Amârnah , Gr. Βηρυτός, Arab. بيروت, Eth. ቤሩት፡

Bahit , the name of a country, "white marble country"; compare Heb. בַּהַט, Esther i, 6.

Baḥt , a suburb of Memphis.

Baḥṭeṭ , Sphinx 3, 239 = **Beḥuṭ** (?)

Bakh, Bekha, Bekhatt , , , , , , , , , , , , , , B.D. 108, 2, 15, the country of sunrise, the East.

Bakhther , Maskhûṭah Stele, Bactria; Pers. , Babyl. .

Bast , , , , , , IV, 432, , , , Bubastis; see **Per Bast**.

Bash , , IV, 800, a Sûdânî country; situation unknown.

Baq , , a name of Egypt.

Bak , , IV, 800, , Ḳubbân Stele 5, , B.M. 138, Rec. 15, 171, , , , , , Rec. 34, 186, a town in Nubia; Gr. 'Αβουγκίς.

Bak (Ḥe-t Bak) , B.D.G. 210, a temple of the hawk (ⲂⲎⲔ) of Horus, Hierakonpolis (?)

Baka nefer-t en Neb-[er]-tcher , Denderah.

Bakem , Rec. 20, 115; see **Bau-Qem**.

Bagarua , Gol. 4, 10, a foreign country; situation unknown.

Batȧntȧ , IV, 786, a district in Syria; situation unknown.

Batȧ Thupar , Anastasi I, 22, 5, a district in Syria; compare Heb. בֵּית־סֵפֶר (?)

Bat Āarmam (Bat Āalmam) , a district in Syria; situation unknown. Alt-K. (385) compares Heb. בֵּית־עוֹלָם.

Batia , IV, 785, a district in Syria; situation unknown.

Batbentȧ , IV, 786; see .

Bat ḥuarn , L.D. III, 252, 24, Beth-horon; compare Heb. בֵּית־חֹרֹן (Josh. x, 10, 11), a city in Ephraim.

Bat shar, Bat shaȧr , , IV, 785, a district in Syria; var. , L.D. III, 131.

Bat shanrȧa , L.D. III, 252, 16; compare Heb. בֵּית־שְׁאָן (1 Kings iv, 12), in Manasseh, west of the Jordan; var. .

Bat tapuḥ , L.D. III, 252, 39, a district in Syria. Alt-K. (389) compares Heb. בֵּית־תַּפּוּחַ.

Bat tarmam , L.D. III, 252, 36, a district in Syria; situation unknown.

Bat-tchabi.... , L.D. III, 252, 45, a district in Syria; situation unknown.

Bathar , Rec. 20, 116, a district in Syria; situation unknown.

Bath āath (?) , L.D. III, 252, 124, a district in Syria; situation unknown.

Bath ānth , L.D. III, 131, , a district in Syria; situation unknown.

Batchana , , IV, 782, a district in Syria; situation unknown.

Bȧa, Bȧat , B.D. 41, 4, , B.D.G. 184, a town in Egypt.

Bȧa-t , a canal near Edfû.

Bȧa-ti (?) , Egypt.

Bȧasta , , Sphinx 14, 160; Copt. ⲂⲈⲤⲒⲀ.

Bȧshu , a town in Lower Egypt.

Bȧket (?) , B.D. 142, 87, , U. 578, , N. 966, a city in the Ṭuat (?)

Bāt (?) Khufu , an estate of Khufu; situation unknown.

Bāḥ , , , , , the capital of the 15th Nome of Lower Egypt (Hermopolites).

Bāḥ Ȧssȧ , , L.D. III, 80, estate of Ȧssȧ, estate of Saḥurā.

Bāḥ , , , B.D.G. 187, 188, the name of several canals.

Bāḥu , the eastern arm of the Nile.

Bi, Bit (?) , B.D.G. 184, a town in Egypt.

Biu , a town in Egypt.

Baut (?) Buut (?) ; var. (?) , IV, 797, a Sûdânî country; situation unknown.

Bu-t ur ent ser neteru , B.D.G. 152, Edfû.

Bu-t beḥen kheftiu , Edfû.

Bu en āḥā , P.S.B. 27, 120; Gr. Βομπαη (?)

Bu-t enti Rā , a solar temple at Denderah.

Bu-t en Rā tchat , the solar temple of Ḥeri-shef neb Ṭeṭ , in the Fayyûm.

Bu-gem ; see **Bau-qem.**

Buṭuṭu, Buṭuitt , , Rec. 2, 140, 19, 22, the city of Naucratis.

Bu tchāmiu , P. 145, M. 182, N. 692, the 19th Nome of Upper Egypt (Oxyrhynchites of the West).

Bu-t Ṭeṭ-ti (Tcheṭ-ti) , Edfû.

Buaiqa , Pap. 3024, 92, Edfû.

Buaiqa en ka nekht user , Edfû.

Bur , Rec. 20, 118, a country conquered by Rameses III.

Buhen , B.D.G. 198, the district of the modern Wâdî Ḥalfah—the Βοῶν of Ptolemy.

[M]bushu (?), IV, 804, a Sûdânî country; situation unknown.

Bukak, IV, 796, a Sûdânî country; situation unknown.

Bebȧ [], IV, 803, a Sûdânî country; situation unknown.

Beber, Bebel, IV, 668, Babylon; Heb. בָּבֶל, Assyr. , Pers. Bâbirush .

Bepset [], IV, 799, a Sûdânî country; situation unknown.

Bemāi (Bum'i?), IV, 781, a district in Syria; situation unknown. Alt-K. (340) suggests that = בָּמוֹת.

Benen, a district of Thebes.

Benu, a temple town of Osiris in Tanis.

Benui (?), a district in Upper Egypt.

Benṭi, a town in Egypt.

Berua, B.D.G. 196, , Nȧstasen Stele 16, Meroë, the capital of the kingdom of the Island of Meroë; var. ; Gr. Μερόη.

Berber (?), a district in Upper Egypt; = κωϲ ϐρϐερ (?)

Berberta; var. , IV, 316, 796, a Sûdânî country; situation unknown.

Bereqna, IV, 786, a district in Syria; situation unknown; Tall al-'Amârnah .

Berget, a town of the god Re-ḥes , in the Fayyûm.

Behen, , capital of the modern district of Wâdî Ḥalfah—the Βοῶν of Ptolemy.

Beḥ, Rec. 3, 50, a town in Egypt.

Beḥ, a town near the modern Al-Ḳâb.

Beḥaa [], IV, 797, a Sûdânî country; situation unknown.

Beḥuit (?) = **Beḥuṭ**, Edfû.

Beḥuk, IV, 802, a Sûdânî country; situation unknown.

Beḥuṭ, Edfû or Udfû.

Beḥuṭ, a district in the Nome Ȧnpu.

Beḥutch, a district in the 6th Nome of Lower Egypt.

Beḥset, Beḥseth, IV, 800, , Rec. 20, 114, a Sûdânî country; situation unknown.

Beḥṭ ur[t] en Beḥuṭ-t, Edfû.

Bekha, Metternich Stele 84, the land of Sunrise, the East; see **Bakh.**

Bekhen; see **Ṭu-en-Bekhan** .

Bekhen, a town which stood on the site of the modern Mît-Ḳamr.

Bekhen ȧrkhen, B.D.G. 203, , a suburb of Busiris.

Bekhen āa nekht: (1) a building of Seti I at Karnak; (2) a name of Tanis.

Bekhen en Biu, B.D.G. 205, a town in Egypt.

Bekhten, Bekhten Stele, an Asiatic country; situation unknown.

Besiṭ, a temple-town in the Nome Metelites.

Best, Bubastis; see **Bast.**

Beq, Rev. 13, 84, Egypt.

Bek, a town near Saïs.

Bekai, Sphinx 14, 164, a town in the Delta.

Bektan (?), IV, 803, a Sûdânî country; situation unknown.

Begshagȧ, IV, 797, a Sûdânî country; situation unknown.

Beta, P.S.B. 14, 238, a town in Egypt.

Bethbeth, IV, 799, a Sûdânî country; situation unknown.

Beṭsh, B.D.G. 212, B.D. 142, 14, a town in Egypt.

Pe, Pi, Pu, N. 11, the town of Buto in the Delta; P. 71, M. 102, N. 10; P. 204.

Pe, Pi, Pu, the temple quarter of the town Per Uatchit, Buto; see Pe-Ṭep.

P-nu-t ur en Ḥeru, Edfû.

Pe-Ṭep, a double town in the Nome Nefer-Ȧment, Buto.

Pa-ȧa en Ȧmen, Sphinx, 14, 160, the capital of the Nome Sma-Beḥṭ.

Pa-ȧner ruṭ, B.D.G. 61, the "sandstone city" *i.e.*, the cemetery.

Pa-ȧra (?), B.D.G. 64, a district in the 11th Nome of Lower Egypt.

Pa-ȧh en penrā (?), Rec. 31, 36, a town in Egypt.

Pa-ȧsḥemu, B.D.G. 72, Rev. 3, 40, a town near Tanis.

Pa-ām'q Āȧatchaȧ, L.D. III, 252, 65 and 66, a district in Syria; situation unknown.

Pa-ā-t en pa uaher, Rec. 23, 49; Copt. ⲡⲓⲛⲡⲟⲱⲣ (?)

Pa-ir, Sphinx 14, 162, a town in the Delta.

Pa-utui, B.D.G. 175, a town in the 17th or 18th Nome of Upper Egypt.

Pa-baiȧa (?), L.D. III, 252, 118, a district in Syria; situation unknown.

Pa-bukh, Ḥeruemḥeb 36, Rec. 19, 18, a district in Syria; situation unknown.

Pa-paȧ, IV, 792, a district in Syria; situation unknown.

Pa-paba, IV, 793, a district in Syria; situation unknown.

Pa-penā, a suburb of Memphis.

Pa-magar, Anastasi I, 19, 2, a district in Syria; situation unknown.

Pa-mu, IV, 798 (Rameses III, , Rec. 20, 114), a Sûdânî country; situation unknown.

Pa-mu en pa Rā, , Sphinx, 14, 163: (1) a canal near Belbês; (2) a canal at Abydos.

Pa-mer, B.D.G. 1064, the region of lake Mareotis.

Pa-nasa, L.D. III, 160, Rec. 8, 137, a district; situation unknown.

Pa-nagbu Åshaḥatȧ, L.D. III, 252, 92 and 93, a district in Syria; situation unknown.

Pa-nagbu Ātchaurḥuth, L.D. III, 252, 84 and 85, a district in Syria; situation unknown.

Pa-nagbu Uahthuarki, L.D. III, 252, 90 and 91, a district in Syria; situation unknown.

Pa-nebs, Nåstasen Stele 29, , Mission 13, 4, , , , , , a town near the modern Wâdî Ḥalfah; Gr. Πνούψ.

Pa-rā, Rec. 17, 120, Abutig, in Upper Egypt; Copt. ⲁⲡⲟⲑⲩⲕⲏ = Ἀποθήκη.

Pa-ruṭ Åment, a town in the Delta.

Pa-ruṭ en pa-Rā, , a town near Tanis (?)

Parbu, Eg. Res. 73, 105, a district in Syria; situation unknown.

Parem, , a canal in the Nome Coptites.

Parekhti, Rec. 11, 146, 12, 24, a town in Egypt.

Pars, II, 128, Persia; see , Old Persian , Baby.

Parqa, L.D. III, 146, 27, a district in Syria; situation unknown.

Pa-ḥaqrȧa Fetiushaȧa, L.D. III, 252, 68 and 69, a district in Syria; situation unknown. In this name and in several following is the Eg. article.

Pa-ḥaqrȧa en Āatchait, L.D. III, 252, 77 and 78, a district in Syria; situation unknown.

Pa-ḥaqer Shanaiȧa, L.D. III, 252, 87 and 88, a district in Syria; situation unknown.

Pa-ḥagrȧa Årqaṭ, L.D. III, 252, 96 and 97, a district in Syria; situation unknown.

Pa-ḥageri Ḥaniniȧu, L.D. III, 252, 94 and 95, a district in Syria; situation unknown.

Pa-ḥager Theruan, L.D. III, 252, 101 and 102, a district in Syria; situation unknown.

Paḥura, IV, 782, a district in Syria; situation unknown.

Pa-ḥuqråa Åabaramā, L.D. III, 252, 71 and 72, "Abram's Field"—a district in Syria; situation unknown.

Pa-ḥer-ḥem (?), a canal in the Nome Latopolites.

Pa-kharm', a canal in the Nome Sethroites.

Pasiu, Rec. 33, 118, a town near Rakoti.

Pasunqa, L.D. III, 88, a district; situation unknown.

Pa-sebti pa-peni, Sphinx 14, 168, a town in the Delta.

Pa-sebti pa ... nuā, Sphinx 14, 164, a town in the Delta.

Pa-sebti pa-setheni, Sphinx 14, 164, a town in the Delta.

Pa-sebt en āameḥ, a part of the town of Sheten.

Pasegnār (?), Rec. 31, 35, a town; situation unknown.

Pa-segerå, Rec. 31, 35, a town; situation unknown.

Pa-shashau-khā, a part of the great temple of Memphis.

Pa-shet en Åneb ḥetch, B.D.G. 59, a part of Lake Moeris.

Pa-qem ur (?), a town in the Eastern Delta.

Pa-ka āa Rā-Ḥeru-åakhuti, a temple of Isis.

Pakākna (?) a district in Syria; situation unknown.

Pa-gem, Per-gem, a town in the south-east Sûdân.

Pa-gem Åten, Nåstasen Stele 36, a seat of the cult of Åten in Nubia.

Pa-gerg, a locality in the Fayyûm.

Pa-ta en Uatchit B.D.G. 148, Alexander Stele, a town in the Nome of Buto; Copt. ⲡⲧⲉⲛⲉⲧⲱ.

Pateb, Demot. Cat. 422, the island of Pathyris; Copt. ⲡⲉⲧⲟⲃ.

Pathen, Pathan, Pethan; see **Pentatehan.**

Pa-tesh en Per Uatchit, a district of Buto.

Patharu, IV, 789, a district in Syria; situation unknown.

Pa-thuf; see .

Pa-thesi, Rec. 12, 24, a town in Egypt.

Pa-ṭmai, a quarter of Thebes.

Pa-tcheṭku, the canal (?) of Avaris.

P-åa uāb, , "holy tomb," or "holy island," *i.e.*, Philae.

P-åa rek, "Island of Rek, or Lek," Philae; Copt. ⲠⲒⲖⲀⲔ.

P-åhi-t, B.D.G. 69: (1) a suburb of Memphis; (2), B.D.G. 68, a town in the Nome Coptites; (3), B.D.G. 69, Edfû.

P-ås-t ent uaher, B.D.G. 160; Copt. ⲡⲓⲛⲡⲟⲱⲣ.

P-ā en p-uaher, Rec. 23, 49; Copt. ⲡⲓⲛⲡⲟⲱⲣ.

Pāpā, B.D.G. 215, a town near Thebes; Copt. ⲠⲀⲠⲎ; Papa of the Itinerary of Antoninus.

Piu = **Pe**.

Pirtau, IV, 788, a district in Syria; situation unknown.

Pi-tchep; see.

Pun, Punt, Palermo Stele, , , , , , a gold-bearing country in the Southern Sûdân, whence came some of the aboriginal Egyptians,

Puntiu, IV, 335.

Pursath, the country of the Philistines;, Thes. 1204, the Philistines; Heb. פְּלִשְׁתִּים, Assyr. and, Rawl. C.I.W.A. I, 35, 1, 12, II, 52, 1, 40.

Purath, IV, 793, a district in Syria; situation unknown.

Puhartå, a canal in the Eastern Delta.

Puqa, a district of Abydos; see.

Puqi, IV, 793, a country and a people in Northern Syria.

Puqiu, IV, 793, a district in Syria; situation unknown.

Putaui, A.Z. 35, 18, an estate in the Oxyrhynchite Nome.

Puther...., Rec. 20, 116, a northern country conquered by Rameses III.

P-mu en Utcha Ḥeru, B.D.G. 183, a canal of Edfû.

P-mu en set en Sebek, a canal in Upper Egypt.

P-mer, a town near Asnâ.

Pemkha, B.D.G. 296, a village near Thebes; Copt. ⲡⲙⲙⲟϣ (?)

P-mesrā, a town in Egypt.

Pen Abṭu, B.D.G. 18, a canal at Abydos.

Peninaåuā; see **Inaåuāā**.

P-nebes, , a town near the modern Wâdî Ḥalfah; Gr. Πνούψ.

Penshāṭ, a canal in the Nome Latopolites.

Penshenu, , a canal in the Nome Patarest.

Pentatehan, , , , a canal in the 21st Nome of Upper Egypt.

Per (?) (Åa-per?), , B.D.G. 120, Crocodilopolis in the Fayyûm.

Per, a town in the Eastern Delta.

Per åau, a part of Memphis.

Per Åakh or **Per sha**: (1) a district near in Upper Egypt; (2) Nåstasen Stele, a town or village in the Sûdân.

Per åakhut, a name of the temple of Hathor at Denderah and of other shrines of Hathor.

Per åakhut Åment, the Osiris temple of Libya-Mareotis.

Per Åār-t Åusāasit, a temple in Ånu (Heliopolis).

Per åāḥu, temple of the Moon.

Per åi, B.D.G. 9, a sanctuary at Sekhem (Letopolis).

Per Åimḥetep sa Pteḥ, the Asklepeion of Memphis.

Per åunr (Påunr?), IV, 793, a district in Syria; situation unknown.

Per Åmen, "house of Åmen," the great temple of Åmen in Thebes and other towns in Egypt and Nubia.

Per Åmenmeri Rāmess āa nekhtut, the town of Rameses in the Eastern Delta; Heb. רַעְמְסֵס, Gen. xlvii, 11.

Per Åmenḥetep, the temple of Åmenḥetep III at Thebes (Luxor).

Per Åmentå, Sphinx 14, 157, a town in the Delta.

Per Åneb, A.Z. 1907, 46, Memphis.

Per Ånpu, Sphinx 14, 156, B.D.G. 59, Rec. 3, 38: (1) a town in the Delta; (2) part of the quarries of Ṭûra; (3), B.D.G. 60, a temple in Alabastronpolis.

Per Ånḥer, B.D.G. 63, a name of This, Sebennytus, etc.

Per åri, Karnak 52, 15, B.D.G. 66, Sphinx 14, 156, A.Z. 1869, 98, a town in the Delta (Prosopis?).

Per Åḥu neb Åmentt, a quarter of the town of Ḥet-neh (Metelis).

Per Åst, the temple of Isis near the Great Pyramid.

Per Åsår, the name of many sanctuaries of Osiris.

Per Åsår, Rec. 31, 35, Demot. Cat. 422, Abûṣîr; Copt. ПОΥCIPI, Arab. ابوصير.

Per Åsår neb Ṭeṭ, Busiris—the capital of the Nome Busirites; Assyr.

Per Åsår Nemur, the temple of Osiris-Mnevis.

Per Åsår Reqeṭ, Sphinx, 14, 161, the temple of Osiris at Rakoti (Pakoϯ).

Per Åsår Khenti-Åmenti, the chief temple of Osiris at Abydos.

Per Åsṭes, B.D. 145, 81, the temple of a form of Thoth.

Per åqer …, Hermopolis in the Delta.

Per åtef Ånḥer-Shu sa Rā …, a name of This.

Per Åtem …, "House of Tem"; …, a town in the Eastern Delta (Succoth); Heb. פִּתֹם, Exod. i, 11, Gr. Πάτουμος 'Αραβίας, Copt. ⲡⲉⲑⲱⲙ.

Per Åten …, the temple of Åten built by Åmenḥetep IV in his town of Åakhut-en-Åten (Tall al-'Amârnah).

Per āa …, "great house," a name of the Necropolis.

Per Āait …, Denderah.

Per Āakheperkarā …, Rechnungen 35, an estate near Memphis.

Per Ānnuit …, Denderah.

Per ānuq …, Rec. 10, 140, the capital of the Nome Maḥetch.

Per ānkh …, Denderah.

Per ānkh …, Rec. 27, 88, the city of the dead, *i.e.*, Deadland.

Per ānkhet …, B.D.G. 126, …, Rec. 17, 119, Bakchis on Lake Moeris.

Per ānkh åru …, "temple of the living," a name of the Necropolis.

Per Āḥa …, a district near Per Mātchet.

Per Uas …, the temple of Åmen-Rā at Napata.

Per Uatchit …, Rec. 31, 35, …: (1) the capital of the 19th Nome of Lower Egypt; (2) a name of Denderah, Buto; Copt. ⲡⲟⲩⲧⲟ, Gr. Βουτώ.

Per uāt …, B.D.G. 140, the temple of Denderah.

Per uāb …, the temple of Osiris at Abydos.

Per Upuatu shemā …, the temple of Upuatu in the south (Lycopolis).

Per Uniu (?) …, B.D.G. 149....

Per Unnut …, B.D. 137, 38, a temple in Hermopolis.

Per unkh …, the temple of Osiris in the 15th Nome of Lower Egypt.

Per ur …, the temple of Osiris in Aphroditopolis.

Per ur en mat …, a temple near the granite quarries at Aswân.

Per ut (?) …, Aphroditopolis.

Per ut (?) …, B.D.G. 174, the burial place of Set.

Per utet en ḥem-t set …, the temple of Denderah.

Per Ba …, B.D.G. 185, a sanctuary of the Ram of Mendes.

Per Ba en Åsår …, a temple near Lake Moeris.

Per Ba neb Ṭeṭ (Tcheṭ) …, Rev. 11, 145, the capital of the 16th Nome of Lower Egypt, Mendes; Assyr. …

Per Baiu , Rec. 10, 142, a town in the Delta.

Per Barȧst , Karnak, 52, 7, a town near the western frontier of the Delta.

Per Bast , , , , Bubastis; Gr. Βούβαστις, Βούβαστος, Copt. ⲡⲟⲩⲃⲁⲥⲧ, Heb. פִּי־בֶסֶת, Arab. تل بسطة.

Per Bast meḥt , Bubastis of the North, *i.e.*, Bubastis in the Delta.

Per Bast shemā , , B.D.G. 207, Bubastis of the South, *i.e.*, of Upper Egypt, or Denderah.

Per bak , , Denderah.

Per bu tcheser , B.D.G. 209, the temple of Smataui, , q.v.

Per Benu , Rec. 10, 141, Farshût.

Per bener enth ta neterit , Denderah.

Per Pekht , temple of Pekht near Beni Ḥasan (Speos Artemidos).

Per Pekht , , , Pekht or Pekhit.

Per pestch neteru , , the temple-town of Osiris in the Mendesian Nome.

Per pestch neteru , , , , , a name of Babylon of Egypt and of many other sanctuaries.

Per peg , P.S.B. 20, 123; Piānkhi Stele 20, a town in Upper Egypt.

Per Pteḥ , , the temple of Ptaḥ and its district at Memphis.

Per Pteḥ shetat , a temple in the Nome of Memphis.

Per fa Ȧsȧr ȧn kaut (?) , B.D.G. 170, : (1) the temple of Denderah; (2) a shrine in the Delta.

Per fa-ā , IV, 1031, a temple of Menu at Thebes.

Per fa mut enth neteru , the temple of Denderah.

Per fefȧ , , Peasant 37, a town; situation unknown.

Per em , a town in Nubia; Primis (?)

Per ma , Karnak 54, 49, A.Z. 83, 66, a temple; position unknown.

Per maākheru en Usrit , Denderah.

Per Manu , A.Z. 35, 18, a district in the West (?)

Per mȧ , an estate in the Delta.

Per M'gu , Mission 13, 117, , a town in the Nome Ka-ḥeseb, .

Per M'tennu (?) , Rec. 1, 52, a town in Egypt.

Per M'tch , , , , Demot. Cat. 422, Oxyrhynchus, the capital of the 19th Nome of Upper Egypt; Copt. ⲡⲉⲙϫⲉ, ⲡⲙϫⲏ.

Per Mut, a town near Hypsele; Muthi of the Itinerary of Antoninus (?)

Per Mut, the sanctuary of Mut at Thebes; varr. , .

Per Menā, , Minyâ in Upper Egypt; Copt. ⲦⲘⲘⲞⲞⲚⲎ.

Per Menu, B.D. 125, 2, 20, , temple of Menu at Âpu (Panopolis); , the canal of Âpu.

Per mennsh Rā (?), Rec. 12, 20, a town in the Delta.

Per Menth, Hermonthis; Copt. ⲁⲣⲙⲁⲛⲑ, ⲁⲣⲙⲟⲛⲑ, Armant; , temple of Mentu in Thebes.

Per mer, , Rec. 10, 140, a town between Asnâ and Al-Ḳâb.

Per mer (Pamer), , , , , , , Mission 13, 8, the temple of Isis at Philae.

Per mer, , , , , , B.D.G. 1177, the district of Mareotis.

Per Merȧu (?), IV, 1123, a town in Upper Egypt.

Per Merit (?), A.Z. 1900, 130, a name of Naucratis.

Per merḥ, the name of several places in Egypt; var. .

Per mes, , , the birth chamber of a god in a temple.

Per Mess, , , the great temple at Abû Simbel.

Per mes-t en Nut, the "birthplace of Nut," *i.e.*, Denderah.

Per mes Rekhit, , Denderah.

Per mes Ḥeru-sa-Ȧst, , , Denderah.

Per Metcha, Rev. 11, 178, Oxyrhynchus; Copt. ⲠⲈⲘϪⲈ.

Per en ȧmi ȧakhut, , , Denderah.

Per Nut, a quarter of Memphis.

Per nub-t, , : (1) the capital of the Nome of Nubt; (2) a town in the Western Delta; Assyr. (?)

Per nubit, , Denderah.

Per Neb ȧam, , , Sphinx 14, 157, , A.Z. 1807, 46, the capital of the 3rd Nome of Lower Egypt.

Per Neb-t neha, , , , a quarter of Memphis.

Per Neb-t ḥetepit, a suburb of Ȧn (Heliopolis).

Per Neb-t ḥetepit, a town near Tanis.

Per Neb khet en Tem, Denderah.

Per nebs, Ḥerusȧtef Stele 21, , Nȧstasen Stele 25, a town near the modern Wâdî Ḥalfah; Gr. Πνούψ.

Per Neb seger, a temple at Thebes.

Per Neb tepu åḥ, Piānkhi Stele, a town in the 17th Nome of Upper Egypt (Aphroditopolis); Copt. ⲠⲈⲦⲠⲒⲈϨ.

Per en pa Mennu, a town in Egypt.

Per en pa Rā en Rāmeses meri Åmen, temple of Rā founded by Rameses II at Memphis.

Per Nefer, a town in Egypt.

Per Nefer ḥer-s, Denderah.

Per nemḥu, Rec. 11, 168, a town in Egypt.

Per ent meḥ, the Necropolis of Saïs; Copt. ⲠⲀⲚⲞⲨϤϨⲎⲦ.

Per en nub, Denderah.

Per ent res, the Necropolis of Saïs; Copt. ⲠⲀⲚⲞⲨϤⲢⲎⲤ.

Per neha, a district of Athribis; Copt. ⲠⲀⲚⲀϨⲞ, Arab. بنها, Benhâ.

Per nehem; see **Ḥet-nehem.**

Per en Ḥeru Neb Måā, the temple of Horus of Måā[m] in Nubia (near Ibrîm, Primis).

Per nekhi en Åsår (Rā), B.D.G. 170, Denderah.

Per Nekhebit, the sanctuary of Nekhebit at Eileithyiaspolis.

Per en Kheper, Sphinx 14, 158, a town in the Delta.

Per nes[er], Palermo Stele, A.Z. 45, 126, a shrine of Uatchit.

Per nesu (?), a name of Saïs.

Per Net, Sni (Asnâ).

Per neterit, a sanctuary of Isis at Sni (Asnâ).

Per Neteru, Denderah.

Per neter ṭuaut, the temple of the high-priestess of Åmen-Rā at Thebes.

Per netchem, a village near Pelusium.

Per netch Rā em ā Āapep, the temple of Denderah.

Per netch Ḥeru em ā Set, the temple of Denderah.

Per Rā, B.D.G. 414, "house of Rā," *i.e.*, Heliopolis; Heb. בֵּית־שֶׁמֶשׁ, Jer. xliii, 13.

Per Rāmessu - meri - Åmen, the town of Rameses II in the Eastern Delta, Gen. xlvii, 11, Exod. i, 11, xii, 37, Numb. xxxiii, 3, 5; Heb. רַעְמְסֵס, LXX Ῥαμεσσῆ.

Per Rāmeses - ḥeq - Ånu, a town of Rameses II in the north of the Delta.

Per ruṭ, a village near Memphis.

Per Repit, Denderah.

Per rema, a district near Edfû.

Per remtu åm en Åsår, Denderah.

Per Rennit, a name of .

Per renput en ta neterit, Denderah.

Per Ruruti, B.D. 78, 30, house of Shu and Tefnut (?)

Per reḥu (?), a district near Oxyrhyncus.

Per rekhit, Denderah.

Per rekh en Åst, the "town of the knowing of Isis," *i.e.*, Denderah.

Per hai-ni en mesu Geb, Denderah.

Per hina, the temple of Åmen at Karnak.

Per ḥa, a town in the Nome Aphroditopolites.

Per Ḥapṭ-re, B.D. 125, III, 13, a temple in Egypt and the Ṭuat.

Per Ḥāp, the capital of the supplementary Nome of Per Ḥāpi .

Per Ḥāpi, a district in the Nome Heliopolites.

Per Ḥebit, capital of the Nome ; Arab. بهبيت = Paḥebit.

Per Ḥep, Nilopolis in the Eastern Delta.

Per Ḥepṭ ur, a town in Egypt.

Per Ḥefau, a town near the modern Gebelên.

Per ḥen, a temple of Osiris in the Nome Ka Kam.

Per ḥenu, B.D.G. 1063, the sanctuary of the Ḥenu Boat of Seker at Memphis.

Per Ḥennu, a sanctuary.

Per Ḥent shemā, Denderah.

Per Ḥeru, IV, 1132, the name of several temples of Horus.

Per Ḥeru åab, Asphynis, the modern Aṣfûn al-Matâ'nah, 18 miles south of Luxor.

Per Ḥeru åment, a name of Ḥesfen ; Arab. اصفون, Tuphium.

Per Ḥeru åti nef ṭesher-t, Denderah.

Per Ḥeru åthi-nef ḥetch-t, Denderah.

Per Ḥeru Bat (?), B.D.G. 186, the temple of Horus in Theb-neter (Sebennytus).

Per Ḥeru Beḥuṭ, a sanctuary built by Usertsen I.

Per Ḥeru merti, a town in the Nome Ka-ḥeseb; Copt. ⲫⲁⲣⲃⲁⲓⲧ, Pharbaethus.

Per Ḥeru merti, the temple of Sheṭen.

Per Ḥeru nub, the capital of the Nome Ṭuf.

Per Ḥeru neb Mesen, a temple of Horus at Edfû.

Per Ḥeru khenti-khat, a temple of the unborn Horus near Athribis.

Per ḥeri neb åabt, Sphinx 14, 164, the modern Faḳûs.

Per Ḥer shefit nesu taui, the temple of Ḥeru-shefit in Ḥensu (Herakleopolis).

Per Ḥet-Ḥer, capital of the Nome P-ṭesh en Per Ḥet-Ḥer; Copt. ⲡⲁⲑⲟⲩⲣⲓⲥ, ⲡⲁⲑⲟⲩⲣⲓⲧⲏⲥ.

Per Ḥet-Ḥer, Denderah.

Per Ḥet-Ḥer, a village near Tanis.

Per Ḥet-Ḥer åst qem (?), a town in the Nome Pathyrites.

Per Ḥet-Ḥer nebt Mafkit, Sphinx 14, 157, a town in the Delta.

Per Ḥet-Ḥer nebt Ḥe-t Sekhem, the temple of Hathor at Diospolis Parva.

Per Ḥet-Ḥer neb-t Tepi-åḥ, the temple of Hathor at Aphroditopolis.

Per ḥetch, a sanctuary near Asphynis and Hermonthis.

Per ḥetcha, P.S.B. 17, 18, a sanctuary in Nubia.

Per khat en ḥem-t-set, Denderah.

Per khebit, a temple in Sekhem (Letopolis).

Per kheper ānkh, Sphinx 14, 155, a town in the Delta.

Per Khemenu, Hermopolis in Upper Egypt.

Per Khen, Palermo Stele, Denderah.

Per Khnem, the temple of Khnemu in Latopolis.

Per Khnemu, a district in the Fayyûm.

Per Khnemu neb Ḥe-t ur-t, the temple of Khnemu in the Nome Maḥetch.

Per Khnemu neb Shasḥetep, the temple of Khnemu in Hypselis.

Per Khensu, the temple of Khensu at Thebes.

Per en Khensu-em-Uas-Nefer-ḥetep, the temple of Khensu Neferḥetep in Thebes.

Per Khensu-pa-åri-sekher-em-Uas, the temple of Khensu, the arranger of destinies.

Per khenti menȧt-f, B.D. 67, 3, a mythological temple (?)

Per khenti Tenen, a temple (?) of Ptaḥ or Osiris in Memphis.

Per kheru, , the name of a canal.

Per kherp āḥ, , a sanctuary.

Per Kherp-kheper-Rā, a town on the great canal that fed Lake Moeris.

Per khet, the temple of Osiris at Mendes.

Pers, Persa, Persu, L.D. 3, 283, , , II, 158, , II, 128, , II, 91, , , Persia; Pers. , Baby.

Per sat, a temple of Uatchit at Letopolis.

Per sai, Met. Stele 8; see **Per sui.**

Per sȧaḥ Rā, a district of Latopolis.

Per sui, Met. Stele, a temple in Nut-ent-Ṭeb , Atfīḥ.

Per Sutekh, a name of Avaris, Pelusium, Ombos, etc.

Per Seb Netert, a town in the Fayyûm.

Per sebkh-t, the Labyrinth .

Per Sebek, , , Crocodilopolis, capital of the Nome Arsinoïtes.

Per Sebek ȧuf ȧri shāit, *i.e.*, Berget , a town in the Fayyûm.

Per Sep, a town near Ȧn (Heliopolis).

Per Sepa, Methen, an estate in the Delta.

Per Sepṭ, , Dream Stele 36, , , Sphinx 14, 165, , a town in the Eastern Delta, Faḳûs(?); Assyr.

Per sensen, Hermopolis Magna.

Per sennu (shennu ?) en nub, Ḥerusȧtef Stele 27, a temple in Napata.

Per seḥep, B.D. 104, 5, a mythological locality.

Per Sekhmit, a name of several temples of this goddess.

Per sekhem en Rā, Denderah.

Per sekhem khenti Khaṭa, Denderah.

Per seshen, a temple in the Nome of Ka-ḥeseb (?)

Per Seker neb Seḥetch, Piānkhi Stele, a temple of the god of the district of Mêdûm.

Per seger, a temple of Osiris in Busiris.

Per Seti, B.D. 125, I, 10, a temple of the fire-goddess.

Per Setem, a temple of Osiris; position unknown.

Per shaā (?) (?), A.Z. 51, 79, a temple; position unknown.

Per Shepset ḥent neterit [hieroglyphs], [hieroglyphs], [hieroglyphs], [hieroglyphs], the temple of Hathor at Denderah.

Per Shentit [hieroglyphs], [hieroglyphs], a temple at Abydos.

Per shesthet [hieroglyphs], Methen, an estate in the Delta.

Per shet erṭu en Ȧsȧr [hieroglyphs], B.D.G. 171, Denderah.

Per sheṭṭȧ en Ȧsȧr [hieroglyphs], Denderah.

Per qen [hieroglyphs], a town in the Nome Ka-ḥeseb.

Per qen Ḥeru utet tef-f Ȧsȧr [hieroglyphs], Denderah.

Per qerȧs Ȧsȧr [hieroglyphs], [hieroglyphs], [hieroglyphs], Denderah.

Per Qerḥit [hieroglyphs], a temple in the Nome Heroopolites.

Per kaut [hieroglyphs], the town Tepi àḥ (Aphroditopolis).

Per Kamkam [hieroglyphs], a temple in Hermonthis.

Per Gebu [hieroglyphs], Sinsin I, 10, a name of the Earth.

Per Gem [hieroglyphs], N. 22, a town in the Ṭuat.

Per gem Ȧten [hieroglyphs], [hieroglyphs], A.Z. 1902, 110, [hieroglyphs], the name of several temples of Ȧten,

Per gerr (gell) [hieroglyphs], [hieroglyphs], Sphinx 14, 167, a town in the Eastern Delta = [hieroglyphs].

Per ta ȧnt [hieroglyphs], B.D.G. 48, a town or district; position unknown.

Pertȧua [hieroglyphs], Maskhûṭah Stele, Parthia; Pers. [cuneiform], Babyl. [cuneiform].

Per tep ṭu-f [hieroglyphs], [hieroglyphs], B.D. 125, I, 13, a sanctuary of Anubis in Ḥebenu.

Per Tefnut [hieroglyphs], [hieroglyphs], [hieroglyphs], Denderah.

Per Tem [hieroglyphs], [hieroglyphs]; see [hieroglyphs], Succoth.

Per Tem Tchak [hieroglyphs], Sphinx 14, 165, Pithom-Succoth.

Per Teḥen [hieroglyphs], the temple of Osiris at Saïs.

Per teka [hieroglyphs], a town in Egypt.

Perth [hieroglyphs], a locality near Memphis.

Per Ṭeḥuti (Tcheḥuti) [hieroglyphs], Hermopolis in Upper Egypt.

Per Ṭeḥuti up reḥui [hieroglyphs], [hieroglyphs], Hermopolis in Lower Egypt.

Per ṭes [hieroglyphs], [hieroglyphs], a town in Egypt.

Per ṭesu [hieroglyphs], Methen, an estate in the Delta.

Per tchatcha [hieroglyphs], Rec. 10, 141, 17, 119, [hieroglyphs], Rec. 21, 13, a town between Per Benu and Gerg (Girgâ); Copt. ⲡⲭⲱⲭ,

Per tcheftchef , a sanctuary of Harmakhis in .

Per tchet , "Everlasting House"—a name of Denderah.

Pehābās , Rev. 11, 185 = Copt. ⲁⲫⲟⲃⲱⲥ.

Peḥanu , IV, 797, a Sûdânî country; situation unknown.

Peḥu , , , , the swampy ground in many parts of Egypt.

Peḥ ȧr-ti (?) , a district in the Delta.

Peḥ ān , , a canal in the Nome Ȧment.

Peḥ Bāḥ , B.D.G. 187, a part of the Nome Ȧm peḥ.

Peḥ neter , , , , the back part of the Nome Aphroditopolites.

Peḥ Qenus , Mission 13, 4, the back part of Nubia.

Pekh-t, Pekhit , , , a temple of , , near Beni Ḥasan (Speos Artemidos).

P-Khann , , a canal in the Nome Pathyrites.

Pekhar ur Nehern , IV, 587, the "Great Bend" in Northern Mesopotamia.

P-serāk , B.D.G. 221, "scorpion town"—a name of , in the Western Delta; Copt. ⲡⲉⲥⲟⲕ.

Pesrun , R.E. 2, 43, a town in Egypt.

P-Serk , , , , , , a town in Nubia, Ψέλχις, Pselchis.

Pesg re , , , [ ], B.D. 142, 94, a town famous for the cult of Osiris; var. .

Pest , R.E. 2, 43, a district; position unknown.

P-shaim' , a village near Memphis.

P-shet ȧshṭ , B.D.G. 75, a lake in Heliopolis.

Peshnu , B.D. 36, 2, a town of Khnemu.

Peq, Pequ , , , , a district of Abydos; see . For , see .

Peq Khāfrā , L.D. II, 12, a district near Memphis.

Peqr , , , , , , , the tomb of Osiris at Abydos.

Peqr-t the canal of Peqr at Abydos.

Peqḥ , a seat of the cult of Isis.

Peg , a district of Abydos; see Peqr .

Pega , B.D. 169, 18, a town in Egypt.

Pegi , Sphinx 14, 164 a town in the Delta.

Peguat , Ṣân Stele, the town of Canopus.

Pegrer , Sphinx 14, 166, a lake in the Delta.

Peges , B.D. 142, II 18, the name of a town and of a god.

Petat (?), a district of Heliopolis.

Petaih (?), B.D.G. 139, a quarter of Memphis.

Petenmut, the capital of a district in Nubia; the Πτεμυθις of Ptolemy.

Petenḥer, Mission 13, 4, a town in Nubia between the Third and Fourth Cataracts; Pontyris (?)

Pet en Kam, "the heaven of Egypt"—a name of Ȧn (Heliopolis).

Petentem, Rec. 20, 114, a country conquered by Rameses III.

Peterti (?), Merti (?), Ȧr-ti (?), the swamp land of the Nome of Ka-ḥeseb; , a town near Ȧnu.

Peterti, Rec. 29, 146, , a mythological locality, and the low-lying land of the Nome (Cabasites).

Petrȧ, , a large canal in the Tanite and Diospolite Nomes.

Pteḥ ān, L.D. 2, 50, a town in Egypt.

Pteḥ men sānkh, a town near Ȧn.

Pteḥ nefer, a town in Egypt.

Pteḥ nefer mer Ȧssȧ, L.D. II, 80, an estate of King Ȧssȧ.

Pteḥ res ȧneb-f, a district of Memphis.

Pteḥ ḥe-t Ka, , a name of Memphis; see **Ḥet Ka Pteḥ**, B.D. 106, 1.

Pteḥ ḥes ȧrt n (?), a town in the Libyan Nome.

Pteḥ ḥetep, a village in the Sebennyte Nome.

Pteḥ sānkh, a town in the Nome of Xoïs.

Pteḥ sruṭ, a town in the Delta.

Pteḥ ṭeṭ sheps, a town near Memphis.

Peṭ, , B.D. 142, II, 12, , a town in Egypt.

Peṭasa, I.H. 211, , Mar. Aby. II, 4; , Rec. 8, 140, a Mediterranean country and people.

Peṭr, IV, 792, a district in Syria; situation unknown.

P-ṭesh en Per Ḥet-Ḥer, a district of Thebes.

Peṭṭi shu, Mar. Mon. 2, 2.

P-tchatcha; ; see ; Copt. ⲡϫⲱϫ.

Fa, a suburb of Memphis.

Fat Ḥeru [ ], B.D. 141, 122, a town of Osiris.

Fariua, IV, 791, a district in Syria; situation unknown.

Fāg, , , , , a temple of Osiris in the 3rd Nome of Upper Egypt.

Fenkhtt, a foreign country; , the two lands of the foreigners.

Fensh; see **Fenkhtt**.

Ferȧm'āa, a district in Syria; Alt-K. (439) compares Heb. פִּרְאָם (Josh. x, 3).

Fek, Fekau, A.Z. 49, 130, , a town in Egypt.

Feka , I, 56 = , Turquoise land—the Sinaitic Peninsula.

Feka , a town near Lake Mareotis.

Fetiushaȧ (?) , Eg. Res. 81, 69, a district in Syria; situation unknown.

Maā-t , , , , a district in the Sebennyte Nome.

Maāti , , , , , : (1) a sanctuary at Letopolis in Lower Egypt; (2) the great Judgment Hall of Osiris.

Maāti (?) , , a sanctuary in the Nome of Libya-Mareotis.

Maāmaā (Mam) , a town in Nubia, Primis (Ibrîm).

Maām, Māȧām (?) , IV, 812, , , , , , , Ḳubbân 6, a district and city in Northern Nubia, Primis (Ibrîm).

Maāt kheru , Rec. 27, 190, a town in the Nome of Sepṭ.

Maikhentka (?) , Nȧstasen Stele 57, a Sûdânî country; situation unknown.

Mauaȧa , Gol. 4, 8, a country; situation unknown.

Mautu ; var. , IV, 799, a Sûdânî country; situation unknown.

Mau-t khenti , a district; situation unknown.

Maat baiu Khufu , an estate of Khufu.

Mabara , Mar. Karn. 52, 11, a district; situation unknown.

Mam , Bubastis 34A, a Sûdânî country; situation unknown.

Manatȧ , Rec. 20, 115, a Sûdânî country; situation unknown.

Ma en Ȧsȧr-Teni , a district near Denderah.

Ma-t en Ḥeṭ-Ḥer , a district in the Nome Pathyrites.

Ma-t en Tarr , a district near Denderah.

Manu , , , , , , , , , , the West, the country of the sunset.

Maanra (?) , , L.D. III, 219, a district; situation unknown.

Marem' , L.D. III, 156, IV, 781, a district in Syria; situation unknown; compare Heb. מָרוֹם.

Maḥetch , , the 16th Nome of Upper Egypt.

Makha taui , , , "balance of the Two Lands"—a name of Memphis.

Mas, Masi , , IV, 800, , Rec. 20, 115, a Sûdânî country; situation unknown.

Masa , I.H. 216, , , ,

R.E. 3, 160, , a country; situation unknown.

Mas khemi , R.E. 11, 122, 12, 29, a town in Egypt.

Masha , Nâstasen Stele 53, a town in the Sûdân.

Magar , Anastasi I, 19, 2, a district in Syria; situation unknown.

Mater (?) Ḥeruȧkau , an estate of King Ḥeruȧkau; situation unknown.

Matha , B.D. 116, 2, a town of Neith.

Maṭ , , , Mar. Karn. 42, 23, , Rec. 32, 65, , , Rec. 32, 65, a suburb of Thebes.

Mȧareth , Rec. 20, 119, a country conquered by Rameses III.

Mȧu , IV, 796, Koller 4, 3, Rec. 20, 118, Mar. Aby. II 2, , L.D. III, 229c, a Sûdânî country; situation unknown.

Mȧn , , , the swamp region of Bubastis; , a town in the Nome of Uatchet, Gau al-Kabîr (?)

Mȧrȧua , , Rec. 12, 53, , Mission 13, 4, Meroë, the capital of the Island of Meroë in the Egyptian Sûdân; var. Berua ; Gr. Μερόη.

Mȧt rehen-t , Rec. 17, 95, Mît-Rahînah (?) near Ṣakkârah.

[Mȧ]ṭi , Rev. 6, 8 (Rosetta Stone 21), a town in Egypt.

M'aur , Demot. Cat. 423, Moeris in the Fayyûm.

M'ȧkhasa (Mȧkhsa) , , IV, 783, a district in Syria; situation unknown.

Māir (M'ir) , Rec. 20, 117, a district in Syria; situation unknown.

M'rrekhnasa , IV, 789, a district in Syria; situation unknown.

Māāu , Rec. 24, 179, a district; situation unknown.

M'urrekhnasa , IV, 789, a district in Syria; situation unknown.

M'urm'r , IV, 792, a district in Syria; situation unknown.

M'urnusa , Rec. 20, 116, a district in Syria; situation unknown.

M'urqa , IV, 794, a district in Syria; situation unknown.

M'ukauḥi , Semnah Stele, a district in the Eastern Desert.

M'uti , IV, 791, a district in Syria; situation unknown.

Māb (?) , R. 22, 2, Andropolis.

M'beg , Rec. 19, 21, a town in Upper Egypt.

M'n , ; see .

M'ngenasa , IV, 790, a district in Syria; situation unknown.

M'nṭar , Rec. 20, 118, a district in Syria; situation unknown.

M'ntchu , Rec. 20, 114, a southern district conquered by Rameses III. The correct reading is Āntchem , , IV, 798.

M'rm', IV, 781, a district in Syria; situation unknown; compare Heb. מָרוֹם.

M'rm'âm, IV, 784,, IV, 784, a district in Syria; situation unknown.

M'rm'r, Rec. 20, 115, a Sûdânî country; situation unknown.

M'haȧ (Mahi), Harris Pap. I, 16B, a country; situation unknown.

M'ḥa,, a district in Nubia near Primis (Ibrîm).

M'ḥanem', L.D. III, 252, 22, Mahanaim; compare Heb. מַחֲנַיִם, Josh. xxi, 38.

M'ḥugȧa (?), L.D. III, 252, 119, a district in Syria conquered by Shishak I.

M'khirp, Alt-K. 494, a town; position unknown.

M'khen,,, a town near Edfû.

M'kher, a country in the Sûdân.

M'sakha, IV, 782, a district in Syria; situation unknown.

M'shaȧr,,, IV, 782; compare Heb. מִשְׁאָל, Josh. xix, 26, xxi, 30.

M'shaua, IV, 792, a district in Syria; situation unknown.

M'shauasha,, Harris Pap. I, 10, 8, the land of the Maxyes.

M'shakasanra, Eg. Res. 68, 76, a district in Syria; situation unknown.

M'qata (Maqta),, IV, 782, a district in Syria; compare Heb. מַקֵּדָה, Josh. x, 10.

M'qrut,, IV, 785, a district in Syria; compare מַעֲרָת, Josh. xv, 59, LXX *Μαγαρώθ*.

M'qerput, IV, 785, a district in Syria; situation unknown.

M'kȧa (Makȧ), Gol. 4, 6, a country; situation unknown.

Māktȧ (M'ketȧ),, IV, 649, 781,, IV, 655,, IV, 781,, Anastasi I, 23, 1, Megiddo; Heb. מְגִדּוֹ, LXX *Μαγεδδώ*, Tall al-'Amârnah.

M'ketȧr,, tower, fort, a fortress in the Eastern Delta; Heb. מִגְדּוֹל, Gr. *Μάγδωλος*, Copt. ⲙⲉϭⲧⲟⲗ.

M'keter, IV, 784, a district in Syria; compare Heb. מִגְדֹּל.

M'keth, IV, 667, a country; situation unknown.

M'kthir (?), Rec. 20, 118, Migdol (?)

M'kṭȧu, L.D. 3, 252, 27, Megiddo; compare Heb. מְגִדּוֹ, 1 Kings iv, 12.

M'g, Rec. 11, 168, Mycia.

M'ga, M'gana,, a town in Egypt.

M'gaṭir, M'gaṭil, Migdol, in the Eastern Delta; see .

M'gaṭen, II, 158, Macedonia; Gr. Μακεδονία.

M'gir (Megir), Rec. 20, 117, a district in Syria; situation unknown.

M'tenu, , , B.D.G. 1041, the 22nd Nome of Upper Egypt (Aphroditopolites).

M'tenu, the capital of the Nome of the same name.

M'tenu ent Sep, a district near Kherāḥa.

M'thna (Methen), IV, 616, , Rec. 20, 116, , IV, 589, a district in Northern Syria; varr. , , Tall al-'Amârnah .

M'ṭi , , Nâstasen Stele 61, a country in the Sûdân; , , the natives of the country = .

M'tch , , a town near Lycopolis.

M'tchana , , IV, 782, a district in Syria; situation unknown.

Muau, IV, 797, a Sûdânî country; situation unknown.

Muȧ, IV, 804, a Sûdânî country; situation unknown.

Mu ent Āntch, Rec. 5, 93, a canal in the Delta.

Mu ent Pteḥ (?), a canal in Edfû; var. .

Mu nesert, a lake of boiling water in the Ṭuat.

Mu neter , , the sacred canal of Edfû.

Muset (?), Rec. 20, 115; see , IV, 798.

Mushanth, Mar. Aby. II, 4, 2, , , Alt-K. 510, a country; situation unknown.

Muqeṭ-t (?), the name of a country (?)

Muka (?), IV, 802, a Sûdânî country; situation unknown.

Mebushu, IV, 798; see and .

Mebutu, IV, 798, , Rec. 20, 114, a southern country conquered by Thothmes III; var. , IV, 798.

Mebeq (Meqeb ?), Ombos I, 130, a district; situation unknown.

Mefki, Sphinx 14, 167, a town in the Delta.

Mefkgi, Rec. 11, 158, a foreign city.

Memu, Memmu (?), a town in the Fayyûm.

Memtu (Memut) [ ], IV, 798, a Sûdânî country conquered by Thothmes III.

Memthu , , IV, 798; see .

Men, Rec. 34, 1, a shrine at Abydos.

Men-t, a canal in the Nome Tekh.

Menȧ, B.D. 142, 3, 19, a town of Osiris.

Menȧs, Rec. 32, 63; varr. and: (1) a town near the modern Tall al-Kabîr; (2) the district of Minyâ.

Menȧs-t, a part of the temple of Edfû.

Menȧsut, the pyramid of Userenrā at Ṣakkârah.

Menānkh, the pyramid of Neferkarā.

Menāt Khufu, "the town of the nurse of Khufu," Minyâ.

Menu, the 9th Nome of Upper Egypt (Panopolites).

Menu khenti, a town with the cult of Menu.

Menut, IV, 803, IV, 799, a Sûdânî country; situation unknown.

Mennu kherp Khākaurā, a fortress built by Usertsen III at Kummah in the Third Cataract.

Mennus, Rec. 19, 18, a district.

Mennu Senmut, the fortress of Biggah.

Menmentt, a region in the Fayyûm.

Menmenu, Rec. 32, 64, a shrine of Ȧmen.

Men nefer, A.Z. 49, 130, Demot. Cat. 423, Memphis, the tomb of Osiris, Τάφος 'Οσίριδος. From this name are derived the Coptic forms ⲙⲉⲙⲃⲉ, ⲙⲉⲙⲃⲓ, ⲙⲉⲛϥⲓ, ⲙⲉϥⲓ, ⲙⲉⲛϥⲉⲱⲛ, Assyr.

Men nefer, the pyramid of King Pepi Meri-Rā.

Men-t Nefer-kheperu-Rā uā-en-Rā Rec. 15, 39, 47, the town of Ȧmenḥetep IV, the modern Tall al-'Amârnah.

Menti-nenu, two rocks in the First Cataract, the Κρῶφι and Μῶφι of Herodotus (?)

Menḥ, a town in the Libyan Nome.

Menḥeb, a town in Egypt.

Men Khufu, an estate of Cheops.

Mensa qebḥ, an estate of King Ṭeṭkarā.

Mensȧu, IV, 798, Rec. 22, 114, a southern country conquered by Thothmes III.

Menqeb Khufu, an estate of Cheops.

Mentheb, a town founded by Cheops.

Mentch, Rec. 11, 79, a town in Egypt.

Mentchefa, an estate of King Kakaȧ.

Mer, B.D. 110, 5, a temple of Osiris in the town of Sheṭen.

Merȧ; see **Ta Merȧ**.

Merȧu (?), IV, 873, a country or nation.

Meråu, B.D.G. 280 = Meroë, capital of the Meroïtic kingdom; Gr. Μερόη.

Meråu, the sacred boat of Athribis.

Meråhetåa, IV, 801, a Sûdânî country; situation unknown.

Mer Åtem, Rec. 11, 155, Pithom (?)

Mer ānkh Åssȧ, an estate of King Åssȧ.

Mer ānkh Rā Åssȧ ḥet, an estate of King Åssȧ.

Meri, Merti, a district in the Nome Sepṭ.

Meri-t, port, harbour of a city, *e.g.*, ; var. B.D.G. 57, the port of Memphis.

Meri-t, Mareotis.

Mer ur, Lake Moeris in the Fayyûm.

Mer maāt a town of Åssȧ in the Nome Metelites.

Mer nefer, a town in the Nome Cynopolites.

Mer nefer Ḥet Saḥurā, a town founded by King Saḥurā.

Mer-t neterit, A.Z. 1907, 46, a town in the Delta.

Merḥu (?), IV, 801, a Sûdânî country; situation unknown.

Mer Ḥerui (?), a canal in the Nome Ka ḥeseb.

Merr ḥe-t ka Åssȧ, the Ka town or temple of Åssȧ.

Mer Sepṭ Kakaȧ, a town built by King Kakaȧ.

Mer Sesheta Ḥeråkau, an estate of King Ḥeråkau.

Merkar, IV, 797, a Sûdânî country; situation unknown.

Mer gerḥ, the name of a locality near the Labyrinth.

Mert Ḥerusåtef Stele 149, a Sûdânî town.

Mer Tem, Mêdûm.

Mehå, IV, 801, a Sûdânî country; situation unknown.

Meḥ, the modern Minyâ.

Meḥ, the temple of Osiris at Elephantine.

Meḥ-t, a canal in the Nome of Maḥetch.

Meḥti åb åātu, Rec. 27, 50, a name of Maghârah.

Meḥi, a canal in the Nome Nefer Åment.

Meḥi, a town in Northern Nubia, Meae (?)

Meḥu, IV, 953, A.Z. 1907, 11, Hymn Darius 29, the northern half of Egypt—the Delta; Copt. ⲉⲙϩⲓⲧ, ⲙϩⲓⲧ.

Meḥen en Meḥurt [hieroglyphs], a name of Sni (Latopolis).

Meḥtchem' [hieroglyphs], IV, 798, a Sûdânî country; situation unknown; var. Metchḥem' [hieroglyphs].

Mekha taui [hieroglyphs], a name of Memphis.

Mekhem [hieroglyphs]; see **Sekhem** (Letopolis).

Mekher [hieroglyphs], a town near Sni (Asnâ).

Mekhsherkher [hieroglyphs], Nåstasen Stele 55, a Sûdânî country; situation unknown.

Mekhtḥenif (?) [hieroglyphs] (*sic*), Ḥerusåtef Stele 97, a Sûdânî town; situation unknown.

Mekhtḥenintiteqth (?) [hieroglyphs], Nåstasen Stele 46, a Sûdânî town; situation unknown.

Mesper en Ma-t ensa Ḥeru ḥer åst-f [hieroglyphs], Denderah.

Mesen-t [hieroglyphs], a sanctuary of Ḥeru-Beḥuṭ.

Mesen-t åabtt [hieroglyphs], a district of Edfû.

Mesen-t åmentt [hieroglyphs], a district of Edfû.

Mesen-t meḥ-t [hieroglyphs], a name of Tanis.

Mesen-t res-t [hieroglyphs], a name of Edfû.

Mesḥet [hieroglyphs], IV, 799, a Sûdânî country; situation unknown.

Meskhen-t [hieroglyphs], Ombos.

Messhes [hieroglyphs], IV, 802, a Sûdânî country; situation unknown.

Mest, Mesth [hieroglyphs], IV, 798, a Sûdânî country conquered by Thothmes III; var. [hieroglyphs].

* **Mesta** [hieroglyphs], A.Z. 38, 18, a town in Egypt.

Mesṭ [hieroglyphs], Piānkhi Stele 122, a town of Lower Egypt.

Mesṭ [hieroglyphs], IV, 800, a Sûdânî country; situation unknown.

Mesha [hieroglyphs], Ḥerusåtef Stele 156, a Sûdânî town; situation unknown.

Mekanu (?) [hieroglyphs], Rec. 13, 62, Lycopolis.

Mekes [hieroglyphs], Rec. 35, 192, a name of the Nome [hieroglyphs].

Mekter [hieroglyphs], Sphinx 14, 169, Migdol; Heb. מִגְדּוֹל.

Mekter pef Brātchapnu [hieroglyphs], Sphinx 14, 169, Migdol of Baal Zephon.

Mekter peḥ Sai (?) [hieroglyphs], Sphinx 14, 169, Migdol behind Sai.

Mekter ta sata (?) [hieroglyphs] (?), Sphinx 14, 169, Migdol of the land of . . . . . .

Megubet [hieroglyphs], Rec. 19, 21, a town near Asyûṭ; Copt. ⲘⲀⲚⲔⲀⲠⲰⲦ, Arab. منقباض.

Metun en ka, Methun en ka [hieroglyphs], Åmenemḥat I, 2, 2, 3, the place where bulls run, arena.

Meturt [hieroglyphs], IV, 797, a Sûdânî country; situation unknown.

Meter [hieroglyphs], a town in Egypt.

Metra, Metla, Rec. 11, 141, Metelis.

Methen shet, a place in the Saïte Nome.

Meṭṭ, Ḥerusȧtef Stele 78, a country in the Sûdân.

Meṭnȧt, Peasant 38, Gol. Ḥamm. 12, 99, a town; situation unknown.

Metch, a sanctuary at Elephantine.

Metcha, IV, 799, a Sûdânî country; situation unknown.

Metchau, Demot. Cat. 20, a district; situation unknown.

Metchar, Nȧstasen Stele, a Sûdânî town.

Naȧskhanḥu, Rec. 14, 66, an island in the Nile.

Naȧrrutf, B.D.G. 1063; see **N-ruṭef**.

Na āui en pa sekh user, a district in the Nome Metelites.

Na āui en Ḥāp, "the gates of Ḥāp"—a district in the Nome Metelites.

Na p n Kamȧ ḥui, Demot. Cat. 423, a place at Pathyris.

Nait, B.D.G. 1064, a town near Tall al-Yahûdîyah.

Naun, IV, 784, a district in Syria; situation unknown.

Nabur, Rec. 20, 117, a district in Syria; situation unknown.

Naap, IV, 791, a district in Syria; situation unknown.

Napit, A.Z. 1865, 28, a country in the Sûdân; it produced root of emerald.

Naruṭ-f; see **N-ruṭef**.

Narruṭf; see **N-ruṭef**.

Nahrina, IV, 36, Anastasi IV, 15, 4; see **Neharna.**

Nakhasa, Anastasi I, 27, 6, a district in Syria; situation unknown.

Naqbesu, L.D. III, 160, a country; situation unknown.

Nagbu; see **Negbu**.

Natuba, IV, 790, a district in Syria; situation unknown.

Natkina, IV, 792, a district in Syria; situation unknown.

Nathana, Anastasi I, 21, 1, a district near Tyre.

Nȧpt, B.D.G. 163, the capital of the Northern Meroïtic kingdom at the foot of the Fourth Cataract, Napata.

Nȧruṭf; see **Neruṭ-f**.

Nāā, a town in Egypt.

Nām'na ⟨hieroglyphs⟩, ⟨hieroglyphs⟩, IV, 784, a district in Syria; situation unknown; varr. ⟨hieroglyphs⟩, ⟨hieroglyphs⟩, ⟨hieroglyphs⟩ ⟨hieroglyphs⟩ (Alt-K. 570); Heb. נַעֲמָן.

Nār ⟨hieroglyphs⟩, ⟨hieroglyphs⟩, ⟨hieroglyphs⟩, ⟨hieroglyphs⟩, Thes. 1251, a district of Ḥensu (Herakleopolis).

Ni ⟨hieroglyphs⟩, ⟨hieroglyphs⟩, IV, 698, 788, 893, a district in Syria; Assyr. ⟨cuneiform⟩.

Niu (Neniu?) ⟨hieroglyphs⟩, Rec. 32, 68, the Equatorial Lakes.

Nirab ⟨hieroglyphs⟩, IV, 790, a district in Syria; situation unknown; Gr. Νήραβος, Akkad. Nēribu (Zimmern, Akkad. Fremdenwörter, 43).

Nishapa ⟨hieroglyphs⟩, IV, 790, a district in Syria; situation unknown.

Nu-t (Nenu-t) ⟨hieroglyphs⟩, ⟨hieroglyphs⟩, ⟨hieroglyphs⟩, ⟨hieroglyphs⟩ the canal of the Nome Ka Kam.

Nui (Nenui?) ⟨hieroglyphs⟩, ⟨hieroglyphs⟩, ⟨hieroglyphs⟩, the great canal of Abydos, which fed the stream into which offerings were thrown near the temple of Osiris; this stream or lake was supposed to represent the primeval watery mass out of which all things were created.

Nu-t (Nenut?) āa ⟨hieroglyphs⟩, ⟨hieroglyphs⟩, the chief canal of the Nome Åm peḥ.

Nu (Nenu?) Set ⟨hieroglyphs⟩, ⟨hieroglyphs⟩, ⟨hieroglyphs⟩ the canal of the Nome of Set.

Nu-t åau ⟨hieroglyphs⟩, B.D.G. 1072, a name of Ån (Heliopolis).

Nu-t Åmen ⟨hieroglyphs⟩, the "town of Åmen," i.e., Thebes; Heb. נֹא אָמוֹן, Assyr. ⟨cuneiform⟩.

Nu-t Åṭeḥ-t ⟨hieroglyphs⟩, "the marsh city"; Gr. Ναθῶ, Assyr. ⟨cuneiform⟩.

Nu-t āa-t ⟨hieroglyphs⟩, ⟨hieroglyphs⟩, the "great city" par excellence, i.e., Thebes.

Nu-t Uast ent Åmen ⟨hieroglyphs⟩ ⟨hieroglyphs⟩, Dream Stele 11, "the city Uast of Åmen," i.e., Thebes in Upper Egypt.

Nu-t urt ⟨hieroglyphs⟩, ⟨hieroglyphs⟩, ⟨hieroglyphs⟩, "great city," i.e., Tanis.

Nu-t meḥt ⟨hieroglyphs⟩, ⟨hieroglyphs⟩, ⟨hieroglyphs⟩, "the city of the North," i.e., Thebes of the Delta (Diospolis Parva); var. ⟨hieroglyphs⟩ ⟨hieroglyphs⟩.

Nu-t mes[t] nut ⟨hieroglyphs⟩, Rec. 33, 18, Demot. Cat. 423, "mother of cities" (metropolis); ⟨hieroglyphs⟩ "city of cities," i.e., Thebes.

Nu-t en Åmen ⟨hieroglyphs⟩, "city of Åmen," i.e., Thebes.

Nu-t ent Bak ⟨hieroglyphs⟩, ⟨hieroglyphs⟩, B.D.G. 186, capital of the Nome Ṭuf.

Nu-t neb-t ḥeḥ ⟨hieroglyphs⟩, "the city, lady of eternity," i.e., Thebes.

Nu-t en Nubit ⟨hieroglyphs⟩, Denderah.

Nu-t ent Ḥep ⟨hieroglyphs⟩, ⟨hieroglyphs⟩, the capital of the Nome Åment.

Nu-t enth ḥeḥ ⟨hieroglyphs⟩, "eternal city"—a name of the Other World.

Nu-t en ka pefs ⟨hieroglyphs⟩, Panopolis.

Nu-t ent thebti ⟨hieroglyphs⟩, B.D.G. 926, "city of the two divine sandals"—the modern Aṭfîḥ, اطفيح.

Nu-t kheper ⟨hieroglyphs⟩, ⟨hieroglyphs⟩, ⟨hieroglyphs⟩, ⟨hieroglyphs⟩, Abydos.

Nu-t Kheper tchesef, Thebes.

Nu-t shesit (?), Lib. Fun. II, 89, a town in Egypt.

Nukartȧ, Sphinx 14, 159, Naucratis; var. , Rec. 24, 184, Annales 1, 186.

Nu-t Tem = **Per Tem**, Ȧn (Heliopolis).

Nub, the Nome Ombites.

Nubit, Nubti, U. 285, M. 210, N. 674, , , , IV, 1127, , , , , , Ombos; Copt. ⲉⲙⲃⲱ, ⲱⲙⲃⲟⲛ, Arab. كوم امبو.

Nub, , Rec. 10, 141, 15, 160, a town near Ballâs (Pampinis ?)

Num'ȧna (Nenum'ȧna), , , IV, 784, a district in Syria; situation unknown.

Nurnas (Nenurnas ?), IV, 793, a country in Syria, situation unknown.

Nuḥtem, , , , IV, 798, , a district in Syria; situation unknown.

Nuges, see **Ȧnȧugasa**, IV, 704.

Nuthana (Nenuthana ?), IV, 792, a district in Syria; situation unknown.

Nebata, a district in Syria; situation unknown; compare Heb. נְבוֹת (Alt-K. 567).

Neb ȧru, a town in the Nome Ȧm-peḥ.

Neb ānkh, , , "Lady of Life"—the Necropolis of Thebes.

Nebit, , , , a town in the Thebaïd (?)

Nebiui, , , a town in the Thebaïd (?)

Nebina, Canopus Stele 9; a mistake for , Ȧuntȧnai, Cyprus; see also **Ȧsi**.

Nebu, Rec 10, 141, Chenoboscion.

Nebut (?), a town near Denderah.

Neb neter, the canal of Edfû.

Nebes Seneferu, an estate of Seneferu famous for its mulberry trees; situation unknown.

Neb-t seger-t, , , the district of Busiris; var. .

Nepau, IV, 805, a Sûdânî country; situation unknown.

Nepi, Sphinx 14, 159, a town in the Delta.

Nepi, Nȧstasen Stele 9, III, 139, , III, 143; see **Nepita**.

Nept, Nepita, III, 139, , , , , , a town situated at the foot of the Fourth Cataract, the capital of the Northern Nubian Kingdom, the Napata of classical writers. Its ruins lie opposite Gebel Barkal.

Neper, B.D. 141, 117, a town of Osiris.

Nepriuriu, IV, 792, a district in Syria; situation unknown.

Nef ur (Tau ur?), B.D. 131, 10, B.D. 142, II, 14, Sinsin II, 6, a quarter of Abydos.

Nefer (?), B.D. 125, II, 39, swamp land in the Delta.

Nefer (?) Åabti, the 8th Nome of Lower Egypt (Heroopolites).

Nefer (?) Åmenti, the 7th Nome of Lower Egypt (Metelites).

Nefer, a town in the Delta.

Nefer, the pyramid of King Åssȧ.

Nefer ȧsut, the pyramid of King Unȧs.

Nefer ȧsut Khāfrā, an estate of King Khāfrā.

Neferāu Åssȧ, an estate of King Åssa.

Nefer ānkh Ḥerȧkau, an estate of King Ḥerȧkau.

Nefer uatu Khākaurā, Rec. 13, 202, a canál made by Usertsen III in the First Cataract.

Nefrus, Rechnungen 77, P.S.B. 13, 516, a town near Minyâ.

Nefer en ḥer (?) Åssȧ, an estate of King Åssȧ.

Nefer ḥer, A.Z. 35, 19, a district in Bȧasta.

Nefer ḥesut Åssȧ, an estate of King Åssȧ.

Nefer ḥetep Khufu, an estate of King Khufu.

Nefer ḥeteput Saḥurā, an estate of King Saḥurā.

Nefer sen, B.D. 153A, 26, a town in Egypt.

Nefer seḥ ȧn, a town in Egypt.

Nem-t, B.D. 125, II, the slaughter house of the god Unemsnef.

Nem-t Sekhmit, the slaughter house of the goddess Sekhmit.

Nemmit, Nemit, a district in the Nome of Set.

Nemnem, Hh. 238, the name of a place (?)

Nemti, the name of the canal of the Nome Coptites.

Nenurm'nnatcha, IV, 789, a district in Syria; situation unknown.

Nerau, a country; situation unknown.

Neruṭ-f, the "place where nothing grows"—a sanctuary of Osiris at Ḥensu.

Neh-t: (1) a district of Memphis; (2) a part of Athribis.

Nehau, a town in Northern Nubia, Noa (?)

Nehaut, B.D. 125, II, 21, a district in Memphis (?)

Nehana-t, Ḥerusâtef Stele 159, a town in the Egyptian Sûdân.

Neharna, Neherna, IV, 710, A.Z. 1880, 82, IV, 649, IV, 698, IV, 870, Mar. Karn. 38, IV, 9, Alt-K. 578, Thes. 1123, a portion of Mesopotamia; Heb. נַהֲרַיִם, Tall al-'Amârnah *mat* Narima (Berl. 91, 32), *mat* Na-akh-[ri]-ma (Bûlâḳ tablet).

Nehi, "sycamore land."

Neḥam, a town near Lake Mareotis.

Neḥim-u, IV, 804, a Sûdânî country; situation unknown.

Neḥestt, IV, 800, Palermo Stele, Ḥerusâtef Stele 5, the Land of the Negro; negroes.

Nekhir (Nekhel), Anastasi IV, 15, 7, stream, river; Heb. נַחַל, Syr., Gr. Νεῖλος. This river is probably the "river of Egypt," נַחַל מִצְרַיִם of Num. xxxiv, 5 = Assyr. (Budge, Esarhaddon, 119).

Nekheb-t, Palermo Stele, U. 459, T. 332, P. 290, the capital of the 3rd Nome of Upper Egypt (Eileithyiaspolis).

Nekhbu, Love Songs 2, 4, low-lying lands.

Nekhen, P. 72, B.D. 15, Litanie 8, IV, 1126, the capital (?) of the 3rd Nome of Upper Egypt (Hierakonpolis), Kôm al-Aḥmar.

Nekhen neshen, Xoïs.

Nekhen neshen, Edfû.

Nesâf, a town near Saïs.

Nes-t ur en neb nebu, the temple of Khnemu in Sni (Asnâ)

Nes ba Ṭeṭ = Ἐσβενδῆτις = Σμένδης.

Nes Menu-ti (?), A.Z. 35, 18, a town in the Hermopolite Nome.

Nes-t neteru, Edfû.

Nes-t en tchet Neb tcherit, Denderah.

Nes-t Rā, Denderah.

Nes-t Ḥer, Edfû.

Nes-t Ḥerui, a temple of Horus and Set at Panopolis.

Nes-t Ḥet-Ḥer, Denderah.

Nes-t taui, "Throne of the Two Lands," *i.e.*, Thebes.

Neserser (Serser ?), B.D. 22, 7, a lake of fire in the Ṭuat.

Nesgestt, P. 332, , M. 635, the name of a country or god.

Nesh-t, Rev. 10, 141, = , Ptolemaïs; Copt. ⲯⲟⲓ, ⲯⲱⲓ, the modern Manshîyah.

Neshau, IV, 805, a Sûdânî country; situation unknown.

Neshat Khufu, an estate of King Khufu.

Neshen, Edfû.

Nega, P. 368, , Rec. 29, 165, a district; situation unknown.

Negba, IV, 890, Southern Palestine; Heb. נֶגֶב.

Negbu, , IV, 783, a district in Syria; situation unknown.

Netauka, Rec. 20, 113, 117, a district in Syria; situation unknown.

Netit (?), see **Neṭit**.

Net em pekhar, Rev. 27, 84, the ocean surrounding the world.

Neter, , , , , , , the temple of Isis, Ἰσεῖον, at Ḥebit , in the Delta; Arab. بهبيت.

Neter-t, , , the temple of Osiris in the Nome Bubastites.

Neter-t (Ḥe-t neter ?), the temple of Denderah.

Neter, , , a sanctuary in the Nome Coptites.

Neterui (?), , , , the Nome of Horus and Set (Aphroditopolites); see **Āntui, Āntchui.**

Neter ȧāu, a town in Egypt.

Neter ȧsut, the pyramid of King Menkauḥer.

Netert Utchat, B.D. 96 and 97, 7, a locality in Egypt.

Neter ḥeb, Rev. 11, 165, a town in Egypt.

Neter-t-khaṭa, a quarter of Denderah; see .

Neter shemā, a name of Coptos.

Neter ta = , see **Ta Neter.**

Neter theb, see **Theb neter.**

Netḥra, , , , , Dendûr, in Northern Nubia; see **Ta ent Ḥer** .

Nethen, P. 609, a town in the Ṭuat (?)

Neṭȧt, P. 8, 476, N. 114, 994, 1263, Rec. 26, 229, a place near Abydos where Osiris was slain; var. , B.D. 174, 5.

Neṭit, B.D. 142, II, 15, Hh. 238; see .

Neṭbit, B.D 141, 112, a town of Osiris.

Netchit, B.D. 142, I, 24, , , , Mett. Stele 7, , a district in the Delta.

Netchit , a town in the Nome Sethroïtes.

Netchfet , a town in the Nome Sethroïtes.

Netchem , a town near Pelusium.

Netchem netchem ānkh , a name of: (1) the temple of Denderah; (2) Elephantine; (3) a temple chamber at Edfû.

Netchem shu , a town near Al-Ḳâb.

Netchert, Netcherȧt , q.v.

Re-au , the quarries of Ṭûrah opposite Memphis; Copt. ⲗⲓⲟⲩⲓ (?)

Re-Ȧabti , B.D.G. 12, a part of the eastern frontier of the 8th Nome of Lower Egypt.

Re-ȧnti , B.D.G. 47, , "mouth of the valley"—a name given to the entrance of several valleys; , Rec. 17, 113.

Re-ȧti , Rec. 3, 45, a canal in the Nome Heliopolites.

Re-ā-ur , B.D. 64, 17, , B.D. 64, 23, a quarter of Abydos; , A.Z. 45, 138, gate of the South Lands.

Re-ānkh , "mouth of the land of life," *i.e.*, the grave.

Re-Āntui , Rec. 5, 86; see **Āntui**.

Rā Ḥeru ḥetep , B.D.G. 441, a sun temple at Ṣaḳḳârah.

Rāqeṭi , Rec. 33, 118, , an ancient town on part of the site on which the city of Alexandria was built; Copt. ⲣⲁⲕⲟϯ, ⲣⲁⲕⲟⲧⲉ.

Rāka (?) , a district in Egypt.

Reiut (?) , IV, 689, a district in Syria; situation unknown.

Reusa , IV, 782, a district in Syria; situation unknown.

Reuȧar , Rec. 20, 118, a district in Syria; situation unknown.

Ruthen , IV, 783, a district in Syria.

Ruṭuāhu , IV, 798, a Sûdânî country; situation unknown.

Rutch , an estate of Seneferu in the Nome Athribites.

Rebaȧu, Rebaȧa , IV, 784, a district in Syria; situation unknown.

Rebaut , IV, 785, a district in Syria; compare Heb. רַבָּה (?); varr. .

Rebana (Lebana) , IV, 781, a district in Syria; compare Heb. לָבָן.

Rebanth (Lebanth) , Rec. 20, 117, , L.D. III, 209, a district in Syria; Heb. לְבָנָה.

Rebar, Nâstasen Stele 50, a Sûdânî country.

Rebarna (Lebarna), Unu-Åmen, , Lebanon; compare Heb. לְבָנוֹן?.

Rebatå, L.D. III, 252, 13; compare Heb. רַבִּית, Josh. xix, 20.

Rebatå, a well on the caravan road to Syria.

Rebu (Lebu), Mar. Karn. 53, 27, , the land of Libya; Heb. לוּבִי; , a Libyan; plur. .

Rebkhenṭen (?), Nâstasen Stele 51, a Sûdânî country.

Rep, Berl. 2296, a town in Egypt.

Reper (?), II, 126, a town in Egypt.

Repeḥ, Anastasi I, 29, 7, , Eg. Res. 57, 16, a district in Syria; Assyr. , Gr. Ῥαφία.

Re-peq, Re-peqr, , , the entrance to a canal at Abydos; , , Re-pequi.

Remaq, Rec. 30, 66, a town in Egypt.

Remath, a town in Egypt.

Rem'nnai, IV, 793, a district in Syria; situation unknown.

Remnen (Lamnen), IV, 719, , IV, 700, Lebanon; Heb. לְבָנוֹן.

Remenui ṭu (?), IV, 388.....

Re mer nefer, , , a town near Mendes (Onuphites).

Renam' (Ranam), IV, 783, a district in Syria; situation unknown.

Renr, L.D. III, 131A, a district in Syria; situation unknown.

Renreka, IV, 792, read Åanraka, a district in Syria; situation unknown.

Re nekhen, see **Nekhen.**

Re en qerr-t åp-t khaut, Ṭuat XI, a circle in the Ṭuat.

Renga, , , a town in Egypt.

Rentånu, IV, 902, a district in Syria; situation unknown.

Rere . . ber, Rec. 20, 115, a district in Syria; situation unknown.

Rerekabra, Rec. 20, 117; see .

Rerti, IV, 788, a district in Syria; situation unknown.

Rehanti, a lake in the Fayyûm.

Rhum, A.Z. 49, 86, Ῥώμη, Rome.

Rehen, the swamp land of the Nome Busirites.

Re-hen, , , a district east of Coptos (Wâdî Ḥammâmât).

Rehrehsa, Ḥerusåtef Stele 73, 100, a Sûdânî country.

Re-ḥa-t, Greene 2, 23, , a mouth of the Nile; plur. , , .

Reḥab, Alt-K. 528, , L.D. III, 252, 17, a district in Syria; compare Heb. רְחוֹב.

Reḥui (?), , B.D. 178, 16, , Hermopolis in the Delta.

Reḥbu, IV, 785, , a district in Syria; compare Heb. רְחֹב.

Reḥburtȧ, Anastasi I, 27, 7, a district; situation unknown.

Re-ḥent, , , , , , , , Al-Lahûn in the Fayyûm.

Reḥer (?), IV, 801, a Sûdânî country; situation unknown.

Reḥsa, , , , , a town near Sekhem.

Reḥtcha, Rec. 20, 118, , a district in Syria; Tall al-'Amârnah.

Rekh-t, , , a lake district in the Mendesian Nome.

Rekhasna, Treaty 27, a district in Syria; Boghaz Keui, Li-ikh-zi-na.

Re-senti, a town in the Fayyûm.

Re-seḥ, Amherst 46, a town in the Delta.

Reshui (?). Rec. 22, 138, a town in the Fayyûm.

Re-set, Re-sthau, , U. 556, , , , , , Ṭuat IV, , , , , , , , Rec. 36, 211, , , , , , , , , , , , Rev. 5, 97, , originally a portion of the Ṭuat of Memphis; later a common name of the grave.

Re-she, an estate of King Khufu.

Reshaut, IV, 373, , Rec. 3, 3, , IV, 385, , , A.Z. 1872, 99, 100; var. , , Rec. 19, 19, , a district in the Sinaitic Peninsula or Arabia.

Resha Qeṭesh, , IV, 783, , Rec. 20 118, a district in Syria; compare Heb. רֹאשׁ־קָדֵשׁ.

Reshit, a name of the Underworld.

Reqatcha, Alt-K. 639, a district in Syria; situation unknown.

Reqrer, a town near the modern Asyûṭ.

Re-qeṭ, , , , , , , , the necropolis of Ṣakkârah.

Reka, , , I.H. 240, a district in Western Asia; Tall al-'Amârnah (Berl. Tablet, 11, 10).

Rekaȧm, A.Z. 1907, 46, a town in the Delta.

Rekares, Rec. 20, 116, a district conquered by Rameses III.

Regaba, IV, 788, a district in Syria; situation unknown.

Regatcha (Legtcha), IV, 784, a district in Syria; situation unknown.

Retam', IV, 792, a district in Syria; situation unknown.

Retam'rka, IV, 783, a district in Syria; situation unknown.

Retȧr (Ratȧl), Rec. 20, 116, a district in Syria; situation unknown.

Retnu, IV, 809, a district in Syria.

Ret shes (?), a town in Egypt.

Rethnu, IV, 689, a district in Syria.

Rethen Ḥert, IV, 907, Upper Rethen.

Rethen Khert, IV, 907, Lower Rethen.

Rethnepen, IV, 800, a Sûdânî country; situation unknown.

Retheq, Nȧstasen Stele 45, a country in the Sûdân.

Retcha, Asien 165, Luz; compare Heb. לוּז.

Retchatcha (?), IV, 794, a Sûdânî country; situation unknown.

Haa, Rec. 20, 114, a district in Syria; situation unknown.

Haubu, IV, 805, a Sûdânî country; situation unknown.

Har, IV, 784, a district in Syria; situation unknown; compare Heb. הַר(?)

Har, a canal near Tanis.

Harm', A.Z. 49, Ῥώμη, Rome.

Har-nemȧta, Anastasi I, 22, 4, a district in Northern Syria.

Haqa, L.D. III, 252, 89, a district in Syria; situation unknown.

Hi en Shu nefer, the temple of Edfû.

Hirana, Rec. 20, 117, a district conquered by Rameses III.

Hikrim, IV, 785, a district in Syria; situation unknown.

Hu, a canal near Edfû.

Hum', IV, 786, a district in Syria; situation unknown; compare Heb. הָם, Gen. xiv, 5.

Heb, the capital of **Kenem**, the Oasis of Khârgah.

Heb-t, the swamp land of Athribis.

Hen, the canal of Saut (Asyûṭ).

Henhen, the lakes near Buto.

Henṭui, Rev. 11, 168, 13, 105, A.Z. 49, 79, India; Copt. ϩⲛ̄ⲧⲟⲩ, Baby.

Herȧr, (var.), IV, 784, a district in Syria; situation unknown; compare Heb. הַרְאֵל.

Herua, Maskhûṭah Stele, A.Z. 49, 78, Herat (?); Pers. Behis. I, 16, Babyl. [ ], l. 16.

Hernefer, Sphinx 14, 160, a town in the Delta.

Herhertȧ, Sphinx 14, 168, a town in the Delta.

Herkhṭi, Maskhûṭah Stele, Arachosia; Pers. [ ], Col. I, 17, Babyl., ll. 7, 79, 83, 84.

Heh, , , a town in Egypt.

Heker, Demot. Cat. 421, a district in Egypt; Copt.

Ḥe-t, , , Diospolis Parva; Copt.

Ḥe-t, a name of Edfû.

Ḥe-t au, a town near Latopolis.

Ḥe-t au ȧb, a temple in the Nome Coptites.

Ḥe-t ȧabbekh, a temple in Hermopolis Magna.

Ḥe-t ȧakhu, the temple of Hathor at Denderah.

Ḥe-t ȧakhut khep[er] em ḥat, Denderah.

Ḥe-t Ȧāḥ, B.D. 153B, 10, , , , the temple of the Moon-god at Panopolis and other places.

Ḥe-t Ȧusāsit, Denderah.

Ḥe-t ȧb, , Athribis.

Ḥe-t ȧbti, , , B.D.G. 18, Unu (Hermopolis).

Ḥe-t ȧbṭ, a sanctuary in Abydos.

Ḥe-t ȧpit, a name of Thebes (?)

Ḥe-t Ȧment, Denderah.

Ḥe-t Ȧnup, Lycopolis.

Ḥe-t Ȧnes, , , B.D.G. 17, Ḥensu (Herakleopolis).

Ḥe-t ȧr, a sanctuary at Kom Ombos (?)

Ḥe-t Ȧḥ, B.D.G. 1064, Aphroditopolis.

Ḥe-t Ȧst, the name of any sanctuary of Isis.

Ḥe-t ȧsut Rā, , the temple of Osiris in the Nome Ka Ahau.

Ḥe-t Ȧsȧr, Mareotis.

Ḥe-t ānkh, , Denderah.

Ḥe-t Āḥa, a town near Thebes.

Ḥe-t Ākhmiu, , B.D. (Saïte) 148, 14, the temple of the Divine Statues.

Ḥe-t Uatchit, a name of the town Buto.

Ḥe-t Uāb, Denderah.

Ḥet uār, B.D.G. 144, , , Avaris, capital of the Nome Ȧment (Libya-Mareotis).

Ḥe-t uār Ȧment, , B.D.G. 144, part of the metropolis of the Nome Ȧment.

Ḥe-t urt, , , , B.D.G. 153, B.D. 178, 28, a town in the Nome Maḥetch.

Ḥe-t ur, , , B.D.G. 153, a town in the Nome Maḥetch.

Ḥe-t Urit , , , , A.Z. 1908, 121, a temple or town of Hathor.

Ḥe-t ur åau , , the temple of the Aged Prince, *i.e.*, the Sun-god, in Heliopolis.

Ḥe-t ur-t Åmenemḥat , Rechnungen 6, a place north of Thebes; position unknown.

Ḥe-t ur ka , , a town of Hathor (?)

Ḥe-t User menu , the temple of the goddess Åpit at Thebes.

Ḥe-t utet , B.D.G. 175, , : (1) a town near Memphis; (2) a temple at Karnak; (3) a name of Edfû.

Ḥe-t utet en Usen , B.D.G. 176, a name of Latopolis.

Ḥe-t Baiu , , a town in the Nome Maḥetch.

Ḥe-t ba Åst , Rec. 10, 141, a town between Ḳanâ and Denderah; Copt. ⲦⲀⲂⲈⲚⲚⲎⲤⲈ.

Ḥe-t Bak , , Hierakonpolis; Gr. Ἱεράκων πόλις (?)

Ḥe-t Benu , , B.D.G. 189: (1) a sanctuary at Heliopolis; (2) the temple of Osiris in the 7th Nome of Upper Egypt; (3) a temple mentioned on the Stele of Piānkhi—Hipponon, Al-Hîbu.

Ḥe-t Benben , , , , Rev. 15, 47, a name given to several temples of the Sun-god, Rā, Åten, etc., in which a stone was worshipped.

Ḥe-t pa Åāni , Sphinx 14, 163, a town in the Delta.

Ḥe-t pa Åten , the temple of Åten at Memphis.

Ḥe-t pāpā-t , Denderah.

Ḥe-t Pepi , a town near Ṣaḳḳârah.

Ḥe-t pestch neteru , , a name of many sanctuaries.

Ḥe-t Pteḥ , a quarter of Thebes to the north of Karnak.

Ḥe-t Pteḥ , , , , B.D.G. 235, the temple town of Ptaḥ at Memphis.

Ḥe-t maākheru , a name of several sanctuaries of Osiris.

Ḥe-t māb (?) , B.D.G. 140, a name of Ombos (?)

Ḥe-t Mut , , Rec. 27, 88, : (1) the temple of Mut at Latopolis; (2) the temple of Mut at Diospolis Parva.

Ḥe-t menå-t , , B.D.G. 255, Denderah.

Ḥe-t menu , the temple of Denderah.

Ḥe-t men uār , the temple of Osiris of the Libyan Nome of Lower Egypt.

Ḥe-t mennu Khāemmaāt , the temple of Åmenḥetep III at Gebel Barkal or Ṣûlb.

Ḥe-t menḥ , the temple of Osiris at Saïs.

Ḥe-t Menth, Rec. 31, 35, a sanctuary of Menthu of Hermonthis.

Ḥe-t Merit, a temple of Osiris at Thebes.

Ḥe-t Meriti, the temple of Osiris at Bāḥ in the Delta.

Ḥe-t Meḥ, a town in the Nome of Maḥetch.

Ḥe-t meḥt, Berl. 2296, a town in Egypt.

Ḥe-t Meḥi, a name of Elephantine.

Ḥe-t mest, a town in the Nome Tekh (?) in the Delta.

Ḥe-t mes-[t] Ḥeru, Denderah.

Ḥe-t meskhenit, Ombos; varr.

Ḥe-t Nut, a section of the temple of Denderah.

Ḥe-t nub, Sni (Latopolis).

Ḥe-t nub, Alabastronpolis in Upper Egypt.

Ḥe-t nub, the temple of Osiris at Memphis.

Ḥe-t nub, the temple of Osiris at Coptos.

ḥe-t nub, the gold foundry of the temple at Denderah; near it was the manufactory of jewellery, or.

Ḥe-t nuṭ, the sanctuary of Rāit taui, at Hermonthis.

Ḥe-t Nebȧ, a town of Hathor in Nubia.

Ḥe-t nebs, Rec. 31, 35: (1) a town in the Nome of Ṭuf; (2) a town in the Nome of Sepṭ.

Ḥe-t nef, a village in the Nome of Edfû.

Ḥe-t nem, a district; situation unknown.

Ḥe-t nemm: (1) a sanctuary at Denderah; (2) the temple of Osiris in the 11th Nome of Upper Egypt; (3) the temple of Osiris in the 2nd Nome of Lower Egypt.

Ḥe-t en Maākheru, a name of the temple of Sni.

Ḥe-t ent Maḥes, Leontopolis; Gr. Λεωντων.

Ḥe-t neh, the temple of Osiris in Metelis.

Ḥe-t nehem, Denderah.

Ḥe-t ent ḥeḥ en renput, "house of 100,000 years"—a name of several temples.

Ḥe-t nekhen, Edfû.

Ḥe-t nekht neteru, Edfû.

Ḥe-t nes-t, a town in the Northern Delta.

Ḥe-t nesu: (1) Alabastronpolis; (2) Diospolis in the Delta.

Ḥe-t nesu ḥent, Inscrip. of Methen 17, a temple.

Ḥe-t Net, the temple of Neith at Saïs.

Ḥe-t en ta åḥ-ṭ, Demot. Cat. 424, the temple of Dêr al-Baḥarî.

Ḥe-t neṭå, Sphinx 14, 163, a town in the Delta.

Ḥe-t neteru, Edfû.

Ḥe-t neter Ån-t, B.D.G. 46, the temple of Pakhit near Beni Ḥasan (Speos Artemidos).

Ḥe-t neter Ånpu, Cynopolis.

Ḥe-t neter en Åsår-Ḥep, var., the temple of Serapis at Memphis.

Ḥe-t neter en Ḥer en Taui, Denderah.

Ḥe-t neter ent Sebek, Crocodilopolis in the Fayyûm.

Ḥe-t netches, Rec. 31, 35, a town in Egypt.

Ḥe-t rekhit, a temple near Heliopolis.

Ḥe-t reshu, Denderah.

Ḥe-t erṭu, B.D.G. 1063, the temple of Osiris in the Nome Åmkhent.

Ḥe-t Ḥāp, the abode of the Apis Bull.

Ḥe-t ḥāu neter, the temple of Osiris in the Nome Lykopolites.

Ḥe-t ḥenmem-t, B.D.G. 36, Denderah.

Ḥe-t Ḥensu, Demotic Cat. 423, the temple and town of Herakleopolis; Assyr. ..., Heb. חָנֵס, Copt. ϩⲛⲏⲥ, Arab. اهناس.

Ḥe-t ḥenk ānkh, Rec. 19, 87, a sanctuary in the Theban Necropolis, a temple of Thoth (?)

Ḥe-t ḥenk ānkh Menkheperrā, Annales 7, 186, a temple of Thothmes III at Thebes.

Ḥe-t Ḥeru, any sanctuary of Horus.

Ḥe-t Ḥeru åu, Edfû.

Ḥe-t Ḥeru uru (?), Edfû.

Ḥe-t Ḥeru mer . . . Åsså, an estate of King Åssa.

Ḥe-t Ḥeru nekht, a temple of Horus at Edfû.

Ḥe-t ḥeri åteb, the temple of Osiris in the Nome Sebennytes.

Ḥe-t ḥertu er ḥai ḥetch, Denderah.

Ḥe-t ḥeḥ, "house of eternity," *i.e.*, the tomb.

Ḥe-t ḥesmen: (1) a chamber in the temple of Thoth at Hermopolis; (2) a chamber in the Ramesseum at Thebes.

Ḥe-t ḥeq , , , , Edfû.

Ḥe-t ḥeka , , the temple of Hathor in Heliopolis.

Ḥe-t ḥetep , the temple of Latopolis (Asnâ).

Ḥe-t ḥetch , N. 669, , , a settlement; site unknown.

Ḥe-t kha , "house of Kha" ; situation unknown.

Ḥe-t khas ; , B.D.G. 1012, , a town in the Delta.

Ḥe-t khastu , Sphinx 14, 163, a town in the Delta.

Ḥe-t khā , , Mendes.

Ḥe-t khā-t , , "the coronation chamber" of the king in a temple.

Ḥe-t khāit , a district in the Nome Lykopolites.

Ḥe-t khā ent Ḥeru , Edfû.

Ḥe-t khā-t en nesu neteru , the temple of Åmen-Rā in the Oasis of Dakhlah.

Ḥe-t Khufu , a temple-town founded by Khufu in the Nome Lykopolites.

Ḥe-t Khufu nefer , a temple-town founded by Khufu.

Ḥe-t Khebit , , , , the temple of Osiris at Saïs.

Ḥe-t Kheper , Edfû.

Ḥe-t Khnemu , Sni (Latopolis).

Ḥe-t Khnemit , , the god's birth-chamber at Denderah.

Ḥe-t Khnemti , a town in the Wâdî Ṭûmîlâṭ, Sile.

Ḥe-t Khnemt ānkh a temple in Western Thebes.

Ḥe-t Khenti , the Island of Philae.

Ḥe-t Khenti , , , , Sunu-Syene-Elephantine-Aswân.

Ḥe-t Khenti , Mission 138, a temple; position unknown.

Ḥe-t Sata , , Denderah.

Ḥe-t sutenit , a name of Xoïs.

Ḥe-t sutenit en Rā , Rec. 27, 190, , Xoïs.

Ḥe-t Sebakh . . . , a name of (Tuphium).

Ḥe-t Sebaq , a town of , a form of Tefnut.

Ḥe-t Sfen , Asphynis; Arab. اصفون.

Ḥe-t smau [ ], IV, 800, a Sûdânî country; situation unknown.

Ḥe-t sma-taui , , , , a temple at Denderah.

Ḥe-t Sems , , a town in the Nome Nefer Åment.

Ḥe-t Sent , Inscrip. of Methen, an estate in the Delta.

Ḥe-t Seneferu , , Palermo Stele, a temple-town of Seneferu.

Ḥe-t Seneferu, Rec. 10, 140, a name of , Asphynis (Tuphium).

Ḥe-t snetchemnetchem, : (1) Pelusium; (2) a portion of the temple of Denderah.

Ḥe-t seḥetep, a town in the Nome of Uatchet.

Ḥe-t Seḥetepȧbrā, a temple founded by Ȧmenemḥat I, in the Nome Unt.

Ḥe-t Sekha-Ḥeru, the temple of Serapis in the Nome Ȧment.

Ḥe-t sekhun, a temple in the Nome Metelites.

Ḥe-t sekhem (Seshesh ?), IV, 1137, Diospolis Parva.

Ḥe-t sekhen enti Ḥep, a sanctuary of Apis at Memphis.

Ḥe-t Seshesh, the temple of Denderah.

Ḥe-t Seshem, Diospolis Parva.

Ḥe-t Seker, Ḥe-t ka Seker, the temple of Seker at Ṣaḳḳârah.

Ḥe-t Seker shemā, a sanctuary on the roof of the temple of Denderah.

Ḥe-t Seti, the temple of Horus at Edfû.

Ḥe-t Shairȧum, a town or village; Copt. ϣⲗⲏⲓⲗⲗⲓ (?)

Ḥe-ṭ shā, a town in the Western Delta.

Ḥe-t Sheb, Denderah.

Ḥe-t Shepsit, Denderah.

Ḥe-t shefit, a temple of Osiris in the Nome Ten (?) .

Ḥe-t Shennu, Gol. Ḥamm. 12, 81, a town in Egypt.

Ḥe-t Sheser (Qeser ?), a temple in Unu.

Ḥe-t shetat, the most holy part of a temple.

Ḥe-t sheṭ ȧbeṭ, Thes. 968, a town near Memphis.

Ḥe-t qa, Denderah.

Ḥe-t Qebḥ, a temple estate at Memphis.

Ḥe-t Qen, Denderah, Edfû.

Ḥe-t Ka, a town in the Eastern Delta.

Ḥe-t Kaka, Rec. 17, 119, a town in Upper Egypt.

Ḥe-t Ka Pepi, a Ka-chapel of Pepi near Ṣaḳḳârah.

Ḥe-t Ka Ptaḥ, B.D. 181, 3, de Rougé I.H. 159, "house of the Double of Ptaḥ," a name of Memphis; Copt. ⲉⲕⲉⲡⲧⲁ (Budge, Misc. Texts, 207).

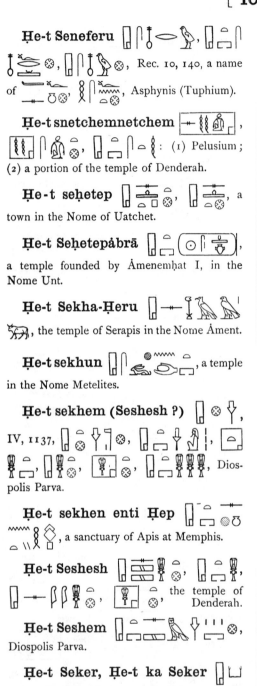

Ḥe-t Ka en Rā, a temple in the Nome of Sȧpi Shemā.

Ḥe-t Ka khnem neteru, Memphis.

Ḥe-t Ka ka, B.M. No. 138, the chapel of Ȧmenḥetep, son of Ḥāp, at Thebes.

Ḥe-t kauit, Panopolis.

Ḥe-t ta neter-t, Denderah.

Ḥe-t ta Ḥeru (?), Rev. 11, 152, a sanctuary of Horus.

Ḥe-t ta ḥer ȧb, the capital of the Nome Ka-kam (Athribis); Assyr., Copt. ⲁⲑⲣⲉⲃⲉ, Arab. اتريب.

Ḥe-t Ti, Rec. 11, 97, Taḥtah (?)

Ḥe-t tu (?), a temple in the Nome Maḥetch.

Ḥe-t tut Rā, a town near Busiris.

Ḥe-t Tef, Rec. 27, 88, Sni (Latopolis).

Ḥe-t Tem, the capital of the Heroopolite Nome (Succoth ?)

Ḥe-t tekh, a part of the temple of Denderah.

Ḥe-t thaui (?), Rec. 27, 191, a temple in Sni (Latopolis).

Ḥe-t Ṭunti, the capital of the Nome Maḥetch.

Ḥe-t ṭebutiu, the "house of the coffined ones," *i.e*, the Necropolis.

Ḥe-t tchefa, the name of a chamber at Denderah and of one at Abydos.

Ḥa, a Sûdânî country; situation unknown.

Ḥa-t (Aḥ-t ?), a town in Egypt.

Ḥa-t, the frontier city, *i.e.*, Elephantine; the 1st Nome of Egypt; the southern frontier.

Ḥaȧanem, L.D. III, 252, 31, a district in Syria; situation unknown.

Ḥai-t en ḥesb āḥā, the temple of Khnemu at Latopolis.

Ḥaiṭbaȧa Ṭuathi, L.D. III, 252, 105 and 106, a district in Syria; situation unknown.

Ḥaiṭbȧa, a district in Syria; situation unknown.

Ḥaiṭbȧa Sharnerȧm, L.D. III, 252, 103 and 104, a district in Syria; situation unknown.

Ḥau, a sanctuary of (Nome Metelites).

Ḥaau [], IV, 806 (var.), a Sûdânî country; situation unknown.

Ḥab, A.Z. 51, 71, Hibis in the Great Oasis.

Ḥap ȧuti, a town in the Nome Ka-kam.

Ḥapu ȧutitt, a name of the Ṭuat.

Ḥap ȧms, a town of Rā-Ȧmen in the Xoïte Nome.

Ḥap nebes, a gate at Abydos.

Ḥap nebes, the Necropolis of Memphis and of Abydos.

Ḥapurmȧa, L.D. III, 252, 18, a district in Syria; compare Heb. חֲפָרַיִם, Josh. xix, 19.

Ḥamatȧ, Anastasi I, 21, 7, , Hamath; Heb. חֲמָת, Assyr. , Rawl. C.I.W.A. III, 11, 1, 51.

Ḥa meḥit, B.D. 112, 2, the 16th Nome of Lower Egypt (Mendesius).

Ḥa meḥit, a district in the Mendesian Nome.

Ḥanani, L.D. III, 252, 99, a district in Syria conquered by Shishak I.

Ḥa-t nu-t, Rec. 27, 87, "first of towns," *i.e.*, Elephantine.

Ḥarkar, IV, 785, a district in Syria; situation unknown.

Ḥaqrȧa. For place-names containing this word see under .

Ḥaqrȧa Fetiushaȧa, Eg. Res. 81, 68, a district in Syria; situation unknown.

Ḥaqrȧa en Āatchait, Eg. Res. 81, a district in Syria; situation unknown.

Ḥaqrm' Āarṭȧat, Eg. Res. 82, a district in Syria; situation unknown.

Ḥaqr-t Shanaiȧa, Eg. Res. 82, a district in Syria; situation unknown.

Ḥaqeṭti, a district in Egypt (?)

Ḥagrȧa Ȧrqaṭ, Eg. Res. 82, 96, a district in Syria; situation unknown. (= article).

Ḥagri Ḥaniniȧa, Eg. Res. 82, 94, a district in Syria; situation unknown.

Ḥagr Thruan, Eg. Res. 83, 101, a district in Syria; situation unknown.

Ḥa-t ta, , the main canal of the Nome Aphroditopolites.

Ḥatchaā (?), a town near Al-Ḳâb.

Ḥāā, , , a town in the Delta.

Ḥāp, , , , , , , , the Nile.

Ḥāp, a locality in the Western Delta.

Ḥāp, a locality in the Fayyûm.

Ḥāp meḥ, , , , a district in the Nome Sȧpi meḥ.

Ḥāp res-t, , , a district in the Nome Sȧpi res.

Ḥuau, Rec. 20, 114, a Sûdânî country; situation unknown.

Ḥuā, Nav. Bubast. 34A, , Rec. 20, 115, , IV, 800, a Sûdânî country; situation unknown.

Ḥuburtȧ, Anastasi I, 19, 6, a district in Assyria (?); Heb. רְחֹבוֹת, reading (Alt-K. 673).

Ḥu em Mennefer, Rechnungen, a royal granary in Memphis.

Ḥu en mu (?), a name of the 11th Nome of Upper Egypt (Hypselis ?)

Ḥur xx, Anastasi III, 2, 9, a lake (?); situation unknown.

Ḥur, a canal in the Tanite Nome.

Ḥuren, Rec. 6, 134, Sphinx 14, 159, a town in the Nome Āntchui.

Ḥurenkar, IV, 74, 665, a district in Syria; situation unknown.

Ḥusfen, Asphynis; Arab. أَصْفُون.

Ḥuqrȧa Ȧbrem, Eg. Res. 81, a district in Syria.

Ḥuthaina, Anastasi I, 27, 4, a district in Syria; situation unknown.

Ḥuṭ-t ȧab-t, B.D.G. 1068; there was a northern part also.

Ḥuṭasath, Rec. 20, 118; var., a district in Syria; Heb. חֲדָשָׁה, Josh. xv, 37, Gr. Ἀδασά, 1 Macc. vii, 40, 45.

Ḥuṭitȧ (?), IV, 784, a district in Syria; situation unknown.

Ḥutchar, IV, 782; varr., a district in Syria; Heb. חָצוֹר, Josh. xi, 1, Assyr., Syr. ܚܨܘܪ, Gr. Ἀσώρ.

Ḥeb, Sinsin II, 2, 5, Heliopolis.

Ḥeb, Ḥebit, Rev. 11, 14, a town near Behbît; Arab. بَهْبِيت.

Ḥebu, IV, 799, a Sûdânî country; situation unknown.

Ḥebnu, Rev. 12, 16, the capital of the Nome Maḥetch.

Ḥebnu, IV, 803, a Sûdânî country; situation unknown.

Ḥeb en sȧs, "city of the festival of the 6th day"—a name of Egypt.

Ḥeb kher, a locality in the Busirite Nome.

Ḥebs, capital of the Nome Kaḥesb (Cabasa); Copt. ⲕⲃⲁϩⲥ, ϫⲃⲁϩⲥ.

Ḥepu (?), Rec. 18, 183, the Nile.

Ḥepḥep (?), B.D.G. 494, a town in Upper Egypt with the cult of Menu.

Ḥef, Rev. 10, 140, Mahallah, between Luxor and Armant; Gr. Τούφιον.

Ḥemamtt, a country in the Sudan.

Ḥemag, a name of any sanctuary of Osiris.

Ḥemit, a town famous for wine near Lake Mareotis.

Ḥemut , IV, 781, Hamath; Heb. חֲמָת, Assyr. .

Ḥemreth (Ḥenreth) , (*sic*) , IV, 798, varr. , , IV, 805, a Sûdânî country; situation unknown.

Ḥen-t , , a canal in the Nome Saïtes.

Ḥen-t , , , the marsh district of the Nome Åm peḥ.

Ḥen , U. 417, , T. 238, , a town in the Ṭuat.

Ḥenḥen , T. 369, a town in the Ṭuat.

Ḥenu , a town in the Sûdân.

Ḥenui ta khartå , Sphinx 14, 168, a lake in the Delta.

Ḥenui ta gerri , Sphinx 14, 166, a lake in the Delta.

Ḥen nefer , A.Z. 1865, 27, Nubia; see .

Ḥensu , Palermo Stele, A.Z. 49, 20, , , Peasant 36, , Rec. 11, 80, , , , , , , , , B.D. 185, the capital of the Nome Åm Khent (Herakleopolis); Heb. חָנֵס, Copt. ϩⲛⲏⲥ, Arab. اهناس, Ahnâs, Assyr. .

Ḥenk , B.D. 141, 119, a city of Osiris.

Ḥen-t taui , "mistress of Egypt," a name of Thebes.

Ḥer , the Pyramid of King Menkaurā.

Ḥer-t , , A.Z. 1908, 118, the Necropolis of Memphis.

Ḥerui , , A.Z. 1906, 120, Denderah.

Ḥerit åb ḥet ka : (1) a town in the Nome Lykopolites; (2) a town in the Nome Libya-Mareotis.

Ḥer-å ḥer Åmen , A.Z. 1907, 1, 4, a place in the Thinite Nome.

Ḥer åst åb shet , a town in the Nome Åtef-peḥ.

Ḥeri p-ṭemåi , a suburb of Memphis.

Ḥer ur, Ḥer urit , Rec. 32, 63, , Rec. 27, 87 , , Metternich Stele, 45, , P.S.B. 13, 511, the capital of the Nome Maḥetch and the Nome Tekh; Copt. ϩⲟⲩⲱⲣ, Arab. هور.

Ḥer menṭ , a necropolis near Edfû.

Ḥer-t ent ḥeḥ , "the everlasting hill," a name of the tomb.

Ḥerit en ḥetch (?) ḥetep , a name of the temple of Latopolis.

Ḥerui , Weill, Décrets, 9, , the Nome Coptites.

Ḥerui , a canal in the Nome Ka ḥeseb.

Ḥeru åabt , the Nome of Horus of the East; , the town of Horus of the East; Copt. ⲫⲁⲣⲃⲁⲓⲧ. See **Per Ḥeru åabt**.

Ḥeru Ȧmenti, Asphynis and its neighbourhood.

Ḥeru ān (Ḥeru em ḥe-t Ān), B.D.G. 121, , , Heroonpolis; Gr. Ἡρωωνπόλις.

Ḥeru uat (?), Gol. Ḥamm. 12, 89, a district in the Eastern Delta.

Ḥeru maāti, Edfû.

Ḥeru em ȧat uāb (?), a town near Heliopolis.

Ḥeru mer, a town of Khnemu.

Ḥeru mer ānkh Userkaf, a temple founded by Userkaf.

Ḥeru mer Khāfrā, a town founded by King Khāfrā.

Ḥeru khenti khati, , , Berlin 12,800, a town near Athribis; it was associated with the unborn Horus (Horus in the belly).

Ḥeru sa Ȧst, A.Z. 35, 18, a town in Egypt.

Ḥeru sma taui, Denderah.

Ḥeru taiu, Rec. 33, 4, "lands of Horus," *i.e.*, temple estates.

Ḥeru-ṭ (?), a town in Egypt.

Ḥeḥ, the district of Semnah in the Second Cataract.

Ḥeḥ, , , a sacred lake in Ḥensu (Herakleopolis).

Ḥeḥ sutenit, a district at Abydos 50 aruras, , in extent.

Ḥes, , , , , a town near Sekhem (Letopolis).

Ḥesb Ka (Ka Beḥes ?), the 11th Nome of Lower Egypt (Cabasites).

Ḥesb Ka (Ka Beḥes ?), , , , Cabasa; Copt. …

Ḥesp-t Maāti, B.D. 1, 17 (Saïte), the domain of Osiris.

Ḥesp-t mert, , , , , Oxyrhynchus; , , , the canal of the town.

Ḥesp-t ent Rā em sep tep, Denderah.

Ḥesp-t ent tchet, Abydos.

Ḥesp ḥa en Ḥeru, Edfû.

Ḥesp ta ȧui, B.D.G. 11, the town of Busiris.

Ḥesp tchatcha-t ent Unnefer maākheru, Elephantine.

Ḥesfen, , Asphynis; Arab. اصفون.

Ḥeser, Thes. 1283, Ḥeruemḥeb 8, , Dream Stele 2, , , , B.D.G. 1063, a quarter of Hermopolis containing a famous temple of Thoth.

Ḥeqȧst (?), a town in Egypt.

Ḥeq āntch (?), U. 293, , B.D. 99, Intro. 9, , , the 13th Nome of Lower Egypt (Heliopolites).

Ḥeq ānṭch (or **ānṭ**), the capital of the 13th Nome of Lower Egypt.

Ḥeqs, a district in the Nome Abetch (Abydos).

Ḥekauhet, Ḥekauheth, IV, 798, a Sûdânî country; situation unknown.

Ḥeka mer ānkh Ȧssȧ, an estate of King Ȧssȧ.

Ḥeken, B.D. 142, III, 13, a suburb of Memphis.

Ḥekha, Rec. 20, 115; see **Ḥekauhet**.

Ḥetau, IV, 797, a Sûdânî country; situation unknown.

Ḥetit, Rec. 31, 35, a city captured by Shashanq I.

Ḥetep, a name of the Nome Sma Beḥuṭ.

Ḥetep em ḥetep, a town of Hathor.

Ḥetep ḥemit (?), P. 423, M. 605, N. 1210, Metternich Stele 90, a district in the Nome Heliopolites.

Ḥetep khet, a district in the Fayyûm.

Ḥetep Khufu, an estate of King Khufu.

Ḥetch, a town near Ḳom Ombos.

Ḥetch Nekheb, Eileithyiaspolis (Al-Ḳâb).

Ḥetch-t Nekhen, Rev. 10, 139, see **Nekhen.**

Ḥetch Ḥeru, a name for Lower Egypt.

Ḥetchi, IV, 801, a Sûdânî country; situation unknown.

Ḥetcheb, P. 506, a town in the Ṭuat (?)

Ḥetcher, a town or village.

Ḥetchrer, a village or estate.

Kha, Hh., a mythological lake.

Khaitu, IV, 792, a district in Syria; situation unknown.

Kha, a town in Egypt.

Kha-t Uast, Denderah.

Khab, a canal in Edfû.

Khabatchana, IV, 784, a district in Syria; situation unknown.

Khabu, the land of the hippopotamus (?)

Khabs, a town in Upper Egypt.

Khanratcha, Anastasi I, 22, 6, the "fortress"; compare Heb. √חלץ, Assyr.

Khar, IV, 712, IV, 665, Demot. Cat. 421, Syria.

Kharr, a region in Western Thebes.

Khari (Khri), Rev. 13, 96 =, Lower Egypt; Copt. ⲉϧⲣⲏⲓ.

Khar en pa sebt, a part of the town of Sheṭen.

Kharb, Alt-K. 736, the desert; Heb. √חרב, Assyr., Tig. Pil. I, VI, 63, Ashurn. Annals III, 28, Heb. חָרָבָה.

Kharbu (Khalbu, Khalpu), IV, 793, Rec. 20, 116, , L.D. III, 153, Aleppo; Assyr. Khalman, Rawl. C.I.W.A. III, 8, 86, Gr. χαλυβον.

Kharm, a canal in the 8th Nome of Lower Egypt; , Lake Timsah.

Kharma, Gol. 4, 6, a district in Syria; situation unknown.

Kharersa (Khalarsa), IV, 789, a district in Syria; situation unknown.

Kha[r]sam, Rev. 13, 105, a district.

Kharqut, IV, 786, a district in Syria; situation unknown; compare Heb. חֶלְקַת (?), Josh. xxi, 31.

Kharkakh, IV, 788, a district in Syria; situation unknown.

Khas, a district in the Nome Gynaecopolites.

Khasȧu, Sphinx 14, 162, Casius on the Mediterranean (?)

Khasu, the capital of the 6th Nome of Lower Egypt; Gr. Ξοΐς, Copt. ⲥϧⲱⲟⲩ, ⲥϩⲟⲟⲩ, ϫⲉⲟⲥ, Arab. Sakhâ سخا.

Khasui (?), B.D. 125, II, 22; varr.

Khasu, Rev. 5, 76, foreign land.

Khaskh-t, IV, 800, Rec. 20, 115, Bubastis 34A, , Karnak 22, 95B, Thes. 1254, foreign land; plur.

Khaskhetu, foreign peoples

Khas (?) seshem, a part of the Nome Metelites.

Khast, see

Khas (?), Sphinx 14, 158, a town on the Libyan frontier.

Khashabu, IV, 783, a district in Syria; situation unknown.

Khat, Khaṭ, a part of Denderah.

Khatȧāi, IV, 789, a district in Syria; situation unknown.

Khatȧthana, Annales 4, 131, a district in Syria; situation unknown.

Khatithet, a Sûdânî country, far to the south.

Khatum', IV, 790, a district in Syria; situation unknown.

Khaathen, IV, 802, a Sûdânî country; situation unknown.

Khathai (read (?)), IV, 781, a district in Syria; compare Heb. חֹסָה, 1 Chron. xvi, 38.

Khathartchau, IV, 789, a district in Syria; situation unknown.

Khathakana, Rec. 20, 117, a district in Syria; situation unknown.

Khaṭṭ, a town in Egypt (?)

Khaṭum', Anastasi I, 17, 7, a district in Syria; situation unknown.

Khatcham', IV, 789, , Rec. 20, 117, a district in Syria; situation unknown.

Khā , , , Mendes.

Khā åsut , a town in Egypt.

Khāi , a Nome in Upper Egypt.

Khāi , Rev. 12, 1, Rec. 37, 70, the capital of the Nome Khāi.

Khāi-t ur-t , Edfû.

Khāi en åakhuti , Edfû.

Khāi-t en mut neter , Denderah.

Khā-t utet qa em ḥat , a name of Karnak and of Thebes.

Khāba , the pyramid of King Saḥurā.

Khāfau , a town in Egypt.

Khā em Maāt , Rec. 20, 42, the temple of Åmenḥetep III at Ṣûlb between the Second and Third Cataracts.

Khā meḥt , an estate of King Khufu.

Khā em ḥebs , a sanctuary at Lycopolis.

Khā nefer , , Memphis.

Khā nefer , , the pyramid of King Merenrā .

Khā nefer ḥe-t Usertsen , the pyramid town of Usertsen I.

Khā neter mesu , a town in Egypt.

Khā resu , an estate of King Khufu.

Khāḥet , IV, 802, a Sûdânî country; situation unknown.

Khā khāb (?) , B.D.G. 562, a lake (?)

Khā Khākheperrā , the name of the pyramid of Usertsen II.

Khā Khufu , an estate of King Khufu.

Khāui (?) Seneferu , Weill, Décrets, 107, the two pyramids of Seneferu.

Khā kau , a sanctuary of Rā.

Khibur , Rec. 20, 118, Hebron; Heb. חֶבְרוֹן.

Khirba (Khalba, Khalpa) , , , , L.D. III, 153, Rec. 8, 134, Aleppo; Assyr. , Gr. χαλυβον.

Khirpa , L.D. III, 146, a Hittite town; Boghaz Keui, Khal-ap.

Khirtha , L.D. III, 144, Rec. 20, 118, Eg. Res. 61, 16, a district in Syria; compare Heb. חֲרֶם, Judges i, 35.

Khisas[khe]pa , L.D. III, 146, Treaty 27, a Hittite district in Syria; Boghaz Keui, Khi-ish-sha-ash-kha-pa.

Khita , , Rec. 11, 71, Heth; Heb. חֵת, Assyr. .

Khu-t khu Kheper , Edfû.

Kheb : (1) a town in the Nome Matenu; (2) , Metternich Stele 65, a town in the Delta; (3) , , , a canal in the Nome Ka Kam.

Khebit , Sphinx 14, 159, , Hymn Darius 29, , , , , , , , , Rec. 30, 190, , , , the swamp land of the Nome Metelites (Chemmis).

Khebs ta āa ḥeb , Berg. 52, a name of Mendes.

Kheppȧ , IV, 802, a Sûdânî country; situation unknown.

Khep[er] em ḥa , , , a name of Denderah and of Edfû.

Kheper , , Denderah.

Kheper , , , a district in the Nome of Thebes.

Kheft ḥer en ȧr Rā , a name of Thebes.

Kheft ḥer en neb-s-t , IV, 834, Rec. 2, 129, , Tombos 3, , , , , , a fortified gate of Western Thebes.

Khem , N. 676, M. 211, , Panopolis, the capital of the Nome Menu; Gr. χέμμις, Copt. ⲭⲙⲓⲙ, ⲭⲙⲓⲛ, ϣⲙⲓⲛ, Arab. الاخميم.

Khemkhem , Karnak 42, 28, a town in Egypt.

Khemik , IV, 802, a Sûdânî country; situation unknown.

Khemenu , , , , , , , , Rec. 31, 25, , , B.M. 280, , , , , , , Demot. Cat. 423, the capital of the Nome Unt (Hermopolites); Assyr. .

Khenbat (?) , Treaty 29, a Hittite town or district.

Khenm Khufu , an estate of King Khufu.

Khensu (?) , , , the 2nd Nome of Lower Egypt (Letopolites). The object represented on the stand of the first example is the placenta.

Khenti , , , the Nubian frontier; , Rec. 27, 191, a land in the Sûdân.

Khent , Thes. 1251, 1287, the estate of Thothmes III in Lebanon.

Khent , a lake district in the Fayyûm.

Khenti , Rec. 14, 21, a town in Egypt.

Khenti Ȧabt , , A.Z. 1913, 124, the 14th Nome of Lower Egypt (Tanites), capital Thar (Tanis).

Khenti Ȧabtt , , , , , , the frontier town of the Nome Tanites.

Khenti ānkhiu , B.D.G. 127, the temple of Osiris in Sheṭnu.

Khenti Menu, Khent Menu , , , , Demot. Cat. 424, Apu (Panopolis, Chemmis); Copt. ϣⲙⲓⲛ.

Khent en Uast , Dream Stele, the foreshore of Thebes (?).

Khent nefer , a town in the Delta.

Khent en Teḥen, the frontier of Teḥen in the Northern Sûdân.

Khent en Thar, , , , a district in the Nome Thebȧḥt.

Khent ḥen nefer, Thes. 1288, the Southern Sûdân.

Khent Shemu (?), a lake in Western Thebes near the Rameseum.

Khent ka Ȧssȧ, an estate of Ȧssȧ.

Khent Ta Sti, the Southern Sûdân.

Khentchi, , a district in the Nome Thebȧḥt.

Kher, the Necropolis of Western Thebes.

Kher, Rec. 1, 52, a town in Egypt.

Kherp, A.Z. 1874, 113, the name of a pyramid.

Kherpantȧris, L.D. III, 146, Treaty 28, a Hittite district (?)

Kherm'u, Rev. 11, 169, Lake Timsaḥ.

Khertuf ḥesutuf, Thes. 1318, a court of Ȧmen at Thebes.

Khekh, , , Rec. 27, 191, B.D.G. 628, Sunu, Syene.

Khesȧu, a name for the grave.

Khesef Ȧntiu, A.Z. 1907, 96, the Island Gazîrat al-Malik in the Second Cataract.

Khesem, , , , B.D. 64, 29, ; see .

Khet, Rec. 19, 22, the Egyptian town called Naucratis by the Greeks.

khet, , a name given to many canals.

Kheta, IV, 701, 727, , , , a district and town of the Hittites; Heb. חֵת, Assyr. .

Kheti, a district of Coptos.

Kheti (Khemti ?), a district of Panopolis.

Khetem, a name of Pelusium.

Khetem, , , a canal in the Nome Edfû.

Khetem, , , , a proper name (Etham ?), literally, "fortress"; compare Heb. אֵתָם, Exod. xiii, 20, Gr. 'Οθομ, 'Οθωμ.

Khetem en Merenptaḥ, the fortress of Menephthah in Theku .

Khetem ur en Uatch-ur, Rec. 22, 106, the Mediterranean fortress, Pelusium (?)

Khetem enti em Thar, the fortress of Tanis.

Khetem Gebti . . . . , the fortress of Coptos.

Khetmen, , , , , the name of a certain kind of land, and of Egypt itself (?)

Khet en bāḥ, the landing place of Neb-ḥeḥ; , the sacred boat of Memphis.

Khet ḥesp-t, , , , a region containing terraced gardens near Coptos.

Khet Thar, Tanis.

Khetchar, , Rec. 12, 53, 57, a district in the Delta.

Khaut, a swampy region in the east of the Delta.

Khaut Ānep, B.D. 112, 1, the swamps of Ānep.

Khakha, a swampy region; situation unknown.

Kha-t åment = .

Kha-t menå, Denderah = .

Kharm, a canal in the Nome Heroopolites.

Kharkhar (?), , , a canal in: (1) the Nome Cynopolites; (2) the Nome Herakleopolites; (3) the Nome Letopolites.

Khas, a district in the Nome Ka khas (?)

Khas Tem, a sacred lake at Denderah.

Khati, , , , a town near Athribis; var. .

Khen, , , , , a canal in the Nome Uthes Ḥeru.

Khen nesu **(p-khen-nesu),** the "Royal Canal" of Edfû.

Khen, B.D. 110, 23, , Rec. 10, 140, , , , , , , , a town near Gebel Silsilah.

Khenu, , , , , a name given to any city in Egypt in which the king and his court resided; Assyr. .

Khenkhen, , , , , , Middle or Upper Egypt.

Khenu-t en Maāt, a district near Busiris.

Khenu Shu, a name of Memphis (?)

Khenbi, IV, 801, a Sûdânî country; situation unknown.

Khnem, , , , a canal in the Nome Ṭuf.

Khnem-t, the famous well at Abydos.

Khnem-t, a well in the Eastern Desert near Sni (Latopolis).

Khnem-t Abetch, the well and temple of Rameses II at Abydos.

Khnem Åaṭen, Edfû.

Khnem-t Åbsaqba a well in the desert between Egypt and Syria.

Khnem-t Åmentet en Kam, B.D. (Saïte) 163, 16, the well of the Åmentet of Egypt.

Khnem-t āa-t ur-t, the Wells of Moses, east of Suez.

Khnem ānkhtt, , , a portion of the Necropolis of Western Thebes called , "the heaven of divine souls."

Khnem ānkhtt en Khemenu, a district of Western Thebes.

Khnem-t (?) uas, the temple of Rameses II at Ḳûrnah.

Khnem Menmaātrā nekhtut, a well dug by Seti I.

Khnem netchem, a sweet-water well on the road between Egypt and Syria.

Khnem resh-t, Denderah.

Khnem reshtu, a temple of Rameses III at Thebes.

Khnem Ḥuthaina, a well near Êthâm and Migdôl.

Khnem-t ḥeru, a famous well in Nubia.

Khnem ḥeḥ, a temple of Rameses III at Thebes.

Khnem Seti Merenpteḥ, a well dug by Seti II Meneph-thah.

Khnem-t qebḥ, the Nilometer shaft at Edfû.

Kherāḥa, P. 605, , B.D. 169, 20, , , , , a town on the right bank of the Nile, the site of which is marked to-day by Fusṭâṭ, or Old Cairo, Babylon of Egypt.

Kheru, , a district in the Nome Nefer Àmenti.

Kher Ṭeḥuti, P. 504, a town in the Ṭuat.

Sa, Sai, U. 556, P. 709, , , , IV, 1134, 1135, , , , , , Saïs, the capital of the Nome Sàpi meḥ; Assyr. , Copt. ⲥⲁⲓ.

Sa em Ta en ḥetch, a name of Sni (Latopolis).

Sai Ta ḥer sept Uatch ur, A.Z. 1871, 12, a tongue of land joining Lake Barullus and the sea.

Sait, , the valley of the cat-mummies near Beni-Ḥasan.

Sau, a district on the western side of the Red Sea.

Saut, N. 649, , T. 275, P. 204, , , , B.D. 125, II, 33, , , , , capital of the Nome Àtef khent; Copt. ⲥⲓⲟⲟⲩⲧ (Asyûṭ).

Sanḥem, B.D. 110, Sinsin I, 4, the Grasshopper City in the Ṭuat.

Sakheb, , a town in the Saïte Nome.

Sātarr, , , Nàstasen Stele, a town in the Sûdân; situation unknown.

Sānkh Sesheta Àssà, an estate of King Àssà.

Su, IV, 800, a Sûdânî country; situation unknown.

Suānu, Sunu, Meux Cat., , Rec. 21, 51, , Rec. 13, 34, , , , , , Syene; Gr. Συήνη, Heb. סְוֵנֵה, Copt. ⲥⲟⲩⲁⲛ Arab. أسوان.

Sun , A.Z. 49, 81, , Pelusium; LXX Σαίν.

Sun , the district of Pelusium (?)

Seben (?) , U. 330, T. 300, a town in the Ṭuat (?)

Sebekh àakhut , the temple of Thek, the capital of the Nome Nefer Àabti.

Sep , the 18th Nome of Upper Egypt (Oxyrhynchites).

Sep , the capital of the Nome Sep (Hipponon).

Sep-Rā , a sun temple near Ṣaḳḳârah.

Sma Āntch-t (?) , a town in the Delta.

Sma Bast , a district near Bubastis.

Sma Beḥuṭ , the 17th Nome of Lower Egypt (Diospolites); , a town in the Nome.

Sma Beḥuṭ , B.D.G. 708, a district near Edfû.

Smen , a town near Gebelên.

Smen Maāt : (1) a town of Hathor near Memphis; (2) a town of Ptaḥ near Sekhem; varr. and .

Smen Ḥer , B.D.G. 1063, the capital of the Nome Àmpeh (Ptolemaïs ?)

Smen Ṭeṭ (Tcheṭ) , a district in the Nome Busirites.

Sni (?) , the capital of the Nome Latopolites (Asnâ).

Senf , a name of Memphis.

Senemtt , Shipwreck 10, , a district in Nubia round about the First Cataract, the modern Biggah.

Senhaqarha , B.D. (Saïte) 163, 2, a town in Nubia (?); var. , ibid. 3.

Senk , B.D. 113, 9, a town in Egypt.

Senti Nefert , the capital of the Nome Nefer Àment (Metelites); Coptic ⲙⲉⲗⲉϫ.

Serà Ḥe-t neha , Saft al-H. Shrine, a locality in the Delta.

Serenkik , IV, 796, a Sûdânî country; situation unknown.

Serq , Pselchis; var. .

Serk , a district in the Nome Nefer Àabti.

Serk (?) ta , , the capital of the district Ḥetep Ḥem.

Seher , P.S.B. 25, 220, a town in Egypt.

Seher sa , a town or district in the Sûdân; situation unknown.

Sekhim = , Letopolis.

Sekhut enth ḥenmemu , a name of the temple and town of Denderah.

Sekheb , , , a town in the Nome Saïtes.

Sekhem , , , , Sinsin 3, 10, , , B.D. 1, 21, , , , , , , , , , , , Rec. 29, 144, , Letopolis the capital of the Nome Khensu (?)

Sesh , , a district in Ḥensu (Herakleopolis); var. .

Sesh en Ȧteḥ , the birthplace of Horus in the Delta.

Sesh en neb Sa , a suburb of Saïs.

Seshesh , Weill, Décrets, 107, the 7th Nome of Upper Egypt (Diospolites Parva); , IV, 957, the capital of the same.

Seshesh , a town in Egypt.

Seshem-t = , Sekhem.

Seshen , , a town in Egypt; varr. , , .

Seshensem , IV, 802, a Sûdânî country; situation unknown.

Sesher , IV, 924, a town in Egypt.

Sesheriut , IV, 689, a district in Syria; situation unknown.

Skarga , a town in the Sûdân. The Σακόλχη of Ptolemy (?)

Seker , , the modern Ṣakkârah.

Seker mer ānkh Ȧssȧ , an estate of King Ȧssȧ.

Segur , Rec. 19, 18, a district; situation unknown.

Set, Seṭ (Sem-t) , , , , , , , desert, necropolis; plur. , .

Set (Sem-t) Ȧmentt , the Necropolis of Western Thebes.

Set (Sem-t) Gebti , the desert of Coptos.

Set, Sti , N. 661, , P. 669, , M. 779, , , the land of the bow, *i.e.*, Nubia—the Sûdân, more fully Ta Sti, . For see B.D. (Saïte) 163, 9.

Sta , , , , the canal in the Nome Ȧtef peḥ.

Setep , , a temple of Thoth.

Setek , , the district of the goddess Pekht near Beni Ḥasan.

Sethu , IV, 799, , Rev. 15, 103, a district in Northern Nubia.

Saȧba, Rec. 20, 118, , Champ. Not. II, 120, a district in Syria; situation unknown.

Saāabu, Westcar Pap. a town in Egypt.

Sauȧb Seneferu, an estate of Seneferu.

Sa Uaḥ-t, Rec. 21, 14, the region of the Great Oasis.

Sauka, Saka, , IV, 784, , P.S.B. 27, 186, a district in Syria; situation unknown.

Sabȧar, Anastasi I, 27, 5, a district in Syria; situation unknown.

Sabur, a town in Egypt.

Saburi ...., Gol. 4, 5, a district in Syria; situation unknown.

Samā (Sam'), Rec. 20, 116, a district in Syria; situation unknown.

Sam'ȧraua, IV, 793, a district in Syria; situation unknown.

Sannur, Rec. 20, 118, a district in Syria; situation unknown.

Sa-t en Sau, the temple of Khnemu at Latopolis.

Sanka, Mar. Aby. II, 2, a country; situation unknown.

Sanger, IV, 700, , , varr. , L.D. III, 88, , Gol. 4, 8, Shinar, Babylonia; Assyr. , Heb. שִׁנְעָר, Arab. سنجار.

Sari, Rec. 20, 116, , a district in Syria; situation unknown.

Sarmertȧ, IV, 791, a district in Syria; situation unknown.

Sarmesk, Rec. 20, 116, a district in Syria; situation unknown.

Sarna, , IV, 782, a district in Syria; Assyr. , compare Heb. שָׁרוֹן, Isaiah lxv, 10.

Sarneg, Maskhûṭâh Stele, Drangiana; Pers. , Behis. I, 16, Babyl. , 6.

Sarresu (?), IV, 793, , Treaty 27, a district in Syria.

Sarsar, Nȧstasen Stele 57, a town in the Sûdân.

Sarka, Gol. 4, 7, a district; situation unknown.

Sarkasha, IV, 788, a district in Syria; situation unknown.

Sartȧ (Saltȧ), , IV, 785, a district in Syria; situation unknown.

Saḥ, IV, 802, a Sûdânî country; situation unknown.

Saḥ, N. 149, a town in the Ṭuat (?)

Sakhpana, Treaty 28, a district in Syria; situation unknown. Boghaz Keui [ilu]za-kha-bu-na-ash.

Saqṭi, Maskhûṭâh Stele, Sogdiana; Pers. , Behis. I, 16, Babyl. , 6.

Saka, capital of the Nome Āntch (Busirites, Cynopolites); Copt. ⲕⲁⲓⲥ.

Sakam, Anastasi I, 21, 6, Shechem; compare Heb. שְׁכֶם, LXX Συχέμ.

Sakakhi, IV, 789, a district in Syria; situation unknown.

Saksakṭi-t, Nȧstasen Stele 42, a town in the Egyptian Sûdân.

Sakath, Rec. 20, 116, a district in Syria; situation unknown.

Sagabaina, Anastasi III, 3, 7, a lake in the Delta.

Satȧ . . . . ., IV, 792, a district; situation unknown.

Satuna, Eg. Res. II, 175, a district; situation unknown.

Satkhebeg, IV, 789, a district in Syria; situation unknown.

Satchḥar, Eg. Res. 54, 15, a district in Syria; situation unknown.

Sȧpi, B.D.G. 996, a name of Saïs.

Sȧpi meḥ, the 5th Nome of Lower Egypt (Saïtes), capital Saïs.

Sȧpi Shemā, the 4th Nome of Lower Egypt (Prosopites).

Sȧna, a district in Syria; situation unknown.

Sȧsȧ, B.D. 98, 7, a fiery district in the Ṭuat.

Sȧti, B.D. 141, 113, a town of Osiris.

Sānkh, a town in Egypt.

Sānkh Taui, a part of Memphis; var.

Suan, Demot. Cat. 423, Syene, Aswân.

Subqa, IV, 789, a district in Syria; situation unknown.

Sumnu, Rec. 28, 168, Sni (Latopolis, Asnâ).

Suna, Rec. 20, 117, a district conquered by Rameses III.

Sur, IV, 792, a district in Syria; situation unknown.

Suhen, Rev. Eg. 4, 95, a fortress in Thebes.

Suḥ, T. 342, P. 221, a town in the Ṭuat (?)

Sukaua, IV, 790, a district in Syria; situation unknown.

Sukbak, IV, 792, a district in Syria; situation unknown.

Suṭen, a canal in the Nome Herakleopolites.

Seb, a town in Egypt.

Sbatt, a mythological locality.

Sba en qerti, "the Door of the Circles" in the Ṭuat, a name of Abydos.

Sebaq, Gol. 12, 81, a district; situation unknown.

Sebma, IV, 805, a Sûdânî country; situation unknown.

Sebkh-t meḥt, a town in Egypt.

Sebkh-t rest, a town in Egypt.

Sebkh-t Sheta, a district in Ȧn (Heliopolis).

Sebek, Crocodilopolis.

Seb Ta kerhet, a quarter of Memphis.

Sebti pāfȧu, Sphinx 14, 156, a town in the Delta.

Sebti en Uast, the fortress of Thebes.

Sebti en Nept, the fortress of Nept (Napata).

Sebṭa, Rec. 24, 160, a district; situation unknown.

Sebṭi-t Årksetres, a name of Alexandria.

Sepṭ (?), the 20th Nome of Lower Egypt (Nomus Arabicus).

Smen tebnut (?), Rec. 22, 2, a town in Egypt.

Sen-t (Ḥe-t Sent (?), Inscrip. Methen, a group of villages in the Delta.

Senu, Rec. 20, 91, B.D. 124, 20, a sanctuary of Menu at Panopolis.

Senger, Mar. Aby. II, 2, L.D. III, 88, Rec. 32, 69, Shinar, Babylonia; Heb. שִׁנְעָר.

Sentchar, a district in Syria; Tall al-'Amarnah

Ser, B.D. 149, a town in the 7th Åat.

Seruṭ Rā Åssà, an estate of King Åssa.

Sernik, IV, 796, a Sûdânî country; situation unknown.

Sehetep, a town near Ån (Heliopolis).

Seḥetep Rā Åssà, an estate of King Åssa.

Seḥtem, IV, 801, a Sûdânî country; situation unknown.

Seḥṭ Ṭeṭefrā, an estate of Ṭeṭefrā.

Seḥetch, Rec. 33, 4, a part of Memphis.

Sekh-t, var., a district in the Nome Menu.

Sekh-t, the Canopic branch of the Nile.

Sekh-t, Sphinx 14, 158, the plain of Baḥêrah.

Sekh-t, a portion of Sni (Latopolis).

Sekh-t åabt, B.D.G. 13, "eastern meadow," a district near Bubastis; "western meadow," a district near Bubastis.

Sekh-t åamit, Rev. 19, 18, the Oasis of Jupiter Ammon (Sîwah).

Sekh-t Åanra (Åaru), "Field of Reeds," the "Elysian Fields" of the Egyptians.

Sekh-t åur, a town near Sni (Asnâ).

Sekh-t Ån, Metternich Stele 89. Horus was stung by a scorpion here.

Sekh-t uāb, a district in the Nome Mātenu.

Sekh-t Mam = Nu-t ent Ḥāp, in the 3rd Nome of Lower Egypt.

Sekh-t Mathu-ḥetep, Hh. 377, a mythological locality (?)

Sekh-t mur (?), a town in the Nome Apollinopolites.

Sekh-t Mefek, Rec. 22, 2, a town near Saïs.

Sekh-t ment, var., a district of Tanis.

Sekh-t en Bast, B.D.G. 207, the territory of the goddess Bast.

Sekh-t en per Ḥeru, the temple estate of Edfû.

Sekh-t ent re Upi, B.D.G. 22, a town near Memphis.

Sekh-t Neter, a district in the Nome Ten (?)

Sekh-t Neter, "Field of God," a name of the Nome Bubastites.

Sekh-t en Tchann, "Field of Zoan," Tanis; Heb. שְׂדֵה־צֹעַן, Psalm lxxviii, 12, Copt. ϪⲀⲚⲎ.

Sekh-t Rā, the estate of a famous sun-temple near Memphis.

Sekh-t resa (?), Rec. 31, 35, a town in Egypt.

Sekh-t Ḥemam, "Salt-field" (Nitriotes, Wâdî an-Naṭrûn).

Sekh-t Ḥetep, a region near Athribis.

Sekh-t Sebek, a district in the 7th Nome of Lower Egypt (Metelites).

Sekh-t Shakkȧ, Demotic Cat. 424, a place near al-Hibah.

Sekh-t Shu, a waste district in the Nome Shens, in Lower Egypt.

Sekh-t shent, a district and canal in the Nome Ȧmpeḥ.

Sekh-t Kenset, P. 175, N. 947, the region of Lower Nubia.

Sekh-t Ṭeṭefrā, an estate of Ṭeṭefrā.

Sekh-t Tchān, "Field of Zoan," Tanis; see **Tchān**; Heb. שְׂדֵה־צֹעַן, Psalm lxxviii, 12, 43, Arab. صان.

Sekhaȧ; see **Ȧat Sekhau**.

Sekhem peḥti, a town in the Eastern Delta near Rameses.

Sekhti (Sekhem-ti ?), Upper and Lower Egypt.

Sessu, Rec. 31, 28, a town in the Fayyûm.

Sessukauar, Gol. 4, 8, a district in Syria; situation unknown.

Sesben, IV, 791, a Sûdânî country; situation unknown.

Seshem, a district in the Delta.

Seshem nefert, an estate in the Delta.

Seshem ḥeḥ, the name of a sacred lake at Ḥensu.

Seshemu taui, Mar. Karn. 52, 9, a royal palace in the Delta (?)

Sek, Maskhûṭah Stele, Scythia, "at the end of the earth," Pers. Sa-ka, Behis. I, 16.

Seg, a village or estate.

Segar; see **Theku**.

Segert, a sanctuary of Osiris at Busiris; see.

Segeḥ, Sphinx 14, 160, a town in the Delta.

Segeq, a town in Egypt.

Set, the country of Set, *i.e.*, Lower Egypt.

Set, the Nome Hypselites.

Statt, Rec. 7, 78, the Necropolis of Memphis.

Ståreḥ, Sphinx 14, 163, Sethroïs (?)

Stit, P.S.B. 25, 220, a town in Egypt.

Sti en sa ḥeb sås (?), Denderah.

Sethebu, Rec. 20, 115, IV, 798, a Sûdânî country; situation unknown.

Seth-t, P. 90, M. 119, N. 698: (1) the district of the First Cataract; (2) Asia.

Seṭ, IV, 799, a Sûdânî country; situation unknown.

She, the lake country, *i.e.*, the Fayyûm.

Sha-t, IV, 618, a country; situation unknown.

Sha-t (?), Stele of Alexander IV, a locality in the Nome.

Shashat (?), a part of the temple of Ån.

Shaåuka, L.D. III, 252, 38, perhaps one of the two towns called Sôkhôh, שׂוֹכֹה in Judah; see Josh. xv, 35, 48.

Shaåna, a lake (?)

Shaånåurgenna, IV, 790, a district in Syria; situation unknown.

Shaåsu resu (shemāu ?), the southern deserts.

Shaås ḥeri, A.Z. 1884, 89, 96, a district in the Sûdân.

Shaås ḥetep, Rec. 27, 87, B.D.G. 1063, capital of the Nome of Set (Hypsele); Copt. ϣⲱⲧⲡ.

Shaā, a canal in the Nome Hermopolites in Upper Egypt.

Shaā, a country in the Sûdân.

Shāshā Åmen (with the article □), a district of Thebes.

Shau (?), B.D. 142, a town of Osiris.

Shaua, Anastasi I, 19, 4, a mountain in Syria.

Shauaṭ, L.D. III, 252, 21, a district in Syria; situation unknown.

Shaurentȧ, IV, 789, a district in Syria; situation unknown.

Shaus, A.Z. 1865, 28; see **Shasu**; **Shaus**.

Shausef, a district in the Nome Busirites; var.

Shab, Rec. 20, 116, a district in Syria; situation unknown.

Shaba, Rev. 13, 108, Sâba (?)

Shabareth Uarkit, L.D. III, 252, 75 and 76, a district in Syria; situation unknown.

Shabareth en gabari, L.D. III, 252, 73 and 74, a district in Syria; situation unknown.

Shabtuna, IV, 784, , a district in Syria; situation unknown; varr. , Rec. 20, 118, .

Shamābu (Shambu), IV, 790, a district in Syria; situation unknown.

Shamāna (Shamna), , , IV, 782, a district in Syria; situation unknown.

Shamāna (Shamna), , IV, 781, a district in Syria; situation unknown.

Shamāshaȧtum, IV, 783, , ibid., a people or district of Syria; var.

Shamāshana, Rec. 20, 118, a district in Syria; situation unknown; compare Heb. שִׁמְשׁוֹן.

Shanamā (Shanam), , , IV, 782, , L.D. III, 252, 15, a district in Syria; Heb. שׁוּנֵם, Josh. xix, 18.

Shanarkai, IV, 790, a district in Syria; situation unknown.

Sharnerȧm, Eg. Res. 83, 104, a district in Syria; situation unknown.

Sharḥana, IV, 4, , P.S.B. 9, 162, , IV, 648, , L.D. III, 252, 125, a district in Syria; Heb. שָׁרוּחֶן, Josh. xix, 6.

Shaḥetep, a part of the Labyrinth representing the Nome Thebȧḥt.

Shasa, , Rec. 11, 60, 25, 194; see .

Shasu, B.D. 3, 127, , IV, 721, the country of the nomads who lived to the east of Egypt; , the Hyksos.

Shasef, , , Rec. 15, 151, a district in the Nome Busirites.

Shas ḥertt, , A.Z. 1884, 96, the port of Berenice on the Red Sea.

Shas ḥetep , , ; and see , , the capital of the Nome of Set.

Shaqan , Rec. 20, 115, a district in Syria; situation unknown.

Shakan , Sphinx 14, 161, Lycopolis; the modern سجين القوم (?)

Shakana , Mar. Karn. 52, 7, a canal in the Delta.

Shagan , Sphinx 14, 161, Lycopolis; the modern سجين القوم (?)

Sha tep . . . . , , a district in the Nome Busirites.

She àu , the sacred lake at Denderah.

She-t àm , a town in Egypt.

Shàs, Shàsti , IV, 800, , Rec. 20, 114, a Sûdânî country; situation unknown.

Shàtchtem , IV, 798, a Sûdânî country; situation unknown.

Shā , , a town near This.

Shāi en per Ḥeru-àr-ti (?) , a district near Edfû.

Shāi qa em Ànu , , the high sandy ridge near the Temple of Àtem in Heliopolis.

She āntcheṭ , B.D.G. 136, a canal in the Nome Mātenu.

Shārr , IV, 794, a district in Syria; situation unknown.

She Āḥa , the sacred lake of Per Āḥa.

Shi en Àst , the Isis-lake at Memphis.

She ur , : (1) Lake Moeris; (2) a canal in Mendes.

She ur , a town in the Nome Busirites.

Shurbana , Rec. 29, 4 = **Qarbana** .

Shusaren , IV, 794, a district in Syria; situation unknown.

Shushugem (?) (?) , IV, 803, a Sûdânî country; situation unknown.

Shushkhen , Alt-K. 153; see **Àshushkhen** .

Sheb , a town in Egypt.

Shebb , IV, 805, Rec. 20, 114, a Sûdânî country; situation unknown.

She Bār , , B.D.G. 186, a lake in the Nome Ṭuf.

Shep , Rec. 5, 86, the Fayyûm district.

Sheps , the Labyrinth.

Sheps Khāfrā , an estate of King Khāfrā.

Sheps Khufu , an estate of King Khufu in the Eastern Delta.

Shefit , a district in the 7th Nome of Upper Egypt.

She Maāti , , , , , the sacred lake at Ḥânês (Herakleopolis).

Shemā , Rec. 13, 96, , Demot. Cat. 425, , Rec. 13, 11, the South, Upper Egypt.

Shemu, a lake near the town of Rameses in the Delta.

Shemu, a quarter of Memphis.

She menȧt (?), a sacred lake or canal in Edfû.

She meḥ-t, the northern portion of Lake Moeris.

Shems, IV, 800; varr., Rec. 20, 114, a Sûdânî country; situation unknown.

Shemshuȧȧtum', IV, 783; see **Shamāshaȧtum'**.

Shemta, Rec. 27, 188, a town in Egypt.

Shenu, the capital of the Nome Maḥetch.

Shenu, a town of Set.

Shenu (?), a sanctuary of Horus at Latopolis.

She en ānkh, B.D.G. 116, the temple-lake at Denderah.

Shenār, P. 589, a town in Lower Egypt.

Shenā khen, B.D.G. 1063: (1) capital of the Nome Herakleopolites; (2) a name of the town Smen Ḥer; Copt. ⲡⲟⲩϣⲓⲛ, Feshn.

Shenit, a sanctuary in the Nome Herakleopolites.

Shenit She en Serser, Ṭuat VIII, the district of the Lake of Fire.

Shen, Shen ur, the irrigated land of Memphis.

Shen ur: (1) part of the Nome Ȧneb ḥetch; (2) part of the Nome Ḥeq ȧmes; (3) part of the Nome Heroopolites.

Shen ur, Rec. 27, 190, the "Great Circle," the Ocean.

Shen-t ur kherp ḥem, the "granary of the high-priest" at Memphis.

Shenp, a district of Edfû.

She en Māam (?), B.D. 17, a sacred lake in Ḥensu (Herakleopolis).

Shenmu, B.D. 160, 3, a town associated with Shu.

She en nesert, a fiery lake in Neruṭef.

Shenrāḥen (?), Nilopolis (?)

She enti Ḥeru, "lake of Horus," a name of Lake Moeris.

Shens, B.D.G. 788, a city in the Eastern Delta, probably in the Wâdî Ṭûmîlât.

She nesu en Beḥuṭ, a name of the canal of Edfû.

Shen qebḥ, B.D.G. 1064, B.D. 79, 3, a Nome and its capital in the Eastern Delta.

She neter, a sacred lake at Abydos.

Shenth Net, Amherst Pap. 46, a town in the Delta.

Sherp, the capital of the Oasis of Sekh-t ḥemam.

Sherhen, a canal in Lower Egypt; var.

She res, "South Lake"—a lake in the Fayyûm.

Sher-t geḥes (?) (?), a district; situation unknown.

She Ḥeru, a town to the north of Thebes, شنهور (?)

She Ḥeru: (1) a canal in the 14th Nome of Lower Egypt; (2) a lake in the 15th Nome of Upper Egypt; (3) a lake at Edfû.

She kharem, Lake Timsaḥ.

She Khufu, an estate of King Khufu.

Shes, a town in the Nome Cynopolites, Ἀλάβαστρων πόλις (?)

Shesp, a town of Osiris; situation unknown.

Shespu àb Rā, a sun temple near Memphis.

Shesp khasha, IV, 788, a district in Syria; situation unknown.

She Seneferu, an estate of King Seneferu.

She Serq, a canal in the 8th Nome of Lower Egypt (Sethroïtes).

She qebḥ: (1) a lake at Heliopolis; (3) the Nile in the First Cataract.

Sheta, U. 560, a town in the Ṭuat.

Shetaṭ, Shetatit, Rec. 11, 182, Rec. 27, 30, the temple of Osiris at Abydos, Busiris, etc.

Sheta, a locality near Denderah.

Sheta, P.S.B. 21, 156, a district; situation unknown.

Shetait, B.D. 125, II, 26, the town of Basti.

Sheta-t àst, a locality in the Nome Heliopolites.

Sheteth, N. 1074, P. 360, a town in the Ṭuat.

Sheṭit, U. 529, P. 711, N. 1359, Rec. 11, 97, B.D. 171, 3, capital of the Nome Arsinoïtes, (Crocodilopolis).

Sheṭit, a canal in the Nome Heliopolites.

Sheṭen: (1) Capital of the Nome Pharbaethites; (2) a town in Libya-Mareotis.

Sheṭ Sebq, Crocodilopolis.

She ṭesher: (1) a part of the Nome of Memphis; (2) a part of the valley of Ḥammâmât.

Sheṭ-t-tà, Rec. 27, 224, a mythological locality (?)

Qa, qaa, qait, a part of the Nome Tekh.

Qaȧnȧu, IV, 782, a district in Syria; situation unknown.

Qai, A.Z. 35, 18, a town in the Nome Aphroditopolites.

Qai en ānkh, the district of Denderah.

Qi qa, Hermopolis.

Qauruputh, Rec. 20, 118, a country conquered by Ramesis III.

Qaurthāntu, Mar. Abyd. 1, 28, a district in Syria; situation unknown.

Qaurthpana, Rec. 20, 118, var., a district in Syria; situation unknown.

Qauḥertȧbarra, Rec. 20, 118, a district in Syria; situation unknown.

Quauḥerthaȧs, Rec. 20, 118, a district in Syria; situation unknown.

Qausanarm', Eg. Res. 61, 13, a district in Syria; situation unknown.

Qausanareth, Rec. 20, 118, a district in Syria; situation unknown.

Qausarā, Rec. 20, 118, a district in Syria; situation unknown.

Qausatȧbarka, Eg. Res. 69, 85, a district in Syria; situation unknown.

Qauthaȧsr, Eg. Res. 60, 8, a district in Syria; situation unknown.

Qaputa, IV, 785, a district in Syria; situation unknown.

Qam'qa, Rec. 20, 118, a district in Syria; situation unknown.

Qam'ṭ, L.D. III, 131, a district in Syria; Assyr. (?)

Qana, Eg. Res. 67, 66, a district in Syria; situation unknown.

Qanefer, the pyramid of Ȧmenemḥat I.

Qarbana, B.D.G. 855, Harris I, 77, 1, an eastern frontier town; Assyr. Karbaniti.

Qarbu, Rec. 17, 150, a town near Abukîr.

Qarbthaqa, Rec. 20, 117, a district in Syria; situation unknown.

Qarmana, L.D. III, 114, Rec. 20, 118, a district in Syria; situation unknown.

Qarm'mu (?), L.D. III, 13, a district in Syria; situation unknown.

Qarḥu, Rec. 20, 118, a district in Syria; situation unknown.

Qarqami'sha, IV, 891, Rev 3, 160, a district in Syria; Assyr., Heb. כַּרְכְּמִישׁ, Isaiah x, 9; the modern Jarâbîs.

Qarqisha, Mar. Abyd. II, 4, a district in Syria; situation unknown.

Qartåānbu, Anastasi I, 22, 4 (a mixture of the two names and), a district in Syria; Heb. קִרְיַת־סֵפֶר, Judges i, 11, LXX Καριασσωφαρ.

Qarthaka, Rec. 20, 118, a district in Syria; situation unknown.

Qasarāa, see .

Qasuna, IV, 782, a district in Syria; situation unknown; compare Heb. קִשְׁיוֹן.

Qatår, Rec. 20, 115, a Sûdânî country; situation unknown.

Qaṭur, Alt-K. 951, a district in Syria; situation unknown; compare Heb. גֶּדֶר.

Qaṭṭhem, L.D. III, 253, 25, a district in Syria; compare Heb. קְדֵמוֹת, Joshua xiii, 18 (?)

Qatchaå, IV, 797, a Sûdânî country; situation unknown.

Qatchatå, Anastasi I, 27, 8, Gaza; Tall al-'Amârnah Azzati, Assyr. Kha-az-zu-tu, Heb. עַזָּה, Arab. غَزَّة.

Qatchir (Qatchil), , IV, 785, , Israel Stele 27, a district in Syria; compare Heb. גֶּזֶר, Tall al-'Amârnah .

Qatchuaṭen, , Rev. 3, 160, , Sallier III, 2 1, a district in Syria; situation unknown; Boghaz Keui alu qi-iz-wa-ad-na.

Qås, Rec. 27, 223, a town in Egypt.

Qāḥ, , Rec. 21, 13, a town in Egypt.

Qin, , IV, 655, , IV, 653, , Anastasi I, 22, 7, a district in Syria; situation unknown; Tall al-Amârnah .

Quina, Rec. 20, 116, a country conquered by Rameses III.

Quburāa, Rec. 20, 118, a district in Syria; situation unknown.

Qebāana, L.D. III, 252, 23, Gibeon; compare Heb. גִּבְעוֹן, Joshua ix, 17, a city in Benjamin.

Qebāu, IV, 786, a district in Syria; situation unknown; compare Heb. גֶּבַע Joshua xxi, 17.

Qebḥ . . . . . , P. 711, , N. 1358 . . . . .

Qebḥ, Rec. 13, 12, , Egypt.

Qebḥui (?), Upper and Lower Egypt.

Qebḥ Ḥeru, Thes. 1218, a name of Upper Egypt.

Qebḥ Set, a name of Lower Egypt.

Qebḥ-t, , , , , the capital of the 1st Nome of Upper Egypt.

Qebḥ, the pyramid of King Shepseskaf.

Qebḥ Khufu, an estate of King Khufu.

Qebsu, Rec. 8, 137, a district in Syria (?)

Qebt, Gebt (varr.), the capital of the 5th Nome of Upper Egypt (Coptites); Copt. ⲔⲈϤⲦ, Arab. القفط; **Merit Qebti**, the port or harbour of Coptos.

Qeb-taui (?), Denderah.

Qepi, the swamp land of the Nome .

Qepu, a district in the Thebaïd (?)

Qefati (?), Ombos I, 130, Crete (?)

Qefnu, B.D. 142, a town of Osiris; situation unknown; var. .

Qem = , Egypt (?)

Qemḥes, a district in the Nome Sept.

Qemtitt, a district; situation unknown.

Qen Àsàr, a quarter of Abydos.

Qen mer, Oxyrhynchus.

Qen ent Rā, Edfû.

Qen enth ḥesu, "the region of the favoured ones"—a district in the Ṭuat.

Qen (?) .... en sekh-t (?), a village in the Eastern Delta.

Qenus, Southern Nubia.

Qenus peḥ, the most southerly part of the same.

Qenb she, a sanctuary on Lake Moeris, associated with Ḥebnu .

Qenqen-t, B.D. 110, a lake in Sekhet-Àaru.

Qenqen taui, a district in Egypt.

Qer-ti, the sources of the Nile at Elephantine.

Qerr, a town in Egypt.

Qeri, a district of Southern Nubia (?)

Qern, a town in Egypt.

Qertnetchna; **Qerthnetchna**, IV, 781, a district in Syria; situation unknown.

Qeḥi, Rec. 12, 91, a suburb of Thebes.

Qeḥs-t, a sanctuary in Edfû; varr. .

Qes, B.D. 114, 3, the capital of the 14th Nome of Upper Egypt, Ἀλάβαστρων πόλις, Κοῦσαι, Cusae; Copt. ⲔⲞⲤ, ⲔⲰⲤ, Arab. القوصيّة.

Qesqes, the capital of the Nome , Apollinopolis Parva.

Qes mer ānkh Åssȧ , an estate of King Åssa.

Qesa (?) , U. 448, T. 260, a town in the Ṭuat.

Qesem , , , Rec. 27, 190, the capital of the Nome Sepṭ, Φάκκουσα; Copt. ⲔⲰⲤ, Arab. فاقوس, Heb. גֹּשֶׁן (?); , the Arabian portion of the town.

Qeṭi , , , , Asien 240 ff., the "Circle" (ⲔⲰⲦⲈ), *i.e.*, the semi-circular North Syrian coast round about the Gulf of Issus. Later it included all the land between the Euphrates and the Mediterranean.

Qeṭem , N. 761, , P. 204, a town in the Delta (?)

Qeṭem' , , , Sa-Neḥat B, 182, 219, the country of the East; compare Heb. קֶדֶם, Josh. xix, 12, 13.

Qeṭna , IV, 696, , Rec. 19, 18, , , L.D. III, 88, a district in Syria; Tall al-'Amârnah .

Qeṭshu , IV, 781, , , IV, 649, 689, , a district in Syria; situation unknown.

Ka , a town in Egypt.

Kainabu , IV, 790, a district in Syria; situation unknown.

Kaau , Unȧ 18, a country in the Sûdân; var. (?) , N. 981.

Kauakaua , A.Z. 35, 18, a town in the Nome Sepṭ.

Kaurm'rarna , Anastasi I, 22, 3, a district in Syria; situation unknown.

Kab , Rec. 20, 115, a Sûdânî country; situation unknown.

Kaban , Sphinx 14, 159, a town in the Delta; Arab. قابيل (?)

Kabuai nefer , Edfû.

Kabur , Rec. 20, 116, a district in Syria; situation unknown; compare Heb. כָּבוּל, Josh. xix, 27.

Kaber , Rec. 24, 160, a district.

Kaf , a locality; site unknown.

Kafr-M'rerna , a district in Syria; situation unknown.

Kaam , , IV, 799, a Sûdânî country; situation unknown.

Kam , B.D. 142, IV, 20, , , , , , , , Egypt; Copt. ⲔⲀⲘⲈ, ⲔⲎⲘⲈ, ⲔⲎⲘⲎ, ⲔⲎⲘⲒ.

Kam , , , Athribis.

Kamm'tȧ , , IV, 781, a district in Syria; Tall al-'Amârnah .

Kami , Rec. 13, 3, , Dem. Cat. 421, Egypt; Copt ⲔⲎⲘⲈ.

Kamit , , the district of Ka Kam.

Kam ur, B.D. 88, 4, a town in the Nome Athribites.

Kam ur, a sanctuary in the Fayyûm.

Kam ur, a canal in the Nomes of Thebes and Coptos.

Kam urȧ, B.D. 64, 13, the great Bitter Lake near Isma'îlîyah.

Kam ur mȧ, the canal that joined the Nile and Red Sea.

Kamru, IV, 792, a district in Syria; situation unknown.

Kam ḥetch, a sanctuary in Sekhem.

Kamsa, Rec. 15, 167, a district; situation unknown.

Kan, IV, 802, a Sûdânî country; situation unknown.

Kanāna, L.D. III, 126, Rec. 11, 55, Israel Stele 26, a district in Syria; compare Heb. כְּנַעַן, Assyr. (Canaan).

Kannu, Rec. 20, 116, a district in Syria; compare Heb. כּוּן, 1 Chron. xviii, 8.

Kanustt, Kanstt, Nubia; var. **Kenstt**.

Kanrut, IV, 789, a district in Syria; situation unknown.

Ka en Ḥeru sheṭ, Latopolis.

Ka en qa renu, Edfû.

Kar, a sanctuary on Lake Moeris.

Kari, Rec. 20, 42, 119, IV, 922, Ḳubbân Stele 5, the district round about Napata (?)

Karbu, Rec. 17, 160, a town in Egypt.

Karpu, L.D. III, 156, a district in Syria; situation unknown.

Karm'im', Rec. 20, 118, a district in Syria; situation unknown.

Karm'n, IV, 785, a district in Syria; see

Karm'ina, Alt-K. 1007, a district in Syria; situation unknown.

Karm'tȧ, IV, 793, a district in Syria; situation unknown.

Karna, Rec. 20, 117, Eg. Res. 65, 20, a district in Syria; situation unknown; compare Heb. גֹּרֶן, Gen. l, 10.

Karkhen, Treaty 29, a Hittite district (?)

Karka, Rec. 20, 118, a district in Syria; situation unknown.

Karkam'sha, IV, 792, Carchemish; Heb. כַּרְכְּמִישׁ, כַּרְכְּמִשׁ, Assyr. The modern Jarâbîs.

Kart, Rec. 21, 226, a town near Daḳḳah in Nubia; Arab. قرطة.

Kart (?), Gol. 4, 9, a district; situation unknown.

Kartâmrut , IV, 791, a district in Syria; situation unknown.

Kartep , Nâstasen Stele, a town in Nubia; situation unknown.

Karth = , A.Z. 1900, 130, Naucratis.

Kahati , Rec. 20, 117, a district in Syria; situation unknown.

Kahni a town in the Nome Athribites.

Ka Ḥeseb , the 11th Nome of Lower Egypt (Cabasites).

Kakham (?) , IV, 789, a district in Syria; situation unknown.

Ka Khas (?) , the 6th Nome of Lower Egypt (Xoïtes).

Kas , , A.Z. 1900, 134, Nubia; Heb. כּוּשׁ.

Kasa , , the capital of the 7th Nome of Upper Egypt (Cynopolites); Copt. ⲔⲀⲒⲤ, ⲔⲞⲈⲒⲤ, Arab. القيس.

Kash Nubia; Heb. כּוּשׁ, Copt. ⲈϬⲰϢ.

Kashpata , Rec. 20, 116, a district in Syria; situation unknown.

Kaqari , L.D. III, 252, 37, a district in Syria; situation unknown.

Kaqeth , Rec. 20, 115, a Sûdânî country; situation unknown.

Kakka (?) , Rec. 17, 119, a town in Upper Egypt.

Ka Kam , T. 84, M. 238, N. 615, the 10th Nome of Lower Egypt (Athribites).

Ka Kam-t , , , Rec. 24, 176, , Gol. 12, 99, the Necropolis of Ṣakkârah; Gr. Κωχώμη.

Kagati , Eg. Res. 66, 49, a district in Syria; situation unknown.

Katarṭ , Nâstasen Stele, a town in the Sûdân.

Kath , Alt-K. 1034, a district in Syria; situation unknown.

Kathar , IV, 793, a district in Syria; situation unknown.

Kathata , Rec. 20, 118, a district in Syria; situation unknown.

Kathini , Rec. 20, 116, a district in Syria; situation unknown.

Kiru , Rec. 20, 116, a district in Syria; situation unknown.

Kirsenpen (?) , Rec. 20, 116, a district in Syria; situation unknown.

Kirshaua (?) , IV, 792, a district in Syria; situation unknown.

Kirkmisha , Carchemish; Heb. כַּרְכְּמִישׁ.

Kitsuna , IV, 781, , a district in Syria; situation unknown.

Kushapat , Eg. Res. 65, 31, a district in Syria; situation unknown.

Kebāsum'n, Kebāsuān , , IV, 782, a district in Syria; situation unknown.

Keben , I, 140, Rec. 27, 224, 225, 29, 146, Gebal; Heb. גְּבַל, Tall al-'Amârnah , Assyr. , Gr. Βύβλος.

Kepuna (Kepen), Anastasi I, 20, 7, , , Rec. 21, 99, Gebal; see **Keben.**

Kefti, IV, 616, , IV, 733, Mar. Aby. II, 2, , , , Rec. 32, 69, , Crete; compare Heb. כַּפְתּוֹר.

Kennarut; var. , IV, 782, a district in Syria; compare Heb. כִּנֶּרֶת, Deut. iii, 17.

Kenaskha (?), IV, 792, a district in Syria; situation unknown.

Kenȧ, Rec. 31, 35, a town in Egypt.

Kennām'u, Anastasi III, 8, 5, Canaan.

Kenem, , , , , , , , , , , the Oasis of Khârgah.

Kenmu, T. 40, a town in the Ṭuat (?)

Kens, U. 178, 419, P. 175, N. 947, , P. 337, , M. 639, , P. 703, , , , , , , , , Nubia.

Kenseth, , IV, 799, Nubia; see **Kens.**

Kentu (?), IV, 783, a district in Syria; situation unknown.

Kentuȧsna, IV, 783, a district in Syria; situation unknown.

Kenthaȧuthȧ, IV, 785, a district in Syria; situation unknown.

Kenthu, , IV, 783, , IV, 784, , IV, 785, a district in Syria; situation unknown.

Kerer (Kelal), , IV, 784, a district in Syria; compare Heb. גְּרָר, Gen. xx, 2.

Krimna, , IV, 783, a district in Syria; situation unknown.

Kerna, Rec. 20, 116, 119; see **Karna.**

Kerka, Rec. 20, 114, a Sûdânî country; situation unknown.

Keha, IV, 802, a Sûdânî country; situation unknown.

Kehek, A.Z. 1883, 88. The were a nomad tribe conquered by Ȧmenḥetep I.

Kes, Kest, IV, 334, , Rec. 26, 76 = , Nubia.

Kesh, , , Rec. 15, 87, a town in the south of the Oasis of Khârgah (Dûsh); Gr. Κύσις.

Kesh (Kash), Mar. Aby. II, 2, , , IV, 733, Jour. E.A., III, 98, Nubia; Tall al-'Amârnah , Assyr. , Heb. כּוּשׁ, Copt. ⲉϭⲱϣ.

Kesh khas-t, IV, 796, Kesh the vile, or Nubia the impotent.

Keshkesh, Coptos 18, a Hittite country.

Keket, , IV, 799, a Sûdânî country; situation unknown.

Ketasha, IV, 792, a district in Syria; situation unknown.

Ketsuna , IV, 781, , IV, 781, a district in Syria; Heb. קְדְשׁוֹן, Tall al-'Amârnah .

Kethnes , IV, 803, a Sûdânî country; situation unknown.

Kethsun , IV, 781, see **Ketsuna.**

Gau , Sanehat, a town in Upper Egypt.

Gauti (?) , , , , , , the town of Canopus.

Gauash, Gash , , , a canal in the Nome Ânpu (Cynopolites).

Gam , Rec. 24, 176, Athribis (?)

Garr , a town in the Egyptian Sûdân (?)

Gahaga , Gol. 4, 1, a country; situation unknown.

Gaqati , A.Z. 1879, 29, a district in Syria; situation unknown.

Gatchai , A.Z. 1879, 29, , IV, 648, Gaza; Heb. עַזָּה, Tall al-'Amârnah , Assyr. , Arab. غزة, Gr. Γάζα.

Gurubu (Gulubu) , , , IV, 797, a Sûdânî country; situation unknown.

Gurses , IV, 796, a Sûdânî country; situation unknown.

Gemit , , Mission 13, 127, a name of Athribis (?)

Gem ur , Rec. 14, 18, a town in Egypt.

Gem baiu-s , , , a town; site unknown.

Gen , , , , a canal in the Nome Maḥetch.

Gen , Rec. 27, 189, a town in Egypt.

Gengen , Sphinx 14, 166, a town in the Delta.

Gennu , , a town in Egypt.

Genp , Canopus.

Genem , = .

Gensh , see **Thegensh** .

Gerb , B.D.G. 49, a town near Canopus.

Gernaȧ , L.D. III, 252, 127, a district in Syria; situation unknown.

Gerses , IV, 796, , Mar. Aby. II, 2; see .

Gerg , an estate of Rameses II near Abydos; , B.D. 99, 30 (Intro.), , Thes. 1253, the property of Osiris at Abydos.

Gerg Rāmessu , Rec. 13, 141, Balyanâ; Copt. ⲦⲠⲞⲨⲢⲀⲚⲎ.

Gergȧmesh , Ombos I, 130, 170, Carchemish; Heb. כַּרְכְּמִישׁ.

Gergubaf , IV, 808, a suburb of Abydos.

Gergbaf , Rec. 22, 138; see .

Gerger , Sphinx 14, 166, a town in the Delta; Arab. قراقرة.

Geḥes, P. 204, Rec. 20, 78, Lib. Fun. II, 57, a town in Egypt (Kôm Yasîn?); var. , P. 683.

Geḥesti, N. 696, , N. 920, , N. 482, the Gazelle country.

Gesa, T. 260, a town (?)

Geṭpeṭkai, Rec. 11, 168, Cappadocia; Pers. , Behis. I, 15, Babyl. , Behis. 6.

Ta, a town of Isis.

Taiu, , IV, 800, a Sûdânî country; situation unknown.

Ta àab, Sphinx 14, 164, the Eastern Delta.

Ta àam, , , B.D.G. 24, a district in the Nome Sep.

Ta àakhu, "land of the spirits"—a country in the Southern Sûdân.

Ta Àmentt, the country to the west of the Nile.

Ta àri, Rec. 16, 118, Asnâ (Latopolis).

Ta àḥ, Mar. Karn. 52, 20, , the Oasis of Farâfrah.

Taiu Àgert, the lands of the Ṭuat of Memphis.

Ta ān, A.Z. 17, 56, a district on the Euphrates (?)

Ta ānkh, a district in the Nome Khensu (?).

Ta ār, Rev. 13, 3 . . . .

Ta uatch, , Mission 13, 4, a town in Nubia near Wâdî Ḥalfah.

Ta uāb, , B.D. 174, 12, the district of Napata (Gebel Barkal).

Ta ur, M. 187, N. 694, , B.D. 40, 5, , A.Z. 1907, 1, 3, the district of Abydos; var. , B.D.G. 158.

Ta utcha, Demot. Cat. 425, a town near Al-Hîbah.

Ta Bati, Rec. 27, 83, Sni (Asnâ).

Ta bar, Eg. Res. 65, 27, Rec. 20, 116, a district in Syria; compare Heb. תָּבוֹר, Josh. xix, 22.

Ta Benr (?), a district near Xoïs.

Ta makhit, Nâstasen Stele 58, a district in the Sûdân.

Ta em ārq ḥeḥ, a name of the Necropolis.

Ta mer, Al-Lahûn, in the Fayyûm.

Ta mer, IV, 805, a Sûdânî country; situation unknown.

Ta merà, , , , , the Land Merà, *i.e.*, Egypt; Gr. Πτίμυρις.

Ta meḥ, A.Z. 1907, 16, , , , , , , Rec. 13, 11, the Land of the North, *i.e.*, the Delta.

Ta meḥi, the district about the Phatnitic mouth of the Nile.

Ta em Thar, the region about Tanis.

Ta nen, a name of Mendes.

Ta nen, a sanctuary of Ptaḥ and Osiris at Memphis; varr.

Ta en Åtem, Tentyra (Denderah), the capital of the Nome Åaṭṭa.

Ta en ānkh, a district of Heliopolis.

Ta nisa(?), Rec. 8, 138, a district in Syria.

Ta en Uatchit, the district of Buto.

Ta en Manu, the West, the land of the sunset.

Ta ent Ḥer, Dendûr in Northern Nubia.

Ta Neḥes, IV, 334, Ḥerusâtef Stele 5, the Sûdân.

Ta en tarer, Tentyris, the capital of the Nome Tentyrites (Denderah); Copt. ⲧⲉⲛⲧⲱⲣⲉ.

Ta Neter, Land of the God, *i.e.*, the Western Coast of the Arabian Peninsula and the African Coast facing it, Somaliland, etc.

Taui Neteru, the desert region between the Nile and the Red Sea.

Tar, Ter, Ḥerusâtef Stele 32, 121, Nåstasen Stele 32, a town in Nubia and a seat of the cult of the goddess Bast; var.

Tarer, Denderah.

Taruṭi peḥ, Nåstasen Stele 40, the region beyond Taruṭi.

Ta rem, B.D. 113, 5, a town in the Delta.

Tarmen, a town in Nubia.

Tarreq, Nåstasen Stele 44, a town in the Sûdân.

Ta ḥetch, a suburb of Thebes (?)

Ta khent, Nubia.

Taiu sa (?), IV, 798, a Sûdânî country; situation unknown.

Ta Sebåk, Crocodilopolis.

Ta semå, IV, 800, Rec. 20, 115, a Sûdânî country; situation unknown.

Ta Set, a district in Upper Egypt.

Ta set, Ta sti, M. 182, N. 661, III, 139, Nåstasen Stele 15,

the land of the bowman (?), *i.e.*, Nubia; , Nubians.

Ta she , , , , , , the Land of the Lake, *i.e.*, the Fayyûm.

Ta shemā , , , , Dream Stele 5, , Rec. 13, 11, the "South land," *i.e.*, Upper Egypt.

Ta shesht, Ta sheshth , , IV, 800, , Rec. 20, 114, a Sûdânî country; situation unknown.

Ta qat , Denderah.

Taqtat (?) , Nåstasen Stele 44, a town in the Sûdân.

Takerhet , a town in Egypt.

Ta tarr , Rec. 15, 159, Tentyris (Denderah).

Ta tham (?) , a foreign country.

Ta tcheser , , , , "holy land"—a name of the Necropolis.

Taȧ , T. 374, M. 190, , M. 125, , N. 694, , Hh. 181, , Hh. 175, the Ṭuat (?)

Ta ȧabȧn , Demot. Cat. 424; Gr. Τιαβωνις.

Ta ȧa-t pa Bast , Rev. 31, 35, a town in Egypt.

Ta ȧa-t thath , Rec. 31, 35, a town in Egypt.

Ta ȧu ȧu , a district of Western Thebes.

Ta ȧmens , a town in Nubia, the modern Kalâbshah; see **Termes.**

Ta ȧhi en Bast , B.D.G. 209, a district in the Nome Theb ȧḥ.

Ta ȧḥ-t pa.... , Sphinx 14, 166, a town in the Delta.

Ta ȧs-t mens , a district of Western Thebes.

Ta ȧs-t en Ṭena , a town in the district of Phathyrites.

Ta ȧs-t ges seshen , a district of Edfû.

Taāanak , IV, 783, , IV, 650, , L.D. III, 252, 14, , , a district in Syria; Heb. תַּעְנָךְ, Josh. xvii, 11, Tall al-'Amârnah .

Ta āt pa-skhenu ... tȧ , Sphinx 14, 162, a town in the Eastern Delta.

Ta āt pa-qen pa-mshā , Rec. 31, 35, a town in Egypt.

Ta āt nehep , a village near Saïs.

Ta āt en Sessu , Anastasi I, 27, 3, a town in the Eastern Delta.

Ta āt en Thar , A.Z. 35, 18, the district of Tanis.

Ta āmi , , Rev. 11, 146, a place; compare Copt. ⲟⲙⲙⲉ.

Ta āmi , Rev. 11, 122, 12, 24, 37, a place.

Ta ān (?), P.S.B. 14, 238, , , a town in the Delta.

Ta ārget, B.D.G. 131, a town near Thebes; Copt. ⲦⲀⲢⲔⲒⲤ, ⲦⲞⲖⲔⲒⲤ.

Ta āḥā en Åmen, B.D.G. 29, A.Z. 1876, 122, a portion of the Necropolis of Thebes.

Taitchai, Rev. 14, 74, a town in Egypt.

Tau (?), Gol. 11, 73, a town near This.

Tau ur, a town near Abydos; see **Nefur**.

Tauḥibit, B.D.G. 160, a town near Memphis.

Tausakh, Gol. 4, 4, a district in Syria; see .

Ta ut, P.S.B. 13, 518, the Necropolis of Ḥe-t-Benu.

Ta utchaȧ, a district in the Nome Sept.

Tab, N. 1360, P. 711, a town in the Ṭuat.

Tabȧ, IV, 802, a Sûdânî country; situation unknown.

Tapun, IV, 785, a district in Syria; compare Heb. דִּיבוֹן Numb. xxi, 30.

Ta ma[it] ȧaṭ-t, B.D.G. 137, a district near Edfu.

Ta mait Åmen, B.D.G. 28, a district in Upper Egypt.

Ta mait ȧser, B.D.G. 72, a district near Edfû.

Ta mait en Penȧi, a district in the Nome Pathyrites.

Ta mait sher, a district near Edfû.

Ta m'khir pet, a town in the Western Delta.

Ta m'ten en Ånep, a suburb of Memphis.

Tam en pa Rā, Sphinx 14, 162, a solar sanctuary.

Tamens, a district of Western Thebes.

Ta mer Rā, Piānkhi Stele, 115, a town near Mendes.

Tamkera, IV, 797, a Sûdânî country; situation unknown.

Ta ner-t en Beḥuṭ, B.D.G. 61, the quarry of Edfû.

Ta[u]nres, IV, 791, a district in Syria; situation unknown.

Tari, B.M. 138, Rec. 15, 171, a district in Eastern Nubia.

Tareb Åmen, P.S.B. 14, 238, a town in Egypt.

Ta res shemā, Demot. Cat. 424, a suburb of Memphis.

Tarshaba, Rec. 20, 116, a district in Syria; situation unknown.

Tar . . . . shemā, Ḥerusȧtef Stele 23, a town in the Sûdân.

Tartcha, IV, 789, a district in Syria; situation unknown.

Ta ḥe-t, , Dabûd, in Nubia (?)

Ta ḥe-t, a town in Lower Egypt, near .

Ta ḥeni pa senb, Sphinx 14, 162, the Serbonian Bog.

Ta kham', a canal in the Nome Herakleopolites.

Ta Kharmush, a canal in the Nome Edfû.

Takheb, N. 1343 = , N. 1360 (?)

Ta kherm'u, a canal in the Nome Sethroïtes.

Tasana [ ], Rec. 20, 115, a district in Syria; situation unknown.

Tasu, P.S.B. 11, 256, a town in Egypt.

Tasth, , IV, 799, a Sûdânî country; situation unknown.

Tashaȧnȧu, a canal near Tanis.

Ta shetaf (?), Pierret, Inscrip. II, 33, a locality in Upper Egypt.

Ta sheṭȧ, Demot. Cat. 424, a place near Thebaïs.

Tasheṭna, L.D. III, 252, 86, a district in Syria; situation unknown.

Taqa, III, 143, a town in Nubia.

Ta qait, , a district in the Nome Set.

Ta qāḥ ḥe-t, , Berlin, 2074, a locality of Eastern Thebes.

Ta qi (?), Demot. Cat. 425, a suburb of Gebelên.

Ta qeḥi, Demot. Cat. 425, a town near Al-Hibah.

Ta kam-t, a town in the Eastern Delta.

Takamsa-t, , , , , Tachompso, the limit of the Δωδεκάσχοινος, on the south, opposite Pselchis; Gr. Ταχομψώ.

Ta kari āa-t pa nefer [ ], Sphinx 14, 165, a town in the Delta.

Tag, a town in Egypt.

Ta get en na sia (?) (var.), a canal near Edfû.

Ta get en ṯa tebt, a canal near Edfû.

Ta Tehen, a fortress in the Nome Ȧnpu.

Tatha, IV, 791, a district in Syria; situation unknown.

Ta then (?), Rec. 31, 35, a town in Egypt.

Ta ṭenȧt, a canal near Tanis.

Ta ṭehen, Rec. 14, 56, the temple of Serapis at Memphis.

Tȧakmers, IV, 791, a district in Syria; situation unknown.

Tȧb, IV, 804, a Sûdânî country; situation unknown.

Tȧbata, Rec. 20, 177, , Rec. 20, 113, a district in Syria; situation unknown.

Tȧmm, IV, 782, a district in Syria; situation unknown.

Tȧm'qur, IV, 794, a district in Syria; situation unknown.

Tȧmenti, Anastasi I, 21, 3, a district in Syria; compare Heb. תִּמְנָה, Josh. xv, 10.

Tȧnai, IV, 733, a district in Syria; situation unknown.

Tȧnep, Rec. 19, 18, Tunep(?) q.v.

Tȧrua, IV, 797, a Sûdânî country; situation unknown.

Tȧrennu, IV, 792, a district in Syria; situation unknown.

Tȧrkha (Talkha), IV, 793, a district in Syria; situation unknown.

Tȧrqaȧr, Anastasi I, 22, 8, a district in Syria; situation unknown.

Tȧkhsa, Anastasi I, 22, 3, a district in Syria; situation unknown; Tall al-Amârnah.

Tȧsakha, Rec. 20, 116; see **Tȧkhsa**.

Tȧsasu, Rec. 20, 114; see **Tȧsurt**.

Tȧsurt, IV, 783, a district in Syria; situation unknown; Tall al-'Amârnah.

Tȧknu (?), IV, 793, a district in Syria; situation unknown.

Tiȧ, IV, 784, a district in Syria; situation unknown.

Tiruaȧa, Gol. 4, 9, a foreign district (?)

Tita, L.D. III, 88, a district in Syria; situation unknown.

Tua, IV, 800, a Sûdânî country; situation unknown.

Tua, B.D.G. Supp. 886, a town in the Nome Maḥetch.

Tuȧub, IV, 790, a district in Syria; situation unknown.

Tui utchai, Piānkhi Stele, a town in the Nome Bu Tchāmui.

Tubakh, a district in Syria (?)

Tubi, IV, 782, Rec. 20, 116, a district in Syria; situation unknown.

Tun, Rec. 20, 115; see **Utent**.

Tunipa, Tunpa, IV, 788, IV, 686, 729, L.D. III, 88, a district in Syria; Assyr.

Tur, Rec. 20, 118, a district in Syria; situation unknown.

Tururek, IV, 797, a Sûdânî country; situation unknown.

Turbi, (*sic*), Eg. Res. 64, 19, a district in Syria; situation unknown.

Turbentȧ, IV, 791, a district in Syria; situation unknown.

Tursi, Rec. 20, 119, a district conquered by Rameses III.

Tuksar, Rec. 20, 118, a district conquered by Rameses III.

Tutina, IV, 781, a district in Syria; situation unknown.

Teban (?), IV, 805, a Sûdânî country; situation unknown.

Tebu, with, B.D. 85, 15, a mythological locality.

Tepasu, P.S.B. 25, 220, a town in Egypt.

Tepi-ȧaut, a name of Edfû.

Tepi Ȧn, B.D.G. 48, a town in Egypt.

Tepi en Ȧn, , , , , "head of the valley," perhaps a proper name.

Tepi ȧḥ, , the capital of the Nome Matenu (Aphroditopolis); Copt. ⲡⲉⲧⲡⲓⲉϩ, Arab. اطفيح.

Tepi uār, , a town, the site of the Northern Fûm al-Khalîg, Babylon of Egypt.

Tepi-t mu (?) a town in Egypt.

Tepi nef, a town in Egypt.

Tepi nekheb, Rec. 20, 115, , , IV, 800, a country conquered by Thothmes III.

Tepi sekh-t, a district near Hermopolis.

Tepi setem, a portion of the Labyrinth which represented the Nome Coptites.

Tepi she maā, a quarter of Thebes.

Tepi shemā, "the head of the South"—the southern frontier of Egypt.

Tepi taui, : (1) a part of the Labyrinth representing the Nome Aphroditopolites; (2) a name of Edfû.

Tepḥen, Sphinx 14, 162, Tahpanhes—a frontier town near Pelusium; Heb. תַּחְפַּנְחֵס, Daphnae, the modern Tall Dafannah.

Tepḥ Nu (Nenu), a sanctuary at Memphis.

Tepḥ tcha, , , , , , a sanctuary in Memphis.

Tepestem, IV, 806, a Sûdânî country; situation unknown.

Tepkenna, IV, 790, a district in Syria; situation unknown.

Teptennu, A.Z. 49, 130, Tebtynis = **Tebtennu**.

Tef ur, see .

Tema, a town in Nubia.

Temi, , , , , the canal of the Nome Bu-tchāmui.

Temmerp, IV, 801, a Sûdânî country; situation unknown.

Temḥ, see .

Tem ḥesi su em peṭ-t pesṭ ṭemṭ, Tombos Stele 10, a fort of Thothmes I in the Third Cataract.

Temesqu, , IV, 781, Damascus; Heb. דַּמֶּשֶׂק, Tall al-'Amârnah, Arab. دمشق, Syr. ܕܪܡܣܘܩ, Gr. Δαμασκός.

Tem qai, a name of Khemenu (Hermopolis Magna).

Ten (?), , the 3rd Nome of Upper Egypt.

Ten (?), the capital of the 3rd Nome of Upper Egypt, Nekheb (Eileithyiaspolis).

Ten, , , Demot. Cat. 424, the capital of the Nome Abydos in Upper Egypt; Gr. Θὶς, Θίνις; varr. , , ; Assyr. .

Tenen, a town in the Delta, Al-Batnûn; Copt. .

Teni, Rec. 11, 147, a town in the Eastern Delta.

Teni, , , , a canal in the Nome Cynopolites.

Tennu, the district of Abydos (?)

Tenuḥi, Rec. 11, 91, a district in Egypt (?)

Tenusuu, IV, 805, a Sûdânî country; situation unknown.

Tent ta ā, a district in the Sûdân.

Tentcham, P.S.B. 7 (plate), a district near Denderah.

Terb, IV, 790, a district in Syria; situation unknown.

Terbu, IV, 791, a district in Syria; situation unknown.

Terbusa, Rec. 20, 117, a country conquered by Rameses III.

Term'nna (?), IV, 788, a district in Syria; situation unknown.

Termems, a town in Nubia, the modern Kalâbshah; see **Termes.**

Termes, Rec. 21, 226, Kalâbshah; varr. , , , Gr. Ταλμις.

Terres, a district in the Sûdân.

Terkhais, Rec. 20, 117, see .

Terter, , , IV, 797, a Sûdânî country; situation unknown.

Tehbȧu, IV, 805, a Sûdânî country; situation unknown.

Tehbebu, IV, 797; see .

Tehen, , , a quarter of the town of Shenākhen in the Nome Arsinoïtes.

Tehni, a temple estate in Memphis.

Tehen ta, see **Tehen.**

Teḥi, Rec. 11, 69, a foreign country.

Teḥnu, M. 766, , IV, 617, , Rec. 11, 68, , Rec. 11, 91, , L.D. III, 229c, , B.D.G. 1064, , Libya.

Tekh, Pap. 3024, 136, a district in Egypt.

Tekht (?), Mar. Karn. 38, a district in Syria (?)

Tekhs, IV, 893, L.D. III, 65A, 17, a district in Syria; Tall al-'Amârnah .

Teser, Rec. 11, 186, a name of the Necropolis.

Teqnen, Ḥerusȧtef Stele 116, a town in the Sûdân.

Tekaru (?), , IV, 796, a Sûdânî country; situation unknown.

Tethnes, IV, 800, a Sûdânî country; situation unknown; varr. , IV, 800, and , Rec. 20, 114.

Tethres, IV, 800, a Sûdâni country; situation unknown.

Thaȧur, Rec. 20, 116, a district in Syria; situation unknown.

Thairsa, IV, 790, a district in Syria; situation unknown.

Thapthar, IV, 788, a district in Syria; situation unknown.

Tham; varr. , the town and Necropolis of Western Thebes; Copt. ϫⲏⲙⲉ, ϫⲉⲙⲏ, ϫⲉⲙⲉ, ϫⲏⲙⲏ; see .

Tham'uka, IV, 792, a district in Syria; situation unknown.

Thanret, IV, 788, a district in Syria; situation unknown.

Thar, a district near Mendes.

Thar, the marshy district of Sma-Beḥuṭ.

Thar: (1) a sanctuary of Ȧn-ḥer in Sebennytus; (2) a sanctuary of Neith in the Delta.

Thar, IV, 647, a frontier fortress in the Eastern Delta, Tanis; Assyr. .

Tharbu, Rec. 20, 115, a country conquered by Rameses III.

Tharnasa, IV, 793, a district in Syria; situation unknown.

Tharḥu, Anastasi IV, 1B, 1, a town in the north-east of the Delta.

Tharkha, IV, 794, a district in Syria; situation unknown; Tall al-'Amârnah .

Thartuna, Alt-K. 1173, a town in Egypt (?)

Thakar (Thakal), IV, 788, a district in Syria; situation unknown.

Thakar, Rec. 21, 77, a district on the Mediterranean coast.

Thakna, Rec. 20, 115, a district in Syria; situation unknown.

Thagerr, IV, 789, a district in Syria; situation unknown.

Thatȧrset, IV, 790, IV, 791, a district in Syria; situation unknown.

Thatha (Thaui?), the Nome Latopolites.

Thatham', Rec. 20, 116, a district in Syria; situation unknown.

Thaṭāa, Alt-K. 1183, a town; position unknown.

Thaṭṭana, Rec. 15, 144, a town; position unknown.

Thȧmens, a town in Nubia (Kalâbshah).

Thinnur, IV, 793, a district in Syria; situation unknown.

Thirna, L.D. III, 209, Rec. 20, 116, a country; situation un known.

Thirsa, IV, 790, a district in Syria; situation unknown.

Thirshakhar, Rec. 20, 116, a district in Syria; situation unknown.

Thisup, Rec. 20, 117, a country conquered by Rameses III.

Thithu, IV, 794, a Sûdânî country; situation unknown.

Thua [ ], IV, 800, see **Tua**.

Thuāu, a district in the south of Egypt.

Thubti, Rec. 20, 117; var. , a district in Syria.

Thufi, , or , a name for the swampy districts in the Delta filled with marsh plants; = Heb. סוּף, Copt. ϫⲟⲟⲩϥ.

Thuna, , Pelusium; Heb. סִין, Ezek. xxx, 15, 16, Tall al-'Amârnah (?)

Thuntchaur, IV, 789, a district in Syria; situation unknown; Tall al-'Amârnah .

Thukhm'raka, Rec. 20, 117, a district in Syria; situation unknown.

Thuka, IV, 788, a district in Syria; situation unknown.

Thuthenau, IV, 790, a district in Syria; situation unknown.

Theb ȧḥ (?), the 12th Nome of Lower Egypt (Sebennytes).

Theben, , B.D.G. 644, Supp. 931, Sphinx, 14 160, a town near Tanis (Daphnae); Arab. تل دفنو.

Theb-neter, , Sebennytus, the capital of the 12th Nome of Lower Egypt; Copt. ϫⲉⲙⲛⲟⲩϯ, Assyr. , Arab. سمنود.

Thmusnuth (?), IV, 797, a Sûdânî country; situation unknown.

Themeḥ, a country to the west of the Nile.

Then, IV, 1131, , IV, 769, , , , the capital of the Nome Abydos in Upper Egypt; Assyr. .

Thenȧs, IV, 803, a Sûdânî country; situation unknown.

Thennu, , Sanehat, a district; situation unknown.

Thennu Ḥer-t, Upper Thennu.

Thenutchaur, IV, 789, a district in Syria; situation unknown.

Thenpu; see **Tunip**.

Thenheqȧb, IV, 801, a Sûdânî country; situation unknown.

Thent remu, Piānkhi Stele, a town in the Eastern Delta; var. .

Therr, IV, 1029, a town in the Delta (?).

Therbu, Rec. 20, 117, a district in Syria; situation unknown.

Thertȧ, , a town in Upper Egypt; Copt. ⲧⲉⲣⲱⲧ.

Theretis, Rec. 20, 115, a Sûdânî country; situation unknown.

Thehbebu, IV, 797, a Sûdânî country; situation unknown.

Theḥenu, IV, 800, a Sûdânî country; part of Libya.

Thes, Rec. 36, 53, a town of Menu.

Thes, a Sûdânî country; situation unknown.

Thes, Edfû.

Thes Uān, IV, 891, "Ridge of Uān," a district in Syria (?)

Thes Ḥeru, the 2nd Nome of Upper Egypt (Apollinopolites).

Thes ḥeḥutt, A.Z. 1866, 36, a name of Åmenti; Gr. Ταστάς.

Thes khā-t en Ṭeḥuti, a name of .

Th-Set, Nāstasen Stele 25 = **Ta Sti** .

Thekansh, a town near Oxyrhynchus.

Theku, capital of the Nome Heroopolites; Heb. סֻכּוֹת (?)

Thetasth, IV, 799, a Sûdânî country; situation unknown.

Thetna, IV, 799, a Sûdânî country: situation unknown.

Ṭapur, L.D. III, 156, a district in Syria; situation unknown.

Ṭarṭeni, Rec. 8, 140, see .

Ṭåum (?), Rec. 20, 114, a Sûdânî country; situation unknown.

Ṭātur, a town in Nubia, Dendûr (?)

Ṭimåi, a name of Antinoopolis.

Ṭint, III, 143, a town in Egypt.

Ṭir, Rec. 21, 77, a town in Syria; compare Heb. דּוֹר.

Ṭirā-t, a district near (Asnâ).

Ṭuat en ba, a crypt at Edfû.

Ṭuat Kherāḥa, the Ṭuat of Babylon of Egypt.

Ṭuat sheta (?), a crypt at Denderah.

Ṭuatchef, Palermo Stele, a town of Egypt.

Ṭu Åmentt, the west bank of the Nile.

Ṭu āa, a name of the Necropolis.

Ṭu āa tes theḥen, the alabaster quarries in the Nome Sep; Gr. Ἀλαβαστρηνὸν ὄρος.

Ṭuu Uaḥ-t (?), the hills round the Oasis of Khârgah.

Ṭu uāb, "holy mountain," *i.e.*, Gebel Barkal at the foot of the Fourth Cataract.

Ṭubakh, Anastasi I, 19, 1, a district in Syria; Tall al-'Amârnah ; compare Heb. טִבְחַת, 1 Chron. xviii, 8.

Ṭu båa, the quarries of Thebes.

Ṭu-f, the 12th Nome of Upper Egypt (Antinoopolites).

Ṭu-f, Rec. 17, 120: (1) a section of the Labyrinth; (2) a town sacred to Horus.

Ṭu manu, the region of the West, the mountain of Sunset.

Ṭu en Up-ta, Rec. 15, 171, A.Z. 1883, 66, "mount of the horns of the earth."

Ṭu en Bekha, , the region of the East—the mountain of Sunrise.

Ṭu en Bekhan, L.D. III, 219E, 12, , the eastern end of Wâdî Ḥammâmât.

Ṭurbantu, Rec. 20, 118, a district in Syria; situation unknown.

Ṭu ḥetch, , "white mountain"—a desert region in Northern Nubia.

Ṭu semt (?), Rec. 13, 37, a mountain district.

Ṭu sheta, , , a name of the Necropolis.

Ṭu sheta ent Unnefer, a Necropolis in the Natron Valley, .

Ṭu sheta en Beḥuṭ, the Necropolis of Edfû.

Ṭu qa, , , a town in the Nome Aphroditopolites.

Ṭu qa Ȧment, the hills of Wâdî Naṭrûn.

Ṭu ṭesher, , IV, 167, "Red Mountain," *i.e.*, the granite quarries of Aswân.

Ṭuh, , IV, 799, a Sûdânî country; situation unknown.

Ṭeb (Tcheb), , , , , , A.Z. 35, 19 (Apollinopolis Magna), the capital of the 2nd Nome of Upper Egypt; Copt. ⲧⲃⲱ, ⲁⲧⲃⲱ, Arab. ادفو.

Ṭeb Userka, Edfû (?)

Ṭeb meḥ: (1) "Ṭeb of the North"—a name of Tanis; (2) a temple of Serapis in the Nome Metelites.

Ṭeb en Ṭebti, , Edfû.

Ṭebi, a name of Naucratis (?)

Ṭebu (Tchebu), the capital of the Nome Uatchet; Copt. ⲁⲧⲃⲱ, Arab. Aṭfîḥ.

Ṭebui, , the marshland of the Nome Ṭuf.

Ṭebennu, Rec. 20, 115; see **Theḥennu**, IV, 800.

Ṭeber, , Edfû.

Ṭebkhu, IV, 781, a district in Syria; compare Heb. טִבְחַת; Tall al-'Âmârnah .

Ṭep, U. 261, , N. 939, , , , , one half of the town of Per Uatchet (Buto); the other half was called Pe.

Ṭepi, Sphinx 14, 159, Buto.

Ṭep-Pe, , , Pe-Ṭep, the two halves of Per Uatchet (Buto).

Ṭepr, a district in Syria, situation unknown; compare Heb. תָּבוֹר.

Ṭemȧi = **Ṭemȧi en Ḥeru**; Copt. ⲡϯⲙⲓⲛϩⲱⲣ. The modern Damanhûr.

Ṭemȧi p-sebt meḥt, a district of Dêr al-Baḥarî.

Ṭemȧi enti ȧst Ḥeru, Edfû.

Ṭemȧi en Ḥeru, a town in the 6th Nome of Lower Egypt (Hermopolis Parva); Copt. ϯⲙⲉⲛϩⲱⲣ, ϯⲙⲉⲛϩⲟⲩⲣ. The modern Damanhûr.

Ṭemȧ en Tchāru; see **Tchāru**.

Ṭemȧ Thebent, Daphnae (?); Heb. תַּחְפַּנְחֵס. The modern Dafanu دَفَنُّو.

Ṭenȧ, a town near Ḥensu (Herakleopolis).

Ṭenȧa, a town near Memphis.

Ṭen Ȧssȧ, an estate of King Ȧssȧ.

Ṭenu, a canal in the Nome Cynopolites.

Ṭenṭeni, see **Ṭerṭeni**.

Ṭeriksu, II, 158, a district; situation unknown.

Ṭerṭeni, Champ. Not. II, 122, de Rougé I.H. 206, the name of a Mediterranean people; Gr. Δάρδανοι (Asien, 355).

Ṭehan, see .

Ṭehan, Demot. Cat. 38, 425; Copt. ⲦⲈϨⲚⲒ; Arab. Al-Hîbah.

Ṭeshau, IV, 797, a Sûdânî country; situation unknown.

Ṭeshert, L.D. III, 140c, the Eastern Desert and Arabia.

Ṭequr, Rec. 20, 115, a district in Syria; situation unknown.

Ṭeqnasa, Rec. 20, 116, a district in Syria; situation unknown.

Ṭegar, Anastasi I, 21, 8, a district in Syria; situation unknown.

Ṭegarȧar, Anastasi I, 21, 8, a district in Syria; situation unknown.

Ṭegnui, P.S.B. 25, 220, a town in Egypt.

Ṭet (?), a town in Nubia (?), situation unknown.

Ṭeṭ (Tcheṭ) Ṭeṭȧ, T. 235, P. 204 + 15, M. 310, N. 846, Rec. 27, 228, Rec. 4, 27, Busiris and Mendes.

Ṭeṭ, a canal in Lower Egypt.

Ṭeṭ ȧs, a sanctuary; situation unknown.

Ṭeṭ ȧsut, B.D.G. 983, Gol. 12, 101 . . . . .

Ṭeṭ ȧsut Tetȧ, the pyramid of Tetȧ.

Ṭeṭnu, a town in Egypt.

Ṭetchuuth, IV, 805 (, Rec. 20, 114), a country conquered by Thothmes III.

Tchaāni, Rev. 11, 128, Tanis; Copt. ϫⲁⲁⲛⲉ, the modern Ṣân صَان.

Tchaitathkharri, Treaty 28, a district in Syria; situation unknown.

Tchaitȧgaȧȧr, Mar. Aby. II, 28, a district in Syria; situation unknown.

Tchaua, Rec. 20, 114, a country conquered by Rameses III.

Tchauar, Rec. 24, 160 = , Tyre.

Tchaur, Rec. 20, 119, Tyre; Tall al-'Amârnah , Assyr. , Heb. צוֹר.

Tchaursu, IV, 788, a district in Syria; situation unknown.

Tchababa, Rec. 20, 119, a district in Syria; situation unknown.

Tchaben, Sphinx 14, 160, Sebennytus; Assyr. , Copt. ϫⲉⲙⲛⲟⲩϯ.

Tchapaqȧa, L.D. III, 252, 80, a district in Syria conquered by Shishak I.

Tchapȧrenṭa, Treaty 27, a district in Syria; situation unknown; Boghaz Keui Zi-ib-la-an-da.

Tchaftȧ, , IV, 786, , IV, 650, a district in Syria; situation unknown.

Tcham, , Rev. 14, 46, 51, Egypt; Copt. ϫⲏⲙⲉ.

Tcham = Metcha (Unȧ, 15), Rec. 19, 88.

Tcham, Rec. 14, 51, a district near Karnak.

Tcham, Denderah.

Tcham'ith, L.D. III, 131, a dictrict in Syria; situation unknown.

Tcham'ra, IV, 689, , Anastasi I, 17, 8, a district in Syria; Assyr. , Gr. Σίμυρα. The modern Ṣumra on the Nahr al-Kabîr.

Tchanu, IV, 806, , Rec. 20, 114, a Sûdânî country; situation unknown.

Tchanriusu, IV, 789, a district in Syria; situation unknown.

Tchar, IV, 891, , Rec. 21, 101, , , , , , Tyre; Heb. צוֹר; Tall al-'Amârnah , Assyr. .

Tchar, Anastasi I, 21, 1, Tyre the port.

Tchar, Nȧstasen Stele, 39, a town in the Sûdân.

Tchar āmu, Anastasi I, 21, 3, a district in Northern Syria.

Tchareb, IV, 788, a district in Syria; situation unknown.

Tcharbasana, Mar. Aby. II, 50, a district in Syria; Assyr. .

Tcharputȧ, Anastasi I, 20, 8, a district in Syria; Assyr. , Heb. צָרְפַת, Gr. Σάρεπτα.

Tcharmam, L.D. III, 252, 56, a district in Syria; situation unknown.

Tcharrum', Alt-K. 1237, a district in Syria; situation unknown.

Tcharta (?), Treaty 28, a district in Syria.

Tchah, IV, 687, 699, 723, 1004, Phoenicia.

Tchahana, Anastasi I, 17, 3, a district in Syria; situation unknown.

Tchas, IV, 803, a Sûdânî country; situation unknown.

Tchat, Tchath, IV, 798, a Sûdânî country; situation unknown.

Tchathakar, IV, 792, a district in Syria; situation unknown.

Tchaṭpther, L.D. III, 252, 34, a district in Syria; situation unknown.

Tchatchasa, IV, 800, Rec. 20, 113, a district in Syria; situation unknown.

Tchān, Rec. 21, 76, the capital of the 14th Nome of Lower Egypt; Heb. צֹעַן, Assyr. (?) Gr. Τάνις, Copt. ϫⲁⲛⲏ, Arab. صان; see **Sekh-t Tchān.**

Tchārit, see

Tchāru, a town which stood near Manṣûrah.

Tchāru, Mar. Karn. 52, 12 . . . . .

Tchārukha, A.Z. 1901, 63, a town in Lower Egypt.

Tchiṭiputȧ, Anastasi I, 22, 5, a district in Syria; situation unknown.

Tchiṭuna, Anastasi I, 20, 8, Sidon; Heb. צִידוֹן, Gr. Σιδών, Assyr.

Tchuḥenu, Rec. 20, 113, a Sûdânî country; situation unknown.

Tchebneter, Rev. 12, 40, Sebennytus; Assyr. , Copt. ϫⲉⲙⲛⲟⲩϯ.

Tchebākher, Palermo Stele, M. 210, N. 675, T. 369, a town in the Delta.

Tchef, B.D. 125, II, 31, the seat of Neb-ḥeru.

Tchefrer, Brugsch, Rec. IV, 69, a district; situation unknown.

Tcheftȧ, IV, 650, a district in Syria; situation unknown.

Tchemnuȧ, IV, 806, a Sûdânî country; situation unknown.

Tcher, a sanctuary of Anubis in the Nome Sept.

Tcherr, IV, 786, a district in Syria; situation unknown.

Tcherit en Tcherti, the temple of Edfû.

Tcherna, Stat. Tab. 9, a lake.

Tcher (Tchert), Rec. 15, 162, , Rec. 10, 116, 32, 65, , , a town opposite Hermonthis (Tuphium); Arab. Taud.

Tches, IV, 800, a Sûdânî country; situation unknown.

Tchestchestt, , , , , the Oasis of Dâkhlah.

Tchesen, Rec. 20, 114, a Sûdânî country; situation unknown.

Tcheser, Rec. 16, 37, 17, 53; see **Ta tcheser.**

Tcheser tcheseru, Rec. 32, 64, the district of Dêr al-Baḥarî.

Tcheqā, , the capital of the Nome Sâpi Shemā.

Tchet (?), Rec. 24, 179, the swamp region—the Delta.

Tcheṭ, U. 425, T. 244, , U. 426 (var.), , U. 426, , T. 244, , U. 254, , N. 906, 993, , P. 189, , M. 354, Busiris (Mendes).

Tcheṭem, a town to the south-east of Thebes.

Tcheṭṭenna, Rec. 21, 84, Sidon; Assyr. 𒀀𒀀𒀀𒀀, Heb. צִידוֹן.

Tcheṭku, a canal in the town of Avaris.

I.

INDEX OF ENGLISH WORDS, NAMES OF GODS AND GODDESSES, ETC.

NOTE.—Reference numbers with letters a and b after them signify that a = first column, b = second column of the Egyptian Dictionary.

A.

a, 105a, 153a.
Āa, god, 108b.
Ȧaȧit, goddess, 17a.
Ȧaau, god, 18a.
Āabi, 110b.
Ȧabit, goddess, 19a.
Āȧbṭ, mythological fish, 113b.
Ȧabtt, serpent, 19a.
Ȧabṭu, mythological fish, 20a.
Ȧabui, god, 19b.
Āagm', 113a.
Ȧagt, town, 26b.
Ȧaḥes, Sûdânî god, 22a.
Ȧaheṭ, god, 22a.
Ȧaḥi, god, 22a.
Āaḥpi, god, 112b.
Ȧāḥ-remt, god, 30a.
Āāḥti, 114a.
Ȧaḥui, god, 22a.
Ȧāḥ-ur, god, 30a.
Ȧai, Ass-god, 17b.
Ȧāi, form of Rā, 28b.
Āai, god, 108b.
Ȧait, 17b.
Āait, goddess, 108b.
Ȧaiu, slayers of Āapep, 17b.
Ȧakebi (Rā), 26a.
Ȧakebi, Circle of, 70a, 888b.
Ȧakebit, Circle of, 26a.
Ȧaker, god, 26a.
Ȧakhabit, 22b.
Ȧākhbu, god, 30a.
Ȧakht, season of year, 22a, 40b.
Ȧakhit, goddess, 22a.
Ȧakhu, Light-god, 23a.
Ȧakhu, Rain-god, 24a.
Ȧakhu, a Dekan, 23a.
Ȧakhu of the gods, 24a.
Ȧakhu of the Ṭuat, 24a.
Ȧakhu, the Four, 24a.
Ȧakhu, the Seven, 24b.
Ȧakhu, the Eight, 24b.
Ȧakhuait, goddess, 22b.
Ȧakhui, 24a.
Ȧakhu-kheper-ur (?), 23b.
Ȧakhu-menu, 22b.
Ȧakhu-neb-s, 24b.
Ȧakhu-nekhekh, a Dekan, 23b.
Ȧakhu-Rā, a dawn-god, 23b.
Ȧakhu-sa-ta-f, god, 23b.
Ȧakhuti, double Horizon-god, 24a, 25a.
Ȧakhut Khufu, 25a.
Āam, god, 111b.
Āām (Nile), 114a.
Ȧamit (Hathor), 20b, 21a.
Ȧammi, title of Rā, 20b.
Āamu, the, 107b, 111a.
Ȧamut, goddess, 20b.
Ȧamuti, god, 21a.
Āān, 114a.
Ȧanait, goddess, 21a.
Ȧānā Ṭuati (Rā), 29a.
Aāni, Ape-god, 2a.
Ȧa-nsernsert, 16b.
Āapef, 111a.
Āapep, 17b, 111a, 212a, 284b, 869a, 875b, 878a, 901b.
Āapep in wax, 154a.
Āapep, associates of, 145b.
Āapep, fetterer of, 40a.
Āa-perti, 109a.
Āapit, 111a.
Ȧaqeṭqeṭ, 26a.

Aaràar, 21b.
Àarr, god, 21b.
Àaru, city, 21b.
Àaru, god, 21b.
Àas, god, 25a.
Āa-saaḥ, 109a.
Àasabatiu, 25b.
Àasakhr, 25b.
Āasek, god, 112b.
Aash, god, 1a.
Āa-shefit, title, 109b.
Āasit, goddess, 112b.
Āasiti-Khar, 112b.
Àast (Isis), 25b.
Àasṭen, god, 25b.
Àasṭes, god, 25a.
Àasu, 25b.
Àat Àakhu, 16a.
Àat, god, 26b ; the Holy, 15b.
Àaṭ, Lake in the Ṭuat, 27b.
Àat of Life, 15b.
Àaṭ, town, the Ṭuat, 27b.
Àat-Àakhu, goddess, 108b.
Āat-Àaṭ-t, goddess, 109a.
Àaṭ-en-Sekhet, 113a.
Àat-en-setcht, 16a.
Àat-ent-mu, 16a.
Àat-ent-Up-uatu, 17a.
Àat-en-uābu, 16a.
Àat Ḥeru, 16a ; north and south, 16a.
Āaṭi, an Assessor, 113a.
Àaṭit, goddess, 27b.
Āaṭiu (Rā), 113a.
Àat Kher-āḥa, 16a.
Āat-qar-uaba, 109b.
Āat-Setkau, 109b, 888a.
Àat-sha, 81a.
Àat-sharà, 16a.
Āa-sti, 109a.
Àats, gods of, 405a.
Āātt, 113b.
Àau, god, 17b.
Āau, 110a.
Àau Nu, Sky-god, 18a.
Àaurmerrā, 18b.
Àb, god, 37b.
Àbait, 39a.
abandon, 528a.
Abaqer, a dog, 5a.
abase, 631b ; abase oneself, 607a.
abased, 174b, 373a, 885b.
abasement, 885b.
abash, 499b.
abate (a tax), 564b.
Ābb (Osiris), 118a.
Abenti, god, 5a.
Àbes, god, 40a.
Ābesh, star, 118b.
Àbeth, god, 40a.
Àbhet, 39b.
abide, 296b.
abiding, 296b, 913b.
ability, 624b, 751b ; abilities, 751b, 779b.
abject, 798b.
Ab-lān āthān-ālbā, god, 5a.
able, 178b, 347b, 621b, 624b, 698a, 751b.
abode, 11b, 32a and b, 34b, 38a, 58b, 62a, 79b, 95a, 107a, 110a, 140b, 178a, 197a, 273b, 297b, 333a, 342b, 347a, 348b, 419a and b, 436b, 440a, 444a, 499b, 725a, 775b, 796a, 856a, 881b, 893a.
abode of peace (tomb), 80b.
abolish (tax), 144a.
abominable, 208a, 228a, 243b, 262b, 329a, 708a, 824b.
abominate, 214b, 622b.
abomination, 208a, 215a, 226a, 260a, 673b.
abortus, 178a.
abound, 538a.
about, 339a, 828b.
above, 30b, 150a, 265a, 498b.
Āb-peq, 116a.
Ābrāskhtiāks, 118a.
abridgment, 683a.
abrogate, 425a.
abruptness, 820b.
abscess, 217a, 222b, 617a, 693b.
absent, 144a.
Āb-shā, 116a.
absolute, 164b.
absorb, 54b, 590b, 645a.
abstain, 131a.
Āb-ta, 116a.
Àbti, god and goddess, 38b.
Àbtha, god, 40a.
Abu (Elephantine), speech of, 335b.
Ābui, 116a.
Àbuit, goddess, 39b.

abundance, 134b, 213b, 278a, 317a, 458b, 545a, 606b, 677a, 783a, 809a, 877b.
abundant, 2b, 102a, 107b, 137a, 148a, 159a and b, 213a and b, 458b, 538a.
abuse, 110a, 185a, 186b, 394a, 540a, 683a, 689a, 727b, 757a, 794b, 805b, 807a, 809b, 895a; term of, 826a.
Ābutt, 116a.
Ȧbu-ur, god, 39b.
Abydos, 19a; Council of, 901a; shaft for offerings at, 439b; goddess, 4a.
abyss, 279a, 332a, 822a, 872a, 893b; celestial, 768b.
acacia, 749a; wood of, 302b, 679a.
acacias, chief of, 84a.
accelerate, 689a.
accept, 291b; accept the person of some one, 101a.
acceptable, 110b, 752a
access (to a woman), 300b.
accident, 595a.
acclaim, 76a, 352b, 381a, 425a, 448a, 515b, 603b, 608a, 619a, 670a, 677b, 678a, 791b.
acclamation, 15a, 17b, 603b, 675a.
accompanyists, 265b.
accord, 725b.
according as, 545a.
according to, 264a, 277a, 414a, 415a; according to law, 266a.
according to that which, 414b.
account, 41a, 118a, 161a, 430b, 510b, 527a.
account books, 129a.
accountant, 79b, 511a, 849a.
accoutrements, 119a.
accursed, 214b, 574b, 669b, 683a.
accusation, 860b.
accuse, 669b.
accused, 612a, 681a.
Achaemenes, 25a.
acquaintance, 430a, 551a.
acquainted with, be, 430a.
acquire, 638a, 752a.
acquittal, 147b; to procure, 601a.
acre, 8a, 22a, 75a, 526b.
acrobat, 539a, 897b.
acrobatic feats, 61a.
act, 67a, 418b, 595a and b; a man's part, 850b; as a deputy, 98b, 103a; as an enemy, 726a; in a lordly manner, 888b; perversely, 637a; prudently, 317a; violently, 899a; with decision, 193b; with partiality, 437a.
act of folly, 180a; of grace, 508a.
action, 418b, 595a, 666b, 698b; of arms, 418b.
active, 66b.
activity, 241a.
actual, 270b, 271a.
add to, 148a; add up, 683a, 828a; add figures together, 880a.
adder, 479b.
addition, 178a, 317a, 449a, 458b, 880a.
addition, sign of, 138a.
address, 95a, 345a, 410b, 824a, 911b.
addressee, 187a.
addresser, 632b.
addresses, 692b.
Adelphoi, 404b, 674a.
adept, 131a.
adhere, 862b.
adherent, 742a, 823b.
adjudge, 41a.
adjudicator, 248b.
adjuration, 745a.
adjure, 527b.
administer, 300b, 486b, 622b, 683b, 699a, 830a, 840b.
administration, 3b, 136a, 622b, 683b, 699a.
admirable, 737a.
admiration, 292b.
admire, 200a.
admit, 441b.
admonish, 486b, 587b.
adoration, 17b, 149b, 603b, 857b.
adore, 149b, 184b, 186b, 352b, 403a, 442a, 515b, 592a, 593a, 608a, 649a and b, 650a, 652b, 677b, 818a, 841b, 871a.
adorer, 479b, 603b; of the god, 403a.
adorn, 574b, 590b, 601b, 602b, 873a.

adornment, 602a b, 671a.
adultery, to commit, 381a, 395b.
advance, 8a, 40a, 135b, 159a, 181a, 193b, 222a, 329b, 400b, 478a, 487b, 498a, 509a, 541a b, 549a, 558a, 641b, 645a, 693b, 710a, 728a, 858b ; advance against, 614a ; advance cautiously, 478a ; advance in, 554a ; advance quickly, 643a, 907a.
advanced in years, 2b, 222a ; in life, 134a.
advance-guard, 272a, 460a and b.
advantage, 22b, 459a, 724b.
advantageous, 622a, 659b.
adversaries, 564b, 572b.
adversity, 802a.
advice, 610b, 694a ; to reject, 615a ; to seek, 410b.
adviser, 495b.
advocacy, 186a.
advocate, 64b, 409b.
adze, 11a, 123b, 351a.
Åf, 22b, 43a b, 186b ; boat of, 23a ; soul of, 199a.
Åfȧ, 43b.
afar, 144a.
Āfat, 119b.
Āfau, Season-god, 119b.
Åf-ermen-ȧri-f, 43a.
affair, 8b, 335a, 525a, 595a, 694a ; affairs, 486b, 561a, 580b ; personal, 525b.
affection, 588b.
affectionately, 658a.
affidavit, 131a.
affirmation, 348a.
afflict, 464b.
afflicted, 14a, 102a, 331a, 396a.
afflicted man, 887a.
affliction, 74a, 270a, 290a, 396a, 431a, 460a, 524a.
Āfkiu, 120a.
Āfmuit, 120a.
aforetime, 554a.
afraid, 499a, 619a, 636a ; to make 697a.
afresh, 264b.
Africa, East, 179a.
after, 73a, 714b, 265a b, 305a, 415a, 494b; after the manner of, 277a.
after-birth, 795b.
afterwards, 305a.
Åfu-Åsȧr, 125b.
Åfuau, 466a.
Åfu-fṭu, 43a.
Åfu-ḥeri-khenṭ-f, 43a.
Åfu-Rā, 46b, 163a.
Åfu-Tem, 43a.
Åga, Ågaȧ, 95b.
again, 122b, 342b.
against, 65a, 414a.
Agaiu, 122b.
agate, 317a.
Ågau (Anubis), 95b.
Agbȧ, 317b.
Agb-ur, 12a.
Ageb, Water-god, 12a.
age, 434a ; past age, 830a ; ages, 134a ; age of man, 133b.
aged, 134a, 387a, 514b, 626b, 747a, 838b, 856a ; aged folk, 17b ; aged man, 838b ; aged one, 108b.
Aged One, 83b, 453a.
Aged One (Rā), 882a.
Aged One (Thoth), 757a.
agent, 103a, 422a, 436b, 849a.
Aggit-ḥebsit-bag, 96a.
aggressive, 839b.
agile, 227a.
agitate, 678a.
agitated, 243a, 393b, 906b.
agree, 291b ; to a proposition, 129b.
agreeable, 50a, 766a.
agreement, 568a ; sign of, 448a.
agriculture, 157b ; office of, 239b.
ague, 393b, 448a.
Aḥa (Menu), 8b.
Āḥā, god, 133a.
Āḥā-ȧb, 133b.
Ahait, Cow-goddess, 7b.
Āḥāit, goddess, 133b, 134a.
Āḥā-neteru, 133b.
Āḥānurṭnef, 133b.
Āḥārer, 133b.
Āḥāsekhet, 133b.
Ahasuerus, 566a.
Āḥatiu, 132b.
Åḥāu gods, 133b.
Åḥemt, 76b.
Åḥes, god, 76b.
Åḥeth, 134b ; chamber, 515b.

Åḥi, god and Assessor and form of Harpokrates, 76a, 450b.
Åḥibit, 76b.
Ahit, goddess, 8a.
Åḥkai, god, 77a.
Åhmesu, 74b.
Åḥ-pet, 75a.
Aḥs, Sûdânî god, 8b.
Åḥti (Osiris), 77a, goddess, 77a.
Aḥu (Menu), 8b.
Åḥu (Tem and Thoth), 76b.
Åḥui, 76a.
Aia, god, 2a.
Åi-em-ḥetep, 30b.
aim blows, 595a, 685b.
Ai-må-seb, 391a.
air, 13b, 82a, 89b, 98b, 280a, 342a, 344b, 346b, 356a, 369b, 377b, 593a, 651b, 683ab, 732a, 750a, 823b, 824a, 849b; to make, 269b, 606a; the open, 554a.
Air-god, 500a, 731b.
Air-goddess, 474b.
air-hole (?), 99a.
airless, 340b.
Åit (Nut), 30b.
Åkanhi, 94b.
Åkbit, 94b.
Åkbiu, 94b.
Åken-åb, 95a.
Åkenh, Åkenha, 95a.
Åken-tau-keha-kheru, 95a.
Åkenti, 95b.
Aker, Earth-god, 11b, 95b.
Akeru, Earth-gods, 11b, 64a, 830b, 835b, 905b; net of, 27a, 519a.
Akerta, god, 12a.
Åkes, 95b.
Akhabi, god, 9a.
Akhabit, goddess, 9a.
Akhabiu gods, 11b.
Ākha-ḥer, 135b.
Ākhauårit, 135b.
Åkhekh, 77b, 135a.
Ākhekhtiu, 135a.
Åkhem-ḥems-f, god, 78b.
Åkhem-hep-f, god, 78b.
Åkhemit, 78a.
Åkhem-sek-f, 78b.
Åkhem-urṭ-f, 78a.
Åkhemu-beṭeshiu, 78b.
Åkhemu-seshåu, 78b.
Åkhkhi, 77b.
Åkhkhu, god, 9a.
Ākhmu, 136a.
Ākhnårtif, 136a.
Åkhniu, 95a.
Åkhpi (Rā), 77b.
Åkhsef, 79a.
Åkhuti, 77b.
Ākriu, 139b
Akriu, 11b.
Åkshit, 95b.
Åku, 94b.
alabaster, 473a, 523b, 751a.
alarm, 395a.
alas! 30b, 104b, 219b.
Alexander the Great, 52b.
Alexandria, 661a.
alien, 541b, 546a, 911a; aliens, 11b, 782a.
alienation (of property), 568a.
alight, 5b, 368b, 480ab, 549a, 617a, 623b, 693a, 700a, 743a, 863a.
alighting, 693a; places of, 148a, 693a.
alike, 826a.
Al-Ḳâb, 62a.
all, 2b, 30b, 357a, 414a, 826a, 834a, 880a, 908b, 909a; all that is, 164b.
all at once, 765b.
all-embracing, 676b.
all eyes (everybody), 313b.
all men, 214a; all peoples, 834a; all persons, 68a.
allegiance, 739b.
allocate, 885b.
allot, 722b.
allotment, 248b, 638a; to make an, 490a.
allow, 865a.
allowance, 248b; 836b.
alloy, to, 736a.
ally, 281a, 282a, 520b, 539b, 540a, 599b, 739b.
almond tree, 411b.
alms, 3a, 518a.
alone, 153ab, 264a, 560a.
along with, 73a, 339a, 489b.
also, 782a, 792a, 799a, 809b.
altar, 117a, 151a, 152a, 191ab, 196a, 220b, 224b, 519b, 529ab, 538a, 572a, 805b, 862b; equipment of, 516b; altar pitcher,

152a ; altar slab, 280a, 817b ; altar table, 328b ; altar vessel, 529b ; laden altars, 725b.
alternatively, 265a.
altogether, 765a, 779b, 822b, 880b.
alum, 5a, 39b.
always, 270b, 450a, 778a, 840b.
Ȧm (Horus), 49a.
Ȧm (Lion-god and Jackal-god), 49a.
Ām, god, 120b.
Amȧ (Rā), 6b.
Ȧma, god, 49b.
Ām-ā, 121a.
Āmāa, 121a.
Amȧ-ȧmi-ta (Rā), 6a.
Āma-āsht, 121a.
Ām-āau, 121a.
Āmāf, 121a.
Āmakhet, 121a.
Ȧmakhiu, 50b.
Ȧmakhu, god, 50b.
Ȧmam, 513a.
Āmam, 122a.
Āmām, Eater of the dead, 120b.
Ȧmam-ȧst, 122a.
Āmamu, 122a.
Āmanḥu, 122a.
amazed, 131a, 209b.
amazing thing, 209b.
Āmemit, 121a.
Ȧmen, god, 7b, 435b ; image of, 826b ; of Khargah, 52b ; of Tehnit, 53a ; of the East, 52a.
Ȧmen, Bull-god, Frog-god, Lion-god and Serpent-god, 53a.
Ȧmen (priest), 51a.
Ȧmen-ȧabti, 52a.
Ȧmen-ȧakhu, 51b.
Ȧmen-ȧpt, 52a.
Ȧmen-em-ȧpt, 52a.
Ȧmen-ḥāu, 51b.
Ȧmen-ḥep, god, 52b.
Ȧmen-Ḥeru, 51b.
Ȧmen-ḥetep IV, 192b.
Ȧmeni (Rā), 51b.
Ȧmenit, goddess, 51b.
Ȧmenit-Rā, 52a.
Ȧmen-kau, 53a.
Ȧmen-khet (Rā), the Great Hand, 51b.
Ȧmen-khnem-ḥeḥ, 52b.
Ȧmen-Menu, 52a.
Ȧmen-meruti, 52a.
Ȧmen-naȧu-ka, 52a.
Ȧmen-neb-khart, 52a.
Ȧmen-neb-nest-taui, 52a.
Ȧmen-neb-Nut, 52a.
Ȧmen Nept, 52a.
Ȧmennu god, 51b, Devil, 51a.
Ȧmennu-āu, 51a.
Ȧmen Qa-ȧst, 53a.
Ȧmen-Rā, an official, 53a ; title of, 19a.
Ȧmen-Rā, 52ab, 435b.
Ȧmen-Rā + Ḥeru-ȧakhuti, 52b.
Ȧmen-Rā + Ptaḥ, 52a.
Ȧmen-Rā + Tem + Kheperȧ + Ḥeru, 52b.
Ȧmen-Rā em Usr-ḥat, 53a.
Ȧmen-Rā Kamutf, 52b.
Ȧmen-Rā-menmen-mut-f, 52a.
Ȧmen-Rā Neb-nest-taui, 52b.
Ȧmen-ren-f, 51b.
Ȧmen-ren-ḥer, 51b.
Ȧmen + Ruruti, 52b.
Ȧmen-sekhem-f-au, 54a.
Ȧmen Sepṭ-ḥennuti, 52b.
Ȧmen-t (Rā), 53b.
ȧmen-t (amulet), 54a.
Ȧment, 8a.
Ȧmen-t (Ȧmenit), 53b, 776a.
Ȧmen-ṭa-f-pa-khepesh, 53a.
Ȧmen-ta-Mȧt, 53a.
Ȧmen-Temu em Uas, 53a.
Ȧmen-t Ḥep-neb-s, 54a.
Ȧmen-t-ḥerit-ȧb-ȧpt, 52b.
Ȧmenti, brow of, 163a ; domain of, 900b.
Ȧmenti, god, 53b.
Ȧmentit, 53b.
Ȧmentiu (the dead), 53b.
Ȧmen-t Nefer-t, 54a.
Ȧmen-t Se[m]-t, 54a.
Ȧmen-t-seshemu-set, 51b.
Ȧmentt-ermen, 54a.
Ȧmen-t-urt, 54a.
Ȧmenui, 51b.
Ȧmen-user-ḥat, the sacred barge, 53a.
Ȧmesta-en-ȧbu, 55b.
amethyst, 471a, 484b, 551b.
Ȧmges, 55b.
Ām-ḥeḥ, 121a.
Ȧmḥit, goddess, 55a.

Åmḥ-t, 54b.
Åmi, Eye of Horus and Fire-god, 50b.
amiability, 20f.
amiable, 309b.
Åmi-bak, god, 46b.
Åmi-beq, god, 46b.
Åmi-besek, 46b.
Åmi-haf, god, 47a.
Åmi-heh-f, 47b.
Åmi-hem-f, 47b.
Åmi-ḥent-f (Rā and Osiris), 47b.
Åmi-hepnen, god, 47a.
Åmi Ḥetchpār (Osiris and Rā), 47b.
Åmi Ḥe-t Serqet Ka ḥetep-t, 47b.
Åmi Ḥe-t-ur-ka (Rā), 47b.
Åmi-kap, 48a.
Åmi-kar, 48a.
Åmi-kehau, 48b.
Åmi-Nenu (Nu), 47a.
Åmi-Net, 47a.
Åmi-Neṭat (Osiris), 47a.
Åmi-neter, 47a.
Åmi-net-f, 47a.
Åmi-Pe, 46b.
Åmi-pet-seshem-neterit, 46b.
Åmi-Qerq-t, 46a.
Åmi-qeṭem, 48a.
Åmi-rerek, 47a.
Åmi-reṭ, 47a.
Åmi-Seḥ (Osiris), 48a.
Åmi-Seḥ-neter, 48a.
Åmi-Seḥseḥ, 48a.
Åmi-Seḥti (Rā), 48a.
Åmi-sepa-f, 48a.
Åmi-Sepṭ-f, 48a.
Åmi-Sheṭ-t, 48a.
Åmi-suḥt-f (Rā), 48a.
Åmit, 49a, 51a.
Åmi-ta, 48b.
Åmi-ta-f, 48b.
Åmi-tchāāmu, 48b.
Åmi Tchebā, 48b.
Åmi-teḥenu (Set), 48b.
Åmi-Ṭep (Horus), 48b.
Åmi-Ṭeṭ (Osiris), 48b.
Åmi-thepḥet-f, 48b.
Åmit-neb-s-Usert, 47a.
Åmit She-t ur-t, 48a.
Åmi-Ṭuat (Horus), 48b.
Åmiu-åmau, 44b.
Åmiu-åsu, 46a.
Åmiu-Baġiu, 46b.
Åmiu-baḥiu, 46b.
Åmi-urt, 46a.
Åmi-ut, 46b.
Åmi-utchat-såakhu-Åtemt, 46b.
Ām-khaibitu, 121a.
Ām-khu, 121b.
Ām-mit, 121a.
among, 44a, 264a b, 265b, 296a, 414a.
amount, 65a, 134a, 221a, 838a, 900a.
Åmset, 55b, 553a.
Åmsi (Menu), 55a.
Åm-t (Åmit), 46a.
Åmtt, 55b.
Āmt-tcheru, 121b.
Amu, 6b.
Āmu, 122a.
amulet, 15a, 37b, 44b, 73a, 105a, 110a, 125a, 128a, 129b, 150b, 180a, 181a, 183b, 194a, 197b, 206a, 217a, 221b, 226a, 256a, 277a, 282a, 289b, 291a, 296b, 301b, 303b, 306a, 330b, 334b, 336a, 376a, 378b, 380a, 387a, 422b, 452b, 461b, 486b, 493a, 512b, 530b, 537b, 541a, 584b, 585b, 621b, 634a, 667b, 698a, 736b, 739b, 755a, 786b, 895a, 914a, 987a ; amulet for child-birth, 431a ; amulets with fluid of life, 193a.
amulet cases, 42b.
amuse oneself, 616b, 692b.
amused, 716b.
amusement, 716b.
Åmutnen, 51a.
Åmu-upt, 46a.
an, 105a.
Ån (On), 23b, 57a, 123b.
Ānā, 124a.
Ån-ā-f, 57a.
Ånana, 59b.
Ån-år-t-Rā, 57a.
Ån-åtf-f, 57a.
anathematize, 490b.
Ånåukar, 60a.
ancestor gods, 11b, 83a, 830b.
ancestors, 4b, 19b, 32b, 45b, 233b, 460a, 621a, 630a b, 909a ; figure of, 907a ; royal, 392b ; of Rā, 11b.

ancestral, 830b ; gods, 909a.
Ancestress (Isis), 909a ; ancestresses, 294b ; the Two, 906b.
ancient, 82a.
and, 32b, 74b, 148b, 466a, 472b, 486a, 492b, 506b ; and so forth, 483b.
Ān-em-ḥer, 123a.
Ȧnenit, 62a.
Ȧnen-reṭui, 57b.
Ānep, 34a, festival, 124a.
Ȧnerti, 62a.
Ȧnes-Rā, 63b.
anethum, 55a.
anew, 58a, 177a, 264b.
angarêb, 467b.
anger, 123b, 550a, 774b, 794b, 907a, 908a.
angle, 563b, 574b, 607b, 766b, 774a, 777b.
angry, 12b, 14a, 228a, 524b, 532a, 536a, 615b, 681a, 689b, 726a, 744b, 774b, 794b, 809b, 817b, 848b, 897b, 907a, 908a ; to make, 689b ; angry man, 615b, 681a, 689b.
anguish, 445b, 569b, 588a, 703b, 887a.
Ȧn-ḥāā, 59b.
Ȧnḥer, 57a, 132b.
Ȧnḥer Shu, 57b.
Ȧn-ḥetep, Ȧn-ḥetep-f, 57b.
Ȧni (Moon-god), 59a.
animal, 16b, 32a, 40b, 90a, 111b, 114b, 118a, 207b, 285b, 440a, 442b, 449a, 473b, 511b, 517a, 550a, 589a, 667a, 850a, 897b, 911a ; demon, 444b ; domestic, 126a, 299a ; dung of, 902b ; fabulous, 665a ; fighting, 132b ; filthy, 75b ; for food, 3b ; gnawing, 798b ; hawkheaded, 627a ; horned, 17b, 33b, 129a ; of Set, 132b ; sacred, 114b, 669b ; sacrificial, 19b, 54b, 538a, 561a, 666a, 754a ; small, 39a ; to stick, 900b; Typhonic, 306b; wild, 226a, 864b ; young, 897a.
animosity, 329a.
aniseed, 279a.
Ȧnit, 59a, 123b.
Ȧnith, 57a.
Ȧn-ken-mut, 59b.
Ȧn-Kenset, 59b.
ānkh, beetle, 125a ; god, 125a.
Ānkh-ȧb, 125b.
ānkham water, 293b.
Ānkh-ȧru-tchefa, 125b.
Ānkh-em-maāt, 125b.
Ānkh-em-nesert, 125b.
Ānkh-f-em-fenṭu, 125b.
Ānkh-f-em-khaibitu, 125b.
Ānkh-ḥer, 126a.
Ānkh-ḥetch, 126a.
Ānkhit, 125b.
Ānkhit-unem-unt, 125b.
Ānkh-neteru, 50b, 126a ; god, 30b ; 31a.
Ānkh-Septit, 126a.
Ānkh-s-meri, 126a.
Ānkh-ta, 126a.
Ānkhti, 126a.
ankle, 618b ; ankle joint, 695b.
anklets, 71a, 531b, 680a.
Ȧnku, god, 64a.
Ȧn-maāt, 57a.
Ȧn-mut-f, 59a, 450a b.
Ȧnmutf-ābesh, 59a.
Ȧn-mutk, 59a.
annals, 808b.
Ȧn-nef-em-hu, 57a.
annihilate, 702b, 704b.
annihilation, 186b.
Ȧnniu, 57a.
anniversary, 594a.
announce, 468b, 610b, 669b, 679b.
announcer, 548b, 598a, 601b.
annoyance, 664b.
annoyed, 32b, 664b, 665a.
annular, 215a.
anoint, 175a, 205b, 249a, 287a, 291a, 315a, 376b, 576a, 627b, 639a, 643a, 657a, 660a, 702b, 706a, 803b, 813b, 843a ; anoint the heart, 643b.
anointed, 205b ; anointed man, 665a ; ones, 175a.
anointings, 803b.
another, 782a, 791b, 792a, 798b.
Ȧnp-heni, 61a.
Ȧnpit, 61a.
Ȧnpu, 588a, 903a ; title of, 162a.
Ānq, 127a.
Ānqit, 127a.
Ānqnāamu, 127a.
Ȧnq-t, 64a.

Ȧnran, 59a.
Ȧn-re-f, 57a.
Ȧn-ruṭ-f, 62b.
Ȧn-sebu, 59b, 830b.
Ȧn-smet, 59b.
answer, 145b, 185b, 186a, 428a, 735b, 874a ; a letter, 564b ; a soft, 597b.
Ȧn-t, 57a, 58b.
Ānt Fish, 124a.
Ȧnṭaf, 57b.
Ȧntȧt, 127b.
Āntch, 128b.
Āntcheṭ, 128b.
Āntch-mer, 128b, 129a.
Āntchi Boat, 152a.
Āntch-ur, 128b.
Ȧnṭebu, 64b.
Ȧntef-āa, 5a.
antelope, 268a, 270a, 275b, 379b, 624b, 751a, 752a, 754b, 803b ; food of, 123a.
ȧntesh, 64a.
Ānthet, 127b.
Ȧntheth, 64b.
Ȧntheti, 64b.
Ānthrtȧ, 127b.
Ānṭi, 128a.
antidote, 247a.
antimony, 673b, 715b.
antiphon, 549a.
antiquity, 830a.
Ȧn-ti Set (Sti), 59b.
Ȧntit, 57a.
Āntit, 127b, 128a.
Ȧntiu, 59b, 64a.
Ānt-mer-mut-s, 123a.
Ȧntriush (Darius), 64a.
Ȧntt, 59b.
Ȧnt-t, 64a.
Ȧntti, 64a.
Āntu, 127b ; Ānṭu, 128a.
Ānu, 36b ; Council of, 901b ; spirits of, 263b.
Anubis, 41a, 46b, 588a, 828b, 901b ; daughter of, 769a ; festival of, 474b ; titles of, 48a, 61ab ; tool of, 352b.
anus, 244a, 274a.
anxiety, 319a, 330b, 428b, 464a, 484b, 889a.
anxious, 319a, 464a.
any, 357a ; anybody, 426a ; anyone, 153a, 823a.
Ȧpa, 426.
Ȧpaȧ-f, 42a.
Ȧpapit, 41b.
Aparius, 5b.
apartments, 154b, 552b ; private, 136a ; royal, 238b, 391b.
Ape, 2a, 28b, 29a, 111b, 114a, 123b, 227a, 296a, 444b, 452b, 786a, 792b, 795b, 802b, 804a, 807a ; dog-headed, 219a ; sacred, 91a.
Ape-god, 2a, 28a, 29a, 40a, 113b, 114a, 191b, 213a, 316a, 408b, 630a, 769b, 794b, 795a, 802b, 911a ; Ape-gods, the Eight, 25b ; the singing, 63a ; Ape-goddess, 29a.
Āper, 119a.
Āper-ḥer, 119a.
aperient, 528b, 697b.
Āperit, 119a.
Āper-peḥ (peḥui), 119a.
Āper-ta, 119a.
Āpert-Rā, 119a.
apex (of obelisk), 470b.
aphorism, 860b, 913a.
aphrodisiac, 325b.
aphronitrum, 7b.
Ȧpi, 42b.
Ȧpi-ȧb-neter, 41a.
Ȧpi-ȧbu, 41a.
Ȧpi-khenti-seḥ-neter (god of 110 years), 41a.
Apis, 111b, 478a ; circuiting of, 245b, 478a ; mother of, 95b ; priests of, 666b ; tomb of, 118b.
Ȧpit, 454b.
Ȧpit, 41b, 42a.
Ȧpit-ȧakhut-theḥen, 42a.
Ȧpi-tchet-f, 41a.
Ȧpit-ḥemt-s, 42a.
Ȧpit-urt-em-khat-Nut, 42a.
Apollinopolis Magna, 800b.
apology, 899b.
apophthegm, 860b.
apostates, 457b.
apparatus, 789b.
apparel, 14a, 34b, 62a, 63b, 155b, 160a, 169b, 230a, 262b, 282b, 324b, 329a, 476b, 629b, 635a, 667a, 712b, 818b, 829b, 836ab,

855a, 857b, 895b ; festal, 476b ; mourning, 252b, 751a ; white, 698b.
appeal, 124a, 668b, 745a ; house of, 136b ; for justice, 668b.
appear, 169a, 240a ; in a procession, 534b ; in the presence, 241a ; make to, 689b.
appearance, 416a, 535a, 615b, 891a ; astronomical, 242a ; distinguished, 630a.
appease, 614a, 684b.
appeased, 28a.
appellant, 868a.
appertaining to, 69b.
applaud, 508a, 798a, 840a.
apple, 832b, 877b, 906a ; of the eye, 217a.
appliance, 180b.
appoint, 66a, 436b, 722b, 841b, 866a, 885a.
appointment, 69b.
apportioning, 538b.
appreciate, 41a.
approach, 28a b, 29a, 390a, 443b, 549a, 565a, 576a, 629a, 638a, 645b, 846a b, 855b, 879a, 891a ; of death, 727b ; in fear, 441b, 447b ; to make, 722a.
approbation, 508a.
approval, 508a.
Āpriu, 119a.
Åpsetch-t, 42b.
Āpshait, 119b, 663a.
Åpsit, 42b.
Åpt, 40b.
Åptches, 43a.
Åp-t ur-t (Karnak), 41b.
Åpt-khatu, 416b.
Āp-ur (Osiris), 118b.
Åput, 42a.
Āqa, 139b.
Aqan, 11a.
Åqauasha, 93a.
Aqbi, 11a.
Aqbut, 11a.
Åqeh, 93b.
Åqen, 93a.
Āqen, 139b.
Āqennu-ḥeru, 139b.
Åqertt, 93b.
Åqeru, 93a.
Åqes, 93b.
Aqeṭqeṭ, 11b.
Āqḥer-åmi-unnut-f, 138b.
Åqhit, 93b.
Åqrit, 93a.
Åqrit-khenti-ḥe-t-set, 93b.
Åqru, 93a.
Āq-t-er-pet, 10b.
aqueduct, 499b, 650b.
arable land, 292a.
Aram, 72b.
arbour, 753a, 905a.
arch (of sky), 793a.
archer, 257a, 416b, 709a, 716a ; naval, 257b.
Archer-god, 859b.
archetype, 604b, 704b.
archiatros, 313a.
architecture, goddess of, 698a.
archives, 619a, 808b.
archon, 460b.
ardeb, 73b.
ardent, 817b.
area, 35b, 147a, 882b, 899b.
arena, 333a.
Årensnuphis, 71a.
Ārf, 131a.
argue, 167a, 366b, 410b.
argument, 854a.
År-ḥes, 73a.
Åri, 72a ; Ka of Rā, 67a ; Dekan, 130b.
āri (fish), 130b.
Åri-Åmen, 67b.
åri ānti, 70a.
åri åru, 70a.
Åri-år-t-tchesef, 70a.
arid, 185b, 340b, 732a.
Åri-em-åb-f, 67b.
Åri-em-āua, 67b.
Åri-en-åb-f, 67b.
Åri-ḥems-nefer, 71a.
Åri-ḥetch-f, 67b.
åri Nekhen, 70b.
Åri-peḥti, 70b.
Åri-ren-f-tchesef, 67b.
arise, 240a.
Åri-sekheru, 66b.
aristocracy, 829b.
Aristonikos, 7a.
Åri-t, 69b.
Ārit, 130a.
Åri-ta, 67b.
Årit-åakhu, 67b.

Årit-åru, 67b.
Åri-tchet-f, 67b.
Åriti, 67b.
Ārits, the Seven, 130b.
Årit-ta-theth, 67b.
Åri-usert, 70b.
Årk, 73a.
Årkanåtchpan, 73b.
Årkhåm, 73a.
arm, 11a, 419a, 425a, 766b, 768a, 802a, 806a, 898b ; arm and shoulder, 544a ; hidden arms, 756a ; the two arms, 806b ; to open the arms, 158b ; arm ornament, 141b ; arm ring, 105b ; arm of canal, 385a ; arm of Horus (censer), 105b ; arm of Nile, 35b ; arm of Orion, 105b ; arm of river, 97b ; arms (of tree), 425a ; to throw up, 898b.
arm oneself, 516a.
Årman, 72b.
armlet, 70a, 105b, 225a, 290a, 302b, 327b, 443a, 698b.
armour, 273b, 324a, 419a b, 535b, 575a, 582a, 684a, 789a.
armoury, 238a, 544a.
arms (weapons), 535b.
Årmu, 72b.
army, 288a, 320a, 897b.
Ārnebs, 129a.
aromatic, 736a ; substance, 862b.
around, 875a.
arouse, 681b.
årqabas (stone), 73a.
Ārq-ḥeḥ, 7b.
Ārq-ḥeḥtt, 131b.
arrange, 486b, 499a, 610a, 679b, 680a, 700b, 715a, 860a, 900a ; arrange laws, 400b ; words, 610b, 860b.
arrangement, 663a, 694a.
arranger, 860b.
array, 169a, 376a, 499a, 613b, 631a, 671b, 714a, 818b.
arrayed, 757a, 835b.
arrears, 193b ; of taxes, 495a.
arrival, 300b, 439a.
arrive, 244a, 300b, 346a, 390a, 517b, 522a, 647b, 661b ; arrive happily, 20b ; in port, 301a b ; to make arrive, 662a.
arrogance, 550b, 639a, 861b.
arrogant, 107b, 189b, 760a, 910a b.
arrow, 132b, 216a, 290a, 563a, 592b, 610b, 647a, 697b, 754a ; bundles of arrows, 545a ; packets of, 75b ; the Two Arrows, 624a.
arrow heads, 390a.
Arsaṭnikus, 7a.
Årsi, 73a.
Arsinfau, 7a.
Arsinoë, 7a, 73a.
År-stau, 71b.
Årsu, 73a.
Årsu, Syrian general, 73a.
Årt, Årtå, 73b.
Ārt, 130a.
artabe, 513b.
Artakhshassha, 7b.
Artaxerxes, 7b.
Artemis, 388a.
artery, 331b.
Årtheth-āa-sti, 73b.
Årti, 69b, 268a.
article, indefinite, 153a.
År-ti-en-tches, 68b.
Årti-f-em-khet, 68a.
Årti-f-em-ṭes, 68a.
artificer, 94a, 392a, 483b, 582b, 777b.
artificial, 67a.
Artikastika, 7b.
artisan, 6a, 158a, 483b, 777b, 784a, 805a.
artists, 122b, 483b ; quarter of, 156b.
Årti-tchet-f, 69a.
År-t-Rā-neb-taui, 68b.
År-t unemi, 68a.
Åru, 69a.
arura, 8a, 457b, 585b, 707a ; the quarter of, 511b.
as, 264a, 277a, 278b, 307b, 339b, 414a, 788b, 815a, 908b ; as far as, 65a, 414a b, 723a ; as long as, 104b, 339a ; as much as, 415a b ; as the result of, 633b ; as well as, 277a.
Ā-saḥ, 105b.
Åsår (Osiris), 83a ; Council of, 901b.
Åsåres, 36b.
Asb, 10a.

Asbit, 10a, 88b.
Asbu, 88b.
ascend, 28a, 29a, 112a, 129a, 234b, 447b, 468a, 498b, 534b, 558a, 689b, 701a, 861a.
ascender, 861a.
ascent, 306a, 861a.
ascribe merit, 508a; blessing, 668b.
Åseb, 88b.
Asenath, 389b.
Åser, 90a.
Åses, 82b.
Åsfa, 89b.
ashamed, 736a.
Ashbu, 10b.
Āsheb, 138a.
Āshemeth, 138a.
Asher, 765b.
ashes, 757a; hot, 618b, 696b.
Åshesp, 92b.
Åshespi-khā, 92b.
Āshḥeru, 137b.
Āshitabu, 137b.
Āshkheru, 137a.
Åshṭ (tree), 92b.
Åshteth, 92b.
Åshtit, 92b.
Āshtkheru, 137b.
Ashtoreth, Ashtoroth, 136b.
Åshṭṭ, 92b.
Ashu, Water-god, 10b.
Asiatic, 111a, 709a, 712b.
ask, 186b, 254b, 382b, 548b, 597a, 662a, 730a, 745a; ask for, 25b, 516a.
Åskhit, 90b.
Åsmet (see Mestå), 89b.
Ås-neteru, 82a, 888a.
asp, 479b.
aspalathus, 902b.
aspect, 243a, 493a, 761b.
asperge, 302b, 629b.
ass, 109b; she-ass, 733b; wild ass, 243b; young asses, 639b.
Ass-god, 17b, 109b, 121a; ass-headed god, 2a.
ass herd, 70a.
assail, 443a.
assarium, 854a, 867b.
assault, 769b; assaulter, 881a.
assemble, 639a, 683a; assembled, 467a, 826a.
assembly, 137b, 570a, 600b, 639a, 818a, 821a, 879a; the Great, 768a.
assent, 441b, 448a; particle of, 823a.
assess, 41a, 510b; what is assessed, 42b.
assessment, 206b, 511a, 521a.
assessor, 511a, 753b; of taxes, 605b.
assign, 889b.
assist, 113a, 865b.
assistance, 141b.
assistant, 248a, 265b, 579b; priest, 79b.
associate, 69b, 76a, 277b, 285a, 540a, 577b, 599b, 742a; associate with, 577b, 674b; associated, 539b.
Åss-t, 82b.
assuredly, 34b, 164b, 336b, 340a, 371a, 415b, 480b, 560a, 602a, 670a, 782a, 786a.
Åst (Rā), 81b; a uraeus, 81b.
Åsṭ (Set ?), 91a.
Åst-āat, 81a.
Āstårtåt, 136b.
Astarte, 136b.
Åstcheṭ, 91a.
Åsṭen, Åsṭenu, 90b, 91a.
Åsṭes, 91a.
Āsthåreth, 136b.
asthma, 547a.
Åsti, 81b.
Åsti-pesṭ-f, 81b.
astonished, 209b.
astragalus, 398a.
Åstsen-åri-tcher, 81b.
astuteness, 781b.
Åsut tcheseru, 80b.
asylum, 38a, 181b, 380a.
at, 65a, 264a, 339a, 414a, 492b, 828b; at all, 371a; at all times, 840b; at any rate, 336b; at hand, 828b; at no time, 340a; at once, 105a, 167a, 265b, 494b, 595b; at one time, 265b; at that time, 704b, 705b; at the back of, 265b, 633b; at the front, 265a; at the head of, 265b; at the moment, 264a; at the point of, 265a; at the rate of, 837b; at the side of, 415a; at what time, 545a.

Åtå, god, 97a.
Åṭa, town, 102b.
Åtar, Dwarf-god, 97a.
Atara, 13a.
Aṭau, god, 14a ; gods, 14b.
Åṭau, god, 102b.
Ātcha, 141b.
Ātcharti, 141a.
Ātchen, 141b.
Ātchnit, 141b.
Atef-crown, 13b.
Åtem, Bow-god, 98b.
Åtem, god, 98a, 103a ; Image of, 826b.
Åtemit, 98b.
Åtemt Kheprå, 98b.
Åten, 28a, 103a.
Åten-ur-nub, 98b.
åter (land measure), 100a.
Ates-ḥeri-she, 14b.
Åtfa-ur, 98a.
Åthabu, 100a.
Athemti, 101b.
Åthep, 101b.
Åthi-ḥeḥ, 101a.
Åthi-hru-em-gerḥ, 101a.
athlete, 704a.
Athpi, 13b.
Athribis, Boat of, 502a ; title of priest of, 477a.
Åṭhu, 104a.
Åti, god, 13a, 97a.
Åti-baiu, 97a.
Åtit-khau, 97a.
Åtru-neser-em-khet 99b.
attached, 389b, 399a.
attachment, 835b.
attack, to, 222a, 398a, 731a, 796b, 839b, 881a, 884a, 907b ; with violence, 908a ; to be attacked, 48b, 881a.
attack, 9b, 135b, 145a, 232a, 240b, 256b, 386b, 396b, 397a, 443a, 445b, 446a, 467ab, 499a, 509a, 528b, 547a, 571b, 633a, 705b, 738a, 753b, 767a, 841ab, 845ab, 847a, 858a, 881a, 885a, 907b, 908a.
attacker, 240b, 841a, 881a, 908a.
attain, 244a, 577b, 747b.
attendant, 718a, 742a, 847b.
attention, 37b ; to pay, 649b.
attestation, 332b.
Åṭṭi, 36b, 102b.
attire, festal, 776b.
attributes, 485b, 630a, 910b.
Åṭu, 102b.
Åtu, god, 97a.
Åtum, 97b.
Åturti, 97b.
Åu, god, 30b, 31ab.
Åu-ā, 3a.
Åua-en-Geb, 32a.
Āuāḥa, 115a.
Åuai (Rā), 32b.
Āuai, 115a.
Āuait, 115a.
Åu-ānkhiu-f, 31a.
Åuā-uā, 33a.
Au-āu-Uthes, 3a.
audience chamber, 535a, 900b.
audit, to, 642b.
Åuf, god, 34a ; frog-headed Ape-god, 34a.
Åufå, god, 34a.
Åugerit, 36b ; Khenti-åsts, 36b.
Åuger-t, 36b.
Åugertt, 36b.
august, 108a, 737a.
Åu-ḥer, 3a.
Åu-ḥer-åptes, 36a.
Åuheṭ, 35b.
Åuḥu, god, 36a.
Åuḥut, 36a.
Auit, 3b.
Åuker, 36b.
Åukhemu :—penḥesb, urṭu, seku, 36a.
Au-matu (?), 3a.
Āun, god, 115b.
Åun-āā-f, 34b.
Āun-åb, 115b.
Åunith, 35a.
Åunut, 35a.
Åupasut, 34a.
Åup-ur, 33b.
Åu-qau, 31b, 36b.
Åurauåaqrsånq Rabati, 35b.
Åusårs, 36b.
Åusāsit, 36b ; Ausāusit, 833b, 834b.
Au-t-ā, 3a.
Aut-åb, 3a.
author, 358a.
authority, 80a, 105a, 163b, 512b, 683b, 697b.

authorized, 722b.
Åuti (Rā), 37a.
Åutiu, 31b.
Aut-maātiu-kheru-maāt, 3a.
Åuuba, 33b.
auxiliaries, 115b, 281a.
avarice, 488b.
avaricious, 115b.
avenger, 64b, 807a.
avenue of trees, 299a, 677a.
avert, 683b.
aviary, 31a, 166a, 441b, 514b.
avoid, 176a, 323b, 481a, 499a.
awake, 381a, 607b, 612a; to keep, 432a, 681b.
award, 304a.
away, 492b; away to the left! 18b.
awe, 34a, 378b, 499b, 738b, 790b; awe-inspiring, 108a.
awning, 576a, 818b.
axe, 11a, 21a, 111b, 123b, 278b, 351a, 407b, 677b, 764b; battle-axe, 11a.
Axe-god, 403b, 404a.
axe-man, 391b; axemen, 11a.

B.

Ba, Bā, god, 200b, 212b.
Ba-åakhu-ḥā-f, 199b.
Baabi, 203a.
Baabu, 202a.
Båa-em-seḥt-neter, 210a.
Båaiti, 209b.
Baal, 202a, 203b, 213a.
Ba'alath, 213a.
Ba-Åment, 198a.
Ba-ānkh, 198b.
Ba-åri, 199b.
Ba-āshem, 198b.
Baå-ta, 210b.
Baåt-erpit, 199a.
Båau, 210b.
Baba, 200b; phallus of, 489a.
Babå, 203a, 210b.
Babai, 200b.
Babait, 202b.
Babau, 203a, 890a.
babble, 185a, 822b, 863a.
Babe (Rā), 525a.
babe, 196a, 284b, 349a, 388a, 525a, 591b, 597b, 632a, 647b, 652b, 664b, 706b, 716b, 798b, 825a.
Babi, 203a.
baboon, 347a.
Babuå, 203a.
Babuu, 203a.
baby, 322a, 548b; babyhood, 388b.
Bachis, 601a.
back, 1a, 13ab, 244a, 249a, 250a, 633b; flat part of, 846b; of head, 275b, 457b; of neck, 244a; backs of leaves, 794a; backs of men, 248a; back of sky, 457b; back (rump), 910a; to turn the, 528a, 633b, 866b; back-hall, 458a.
backbiter, 739b.
backbone, 15b, 249ab, 250a, 859b; of Osiris, 914a.
backside, 794a.
backwards, 30b.
bad, 133a, 145b, 203a, 216b, 226a, 343ab, 469b, 524a, 635a, 778b, 868b, 869a; bad act, 14b; bad deeds, 398a; bad man, 211a, 869a; bad place, 80b; bad year, 802a.
badge (of regiment), 647b.
badness, 214b, 216b, 641a, 868b.
Ba-em-uār-ur, 199b.
Bafermit, 198b.
bag, 102a, 131a, 209a, 256b, 484b, 568b, 647a, 803a, 805a, 819b, 835b, 873b, 895b; for clothes, 801b; leather, 528b, 529a.
Bages, 207b.
baggage, 209a.
Bāḥ (Nile), 213a.
Baḥeka, 200a.
Baḥrîyah, 84b.
Båi, 197a, 200b, 202ab, 212b.
bail, to go, 825b.
bailiffs, 562a, 652b.
Ba-irqai, 198b.
bait, 155a.
Bait, Baiti, 197b, 198a, 202b.
Baiu, 200a.
Baiu-Åment (Åmentiu), 198a.
Baiu-ānkhiu, 200a.
Baiu-Ånu, 198a.
Baiui, 200a.
Baiu-Khemenu, 199a.
Baiu-periu, 198b.
Baiu-Pu, 198b.
Baiu-shetau, 199a.

Baiu-ta, 199a.
Bȧk, 896a ; a Dekan, 206b.
Bakȧ (Rā), 206b.
bake, 232b, 261b, 355b, 593b, 769b, 822b ; bake pottery, 775b ; baked, 236a.
bakehouse, 440a.
baker, 247b, 559a ; baker's shop, 106b ; bakery, 334b, 786b.
Bakha, 869b.
Bakhai, 205a.
Ba-khati, 199a.
Bakhet, 150b.
Bȧkt, 211b.
Baktiu, 206b.
Bȧkui, 211b.
balance, 4a, 225a, 320a, 330a, 622a, 688a, 894a ; of the earth, 285b, 614b ; strike a, 716a.
balance, to, 194b, 614b ; balance the tongue, 236b.
balcony, 112a, 625a, 701b.
bald, 184b, 186b.
baldness, 167a, 344b, 799a.
bale a boat, 237a ; baler, 338a.
baleful, 221a, 778b.
balk of timber, 637a, 789a.
ball, 140a, 217a, 255b, 256b, 481b, 484a, 490b, 593a, 653a, 910a.
balsam, 4a, 5b, 110b, 282a, 378a, 650b, 706a ; balsam plant or tree, 14b, 50b, 113a, 348b, 566b, 810a.
Ba-merti, 198b.
ban, 649b, 745a; to be under a, 766a.
Bȧn, 211a.
Banȧathana, 203b.
Ban-Āntȧ, 203b.
band, 156a, 164a, 202a, 282b, 313b, 396b, 399b, 422a, 479a, 486b, 599b, 607b, 750b, 844b, 852b, 859b ; for a bow, 443a ; leather, 324a, 728b.
bandage, 37a, 71b, 92b, 169b, 234b, 249a, 301a, 305a, 313b, 399b, 419b, 517a, 606a, 607b, 629b, 701b, 728b, 758b, 835b, 904b.
bandage, to, 188a, 713a, 846b, 904b, 909b ; bandager, 103b ; bandaged, 909b ; Bandaged One, 818b.
banded, 63a, 324b.
bandlet, 27a, 90a, 103b, 110a, 120a, 131b, 164a, 169b, 174b, 228a, 234b, 243a, 249a, 276b, 278b, 279a, 282b, 289a, 304b, 319a, 323b, 372b, 377b, 381b, 399b, 421b, 450a, 622b, 625a, 631a, 635a, 654b, 678a, 693b, 695b, 698b, 701b, 714a, 741b, 755a, 756a, 776a, 835b, 840a, 849a, 852a, 855a, 858a, 870a, 876b, 904b ; coloured bandlets, 63b, 150b, 304b ; festival, 742a ; of crown, 535a.
bandy-legged, 260b.
Ba-neb-Ṭeṭ, 200a.
Baneteru, 200a.
bangles, 105b.
banished men, 574b.
bank, 128a, 409a, 421b, 544b, 597a, 693b ; of river or canal, 37b, 106a, 195a, 272b, 332a, 434a, 861b ; of Nile, 140b.
banner-bearer, 849a.
Bȧnrrat, 211a.
Bant-Ānt, 203b.
Bānti, 213a.
Ba-Pu, 198b.
Baqbaq, 206a.
Baqeṭt, 200a.
Baqt, 206a.
bar, 583b, 726a, 750a, 769b, 892b.
Ba-Rā, 198b.
Barȧst, 203b.
barbarian, 2a, 256a, 533b, 764a.
barber, 534a.
bare, 186b.
bargain, 723b.
barge, 211b, 640a, 685b, 762b, 764a, 767a, 877a, 894b, equipment of, 119a ; Barge of Ȧmen, 53a, 170a ; of Ȧmen-ḥetep III, 98b ; of state, 762b ; royal, 152a, 391b ; sacred, 182a.
bark, 178a, 221a, 343a, 832a.
bark (a tree), 511a ; make an incision in, 219a.
bark (cassia), 781a ; medicinal, 35b, 231b ; Nubian, 798b ; of a tree, 814b.
Barkatȧthaa, 204b.
barley, 50b, 215b, 227b, 468a, 611a, 821b.

barm, 611b.
Bār-m'hr, 213a.
barn, 286b, 490a, 746b ; floor of, 567a.
barracks, 419a, 850b, 852a.
barrage, 882a.
barren land, 340b, 730a.
Barst (Bast), 242a.
barter, 874a, 904a.
Basa, god, 205b.
basalt, 62a, 221b ; black, 210a.
base, 156a, 207a, 229a, 289a, 831a ; bases, 662b ; base of obelisk, 244a ; of pyramid, 180a ; of statue, 298a.
Baseḥ, 200a.
basement, 847a.
Basheftḥat, 200a.
basin, 94b, 95a, 97b, 354a, 366a, 421a, 431a, 473a, 511b, 574a, 596b, 731b ; libation, 629b ; of harbour, 307b ; of water, 307b.
basis, 675b.
basket, 124a, 202b, 219b, 256b, 307b, 354a, 366ab, 519b, 549b, 736a, 757a, 764a, 790a, 800b, 805a, 838a, 882a ; basket-bearer, 259a.
bast, 351a.
Basti, 205b.
bastinado, 26a, 112b, 208b, 280b, 468b, 614a, 685b ; bastinadoed, 468b, 686a.
bastion, 862a.
Bast-sheshȧ-ȧrit, 205b.
Bastt, 205a.
Bastt Tar, 205b.
bat, 717b, 868a, 885a, 891b.
Bȧt, 209a.
Ba-ta, 199a, 208a.
Bata-āntȧ, 208a.
Baṭaṭa, 200a.
Ba-tau, 199a.
Baten, 208b.
Batgeg, 208b.
bath, 79b, 80b, 155b, 702a, 768b ; of Rā, 308b ; natron, 456a ; house, 702a ; master of, 768b.
Bȧth, 212a.
Bathaḥ, 208b, 212a.
bathe, 27b, 217b, 374b.
Bathit, 208b.
Bathresth, 208b.
Bȧti, 212a.
Bati-erpit, 198b.
Bȧtiu, 212a.
baton, 83a, 726a.
Batr, 208b.
batter down, 452b.
battle, 132a, 154b, 670a, 704a, 772ab ; to do, 611a.
battle-axe, 11a, 21a, 333b, 459a ; battle cry, 447a ; battlefield, 240b ; battleships, 134b.
battlement, 175a.
Bau, 203a.
Bautcha, 203a.
Ba-utcha-ḥāu-f, 199b.
Bautchȧru, 198b.
bay, to, 178a, 203a, 343a.
bazaar (bazār), 549b ; to make, 733a.
be, 30ab, 164b, 230b, 542b ; make to be, 650a, 685b, 690a, 866b.
beacon tower, 274b.
bead, beads, 219b, 428a, 507a, 572b, 593a, 640b, 650a, 723a, 728a, 734b, 849b, 910a ; white, 651a.
beak of bird, 533a, 861b.
beaker, 605b.
beam, 49a, 79b, 124a, 164a, 215a, 583b, 590a, 635b, 644b, 789a, 818b, 908a ; of boat, 506b ; of plough, 127a ; of roof, 179b ; of scales, 425b.
beans, 21a, 69a, 112a, 235a ; Syrian, 35a.
bear, to, 18a, 35b, 91b, 145a, 205a, 258a, 260a, 321a, 676a, 849a, 852b, 853a, 872a, 873a ; bear children, 233b ; bear in mind, 274a, 396a, 861a ; on shoulders, 425a, 521b ; bear testimony, 334a ; bear up, 189b, 632b, 684a, 712a, 823b, 861a.
beard (of grain), 186b.
beard, 531a, 540b ; of Menthu, 306b ; plaited beards, 307a.
bearer, 258ab, 260a, 287a, 321a, 425b, 591a, 643a, 849a ; of a message, 200b ; in chief, 258b ; funerary bearers, 93b ; of loads, 13b.

bearing-pole, 60a, 89a, 274a, 773b, 851a, 859b.
beast, 111b, 868b ; four-footed, 114b ; ration of, 41b ; beast of a man, 114b, 705a ; beast-like, 488b.
beastly, 12b, 470a, 708a.
beat, 90b, 110a, 112b, 140a, 163b, 206a, 280b, 282a, 295b, 320b, 387a, 439a, 468b, 612b, 625b, 702b, 772ab, 776a, 779a, 799b, 821a, 827a, 841a, 842b, 851b, 887b, 902b ; beat a drum, 381b, 685b, 706a, 843b, 887b, 902b ; beat down, 91a, 179b, 253a, 868a ; beat flat, 185a ; beat out, 396a, 621a ; beat small, 452b ; beat to death, 135b ; beat to pieces, 685b ; beaten, 468b, 564b, 772a ; beating, 285a, 468b, 614ab, 685b, 772b, 821a ; place of, 772b.
beat (of the heart), 876b.
beater, 468b, 772b.
beatified, 93a, 197b.
beauties, 372b, 644b.
beautiful, 123a, 342b, 370b, 912a ; Beautiful Boy, 848b ; Beautiful Face, 371a.
beautify, 602b, 632b, 644b, 645a, 670b, 677a, 719ab, 912a.
beauty (a woman), 123a.
beauty, 123a, 141a, 370b.
Beb, 216a.
Bebi, 216a, 900b.
Bebti, 216a.
because, 56a, 79a, 339a, 399b, 414b, 492b, 536a, 815a, 908b ; because of, 493a, 579b, 904ab.
become, 164b, 736a ; to make become, 616a ; become many, 148a ; becoming, 304a.
bed, 13ab, 43ab, 111b, 289a, 374b, 375a, 467b, 492a, 600b ; death, 301a ; funeral, 457a, 739a ; of baby, 326b ; string, 368a ; bed-chamber, 375a ; bedclothes, 43b, 375b ; bed and linen, 43b.
bedaub, 801a.
bedew, 804a, 814a.
bedstead, 43b, 467b.
bee, 119b.
beer, 100b, 137a, 408a, 474a, 491b, 510b, 513b, 531b, 551b, 553b, 671b, 823a ; celestial, 514a ; everlasting, 514a ; of Maāt, 514a ; beer pot, 467a.
beerhouse, 140b, 513b, 651a.
beer-shop, 106b.
beetle, 28b, 118ab, 119b 295a, 541b, 543a ; medicine, 543b.
Beetle-god, 522b, 543a.
Befen, 216b ; Befent, 216b.
before, 105a, 205a, 264b, 265a, 316a, 339a, 414b, 415a, 460a, 494b, 545a, 554a, 560a, 580a, 738b, 828b, 683a, 909a.
beg, 254b, 472b, 577b, 606b, 607a, 677b, 730a, 733b, 809a.
beget, 65a, 101b, 188b, 189b, 217a, 609ab, 628a, 708a, 712a, 717a, 770b, 826a, 866b, 898a, 907a.
begetter, 84a, 316a, 322a, 331a, 648a ; begetting, 316a.
Begetter (Rā), 188b.
beggar, 472b, 552a, 584b, 723b, 734a, 824a, 876a ; wandering, 380b ; begging, 607a.
begin, 723a, 734a.
beginning, 460ab, 554a, 752a, 828a, 909a ; of time, 231a, 830a ; the first, 230b ; from beginning to end, 460a.
begotten, 186a, 217a.
behave, 794b ; rightly, 139a ; well, 770a.
behaviour, 595a, 694a, 698b.
Beḥen-t, 221a.
behest, 190b.
behind, 30b, 122b, 265ab, 339a, 457b, 567b, 580a.
behold, 79b, 266a, 279b, 289a, 330b, 385a, 712a, 824b.
Behthu, 220a.
Beḥuka (Libyan dog), 220b.
Beḥuṭit, Beḥuṭ-t, 220b.
Beḥuṭti, 220b.
being (existence, coming into), 164b, 542a ; the act of, 30b ; beings, 230b, 542b, 909a ; celestial, 494a ; human, 67a ; of former time, 45b ; of light, 9a, 77b ; primeval, 230b.
Bekat, 225b.
Bekh, 221b.

Bekha, 601a.
Bekhbekh, 221a.
Bekhen, 221b.
Bekhkhi, 221a.
Bekhkhit, 221a.
beleaguer, 743b.
belief, 382b.
belittle, 624a, 679b, 694b.
bellow, 375a, 447a.
belly, 224b, 346a, 416b, 570a, 571b, 773ab; disease of, 151a, 175a, 176b; of heaven, 570a; opener of, 584a; slave of, 583a.
belly-dance, 854a.
belongings, 444b, 525a, 580b; belonging to, 69b, 348a, 389b, 415b, 818b, 824b, 839b.
beloved, 107b, 310a.
belt, 113a, 164a, 217a, 324a, 540a, 631a, 676b, 701b, 715a; Belt of Orion, 99b; belt-knife, 666a.
Bêltis, 213a.
Ben, Benut, 216b.
Benben, 217b; Benbeniti, 217b.
bench, 289a, 328b; carpenter's, 539a.
bend, 156b, 429b, 448a, 530a, 531a, 539b, 572ab; bend down, 195a; bend a bow, 251b, 256ab; to make, 539b, 571b.
Bend of Amente, 216a.
bend (of a stream), 71b, 156b, 247a, 766b.
beneath, 494b.
Beneb, 218a.
benefactions, 148a, 304a.
benefactor, 285a, 305a.
beneficent, 304a, 305a, 343b.
beneficial, 22b.
benefit, 22b, 23a, 304a, 459a, 596b, 722b, 724b.
Benen, 217a.
benevolent, 20b, 310a, 343b, 346b, 517b.
Benf, 218b.
benighted, 529b.
Benn, 217a.
Benni, 217a.
Benr, 218b.
bent, 530a.
Bent, 219a.
Benti, 219a.
Benti-ȧri-ȧḥet-f, 219a.
Bentiu, 219b.
Benu bird, 218a.
Beq, 224a.
Beqenqen, 224b.
Beqtiu, 225a.
bequeath, 654a.
Berqer, 219b.
berry, 21a, 204a, 566b, 636a, 736a, 745b, 753a; berries, juniper, 237a.
Bes, 125b, 205b, 223a, 462a, 465ab.
Besa, 223a.
Bes-ȧru, 222b.
beseech, 124a, 186b, 352b, 382b, 577b, 602b, 662a, 671b, 809a.
Besek, god, 223b.
Besi, god, 222b; Besit, 222a.
Besi-ā, 222b.
besides, 148a, 264a, 492b, 493a.
besiege, 7a, 485a, 801b, 805a; besiegers, 908b.
Besi-em-ḥet kauit, 222b.
Besi-neḥeḥ, 222b.
Besi-sāḥu, 222b.
bespatter, 1b.
best, 214a, 461a, 828b, 829b; for the, 371a; best possible, 830a; the very, 828b.
Best-ȧru, etc., 222b.
bestial, 488b, 677a.
bestow, 260a, 291b, 474a, 487a, 490a.
Besu-aḥu, 222b.
Besu-Menu, 222a.
betake oneself to, 193b.
Bêt al-Mâl, 108b, 193b.
Beṭbeṭ, 227b.
Betch, 228b.
Beṭen, 228a.
Beṭesh, 228b.
Bethel, 208a.
Bet-neters, 226b.
betrothed, 756b.
Beṭsh-āui, 228a.
Beṭshet, 228a.
Beṭshu, 228b.
Beṭti, 227b.
Beṭu, 227b.
between, 32b, 37a, 44a, 331a, 414a.
bewail, 549b, 773a.

beware of, 586a.
bewitch, 247a, 434a, 464b, 514b.
bewitchment, 515a, 647b.
beyond, 244a, 308a.
Bi, 213b.
bier, 13a, 15b, 289a, 301a, 328a, 374b, 375ab, 378a, 457a, 600b, 71[illegible]b, 739a, 777a.
bifurcation, 156b.
bile, 1b, 82b.
billow, 145a, 440a, 441b.
bind, 1b, 20a, 58a, 99a, 113b, 120a, 124a, 131b, 156a, 203b, 228a, 285b, 291a, 338b, 347b, 351a, 355a, 399b, 409a, 446b, 606a, 607b, 645a, 662a, 675b, 676ab, 762b, 763a, 765a, 766a, 774a, 775a, 801b, 808a, 813b, 818b, 836ab, 840b, 850b, 859b, 878b, 883a, 912a, 915b ; bind on, 701a ; bind up, 313b ; bind a crown, 853a ; bind a sacrifice, 17a ; bind the toes, 64a ; bind together, 878b ; bind to stakes, 290b ; bind with spells, 219b.
binding, 58a, 99a, 164a, 607b, 745a, 765a, 863a ; of a bow, 287b.
bird, 5b, 9b, 19b, 21b, 70b, 73b, 100b, 102a, 116b, 124a, 129b, 134b, 135b, 147a, 152b, 163b, 176a, 195b, 219a, 230a, 231b, 234b, 235a, 243a, 304a, 315a, 324a, 330a, 347b, 354b, 382b, 385b, 397b, 431a, 433b, 439b, 444a, 469a, 490a, 508a, 541b, 564a, 569b, 579a, 593a, 613b, 633a, 639b, 666a, 682b, 697b, 738b, 746a, 758b, 795b, 804a, 806a, 808a, 809b, 810a, 839a, 848b, 857a, 872b, 870a, 895b, 897a, 902a, 907a, 910b ; fat, 138a ; fattened, 795a ; for breeding, 137b ; green - breasted, 151a ; marsh, 181b, 714b ; netted, 186b ; of prey, 247b, 322b.
birdcage, 854a.
bird catcher, 475a, 514b.
bird houses, 441b.
bird snarers, 181b.
Birds, the Two, 840b.
birth, 205a, 321ab ; at one, 570a ; to give, 321a, 865b ; of five gods, 321b ; second, 323a.
birth chamber, 326b.
birthday, 321b, 438b, 450b.
birth goddess, 145a, 234a ; Birth goddesses, the Four, 326b.
birthplace, 326b.
birthstones, 326a.
Bit, 213b.
bit, 245b.
bitch, 722a, 862a.
bite, 169b, 185b, 249a, 392b, 538a, 706b, 914b ; of insect, 248a ; biters, 39b ; bitten, 878a.
bitter, 686a, 887a.
bittern, 714b.
bitterness, 290b, 536b.
bitumen, 302b, 423b, 428a, 647b.
black, 243b, 787b, 789a ; dead black, 389a ; shining black, 787b ; strong black (i.e., jet black), 787b ; black powder, stone and wood, 788a ; blacken, 704b.
Black Pig (Set), 428a.
Black-Face, 788a.
blackness, 798a.
Blacks of Sûdân, 344a.
blacksmith, 160b, 325a ; of Edfû, 505b.
blade, 390a.
blains, 11b, 320a, 565b, 698b, 709b, 791a.
blandishments, to use, 650b.
blaspheme, 60a, 110a, 145b, 154b, 745a, 794b.
blasphemers, 145b, 707b.
blasphemy, 145b.
blast, 696a.
blaze, 49a, 160a, 164a, 177b, 221b, 222a, 295a, 393a, 572b, 601b, 664b ; make a, 696b.
blazer, 160a, 393a.
blazon, 681b.
bleach, 700b.
bleached linen, 685b, 700b.
blear-eyed, 459b.
blemish, 441b, 895a.
bless, 204a, 207a, 598b, 666b.
blessings, 23a, 666b.
blind, 203b, 340b, 736b, 789a ; of the blind, 736b ; blinded, 914a.

blindness, 736b.
block, 298a, 654a, 874a; of execution, 373a; in Ṭuat, 39b; the god's, 402b; of Osiris, 775b.
block up, 103b, 643b, 750a, 873b, 905a; blockaded, 800a.
blockade, 801b, 805a.
blocked, 524a, 624a, 803a, 905a; of artery, 491a.
Block-god, 39b.
blockhouse, 569a, 660b.
blood, 606a, 676a, 677a, 889b; drinker of, 109a; flux of, 606a.
bloody-eyed, 606a.
bloom, 8b, 22a, 243b, 464a, 467a, 472b; afresh, 375a.
blooming, 148b; Blooming One, 841b.
blossom, 8b, 146a, 148b, 354a, 372b, 384b, 500a, 903b.
blot out, 591a, 884a.
blow, 159b, 397b, 468b, 489ab, 527b, 614b, 615a, 685b, 698a, 723b, 734a, 751a; of Fate, 724a.
blow, to, 348b, 409a; blow at, 369b; blow hot and cold, 681a; of flowers, 639a.
blow-pipe, 72b.
blue, 330b, 564a, 569b; cloth, 69b, 564a; porcelain, 842a.
bluish, 564a, 569b.
blunder, 675a.
board, 88b, 149a, 566a; writing, 123a.
board of guardians, 901a.
boast, 651b, 723b, 724a, 910b; boaster, 651b, 911a; boastful, 108a; man, 824a.
boat, 13a, 16a, 49b, 60b, 97b, 134b, 139b, 152a, 174a, 180b, 202b, 203a, 204a, 211b, 235b, 273a, 289a, 308a, 328b, 356b, 374a, 425b, 433a, 448a, 467a, 470b, 475b, 478b, 479b, 540a, 561b, 565b, 576b, 590a, 602b, 612b, 671b, 682b, 762b, 764a, 767a, 778b, 786a, 789b, 791b, 832a, 851b, 877a, 892a, 894b, 895a, 900a; boat and crew, 119a; basket-shaped, 202b; for bird transport, 134b; broad, 183b, 685b; cattle, 576b, divine, 832a; fare, 90a; magical, 17a, 28a, 38a, 69b.
Boat of Åf, 5a.
Boat of Byblos, 661a, 757a.
Boat of Herr, 152b.
Boat of Kheperȧ, 152b.
Boat of Millions of Years, 152b.
Boat of Neh, 152b.
Boat of Rā, 30b, 31a, 152b.
Boat of Sunrise, 140b.
Boat of Tem, 152b.
Boat of Ṭesṭes, 152b.
Boat of the Earth, 152b.
Boat of the Father, 152b.
Boat of the king, 152a.
Boat of the morning Sun, 291a.
Boat of the setting Sun, 328a.
Boats of the Sun-god, 152a.
Boat of Truth, 272a.
Boat of Truth, 152b.
boat, parts of a, 11a, 40a, 187a, 192b, 226a, 231b, 268b, 275a, 276a, 547b, 562b, 610b, 657b, 680a, 828a, 902a; pleasure, 310b; river, 290a; rope of, 559a; sacred, 108b; 357b, 358a, 385b, 699b; sea-going, 305b, 793a; Sûdânî, 152a; swift, 643a; tackle of, 9a.
boats, treasure, 417a; festival of, 474a; procession of, 576b.
boatman, 93b, 290b, 769a, 877a; boat-master, 154b.
body, 34a, 75b, 165a, 222b, 424b, 570a, 571b, 633a, 722b, 773ab, 778a, 893a; complete, 659b; dead, 528b, 570b; divine, 893a; embalmed, 158a, 188a; hidden, 43a; human, 466a; invisible, 755b; mummified, 570b, 778b; of a man, 878b; of Osiris, 24b; of Rā, 23b; body of the god, 33a, 106a, 402b; One body, 466a; part of the, 21a, 32b, 150a, 220a, 324a, 417b, 612b, 682a, 697b, 851b; solid parts of, 848b; substance of, 528a; lower part of, 910b.
bodyguard, 33a, 742ab; divine, 742b; king's, 392b; of the god, 403a.

boil, 11b, 124a, 134b, 140b, 204a, 217a, 222b, 231a, 247b, 248a, 261b, 320a, 356a, 382b, 565b, 597b, 676a, 681a, 698b, 709b, 791a, 817b, 841b ; boiled meat, 247b ; boiling lake, 539a ; boil away, 899a.
boil, a hard, 381a, 836b.
bold, 193b, 259a, 289a, 297a, 307a, 382b, 433b, 702b, 772a, 851a, 857a, 861b, 899a ; bold-faced, 691a ; bold-hearted, 690b ; of speech, 690b.
bolt, 93b, 139b, 140a, 219a, 246a, 583b, 600b, 757a, 762a, 763b, 764a, 769b, 777b, 810a, 896b ; of door, 244b, 473b, 516a, 775b.
bolt in, 5a ; bolt together, 803a ; bolting (of food), 645a.
bolt-peg, 267a, 464b, 769a, 871b ; bolt-socket, 126a.
bolus, 203b, 237a, 256b, 490b.
bon à merveille, 209b.
bonds, 11b, 118a, 146a, 305a, 355a, 521a, 587a, 653a, 750a, 765a.
bone, 9a, 765a, 778a ; bone and flesh, 28a ; bone-chamber, 595a ; counting of bones, 41a ; sacred, 249b.
bonnet, 458b.
book, 71b, 99a, 129a, 131b, 200b, 337b, 377b, 619a, 722b, 725a, 738b, 739a, 755a, 836b, 848a, 880a, 885a, 896b, 898b ; account or day book, 129a ; closed books, 619b ; magic books, 619b ; sacred, 402a, 403a, 525b ; Book of Praise, 337b ; Book of the Festival, 474b ; Book of the praises of Rā, 337b ; Book of the Words of the God, 337b ; Book of traversing Eternity, 337b.
book-box, 255b.
book-learned, 120a.
boomerang, 97a, 122a, 770a, 800b, 856b ; to throw, 111b, 121b, 770a.
boon companion, 739a.
boor, 180a.
booth, 92b, 238b, 475a, 511b, 682a, 700b, 753a, 801b ; to build a, 695a.
booty, 283b, 464b, 512b.
border, 50a, 248a, 488a, 881b, 819b, 908b.
bore, 191b, 189a ; boring tool, 452a.
born, 55a, 221b, 233b, 240a, 241a, 321a.
borne, 894b.
bosom, 212b, 307a, 777b.
boss, 369a.
bottle, 94b, 281b, 292b, 485a, 801a ; skin, 62a, 568b, 576a.
bottom, 609a ; bottom side uppermost, 580a.
boulders, 789b.
bound, 15b, 273a, 759a, 899a.
boundary, boundaries, 50a, 104b, 133b, 248b, 297b, 411a, 488a, 773a, 818a, 819b, 820b, 844b, 852a, 881b, 908b ; door, 908b ; mark, 301a ; stone, 192b.
boundless, 908b.
bounty, 213b.
bouquet, 118a, 287a, 328a, 563a ; carrier, 259a ; funerary, 518a.
bow, to, 94b, 441b, 448a, 476a, 530a, 531a, 539b, 572b, 603a, 791b, 797ab ; in homage, 879a ; the head, 147b, 828a ; the knee, 204b.
bow down to, 178b, 544b, 590b.
bow, 96a, 253b, 256a, 257a, 516b, 572a, 795b, 832b, 877b ; amulet of, 256a ; divine, 741b ; Land of the, 22a ; Nine Peoples of the, 257a ; the Nubian, 59b ; of heaven, 741b ; Syrian, 256a ; to draw a, 13b ; to string, 100a ; to ground, 79a ; bearer, 70b, 99a ; master, 70b ; bow-shaped, 274b.
bow (of ship), 750a, 828b.
bowed, 441b, 530a, 763a.
bowels, 181b, 224b, 599a, 769b.
bowings (homage), 94b, 448a, 797a.
bowl, 2a, 28ab, 94b, 95a, 114a, 218a, 253a, 318b, 324b, 422a, 485a, 527a, 529b, 558b, 649a, 652a, 842b, 852a, 856b, 878b, 892a, 895b.

bowman, 257a, 416b, 709a, 848a, 903a; divine, 535a; bowmen (foreign), 256a; naval, 257b; the Nine, 251a; of Horus, 257a.
Bowman, god, 256b.
bowstring, 421b, 422a.
bowstringer, 422a.
box, 43ab, 63b, 120a, 155a, 166a, 203b, 255b, 256b, 263a, 302a, 447b, 514a, 581b, 604b, 605a, 675b, 685a, 805b, 812b, 827b, 832a, 836b, 839a, 873b, 874b, 876b, 904b; box of head of Osiris, 19a.
boy, 61a, 110b, 141ab, 303a, 466a, 471a, 487b, 525a, 545b, 573b, 597b, 647b, 749b, 798b; of the South, 472a.
bracelet, 33b, 70a, 105b, 217a, 302b, 303a, 428b, 443a, 451b.
bradawl, 123b, 452a.
brag, 651b.
braid, 82a.
brain, 190b.
brainpan, 448a.
branch, 17a, 60a, 90a, 138a, 262a, 487b, 566a, 600b, 637b, 892b, 903b; of the Nile, 714a.
brand, to, 4b, 19a; branded cattle, 569b.
brandish, 662b.
brass, 533a, 842a.
brave, 107b, 241a, 289a, 297a, 772a, 838b, 839a, 841b, 855a, 857a; braves, 772a, 841b, 857b.
brave man, 314a, 841b.
bravery, 241a, 245a, 330b; prize of, 259a.
bray in a mortar, 411a, 480b.
brazier, 135a, 178a, 286a, 582a.
breach, 26b, 397b, 630b, 713b.
breach a wall, 189a, 191b, 689a, 693b, 700b, 713b.
bread, 2b, 3b, 8a, 31a, 33b, 37b, 39a, 43a, 62b, 119b, 138b, 139a, 143a, 168b, 221b, 230b, 233a, 234a, 235a, 253a, 262b, 276a, 330a, 372b, 401a, 465b, 487a, 534ab, 551b, 590b, 605a, 621b, 717b, 722b, 730b, 734a, 750b, 767a, 769b, 776b, 786b, 790a, 793a, 796ab, 802b, 804a, 813b, 815a, 817a, 822b, 823a, 833a, 844a, 846a, 908a; bread and beer, bread and wine, 842b; crumby, 423b; everlasting, 817b; fancy, 645a, 862a; for journey, 894b; great-great, 817a; holy, 817a; incorruptible, 817a; of angels, 817b; of eating, 817a; of fine flour, 771b, 817b, 851b; of Memphis, 817b; of Menu, 817a; of the field, 817b; of the highest quality, 817b; of the moon, 817a; of the morning, 817b; of the month, 817b; sacrificial, 817a; stamped, 568b; wheaten, 788b, 789a; white, 523b, 866b; to make, 774a.
breadcake, 113a, 138b, 139b, 390b, 415b, 457a, 506b, 545a, 614a, 739b.
bread offering, 144a, 245b, 823b.
bread oven, 822a.
bread store, 238a.
breadth, 182b, 615b, 685b.
break, 91ab, 114b, 178a, 220b, 261b, 398b, 452b, 517a, 539a, 547a, 565b, 587a, 593b, 630b, 633a, 685b, 706b, 713b, 716a, 764b, 765ab, 801b, 808a, 821a, 822b, 842b, 844b, 902a; down, 528b; forth, 795b; ground, 29b, 302a, 488b; in, 765a, 854a; into, 185a, 841a; into flame, 439b; open, 158a, 253a, 347b, 388a, 571b, 625b, 702b, 716a; peace, 845a; seal, 665b; through, 201a; up, 411a, 613b, 683b.
breakers, 587a.
Breaker of bones, 714a.
breast, 203a, 207b, 217a, 307a, 329a, 460a, 461a, 516b, 746b, 763a, 768a, 773b; breasts of woman, 763a; pendent, 307a, 695b; the two, 219b, 306ab, 307a; breasts with milk, 225b.
breast bone, 773b.
breast cover, 853a.
Breast-god, 202a.
breast offering, 616b.
breast ornament, 183b.
breast plate, 193b, 216a.

breath, 82a, 280a, 348b, 369b, 377b, 451b, 551a, 605a, 618b, 651b, 697a, 823b, 824a, 849b.
breath of life, 370a ; of serpent, 348b.
breathe, 348b, 369b, 394a, 603b, 612ab, 618a, 675a, 681b, 695b, 697a, 832a, 854b ; an odour, 551a ; easily, 10a ; into 451b ; with difficulty, 807b.
breathing, 603b, 618b, 697a ; difficulty in, 547a.
breathlessness, 547a.
breeze, 82b, 89b, 130b, 141b, 273a, 342a, 344b, 346b, 377b, 445a, 605b, 648b, 836b.
brethren, 674a.
brew, 100b, 735a.
brewer, 100b ; brewers, 140b.
brewery, 156a.
bribe, to, 262a, 904a.
brick, 42a, 654a, 819b, 827b, 874a, 905a ; of metal (ingot), 827b.
brick base, 875a.
brick kiln, 118b.
bricklayer, 538b.
brickmaker, 201a, 538b.
brickmaking, tools for, 56b.
bricks, to make, 233b, 234b, 235ab ; the Four, 874a.
brickwork, 905a.
bride, 756b.
bridle, 552a.
brigand, 115a.
bright, 160a, 180b, 206a, 212b, 215b, 224ab, 522b, 628b, 635a, 736b ; to be, 22b, 225a, 820b ; become, 522a ; to make, 589b ; something that is, 3b.
brightness, 9a.
brilliance, 23a, 31a, 142b, 160a, 274a, 459b, 522b, 535a, 914a.
bring, 7a, 56a, 113b, 260a, 286b, 301b, 324a, 591a, 616a, 640a, 690a, 707b ; bring forth, 1a, 233b ; bring forward, 152a, 558a ; gifts, 562a ; in, 735a ; low, 256b ; report, 56b ; to an end, 129b, 138a, 546a, 626a ; together, 879a ; up, 591a, 645ab ; 655a ; bring up children, 677b, 690a ; bringer, 56a, 645b, 707b.
bristle, to, 167a ; bristling (of the hair), 726b.
bristles, 716b, 726b.
broad, 180b, 260a, 635b ; to make, 652a.
broaden, 697a.
broken, 181a, 778a, 802a.
Broken-hearts, 716a.
bronze, 132b, 188b, 512a, 602a.
brood, to, 319a, 387b.
brook, 576a.
brother, 674a ; brothers and sisters, 674ab.
Brother-gods, the Two, 674a.
Brother-kings, 392a.
brought forth, 321a.
brow of Åmenti, 163a.
brow of the water, 293a.
bruise, 140b, 253a, 571a, 688b.
Bu (devil), 197a.
Bua-tep, 215b.
bubble up, 476a, 833a.
bucket, 186b, 881b ; sacrificial, 185b.
buckler, 93a, 95a, 324a, 776a, 788a, 810a, 851b, 853a.
bud, 246a, 385b, 394a.
buffoon, 294b.
Bu-ḥeḥ, 214b.
build, 1b, 94a, 144a, 164a, 366b, 375b, 432b, 535b, 536a, 538a, 563b, 578a, 597a, 611a, 642b, 662b, 676b, 689b, 728a, 730a, 769b, 778a, 779a.
builder, 60b, 535b, 563b, 578a, 779a.
building, 99a, 132a, 164a, 181a, 298a, 438a, 563b, 731b, 734a, 914b ; government, 881b ; high, 134a ; memorial, 192b ; pillared, 58b ; site, 147a ; strong, 38a ; walled, 633b.
bulge, 225a.
bull, 39a, 275b, 299a, 379a, 396b, 397b, 398a, 669a, 774a, 800b ; a " cut," 784b ; divine, 393a ; fighting, 132a ; for sacrifice, 400a ; red and white, 75a, 784a ; parts of, 559b ; stud, 26b ; wild, 636b.
Bull in Ṭeṭ, 886b.
Bull of Maāt, 886b.
Bull of the Gods, 784b.

Bull, name of a boat, 668a.
bull calf, 784a.
bull cakes, 730a.
Bull-god, 7b, 109a, 127a, 228b, 374a, 398a, 707b, 912b ; of Hermonthis, 221b ; with two faces, 208a.
bull's skin bier, 327b, 328a.
Bulls, the Two, 667a, 674b ; the Four of Tem, 151b, 159a.
bulwark, 164a.
Bun, Bunā, 215b.
bunch, 347b, 814a, 915a ; of flowers, 257a.
bundle, 124a, 131a, 313b, 347b, 519b, 561b, 563a, 735a, 764a, 792b, 814a, 844b, 866b, 915a ; of grain, 773b ; of reeds, 377b ; of vegetables, 563a ; to tie up in, 563a.
burden, 13b, 206b, 338a, 883b ; burdened, 531a.
burdensome, 507a, 882a.
bureau, 80b, 510b, 526b.
burial, 375ab, 599a, 667b, 669a, 764b, 776a, 777a, 778b, 783a, 860a ; day of, 450b.
buried, 550a, 777a, 909b.
burn, 6a, 9b, 10b, 17a, 19a, 25b, 49a, 140a, 145b, 146b, 160a, 164a, 187a, 189a, 190b, 221a, 227b, 237a, 275b, 295a, 320a, 367a, 388a, 390a, 393a, 420b, 429b, 434ab, 439b, 445a, 510a, 517a, 526a, 547a, 588b, 628a, 630b, 635a, 636b, 639b, 672a, 695b, 724b, 774a, 817b, 832a, 897b, 899a, 900b ; incense, 227b ; to make to burn, 645b, 708a ; up, 163b, 177b, 268b, 285b, 392b, 439b, 550b, 605b, 639a, 670a, 676a, 726a ; burnt out, 429b ; up, 186b, 750b.
burned, 187a, 215b, 388a, 429b.
burner, 160a, 284b, 367a.
burning, 131a, 434a, 531a, 588b, 817b.
burnt offering, daily, 92b.
burst, 22a, 639a.
bury, 599a, 815b, 837a.
bush, 89a, 167b, 197a, 202a, 209a, 344a, 539b, 636a, 695a, 833a ; "bush," 765b.
business, 8b, 160b, 335a, 438a, 486b, 525a, 580b, 622a, 650b, 694a, 733a.
Busiris, 15b, 238b, 852b ; title of priest of, 389b.
bust, 494b.
but, 79a, 96a, 160b, 480b, 809b ; but not, 79b.
butcher, 54b, 303b, 575b, 653b, 665a, 666a, 669a, 711a.
Butcher-gods, 489b.
butler, 19b, 71a, 158a, 843a ; royal, 391b.
But-Menu, 215a.
Buto, 406a.
butt, to, 386b, 445b, 447b, 777b.
butter, 610b, 669b.
buttocks, 244a, 298b, 513b, 544b, 909b.
buying, 650b.
by, 56a, 65a, 339b, 414a, 492b, 560a, 762b, 813a, 828b ; by all means, 336b ; by means of, 279b, 492b ; by no means, 835a ; by the, 277a ; by the hand of, 279b ; by the side of, 415a ; by way of, 492b.
Byblos, boat of, 661a, 768b, 787a.
byre, 337a.
byssus, 252ab, 440b, 648b, 653b, 697b, 751a, 840a, 884b.
bystander, 813a.

C.

cabin, 549b, 605a, 678ab, 746b ; of boat, 34b, 130b, 573a, 575b.
cabinet, 37b, 286a ; royal, 312a.
cabinet maker, 289b.
cackle, 348a, 398a, 800b.
cackler, 398a.
Cadmus, 766a.
Caesar, 841b.
cage, 204a, 514b, 521a, 729a, 757a, 875a, 905a.
cajole, 650b.
cajolery, 650b.
cake, 2b, 7a, 8a, 31a, 33b, 36b, 37b, 39a, 43a, 62b, 100b, 138b, 143a, 151a, 152a, 168b, 174a, 186a, 191a, 202a, 203b, 209a, 218a, 221b, 230b, 231b, 232b, 233a, 234ab, 235a, 247b, 248a,

253a, 259b, 261b, 283ab, 324a, 330a, 332b, 385b, 422b, 429b, 442b, 457a, 465b, 487a, 516a, 521b, 533a, 536b, 551b, 568b, 591a, 617a, 621b, 635b, 653a, 729b, 734a, 736a, 750ab, 754b, 765b, 769b, 786b, 790a, 792b, 793a, 796a, 802b, 804a, 813b, 815a, 817a, 822b, 833ab, 844a, 846a, 851b, 862b, 882b, 894b, 897b, 900a ; baked, 20a ; bull, 730b ; evening, 323b ; goose, 730b ; hard baked, 441b ; medicinal, 550b ; obelisk, 730b ; round, 42a ; sacrificial, 435b, 476a, 531b, 550b, 823b, 825b ; sweet, 730b ; white, 730b.
cakes, the Four, 817a ; the Seven, 817a.
cake offering, 55b, 100b, 102a, 186a, 191a, 796b.
calamint, 39b, 344b, 345a.
calamity, 2a, 2b, 14ab, 31b, 74a, 103b, 120a, 127b, 142a, 170a, 214b, 296b, 379b, 386b, 395a, 450a, 461b, 489a, 527b, 549b, 577ab, 595ab, 632a, 698a, 715a, 717b, 772b, 778b ; day of, 451a.
Calasirites, 315b.
calculate, 510b, 735b, 838a.
calculation, 297b, 510b, 856b.
caldron (see cauldron).
calf, 37b, 170a, 205a, 221a, 426b, 428a, 477b, 509b, 854a, 864b ; bull, 323a ; of Kherȧ, 220b ; star, 220b.
call, 17a, 25b, 60a, 79b, 136b, 333a, 345a, 587b, 658a, 790a, 872b.
call out, 136b, 705b, 782b.
call to mind, 90b, 688a.
call up troops, 677b.
called (i.e., named), 187b.
calling, 345a.
calm, 570a ; weather, 898b.
calumniate, 642a.
calumny, 419a, 420a.
Cambyses, 763b, 793a, 794b, 795a, 808a.
camel, 786a, 788b, 808a, 882b.
camel cloth, 330b.
camels' hair, 22a ; tents of, 74b.
camel stick, 856b.
camp, 7b, 21a, 32a, 74b, 114a, 120a, 235a, 297b.
campaign, 193a.
camping ground, 718b.
camwood unguent, 890a.
canal, 8b, 22a, 35b, 99b, 114a, 115b, 202a, 212b, 257b, 293a, 307b, 308a, 343a, 349b, 400a, 407b, 416a, 424b, 461b, 488b, 499b, 516b, 526b, 533a, 650b, 707b, 714a, 731b, 758a, 759b ; of Heliopolis, 16a ; the old, 882b ; the small, 750a.
cancer, 160a.
Cancer, 543a.
candlestick, 582a.
cane, 277a.
canon, 271b, 400b, 566a, 753b.
canopy, 13b, 678ab.
cap, 40a, 119b, 458a.
capable, 129b.
cape, 773b.
capital (money), 829a.
capital city, the, 575b.
capital of pillar, 210b.
capsize, 232b, 236b, 647a, 661b.
captain, 71a, 154b, 311b, 370a, 461a, 494a, 495a, 562b, 825b, 860ab, 896a ; of boat, 694a ; of ten, 312b ; to act as, 117b.
captives, 464b, 512b, 550a, 552a, 648a, 702ab, 705b ; to take, 597b.
captivity, 412b.
capture, 100b, 435b, 449a, 464b, 473a, 512b, 545a, 702b, 794a.
captured, 7a.
Capturer, 794a.
caravan, 106a ; chief of, 311b ; leader, 671a, 791b.
caravan march, 499a.
caravanserai, 297b.
caraway seed, 296a.
carbuncles, 681a, 709a, 791a.
carcase, 32b, 34a, 530a.
cardinal points, gods of, 556b.
card wool, 114a.
care, 3b, 319a, 351b, 428b, 464a, 484b, 866a.
care for, 319a, 351b, 381a, 386a, 421a, 433a.
careless, 176b, 180a, 289b.

caretaker, 351b.
cargo, 594a.
carnage, 730a, 731b.
carnelians, 471a, 485b, 612b, 682a.
carobs, 131b, 153a, 891b, 900a; dried, 470b.
Carob wine, 839a.
carpenter, 11a, 304b, 320a, 413a, 483b, 567a; to work as a, 11a.
carpet, 195b, 249a, 773a.
carriage, 649b.
carried, 894b.
carrier, 56a, 258ab, 260a, 425b, 591a, 645b, 670b, 676a, 763a, 764a, 849a; of gold, 792b; of the book, 849a.
carroty, 889a.
carry, 18a, 35b, 91b, 113b, 149b, 189b, 258a, 260a, 425a, 640a, 673a, 676a, 705b, 849a, 852b, 853a, 872a; away, 105a, 531b, 538b, 713a, 757b; off, 63b, 100b, 101a, 146a, 212a, 298a, 385a, 420b, 550b, 590a, 703b, 747b, 750b, 796a, 849a, 865b, 867b; on, 846b; out, 65b.
carrying pole, 859b.
carthamus silvestris, 810b.
carthamus tinctorius, 791a.
cartonnage, 188a.
cartouche, 305b.
carve, 9a, 186a, 220a, 304b, 323a, 527b, 587b, 639b, 644a, 660b, 777b, 836a; patterns, 571b; statue, 279a, 645b.
carved, 567b; work, 19b.
carver, 323b.
case (affair), 525a, 581b, 595a, 675b, 685a, 836b; at law, 595ab, 685a, 745a, 818a.
case (box), 2a, 604b, 605a; for amulets, 42b; for arms or tools, 2a; for spells, 390b; leather, 728b.
casket, 155a.
casque, 139b.
Cassandra, 804b.
cassia, 533b, 563b, 574a, 781a.
cast, 189b, 470ab, 688b, 708a; cast a line or net, 178b, 490b; aside, 89b, 157b, 528a, 628b; away, 770a; evil glances, 806b; down, 79a, 247ab, 255a, 476a, 744b, 758b, 599b; out, 91a, 190a, 219b, 437a; spells, 745a; up, 753a, 477a.
castanets, 76a, 344a.
caster of metal, 325a.
castle, 633b, 205b.
castor oil plant, 891b.
castrate, 472a, 485b, 645a.
castrated, 656b; animal, 641b, 654b, 777b; man, 481b.
cat, 49b, 50b, 269b, 273b, 277b, 278a; he, 278a; she, 278a.
Cat, the Great, 92b.
cat of Bast, 278a.
Cat-god, 273b, 278a; goddess, 205b, 232a, 246a.
catalogue, 45b, 106b, 161a, 346a, 430b, 683a.
cataplasm, 387b.
catapult, 528b.
cataract, 768b.
catch, 466a, 802b; fish, 244a, 433a, 482a; in a net, 75a, 437b.
cattle, 15a, 16b, 18a, 32a, 74b, 114a, 123b, 165a, 299a, 379a, 521a, 805a, 822a, 824b, 829b, 832a, 868b; black, 787b; branded, 569b; fattened, 185a; foreign, 75a; hornless, 170a, 493a; sacred, 111b; sacrificial, 69a, 116b, 537b, 569b, 658a; selected, 713a; stud, 27b; turned out to graze, 193a; young, 284b, 428a.
cattle-boat, 786a.
cattle-farms, 587a.
cattle-men, 306a, 351b.
cattle-pen, 32a, 337a.
cattle-pounds, 60b.
cattle-runs, 27a.
cattle-shed, 74b.
cauldron, 137a, 429a, 535b, 791a, 847b.
cause, 102b, 436b, 525a, 865a; to be, 865b; to do, 865b; to make, 590a.
cavalry, 105a, 288a, 372b, 408a, 521a, 772a, 839b.
cavalrymen, 521a.
cave, 38a, 201ab, 216a, 225b, 290a, 477b, 538b, 539b, 774b, 775a, 832b, 854b, 857a, 877b.

cavern, 201a b, 216a, 337a, 464a, 465b, 477b, 539b, 774b, 775a, 832b, 854b, 877b.
cavity, 216a.
cease, 4b, 19a, 38b, 65a, 141b, 176a, 420a, 703b, 810b ; cease from, 420b, 433b ; make to, 680b.
ceaselessly, 4b, 19a, 340a.
cedar, 137a, 156a, 654a ; fruit, 156a ; ointment, 137a ; valley of, 58a ; wine, 72b ; wood, 137a.
ceiling, 110a, 419b, 440b.
celebrate a festival, 66a, 689b, 767a, 825a.
celestial, 689b.
cell of a god, 99a.
cellar, 374b, 763b ; wine, 238a.
cemetery, 58b, 71b, 80a, 402b, 498b, 511b, 561b, 580a, 599a, 708a, 756a, 776a, 816a, 900b.
cense, to, 66b, 609b, 678b, 786b ; censing, 227b, 786b.
censer, 105a b, 227b, 407b, 614a, 652b, 684b, 804b.
censer, incense and vase of, 2a.
census, 41a, 161a, 838a ; of cattle, 856b.
cerastes, 584b.
cercopithecus, 802b.
cerebellum, 307b.
cerebrum, 190b.
ceremony, 69a, 93a, 270b, 484b ; ceremonies, 400b, 407b ; to perform magical, 710b.
certainly, 30b, 34b, 336b, 480b, 782a.
cessation, 4b, 38b, 175b.
chagrin, 796b.
chain, 64a, 292a, 408b, 652b ; of Āapep, 64a, 323a ; chains for jewellery, 119a.
chair, 13b, 234a, 367b, 773b ; of state, 235b, 559b, 773a, 850a, 851a, 857a b, 898b.
chair bearer, 13b.
chalk, 10a.
challenge, 699b.
chamber, 11b, 32b, 33a, 74a, 75a, 77a, 79b, 106a, 110a, 120a, 130a, 148b, 149a, 157b, 166a, 174b, 183a, 190b, 275a, 286a, 348b, 417b, 419a, 468a, 484b, 492a, 526a b, 540a, 605a, 608a, 613a, 615b, 617b, 621a, 675b, 682b, 685b, 709a, 712b, 719b, 740b, 744a, 753a, 763b, 821b, 860a, 881b, 882a, 885a, 897a, 909b, 910b ; audience, 900b ; coffin, 378a ; dissecting, 106b ; of embalming, 46b ; of execution, 373a ; for statues, 454a ; funerary, 238a ; incense, 227b ; inner, 34b, 874b ; magical, 710b ; of mummification, 300a, 613a ; observation, 275a ; of sickness, 225b ; private, 154b ; rectangular, 774a ; roofed, 419b ; sacrificial, 454a ; of temple, 685a, 759a, 896b ; of tomb, 238b ; underground, 351a ; vaulted, 462b ; vestment, 455a.
chance, 898b.
chancellor, 568b.
chancery, 79b, 81b, 238b ; royal, 392a.
change, 30a, 191a, 246b, 420b, 542b, 735a b ; direction, 195a ; of apparel, 476b ; changed, 108a.
channel, 56b, 144b, 758b.
chant, 508b, 509a.
chants, the 70 of Rā, 509a.
chapel, 18b, 92b, 132a, 523b, 774b, 789b, 796a, 801a, 804b, 812b, 912a ; of tomb, 81b.
chaplet, 275a, 728b ; of flowers, 677a.
chapter, 415b, 457a ; Chapters, i.e. Books, 416a.
character, 209b, 694a, 779b, 782b, 804b.
characteristic, 34b, 200a, 209b, 261b, 430a, 595a.
charcoal, 491a.
charge, 338a, 449a, 586b, 633a ; make a charge against, 1b, 837a.
charge sheet, 739a.
chariot, 112b, 115b, 131b, 174b, 204a, 208b, 283b, 289b, 462b, 825b ; parts of, 131b, 655a, 714b, 875a, 905a ; pole of, 106a, 115b, 884b.
chariot, Hittite, 853a.

charioteer, 115b, 791a b.
charm, charms, 289b, 518a, 537b, 860b ; magical, 647b ; to use, 514b.
Charon, 894b.
charter, 106b.
chase, 221a, 658a ; away, 420b, 531b, 787a ; chased, 711b.
Chase-god, 213a.
chastise, 103b.
chattels, 525a.
chatter, 822b, 844a, 852b, 863a ; foolishly, 797b.
chatterer, 335a, 648a.
cheat, 165b.
cheater, 641b.
check, 642b.
cheek, 206a, 215b ; bones of, 139a.
cheese, 610b.
chest, 13b, 43b, 91a, 120a, 203b, 209a, 255b, 256b, 311a, 447b, 514a, 796a, 800b, 805a, 812b, 827b, 832a, 836b, 839a, 896b, 909b ; for linen, 447b ; for papers, 447b.
chest, funerary, 174a, 874b, 910b.
chew, 185a b, 187a, 262b, 479b, 572b, 631a b, 715a ; chew up, 615a.
chick-pea, 490b.
chicory, 355a.
chief, 97a, 101b, 107a, 108a, 128b, 161a, 164a, 170b, 215b, 224b, 283a, 323b, 331b, 417a, 423a, 433b, 461a, 473b, 494a, 519b, 554a, 562a, 588a, 604a, 679b, 690b, 828b, 829b, 851b, 860b, 862a, 901a ; chiefs, captive, 315a.
chief in command, 829b ; of a caravan, 311b ; of the Nome, 460b ; of a port, 108b ; of a tribe, 290b.
chief priest, 155a.
chief steward, 312a.
chieftain, 494a.
chieftainess, 423a, 460b, 494a, 496a, 513a, 860b.
child, children, 3b, 27a, 31a, 49a, 61a, 130b, 141b, 152a, 165a, 196b, 279a, 290a, 321a b, 322a, 349a, 372b, 386b, 388a b, 413b, 428a, 466a, 507a, 525a, 532a, 545b, 548b, 570a, 573b, 575a, 591b, 597b, 632a, 644b, 647a b, 664b, 716b, 731b, 749b, 798b, 825a, 907a ; divine, 76b ; in arms, 616b ; royal, 76b, 392a ; sucking, 547b, 652b.
Child, i.e. Rā, 76a.
child, to be with, 206a, 224b, 450a.
childbirth, 321b, 326b.
Childbirth-goddess, 59a, 327a.
childhood, the second, 387a.
Children, the Two, 598a, 632a.
chin, 60a, 531a.
china, 909b.
chip, 14b.
chisel, 205b, 223a, 304b, 337b, 452a, 519b.
choice (of bread), 710b.
choicest, 710a, 829b.
choir, 548b, 741b, 835b, 872b, 878b, 879a b.
choirs of the Ṭuat, 448a.
choke, 64a ; choked, 763b, 769b, 800a, 805a.
choose, 628b, 696b, 710b, 713a.
chop, 338a, 390a, 488b, 613b ; chop up, 186a, 288b, 482a, 911b.
choristers, 835b.
chosen (of a person), 710b.
cincture, 217a.
circle, to, 232a, 875a, 796b.
circle, 76b, 99a, 247a, 266a, 743b, 744a, 779b, 780a, 827b, 875a ; to mark out, 796b.
circle, hidden, 775a ; in Ṭuat, 26a, 774b ; of sky, 831a ; the Great, 743b.
Circles, the Two, 743b.
circler (Nile), 452a.
circuit, to, 246a b, 251b, 701a.
circuit, 134a, 246b, 252a, 743b, 744a, 768a, 780a, 827b, 832a ; to make a, 875a, 251b ; of earth, heaven and solar disk, 743b, 746a.
circuit wall, 910a.
circuiting, a, 743b.
circular, 476a, 875a.
circulate, 216a.
Circumcision-god, 862a, 870a.
circumcision, knife for, 870a.

circumference, 134a, 743b, 875a.
circumstances, 580b, 693b.
circumvent, 30a.
cistern, 106b, 307b, 491a, 579a, 720a, 724b, 733b, 758a.
citadel, 164a, 526a, 660b.
citizen, 124b ; citizens, 350b.
city, 206b, 350b, 764b ; the everlasting, 351a ; walled, 60b.
City of Eternity, 507b.
City of the god, 350b.
City of Night, 288a.
claim, 334b.
clamour, 838b.
clamp, 246a.
clan, 284a, 316a, 320a.
clap, 5a, 275a, 468b, 795a.
clapper, 76a, 304b, 344a.
clapping, 275a.
clarias anguillaris, 347a.
clarify, 598a, 628b, 631b.
clasp, 111a, 273a, 446a, 484b.
class, 585b.
classes, the upper, 774a.
claw, 20a, 112b, 123b, 128b, 140a, 142b, 176b, 180a, 215b, 218a, 351a, 722a, 800b, 840b.
clawless, 835a.
claw-sheath, 639b.
clay, 10a, 11a, 49b, 122a, 604b, 643b, 816a, 875b ; like, 49b.
clean, 155a, 329b, 346a, 825a, 873a ; to make, 117a ; clean out, 700b ; clean-handed, 155a, 825a ; clean-mouthed, 155a ; of speech, 155a.
cleaning, substance for, 531b.
cleanness, 214a.
cleanse, 407b, 644b, 653b, 710a, 825a, 858a.
cleansing, 117a, 155a, 726b.
clear, 206a, 711a ; a way, 631b ; clear up, 685a ; to make, 600b, 796a.
cleave, 195a, 248b, 251b, 252ab, 480b, 598a, 665a, 705a, 713b, 844b, 881a.
cleaver, 246a.
cleft, 207a.
clement, 598a.
clepsydra, 735b.
clerk, 620b, 852b ; of works, 67a, 313a ; room of, 80b.
clever, 624b, 682b.
client, 285a, 824a.
climbing pole, 646b.
clippings (of hair), 594a.
cloaks, 141a.
cloisters, 247a.
close, 98a, 265a, 568a, 708a, 750a ; bring to a, 704b ; close the eyes, 135b ; close up, 64a, 569b, 874b.
close by, 438b.
closet, 286a.
cloth, 19b, 49b, 62a, 63b, 97a, 128b, 160a, 243b, 289ab, 290a, 291b, 300a, 304b, 305b, 328b, 368b, 408b, 411a, 440b, 458b, 476b, 536b, 623b, 635a, 641a, 652a, 667b, 747b, 756b, 773b, 776a, 791b, 840a, 866b, 884b, 895b, 896b, 897a, 915a ; black, 300a ; coarse, 773b ; flax or linen, 234b ; painted, 122b ; a square, 631a, 715a ; Sûdânî, 332b ; to weave, 66a ; white, 523b.
clothe, 282b, 356b, 376a, 476b, 629b, 682b, 713a, 714a, 818b, 849a, 850b, 904b ; clothed, 826a ; clothed in armour, 422a.
clothes, 324b, 525a ; chamber for, 613a ; chest for, 13b ; dirty, 726b ; old, 82a ; wrap for, 256b.
clothing, 141a, 160a, 169b, 476b, 477a, 818b.
cloud, 96a, 368a, 793b ; cloudy, 789a.
Cloud-gods, 669a.
club, 17a, 32b, 83a, 141a, 202a, 274a, 300a, 320b, 366b, 367a, 459a, 470a, 523b, 566b, 643a, 672a, 684a.
clutch, 124a.
coast, 354a.
coast region, 587b.
coat, 652a ; of leather, 324a.
codify, 400b.
coerce, 850a.
coffer, 91a, 99b, 120a, 238a, 263a, 285a, 311a, 447b, 489b, 630a, 796a, 800b, 805a, 827b, 832a, 839a, 860a, 873b, 874b, 875b, 876b, 904b, 909b, 910b.

coffin, 120a, 188a, 284a, 357b, 447b, 457a, 489b, 566b, 626b, 756a, 757a, 777a, 796a, 800b, 832a, 873b, 874b, 904b, 909b; chamber, 904b; coffined one, 756b, 904b; coffins of the Ṭuat, 447b.
cogitate, 330b, 398a.
cognizance, 681b.
cohabit, 66b.
coiffure, 526b.
coign, 766b.
coil, 859b; coils, 763a; of serpent, 380b, 768a, 793a.
coin (copper), 854a.
coin a proverb, 469a.
coinciding with, 332b.
coition, 316a.
cold, 474a.
collapse, 122b, 180b, 471a, 594b, 657b, 806a.
collar, 71a, 75b, 183b, 184a, 207b, 216a, 226a, 278b, 282a, 306a, 408b, 446a, 452a, 575a, 734b, 764a, 862a; amulet of the, 171b; beaded, 734b; of Eternity, Khensu, Mut and Uatchit, 183b.
colleague, 674a.
collect, 131a, 544b, 598b, 613b, 625a, 628b, 639a, 659b, 664b, 683a, 701b, 710a, 826ab, 847a, 878b, 914b; by force, 841a; taxes, 794a; the eyes, 826a; the heart, 639b, 826a; collected, 467a, 853b.
collection, 683a; of Sayings, 880a.
collectively, 779b.
college, 106b, 124b, 238a, 239a, 901a; of priests, 454a; Royal College, 901a.
colonize, 812a.
colonnade, 58b, 109b, 134a, 148b, 151a, 179b, 640b.
colossal, 298a.
colour, 34b, 49b, 63a, 346a, 419b, 581b, 821b, 825b, 840b, 857b; coloured, 122b, 855b.
colour-bearer, 851b.
column, 16b, 58b, 151a, 526b.
columns (of a book), 619a.
comb, to comb, 28b, 114a.
combat, 670a, 762a.
Come! 48b, 266b, 280a, 292b.
come, 1ab, 15a, 30a, 31a, 83a, 93a, 101b, 193b, 216b, 217a, 222a, 339b, 346a, 351b, 400b, 517b, 576a, 640a, 647ab, 661b, 827a, 846b, 891a; forth, 156b, 215a, 597a; make to come forth, 661b; near to, 879a; on, 222a; out, 97b; to an end, 10b, 19a, 181a, 398b; towards, 28b; up, 129a, 240a.
comer, 31a, 240b.
comers, i.e., posterity, 30a.
comet, 155a, 701a.
comfort, 493a, 610b.
coming, a, 31a; the act of, 804b; forth, 449a.
command, 136b, 161a, 187b, 190b, 191b, 270b, 289b, 335a, 382b, 449a, 470a, 486b, 487a, 597a, 613b, 677b, 683b, 860a, 862a, 896a, 900a; to be in, 683b; to give a, 37a; to issue, 187b.
commandant, 290a, 860a.
commander, 190b, 312a, 417a, 487a, 613b, 896a.
commander-in-chief, 312a, 495b, 638a.
commemorate, 614b, 688a.
commemorative formulas, 688a.
commend, 508a.
commendation, 508a.
commerce, 733a.
commission, 161a, 697b, 722b; royal, 161a.
commit, 642b; a crime, 141a; a sin, 165b; violence, 32b.
common, 247a.
commotion, 577b; to cause a, 549b.
commune, 145b.
community, 350b.
compact, 836a.
companion, 45b, 69b, 71ab, 277b, 530b, 548a, 551a, 577b, 636a, 674a.
company, 585b, 599b, 768a, 968a, 818a, 878b, 879a; a large, 137b; of the gods, 231b, 880b; of troops, 18b; in company, 39a.

comparative, sign of the, 415a.
compare, 628b, 707b, 713b.
compass, 134a.
compassionate, 597b.
compatriot, 306b.
compel, 92b, 521a, 705b, 802b.
competent, 178b.
compilation, 880a.
complain, 382b, 386b, 419a, 465a, 642a, 662a, 778b.
complaint, 386b.
complete, 129b, 131a, 305b, 521b, 522a, 670b, 704b, 719b, 770a, 773a, 787b, 834a, 878b, 910a; to make, 626a.
completely, 834a.
completeness, 214b.
completion, 787b, 818b.
complexion, 58a.
compose, 610b, 860b.
composition, rhythmical, 509a.
compound, 6b, 178a, 235a, 837a.
comprehend, 121b.
compress, 113b, 228a, 836a.
computation, 856b.
compute, 510b, 899a.
conceal, 51a, 463a, 470b, 624b, 682b, 787a; concealed, 325b, 463a.
concealment, 786b.
conceit, 189b.
conceive, 35a, 65b, 143a, 146b, 450a, 752a; to make, 650a; conceived, 142a, 698b; be conceived, 32b; the child, 35a.
conception, 35a, 450a.
concern, 525a, 561b, 622a.
concerning, 414a.
conclude, 131a.
conclusion, 214b, 274a; of a matter, 131b.
concubine, 74b, 331b, 412a, 552b, 558a, 599b, 785b.
condemnation, 335b.
condemned, 260a, 855b.
condition, 106a, 133b, 561b, 595a, 694a, 697b, 698b, 761b, 766b; good, 128a; of peace, 805a.
conduct, 56b, 593b, 698b, 729a.
conduct, to, 55a, 707b, 713a; a service, 699a.
conductor, 594a; of a caravan, 334b.
confectioner, 103a, 140b, 356a, 219a, 247b, 448b.
confectionery, 138b, 440a.
confederate, 530b, 599b, 739b.
confer, 304a.
confess, 441b.
confidant, 577b, 666b.
confide, 158b.
confidence, 769b.
confidential, 701a.
confine, 900b; confined, 557b.
conflagration, 588b.
confluence, 878b.
conflux, 878b.
conform, 448a.
conformable, 264b, 332b.
conformably to, 266a, 269b.
confound, 499b.
confuse, 683a; confused, 651b, 844a; of speech, 844a.
confusion, 577a, 682a, 844a.
congratulate, 619a.
conjunction, 79a, 492b, 578a; enclitic, 79a.
conjure, 154b, 745a.
connection, 599b.
conquer, 100b, 142a, 384a, 564b, 723a, 769a, 772a, 884a.
conqueror, 100b, 378b, 527b, 677b, 703a.
conquest, 677b, 775b.
consider, 42b, 209b, 330b, 393a.
console, 610b.
consolidate, 702b.
consort, 599b.
conspicuous, 630a.
conspirators, 113a.
conspire, 398b.
constellation, 193b.
constrain, 100a, 412b, 626a, 633a, 705b, 867a, 910a, 915b; constrained, 805a.
constraint, 868a.
constricted, 492a, 800a.
construct, 375b, 779a, 909b.
construction, 94a.
consult, 410b.
consultation, 410b.
consume, 6a, 9b, 186a, 390a, 392b, 434b, 588b, 639a, 670a, 672a, 851a, 898b; consumed, 34a, 186b.
consumer, 392b.

contagion, 295b.
contain, 547b, 616b, 693a.
contemporary, 45b, 47a, 438b.
contempt, 621a.
contemptible, 243b, 373a.
contend, 285b, 626a, 727b, 729a, 734b.
content, 124b, 148b, 291b, 292a, 333a, 449b, 517b, 612b, 682a, 727a, 766a.
contented disposition, 449b.
contentious, 682a.
contentment, 449b.
contents (of document), 430b.
contest, 241a.
continue, 296b, 649b.
continuously, 297a.
contract, 204b, 568b.
contracted, 659b, 782b.
contraction, 800b.
contradict, 116b, 122b, 212b, 410b, 437a, 533a.
contradiction, 116b, 212b.
contrary, 122b.
contrition, 91b.
controller, 511a.
converse, 212b, 410b, 650b.
conversely, 247a.
convey, 56a.
conveyance (a deed), 45a.
convulsion, 887b.
cook, 115b, 134b, 189a, 140b, 237a, 247b, 248a, 261b, 356a, 578a, 696b, 822b, 841b.
cook, to, 232b, 236a, 355b, 356a, 427a, 593b, 597b, 664b, 676a, 896b.
cooking pot, 799a.
cool, 28a, 570a, 625b, 702a b, 767b, 768b ; to be cool, 768b ; to make cool, 697a.
cool, of a breeze, 767b ; of the heart, 767b ; place, 305b, 767b ; water, 767b, 768b.
cooled, 411b.
cooling, 767b.
coolness, 240a, 768b ; place of, 768b.
copper, 210a, 485b, 842b ; object of, 809a ; Asiatic, 486a ; black, 486a ; fittings of, 482b ; ingots of, 485b ; ore of, 486a ; preparation of, 482b ; sulphate of, 150b ; smelted, 486a ; weapon, 485b.
coppersmith, 324b, 486a.
Coptos, necropolis of, 407b.
copulate, 164a, 217a, 219b, 257b, 303a, 345b, 381a, 396b, 443a, 465b, 599a, 630b, 898a.
copulation, 396b, 818a.
copy, to, 171b, 604b, 628b, 675b, 779a, 841a ; to make, 66b, 710a.
copy, 277b, 307b, 604b, 619a, 642b, 673a, 675b, 677b, 698b ; an ancient, 831b.
copyist, 191b, 619b, 852b, 853a ; of texts, 620a ; room of, 81b.
cord, 58a, 64a b, 75b, 82a b, 97a, 113a, 123a, 139a, 167a, 202a, 254b, 279a, 282a, 305a, 332b, 333a, 337a, 351a, 352b, 355a, 356b, 372b, 396b, 399b, 408b, 419b, 421b, 422a, 484b, 486b, 510a, 521a, 527a, 587a, 593b, 628a, 629b, 652b, 658a, 693b, 707a, 745a, 750b, 751a, 758b, 790b ; for vegetables, 563a.
cord, measuring, 146b, 527a, 753b.
cord of book, 100a, 102a, 443a, 625a, 701b ; of magic net, 146b ; of rule, 751a ; of a seal, 27a.
cordage, 64a b, 102a, 132a, 258a, 273a, 355a, 790a, 867a, 868a.
core, 531b.
coriander, 169b, 242b, 243b, 296a.
corn, 97a, 126a b, 242b, 368b, 369a, 431b, 592a, 648b, 701a, 850b ; store of, 369a.
corn bin, 369a.
Corn-god, 223a, 369a, 831b.
corn-grinder, 218a.
corn-land, 237b, 368b, 369a ; god of, 490b.
corn-measure, 41a, 42b, 573a.
corn-rack, 573b.
corn-stalk, 208a.
corner, 563b, 766b, 774a, 777b ; corners of the earth, 774a.
coronation, 392a, 535a, 615b, 689b ; chamber, 535a ; festival, 535a.

corps of soldiers, 570a, 585b.
corpse, 570b ; corpses on battle-field, 477b.
correct, 139a, 304a, 332a, 333b, 601a, 668a, 866a, 894a ; arrangement, 332a ; measure, 510b.
correction, 594b, 652b, 655b ; place of, 588b.
corresponding to, 414b, 545a.
corridors, 629b.
corrupt, 741b, 805a ; to become, 55b.
corruption, 137a, 470a, 592a, 634b, 762a, 774b.
corselet, 532a, 552a.
coruscate, 630a, 842a.
corvée, 206b, 258b, 303b, 439a, 495a, 511a, 867a ; chief of, 290a ; gang, 290a ; land of, 278b ; royal, 108b.
Cosmic Egg, 805b.
cost, 443b, 446b.
cotton plant, 566b.
couch, 13ab, 43b, 289a, 374b, 375ab, 409b, 492a, 596a, 600b, 773a, 884a ; funeral, 301a ; royal, 559b.
Council, 570a ; the Great, 818a, 901a ; of the city, 818a ; of the land, 818a ; of Abydos, 901a ; of the dead, 901b ; of statesmen, 901a ; the double, 901a.
Council Chamber, or Hall, 80b, 238b, 403a.
councillor, 410a, 495b.
counsel, 410b, 682b, 717a ; to take, 145b, 410b, 613a.
counsellor, 131a.
count, 41a, 477a, 510b, 838a, 856b.
countenance, 545a.
counter, 605a ; of hearts, 41a.
counterpart, 674a, 710a, 821b.
counting, 465b ; of bones, 41a.
counting-house, 510b.
counting-sticks (tallies), 511a.
countless, 41a.
country, 598b, 661b, 815a ; deadly, 26b ; enemy's, 657b.
countryman, 686a.
courage, 37b, 197a, 861b ; to be of small, 524a ; to inspire, 645a.
courageous, 382b, 690b, 738a.
courier, 245b, 688a ; a swift, 715b.
course, 166a, 324b, 478a, 734b, 813a, 856a ; of action, 277b ; of the Disk, 31a ; of events, 580b ; of the law, 831b ; on the river, 703a.
courses, 621a, 167b.
court (courtyard), 32a, 34b, 175a, 272b, 420b, 744a ; of temple, 147a, 183a, 910b.
Court, the, 136a, 557b, 575b, 744a ; to visit the, 67a.
Court, of Judges, 901a ; of Justice, 238b, 454a ; of Law, 194b, 453b, 454a ; of Rā, 158b ; of the Six, 456a ; of the Thirty, 281b.
courtesy, 347a.
courtiers, 557b, 610a, 744a.
courtyard, 63a, 74b, 115a, 158b, 438a, 529b, 744a.
cousins, 599b.
covenant, 204b.
cover for chariot, 476b ; for sarcophagus, 107a ; for vessel, 477a.
cover, to, 380b, 386a, 576a, 703b, 899a.
cover over, 131b, 220a, 463a, 470b, 476b, 576a, 590b, 626a, 650a, 651b, 701a, 787a, 837a, 843b, 850b, 874b, 887b ; covered, 757a.
covering, 58a, 63a, 220a, 256b, 260a, 288b, 458b, 463a, 476b, 576a, 672a, 689a, 755a, 791b, 835b, 850b, 852a, 867a ; for bread, 376a ; for floor, 195b ; for phallus, 776b.
coverlet, 43b, 222a, 492a.
covet, 627a.
covetous, 115b.
cow, 7b, 75a, 170a, 299a, 314a, 398a, 481b, 785b, 854a, 857a ; black, 787b ; milch, 12b, 69a, 302a, 331b ; sacred, 25a ; stud, 27a ; young, 372b, 426b ;
Cows, the Two, 785b.
Cows, the Seven, 36b, 785b.
cow byre, 74a.
Cow-goddess, 7b, 422b, 425b, 510a.

cow-keeper, 379a.
coward, 220a, 215b, 481b, 483b, 491a, 534b, 548a, 574a, 575a.
cowardice, 252b, 481b, 574a.
cowardly, 472b.
cradle, 325a, 326b, 800b ; songs, 549a.
craft, 383b, 781b ; of the artist, 122b.
craftsman, 430a, 762b, 784a.
craftsmanship, 483a.
crafty, 335b.
cramp, 777b.
crane, 100b, 134b, 348b, 395a, 809b, 833b, 842b, 895b, 896a, 897a.
crate, 124a, 519b.
crave, 309b.
crawl, 262b, 491a.
crayfish, 804b.
cream, 669b.
create, 65a, 118a, 260b, 541a, 542a, 616a, 690a, 770b.
created things, 609a, 771a.
creation, 149b, 231a, 770b.
Creator, the, 543a, 770b, 771a.
creature, 67a, 609a, 770b ; fattened, 542a ; mythological, 681a.
credit, 22b.
creep, 491a.
crescent, 530a.
crew, 93b, 119a, 780a.
crier, 187b, 330b, 389a, 678a, 872b.
Crier (Set), 25b.
cries (see cry), 29a, 438a, 442b, 549a ; of acclamation, 73b ; of joy, 15a, 149b, 440a, 487a ; of pain, 136b ; to multiply, 646b.
crime, 31b, 89b, 180a, 226ab, 243a, 352b, 396b ; to commit, 591b, 647a.
criminals, 89b, 398a, 540a, 561a.
cringing man, 886a.
cripple, 64a, 470b, 641b.
critical state, 80b.
crockery, 252a.
crocodile, 12b, 14a, 119b, 120a, 289a, 308a, 324a, 325b, 331a, 429b, 472a, 485b, 558a, 559b, 589a, 625a, 634b, 758b, 910a ; members of the, 325b ; mouth of the, 831a ; of Set, 488b ; the fiend, 76a.
Crocodiles, the Four, 325b.
Crocodiles, the Seven, 325b.
Crocodile-god, 97a, 208b, 261b, 417a, 558a, 650a, 657b, 660a, 724b, 900b.
crocus, 810b.
crook, 114b, 512b ; of Osiris, 328a.
crops, 150a, 240b, 292a, 324a, 667a, 914b.
cross, to, 459b, 841b, 850a, 894b.
cross-examine, 186b.
crouch, 246a.
crowd, 137b, 284a, 818a, 823a ; crowded, 241a.
crown, 23a, 55a, 77b, 119b, 146b, 148b, 192b, 274a, 279a, 319a, 326a, 336b, 371a, 393a, 496a, 515a, 525b, 528a, 530a, 535a, 544a, 579b, 595a, 615b, 635b, 683a, 684a, 689b, 693b, 701b, 715b, 790a, 810b, 853ab ; festival of, 701b ; of earth, lake and sky, 163a ; of feathers, 701b ; of flowers, 595a ; of innocence, 271b ; of North, 171b, 189b, 320a ; of South, 172a, 653b, 692b ; of South and North, 171a, 358a ; parts of the, 20a, 147b, 355b, 540b, 572a, 658a ; of the Double, 599b ; sides of the, 146b ; the Double, 617a ; the Green, 150b ; the Red, 399b ; the Triple, 447b ; the White, 372b, 628b, 629a, 630b, 711b.
crown of the head, 163a, 771b, 808b.
crowned, 534b ; crowned one, 689b.
cruel, 395b.
cruelty, 314b.
crumbling, 149a.
crush, 9b, 114b, 140b, 185a, 186a, 253a, 292b, 347b, 397b, 411a, 441a, 452b, 468b, 480b, 538a, 571ab, 601b, 612b, 613a, 626a, 643a, 703b, 795a, 808a, 844b, 900a ; under foot, 821a ; crush up, 683b ; crushed, 181a, 186b, 763a ; of foes, 395b ; something crushed, 6b ; crushing, 821a.

crusts, 596b.
cry, 25b, 31b, 34b, 49a, 74b, 94ab, 124a, 209a, 211a, 225a, 385b, 386b, 447a, 537b, 595a, 609b, 648a, 658a, 705ab, 766b, 821b, 838b, 896b ; cry out in pain, 447a ; in shrill tones, 877b ; of death, 94a ; of birds, 658b, 800b, 814a, 853b ; of grief, 22a, 74b, 658b ; of joy, 74a ; to raise a, 627a ; cry out, 12b, 15a, 17a, 25b, 30c, 31b, 49a, 94b, 106b, 113b, 115a, 124a, 136b, 138a, 149b, 154b, 178a, 184b, 186b, 224b, 225b, 345a, 385b, 386b, 419a, 438a, 527b, 548b, 587b, 642a, 658a, 671b, 702a, 766b, 782b, 790b, 809a, 821b, 838b, 841b, 872b, 896b ; cry out for joy, 472b ; cry out noisily, 536a.
crying, 424a ; crying men or women, 462a.
crypt, 351a, 758b.
crystal, 111b, 842a, 858b ; sceptre of, 150b.
cubit, 25a ; royal, 316a ; great and little, 316a; the square, 567a.
cubit, gods of the, 316a.
cucumber, 92a.
cudgel, 17a, 115b, 140a, 208b, 283a, 284b, 467a, 470a, 516b, 643a, 862b.
cudgels, Sûdânî, 202a.
cuirasses, 422a.
culmination (of star), 139a, 904a ; time of, 12b.
cult, 112a ; to perform a, 742a.
cultivate, 302a, 697a, 833a.
cultivators, riparian, 195b.
cumin, 832a.
cuminum, 832a.
cummin, 296a, 808a.
cunning, 682b, 698a, 751b, 781b ; of hand, 430b.
cup, 2a, 43a, 186a, 230b, 366a, 797a, 850b ; lily-shaped, 623b.
cupbearer, 843a ; royal, 391b.
cupboard, 475b.
curb, 490b.
curious, 755b.
curl, 323b, 854a.
current, 441b ; of stream, 294a.
curse, 110a, 136b, 153a, 185a, 202a, 246a, 335a, 356a, 490b, 613b, 615b, 642a, 646b, 649b, 652a, 683a, 689ab, 745a, 757a, 778a, 794b, 805b ; the king, 145b.
cursings, 185a, 794b.
curved, 274b.
Cusae, priestess of, 548b.
cushion, 13a.
Cushite, 95b.
custodian, 585b.
custody, 83a.
custom, 400b, 446a, 516b, 609a, 666b, 678b, 694a, 722b ; ancient, 831b ; to observe, 628b, 710a ; customary, 332a, 826a.
cut, 19b, 31b, 57b, 90b, 91b, 93b, 127b, 149a, 168a, 182b, 186a, 195a, 205b, 208b, 219a, 220a, 221b, 237a, 251a, 262a, 263ab, 274b, 275b, 282b, 290b, 291b, 304b, 323a, 325b, 336b, 344a, 393b, 395b, 398b, 400a, 480b, 508a, 511a, 516b, 519b, 527b, 533a, 538a, 571ab, 587b, 591b, 596a, 597b, 598a, 601a, 603b, 606a, 615a, 629a, 630b, 631b, 647a, 648a, 656b, 660b, 664a, 668b, 684a, 685b, 694a, 696b, 703a, 705a, 706b, 710a, 711a, 713b, 727b, 730a, 731a, 735b, 771a, 836a, 837b, 845a, 867a, 881ab, 888a, 907b, 911b ; an inscription, 878a.
cut away, 36a, 665b ; down, 538b, 648b, 678b, 703b, 730a, 801b, 883b.
cut flowers or fruit, 492a ; the hair, 850a ; reeds, 575a ; wheat, 637b ; a pattern, 571b ; stone, 178a, 777b ; the nails, 123b ; a throat, 592a, 990b.
cut in pieces, 220b, 465b, 482a, 567b, 713a, 715a, 881a.
cut into, 567b, 592a, 846a.
cut off, 31b, 89a, 184a, 195a, 246a, 263b, 397b, 512b, 539b, 566a, 587a, 629a, 665b, 685b, 710a, 730a, 881a.
cut open, 187b, 397b, 603b.
cut through, 245b, 878a, 907a.
cut up, 201a, 664b, 867b ; cut up small, 390a.

cutter, 291a.
cutting, 201a, 459a, 603b, 730a, 881a, 878a.
cutting board, 539a.
cuttle fish, 347a.
cycle, 827b ; of time, 827a.
cylinder, 789b.
cyperus, 804a, 805a ; ointment, 801a ; seed, 801a.
cyperus esculentus, 370a.
cypress tree, 29b, 115b, 169a, 204a, 793a.
Cyprus, Queen of, 465a.
Cyrus, 784b.

D.

dagger, 91a, 141a, 208a, 226a, 275b, 276b, 287a, 325a, 333b, 338b, 351a, 390b, 665a, 666ab.
ḍahabîyah, 682b.
daily, 264ab, 278b, 297a, 339a, 417b, 450a ; affairs, 580b ; gift, 297b.
dainty (food), 737a.
dam, 106a, 291a, 308a, 715b, 882a.
damage, 140b, 263b, 605a, 772b.
damned, the, 94a, 97a, 98a, 197b, 295b, 314b, 340a, 345b, 377a, 520a, 538b, 560b, 571a, 617b, 618a, 695b, 835b ; damned person, 837a.
damned, abode of the, 520a ; roads of the, 144b.
damp, 470a.
damûr cloth, 304b.
dance, 38b, 61a, 93a, 118a, 141a, 147a, 448a, 539ab, 549a, 566a, 597a, 662b, 726a, 734b, 769b, 789a, 797b, 798b, 852b, 854ab, 857a, 858a.
dance of the god, 38b.
dancer, 38b, 74a, 539a, 789a, 897b.
dancing, 38b, 74a, 797b.
dancing girl, 549a.
dancing woman, 60a, 74b, 539ab ; foreign, 234b.
dandle, 426a, 428a, 858a.
danger, 445a, 744b.
Danuna, 867a.
Darius, 64a, 408a, 409ab, 820a, 827b, 884b.
dark, 787a, 789a ; to become, 76a ; to make, 626a.
dark water, the, 798b.
darken, 626a, 652a.
darkness, 8b, 36a, 77b, 94b, 96a, 107a, 128a, 135a, 179b, 184b, 185a, 323b, 529b, 563a, 592a, 608b, 621b, 622a, 624b, 642b, 649a, 751b, 761b, 776b, 778b, 791a, 795ab, 797a, 798ab, 803b, 810b, 897a ; thick, utter, outer, 600b, 798a.
darling, 44b, 50a, 310a.
dart, 390a, 490b, 516b, 754a ; dart out, 190a.
dash water, 468b ; dashed in pieces, 802a.
date flour, 56b.
date palm, 20a, 50a, 203a, 218b, 849b.
date shop, 106a.
date wine, 217b, 218b.
dates, 49b, 211a, 218b.
daub, 847b.
daughter, 584a, 750a ; king's, 392a.
Daughters, the Two, 584a.
dawn, 77a, 159b, 193b, 381a, 522b, 586a, 634a, 685a, 752b, 815b, 840b, 870b ; the earliest, 829b ; to prevent the, 562b.
Dawn-god, 13b, 49b, 133b, 145a, 198a, 861b.
dawn wind, 370a ; goddess of, 661b.
day, 10b, 438b, 442a, 444b, 450a, 622b, 648b, 696a ; the matter of the, 8b ; lucky and unlucky, 451a.
day and night, i.e., for ever, 417b, 450a.
day before yesterday, 664b.
day of judgment, 450b.
day, turn of the, 246b.
day-books, 129a, 450a, 499b.
daybreak, 522b, 815b.
day-couch, 333b.
Day-god, 109a ; Day-gods, the Thirty, 450a.
daylight, 731b.
days, the Five Epagomenal, 427b, 451a, 868b ; the Fifty hot, 547a.
day's work, 316b.

daytime, 622b.
dazed, 651b.
dazzle, 206a.
dead, 197b, 295b, 314b, 334b, 544b, 862a, 879a, 904b ; the dead, 155b, 207b, 235b, 293a, 295b, 301a, 371b, 560b, 571a, 632b, 706a, 713b, 718b, 756b, 835b, 836b, 854b ; the beatified, 744a ; the blessed, 508b, 518a, 718b ; the divine, 527b ; the righteous, 271a ; the sainted, 24a ; the venerable, 50a ; festival of the dead, 474b, 645b.
dead body, 280b, 713b, 893a ; bodies, 806b.
dead man, 51a, 67a, 399a, 594a.
dead, offerings to, 518a.
dead (of colours), 389a.
Dead-land, 53b, 571a.
deadly, 221a, 345b.
deaf, 54b, 72a, 102a, 341a, 614a, 615a, 688b, 689b, 705a, 883a.
deaf ear, to turn a, 615a.
deaf man, 614b.
deafness, 102a, 615a, 686a ; mental, 451b.
deal kindly, 20b.
dearest, 561b.
death, 7a, 102a, 145b, 188a, 266b, 295b, 301a, 314b, 331a, 386b, 541b, 546b, 602a, 703b, 835a, 872a ; the second, 177a.
death bed, 301a.
death blow, 489a.
death cry, 74a, 301a, 386b, 450b, 469a.
Death-god, 55a, 71b, 255a, 435a, 626b ; Boat of the, 490a.
deathless, 301a.
death rattle, 411b.
death sentence, 74a, 160b, 335b.
death trap, 245b.
debate, 410b.
debility, 7b.
decapitate, 90b.
decay, 55b, 61a, 72b, 82b, 176b, 177b, 181a, 262b, 263a, 420a, 470a, 520a, 565b, 566a, 592a, 594a, 604b, 621a, 624b, 640b, 693b, 774b, 787b, 865b ; decayed, 149a, 176a, 184b ; decaying, 463a.
deceit, 31b, 82a, 141a, 488b, 530a, 540a, 572a, 776b, 777a, 790a, 874b.
deceitful, 90b, 224b, 335b.
deceive, 141b, 538b, 797b, 839a, 647a.
deceiver, 641b.
December, 5b.
decide, 160b, 194b, 195a, 722b.
decipher, 178a.
decision, 131b, 157b, 194b, 753b ; judicial, 146b ; legal, 596b.
deck out, 613b, 590b, 904b.
deck of a boat, 689a.
declaim, 758a, 835b.
declaration, 332b, 669b, 860b, 886a.
declare, 253b, 276b, 673a, 796a, 913a.
decorate, 333b, 530a, 572a, 574b, 590b, 601b, 615b, 644b, 677a, 680a, 689a, 701a, 755a, 873b, 904a ; decorated, 689a, 731a, 755a.
decoration, 387b, 575a, 602a, 615b, 644b, 776a, 904a.
decoction, 292b, 328a, 762a.
decree, 3a, 19a, 34b, 37a, 76b, 131b, 160b, 161a, 190b, 191b, 192a, 335a, 337b, 431b, 470a, 567b, 619a, 679b, 683b, 688a, 692b, 697b, 710a, 722b, 754a, 831b ; of doom, 837a ; royal, 391b ; to pass a, 654a.
decry, 631a, 715a.
dedicate, 601a, 668a, 841b, 885b.
dedication, 574b.
deed, 67a, 106b, 337b, 387b, 440a, 666b ; glorious deeds, 23a ; deeds of violence, 127b.
deed (document), 129a.
deep, to be, 337a, 822a.
deep, 475b, 768b ; deep place, 337a.
deer, 624b.
defaced, 420a.
defame, 631a, 715a.
defaulter, 176a.
defect, 140b, 256b, 293a, 528b, 560b, 685b, 694a, 715b, 768a, 772b ; defeated, 560b, 617b.
defect, 26b, 165b, 180a, 441b, 540a, 809a, 853a ; of body, 574a.
defection, 434a.

defective, 141b, 165b, 802a.
defence, 164a, 380a, 823b, 860b, 868a.
defenceless, 558a.
defend, 324b, 354a, 366b, 381a, 409b, 591b, 715b.
defendant, 612a, 681a.
defender, 64b.
defile, 704b, 801b, 818a.
defilement, 825b.
define bounds of, 194b.
deflect, 18a.
deformed, 806b.
defraud, 373a, 451b, 473a, 538b.
degradation, 411b.
degrees, 379b.
deify, 66a, 401b.
dejected, 476a, 861b.
Dekan, the Thirty-six Dekans, 23a, 42b, 57b, 405a, 409b, 530b, 572a, 585b, 656a ; Keeper of the, 71b.
Dekan-god, 109a.
delay, 9b, 10a, 57b, 90b, 174b, 191a, 195b, 283b, 315b, 377b, 499b.
delete, 315b.
deliberate, 145b.
delicate, 764a, 774b.
delight, 693a, 776b, 728b, 729a.
delighted, 412a.
delightful, 123a, 412a.
delights, sexual, 412a.
delimit, 490a.
delimitation, 133b.
deliver, 385a, 608a, 757b ; deliver a woman, 602b, 671b.
deliverance, 385a.
deliverer, 385a.
delivery, 683b.
Delta, 103b, 318a, 816a ; dwellers in marshes of, 820a ; man of, 103b; speech of, 335b; woman of, 820a.
deluge, 12a, 49b, 544b, 644a.
demand, 334b, 577b, 643a, 745a, 756b.
Demetria, 880b.
Democritus of Abdera, 91a.
demolish, 499b, 810a.
demon, 30b, 197a, 468a, 657a, 731b, 740a b, 741a, 820a, 895a ; female, 112a.
demonstrate, 235b.
demotic, 619b.
den, 201a b, 216a, 275b, 419b, 538b, 539b, 775a, 832b, 857a.
Denderah, gods of, 132b.
denial, 435a.
denizens of earth, 71b.
dense, 164a, 601b ; of heart, 37b, 164a.
denseness, 164a.
denude, 793b.
depart, 149b, 153a, 156b, 212a, 240a, 351b, 420a b, 499a, 587b, 632a, 633a, 716b, 737b, 844b ; to make, 696a.
departure, 670b, 716b.
dependant, 293a, 311a, 824a ; dependants, 893a.
dependent upon, 293a.
depict, 346a.
depose, 868b.
deposit, 131b.
deposition, 186a, 416a, 758a.
depravity, 467b.
depressed, 64b, 744b.
depression, 140b.
deprivation, 176a.
deprive, 793b.
deprived, 176a, 184b, 800a.
depth, 216a, 827a.
deputy, 80b, 98b, 101b, 103a, 579b, 580a.
deputy confectioner, 103a.
deputy general, 103a.
deputy master of horse, 103a.
deputy sealer, 103a.
descend, 27a, 224b, 387b, 439a, 444a, 528b, 532b, 612b.
descendant, 243a, 331b, 439b, 567b, 898a.
descent, 682a.
describe, 387b, 719b.
description, 719b.
desert, 185b, 311a, 340b, 532a, 533b, 598b, 732a, 889b, 902a ; dwellers in the, 609b, 730a, 841a ; the Eastern, 59b.
desert, to, 205b.
deserter, 587b.
desertion, 587b.
design, to, 290b, 619a, 694a, 753b, 779a.

design, 94a, 346a, 570b, 572a, 698b, 722b, 753b, 779b, 798b, 855b ; crafty, 860b ; mural, 619b ; to make a, 122b.
designer, 619b, 780a ; of Ptaḥ, 620a, 662b.
desire to, 118a, 309b, 723b, 726a, 729a.
desire, 4b, 19a, 37b, 309b, 310a, 417b, 561b, 865a ; of the heart, 752a ; desired, 118a.
desolate, 27b.
de sorte que, 331a.
despair, 263a, 290a, 703b, 807b.
despairing, 461a.
despatch, 180a, 184a, 440b, 445a.
despicable, 574b.
despise, 260a, 621a, 622b.
despoil, 285b, 552b, 698a, 794a.
destine, 722b.
destinies, to arrange, 66b.
Destiny, 326b, 561a, 694a, 722b ; lords of, 561b ; Tablet of, 326a.
destitute, 12b, 128a, 129b, 174b, 186b, 204b, 225b, 339b, 340ab, 375b, 379b, 472b, 546a, 734a, 833a.
destitution, 7b, 127b.
destroy, 12a, 57b, 103b, 135b, 138a, 139a, 145a, 176b, 177b, 181a, 182b, 187b, 256b, 261b, 262a, 263b, 281b, 305b, 315b, 337b, 390a, 435a, 459a, 523b, 532a, 538b, 539ab, 540a, 544b, 547a, 560b, 562b, 567b, 568a, 573a, 575a, 587a, 591ab, 592b, 596a, 607b, 613b, 618b, 619a, 622a, 626a, 627a, 633a, 637b, 641b, 644a, 645b, 647a, 660b, 684b, 696b, 697a, 701b, 702b, 703b, 704b, 741b, 750b, 810a, 822a, 824a, 840ab, 847a, 858a, 865b, 884a, 909b ; destroy by fire, 392b, 696a.
destroyed, 39a, 94a, 149a, 184b, 388b, 398b, 439b, 473a, 520a, 536b, 544b, 552b, 560b, 702a, 792b, 862b.
destroyer, 98b, 373a, 375b, 520a, 538b, 547a, 587a, 641b, 684b, 740b, 884a.
Destroyer of Sin, 103b.
destruction, 10b, 11b, 82b, 92b, 102a, 103b, 145b, 163b, 168a, 188a, 243b, 263b, 375b, 440a, 489a, 520a, 524a, 538b, 539a, 561b, 577b, 612b, 648a, 650b, 652a, 666a, 697a, 703b, 840a, 872a ; place of, 538b, 520a.
destructive, 212a.
detach, 261b.
detain, 643b, 653b.
determination, 139a.
determine, 722b.
determined, 297a.
detestable, 778b.
develop, 649b.
device, 694a.
devil, 197a, 208a, 211a, 345b, 377a, 419a, 470a, 599b, 621a, 624a, 657a, 694b, 708a, 740b, 820a, 895ab.
Devil, the, 657a.
devise, 66b, 145b, 398a, 782b.
devoted, 147b, 399a, 793b.
devour, 120b, 122a, 168b, 215b, 248a, 390a, 392b, 606b, 688b, 851a, 896b, 898b.
devourer, 338a, 392b, 590b, 602a, 615a, 645a ; the crocodile, 877a.
devouring, 34a.
dew, 27a, 97a, 101b, 142a, 143b.
Dhu'l-Ḳarnên, 52b.
dhurra, 223b, 227b, 390b.
diadem, 119b, 326a, 496a, 515a, 528a, 683a, 701b.
diaphragm, opening in, 416b.
diarrhœa, 61b, 169b.
diary, 450a.
didrachma, 781a.
die, 10b, 293a, 301ab, 314b, 334b, 632a, 654a, 716b, 835a, 866b ; die off, 865b ; die out, 520a.
difference, 711a, 825a.
differentiate, 629a, 630a.
difficult, 145a, 753b.
difficulty, 99a, 755b, 861b.
diffident, 754b.
dig, 29b, 201a, 668b, 729b, 881b ; dig foundations, 201a ; dig into, 388a ; dig out ore, 158b, 209b, 282b, 626a, 757b ; dig up, 540a ; by the roots, 263a.
digging up the earth, ceremony of, 540b.

digger, 531a, 540a, 759b.
dignitary, 18a.
dignity, 15a, 18a, 32a, 883b ; dignities, 829b.
dilatation of heart, 3a.
diminish, 10b, 116a, 127b, 138a, 355a, 451b, 538b, 539b, 640b, 703b, 858a ; diminished, 379b, 749b.
diminution, 12b, 409b, 539b.
diminutive, 226a.
dimness, 753a.
dining room, 168b, 613a.
diorite, 221b.
dip, 596a, 897b ; dip in water, 27b, 820a, 843a.
direct, 117b, 285a, 411a, 482a, 486b, 512b, 562a, 582a, 610b, 622b, 679b, 683b, 694a, 699a, 860a, 862a, 896a ; a course, 837a ; the mind, 699a ; the feet, 866a.
direction, 28a, 699a.
direction, rubrical, 487a, 861a.
director, 98b, 311b, 351b, 417a, 487a, 513a, 562a, 666b, 699a, 862a.
director of ceremonies, 699b.
director of corvêe, 108b.
director of festival, 71a.
dirt, 119b, 179b, 470a, 476a, 537b, 635a, 763b, 822b.
dirty, 260a, 470b, 524a, 726a, 787a, 883a.
disaffected, 227a.
disagree, 410b.
disappear, 477b, 520a, 560a, 787b.
disappearance, 451b.
disapprove, 446a, 540a.
disarrange, 577b, 683a, 844a.
disaster, 8a, 31b, 214b, 269ab, 379b, 395a, 419a, 577b, 595b, 631b, 632a, 698a, 715a, 717b.
discharge a debt, 601a, 668a, 717b, 874b, 904a.
discomfort, 524b, 895b.
discontented, 227a.
discord, 844a.
discouragement, 262b.
discourse, 549a.
discover, 96a, 468a, 807a.
discuss, 145b, 410b, 613a.
disease, 27a, 39b, 72a, 81a, 91b, 160a, 168b, 195b, 212b, 222b, 275b, 288a, 296b, 324a, 383a, 390b, 393b, 434a, 444a, 459a, 462a, 469a, 484ab, 485a, 489b, 522a, 529a, 550b, 553a, 571a, 610a, 836b, 646b, 649a, 680b, 682b, 696b, 711a, 737b, 747a, 805b, 813b, 824a, 839b ; deadly, 295b ; devil of, 212a ; fatal, 314b ; of belly, 82a, 151a ; of the bladder, 178a ; of the ears, 883b ; of the eyes, 14a, 120a, 149b, 725a, 753a ; of the feet, 812b ; of the genital organs, 109b ; of the leg, 806b ; of the mouth, 185b ; of the skin, 149b, 390b ; of the womb, 9a ; diseased, 383a.
disembark, 677b.
disembowel, 757b.
disentangle, 43b, 178b.
disgrace, 7a, 31b, 541b, 544b, 612b, 682a, 731b, 737b.
disgraceful, 535b, 541a.
disguise, 65b.
disgust, 64b, 262b, 263a, 383a, 618b, 638a, 744b, 796b ; to feel, 258a ; disgusted, 260a, 664b, 665a, 714a.
disgusting, 383a, 819b.
dish, 178a, 208b, 558b, 856b, 892a.
disheartened, 261a, 263a, 524ab.
dishevelled, 393b, 727a.
dishonour, 564b, 895a.
disk, 234a ; of sun, 26b, 27ab, 98b, 101b, 622b, 820a.
disk, winged, 111a, 474a, 536a.
disks of Rā, the Seven, 98b.
Disk-goddess, 134a.
dislike, 541a.
disloyal, 227a.
dismantle, 793b.
dismayed, 464a, 524a.
dismember, 393b, 512b.
dismiss, 190a.
disobedient, 341a.
disorder, 577a, 736a, 844a.
dispel, 787a.
dispensation, 694a.
disperse, 420b, 787a.
disposal, 679b.
dispose, 679b.

disposer, 860b.
disposition, 34b, 37b, 50b, 209b, 460b, 461a, 637a, 703a, 770b, 779b, 782b ; good, 34b ; happy, 168a.
disputant, 745a.
dispute, 167a, 727b, 744b, 852b, 854a.
disquieted, 744b.
disregard, 289b, 546a, 633b.
dissemble, 51a.
dissolve, 228a, 899a ; dissolved, 216b.
distant, 144b.
distil, 409b, 863b.
distinction, 630a, 711b.
distinguish, 629a, 630a, 711a, 837b, 856a ; distinguished, 153b, 336b, 711b, 713a, 838a, 841b, 856a, 880b.
distorted, 344a.
distract the mind, 685b.
distress, 650b ; to be in, 800a.
distribute, 235a, 248b, 251a, 881b.
distribution, 538b.
distributor, 248b.
district, 79a, 144a, 289a, 420b, 444b, 511b, 533b, 605b, 738b, 781b, 783b ; inspector, 311b ; walled, 60b.
disturb, 549b, 577a, 710a, 845a.
disturbance, 549b, 557a b.
disturbed, 344a, 393b, 464a, 630a ; disturbed times, 887b.
disturber, 7b, 549b, 577a.
ditch, 21b, 142a.
ditcher, 444b, 729a, 758a.
diuretic, 528b.
diver bird, 541a.
divers, 736a.
divert, 680b, 793b.
divide, 37a, 235a, 237b, 243b, 245b, 246a, 248b, 251a b, 325b, 662a, 755a, 837b, 838a, 881b, 844b, 888a, 907b, 911b.
divider, 248b.
divine, 356a, 401b ; be or become, 401b.
divinity, 402a.
division, 103b, 235a, 248b, 251b, 252a b, 511b, 538b, 621a, 695a, 881a, 882b.
divisionless, 341a.
divorced, 481a.
dîwân, 13a, 108b, 190a, 526b, 596a.
do, 65a, 418b ; do away, 89b, 103b, 181a, 425a, 847b ; do battle, 132a ; do continuously, 66a ; do good to, 65a ; do homage, 96a ; do honour, 147b ; do not, 44a ; do nothing, 78a, 225b, 377a ; do well, 66a ; do what is obligatory, 65b ; do the will of, 65b ; do wrong, 369b, 637a.
dock, 74a, 180b.
dockyard, 180b.
doctor, 592b.
doctrine, 655b.
document, 90b, 106b, 129a, 144a, 161a, 180a, 184b, 200b, 337b, 387b, 440a, 619a, 622b, 661a, 644a, 701b, 722b, 725a, 738b, 755a, 774a, 836a b, 841a, 848a, 849a, 855b, 882a, 885a, 898a ; documents, old or ancestral, 345a, 830b.
Doer of right, a title, 67b.
doers, 67a.
dog, 4a, 10a, 25b, 31b, 33b, 147b, 149a, 177b.
dog, the fighting, 179b, 221a, 722a ; the house, 177b ; the Libyan, 5a.
dog of Ȧntef-āa, 243b.
Dog-god, 70a, 699b.
dog-headed, 862a.
dog-skin, 722a.
Dog-star, 664a.
dolphin, 643a.
dolt, 546a.
domain, 95a, 106a, 107a, 144a, 409a, 457b, 490a, 667a, 861a, 897a, 900b ; domains of Horus and Set, 16a.
domestic, 568a.
domicile, 910b.
domination, 468a.
dominion, 496a, 512b.
done, 67a.
donkey (see ass).
donkey-herd, 586b.
doom, 160b, 520a.
doomed, 345b.

door, 107a, 130b, 222a, 275a, 371b, 393a, 416a, 419a, 521b, 522a, 588b, 594b, 647a, 654b, 658b, 659a, 723b, 819a, 822a, 823a ; boundary, 908b; false, 420b ; folding, 655a ; leaves of, 129a ; of the earth, 416a ; two sides of, 821b.
door-bolt, 618b, 775a ; of Maāti, 842b.
door-chamber, 526b.
door-fitting, 283a.
door-gods, 107b, 655a.
doorkeeper, 70a, 71a, 107b ; of heaven, 70a ; of Osiris, 70a ; of the Ṭuat, 107b.
door-post, 351a, 520b ; of Maāti, 388b.
doorway, 159a, 275a, 393a, 417b, 419a.
dose, 661b.
double, 548b, 782b ; of the East, 19a.
double, to, 93a, 763a, 768a.
double-plumed, 18a.
doubler (of years), 768a.
dough, 230b, 534ab, 776b, 844a.
dove, 54b, 234a, 299b, 300a, 301b, 809b, 810b.
dovecot, 166a.
downcast, 861b.
downwards, 493a, 532a, 579b.
dowry, 286b, 544a, 736a, 774ab ; in silver, 215b.
doze, 113b.
drachm, 706a.
drachma, 781a.
draft, 94a, 337b.
draftsman (see also draughtsman), 689b.
drag, 100a, 184a, 324a, 327b, 628b, 629b, 707b, 713a, 827a ; drag a stream, 490b ; drag away, 752b ; drag down, 177b ; drag out, 787b ; drag with ropes, 3b.
dragoman, 106a, 177a.
draper, 356b.
drapings, 476b.
draughtboard and draughts, 604b, 628b, 630a.
draught box, 302a.
draughts, to play, 476a, 604b.
draughtsman, 38a.
draughtsman (artist), 358a, 780a ; craft of the, 779b.
draw, 90b, 100a, 104a, 184a, 346a, 619a, 703b, 707b, 827a.
draw and quarter, 873a ; draw game, 287a ; draw geese, 187b.
draw bolts, 620b, 690a.
draw a bow, 13b.
draw a design, 610b, 662b.
draw near, 565a, 638a, 846ab, 891a.
draw off, 747b.
draw out, 894a.
draw a sword, 827a.
draw thread, 346b.
draw up a list, 190b.
drawers, 565b, 749a.
drawing, 346a, 555a, 779b.
dream, 163b, 432b ; a bad, 652a.
dregs, 411b, 611b, 677b, 820b.
drench, 223b.
dress, 34b, 169ab, 282b, 356b, 476b, 537b, 606a, 613b, 629b, 631a, 671b, 703b, 714a, 787a, 818b, 850b, 904b ; dressed, 757a, 826a, 835b.
dress a god, 670a.
dress the hair, 850a.
dresser, 714a ; of the dead, 158a ; of a god, 667b.
dressing room, 240a.
dribble, 351b.
dribblings, 620b.
dried (see also dry), 764b ; dried up, 186b.
drill, 452a.
drill-bow, 166a.
drink, to, 168b, 350b, 592a, 593a, 642a, 648b, 651a, 695b, 710a, 842b, 887b, 889a ; give to drink, 696b, 866b ; drink oneself drunk, 887b.
drink, 58b, 92b, 140a, 202a, 230b, 409a, 485b, 491b, 572b, 616a, 621a, 631b, 637b, 648b, 651a, 722a, 723a, 726a, 735a, 751b, 759b, 761b, 773b, 801a, 817a, 823a, 843a, 857a, 872b ; fermented, 115a ; holy, 912b ; made of red grain, 889a ; pots of, 776a ; to prepare, 735a ; sacrificial, 690a.

drinker, 593a, 651a.
drinking, the act of, 804b; pot, 775b.
drinking companions, 651a.
drinking festival, 859a, 889a.
drink offering, 474a, 516b, 525a, 538a, 709b, 872b.
drip, 708b, 906b; drip away, 636a.
drive, 443b, 470a; a furrow, 564a; ashore, 74ab.
drive away, 40a, 57b, 145a, 262a, 370b, 381a, 393b, 417b, 420ab, 440b, 531b, 533b, 564b, 565b, 613b, 683b, 684a, 696a, 707b, 794a, 810a, 846a, 896b; drive pegs, 140a.
drive back, 487b, 614b, 676b, 746a, 747a.
drive cattle, 564b, 841b.
drive off, 787a.
drive in, 72a.
drive out, 563b, 564a, 884a; drive out pain, 445b.
driver, 766a, 791ab.
dromos of temple, 545a.
drop, 227a, 409b, 575b, 849b; drop back, 116a; down, 549a; of the jaws, 568a; out, 568a; tears, 906a; with fatigue, 802a.
droppings, 366b, 409b; from eye, 61b; from nose, 608a.
dross, 714a, 820b.
drought, 652b, 697b, 723b, 732a.
drover, 351b, 586b.
drown, 140a, 442b; drowned, 95b, 317b, 451a, 897b.
drowning man, 139b.
drowsy, 113b.
drug, 128b, 186a, 247a, 300a, 771a; aromatic, 346b; to treat or be treated with a drug, 180b, 631b, 710a, 712a, 715a; drugged beer, 719a.
drum, 10a, 610b, 680a, 827ab, ; to beat a, 843b.
drunk, 355b, 887b.
drunk, to be or become, 842b; to make, 776a.
drunkards, 436a, 593a, 626b, 651a, 705a, 843a; habitual, 843a.
drunken man, 634b.
drunkenness, 355b, 634b, 843a; day of, 451a; festival of, 475a.
dry, 185b, 547a, 590a, 724b, 732a, 798a; dry land, 898a; dry rot, 565b, 566a; dry tears, 132a; dry up, 91b, 698a.
dryness, 441a, 652b, 697b, 724b.
dual, mark of the, 152a, 157b, 821a.
duck, 5b, 100b, 256b.
duck-headed, 165b.
due, 882b.
dues, 511a, 521a, 580b, 722b; of temple, 195b.
dumb, 705b.
dûm palm, 269b; fruit of the, 473b.
dung, 27b, 30b, 37a, 289b, 451b, 467a, 473a, 509b, 571b, 624a, 700b, 786a; of crocodile, 325b; fuel, 902b.
duplicate, 177a, 604b, 675b.
durable, 632a.
during, 815a.
dust, 37a, 99a, 179b, 223b, 253a, 347b, 396a, 469a, 536b, 571b, 723b, 731a, 763b, 815a; of alluvial gold, 353a; storm, 544b; white, 751a.
dust heap, 15b.
duty, 69b, 161a; daily, 160b; place of, 80b; regular, 167a.
duties, 586b.
dwarf, 294b, 374b, 470b, 867b, 868b, 883b; dancing, 883b.
Dwarf-god, 867b.
dwell, 374b, 485ab, 864a.
dweller, 485b, 774b; dweller in, 573a.
dweller on the earth (i.e., the living), 828b.
dweller on the mountain (i.e., the dead), 826b.
dwelling, 41b, 42a, 62a, 273b, 499b, 571b, 632b, 725a, 909b; dwelling place, 750b.
dye, 693b, 791a.
dyke, 106a, 758a, 759b, 767b, 838b, 861b, 882a, 907b; to build a, 882a.

E.

each, 357a, 828a, 856b, 882b.
eagle, 135b, 910b.
ear, 103a, 126b, 329b ; the two ears, 508a ; running of the, 644a.
ear, of corn, 548a, 573a, 726b, 728a, 743a, 794b, 795a ; of a door, 126b ; of a god, 126b.
early, 351a, 870b.
earring, 356a, 728b.
earth, 10a, 11a, 13b, 16b, 25a, 30b, 37a, 83a, 99a, 118b, 220a, 253a, 537a, 585b, 609a, 627b, 666a, 763b, 764b, 766b, 806a, 815a, 816a, 835a ; coloured, 773b, 910a ; crown of the, 163a ; for faïence, 753a ; for sealing, 643b ; red and white, 558b, 752a.
earth amulet, 750a.
earth creatures, 584b.
Earth-destroyer, 641b.
earthenware, 114a, 252a.
earth, fullers', 866b.
Earth-god, 11b, 95b, 175b, 199a, 255a, 498a, 805b, 819b, 831a, 838a, 848b.
Earth-goddess, 819b, 868a.
earth-iron, 210a.
earth lightening, 815b.
earthquake, 298b, 447a, 762a.
Earthquake-god, 631a, 714b.
earthwork, 758a, 858a.
ease, to be at, 610a, 679a.
east, 18b, 19a, 20a, 815b ; Bull of the, 221b ; goddess of the, 19a ; wise men of the, 430b.
eastern, 18b.
east side, 106a.
east wind, 449a.
easy, 516a.
easy-going, 898b.
eat, 10a, 28b, 48b, 49b, 120b, 122a, 168b, 184b, 185b, 186a, 187a, 215b, 248a, 261b, 392b, 393a, 572b, 600b, 631b, 762a, 772b, 778b, 814a ; eat into, 395a ; eat ravenously, 606b ; eat the heart, 120b ; to make to, 592b, 645a ; eat up, 392b.
eater, 168b, 392b.
Eater of foes, 121b.
Eater of heart souls, 169a.
Eater of many, 121a.
Eater of the Arm, 120b.
Eater of the Ass, 121a.
Eater of the Dead, 121a.
Eater of sinners (Osiris), 120b.
Eater of souls, 121a.
eating, 105b, 804b.
eavesdrop, 471a, 672b.
ebony, 142b, 441a, 445b, 446a.
eclipse, 395a, 838b.
eclipsed, 395a.
Ecliptic-god, 479a.
ecstasy, 593a ; fall into an, 530a ; religious, 480b.
eddy, 247a.
Edfû, priestess of, 460b.
edge, 243b, 662b ; of sword, 878a ; of the water, 662b.
edict, 106b, 192a, 337b, 346a, 400b, 441a, 692b, 710a, 849a ; of slaughter, 631b ; righteous, 668b.
edition, 683a.
Edomite, 102b.
educate, 655a, 757b ; educated, 634a.
education, 655ab.
eel, 480b.
efface, 840a ; effaced, 184b.
effect, to, 807a, 900a.
effective, 20a.
effeminacy, 574a.
efficient, 129b.
effigy, 19a.
efflux, 91b, 419b, 766a.
effusion, 708b.
egg, 119a, 121b, 593a, 649b, 651b, 683a.
eggshell, 62a.
Egypt, Lower and Upper, 97b, 99b, 248b, 431b, 523a, 675b, 741a, 771b, 815a.
Egypt, Middle, 575b.
Egypt, speech of, 416a.
Egyptians, 787b, 815b.
eight, 547b, 548a ; eight-day cloth, 547b ; eight-day period, 547b.
Eight Gods, the, 548a.
eighteen, 331a.
eighty, 485a, 548a.

Eileithyia, 388a.
Eileithyiaspolis, 403a, 522b.
ejaculation of spells, 190b.
eject, 659a, 708ab, 833a; fluid, 394b, 561b.
ekbolic, 528b.
elbow, 766b.
elder, 679b.
eldest, 107a, 170b, 601b, 602b, 672a, 828b.
elect, 696b.
elephant, 4a.
elephant grass, 4a.
Elephantine, priest of, 628a; speech of, 335b.
elevate, 92a, 537b.
elevation, 424b.
eloquent, 410b, 626a.
Elysian Fields, 183a.
emanation, 419b, 821b, 852b; divine, 821b; liquid, 437a.
embalm, 117a, 188a, 512a, 593b, 631a, 652a, 653b, 654a, 680b, 710a, 715a; embalmed, 158a, 180b.
embalmer, 158a, 188a, 190b.
Embalmer (Anubis), 593b.
Embalmers, the Four, 188a.
embalmment, 46b; chamber of 803b.
embank, 882a.
embankment, 882a.
embarcation, 439a.
embark, 7a, 74a, 439a.
embassy, 31a, 161a, 671a.
embers, 896b, 897b.
embrace, 15b, 63a, 64a, 252b, 317a, 446a, 451b, 463a, 470b, 479a, 531a, 548a, 577b, 603b, 616b, 693a, 773ab, 851a, 889a.
embroider, 833a.
emerald, 39b, 89b, 204b, 296a, 741a; root of, 150b.
Emerald Field, 686b.
emery, 602b; powder, 89b.
eminence, 830a.
eminent, 713a.
emission, 91b, 218a, 223a, 332a, 366b, 387ab, 394ab, 400a, 437b, 571b, 820b, 864b; divine, 331b; of body, 722b; of seed, 868a.
emit a cry, 190a; a fluid, 395a; seed, 118a, 609a; a smell, 551a.
emotion, 241a; supreme, 44b.
emphasis, 56a, 79a.
employês, 579b.
emptiness, 181a, 184b, 186b, 698a.
empty, 181a, 182b, 184b, 186b, 204ab, 207b, 226a, 237a, 622b, 732b, 771b, 800a; to make, 698a; empty of, 339b; empty oneself, 133a; places, 872a; the belly, 262b; handed 732b.
encampment, 178a, 179a, 235a.
enchant, 464b.
enchanter, 514b, 585b.
enchantments, 247a; god of, 162b; to work, 247a.
encircle, 246a, 743b; with walls, 477a; encircled, 706b.
encirclers, 63a.
enclose, 63a, 75a, 131a, 743b, 769b, 808a, 850b, 851a, 910a; enclosed, 557b, 574b, 852a.
enclosure, 19b, 63a, 286b, 600b, 778a, 813a, 878b; walled, 38a, 575b, 851a.
encompass, 92a.
encourage, 702b.
encroach, 509a.
end, to, 305b, 560a, 787b.
end, 131b, 145b, 244a, 306a, 414a, 488a, 703b, 787b, 835a; of a period, 131b; ends of leaves, 244b; ends of the earth, 131b, 773a; bring to an, 703b, 715b, 770a, 909b; come to an, 834a; to make an, 645b, 703b, 711a, 773a, 822a, 833b; put an end to, 790a.
endless, 488a, 787b.
endow, 88b, 262a, 487a, 602b, 654a, 670b, 885b; endowed with spirit or zeal, 23b, 38b.
endowment, 518a, 609b.
endure, 413b, 665a; to make, 704b; endured, 140a.
enduring, 913b.
endwise, 264b.
enemy, 1a, 11b, 12b, 27b, 79a, 101b, 116a, 203a, 208b, 227a, 228a, 289b, 302a, 329ab, 345b, 348b, 356a, 369b, 388b, 411b, 434a, 531a, 545b, 546b, 561a,

572b, 574b, 636a, 642a, 657a, 676a, 678a, 708a, 738b, 740b, 762a, 787a, 817b, 819a, 820a, 894a, 895a b, 899a ; defeated, 806b.
Enemy (the Devil), 657a.
enemy, to act as an, 657a.
energy, 738a.
enforce, 300b.
engrave, 9a, 186a, 190b, 254b, 521b, 527b, 567b, 610b, 662b, 680a, 777b, 836a, 867a ; engraved, 290b, 567b ; engraved objects, 206a.
engraver, 223a, 291a, 567b, 645b.
enjoy, 147a, 205a, 628b, 833b ; a dignity, 65a, 410b ; food, 606b ; oneself, 558b, 716b.
enlarge, 181b, 652a, 697a, 837b.
enlarger, 587b.
enlighten, 376b.
enmity, 328b, 461b, 642b, 657a, 678a, 744b, 874b, 895b.
ennobled, 591a.
enquire, 548b ; after, 186b ; for, 179b ; into, 462a, 642b, 673a, 745a.
enquirer, 672b.
enquiry, 642b, 695a, 745a ; judicial, 745a.
enroll, 662b ; a name, 65b.
enslave, 607a.
enter, 5a, 9a, 25b, 30a, 93b, 138a b, 158b, 439a, 447a, 576a, 688b, 690a, 845a, 846a ; make to, 641b, 646b.
enterer, 846a.
entertainer, 509a.
enthronement, 485b.
entire, 834a, 880a.
entirely, 414a, 415a, 634a, 779b.
entrails, 189b, 585a.
entrance, 138b, 158b, 284b, 416a, 417b, 419a, 420b, 439a, 576a, 647a, 885a ; and exit, 138a ; to a path, 416b.
entreat, 124a, 468a, 597a, 603a, 650b, 668b, 745a, 876a.
entreater, 745a.
entreaty, 2a, 8a, 382b, 607a, 650a, 658a, 857b, 876a.
entrust, 683b ; entrusted, 384a.
entwine, 282a.
enumerate, 41a.
envelop, 91a, 463a, 651b, 717a, 849a, 909b.
environs, 638a.
envoy, 33b, 42a, 161a, 170a, 245b, 289b, 594a, 688a, 854b ; royal, 391b, 742b.
envy, 388a, 774a.
epagomenal days, 427b.
epidemic, 27a.
Epiphanes, 241b, 403b, 404b ; the two gods, 23a.
Epiphi, 674b, 740a.
epistle, 337b.
equal, 227b, 595a.
equilibrium, 139a, 563a.
equinox, 543a.
equip, 28b, 291b, 601a, 631b, 661a, 715a, 811b, 904a.
equipment, 282b, 487a, 660b, 715a, 796b, 812a, 885b, 904a ; funerary, 904b.
equipped, 118b, 796b.
equivalent, 88b.
eradicate, 237a.
erase, 884a.
erect, to, 591b, 646a.
Erpit, 84a.
err, 176a, 83a.
errand, 31a, 161a.
error, 141b, 165b, 373a, 797b.
Erṭa-ḥen-reqaiu, 437a.
Erṭa Sebanqa, 437b.
escape, 14b, 118b, 156b, 176a, 193a, 212a, 216b, 240a, 373b, 380b, 409a, 472a, 481a, 519b, 612b, 793b, 864b.
essence, 280a, 293a, 317b, 398b ; divine, 293b ; of god, 821b.
establish, 436b, 609a b, 649b, 678a b, 694b, 811b ; oneself, 437a ; established, 54a, 602a, 670a, 671a, 812a, 913b.
establishment, 609b, 900a.
estate, 1a, 10b, 22a, 72a, 79a, 94a, 95a, 97b, 106a, 107a, 118b, 121b, 144a, 440b, 453a, 459b, 490a, 510b, 537b, 579a, 638a, 661b, 712b, 720a, 721b, 723a, 758a, 769a, 773a, 781b, 835b, 854a, 861b, 900b ; in Åment, 8a ; landed, 467a.

estate officer, 526b.
estate rolls, 41a, 474b.
estimate, 510b, 838a.
et cetera, 158a, 483b.
eternal, 343b ; eternal home (the tomb), 80a.
Eternal, the, 507b.
eternity, 264a, 355b, 383ab, 507b, 744a, 893a ; amulet of, 183b ; begetter of, 189a ; god of, 52b, 383a ; house of, 239ab, 240a ; place of, 214b ; seed of, 331b ; soul of, 199b.
êtui, 581b.
Euergetai, 340a, 404b.
eunuch, 481b, 822b.
Eupator, 833a.
evacuate, 91b, 180a, 184a, 195b, 260b, 262b.
evacuation, 184ab.
evade, 240a.
even, 96a ; even as, 826a ; even though, 786a.
evening, 10ab, 22b, 100a, 287a, 288a, 296b, 330a, 420b, 421a, 429a, 529b, 537a, 608b, 621b, 622a, 624b, 648b, 649a, 840b, 897a.
evening bread, 323b ; evening meal, 91b, 330a.
event, 163b, 542b, 548b, 561b, 580b, 614b, 617a, 690a, 693b.
eventide, 323b.
ever and ever, 383a.
everlasting, 893a.
Everlasting Rā, 418a.
everlastingly, 264a, 414b.
everlastingness, 383a, 893a.
ever living, 124b.
every, 357a, 414a, 838a, 856b, 882b.
everybody, 37b, 68a, 154a, 214a, 260b, 313b, 357a, 426a, 435a, 436a, 493a, 583b, 633a, 880a.
everyone, 154a, 357a, 640b.
every place, 214a.
everything, 475b, 525b.
everywhere, 214a.
evidence, 332b, 544b ; damning, 334a ; false, 141b ; to give, 334a, 694b.
evident, 265b.
evidently, 265b.
evil, 8a, 31b, 120a, 141a, 203a, 208a, 211a, 212a, 214ab, 216b, 226a, 260a, 343a, 345a, 356a, 434a, 459a, 472ab, 490a, 524a, 536b, 538b, 540a, 582a, 594a, 635a, 634b, 641a, 644b, 649a, 678a, 744b, 751a, 778b, 808a, 868b, 869a, 895b.
evil beings or things, 164b, 462b, 744b, 778b, 824a.
evil disposed, 227a.
evil doer, 12b, 165b, 369b, 373a, 375b, 434a, 462b, 541a.
evil eye, 30a, 217a.
evil, form of, 138a.
evil glance, 807a.
evil, god of, 713b, 869a.
evil hap, 30b, 170a.
evil-hearted, 165b, 216b, 434a.
evil men, 88b, 89b, 869a.
evil natured, 209b.
evil one, 216b, 369b, 677a.
evil personified, 111a, 211a.
evil plight, 80b.
evil quality, 95a.
evil, secret powers of, 625a.
evil, serpent of, 657a.
Evil (i.e., Set), 629a.
evil spirit, 228a, 377a.
evil thing, 459a.
evil, to be or to do, 141a, 211a, 373a, 488b, 591b.
evilly entreated, 606a.
exact, 139a, 332a, 333b.
exactly, 139a.
exaggerate, 651b.
exalt, 28a, 110a, 625b, 629a, 630a, 680a, 684a, 702a, 711a, 713b, 733a, 837b.
exalted, 7a, 93a, 344a, 713b, 760a, 767a, 912a ; state, 554a.
examine, 158b, 178a, 203a, 266b, 642b, 673a, 716a, 846b, 891a.
Examiner (Osiris), 642b.
examining, 754a.
example, 595a.
exasperate, 689b.
excavate, 178a, 757b.
excavation, 756b.
exceedingly, 108a, 181a, 266a, 414ab, 431b, 459a.
excel, 562a.
excellences, 23a, 214a, 304a.

excellent, 22b, 93a, 211a, 304a, 305a, 370b.
except, 160b, 340a, 493a.
exception, 160b, 537a ; to make an, 537a ; without any, 537a.
excess, 189a, 470a.
exchange, 735a b, 874a, 904a ; speech, 410b.
excitable, 861b.
excited, 159a, 419a, 570a.
excitement, 378a.
exclaim, 49a.
exclamation, 142a, 157b.
exclusive, 546a.
excrement, 184a, 289b, 476a, 528b, 624a, 700b, 786a, 822b.
excretions, 38b, 222b ; bodily, 307b ; foul, 459a.
excuse, 185b, 899b.
execute, 910a.
executioner, 195a, 303b, 373a, 575b, 644a ; of Osiris, 57a.
exercise functions, 65a.
exert pressure, 521b.
exhaust, 622a.
exhausted, 10b, 175b, 176b, 207b, 225b, 228a, 522a, 534b, 570b, 574a, 598a, 666a, 753a, 800a, 802a.
exhaustion, 207b, 534a, 666a.
exile, 574b, 598a.
exist, 164b, 230b, 542a, 690a, 717b ; to make, 616a.
existence, 164b, 694a ; god of, 165a.
exit, 138a b, 218b, 219b, 240b.
exorcise, 490b.
exorcist, 155b.
expand, 681b.
expansion, 257a.
expedient, 595a.
expedition, 193a ; set out on an, 192b.
expel, 696a, 801b, 884a.
expend, 604a.
expenditure, 438a.
expenses, 240b, 438a, 443b, 446b.
experience, 899a.
expert, 131a, 284b.
expire, 240a.
explain, 178b, 212b, 235b, 252b, 253b, 685a.
explanation, 401a ; mark of, 79a.
explore, 903b.
expunge, 884a.
extend, 3a, 184b, 191a, 450a, 597b, 635b, 652a, 804b, 873a, 894a.
extended, 255b.
extension, 894a.
extent, 134a, 838a.
external, 420b.
extinguish, 2a, 135b.
extol, 733a.
extortion, 141b.
extortioner, 635a.
extract, 292b.
extraordinary, 209b.
exudation, 27a, 61b, 218a, 820b, 852b, 876b.
exude, 877b.
exult, 6a, 466b, 713b.
eye, eyes, 194a, 219b, 306a, 313a, 351a, 408b, 409b, 702a ; disease of, 14b, 149b, 212b, 421b, 459b, 831a, 843b, 906b ; every, 68a ; inflammation of the, 14a ; the evil, 30a ; the King's, 68a ; right, 53b ; the two eyes, 68a, 275a ; eye to eye, 68a.
Eye-in-his-belly, 224b.
Eye of Horus, 23a, 119a, 125b ; an offering, 68b ; the black, white, and green, 68b.
Eye of Heaven, the left, 18b.
Eye of Khnemu, 68b ; a boat, 68b.
Eye of Rā, 23a, 68b, 80a ; the left, 4b, 18b.
Eye of Shu, 68b.
Eye of Teb, 68b.
Eye of Tem, 68b.
Eye, the One, 68a.
Eyes, the Two divine, 267a.
eyeball, 217a ; the Two Eyeballs of Rā, 840a.
eyebrows, 49b, 58a, 63a, 273a.
eyelashes, 630a, 713b.
eyeless, 340b.
eyelids, 574b, 670a, 671b, 672b, 713b.
eye paint, 19b, 20a, 150b, 192b, 329a b, 603a, 672b, 673b, 715b.

F.

fabrics, 487a.
face, 460a, 493a. 545a, 554a; downwards, 579b; opening the, 116b, 650a; the Hidden, 755b; face to face, 116b, 493a; pure faces, 155a; face cloths, 850b.
face, to turn the, 866a; to face some one, 116b.
facing, 158a, 264a, 339a, 493a.
fact, 525a.
factory, 81b, 483a.
Fāgit, 260a.
Fai, 259a b.
Fai-ā, 259b.
Fai-ākh, 259b.
faïence, 842a; blue glazed, 858b, 887a.
Fai-Ḥeru, 259b.
fail, 10b, 26b, 141b, 176a, 227a, 261b, 433b, 802a, 806a, 839a, 891a.
failing, 587b.
failure, 12b, 176a, 177b, 262b, 352b, 595a, 703b, 838b.
Fai-m'khat, 259b.
faint, 227a, 471a, 480b, 803a.
faint-hearted, 680a.
fainting, 175b.
Fai-pet, 259b.
Fait, 259a.
faith, 382b.
Faiu, 259a b.
Faku, 260a.
falcon, 909b.
fall, 227a, 255a, 425b, 439a, 440a, 444a b, 447a, 560b, 694b, 813b; away, 433b, 587b, 803b; down, 439a b, 572b, 624a, 749b; in with, 129b; out (of hair), 184b; to make, 79a, 104a, 693b.
fallâḥ, fellâḥ, 75a, 111a, 489a.
fallen, the, 79a.
falsehood, 124a, 141b, 335a, 604b, 803a, 810a, 812a, 813b.
falseness, 675a.
falsify, 647a.
fame, 245a, 724a.
familiarity, 278b.
family, 105b, 284a, 316a, 322a, 438b, 443b,
famine, 514a, 772b; goddess of, 514b; years of, 732b.
famous, 115b, 508b, 837b.
fan, to, 269b, 606a.
fan, fans, 204b, 220a, 318b, 370a, 537b, 610b, 611a, 643b, 647b, 680b; cook's fan, 370a.
fan bearer, 647b, 849a; fan for fire, 237a, 248a.
fancy, to let run free, 38a.
fare, 832a.
fare collector, 446b.
far from, 499a.
farm, 1a, 74a, 99a, 457b, 758a, 767a; labourer, 457b; land 234a; Pharaoh's, 526b.
farm folk, 638b.
farmers, 32b, 111a, 489a.
far off, 417b.
far reaching, 181a.
fascinate, 509b.
fashion, 65a, 95a, 118a; to fashion, 321a, 323a b, 353b, 366b, 384b, 542a, 616a, 628b, 688b, 689b, 690a, 710a, 730a, 770b, 779a, 909b.
fashioner, 384b.
fasten, 147b, 355a.
fastened, 304b, 776a.
fastening, 273a, 516a, 563b, 600b.
fat, 102a, 113a, 128a b, 140a b, 189a, 260a, 315a, 542a, 550a, 824b, 828a, 913a, 914b; goose fat, 758b.
fat, to be, 772b; to put on, 702b.
fate, 595a, 722b, 724a.
Fate, 326b, 724a.
father, 5a, 19b, 98a, 143b, 832b; divine, 402a; of mankind, 98a.
Father-gods, 402a, 832b.
father-in-law, 739a; of the king, 98a, 402a; of the god, 98a, 402a.
fatigue, 142a, 296b, 644b, 802a.
fatten, 757b; birds, 593b; geese and cattle, 185a.
fattened, 773b; geese, 914b.
fault, 89b, 143b, 165b, 226a, 328a, 367a, 595a.
faultless, 340a, 732b.
favour, 219a, 283a, 347a, 508a, 528a; by favour, 370b; mark of, 508b; to show, 508a, 813a; unjustly, 437a.

favoured one, 508b.
favourite, 153a, 561b.
Fayyûm, 816b; Osiris of the, 104a.
fealty, 50a.
fear, 34a, 445a, 452a, 473b, 479b, 480a, 490b, 499b, 507a, 588a, 589a, 609b, 636a, 678ab, 679a, 887a, 898b.
fearful, 108a, 905b.
fearless, 193b.
feast, 287a, 449b, 474a; to keep the, 474a.
feast-day, 451a.
feather, 311b, 352b, 607b, 733a; of goose and hawk, 733b; of south, 733b; of Thoth, 733b; pair of feathers, 733b.
feather crown, 319a.
feathered headdress, 528a.
fecundate, 387a, 629b.
fed, 394a.
fee, 90a.
feeble, 22a, 78a, 149a, 152b, 207b, 225b, 226a, 227a, 260b, 574a, 587a, 661a, 771b, 802a, 898b.
feebleness, 226a, 874a, 898b.
feed, 77b, 139b, 166b, 179a, 213b, 261b, 590a, 592b, 601a, 606b, 607a, 632a, 645a, 677a, 678a, 696a, 717b, 772b; feed on, 186a.
feel, 527a.
feeling, 783b.
feet (see also foot), 638a, 807a.
feign, 65b; feign ignorance, 546a.
Fekhti, 261b.
feldspar, 150b.
felicity, 214b.
fell a tree, 338a, 894a.
fellow, 71b, 277b, 603a, 674a.
fellow worker, 277b.
female, 785b; females (children), 322a.
female spirit, 24a.
fen district, 103b.
fen man, 103b.
fence, 380b.
Fenkhu, 150b, 260b; fire of the, 222a.
Fenkhu cakes, 260b.
Fentchi (Thoth), 261a.
Fenti, 260b, 261a.
Fenti-en-Ānkh, 260b.
Fenṭ-ket, etc., 261a.
ferment, 49b, 72b, 115a, 758b.
ferocity, 433b.
ferry, 576b, 704a.
ferry boat, 286a, 295b, 320b, 576b, 814b.
Ferry-god, 267b, 320b, 354b.
ferryman, 267b, 576b, 850a, 895a; craft of, 286b; of truth, 894b.
fertile, 150a, 189b, 593a, 649b, 651a.
fervent, 320a.
festal apparel, 602a.
festival, 74a, 117b, 158b, 161b, 166b, 249b, 268a, 310b, 323b, 346b, 438b, 449b, 462b, 474a, 476b, 525b, 616b, 640a, 675a, 840b; annual, 594a; book of the, 474b; the drunken, 843a; the 15th day, 331a; the great, 474b; hall, 183a; Karnak, 474b; monthly, 40ab, 640ab; half-monthly, 673a; quarter monthly, 881b; of last quarter, 907b; of several gods, 242a; of Khârgah, 175b; of the tail, 714a; of the Two Bulls, 624b; sailing, 752b, 893b; Sixth day, 643b.
festival, to keep the, 438b, 462b, 613b, 615b.
festivity, 474a.
fetter, to, 273a, 313b, 338a, 607b, 643b, 662a, 762b, 763a, 764b, 765a, 769a, 774a, 778a, 883a.
fetter, 11b, 58a, 64ab, 72a, 82b, 91a, 118a, 146a, 156a, 282a, 290b, 292a, 355a, 408b, 479a, 529a, 587a, 593b, 607b, 611b, 631b, 750a, 764b, 766a, 818b, 858a, 883a; of Set, 587a.
fettered, 533a, 680a, 702b.
feud, 459a.
fever, 81a, 443a, 471a, 517a, 531b, 740a; patient, 584b.
few, 379b, 397b, 438a, 659b.
fibre, 573b.
ficus carica, 380a.
field, 1a, 8a, 22a, 27a, 30a, 75a, 100a, 128ab, 195a, 440b, 449b,

457b, 490a, 585b, 667a, 686a, 720a, 767a, 861b, 881b, 882ab; labour, 206b; labourer, 30a, 75a, 76ab, 201a, 489a, 686a; of flax, 8a.
field bread, 686a.
Field-god, 686a.
Field, Holy, 687b.
Field of Eternity, 687a.
Field of Fire, 687b.
Field of Horus, 687a.
Field of Offerings, 687b.
Field of Rā, 687a.
Field of Reeds, 183a, 686b.
Field of the Beetle, 687b.
Field of the Bull, 687b.
Field of the Chief, 687b.
Field of the Gods, 687a.
Field of the Grasshoppers, 687b.
Field of the Ka, 687b.
Field of the Twin Gods, 687a.
field, offering of, 8a; produce, 242b, 451b, 667a; segment of, 464b; service, 742a; woman's, 526b.
fiend, 12b, 64a, 79a, 89b, 97a, 99a, 116a, 208a, 227a, 228a, 377a, 419a, 434ab, 546b, 552a, 600a, 618a, 642a, 676a, 694b, 695b, 708a, 731b, 819a, 820a, 895ab.
fierce, 499a, 510a.
fierce looking, 509ab.
Fierce-mouth, 417a.
fiery, 221a, 390a, 817b.
Fiery-eyed, 295a.
Fiery-eyes, 68a.
Fiery-hands, 190b.
fiery man, 817b.
Fiery Mouth, 817b.
Fiery One, 130b.
Fiery-Soul, 636b.
fifteen, 331a.
fifth, 868b.
fifty, 819a.
fig, 825a, 874a; bundle of, 867a; persea, 725a; syrup, 380a; tree, 380a, 792b, 825a, 867a; wine, 874a.
fight, to, 90b, 285b, 315b, 515b, 611a, 729ab, 731a, 744b, 752a, 757a, 772b.
fight, 75b, 116a, 132a, 154b, 280b, 285b, 292b, 315b, 320ab, 459a, 461b, 467b, 531b, 563b, 626a, 627b, 639b, 661a, 670a, 702b, 704a, 772ab.
fighters, 19b, 132a, 241a, 285b, 286a, 459a, 461b, 468b, 492b, 604a, 639b, 640a, 684a, 703a, 704ab.
Fighters, the, 132b.
Fighter-gods, the Two, 429b, 577b.
fighting, 461b, 735b; dogs, 221a; gods, 241b; men, 903a.
Fighting Faces, 19b, 132b.
figure, 19a, 69a, 222b, 542a, 557b, 572a, 577a, 602a, 604b, 609a, 616a, 624b, 675b, 752b; magical, 823a; of animal, 135b; sacred, 138a.
figured (of bronze), 619a.
figures, wax, 303b.
filch, 523b.
file, to, 608a.
fill, 316b, 411b, 490a, 607a, 671b, 690a; fill full, 54b, 83a, 602b; fill the bosom, 317a; the ear, 316b; to overflowing, 813a; with food, 696a; with water, 902a.
filled, 316b, 467b, 520a; be filled, 490a; with soul, 38b.
fillet, 228a, 304b, 313b, 319a, 376a, 399b, 450a, 607b, 623b, 658a, 859b, 876b; white, 698b.
fillets (of fish), 187b.
filling, 690a.
filly, 695b.
filth, 9b, 11a, 49b, 113b, 119b, 177b, 227a, 459a, 467a, 469a, 470a, 473a, 476a, 509b, 571ab, 635a, 683a, 708a, 786a.
filthy, 31b, 208a, 470ab; people, 762a.
find, 770a, 807a; a mouth, 807a; find out, 527a.
fine, to, 865b.
fine, 22b; garments, 710b; gold, 370b; linen, 779a.
finest, 461a, 829b.
finger, 104b, 874b, 902b, 905b; of Set, 905b.
fingernails, 523b.

finish, 19a, 129b, 131a, 305b, 306a, 568a, 591a, 626a, 645b, 704b, 773a, 787b, 834a, 878b, 909b, 910a ; of a matter, 703b.
finished, 131b, 787b.
fir-cones, 793a.
fire, 6a, 9b, 14a, 17a, 22b, 49a, 78b, 92a, 110a b, 130a, 146a, 163b, 174a, 182b, 221a b, 222a, 234a, 276a, 284b, 285b, 290a, 310b, 345a, 366b, 367a, 377b, 380c, 387b, 390a, 391a, 392b, 393a, 417a, 429a, 434a b, 439b, 447a, 451b, 452a, 465b, 510a, 517a, 526a, 531b, 538a, 539a, 547a, 588b, 589b, 609b, 611b, 618b, 628a, 631a, 632b, 649a, 653a, 680a, 681a, 695b, 696b, 702a, 709a, 714b, 716a, 724b, 725a, 731b, 740a, 764b, 765a b, 774a, 775b, 795a, 803a, 817b, 823a, 832a, 845a b, 864b, 897b, 900b, 911b, 915a ; a consuming, 168b ; divine, 163b; lake of, 71b, 687a ; liquid, 400a ; place of, 80b ; region of, 16a ; sacred, 373a ; slow, 373a ; to light a, 247b, 628a, 676b, 708a, 709a, 712b ; to set on, 648a.
fire altar, 135a, 147b, 179b, 286a.
fire bringer, 56b.
fire drill, 590a, 850a.
fire flash, 267b.
fire festival, 147b.
Fire-god, 10a b, 49a, 70b, 166b, 186a ; gods of Ṭuat, 434b.
Fire-goddess, 163b, 393a, 428a.
firelight, 695b.
fireman, 70b.
fire offering, 10a, 135a, 196a, 217b, 594a, 639a, 775b.
fire pits, the Five, 465a.
fireplace, 135a, 147b, 290a, 535b.
fire stand, 137a.
fire stick, 56b, 222a, 238a, 590a, 894a.
firewood, 566b, 590a.
firm, 128a b, 164a, 297a, 680b, 893b, 914b ; to make, 49b.
firm-handed, 193b.
first, 316a, 460a b, 473b, 554a, 562a, 597b, 734b, 828b ; to be, 381a.
firstborn, 107a, 160b, 584a, 601b, 642b, 672a, 723a ; of Osiris, 216a.
first fruits, 829a.
First Image, 826b.
First Lady, 829b.
firstling, 160b.
first part, 460b.
fish, to, 463a, 465a, 475a, 484a.
fish, 5a b, 13a, 25a, 30b, 32a, 115a, 128a, 148a, 154b, 176b, 179a, 203a 207a, 214b, 220b, 225b, 226b, 233a, 236b, 262b, 318a, 376b, 419a b, 423b, 424 , 428b, 433a, 437b, 440b, 462b, 475b, 536b, 537b, 542a, 549b, 550b, 569b, 592b, 661b, 624a, 651a, 737b, 757a, 767a, 835b, 837a, 902b, 914b ; dead, 273b ; fighting, 132b ; latus, 152a ; mythological, 19b, 141b ; pilot of Rā, 20a ; red, 192b ; spotted, 58b ; voracious, 832a.
Fish-city, 424b.
fisherman, 142b, 148b, 178b, 179a, 318a, 463b, 514b, 535b, 538b, 897b.
Fish-god, 424b, 431a, 699b.
fishing, festivals of, 179a; net, 745b ; tackle, 931a.
fish line, 421b.
fish offal, 594a.
fish pond, 76a, 170b, 758a, 812a.
fish pool, 814b.
fish scales, 394b.
fish spawn, 21b, 606b, 657b, 741a.
fish tanks, 720a, 766b.
fist, 6a, 120a, 545a.
fistful, 545a.
fistula, 736a.
fitting, 722b, 819b, 837a ; order, 193a.
fittingly, 332a.
fittings, 119a.
five, 868b.
Five Days, the epagomenal, 451a.
fix, 602a, 722b ; the attention, 274a ; the eyes, 826a.
fixed, 1b, 296b.
flabby, 152b.

flag, 523b, 594b, 647b ; coloured, 69b.
flagbearer, 851b.
flagstaff, 583b, 675b.
flail, 139b, 387a, 449b.
flame, 6a, 9b, 14a, 17a, 49a, 63b, 92a, 110ab, 130a, 131a, 146a, 174a, 182b, 221ab, 222a, 234a, 276a, 284b, 285b, 300b, 345a, 366b, 367a, 377b, 380a, 387b, 390a, 391a, 392b, 393a, 419a, 429a, 434ab, 439b, 445a, 451b, 452a, 465b, 510a, 526a, 538a, 539a, 589b, 609b, 611b, 628a, 631a, 632b, 649a, 653a, 664b, 680a, 681a, 709a, 716a, 725a, 740a, 775b, 798a, 817b, 832a, 841a, 845b, 846b, 897b ; divine, 49a ; flame up, 159a, 221b, 367a ; Island of, 16b.
Flame-god, 241b.
Flame-goddess, 23a.
flamer, 367a, 393a.
Flaming-Eye, 24b.
flap the wings, 797b.
flare up, 191a.
flash, lightning, 842a.
flask, 282b, 462b.
flat, river, 272b.
flat (transport), 764a.
flat drum, 875b.
flatter, 224b, 643b, 650b, 804a.
flattery, 15a, 650b.
flatulence, 732a, 813b.
flax, 17a, 110b, 136a, 155a, 252a, 284b, 319a, 484b, 589a, 661a ; hot-presser of, 247b.
flax cloth, 234b.
flax fields, 8a.
flea, 234b, 235a.
flee, 14b, 43b, 44a, 216b, 220a, 255b, 275a, 420ab, 481a, 519b, 612b, 633b, 688a, 695b, 750b, 857b, 864b ; flee in terror, 810a.
fleet, 314b ; inspector of, 642b.
flesh, 30a, 31a, 34a, 43a, 75b, 76a, 120b, 602a, 652b, 746a ; divine, 33a, 402b, 466a.
flesh and bone, 28a, 33a, 113b, 154b.
flesh of Osiris, 43a ; of Rā, 43a ; of Tem, 43a.
flesh food, 120b.
flexible, 256b.
flier, 118ab.
flight, 105b, 156b, 258a, 263b, 420a, 462b, 465b, 633b, 688a, 866a ; put to, 658a ; take to, 255b.
flint, 218a, 630b, 777b, 888a ; knives, 842a.
Flint-eyes, 68a.
float, 374a.
flock, 18a, 114b, 299a.
flood, to, 12a, 22a, 213a, 368b, 544b, 602b, 626b, 644a, 671b, 843a.
flood, 12a, 27b, 31b, 35b, 36a, 49b, 95b, 96a, 97b, 142b, 174b, 195b, 203a, 211a, 212b, 253b, 293a, 297b, 307b, 370b, 459b, 475b, 589a, 607a, 611b, 612b, 653b, 806b, 807a, 814a ; new, 349a ; rising, 370b.
Flood, the, 317b.
flooded, 213a.
flooding, 602b.
floor, 83a ; of chariot, 246a.
floral crowns, 275a.
flour, 32b, 356b, 411a, 704a ; fine, 395b, 853a ; fine wheaten, 771b ; offerings of, 56b.
flour of dates, 56b.
flour of millet, 223b.
flourish, 22a, 77b, 110a, 147a, 148b, 150a, 175a, 224b, 282b, 421b, 436b, 680b ; to make, 649b.
flourish a knife or stick, 17a, 394b.
flourishing, 148b, 193a, 422a, 423a.
flout, 334b.
flow, 32b, 69a, 97b, 223a, 224b, 293a, 329b, 400a, 541a, 697b, 736a, 793b ; flow away, 157a, 343b ; of poison, 736a ; of water, 725b ; flow out, 889a ; flow quickly, 9b.
flower, 10b, 54b, 55a, 105a, 126b, 146a, 151b, 167b, 179a, 192b, 209a, 216a, 226b, 243b, 372b, 374b, 383b, 384b, 385b, 423b, 464a, 467a, 472b, 487b, 500a, 531b, 645a, 721a, 722b, 750b, 900a, 903b, 905a.

flower basket, 248a.
flower for a wreath, 126b, 275a.
flowers, of heaven, 8b, 77b ; of the south, 388a ; of speech, 667a.
flower stand, 248a.
flowering shrub, 721b.
flowing, 541a, 708b.
fluid, 400a ; of life, 193a, 585b.
flute, 147a, 152a, 273b, 594a, 654a.
flutter, 5b, 386b, 393b, 549a, 604a.
flux, 138b, 387a, 604b.
fly, 111a, 118a, 119b, 465b, 472b, 480a, 552a.
fly, to, 42a, 118b, 135a, 136a, 203a, 230a, 234b, 235a, 462ab, 498b, 532a, 645a ; fly away, 541a ; into the air, 824b ; into a rage, 849a ; to make, 661b ; over, 552b ; through veins, 381a.
fly flapper, 318b, 537b.
fly whisk, 647b.
foal, 323a, 705a.
foam, 7b, 629a, 738b.
fodder, 49a, 532a, 709b, 711a.
foe, 27b, 101b, 227a, 228a, 285b, 289b, 302a, 329ab, 345b, 369b, 434ab, 545b, 546b, 561a, 574b, 636a, 657a, 676a, 740a, 817b, 895b.
foetid, 822b.
foetor, 294b, 553a.
fog, 96a.
fold (of flock), 813a.
fold, 286b ; in the arms, 616b, 693a ; the wings, 616b.
folds of serpent, 763a.
foliage, 34a, 90a, 146a, 167a, 343a, 600b, 631a, 669a, 733a, 745b, 802b, 806b, 897a, 905a, 911a.
folk, 170a, 435b, 436b, 465b, 525a, 583b, 815b, 880a ; aged, 17b ; young, 898a.
follow, 245b, 467b, 568a, 675b, 742a ; about, 246b ; a road, 891b ; closely, 338a ; to make, 623a.
follower, 45b, 293a, 457b, 567b, 742a.
Followers of Ḥāp, Hathor, Horus, Rā, 743a.
following, 742a ; to be in the, 164b.
folly, 140a, 180a, 419b, 648a; to commit, 369b.
food, 3b, 8a, 28a, 43a, 49a, 72b, 77a, 91b, 119b, 120b, 126ab, 134b, 137a, 138a, 139b, 140a, 142a, 148a, 168b, 179a, 185b, 186a, 202a, 230b, 234a, 247b, 252a, 253a, 255b, 259b, 261b, 262b, 283b, 286b, 323b, 369a, 433a, 450a, 468a, 469a, 525a, 528b, 532a, 538a, 606b, 612b, 624a, 632a, 676a, 677a, 717b, 722b, 725b, 734a, 735a, 747a, 761b, 762a, 730b, 783b, 822b, 832a, 833a, 884b, 904a, 908a, 915b ; celestial, 906b ; cooked, 236a ; daily food, 278b, 663a ; mixed, 885b, 887b ; for journey, 446b ; roasted, 906a.
Food-gods, 71a.
food offering, 735a.
foodstuff, 566b.
fool, 340b, 419b, 528a, 546a ; to play the, 546a.
foolish, 180a, 431a, 649b, 652b.
foolish man, 640a.
foot (see also feet), 156b, 233a, 435a ; ring for, 302b.
footboard, 253b.
foot cases, 106b.
footman, 255b.
footsoldier, 6a, 255b.
footstep, 873b, 891b.
footstool, 253b, 443a, 452ab, 786b.
for, 56a, 339a, 492b, 536a, 545a.
for ever, 339ab, 415a, 450a, 787b.
for the sake of, 30b.
for why, 77a.
forage, 101a.
forager, 101a.
forbear, 830a, 909a.
forbearing, 180b.
force, to, 201a, 292b, 521a ; a door, 219b, 650a; a passage, 480b ; a way, 20a, 117b, 158b, 201a, 347b ; open, 539a, 592a ; a woman, 571b, 797a ; to use, 867a.
force, 388b, 401b, 528b, 738a, 795b, 802b ; forces, 389a, 772a.
ford, 288a, 330a, 569a.

forearm, 105a b, 120a, 326a, 327a, 726a, 736b, 737b.
forecourt, 158b, 419a, 443b.
forefathers, 4b.
forehead, 273a, 416b, 554a, 820a, 841b, 885b.
foreign, 214b, 420b, 911a ; lands, 533b, 534a, 815b ; speech, 335a.
foreigner, 2a, 11b, 90a, 113b, 214b, 260b, 343b, 533b, 541b, 740b, 741a b, 782a, 911a.
fore-knowledge, 896a.
fore-leg, 544a, 559b, 597b.
foreman, 311b, 473b, 562a, 901a.
foremost, 828b.
forepart, 460a, 461a, 554a ; of boat, 461b.
forequarter, 460a.
forerunner, 554a.
foreskins, 764a b.
forest, 755a.
forge, 368b, 484a, 544a, 708a.
forget, 5a, 283b, 315b, 616a, 671b, 692b, 851a ; to make, 602b, 671b.
forgetfulness, 283b.
fork (of the legs), 162a.
form, 19a, 21a, 65a, 69a, 93a, 222b, 321a, 323b, 353b, 366b, 534b, 542a, 542b, 598a, 616a, 624b, 632a, 666b, 670b, 672b, 673a, 688b, 689b, 690a, 698b, 716b, 730a, 761b, 765b, 770b, 771a, 779a b, 804b, 821b, 847a, 853b ; bodily, 466a, 893a ; divine, 402a, 577a ; hidden, 775b.
former, 820a.
formerly, 554a, 580a.
formulae, 22b, 346a, 400b, 623a, 831b, 860b, 862a ; commemorative, 589b ; for spirit-souls, 635a ; magical, 448a, 515a, 745a ; to recite, 22b.
forsake, 528a.
fort, 100a, 297b, 338b, 526a, 557b, 569a, 595a, 633b, 660b, 705b, 706a, 718b, 840a, 903b, 910a.
forthwith, 265b, 495a, 595b.
fortification, 60b, 605b.
fortified, 851a, 852a.
fortify, 54a, 104b, 690a, 772a, 910a.
fortress, 60b, 104b, 166a, 290a, 297b, 389a, 569a, 650b, 705b, 706a, 851a, 878b, 903b.
Fortress of the Father, 878b.
fortunate, 595a.
fortune, 693b, 724a ; good, 617a.
forty, 480b.
fosterer, 809b.
foster mother, 428a.
foul, 143a, 145b, 343b, 382b, 383a, 470a, 537b, 644a, 725b, 726a, 762a, 787a, 883a.
Foul-Face, 459b.
found, 609b, 629a, 678a b, 778a, 807a, 810a, 811b, 812a, 884a.
foundation, 207a, 325b, 602a, 605a, 609a b, 670b, 675b ; to lay a, 609a.
founded, 189b.
founder, 678b ; of the earth, 812a.
foundry, 312a, 323b, 325a, 544a.
foundryman, 354a.
fountain, 110a, 123b, 233a, 280a, 490b, 579a, 724b, 863a.
four, 44a, 258a, 263a.
fourfold, 548b ; garment, 44a.
four-horned, 398a.
four-legged, 255b.
fourth, 263a.
fowl, 186b, 230a, 235a, 573a, 848b.
fowler, 178b, 463a b, 475a, 618a, 695a, 769a ; chief, 475a.
fractions, mark of, 415a.
fragment, 252a, 392b, 772b.
frame, 206b, 859b ; framed, 324b.
framework, 835b, 859b.
frankincense, 348b, 377b, 378a.
fraternize, 89b.
fraud, 14b, 472b, 488b, 530a, 540a, 572a, 777a, 790a.
free, to free, 369b, 472a, 591a, 621a, 622b, 727a.
free born, 591a.
freedom, 370a.
freeman, 646a.
freight, 594a.
frenzy, prophetic, 530a, 647b.
frequenters, 138b.
frequently, 595b.
fresh, 150a.

fretwork, 304b.
friend, 69b, 285a, 310a, 366b, 442a, 449b, 540a, 548a, 551a, 552a, 554a, 577b, 636a, 809b; intimate, 430a; to be, 520b, 539b, 674b; to behave as a, 551b.
"Friendlies," 386a.
friendship, 552a, 624b.
fright, 395a, 499b, 839a.
frighten, 393b, 395a, 420a, 499a, 577a, 693b, 712b, 866b.
frightening, 887b.
fringe, 631a.
frisk, 854a, 858a.
frizz the hair, 849b.
frizzle, 550b.
frog, 118a, 764a, 775b, 789a.
Frog-goddess, 80b, 514a.
from, 65a, 100b, 264a, 279b, 414a, 560a; from —— to, 851b.
from of old, 909a.
from this day, 100b.
front, 220a, 460a, 461a, 494b, 545a, 554a, 580a, 878b, 879a; to be in, 562a; put in, 693b.
frontier, 158a, 488a, 820b, 844b, 852a; guard of, 246b; to cross, 439a.
frontier stones, 81b.
Front-land (South), 575b.
froth, 7b, 509b, 738b, 820b; of beer, 629a.
fruit, 49b, 60a, 61a, 72a, 195a, 201b, 233b, 242b, 252a, 273b, 380b, 411b, 427a, 470b, 547a, 563b, 586a, 621b, 641a, 688b, 689a, 745b, 746b, 747a, 753a, 762a, 767a, 785b, 788a, 796b, 798a, 804a, 814b, 827b, 833a, 839b, 842a, 845b, 876b, 890b, 900a; Sûdânî, 728b; cake, 817a; of sycamore fig, 797b; tree, 49b, 63a, 269b, 797b, 892a.
fruit-bearing trees, 890b.
fry, 550b.
Fṭu-ḥeru, 263b.
fuel, 702a, 902b.
fugitives, 9b, 156b, 215b, 220a, 255b, 618a.
fulfil, 129b.
full, 2b, 316b, 489b, 520a, 587b, 634b, 834a.
fuller, 318a, 435a.
fullers' earth, 866b.
fulling, 726b.
full moon, 29b.
fullness, 314b, 316b, 545a, 634b, 647a.
fume, 131a, 516b.
functions, 486b, 487a.
fundament, 244a.
funeral, 301a, 772a, 860a.
fur, 631a.
furious, 615b, 689b, 774b.
furl, 735b; a sail, 725b.
furnace, 135a, 464a, 499b, 506b, 535b, 708a, 775b, 786b, 803a, 819ab, 840a, 841b, 885b.
furnaces, the Five of the Ṭuat, 465a.
furnish, 92a, 810a, 811b, 904a; furnished, 118b.
furnishing, 119a, 282b, 812a.
furniture, 43a, 79b, 90a, 136a, 229a, 234a, 462b, 525a, 640a, 715a, 789b, 812a, 876a.
furrow, 191a.
further, 809b.
fury, 395a, 536b, 908a.
futurity, 265b.
"fuzzy-wuzzies," 368a.

G.

Ga àsut, 800b.
Gaf, 802b.
gag, 729b; gags of leather, 729b.
Gagait, 801a.
Gai, 801a.
gain the mastery, 531a, 690b.
gainsay, 116b, 122b; gainsaid, 34a.
Gait, 801a.
gait, 373b.
gale, 174a, 683a, 902a.
gall, 1b, 82b, 689b.
gall bladder, 9b.
gall duct, 9b.
gallop, 852b.
gamble, 858a.
game, 25b, 221a; from the desert, 114b.

ganders, 848a.
gang, 599b.
gang of five, 864a.
gang of labourers, 82a, 585b.
ganger, 495a.
gangrene, 160a, 217a.
gangway plank, 157a.
gap, 252b.
Gaqit, 804a.
garb, 169b.
garden, 19b, 122a, 146a, 148b, 192b, 240a, 499b, 529b, 559a b, 721b, 722a, 723a, 725a, 745b, 749a, 770a, 788b, 789a, 808a, 891b, 905a; water-garden, 720a.
gardener, 559a, 788b, 789a, 789b ; date tree gardener, 269b.
gardeners, the twelve, 69b.
garden house, 700b.
garden land, 558b, 614b.
garden plants, 722a, 808a.
garden stuff, 709b.
garden tent, 475a.
garden walk, 144b.
garland, 146b, 169a, 192b, 275a, 279a, 287a, 319a, 602b, 701b, 810b ; of triumph, 271b ; to put on, 701a.
garlic, 473b, 822b.
garment, 14a, 34b, 49b, 62a, 92b, 95b, 103b, 104a, 110a, 119a, 121b, 139a, 164a, 169b, 170a, 174b, 205a, 230a, 236a, 252b, 260a, 262b, 282b, 289b, 300a, 329a, 393b, 407b, 424b, 440b, 458b, 476b, 483b, 532b, 579b, 582a, 591b, 606a, 618b, 624a, 629b, 635a, 641a, 649b, 652a, 672a, 678a, 695b, 711a, 711b, 712b, 714a, 718a, 750b, 755a, 757a, 768a, 773b, 776a, 791b, 818b, 840a, 864a, 867a, 868a, 870a, 875b, 879a, 895b, 897a, 904b ; funerary, 832b ; linen, 615b ; night, 667a ; nobleman's, 646a ; skin, 200b ; white, 698b ; whole, 896b.
garrison, 55b, 557b.
garrulous, 335a.
gash, 561a, 730a, 867b.
Gasut, 803b.
Gaṭa, 804a.
gate, 130b, 275a, 371b, 416a, 419b, 443b, 658b, 659a, 660b, 723b, 819a ; at Philae, 108b ; title of king, 659a ; a tomb, 819a.
Gates, keeper of the Two, 70a.
Gates of hell, horizon, palace, 655a.
gate-house, 221b.
gatekeepers, 71b.
gate-sockets, 113a.
gate-tower, 275a, 658b.
gateway, 130b, 219b ; fortified, 633b.
gather, 575a, 683a, 701b, 710a, 914b ; grapes, 734b ; together, 64a, 613b, 625a, 628b, 639a, 659b, 664b, 683a, 826a b, 878b.
gathering, 600b, 639a ; of people, 848a.
gaze, to, 158b ; intently, 826a.
gazelle, 33b, 40a, 129a, 268a, 270a, 441b, 442b, 443b, 777b, 803b, 812b ; white, 275b ; young, 426b ; the Four, 439b.
Gazelle-god, 122b, 555a.
gazelle-herd, 586b.
Geb, god, 800b, 805b, 831a, 848b ; a form of Rā, a stake, an ithyphallic god, 806a ; head of the gods, 806a.
Geb, the Four Sons of, 263b.
Geb, god of celestial ocean, 806a.
Geb, Hall of, 183a,
Geb in Shentch, 806a.
Geb (Nile), 806a.
Geb-qenbti, 806a.
Geb, soul of, 200a, 669a.
Geb-ur (Horus), 806a.
Gebb, 805b.
Gebel Barkal, 869b.
Gebel Zâbarah, 154b.
Gebi, 806a.
Gebit, 806a.
geese, 14b, 829b ; drawn, 187b ; fattened, 185a, 415b ; gall of, 689b ; mixed food for, 885b, 887b.
Gefut, 807a.
Geḥsit, 812b.
gem, 344b, 394b, 521b.
Gem-ḥesu, 807b.
Gemi, 807b.

Gemu-ḥeru, 807b.
Gemut, 807b.
general, 247a, 312a, 638a, 860ab.
generation, 284a, 331b ; first, 570a.
generation-god, 189a.
generations of men, 898a.
generator, 462b.
generous, 305a.
genetrix, 321a.
Gengen-ur, 809a.
Gen-ḥesu, 809a.
genital organs, 848a.
genitals, 481b.
genitive, mark of, 339a, 344b, 348a, 349a.
genius, 782b.
gentle, 597b, 598a, 809a ; of winds, 517b.
gentleman, 538b, 591a, 646a, 737a ; son of a, 584b.
gentleness, 273b, 680b.
gentlewoman, 422b, 737a.
gently, to act, 796b.
genuine, 271a.
genuineness, 270b.
Genur, god, 809a.
Gen-urit, 809a.
geometry, term used in, 464b.
Gerbatus, 810b.
Gerḥ, 811a.
Gerḥit, 811a.
germ, 651b.
Gersi, 811b.
Gerteka, 810a.
Gerṭes, 810a.
Gesi, 813b.
Geseptiu, 813b.
Geshi, 814b.
Gestȧ, 814a.
Getȧ, 814b.
get back, 43b.
get round, 30a.
get up, 258a ; get up early, 562b.
giant, 389a.
Giant (Orion), 389a.
gift, 3a, 4a, 5b, 56b, 117a, 148a, 191a, 204b, 206b, 262a, 270b, 283b, 286b, 304a, 343a, 438a, 487a, 491b, 508a, 514b, 518a, 521b, 544a, 813b, 865a, 868a, 884b.
gills of fish, 572b, 907a.
Gilukhipa, 792b.
giraffe, 282a, 592a, 610b.
gird, 574b ; gird on, 169a, 701a ; gird round, 64a; girded, 451b.
girdle, 15b, 75b, 113a, 131b, 164a, 217a, 282b, 304b, 313b, 319a, 324a, 338b, 395b, 419b, 540a, 625a, 631a, 654b, 676b, 701b, 715a, 862b, 911a.
girl, 32b, 102a, 110b, 141b, 303a, 426b, 471b, 545b, 573b, 584a, 798b; little, 750a.
girt, 253a.
give ! 50b, 279b.
give, 102b, 115a, 139b, 270b, 436b, 562a, 654a, 815a, 840b, 864a, 865a ; a command, 57a ; birth, 55a, 89b, 221b, 233b, 387b, ground, 889a; light, 204b, 212b ; make to, 681b ; order, 191b ; thanks, 403a ; the hand, 865b ; the lie to, 437a.
give quarter, 9a.
give way, 889a, 891a.
given, 436b, 774b.
giver, 865a, 868a ; of winds, 437a.
glad, to be, 74b, 145a, 168a, 412a, 433a, 466b, 499a, 517b, 689a, 833b ; to make, 592b, 613b, 683a.
gladden, 635b, 679b, 682b.
gladness, 3a, 37b, 74a, 77b, 160b, 168a, 260a, 310b, 326a, 426b, 433a, 444a, 466b, 858b.
glance, 68a, 123a, 254a, 357a, 808a, 891a ; evil, 807a ; to shoot a, 708b.
gland, 201b ; of throat, 110a.
glaucoma, 736b.
gleam, 681b.
gleanings, 596a.
glede, 909b, 910ab.
glib, 533a.
glide, 136a, 370b.
glimpse, 254a.
glitter, 820b, 858b.
globule, 234b, 237a, 256b, 650a, 880b.
gloom, 600b, 795b, 798a.
gloomy, 789a.
gloomy-faced, 798b.
glorification, 635a, 680a.

glorify, 17a, 589b, 635a, 710a.
glorifyings, 824a.
glorious, 22b, 245a, 737a ; deeds, 23a.
glory, 3b, 245a, 724a, 822b, 912a ; glory be to ! 15a.
glow, 436b, 817b, 896b.
glue, 32b.
glutted, 634b.
glutton, 5b, 111a, 120a, 626b, 705a.
gluttonous, 626b.
gluttony, 5b, 119b.
gnat (mosquito ?), 550a, 552a, 900a.
gnaw, 168b, 169b, 185b, 248a, 731a, 882b.
go, 8a, 9a, 11b, 30a, 31a, 74b, 118b, 193b, 216b, 235b, 272b, 287a, 289b, 324b, 330a, 346a, 377b, 429a, 451b, 541a, 624b, 632a, 633a, 637a, 640b, 647a, 654a, 716b, 723a, 725a, 737b, 739a, 740b.
go about, 195a, 232a, 288b, 351b, 376b, 415b, 417a, 478a, 875a.
go against, 145a.
go astray, 839a.
go away, 144a, 157b, 187b, 240a, 417a, 420a, 449b, 587b, 633a.
go back, 28b, 457b, 569b, 618a ; make to, 684a, 694b.
go beyond, 604a.
go down, 444b, 528b, 633a ; make to, 682a.
go forth, 193b, 240a.
go forward, 593b.
go in, 118b, 138a b, 576a ; in front, 381a.
go off, 841a.
go on, 196b, 216b ; a journey, 32a.
go out, 118b, 240a ; of the way, 883a.
go round, 216a, 246a b, 428a, 743b, 780a ; to make to, 662b, 680a.
go softly, 449b.
go through, 567b.
go to waste, 439b.
go up, 7a, 28a, 129a, 449b.
goad, 40a, 386b, 516b, 680a, 792a.
goats, 18a, 39a, 107a, 114a, 126a, 129a, 142a, 154b, 170a, 299a, 624b, 762a, 786a, 792a, 796a, 897b ; wild, 514b.
goat hide, 140a,
God, 546a, 401a.
god, 170b, 401a, 408b ; an everlasting, 78b ; composite, 109a ; ears of the, 126b.
god, dance of the, 38b.
god, dog-faced, 121a, 406a.
god, field of the, 403a.
god, four-headed ram, 494a.
god, great, 108b.
god, house of the, 402b.
god, letter of, 108b.
god, mouth of the, 831a
god of olden time, 830a.
God One, 403b.
god, the limitless, 413a.
god, the old, 17b.
god, the primeval, 231a.
god, way of the, 144b.
god, young, 76b, 749b.
goddess, 182a, 401b, 408b, 486a, 494a, 690b, 737a, 826a.
goddess, the Hittite, 25b, 127b, the nude or Syrian, 781b, 794b ; the Two Nursing Goddesses, 551b.
gods, 409b.
gods of the Boat of Earth, 405b.
gods of the Circles, 407a.
gods of earth, 407a.
gods of heaven, earth, Ṭuat and Nile, 405b.
gods of the east, 405a.
gods of the exits, 406a.
gods of the funerary mountain, 407a.
gods of the Great Bear, 406a.
gods of the Great House, 406a.
gods of Ḥet-Benben, 406b.
gods of the horizon, 405a.
gods of the House of Fire, 406a.
gods of the Lake of Fire, 405b.
gods of Meḥen, 405b.
gods of the months, 40b.
gods of Nekhen, 406a.
gods of the Nile Caverns, 407a.
gods of the nomes, 406b.
gods of the North, 406b.
gods of 1,000 years, 404a.

gods of one (i.e., the same) shrine, 237b, 588b, 789b.
gods of Osiris, 407a.
gods of Pe, 406a.
gods of roads, 406a.
gods of Saa-Set, 405b.
gods of Seti, 407b.
gods of slaughter, 71b, 117b.
gods of the shrine of Osiris, 405b, 406a.
gods of Sinai, 406b.
gods of the South, 406b.
gods of towns, 406b.
gods of the train of Osiris, 405b.
gods of the Ṭuat, 406b, 407a.
gods of the West, 406b.
gods, the ancestor, 830b.
gods, the avenging, 669a.
gods, the Eight of Khast, 407a.
gods, the endowed, 407a.
gods, the false, 407b.
gods, the father, 406a.
gods, the Four, Seven, Eight and Nine, 404b.
gods, the Forty-two, 405a.
gods, the gracious, 20b.
gods, the groups (tetrads) of, 263ab.
gods, the guides of Ṭuat, 407a.
gods, the little (false), 406b; the Nine Little, 405a.
gods, the lesser, 750a.
gods, the mummied, 97a.
gods, the Nine, 250b, 405a.
gods, the old, 17b.
gods, the primeval, 406a.
gods, the senior, 407a.
gods, the Seven, 406b; the Seven Wise, 896a.
gods, the Twelve Fetterers of Āapep, 407a.
gods, the twin, 404a.
gods, the Two and Three Companies of, 250b, 405a.
gods, the Two Devourers, 404b.
gods, the Two Lion-, 404a.
gods, the Warrior, 26a.
gods who are on pedestals, 405a.
gods who follow their doubles, 407a.
gods who rejoin limbs, 405a.
gods who weep not, 78b.
gods who weigh, 406b.
God-city, 407b.
God-house, 239a.
goers, 31a, 723a, 739a.
going, 31a, 105b, 723a, 739b; back, 236b; in and out, 138a.
gold, 635b.
gold, fine, 353a, 781b, 791a.
gold, green, 353a.
gold, mountain, 353a.
gold, river, 353a.
gold, thrice refined, 353a.
gold, to work in, 353b.
gold, water, 353a.
gold, white, 353a, 903a.
gold of praise, 353a.
gold of valour, 353a.
gold-beaters, 140b.
gold carriers, 763a.
golden, 353a.
Golden Lady, 353b.
Golden One (Rā), 353b.
gold foundry, 353b.
gold house, 238b.
goldsmiths, 354a; craft of, 354a; quarter of the, 455a; shop of, 455a.
goldwashers, 28a.
gold worker, 354a.
gold workshops, 239a.
good! 296a.
good, 22b, 211a, 304a, 305a, 342b, 346b, 370b, 570b.
good, doubly, 370b.
good, to do, 517b, 635a; to make good, 129b.
Good Being, 84a, 371b.
good-hearted, 20b, 371a.
good luck, 724a.
goodness, 343b.
goods, 77a, 91b, 164b, 395b, 396b, 487a, 525a, 561a.
good, 580b, 724b, 789b.
Good Shepherd, 586b.
goose, 5b, 42b, 43a, 119a, 163b, 223a, 256b, 324a, 415b, 462b, 478a, 531a, 532b, 541b, 568a, 583b, 588b, 602a, 610b, 611a, 633a, 670b, 680a, 790b, 802b, 805b, 806b, 825b, 840b, 848a, 854b, 858a, 884ab, 885b; cry of, 658b; egg of, 119b.
goose, green, 5b, 151a.
goose, white, 523b.

goose-cakes, 730b.
gooseflesh, 898b.
goose food, 126b.
Goose-god, 12b, 98b, 358a, 393a, 611a, 628b, 768a, 809a, 824b.
Goose-goddess, 398a, 809a.
goose herd, 301b.
Goose-lake, 350a.
goose pens, 31a, 778a.
goose pond, 449b.
gore, 116a, 443a, 445b, 447b, 889a b.
gorge, 207a.
gorgeous, 737a.
goslings, 671b.
gossip, 335b, 478b, 852b, 863a.
gourd, 803a.
govern, 25b, 512b, 622b, 699a, 753b, 845a.
government, 378b, 447b, 512b.
governor, 108a, 128b, 145b, 147a, 331b, 433b, 494a, 513a, 562a, 595b, 828b ; of priests, 848b.
Governor of the North, 848b.
Governor of the South, 848b.
Governor of the Two Lands, 848b.
Governor-General of Egypt, 848b.
Governor-in-Chief, 846b.
governorship, 679b.
grace, 49b, 528a.
graceful, 660a, 547b.
gracefulness, 49b.
gracious, 20b, 50a, 123a, 211a, 217b, 304a, 346b, 370b, 449a b, 517b, 597b, 646b, 665a, 809a.
graciousness, 20b, 49b, 346b, 588b ; to show, 643a.
grain, 34a, 36a, 50b, 69b, 74b, 77b, 117a, 126a b, 129b, 139b, 142a, 143b, 148a, 157b, 164a, 179a b, 186a, 187b, 188b, 204a, 209a, 210b, 215a, 226b, 234a, 242b, 245b, 279a, 284b, 292a, 307a, 324a, 329a, 343b, 344a, 368b, 369a, 372b, 386b, 390b, 393a, 413a, 421a, 431b, 465b, 466a, 468a, 470b, 472b, 482b, 488a, 529a, 533a, 566b, 592a, 611a, 612b, 616a, 621b, 637b, 648b, 654b, 672b, 690a, 697b, 701a, 747a, 750b, 781a, 788b, 827b, 839b, 845b, 849b, 850b, 877b, 885b, 890b, 910b; boiled, 730b ; crushed, 411a ; for beer, 243a ; for cakes, 243a ; heap of, 567a.
grain, black, 243a.
grain, golden and light, 243a, 353a.
grain, green, 697b.
grain, red, 243a.
grain, white, 523b, 697b, 751a.
Grain-god, 117a, 368b, 369a ; birth of the, 321b.
grain measure, 33b.
grain plant, 146b, 788a.
grain store, 567a.
grain, to measure, 513b.
grain, to tread in, 756b.
granary, 81b, 180b, 286b, 369a, 723a, 746b, 747a.
granary men, 243a.
grand, 108a, 737a.
grandfather, 833a.
grandmother, 294b ; great-grand-mother, 294b.
grandparents, 4b.
grandson, 584a, 749b.
grandsons of Horus, 24b.
grange, 767a.
granite, 62b.
granite, black, 62b.
granite, red, 276b.
grant, 102b, 260a.
grant ! 50b, 279b.
granule, 248b.
grape, grapes, 21a, 72a, 124a, 536b, 915a ; seeds, 72a.
grapes, dried, 698b.
grasp, 6a, 20a, 64b, 79a, 102a, 111a, 120a, 131a, 145a, 261b, 266b, 381b, 412b, 459a, 484b, 531a, 545a, 547a, 572b, 614a, 636b, 738a, 738b, 794a, 808a, 849a.
grass, 25a, 135b, 143a, 421a, 550b, 658a, 667a, 709b, 745b, 765b ; coarse, 770a.
grasshopper, 225a, 588b, 608a, 687b.
Grasshopper-city, 588b.
grass land, 77a.

grass ropes, 355a.
grateful (to the senses), 218b.
gratification, 508a.
gratified, 549b.
gratify, 28a, 442a, 592b, 669a, 677a.
grave, 1b, 15b, 28a, 39b, 58b, 134a, 174b, 225b, 239a, 278a, 285a, 371b, 377a, 457a, 561b, 571a, 587a, 598b, 708a, 709a, 729a, 756a, 816a, 914a.
grave of demeanour, 883b.
gravel, 62a, 394a.
graven objects, 849b.
graver, 205b, 223a.
gravid, 849b.
grease, 113a, 128ab, 189a, 315a, 824b, 825a,
grease pot, 582a.
great, 107b, 108a, 170b, 171a, 215a, 342b, 343a, 344a, 347b, 856a ; doubly, 108a ; great-great, 172b ; greater, 170b ; greatest, 830a.
great, to make, 590b.
great man, 170b, 423b, 806b ; great one, 107a.
Great Bear, 326a, 327a, 544a.
Great Bend, 247a.
Great Boat, 895a.
Great Body, 570b.
Great Bread, 138b.
Great Cackler, 800b, 805b.
Great Circuit, 247a.
Great Cooler, 767b.
Great Counting, the, 41a.
Great Door, 107b.
Great Examination, 642b.
Great Field, 686b.
Great Flower (Rā), 388a.
Great Gate, 659a.
Great God, 172a.
Great Green Water, 151a.
Great Hand, 29a, 908b.
Great Heat, festival of, 484b.
Great House (Pharaoh), 238a.
Great Illuminer, 685a.
Great Judge, 588a.
Great Lake, 720b.
Great Leg, 71a.
Great Light, 23a.
Great of Names, 108a.
Great Oasis (see also Khârgah), 148b.
Great One, the, 768b.
Great Place (Heaven), 796.
Great Power (Osiris), 691b.
Great Protectress, 747b.
Great Quaker, 714b.
Great Raiser, 190a.
Great River, 35b.
Great Scales, 285b.
Great Stairs, 436b.
Great Wall of Egypt, 595a.
Great Water, 293b.
greatly, 414a, 470a.
greatness, 34b, 170b.
greatness of eye (i.e., pride), 203b.
Greece, 157b.
greed, 5b, 488b.
greedily, 164a.
greediness, 606b, 608b.
greedy, 111a, 115b, 120a, 411b.
greedy man, 5b, 488b, 608b.
Greek, 157b, 312b, 318b, 463b.
Greek language and writing, 619b.
green, 8b, 75a, 77b, 147a, 148b, 150a, 175a, 195b, 593a, 640b ; to make, 649b, 651a.
green, i.e., new, 188b.
Green-Face, 151b.
Green Field, 686b.
Green Land (Delta), 150a.
green substance, 873a.
green things, 150a, 188b.
greet, 141a, 149b, 186b, 341b, 348b, 354b, 727a, 752a, 791b, 841b, 911b ; greet kindly, 66b.
greeting, 193a ; in a letter, 654a.
grey-haired, 626b, 704b.
grey-haired god, 705a.
greyhound, 862a.
greyness, 704b.
grief, 7b, 8a, 40a, 64b, 74b, 89a, 219b, 290ab, 314b, 319a, 330b, 386b, 459a, 475b, 476a, 605b, 648a, 677a, 755a, 778a, 790b, 803b, 807b, 831a ; cry of, 22a.
grief, to suffer, 64b.
grieve, 6a, 8a, 26a, 314a, 396a, 397b, 464a, 469b, 475b, 606b, 609b, 623b, 642b, 677a.
grievous, 507a, 778b.
grind, 351b, 395b, 589a, 683b, 704a.
grinder, 757a.

grip, 124a, 381b, 610a.
grist, 97a.
groan, 8a, 49a, 136b, 219b, 771a.
groaning, 74b, 225b.
groom, 280b, 283a.
groomed, 423b.
grotto, 775a.
ground, 1a, 3b, 10a, 13b, 16b, 25a, 27a, 30b, 37a, 82b, 83a, 99a, 104b, 118b, 128a, 156b, 201a, 220a, 237a, 247a, 315b, 440b, 537b, 585b, 592a, 609a, 627b, 666a, 675b, 709a, 763b, 764b, 766b, 806a, 815a, 838a, 880b, 896b ; for a camp, 235a ; for recreation, 475b.
ground, high, 215a.
ground produce, 890b.
ground, rising, 559b.
ground, terraced, 421b.
ground, triangular plot of, 664a.
group, 683a, 768a.
grove, 299a, 558b, 559a, 723a, 745b.
grovel, 476a, 878b, 879a.
grow, 90a, 148a, 222a, 421ab, 640b ; of the moon, 107a ; grow large, 171a ; grow old, 387a ; to make, 651a, 680b.
grown up, 344a.
growth, 31a, 148a, 761b.
growthless, 340b.
grumble, 778b.
gryphon, 135a.
guarantee, 32b.
guard, 45a, 83a, 175a, 381a, 351b, 506b, 586b, 648b, 656b, 704a, 746b.
guardian, 230a, 281a, 351b, 386b, 410a, 586b, 746b, 757b, Nubian, 333a.
guess, 328a.
guidance, 622b, 699a ; true, 139a.
guide, 161b, 162a, 228b, 290b, 291a, 314a, 334b, 351b, 512b, 593b, 594a, 622b, 697b, 699a, 737b, 840a, 899a.
Guide of the Two Lands, 666b.
guild of priests, 671a.
guile, 14b, 530a, 572a, 776b, 777a, 790a.
guileless, 732b.
guilt, 895b.
guiltless, 155a.
guilty, 141a.
guitar, 373a.
gulf, 727a, 729b, 832b.
Gulf of Issus, 780b.
Gulf of Ṭuat, 337a.
gullet, 112b, 137a, 492a, 515b, 517a, 521b, 768a.
gum, 249a, 300a, 301b, 302b, 528a, 677a, 771b, 786a ; sweet-smelling, 74b.
gum, Arabian, 771a.
gum, myrrh, 771a.
gunwale, 530a.
gush, 400a.
gut, 223b, 599a.
gut, to, 187b, 223b, 257a.
gymnastic feats, 539a, 549a, 566a.
gymnasts, 539a.
Gynæcopolis, 80b.
Gynæcopolites, 15b.

H.

Ḥa, god, 460a.
Ḥāā-ȧakhu, 466b.
Ḥāā-ȧb-Rā, 466b.
Haȧker, 440a.
Ḥaȧs, 461b.
Ḥāā-tem-sepu-s, 466b.
Ha-Bāru, 440b.
Habemat, 441a.
habit, 595a, 678b, 694a.
habitation, 297ab, 438a, 444a, 775b, 796a.
habitation of Horus and Set, 59a.
hack, 90b, 201a, 220a, 393b, 684a, 711a, 878a, 911b, ; hack at, 263ab ; in pieces 262b, 288b, 888a.
hacking, 201a, 396b.
Hades, 443a.
haematite, 276a.
Ḥafemḥaf, 458a.
Haga-haga-ḥer, 442b.
haggle, 723b, 733a.
Hahaiu, 439b.
Ha-ḥetept, 439b.
Hahuti-am, 442b.
Hai, 439a, 458a.
Ḥai (Bes), 462a.
Ḥai (priest), 462a.

Ḥāi (Rā), 466b.
Ḥaika, 462b.
hail! 15a, 30b, 73b, 438a, 440a, 443b, 444a.
hail, to, 79b, 141a.
hailstorm, 746a.
hair, 7a, 58ab, 76a, 146a, 167a, 260a, 280b, 287a, 600b, 621b, 629b, 631a, 634b, 636b, 648b, 667b, 716b, 733a, 745b, 802b, 808b, 897a.
hair, to tear the, 469b, 606b.
hair, goats', 635b.
hair of the temples, 808b, 827b.
hair ornament, 184b.
hair, tail of, 154b.
hair, white, 754b.
hair cloth, 640a, 701b.
hairdresser, 67a.
hairless, 184b.
hair tree, 566b.
hairy, 174b, 491a, 745b.
hairy hide, 887a.
Ḥait, 462a.
Ḥȧit (Bes), 465b.
Ḥait (Tefuut), 460a.
Ḥait-enth-Ȧāḥ, 462b.
Haker, 442b, 811a.
Haker festival, 66a, 442b.
Ḥakhau, 461a.
Ha-Kheru, 439b.
half, 248b, 812b.
half-way, 248b.
half-witted, 652b.
hall, 34b, 92b, 99a, 130ab, 147a, 148b, 149a, 164a, 174b, 181ab, 183ab, 348b, 438a, 440a, 444a, 451b, 462b, 468a, 475a, 484b, 526ab, 549b, 613a, 614b, 615b, 682b 685b, 719b, 900b.
hall-keeper, 495a.
hall of columns, 58b, 148b.
Hall of Maāti, 32a.
hall of offerings in a tomb, 183a.
hall of temple, 557b.
hall of tomb, 58b, 453a, 465a.
hall, an outside, 183a.
hall with pillars, 151a.
hall with plants, 148b.
halt, 133a, 549a, 670a, 693a.
halting place, 179a.
Ḥām, 467b.
Hamemu, the, 441b.
hamlet, 350b, 787a, 879b.
hammer, 140a, 368b, 468b, 483b, 803a, 842b.
hammer out, 777b.
hammer, Chief of the, 172a.
hamper, wicker, 729a.
Han, 441b.
Ḥanā-ȧru-ḥer-ḥer, 463b.
hand, hands, 1b, 105ab, 752b, 805a, 864a, 908b; by the, 266a; clenched, 545a; hands of enemies cut off, 793a, 864a; the open, 3a, 166b; to clap the, 5a.
Hand, the Great, 29a, 51b.
handbreadth, 752b.
handful, 814b, 894a.
handicraft, 483a.
handicraftsman, 483a.
handle, 106a, 280b, 808a; of quiver, 105b.
handmaiden, 158a, 482b, 525a.
hand scales, 36b.
handwriting, 619a.
Ḥa-nebu, 463b, 619b.
hang, 387b.
hang down, 885b.
hang out, 135a, 143b.
hanging, 387b.
hangings of a shrine, 631a, 715a.
Ḥantus, 465b.
hap, 548b, 595a, 693b; evil, 450a.
Ḥāp, Followers of, 743a.
happen, 137a, 542a, 617a.
happening, 163b, 617a.
happily, 517b.
happiness, 214a, 371a, 595b.
happy, 206a, 282b, 370b, 412a, 517b, 558b, 595a, 610a, 679a, 716b; to make, 601b, 670a, 677a.
Ḥap-seshemu-s, 463a.
Ḥap-tcheser, 463a.
Ḥap-tchesert, 463a.
Ḥap-tchetf, 463a.
Ḥapṭre, 463a.
Ḥapu-ȧntitt, 463a.
Ḥar, 464a.
harbour, 105a, 180b, 300b, 307b, 531b.
harbour master, 108b, 312a.
hard, 134b, 219b, 442a, 507a, 680b, 836a, 899b.

hard of hearing, 49b.
hard to understand, 755b.
hare, 165a, 688b.
Hare-goddess, 165a.
Hȧri-Au, 443b.
ḥarîm, 42a, 79a, 239ab, 550a, 557b; royal, 41b.
ḥarîm woman, 552b, 558a.
harlots, 412a.
harm, 12b, 31b, 115a, 345a, 354b, 524a, 695a.
harm, to do, 1b, 488b, 523b.
Harmakhis, 501b.
harmful, 523b.
Harmes (Roman), 442b.
harness, 64a, 100a, 355a, 532a, 536b, 552a, 286a.
harp, 202b, 203b, 211a, 216b, 795a, 902a.
harper, 509a, 902a.
harpers, 839a.
Harpokrates, 76a, 501b (of Busiris), 515b.
harpoon, 47a, 110b, 281b, 708b, 905a.
Harpoon-gods, 281b.
harpoon-lord, 57b.
Ḥarpugakasharshabiu, 464a.
harshness, 820b.
Ḥarti, 464a.
harvest, 8b, 178a, 268b, 426b, 740b.
Harvest-god, 319b.
Harvest-goddess, 426b.
Hasau, 442b.
Ha-ser, 439b.
haste, 9b, 82b, 392b, 487b.
hasten, 9b, 25a, 90b, 143b, 212a, 217a, 227a, 255b, 275a, 393b, 471a, 531b, 533ab, 562b, 563ab, 590a, 612b, 615b, 618a, 640b, 643a, 689a, 694b, 727b, 750b, 754b, 877b; away, 481a.
hastening, 688a.
hasters, 9b.
hasty of speech, 533a.
hat, 119b, 635b.
Ḥat, 460a.
Ḥatȧbu, 465a.
Hȧtȧtȧbȧtȧsheraḥafgt, 443b.
Ḥātcha, 467b.
Ḥatchat, 461a.
hatchet, 111b, 632a, 717a.
hate, 140a, 214b, 328ab, 329ab.
hated, 328a.
hateful, 214b, 329a, 657a, 704b, 899a.
Ḥatemtauis, 467a.
hater, 329ab.
Hatestt, 443a.
Hathor, 7b, 20b, 41b, 159b, 235a, 455b, 770a, 820a, 914a.
Hathor, Followers of, 743a.
Hathors, the Seven, 164b, 455b.
Ḥat-meḥit, 461a.
hatred, 328a, 329ab, 794b.
Hat Sett, 439b.
Ḥatti, 465a.
Hȧu, god, 443b.
Ḥau (Rā), 462b.
Ḥau gods, 459a.
Hȧu, country, 443b.
Ḥāuau, 466a.
Ḥāu-em-nubit, 466a.
haughtily, 639b.
haughty, 189b, 562a, 633b, 760a, 861b.
Hȧuk, 443b.
Ḥaukar, 458a.
haul, 3b, 100a, 104a, 628b, 827a.
haulers, 707b, 713a.
haunch, 33b, 129b, 559a.
haunt, 120a.
Ḥauq, 462b.
have, 580a.
have nothing, 78a, 127b.
have power over, 54b.
haven, 137b, 300b, 531b, 579b.
hawk, 206a, 210b, 211b, 225a, 395a, 909b, 910b; amulet of, 206a.
Hawk-boat, 211b.
Hawk-city, 84b.
hawk-collar amulet, 183b.
Hawk-god, 208b, 210b, 211b, 225a, 295b, 897a.
Hawk-goddess, 211b, 225a.
hay, 658a, 725b.
he, 258a, 306b, 401a.
he who, 15a, 233b, 237b.
he who is there (i.e., the dead), 399a.
head (i.e., chief), 554a.
head, 417b, 433b, 443a, 464a, 828a, 901a; part of, 146a, 482b; back of, 457b.

head downwards, 694b, 695a.
head, hairy, 174b.
head (of a stream), 108b.
head, set up the, 694b.
head to feet, 828a.
head, to stand on the, 618a.
head, top of the, 827b.
headache, 696a.
head attire, 528a, 575a.
head-box of Osiris 19a.
head-cloth, 43b, 104a, 120a, 376a, 458b, 528a, 623b, 631a, 714a, 776a.
headcovering, 163a, 458b, 827b.
headdress, 40a, 55a, 120a, 123b, 216a, 368a, 525b, 776a, 810b.
headland, 417b.
headless, 184b.
headman, 848b, 885b.
headrest, 147a, 175a.
heads (of a book), 828a.
headsman, 373b, 417a, 644a.
headstrong, 650a.
heal, 65b, 593b, 643a, 654a, 679a, 697a.
healed, 420b.
healing, pills of, 247a.
health, 633a, 676ab, 893b.
health, to wish good, 676b.
healthy, 128ab, 193a, 422a, 676a, 697a, 893b ; to make, 654a.
heap, 809a, 814b, 915a ; heaps of grain, 134b.
heap together, 598b.
heap up, 181b, 485a, 544b ; heaped up full, 348b.
hear, 27a, 400b, 629a, 672b, 715b, 717b ; to make, 619a.
hearer, 718a.
hearing, 718a, 783b.
hearken, 717b.
hearsay, 416a.
heart, 37b, 158a, 460a, 460b, 516b ; dense, 37b ; desire of, 37b, 79b, 864a ; dictates of the, 37b ; place of rest of, 80b ; to sacrifice a, 57a ; to vivify, 645a ; to wash the, 28a.
heart of Rā, 37b.
heart of the soul, 37b.
heart-ache, 460a.
heart-amulet, 37b.
heart-disease, 14a.
heartless, 461a, 732b.
hearts, house of, 238a, 239a.
heart soul, 197ab.
heart support, 289a.
heat, 110a, 115b, 189a, 221a, 300b, 429a, 434a, 434b, 439b, 447a, 451b, 471a, 510a, 526a, 531b, 547a, 611b, 612b, 623a, 649a, 664b, 676a, 681a, 700a, 731b, 732a, 740a, 765b, 774a, 798a, 841a, 911b.
heated, 570a, 817b.
heave, 765a.
heaven, 80a, 144b, 150a, 156a, 190a, 194a, 210b, 224a, 229a, 234ab, 238b, 307b, 403a, 498b, 536a, 630b, 733a, 769a, 867b.
heaven, belly of, 570a.
heaven, festival of creation of, 474b.
heaven, nether, 685a.
heaven of stars, 685a.
heaven, two halves of, 229a, 251b, 314a, 834a.
heaven, watery mass of, 768b.
heavenly beings, 229a.
heaviness, 473a.
heavy, 189b, 191b, 507a, 838b, 839b, 882a, 883b, 908a.
heavy-handed, 191b.
Heb, 52b, 445a, 474b.
Hebai, 445b.
Ḥebbt (Nile-god), 475b.
Heben, great and little, 446a.
Hebi, 445b.
Ḥebi, god, 475a.
Hebit, 445b.
Ḥebit, 474b.
Hebrews, 119a.
Ḥebs, 477a.
Ḥebs-an, 477a.
Ḥebsit, 477a.
Ḥebs-kheperu, 477a.
Ḥebs-nebs-etc., 477a.
Ḥebtch, 477b.
Ḥebṭre, 477b.
Ḥebṭref, 477b.
hedge, a green, 677a.
heed, to pay, 615a, 681a.
Ḥefa . . . god, 479b.
Ḥefait, 479b.

Ḥefaiu, 479b.
Ḥefau, 480a.
Ḥefnent, 480a.
Ḥefnu, 480a.
Ḥeft-ent- . . . , 480a.
ḥeget, the quadruple, 41b.
Ḥegit, 513b, 514a.
Ḥeḥ, a god, 507b.
Ḥeḥ (Nile), 507b.
Ḥeḥ of Ḥeḥ-ta, 508a.
Ḥeḥit, 507b.
Ḥeḥtt, 507b.
Ḥeḥu, god, 507b.
heifer, 426b.
height, 2b, 11a, 190a, 424b, 761b, 762b ; of heaven, 760a ; of misery, 778b.
heir, 31a, 33a, 113ab, 154b, 423a, 584a.
Hekȧ, 452a.
Ḥeka, 515a.
Ḥekab, 515b.
Ḥeka-ka-en-Rā, 515b.
Ḥeka-p-khart, 515b.
Ḥekaui, 515a.
Ḥeka-ur, 515a.
Ḥekau-ur, 515a.
Ḥeken-em-ānkh, 515b.
Ḥeken-em-benf, 516a.
Ḥeken-kheperȧ, 516a.
Ḥeken-Rā, 516a.
Heker country and festival, 452a.
Heker-t, 452a.
Ḥekka, 515b.
Ḥeknit, 515b.
Ḥeknit-em-ba-s, 516a.
Ḥeknit-em-tep-Ḥeru, 516a.
Ḥeknith, Ḥeknithth, 516a.
Ḥekniu, 515b.
Ḥeknu, 516a.
Ḥeknutt, 575b.
Hekru, 452a.
Heliopolis, canal of, 16a.
helmet, 119b, 544a, 827b, 875b.
help, 113a, 141b, 166a, 865b, 866b.
helper, 248a, 281a, 282a.
helpless, 39a, 111a, 174b, 186b, 207b, 208b, 225b, 227a, 228a, 260b, 375b, 377a, 393b, 506b, 520a, 531a, 537b, 574a, 575b, 594b, 622b, 627b, 634b, 652b, 675a, 706a, 732b, 733b, 744b, 771b, 798b, 802a, 803a, 806a, 809a, 812b, 833a, 834a.
helpless folk, 806b.
helpless man, 574a, 809a.
helpless ones, i.e., the damned, 377a.
helplessness, 76b, 226a, 802a ; of old age, 187b ; place of, 225b.
Hem, 447a.
Ḥem, god, 480b.
hem in, 676b.
Ḥemag, god and city, 484b.
Ḥem-ba, 450b.
Hememt, 447a.
Ḥemen, 471a, 485a.
Ḥemfṭesf, 483b.
Hemhem, 447a.
Hemhemti, 447b.
Ḥem-Ḥeru, 483a.
Ḥemit, 481ab.
Ḥemmit, 484a.
Ḥem-nenu, 481b.
Ḥemnit, 485a.
Ḥemnuba, 483a
Ḥem-pestchet, 483a.
Ḥemsbeqsnȧrit, 485b.
Ḥemṭ (Set), 486a
Ḥem-taiu, 483b.
Hemthet, 447b.
Hemti, 446b.
Ḥemti, 481b.
hen, 792b, 802b.
Ḥenātiu, 489b.
Ḥenb, 490b.
Ḥenbethru, 490b.
Ḥenbi, 490b.
Ḥenbiu, 490b.
Ḥenbrequ, 490b.
Ḥenbu Boat, 490b.
Ḥenemit, 490b.
Henen, 448b.
Ḥeng, god, 492a.
Ḥeng-re, 492a.
Ḥenḥenith, 489b.
Heni, 449a.
Henit, 448b.
Ḥenit-heteput, 486a.
Ḥenit-netit, 486a.
Ḥenit-ṭeshert, 486b.
Ḥenkherth, 491a.
Hennȧ, 449a.
Hennȧthf, 449a.

Hennit, 448b.
Ḥennu Boat, Festival of, 474b.
Ḥennu-Neferit, 489a.
Ḥenq, 491b.
Ḥensektit, 491b.
Ḥensektiu, 491b.
Ḥensit, Festival of, 475a.
Ḥent, 488a.
Ḥenti, god, 492b.
Ḥenti, Osiris, 488b.
Ḥenti, period, 488a.
Ḥenti-nekenf, 492b.
Ḥenti-requ, 492b.
Ḥentnuts, 489a.
Ḥent-she, 488b.
Henu Boat, 455b, 490a.
Ḥenu, i.e., Seker, 489b.
Ḥenui-Shu, 487b.
Ḥenuit, 489b.
Ḥep (Apis), 478a.
Ḥep, day-god, 478b.
Ḥep, god of offerings, 478a.
Ḥep, 477b.
Ḥep, son of Horus, 478a.
Hepa, 446b.
Ḥepā, 479a.
Hepaf, 446b.
Hepath, 446b.
Hepȧu, 446b.
Hepȧuu, 446b.
Ḥepemḥepf, 477b.
Hepenu, 446b.
Ḥeper, Nile-god, 479a.
Ḥepḥep, 479a.
Ḥepi, 478b.
Ḥepit, 478a, 479a.
Ḥepit-Ḥeru, 479a.
Hepmentȧ, 446b.
Ḥep-seshemus, 874b, 880a, 888b.
Ḥeptcheserit, 478b.
Hepṭes, 446b.
Ḥepti, 478a, 479a.
Ḥepti (Rā), 478b.
Ḥeptitaf, 478a.
Ḥeptkhet, 479a.
Ḥept-tef, 478b.
Ḥepṭur, 479b.
Ḥep-ur, 479b.
Ḥeq, god, 513a.
Ḥeq-ȧrti-tefef, 573b.
Ḥeqau, god, 515a.
Ḥeqenbit, 514a.
Heqes, 451b.
Ḥeqes, god, 514b.
Ḥeq-ḥesi, 513b.
Ḥeq-nek-mu, 513b.
Ḥeq-neterut, 513b.
Ḥeqrer, god, 514b.
Ḥeqrit, 514b.
Ḥeq-sa-neter, 513b.
Ḥeqsi, god, 514b.
her, 234ab, 818b.
herald, 56b, 176b, 177a, 391b, 601b, 669b ; of god, 402a.
Ḥer-Ȧten, 493a.
herb, 8a, 17a, 25a, 46a, 60b, 61a, 77b, 82a, 95b, 110b, 121b, 122a, 140a, 146b, 150a, 175a, 202a, 209a, 216a, 223a, 227b, 232a, 278b, 328a, 336a, 343a, 352b, 370b, 407b, 437b, 451b, 452a, 484a, 527b, 553a, 598b, 647b, 667a, 714b, 738b, 749a, 752a, 784a, 799b, 805a, 808a, 823b.
herbs, aromatic, 547a.
herbs, sweet, 527b.
herbage, 667a, 733b, 745b.
herd, herds, 18a, 32a, 203a, 283a, 299a, 586b.
herd, to, 301a, 379a.
herdsman, 111a, 185a, 226b, 301b, 351b, 379a, 435b.
here, 107a, 868a.
hereabouts, 107a.
Ḥerenba, 493b.
Herer, 888b.
Herer, Boat of, 3a.
Ḥerfḥaf, 493b.
Ḥerfāuif, 493b.
Ḥerf-em-gebf, 493b.
Ḥerf-em-khentf, 493b.
Ḥerf-em-shet, 493b.
Ḥerf-m-mḥaf, 493b.
Ḥerḥerḥer, 493b.
Ḥeri, god, 496a.
Ḥeri-ȧau, 496a.
Ḥeri-ȧb-ȧrt-f, 496a.
Ḥeri-ȧb-karȧf, 496b.
Ḥeri-ȧb-khentu, 496a.
Ḥeri-ȧbt-nut-s, 496a.
Ḥeri-ȧbt-shait, 496a.
Ḥeri-ȧb-uȧa, 496a.
Ḥeri-ȧb-uȧa-f, 496a.
Ḥeri-ȧbt-uȧa-set, 496a.
Ḥeri-ȧb-uu, 496a.

Ḥeri-agbaf, 496a.
Ḥeri-ākhut, 496b.
Ḥeri-ȧmi-ȧbu, 500b.
Ḥeri-ānkhiu, 496b.
Ḥeri-ȧriu-āā, 496b.
Ḥeri-ȧst-f-urt, 496b.
Ḥeriāt, 496b.
Ḥeri-bat, 497a.
Ḥeri-beḥ, 497a.
Ḥeri-ḥatentiu, 497b.
Ḥeri-ḥerit, 497b.
Ḥeri-ka, 498a.
Ḥeri-kau, 498a.
Ḥeri-khent, 497b.
Ḥeri-khenṭu-f, 497b.
Ḥeri-khu, 497b.
Ḥeri-maāt, 497a.
Ḥeri-meḥt, 497a
ḥeri-nest, a title, 495a.
Ḥeri-qatf, 498a.
Ḥeri-qenbt-f, 498a.
Ḥeri-remen, 497a.
Ḥeri-ret-f, 497a
Ḥeri-retitsa, 497a.
ḥeri sa, a title, 495a.
Ḥerisau, 497b.
Ḥeri-sefus, 497b.
Ḥeri-sep-f, 497b.
Ḥeri-Serser, 497b.
Ḥeri-shāf, 497b, 498a.
Ḥeri-shafit, 498a.
Ḥeri-shata-taui, 498a.
Ḥeri-shemā, 498a.
Ḥerit, 500a.
Ḥerit (Nut), 496a.
Ḥeri-ta, 498a.
heritage, 33a, 154b.
Ḥerit-āshm, 496b.
Ḥerit-ast, 496b.
Ḥeri-tchatchasenuf, 498b.
Ḥeri-tchatcha-taui, 498b.
Ḥeri-ṭeba-f, 498a.
Ḥeri-ṭesu-f, 498a.
Ḥerit-em-ḥetepit, 502a.
Ḥerit-ḥaṭus, 497b.
Ḥerit-hertu, 498a.
Ḥeriti-senti, 495a.
Ḥerit-ketuts, 498a
Ḥerit-nebt-uu, 502b.
Ḥerit-neferu-en-nebs, 497a.
Ḥerit-nemmtits, 497a.
Ḥerit-neqef, 497a.
Ḥerit-nest, 497a.
Ḥerit-neteru, 497a.
Ḥerit-remen, 497a.
Ḥerit-shās, 498a.
Ḥerit-tchatcha-ȧḥ, 498b.
Ḥerit-tchatcha-āḥa, 498b.
Ḥerit-tchatcha-nebs, 498b.
Ḥerit-tchatcha-ṭuatiu, 498b.
Ḥeriuā, 496b.
Ḥeri-uāf, 496b.
Ḥeriu-ākhusen, 496b.
Ḥeriu-āmāmti, 496b.
Ḥeri-uaref, 496b.
Ḥeriu-ārit, 496b.
Ḥeri-uatchtf, 496b.
Ḥeriu-ḥatu, 497b.
Ḥeriu-metut-ḥekaiu, 497a.
Ḥeri-uru, 497a.
Ḥeriu-senemu, 497b.
Ḥeriu-set, 497b.
Ḥeriu-shā, 495b.
Ḥeriu-tuf, 497a.
Ḥeriu-unut, 497a.
Ḥerk-em-maāt, 494a.
Hermopolis, 16b, 417a ; of South and North, 46a.
hero, 241a, 243a, 314a, 855a.
heron, 746a.
Herpiu, 451a.
Herr, 449b.
Ḥerratf, 506a.
Ḥerrit, 500a.
hers, 229b, 234b, 342b, 818b, 819a.
herself, 911b.
Ḥersen, 494a.
Ḥerset, 44b.
Herti, 449b.
Ḥeru (Horus), 500a.
Ḥer-uā, 493a.
Ḥeru-ȧa, 500a.
Ḥeru-ȧabtȧ, 500b.
Ḥeru-ȧakhuti, 40b, 500b.
Ḥeru-ȧakhuti-Kheperȧ, 500b.
Ḥeru-ȧakhuti-Temu-Ḥeru-Kheperȧ, 500b.
Ḥeru-ȧmi-ȧthen-f, 500b.
Ḥeru-ȧmi-Ḥenu, 500b.
Ḥeru-ȧmi-Khent-n-ȧrti, 500b.
Ḥeru-ȧmi-u (?), 500b.
Ḥeru-ȧmi-uȧa, 500b.
Ḥeru-ȧmi-Uatchur, 500b.
Ḥeru-Baȧt, 501b.
Ḥeru-Beḥut, 501b.

Ḥeru-Beḥuṭet, 4a.
Ḥeru-em-àakhuti + Kheperà + Rā + Tem, 501b.
Ḥeru-em-Khebit, 502a.
Ḥeru-em-saḥt, 502a.
Ḥeru-em-sau-àb, 502a.
Ḥeru-ḥenb, 503a.
Ḥeru-Ḥennu, 503a.
Ḥeru-ḥeri-ā-f, 503a.
Ḥerui (Horus and Set), 500a.
Ḥerui-fi, 493b.
Ḥeru-Keftà, 505b.
Ḥeru-Khenti, 503b.
Ḥeru-Khenti-khaṭit, 40b.
Ḥeru-meri-tef, 502a.
Ḥeru-merti, 502a.
Ḥeru-m'thenu, 502a.
Ḥeru-neb-au-àb, 502b.
Ḥeru-netch-àt-f, 502b.
Ḥeru-netch-f-àtf, 501a.
Ḥeru-netch-her-tef-f, 503a.
Ḥeru-netch-tef-f, 503a.
Ḥeru-p-Rā, 501b.
Ḥeru-Qebḥ, 505b.
Ḥeru-seqi-ḥāu, 505a.
Ḥeru-sethen-ḥer, 505a.
Ḥeru-Shāu, 505a.
Ḥeru-Shemsu, 505b.
Ḥeru-Shest-tà, 505b.
Ḥeru-Sheta, 505b.
Ḥeru-Sheta-taui, 505b.
Ḥeru-Sheṭ-ḥer, 505b.
Ḥeru-Sheṭti, 505b.
Ḥeru Shu, 505b.
Ḥeru-Skhait, 505a.
Ḥeru-Smai-en-nub, 505a.
Ḥeru-Smai-taui, 505a.
Ḥeruṭaṭaf, 506b.
Ḥeru-tauseru, 506a.
Ḥeru-tcham-ā-ā, 506b.
Ḥeru-tchatcha-nefer, 506a.
Ḥeru-tema-ā, 506a.
Ḥeru-Ṭemam, 506a.
Ḥeru-thema-ā, 506a.
Ḥeru-Ṭuati, 506a.
Ḥeru-uātt, 501a.
Ḥeru-ukhakhat-tà, 501b.
Ḥeru-unemi-àfu, 500b.
Ḥeru-Unnefer, 501a.
Ḥeru-ur, 501a.
Ḥeru-ur, Eye of, 194a.
Ḥeru-ur, priest of, 45a.
Ḥeru-ur-shept, 501b.
Ḥeru-uru, 501a.
Ḥeru-Usāsit, 501b.
Ḥesà, 509a, 510a.
Ḥesamut, 510b.
Ḥesbi-āḥā, 511a.
Ḥesbi ànu, 511a.
Ḥeser, 512a.
Ḥes-ḥer, 509b.
Ḥesit, 509b.
hesitate, 90b, 283b, 499b, 839a, 847b.
hesitating, 746b.
hesitation, 280b, 315b, 352b.
Ḥesq, god, 512b.
Ḥesqit-Kheftiu-Set, 512b.
Ḥes tchefetch, 509b.
Ḥet, god, 516b, 576b.
Ḥetàḥt, 453b.
Ḥet-ākhmiu, 454a.
Ḥet Åment, 453b.
Ḥetān, 454a.
Ḥet Ånes, 453b.
Ḥet ānkh, 454a.
Ḥet Åptt, 453b.
Ḥet Åsàr, 453b.
Ḥet Åsàr-ḥemagat, 453b.
Ḥet Āshemu, 454a.
Ḥet àt, 453b.
Ḥet àtu, 453b.
Ḥet Ba, 454b.
Ḥet Baiu, 454b.
Ḥet Banban, 454b.
Ḥet Bast, 454b.
Ḥet Bàti, 454b.
Ḥet-Benben, 51a, 454b.
Ḥet Benu, 455a.
Ḥet Berber, 455a.
Ḥetch-ā, 523a.
Ḥetch-àbḥu, 523a.
Ḥetchfu, 524b.
Ḥetchḥetch, 452b, 522b.
Ḥetchi-ḥeru, 524a.
Ḥetchit, 522b.
Ḥetchit-àṭi, 523a.
Ḥetch-nāu, 523a.
Ḥetch-re-pesṭ-tchatcha, 523a.
Ḥetchtch, 522b.
Ḥetch-tchatchau-etc, 523a.
Ḥetchtchiti, 524b.
Ḥetchtchut, 523a.
Ḥetch-ua, 523a.
Ḥetchu-kau, 524a.
Ḥetch-ur, 523a.

Ḥetchuti, 522b.
Ḥetem-ȧb, 520b.
Ḥetemit, 520a.
Ḥetemit-ȧakhu, 520b.
Ḥetemit-baiu, 520b.
Ḥetemith, 520b.
Ḥetemit-ḥer, 520b.
Ḥetemit-khemiu, 520b, 888b.
Ḥetem-ur, 520b.
Ḥetennut, 452b.
Ḥet ent Gemḥeru, 455b.
Ḥetep, city of, 518b.
Ḥetep, god, 518b.
Ḥetep, Lake of, 518b.
Ḥetepet-neb-per-s, 49a, 888b.
Ḥetep-ḥemt, 579a.
Ḥetepi, 518b, 519a.
Ḥetepit, 518a.
Ḥetepit-ȧb-neb, 519a.
Ḥetepit-em-ȧakhuts, 519a.
Ḥetepit-nebt-pers, 519a.
Ḥetep-ka, 579a.
Ḥetep-Khenti-Ṭuat, 519a.
Ḥetep-mes, 519a.
Ḥetep-neteru, 519a.
Ḥetep-sekhus, 519a.
Ḥetep-ta, 519b.
Ḥetep-taui, 519b.
Ḥetep-tebes, 519b.
Ḥetep-ṭet, 519b.
Ḥeteptiu, 518a.
Ḥeteptiu-Kheperu, 519a.
Ḥeteptiu-kheriu-aaut, 519a.
Ḥeteptiu-ṭuaiu-Rā, 519b.
Ḥetep-uȧa, 519a.
Ḥetepu-ḥetepit, 519a.
Ḥetepui, 518b.
Ḥeteputiu, 40b.
Ḥet-erṭu, 455b.
Ḥet-Ḥer, 40b.
Hethet, 452b.
Ḥet Ḥet Baiu, 454b.
Heththi, 452b.
Ḥetit, 453a, 517a.
Ḥet ka, 456b.
Ḥet ka Seker, 456b.
Ḥet kau Nebt-er-tcher, 456b.
Ḥet menkh, 455a.
Ḥet ment, 455a.
Ḥet meritit, 455a.
Ḥet mesnekhtit, 455a.
Ḥet Mut-ānkh, 455a.
Ḥet Nefert, 455a.
Ḥet nemes, 455a.
Ḥet qa, 456b.
Ḥet Renrenui, 455b.
Ḥet Sȧp, 456a.
Ḥet Sekha-Ḥeru, 456a.
Ḥet Sekhemu, 456a.
Ḥet Sekhmit, 456a.
Ḥet Sekht, 456a.
Ḥet Sekhuut, 456a.
Ḥet Septt, 455b.
Ḥer Ser, 456a.
Ḥet Serqit, 456a.
Ḥet shāt, 456b.
Ḥet shent, 456b.
Ḥet stau, 456b.
Ḥet sutenit en Rā, 456a.
Heṭṭ, 452b.
Hettȧ, 452a.
Ḥet Ṭat-ānkh, 456b.
Ḥet-Ṭebutiut, 456b.
Ḥet ṭemṭt Rā, 456b.
Ḥet Ṭesheru, 456b.
Ḥet Ṭeṭ, 457a.
Ḥet-ṭuau-Rā, 456b.
Ḥeṭṭit, 522a.
Ḥeṭṭut, 452b.
Hetu, 452a.
Ḥetu, 517b.
Ḥet Uhem-ḥer, 454a.
Ḥet urt, 454a.
Ḥet-usekh-ḥer, 454b.
Ḥet User Menu, 454b.
Ḥet utett, 454b.
heure, de bonne, 351a.
hew, 158b, 178a, 220a, 282b, 291b, 338a, 397b, 639b, 703a, 765b ; hew stones, 201a, 725b.
hewer, 395b.
Hi, 444a.
Ḥi, an Assessor, 467b.
Ḥi, water-god, 467b.
Ḥi-ȧakhu, 468a.
Ḥiāt, 468a.
hidden, 51a, 325b, 463a, 477b, 755b, 891a.
hidden chamber, 107a.
hidden countries, 756a.
hidden (of face), 755b.
hidden (of mummies), 265b.
hidden (of soul), 755b.
hidden place, 51a, 756a.
hiddenness, 335b.

hide, 51a, 62a, 327a, 400b, 463a, 470b, 477b, 536a, 576a, 624b, 631b, 682b, 701a, 716a, 747b, 751a, 787a, 813b, 837a, 843a b, 847b, 866a, 887b.
hide oneself, 629b, 631b, 712a, 891a.
hide the heart, 51a.
hide (i.e., skin), 55a, 160a, 390b, 530a, 571a, 859a, 887a ; dressed, 887a.
hiding place, 120a, 216a, 477b, 793b, 843a.
hieroglyphic, 335b.
hieroglyphs, 402a, 403b, 619b.
Higer, 444b.
high, 7a, 93a, 525a, 529a, 536a, 537a, 760a, 767a, 783b, 786a, 861a, 880b.
high banks, 828a.
high building, 761a.
high crown, 760a.
high ground, 536a, 828a, 861b.
high land 761a.
high-lying, 498b.
high offices, 18a.
high place, 11a, 80a, 215a, 216b, 424b, 536a, 761a b, 805a.
high position, 557b.
high priest, 132a, 155a, 483a ; of Coptos, 598b ; of Heliopolis, 171a ; of Panopolites, 598b ; of Ptaḥ, 172a ; of Thoth, 172a ; of Saïs, 171a.
high rank, 591a.
high rock, 215a.
high-backed, 13a, 633b, 760b.
high-handed, 241a.
high-pitched, 560b.
high-shouldered, 760a.
high-voiced, 536a.
highway, 529b ; the common, 144b.
hill, 133b, 215a, 417b, 449b, 598b, 636a, 761a, 869a, 872b ; of east, west and spirit border, 598b ; prominent, 885b.
Hill of Life, 761b.
Hill of Stone, 298a.
Hill of Truth, 598a.
hill-country, 106a, 598b.
hill-men, 59b.
hill top, 105b.
him, 401a.
himself, 889b, 911b.
hind, 411a.
hinder, to, 82b.
hinder parts, 244a, 567b, 633b, 794a.
hindrance, 64a.
hip bones, 275b.
hippopotamus, 382a, 428a, 530b, 531a, 539a, 827a, 873b, 877a, 832a, 839b.
Hippopotamus goddess, 125b, 295a, 371b, 428a, 551b, 819b, 882a.
hire, 90a, 642a, 650b, 729a ; of boat, 446b.
his, 229b, 234a b, 258a, 342a b, 401a, 818b, 819a, 824b, 847b.
Ḥit (Besit), 468a.
hither, 296a.
hitherto, 100b.
Ḥitiu, 468a.
hoe, 95a, 489a, 492a, 540a, 632a, 717a.
hoist, 259a.
hold, 412b, 547b, 614a, 616b, 693a ; back, 30a ; fast, 412b ; lightly, 28a.
holdall, 256b.
holder, 581b.
holding, a, 638a.
hole, 539b, 756b, 763b.
hole in the ground, 201a, 216a, 775a, 854b, 877b.
hole (of serpent), 837b.
holiday, 693a.
hollow, 763b, 774b, 832b, 872a.
hollow of hand or foot, 786b, 793a, 894a.
hollow out a boat, 11a, 730a.
holy, 88b, 108a, 155a, 737a, 912a ; to account, 912a.
Holy Land, 81a, 817a.
holy man, 155a.
Holy Mountain, 869b.
holy of holies, 546b, 616a.
holy place, 80b, 88b, 117b, 214b, 238b, 912a.
holy thing, 38b, 912a.
homage, 96a, 565a, 633a, 675a, 787a.
homage to thee ! 410a.

homage, to do, 204b, 348b, 352b, 377b, 476a, 530b, 586a, 603b, 675a, 797ab, 885a.
homage, to pay, 200a, 603b, 841b.
homage, payers of, 571b.
home, 32a, 34b, 62a, 226b, 754b.
homestead, 74a, 638a, 812a.
honey, 39a, 201b, 202a, 209a.
honey, wild, 768a.
honeycomb, 343b.
honey fly, 119b.
honey plant, 539a.
honey wine, 72b.
honour, 50a, 508a, 591a, 622b, 637a, 737a, 805b, 824a, 871a, 883b, 912a.
honour, held in, 912a.
honour, to pay, 646a, 840a.
honour, to receive, 646a.
honour, worthy of, 50a.
honourable, 737a, 837b.
honourable lady, 737a.
honourably, to act, 637a.
honoured, 737a.
honourings, 824a.
hoof, 63b, 112b, 140a, 176b, 311b.
hook, 180a, 273a, 435b.
hoopoe, 767a.
hop, 833ab, 854a, 862b.
hopeless, 874a.
Hophra, 466b.
hopper (a bird), 833b.
hoppings, 833a.
Horapollo, 197a.
horizon, 24b, 99a ; dwellers on the, 70a.
horizon of Manu, 24b.
horizon, the eternal, 25a.
horizon, the secret, 25a.
horizons, the two, 616b.
horn, 115b, 311b, 355b, 488b, 853a, 873b.
horns of a bow, 873b.
horns, the four, 116a.
horns, the two, 796a.
horoscope, 45a.
horoscopist, 45a, 167b.
horrible, 541a, 889b.
horror, 208a, 395a, 541a.
horse, 39a, 517a, 521a, 598b, 618b, 667a, 695b, 696ab, 774a, 801b, 830a.
horses, appertaining to, 408a ; pair of, 696b.
horse of Rameses II, 295a, 389a.
horse of Seti I, 53a, 772a.
horse, young, 372b.
horseman, 408a.
horse soldier, 839b.
Horus, 3a, 15b, 39b, 42b.
Horus Jupiter, 505a.
Horus Saturn, 505b.
Horus Set, 172b, 429b, 493b, 505a, 555b, 577b, 674a.
Horus Shu, 505b.
Horus Sothis, 505a.
Horus Thoth, 506a.
Horus, the Blind, 500b, 502a.
Horus, the Blue-eyed, 504b.
Horus, the Bold, 501a.
Horus, the Bull, 501b, 505b.
Horus, the Child, 388b, 504b.
Horus, the crocodile, 500b.
Horus, Destroyer of Rebels, 501a.
Horus, the Dog-Star, 505a.
Horus, the Fire-god, 504b.
Horus, the Lightning, 506a.
Horus, the Look-out (i.e. Pilot), 503b.
Horus, Lord of men, 502b.
Horus, the Pillar, 501a.
Horus, the Red, 656a.
Horus, the Rejuvenator, 502b.
Horus, the Singer, 503b.
Horus, the Slaughterer, 505a.
Horus, Smiter of the Nine Bows, 503a.
Horus, Son of Hathor, 504b.
Horus, Son of Isis, 504b.
Horus, the Soul of Ṭeṭ, 501b.
Horus, the Sun-god, 500b.
Horus, the two-headed, 502a.
Horus, the unborn, 503a, 504ab.
Horus, the Winter, 505a.
Horus, the Young, 502b.
Horus of Antaeopolis, 502a.
Horus of Behen, 502b.
Horus of Dâkhlah, 503b.
Horus of Edfû, 503b.
Horus of gold, 502a.
Horus of Hermonthis, 503a.
Horus of Hierakonpolis, 502ab.
Horus of hundreds of thousands of years, 504b.
Horus of Khaṭṭ, 505a.

Horus of Letopolis, 504b.
Horus of Mābiu, 502b.
Horus of Sothis, 501a.
Horus of Thes-Ḥeru, 503b.
Horus of the Ȧtebui, 501a.
Horus of the bandages, 112a.
Horus of the bandlet, 504a.
Horus of the Crown, 502b.
Horus of the drowned, 502b.
Horus of the East, 500b, 502b, 656a.
Horus of the First Cataract, 505b.
Horus of the Ḥenu Boat, 500b.
Horus of the horizon, 500b, 502b.
Horus of the North, 16a.
Horus of the oars, 503a.
Horus of the Oases, 503a.
Horus of the Red Eyes, 506a.
Horus of the Scales, 503b.
Horus of the Sceptre, 503b.
Horus of the Serekh, 501a.
Horus of the South, 16a.
Horus of the Spirit-souls, 504a.
Horus of the Swamps, 502a.
Horus of the temples, 504a.
Horus of the thighs, 504a.
Horus of the throne, 503b.
Horus of the Tomb, 504a.
Horus of the Ṭuat, 500b.
Horus of the Ṭuat and its Lakes, 503b, 506a.
Horus of the Two Sceptres, 503b.
Horus of the Two Years, 503a.
Horus with his eyes, 501b.
Horus without his eyes, 504a.
Horus, Blacksmiths of, 325a.
Horus, Boat of, 207a.
Horus, double form of, 850b.
Horus, Eye of, 23a, 194a, 224a, 313b, 407b.
Horus, the two Eyes of, 407b.
Horus, festival of, 742a.
Horus, Followers of, 505b, 743a.
Horus, the Four Ȧats of, 16a.
Horus, the Four Grandsons of, 24b, 323a.
Horus, the Four Sons of, 24b, 322b.
Horus, grandson of, 67b.
Horus, greyhounds of, 862a.
Horus, the lands of, 506b.
Horus, mother of, 7b, 36a.
Horus, Realm of, 815a.
Horus, uraeus of, 1a.
Horus in the Disk, 500b.
Horus in hearts, 500b.
Horus of travellers, 500a.
Horus, eater of flesh, 500b.
Horus of the Mediterranean, 500b.
Horus, kitchen of, 455b.
Horus, locks of, 491a.
host, 288a, 897b.
hostile, 1a, 27b, 329a, 343a, 657a, 744b ; in intent, 227a.
hostility, 488b, 657a, 749a.
hostilities, 895b.
hot, 6a, 140a, 145b, 146b, 221ab, 320a, 434b, 447a, 510a, 531b, 547a, 572b, 611b, 623a, 681a, 724b, 732a, 739b, 740a, 741a, 750b, 769b, 798a, 817b, 896b, 897b, 915a ; to make, 688b, 692b.
hot and cold, 767b.
hot drink, 681a.
hot presses, 247b.
hot-weather festival, 434b.
hot wind, 740a.
hour, 12b, 27a, 167a, 351a, 378a.
Hour-god, 167b.
Hour-goddess, 169b.
hour gods, 175b.
hour priest, 45a.
house, 21a, 30b, 32a, 33a, 41b, 42a, 50a, 106a, 107a, 110a, 125a, 140b, 174ab, 201a, 202b, 208a, 213b, 226b, 231b, 237b, 250a, 313b, 333a, 342ab, 347a, 348b, 357b, 444a, 499b, 523b, 537a, 540a, 570b, 571b, 575b, 731b, 734a, 740b, 893a; houses above, 239b.
house, ancestral, 454b, 830b.
house, country, 148b.
house, double, 237b.
house, great, 453ab.
house, large, 132a.
house, mistress of, 237b.
house, royal, 391b.
House of Aged One, 453a.
house of apparel (i.e., wardrobe), 136b.
house of call, 114b.
house of copies, 239a.

house of eternity (i.e., tomb), 239a.
house of flame, 239a.
house of gold, 455a.
house of Life, 238a, 848a.
house of one thousand years, 239b.
house of speech, 238b.
house of the North, 319b.
houses, god's, 402a.
houses of the stars, 570b.
house boat, 11a, 682b.
house-dwellers, 201b.
household, 201b, 438b, 444b, 449b.
household staff, 823b.
house lord, 357b.
house master, 683b.
house steward, 312a.
housewife, 289a.
hover, 143b, 368b, 480b, 693a, 743a.
hover over, 393b, 549a, 623b.
how, 77a, 277a; how many? 279b.
however, 96a, 480b.
howsoever many, 158a.
Hu, hour-god, 469b.
Ḥu, Nile-god, 469a.
Ḥu, the Sphinx, 469b.
Ḥu (Taste), 469b.
Ḥuȧḥuāa, 469a.
Ḥuaiti, 470a.
Ḥuaur, 470a.
hug, 479a, 773a, 773b.
Ḥuḥu, 469a.
Ḥui-Nu, 469a.
Ḥuit, 470b.
Ḥuiti (Rā), 470b.
Ḥuitiu, 470b.
Ḥuit-Rā, 469a, 470b.
Hukheru, 445a.
human being, 164b, 165a, 233b.
human race, 898a.
human sacrifice, 731a.
human victim, 846a.
humble, 480a, 502b, 631b.
humble oneself, 607a, 677b.
Ḥumen, 471a.
humiliation, 895a.
humility, 388b, 476a.
humours, 222b, 263a, 387b, 437b.
Ḥun, Ḥunu, 471b.
Ḥunb, 472a.
hundred, 721b; two hundred, 756b.
hundred thousand, 480a.
hundred thread stuff, 721b.
Ḥunesmit, 469a.
hunger, 473b, 514a b, 684a; to let hunger, 614a.
hunger, years of, 514a.
hungry, 411b, 514a; to keep, 614a, 684a.
hungry man, 464b, 514b.
Ḥunit goddesses, 471b, 472a.
Ḥunit Pe, 472a.
Ḥunit urit, 472a.
Ḥunnu Shu, 472a.
Ḥun-sāḥu, 472a.
Ḥun-shemā, 472a.
hunt, 221a, 292a, 484a; with nets, 40a.
Hunt-god, 475a.
hunt master, 351a.
hunter, 178b, 221a, 257b, 292a, 351a, 463b, 475a, 618a, 695a, 787a, 793b, 810a.
hunter, the divine, 592b.
Hunter-god, 212a.
Ḥuntheth, 472a.
hunting, god of, 61b, 78a.
hunting, goddess of, 112b.
hunting ground, 351a.
huntsman, 351a; chief, 562a.
Ḥunut, 472a.
Ḥurit urit, 472b.
hurl, 91a, 770a; a weapon, 116a.
hurrah! 73b.
hurricane, 246a, 395a, 573b, 700b, 746a b, 775b, 902a.
hurry, 9b, 374a, 393b, 689a.
hurry towards, 9b.
hurt, 27b, 100b, 180b, 538b.
hurtful, 100b.
husband, 439a, 443a, 444a; to act the, 439a.
husbandman, 32b, 292a.
husbandry, 157b.
hush, to, 706a.
hut, 22a, 753a.
Ḥu-tepa, 469a.
hyena, 220a, 296a, 520b, 521b, 868a.
hymn, 508a, 515b, 516b, 608a; of praise, 871a.
hymn to Uraei, 206a.

hyoscyamus, 597b.
hypnotism, 647b.
hypnotized, 647b.
Hystaspes, 185b.
I, 15a, 60b, 344a, 352b, 356a, 824b.
Iāa (Jāh), 142a.
ibex, 129a, 344b, 352b, 379b, 400b.
ibis, 343a, 440b, 445a, 842b, 844a.
Ibis-god, 185b, 440b, 445a, 663b, 886a.
ichneumon, 524b, 534b.
Ichneumon-god, 432b, 575a, 700a.
icy (winds), 767b.
idle, 181b, 341a.
idleness, 181b, 425b, 727a, 898b.
idler, 377a.
if, 64b.
ignominious, 728a.
ignominy, 564b, 612b, 737b.
ignoramus, 180a.
ignorance, 276b.
ignorant, 78a, 180a, 276b, 340b, 546a b, 548a.
ignorant man, 46a.
ignorantly, 265a.
ignore, 615a, 692b.
Ihit, 143b.
ill, 592b, 744b.
illegible, 807b.
ill-feeling, 774a.
ill-luck, 30b, 31b, 595a, 723b, 724a.
illness, 314b, 443b, 484a b, 553a, 744b.
ill-temper, 737b.
ill-treat, 851b, 867a.
illumination, 230a, 470b.
illumine, 159a, 163b, 204b, 221b, 225a, 227b, 234a, 249a, 249b, 250a, 376b, 522a, 601b, 614a, 685a, 734a, 876b.
ill-will, 329a, 737b.
ill-wish, 615b, 689a b.
image, 37b, 69a, 135b, 222b, 277b, 298a, 367a, 377b, 422b, 494b, 530b, 534b, 542b, 545a, 557b, 577a, 598a, 602a, 604b, 622b, 632a, 666b, 670b, 671b, 675b, 699a, 710a, 716b, 752b, 761b, 770b, 771a b, 779b, 782b, 788a, 821b, 826b, 847a, 853b.
image, divine, 402a.
image, myrrh, 127b.
image of a god, 176a.
Image One, 826b.
image, to make an, 628b.
imagine, 38a.
immediately, 105a, 264a, 494b, 830a.
immerse, 443b, 897b.
immersed, 539b.
immobility, 175b.
immovable, 207b, 894a.
immutable, 340a.
impaled, 566b.
impartial, 866a.
impassable, 755b.
impede, 487b.
imperishable, 78b, 340a.
implement, 333a, 535a, 673b, 715a, 876a.
implore, 662a.
important, 108a.
importunity, 143b.
impost, 338a, 516b, 580b, 655b, 722b, 838a.
impostor, 641b.
impotence, 897a.
impotent, 228a.
impotent beings, 228b.
impoverish, 698a.
imprecation, 246a, 658a.
imprison, 435b, 437b, 566a, 910a, 915b.
imprisoned one, 137b.
imprisonment, 412b, 587a.
impudence, 639a.
impudent, 433b.
impure, 818a.
impure man, 895b.
impurity, 690a, 825b, 895a.
in, 56a, 264a, 339a, 545a, 828b.
in a body, 779b.
in accordance with, 265b, 415a.
in addition to, 148a, 264a, 339a, 414b, 459a, 492b, 494b.
in all, 880b.
in any case, 336b.
in charge of, 37a.
in front of, 266a, 333b, 414b, 415a, 545a.
in order that, 264b, 339a.
in order to, 4b.
in proportion to, 277a, 415b.
in respect of, 339a, 492b.
in return for, 88b, 264a, 414a, 874a, 904a.

in that case, 229b.
in the capacity of, 264a.
in the charge of, 415a.
in the condition of, 264a.
in the face, 265a, 415a.
in the following of, 265b, 415a.
in the form of, 277a.
in the likeness of, 264b.
in the manner of, 264a.
in the midst, 266a.
in the presence of, 105a, 264b, 339a, 494b.
in this wise, 277a.
inactive, 207b, 377a, 398b, 546a, 574a.
inactivity, 377a, 425b.
inasmuch, 279b ; inasmuch as, 277a, 414b, 545a.
inattention, 451b.
inattentive, 451b.
inaugurate, 900a.
incantation, 209a, 246a, 515a, 693a, 739a, 745a, 758a, 860b.
incantations, to use, 386a, 514b.
incapable, 140b.
incense, 4a, 8a, 13b, 14b, 37a, 54b, 74b, 90b, 101b, 111a, 116a, 123b, 177b, 209a, 215b, 220a, 223b, 256a, 257b, 268b, 288a, 302b, 407b, 528a, 536a, 541b, 561a, 563b, 590a, 593a, 601b, 602a, 609b, 669b, 670b, 678b, 679a, 713b, 720a, 732b, 735a, 739b, 750b, 765a, 767a, 774a, 786b, 790b, 810a, 907a ; green, i.e., fresh, 678b ; cake of, 233b ; ingredients of, 22a.
incense, burning, 517a, 526a.
incense, chamber of, 455a.
incense, festal, 709b.
Incense-god, 669b.
incense plant, 452b.
incense trees, 380b.
incident, 614b.
incision, 219a.
incite, 689b.
inclination, 703a.
incline, to, 247a, 434a, 441b, 448a.
inclined (plane), 89a, 390a, 435a.
inclined way, 707b.
income, 56b, 138b, 161a, 487a, 521b, 906a.
incomer, 576a.
incontrovertible, 340b, 410b.
incorruptible, 82b, 341a.
increase, 56b, 148a, 171a, 317a, 458b, 651a, 768a, 813a, 837b.
increment, 148a, 178a, 317a, 458b.
indeed, 164b, 270b.
indemnify, 874a, 904a.
indescribable, 341a.
indestructible, 341a.
indicate, 696b.
indictment, 837a.
indigent, 340b, 379b, 732b.
indigestible, 883b.
indigestion, 577b.
indignation, 618b, 794b.
indignity, 885b.
indisputable, 340b.
indissoluble, 27b.
individual, 828b.
indolence, 377a.
indolent, 665a.
induct a priest, 222a.
induction (of king), 222a.
ineffaceable, 315b.
inert, 78a, 225b, 377a, 574a, 706a, 771b.
infallible, 12b.
infancy, 388b.
infant, 165a, 647a, 716b, 731b.
infantry, 255b, 641b.
inferior, 535b.
infinitive, mark of, 492b.
infirm, 675a.
infirmity, 82a.
inflame, 615b, 866a.
inflamed, 180b, 848b.
inflammation, 160a, 180b, 726b ; of eyes, 14a.
inflated, 423b.
inflict pain or injury, 6a, 140a, 451b, 671a.
influence, to have over, 531a.
inform, 274b, 437a, 622a, 667b, 669b, 693b, 865b, 866a.
inform against, 669b, 681a.
information, 681a.
infringe, 841a.
infuriate, 689b.
ingoers, 138b.
ingots, 210a ; of gold, 353a, 827b, 905a.

ingratiate, 643a.
inhabit, 485a.
inhabitants, 165a, 485b, 774b, 815b, 879b.
inhabited, 866a.
inhabited, to make, 866a.
inhabited district, 207a.
inhale, 204b, 394a, 550b, 595a, 660b, 681b.
inhaler, 394b.
inheritance, 33a, 113b ; to settle one in an, 654a.
inheritor, 33a.
inimical, 657a, 744b.
iniquity, 9b, 214b, 226a, 895b.
injure, 6a, 27b, 114b, 396b, 476a, 488b, 523b, 528b, 571b, 714b, 727a, 792a.
injured, 92b, 345b.
injurious, 523b, 778b.
injury, 12b, 26b, 31b, 92b, 94a, 115a, 140b, 141b, 345a, 354b, 396ab, 397ab, 524a, 605a, 648a, 651b, 695a, 751a, 772b, 792a, 849b.
injury, to suffer an, 14a.
injustice, 14b, 30b, 141b, 896a.
injustice, to do an, 369b.
ink, 346a, 417b, 419b, 620b.
ink, green, 417b.
ink jar, 235a.
inlaid, 317a, 590b, 645a.
inlaid work, 304b.
inland (tribes), 576a.
inlay, 212b, 353b, 474a, 521b, 590b, 822a, 833a, 891b.
inlay an inscription, 884b.
inlayings, 286a, 590b, 673b, 696a.
inner (part of the body), 575b.
innermost, 769b.
innocent, 155a, 271b, 601a, 668a.
innumerable, 340b.
inquire into, 160b.
inscribe, 190b, 597a, 836a.
inscribed, 290b, 291b, 527b, 567b.
inscribed tablet, 855b.
inscription, 291a, 387b, 619a, 836a, 863b, 885a.
insect, 118a, 119b, 253a, 439b, 564a, 682b, 845b ; flying, 552a, 897a ; gnawing, 798b.
insert, 822a.
inside, 265a, 494b.
inside and outside, 339b.
insignificant, 749b.
insincere, 224b.
insistent, 292b.
insolent, 108a.
insolent speech, 690b.
inspect, 178a, 266b, 288b, 468a, 642b, 673a.
inspection, 266b, 642b.
inspector, 157a, 287b, 311b, 421a, 422a, 468a, 495b, 642b, 646b, 685a.
instability, 341a.
instant, 906a.
instantly, 414b, 494b.
instead of, 904a.
instruct, 121b, 289b, 587b, 655a, 697b.
instructed, 655a, 682b.
instructed folk, 23a.
instruction, 655ab, 831b ; place of, 655b.
instructor, 222a, 290a, 655b.
instrument, 19b, 180b, 210a, 228b, 292ab, 304b, 344b, 352b, 419a, 469a, 480a, 613a, 661a, 728b, 789b, 791b, 894a, 907b, 914b ; cutting, 351a ; grinding, 711b ; pointed, 680a ; wooden, 74b, 841a.
instrument of music, 381b, 419a, 795a.
insult, 334b, 433b.
insurrection, 801a.
intact, 193a, 341a.
integrity, 65b, 270b, 271b, 332a, 334a.
intelligence, 37b, 637a.
intention, 37b, 351b, 694a.
intercourse, daily, 278b.
intercourse, sexual, 66a, 718b.
interest, 324a.
interest on money, 258b, 829a.
interior, 6b, 37b, 108a, 494b ; of body, 763a.
interjection, 56a, 74b, 77a, 153a, 157b, 438a, 440a, 443ab, 444a, 451b.
interpreter, 2a, 106a.
interrogate, 186b, 882a.
interrogation, legal, 745a.
intertwine, 561b.
interval, 134a, 351a.

intestine, 21a, 45b, 121b, 181b, 238b, 286a, 320a, 378a, 494b, 512a, 570a, 585a, 599a, 763a, 767b ; the great, 55a.
intimate, 442a, 554a.
into, 264a, 414a, 545a ; into the presence of, 65a.
introduce, 83a, 88a, 642a, 646b.
introducer, 646b.
introduction, 647a.
Inu, 143a.
inundate, 22a, 35b, 626b, 740a.
inundation, 211a, 241a, 253b, 293b, 307b, 308a, 332a, 349ab, 370b, 459b, 462a, 467b, 469a, 507b, 611b, 653b, 695a, 740a, 804a, 807a, 811a, 824b, 836b.
Inundation-god, 318a, 475b.
invade, 93b, 138b, 156b, 439a, 441a, 841a, 845ab, 851b, 858ab, 881a, 885a, 891a, 907b.
invader, 629b, 712a, 841a, 845b, 858a.
invasion, 841a.
inventory, 45a, 161a, 346a, 863a, 701b, 882ab.
inventory, to make an, 607b.
invert, 563b.
investigate, 673a, 807b, 903b.
investigation, 642b, 695a.
investigator, 672b.
invisible, 340b, 755b.
invite, 25b.
invocation, 136b, 345a, 382b, 549a.
invoke, 176b, 345a, 745a, 838b.
invoker, 745a.
involved, 208b, 844a.
invulnerable, 345b.
Ionians, 463b.
Ionian Sea, 463b.
irascibility, 615b, 689b.
irascible, 817b, 861b.
Irene, 33b, 444b.
iron, 203b, 218a, 232a.
iron of the sky, 210a.
Irqai, 143b.
irrational, 637a.
irresistible, 341a.
irrigate, 22a.
irrigated land, 758a.
irrigation, 207a.
irrigation, officers of, 213a.
irrigation, to work the, 65b.
irrigation channels, 727a.
irrigator, 558b, 559a.
Ishtar, 136b.
Isis, 9a, 24a, 29a, 36a, 81a, 402a, 633a.
Isis, acacia of, 749a.
Isis, amulet of uterus of, 847b.
Isis, ceremony of, 766b.
Isis, forms of, 81a.
Isis, the Seven Scorpions of, 179a, 216b.
Isis, tear of, 459b.
Isis and Anubis, 81a.
Isis and Nephthys, 422b, 429b, 431a, 449b, 462a, 491b, 840b, 848b.
Isis-Hathor, 208b.
Isis of Seker, 81a.
Isis-Sothis, 23a, 81b, 430b.
Isis, the clother, 91a.
Isis, the Great, 81a.
Isis, the Wide-tailed, 2b.
island, 6a, 16a, 269a, 270a, 273b, 375a.
Islands, the Greek, 875b.
Island of Flame, 16b.
Islands of Mediterranean, 16b.
Island of Seneferu, 16b.
Israelites, 143b.
issue, 223a, 240ab, 400a, 570a ; an order, 192a.
it, 36a, 306a, 389b, 408a, 409b.
itching, 185b.
its, 258a, 847b.
Itua Bār, 143b.
Iuba, 142b.
Iubani, 142b.
ivory, 4a, 19b.

J.

jackal, 4a, 10a, 25b, 31b, 33b, 40a, 588a, 593b, 636a, 813a, 868a.
Jackal-god, 49a, 92a, 173b, 259b, 588a, 636a, 641b, 884b, 912b.
Jâh, the Great, 142b.
jar, 134b, 281b, 305a, 318b, 332b, 446a, 448b, 569b, 605b, 606a, 626ab, 713a, 725a, 767a, 850b.
jars, the Four, 644b.

javelin, 211a, 305a, 573a, 704b, 905a.
jaw-bone, 129b, 139a, 187b, 206a; the two, 71b.
jawbones of bull, 279b.
jaw, the lower, 129b.
jaws, the two, 617b.
jealous, 291b, 842a.
jealousy, 887a.
jerkins, leather, 422a.
jest, 141b, 476a, 632a, 657b, 716b, 717a, 719b, 797b.
jester, 294b.
jestingly, 476a.
jewellery, 302b, 303a, 575a, 644b.
jewels, 282b.
jibe, 657b.
join, 116b, 577b, 614b, 715b, 747b, 836ab, 879a.
join battle, 5a.
join oneself to, 599a.
join together, 520b.
joined to, 883b.
joiner, 289b.
joinless, 341a.
joint, 32b, 33ab, 43a, 174a, 237a, 400a, 662a, 735a.
joke, 141b, 632a, 693a, 717a.
jolly, 412a.
journal, 450a.
journey, 42a, 65b, 92a, 107a, 118b, 144b, 166a, 192b, 193b, 245b, 246b, 272b, 288a, 324a, 346ab, 366b, 373b, 420a, 440b, 589a, 617a, 653a, 659b, 703a, 713a, 723a, 734a, 739a, 817a, 891b, 894b; upstream, 565a.
journeyings, 1b, 105b.
joy, 3a, 28a, 37b, 73b, 74a, 77b, 113b, 160b, 168a, 326a, 419b, 426b, 433a, 442b, 444a, 449b, 466b, 517b, 727a, 858b.
joy, cries of, 15a.
joys of love, 412a.
joyful, 257a.
judge, to judge, 160b, 161a, 163b, 194b, 285a, 588a, 624b, 748a, 753b, 844a, 901a.
judge, the chief, 588a.
judge, the divine (i.e., Thoth), 886a.
judge of hearts, 61a.
Judges, the Two, 901a.
Judges, the Thirty, 281a.
judge hastily, 9b.
judge hearts, 195a.
judge wrongly, 437a.
judged ones, 194b.
judgment, 42b, 146b, 157b, 160b, 194b, 450b.
Judgment, the Last, 41a.
Judgment, Hall of, 130b, 183a, 454a, 642b.
judgment, place of, 194b.
judgment seat, 80b.
jug, 305a, 888a.
juice, 58b, 292b, 491b.
jump 274b, 577a, 662b.
jump up, 44a.
jumpings, 833a.
junction, 725b.
juniper, 157a, 237a.
Jupiter, 501a, 504a, 656b, 673b.
Jupiter Ammon, Oasis of, 20b.
just, 333b.
just as, 826a.
justice, 139a, 270b, 271b, 332b, 446b; even-handed, 139a; regulation of, 842b.
justice, court of, 613a.
justified, 271b.
justifier, 668b.
justify, 601a, 668ab, 682a.

K

Ka, god, 783a.
ka, the, 782b.
ka-chapel, 456b, 753a.
ka-minister or priest of the ka, 483a, 783a.
Ka, master of Wisdom, 896a.
Ka, son of Meḥurit, 784b.
Kaa, god, 782b.
Ka-ȧakhu, 784b.
Ka-Ȧmentt, 784b.
Kaȧrik, 786a.
Ka-ānkh, 784b.
Ka Ȧnu, 784b.
Ka-ȧru, 784b.
Ka-Ȧsȧr, 784b.
Ka-Āshemu, 784b.
Kaau gods, 783a.
Kab, 786a.
Ka-chapel, keeper of the, 312b.
Ka-em-ānkh-neteru, 783b.

Kafiyyah, 528a, 631a.
Kaharsu, 790b.
Ka-hemhemt, 785a.
Ka-henti, 755a.
kaḥerka, 40b, 783b.
Ka-ḥetep, 783b.
Ka-house of Ptaḥ, 84b.
Kai, 784b.
Kait, 783a.
Kaiu gods, 782a.
Kak, 790b.
Kaka, 791a.
Kakau, 418a.
Ka-Kamur, 785b.
Ka-Khepreri, 785a.
Kalasirian, 796ab, 811b.
Kam-ā, 788a.
Kamȧmut, 788a.
Ka-meshru, 785a.
Kam-ḥer, 788a.
Kam'itha, 789a.
Kamit-urit, 788a.
Kam-neb-mesent, 788a.
Kam-ur, god, lake and town, 788a.
Kam-ur (Red Sea), 788a.
Ka-mutf, 785a.
Ka-Nekhen, 785a.
Ka-n-erṭa-neba-f, 755a.
Ka-neteru, 785a.
Ka-Nut, 785a.
Kap, 787a.
Ka-pest-neteru, 785a.
Kapu, 787a.
Kapur, 787a.
Ka-Rā, 785a.
Karȧmemti, 789b.
Karȧstt, 780a.
Ka-renp, 785a.
Karnak, 390a; temple and its gates, 41b.
Karpus, 790a.
karwânsarai, 549b.
Kash, prince of, 392a.
Ka-shespt, 785b.
Ka-Shu, 783b.
Kasika, 790b.
Ka-taui, 785b.
Ka-ṭer, 785b.
Ka-thai, 785b.
Ka-Ṭuat, 785b.
Kauarsh, 784b.
Kau of Rā, the Fourteen, 782b, 783a.
Kaui, 784b.
Ka-ur, 785a.
Ka-ur-ḥu-Kens, 785a.
Kau-urit, 783b.
Kebit, 793a.
keel of magical boat, 157a.
keen, 291b.
keep, to, 656b.
keep alive, 865b.
keep away, 748a.
keep count, 89a.
keep festival, 683a.
keep guard, 386b.
keep in order, 486b.
keep in restraint, 1b.
keep off, 417b, 747a.
keep the mean, 139a.
keep together, 351b.
keep watch, 175a, 473a.
keeper, 69b, 586b.
keepers of books, 586b.
keepers of cemeteries, 71b.
keeper of drowned, 70b.
Keeper of Great Leg, 71b.
Keeper of Lake of Fire, 71b.
Keeper of the Seals, 906a.
keeper of tackle, 70b.
keeper of virgins, 70b.
keeper of wardrobe, 70b.
Kefaiu, 794a.
Kefi, 794a.
Kef-pesesh, 793b.
Kefni-ur, 15a.
Keft, 794a.
Keftenu, 794b.
Kehab (Set), 796b.
Kehai (Set), 796b.
Keḥau, 796b.
Keḥkeḥit, 797a.
Kek (Nile-god), 798b.
Keki, 798a.
Kekr, 798b.
Kektiu, 798a.
Keku, 798a.
Kem, ka of Rā, 794b.
Kemkem, 794b.
Kemnu, 794b.
Kenȧt, 795a.
Kenem, 795b.
Kenemmti, 795b.
Kenemti, 795a.
Kenemtiu, 795b.
Kenkenemmti, 795a.

Kenmen, 795b.
Kenmet, 795a.
Kenmut, 795b.
Kep-ḥer, 793b.
kept back, 345b.
Ker, god, 796a.
Kerāsher, 796a.
Kerent, 796a.
Kerit, 796a.
kernel, 354a, 531b.
Kerrshaā, 796b.
Kes, god, 797b.
Kesem-heh-Ȧmentt, 797b.
Kesht, 798a.
Keshtt, 798a.
Kesmiu-nent, 797b.
Ḳetits, 465b.
kettle, 178a, 429a, 791a.
Ketuiti, 797b.
Ketuitt, 799b.
Kha, 526a.
Kha, Lake of, 526b, 763a.
Khā-ȧakhut, 535a.
Khāȧ-tau, 535a.
Khabestiu, 540b.
Khabiu, 572a.
Khabsit, 530b.
Khabsu (Dekans), 572a.
Khā-em-Maāt, 535b.
Khā-em-Mennefer, 535a.
Khā-frā, pyramid of, 172a.
Khai (Rā), 529a.
Khaibittiu, 529b.
Khait, 529a.
Khāit, 535a.
Khaitiu, 529a.
Khak-ȧb, 574b.
Khakerit, 575a.
Khakerit-ḥat, 575a.
khamâsîn, 547a.
Khā-mut-f, 535b.
khân, 102b, 549b.
Khā-nefer Mer-en-Rā, 535a.
Khā-neferu-en-Rā, 535b.
Khânês, 342a.
Khanr (Āapep), 531b, 532a.
Khapri, 572b.
Kharbṭu, 532b.
Khârgah, Oasis of, 52b, 84b, 795b.
Kharkhar, 573b.
Kharstȧ, 533a.
Khast, 574a.
Khastiu, the Four, 534a.
Khast-shemu-ruṭ, 574a.
Khatȧthana, 534a.
Khateb-mut-f, 575a.
Khati gods, 534a.
Khat-Kheprer, 570b.
Khatri, 575a.
Khatt-Satt, 534a.
Khatu gods, 575a.
Khau, 526b, 528a.
Khā-urit, 535b.
Khebetch, 541a.
Khebetchtch, 541a.
Khebit-ḥeri-snef, 539a.
Khebitt-sāḥt-meter, 539b.
Khebnit, 540a.
Khebsit, 540b.
Khebsi-ta, 540b.
Khebs-ta, Council of, 901b.
Khefāt, 545a.
Kheftes-ḥȧu-etc., 545b.
Kheft-ḥer-neb-set, 545b.
Kheft-ta, 545b.
Khekh, god, 563a, 896a.
Khekh-nemmt, 563a.
Khem (Menu), 546b.
Khemenit, 547b.
Khemenu, dweller in, 886a.
Khemi, 547a.
Khemit, 547a b.
Khemiu-ḥemu, 546b.
Khemiu-ḥepu, 546b.
Khemiu-seku, 546b.
Khemkhem, 547a.
Khen, god, 549b.
Khenf, god, 550b.
Khen-ḥer, 576a.
Khennu, 577a.
Khen-n-urt-f, 577a.
Khen-pet, 576a.
Khenp-shānu festival, 550b.
Khen-remenes, 549b.
Khensit, 552b.
Khensu, 40b, 183b, 553a, 821b.
Khensu-Beḥeṭ, 553a.
Khensu-em-Uast, 553a.
Khensu-ḥeri-ȧb-Benn-t, 553b.
Khensu-ḥunu, 553a.
Khensu-Nefer-ḥetep, 553b.
Khensu-Nefer-ḥetep-Ḥeru, 553b.
Khensu-Nefer-ḥetep-Ṭeḥuti, 553b.
Khensu-pa-ȧri-sekher, 553a.
Khensu-pa-khraṭ, 553a.

Khens-ur, 552b.
Khensu-Rā, 553b.
Khensu-sa-Tekhit, 553b.
Khensu-Sepṭ, 553b.
Khensu-Shu, 553b.
Khensu-Ṭeḥuti, 553b.
Khensu-ur, 553a.
Khenṭ-Ḥepui, 559a.
Khenti, god, 554b.
Khenti-Åabtt, 554b.
Khenti-åakhut-taui, 554b.
Khenti-āat, 555a.
Khenti-åau-t-f, 554b.
Khenti-Åmenti, 554b.
Khenti-Åmenti-Rā, 555a.
Khenti-Åmentiu, 554b.
Khenti-Åmentt, 554b.
Khenti-Ån, 555a.
Khenti-ānkhiu, 555a.
Khenti-ånt-s, 555a.
Khenti-årti, 555a.
Khenti-åst-f, 558b.
Khenti-āt-Åment, 555a.
Khenti-Åturti, 555a.
Khenti-em-ṭeft, 555b.
Khenti-en-Sat, 556a.
Khenti-ḥeḥ, 556b.
Khenti-ḥeḥ-f, 556a.
Khenti-ḥensekt, 556a.
Khenti-ḥenthau, 556b.
Khenti-Ḥeq-āntch, 556b.
Khenti-ḥeri-åb-etc., 556b.
Khenti-ḥerit, 556b.
Khenti-ḥesert, 556b.
Khenti-ḥespu, 556b.
Khenti-ḥet-Ånes, 556a.
Khenti-Ḥet-res-utchat, 556a.
Khenti-kau, 557a.
Khenti-Khas, 556b.
Khenti-khat-ånes, 556b.
Khenti-khati, 556b.
Khenti-Kheri, 557a.
Khenti-meḥt-agbå, 555b.
Khenti-men, 555b.
Khenti-menåt-f, 555b.
Khenti-Menṭ, 555b.
Khenti-Mentchet-ti, 555b.
Khenti-ment-f, 555b.
Khenti-Naåruṭef, 555b.
Khenti-n-årti, 556a.
Khenti-nefer, 556a.
Khenti-Nunut, 556a.
Khenti-nut-f, 556a.
Khenti-petchu, 555b.
Khenti-Qerr, 557a.
Khenti-Rastau, 556a.
Khenti-sebkhet, 557a.
Khenti-seḥ-kaut, 557a.
Khenti-seḥ-neter, 557a.
Khentit-seḥ-neter, 557a.
Khenti-Sekhem, 557a.
Khenti-senut-s, 557a.
Khenti-she-f, 557a.
Khenti-shenen, 557a.
Khenti-shet-āa-perti, 557a.
Khenti-ta-shemā, 557b.
Khenti-temt, 557b.
Khenti-Ṭeshert, 557b.
Khenṭit-ḥer, 559a.
Khenti-thethef, 557b.
Khenti-uas-f, 555a.
Khentiu-Ḥen-Nefer, 554b.
Khenti-un, 555b.
Khentt-sekhet-s, 557a.
Khentt-shepsit, 557a.
Khentt-thes, 557b.
Khentu, 554b, 558a.
Khentui, 555b.
Khenub, 550a.
Khenuf, 550a.
Khen-unnut-f, 577a.
Khenup, Nile-god, 550a.
Khenu-set, 577a.
Khep, Nile-god, 541b.
Khepå, 541b.
Khepau, 544b.
Kheper = God, 543b.
Kheper, spirit, staff, standard, winged disk, 543a b.
Kheper-Rā, 543b.
Kheper, Image of, 828b.
Kheper-ānkh, 543b.
Kheper-keku-khā-mesut, 542b.
Kheper-Khenti-Åmentt, 543b.
Kheper-khesef, 543b.
Khepesh, Great Bear, 544a.
Khepi, 542a.
Kheprer, 543a.
Kheprer = Rā, 543a.
Khepri = Rā, 542a, 543b.
Khepri, a serpent-boat, 47b, 543b.
Kheprit, 543a.
Khepru, 543b.
Kher, a god, 560b.
Kher (Āapep), 561a.

Kherȧ, 561b.
Kher-āḥa, god and city, 581a.
Kherefu, the, 562b.
Kheri-beq-f, 581a.
Kheri-ermen-Saḥ, 581a.
Kheri Kenem, 581b.
Kheri-Khepti, 581b.
Kheri-khepti-Kenemut, 581b.
Kheri-khepti-Serit, 581b.
Kheri-She, 581b.
Kherit, goddess, 580a.
Kheritȧ, 582b.
Kheri-ṭesu, 581b.
Kherit-khenti-Sekhem, 581b.
Kherit-teka, 581b.
Kheriu, 561a.
Kheriu-ȧakhu, 581a.
Kheriu-āmu, 581a.
Kheriu-autu, 581a.
Kheriu-ḥeteput, 581b.
Kheriu-metaḥu, 581a.
Kheriu-nuḥ-en-Ṭuat, 581a.
Kheriu-Nutchi, 581a.
Kheriu-sebu, 581b.
Kherm'u, 562b.
Khermuti, 562b.
Kherp, 562b.
Kherp Ḥeru-em-ḥetep, 562b.
Kherp-neteru (Osiris), 562b.
Kherp-seḥ, 562b.
Kherru, 562a.
Khersek-kek, 563a.
Khersеrȧu, 562b.
Kherset-Shu, 563a.
Khertt-neter, 580a.
Kheru-ȧb, 561b.
Kheru-qerȧ, 560b.
Khesbetch, 564a.
Khesbetch-ȧrti, 564a.
Khesef-Ȧntiu, 564b.
Khesef-aṭ, 564b.
Khesef-hai-etc, 565a.
Khesef-ḥer, 564b.
Khesef-ḥer-āsh-Kheru, 564b.
Khesef-ḥer-khemiu, 565a.
Khesef-khemit, 565a.
Khesef-khemiu, 565a.
Khesef-nerit, 564b.
Khesef-neteru, 564b.
Kheser-Pek, 565b.
Khesfit-seba-em-perit-f, 565a.
Khesfit-smait set, 565a.
Khesfu, 564b.
Khesfu-āus, 564b.
Khessi, 36b, 563b.
Khet, god, 526a.
Khet-ānkh-ȧm-f, 526a.
Khet-ānkh-uȧa-f, 526a.
Khetasar, 568a.
Khetchtch, 569b.
Khet-em-Ȧmentiu, 526a.
Kheti, 526a, 568a.
Kheti, the "Worm," 6a, 281b.
Khetiu-Geb, 568a.
Khetiu-ta, 568a.
Khet-Kheperȧ, 526a.
Khetrȧ, 569a.
Khett-nebt-rekhu, 526a.
Khet-uat-en-Rā, 526a.
Khi, God and "god," 536a.
Khirpasar, 536b.
Khit, 536a.
Khnem, 578a.
Khnem-ānkhtt, 578a.
Khnem Ḥeru-Ḥetep, 578b.
Khnemit, 551b.
Khnemit goddesses, 578a.
Khnemit-em-ānkh-Ȧnnuit, 578b.
Khnemit-urt, 578a.
Khnemiu gods, 578a.
Khnem-Khenti-ȧneb-f, 578b.
Khnem-Khenti-netchemnetchem-ānkht, 579a.
Khnem-Khenti-per-ānkh, 579a.
Khnem-Khenti-taui-neteru, 579a.
Khnem-Khenti-uār, 578b.
Khnem Neb, 578b.
Khnem Neb-per-Meḥti, 578b.
Khnem Neb-Peshnu, 578b.
Khnem Neb-Smen, 578b.
Khnem Neb-ta-ānkhtt, 578b.
Khnem Neb-Tcherur, 578b.
Khnem Neb-Uāb, 578b.
Khnem-nefer, 551b.
Khnem-neḥep, 578b.
Khnem-qenbti, 579a.
Khnem-qeṭ-ḥeru-nebu, 579a.
Khnem-Rā, 578b.
Khnem-renit, 578b.
Khnem-sekhet-ȧsh-f, 579a.
Khnemtit, 551b.
Khnemu, 450b.
Khnemut goddesses, 578a.
khôr, 58a.
Khuait, 538a.
Khufu, pyramid of, 25a.

Khu-Ḥeru, 537b.
Khuit, priestess, 537b.
Khuit-mu, 537b.
Khuràb, 538a.
Khurrti, 562a.
Khu-tchet-f, 537b.
Khutt, 537b.
Khut-Tuat, 537b.
Ki, god, 792b.
kick, 386a.
kidney, 55a, 117b.
kidney, to be of the same, 164b, 277b, 293a, 518a.
kill, 156a, 210b, 220a, 223b, 270a, 273a, 274b, 291b, 388a, 400a, 431a, 435b, 468b, 512b, 534a, 535b, 538a, 539a, 575a, 597b, 598ab, 601b, 629ab, 632a, 653b, 664b, 665a, 666b, 667b, 668b, 711b, 717b, 727b, 734a, 756b, 757b, 799b, 844a, 876b, 884a.
kill men for dead chief, 302a.
kill oneself, 295b, 429b.
killing, a, 878a.
kiln, 118b, 708a, 819a.
kin, 739a.
kind, i.e., species, 595a, 694a.
kind, 4b, 20b, 50a, 283b, 297b, 598a, 666b, 673a, 779b, 801b.
kind-hearted, 371a.
kindle, 20a, 259a, 866a, 434a, 601b, 636b, 676b, 685b, 709a, 845b.
kindling, 601b.
kindly, 305a.
kindly man, 665a.
kindness, 680b.
king, 45a, 63b, 97a, 128b, 171a, 390b, 391a, 653a, 754b, 823a.
king, house of, 239a.
king, place of in temples, 79b.
king, to act the, 646a.
king, the two eyes of, 391b.
king of the North, 203a, 211b.
king of the South and North, 391b.
kingdom, 653b.
kingdom of Horus, 16a.
kingdom of Set, 16a.
king's highway, 529b.
kingship, 653b.
kinsfolk, 4b, 27b, 55b, 812a.
kinsman, 599b, 637a, 674a.
kinsman, royal, 392a, 430b.
Kirgipa, 792b.
kiss, to, 89b, 548b, 603b, 675a.
kiss the earth, i.e., do homage, 89b, 601b, 675a.
kiss the feet, 675a.
kiss the hand, 603b.
kitchen, 455b.
kite, 909b, 910ab.
kith and kin, 284a.
Kkhert (?), 797a.
knap and flint, 664b, 685b.
knead, 605a, 676a, 774a, 802b, 879a.
knee, 12a, 255b, 305a, 709b.
knife, to, 888a, 911b.
knife, 57b, 72a, 91a, 98b, 123b, 138a, 205a, 226a, 234a, 275b, 288b, 325a, 333b, 334b, 336b, 345b, 387a, 390a, 390b, 511ab, 512a, 536a, 541b, 597b, 606a, 615a, 664b, 665a, 666a, 667b, 730a, 731a, 793b, 844a, 867b, 870a, 878a, 887a, 888a, 911b.
knife, broad, flat, 846b.
knife, butcher's, 575b, 730a, 792a.
knife, reed-cutter's, 665a.
knife, sacrificial, 71b, 527b, 575b.
knife-hearted, 291b.
knight, 861a.
knob of crown, 204a.
knock, to, 902b.
knock over, 528b.
knots, 99a, 859b.
knots, the seven, 859b.
knotted, 491a.
know, 6a, 73a, 120a, 121b, 128a b, 274b, 430a, 433a, 583b, 587b, 633b, 640b, 641a, 649a, 650b, 896a; to make to, 612a, 681a, 866a.
know by sight, 641b.
know carnally, 430a.
know the water, 293a.
knower, 143b.
knowing, 739a, 852b.
knowingly, 265a, 430a.
knowledge, 430a, 621b, 634a, 640b, 643b, 751b, 896a.
knowledge personified, 430b.
Knowledge-god, 896a.
Knufi, 795a.

koḥl, 673b.
koḥlstick, 201b.
kyphi, 862b, 902b, 906a.

L.

laboratory, 81b, 455b.
labour, 206a, 225a, 232b, 439a, 784a.
labour, forced, 258b.
labour, to be in, 296b.
labourer, 30a, 94a, 105b, 206b, 302a, 487a, 547b, 747b, 784a; skilled, 483a.
Labyrinth, 456b.
lace, 91a, 790b.
lace up, 146b.
lack, 12a, 19a, 26b, 127b, 181a, 184b, 186b, 382b, 397b, 469b, 539b, 800a, 874a.
lack of, 635a.
lacking, 37a, 78a, 395b, 539b, 732b, 778b.
lacuna, 184b.
ladder, 110a, 174a, 225a, 233a, 276a, 288b.
Ladder, the Celestial, 10b.
ladder, rope, 422a, 765a.
ladder, two sides of a, 280b.
ladder of Osiris, 276a.
laden, 13ab, 97b, 274a, 357ab.
lady, 422b, 463b, 486a, 742b, 860b.
lady, great, 107a.
lady, royal, 391b.
laid out, 713b.
laid waste, 702a.
lair, 201b, 216a, 275b.
lake, 22a, 97b, 128b, 146b, 174a, 204b, 212b, 257b, 280a, 285a, 293a, 307b, 308a, 325b, 349b, 374a, 442ab, 449b, 488a, 574a, 576a, 592b, 640a, 642a, 650b, 653b, 704a, 720a, 731b, 733b, 744a, 758a, 814a, 896b, 915b.
lake for waterfowl, 768b.
lake, celestial, 307b.
lake, crown of the, 163a.
Lake-god, 184b.
Lake Moeris, 720a.
Lake of Aqeb, 720b.
Lake of Boiling Water, 309a.
Lake of Celestial Beings, 721b.
Lake of Cold Water, 721a.
Lake of Destruction, 308b.
Lake of Fire, 71b, 308a, 720ab, 721a.
Lake of God, 721a.
Lake of Ḥepu, 309a.
Lake of Ḥetep, 309a, 721b.
Lake of Ḥi, 721b.
Lake of Horus, 308b, 720b.
Lake of Jackals, 309a.
Lake of Kenstȧ, 309b.
Lake of Kha, 309a.
Lake of Life, 308a, 720b.
Lake of Light, 721a.
Lake of Maāt, 308b.
Lake of Menā, 308b.
Lake of Natron, 308b, 721a.
Lake of Nu, 309a, 721a.
Lake of Nubia, 263b.
Lake of 100,000 years, 309a.
Lake of 1,000,000 years, 721b.
Lake of Osiris, 720a.
Lake of Perfection, 720b.
Lake of Propitiation, 309a, 721a.
Lake of Reeds, 308b, 720b.
Lake of Sȧsȧ, 308b, 309a.
Lake of Seḥseḥ, 309b, 682b.
Lake of Sekhmit 309b.
Lake of Serser, 349a.
Lake of Sharu, 721b.
Lake of Shesh, 309b.
Lake of Ṭattȧ, 721b.
Lake of Testes, 309a.
Lake of the Geese, 309a.
Lake of the God, 309a.
Lake of the horizon gods, 308b.
Lake of the Jackal, 721a.
Lake of the Kha geese, 721a.
Lake of the Kharu geese, 721b.
Lake of the Ṭuat, 309b.
Lake of the Ụraei, 308b.
Lake of the Wicked, 721a.
Lake of Truth, 308b, 720b.
Lake of Truth-speakers, 720b.
Lake of Turquoise, 308b, 720b.
lamb, 790a.
lame, 356b, 806b.
lament, 6a, 36a, 74a, 94b, 136b, 279a, 385b, 386b, 396a, 397b, 398b, 475b, 549b, 763b, 771ab, 772a, 773a, 786a, 821b, 896a.

lamentation, 225b, 386b, 438a, 450a, 469b, 475b, 648a, 658a, 705b, 727a, 786b, 794b, 821b, 821b, 896a.
lamp, 530b, 533b, 540b, 845a b.
Lamps, i.e., the Dekans, 530b.
lamp stands, 809a.
lamp wicks, 82a, 533b.
lance, 154b, 281b, 283a, 366b, 459a, 516b, 573a.
land, to, 281b, 638a, 868b, 885a.
land, 6a, 13a, 25a, 72a, 94a, 97b, 99a, 104b, 122a, 247a, 409a, 423b, 453a, 457b, 490a, 533b, 667a, 712b, 759b, 815a, 835b, 855a, 990b, 896b.
land, arable, 369a, 490a, 755b.
land, cultivated, 8a, 128a, 146a, 758b.
land, fertile, 77a, 113a.
land, flooded (or irrigated), 843a.
land, irrigated, 8b, 102b.
land, lighting up of, 522b.
land, low-lying, 269a.
land near a canal, 882b.
land, ploughed, 276a, 704b.
land prepared for building, 388a.
land, salt, 750b.
Land, the Beautiful, 816b.
Land, the Eternal, 507b.
Land, the Hidden, 816b.
Land, the Holy, 816b.
land, uncultivated, 816a.
land, unenclosed, 815b.
land, waste, 732a, 815b.
land, watered, 99b, 368b.
land, wooded, 661b.
Land of Eternity, 816a, 817a.
Land of Life, 125a, 816a.
Land of refreshing, 816b.
Land of Seker, 816b.
Land of the Bow, 22a.
Land of the God, 816a.
Land of the Lake, 816b.
Land of the North, 816a.
Land of the Spirits, 815b.
Land of Truth, 816b.
Land of Truth-speaking, 816b.
landing, 301a.
landing-place, 137b, 281b.
landing-stage, 80a, 308a, 544b, 647b.
landlord, 562a, 812a.
landlord of Egypt, 812a.
landmark, 133b, 192b.
landsmen, 815b.
lane, 313b.
language 913a ; the finest, 830a.
language, the Egyptian, 335b, 416a.
language, the Sûdânî, 913a.
languid, 122b.
languor, 550b, 553a.
lap, 212b.
lapis-lazuli, 564a, 565b, 574b, 754b.
lapis-lazuli, artificial, 564a.
lapis-lazuli, real, 564a, 566a.
lapis-lazuli of Babylon, 564a.
large, 2b, 107b, 644b.
largeness, 2b.
largesse, 343a.
lascivious, 709a.
lash the tail, 795a.
lasso, to, 597a, 662a.
lassoer, 351b.
Lasso-god, 36a, 498a.
last, 131b, 527b, 579b.
Last Judgment, 642b.
last year, 606a.
lasting, 912b.
lattice, 852a, 905a.
latus fish, 132b, 152a.
laugh, 411a, 616a, 656b, 657b, 660b, 717a ; to make, 696b.
laugh at, 215b.
laughing matter, 632a.
laughingstock, 693a.
laughter, 660b.
laundryman, 136a, 170a.
laurier rose, 347a.
laver, 720a.
law, 82a, 192a, 270b, 271b, 346a, 400b, 441a, 446ab, 487a, 831b, 844b ; course of the, 831b.
law court, 453b.
law, personification of, 271b.
law, to employ, 66a.
law, words of, 335b.
lawgiver, 682a.
lawmaker, 860b.
laxity, 207b, 574a.
laxness, 574a.
lay, 190a, 631a.
lay bare, 793b.
lay charge on, 866a.

lay down arms, 147b.
lay eggs, 321b.
lay hands on violently, 101a, 849a.
lay hold on, 547b.
lay oneself flat, 864a.
lay open, 252b.
lay snare, 75a.
lay to heart, 437a.
lay under tribute, 562a.
lay waste, 204a, 256b, 538b, 716a.
laymen, 167b.
lay priest, 176b.
laziness, 181b.
lazy, 181b, 377a.
lead, 56b, 83a, 324a, 381a, 493b, 562a, 593b, 594a, 616a, 622b, 629b, 642a, 690a, 694a, 699a, 707b, 713a, 842a, 886a, 887a, 911a.
lead astray, 37a, 629a, 630a, 711b, 713b.
lead forward, 286b.
lead, block of, 355b.
leaden objects, 887b.
leader, 31a, 45b, 161a, 164a, 190b, 290b, 351b, 461a, 554a, 562a, 604a, 622b, 697b, 699a, 707b, 776a, 828b.
leaf, leaves, 34a, 343a, 400b, 600b, 625b, 771b, 802b, 806a, 808b, 911a.
leaf, of a door, 107a, 718a.
leaf-work, 771b.
league, 97b.
league, to make a, 540a.
lean (of years), 778b.
lean, 429a, 448a.
leap, 166a, 212a, 243a, 274b, 734b ; of an animal, 439b ; of fish, 262b, 628a, 837a.
leap away, 44a.
leap for joy, 147a.
leapings, 833a.
learn, 655a.
learned, 35b, 659b, 751b.
learned man, 430b, 650b, 848a, 852b, 900a.
learning, 430a, 525a, 634a, 655b.
learning, goddess of, 698a.
leather, 55a, 282a, 327b, 563b, 773b, 887a.
leather-worker, 853b.
leathers, magical, 67b.
leather objects, 182b, 327b, 790b.
leather roll, 129a, 753a.
leather strap, 911a.
leave, 261b, 528a, 702b, 792a, 844b.
leave behind, 147b.
leave the country, 240a.
leaves of door, 129b, 420b, 522a, 823a.
leaves of tablet, 129b.
leaven, 348a.
ledge, 243b.
ledger, 450a.
leech, 480a.
leek, 26a.
lees, 611b, 637b, 820b.
left, 18b, 20a.
left hand, 602b, 671ab.
leg, 156b, 298b, 305a, 329a, 393b, 436a, 589ab, 597b, 638a, 659b, 709b.
leg, fork of, 162a.
leg, part of, 6a.
leg of chair, 367b, 639a, 693a.
legs of a vessel, 617a.
legal, 91b.
leg-bands, 680a.
leg-bones, 274a.
legend, written, 291a.
leisure, 611b, 681a, 693a.
Lêlat an-Nukṭah, 459b, 811a.
length, 2b.
lengthen stride, 652a.
lentils, 112a, 113a, 484a.
leopard, 4ab, 19b, 233a, 274b, 367b.
leopard of South and North, 4b.
Leopard-god, 200b.
leopard skin, 200b.
less, 576a.
less, to make, 624a.
let (imperative), 50b.
let fall, 180a.
let fly arrow, 74a.
Letopolis, 46a ; title of high-priest of, 483a.
letter, 180a, 184a, 337b, 619a, 725a, 730b.
letter of invitation, 122b.
letters (books), 730b.
letters (writing), 688a.
letters, god and goddess of, 211b, 665b.

letters, love, 310a.
lettuce, 38b.
level, a, 563b.
level, to, 563a, 668b.
levies, 516b, 860b.
levy, to, 860a.
levy taxes, 521a, 522a, 655a, 757b.
lewd, 649b.
liability, 248a.
liar, 90b, 330b, 812b.
libations, 117a, 155b, 768b, 872b.
libation chamber, 239b.
libation, to make or pour out a, 28b, 148a, 629b, 884b.
libation jar, 510a.
libation priest, 148a.
libation vessel, 148a, 605b.
libationer, 108b, 155a, 768b; royal, 391b.
librarian, 358a, 586b.
librarian, chief, 495a.
library, 80a, 238b, 526b.
Libya, chief in, 554b.
Libya-Mareotis, title of high priest of, 427a.
Libyan god, 855a.
Libyans, 422b, 842a, 859a; in the Ṭuat, 855b.
lick up, 615a.
lie, to lie, 55a, 82a, 124a, 335a, 540a, 604b, 675a, 776a, 797b, 803a, 812a, 913a.
lies, highly coloured, 812a.
lies, tissue of, 860b.
lie, 141b, 810a, 812a.
lie at full length, 713b.
lie down, 374b, 375b, 629b, 632b, 718b.
lie on the back, 862a.
lie prone, 713b.
lie prostrate, 570a.
lier in wait, 787a.
lieutenant, 154b.
life, 112a, 124b, 127a; to spare, 866b.
Life, Åat of, 15b.
life, fluid of, 193a, 585b.
life, plant of, 487b.
life, tree of, 20b.
life time, 133b, 134a.
lift, 536a, 833a.
lift away, 861a.
lift oneself up, 823b.
lift the face, 259a.
lift the hand, 166a.
lift up, 189b, 258a, 529a, 630a, 646b, 698a, 713b, 733a, 827a, 852b, 856a, 861a, 873a.
lifted up (in a bad sense), 189b.
ligament, 422a.
ligature, 301a, 322b, 521a, 859b.
light, 5a, 9a, 10b, 23a, 31a, 49a, 93b, 128ab, 130b, 146a, 157b, 159a, 160a, 167a, 200a, 224b, 225a, 274a, 419a, 459b, 470b, 488a, 512b, 530b, 622b, 685a, 698b, 708ab, 712b, 731b, 736b, 753a, 764b, 783a, 914a; to emit or give, 163b, 249a, 269b, 700b.
light (i.e., dawn, morning), 225a, 381a.
light, beings of, 9a, 23a.
light-circle, 701a.
light-emitter, 708b.
light-giver, 459b, 522b.
Light-givers, the two, 459b.
Light-god, 23ab, 24b, 25a, 77b, 217a, 274a, 622b, 830b.
Light-god, eye of, 194a.
Light-goddess, 163b, 774a.
Light, the Great, 23a.
light, to be, 9b; to become, 522a.
lighten, 8b, 215b, 631b.
light a fire, lamp, or light, 609a, 712a, 845b.
light up, 221b, 614a, 685a.
light upon, 560b.
light in weight, 82a.
light of foot, 764a.
light (i.e., weak, worthless), 165b, 774b.
light-minded, 82a.
lighter (boat or barge), 640a, 685b.
lightning, 631b, 842a.
Lightning-god, 433b.
lightning-stone, 858b.
like, 50b, 177a, 264a, 269b, 277a, 278b, 307b, 339a, 414a, 595a, 779b, 788b, 804b, 826a.
like, to be, 277b, 385b, 826a.
like this, 265a.
like what? 77a, 277a.

likeness, 269b, 277b, 307b, 377b, 414b, 422b, 545a, 577a, 604b, 609a, 666b, 673a, 675b, 698b, 779b, 821b, 826b, 847a.
likeness, to make a, 321a, 675b.
likewise, 264b.
lily, 355b, 383b, 388a, 608a, 622a, 623b, 681a, 700b.
lily buds, 385b.
lily-field, 700b.
Lily-god, 207b.
lily knosps, 700b.
lily of Nefer-Tem, 624a.
lily-water, 700b.
limb, limbs, 30a, 31a, 75b, 76a, 106b, 134b, 315b, 368b, 392b, 465b, 466a, 583b, 746a.
limestone, 62b, 123a.
limit, 15b, 100a, 104b, 150a, 411a, 488a, 554b, 825a, 908b.
limit, to the, 414b ; to the uttermost, 415a.
limitless, 908b.
limits of earth, 479a.
limner, 620b.
limp, 809a.
line, measuring, 146a.
linen, 110b, 289a, 300ab, 319a, 661a, 680b, 866b, 884b.
linen, blue, 624b.
linen, fine, 252ab, 461a, 751a.
linen, royal, 653b, 751a.
linen, Sûdânî, 332b.
linen bandlet, 884b.
linen-chest, 475b.
linen closet, 455b.
linen cloth, 43b, 234b, 458b, 476b.
linen thread, 319a.
linger, 90b, 499b.
lintels of Hall of Maāti, 492a.
lion, 21ab, 129a, 211a, 245a, 268a, 269b, 278a, 419ab, 422b, 424b, 541b, 746b, 851a, 870a.
lion, fierce, 268b.
Lion (of Zodiac), 154b.
Lion-god, 46b, 268b, 270a, 273b, 562b ; of Manu, 419b.
lioness, 268a, 422b ; young, 372b.
Lioness-goddess, 70a, 116a, 165b, 168b, 169a, 232a, 246a, 247b.
lip, lips, 597a, 662b.
liquefy, 597b, 664b.
liquid, 36a, 73b, 92a, 122a, 202a, 293a, 400a, 435a, 636a, 795a.
liquid, embalming, 328b.
liquor, 77a, 230b.
liquor, fermented, 611b.
list, 41a, 106b, 161a, 346a, 430b, 604b, 642b, 661a, 683ab, 701b, 738b, 739a, 855b, 882ab.
list, daily, 450a.
list of names, 45b.
listen, 291b, 672b.
listen attentively, or carefully, 316b, 718a.
listener, 718a.
literature, 525a, 619a, 730b, 885a.
literature, divine, 337b, 401b.
Literature, Egyptian, 787b.
litigant, 745a.
litter, 258b, 773a, 773b, 884a.
little, 226a, 379b, 409b, 411b, 413b, 538b, 546a, 657a, 659b, 660b, 692b, 734a, 734b, 746a, 749b, 798b.
little-bread, 138b.
little by little, 379b.
Little-cat, 278a.
little child, 734b.
Little Heat, 434b.
littleness, 411b.
little one, 767a.
liturgy, 200b, 337b, 346a, 400b, 563b, 758a.
live, 112a, 124b, 127a.
live with a wife, 481a.
liver, 6b, 273b, 279a, 328a.
livers of the dead, 216a.
livid, 113a.
living, 766b, 804b.
living, the, 29a, 125a.
Living One, i.e., Osiris, 83b.
Living Ones, i.e., the 36 Dekans, 125a.
lizard, 472a, 490a, 492b, 667a.
Lizard-god, 328b.
lo ! 330b, 712a, 824b.
load, 13ab, 14b, 35b, 97b, 102b, 258b, 274a, 288b, 594a, 883b.
load a ship, 34b.
loaded, 14b, 35b, 441b.
loaded heavily, 883b.
loader, 594a.
load-carrier, 147b.
loading-up-place, 102b.

loaf, loaves, 151a, 152a, 186a, 202a, 209a, 218a, 233a, 232b, 234 ab, 247b, 259b, 261b, 283a, 324a, 415b, 422b, 442b, 516a, 521b, 533a, 534b, 545a, 635b, 722b, 730b, 734a, 750ab, 765b, 767a, 790a, 792b, 796a, 799b, 815a, 817a, 822b, 846a, 862b, 867a, 882b.
loaf, pyramidal, 219b.
loathe, 541a, 665a, 714a, 825b.
loathing, 262b, 263a, 383a.
loathing, to cause, 638a.
loathsome, 215a, 226a, 383a.
lobster, spiny, 804b.
locality, 269a.
lock, 280b, 600b, 636b, 808b.
lock of hair, 7a, 21b, 327b, 343a, 367b, 368a, 369a, 491a, 594a, 621b, 625a, 854a, 875b.
locust, 499b, 588b, 608a.
lodge, 753a.
lofty, 108a, 450a.
log, 249a, 329b, 615b, 789a, 796a, 856b.
loin band, 223a.
loincloth, 170a, 565b, 641a, 652a.
loins, 55a, 544b.
loneliness, 153b.
long, to or for, 4b, 309b.
long, to be, 2b, 760a.
long life, 760a.
long-armed, 181a.
long-bearded, 531a.
long-clawed, 760a.
long-haired, 2b.
long-nailed, 760a.
longsuffering, 33b, 180b, 598a, 664b.
Long Phallus (Osiris), 291a.
look, 68a, 158b, 211a, 254a, 351a, 672a, 716a, 762b, 771b, 801a, 808a, 890b, 891a.
look at, 216b, 266b, 702a, 846b, 891a.
look fierce, 509b.
look maliciously, 509b.
look most carefully, 891b.
look upon, 544b, 802b.
look-out, 266b ; to keep a, 273a.
look-out for, 903b.
look-out man, 382a.
look-out place, 254a, 273a.
look with curiosity, 814b.
look with evil design, 802a.
loom, 121b.
loops for pectoral, 510a.
loose, 152b, 598a, 622a.
loosen, 178b, 296a, 401a, 606a, 665b, 697a.
lord, 215b, 283a, 357a, 359b, 862a, 867b.
lord it over, 772a.
Lord Creator, the, 357b.
Lord of names, 426a.
Lord of Spirit-souls, 24b.
Lord of Things, 24a.
lose, 92b, 181a, 379b.
lose the way, 711b, 797b, 839a.
loss, 7b, 12b, 25b, 92b, 140b, 379b, 539b, 648a.
loss, to suffer, 14a.
lost, 94a, 536b, 552b.
lot, 248b, 251b, 252a, 821b.
lote tree, 368a.
lotion, 36a.
lotus, 355b, 383b, 384b, 388a, 394a, 539a, 608b, 622a, 623b, 700b.
lotus, extract of, 700b.
Lotus-god, 207b.
loud-voiced, 760a.
louse, 230a, 594a.
lovable, 310a.
love, 4b, 19a, 54b, 62a, 118a, 309b, 310a, 412a.
love, to make, 412a.
love, pleasures of, 412a.
love of books, 655b.
love-apple, 850a.
loved one, 310a.
love-letters, 310a.
lovely, 309b.
lover, 310a.
love-song, 509a.
love-spells, 310a.
love-women, 74b.
loving mankind, 310a.
low (of cattle), 375a.
low, 476a.
low (of the Nile), 409b.
lower, 532a, 579b.
lowering, 789a.
lowing (of cattle), 345a.
lowly, 388b, 885b.
low-lying, 244b, 561a.

loyal 164b, 304a, 357b, 793b.
Lucina, 388a.
Luck, 326b, 595a.
luck, good, 193b, 371a.
luck, ill, 724a, 370b.
lull to sleep, 448a.
luminary, 159b, 163b, 459b, 530b, 540b, 809b.
lung, the, 77a, 163b.
Lung-god, 83b.
lurker, 787a.
lust, 37b, 419b.
Lycopolis, priest and priestess of, 403a, 425b.
lying, 95a.
lynx, 274b, 491a.
Lynx-god, 274b.
lyre, 902a.

M.

Maa-ā, 267a.
Maā-ȧb, 272a.
Maa-ȧb, 267a.
Maa-ȧntuf, 267a.
Maa-ȧri-f, 267a.
Maāāt Boat, 273b.
Maa-ȧtf- etc. 267a.
Maa-ȧtht-f, 267a.
Maā-ennuḥ, 272a.
Maa-en-Rā, 267b.
Maa-f-ur, 267a.
Maa-ḥaf, 267b.
Maa-ḥeḥ- etc., 267b.
Maā-ḥer, 272b.
Maā-ḥer-Khnemu, 272b.
Maā-ḥer-pesh- etc., 272a.
Maait, 267a.
Maait-neferu, 267b.
Maaiusu (?), 267b.
Maā-kheru, 271b.
Maa-mer-f, 267a.
Maa-mer-tef-f, 267a.
Maa-m-gerḥ, 267b.
Maa-neb- etc., 267b.
Maa-neferut-Rā, 267b.
Maa-neter-s, 267b.
Maa-setem, 268a.
Maȧs (? crown), 270a.
Maasas, 267b.
Maāstiu, 273b.
Maatcheru, 268a.
Maateff, 268a.
Maa-tepu-neteru, 268a.
Maatet, 268a.
Maāt goddess, 271b.
Maāti goddesses, 272a.
Maāti (Nile-god), 272b.
Maāti (in the Ṭuat), 272b.
Maāti Boat, 290b.
Maāti, Hall of, 183a.
Maȧu, 269b.
Maāuatu (Rā), 272a.
Maȧu-ḥes, 269b.
Mābit, 47a, 281b.
mace, 17a, 27a, 32b, 83a, 90a, 202a, 459a, 523b, 672a.
mace, ceremonial, 19a.
macerate, 204a, 597b.
mad, 647b ; with terror, 531b.
madness, 419b, 648a.
Maft, god, 274b.
Māg, 289b.
magazine, 130a, 238a, 286b, 415b, 445b, 900a.
Mȧgeb, 266a.
maggoty, 153a.
magic, 515a.
magic, divine, 401b.
magic, malign, 712a.
magic, to work, 66a, 244a, 434a, 515a.
magical strength, 634a.
magician, 171b, 514b, 580b.
magistracy, 679b.
magnate, 215b.
magnet, 862b.
magnificence, 912a.
magnificent, 719b, 837b, 912a.
magnify, 215a, 590b, 644b, 651a.
Magnus, 288b.
Mahar-Baal, 284a.
Mȧi, 278a.
maiden, 17a, 32b, 102a, 110b, 303a, 471b, 573b, 750a.
maid servant, 206b, 525a.
maintenance, 286b.
majestic, 737a.
majesty, 214a, 483a, 737a, 783a.
major-domo, 108b, 312a.
majority, 126b, 137b.
make, 65a, 102b, 118a, 542a, 590a, 618a, 770b.
make to advance, 40a ; to approach, 88a ; to arrive, 42b, 54a ; to bow, 535b ; to cease,

435a, 539b ; to enter, 591b, 592a ; to fly, 42a ; to follow, 92a ; to go, 74a, 92a ; to know, 73a ; to open, 34a, 90a ; to recover, 65b ; to rise, 40a ; to rise on throne, 77b ; to see, 235b ; to travel, 50a ; to tremble, 91a.
make away with, 420b.
make bricks, 234b.
make copy or model, 604b.
make end of, 98a, 131a, 541a, 591a.
make eyes at, 801a.
make a defence, 185b.
make firm, 54a, 89b.
make friends with, 89b.
make great, 171a.
make haste, 82b.
make libations, 28b.
make like, 103a.
make magical passes, 67a.
make offering, 28b, 189a, 191a, 491b.
make oneself like, 65b.
make order, 37a.
make possession, 91b.
make strong, 38b, 104b.
make voyage, 55a.
make water, 133a.
makers, 67a.
Makhi, 275b.
Mākhiu, 286a.
malachite, 262a, 296a.
malady, 650b.
male, 188b, 217a, 292a, 331a, 473b, 583a, 848a, 850b.
male animals, 398a.
male child, 584a.
male deities, 401a.
Male, i.e., Geb, 848b.
male (heir), 33a.
males and females, 848a.
malefactor, 397b, 398a.
malice, 388a, 419a, 420a.
malignant, 213b.
malign glance, 802a.
mallet, 672a, 772b.
Mām, 281b.
man, 124b, 152a, 217a, 233b, 331b, 415b, 425b, 439a, 495b, 570a, 583a, 633a, 650b, 848a.
man, devilish, 621a.
man, educated, 131a.
man, learned, 621b.
man, living, 164b.
man, wise, 131a.
man of culture, 123a.
man of eternity (i.e., dead), 583a.
man of god, 423b.
man of means, 165a.
man of olden time, 830a.
man of truth, 423b.
man of war, 132a, 240b, 772a.
man, old, 26a.
man, Pharaoh's, 238a.
man, young, 17a, 27a, 303a, 372b, 471a.
manager, 860b.
man child, 848a.
mandragora, 850a.
Māngabtȧ, 282a.
Man-god, 834a.
man-hawk-god, 374b.
manicurist, 65b.
manifest, 166b.
manifest oneself, 240a.
manifestation, 240b, 534b, 542b.
manifold, 646b.
Mānkhti, 282a.
mankind, 67a, 233b, 322a, 379a, 423b, 426a, 429a, 430a b, 435a b, 493a, 570a, 617b, 717b, 834a.
mankind, three classes of, 436a.
Mānn, 282a.
manna, 300a.
manna of Tchah, 300a.
manna, white, 300a.
manna tree, 50b.
manner, 34b, 37b, 77a, 297b, 435a, 595a, 598a, 666b, 673a, 694a, 698b, 761b, 765b, 766b, 779b, 801b, 804b, 819b.
manner (of country), 766a.
manner of yesterday, 804b.
man servant, 206b ; young, 582b.
mansion, 174a.
mansions, celestial, 239b.
Māntchit, 282b.
mantis, 4b, 19b, 202b, 239b.
Mantis-god, 39a.
Mānṭit Boat, 282b.
mantle, 119a.
Manu, 24b, 274b, 869b.
manure, 128a, 262a.

manuscript, 337b.
many, 137a, 278a, 341b, 342b, 722a, 882b.
many-eyed, 313a.
many-faced, 137b.
many-formed, 107b, 137b.
Māpu, 281b.
Mārȧiu, 283a.
marauder, 841a, 845b.
march, 6a, 8a, 97b, 118b, 189b, 192b, 235b, 243b, 287a, 289b, 330a, 422a, 451b, 541a, 559a, 559b, 640a, 653a, 739a, 891a.
march after, 568a.
march against, 753b.
march at double, 289b.
march back, 567b.
march in front, 593b.
march southwards, 558a.
march through, 445b.
marches of a country, 256b.
mare, 618b, 695b, 696b.
Mareotis, 307b.
Mārerar, 281a.
margin of book, 766b.
margin of lake, 662b.
margin of road, 746b.
Māri, 281a.
mariner, 154b.
marines, 108b.
mark, 19a, 290b, 694a.
marks, cattle, 685b.
mark, distinguishing, 261b.
mark of quotation, 913a.
mark on beasts, 19b.
mark out, 256a, 711a.
mark, to be made a, 855b.
mark, to shoot at, 475b.
market, 314a, 778b.
market-place, 313b, 549b.
Mārqati, 283b.
marriage, 303a.
marry, 520b, 548b, 812a, 866a.
Mars, 656a.
Mārsar, 283b.
marsh, 3b, 27b, 103b, 104b, 244b, 272b, 334b, 442b, 526b, 533b, 539a, 571a.
marsh flower, 75b, 654a, 803a.
marsh land, 27a, 100b.
marsh plants, 107b, 641b.
marsh man, 769a.
marsh vegetation, 100b.
marshal, to, 607b, 677b.
marshal of court, 108b.
Mart, 275a.
marvel, 39a, 202b, 209b, 215a b.
marvellous, 215a.
masculine, 473b, 848a, 850b.
Maskhemit, 276a.
Mȧskhent, 279a.
mason, 26a, 60b, 94a, 578a, 582b, 779a, 805a.
mason, funerary, 582b.
mason, mortuary, 402b.
masonry, 725b, 764b.
mass, 570b, 915a.
mass of people, 164a.
mass of water, 174b, 317b.
massacre, 528b, 571a, 730a, 768a, 843a.
Mȧst, 279a.
mast, 58b, 276a, 566b, 583b, 675b, 757b ; of magical boat, 57a.
masts with sails, 517a.
master, to master, to be master, 145a, 154b, 357a, 494a, 562a, 588a, 810a, 851b, 860a b, 862a, 378b, 381a, 562a, 772a, 774b, 896a.
master mariner, 154b.
master of design, 358a.
master of the house, 495a.
master of scythes, 71a.
Masters of Wisdom, the Seven, 896a.
master of words of power, 886a.
mastery, 648a, 812a.
Mast-f, 276a.
masticate, 185a b.
Mastiu gods, 275b.
masturbate, 66a, 355b, 378a, 635b, 818a, 892b.
masturbation, 864b.
Māt, 280a.
mat, 146b, 249a, 586a, 600b, 773a, 796b, 835b, 836a b, 855a, 878b, 879a.
mat, grass, 541a.
mat, palm leaf, 647b.
mat, plaited, 368a.
mat covering, 202b.
Matȧit, 276b.
Matȧuahar, 276b.
mate, 579b.

material for rope, 351a.
maternal, 621a.
mathematical term, 703a.
Mathit, 276b.
Mȧti, 278b.
Matit, 276b.
Maṭiu priests, 276b.
matrix, 481b.
Māṭt, 290a.
matter, 201b, 230b, 233a, 525a.
matter, the daily, 8b.
matter, foetid, 222b.
matter, inert, 525b.
matter, what is, 77a.
matters, 438a, 580b.
mattocks, 492a.
maturity, 838b.
matutinal, 870b.
Mau, 273b.
Mȧu, 278a.
Mȧu-āa (Rā), 278a.
Ma-ur, a high priest, 266b.
M'au-taui, 280b.
Māuthenre, 281a.
Mauti, 278b.
maxim, 335a.
mayor, 312b.
me, 15a, 344a.
meadow, 27a, 423b, 686a, 721b, 770a.
meadow land, 201a.
meal, 6b, 8a, 91b, 137a, 411a, 704a.
meal, evening, 323b.
meal of reconciliation, 717a.
meal of wheat, 395b, 396a.
meals for the dead, 186a.
meals, sepulchral, 3b, 518a.
meals, the three, 817a.
meals, the two, 817a.
mean, 373a, 434a, 538b.
mean, the true, 139a.
means, 106a, 595a; to find, 807a.
measure, to, 41a, 285a, 526b, 563a, 753b, 813b, 899a.
measure land, to, 490a, 707a.
measure time, to, 315b.
measure, 1b, 2a, 41a, 43a, 73b, 107a, 131b, 139b, 186b, 220a, 237a, 253a, 301b, 390b, 400b, 448b, 486b, 527a, 542a, 544a, 652b, 659a, 722a, 731a, 736a, 752b, 767a, 790a, 814a, 827b, 850a, 854a, 863a, 867a, 868b, 882a, 895b, 913a, 915a.
measure (ἀρτάβης), 28b.
measure, dry, 442a, 855b.
measure of beer, 736b.
measure of capacity, 337a.
measure of cloth, 256a.
measure of corn, 33b, 41b, 42b, 876a.
measure of dates, 735b.
measure of fish, 328b.
measure (*hen*), 448b.
measure ($\frac{1}{4}$ hen), 235a, 446a.
measure ($4\frac{1}{2}$ hen), 201b.
measure (10 henu), 513b.
measure (160 henu), 579b.
measure of land, 3b, 71b, 97b, 567a, 573a, 585b, 707a, 717b.
measure of length, 614b, 648b.
measure, linear, 425a.
measure, liquid, 201b, 442a, 786b.
measure of time, 315b.
measure of weight, 253a.
measure, wine, 300a, 709b.
measuring cord, 527a, 652b, 707a.
measuring stick, 510b.
meat, 34a, 43a, 525a.
meat, cooked, 247b.
meat, joint of, 466b, 648b.
meat, pieces of, 730a, 735b.
meat, raw, 150a.
meat, selected, 713a.
meat and drink, 469a.
meat offering, 155b, 394b, 466b, 648b, 735b.
meat ration, 174a.
Medes, 336a.
medicament, 149b, 186a; to rub in, 643a.
medicine, 5b, 8a, 140a, 149b, 230a, 247a, 379b, 428b, 570b, 697b, 746b.
medicine, astringent, 160a.
medicine for eyes, 43b.
medicine for heart, 3a.
medicine pot, 284a.
medicine, science of, 592b.
medicine vessels, 300a.
medimnus, 337a.
meditate, 145b, 398a, 782b.

Mediterranean, 16b, 151a, 463b, 469b, 875b.
meek, 664b.
meet, 28b, 116b, 299a, 451b, 560b, 565a, 674b, 858b.
Mega, 331a.
Mehȧt, 315b.
Meḥen, 43a, 319b.
Meḥen-ȧpni, 319b.
Meḥenta, 319b.
Meḥenti, 319b.
Meḥ-f-meṭ, 317a.
Meḥi, 317a, 742b.
Meḥi (a canal), 317b.
Meḥi, Osiris, 318a ; Thoth, 318a.
Meḥit, 317a.
Meḥit, the Nile, 318a.
Meḥit and Tefnut, 317a.
Meḥiu, god, 317a.
Meḥ-maāt, 317a.
Meḥni, 319b.
Meḥnit, 319b.
Meḥnuti, 319b.
Meḥtit, Boat of, 152b.
Meḥtiu, 318b.
Meḥt-urit, 318a.
Meḥun, 319b.
Meḥ-urit, 826b.
Meḥ-urit, Seven Sons of, 119a.
Mekhir, 286a.
melon, 725a ; dried plants of, 725b.
melon plant, 722a, 725a.
melt, 10b, 356b, 597b, 612b, 696b.
melt away, 156b, 636a.
Melul (Merur), 315a.
Mema-āiu, 296b.
member, 30a, 31a, 43a, 75b, 106b, 134b, 368a b, 392b, 416a, 583b, 602a, 746a.
member, the, 141a, 204b.
member of the body, 7b, 315b, 465b, 466a, 609b.
member of a bodyguard, 45b.
member of council, 410a, 901a.
members of crocodiles, 525b.
members, pair of, 106b, 670b.
membrane, mucous, 222b.
Memḥet, 296b.
Memḥit, 296b.
memorandum, 614b, 688a, 808b.
memorial, 614b, 688a b, 808b.
memorial slab, 134a.
memorial tablet, 81b, 151a, 192b.
memory, 274a.
Memphis, 30b, 118b, 417a.
Memphis, title of high priest of, 483b.
Memphis plant, 126b.
Memu, 296b.
men, 164a, 205a, 214a, 270b, 423b, 429a, 430a, 435a b, 436b, 584a, 717b, 815b.
men, any group of, 33a.
men, festival of, 495a.
Men, the Two, 429b.
men, wax figures of, 436a.
men, ways of, 617b.
" men," i.e., Egyptians, 436a.
men of foreign speech, 782a.
men of high rank, 552a.
men of nothing, 546b.
men of wealth, 737a.
men on an estate, 676a.
men who know, 35b.
men and women, 125a, 165a, 170a, 233b, 249a, 379a, 430b, 447a, 481a, 491a, 542b, 681b, 815b, 834a, 848a.
Men-ā, 297a, 302a.
Men-ānkh, 302a.
Menant-urit, 301b.
Menȧt, a star, 301b.
Menȧt, 301b.
Menȧt-urit, 301b.
Menȧtiu, 301b.
Mendes, 15b, 111b.
Mendes, ram of, 408b.
Mengabu, 306a.
Men-hesȧu, 303a.
Menḥi, 303b.
Menḥit, 304a.
Menḥi-khenti-Seḥetch, 304a.
Menḥu, 303b.
Meni, 299a, 302a.
Menkerit, 306a.
Menkh, god, 305a.
Menkhet, 40b.
Menkh-qa-haḥetep, 305a.
Menmenit, 298b.
Menmenuā, 298b.
Menmutf, 298b.
men-nefer, 303a.
Mennu, 302b.
Mennui, 302b.

Menqeb, 305b.
Menqebȧ, 305b.
Menqit, 305b.
Menrir, 303a.
menses, 138b.
Menset, 305a.
menstruate, 512a.
Ment, 297a, 298a, 299a, 300a.
Menṭeft, 307a.
Mentha, 306b.
Menthesuphis, 306b.
Menthu, god, 306b.
Menthu nomads, 306b.
Mentit, 306b.
Mentsafi, 306b.
Mentu god, 306b.
Menu, 8b, 40b, 55a, 217a, 242a, 259b, 299a, 514b, 806a.
Menu-ȧāḥ, 299b.
Menu-ȧb, 297a.
Menu-Ȧmen, 299b.
Menu-fai-ā, 299b.
Menu Ḥeru, 299b.
Menu Ḥeru-fai-ā, 299b.
Menu Ḥeru-netch-tef-f, 299b.
Menu Ḥeru-sa-ȧst, 299b.
Menui-ḥer-pet, 298b.
Menu-nesu-Ḥeru, 299b.
Menu-qet, 299b.
Menu-ur, 302b.
Menu-urit, 297a.
Mer, 308a, 314b.
Merȧ, 315a.
Mer-ȧakhu, 313b.
mercenaries, 495a.
Merchant, 56b.
merchant, 289b, 733a.
Mercury, 654b, 657a, 660b, 673b, 707a.
Mer-en-āui-f, 311a.
Mer-en-Rā, pyramid of, 535a.
Mer-ent-neteru, 311a.
Meres, 315b.
Merḥi, 315a.
Merḥu, 315b.
Merḥuit, 315b.
Merifṭa, 310b.
Meri-fuā, 310b.
Meri-Maāt, 310b.
Meri-mut-f, 310b.
Merit, 308a, 314b.
Meritef, 311a.
Merit-erpā-neteru, 311a.
Meriti, 310b.
Merit-nesert, 314b.
Mermer, 315a.
Merqet, goddess of, 272a.
Merr, 310b.
merry, 419b, 858b.
merry, to make, 412a.
Mer-segrit, 311a.
Mer-sekhuit, 309b.
Mer-setau, 311a.
Merti, 308a, 310b, 313b.
Merti, the Two, 429b.
Merti-seti, 313b.
Meruā, 310b.
Merur, 314a, 315a.
Mesānuit, 324b.
Meseḥ, 325b.
Mesen, 325a.
Mes-en-Ḥeru- etc, 322b.
Mesenti, 325a.
Mesetchtch-qeṭ-f, 329b.
Mesit, 324b.
Mesit-tcher-s, 323a.
Meskat, 327b.
Meskhat-kau, 326a.
Meskhen, 326b.
Meskhenit, 326b.
Meskhenit-Āait, 326b.
Meskhenit-Menkhit, 327a.
Meskhenit-Menkhit-Nebt-ḥet, 327a.
Meskhenit-Neferit, 327a.
Meskhenit-Nefert-Ȧst, 327a.
Meskhenit-Nefertit, 327a.
Meskhenit-Nekhtit, 327a.
Meskhenit-Sebqit, 327a.
Meskhenit-Uatchit, 327a.
Meskhenit-Urit-tef-set, 327a.
Meskhent instrument, 326a.
Meskhenut, 326b.
Meskhti, 326a.
Mesktt, 328a.
Mes-nekhtit, 325b.
Mesnui, 325a.
Mesopotamia, 72b.
Mesore, 321b, 740a.
Mes-peḥ, 322b.
Mesper, 324b.
Mesperit, 324b.
Mes-pet-ȧaṭ- etc, 322b.
Mes-Ptaḥ, 322b.
Mes-qas, 323a.
Mesqatt, 327b.

Mesqen, 327b.
Mesqt, 327b.
Mesqt-Seḥṭu, 327b.
message, 19a, 161a.
messenger, 33b, 42a, 161a, 170a, 245b, 445a, 538a, 854b.
messenger, divine, 402a.
messenger, king's, 161b.
Messenger-god, 42a.
Mes-sepeth, 323a.
messman, 356a.
Mest, 328a.
Mestȧ, son of Horus, 328b.
Mest-Ȧsȧr, 328a.
Mestet, 328a.
Mestet-f, 328b.
Mestcher-Saḥ, 329b.
Mestcherti, 329b.
Mestcheriu, 329b.
Mesth, 328b.
Mesti, 328b.
Mesṭt, 329a.
Mesu Ḥeru, 322b.
Mesu-qas, 323a.
Mesu-Set, 323a.
Mesu-Temu, 323a.
Mesut-Rā, 321b.
Meṭȧ, 336a.
metal, 93b, 126b, 210a, 270a, 311b, 366b, 486b, 537b, 598b, 842a b, 846b, 903a, 907a.
metal, white, 75b, 523a.
metal, to plate with, 323a.
metal carriers, 764a.
metal fastening, 273b.
metal objects, 325a, 327b, 345a.
metal weapons, 394a.
metal work, 287a ; chased, 619a.
metal worker, 325a, 482b.
metal working, 354a.
metals, office of, 239b.
Metcha, 337b.
Metcher, 338a.
Metcheṭȧt, 338b.
Metcht-aa-utchebu, 337a.
Metcht-nebt-Ṭuat, 337a.
Metelis, Metelites, title of high priest of, 432a, 602b.
Meṭ-en-Ȧsȧr, 336a.
Meṭes, 336b.
Meṭes-ȧb, 336b.
Meṭes-ḥer, 336b.
Meṭes-ḥer-ȧri-she, 336b.
Meṭes-en-neḥeḥ, 336b.
Meṭes-mau, 336b.
Meṭes-neshen, 336b.
Meṭes-Sen, 336b.
Methen, god, 334b.
Meṭ-ḥer, 336a.
methods of procedure, 246b.
Meti, 333a.
Meṭi, 336a.
Meṭiu, 336a.
Meṭni, 336b.
Metrit, 334a.
Metrui, 334a.
Metsȧs, 331a.
Meṭt-qa-utcheba, 336a.
Meṭu-ȧakhut-f, 335b, 336a.
Meṭu-ta-f, 336a.
M-Ḥāp, 266a.
mice, 341b.
micturate, 133a, 260b, 652b.
midge, mosquito, 550a, 552a, 900a.
mid-day, 332a, 333b, 450a, 494b, 840b.
middle, 37b, 139a, 332a, 494b, 763a.
midnight, 248b, 494b.
midst, 494b, 819b.
midwife, 321a, 671b, 855b.
midwife, divine, 412b, 865b, 866a.
might, 5b, 182a, 197a, 245a, 288a, 379a, 388b, 563a, 592a, 608b, 621b, 690b, 738a, 772a, 805b, 822b.
mighty, 107b, 108a, 181b, 347b, 379a, 386b, 388b, 690b, 772a, 845a, 899b.
mighty, to be, 378b.
mighty bull (i.e., King), 784b.
mighty man, 241a, 287b, 389a.
mighty one, 182a, 215b.
mighty woman, 182a.
mild (of manner), 436a, 597b, 598a.
military, the, 125a.
militia, 620a.
milk, to, 65b, 615b, 659a, 700b.
milk, 21b, 60a, 69a, 73b, 127a, 223a, 510a, 523b, 857a, 882b.
milk, first, of a woman, 857a.
milk, sour, 305a.

milk-calves, 284b.
milk-can, 284a.
milk-carrier, 259a.
milkman, 284a, 316a.
milk pot, 284b, 314a, 316a, 422a, 431a, 442a, 467a.
milk vessel, 450a.
Milky Way, 510a.
mill, 531b.
millet, 223b, 227b.
millet, red, 227b.
millet, white, 227b.
million, 507a.
mina, 301b.
mince, 201a, 390a.
mince matters, 416a.
mind, 37b, 274a, 460b.
mine, possessive pron., 229b, 253b, 571a, 818b.
mine, 571b, 869b.
mine of the god, 402b.
mine-region, 210b.
miner, 402b, 535b, 770b.
mineral, 73a, 93b, 207a, 429a, 483b, 662a, 753a, 768a, 797b, 820b.
mineral, medicinal, 520b.
mineral unguent, 767a.
mingle, 598a.
mingled, 20a.
ministrant, 13a, 298b, 742a.
minium, 305b.
minority, 127b.
mint, 139b, 344b, 345a.
minute, 12b.
miracle, 544a.
mirror, 98b, 143a, 166b, 267a.
mirror, amulet of, 126b.
mirror in case, 126b, 238a.
mirthful, 412a.
miscarriage, 180a.
miscellaneous, 736a.
mise en livre, 767a.
miserable, 94b, 114b, 174b, 202b, 226a, 270a, 273a, 319a, 413b, 472b, 476a, 524b, 550a, 574a, 601a, 604a, 652b, 669a, 675a, 733b, 802a, 899b.
misery, 3b, 7b, 21b, 64b, 74a, 102a, 181a, 211a, 214a, 226a, 227a, 270a, 277b, 476a, 514a, 569b, 631b, 644b, 715a, 778a b, 802a, 815a, 906a b.
misfortune, 142a, 214b, 527b, 549b, 577a, 632a, 698a, 717b, 751a, 772b.
Misheps, 293a.
mislead, 629a, 711b.
mission, 32b, 161a, 440b, 441a, 487a.
mission, annual, 161a.
miss the mark, 176a.
mist, 27a, 96a.
mistake, 141b, 165b, 325a, 373a, 675a.
mistress, 107a, 157a, 357a, 463b, 486a, 494a ; a man's, 551a.
misty, 789a.
Mithras, 291a.
Mithrashamā, 291a.
mitre, 511b.
mix, 5a, 6b, 38a, 186b, 330b, 571a b, 573b, 598a, 600b, 735a, 736a, 837a.
mix drink, 859a.
mix unguent, 813b.
mixed, to be, 736a.
mixture, 330b.
Miysis, 270a.
M'kam'r, 289a.
M'katu, 289a.
M'ket-åri-s, 289a.
M'khan, 286a.
M'khenti, 286b.
Mkhenti-årti, 320b.
Mkhenti Sekhem, 320b.
Mkhenti-Ṭefnut, 320b.
M-Khenti-ur, 320b.
M'kheskhemiut, 286b.
M'khiår, 286a.
M'khiåru, 286a.
M'k-neb-set, 289a.
M'neniu, 282a.
Mnevis, 111b, 450b.
moan, 73b, 219b, 225b, 447a, 771a.
mob, 137b, 284a, 818a, 823a.
mock, 200b.
mock at, 215b.
mockery, 657b, 716b.
mode, 435a, 595a, 766b.
model, to, 323a, 353b, 849b.
model, 604b, 644a ; models, 135b.
modeller, 385b, 779a.
modesty, 798b.
moist, 39b, 189b, 635b.

moisten, 35b, 40a, 211b, 407b, 843a, 857b.
moisture, 27a, 69a, 73b, 97a, 394a b, 470a, 708b, 795a, 843a, 877b, 906a.
mole, 809b.
Mole-god, 580a.
moment, 12b, 14a, 15a, 17b, 27a, 351a, 438b, 517a, 753a, 815a.
money, 729a.
money deposit, 131b.
money, ring, 622a.
monkey, 795b, 804a, 807a.
monkey, long-tailed, 802b.
monkey, sacred, 769b.
monolith, 62a, 106b, 695a.
monster, composite, 121a.
month, 1b, 40b ; first day of, 829a ; first day of half-month, 829a ; priest of, 44b, 155b ; 25th day of, 450b.
month, Macedonian, 1b, 868a.
month, the half, 673a.
months, gods of, 40b.
monument, 28a, 274b, 298a, 670b ; funerary, 733b.
monuments, colossal, 298a.
moon, 18b, 23a, 29b, 68a, 75b, 132a, 177b, 194a, 659b ; the full, 29b, 316b ; at noon, 29b ; first quarter of, 881b ; third quarter of, 124a ; shining eye of, 657a.
moon, festival of, 75b, 250a.
Moon-god, 29b, 59a, 75b, 112b, 148a, 553a.
moored, 300b.
moral of a tale, 274a.
more, 384a, 449a, 469b.
more than, 64b, 459a.
moreover, 321a, 492b, 782a, 792a, 809b.
morning, 100a, 207a, 225a, 586a, 634a, 819a, 824b, 870b ; to do in the, 870b ; to pass the, 715a.
morning, to-morrow, 870b.
morning and evening, 840b.
morning meal, 28a, 91b.
morning star, 403b.
morsel, 233b, 245b.
mortals, 834a.
mortar, 331a, 757a.
morus tree, 314b.
mosaic, 203b ; pavement, 585a.
Moschion, 280b.
Moses, 324b.
mosquito, 552a.
most certainly, 415b.
mother, 294b, 331b, 334b, 771a, 785b ; of Horus, 7b ; of the god, 295a, 402a ; king's, 391b.
Mother (proper name), 50b.
mother-cow, 295a.
mother-gods, 41b, 402a.
mother goddess, 388a.
mother-in-law, 294b, 739a.
motherless, 340b.
mother-of-emerald, 262a, 394b.
mother-of-pearl, 593a.
motion, to set in, 607b, 690a.
motionless, 175b, 651a.
mould, to, 235a ; bricks, 695a.
mould, 226b, 353b, 779a.
mould of Osiris, 228a, 776b.
mould, to make a, 277b.
mould, two halves of, 910a.
moulder, 233b, 779a.
mouldiness, 78a.
mouldy, 78a, 566a.
mound, 857b, 858a.
mound, to cast up a, 477a.
mount, to, 212b, 701a, 824b, 873a.
mount up, 135a, 366b, 852b.
Mount of Sunrise, 47b.
Mount Seḥseḥ, 682b.
mountain, 129b, 261a, 298a, 311a, 442a, 449b, 636a, 823b, 841a, 869a, 872b, 904a.
mountain, funerary, 174b, 707b.
mountain of God, 449b.
mountain, the double, 600a, 869b.
mountain pass, 801a.
mountaineers, 869b.
mounted soldier, 861a.
mourn, 6a, 381b, 396a, 398b, 475b, 606b, 677a, 763b, 786a, 808b.
mourners, 6a, 26a, 94b, 348a, 396a, 397b, 424a, 446a, 457a, 509a, 763b, 807b.
mourner, professional, 462a.
mourning, 22a, 26a, 74a, 296b, 786b, 803b, 807b.
mouse, 236a b.

mouth, to, 351b.
mouth, 416a, 831a.
mouth, Opening the, 34b, 158b, 161b, 793b.
mouth, disease of the, 185b.
mouth, to steal a, 385a.
mouth of the people, 423a.
mouth to mouth, 416a.
mouthful, 316b.
move, 11b, 82b, 166a, 189b, 298a, 351b, 356b, 377b, 420b, 446b, 479a, 541a, 618b, 670b, 673a, 767a, 777b, 791b, 792b.
move, to make, 602a.
move about, 854b.
move away, 499a.
move onward, 478a.
move quickly, 343a, 827a.
move rapidly, 754b, 814b.
move up and down, 375a.
mover of stone, 439a.
Mqeṭqeṭ, 330b.
M'shaken, 287b.
M'shashar, 287b.
M'shauasha, 287b.
M'tchaiu, 291a, 495a.
M'tcheṭ, 292b.
M'ṭes, 291b.
M'ṭes-ab, 291b.
M'ṭes-årui, 291b.
M'ṭes-sma-ta, 291b.
M'tharima, 291a.
M'thenu, 291a.
M'thra, 291a.
M'ṭiṭi, 336a.
Mu, god, 293b.
much, 137a, 170b, 181a, 772a.
much, to be, 137a.
mud, 30b, 123b, 275b, 421a, 424b, 765b ; workers in, 201a ; mud of a stream, 880b.
mud flat, 836b.
muddle, 844a.
mudîr, 513a, 848b.
M'uit, 281a, 293b.
mulberry bread, 817a.
mulberry tree, 314a, 368a.
mulct, 865b.
mule, 792a, 796a.
mullet, 203b, 204a.
multiplication, 147b, 595a.
multiply, 177b, 591b, 595a, 646b, 763a.
multitude 137b, 768a, 880a.
multitudinous, 102a, 137b.
mummify, to, 188a, 613b, 631a b, 647b, 712a.
mummy, 280b, 758b.
mummy bandages, 188a.
mummy case, 152a, 188a.
mummy chamber, 777a.
mummy equipment, 777a.
mummy swathings, 71b, 818b.
muniment room, 526b.
M-up-tef, 266a.
murder, 396b, 398a.
murderer, 397b, 398a, 704a.
murmurs, 442b.
music, 444a.
musicians, 509a, 741b, 747a, 843b, 910b.
must (of wine), 759b.
Musta, 295b.
mustard, 611b.
muster, 607b, 677b, 841a, 841b.
musty, 470a.
Mut, collar of, 183b.
Mut, goddess, 150a, 295a.
Muthenith, 296a.
mutilation, 512b.
mutter spells, to, 209a, 386a, 758a.
Mut-urit, 295a.
muzzle, 729b.
my, 15a, 229a b, 234a, 253b, 342b, 344a, 818b.
myriads, 905b.
myrrh, 29a, 128a, 187b, 293b, 561b, 250b, 890b.
myrrh, dry, 127a.
myrrh, fresh, 127a.
myrrh of women, 127a.
myrrh, moist, 127a.
myrrh, ceremony of, 742a.
myrrh, image of, 127b.
myrrh box, 29a.
Myrrh-god, 83b, 127b.
myrrh seed, 127b.
myrrh shrub, 127b.
myrrh store, 127a.
myrrh tree, 380a, 771a, 890b; terraces of, 567a.
myrrh valley, 58a.
myrtle plant, 82a.
myself, 911b.
mysterious, 51a, 470b, 755b.
mystery, 624b, 701a, 755b.

N.

Nā, 346b.
Naȧb, 342a.
Naȧrik, 342a.
Naȧrruṭ, 341a b, 342a.
Naȧruṭ-f, Council of, 901b.
Nāȧu, 346b.
Nȧbḥer, 345a.
Nabkhun, 343a.
Nabti, 343a.
Naḥsu, 344a.
Nāi, 346b, 347a.
nail, to, 140a.
nail, 112b, 123b, 128b, 139b, 140a, 180a, 215b, 218a, 351a.
nails, to pare or cut, 621a.
nails, worker on, 65b.
Nāit, 346b, 347a.
Nāi-ur, 347a.
Nȧk, 345b.
naked, 383b, 458a, 469b, 794a.
naked man, 458a.
nakedness, 458b.
Nȧkh, 345a.
Nȧkit, 345b.
Nȧkiu-menȧ-t, 345b.
Namart, 343b.
name, to, 187b, 345a, 387b, 877b.
name, 426a, 782b.
Name, the Great, 426a.
names of limbs of Rā, 426a.
named, 345a, 387b, 877b.
namely, 79a.
Na-nefer-ȧri-sheṭit, 343b.
Na-nefer-sheṭi, 343b.
naos, 773b, 777b.
nape of neck, 123b, 124a b.
napkin, 243b.
Nāq, 347b.
Narḥ, 343b.
Nāri, 36b, 347a.
Nȧri-nef-nebȧt-f, 341a.
Nārit, 347a b.
narrate, 176b, 717a, 719b, 913a.
narrator, 176b, 719b.
narrative, 669b, 719b.
narrow, 491a, 492a, 782b, 800a.
Nārt, 347a.
Nārti-ānkh, etc., 347b.
Nȧs, 345b.
Nasaqbu, 344a.
Nā-shep, 347a.
Nashutnen, 344a.
Nȧs-Rā, 345b.
Nȧsṭ-taui-si, 345b.
nasty, 537b.
Nāṭai, 348a.
Nāṭi, 348a.
native, 350b, 583a.
Natkarti, 344a.
Nȧṭnȧṭu, 346a.
natron, 76b, 227b, 294a, 407b, 409b, 464b, 485a, 512a, 713b.
natron, chamber of, 456a.
natron of South and North, 408b.
Natron-god, 512a.
nature, 6b, 34b, 50b, 297b, 561a.
Nȧu, 344b, 345a.
naught, 835a.
nausea, 152b, 258a, 262b, 263a, 577b, 611a, 680b, 696b, 745a, 807a.
nauseated, 262b.
Nāutȧ, 347a.
navel, 533a.
navel string, 572b.
navigate, 93b, 576b.
near, 265a, 414a, 415a, 438b, 712a, 762b, 813a, 907a, 908a.
Neb, devil, 367a.
Neb-ȧa, 358b.
Neb-ȧakhut, 358b.
Neb-Ȧatit, 358b.
Neb-ȧbu, 358b.
Neb-ābui, 359a b.
Neb-āḥa, 359b.
Neb-ȧmakh, 358b.
Neb-Ȧmentt, 358b.
Neb-ānkh, 359b.
Neb-ānkh-em-pet, 359b.
Neb-ānkh-taui, 359b.
Neb-āqt, 360a.
Neb-āui, 359a.
Neb-ȧui, 367a.
Neb-aut-ȧb, 358a.
Neb-baiu, 360b.
Neb-er-ȧri-tcher, 362a.
Neb-er-tcher, 362a, 742b.
Neb-ḥeḥ, 363a.
Neb-ḥer, 367b.
Neb-ḥeru, 362b.
Neb-ḥer-uā, 363a.
Neb-ḥet-ā, 362b.

Neb-khāu, 363a.
Neb-kheper-Khenti-Ṭuat, 363b.
Neb-kheperu, 363a.
Neb-khepesh, 363b.
Neb-Khert-ta, 363b.
Neb-khet, 363a.
Neb-Maāt, 361a.
Neb-Maqt, 361a.
Neb-mau, 361a.
Nebneb, 354a, 367a.
Neb-nebu, 361a.
Neb-nefu, 361b.
Neb-neḥeḥ, 361b.
Neb-nekht-Khensu, 361b.
Neb-nemmt, 361b.
Neb-nerau, 361b.
Neb-neru, 361b.
Neb-neru-āsh-kheperu, 361b.
Neb-net, 362a.
Neb-neteru, 362a.
Neb-Pai, 360b.
Neb-Pāt, 360b.
Neb-qebḥ, 365a.
Neb-qerst, 365a.
Neb-Rasta, 362a.
Neb-rekeḥ, 362a.
Neb-rekhit, 362a.
Neb-renput, 362a.
Neb-Sakhb, 363b.
Neb-Sau, 363b.
Neb-sebt, 363b.
Neb-Seger, 364b.
Neb-sekhab, 364a.
Neb-sekht, 364a.
Neb-sekhut-uatcht, 364a.
Neb-senku, 363b.
Neb-settut, 364b.
Neb-shefit, 364b.
Neb-sherat, 364b.
Neb-shespu, 364b.
Neb-shuti, 364b.
Neb-Ta-ānkhtt, 365b.
Neb-taiu, 365a.
Neb Ta-tchesert, 365b.
Neb Ta-ṭesher, 365b.
Neb-tau, 365b.
Neb-tchefa, Neb-tchefau, 366a.
Neb-tcher, 366a.
Neb-tcheser-sesheta, 366a.
Neb-tchet, 366a.
Neb-ṭebui, 365b.
Neb-ṭemat, 365b.
Neb-temu, 365b.
Neb-ṭesher, 366a, 896a.
Neb-tha, 365b.
Neb-thafui, 365b.
Neb-Ṭuatiu, 365b.
Neb-uā, 360a.
Neb-uāb, 360a.
Neb-Uast, 360a.
Neb-un, 360a.
Neb-urrt, 360a.
Neb-user, 360a.
Neb-utchatti, 360b.
Nebȧ, 241b, 366b, 367a.
Nebȧ-ȧakhu, 367b.
Nebȧ-per-em-khetkhet, 367b.
Nebȧts-kheper, 367a.
Nebȧu, 367b.
nebeḥ bird, 367b.
Nebetch god, 368b.
Nebs, god, 368a.
Nebses, 364a.
Nebt, 368a.
Nebt-ȧakhu, 358b.
Nebt-Ȧamu, 368b.
Nebt-ȧāshemit, 358b.
Nebt-Ȧat, 358b.
Nebt-Ȧaṭt, 358b.
Nebt Ȧat-Then, 358b.
Nebt-āāu, 359a.
Nebt-ābui, 359a.
Nebt-āḥāu, 360a.
Nebt-ȧkeb, 359a.
Nebt-ȧm, 358b.
Nebt-ȧnemit, 358b.
Nebt-Ȧnit, 359a.
Nebt-ānkh, 359b.
Nebt-ānkhiu, 359b.
Nebt-Ānnu, 359b.
Nebt-āremuȧa, 359b.
Nebt-ȧrit-qerrt, 359a.
Nebt-ȧrit-tcheṭfiu, 359a.
Nebt-ārui, 359b.
Nebt-ȧs-ḥatt, 359a.
Nebt-ȧst-enti-mu, 359a.
Nebt-Ȧter-Meḥ, 359a.
Nebt-Ȧter-Shemā, 359a.
Nebt-Ȧṭu, 359a.
Nebt-ȧur, 358b.
Nebt-ȧut, 358a.
Nebt-ȧut Khenti-Ṭuat, 358a.
Nebt-Bȧat, 360b.
Nebt-em-shen, 361a.
Nebt-en-sheta, 361b.
Nebt-ent-ḥet, 361b.

Nebt-er-tchert, 362a.
Nebt-ġem-åb, 365a.
Nebt-Gerġ, 365a.
Nebt-ḥa-Rā, 362b.
Nebt-ḥebb, 362b.
Nebt-ḥekau, 363a.
Nebt-Hen, 362a.
Nebt-ḥent, 362b.
Nebt-ḥep, 362b.
Nebt-ḥep-neteru, 362b.
Nebt-ḥeru, 362b.
Nebt-ḥet, 362b.
Nebt-ḥet Ānqit, 362b.
Nebt-ḥetep, 363a.
Nebt-ḥetept, 363a.
Nebt-ḥuntt, 362b.
Nebt-Kepen, 365a.
Nebt-Khasa, 363a.
Nebt-khat, 363a.
Nebt-khaut, 363a.
Nebt-Khebit, 363a.
Nebt-Kheper, 363a.
Nebt-Kheriu, 363b
Nebt-Måt, 361a.
Nebt-m'kt, 361a.
Nebt-mu, 361a.
Nebt-nebå, 361a.
Nebt-nebt, 361a.
Nebt-Nehemt, 361b.
Nebt-neḥep, 361b.
Nebt-Neht, 361b.
Nebt-Nekhen, 361b.
Nebt-nerit, 361b.
Nebt-neser, 361b.
Nebt-neshå, 361b.
Nebt-Netchemtchem, 362a.
Nebt-Netit, 362a.
Nebt-Nut, 361a.
Nebt-Pe, 360b.
Nebt-peḥti, 360b.
Nebt-peḥti-petpet-sebåu, 360b.
Nebt-peḥti-thesu-menment, 360b.
Nebt-Per res, 360b.
Nebt-peru, 360b.
Nebt-Pesṭt, 361a.
Nebt-pet, 360b.
Nebt-petti, 360b.
Nebt-qebḥ, 365a.
Nebt-Qeṭ, 365a.
Nebt-reṭui, 362a.
Nebt-Sa, 363b.
Nebt-Såf, 363b.
Nebt-sam, 363b.
Nebt-San, 363b.
Nebt-Sauta, 363b.
Nebt-sebu, 363b.
Nebt-Seher, 364a.
Nebt-Seḥt, 364a.
Nebt-Sekhemu, 364a.
Nebt-Sekri, 364a.
Nebt-senkt, 363b.
Nebt-senṭt, 364a.
Nebt-Septi, 363b.
Nebt-Seqaiu, 364b.
Nebt-Seshemu-nifu, 364a.
Nebt-Seshent, 364a.
Nebt-sesheshuta, 364a.
Nebt-seshta, 364a.
Nebt-seṭau, 364b.
Nebt-setchef, 364b
Nebt-Shas, 364b.
Nebt-shāt, 364b.
Nebt-Shefshefit, 364b.
Nebt-shem, 364b.
Nebt-shemās-urt, 364b.
Nebt-sheser, 364b.
Nebt-shesh- etc., 365a.
Nebt-sres, 364a.
Nebt-Ta-åmen, 365b.
Nebt-taui, 365a.
Nebt-taui-em-kara, 365b.
Nebt-tcheser, 366a.
Nebt-tchet, 366a.
Nebt-teḥen, 365b.
Nebt-Tem, 365b.
Nebt-ṭemat, 365b.
Nebt-Ṭennu, 366a.
Nebt-Ṭens, 366a.
Nebt-Ṭenṭen, 366a.
Nebt-Tep, 365b.
Nebt-Tep-åh, 365b.
Nebt-uåa, 360a.
Nebt-uauau, 360a.
Nebt-uġat, 360b.
Nebt-Un, 360a.
Nebt-unnut, 360a.
Nebt-usha, 360b.
Nebt-uut, 360a.
Nebṭ, 368a.
Nebtå, 357a.
Nebṭ-åb-f, 368b.
Nebti, 357a, 358a.
Nebti of Nenu, 189a.
Nebṭuqeṭ, 368a.
Nebu, 358a.
Nebu-en-Meḥt, 361b.

Nebui-ȧrt, 359a.
Nebu-Kau, 365a.
Nebu-Khert, 363b.
Nebu-Meḥt, 619b.
necessary, 876a ; what is, 885b.
neck, 22b, 77a, 212b, 226a, 285b, 332b, 384a, 530a, 533a, 536a, 563a, 572a, 573b ; back of, 458a, 461b.
neckband, 446a, 799b.
necklace, 148b, 184a, 202a, 207b, 226a, 408b, 507a, 728b, 734b, 849b, 862a.
necklet, 71a, 75b.
neck ornament, 282a, 484b.
neck stick, 619a.
necropolis, 113b, 131b, 238a, 298a, 507b, 561b, 580a, 687a ; in hill, 533b.
necropolis of Abydos, 156b ; of Denderah, 534b ; of Hermopolis, 16b ; of Philae, 16b ; of Thebes, 667a.
need, 382b, 561b, 580b, 732b, 800a, 897a.
need, to be in, 64b, 375b, 800a.
needle, 320a.
needle (koḥlstick), 201b.
needy, 207b, 379b, 569b, 604a, 674b, 732b.
needy man, 653a, 800b.
Nefer-ȧat-mek-ȧrt, 371b.
Nefer-ȧitȧ, 371b.
Nefer-em-baiu, 370a.
Nefer-ḥat, 371b, 896a.
Nefer-ḥerit-tchatchat, 372a.
Nefer-ḥetep, 372a.
Nefer-ḥetep-pa-āa, 372a.
Nefer-ḥetep-pa-khart, 372a.
Nefer-ḥetep-pa-neter-āa, 372a.
Neferit-khā, 372a.
Nefer-neteru, 371b.
Nefer-peḥiu, 896a.
Nefer-Shuti, 372a.
Nefert, 371b.
Nefer-Tem, 372a.
Nefer-Tem-kau, 372a.
Nefer-Tem-khu-taui, 372a.
Nefer - Tem - Rā - Ḥeru - ȧakhuti, 372a.
Neferu-kau, 372a.
Nefer-usr, 371b.
Nef-ḥati, 370b.
Nefnef, 370b.
Nefrit, 371b.
Nefur, 370a.
Neġ, 398a.
Neġaġa-ur, 398a.
neġation, 213b ; mark of, 266a ; particle, 339b, 345a, 348a, 349a.
neġative, 209a ; a stronġ, 371a.
Neġau, 398a.
Neġeb, 398b.
Neġ-en-kau, 398a.
Neġġ-ur, 398a.
Neġit, 398a.
neġlect, 283b, 289b.
neġlectful, 180a.
neġliġent, 289b.
Neġneġ-ur, 398a.
Neġnit, 398b.
neġress, 386a.
neġro, 355b, 386a.
Neġro-land, 913a.
Neḥ, 383a.
Neḥȧ, 383b.
Neḥȧ-ḥa, 383b.
Neha-ḥer, 380b.
Neḥa-ḥer, 383b, 561a, 861b.
Neḥait-ḥer, 383b.
Neha-Kheru, 380b.
Nehap, 380b.
Neha-ta, 380b.
Neḥeb-kau, 384a.
Neḥeb-nefert, 384a.
Neḥebsa, 384b.
Neḥebti, 384a.
Neḥeḥ, 383a.
Nehem-kheru, 381b.
Neḥemt-āuait, 385a.
Neḥemu, 385a.
Nehen, 381b.
Nehenut, 381b.
Neḥep, 46b, 47b, 385a.
Neher, 381b.
Neḥer-tchatcha, 386a.
Neḥerti, 385b.
Nehes (Set), 382a.
Nehesȧ, 382a.
Nehes-ḥer, 382a.
Neḥesu, 386a.
Nehet, 380a.
Neḥi, 382b.
Neḥit, 383a.
Nehp, 381a.

Neḥru, 385b.
Neḥsit, 386a.
Neḥsiu-ḥetepu, 386a.
Nehti, 380a.
Nehui, 381a.
neighbour, 438b, 444b, 449b, 539b, 638b, 674a.
neighbourhood, 27a, 265a, 438a, 638a.
Neith, 399b ; festival of, 161b ; temple of, 80a.
Nekȧ (Set), 398a.
Nekait, 398a.
Nekentf, 397b.
Nekhȧ, 387b.
Nekhben, 388a.
Nekhbit, 388a.
Nekhbu ur, 388a.
Nekheb, 388a.
Nekhebet, 522b.
Nekhebit, 183b, 522b, 756a, 860b.
Nekhekh (Rā), 387a.
Nekhekh-ur-Ȧten, 387a.
Nekhen, an Assessor, 388b.
Nekhen, judge from, 588a.
Nekhen (Babe), 388b.
Nekhenit, 388b.
Nekht-ā, 389a.
Nekht, a ka of Rā, 389a.
Nekhtit, 389a.
Nekht-ti, 389a.
Nekhtu-nti-setem-nef, 389a.
Nekhtut-em-Uas, 389a.
Nekit, 396b.
Neknit, 397b.
Neknits, 465b.
Nem, 374a b.
Nemȧt, 374a.
Nemit, 374a.
Nemmȧ, 374b.
Nemmt, 373a.
Nemtit-set, 465b.
Nem-ur (Mer-ur), 67b, 374a.
Nen, 376b.
Nenā, 377b.
Nenḥa, 378a.
Neni, 348a, 377b.
Nenit, 348a, 351a, 376b.
Neniu, 377a b.
Nenkar, 356a.
Nenr, 378a.
Nent, 350a.
Nentchā, 378b.
Nenu, 348a.
Nenu, Sky-god, 349b.
Nenu (Āapep), 349b.
Nenu, the Nile, 350a.
Nenui, 378a.
Nenunser, 378a.
Nep, god, 368b.
Nepȧ, 369a.
Nepen, 369a.
Nepertiu, 369a.
Nephthys, 24a, 29a.
Nep-meḥ, 369a.
Nepnept, 369a.
Nepr, Neprȧ, 369a.
Neqāiu-ḥatu, 396a.
Neqeht, 396a.
Ner, 378b.
Nerȧt, 378b.
Neri, 379a.
Nerit, 378b, 379a.
Nerit-ābui, 379a.
Nerta, 379b.
Nerṭa-nef-bes-f, 341b.
N-erṭa-nef-nebt, 341b, 379b.
Nerti, 378b.
Nesa, 390b.
Nesȧsȧ, Lake, 721a.
Nesb-ȧmenu, 392b.
Nesbit, 392b.
Nesb-kheper-ȧru, 392b.
Nesem, 393a.
Nesereh, 393b.
Neserit, 393a.
Nesermer, 393a.
Neserser, Lake of, 721a.
Nesh, 393b.
Neshem, 394b.
Neshemit, 394b.
Neshenti (Set), 395a.
Neshm-t-Boat, 394b.
Nesh-renpu, 394a.
Nesht, 395b.
Nesiu fiends, 390b.
Nesmekhef, 389b.
Nesrem, 393a.
Nesrit-ānkhit, 393a.
Nesru, 393a.
Nessf, 393a.
Nesst-naisu, 389b.
nest, 32a, 34b, 288a, 319a, 621b, 754b.
Nestȧ, 390b.
Nesti-Khenti-Ṭuat, 390b.

Nestiu-gods, 390b.
Nesttauit, 390b.
net, 27a, 33b, 40a, 41a, 75a, 97a, 102a, 116b, 118a, 122a, 132a, 259b, 412b, 514b, 527a, 618a, 695a, 835b ; cord of, 194b.
net, fishing, 458b, 465a.
net for snaring souls, 27a, 64a.
net, fowling, 127b.
net, hands of, 105b.
net, hunting, 456a.
net, magical, 123b, 905b, 906a.
net of the Åkeru-gods, 905b.
net, pegs of, 38a.
net, to, 121b, 695a.
net, to cast a, 465a ; to draw a, 613a.
net, to hunt with, 40a.
Net-gods, 118a.
Net-Ḥetchet, 399b.
Net-Ḥetut, 399b.
Net-Shert, 399b.
Net-tepit-Ån, 399b.
Net-Ṭeshert, 399b.
Net-Tha, 399b.
Netȧ, 400b ; Osiris, 24b.
Net-Åsȧr, 400a.
Netchȧtf, 410a.
Netch-baiu, 410b.
Netchebȧbf, 411b.
Netcheḥnetcheḥ, 413a.
Netchem, 412a.
Netchem-ȧb, 412a.
Netch-em-ānkh, 412a.
Netchemnetchmit, 412b.
Netcher, 412b, 413a.
Netcherf, 413a.
Netchertt, 412b.
Netchesti, 413b.
Netchft, 411b.
Netch-ḥer, 410a.
Netch-Nu, 410b.
Netchrit, 413a.
Netchses, 413b.
Netchti, 410a.
Netchti-ur, 410a.
Neter, a god, 403b.
Neter-āa, 403b.
Neterit-nekhenit-Rā, 404a.
Neter-ka-qet-qet, 404a.
Neter-neferu, 404a.
Neter-neteru, 404a.
Neter-sepṭ-f, 404a.
Neter-tchai-pet, 404a.
Neterti, 403b ; Isis and Nephthys, 404b.
neterti instrument, 407b.
Nether, 408b.
Netherit, 408b.
Netheth, 408b.
Netit, 400a.
Net-net uā-kheper-aut, 400a.
Netneṭit, 409a.
Net-qa- etc., 408a.
Net-Rā, 400a.
Netrit festival, 407b.
Netrit-ta-ȧakhu, 404a.
Netrit-ta-meḥ, 404a.
Neṭru, 409b.
netted, 7a.
Netter, 64a.
nettle, 611b.
Netu, 400a.
never, 340a, 341a.
never again, 596b.
never before, 230b, 341b.
never-failing, 78b, 341a.
new, 269a, 273b, 375a ; to be, 150a.
new thing, 269b, 375a.
new wine, 231b.
New Year's Day, 76a, 161b, 379a, 427b, 450b, 829a.
New Year's tax, 521a.
newly, 269b.
N-ger-s, 341b.
N-ḥeri-rtitsa, 341b.
Ni, 348a.
nibble, 731a.
nice, 218b.
niche, 92b, 701b.
night, 8b, 22b, 36a, 77b, 94b, 107a, 135a, 179b, 184b, 185a, 296b, 377a, 537a, 622a, 624b, 649a, 751b, 761b, 776b, 778b, 791a, 795b, 796a, 797a, 803b, 810b, 897a ; deepest, 244a ; early, 529b ; the whole, 811a.
night personified, 77b, 135a.
Night of counting the dead, 811a.
Night of counting years, 811a.
Night of erecting the pavilion, 811a.
Night of fights, 811a.
Night of Haker, 811a.
Night of Horus and Set, 811a.

Night of Judgement, 811a.
Night of ploughing the earth, 811a.
Night of the resurrection of Horus, 811b.
Night of secret ceremonies, 811b.
Night of setting up Ṭeṭ, 811b.
Night of the Drop, 459b, 811a.
Night of Weighing Words, 811a.
night, provisions for the, 323b.
night, to pass the, 188b, 718b.
night festivals, Great and Little, 796a.
Night-god, 109b.
night-season, 840b.
Nile, 12a, 69a, 99b, 218b, 452a, 467a, 470b, 506b, 767b.
Niles, the, 467b.
Nile, arm of, 35b ; Canopic arm of, 97b.
Nile deposit, 411b, 499b.
Nile, mouths of the, 416a.
Nile of Ṭuat, 467a.
Nile, source of the, 774b, 775a.
Nile banks, 102b.
Nile festivals, 99b.
Nile flood, 95a, 174b, 462a, 467a b, 507b, 744a, 836b.
Nile-god, 76a, 128a, 130b, 177a, 184a b, 187a, 253b, 255a, 257b, 385a, 400a, 404a, 467b, 477b, 479a, 506b, 611b, 629a, 631b, 637b, 695a ; emission of, 332a.
Nile-Red Sea road, 113a.
Nile-swamp, 272b.
Nile water, 263a, 293b.
Nimrod, 343b.
Ninarruṭf, 349a.
nine, 249b, 250a.
Nine gods, the companies of the, 251a.
Nine goddesses, the, 251a.
Nine hands, 533b.
nine thread stuff, 250a.
ninety, 250a.
Ningal, 60a, 356a.
ninth, 250a.
nip, 795a.
nipple, 302b, 768a, 963a.
nitrum, 407b.
Nnaruṭf-t, 341a.
Nn-rekh, 341b.
no, 124a, 339b, 349a, 376b, 835a.
no one, 213b, 340a.
no time, 341a.
nobility, 591a, 737a, 830b ; title of, 671a.
noble, 108a, 123a, 170b, 591a, 610a, 737a.
noble, to be, 646a, 737a.
noble attributes, 370b.
noble words, 698b.
nobleman, 215b, 643b, 646a, 671a, 679b, 737a.
nobles, 460b, 867b ; at Court, 744a.
Nobles, the Two, 202b.
nod, 441b, 448a.
noise, 419b, 607b, 668b.
nomad, 111a, 292a, 306a b, 373b, 752a.
nomads of Sûdân, etc., 179a.
nomads, village of, 179a.
nome, 477b, 511b, 596b, 661b, 835a, 844b.
nome, dwellers in, 844b.
nome of Eternity, 511b.
nome, recorder, of, 176b.
non-combatant, 517b.
non-existent, 164b, 340a, 542a, 835a.
none the less, 415b.
nook, 774a.
noon, 134a, 332a, 333b.
north, the, 318a, 816a ; king of, 212a ; festival of, 212a.
northern, 318a.
North-house, 318b.
North-land, 815a.
northwards, 286a.
north-west, 318b.
north wind, 707b ; god of, 767b.
nose, 260b, 261a, 554a, 729b, 750a.
nose, disease of, 433b.
Nose-of-life (Osiris), 261a.
nostrils, 261a, 329a, 375a, 551a, 572b, 573a, 579b, 747b, 750a.
not, 6a, 12b, 44a, 98a, 213b, 216b, 282a, 339b, 341b, 349a, 376b, 414b, 835a.
not allowable, 340b.
not any, 835a.
not at all, 835a.
not possessing, 265a, 339b.
not so, 124a, 339b.

not to have, 296b.
not yet, 264b.
notable, 644b, 713a.
note, 180a.
notes of a case, 604b.
nothing, 184b, 835a.
nothingness, 339b, 835a.
nourish, 13b, 284b, 607a, 645a, 678a.
nourishment, 612b, 832a.
now, 96a.
now behold, 782a.
Nqeṭqeṭ, god, 396a.
Nsekf, 341a.
N-tcher-t, 341b.
Nti-ḥer-f-mm-masti-f, 399a.
Nti-she-f, 341b.
Ntiu gods, 399a.
Ntuti, 400b.
Nu, 242a, 349b, 600a, 777a.
Nu (Ȧmen-Rā), 350a.
Nu (Nile), 350a ; festival of, 474b.
Nu, gods of this name, 350a.
Nua, 352b.
Nub, 354a.
Nubȧ-neb-s-ȧms, 353b.
Nub-ḥeḥ, 353b.
Nub-ḥetepit, 353b.
Nubia, 22a.
Nubia, Lake of, 263b.
Nubia, Nine Peoples of, 832b.
Nubia, viceroy of, 392a.
Nubian, 95b.
Nubian (adj.), 95b, 187a.
Nubians, 495a, 554b, 709a, 712b, 790b, 795b.
Nubit, 353b.
Nubit-ȧith, 353b.
Nubit-neterit, 353b.
Nub-neteru, 353b.
Nubnub, 354a.
Nubti (Set), 354a.
nudity, 458b.
Nuenrā, 350a.
Nuḥ-ḥatu, 355a.
Nuit, 350a b.
Nuit-Rā, 350a.
Nukar, 356a.
number, 41a, 134a, 415a, 838a, 856b, 857b, 882b.
number, a great, 507a.
numbers, goddess of, 665b.
number, sign of ordinal, 316a.
numbering, a, 41a.
numberless, 340b, 415a.
numerous, 137a, 646b.
Nun, god, 354b.
Nunu, 350a.
Nunuiu, 350b.
Nunun, 354b.
Nunut, 350a.
Nunuth, 356b.
Nurkhata, 354b.
nurse, 13b, 15b, 69a, 302a, 428a, 551a, 616b, 747b, 820b, 847b.
nurse, divine, 20b.
nurse, to, 13a, 122a, 426a, 428a, 551a, 757b.
Nurse goddess, 302a, 426a.
nursling, 428a.
N-urtch-nef, 341b.
N-urṭ-f, 341b.
nurture, to, 645a.
Nuru, god, 354b.
Nut, 25a, 46a, 193b, 349a, 422b, 720a, 777a.
Nut, Five Children of, 322b.
Nut, title of, 725b.
Nut goddesses, 350b.
Nutchi, 357a.
Nuth, 356b.
Nut-hru, 351b.
Nuti, 351a.
Nuṭiu, 356b.
Nuti-urti, 351a.
nuts, 411b.
Nut-Shesit, 351a.
Nut-urit, 350a.
Nut-urt, 351a.

O.

O, an interjection, 7b, 15a, 30b, 73b, 74b, 143b, 438a, 440a, 443b, 444a, 451b.
O that ! 292b, 441b, 457a, 464a.
O then, 782a.
Oak tree, 62b.
oar, 182b, 279a, 281a, 284b, 295a, 393b, 478b, 631a, 877a.
oar, steering, 315a.
oar, stroke of, 688b.
oar, toil at, 143b.

oarsman, 780a.
Oasis country, 148b.
Oasis of Khârgah, 52b.
Oasis of Jupiter Ammon, 20b.
oath, 112a.
oath (so help me God !), 752b.
oath, to fulfil an, 65b ; to take an, 65b.
oath of king, 126a.
obeisance, 885a.
obelisk, 85a, 217a, 843b, 887b.
obelisk cakes, 730b.
obelisks of Rā, 843b.
obelisks, pair of, 839b.
obey, 291b, 292a, 717b.
object, 525a, 580b, 595a, 789b.
object, bronze, 670b.
object, sacred, 289b.
object that protects, 193a.
object, wooden, 40a, 542a, 571b, 756b, 837b.
objection, 643a.
oblation, 3a, 518a, 725a.
oblique-eyed, 641a.
obliquity, moral, 530a, 540a, 572a.
obliterate, 57b, 315b, 840a.
oblivion, 492b, 550a.
oboli, 867b.
obolus, 781a, 854a.
obscure, 652a.
obscurity, 458a, 475b, 600b, 761b, 795b, 798a.
observatory, 175a.
observe, 351a, 548a, 903b.
observe astronomically, 175a.
observe laws, 412b.
observer, 175a.
obsidiȧn knives, 842a.
obstacle, 564b, 750a.
obstinate, 164a, 650a, 746b, 760b, 838b.
obstruct, 36b, 103b, 487b, 646b, 743b, 750a, 905a.
obstructed, 800a.
obstruction, 64a, 491a, 750a.
obvious, 34a.
occasion, 595b.
occupation, 18a.
occupied, 316b, 531a ; of mind, 883b.
occupy, 333a, 811b ; an office, 65a.
occurrences, 542b, 617a, 690a.
ocean, 151a.
ochre, 3b, 189b, 417b, 558b, 581b, 773b, 774a, 837a, 910a.
ochre, red, 283b.
ochres for ink, 620b.
odour, 551a, 627b, 629b, 631a, 648a, 675a, 712b, 747b.
odour, bad or foul, 709b.
of, 264a, 279b, 348a, 408a.
of old time, 205a, 264b, 460a, 830a.
offal, 31b, 470a, 708a ; of fish, 594a.
offence, 31b, 165b, 226a, 398a, 772b, 849b, 853a, 895b ; criminal, 595b.
offend, 694a.
offender, 165b, 540a.
offer, 3a, 147b, 270b, 301b, 472a, 550b, 562a, 582a, 592a, 898b.
offer sacrifice or thanksgiving, 425a, 431a.
offer up, 741a.
offered, 89a.
offering, 3a b, 4a, 5b, 9b, 28a b, 56b, 91b, 110b, 112b, 117a, 141a, 148a, 155b, 156a, 157b, 189a, 191b, 195b, 215b, 230b, 251b, 257b, 259b, 270b, 286b, 304b, 318b, 387b, 487a, 491b, 506b, 518a, 521b, 545a, 562b, 601a, 606b, 621b, 623b, 634b, 643b, 644a, 652b, 654a, 657a, 675a, 733b, 734b, 754b, 759b, 810a, 857a b, 876a.
offerings, to heap up, 667a.
offerings, to make, 117a, 259a, 677a, 775a, 884b.
offerings, burnt, 764a, 796a.
offerings by fire, 10a.
offerings, chamber of, 239b.
offering, the daily, 54a, 138b.
offering, evening, 191a.
offering, festal, 474a.
offering, funerary, 241b, 242a.
offering, king's, 392a, 518a.
offering, obligatory, 332b.
offerings of birds and fish, 5b.
offering of sand, 730a.
offerings, propitiatory, 402b.
offering, spice, 38b.
offerings, table of, 876a.
offering-bearer, 287a.

offering slab, 117a.
office, 69b, 79b, 80b, 510b, 526b, 531b, 540a, 557b, 755a.
office of mayor, 526b.
office building, 881b.
office, draughtsman's, 780a.
office, Government, 902a.
officer, 108a, 144a, 154b, 184a, 284a, 311b, 436b, 444a, 473b, 487a, 604a, 613b, 685a, 718a, 828b.
officer, chief, 646b, 851a, 860a.
official, 19b, 74b, 154b, 187b, 639b, 747a, 774a, 852b.
official, cemetery, 828b.
official, title of, 399a, 417a.
officials, court, 444a.
officials of palace, 45b.
offspring, 240b, 331b, 583b, 903a ; of animals, 33a.
often, to do, 177a.
ogle, 801a.
Oh ! 74b, 106b, 438a.
oikoumenê, 538a.
oil, 112b, 113a, 140b, 205b, 315a, 318b, 337a, 382b, 383a, 388b, 473b, 507b, 626b, 705a, 706a, 765b, 767b, 813b, 846a.
oil, circumcision, 845a.
oil for grey hair, 704b.
oil for kyphi, 913a.
oil, holy, 395a, 666a, 872b.
oil, medicated, 40a.
oil, perfumed, 706a.
oil, prepared, 356a.
oil, sacred, 597b.
oil, scented, 665a, 824a.
oil the hair, 169b.
oil-boiler, 236a.
oil-bottle, 222b.
oil plant, 767b.
oil seed, 786b.
oil tree, 206a.
oily-hearted, 224b.
ointment, 39b, 40a, 55b, 205b, 233a, 263a, 283a, 292b, 337a, 377a, 643b, 706a, 767b, 804a.
ointment, copper, 150b.
ointment, festal, 712b.
old, 3b, 9b, 17b, 82a, 134a, 778a, 838b.
old, to be or grow, 17b, 387a, 626b, 677b, 797a, 838b, 856a.
old, of, 830a.
old age, 17b, 32b, 82a, 514b, 797a, 838b, 856a, 881b, 882b.
old canal, 838b.
Old God, 387a.
old home, 226b.
old man, 15a, 17b, 26a, 32b, 33b, 387a, 514b, 532a, 626b, 714b, 797a, 882b.
old woman, 15a, 18a.
olive, 206a, 207a, 849b, 850a, 897a, 913b.
olive oil, 207a, 224a, 903b ; fresh, 224a ; sweet, red, 224b.
olive tree, 224a, 897a, 913b.
omission, 184b.
on, 264a, 492b, 826b.
on account of, 339a, 492b.
on behalf of, 493a, 545a.
on both sides, 813a.
on the contrary, 265a.
once again, 273b, 792a.
oncomer, 439b.
one, 105a, 153a.
one, the impersonal, 333a.
One (i.e., God), 153a.
one (i.e., king), 823a.
one (i.e., Rā, Osiris, etc.), 154a.
One, the Lord, 360a.
one and the other, 153b.
one at a time, one by one, 595a.
one to one, 153b.
one who is in front, 45a.
one-armed, 184b.
one-handed, 184b.
onion, 26a, 288b, 473b, 523b ; seed, 26a.
only, 340a.
only one, 153a b.
Onouris, 57a.
onyx, 273a.
ooze, 424b.
open, 33b, 34a, 39a, 90a, 157b, 158b, 160b, 166a, 167a, 235a, 252b, 254b, 388a, 598a, 604a, 608a b, 612a, 620b, 623b, 624a, 629a, 678a, 697b, 700b, 701a, 793a.
open, to force, 592b ; to make, 619a, 697a.
open a way, 178b, 621a, 650a.
open a well, 158b.

open out, 255b.
open the arms, 248b, 255b.
open the bowels, 662a.
open the eyes, 158b.
open the face, 34b.
open the hands, 118a.
open the heart, 158b.
open the way, 161b.
open up, 116b, 158b.
open wide, 184a.
opened, 235a, 731a.
opener, 166b.
opener of the body, 697b.
opener of the roads, 162a.
open-handed, 166b.
opening, 99a, 167a, 416a, 521b, 697a, 713b ; to make, 592b.
opening for light, 764b.
opening in diaphragm, 416b.
opening in wall, 701b.
opening (of years), 379a.
opening the face, 650a.
opening the mouth, ceremony of, 161b ; to perform, 34b.
openwork, 254b.
opinion, 416a, 430a, 694a, 745a.
opponent, 434a, 493a, 545a, 564b, 707b, 894a.
opportunity, 335a, 595a.
oppose, 82b, 116a, 564b, 764b, 885a, 894a.
oppose in speech, 116b.
opposite, 116b, 139a, 158a, 264a, 265a, 339a, 414a, 415a, 493a, 708b.
opposition, 2a, 18a, 116a, 224a, 577a, 612b, 643a, 705a, 894a.
oppress, 1b, 27b, 112b, 141a, 156a, 442a, 451b, 464b, 601a, 787a, 867a b.
oppressed, 27b, 64b, 69b, 102a, 270a, 273a, 524b, 637b.
oppression, 102a, 112b, 141b, 744b, 867a, 868a, 909b.
oppressor, 115b, 181b, 422a, 635a, 637b.
opulent, 538b.
or, 33b, 265a, 415b.
oracle, divine, 831a.
oration, 549a.
orator, 176b ; to play the, 410b.
orbit, 333b, 701a, 743b, 780a.
orchard, 559a b, 723a, 749a, 755a.
ordain, 697b, 722b.
order, 82a, 136b, 161a, 190b, 192a, 270b, 271b, 335a, 337b, 346a, 400b, 446a, 449a, 489a, 597a, 602a, 610b, 669b, 670b, 679b, 683b, 697b, 768a, 849a ; a written, 106b.
order of priests, 585b.
order, to, 187b, 190b, 289b, 410b, 470a, 610a b, 679b, 680a, 683b, 850a, 900a.
order, to set in, 647a.
ordinance, 346a, 400a b, 409a, 487a, 661a, 753b, 831b, 844b, 912b.
ore, 218a, 226b ; copper, 486a ; silver, 523a.
organ of the body, 103b.
organs, genital, 544b ; disease of, 122a.
original (place), 226b.
originally, 580a.
Orion, 99b, 118b, 124a, 389a, 393a, 402a, 446b, 638b, 682b.
Orion, arm of, 105b.
Orion, boat of, 625b.
Orion, stars of, 42b, 638b, 757a.
ornament, 92a b, 119a, 121b, 282b, 296b, 387b, 428a, 443a, 575a, 644b, 680a, 689a, 728b, 880b.
ornament, annular, 215a.
ornament, lion-shaped, 367a.
ornament, metal, 219b.
ornament of crown, 279a, 568b.
ornament of dress, 452a.
ornament, the royal, 535a.
ornament, to, 615b.
ornamental water, 812a.
Orontes, 63a, 73a.
orphan, 375b, 376a, 598a, 833a.
oryx, 270a.
Osirians, 83b.
Osiris, 41a, 83a.
Osiris, backbone of, 249b.
Osiris, birthday of, 450b.
Osiris, body of, 24b.
Osiris, carrier of Horus, 84a.
Osiris, children of, 322b.
Osiris, crown of, 13b.
Osiris, day of, 450b.
Osiris, dead body of, 43a.
Osiris, death day of, 242a.
Osiris, firstborn of, 200b.

Osiris, foes of, 545b.
Osiris, followers of, 742b.
Osiris, form of, 83b ff.
Osiris, form of his name, 181a.
Osiris, Four Obelisks of, 843b.
Osiris, gardeners of, 67b.
Osiris, garment made by, 897a.
Osiris, grave of, 416b.
Osiris, head-box of, 19a.
Osiris, Kingdom of, 15b.
Osiris, left shoulder of, 766b.
Osiris, lock of hair of, 574b.
Osiris, phallus of, 429b.
Osiris, pillar of, 59b.
Osiris, secretary of, 777b.
Osiris, shrine of, 99b, 453a.
Osiris, stars of, 656a.
Osiris, Two Feathers of, 733a.
Osiris, Two Tombs of, 15b.
Osiris, vertebræ of, 667b.
Osiris-Akhem, 84a.
Osiris-Ȧn, 83b.
Osiris-Anubis, 83b.
Osiris-Harmakhis, 89a.
Osiris-Harmakhis-Temu, 89a.
Osiris in Henȧ, 85b.
Osiris Khenti Ȧmentt, 87a.
Osiris-Mnevis, 89a.
Osiris pa-meres, 84a.
Osiris-Ptaḥ, 84a.
Osiris-Saḥ, 88a.
Osiris-Seker, 88a.
Osiris-Sep (or Sepȧ), 88a.
Osiris-Unnefer, 84a.
Osiris the Aged One, 83b.
Osiris the Almighty, 86b.
Osiris the Bull-god of Ȧmentt, 7b, 88a.
Osiris the Eternal, 86b, 87a.
Osiris the Executioner, 88a.
Osiris the Grain-god, 87b.
Osiris the Living, 86b.
Osiris the Moon, 83b.
Osiris the Shepherd, 87b.
Osiris of Abydos, 83b, 84b.
Osiris of Āķesh, 84b.
Osiris of Ȧmentt, 86b.
Osiris of Āntch, 84b.
Osiris of Āper, 84b.
Osiris of Asher, 84a.
Osiris of Ȧtefur, 84b.
Osiris of Athribis, 109a.
Osiris of Bakt, 84b.
Osiris of Benben, 85a.
Osiris of Benr, 85a.
Osiris of Busiris, 84a.
Osiris of Buto, 85a.
Osiris of Erpit, 84a.
Osiris of Ḥeken, 85b.
Osiris of Heliopolis, 83b.
Osiris of Ḥemaġ, 85b.
Osiris of Ḥensu, 85a.
Osiris of Ḥeser, 85b.
Osiris of Maāti, 85a.
Osiris of Memphis, 84b.
Osiris of Menȧ, 85a.
Osiris of Nefer, 87b.
Osiris of Nefur, 85a.
Osiris of Neṭbit, 85b.
Osiris of Netch, 85b.
Osiris of Neṭit, 85a.
Osiris of Netr, 85a.
Osiris of Pesġ-Rā (?), 85a.
Osiris of Peṭ, 85a.
Osiris of Qefṭenu, 86a.
Osiris of Reḥnen, 85b.
Osiris of Rustau, 84a.
Osiris of Sȧ, 86a.
Osiris of Sȧti, 86a.
Osiris of Sau (Upper and Lower), 86a.
Osiris of Sekrit, 86a.
Osiris of Sesh, 86a.
Osiris of Shau, 86a.
Osiris of Shenu, 86a.
Osiris of Shetat, 83b.
Osiris of Sunu, 86a.
Osiris of Tenen, 87b.
Osiris of Ṭesher, 86b.
Osiris of the Cows, 87b.
Osiris of the Earth, 86b.
Osiris of the Great Ȧat, 84a.
Osiris of the Great House, 85b.
Osiris of the Lake, 87b.
Osiris of the Northern Oasis, 84b.
Osiris of the river (?), 84b.
Osiris of the Sekti Boat, 86a.
Osiris of the Southern Oasis, 84b.
Osiris of the World, 86b.
Osiris of Un, 87b.
ossify, 219b.
ostrich, 343a, 344b, 348b, 379b; eggs of, 651b.
other, 187b, 792a b, 799a.

other side, 308a.
other things, 798b, 799a.
Other World, 93b, 113b, 125a, 131b, 156b, 214b, 492a, 511b, 687a, 865a, 872a, 900b.
Other World, Nile of, 467a.
otherwise said (i.e., a variant reading), 913a.
our, 229b, 339a, 342a b, 818b, 824b.
out from, 264a.
out of danger, 282a.
outbreak, 240b.
outcast, 194b, 483b.
outcry, 29a, 31b, 130a, 381a, 658a, 790a, 838b, 882b, 896b.
outfit, woman's, 119a.
outflow, 621a.
outgoings, 240b.
outhouse, 74a.
outlive, to, 779a.
outpourings, 91b, 708b.
outrage, 396b ; to commit an, 398a.
outside, 214b, 218b, 219b, 265a, 339b, 414a b, 420b, 428b, 458a, 494b, 554a, 723b.
oval for royal name, 305b.
oven, 290a, 464a, 708a, 775b, 786b, 819a b, 840a, 841b, 885b.
ovens of the Ṭuat, 465a.
over, 492b.
over, he who is, 828b.
over and above, 414b.
over against, 414b, 444b.
overabundance, 469b.
overargue, 375a.
overcome, 400a, 772a, 858a, 884a, 899a.
overeat, 49a.
overflow, 159b, 203a, 343b, 366b, 368b, 398b, 597b, 602b, 621a, 665a, 708b, 766a, 813a.
overfull, 545a.
overlay, 474a ; with metal, 368b, 689a.
overloaded, 398b.
overlord, 215b, 357b, 812a.
overmuch, 137a.
overpower, 386b.
overseer, 71a, 157a, 224b, 287b, 311b, 312b, 323b, 417a, 422a, 468a, 494a, 562a, 585b, 685a.
overspread, 889a.
overstep, 877a.
overthrow, 176b, 177b, 187b, 236a b, 256 b, 261b, 375b, 409a, 447b, 480a, 522a, 527b, 528b, 544b, 547a, 561b, 575a, 603b, 611b, 612b, 617a b, 618a, 624a, 626b, 633a, 644b, 647a, 651b, 662b, 676b, 682a, 685b, 689a, 693b, 694a, 695b, 700b, 703b, 704b, 715b, 718b, 741b, 757b, 768a, 770a, 792a, 796b, 806b, 884a, 887b.
overthrown, 606a, 617b, 657b, 802a, 806b.
overturn, 175a, 219b, 232b, 236b, 247b, 661b, 682a, 770a, 800b.
overturned, 232b.
overweighted, 524b.
overwhelmed, 763a.
ovis longipes, 200a.
ovis platyura, 649a.
owner, 357a, 820a.
ox, oxen, 32a, 74b, 170a, 398a, 516b, 645a, 654b, 777b, 864b.
ox, full-grown, 461a.
ox, hornless, 507a.
ox, lassoed, 333a.
ox of heaven, 75a.
ox for ploughing, 384a, 704b.
ox, stalled, 2b, 69a, 337a, 351a, 550a.
ox (yoke), 355b.
ox, young, 426b.
ox-fat, 140a.
oxen, pair of, 521a.
oxen, sacred, 132a.
oxen, white, 523b.
oxen, yoke of, 648a.
ox hides, 887a.
oyster, pearl, 790b.

P.

Paȧh-nersmen, 230a.
Paȧri-sekhi, 229b.
Paāt, 231b.
Pa-Bār, 230a.
Pa-bekhennu, 230a.
Pabekht- etc., 230a.
pace, 446a.
Pachons, 740a.
pacification, 682a.

pacifiers, 684b.
pacify, 612a, 614a, 682a, 684b, 706b.
packet, 131a, 581b.
packets of arrows, 75b, 132b.
packets of natron, 76b.
pack-saddles, 288b.
padded, 164a.
paddle, 75b, 182b, 279a, 281a, 284b, 295a, 315a, 373a, 375b, 478b, 482a, 576b, 638b.
paddle, to work a, 66a, 75b, 478a b, 482a, 877a.
paddler, 478b, 576b, 703a, 877b.
paddles of magical boat, 905b.
paddles, pair of, 877a.
paddling, sound of, 75b.
pagari, 631a.
Pāhā-aref, 234a.
Pai, god, 231b.
paid, 262a.
pail, 2a.
pain, 3b, 7b, 15b, 64b, 89a, 94a, 180b, 314b, 330b, 465b, 527b, 569b, 697a, 703b, 895b.
pain, to be in, 11b, 413a, 592b, 678a.
pain, cries of, 136b.
Pain, Lake of, 231b.
painful, 180b.
paint, 49b, 346a, 417b, 419b, 558b, 821b, 825b, 840b, 857b.
paint, to, 122b, 346a, 807b, 857b; pictures, 855b.
paint the eyelids, 603a, 715b, 718b.
painted, 122b, 346a.
painter, 346a.
painting, 346a, 411a, 486, 784a, 837a, 857b.
painting, goddess of, 665b.
pair, 105a, 180a; of horses, 521a; of wings, 522a.
Pais, 231b.
Pait, 231b.
Paium'-Åsår, 230a.
Pakhenmet, 232a.
Pakhet, 232b.
Pakhit, 232a.
Pakht, boat of, 48b.
palace, 30b, 41b, 60b, 81b, 106a, 132a, 174a, 237b, 238a, 239a, 313b, 391b, 444a, 537a, 576b.
palace affairs, 335b.
palanquin, 89a, 773b.
pale, 113a.
paleness, 113a.
Palestinian, 532b.
palette, 123a, 328b, 814a.
palings, 910b.
Palinurus, 804.
palisade, 910b.
pallor, 58b, 113a.
palm, date, 20a, 49b, 211a.
palm branch, 208a.
palm cord, 146a.
palm fibre, 202a, 745b.
palm garland, 209a.
palm leaves, 60a.
palm labourer, 218b.
palm-leaf mat, 773a.
palm nuts, 767a.
palm shoots, 217b.
palm sticks, 202a, 216b.
palm tree, 20a b.
palm wine, 20b.
palm wood, 212b.
palm of the hand, a measure, 541a, 736a, 752b, 894a, 908b.
palpitate, 833a.
palsy, 393b, 631a, 714b.
Pån, 233b.
pan of scales, 492a.
panegyric, 474a, 576b.
Panemmå, 230a.
Pānkhi, 234a.
pannier, 790a.
Pannṭu, 232a.
panther, 19b, 367b, 827b; skin of, 205b.
Pantibaf- etc., 232a.
pantry, 238a.
Paoni, 236b.
Paophi, 255a.
Paopi, 236b.
papers, 619a.
papyrus, 9a, 13b, 41a, 75b, 82a, 100a, 143b, 302b, 303b, 355a, 459b, 733a, 853a, 893b, 897a, 898a.
papyrus, bundles of, 563a.
papyri, hieroglyphic, 337b.
papyrus nilotica, 770a.
papyrus plant, 854b.
papyrus roll, 200b, 619a, 733a.
papyrus shoots, 188b.
papyrus swamp, 14b, 27b, 180b.

Paqrer, 233a.
Pa Rā, 230a.
parable, 178b.
paragraph, mark of, 425a.
paralyse, 395a, 641b.
paralysed, 809a.
paralysis, quaking, 631a, 714b.
paralytic, 10b.
paraschistes, 205a.
parasol, 647b.
parcel of land, 75a, 121b, 125a, 136a, 631a.
parch, 441a.
parched, of land, etc., 185b, 186b, 724b, 732a b, 750b, 764b, 898a.
parchment, 129a.
pare the nails, 621a.
parent, 771a.
Parhaqa, 232a.
Parhu, 232a.
park, 457b, 725a.
paroxysm, 841b.
parsley, wild, 810b.
part, 103b, 248b, 251b, 252b, 334b, 815a, 821b, 881b, 882b.
partheno-genesis, 295a.
partiality, to show, 813a.
participate, 248b.
particle, 18b ; of asseveration, 792a ; causative, 583a ; conditional, 56a, 64b ; conjunctive, 321a, 339a, 818b ; demonstrative, 235b, 236a, 341b, 369b, 370a, 376b, 823a ; emphatic, 1a, 64b, 72b ; exclamatory, 142a, 143b ; explanatory, 88b, 90b, 91b ; grammatical, 550a ; interrogative, 7a, 56a, 77a, 92b, 253b, 583a, 591b, 593b ; 750b ; negative, 56a ; optative, 292b ; prohibitive, 307a.
particular, 595a.
party (in law case), 745a.
Paru (Rā ?), 232a.
Paseru, 232b.
Pasetu, 232b.
Pashakara, 232b.
Pa-shemt-en-Ḥer (Pashons), 232b.
Pashons, 40b.
pass, 377b, 592a, 605a, 618b, 622a, 649a, 653a, 676a.
pass a limit, 240a.
pass away, 216b, 568a, 592a, 604a, 649a, 787b, 864b.
pass in front, 604a.
pass into, 286b.
pass on, 222a, 286b, 592a.
pass over, 604a.
pass quickly, 605a.
pass sentence, 194b.
pass the day or night, 66a, 632b.
pass the time, 65a, 175a, 661b.
pass through, 593b, 620b, 654a.
pass up, 222a.
passage, 105b, 252b, 287a, 330a, 569a, 621a, 894b ; to make a, 621a, 894b.
passage by boat, 894b.
Passage of the god, 895a.
passages of tombs, 629b.
passengers, 31a.
passers-by, 31a.
passes, to make magical, 66a b.
passing away, 604b.
passion, 729a.
passionate, 615b, 689b.
passive, mark of the, 823a.
paste, 511a.
paste, to rub down into, 676a.
paste, sycamore, 669b.
paste, turquoise, 281b.
paste, vegetable, 538a.
pastille, 42a, 381a, 572b, 650b.
pastry cook, 140b.
pastures, 27a, 54b, 75a, 128b, 343a, 667a.
pasture flocks, 83a.
pasture land, 712b.
pasturer, 185a.
Pāt, 233b.
path, 28a, 38b, 80a, 144b, 202a, 276b, 277b, 280b, 290a b, 293a, 333b, 334b, 499a.
Patheth, 233b.
patience, 664b.
patient, 49b, 94b, 451b, 598a, 665a ; to be, 33b.
patient, the, 580a, 664b.
patter, 906b.
Pau, god, 231a.
pause, 134a.
Pauti, 231a, 250a.
Pauti-taui, 231a.
Paut-then-ta, 231b.

paved walk, 202a.
pavement, 209a, 585a b ; blocks for, 566a.
pavilion, 298a, 647b, 682a, 839b ; of a ship, 531a.
paw, 255b.
pay, 193b, 874b, 904a.
pay a due, 601a, 668a.
pay back, 304a, 874a.
pay for, 904a.
pay heed to, 147b.
paymaster, 172a, 650b.
payment, 9b, 88b, 193b, 264a, 266a, 729b, 874a b, 904a.
payment, forced, 521a.
payment, part, 821b.
Payni, 740a.
peace, 449b, 517b, 727a.
peace, to be at, 449b, 517b, 706b ; depart in, 716b.
peace-cakes, 518a.
peaceful, 517b, 727a.
peacemaker, 699a.
peak, 433b.
peak of the mountain, 885b.
Peak of the West, 885b.
peals of thunder, 447a.
pearl beads, 186a.
pearls, rope of, 70b.
peas, 235a.
peasant, 30a, 76a, 302a, 311a, 411a, 413b, 457b, 686a, 860b, 893a.
Pebaf, 235b.
pebble, 62a, 112a, 115b, 129b, 218a, 394a.
pectoral, 70a b, 183b, 193a, 202a, 216a, 306a, 446a, 452b, 575a, 734b.
pedestal, 156a, 253b, 298a, 388a, 675b, 875a ; of a god, 220b.
peep, 762b, 814b.
Pefi, 235b.
Pefset-ākhu-f, 236a.
peg, 139b, 140a, 246a, 367a, 565a, 777b ; of a boat, 101a, 187a ; of a net, 38a.
Pega, 252b, 253a.
Peḥ-ȧm, 245a.
Peḥ-ȧrti, 245a.
Peḥ-Ḥerui, 245a.
Peḥ-khau, 244b.
Peḥreri, 245b.
Peḥ-reṭui, 245a.
Peḥ-sekhet, 245a.
Peḥ-Sepṭ-f, 244b.
Pehtes, the dog, 243b.
Peḥui-ḥer, 244b.
Peḥui-utchait, 244b.
Peḥ-ustt, 245a.
Pekharer, 246b.
Pekhari, 246b, 428b.
Pekharit, 246b.
Pekhariu, 246b.
Pekharu, 428b.
Pekhat, 246a.
Pekhit, 246a.
Pekht, 247b.
pelican, 184b, 441b, 547b.
pellet, 42a, 129b, 849b, 880b, 910a.
pelt, 62a, 400b.
Pelusium, 605b ; wine of, 676a.
pen for cattle, 337a.
Pen, god, 236a.
pen, sheep's, 817a.
penalty, the death, 655b.
Penȧnt, 236b.
Penȧpt, 236b.
Penāt, a boat, 236b.
Penāt boat, 152a.
pendant, 282a.
pendent, 387b ; of the breasts, 398a, 885b.
penetrate, 5a, 19b, 49b, 117b, 158b, 191b, 567b, 592a, 630b, 650a, 845a, 846b.
Penḥesb, 237a.
Penḫuba, 237a.
penis, 489a.
Penn-Khenti-Ȧmenti, 237a.
Penramu, 236b.
Penrent, 237a.
Penṭ, 237b.
Pentauru, 237b.
Pentch, 237b.
Pentchen, 237b.
Penṭen, 237b.
Penṭer, 237b.
Penti, god, 237b.
Penṭṭȧ, 237b.
people, 117b, 165a, 170a, 197a, 205a, 233b, 249a, 269a, 313b, 423b, 426a, 429a, 430a, 435b, 436b, 447a, 465b, 466a, 525a, 570a, 584a, 681b, 880a, 900b ; all people, 357a.

people, foreign, 6b.
people of a country, 815b
People of the Two Lands (i.e., Egyptians), 815b.
peoples on the land, 774a.
pepper (?), 235b.
peppermint, 139b.
Peqȧ, festival and temple of 252a.
Peqert, 252a.
peqer tree, 252a.
peqer wood, 252a.
Per-Ȧmen, 238a.
perceive, 121b, 128a, 266b, 771b, 802b, 808a.
perception, 783b.
perch, 13a, 373a.
perdition, 120a, 520a.
Per em hru, 241a.
perfect ! 296b.
perfect, 93a, 304a, 522a.
perfect, to be, 900a.
perfect, to make, 521b ; 644a, 670b, 773a.
perfected, 671a.
perfection, 214a b, 304a.
perforate, 220b, 249a.
perform, 411a.
perfume, to, 610a, 786b.
perfume, 36a, 54b, 112a, 256b, 257b, 374b, 631a, 670b, 705b, 712b, 899b ; festival of, 628a ; Nubian, 536a.
perfumer, 91b, 315a.
Pergasides, 243b.
pergola, 219b, 396b, 762a.
perhaps, 130b, 328a, 548b.
Per-Ḥenu, 239b.
Peri-em-ḥat-f, 241b.
Peri-em-khet- etc., 241b.
Peri-em-qenbt, 241b.
Peri-em-tep-f, 241b.
Peri-em-thet-f, 241b.
peril, 445a.
perimeter of a town, 317a.
Perimu (?), 241b.
perinaeum, 795b.
period, 133b, 434a, 440b, 588b, 696a, 778a.
period, the ḥenti, 488a.
period of time, 875a.
Period, Pre-dynastic, 830a.
period, recurring, 594a.
period, the ten-day, 134a.
periphery, 747b.
periplus, 576b.
perish, 10b, 163b, 240a, 315b, 520a, 565b, 627a, 703b, 792b, 805a, 835a.
peristyle of court, 247a.
Perit, 241a, 242b.
Perit-em-up-Rā, 241b.
Periu, 241b.
Per-Keku, 240a.
Per-Kemkem, 240a.
permanent, 296b, 297a, 413b, 422a, 632a, 913b.
Per-Manu, 238b.
Per-mȧu, 81a.
permeated, 20a.
permit ! 279b.
Per-mit, 238b.
Per-nefer, 239a.
Per-neferu- etc., 243a.
Per-neser, 239a.
Per-neter, 239a.
perpetually, 264a.
Per-Qebḥ, 240a.
Perru, 241b.
Per-Saḥ, 239b.
persea, 92b, 734a.
persecute, 373a.
Per-Seker, 240a.
Per-seshep, 239b.
Per-sha-nub, 240a.
persistent, 297a.
person, 153a, 466a, 583a, 633a, 640b, 782b, 828b, 893a.
person, great, 108a.
persuade, 650b.
Pert, season of, 40b, 242b, 829a.
per Ṭuat, 240a.
perturbed, 380a.
perverse, 637b.
perversity, 637a.
pervert, 741b.
Pesekhti, 248b.
pesesh Kef, 249a.
pesh-en-kef, 251b.
Peshf-ḥeteput, 251b.
Peshnȧ, 251b.
Pesit, 248a.
pesiu, 248a.
Pestchet, 250a.
Pesṭ-em-nub, 249b.

Pestit, 249a.
Pesṭit, 249b.
Pesṭit-khenti-ḥert, 249b.
Pest-taui, 249a.
Pesṭ-taui, 249b.
Pesṭti, 249b.
Pesṭu, 249b.
Pet (Ptaḥ), 253b.
Pet-ā, 256a.
Peṭ-āḥāt, 256a.
Petch-āḥā, 257b.
Petch-taiu, 257b.
Petchu, 257b.
Pe-Ṭep, Council of, 901b.
Peti, god, 237b, 253b.
Petit, 253b.
Peṭit-ȧbut, 256a.
petition, 8a, 382b, 465a, 596a, 607a, 645b, 658a, 662a, 668b, 670a, 745a, 824a.
petition, to, 382b, 650b.
petitioner, 662a, 809a, 824a, 866a, 896a.
Petr, 254a.
Peṭ-ra, 256a.
Petrȧ, 254a.
Petrȧ-Ba, 254a.
Petrȧ-neferu- etc., 254a.
Petrȧ-sen, 254b.
Petrȧt, 254a.
Pet-she, 256a.
Peṭsu, 256b.
Peṭti, 255b.
Peṭu-she, 256a.
phallus, 164a, 204b, 217a, 219b, 291a, 292a, 331a, 372a, 448b, 485b, 489a, 599b, 721b.
phallus, knife-shaped, 43a, 81a, 121a.
phallus of Osiris, 429b.
phallus, skin cases for the, 489a.
Phallus-god, 110a, 200b, 217a.
Phamenoth, 236b.
phantom, 473a.
phantom-island, 783a.
Pharaoh, 109a, 238a ; his apartments, 136a.
Pharmuthi, 237a.
phase, 761b.
Philadelphus, 674a.
Philae, 36a ; necropolis of, 166a.
philander, 66b.
Philometor, 295a.
Philometores, 404b.
Philopator, 98a, 833a.
Philopatores, 404b.
Phoenicia, 794a.
phoenix, 213b, 218a.
phylactery, 585b.
phylarch, 108b, 585b.
physician, 592b, 605b ; chief, 172a.
physician, craft of, 592b.
Physician-god, 30b.
pick, 95a.
pick (of the stable), 710b.
picked (words), 710b.
picket, 565a.
picture, 666b, 885b ; of a god, 698b ; to make, 779a.
piece, 91b, 105a, 106b, 154a, 245b, 252b, 392b, 396b, 838a ; broken pieces, 772b ; of flesh, 32b ; of ground, 156b.
pied, 278b.
pierce, 19b, 220b, 395a, 441a, 446a, 567b, 592a, 608b, 630b, 650a, 694a, 713b, 845a, 846a b, 878a, 889a, 905a, 914b.
piercer, 166b.
piercing (of the eye), 509b.
pig, 42b, 174a, 428a, 722a.
pig, black, of Set, 722a.
pig in the boat, 121a.
pig, mythological, 120b.
pigeon, 231b, 299b, 803b, 809b, 810b.
pigeon tower, 319b.
pigment, 34b.
pike, 281b, 351a, 338b ; soldier's, 635b.
pilaster, 179b.
pile, 814b.
pilfer, 538b.
pilgrim, 810b.
pill, 42a, 129b, 203b, 234b, 237a, 248b, 256b, 428a, 490b, 650a, 910a.
pillage, 459a, 729b, 796b.
pillaging, 461b.
pillar, 58b, 109b, 121b, 133a, 151a, 179b, 192b, 274b, 583b, 617a, 635b, 693a, 823b, 861a, 872a, 914a.
pillar of a balance, 272a.
pillar, sacred, 914a.

pillar-scales, 320a.
pillars of heaven, the Four, 550a, 617a, 639a, 693a, 861a.
pillow, 175a, 541a.
pilot, 30a, 44b, 93b, 170b, 739a.
pilot of Rā, 20a, 58b.
Pineter-ṭuau, 234b.
pinion, 298b, 522a, 733b, 878b, 907b.
pint, 442a.
pioneers, 272b.
pipe, 147a.
pipe, to, like a bird, 100b.
piping, 853b.
Pit, 234b.
pit, 187b, 337a, 444b, 464a, 754b, 758b.
pit of fire, 58a.
pit of a tomb, 8a.
pitch, 423b, 428a, 647b, 666a.
pitch a camp, 147b ; a tent, 499a.
pitcher, 856b ; pitcher and stand, 645b.
pitiful, 597b, 598a.
pity, 348a ; to show, 66a, 346b.
place, 27a, 79b, 82b, 106a, 114a, 133b, 174b, 190a, 197a, 207a, 213b, 215a, 220a, 226b, 272b, 278a, 289a, 297b, 330b, 419a, 436b, 448b, 479a, 583b, 731b, 734a, 783b, 856a, 893a.
place, accustomed, 80a.
place behind, 458a.
place below, 214b.
place for drawing water, 287a ; for exercising horses, 851b ; for fattening animals, 185a ; for fighting, 516a.
place, holy, 155b.
place of honour, 79b.
place of law, 80a.
place of protection, 38a.
place of purity, 79b.
place of rest, 35a, 409b.
place of slaughter, 26b.
place of the feet, 80a, 214a.
place, secret, 477b.
place, to, 22a, 147b, 180a, 436b, 631a, 707b, 864a, 865a.
placenta, 795b.
plague, 27a.
plain, 311a, 721b.
plainly, 265b.
plaintiff, 662a, 745a, 866a.
plait, 261b, 615b.
plait, to, 368a, 859b.
plaiter, of baskets, 368b ; of crowns, 292b.
plan, 94a, 510b, 617b, 624a, 694a, 700b, 779b, 855a, 860b.
plan, to, 694a, 708b.
plane, inclined, 390a.
planet, 546b, 701a.
plank, 79b, 88b, 314a, 469b, 566a, 590a, 615b, 644b, 765a, 856b.
plant, 5a, 8a, 14b, 15a, 17a, 21b, 25a b, 30b, 32b, 33b, 34a, 38b, 40a, 41a, 54b, 55a, 60a b, 61a, 63b, 64a, 75b, 77b, 79a, 93b, 95b, 99a, 102a, 105a, 111b, 113b, 119b, 121b, 122a, 125a, 136a, 138a, 139b, 140a, 141a, 146a b, 147b, 150a, 159b, 167b, 168a, 169b, 179a, 188b, 197a, 202a, 209a, 213a, 224b, 226b, 232b, 242b, 245b, 247b, 259b, 262b, 263a, 278b, 279a, 280a, 290a, 299a, 322a, 330b, 343a b, 348b, 354a, 355a b, 370b, 372b, 377b, 380b, 383b, 389b, 390a b, 394a, 396a, 407b, 437b, 452b, 464a, 466a, 471a, 472a b, 475b, 479a, 482b, 484a, 487b, 489a, 527b, 531b, 539b, 544a, 545a, 553a b, 563b, 566a, 589a, 590b, 594b, 597b, 598a, 600b, 605b, 612a, 615a, 635a b, 636b, 637a b, 638a, 644b, 645a b, 659a, 676a, 677a, 681b, 695a, 697a, 711a b, 714b, 727b, 728a, 735b, 736b, 741a b, 746b, 752a, 753a, 785b, 791a, 798b, 799b, 803b, 804a, 805a, 808b, 809a, 810b, 811b, 818a, 825a, 827b, 828a, 832a, 839a b, 842a, 846b, 850a, 858a b, 872a, 873a, 886a, 887a, 888a, 891a, 892b, 896a, 897a, 899b, 900a, 913a.
plant, aromatic, 160a, 344a, 398a.
plant, earshaped, 883a.
plant, flowering, 884a.
plant, the frankincense, 377b.
plant, to, 867b, 891b.
plant, medicinal, 35a.

plant of life (i.e., grain), 126b, 487b.
plant of smell, 388a.
plant of spring, 427a.
plant, oily, 802b.
plant, resinous, 367b.
plant, river, 13b.
plant, strong-smelling, 26b.
plant, sweet-smelling, 574a.
plant used in making boats, 648b.
plant, water, 22b, 302b, 303b.
plant with gummy juice, 398a.
plantation, 299a, 558b, 755a.
Plant-god, 180b.
plants, growing, 421b.
plants, kinds of, 192b.
plaque, 42a, 123a, 317a, 511a, 827b.
plaques, the Four, 827b.
plaster, 1b, 36b, 702a.
plate, 208b, 223b, 708a, 762a.
plate, to, 212b, 353b, 368b, 474a, 590b, 650a, 659a, 717b, 891b.
plate with metal, 183b, 409b.
plated, 324b, 617b.
platform, 207a, 600b.
plating, metal, 717b.
plaudits, 275a, 442a.
play the fool, 180a.
play, to, and play musical instruments, 475b, 476a, 541b, 771b ; the flute, 588a, 594a ; harp, 211a, 614a, 836a ; sistrum, 66b ; tambourine, 42b, 887b ; zither, 685b, 741b, 843b, 857a, 887b.
player, 475b, 741b, 843b ; of music, 535b.
playfully, 476a.
playing, 887b.
pleader, 745a.
pleading, 868a.
pleasant, 111b, 123a, 211a, 219a, 347a, 370b, 412a, 449a, 516a, 610a, 876b.
pleasant, to make, 658a, 679a ; to make oneself, 643a.
pleasantness, 421a.
please, 66b, 110b, 442a, 601b, 658a, 669a, 670a, 677a.
pleased, 333a, 549b, 658a, 752a.
pleasing, 449b, 660a.
pleasure, 3a, 19a, 20b, 155a, 508a, 616b, 682a, 776b, 865a.
pleasure ground, 559a.
pleasure, to feel or to have, 688a, 693a, 717a.
pledge, 32b, 131b.
plentiful, 148a.
plenty, 469b, 606b, 677a.
plinth, 253b, 662b, 675b, 875a.
plot, 145b, 694a, 860b.
plot of ground, 10b, 43b, 106a, 175a, 424b, 449b, 479b, 568a, 758a, 881b, 915a.
plough, 29b, 66b, 90b, 95a, 127a, 445b, 488b, 489a, 540a, 626a.
plough, to, 201a, 302a, 441a, 445b, 468b, 488b, 540a, 559b, 564a, 704a b, 751b.
ploughed land, 276a, 540b.
ploughman, 75a, 201a, 302a, 489a, 540a, 704b.
ploughshare, 604a.
plover, 891b.
pluck, 262a, 263a.
pluck a bird, 186b, 395a.
pluck away, 796a.
pluck out, 550b, 688b, 801b ; hair, 167a, 458a.
plum tree, 102b.
plumage, 887a.
plume, 319a.
plumed, double, 18a.
plumes, the Two, 596b, 662b, 725a.
plummet, 842b.
plunder, 100b, 101a, 110b, 114b, 115b, 464b, 467b, 473a, 550b, 572b, 750b, 794a, 849b.
plunder, to, 467b, 545a.
plunderer, 464b.
plunge, 442b, 613a, 642a, 820a, 843a.
pluralist, 131a.
P-neb-taui, 236b.
P-nefer-nehem, 236b.
poignard, 226a, 276b, 333b.
point, 525a, 554a, 828a.
pointer of the scales, 842b, 887b.
poised in air, 135a.
poison, 300b, 332a ; of serpent, 348a.
pole, 1b, 17a, 60a, 89a, 115b, 129b, 274a, 347a, 467a, 470a, 566a, 583b, 635b, 638b, 675b, 847b, 851a.

pole, carrying, 367b, 630b.
pole, chariot, 106a, 864b.
pole for working a boat, 670a.
pole, impaling, 566b.
pole of net, 835b.
pole, steering, 373a, 375b, 478b.
police, 292a.
Police, Sûdânî, 386a.
policeman, 333a, 588a.
polish, 329b, 356a, 395b, 622b, 682a.
polished, 753a.
pollute, 642b, 818a.
pollution, sexual, 818a.
poltroon, 481b, 548a.
pomade, 337a, 433b, 516a, 824a.
pomatum, 626b.
pomegranate, 62b, 63a, 222b, 876b.
pond, 22a, 204b, 293a, 442a, 449b, 768b.
ponder, 274a, 285a, 330b, 393a.
ponderous, 838b, 839b.
pool, 78b, 121b, 128b, 140b, 187b, 202a, 204a b, 212b, 285a, 307b, 325b, 349b, 431a, 569a, 574a, 576a, 592b, 640a, 642a, 650b, 720a, 758a, 814a.
pool, the upper, 579a.
pool with plants in it, 148b.
poor, 12b, 375b, 379b, 733b, 899b.
poor folk, 476a.
poor man, 270a, 413b, 472b, 734a, 810a.
poor, the, 128a, 340a, 376a.
poor, to be, 472b.
poor-spirited, 472b.
poppy-seed, 252a.
population, 815b.
porcelain, blue, 842a.
porch, 420b, 701b.
porphyry, 62b.
port, 105a, 1376, 180b, 230a, 300b, 307b, 308a, 647b.
port-master, 312a.
port side, 45a.
portal, 371b, 819a.
portals, the Two, 552b.
porter, 56a, 70a, 260c, 425b, 591a, 629b, 643a, 645b, 670b, 712a, 767a, 776a.
portico, 58b, 179b, 420b.
portion, 245b, 248b, 251b, 252a b, 263b, 334b, 392b, 580b, 693b, 815a, 821b, 835b, 881b.
portrait, 577a.
portrait painter, 645b.
portulaca, 288b.
position, 133b, 297a, 737a; official, 18a.
possess, 317b, 547b, 580a, 638a, 707a, 772a.
possessing, 579b.
possession, 79a, 91b, 638a; to take, 333a.
possession, demoniacal 419a.
possessionless, 12b, 340b.
possessions, 77a, 296b, 395b, 396b, 487a, 525a, 561a, 580b, 720, 724b, 812a; of the god, 525b.
possessor, 357a, 580a, 810a, 812a.
post, 133b, 141a, 301a, 347a, 635b.
post, mooring 301a.
post of door, 479b.
post on a boat, 540a.
posterity, 30a, 31a, 33a, 113b, 243a, 265b, 331b, 443b, 542b, 567b, 812a, 898a.
pot, 28a b, 43a, 72a, 94b, 104a, 107a, 118a, 128a, 131a, 137a, 143a, 178a, 186a, 204a, 208b, 213b, 230b, 276b, 278a, 282b, 284a, 292b, 295a, 300a, 301b, 314a, 354a, 355b, 374b, 376a, 394a, 400b, 433a, 449b, 486b, 499b, 510a, 512b, 516b, 529b, 537b, 539b, 544a, 558b, 603a, 605b, 606a, 672b, 676a b, 716b, 731a, 725a, 754b, 758a, 763b, 767b, 790b, 791b, 809a, 838b, 847b, 850b, 851b, 852a, 854a, 857a, 868b, 872b, 876a, 877a b, 884a, 888a, 892a, 895b, 911b; boiling, 791a; cooking, 228b; metal, 41b, 764b.
pot for grain, 596a.
pot for shoulders, 425b.
pot of beer, 350b.
pot of Khoiak festival, 783b.
pot of palette, 232b.
pot, unguent, 356b.
pot-herb, 8a.
potentate, 690b.
Potiphar, 256b.
potsherd, 252a.
pottage, 6b, 8a, 36b.

potter, 143b, 384b, 779a.
potter, craft of, 384b.
potter, table of, 384b.
Potter, the Divine, 385a, 779a.
potter's clay, 10a.
pouch, 33b, 835b.
poultry, 573a.
poultry yard, 316b.
pound, to, 140b, 185a, 480b, 571a, 573b, 613a, 683b, 704a, 757a, 844b ; drugs, 605a ; together, 186a, 411a.
pound up, 441a, 446a.
pounded things, 331a.
pounding, 285a.
pour out a libation, water, oil, etc., 35b, 91b, 99b, 101b, 118a, 155b, 185a, 195b, 224b, 228a, 237a, 252a, 302b, 387a, 400a, 401a, 541b, 561b, 589a b, 597b, 598a, 609a, 665a, 666a, 697b, 702a, 708a, 729b, 793b, 804a, 814a, 833a b, 854b, 862b, 906b.
poverty, 7b, 270a, 800b.
powder, 347b, 386b, 395b, 396a, 469a, 534a, 752a ; to reduce to, 347b.
powder, white, 751a.
powdered substance, 186b.
power, 182a, 197a, 241a, 245a, 306a, 379a, 388b, 402a, 537b, 544a, 690b, 738a, 769b, 772a, 783a, 822b ; personified, 691a.
Power, Divine, 389a, 401b, 691a.
power, to have, 18a, 145a, 163b, 317b, 772a.
power, words of, 22b.
powerful, 107b, 388b, 697a.
powerless, 8a, 228a.
Powers, the, 691a.
Powers, the Two, 691a.
P-peshṭit-neteru, 235b.
practice, 666b.
praise, 6a, 15a, 17a b, 68b, 102b, 149b, 184b, 381b, 358b, 440a, 442a, 449a, 451b, 479a, 485a, 487a, 515b, 586a, 589b, 592a, 608a, 633a, 639a, 649b, 652b, 677b, 680a, 696a, 798a, 805b, 822b, 824a, 871a ; words of, 3b ; praised, 508b.
praise, the gold of, 353a.
praise, to, 65a, 66a, 138b, 141a, 149b, 152b, 166b, 379b, 438a, 442a, 444b, 448a, 508a, 515b, 516a, 593a, 603b, 608a, 622b, 635a, 678a, 801b, 833b, 835b, 858a, 871a.
praises, to sing, 508a.
praisers, 442a, 448a, 871a.
praisings, 824a.
prance, 701a.
pratas monkey, 802b.
pray to, 186b, 187a, 254b, 382b, 385a, 436b, 597a, 598b, 601a, 602b, 606b, 607a, 624a, 649a, 668b, 671b, 677b, 726b, 740b, 741a, 758a, 824a, 835b, 876a.
prayer, 80a, 254b, 382b, 607a, 658a, 662a, 711b, 726b, 857b, 876a.
prayer, pure, 825a.
preach, 468b.
precept, 409a, 679b, 719b, 831b, 860b.
precinct, 207a ; of temple, 511b.
precious, 93a, 110a.
precipice, 727a, 729b.
predecessors, 45b, 830a, 909a.
predestinate, 722b.
predict, 610b.
pre-eminence, 554a.
pre-eminent, 828b.
prefix, causative, 633a.
pregnant, 35a, 165b, 206a, 207a, 215b, 225b, 651a.
pregnant, to make, 590a, 594b, 642a, 656b, 660a.
pregnant woman, 35a, 658a.
prejudice, 2b, 8a, 12b.
preparation, 660b, 663a.
prepare, 269a, 618b, 661a, 696b, 710a, 715a, 811b ; a bed, 14a ; food, 65b ; path, 912a.
prepared, 597b, 645a, 663a.
preparedness, 660b, 783b.
preposition, compound, 749a.
prepuce, 220a, 264b, 776b.
prescribed, 487a.
prescription, 563b, 831b ; to make up a, 140b.
presence 333b ; presence of 205a.
present, 3a, 5b, 115a, 117a, 204b, 270b, 333b, 343a, 487a, 550b, 582a, 736a, 862a.
present, to, 28b, 152a, 259a, 301b, 562a, 592a, 694b.

presentation to the dead, 259a.
preserve, 594b.
preserved, 180b.
preserves of birds, 778a.
president, 331b, 494a, 562a; of priests, 331b; of the Thirty, 281a.
press, to, 292b, 338a b, 491b, 492a, 707b; oil or wine, 28b, 114a.
pressing, 356b.
pressure, 338a.
pretend, 65b.
pretty, 123a, 341b, 370b, 371a.
prevail, 690b, 794b.
prevent, 36b; the dawn, 562b.
previously, 554a.
prey, 243b.
price, 88b, 206b, 286b, 642a, 643b, 649a, 650b, 904a.
prick the ears, 589a.
prick, to, 249a, 344a.
pride, 189b, 203b, 241a, 861b; words of, 335b.
priest, 44b, 116a, 138b, 155a, 158a, 298b, 402b, 482b, 483a, 548b, 580b, 598b, 677a, 690b, 711a; assistant, 715b; chief, 581a; courses of, 167b; funerary, 558a; in ordinary, 167b.
priest of Ȧn-ḥer, 132b.
priest of a tomb, 44b.
priest of the hour, 45a, 402b.
priest of the month, 44b.
priest of Rā and Mnevis, 174b.
priest of resurrection, 262a.
priest of the people, 580b.
priest, royal, 392a.
priest, sacrificial, 54b, 166b, 303b, 325a, 665a.
priest, the *sem* or *setem*, 666b.
priest, titles of, 39b, 409b.
priest who "opened the mouth," 166b.
priestess, 483a.
priestess of Busirite Nome, 171b.
priestess of Heliopolis, 172a.
priesthood, 483a.
primeval, 830a; beings, 230b.
prince, 61a, 97a, 170b, 323b, 392a, 423a, 460b, 513a, 584a, 610a, 679b, 715b.
Prince, Everlasting, 610a.
prince, hereditary, 423a.
Prince, Great (i.e., Rā), 610a.
princess, 392a, 422b, 460b, 513a, 584a.
principal (money), 829a.
prison, 75a, 99a, 100a, 101b, 342a, 412b, 465a, 499b, 539a, 550a, 569a, 690a, 723b, 758b, 789b, 875a, 903b, 915b.
prisoner, 12b, 90a, 100a, 101b, 317b, 464b, 550a, 552a, 648a, 702b, 705b, 752a; living, 625b; of war, 702a; to take, 464b.
prison-house, 557b.
prithee, 279b.
private apartment, 573a, 575b.
private parts, 550a.
private soldier, 436a.
privilege, 605b.
prize-bearer, 259a.
prize of victory, 736a.
problem, 178b.
procedure, 698b.
proceed from, 240a.
procession, 242a.
procession of boats, 576a.
procession, festal, 166b.
procession, royal, 535a.
procession-boat, 703a.
proclaim, 34b, 40a, 276b, 343b, 344a, 345b, 468b, 632b, 642a, 722b, 745a, 756b.
proclaim the name, 411a.
proclaimer, 176b, 548b.
proclamation, 192a, 344a, 669b.
procreation, 188b.
procreator, 826a.
produce, 65a, 72a, 188b, 221b, 246a, 490a, 616a, 840a, 868a, 914b, 915b.
produce, annual, 580b.
produce (food), 747a.
produce of a country, 722b.
produce of field or garden, 647b, 711a.
produce, to, 56a, 321a, 639b, 690a.
produced, 221b.
producer, 321a.
product, 56b, 72b, 77a, 206b, 230b, 251b, 270b, 489a, 525a, 561b, 825a; natural, 770b.

product of enchanted island, 723b.
product of Sûdân, 287a.
production, 149b.
production, literary, 242b.
profane, 262b.
professional men, 212a.
professional occupation, 18a.
profit, 443b, 453a, 722b.
profitable, 458b, 659b.
profondeur, 297b.
progenitor, 830a.
progeny, 33a, 243a, 439b, 443b, 466a.
progress, 222a, 478a.
progress, to, 370b.
prohibition, 441a ; particle of, 307b.
project, 470b.
prolific, 189b.
prolong, 450a, 702a ; life, 625b, 677b.
promenade, 80a b, 272b.
prominent, 105a, 554a, 557b, 630a, 713a.
promise, to, 723b.
promote, 558a, 693b, 719a, 837b, 841b, 856a, 885a.
promulgate, 3a, 690a ; edict, 192a.
prong, 803b.
pronoun, 229a, 233b, 234b, 253b, 610b.
pronounce, 758a, 877b.
proof, 444b, 643b.
prop, 190a, 637a, 861a ; of sky, 133a ; of vine, 473a.
propagate, 260b.
proper, 139a, 304a.
property, 77a, 79a, 164b, 389b, 396b, 403a, 487a, 525a b, 561a b, 580b, 631b, 724b, 798b.
property, cemetery, 525b.
property, divine, 518b.
property, funerary, 893b.
property, landed, 638a, 773a, 900b.
property, paternal, 525a.
property, royal, 239a.
property, sacred, 70b, 312a.
prophecy, 679b.
prophesy, 530a, 593a.
prophet, 166b, 548b.
propitiate, 614a, 684b.
propitiation, 656b ; offerings of, 614a, 684b ; place of, 519b.
propose, 753b.
Prosopite, 23a, 132a, 489b.
prosper, 77b, 150a, 282b, 371a, 421b, 596b.
prosperity, 214a, 371a, 680b.
prosperous, 128a, 206a.
prostrate oneself, 550a, 572a, 885a.
prostration, 719a.
protect, 65b, 66a, 67a, 175a, 273b, 288b, 324b, 354a, 366b, 381a, 386b, 409b, 410a, 473a, 477a, 537a, 586b, 591b, 643a, 654a, 656b, 658b, 676a, 700a, 701a, 715b, 814a, 843a b.
protect oneself, 586b.
protected, 206a, 710b, 747b, 851a.
protection, 22b, 214b, 288b, 330b, 380a, 537a b, 585b, 586b, 602a, 634a ; places of, 330b.
protective formulae, 22b.
protector, 64b, 273b, 281a, 288b, 366b, 386b, 410a, 458a, 537a, 552a, 592a, 648b, 717a.
protectress, 288b, 410a.
proud, 107b, 189b, 633b, 861b.
prove, 444b, 644a, 668b.
provender, 49a, 259b.
proverb, 335a, 860b, 913a.
proverb, to coin a, 469a, 632b.
provide, 376b, 487a, 607a, 618a, 631b, 683b, 689a, 690a, 709b, 710a, 715a, 717b, 904a, 906b ; provide for, 632a ; offerings, 840b.
provided, 118b, 520a, 663a.
province, 649a.
proving, 754b.
provision, to, 632a, 710a, 717b.
provisions, 134b, 179a, 278b, 286b, 289a, 323b, 426b, 433a, 490a, 580b, 594b, 606b, 609b, 612b, 632a, 663a, 690a, 696a, 715a, 735a, 783b, 866b, 884b, 904a ; house of, 80b.
prudent, 246a.
prune vines, to, 178a.
pry into, 332b, 762b, 814b, 903b.
P-seb-uā, 248a.

Ptaḥ (see also Pteḥ), 30b, 40b, 118b, 432a ; claw of, 123b ; high priest of, 672a ; priests of, 666b ; title of, 432a.
Pteḥ, the god, 254b.
Pteḥ-āa-resu-ȧneb-f, 254b.
Pteḥ-Ḥāp, 255a.
Pteḥ-Nefer-ḥer, 254b.
Pteḥ-Nu, 254b.
Pteḥ-re, 254b.
Pteḥ-Seker, 255a.
Pteḥ-Tenen, 255a.
Pteḥ-Ṭeṭ, 255a.
Pteḥ-ur, 254b.
publicity, 166b.
publish, 610b.
published, 632b.
pudenda, 217a, 466a, 481b, 489a, 544b.
puff of wind, 82b, 273a, 445a.
puffed up, 545a.
pull, 100a, 104a, 628b, 629b, 703b, 713a, 827a.
pull down, 443a, 499b.
pull off, 262a, 793b.
pull up, 827a.
pulse, 490b.
pulse (herbs), 625b.
pump, 292a.
pumpkin, 803a.
punish, 1b, 82b, 102b, 163b, 375b, 564b, 568a, 644b, 648a.
punished, 564b.
punishment, 9b, 568a, 594b, 614b, 648a, 655b, 664b, 685b, 904b ; hall of, 80b.
punt, to, 93b.
Puntites, 809b.
pupil, 49a, 652a.
pupil of eye, 68a, 102a, 307a, 471b, 481b, 893a, 906b, 907a.
pure, 155a, 711a, 714b, 825a.
Pure Land, 816b.
pure thing, 38b, 711b.
purge, 180a, 246a, 711a ; nitre, 512a.
purification, 117a, 486b, 711b, 868a ; place of, 623b.
purified, 155a, 825a.
purify, 117a, 155a, 407b, 592a, 598a, 609b, 631b, 644b, 653b, 678b, 703b, 825a, 858a, 865b, 873a.
purifying, 868a.
purity, 214a.
purple linen, 58b.
purpose, 595a, 753b.
purpose, to, 753b.
purse, 131a, 803a.
purslane, 286a, 288b.
pursue, 253a.
pus, 217a, 222b, 294b, 459a, 553a, 822b ; bloody, 100b.
push, 190a ; aside, 99a, 101b, 631b ; away, 116b ; back, 90a ; open, 631b ; out of the way, 866a ; over, 547a.
pussy, 278a.
pustules, 11b, 217a, 222a, 256b, 738b, 791a, 824a.
put, 190a.
put an end to, 135b.
put aside, 7a, 153a.
put a stop to, 437a.
put before, 866a.
put behind, 289b.
put forth shoots, 8b.
put in restraint, 7a.
put into writing, 56b.
put off clothes, 665b.
put on, 131b, 376a, 476b ; apparel, 169a ; armour, 574b.
put out a fire, 2b.
put outside, 437a.
put to earth, 865b.
put together, 578a.
putrefaction, 470a, 553a.
putrefy, 49b.
putrid, 176b, 470a, 762a.
putridity, 554a.
putting forth, 894a.
Putukhipa, 235b.
pygmy, 374b, 883b.
pylon, 174b, 205a, 221b, 588b, 658b, 659a, 847a.
pylon keeper, 70b.
pyramid, 113b, 217a, 219b. 314b
pyramid, base of, 180a.
pyramid of Ȧmenemḥat II, 54a.
pyramid of Userkaf, 156a.
pyramid tomb, 5a, 118b, 217b, 314b.
pyramid-town, 351a.
pyramidion, 217b, 813a.
Pyrrhides, 243b.

Q.

Qa, god, 760b.
Qa (Temu), 761b.
Qaȧ, 760b.
Qa-ā, 760b.
Qa-āau, 760b.
Qa-ȧb, 760b.
Qaȧsu, 762b.
Qa-ba, 760b.
Qab-en-Ȧment, 763a.
Qabi, 763a.
Qabt-ent-Shu, 763b.
Qa-ha-ḥetep, 761a.
Qahaqu, 764b.
Qa-ḥer-ȧst-f, 761a.
Qa-ḥer-f, 761a.
Qaḥu, 765a.
Qai, 762b.
Qaiqashau, 762b.
Qait, 761b.
Qa-meri-mut-f, 760b.
Qa-mertu-neb, 760b.
Qān, 766a.
Qa-neb, 761a.
Qaq, 765a.
Qaqa, 761b.
Qār, 766a.
Qart, 763b.
Qa-serpit, 761a.
Qa-shefshef, 761a.
Qa-shuti, 761a.
Qat, 263b.
Qaṭ, 765b.
Qatȧ, 765a.
Qat-ā, 760b.
Qatcharti, 765b.
Qat-em-ȧakhu-s, 760b.
Qat-em-sekhem-s, 760b.
Qat-em-sepu-s, 760b.
Qa-ṭemt, 761a.
qaṭit, 765b.
Qat-kheru, 761a.
Qau, 761b.
Qeb, 767b, 768a.
Qeb Ȧmentt, 768a.
Qebak, 768a.
Qebḥ (pyramid), 769a.
Qebḥit, 768b, 769a.
Qebḥit-urit, 769a.
Qebḥ-neteru-ḥet, 769a.
Qebḥ-senuf, 769a.
Qebḥ-senui-f, 769a.
Qebḥu, 769a.
Qebḥut, 769a.
qebti, a title, 769b.
Qeftenu, 769b.
Qefṭenu, 770a.
Qeheq, 777b.
Qem-baiu-s, 770a.
Qem-baiu-set, 770a.
Qem-ḥes, 771b.
Qen-ȧb-f, 772a.
Qen-Ȧmen, 772a.
Qen-qen-t, 773a.
Qenqentiu, 772b.
Qenqentt, 772b.
Qenti, 773a.
Qeq-ḥa, 778b.
Qeq-snef, 778b.
Qerȧ, 775b.
Qerȧstt, 776a.
Qeraut, 777a.
Qerḥap, 776b.
Qerḥit, 776b.
Qerner, 776b.
Qerpiais, 776a.
Qerqer, 777b.
Qerr, Qerrȧ, 775b.
Qerrt, 775a.
Qerrt Sar, 775a.
Qersu, 777a.
Qerti, 122a, 775a.
Qertiu gods, 775a.
Qeṭ, 780b.
Qeṭ, devil, 781b.
qeṭ, a weight, 781a.
Qeṭi, god, 780b.
Qeṭ-ka, 780b.
Qeṭ-kha, 780b.
Qetqet, 779a.
Qeṭqeṭ, 780b.
Qeṭshit, 794b.
Qeṭshu goddess, 781b.
Qeṭ-t, Sea of, 142b.
Qettbu, 779a.
Qeṭṭ-ka, 780b.
Qett-Ṭent, 779a.
Qeṭu, the "Circle," 780b.
Qi, god, 766b.
Qitaui, 767a.
quack, 100b, 398a, 705b.
quadrupeds, 14b.
quake, 12b, 298a, 352b, 356b, 380a, 628a, 631a, 636a, 640a, 714b, 799b, 864b.

quaking, 588a, 589a b, 716a, 864b.
qualities, 485b, 779b, 829b, 910b ; distinguishing, 630a ; good, 635a.
quality, 34b, 200a, 209b.
quality, finest, 461b.
quantity, 134a, 221a, 838a, 856b ; small, 379b.
quarrel, 461b, 729b, 744b.
quarrelsome, 639b, 682a.
quarry, to, 158b, 178a, 729b.
quarry, 571a b ; works, 755a.
quarryman, 36b, 94a, 158b, 402b.
quarter, 529b ; to give, 9a.
quarter of month, 881b ; of town, 32a, 77b, 156b, 313b, 314a ; of a city, 532a.
quarters, 136a.
quay, 80a, 137b, 300b, 307b, 308a, 354a, 544b.
queen, 107a, 171a, 391a, 392a, 481a, 486a, 513a.
quench, 135b.
quern, 218a.
quest, 745a.
question, to, 445a, 882a, 911b.
quick, 563a, 827b.
quick spoil, 82b.
quickly, 754b.
quiet, 95b, 767b.
quiet, to, 252b, 682a, 706b ; to be, 291a ; to keep, 575b.
quieter, 612b.
quietness, 896b.
quite, 181a.
quiver, 89a, 640a, 728b ; handle of, 105b.
quotation, mark of, 1a, 913a.

R.

Rā, 230a, 417b, 418a.
Rā Åfu, 418a.
Rā Åsår, 418a.
Rā-åst-åb, 417b.
Rā Åtni, 418a.
Rā-em-åten-f, 418a.
Rā-em-ḥetep, 418a.
Rā-em-nu, 418a.
Rā-em-ta-en-Åtem, 418a.
Rā-en-ḥequ, 417b.
Rā-er-neḥeḥ, 418a.
Rā-Ḥeru, 418b.
Rā-Ḥeru-åakhuti, 418b.
Rā-Khenti-ḥet-Mesq, 418b.
Rā-Kheper, 418b.
Rā-Nekhen, 418a.
Rā-nub, 418a.
Rā-sa-em-åkhekh, 418b.
Rā-sesh, 418b.
Rā-sherå, 418b.
Rā-shesp-åb, 418a.
Rā-Tem, 418b.
Rā-Tem-Kheper, 418b.
Rā-tem-åb, 418a.
Rā-ur, 418a.
Rā, ancestors of, 11b, 830b.
Rā, Boat of, 30b, 31a, 403b.
Rā, Body of, 23b.
Rā, Chief of Followers of, 830a.
Rā, dead body of, 43a.
Rā, eye of, 23a, 154a, 194a, 408b, 475a.
Rā, Followers of, 743a.
Rā, harpoon of, 47a.
Rā, left eye of, 18b, 68a.
Rā, masturbations of, 386a.
Rā, right eye of, 68a, 168a.
Rā, phallus of, 489a.
Rā, pilot of, 20a.
Rā, products of, 352b.
Rā, the Seventy-five Addresses to, 337b.
Rā, title of, 20b.
Rā, Two Aspects of, 461a.
Rā, Two Obelisks of, 843b.
Rā, Two Pillars of, 698b.
Rā, woman of, 471b.
race, 322a.
radiance, 23a, 31a, 128b, 146a, 225a, 274a, 459b, 522b, 535a, 622b, 685a, 708a b, 712b, 736b, 753a, 914a.
radishes, 786a.
raft of reeds, 905a.
rafters, 215a.
rag, 82a, 516b, 517a, 589b, 596b, 652b, 810a.
rage, 395a, 536b, 602a.
rage at, 14a.
rage, to, 381b, 536a, 744b, 774b, 884a, 908a.
raging of the sea, 774b.
raid, 441a, 461b.
raid, to, 138b, 158b, 261b, 441a, 459a.

raider, 858a.
raiding, 461b.
rail, 723b.
railing, 723b.
raiment, 476b, 606a, 757a.
raiment, change of, 304b.
raiment, festal, 670a, 712b.
raiment, fine, 282b.
raiment, holy, 155b.
raiment, ornamental, 671b.
rain, 122b, 293b, 459b, 467b, 469a, 571a, 806b.
rain channel, 144b.
rain cloud, 465a.
rain flood, 95a.
rain, heavy, 465a.
rain storm, 27a, 95b, 317b, 465a, 571a, 642b, 746a, 775b, 814a.
rain, thunder, 607a.
rain torrent, 294a.
raise, 189b, 536a, 837b, 856a, 861a, 873a.
raise a song, 630a.
raise taxes, 860a.
raise up, 92a, 135a, 618a, 646b, 880b.
raise up children, 101b.
raised, 880b.
raisins, 49b.
Rāit, 418a, 780a.
Rāit-taui, 418b.
ram, 129a, 200a, 444a, 587a, 610a, 611a, 737b.
Ram (Dekan), 640b.
Ram of Ȧmen, 429a.
Ram of Mendes, with four faces, 111b, 200a, 408b, 493b.
Ram-god, 181b, 199b, 424b, 498a, 578a ; the four-headed, 738a.
Ram-gods, the Four, 260a.
Rameses II, 696a.
ramp, 435a, 707b.
range, 134a.
ranger, 157a.
rank, 15a, 18a, 32a, 387b, 554a.
rank, royal, 646a.
Rapan, 234a.
rape, to, 396b.
rapidly, 754b.
rapids, 236b.
rare, 110a, 755b.
Rastau, Council of, 901b.
rat, 236b, 809b.
Rȧtȧt, 417b.
ratepayers, 838a.
ration, 91b, 174a, 245b, 248b, 251b, 663a, 696a, 838b, 866b.
ration, for beasts, 41b.
rational beings, 430a b.
rat's bane, 25b, 236b, 589a.
rat's tail (herb), 714a.
rattle, to, 66b.
ravager, 115b.
ravenous, 411b.
ravine, 58a, 252b, 533a.
ravish, 849a.
ravisher, 101a.
rays, 49a, 124a, 249b, 608b, 685a, 698b, 708b.
rays of light, 3b, 159b.
razor, 534a, 572a.
Re-āa-ur, 416b.
Re-Ḥāp, Re-Ḥep, 416b.
Re-Khemenu, 417a.
Re-nen, 416b.
Re-pān, 416b.
Re-peq, 416b.
Re-Peshnȧ, 416b.
Re-Qerrt, 417a.
Re-stau, 417a.
reach, 244a, 577b, 638a.
reach out, 712a, 804b, 873a, 894a, 896b.
reach the shore, 638a.
reach up, 28a.
read, 722b, 758a b.
ready, 645a, 663a ; be ready, 597b ; make, 269a, 715a, 811b.
ready of mind, 533a.
ready of tongue, 633a.
real, 270b, 271a.
really, 170a, 602a ; and truly, 271a.
reap, 8b, 10a, 36b, 90b, 114b, 178a, 263b, 268b, 274b, 614b, 685b.
reaper, 527a, 567b.
Reapers, the Seven, 71a.
reaping, 110b.
rear guard, 244a.
rear, to, 468a, 677b, 757b, 865b.
rearing, of cobra, 259a.
rearward, 264b.
Rebasunna, 422a.
Rebati, 422b.

rebel, 12b, 88b, 99a, 101b, 116a, 145b, 208b, 209a, 216b, 227a, 251b, 322b, 356b, 357b, 434a, 549b, 574b, 682a, 704a, 707b, 735b, 755a, 899a.
rebel, to, 3b, 224a, 433b, 577a, 690a.
rebellion, 145b, 207b, 224a, 531b, 597a, 657a, 682a, 796b.
rebellious, 227a, 735b.
rebels, foreign, 227a.
Rebu (Lebu), 422b.
rebuild, 601a, 668b.
Rebu-inini, 422b.
rebuke, 644b, 652b.
receive, 622b, 698b, 701a, 752a.
receptacle, 473a, 707b, 800b.
recitation, 758a, 758b.
recite formulae, 22b, 574b, 589b, 745a, 814b.
recite, to, 106b, 176b, 601a, 635a, 692b, 717a, 758a b, 913a.
recited, 877b.
reciter of spells, 585b.
reckon, 345a, 477a, 510b, 838a, 856b.
reckon up, 41a, 79b, 89a, 807b, 888a.
reckoning, 41a, 465b, 510b, 856b; make a, 716a; method of, 134a.
reclaim, 289a.
recluses, 552a.
recognize, 641b, 649a.
recoil, 152a.
recollection, 688a.
recommend, 448b.
recompense, 33a, 88b, 304a, 508a, 898b, 904a.
reconstitute, 859b.
record, 192a, 688a, 808b.
record office, 80a, 526b.
recorder, 176b, 688a.
recount, 176b.
recover, 370b.
recreation, 693a.
recruits, 269a, 680b, 898a.
rectangle, 43b.
rectify, 194b.
rectitude, 277b, 280a.
rectum, 599a.
red, 845a, 889a.
red calf, 890b.
red cloth, 58b, 97a, 98b, 103a.
red clouds, 890a.
red cow, 845a.
Red Crown, 890a.
Red Ear, 890a.
red earth, ochre or paint, 558b.
Red-Eyes, a god, 890a.
Red-Faces, gods, 890a.
Red Festival, 890a.
red fiends, 889b.
Red-Fish, 890b.
red flame, 889b.
red grain, 889b, 890b.
red hair, 890a.
red-haired devils, 208a.
red hot, 817b.
red land, 889b.
Red-Land, 890b.
Red Mountain, 870a.
red ones, 889b.
red plants, 889b.
red pomade, 890a.
red sand, 890b.
red stone, 551b.
red thing, 715b, 889b.
red vases, the Four, 890a b.
red wing, 890a.
red wood (cam wood ?), 566b.
redden, 715b.
reddish, 889a.
redness, 845a.
reduce, 57b, 607a, 635a, 644a, 858a.
reduce to powder, 9b.
reed, 2b, 8b, 9a, 21b, 25a, 29b, 36b, 82a, 92b, 103b, 129a, 135b, 139b, 147a, 167a, 189b, 293b, 421a, 431b, 636a, 641b, 654a, 722a, 733b, 735b, 773a, 779a, 778b, 795a, 803a, 804a, 808b, 814b, 825b.
reed basket, 700b.
reed case, 63b.
reed mat, 747b.
reed pipe, 152a.
reed, writing, 129a, 347a.
reed work, 790b.
refined, 711a, 773a; of gold, 41b.
refineries for gold, 455a.
refresh, 625b, 654a, 697a, 702a b, 767b.
refresh oneself, 471a, 681a, 768b.

refreshed, 681b.
refreshing, 767b, 768b ; place of, 80b.
refreshment, 240a.
refuge, 181b, 380a, 534b, 793b ; to take, 629b, 712a.
refuse, 261b, 348b, 571b, 628b.
regard for, 840a.
regiment, 860b.
region, 1a, 3b, 13a, 16b, 27a, 106a, 207a, 270a, 289a, 479a, 592a, 649a ; celestial, 498b.
regions, the two, 79a.
register, 45b, 65b, 71a, 82a, 106b, 129a, 161a, 303a, 450a, 499b, 597a, 607b, 619a, 662b, 855b.
register, daily, 442a.
register of lands, 41a.
registers, old, 619b.
registrar, 511a, 619a b.
registrary, 176b ; of sins, 71a.
registration office, 899a.
registry, 238b, 882a.
regular, 333a.
regularly, 270b, 297a.
regulate, 607a.
regulations, 82a, 161b, 400b, 409a, 441a, 446a b, 487a, 844b.
Reḥar, 429b.
Reḥen, 429b.
Reḥent, 429b.
Reḥnen, 429b.
Reḥti, 429b.
Reḥu, 429b.
Reḥui, 429b.
reign, 512b ; to make, 618b.
reincarnation (?), 222b.
reins, 55a, 552a.
reject, 166a, 344b, 470b, 528a, 615a, 628b, 810a, 823a, 825b, 846a, 857a.
rejected, 528a, 758b.
rejoice, 3b, 6a, 63b, 74b, 76a, 104a, 110a, 114a, 118a, 141a, 147a, 157b, 168a, 247b, 289a, 326a, 355b, 380b, 381b, 385b, 412a, 433a, 440a, 442a, 457a, 464a, 466b, 474a, 492b, 499a, 507b, 559a, 613b, 616b, 635b, 689a, 692b, 820a, 833b, 858a b, 877b, 900a, 907a ; make to, 682b.
rejoicing, 161b, 381b, 426b, 449b, 466b, 717a, 858b, 863b.
rejoinder, 122b.
rejuvenate, 423a, 427a, 611b, 615b, 618a, 677b, 694b.
rejuvenation, water of, 294a.
Rekeḥ netches, 40b, 435a.
Rekeḥ-ur, 40b, 434b.
Rekem, 434b.
Rekes, 435a.
Rekh, 430b.
Rekhi (Rā), 434b.
Rekhit, 430a b.
Rekhit, fire-goddess, 434b.
Rekhit-Åpit, 431a.
Rekhit-besu, 435a.
Rekhsi, 36b, 431a.
Rekhti, Council of, 901b.
Rekhtti, 431a.
Rekhtti-Merti, 431a.
Rekit, 434a.
Rekkt, 435a.
Reku, 434b.
relate, 745a.
related, 560a.
relation, 284b.
relationship, 703a.
relative, 284a, 404b, 739a ; female, 599b ; male, 599b.
relax, 261b, 665b.
release, 178b, 296a, 525a, 862b.
relief, 412a, 606a.
relight, 56b.
relish, 628b.
rely, 517b.
Rem', 425a.
remain, 296b, 868a.
remain over, 596a.
remainder, 193b, 596a, 661a, 894a.
remains, 596a.
remedy, 247a.
remember, 90b, 274a, 396a, 614b, 688a.
remembrance, 652a.
remembrancer, 688a.
Remen-ḥeru, 425b.
Remen-kheru, 425b.
Remen-ta, 425b.
Remenu, 425b.
Remenui-Rā, 425b.
Remi, Fish-god, 424b.
Remi, Remit, 424a.

Remi-ur-āa, 424b.
remit, 417a ; a tax, 144a, 355a, 564b.
remnant, 244b.
Rem-neteru, 424b.
Remnit, 425b.
remorse, 120b.
remote, 144a, 417b, 499a.
remote ages, 230b.
remote event, 144b.
remote time, 277a.
removal, 7a.
remove, 7a, 28a, 37a, 71b, 100b, 103b, 144a, 152a, 177b, 298a, 420b, 532a, 646b, 670b, 689b, 705b, 713a, 757b, 846b.
removed, 97b, 420a.
Remrem, 424b.
Remtit, 425a.
Remu, 424b.
Remuiti, 424a.
remunerate, 508a.
remuneration, 88b, 758b, 904a.
rend, 243b, 255b, 351b, 755a.
render, to, 803a.
Renent, 49a.
Renenti, 130a, 426b.
renew, 176b, 177a b, 269a, 601a, 668b.
renew youth, 66a.
renewed, 269b.
Renfreth, 427b.
Rennit, 426a.
Rennit-nefrit, 426a.
Renniu, 426a.
Renn-sebu, 426a.
Rennutet, 40b.
Rennutt, 426b, 427a ; uraeus of, 427a.
renown, 22b, 245a, 724a.
renowned, 115b, 508b.
Renpit, 427b.
Renpu, 427b.
rent, 77a, 729b, 838a, 882b.
Rentheth, 428a.
Renti, 426b.
Repā (Geb), 423a.
repair, 129b, 601a, 668b, 801b ; out of, 803b.
repairing, 351b.
Repātt, 423a.
repeat, 66b, 120b, 122b, 176b, 177a b, 179b, 782b.
repeating, 264a.
repel, 87b, 101b, 247b, 509b, 676b.
repeller, 57b.
repetition, 177a, 277b, 595b.
Repit, 422b.
Repit Ȧnu, 422b.
Repit Ȧst, 423a.
replace, 904a.
repletion, 696a.
reply, 874a ; making a, 104b.
report, 90b, 430b, 549a, 604b, 669b, 670a, 694a.
report, to, 667b, 669b, 824a.
reporter, 601b, 669b.
repose, 7a, 43b, 374b, 448a, 449b, 517b, 611b, 681a, 693a.
reprehensible, 895b.
reptile, 62b, 118a, 417a, 758b, 799b, 900b.
repulse, 33b, 99a, 481a, 563b, 564b, 605a, 618a, 682a, 684a, 694b, 698a, 746a b, 748a, 824a, 896b.
repulser, 385b, 684a.
repulsiveness, 746b.
repulsive man, 2a.
repurchase, 707a.
reputation, 209b.
Requ, 434a.
request, 382b, 662a.
required, 876a.
requite, 508a, 874a, 898b, 904a.
requiter, 827b.
Rer, 428a.
Rerȧt, 428a.
Rerek, 309a, 428b, 788a.
Reri, 428b.
Rerit, 428a.
Rerp, 428b.
Rerti Nifu, 428b.
Reru, 428b.
Res-ȧb, 432a.
Res-ȧfu, 432a.
rescue, 385a, 608a.
resemblance, 277b.
resemble, 385b, 666b, 667b, 826a.
Resenit, 433a.
reservation, 537a.
reserve, 537a.
reservoir, 307b, 308a.
Res-ḥer, 432b.
Reshitt, 433b.
Reshpiu, 433b.

Reshpu, 97b, 433b.
Resi-åneb-f, 432a.
residue, 894a.
resin, 95a, 226b, 300a, 301b, 650b, 771a, 833b.
resist, 99a, 116a, 564b, 746b, 818b, 894a.
resistance, 2a, 116a, 224a, 894a.
resister, 26b, 894a.
resistless, 564b.
Resit, 432a b.
Resit-neterit-kheper, 432a.
resolute, 297a.
respect, 724a.
Res-pet, 432b.
respiration, 849b.
responsibilities, 586b.
rest, 7a, 43b, 175b, 291a, 375b, 377a, 423b, 429a, 448a, 449b, 517b, 549a, 611b, 627b, 679a, 681a, 803b, 896b.
rest, festival of, 719a.
rest, place of, 35a, 802a.
rest the heart, 442a.
rest, to be at, 449b, 473a, 610a ; to come to, 617a, 693a, 810b.
rest upon, 429b.
rest (i.e., what remains), 193b, 661a, 894a.
Res-tchatcha, 432b.
rest house, 38a.
resting place, 13a, 95a.
restitution, 874a b.
restless, 386a, 577a.
restore, 866a, 874a, 904a ; to health, 65b.
restrain, 1b, 30a, 64a, 100a, 245a, 338a, 412b, 550a, 610a, 646b, 850a.
restrained, 805a.
restraint, 4a, 83a, 101b, 131a, 275b, 465a, 587a, 680a, 867a, 868a, 909b.
restraint, house of, 550a ; place of, 499b, 789b, 805b, 915b.
restraint, to keep in, 552a ; to put under, 805a.
restricted, 491a.
restriction, 441a, 446a.
Resu, god, 432a.
Resu warders, 432a.
Resu-khā, 432a.
result, 240b, 292b, 510b, 880a.
resurrection, 381a, 824b ; chamber of, 239a ; country of, 190a ; places of, 327b.
Resurrection, the triune god of, 255a.
Res-utcha-Khenti-ḥeḥ, 432b.
Res-utcha (Ptaḥ), 432a.
Reṭ-ā, 437b.
Retas-shaka, 435b.
Reteb-mut-f, 435b.
Rethnu, 436a.
Reth-uarekh, 435b.
Reti, 435b.
retinue, 742b, 823b.
Retnu, Northern and Southern, 435b.
retrace, 478b.
retract, 123b.
retreat, 120a, 246b, 377b, 457b, 481a, 487b, 567b, 569b, 594b, 657b, 713a.
retreat, a, 481a.
retreatings, 883a.
retribution, 88b, 136b, 904b ; place of, 80b, 904a.
Rett-Shesit, 435b.
Retui-en-Åsår, 435b.
Reṭuk, 437b.
return, 28b, 63b, 88b, 122b, 675b, 775b, 780b ; in the evening, 178b.
return for, 266a.
reunion, 600b, 652a.
reveal, 253b, 650a, 767b, 810b ; oneself, 166b.
revel, 287a.
revellers, 474b.
revenue, 56b, 77a, 138b, 161a, 487a, 521b, 580b, 722b, 906a.
revenue officer, 71a.
revere, 178b, 840a b.
revered one, 50a.
reverence, 34a, 479b, 499b, 724a, 857b.
reverse, to, 236b, 862b.
revile, 185a, 394a, 613b, 615b, 689b, 757a, 794b, 807a, 809b.
reviler, 394a.
revilings, 185a, 683a, 757a, 794b.
revise, 642b.
revision, 642b.
revolt, 99a, 116a, 207b, 209a, 224a, 433b, 434a, 549b, 577a, 711b, 756b, 861a.

revolt, children of, 322b.
revolution, 743b, 780a, 887b; of a star, 177a; of time, 247a.
revolve, 43b, 216a, 232a, 246a, 251b, 452a, 680a, 701a, 827b, 875a.
reward, 33a, 88b, 102b, 206b, 262a, 264a, 304a, 333b, 508a, 736a, 758b, 874a b, 892b, 904a.
rewarded, 262a.
rework, 803a.
rheum, 249a, 906b; in the eye, 353a, 459b.
rheumy, 843b.
rib, 662a; of boat, 42b, 325b, 469b.
ribbons, 326a.
rich, 102a, 137b, 171a, 181b, 736a.
rich folk, 436a.
rich man, 358a, 423b, 538b.
rich, to be, 535b.
riches, 134b, 182a, 214a, 260a, 525a, 622a.
riddle, 63a, 178b.
ridge, 861b.
rigging, 517a.
right, 332a, 333b, 605b.
right disposition, 304b, 332b.
right feeling, 286a.
right hand, 53a, 168a.
right-hearted, 138b.
right mind, 139a.
right-mindedness, 637a.
right order, 332a.
right, the, 270b.
right, to be, 139a, 332a, 333b.
right, to do, 65b.
right, to exercise, 517a.
right, to make, 647a.
righteous, 271a, 399a.
righteousness, 139a, 271b, 332a, 598b; goddess of, 385b.
rightly, 266a, 332a.
rigor, 608a.
rim, 643a, 662b.
rimmed, 63a.
ring, 33b, 76b, 123b, 191a, 215a, 217a, 277b, 280b, 302b, 356a, 451b, 476a, 622a, 697b, 728b, 729a b, 764b, 804a, 880b, 897b.
ring, finger, 812b.
ring-fastening, 273a.
ring money, 568b, 622a, 697b, 729a b.
ring of a balance, 191a.
ring-weight, 356a.
riot, 207b, 682a.
rip open, 906a.
rip up, 223b, 263b.
rise, 28a, 40a, 351a, 447b, 861a.
rise, early, 381a.
rise, of a flood or the Nile, 222a, 467b, 468b, 525a, 536a, 558a, 682b.
rise, of Rā, 534b.
rise, of star, 159a.
rise, of the sun, 242a, 380b.
rise, to make, 615b, 664b.
rise up, 129a, 166a, 468a, 733a, 824b, 833b, 853a, 873a; to make to, 689b.
rising, 534b, 535a, 615b, 804b, 861a.
rising of a flood, 824b.
rising of evil, 825a.
Rit, 419b.
rite, 69a, 270b, 563b.
rite, to perform a, 589b, 635a.
ritual, 563b.
rival, 329a.
river, 3b, 35b, 69a, 97b, 99b, 142a b, 143a, 212b, 231b, 343a, 387b, 467b, 840b.
river bank, 37b, 136a, 195a, 293a, 308a.
river flood, 148a.
river gate, 272b.
River of Fire, 121a, 208b.
river plants, 13b.
road, 28a, 32a, 38b, 144b, 277b, 280b, 290a b, 291a b, 333b, 334b, 499a, 604a.
road clearers, 746b.
Road-god, 334b.
road man, 291a.
road of all men (i.e., highway), 144b.
road-side, 599a, 746b.
road, strong, 887b.
roam, 192b, 354b.
roar, 375a, 381b, 447a, 472b.
roar of people, 447a.
roar of sky, 447a.
roar of thunder, 560b.
roars of a lion, 882b.

roarer, 381b, 447a.
Roarer (Set), 25b.
roaring, 109a.
roast, to, 261b, 248a, 276a, 896b, 897b, 902a.
roasted, 236a, 898a.
roasted thing, 10b, 92b, 236a, 237a, 247b, 355b, 356a, 427a, 593b, 695b.
rob, 72a, 110b, 114b, 115b, 141a, 464b, 467a b, 471a, 473a, 550b, 647a, 769b, 845a.
robbed, 115a, 176a, 184b, 536b.
robber, 71b, 100b, 101b, 115a b, 141a, 437b, 464b, 550b, 845b, 849b ; desert, 306a.
Robber (Set), 473a.
robbers, a game, 849b.
robbery, 115a b.
rock, 129b.
rod, 4a, 17a, 140a, 475b, 726a, 900b ; for measuring, 41a ; of authority, 6b.
roe deer, 624b.
roe of fish, 121b.
roll, 106b, 129a, 131b, 180a, 184a, 519b, 739a, 777b, 789b, 836b, 849a.
roll away, 594b, 626b.
roll of papyrus, 337b, 898a.
roll, skin, 71b.
roll up, 73a, 701a.
rolled, 428a.
rolls (deeds), 41a, 144a.
Roman, 445a.
roof, 32b, 110a, 315b, 419b, 438a.
room, 79b, 149a, 157b, 164a, 166a, 184a, 468a, 621a, 675b, 740b, 821b, 860a, 910b.
room, middle, 37b.
room, private, 909b.
room, sleeping, 331b.
root, 299a, 351a, 753a.
root up, 531a, 560b.
rope, 58a, 64a b, 75b, 82a b, 118a, 123a, 139a, 146a, 167a, 282a, 292a, 332b, 333a, 337a, 351a, 352b, 355a, 356b, 372b, 396b, 419b, 479a, 484b, 486b, 491b, 510a, 527a, 631b, 745a, 751a.
rope, magical, 545b.
rope, measuring, 146b.
rope of a boat, 46a.
rope of a ladder, 422a.
rope, towing, 244b.
rope up, 58a.
ropes, grass, 355a.
ropes of a net, 421b.
ropes of magical boat, 38a, 581b.
ropework, 132a, 790a.
rose, 147a.
rot, 49b, 72b, 176b, 693b.
rotten, 176a.
round, 204a, 476a, 753a, 789b.
round about, 264b, 265b, 266a, 438b, 875a, 907a.
round things, 897b.
round up, 841b.
rouse, 382a, 386a.
rout, to, 682a.
row, to, 66a, 93b, 576b, 688b, 877a.
rower, 182b, 482a, 576b, 877a.
royal, 653b.
royalty, 89a, 653b, 882b.
Ru, 419b.
rub, 329b, 590a, 613a, 643a.
rub away, 263b, 613b, 726b.
rub down, 6b, 123b, 185a, 346a, 351b, 395b, 411a, 620b, 480b, 565b, 571a, 589a, 643a, 664b, 797b, 844b.
rub off, 726b.
rub with oil, 205b ; with unguent, 175a.
rubbed, 813b.
rubbing stone, 757a.
rubbish, 711b.
rubbish-heap, 16b.
rubble, 765b.
ruby, 605a, 675b.
rudder, 18b, 75b, 182b, 279a, 482a ; part of, 39a ; handle of, 898b.
rudder, two-faced, 482a.
rudders of heaven, the four, 23b, 246b, 482a, 692a, 875b.
ruffians, nomad, 741a.
ruffled, 727a.
rug, 773a.
Ruḥu, 429b.
ruin, 2a, 3b, 7b, 10b, 92b, 168a, 176a b, 177b, 181a, 243b, 420a, 439b, 440a, 492b, 528b, 652a, 689a.
ruin, to, 261b, 607b, 644a, 741b.

ruined, 82a, 149a, 184b.
Ru-Iukasa, 420a.
rule, 25b, 82a, 271b, 346a, 378b, 400b, 468a, 512b, 537b, 653b, 831b, 845a.
rule, to, 486b, 562a, 582a, 653a, 683b ; make to, 614a, 684a.
ruler, 513a, 690b ; hereditary, 423a.
ruminate, 715a.
rump, 13b, 129b, 244a, 630b, 714a, 794a, 909b, 910a ; steak, 244a.
run, 9b, 14b, 82b, 166a, 169b, 212a, 232a, 245b, 320a, 374a, 420a, 429a, 446b, 452a, 487b, 615b, 618a, 694b, 729b, 813a, 814a, 852b, 857b, 896b.
run against, 509a, 633a.
run aground, 10b, 74a, 657b, 715a.
run away, 166a, 220a, 255b, 587b, 810a, 857b, 889a.
run down, 715a.
run out, 240a, 736a.
run quickly, 169b, 227a, 891a.
run swiftly, 243a.
run the head against, 885a.
run, to make, 616a, 690a.
run towards, 576a.
rungs of ladder, 670b.
runner, 245b, 253a, 274b, 478b, 533a, 618a, 643a, 694b, 791a.
runners (infantry), 246b.
running, act of, 804b.
running of the nose, 344b.
running water, 9b.
Ru-Rā, 420a.
Ruru, 419b.
Ruru-tȧ, 420a.
Ruruti, 420a.
rush, 129a, 337b, 550b, 594b, 814b.
rush, to, 885a ; against, 509a ; in, 93b ; forward, 487b ; out upon, 393b.
rusk, 441b.
russet, 889a.
rust, 58b, 565b, 566a, 571a.
Ruṭ-en-Ȧst, 421b.
Ruti Ȧsȧr, 420b.
Ruṭu-nu-Tem, 421b.

S.

Sa (Āapep), 587a.
Sa, a crocodile, 634b.
Sȧ, Bull-god, 589b ; fem. Sȧt.
Sȧ, city, 640b.
Sa, god, 586a, 634a.
Sȧa, 634a, 635a, 641a.
Sȧa, Thoth, 640b.
Sȧa-ȧbu, 641a.
Sȧa-Ȧmenti, 641a.
Sȧa-Ȧmenti-Rā, 641a.
Sāaba, 590a, 590b.
Sȧa-Ḫeru, 641a.
Sȧait, 641a.
Sȧa-mer-f, 584a.
Sȧamiu, 589b, 641b.
Sȧar, 635b.
Sȧater, 641b.
Sȧatiu, 589b, 641b.
Sȧaṭt-ta, 641b.
Saba, 635a.
Sabs, 636a.
sack, 209a, 248a, 484b, 647a, 773a, 801b, 805a, 819b, 820b, 835b, 836a b, 843b, 895b.
sacks of grain, 806a.
sackcloth, 105a.
sacking, 701b, 773b, 790a, 834b, 878b, 879a.
sacrifice, a, 11a, 79a, 89b, 110b, 270b, 373b, 560b, 667b, 669a, 810a.
sacrifice, human, 731a.
sacrifice, place of, 80a.
sacrifice, the daily, 54a b.
sacrifice, to, 66b, 303b, 431a, 666a.
sacrosanct, 403a.
sacrum, 914a.
sad, 11a, 55b, 139b, 314a, 887a.
sadden, 643b.
saddle gear, 288b.
sadness, 3b, 7b, 64b, 74a, 290a, 850a, 906b.
Sa-em-Geb, 587a.
safe, 7b, 193a, 307a, 514a, 893b.
safflower, 268b.
saffron, 141b, 810b.
Sag, a fabulous animal, 589a.
sage, 430b, 613a, 634a, 848a, 896a.
sages, 848a, 852b.

Sāḥ (Orion), 591a, 638b, 646a.
Sāḥ-àb, 591b, 646a.
Saḥ-en-nut-f, 638b.
Saḥ-ḥeq, 646a.
Saḥit, 638b.
Saḥtni, 638b.
Saḥu, the Twelve, 638b.
Saḥurā, 417b.
Sai, 587a.
sail, 409a, 428b, 459b, 473b, 517a, 776a, 818b, 894b.
sail a boat, 354a, 566a, 576b, 722b.
sail down stream, 346b, 568a, 569a, 572a, 575b.
sail over, 552b.
sail southwards, 558a, 693b.
sail, to, 273a, 346a, 374a, 449a, 541a, 576b, 589a, 625b, 702a b, 703a, 705a ; to make, 695b.
sail upstream, 473b, 558a, 559a, 565a.
sailcloth, 517a.
sailing, 346b, 565a, 642a, 703a, 894b.
sailor, 33b, 93b, 314b, 370a, 478b, 576b, 703a, 780a, 875a.
sailor folk, 476a, 583a.
sailors, divine, 93b, 780a ; Egyptian and Syrian, 780a.
sails of a boat, 679a.
Saïs, Lower and Upper, 587b.
Sȧit, 584b, 586a.
Sait-ta, 586a.
Saiu gods, 586a.
Sȧ-kam, 589b.
Sakhiu, 639a.
Sakhmit-urr-peḥ, 639a.
Sāks, 591b.
salaam, to, 727a.
salary, 650b.
salesman, 285b.
saliva, 38a, 91a b, 223b, 249a, 347b, 394a.
salt, 484a.
salt land, 484a.
salt of the North, 484a.
salt water, 272b, 280b.
saltpetre, 227b.
salutation, 64b.
salutations, 193a.
salute, 95a, 186b, 345a, 727a, 841b, 885a.
salve, 39b, 55b, 63a, 205a b, 233a, 292b, 318b, 336a, 337a, 352b, 377a, 626b, 643a, 669b, 743b, 804a.
salve box, 581b.
salve, cedar oil, 137a.
Sa-maāt, 584b.
Samārtasa, 637a.
Samba, 636b.
same, 265a.
Sām-em-qesu, 590b.
Sām-em-snef, 590b.
Sāmta, 590b.
Samur, 636b.
Sân, 896a.
Sȧn, 590a.
sanctify, 632b.
sanctuary, 20a, 34b, 51a, 79b, 80b, 107a, 117b, 155b, 166a, 214b, 238b, 239a, 479a, 490a, 494b, 546b, 557b, 565b, 573a, 575b, 633b, 731a, 756a, 768b, 789b, 790a, 839b.
sand, 723a, 730a.
sand, dwellers on, 373b, 730b, 895b.
sand, festival of strewing, 759b.
sandal, sandals, 60b, 105a, 106b, 180a, 666a, 793a, 823b, 826b, 853a b, 864a, 873a b.
Sandal-gods, 263b.
sandal-maker, 853b.
sandals, pair of, 528b, 821b, 827a.
sandals, white, 523b.
sandbank, 276a, 836b.
sandstone, 62b.
sandstone, quartzite, 421b.
sandstone, red, 62b.
sandstone, yellow, 62a.
sandy soil, 730a.
Sānkhi-khaibitu, 645b.
Sānkhiu-gods, 645b.
Sȧnut, 643b.
sap, 58b.
Sapanemma, 584b.
Saparar, 636b.
Sapȧthar, 588b, 636b.
Sapertagessu, 636b.
Sȧpit, 642b.
Sapt-Khenti, 636b.
Saq-baiu, 639b.
Saqeṭ, 585a.

Saq-ḥa, 639b.
Saqnaqait, 639b.
Sar (Osiris), 588b ; limbs of, 466a.
Sārȧut, 591a.
sarcophagus, 43b, 120a, 284a, 357b, 447a b, 566b, 756a, 757a, 777a, 860a, 873b, 874b, 875b, 904b ; chamber, 777a ; chambers for, 238b.
Sarem, 637b.
Sarisa, 635b.
Sārit, 645b.
Sārit-maāt, 645b.
Sārit-neb-s, 591a.
Sariu-gods, 637b.
Sarma, 589a.
Sār-neb-s, 645b.
Sarqit, 637b.
Sasȧt, 585a.
Sa-semt, 585a.
Sa-semu, 585a.
Sa-sert, 585a.
Sa-seshem, 585a.
Sȧshesa, 644a.
Saspa, 585a.
Sat, Dekan, 635a.
Sata, 585a, 586a.
Satȧ, 640a.
Sat-Ȧmenti, 584b.
Satȧrna, 640a.
Sa Tathenen, 585a.
Sȧt Baqt, 589b.
Sat Ḥetḥert, 584b.
sate, 696a.
Sȧthasiu, 590a.
Sathtȧ, 640a.
Sati, fire-god, 589a.
satiety, 634b, 647a.
Sati-qet, 585a.
Sati-Sȧt, 585a.
Sati-Sert, 585a.
satisfaction, 449b, 517b, 682a.
satisfactorily, 265a.
satisfied, 333a, 394a, 449b, 517b, 587b, 694b.
satisfy, 83a, 606b, 671b, 677a, 682a, 696a.
Satit, 589a.
Sat-kamt, 589b.
satrap, 566a.
Saturn, 404a, 501b, 656a.
Sau, 634a.
Sau, city, 587b.
Sȧu, gods, 642a.
Sȧu, serpent, 642a.
Sa-ur, 586a, 634a.
savage, 509a.
save, 385a, 593b, 654a, 757b.
Saviour-god, 653b.
saw, to, 149a, 163b, 181a, 221b, 320b, 648b, 833a.
saw wood, 376b.
sawdust, 181a.
say, 67a, 253b, 335a, 560a, 717a, 782b, 913a.
sayings, 632b, 719b, 860b, 913a b.
Sayings of the Fathers, 913a.
Sba (Āapep), 656b.
Sba-en-sethesu-Shu, 655a.
Sbai, 655a.
Sbait, 656a.
Sbait-nebt-uȧa, 656a.
Sbaiu-Rā, 656a.
Sbaiu shepsu, 656a.
Sbaiut, 656a.
Sbȧk, 657b.
Sbakh-senu, 656b.
Sba-Rā, 594b.
Sbasit, 656b.
Sbȧt, 657a.
Sba-tcheser, 655a.
Sbatt, 655a.
Sba-uāti, 656a.
Sba-ur instrument, 655b.
Sbeg, Sbega, 660b.
Sbek, Crocodile-god, 660a.
Sbekhar, 659a.
Sbekhekhth, 659a.
Sbekht-ȧakhut, 658b.
Sbekht-Ȧgert, 659a.
Sbekhti, 658b.
Sben-ḥesq-khaibiut, 658a.
Sbenqa, 658a.
Sbeq, god, 659b.
Sbeq-en-Shesmu, 659b.
Sbeq-en-Temu, 659b.
Sbeq-ḥer, 659b.
Sbeqit, 659b.
Sbesanka, 659a.
Sbeshes, 659a.
Sbeshes-mer, 659b.
Sbeshta, 659b.
Sbi, 655a.
Sbut, city, 657b.
scabbard, 268b, 333a.

scabby, 736b.
scaffold, 880b.
scald, 160a.
scalded, 215b.
scale, of metal, 58b.
scale walls, 689b.
scale work, 617b.
scales, 4a, 225a, 330a ; part of, 529b.
Scales, Bearer of the, 259b.
scales for heavy objects, 285b.
scales, hand, 36b.
scales, master of the, 70b.
scales of armour, 223b.
scales of fish, 394b.
Scales of Rā, 285b.
scales-room, 285b.
scalpel, 541b, 870a.
scar, 9a.
scarab, 28b, 118b, 295a, 320a, 532b ; flying, 118a.
scarabeus sacer, 543a.
scare, to 577a.
scatter, 185a, 527b, 533b, 689a, 716a, 765b, 862b, 863b.
scatter seed, 10b.
scattered, 473a.
scatterers, 166b.
scene, 80a.
scent, 307b, 486b, 627b, 629b, 631a, 712b.
scent, festival, 628a.
scent, foul, 709b.
scent, the divine, 709b.
scent-pot, 433b.
scented woman, 660a.
sceptre, 4a, 6b, 10a, 13a, 17a, 19a, 38b, 41a, 54b, 55a, 114b, 117b, 148b, 182b, 195a, 253b, 295b, 330b, 384b, 468a, 469a, 475b, 506b, 510a, 566a, 589a, 692b, 898a, 903a, 907a.
sceptre amulet, 6b, 181a.
sceptre, magical, 171b.
sceptre of crystal and feldspar, 150b.
sceptre of Isis-Hathor, of Ḥeru-Beḥuṭi, Osiris, 336a.
sceptre-bearer, 55a.
schedule of furniture, 45a.
scheme, 510b, 684a.
schoenus, 7a, 35a, 100a.
school, 106a, 238a, 239a.
schoolmaster, 222a.
schoolroom, 655b.
science, 430a.
scimitar, 544a, 657a, 737b.
scintillate, 629a, 630a, 842a, 848b.
scoffing, 657b.
scorch, 605b, 639b, 696a.
scorching, 696b.
scoriae, 820b.
scorn, 200b ; to scorn, 621a.
scorn God, 634b.
scorpion, 115b, 125b, 176a, 179a, 472b, 516b, 522a b, 611a, 612b, 819a, 839b, 899a.
scorpions, the Seven, 179a.
Scorpion-goddess, 81b, 509b, 522b, 612a, 681b ; the double, 681b.
scour, 346a.
scourge, 449b.
scout, 245b, 334a.
scrape, 9a, 356a, 836a.
scraper, 915a ; stone, 664a.
scrapings, 181a.
scratch, 836a.
screams, 136b.
screen, to, 477a.
scribe, 337b, 358a, 619b, 852b, 853a.
scribe, chief, 495a, 620a.
scribe, deputy, 620a.
scribe, divine, 619b, 620b.
scribe, female, 619b.
scribe, king's, 391b.
scribe, magistrate's, 620b.
scribe of a temple, 620a.
scribe of collectings, 620b.
scribe of estates, 619b.
scribe of grain, 620a.
scribe of produce, 242b.
scribe of the altar, 620a.
scribe of the Book of Horus, 620a.
scribe of the god, 403a ; of the gods (i.e., Thoth), 886a.
scribe of the militia, 620a.
scribe of the offerings, 620a.
scribe of theological works, 620a.
scribe of the Record Office, 893b.
scribe of the seal, 620a.

scribe of wages list, 620a.
scribe, royal, 620b.
scribe, to act as, 66a.
scribe who wrote at dictation, 620a.
scribe, writing box of, 581b.
Scribes, the Two, 619b.
scroll, 129a.
scrotum, 580a, 873b.
scrub, 89a, 344a, 765b.
scrutinize, 203a, 808a, 891a, 899a.
scrutiny, to make a, 642b.
sculpt, to, 323a.
sculptor, 325a, 395b, 639b, 644a, 645b.
sculpture, 287a, 784a ; on wall, 567b.
scum, 820b, 861b.
scythe, 572a.
scythe of Osiris, 71a.
sea, 142b, 143a, 151a, 280a, 488a, 704a.
sea, celestial, 151a.
sea-bull, 643a.
sea coast, 308a.
sea salt, 484a.
seal, 123b, 126b, 568b, 717a, 905a, 906a.
seal bearer, 212a, 568b.
seal, cord of, 27a, 254b.
seal, engraved, 567b.
seal, great and little, 906a.
seal, keeper of the, 312b.
seal maker, 568b.
seal of office, 906a.
seal of the god, 403a.
seal ring, 764b, 906a.
seal, royal, 911b.
seal string, 510a.
seal up, 568a.
sealed, 906a.
sealed document, 568b.
sealer, 103a.
sealing, a, 568b.
search for, 507b ; into, 757b, 903b ; out, 807b.
Searcher of the Reins, 903b.
season, 100a, 101b, 438b, 595a, 696a, 857b, 840b, 884b.
season, to, 512a.
Seasons, god of the, 259b, 383b.
Seasons of the Year, First, Second and Third, 8b, 22a.
seat, 1b, 25b, 79b, 88a, 89a, 90b, 190a, 220b, 221a, 234a, 289a, 298b, 328b, 367b, 408b, 467b, 509b, 583b, 650b, 706b, 773a, 805a, 855a, 900b, 901a b.
seat in a chariot, 369b.
seat of Horus, 80a.
seat of law, 80a.
seat of the Government, 237b.
seat of the happy, 80a.
seat oneself, 76b, 485a, 679a, 822a.
seat, raised, 258b.
seat, royal, 390a.
seat, to occupy, 643b.
seat with steps, 485a.
seated, 887b.
Seb (Mercury), 654b.
Sebȧ, 594b, 657a.
Sebek, title of, 46b ; title of priest of, 495b.
Sebek of Kamur, 424b.
Sebennytus, 132b.
Sebeshsen, 595a.
Sebḥut, 658b.
Sebit, 594a, 654b.
Sebkhas, 595a.
Sebsebā-Menu, 654b.
Sebṭi (Alexandria), 661a.
Sebu-gods, 594b.
Sebut, 640a.
seclude, 550a, 552a.
seclusion, place of, 557b.
second, 177a, 316a, 603a, 673b.
second, of time, 17b, 459b.
second, third of a, 58a.
second time, 105a, 177a, 264a, 673b.
secret, 51a, 63a, 624b, 755b ; to keep, 624b ; to make, 701a.
secret chamber, 756a.
secret place, 477b.
secret properties, 755b.
secretary, 495b, 620b, 853a.
secretions, 263a, 366b, 400a.
secretive, 570a.
secretly, 265b, 442b.
section, 730a ; of a book, 415b, 457a.
secure, 307a.
security, 7b.
sedan chair, 258b.
sedge, 135b.

sediment, 611b, 637b, 820b.
sedum, 288b.
see ! 60a, 266a.
see, to, 6b, 68a, 118a, 121b, 211a, 216b, 224a, 225b, 243a, 254a, 266b, 273a, 274b, 279b, 289a, 344b, 348a, 352a, 544b, 605b, 702a, 712a, 751a, 771b, 794b, 801a, 802b, 808a, 845b, 846b, 855a, 890b, 891a ; to make, 601a, 627b, 706a.
seed, 26b, 36a, 38b, 40a, 42b, 69b, 112b, 113b, 121b, 140b, 143a, 146ab, 159b, 179a, 186a, 188b, 201b, 204a, 210b, 215a, 233a b, 226b, 231b, 234a, 245b, 249a b, 251b, 252a, 259b, 269a, 278b, 279a, 284b, 307a, 329a, 331b, 344a, 348b, 354a, 369a, 372a, 383b, 390a, 398b, 413b, 443b, 472b, 482b, 484b, 487b, 488a, 493a, 538a, 586a, 612b, 624b, 632a, 639a, 605a, 641a, 672b, 689a, 697b, 708b, 712a, 716a, 724b, 726a, 728b, 736a, 738b, 746b, 753a, 762a, 773a, 777a, 785b, 788a, 791a, 796b, 798a, 801b, 804a, 809a, 813b, 833a, 839b, 842a, 846b, 847b, 853b, 877b, 891b, 896a, 899b, 902b, 910b.
seed, divine, 280a.
seed, edible, 828b.
seed for early crops, 750b.
seed for sowing, 828b.
seed, human, 243a, 280a, 293a.
seed of eternity, 331b.
seed of plant, 475b.
seed, royal, 280a.
seed, to eject, 628a.
seed, to sow, 628a.
seed-land, 777a.
seedlings, 892b.
seeds, bundles of, 563a.
seeing, 68a.
seek, 179b, 507b, 527a, 730a, 903b.
seek after, 148b, 507b.
seek for, 575a.
seeking, a, 745a.
seemly, 722b, 829b, 837b.
seen, 266b.
seer, 266b, 678b.
Seer, god, 267a, 891a.
Sef, 664b.
Sefer, Sefert, 665a.
Sefi-peri- etc., 595a.
Sefkhit, 665b.
Sefkhit-ābut, 665b.
Sefkhit-neb-s, 666a.
Sefsef, 664b.
Sefus, 465b.
Seg, 627a.
Sega, 627a.
Seges, 706b.
Segi, 627a.
Seḥenti-requ, 684a.
Seḥeptt, 683b.
Seḥerit-tu, 614a.
Seḥert baius, 614a, 888b, 909b.
Seḥeṭ, 685a.
Seḥetch-khatut, 685a.
Seḥetch-renpu, 685a.
Seḥetch-ur, 685a.
Seḥetemt, 684b.
Seḥetep-ḥemts, 614a.
Seḥetep-taui, 684b.
Seḥetpit, 614a.
Seḥith, 683a.
Seḥpu, 613b.
Seḥrȧt, 682b.
Seḥrit-tu, 684a.
Seḥseḥ, Lake and Mountain of, 682b.
Seḥtt, city, 684a.
Seḥu, 613a.
Seḥur, 683a.
seize, 6a, 20a, 26b, 54b, 64b, 79a, 100b, 101a, 102a, 111a, 122a, 189b, 212a, 261b, 317b, 327b, 385a, 412b, 443a, 449a, 459a, 464b, 490b, 491b, 531a b, 545a, 547b, 550b, 560b, 572b, 590a, 627a, 636b, 738a b, 747b, 757b, 793b, 794a, 796a, 802b, 808a, 849a.
seize prey, 124a.
seized, 446b.
seizer, 100b, 849b.
seizure, 459a, 461b, 794a.
Sek, a god, 704a.
Seker, 255a, 626b.
Seker festival, 475a, 627a, 742a.
Seker, kingdom of, 55a.
Seker, sanctuary of, 856a.
Seker-em-Shetait, 627a.

Seker-Khenti-Petchu, 627a.
Sekhem, Council of, 201b.
Sek-ḥer, god, 703b.
Sekhet Åaru, 16a.
Sekhit-ḥetep, 687b.
Sekhmit, 24b, 36b, 40b, 109a, 469a.
Sekhmit of Temeḥtt, 515b.
Sekhmit-Bast-Rā, 51a, 295a.
Sekht-Åakhu, 686b.
Sekht-åanru, 686b.
Sekht-åarru, 686b.
Sekht-Åaru, 686a.
Sekht-āat, 686b.
Sekht-ānkh, 686b.
Sekht-en-Sersert, 687a.
Sekht-ḥer, 614b.
Sekht-ḥeteput, 687a.
Sekht-khetf, 687b.
Sekht-mafkat, 687a.
Sekht-nebt-ḥeteput, 687a.
Sekht-neḥeḥ, 687a.
Sekht-Nentå, 687a.
Sekht-neteru, 687a.
Sekht-Paāt, 686b.
Sekht-Rā, 687a.
Sekht-Uatchit-nefert, 686b.
Sekht-uatchu, 686b.
Sekht-Tcher, 687b.
Sekhti, 614b.
Sekhti, Sekhtit, 686a.
Sekhut-åmiut-Åasu, 686b.
Sekhut Khakha, 687b.
Sekhut-uatcht, 686b.
Seki, 626a.
Sekkes, 705a.
Sekktiāks, 627a.
Sek-re, gods, 703b.
Sekri, 626b ; bodies of, 571a.
Sekri-ḥeri-shāf, 627a.
Seksek, 626a.
Seksekit, 626a.
Seksen, 627a, 705a.
Sekt, 627a.
Sekti, 627a.
Sekti Boat, 152a.
Sektit Boat, 705a.
Sektt, 627a.
Seku, stars, 704a.
select, 628b, 710b, 713a.
selected, 689b ; of meat, 710a.
selections from books, 710b.
self, 453a, 466a, 470b, 889b, 911b.
self-begetter, 826a.
self-begotten, 543b.
self-builder, 779a.
self-evident, 34a.
self-existent, 231a.
self-made, 542a.
self-produced, 542a.
sell, 650a, 866a.
Sem, 242a, 666b.
Sememti, 602b.
semen, 398b.
Semites (nomads), 728a.
Semkett Boat, 672b.
Semseru, 672b.
Semsit-set-nekhenkhent, 672a.
Sems-neb-åakhu, 672a.
Semthek, 603a.
Semti, 598b.
Senå, god, 674a.
Senån, 605a.
Senbit-åb, 676b.
Senb-Kheperu, 676b.
Senbu, god, 676b.
send, 147a, 440b, 475b ; away, 440b ; back, 862b ; out, 192b, 445a.
send a messenger, 74a.
Seneferu, Island of, 16b.
Senen, 604b.
Senfiu, blood-gods, 606a.
senility, 797a.
senior, 26a, 170b.
Senk, Senki, Senkit, 608a.
Senk-ḥer, 609a.
Senktett, 609a.
Senktiu, 609a.
Sen-nefer, 674b.
Senq, 608b.
Sensåbt, 608a.
sense, 37b.
senseless, 184b, 340b, 461a, 732b.
Sensent, 604a.
Senshit, 608a.
sensible, 436a.
sensual, 216b.
Senṭ, 609b, 679a.
Sentå, 674b.
sentence, 160b, 335a, 860b.
Senthes, 609b.
Senthit, 609b.
Senthi-ur, 678b.
Senṭit, goddess, 679a.
Senṭ-nef-Åmentiu, 679a.

Sent-Rā, 604b.
Senu, gods, 605b.
Sep, god, 596b, 661a.
Sepa, 24b, 596b.
Sepa-ḥer, 596b.
Sepa-Ḥeru, 596b.
Sepa-shāit, 596b.
Sepa-ur, 596b.
separate, 35a, 37a, 178b, 235a, 237b, 243b, 246a, 251a b, 252b, 344a, 511a, 512b, 662a, 838a, 862b, 881b ; separate from, 350b.
separated, be, 844b.
separation, 248b, 420b.
Sepen, 597a.
Sep-ḥer, 596a.
Sepi, 597a ; festival of, 661a.
Sepit, 596b, 661a.
Sepkh-kenmem, 597a.
Sep-Rā, 596a.
Sepsu gods, 597a.
Sept, god, 662b.
Sepṭ Worm, 664a.
Sept-ȧb, 663b.
Sepṭ-ȧbeḥu, 663b.
Sepṭ-ābui, 663b.
Sepṭat-ānkh, 664a.
Sept-en-tchett, 661b.
Sepṭ-ḥennuti, 52b, 663b.
Septi-khenu, 662b.
Sepṭit (Sothis), 664a ; Queen of the Dekans, 664a.
Septi-ṭenb, 663a.
Sepṭiu gods, 664a.
Sepṭ-masti-ent-Ruruti, 597b.
Sepṭ-metu, 597b.
Sepṭt-uauau, 663b.
Sepṭt, 242a.
Sepṭu, god, 663b ; one of the Fourteen Kau of Rā, 663b.
Sepṭu, the, 664a.
Sepṭu-Gemḥes, 664a.
Sepṭu-ḥennuti, 663b.
Sepṭu-ḥer, 663b.
Sepṭu-kesu, 663b.
Sepṭu-kheri-nehait, 663b.
Sepṭu-meṭut, 663b.
Sepṭu-Shu, 664a.
sepulchral meals, 3b, 110b.
sepulchral stele, 134a.
sepulchre, 15b, 28a, 201a, 285a, 319a, 465a, 557b, 571a, 914a.
sepulture, 188a, 776a, 777a.
Seqa-nu-baiu-petes-ḥeḥ, 625b.
Seqbeb, 625b.
Seqbit, 625b, 702a.
Seqeṭ-ḥati, 626a.
Seqrȧ-tchatchau, 625b.
Seq-uarf, 625b.
Ser, god, 680a.
Serapeum of Letopolis, 455a ; of Prosopites, 455b ; of Saïs, 454b, 455a ; of Ṣaḳḳârah, 455b.
Serȧt, 610a.
Serȧt-beqt, 611a.
Serȧu, 680b.
Seref, 611b.
Serekhi, 612a.
Serem, 611b.
Serem-taui, 611b.
serenity, 148b, 913b.
Seresh-en-mau, 612a.
Seres-ḥer, 612a.
Seres-tepu, 612a.
serf, 33a, 50a, 411a b, 436a, 597b, 673a, 893a.
serfs of the Ṭuat or of Osiris, 50b, 392b.
Seri, 611a.
series, 768a.
Ser-kheru, 610b.
Serkhi, 681a.
serpent, 29a, 43b, 112a, 144a, 221a, 237b, 260b, 261a, 323b, 346b, 417a, 471a, 479b, 497b, 499b, 522b, 596a, 641a, 776b, 791a, 799b, 878a, 882b, 893a, 914b.
serpent amulet, 29b, 73a, 893a.
serpent boat, 543b.
serpent, everlasting, 480a.
serpent, fiery, 109a.
serpent-god, 88b, 105b, 118b, 332b, 428b.
serpent on crown, 98a, 297a.
serpent, two-headed, 210b.
Serpents, the Seventy-five, 479b.
serpents, young, 388b.
Ser-pu-āa, 679b.
Serq, 612a.
Serqi, 612a.
Serqit, goddess, 681b.
Serser, 611a.
Sert, 610a.
Ser-tchatchat, 679b.

Serṭiu, 612b.
Sert-nehepu- etc., 680a.
Seru, 611a.
Seru, god, 180a.
servant, 39a, 67a, 82a, 93b, 158a, 206b, 220a, 255b, 281a, 283a, 311a, 436a, 457b, 482b, 532a, 546b, 568a, 579b, 585b, 603a, 673a, 718a, 732b, 742a, 809b, 823b, 864b.
servant of the Court, 167b.
servant of the god, 402b, 482b.
servant of the temple, 453a.
servant woman, 411a.
servants, armed, 704a.
servants, domestic, 201b.
servants, hereditary, 311a.
serve, 206a, 726b ; as soldier, 65a.
service, 5a, 112a, 167a, 200b, 206b, 698b, 742a.
service book, 563b.
service, daily, 725a.
service, hourly, 167b.
service, to do, 206a.
serving woman, 497a.
Ses, king, 695b.
Sesa, god, 618b.
sesame seed, 94a, 252a, 740a.
Sesba, 618b.
Sesent-åakhut, 619a.
Sesenu, 697a.
Seser, 697a.
Sesh, 621b.
Seshaå, 698a.
Seshait, goddess, 698a.
Seshem-Åf, 699a.
Seshem-Åffi, 699b.
Seshem-ānkh, 699b.
Seshem-årānbfi, 699b.
Seshem-Åsår, 699b.
Seshem-Åst, 699b.
Seshem-Ba-neteru, 699b.
Seshem-em-Tem, 623a.
Seshem-Geb, 700a.
Seshem-Ḥeru, 700a.
Seshem-Ka-Åmenti, 700a.
Seshem-Khatri, 700a.
Seshem-Khepera, 700a.
Seshem-Nebt-ḥet, 699b.
Seshem-nesf, 699b.
Seshem-neter, 699b.
Seshem-netherit, 623a.
Seshem-Nut, 699b.
Seshem-semu-neteru, 700a.
Seshemseshem, 623a.
Seshem-shet, 700a.
Seshem-Shu, 700a.
Seshem-Tathenn, 700a.
Seshem-Tefnut, 700a.
Seshen-neteru, 623a.
Seshen-uab, 624a.
Seshen-ur, 623b.
Seshesp-taui, 624b.
Sesheta, 619b, 888b.
Seshit, 620b.
Seshit-m'kt-neb-s, 621b.
Seshmi, 623a.
Seshmi-en-uat-ṭesert, 623a.
Seshmi-pet, 623a.
Seshmit, moon-goddess and Dekan, 699a.
Seshmit-ḥeri-åb-t, 623a.
Seshmu, 623a.
Seshmu-Ḥeḥ, 700a.
Seshmu-taui, 700a.
Seshmu-Ṭuat, 623a.
Sesh-netch, 620b.
Seshnit, 624a.
Seshnnit, 624a.
Seshpi, 622b.
Seshshå, 622a, 698a.
Sesht, goddess, 697b.
Seshta, 625a.
Seshta Åsår, 625a.
Seshta-baiu, 625a.
Seshtai, 625a.
Seshtait, 625a.
Seshtait-åru, 625a.
Seshta-ren, 625a.
Seshtau-åru, 625a.
Seshu, 622b, 698a.
Sesi, 618b.
Sessi, 17b.
session, 485b.
Sesu (Usertsen III or Rameses II), 696a.
set (or inset), 822a.
set apart, 153b, 512b.
set aside, 152a, 166a, 289b, 298a, 344b, 417a, 861a, 866a.
set at rest, 252b.
set away, 867b.
set behind, 457b.
set down, 180a, 298a.
set fire to, 20a, 160a, 601b.

set free, 36a, 178b, 401a, 665b, 710a, 862b.
set in metal, 218a.
set in motion, 54a.
set in order, 321a, 499a, 602b, 642b, 670b.
set oneself on one side, 813a.
set on the way, 865b.
set out, 101a, 597a, 752a, 894b.
set sail, 259a.
set the feet on, 437a.
set the mind, 147b.
set, to, 22a, 147b, 190a, 436b, 864a, 865b.
set up a memorial, 298a.
set up statue, 812a.
set up straight, 646a.
set up the Ṭeṭ, 591b.
set upright, 591b.
Seṭ, 713b.
Set, the god, 15b, 19b, 24b, 25b, 171b, 197a, 203a, 213a, 598b, 627b, 670a, 706b, 787a, 839b, 869a, 875b.
Set and Thoth, 674a.
Set, black pig of, 722a.
Set, bull-god, 627b.
Set, children of, 707a.
Set, crocodile of, 787a.
Seṭ Festival, 183a, 714a.
Set, hide of, 327a.
Set, hippopotamus of, 882a.
Set of the Acacias, 707a.
Set, realm of, 815a.
Set, red associates of, 889b.
Set, soul of, 326a.
Set, star of, 707a.
Set-Ȧmentt, 598b.
Set-em-ȧst-f, 628a, 709b.
Set-em-ḥer-f, 628a.
Set-ḥeḥ, 628a.
Set-ḥer, 709b.
Set-nehsi, 629b.
Seṭ-qesu, 630b.
Setcha animal, 716b.
Setcheḥ, 632b, 719a.
Setchen-em-sen-f, 718a.
Setchemi, 718a.
Setcheri-ur, 632b.
Setcher-ur, 719a.
Setchfet, 632a.
Setchit-usrit, 716b.
Setchriu, 719a.
Setchti, 632b, 716b.
Setekh, 629a, 707a.
Setem, 242b.
Setesh=Set, 16a, 29b, 627b, 629a, 706b, 712a.
Seṭfit, 795a.
Seth-ȧb, 713a.
Sethasiu, 629b.
Sethen-ḥat, 630a.
Sethen-ḥath, 630a.
Sethenit, goddesses, 630a.
Sethenu, god, 630a.
Sethenu-tep, 630a.
Seth-ḥer, 712b.
Sethu, god, 629b.
Seṭti, 632a.
setting of a star, 175b.
settle accounts, 570b.
settle a country, 811b.
settlement, 207a, 350b, 812a, 873b; foreign, 179a.
seven, 665b, 690a.
seventh, 665b.
seventy, 665b.
sever, 512b.
severe, 639b.
sexual pleasures, 412a.
Sfȧ, 598a.
Sgeb, god, 705b.
Sger, 706a.
Sgerḥet, 706b.
Sgert, 706a.
Sha animal, 722a.
Shaāit, 723a.
Shabti, 185b.
Shabti figure, 725a b.
Shabu, god, 725b.
shackles, 764b.
shade, 529a, 729b, 732b, 734a b.
shadow, 475b, 529a, 530a, 602a, 657b, 729b, 732b, 734a b; judge of shadows, 162b.
shadow, turning of, 246b, 732b.
Shadow-god, 434b.
shadow house, 529a.
shaft of a pillar, 799a.
shaft of a spear, 778a.
shaft of a tomb, 8a.
shaft of an obelisk, 58b.
shaft of mine, 517a.
Shahab, 727b.
Shai, god, 724a.
Shait, 724a.

Shaka-Ȧmen-Shakanasa, 729a.
Shakanasa, 729a.
Shakarshau, 729a.
shake, 90b, 343a, 351b, 356b, 380a, 487b, 589b, 602a, 678a, 767a, 799b, 854b, 864b.
shake down the hair, 597a.
shake, to, 898b.
shaken, 393b, 630a.
shakers, 714b.
Shakershau, 729a.
shaking, 716a.
shaking sickness, 714b.
shallow, 1a, 276a.
Sham'bār, 726a.
shambles, 390a.
shame, 541b, 564b, 569b, 612b, 731b, 737b, 887a, 895a.
shame, put to, 499b, 612b, 682a.
shame, the, 544b.
shameful, 214b, 459a, 535b, 544b.
shameless, 437b.
shape, 542b.
Shapu-neter-ȧrt-ka, 726a.
shard, 233a.
share, 248b, 251a b, 252a, 280b, 693b, 821b, 881b, 882b.
sharp, 291b.
sharpen, 256b, 387a, 394b, 413a, 608a, 618b, 665a, 696b, 878a.
sharp-eyed, 291b.
Sharshar, 727b.
Sharsharkhat, 727b.
Sharshatȧkatȧ, 727b.
Sharṭana, 727b.
Sharṭenu, 727b.
Sharṭina, 727b.
Sharṭshaq, 727b.
Shār-ur, 731a.
Shasi, god, 728b.
Shasu (nomads), 728a.
Shat, 722a.
Shaṭ gods, 731b.
Shatbaka, 729b.
Sha-ṭesui, 720a.
shatter, 208b.
Shat-urt, 720a.
Shau, God of Luck, 724b.
Shau, city, 724b.
shauabti figure, 725a.
shave, 182b, 533a, 571b, 731a, 754b, 849b, 850a.
shave off, 9a.
shaved, 167a.
shaven, 262a, 344b.
shawl, 43b, 776a.
she, 36a, 389b, 408a, 409b, 706b.
sheaf, 773b.
she-ass, 109b.
Shebb-en-Mesti, 735a.
Shebtiu, 735b.
shed, 753a ; shed blood, 400a.
sheep, 18a, 39a, 114b, 200a, 299a, 583b, 587a, 642a, 649a.
sheep and goats, 32a.
sheep-fold, 432a.
sheet, 43b, 300a, 818b, 866b, 867a.
sheet of calculations, 898a.
sheet of water, 442a, 448b.
Shefbeti, 40b.
Shef-ḥer, 738b.
Shefi, 738a.
Shefit-ḥat, 738a.
Shefshefit, 738a.
Sheft-beṭ-f, 738b.
Sheftṭ-beṭ-f, 738b.
Shefut, 738a.
Shehbi, 750b.
Shekershau, 755a.
Shêkh, 291a, 311b.
shell, 233a, 892a.
shell of a fish or animal, 252a.
shell of an egg, 62a.
shelter, 286b, 452b, 587a, 786b.
shelters for cattle, 337a ; on river, 320a.
Shemerthi, 742a.
Shem-Rā, 739b.
Shemshem, 739b.
Shemsu, 742b.
Shemsu Ḥāp, Ḥeru, Ḥet-Ḥer, Rā, 743a.
Shemti, 162a ; Rā and Serpent, 739b.
Shemtt, 743a.
Shemu, god, 740a.
Shemu, season of, 40b.
Shenit, 744a, 746a.
Shenit-urit, 744a.
Sheniut chambers, 744a.
Shennu gods, 744a.
Shent-amm, 743a.
Shenthet, 749a.
Shenṭi (Set), 749a.
Shen-ur, 743b, 744a.

Shepesh, 737b.
Shep-ḥer, 776b.
shepherd, 111a, 226b, 301b, 351b, 586b, 592a.
Shepherd, the, i.e., Osiris, 587a.
shepherds' pens, 813a.
Shepi, 736b, 752b.
Shepit, 736b.
Sheps, 737b.
Sheps, god of the boomerang, 737b.
Shepsi, 737b.
Shepsit, 737b.
Shepsu, 737b.
Sheptui, 737b.
Sherit, 750a.
Sherm, 750b.
Shesa, 751b.
Shesatheth, 752a.
Shesat-māket-neb-s, 751b.
Shesemtt, 753a.
Shesm, 753a.
Shesmā, 753b.
Shesmit, 753b.
Shesmu, star-god and Dekan, 753b.
Shesp-Ȧmen, etc., 752b.
Shespi, 752b.
Shespit, 752b.
Shespiu, 752b.
Shesrȧ, 754a.
Shesshes, 751b.
Shest, 754a.
Shestȧ, 754a b.
Shest-sett, 754b.
Shestt, 754b.
Shest-tȧ, 754b.
Shest-tcha, 754a.
Shet, 755a.
Sheta, 755a.
Sheṭau, 758b.
Sheṭ-ba, 757b.
S-ḥetep-Neterui, 684b.
S-ḥetep-Sekhmit, 684b.
Shethu, 757a.
Sheṭ-Kheru, 758a.
Shetshet, 755a.
shew favour, 101a.
shield, 93a, 94a, 324a, 659a, 776a, 788a, 810a.
shift, 153a.
shimmer, 224b.
shin bones, 632a b, 717b, 719a.
shine, 22b, 90b, 92b, 117b, 159a, 160a, 168b, 180b, 212b, 215b, 224a b, 225a b, 226b, 227b, 234a, 239a, 242a, 249a b, 250a, 351a, 463b, 530b, 534b, 564a, 590a, 621b, 698b, 820b, 858b, 876b, 887a ; to make, 594b, 700b.
shining, 206a, 215b, 589b, 628b, 635a.
shining one, 319b.
ship, 49b, 152a, 204a, 314b, 425b, 467a, 540a, 561b, 602b, 704a, 894b, 895a, 900a ; part of, 42b, 146b, 228b, 233b, 245b, 278a, 336a, 347a, 390b, 548b, 559b, 573b, 627b, 669b, 677a, 688a, 706b, 729b, 753a, 812a, 846a, 854a.
ship of Byblos, 768b, 793a.
ship of Keft, 794a.
ship of 100 cubits, 316b, 872a.
ship of war, 132b.
ship, sailing, 346b.
ship, sea-going, 307b.
ship, to load a, 34b.
shipping import, 348a.
shipwreck, 207a.
shipwrecked man, 32a, 225b.
shirt, 516b.
Shishak, 728b.
shiver, 12b, 898b.
shivering, 510b.
Shma (Horus), 740b.
Shmȧau-mes, 740b.
Shmāit, 741a.
Shmait-ȧakhu, 740b.
Shmentheth, 741b.
Shnār, 747a.
Shnārit, 747a.
Shnȧt, 746a.
Shnȧt-neteru, 746a.
Shnȧt-pet- etc., 746a.
Shnep, 747b.
Shnu, 747a.
shoal, 276a.
shod, to be, 827a.
shoe, 180a, 826b.
shoe, to, 827a.
shoemaker, 842b.
shoot, 91a, 246a, 298a, 369b, 708b, 754a.
shoot a glance, 708b.
shoot out, 190a b.

shoot venom, 470b.
shooter, 709a.
shooting, a, 754a.
shooting star, 647a, 701a.
shoots of plants, 421b, 422a.
shop for dates, 106a.
shore, 272b, 354a, 421b, 544b, 597a, 662b, 659b.
short of, to be, 397b.
short weight, 802a.
shortbread, 138b.
shorten, 539b ; sail, 725b, 735b.
shortened, 379b.
shot, as of silk, 117b.
shot with stars, 190a.
shoulder, 11a, 424b, 425a, 521b, 522a, 530a, 766b, 768a.
shoulders, the two, 298b, 793a.
shout, 73b, 113b, 149b, 440a, 627a, 858a.
shout down, 375a.
shout for joy, 141a, 683b.
shovel for fire, 288b.
show, 121b, 253b, 644a.
show different colours, 117b.
show oneself, 34b, 166b, 866b.
shower, 571a.
shower, to, 35b.
shred, 596b.
shrew-mouse, 43b, 522a, 798b.
shrine, 20a, 34b, 99a, 117b, 130a, 191a, 284a, 298a, 374b, 443a, 519b, 522a, 523b, 546b, 548a, 557b, 565b, 616a, 633b, 678b, 699b, 731b, 734a, 740b, 746b, 756a, 773b, 774b, 777b, 789a b, 790a, 796a, 800b, 801a, 804b, 808b, 812b, 839b, 873b, 874b, 909b, 914a.
shrine of Osiris, 484b.
shrine, part of, 342a, 725a.
shrine, portable, 18b.
shrine, secret, 351a.
shrine, the Southern, 433a.
shrink, 843b ; back, 635b ; from, 839a.
shrinking, 839a.
shrivel, 605b.
shroud, 463a, 755a, 874b.
shrub, 55a, 82a, 129b, 136a, 138a, 139b, 140a, 168a, 169b, 220a, 226a, 283a, 355a, 475b, 566b, 833a, 873a, 874a ; prickly, 714b.
shrubs, wall of, 677a.
shrubbery, 299a, 558b, 762a.
Shta, 755b, 756a.
Shta-ȧb, 756a.
Shta-Ḥer, 756b.
Shtai, 755b, 756a.
Shtait, 756a.
Shtait-em-Ṭuat, 756b.
Shta-Mesutt, 756b.
Shtat, 756a.
Shtat-besu, 756b.
Shtȧti, 756a.
Shtau-Ȧsut, 756a.
Shtau-āu, 756a.
Shtau-ḥeru, 756b.
Shṭit-shemāt, 758a.
Shṭu, god, 758b, 759a.
Shu, 168a, 242b ; blossoms of, 488a.
Shu, a tribe, 732b.
Shu and Tefnut, 420a, 632a, 674a, 848b, 873a.
Shu, forms of, 732a.
Shu, Hall of, 183a.
Shu, phallus of, 489a, 834b.
Shu (Reḥu), 429b.
Shu, Seven Children of, 472a.
Shu, soul of, 198b, 200a.
Shu, supports of, 630b.
Shu, temple of, 41a.
Shu-em-ḥerit, 732a.
Shu-enti-em-Ȧten, 732a.
Shui, 734a.
Shu-neb-Maāt, 732a.
shun, 481a.
Shut, 732a.
shut, 98a, 768a, 834a ; a door, 56b ; the eyes, 136a, 878a ; the mouth, 834a.
shut in, 5a, 60b, 72a, 275b, 435b, 552a, 594b, 800a, 805a, 915b.
shut up, 7a, 557b, 568a, 708a, 729b, 743b, 805a, 874b, 900b ; to be, 550a.
Shut-ent-bȧk, 733b.
Shuti, 732a.
Shutt, 732a.
Shut-tar-na, 648a.
shuttle, 121b, 754a.
shutters, 852a.
Shu-ub-bi-lu-li-u-ma, 636b.
shyness, 569b.
Si, 591b.

sick, 296b, 574a, 577a, 674b, 744b, 802a ; to be, 223b, 314a, 696b ; to make, 286a.
sick man, 296b, 744b.
sickle, 10a, 572a.
sickly, 187a.
sickness, 39b, 58b, 180b, 296b, 314b, 390b, 443b, 465b, 517a, 529a, 571a, 611a, 650b, 680b, 719a, 766a, 807a, 887a ; devil of, 853a.
sickness, god of, 900a.
sickness, mental, 744b.
sickness, shaking, 714b.
sickness, the falling, 444a.
side, 128a, 417b, 425a, 766a ; at the, 495b.
side, disease of, 421a.
side, east, or left, 671b, 812b.
side of field, 599a.
side, south, 813a.
side, west, 812b.
side-locks, 491b, 827b.
sides of ladder, 110a, 425a.
sides of ship, 60b.
sieve, 296a, 689a, 903b.
sift, 396a, 903b.
siftings, 396a.
sighing, 225b.
sign, 19a ; make a, 899b.
signal, 448a, 648a.
signet, 123b, 804a.
sight, 68a, 243a, 254a, 266b, 688b, 678b, 783b, 808a, 891a.
sighter, 612a.
sightless, 340b.
silence, 80b, 627b, 706a ; put to, 626b, 706a ; city of, 706a.
silent, 531a, 627b, 706a, 757a, 810a, 819b ; to make, 610a.
silent man, 810a.
silent-mouthed, 810a.
silent ones, 706a.
silly, 528a, 652b ; to make, 593a.
silo, 81b.
silver, 75b, 131b, 523a, 353b.
similar, 277b.
similarity, 779b.
similarly, 264b.
similitude, 19a, 277b, 534b, 542a b, 673a, 698b, 779b, 826b.
simple, 180a.
simpleton, 180a.
sin, 21b, 31b, 82a, 89b, 114b, 140a, 143b, 211a, 226a, 243a, 367a, 369b, 441b, 540a, 726a, 853a, 895b.
Sinai, 150b, 296a ; mines of, 210b.
since, 100b, 266a, 277a, 339a, 815a, 908b.
sincere, 246a.
sinews, 22b.
sing, 111b, 448a, 449a, 508b, 515b, 741b, 771b, 782b, 800b, 801b, 803a, 835a.
sing praises, 443b.
sing to a dance, 857a.
sing to a harp, 509a.
sing to a sistrum, 508b, 800b.
sing to a tambourine, 795a.
sing to the heart, 509a.
singer, 157a, 509a, 515b, 548b, 630b, 741b, 835b.
singing god, 72a, 263b ; goddess, 70b.
singing men and women, 548b, 741b.
singing voices, 560a.
single, 153a.
sink, 116a, 480b, 820a.
sink down, 819b.
sink into the ground, 116b ; into the heart, 451a.
sinner, 31b, 89b, 165a, 369b, 457b, 538b, 540a, 637b.
sins, register of, 115a.
sip, 212b.
sirocco, 740a.
Sirsa, 647b.
sister, 674b ; king's, 392a.
sister-wife, 674b.
Sisters, The Two Combatant, 429b.
sistra, statues with, 621b.
sistrum, 38b, 616a, 621b, 692b, 754b, 854a ; to play or rattle a sistrum, 621b, 692b.
sistrum bearer, 75b.
sistrum of the god, 403a.
sistrum player, 74a.
sit, 43b, 76b, 374b, 485a, 610a, 682b, 822a, 868a, 887b.
sit down, 679a.
site, 147a, 638a.
situated, 444a.

situation, 595a.
six, 643b.
six-ply stuff, 681b.
sixth, 643b.
sixth-day festival, 696a.
sixty, 635b.
size, great, 170b.
Skamu, god, 704b.
skeleton, 778a.
Skemu-nent, 626b.
Skenu, 626b.
Skhabes, 615a.
Skhabsenfunen, 615a.
Skhāit-baius, 615b.
Skhait-Ḥeru, 614b, 688b.
Skhat-pet, 615a.
Skhaut, 615a.
Skhem, 691a.
Skhem-ā-kheftiu, 691b.
Skhem-en-ȧb-f, 692a.
Skhem-ḥer, 692a.
Skhemit, 616b, 691b.
Skhemit-Bast-Rā, 691b.
Skhemit-em-kheftiu-s, 692a.
Skhemit-en-ȧakhus, 692a.
Skhemit-en-ṭesu-sen, 692a.
Skhemit-meṭu, 692a.
Skhemit-ren-s-em-ḥemit, 692a.
Skhemit-ṭesu, 692a.
Skhemit-Uast, 691b.
Skhemit-Uatchit, 691b.
Skhem-neteru, 692a.
Skhem-shut, 692a.
Skhem-taui (Anubis), 692a.
Skhemti, 692b.
Skhemiu, 691a.
Skhem-ur, 691b.
Skhenȧ, 616b.
Skhen-ba, 617a.
Skhenef, 691b.
Skhen-em-pet- etc., 692a.
Skheni, 616b.
Skhenit, 616b.
Skhen-khaibut, 617a.
Skhen-maāt, 693a.
Skhen-neter, 617a.
Skhen-rekhtt, 617a.
Skhen-ṭuatiu, 617a.
Skhenu, 616b.
Skhen-ur, 616b, 693a.
Skheper-khaut, 690a.
Skhep-kenmem, 616a.
Skhepti, god, 690a.
Skhepti-rest, 616a.
Skher, 694a.
Skher-ānṭ-f, 617b.
Skheriu, 617b.
Skher-remu, 694a.
Skher-reremu, 617b.
Skher-shetau-urā, 617b.
Skhet, god, 695a.
Skheṭ-ḥer-āsh-ȧru, 695b.
Skheṭiu, 618a.
Skhetiut, 695a.
Skheṭui, 618a.
Skhi, Skhit, 615a.
Skhui, 689b.
Skhuni, 616a.
skiff, 576b, 589b, 892a, 900a.
skilful, 621b, 624b, 698a, 751b.
skilfully, 178b.
skill, 751b.
skilled, 284a, 430a, 482a, 613a, 622a, 624b, 682b, 751b.
skilled, be, 284b, 483a.
skilled in speech, 430b, 626a.
skilled workmen, 430a b.
skin, 49b, 55a, 58b, 62a, 63a, 160a, 250a, 327a, 400b, 530a, 536a, 571a, 573a, 576a, 610b, 747b, 813b, 819b, 847b, 861b, 887a.
skin, animal, 753a, 859a.
skin, a sacred, 795b.
skin bottle, 62a.
skin, cap of, 62b.
skin, disease of, 617a, 693b, 899a.
skin dress, 160a.
skin, house of, 327b.
skin rolls, 129a.
skins (i.e., human beings), 62a.
skip, 597a, 662b, 789a, 833a, 854a, 862b.
skippings, 833a, 852b.
skull, 163a, 416b, 448a, 496a, 827b, 907a, 910a.
skull box, 447b.
sky, 77b, 150a, 174b, 183a, 190a, 194a, 210b, 224a, 229a, 238b, 245a, 297a, 307b, 327b, 381a, 419b, 448b, 454a, 498b, 462b, 536a, 630b, 733a, 769a, 775a, 867b.
sky, back part of, 457b.
sky, crown of, 163a.

sky, day and night, 229a.
sky, four quarters of, 229a.
sky, morning, 225a.
sky, night, 504a.
sky of the Ṭuat, 685a.
sky, two halls of, 438a.
sky, two halves of the, 350a.
Sky-god, 18a, 26b, 27b, 47a, 210b, 349b, 500a ; the Eyes of, 194a.
Sky-goddess, 46a, 193b, 163a, 190a, 256a, 318a, 350a, 356b.
sky-water, 459b.
slab, 113a, 117a, 188b, 298a, 566a, 725a, 817b, 819b.
slackness, 207b.
slain, 528b, 560b, 806b.
slain in the Ṭuat, 629b.
slain, the, 58b, 345b, 477a, 512b, 571a, 669a, 802a, 827a.
slander, 739b.
slanderer, 739b.
slashings, 396b.
slaughter, 3b, 19b, 89b, 140b, 154b, 293a, 373b, 528b, 561a, 571a, 602a, 667b, 668b, 669a, 704a, 723b, 730a, 731a b, 757b, 843a, 876b, 878a, 884a.
slaughter, gods of, 54b, 71b.
slaughter, place of, 26b, 376b.
slaughter chamber, 10a.
slaughter house, 26b, 71b, 239a, 373b, 390a, 445b, 455b, 538b, 685b, 689b, 704a, 880b.
slaughterer, 102a, 303b, 601b, 604a, 606a, 653b, 666a b, 667b, 668b, 731b.
slaughterer, chief, 172a.
slaughterings, 392b, 459a, 606a.
slave, 33a, 39a, 67a, 111a, 206b, 311a, 482b ; hereditary, 673a.
slave office, 239b.
slave, woman, 206b, 411a.
slay, 19b, 127b, 154b, 156a, 168a, 179b, 186a, 205a, 206a, 210b, 220b, 223b, 269a, 270a, 273a, 288b, 324a, 325b, 337b, 369b, 388a, 395b, 397b, 398b, 431a, 435a b, 446a, 512b, 522a, 528b, 534a, 535b, 538a, 546b, 559b, 575a b, 590b, 591b, 596a, 597b, 598a, 601a b, 606a, 629a b, 631b, 632a, 661a, 662b, 664a b, 665a, 666a b, 667b, 668b, 677b, 710a, 711a b, 713a, 715a, 717b, 730a, 731a, 735b, 806b, 844a, 845a, 876b.
slayer, 303b, 527b, 528b, 603b, 723b, 731b, 878a, 889b.
sledge, 89a, 136a, 169b, 835b.
sledge of Ḥenu Boat, 285b.
sleep, 1a b, 113b, 115b, 135b, 136a, 163b, 250a, 344a, 374b, 375b, 396a, 559b, 632b, 718b, 780b.
sleeper, 780b.
sleepers (i.e., the dead), 718b.
sleeping draught, 719a.
sleeping room, 106a.
Sleepless One, 718b.
slender, 547b.
slice, 245b, 263b ; of flint, 387a ; of meat, 174a, 400a.
slide, 370b.
slight, 546a.
slime, 275b, 424b.
sling, 528b, 529a.
slink, 491a ; along, 478a.
slip away, 528a.
slip behind, 568a.
slip, to, 356b, 894b.
slippery, 536b.
slit, 187b, 205b, 248b, 603b, 771a, 809b, 867b.
slit open, 566a.
slope, 89a ; of a pyramid, 243b.
sloth, 181b.
slothful, 180a, 181b.
slow, 451b.
slowly, to act, 796b.
sluggard, 180a, 377a.
sluggish, 377a.
sluggishness, 181b.
Slughi, 5a.
sluice, 291a.
slumber, 1a b, 115b, 374b, 665a, 780b.
Sma, god, 667b.
Smaā-ḥuti, 668a.
Smaar, 176a.
Smai, 668b.
Smai-Nu, 600a.
Smai, Smait, 600a.
Smait, 599b, 668a.
Smai-ta (Rā), 600a.
Smai-taui, god, 600a b.
Smaiti, 600a.
Smait-urit, 668a.

Smaiut, 600a.
Sma-kheftiu-f, 601a.
small, 411b, 546a, 657a, 659b, 660b, 746a, 798b.
small, to be or become, 413b, 749b.
Smam, Bull-god, 601b.
Smami, 669a.
Smamit, 601b, 669a.
Smamit-urit, 669a.
Smam-ti, 669a.
Smamu, 669a.
Smam-ur, 601b, 669a.
Smȧn, god, 669b.
Smant-urt, 669a.
smash, 114b, 145a, 154b, 185a, 411a, 630b, 713b, 765b, 801b, 808a, 821a, 854a.
Smati, 600a, 668a.
Smatit, 669b.
Smati-uati, 600a.
Smatt-Bast, 600a.
Smaur, 601a, 668a.
smear, 212b, 376b, 643a, 689a, 702a, 801a, 803b, 847b, 900a.
smear with oil or stibium, 328b, 813b.
smell, 89b, 551a b, 572b, 573a, 595a, 603b, 608a, 618a b, 627b, 629b, 648a, 660b, 675a, 678a, 695b, 697a, 712b, 747b, 749b.
smell, bad, 559b, 709a.
smell, strong, 631a.
smell the earth (i.e., do homage), 89b, 603b, 675a.
smell the stick (i.e., be beaten), 551a.
smelt, 195b, 196a, 275b, 353b, 366b, 664b, 696b, 792b.
smelter, 171b, 212b, 354a.
smelting houses, 455a.
Smen, Goose-god, 602a, 670b.
Smenkhit, 602b.
Smen-maāt-em-Uast, 670b.
Smennu, 602a.
Smentt, 670b.
Smenu, 670b.
Smen-user, 670b.
Smer-nesert, 671a.
Smet, 603a, 672b.
Smeṭ, 603a, 673a.
Smetȧ, 672b.
Smet āqa, 603a.
Smeti, 672b.
Smeṭ-sert, 673b.
Smeṭsmeṭ, 673b.
Smett, 672b.
Smetti, 603a.
Smetu, 672b.
Smi (Set), 670a.
smile, 636a, 660b; to make, 696b.
smite, 19b, 75b, 76a, 79a, 102a, 145a, 154b, 208b, 253a, 396b, 397b, 467b, 508a, 573a, 596a, 617b, 701b, 705a, 723a, 725b, 734a, 794b, 796b, 804a, 821a, 899b.
smiter, 233b, 468b, 492b, 864b.
smiting, 397b.
smitten, 734a, 891b.
Smiu fiends, 670a.
smoke, 6a, 516b, 609b.
snake, 29a, 237b, 374a, 479b.
snake, two-legged, 479b.
snake-goddess, 29a, 77b.
snare, 40a, 186b, 245b, 246a, 458b, 465a, 466a, 475a, 539a, 618b, 632b, 695a ; pegs of, 38a.
snare game, 433a.
snare, to peg out a, 695a.
snarer, 618a, 695a, 787a, 793b.
snatch, 385a, 757b ; away, 100b, 101a.
snatched, 446b.
sneer, to, 200b.
Snehaqarha, 607b.
Sneh-Rā, 607b.
Snem, 607a.
Snemf, 607a.
Snemkhef, 607a.
Snemmti, 607a.
Sneterba, 678b.
sniff, 89b, 551a, 573a, 832a, 877a, 747b.
sniffings, 750a.
snout, 554a.
snow, 637b.
snuff the air, 394a, 603b, 612b, 832a, 854b, 877a.
snuff up, 204b.
so and so, 297b.
so that, 56a, 339a, 414a b.
so that not, 835a.
soak, 35b, 240a.
soar, 135a.
society, 170a.

socket, 156a, 253a, 521b, 544a ; rectangular, 43b.
soda water, 280b.
sodomite, 396b.
sodomy, 395b ; to commit, 396b.
soft, 577b, 803a, 898b ; of bread, 423b ; of speech, 449b.
softness, 273b.
soil, 25a, 128a, 585b, 627b, 815a.
soldier, 11a, 33a, 115b, 132a, 224b, 240b, 241a, 257a, 272b, 288a, 292a, 302a, 303a, 303b, 330a, 333a, 442a, 581a, 639b, 640a, 704a b, 751a, 772a, 794a, 841b, 848a, 857b, 897b ; companies, 768a,
soldier, young (recruit), 342b, 347b, 372b, 491b.
soldiers, Libyan, 343a, 862b.
soldiers, time-expired, 882b.
sole, 153a b.
sole of the foot, 63b, 75b, 368b, 481a, 786b, 826b, 827a, 853a b, 873a b.
solid, 304a, 305a, 680b, 914b.
solitary, 153a.
solstice, 478b, 479a.
solstice, summer, 111a, 118b.
solstice, winter, 351a.
solution, 292b, 293b, 401a.
solution, medical, 328a.
solve difficulties, 99a, 630b.
solve a riddle, 178b.
some, 379b, 444b.
something that is, 164b.
son, 321b, 349a, 583b, 647b, 749b.
son, king's, 392a.
son of Horus, 24b.
son-of-Rā, title, 584b.
son of the heart, 583b.
son's son, 749b.
song, 94a, 448a, 508a b, 509a, 515b ; of praise, 635a.
Song-god, 19b.
soot, 491a.
sorcerer, 514b, 515a, 585b.
sorcery, 515a.
sore, 11b, 124a, 159b, 160a, 296b, 320a, 487b, 688a b.
sorrow, 3b, 7b, 64b, 296b, 314b, 330b, 386b, 450a, 459a, 527b, 606b, 677a, 755a, 790b, 831a, 850a ; to feel, 11b.
sorrower, 604b.
sorrowful, 464a, 469b, 807a.
sorry, 37b, 319a.
sort, 595a.
Soteres, 404b, 410b.
Sothis, 48a, 242a, 656a, 664a ; soul of, 125a.
soul, to have, 197a.
soul, beatified, 197a ; damned, 23b, 197a.
Soul, the dual, 84a.
Soul of Bast, 270a.
soul of gold, 197b.
Souls of Ȧnu, Pu, Nekhen, etc., 198a b.
Souls of the gods, 198a.
souls, passage for, in the Ṭuat, 157a.
Soul-god, 197b ; of the East, 198a.
Soul-goddesses, 198a.
sound, 128b, 140b, 148b, 305a, 422a, 697a, 851a, 893b.
sound (of weeping), 560a.
sound, to be, 128a, 192a, 421b, 676a.
soundness, 893b.
sour, 115a, 122a ; to go, 121b.
source, 216a, 723a ; of river, 202a ; of spring, 475b.
sourness, 78a.
south, 431b, 575b, 741a, 816a, 831b.
south, books of, 741b.
South, chief of, 431b.
South, crown of, 372b, 431b, 653b, 741b.
South, dwellers in, 554b.
South, garments of, 431b.
South, goddess of, 432a.
South, grain of, 741a.
South, hand of, 554a, 771b, 815a.
South, linen of, 431b.
South, plant of, 648b.
South, precious stones of, 741a.
South, stone of, 741a.
South, tribes of the, 431b.
South, wind of the, 431b, 727b, 750b.
southern, 431b.
sovereign, 97a.
sovereignty, 512b, 653b.

sow, 167a, 428a, 628a, 631a, 707a, 708a, 712a, 716a.
sow, white, 722a.
sow, young, 303a.
Spa, 661b.
space, 147a, 184b ; open, 35b, 532a.
spacious, 2b, 107b, 182b, 255b, 652b, 894a.
span, 722a, 752b ; of life, 724a.
spare, 866b.
spark, 234a, 823a, 845a b.
sparkle, 196a, 215b, 530b, 629a, 630a, 711b, 820b, 842a, 858b.
sparkle-stone, 842a.
sparkling, 858b.
spawn of Āapep, 850a.
spawn of fish, 606b.
speak, 104b, 335a, 560a, 719b, 745a, 782b, 807a, 823a, 913a ; make, 673a.
speak again, 176b.
speak against, 416a.
speak arrogantly, 861b.
speak evil, 145b, 739b.
speak firmly, 193b.
speak freely, 158b.
speak loudly, 106b, 113b.
speak scornfully, 416a, 894a.
speak violently, 110a.
speaker, 635a, 913b ; of fair things, 218b.
spear, 75b, 110b, 132b, 154b, 211a, 281b, 283a, 305a, 351a, 390a, 459a, 489b, 523b, 573a, 640a, 754a, 778a, 905a, 914b.
spear fish, 708b, 712b.
spear-handle, 268b.
spear-maker, 281b.
spearman, 325a.
spear thrower, 528b.
speciality, 483a.
species, 694a.
speckled, 117b, 278b.
spectacle, 80a.
speculation, 745a.
speech, 26b, 35b, 104b, 240b, 332b, 335a, 416a, 433b, 549a, 632b, 635a, 669b, 679b, 717a, 719b, 735b, 754a, 831a, 860b, 862a, 913a.
speech, deified, 913b.
speech, fair, 335b.
speech, flowers of, 667a.
speech, foul, 335b.
speech in defence, 186a.
speech, occasion for, 80a.
speech of all men, 335a.
speech of Negroland, 913a.
speech of the god, 403b.
speech, to make a, 67a, 913a.
speechless, 531b.
speedy, 9b, 533a ; remedy, 494b.
Speḥ, 662a.
Speḥt-urt, 662a.
spell, 22b, 173b, 246a, 509a, 515a, 623a, 647b, 693a, 739a, 745a, 758a, 860b.
spell, to cast a, 464b, 514b.
spell-bound, 809a.
spell-case, 390b.
spells, beneficent, 515a ; love, 310a.
spelt, 148a, 208a b, 227b, 442b, 827b.
spend, 438a.
Speos Artemidos, 232a.
Spert-neter-s, 661b.
Spes, 662b.
spew, 778a.
Sphinx, the, 469b, 752b ; temple of the, 239a.
spice, 13b, 112a, 288a, 528a, 561b ; bags of, 754a.
spice, bundle of, 806a.
spice offering, 38b.
spies, 334a.
spill, 804a.
spin, 323b, 325a.
spindle, 563b.
spine, 859b.
spirit, 24a, 30b, 77b, 537b.
spirit, a lying, 141b.
spirit, ancestral, 24b.
spirit, divine, 9a.
spirit, equipped, 24a.
spirit, evil, 740b.
spirit, female, 24a.
spirit, glorified, 24a.
spirit, height of a, 2b.
spirit, primeval, 24b.
spirit, to be or become a, 23b.
spirit-body, 646a.
spirit-soul, 23b, 24b.
spirit-souls, domain of, 900b ; number of the, 24a.

spirits nine cubits high, 24b.
Spirits of Set, 24b.
spirits of the Seven Guardians, 24b.
spirits, reunion of, 652a.
Spirits, the Four, 491b.
spit, 104a, 235a, 248a, 249a, 253a, 409a, 833a b, 854b, 876b, 877b, 906a.
spit out, 91b, 778a, 793b.
spittings, 762b.
spittle, 91a, 223b, 248a, 249a, 252b, 253a, 347b, 394a, 876b, 877b.
spleen, 378a.
splendid, 22b, 123a, 225b, 737a, 888b ; to make, 719a.
splendid acts, 23a.
splendid rank, 912a.
splendour, 3b, 9a, 23a, 128b, 142b, 146a, 159a, 200a, 212b, 225a, 242a, 274a, 326a, 371a, 522b, 535a, 708a b, 712b, 736b, 753a, 912a.
splinter, 14b, 246a.
split, 89b, 186a, 195a, 205b, 235a, 237b, 243b, 245b, 246a, 247a, 248a b, 251a b, 252a, 287a, 571b, 603b, 629a, 665a, 705a, 731a, 844b, 881a.
split open, 187b.
splitting of words, 246a.
spoil, 82b, 464b, 471a, 532a, 753b.
spoil, to, 464b, 591b.
spoken, 877b, 913a b.
spokesman, 913b.
spoon, 114a.
sport, 693a ; sport with, 28a.
spotted, 117b.
spouse, 303a, 599b.
spout, 775a.
sprawl about, 842a.
spread, 185a, 249b, 620b, 621a, 863b ; spreading, 777b, 894a.
spread a net, 75a.
spread out, 182b, 252b, 255b, 256b, 436b.
spread the wings, 220b, 251b, 465b.
spring of water, 144a, 490b, 579a.
spring, the, 543a ; flowers, fruits and plants of, 423b, 427a.
spring up, 166a, 274b, 436b, 833a b.
sprinkle, 35b, 40a, 387b, 393b, 400a, 401a, 409b, 451a, 620b, 716a, 798a, 804a, 814a, 857b, 862b, 863b, 867b, 906b ; sprinkled, 798b.
sprinkling, 155b.
sprout, 242b, 510a ; divine, 167b.
spume, 509b.
spy, spies, 463a, 468a, 862b, 899a.
spy into, 158b, 462a, 471a.
Sqai-nu-baiu, 702a.
Sqaiu, 625b.
square, a, 478a.
squat, 590b.
Sqeb, 702a.
squeeze, 28b, 114a, 292b, 491b, 492a, 689a, 795a, 836a ; squeezing, 356b.
Sqerit, 703a.
Sqer-tchatchau, 703a.
Sqeṭi-ḥer, 626a, 703b.
squint, 464a, 641a.
Sta, god, 628b, 707b.
Sta-en-Åsår, 707b.
stab, 26b, 149a, 166a, 168a, 179a, 187b, 220b, 291b, 344a, 369b, 446a, 549b, 592a, 665a, 845a, 876b, 889a, 905a, 914b, 915a.
stabber, 18a, 166b.
stability, 297a, 670a, 783b, 913b.
stable, 74a, 75a, 77a, 193b, 521a, 723b, 740b, 913b.
stable, to be, 296b.
stablish, 54a, 89b, 602a, 646b, 670a, 716a.
stablished, 296b.
stablisher, 670a.
stablishing, 670a.
stade, 97b.
staff, 1a b, 4a, 5b, 6b, 17a, 49a b, 54b, 90a, 114b, 117b, 121b, 126b, 133a, 140a, 141a, 154b, 168a, 202a, 208b, 228b, 235a, 253b, 268b, 274a, 277a, 284b, 314a, 334a, 336a, 366b, 367a, 379b, 462a, 470a, 475b, 516b, 566a b, 630b, 725b, 789b, 815a, 821a, 823b, 825b, 844a, 850b, 862b, 892b, 896b, 902b ; forked, 304b.
staff bearer, 849a.
staff, magical, 171b.

staff of authority, 330b.
staff of life (wheat), 566b.
staff of office, 55a, 99a.
staff of protection, 193a.
stag, 2b, 441b, 448b.
stag beetle, 804b.
stage of a journey, 179a.
staircase, 42a, 129a, 130a.
stairs, 42a, 129a, 130a, 206a, 207a, 220b, 224b, 225b, 421b, 436b, 596a, 841a.
stairs of Sebek, 436b.
stairway, 224b, 421b, 436b, 885a.
Stait, goddess, 707b.
stake, 347a, 467a, 589a, 672a, 715a.
stake, execution, 290b, 301a.
stakes of a net, 38a.
staleness, 78a.
stalk, 126b, 129a, 262b, 268b, 299a, 354a, 902b.
stall, 75a, 77a, 521a ; cattle, 337a.
stalled ox, 2b.
stallion, 39a, 774a, 801b.
stammer, 346a, 799b.
stamp upon, 821a, 852b.
Stån, god, 628b.
stand, 133a, 253b, 289a, 422a, 297a.
stand, a, 16b, 133a, 140a, 659a, 809a.
stand on end, 393b.
stand still, 133a, 429a, 617a, 670a, 693a, 868a.
standard, 13a, 49a, 285a, 490a, 915b.
stanza, 457a.
staple, 273a, 516a.
star (Ἀστὴρ), 77b, 116a, 125a, 155a, 168b, 262a, 270a, 409b, 528a, 530b, 540b, 647a, 655b, 695b, 809b, 913b ; stars the flowers of heaven, 8b.
star, double, 647a.
star, light-shooting (comet ?), 625a.
star, morning, 220b, 403b, 647a, 656b, 870b.
star of Āri, 130b.
star of the Calf, 220b.
star of the god, 871a.
star of thousands, 656a.
star of the water, 656a.
starboard, 815b.
Star-god, 332b, 655b.
star-gods, 374a, 594b.
stars, circumpolar, 546b.
stars, the Eight, 758b.
stars, fixed, 478b.
stars, imperishable, 24b, 36a, 78b, 92a.
stars, never-resting, 78a.
stars, never-setting, 78a.
stars, non-retreating, 481a.
stars, northern, 656a.
stars, polar, 78b.
stars, the seven of Orion, 42b.
stars, shooting, 647a.
stars, the unresting, 36a, 546b.
stars, wandering, 374a, 626a.
start, to, 288a.
starvation, 897a.
starve, 614a, 684a.
Sta-ta, 631a.
state, 106a, 133b, 561b, 761b, 698b, 765b, 766b.
stately, 737a.
statement, 186a, 297b, 430b, 434b, 860b.
stater, 712a, 781a.
station, 21a, 102b, 114a, 133b, 289a, 297b, 330b, 419a.
statue, 19a, 37b, 277b, 367a, 422b, 466a, 494b, 557b, 577a, 604b, 609a, 616a, 622b, 670b, 675b, 752b, 770b, 771a b, 788a, 826b, 907a.
statue, colossal, 298a.
statue, divine, 323b.
statue, funerary, 737b.
statue of the god, 698b.
statues, the two, 847a.
statute, 192a, 400b.
stave, 1a, 35b, 115b, 208b, 274a, 333a, 467a ; bent, 592a.
stay, 190a, 468b.
staying power, 297a.
steal, 100b, 101a, 110b, 114b, 115b, 298a, 420b, 425a, 437b, 474a, 523b, 550b, 572b, 729b, 849a, 895a.
steal the mouth, 385a.
stealer, 101a, 385a.
steel, 417a, 419b.
steep, to, 35b, 539b, 597b, 843a.
steer, to, 66a, 182b, 481b, 722b.

steering pole, 18b, 75b, 139b, 182b, 428b, 482a.
steersman, 70b, 71a, 290b, 482a, 562b.
Stef, 711a.
Sṭef, 631b.
Sṭefit, 631b.
Sṭefiu, 631b.
Sṭeg, 716a.
Sṭega-khatt, 632a.
Stekh (Set), 712a.
stela, stelæ, 81b, 133b, 151a, 158a, 190b, 192b, 274b, 420b, 421a.
stem, 299a, 902b.
Stenit, 711b.
Stennu, 629a.
Sten-taui, 629a.
step, 11a, 42a, 129a, 130a, 206a, 207a, 224b, 225a b, 324a, 417b, 421b, 436b, 446b, 451b, 541a b, 596a, 805a, 884a ; mincing, 536b ; timid, 479b.
step, to, 607a.
step out, to, 184a, 376b.
step over, 833a.
stepped throne, 567a.
steps of a tomb, 538b.
Steps, the, 537a.
stern of a boat, 244a, 828b.
stern rope, 461b.
steward, 108b, 312a.
stew pan, 208b.
Sthȧit, 712b.
Sthethi, 713a.
Sthit, 712b.
Sthit-s-mm-Nu, 712b.
Sthu, 713a.
Sti (the god Set), 709a b.
Sti, crown of, 535a.
Sti, Fire-god, 709b.
Sti-ȧru, 709a.
stibium, 329a b, 715b.
stick, 1a b, 4a, 17a, 41a, 49a, 89a, 115b, 117b, 126b, 133a, 140a, 151a, 168a, 202a, 208b, 212b, 228b, 235a, 276a, 277a, 283a, 334a, 336a b, 367a b, 470a, 475b, 516b, 566a, 725a b, 726a, 789b, 847b, 850b, 879b, 896b, 900b, 902b.
stick for bastinado, 290a.
stick an animal, 900b.
stick, to, 862b, 914b, 915a.
stick with curved end, 114b.
sticker, 18a, 31b.
sticks of incense, 223b.
sticks, tally, 129b.
sticks, walking, 822a.
storm, 902a, 577b.
strike, 701b.
stiff, 134b, 803b.
stiff-necked, 13a, 760a b, 803b.
stifle, 64a, 873b.
Sti-ḥer, 628a.
still, 627b, 706a, 810a.
Still-heart (i.e., Osiris), 175b, 176a.
stillness, 706a.
stimulate, 689b.
sting, to, 160a, 179a, 248a, 913a, 914b, 915a.
sting of insect or scorpion, 538a, 914b.
stink, 61a, 145b, 383a, 470a, 553a, 554a, 565b, 683a, 712b, 726b ; make to, 617b, 693b.
stinking, 145b, 343b, 470a, 726b, 868b.
Stinking Face, 383b.
stinking fish, 280b, 746a.
stinkingness, 554a.
stipulations, 400b.
Sti-reh-pet, 708b.
stir up, 689b ; wrath, 615b.
Stit, goddess, 709a.
Sti-ṭesui, 709a.
Stiu, 609a.
stock, 487a.
stoker, 70b.
stomach, 416b.
stomach, to turn the, 286a.
stone, 17a, 20a, 58a, 60a, 62a, 63b, 95a, 111b, 112a, 114a, 115b, 117a b, 121b, 124a, 143a, 189b, 191b, 208b, 218a, 220b, 221b, 243b, 260a, 298a, 303a, 315a, 317a, 319b, 329a, 344b, 384b, 464b, 473a, 479a, 483b, 605a, 624a, 630b, 664a, 706b, 777b, 778a, 813b, 817b, 836b, 843a, 844b, 879b, 888a.
stone, coloured, 821b.
stone for amulets, 375b.
stone for inlaying, 790a, 792a.
stone, green, 150b.

stone in the bladder, 178a.
stone, large, 888b.
stone, Nubian, 129b.
stone of Åbhet, 39b.
stone of price, 110a.
stone of the Sun-god, 217a.
stone of truth, 62b.
stone, precious, 39b, 204b, 224b, 259b, 276a, 415b, 435a, 473b, 475a, 507a, 516a, 675b, 729a, 752a, 766a, 795b, 804b, 808a, 837a, 844a.
stone, prepared, 62b.
stone, pyramidal, 219b.
stone, rectangular, 43b.
stone, sparkling, 844a.
stone, to face with, 477a.
stone, variegated, 419a.
stone, white, 251a, 523b, 754b.
stone, white calcareous, 62b.
stone, worked, 62a, 725b, 764b.
stone-breaker, 158b.
stone-cutter, 26a, 344a.
stone mason, 94a, 119a, 402b, 535b, 850b.
stone quarry, 94a.
stool, 13b, 367b, 509b.
stop, to, 4b, 38b, 82b, 176a, 429a, 708a.
stoppage, 746b; to make a, 65a.
stoppage of bowels, 747a.
stopped, 624a ; stopped up, 769b.
stop up, 750a, 873b.
store, 134b, 487a, 649a, 663a, 909b, 914b.
store chamber, 320a.
store-city, 238a.
storehouse, 80b, 108b, 130a, 193b, 239b, 286b, 289a, 415b, 419a, 561b, 723a, 900a ; men of the, 813a.
store-keeper, 71a.
store room, 374b.
store up, 160a, 641b.
stores, office of, 239b.
storey, 640b.
stories (see also story), 632b, 719b.
storm, 93a, 95a, 122b, 174a, 180a, 395a, 459b, 465a, 549b, 573a, 606b, 607a, 608b, 631b, 700b, 722b, 746a b, 807a.
storm cloud, 745b.
Storm fiend, 608b.
Storm-god, 378b, 411b ; gods, 714b.
storm wind, 393b.
stormy, 797b.
story, 291a, 669b, 719b.
story tellers, 648a, 719b.
straggler, 244a.
straight, to make, 653b, 668b.
straighten, 650b.
straightness, 271b.
straightway, 414b, 494b, 495a, 830a.
strain, to, 114a, 347b, 598a, 613a ; through a rag or sieve, 140b, 689a, 800b.
strainer, 347b ; linen, 476b.
straits, to be in sore, 800a.
strange, 541b ; of speech, 911a.
stranger, 214b, 430a, 541b, 546a, 740b, 741a b, 782a.
strangle, 7a.
strap, 282a, 532b.
straw, 528a, 886a, 902b.
stray, 192b.
streaked, 4a, 278b.
stream, 12a, 31b, 35b, 49b, 95b, 99b, 115b, 142a, 145a, 187b, 195b, 202a, 212b, 231b, 257b, 293a, 307a, 349b, 387b, 400a, 407b, 424b, 475b, 488b, 516b, 526b, 569a, 576a, 612b, 725b, 840b, 882b.
street, 77b, 313b, 529b, 532a, 764b.
street corner, 314a.
strength, 5b, 22b, 49b, 115b, 182a, 193a, 197a, 214a, 240b, 241a, 245a, 306b, 338b, 344a, 347b, 376b, 379a, 388b, 389b, 401b, 544a, 690b, 738a, 769b, 772a, 783a, 807b, 822b, 839a, 851a, 883a, 896b ; to use, 910a.
strength, vital, 782b.
strength and good luck, 193b.
strengthen, 49b, 90b, 593a b, 608a, 618a, 650a, 677b, 690a b.
strenuous, 338a b.
strenuously, 292b.
stretch, 3a, 184b, 597b, 613a, 814a.
stretch measuring cord, 178b, 256a.

stretch of land, 256a.
stretch out, 191a, 243b, 256b, 804b, 873a ; a hand, 766a ; hands in prayer, 766a ; the sky, 685b ; to sleep, 374b ; stretched out, 713b.
stricken, 772a.
strict, 139a, 639b.
stride, to, 149a, 184a, 345a, 373b, 375a, 376b, 559b, 593a, 652a, 666a, 813a, 814a.
stride over, 552b.
strider, 255b, 257a, 373b, 374a.
stridings, 324a, 559a.
strife, 18a, 286a, 315a, 459a, 577a, 639b, 642b, 744b.
strike, 64b, 76a, 140a, 185a, 280b, 282a, 285b, 295b, 320b, 336a, 338b, 369b, 387a, 397b, 439a, 452b, 453a, 459a, 467b, 468b, 540a, 573a, 614a, 617b, 625b, 626b, 627b, 685b, 702b, 715b, 734a, 751a, 772a b, 776a, 779a, 790b, 796b, 804a, 827a, 841a, 845a, 887b, 899b.
strike down, 894a.
strike harp, 468b, 881b.
strike the footsteps of, 412b.
strike a light, 685b.
strike the lyre, 614a, 836a.
strike up a tune, 758a.
striker, 385b.
striking, 468b.
string, 355a, 396b, 408a, 421b, 510a, 628a, 629b, 701b, 707a, 751a.
string a bow, 100a, 251b, 872b.
stringer of bows, 99a.
strip, 243a, 261b, 511a, 682b, 793b.
strip naked, 458a.
strip off, 696a.
strip of cloth or linen, 234b, 249a, 596b, 606a, 652b, 810a.
stripe, 159b, 489b, 614b, 685b, 698a, 734a.
striped, 4a, 117b, 346a, 837a, 855b.
stripling, 76b.
stripped, 176a.
strive, 366b, 467a.
striver, 286a, 744b.
stroke, 489a, 527a, 615a, 685b, 723b.
strong, 1a, 3a, 20a, 102a, 108a, 128b, 140b, 177b, 181a b, 190b, 193a, 208b, 216a, 342b, 347b, 356a, 375a, 382b, 388b, 389a b, 395b, 402a, 421b, 422a, 680b, 690b, 697a, 772a, 774b, 794b, 839a, 845a, 851a, 855a, 857a, 893b, 899b.
strong, to be, 378b, 615a, 690b, 698a, 718b, 772a, 839b, 851a, 899a.
strong, to make, 645b, 654a, 718b, 772a.
strong-arm, 389a.
strong building, 632b, 852a.
Strong-heart, 182a.
strong man, 389a, 690b, 704a, 772a.
strong one, 347b, 632b, 910a.
strong place, 706a, 718b, 840a.
strong-smelling, 279a, 729a, 740a ; objects, 17a.
strong sword, 389a.
strong thing, 851a.
strong-voice, 389a.
strong-willed, 173a, 608b, 678a.
stronghold, 55b, 297b.
strophe, 457a.
struggle, 241a, 280b, 531b, 563b, 679b, 704a, 734b.
Stu, god, 628b.
stubble, 528a, 765b, 838b.
stuck, 914b.
stud, 369a.
stud bull, 26b, 103b.
stud cattle, 27b, 100a.
stud cow, 27a.
stud farm, 740b, 830a.
studded, 164a, 424b.
study, to, 757b.
stuff, 49b, 113a, 164b, 230b, 236a, 294b, 300a, 305b, 321a, 328b, 372b, 377b, 395b, 407b, 408b, 411a, 435a, 440b, 532b, 536b, 547b, 579b, 618a, 624a, 641a, 724b, 726a, 765b, 840a, 857b, 879b, 895b, 896b, 897a, 904b, 911a.
stuff, green and yellow, 879b ; inlaid or embroidered, 439b.
stuff, piece of, 43b.
stuff, six-threaded, 643b.
stung, 838a.

stupefied, 131a, 593a.
stupid, 180a, 184b, 276b, 461a, 525a, 546a, 732b, 910b.
stupidity, 276b.
stutter, 799b.
style, 761b, 801b.
stylus (stilus), 519b, 915a.
styrax, 378a ; wood, 348b.
Suatcheb, 592a.
Suatchi, 649b.
Suatchit, 649b.
Suau gods, 649a.
subdue, 95b, 96c, 140b, 452b, 677b, 703b, 706b, 769a, 847b, 884a.
subject, 525a, 595a.
subject (serf), 411b, 579b, 824a.
subject, for discussion, 186a.
subjection, 411b.
subjects, men, 810a.
subjugate, 384a.
subjugation, 613a.
submerge, 213a, 442b, 443b, 509b, 602b, 642a, 671b, 681a, 820a, 897b.
submerged, 317b, 451a, 509b ; land, 317b.
submersion, 820a.
submissive, 49b.
submit, 441b, 531a, 797a.
subordinate, 321a, 580a, 603a, 673a.
subservient, 579b.
subside, 480b.
subsidize, 262a.
subsist, 542a, 717b.
subsistence, 433a ; means of, 580b.
substance, 201b, 230b, 233a, 545a, 561a, 621a, 703a.
substance, aromatic, 506b.
substance, sacrificial, 140a.
substance, strong-smelling, 27b, 473a.
substance, vegetable, 588b.
substitute, 846a.
substitution, 88b.
subterranean, 337a.
subtract, 122b, 538b.
subtraction, sign of, 240a.
succeed, 371a, 421b.
success, 283b, 371a.
successfully, 265a, 414b, 517b.
successor, 80b, 246b, 428a.
such and such, 297b.
suck out, 550b.
sucking-calf, 221a.
sucking-child, 284b.
suckle, 284b, 608b, 678a, 757b, 820b.
suckler, 757b.
suckling, 616b.
Sûdân, mines of, 210b.
Sûdânî man, 386a, 790b.
suddenly, 265b, 689a.
sue for mercy, 727a.
suet, 315a.
suffer, 27b, 296b, 314a, 373a, 413a, 533b, 650b, 671a, 772b.
suffer loss, 379b.
suffer pain, 131a ; patiently, 665a.
suffered, 140a.
sufferer, 379b, 580a, 604a b, 674b.
suffering, 296b, 650b.
suffice, 433b.
sufficiency, 696a.
sufficient, 433b.
suffocate, 873b.
suffocated, 400a, 763b, 800a.
Sugaṭi, 652b.
Suḥit, 593a.
Sui, god, 650a.
suicide, 295b.
suit of apparel, 476b.
suitable, 332b.
Sukhṭu, 652a.
sum, the, 274a.
sum total, 134a, 519b.
sum up, 683a.
summary, 430b, 683a b.
summation, 465b, 880b.
summer, 740a.
summer house, 92b, 106b, 238b, 571b, 707a, 753a.
summit, 433b.
summon, 136b.
sumptuous, 737a.
sun, 23a, 68a, 194a, 417b, 459b, 731b.
sun, disc of, 26b, 27a ; winged, 522a.
sun, the new-born, 664b.
sun, revolution of, 247a.
sun, rising, 118b, 543a.
sun, the spring, 491b, 541b.

sun, the summer, 418a.
sun, the winter, 418b.
sun and moon, 125b.
sun-egg, 398a
Sun-god, 24b, 418a, 685a, 731b ; stone of, 217a ; of night, 198a.
Sun-god, carcase of, 43a.
Sunḥat, 592b.
sunk, 442b.
sunrise, 138a, 159b, 207a, 224b.
sunrise, door of, 655a.
sunrise, land of, 205a.
sunrise, mount of, 47b, 869b.
sunrise, place of, 159b.
sunset, 110a, 138a, 185a, 478b.
sunset, mount of, 869b.
sunshine, 708b.
Sun-stone, 217b.
sun-temple, 596a, 687a.
Sunth, 592b, 651a.
Sunu, 650b.
superabundance, 458b.
superfluity, 179a, 458b.
superintend, 562a.
superintendent, 311b, 422a.
superior, 170b, 494a b, 562a.
supervise, 285a.
supervision, 80a.
supineness, 181b, 898b.
supper, 323b, 330a.
suppliant, 382b, 603a, 876a.
supplicate, 187a, 382b, 596a, 606a, 607a, 650b, 668b, 876a.
supplication, 382b, 607a, 658b, 670a, 711b, 876a.
supplied, 520a.
supply, 3b, 487a, 618a, 631b, 632a, 689a, 715a, 717b, 783b, 884b, 904a, 906b.
supply, daily, 161a.
support, 16b, 133a, 151a, 189b, 190a, 258b, 425a, 536a, 617a, 632b, 637a, 639a, 645a, 693a b, 815a, 821a, 823b, 844a, 861a, 872a.
support oneself, 429b.
supports, the Two, 16b ; the Four, 713b.
supporter, 258b, 366b, 823b.
suppose, 38a.
suppress, 57b, 140b, 452b, 535b, 571b, 787a.
suppression, 140b.
suppurate, 383a.
suppuration, 383a.
sure, 7b.
surely, 265a.
surplus, 469b.
surprise, 209b.
surround, 63a, 75a, 124a, 662b, 676b, 731a, 743b, 851a ; with walls, 60b.
surrounded, 246b.
survive, 189a.
Susek, 652b.
Sush Ḥerui, 593b.
suspend, 143b, 854a.
suspended, 135a.
sustainer, 645a.
sustenance, 286b, 612b, 783b, 884b, 908a.
Susu, 592a.
Sut,. 653a.
Sutekh, 627b, 653b.
Suter (Soter), 653b.
Suti, 653a.
suzerain, 97a.
swaddling band, 356b.
swallow, a bird, 217b.
swallow, to, 6a, 28b, 120b, 186a, 187a, 203b, 299b, 300a, 301b, 590b, 615a, 616a, 645a, 688b.
swallowers, 645a.
swallowing, 645a.
swamp, 3b, 103b, 104b, 244b, 307b, 334b, 526b, 533b, 561a, 571a, 621b.
swamp, papyrus, 14b, 100b.
swamp-dweller, 103b.
Swamp-god, 660a.
swamp-land, 27b, 102a.
swamps of Buto, 244b.
swamps of Eastern Egypt, 244b.
swathe, 61a, 188a, 758b.
swathed, 776a, 909b.
swathing, 37a, 71b, 103b, 188a, 203b, 301a, 635a.
swear, 757a ; an oath, 112a, 126a, 131a, 148a.
sweat, 262b, 263a, 820b, 843a ; break into a, 468b.
sweat, divine, 44a.
sweatings, 91b.
sweep away, 187b.
sweep out, 700b
sweet, 111b, 211a, 412a, 449a ; be, 211a, 218b.

sweet thing, 412a.
sweetheart, 310a.
sweetmeat, 440a ; maker of, 219a ; seller of, 356a.
sweet-mouthed, 218b.
sweetness, 211a, 217b, 219a, 412a, 473a.
sweet-smelling, 412a, 697a.
sweet-tongued, 218b.
swell, 222a, 225a, 473a, 533b, 711b, 726a, 738b ; of a boil or sore, 381a.
swell up, 423b.
swelling, 381a, 709a, 726a, 738b, 776b, 824a ; an inflamed, 11b ; in body, 222b ; of heart, 3a.
swift, 227a, 531b, 533a b, 563a, 727b, 764a, 827b.
Swift-foot (Rā), 563a.
swill, 350b.
swim, 354a, 366b, 374b ; to make, 606a.
swimmer, 366b ; in the Ṭuat, 354a.
swimming, 366b.
swindler, 641b.
swollen, 467b, 545a ; of the arms, 222a.
swoon, 480b.
swoop, to, 536b.
sword, 57b, 287a, 351a, 390a, 473a, 508a, 544a, 615a, 636b, 642b, 657a, 665a, 666a b, 667b, 812b, 878a; drawers of the, 848a.
sycamore, 32b, 347a, 355a ; heart of, 570a.
sycamore fig, 92b, 380a, 797b.
syce, 280b, 283a.
Syene, wine of, 72b.
symbol, 116a, 135b, 136a, 138a.
symbolize, 628b, 710a.
sympathize, 346b.
sympathy, 314a.
synodontis shall, 179a.
Syria, 435b, 436a ; hills of, 700a.
Syrian, 72b, 532b.
syrup of figs, 380a.

T.

Tȧ, 821b.
Ta, god, 816a.
Ta-Ȧabetch, 815b.
Ta-ȧakhu, 815b.
Ta-ȧakhut, 816a.
Ta-āa-t-pa-khent, 818b.
Ṭaȧnȧuna, 867a.
Ta-ānkhit, 865b.
Ta-ānkhtt, 816a.
Ta-ȧḥt, Oasis of, 115b.
Ta-Ȧpt (Thebes), 41b.
Taȧtt, 818a.
tabernacle, 475a.
table, 693b, 846b, 862b ; for offerings, 117a, 191b, 280a, 529a b.
table of holy offerings, 28b, 196a, 874b, 912b.
table-maker, 289b.
tableau, 266b.
tablet, 42a, 133b, 190b, 234b, 255b, 381a, 566a.
tablet for calculation, 511a.
tablet for offerings, 151a, 220b, 519b.
tablet for writing, 123a.
tablet, medicated, 550b, 572b.
tablet, memorial, 192b.
tablet of destiny, 326a.
tablet of incense, 209a.
tablet, round, 234a.
tablet, sacred, 226b.
tablet, wooden, 711b.
tackle, 64a b, 132a, 258a, 661a, 750b, 756b ; to work, 661a.
tackle, fishing, 579a.
tackle of boat, 9a, 244b, 334a, 596a.
tackle of sail, 370a.
tadpole, 480a.
Ta-en-maā-kheru, 816b.
Ta-en-Maāt, 816b.
Ṭafnut, 867b.
Ṭag, 867b.
Ta-ḥer-sta-nef, 816b.
Ta-ḥet-ānkh, 816b.
tail, 129b, 224b, 540b, 629b, 630b, 706b, 714a, 716b, 794a.
tail, festival of the, 475a, 628a, 714a, 716b.
tail in mouth, 706b.
tail of hair, 154b.
tail worn as ornament, 306a.
Ṭait, 865a.
Tait, Taitt, 819a.
Taiu Rekhti, 816a.

Ṫakamāit, 822b.
Ṫakȧ-taḥa-meru, 822b.
take, 752a, 757b, 849a.
take an affidavit, 131a.
take an oath, 126a.
take away, 552b, 756b.
take care ! 449b.
take care of, 586b.
take heed, 586b.
take in pledge, 32b.
take off clothes, 458a.
take out, 755a.
take over, 811b.
take to flight, 156b.
Ta-kharu, 816a.
Takmit, 822b.
tale, 632b, 719b.
talent, 796a.
talisman, 289b, 537b, 585b.
talk an alien speech, 910b.
talk, divine, 104b.
talk over, 145b, 410b, 613a.
talk someone over, 650b.
talk, to, 335a, 549a.
talk too much, 389b, 416a.
talkers, 648a.
tallies, 511a.
tally, 345a, 902b.
tally sticks, 129b.
talon, 20a, 123b, 128b, 215b, 218a, 722a, 840b.
tamarisk, 25b, 90a, 374b, 563b.
tambourine, 610b, 680a, 771b, 827b, 875b.
tambourine, to beat or play, 42b, 381b.
tambourine woman, 371b, 680b, 838b, 887b.
tame, to, 764b.
Ta-mer, 46a.
Ta-merȧu, 815b.
Ta-mer-tchet, 816b.
Ṭamṭ, 867b.
Ṫanasasa, 822a.
Ta-neb-ta-ur, 819b.
Ta-nefer, 816b.
Tanen, 255a, 819b.
Tanent, 819b.
Ta-Neter, 403a, 816a.
Tanett-em-khenu-ȧa, 820a.
tank, 78b, 569a, 592b, 650b, 720a, 724b, 733b, 758a.
tank for libations, 307b.
Ṭa-nubit, 866a.
tape, measuring, 527a.
Ta-qebb, 816b.
Tar, in Arabia, 205b, 820a.
Tarȧush, 820a.
Ta-re, 817b.
Ṫargannasa, 822a.
target, 475b.
Ṫarimāus, 822a.
Tariush, 820a.
tarry, 195b, 377b, 653b, 685b.
Ṫarsha, 822a.
Ṭarṭeniu, 867b.
Tar Tiseb, 820a.
Tarush, 820a.
Tasakhrit, 820b.
Ta-Sekri, 816b.
Ta-sent-nefert, 820b.
Ta-shemā, 816a.
Ta-shet, 816b.
task, daily, 66b.
taskmasters, 901a.
Ṭasmabaerkhat, 866b.
tassel, 278b.
taste, 102b, 783b, 832a, 876b, 877a b.
Tat, 818a.
Ṫat, 821b.
Tāt, the, 822b.
Ṭat (Ṭuat), 865a.
Ta-tanen, the Four forms of, 542b.
Taṭar, 823a.
Taṭara, 821a.
Ta-tcheser, 817a.
Ta-tchet, 817a.
Ta-tebu, 816b.
Ṭaṭemtch, 868a.
Tatenen, 821a.
Tatenent, 868a.
Ta-ṭeser, 816b.
Tathenen, 821a.
Tathunen, 821a.
Tatiu, 816a.
Ṭatiu, 865a.
Ṫat-sheta, 821b.
Tatt, 821a.
Ta-Ṭuat, 816b.
Tatuinen, 821a.
Tatunen, 821a.
Tau, god, 819a.
Ta-uāb, 816b.
Taui Ager, 816a.

Ta-ur, 816b.
Tau-reṭ, 818a.
Taurit, 819b.
tavern, 32a, 651a.
tax, New Year's, 521a.
tax, perpetual, 521b.
tax, taxes, 41a, 42b, 206b, 248a, 338a, 446b, 510b, 511a, 516b, 521a, 521b, 580b, 655b, 722b, 729a, 838a, 882b ; to levy, 521a.
tax-gatherers, 287b.
tax-payers, 206b, 838a.
Tchā, 902b.
Tcha-agru, 894a.
Tchaȧsu, the Seven, 896a.
Tcha-ati, 894a.
Tchaȧui, 894b.
Tcha-bennu-Åsȧr, 895a.
Tchābu gods, 902b.
Tchahar, 900a.
Tchai, 895b.
Tchamaā, 898a.
Tchāmtiu, 903a.
Tchāmuti, 903a.
Tchan, Lake of, 897a.
Tchant, 898b.
Tchanti, god, 897a.
Tchanu, the Four, 898b.
Tchapr, 897b.
Tchart, 899b.
Tchārukha, 903b.
Tchau-ȧb, 893b.
Tcha-unnut, 895a.
Tchat, 895a.
Tchatchaui, 831b.
Tchaṭiu, 900b.
Tchātt, 903b.
Tchat Ṭuat, 895a, 900b.
Tcheb, 905a.
Tcheba, 815b.
Tchebā, 905b, 906a.
Tchebatiu, 973b.
Tcheb-ḥer, 876a.
Tcheb-neter, 905b.
Tchebti, 904b.
Tchef, 906b.
Tchefit, 906b.
Tcheḥer, 911b.
Tcheḥes, 911b.
Tcheḥtcheḥ, 911a.
Tcheḥuti, 886a, 911a.
Tchemtch-ḥātu, 907a.
Tchenerti, 907b.
Tchennutt, 907b.
Tchentchen, 908a.
Tchenti, 908a.
Tchenṭru, 908a.
Tchenṭtchenṭes, 908a.
Tcherȧ, 910a.
Tcher-ȧakhu, 909b.
Tcherȧt, 909a, 910a.
Tcher-ȧtf, 909b.
Tcherit-pet, 909b.
Tcherti, 909b.
Tcherut, 909b.
Tchesef, 911b.
Tcheser-ā, 912b.
Tcheserȧ-ȧru, 912b.
Tcheser-em-per-f, 912b.
Tcheserit, a goddess, 912b.
Tcheserit, Eye of Horus, 912b.
Tcheserit-hent, 912b.
Tcheser-seshetait, 912b.
Tchesert, 912b.
Tcheser-tcheseru, 912a.
Tcheser-tep, 912b.
Tcheser-tep-f, 913a.
Tcheser-ṭeṭȧ, 913a.
Tchesertt, 912b.
Tcheseru, 912b.
Tcheses, 911b.
Tchesrit, 912b.
Tchet (Eternity), 893a.
Tcheṭ, Ka of Rā, 914a.
Tcheṭ, pillar, 914a.
Tchefȧt, 914a.
Tcheṭbi, 914b.
Tchetchi, 914a.
Tcheṭ-ḥeft, 914a.
Tcheṭit, 914a.
Tcheṭit-tent, 914a.
Tcheṭmit, 915a.
Tcheṭ-pa-neter-ȧuf-ānkh, 914b.
Tchet-s, 913a.
Tcheṭ-t Boat, 915a.
Tcheṭṭi, 914a.
Tcheṭu, 914a.
Tcheṭun, 914b.
Tcheṭut, 914a.
Tchit, 893a.
Tchuā, 904a.
Tchun, 904a.
teach, 655a, 587b.
teacher, 222a, 655b.
teaching, 655a b.

tear out, 263a, 906a.
tear the hair, 94b, 469b, 606b.
tear, to, 220b, 255b, 606a, 755a.
tear up, 517a.
tearer, a bird, 220a, 247b.
tears, 293b, 419b, 424a, 428b.
tears of gum, 541b.
tears of Isis, 459b, 811a.
tease, 768a.
teat, 768a.
Teb, 827b.
Tebȧ, 827b.
Ṭeba, 874b.
Ṭebai, Ṭebait, 874b.
Ṭeba-temt, 874b.
Ṭebati, 874b.
Ṭebatiu, 873b.
Ṭebat-neteru-s, 874b.
Tebeḥ, the Seven, 828a.
Ṭeben-pekhar-meḥ-nebu, 875b.
Ṭeben-semu-taui, 875b.
Ṭeben-ur, 875b.
Tebha, 828a.
Ṭebha, 875b.
Ṭeb-ḥer, 876a.
Ṭeb-ḥerk, 876a.
Ṭeb-ḥer-kehaat, 876b.
Ṭebḥes, 876b.
Ṭebi, 875a.
Ṭeb-mesthumut, 875a.
Tebsu, 828a.
Tebteb, 827a.
Ṭebu, 875a.
teeth, 39b, 320a, 536b, 861b.
Tefen, 833b, 877b.
Ṭef-mat-er-nenu-f, 877b.
Tefnit, goddess and form of Rā, 833b.
Tefnut, 460a, 790a, 833b.
Tefnut, vagina of, 785b.
Tefnut, womb of, 834b.
Teftef-Nu, 833a.
Tefu, gods, 832b.
Ṭegas, 891b.
Teḥent, 842a.
Teḥentiu, 842a.
Ṭeḥi (Thoth), 886a.
Tehni Ȧmentt, 885b.
Ṭeḥṭeḥ, 885b.
Ṭeḥuti (Thoth) 886a ; forms of, 886b.
Ṭeḥuti-Ḥāpi, 886b.
Ṭeḥuti-ḥeri-khenṭ-f, 886b.
Ṭeḥuti-khenti, 886b.
Ṭeḥuti-sa-Ȧner, 886b.
Ṭeḥuti-seḥetep-nesrit, 887a.
Tekaharsa- etc., 845b.
Teka-ḥer, 845b.
Ṭekait, 890b.
Tekait, Fire-goddess, 845b.
Tekait, wife of Maa-ḥes, 845b.
Tekem, 846a.
Teken-en-Rā, 846a.
Tekhi, 40b, 842b.
Tekhit, 842b.
Tekhtekh (Āapep), 844a.
Tekneru, 846b.
Ṭekṭek, 891a.
Telemachus, 822a, 825a.
tell a dream or story, 176b.
tell out, 782b.
tell, to, 719b, 745a, 913a.
teller, 176b.
Tem, Temu, 834a b ; of Ȧnu, 36b.
Temu, the Eight Children of, 323a.
Temu, the Four Bulls of, 151b, 159a, 859a.
Tem, a Dekan, 834b.
Tema, 836a.
Tema-ḥert, 836b.
Temam, 836a b.
Ṭemamm, 879a.
Temamti, 836a.
Tem-Ȧsȧr, 834b.
Ṭemathth, 879a.
Tematheth, 48b.
Temati, 834b.
Ṭemat-stit, 878b.
Ṭemau, 878b.
Temeḥtt, 515b.
Tem-Ḥeru-ȧakhuti, 834b.
Temḥit, 837a.
Temḥu, 837a.
Temit, 834b.
Temit-mut-set, 880a.
Tem-Kheperȧ, 834b.
Tem-Kheprer, 834b.
Tem-pesiu, 835a.
tempest, 96a, 395a, 549b, 571a b, 573b, 607a, 722b, 746a b, 775b, 903b.
temple, 32a, 72b, 106a, 193b, 238b, 269a, 402a b, 423a b, 440a, 444a, 453a, 455b, 570b.
temple estate, 423a.

temple of hundreds of thousands of years, 455b.
temple of the head, 273a, 600b, 667b.
temple, property of, 269a.
temple, service book of, 403a.
Tem-Rā, 834b.
Tem-sa-ȧru, 835a.
Tem-sep, 835a.
Tems-Khentt, 837a.
Tem-Ṭeḥuti, 835a.
Ṭem-ṭesi, 878a.
Ṭemṭ-ḥā-t, 880a.
Ṭemṭit, 880a.
Ṭemṭiu, 880a.
Ṭemṭu, 880a.
Temu-sma-khebit, 835a.
Ṭemur, 878a.
Ṭen, king, 598b.
ten, 331a.
Ten Chiefs, 171b, 331a.
Ten, the House of the, 331a.
ten thousand, 905b.
ten-day period, 829a.
Ṭenȧ, 881b.
Tenait, 838a.
tenants, 838a.
Ṭenānu, 882a.
Ṭenȧs, 882a.
tend, 351b.
tend (trees), 833a.
tendril, 202a, 443a.
Ṭenem, 882b.
Ṭenemi, 883a.
Tenemi, Tenenit, 839a.
Tenen, 255a.
Ṭenḥ-uā, 883a.
Ṭeni (Rā), 882a.
Ṭenit, 881a.
Tenn, 838a.
Ṭenn, 881a.
Tennit, 838a.
Tennit-Ȧnit, 838a.
Tennu, 838a b.
tenons, 112a.
Ṭenpu, 882b.
Ṭens-Sma-keku, 883b.
Ṭenṭ, 884a.
tent, 21a 22a, 50a, 114a, 120a, 576a ; of camel's hair, 22a, 74b.
tent pole, 179b.
Ṭent-baiu, 881a, 884a.
Ṭentchen, 884a.
Tenṭen, 839b.
Ṭenṭen, 881a.
Ṭenten, 883b.
Ṭenṭenȧ, 881a.
Ṭenṭenit serpent, 881a.
Ṭenṭenit-uḥesq- etc., 881b.
tenth, 331a.
Ṭenti, 883b.
Tep, a lake, 828a.
Ṭepait, 877a.
Ṭepan, 877a.
Tepḥitnebs, 832b.
Tepḥit-shetait, 832b.
Tepḥit-tchet, 832b.
Tepḥut-Ḥāp, 832b.
Ṭepi, 877a.
Ṭepi, 40a.
Tepi, Tepit, 831b.
Tepi-ā-Ȧakhu, 830b.
Tepi-ā-baiu, 830a.
Tepi-ānkhiu, 829b.
Tepi-ȧtru, 829b.
Tepi-āui-Kenmet, 831a.
Tepi-āui-khent, 831a.
Tepi-āui-qerr-en-pet, 831a.
Tepi-āui-Sepṭit, 831a.
Tepi-āui-Smeṭ, 831a.
Tepi-ḥet, 830a.
Tepi-khu-f, 831b.
Tepi-sekht-f, 831b.
Ṭepit, goddess of Ṭep, 877a.
Tepit-besses, 831b.
Tepi-thrȧ, 831b.
Tepit-netchemu-seth, 831b.
Tepi-ṭu-f, 828b.
Tepi-ṭus, 829a.
Tepiu-āui Akhabiu, 830b.
Tepiu-āui-Ȧnsebu, 830b.
Tepiu-āui-Geb, 831a.
Tepiu-āui-Rā, 830b.
Tepiu-āui-renp-t, 831a.
Tepiu-shetau, 831b.
Tepṭ, god, 832b.
Ṭep-ta, 877a.
Teptiu, 832b.
Tepu, Grain-god, 831b.
Tepui, 831b.
Tepui-sa-then, 831b.
Ṭepu-neteru, 877a.
Teqer, a Libyan dog, 845a.
Teqq, a god, 890b.
terebinth, 129b.

Ṭeri, 884b.
Ṭeri-Kheftiu, 884b.
Ṭerit-neshnut, 884a.
Ṭeriush, 884b.
term, an astronomical, 12a.
term of Osiris, 88a, 192a.
Termuthis, 403b.
terrace, 559b, 724a, 805a, 885a.
terrace for myrrh trees, 567a.
terraces of Lebanon, 537a.
terrestrial beings and things, 579b.
terrible, 108a, 499a, 541a, 887b, 889b.
terrified, 352b, 380a, 640a, 651b.
Terrifier (Set), 393b.
terrify, 66b, 378b, 395a, 499a, 577a, 619a, 668b, 693b, 697a, 712b, 866b, 889b.
terrifying, 499a.
territory, 1a, 97b, 247a, 409a, 457b, 574a, 649a.
terror, 4a, 108a, 172a, 395a, 445a, 490a, 499b, 589a b, 640a, 710b, 887a.
terror-stricken, 322a, 678b.
Ṭert, 884a.
Ṭerṭeniu, 885a.
Tertiu, 841a.
Ṭer-ṭu, 884b.
Ṭeru, 884b.
Ṭes, Lake of, 888a.
Ṭes-àakhu, 888a.
Ṭes-āḥā-ser-Tathenen, 888a.
Ṭes-ākhem-baiu, 888a.
Ṭes-am-uriti- etc., 888a.
Ṭes-em-ḥer-f, 888b.
Ṭeser-ā, 889a.
Ṭeser-àabt, 888b.
Ṭeser-àri, 889a.
Ṭesert-ànt, 889a.
Ṭesert-baiu, gate and district, 888b.
Ṭesert-tep, 889a.
Ṭesh, god, 844b.
Ṭesh, god, 889a.
Ṭesher, 890a.
Ṭesher-àrui, 890a.
Ṭesher-mestcher, 890a.
Ṭeshert, 889b.
Ṭeshesh, 889a.
Ṭeshrit, 890a.
Ṭeshrut, 889b.
Ṭesht, 889b.
Teshtesh, 755a, 844b, 889a.
Ṭeshṭesh, 889a.
Ṭes-hut, 889b.
Ṭesi-ruṭu-en-neter, 888a.
Ṭes-khaibitut-ṭuatiu, 888b.
Ṭes-neb-terer, 888b.
Ṭes-Rā-kheftiu-f, 888b.
Ṭes-sekhem-àru, 888b.
Ṭes-sepṭ-nesut, 888b.
Ṭes-sheta-theḥen-neteru, 888b.
Ṭes-sma-keku, 888b.
test, 642b, 643b, 902b, 903b ; a bow, 647a.
testament, 45a, 192a.
Ṭest-baiu, 888a.
Ṭest-ermen-ta, 888b.
testicle, 9b, 88b, 117b, 217a, 269a, 291a, 481b, 484a, 580a, 599b, 651b.
testifier, 332b.
testimony, 332b ; false, 334a.
testing, a, 754a.
Ṭesu-em-àrit-f, 888b.
Ṭesu-em-nes-f, 888b.
Ṭeṭ, 892a ; to set up the, 591b, 646b.
Tetà, 847b.
Tetàān, 847b.
Ṭet Àmen, 864a.
Ṭet-ent-Àst, 864a.
tether, 300b.
Tetti-àb, 847a.
Ṭeṭu, Council of, 902a.
Ṭeṭun, 472a, 892b.
Thabu, 850b.
Thakar-Bāra, 852a.
Thakaretha, 852a.
Thakaru, 852a.
Thakasa, 208b.
Thamaā, 850b.
Thamākana, 851a.
Tha-nefer, 848b.
thank—to thank God, 871a.
thanks, to give, 710a.
thanksgiving, 408a, 871a.
Thàref, 852b.
that, 231b, 235b, 370a, 853a ; that is to say, 79b ; that which, 15a, 399a.
Thàt, 852b.
Thathait, 852a.
Thatmār, 850a.

Thauathasa, 850a.
Thau-uru, 848b.
the, 864b.
Theba, 854a.
Thebeh, 854a.
Thebes, 41b ; god of, 898a ; nursing mother of, 41b ; personified, 149a.
Thebti, 854a.
thee, 306b, 396b, 398b, 408a, 409a b, 782a, 815a, 824b, 848a, 862b.
Thefnut, 854b.
theft, 115a, 467b, 849b, 895a.
Theḥbith, 858b.
Theḥen, 858b.
Theḥen-àtebu, 859a.
Theḥḥut, 858b.
Theḥnit-tepà-khat, 859a.
their, 144a, 164a, 229b, 253b, 342a b, 603a, 673b, 818b.
Thekem, 862b.
them, 144a, 164a, 339a, 349a, 408a, 603a, 673b, 706b.
Thema, 855a.
Thema-re, 855a.
Themà-taui, 855a.
Themath, 855a.
Themat-ḥert, 855a.
Themat-Khert, 855a.
Themeḥ, 855a.
Themes-en-khentt, 855b.
Themmit, 855a.
themselves, 911b.
then, 79a, 229b, 408a, 704b, 705b.
Thenà, 856b.
Thenàru, 856a.
Thenem, 857a.
Thenemi, 857a.
Thenen, 856a.
Then-neteru, 856a.
Thennit, 856a.
Thennui, 856b.
Then-set, 856a.
Thenther-neteru, 857b.
Thenti, 857b.
Thenut, 856b.
Thepḥt-shetat, 854b.
Thepḥut-petriu, 854b.
there, 868a.
thereafter, 494b.
thereby, 348a.
therefore, 492b.
therewith, 264b.
Therit, 857b.
Thertà, 858a.
Therut, 858a.
Thes-ām, 859b.
Thes-ārq, 860a.
Thesbu, 862a.
these, 42b, 342a b, 349a, 354b, 832b.
these two, 42b, 43a, 349a.
Thes-ḥeru, 860a.
Thesi-en-khentt, 859a.
Thesi-khā-neteru, 861b.
Thesi-tchatcha, 861b.
Thesi-tchatchau-neteru, 861b.
Thesi-Ṭeshert, 860a.
Thesu, the Seven, 859b.
Thesupt, 860a.
Thes-ur, 861b.
Thes-usfu, 860a.
Thesu-urut, 861a.
Theth-meteru, 852b.
Thethu, 863b.
Thett, 862b.
they, 144a, 164a, 349a, 408a, 592a, 603a, 633b, 706b.
thick, 164a.
thicket, 89a, 202a, 209a, 636a.
thickness, 164a.
thief, 115a, 437b, 464b, 674b, 683b, 849b.
thieve, 437b.
thigh, 120a, 156b, 275b, 298b, 326a, 328a, 329a, 544b, 594b, 597b, 659b, 736b.
thighs, the two, 8a, 147a, 244a, 275b, 298b, 559a b.
thine, 229b, 252b, 818b.
thing, 8b, 77a, 91b, 164b, 170a, 179b, 335a, 395b, 396b, 398a, 487a, 525a, 721b, 789b.
things, good, 635a ; pleasant, 20b.
Things, Lord of, 24a.
things of earth, 525a.
things of Horus, 525b.
things of Osiris, 525b.
things on altar, 525b.
things proved, 544b.
things seen, 266b.
things, strange, 541b.
things washed away, 28a.
think, 38a, 42b, 145b, 274a, 396a, 398a, 548a, 614b, 688a.
think out, 614b, 688a, 782b.

third time, 548b.
thirst, 38a, 642a.
thirsty, 4b, 38a, 898a.
thirsty man, 38a.
thirty, 281a.
Thirty-Judges, Court of, 281a.
this, 42b, 229a, 236a, 253b, 342b, 349a, 352b, 354b, 815a, 818a, 824b, 832b, 837b, 856a, 880b.
this and that, 370a.
This (Abydos), 57a.
thong, 532b, 790b ; of whip, 421b.
thorn, 680a, 765b, 844a.
thorn bush, 714b.
thorn growth, 89a.
thorn plant, 637b.
those, 70a, 229b, 348b.
those who are, 342a, 400b, 541a.
Thoth, 3a, 15a, 29b, 37b, 41a, 107a, 108a, 113b, 116a, 189b, 361a, 619b, 629a, 672a, 704a, 742b, 817b, 886a, 911a.
Thoth, ape-god of, 2a.
Thoth, bringer of the Eye, 886b.
Thoth, Company of, 91a, 548a.
Thoth, Eight Ape-gods of, 25b.
Thoth, festival of, 451a, 886b, 887a.
Thoth, form of, 76b.
Thoth, incarnation of, 91a.
Thoth, magical form of, 22b.
Thoth the Great, 886b ; the Twice Great, 886b.
Thoth, the holy, 887a.
Thoth the magician, 886b.
Thoth, titles of, 886a ; title of priest of, 161b.
Thoth, wife of, 81b.
Thoth, words of, 335b.
thou, 94a, 279a, 306b, 396b, 398b, 408a, 409a b, 782a, 815a, 826a, 848a, 852b, 862b.
Thoueris goddesses, the Twelve, 42a.
though, 786a.
thought, 37b, 45b, 241a, 319a, 351b, 398a, 779b, 782b, 798b, 801a.
thousand, 526a.
thread, 254b, 351a, 377b, 399b, 408a, 510a, 596b, 628a, 707a, 859b.
threads of flax, 234b.
threaten, 394a.
threatenings, 499b.
threats, 499b.
three, 548b.
three ply, 548b.
thresh, 468b, 772a.
threshing floor, 907a.
threshold, 585b, 819a.
thrive, 150a, 421b, 596b.
throat, 77a, 112b, 137a, 212b, 468a, 492a, 515b, 517a, 521b, 536a, 563a, 572a, 573b, 728b, 735a, 754b, 768a.
throne, 1a, 79b, 88b, 89a, 90b, 190a, 220b, 228a, 390a, 393b, 408b, 474a, 485a, 558a, 559b, 583b, 612a, 650b, 681b, 704b, 706b, 737a, 773a, 805a, 806b, 839b, 851a, 852a, 855a, 857a b, 884a, 896a, 898b, 900b, 902a b, 908a.
throne, directors of, 562a.
throne, double, 221a, 850a ; the two thrones, 390a.
throne, royal, 80a.
throne, scribe of the, 855a.
throne, the divine, 70a.
Throne, the Great, of Osiris, 567a.
throne attendant, 70a.
throne-bearers, 773a.
throne-chamber, 681b, 806b, 857a, 896a, 900b, 902a.
Throne of the Two Lands, 390a.
throne on a boat, 857b.
throne pavilion, 839b.
throne room, 392a, 600a, 857b, 908a.
thronged, 241a.
through, 279b, 492b, 493a.
through which, 348a.
throughout, 2b, 856a.
throw, 190a, 470a b, 528a, 770a, 796b.
throw away, 157b.
throw down, 247b, 256b, 560b, 617b, 618a, 799b.
throw open, 604a.
throw up the arms, 898a.
throw-stick, 800b.
thrust, to, 190a, 889a.
thrust aside, 247b, 468b.
thrust away, 689b.
thrust forward, 592a, 885a.

thrust together, 236a.
thrust with horns, 445b, 766a ; with phallus, 387a.
Thruster (Rā), 159b.
Th-senȧt-nefer, 862a.
thunder, 66b, 335a, 447a, 560a b, 714b.
thunderstorm, 246a, 395a, 573b, 775b.
thurifer, 849a.
Thuthu, 853b.
thwart, 845a.
thy, 229b, 234a b, 252b, 342b, 396b, 782a, 818b.
thyself, 911b.
tiara, 279a, 323b, 376a, 528a, 579b, 625a, 683a, 693b, 701b, 776a, 855a, 876b.
tie, 1b, 20a, 64a, 72a, 82b, 91a, 99a, 113b, 120a, 124a, 131b, 156a, 203b, 219b, 228a, 282a b, 285b, 291a, 305a, 313b, 336b, 351a, 355a, 399b, 409a, 421b, 479a, 486b, 490a, 535a, 593b, 606a, 607b, 645a, 633a, 676a b, 695a, 701a, 745a, 750a, 765a, 766a, 769a, 774a, 778a, 801b, 813b, 840b, 859b, 863a, 878a, 852b, 883a, 912a, 915b.
tie of the Green Crown, 735b.
tie the hair, 368b.
tie together, 313b, 745a, 878b.
tie up, 58a, 131b, 146b, 188a, 561b, 745a, 909b ; a boat, 300b ; in linen, 758b ; tie up to, 854a.
tied, 253a, 304b, 334b, 491a, 776a, 899a ; tied up, 759a.
Ṭifnut, 867b, 868b.
tight, 782b.
tightness of chest, 805b.
tilapia Nilotica, 58b.
tile, 42a, 188b, 819b, 874a.
tile-kiln, 118b.
till the ground, 132a, 302a.
tillage, 75a, 704b.
timber, timbers, 79b, 89a, 164a, 249a, 566a, 851a.
timber, dressed, 11a.
time, 14a, 100a, 101b, 133b, 163a, 167a, 351a, 434a, 438b, 440b, 444b, 588b, 595a, 696a, 778a, 815a, 821a, 840a b, 857b, 884b.
time, ancestral, 778a.
time, a stated, 880b.
time, beginning of, 231a.
time, course of, 247a.
time, endless, 744a.
time, masters of, 581a.
time of judgment, 596a.
time, of old, 205a, 909a.
time, portion of, 12b.
time, period of, 648b.
time, primeval, 230b, 596a, 830a.
times, the two, 840b.
Time-divider (Thoth), 704a.
Time, god of, 125b, 383b.
Time-gods, 377b.
timid, 252b, 461a, 472b, 479b, 514b, 534b, 575a, 678b, 746b, 905b.
timid man, 609b, 679a.
timidity, 574a, 678a, 798b.
tincture, 128b.
tinder, 618b, 696b.
tip, 433b, 554b, 828a ; of horn, 766b ; of nose, 105b ; of wing, 128b.
tippler, 651a.
tired, 10b, 207b, 225b, 260b, 262b, 377a, 533b, 534b, 802a b.
tiredness, 574a.
tiring woman, 712b.
Tirku, 823a.
tissue, 806b.
Ṭitenent, 868a.
Ṭith, 868b.
Ṭiṭi, 868b.
Titiu, 822b.
title, 384b, 387b, 535a, 757b.
title, official, 315a, 387b.
title of honour, 235b, 387b.
title of priest, 318a, 513a.
title, priestly, 193a, 202b, 262a.
title, to bestow, 877b.
title-deeds, 45a, 345b, 619a, 638a.
Tiṭur, 823a.
Ṭius, 868a.
to, 56a, 65a, 339a, 414a, 590a ; to the back of, 633b ; to wit, 79a.
toad, 118a.
toast, 138b ; offering, 817a.
to-day, 232a, 438b, 450a ; god of, 870b.

toenail, 112b, 523b.
together, 214a, 822b.
together with, 116b, 264a, 277a, 279b, 472b, 486a.
toil, 158a, 206a, 232b, 439a, 784a.
toiler, 440b.
toilet case, 812b.
toilette, to make the, 169b.
tolerant, 180b.
toll-house, 239b.
tomb, 1b, 11a, 15b, 25a, 28a, 35a, 39b, 79b, 80a b, 81b, 113b, 125a, 134a, 140b, 143b, 156a, 183a, 192b, 201a, 217b, 239a, 278a, 285a, 319a, 402b, 453a, 457a, 465a, 498b, 507b, 561b, 587a, 706a, 756a, 874b, 900b, 914a ; gods of the, 15b.
tomb, perpetual, 81b.
tomb, pit or shaft of, 8a.
tomb priest, 44b.
Tombos, 45a.
to-morrow, 381a, 432b ; morning, 225a.
tongue, 97b, 389b, 432b, 751b, 803a.
tongue of a bell, 304b.
tongue of the scales, 842b.
tongue of the sea, 390a.
tongue, perfection of, 626a.
tool, 163b, 180b, 223a, 228b, 292a b, 300a, 304b, 333a, 338b, 345b, 352b, 354b, 419a, 469a, 480a, 483b, 487a, 528b, 535a, 613a, 673b, 710a, 715a, 726a, 728b, 739b, 747a, 789b, 791b, 810a, 845a, 876a, 907a b, 914b.
tool, brickmaking, 56b.
tool, cutting, 13b, 205b, 351a, 387a, 894a.
tool, digging, 95a, 202b.
tool, farming, 710a.
tool, goldworkers', 336a.
tool, graving, 519b.
tool, tillage, 488b.
tool, wooden, 531b.
tool bag, 528b.
tool case, 2a.
tooth, 5a, 39b, 210b, 386b, 413a, 552b, 723b, 789a.
top, 266a, 433b, 828a.
top of head, 163a, 907a.
top of hill, 105b.
top of mast, 828a.
tops of plants, 244b.
toper, 593a, 657a.
topsy-turvy, 604b, 844a.
torch, 276a, 823a, 845b.
torches, the four holy, 845b.
torment, 101a.
torn, 589b.
torrent, 95a, 611b, 637b.
tortoise, 119b, 755a.
Tortoise, body of the, 767a.
Tortoise, Constellation of, 755a, 758b.
tortoise-shell, 233a.
torture, 373b ; instrument of, 715a.
torture chamber, 173b, 538b.
torture ground, 772b.
total, 134a, 274a, 510b, 794b, 880a b.
totality, 2b, 779b.
totter, 487b.
tottering, 152b.
touch, 527a, 808a, 858b, 879a, 891a, 892a, 900a ; to examine a patient by touch, 527a.
touch the earth, 841b.
tow, to, 93b, 100a, 184a, 444a, 625b, 629b, 707b, 713a.
tow-line, 372b.
tow-rope, 139a, 244b, 461b.
towards, 65a, 265a, 414a b, 560a, 633b.
towers of boat, 629b, 707b, 713a.
tower (citadel), 164a, 289b, 290a, 330b, 338b, 705b, 852a, 862a ; of a pylon, 221b.
town, 137b, 206b, 350b, 453b, 764b, 780a, 836b, 868b, 879b.
town, fortified, 221b.
Town-god, 350b, 404a.
town-guard, 292a.
townsfolk, 350b.
townsman, 350b, 836b, 879b.
trace, 355a, 694a.
trace (plans), 610b.
traces of chariot, 287b.
trace of something, 596a.
tract of land, 256b.
trade, 650b, 733a ; a man's, 483a.

tradesman, 718a, 739a.
trafficker, 733a.
train, a, 742b.
train, to, 655a, 757b.
trained, 613a, 622a, 682b ; of mind, 483b.
trained workman, 430a.
training, 655a b.
tramp, 380b.
tramp the earth, 884a.
trample, 253a, 443a, 445b, 868a.
trample upon, 452b, 725a, 821a.
tramplings, 118b.
Tranquilliser, the, 706b.
transcript, 604b, 675b ; to make a, 675b.
transfer, 100b, 324a, 538b, 644b, 803a ; a house, 685a.
transform, 66b, 842a.
transformations, 21a, 30a, 108a, 530b, 542b.
transgress, 153a, 841a, 851b, 858a, 877a.
transgressions, 143b, 396b, 397a.
transgressor, 165b, 841a.
transit, 617a.
translate, 803a.
transmit, 440b.
transmittal, 649b.
transport, 28a, 71b, 495a, 576b, 649b, 713a, 757b, 894b ; the dead, 599a ; by boat, 704a.
transport man, 703a.
transportation, 576b.
trap, 40a, 246a, 539a ; for game, 446a.
trappings, 282a, 285b, 422a, 536b.
travel, 32a, 55a, 65b, 83a, 90a, 92a, 107a, 114b, 118b, 169b, 192b, 288b, 289b, 324a, 346a, 373b, 442b, 446b, 478a, 487b, 541a, 559a b, 593b, 615a, 625b, 653a, 659b, 713a, 723a, 728a, 734a, 739a, 741a, 891b, 894b.
travel by boat, 374a, 703a.
travel by sea, 439a.
travel over, 552b.
travel through, 37a.
traveller, 1b, 122a, 144a b, 289b, 420a, 478b, 495a, 552b, 653a, 659b, 728a, 739a ; a benighted, 529b.
Traveller (Khensu), 553a.
Traveller (Rā), 541b.
traverse, 42a, 245b, 246a, 445a b, 552b, 559a, 593b, 726b.
traverser, 594a.
tray, 838b.
tread, 292b, 756b, 891b ; grapes, 468b ; in the footsteps of someone, 891b.
tread out, 480b, 757b.
treading, 728a.
treasure, 417a, 568b, 618a, 722b, 737a.
treasure house, 239b, 284b.
treasurer, 568b, 906a.
treasury, 130a, 239b, 312a.
treat kindly, 20b.
treat lightly, 28a.
treat with contempt, 564b.
treaty, 568b.
tree, 13b, 20a, 32b, 75b, 79a, 124a, 129b, 189a, 207a, 221b, 274a, 283a, 305b, 372b, 442a, 566a, 600b, 615b, 677a, 734a, 735b, 736b, 745b, 776b, 806b, 852a, 856a, 874a, 906b, 907b.
tree, balsam, 566b.
tree, sacred, 39b, 90a, 496a, 836a.
tree, spice, 566b.
Tree of Life, 20b.
Tree-goddess, 276b.
Tree-trunk, sacred, 914a.
tremble, 10a, 90b, 91a, 143b, 167a, 343a, 352b, 356b, 393b, 487b, 589b, 628a, 631a, 640a, 714b, 864b, 906b ; make to, 104a.
tremblers, 195a.
trembling, 510b, 589a, 716a, 864b, 906b.
trepidation, 471a.
trespass, 595b, 841a, 853a.
tress, 7a, 21b, 280b, 343a, 367b, 368a, 491a, 594a, 600b, 621b, 634b, 656b, 802b, 808b.
tresses, pair of, 879a.
trial, 444b, 595a, 643b.
triangle, 664b ; base of a, 831a.
tribe, 284a, 316a, 320a, 725b.
tribes, desert, 495b.
tribesman, 284a.
tribulation, 898b.

tribunal, 80b, 774a, 818a.
tribune, 225a.
tribute, 42b, 56b, 204b, 206b, 283b, 286b, 487a, 521a and b, 562b, 865a, 907b.
tribute, annual, 521b.
tribute, to levy, 521a.
tribute, pay, 206a.
trickster, 641b.
trident, 548b.
triple, 548b.
triturate, 844b.
triumph, 474a.
Troglodytes, 59b.
troop, 33a, 269a, 288a, 389a, 599b, 772a, 794a, 860b.
trouble, be troubled, 5b, 7b, 64b, 74a, 127b, 226a, 296a, 324b, 577a, 618b, 631b, 745a, 778a, 809a, 841a b, 861b, 906a.
trouble oneself, 13a.
trouble, to stir up, 549b.
troubled, 5b, 7b, 226a, 464a, 665a, 685a, 813b, 843a, 916a ; of water, 224a.
troubled one, 69b.
trough, 511b, 596b, 720a ; drinking, 642a.
truce, 2b.
true, 139a, 270b, 332b, 601a, 668a ; to make, 601a.
true-hearted, 139a.
true of heart, 271a.
true of voice, 271b.
true witness, 332b.
truly, 105a, 271a, 602a, 670a.
trumpet, 853a ; to sound the, 143b.
trumpet-bearer, 853a.
trumpeter, 853a.
trunk of elephant, 864b.
truss a bird, 883a.
trusted one, 44b.
trustee, 410a, 757b.
trustworthy, 139a.
truth, 214a, 270b ; in truth, 34b ; very truth, 164b.
Truth, Boat of, 272a.
truth, stone of, 62b.
truth, words of, 335b.
truthful, 107b, 270b.
Truth-goddess, 271b.
try, 444b, 899a, 902b, 903b.
try a matter, 160b.
try by fire, 10b.
try by taste or touch, 808a.
try cases, 194b.
Ṭu-ā, 870a.
Ṭuaānu, 871b.
Ṭuaȧu, 872b.
Ṭuai, 870b, 871a.
Tuait, 823b.
Ṭuaiti, 870b.
Ṭuaiu-gods, 871b.
Ṭu-Ȧmenu, 869b.
Ṭu-ȧmi-Khert-neter, 869b.
Tuamt, 824a.
Ṭuamutf, 871b.
Ṭuat, a Circle, 872a.
Ṭuat, Council of the, 901b, 902a.
Ṭuat, doors of, 655a, 659a.
Ṭuat Neter, 870b.
Ṭuat of Heliopolis and Memphis, 816a.
Ṭuat, the everlasting and hidden, 439b, 816b, 865a, 871b, 893b.
Ṭua-taui, 872a.
Ṭuatheth, 872b.
Ṭuati, god and gods, 871b, 872a.
Ṭuati-m'ketit-en-neb-s, 871b.
Ṭuatiu, 872a.
Ṭuau, 870b.
Ṭua-ur, 870b.
tub, 511b.
Tuba, 824b.
tube, 167a, 654a.
Ṭu-en-Āmau, 869b.
Ṭu-en-Bakha, 869b.
Ṭu-en-Bekhan, 869b.
Ṭu-en-Kenmut, 870a.
Ṭu-en-Kesh, 870a.
Ṭu-en-khent, 870a.
Ṭu-en-Khert-neter, 870a.
Ṭu-en-maātiu, 870a.
Ṭuf, 869b.
tug, 827a.
Ṭu-Ḥeru-nub, 870a.
Ṭu-ḥetep, 869a.
Tui, 824b.
Ṭui, 869a, 872b.
Ṭui-qaui-āaui, 870a.
Ṭuit, 869b, 872a.
Ṭu-menkh-Rerek, 869b.
tumbling girls, 539b.

tumour, 110a, 381a, 533b, 738b.
tumult, 682a.
Tunābui, 825a.
Tunȧḥ, 825a.
Ṭunānu, 833a.
Tunḥat, 825a.
Ṭun-ḥat, Ṭun-ḥati, 873a.
Ṭuniǡ, 873a.
tunic, 113b, 223a, 325a, 516b, 635a, 649b, 749a, 799b ; leather, 822a ; war, 535b.
tunics, keeper of, 749a.
tunnel through the earth, 95b.
Ṭunn-Maāu, 833a.
Ṭun-peḥti, 873a.
Ṭu-qeṭu, 869a.
Turaush, 825b.
turban, 243a, 323b, 701b.
Turimkus, 825b.
turn, 43b, 123b, 191a, 251b, 320a, 339b, 478b, 780b, 847b ; a bad, 595b.
turn about, 325a, 452a.
turn a glance, 123a.
turn aside, 18a, 435a, 612b, 630a, 682a, 710a, 711a, 713b, 797b, 839a.
turn away, 219a, 325a, 344b, 713b, 746a, 680b, 684a, 801b.
turn away from, 140a, 348b, 857a.
turn back, 57b, 122b, 166a, 245a, 325a, 487b, 567b, 605b, 613b, 614a, 630a, 645a, 657b, 683b, 684a, 694b, 711a, 713b, 747a, 748a, 824a, 857a, 883a.
turn backwards, 246b.
turn down, 612b.
turn from, 825b.
turn of the day, 246b.
turn oneself round, 325b.
turn round, 191a, 195a, 274b, 323b, 420a, 428a, 478b, 780a.
turn the back, 289b.
turn the back on, 437a.
turn the stomach, 286a.
turn towards, 837a.
turn upside down, 563b.
turner back, 122b.
turning, 478b.
turning of the shadow, 246b.
Turper, 825b.
turquoise, 150b, 262a, 281b, 289b. 296a, 475a.
Turquoise Field, 687a.
Turquoise Land, 296a.
Turshau, 825b.
turtle, 119b, 755a.
Turtle-god, 119b, 169a, 778b.
turtle meat, 345b.
turtle shell, 233a.
Ṭu Seḥseḥ, 870a.
Ṭu Semi, 870a.
tusk, 4a, 116a, 220a, 386b, 413a, 552b.
tusk of elephant, 115b, 227a.
Ṭut, 869a.
Tutānkh-Ȧmen, 16b.
Tut-en-ȧrit-Rā, 826b.
Ṭu-Ṭesher, 62b, 870a.
Ṭuti, 869a.
tutor, 757b.
Tutu, 826b.
Ṭuṭu, 869a, 870b.
Ṭuṭuf, 869a.
Ṭuṭu-ḥer, 869a.
Ṭuṭus, 869a.
Ṭu-uāb, 869b.
Ṭuuti, 868b.
twang a lyre, 685b.
twentieth, 897a.
twenty, 897a.
twice, 595b.
twice great (Thoth), 107a.
twig, 17a, 60a, 151a, 343b, 566a, 600b, 637b, 903b.
twilight, 529b, 829a.
twins, 520b ; to be, 520b.
twin-gods, 848b ; lakes and pools, 520b.
twine, 131a, 859b.
twinkle, 629a.
twinkling of the eye, 58a.
twist, 43b, 156a, 274b, 291a, 368a, 645a, 695a.
twisted, 530a.
twitch, 858b.
twitter, 100b, 211a.
twittering, 853b.
two, 673b.
Two-faced (Bat), 494a.
two hands, 815a.
two-legged, 255b.
Two Thrones, Director of, 390b.
Tybi, 738b.
type, 277b.
Typhon, 25b, 839b, 854a.
typify, 628b, 710a.

U.

Uāau, 154b.
Uābit, 156a.
Uābt, 156a.
Uāb-ur, 156a.
Uā-em-uā (Osiris), 154a.
Uaġ festival, 149b.
Uaḥit, 148a.
Uai (Āapep), 145b.
Uaiput, 146a.
Uakh, 148b.
Uamemti, Assessor and Serpent-ġod, 146b.
Uamemtiu, 146b.
Uā-menḥ (Āapep), 154a.
Uamti, 561a.
Uȧnṭit, 153a.
Uā-pesṭ-em-Ȧāḥ, 154a.
Uarkaṭar, 147a.
Uārt, Dekan, 156b.
Uārt at Abydos, 156b ; at Kher-Āḥa, 157a ; in the Ṭuat, 157a.
Uārt of stars, 157a.
Uartȧ, 147a.
Uārt-ent-bȧa, 157a.
Uārt-ent-ma, 157a.
Uārt-ent-she, 157a.
Uas, Uasit, 149a.
Uasȧr (Osiris), 149a.
Uā-seqeb, 154a.
Uashba (Rā), 149b.
Uasheshu, 149b.
Uash-neter, 402a.
Uatch, 151a.
Uatchān, 150b.
Uatchȧrti, 150b.
Uatch-ȧu-mut-f, 151b.
Uatch-ḥer, 151b.
Uatchit, 151b, 183b ; her Seven Companions, 151b.
Uatchit, Land of, 151b.
Uatchit-nebt-kek, 151b.
Uatchit-tcheserit, 151b.
Uatch-nesert, 151b.
Uatch-neterit, 151b.
Uatch-reṭ, 151b.
Uatchti, 151b.
Uatch-ur, 151a.
Uȧth-ȧb (?), 153a.
Uat-Ḥeru, 219a.
Uauaiu, 146a.
Uauamti, 146a.
Uā-uben-em-Ȧāḥ (Osiris), 154a.
Uāuti, 154a.
Ubȧ, 159a.
Ubaemṭut, 159a.
Ubata, 159a.
Ubataiu, 159a.
Ubekht, 160a.
Uben (Rā), 159b.
Uben-ȧn (Rā), 159b.
Uben-em-nubit, 159b.
Ubenit, 159b.
Ubennȧ, 159b.
Ubentiu, 160a.
Uben-urr, 159b.
Ubes-ḥer, 160a.
Ubesu, 160a.
udder, 369b.
Ufȧ, 163b.
Uġa, 187a ; festival, 187a.
Uḥa, 178a.
Uḥāḥat, 178b.
Uhem-ānkh, 177a.
Uhem-ḥer, 177a.
Uhemi, 177a.
Uhemt-ṭesu, 177a.
Uhemu, 177a.
Ukeshti, 187a.
Ukh, 179b.
Ukhikh, 180b.
ulcer, 124a, 487b, 565b, 698b, 709b, 776b.
umbilicus, 572b.
umbrella, 643b, 647b.
umbrella bearer, 647b.
Un, ġod, 165a ; ancestor of, 830b.
unanimously, 265b, 416a, 779b.
Unȧs, pyramid of, 167a.
Unb (Rā), 167b.
unbind, 665b.
unbolt, 388a, 608a, 624a, 677b, 697b, 701a, 707b.
unbolted, 665b.
Unb-per-em-Nu, 168a.
unceasinġ, 340a.
uncle, 674a.
unclean, 226b, 883a.
unclothe, 793b.
unconquered, 690b.
uncouth, 509b.
uncover, 168a, 769b, 793b.
uncovered, 458a, 794a.
uncreate, 340b.
uncultivated (land), 816a.

under, 214b, 494b, 560a, 579b.
under authority, 80a.
under favour, 579b.
undergrowth, 89a, 167b, 202a.
underling, 413b, 603a, 673a.
underrate, 694b.
understand, 6a, 120a, 121b, 400b.
understanding, 37b, 178b, 430a, 637a, 666b.
underwood, 635b.
Underworld, 477a.
undiminished, 138a.
undiminishing, 341a.
undo, 168a, 741b.
undone, 544b, 665b.
undoubtedly, 336b.
undress, 261b, 458a, 598a, 665b, 682b, 696a ; of the hair, 393b.
undressing chamber, 666a.
Unem-besku, 169a.
Unem-ḥa, 778b.
Unem-ḥuat, 169a.
unemployed, 341a.
Unem-snef, 169a, 778b.
unenclosed land, 815b.
unequalled, 177a.
Unermenṭu, 169a.
Uneshit, 169b.
unfailing, 340b.
unfavourable, 133a.
unfeigned, 119b.
unfetter, 166a.
unfettered, 621a.
unfold, 252b, 793b.
unfortunate (man), 213a.
unfriendly, 657a.
unfruitful (of ground), 569a, 732a.
Ung, the Egyptian Atlas (?), 170a.
Ungit, 170a.
ungracious, 213b.
unguent, 3b, 4a, 8a, 22a, 39a b, 55b, 63a, 74b, 90b, 91b, 92a, 110b, 111a, 126b, 128a, 140a, 175a, 192b, 205a b, 224a, 256a, 282a, 287a, 288a, 292b, 315a, 318b, 332b, 336a, 337a, 352b, 356b, 374b, 383a, 395a, 398a, 409b, 435a, 478a, 507b, 516a, 522a, 528a, 536a, 538a, 550a, 574a, 592b, 626b, 643b, 665a, 669b, 705a, 754a, 763b, 765b, 771b, 800b, 804a, 813b, 814a b, 829b, 862b, 872b, 913a.
unguent case, 581b.
unguent, cyperus, 801a.
unguent, festal, 474a.
unguent, Libyan, 859a.
unguent, medicated, 803b.
unguent, scented, 810a.
unguent, to apply, 643a.
unguent vases, 222b.
unguents, sweet-smelling, 13b.
unguentarius, 315a.
unharness, 401a.
Unḥat, 166b.
unheeded, 633b.
Unifier of Egypt, 600a.
unimaginable, 341a.
union, 725b, 879b ; with earth, 599a, 667b.
unique, 341a, 595b.
Uni-sheps, 165b.
unison, 725b.
Unit, 167a.
unite, 5a, 116b, 520b, 599a, 667b, 674b, 715b.
unite with, 577b, 614a, 684b, 747b, 878b, 880a b.
united, 879a, 883b.
universal, 247a.
unjust, 344a.
unjustly, 141a.
unknowing, 340b, 341a.
unknown, 340b, 546a, 633b, 835a.
unlearned, 546a.
unless, 340a.
unlettered, 180a.
unlimited, 908b.
unload, to, 281b, 677b ; a boat, 606a, 733a.
unloose, 43b, 168a, 261b, 665b.
unlucky, 30b, 133a.
unmatched, 595b.
unmindful, to be, 616a, 692b.
Un-Nefer, 36a, 84a ; and Rā, 165b.
Unn-em-ḥetep, 165b.
Unnit, 165a.
Unn-Nefer (Osiris), 165b ; and Harmachis, 165b.
Unnu, 165b.
Unnuit, 165a.
unobserved, 340b.
unoccupied, 727a.
unopposed, 564b.

Unpept-en-Ḥetḥert, 168a.
Unpi, 168a.
unpick, 43b ; a knot, 178b.
unplated, 340b.
unpleasant, 143a, 213b, 507a, 778b, 899a.
unquestionable, 410b.
unquiet, 577a.
unravel, 178b, 630b.
unreliable, 82a.
unrepulsed, 341a.
unresting, 340a.
unrighteousness, 340b.
unrivalled, 154a.
unroll, 43b, 252b.
unsatisfied, 835a.
unseasoned, 341a.
unseeing, 340b, 736b.
unseen, 340b.
unsettle, 602a.
unsheath, 845a.
Unshet, 169b.
Unshtȧ, 169b.
unslit, 341a.
unsplit, 341a.
unstable, 82a, 341a.
unstopped, 243a.
Unt, 166a.
Untā, 165a.
Unt-ābui, 165a.
Unt-baiusit, 165a.
Unth, 170a.
Unti, 165a b.
Unti, Light-god, 167b.
untie, 43b, 99a, 178b, 296a, 373a, 401a, 606a, 630b, 665b, 677a.
untied, 622a.
until, 30b, 65a, 297a, 414a, 415a, 449a, 723a.
untiring, 340a.
untitled, 732a.
unto, 297a.
untold, 341a.
untrained, 546a.
untrue, 813b.
untruth, 55a, 812a.
Unṭu, 170a.
Unu, South and North, 46a.
Ununt, 165a.
unusual, 341a.
unused, 727a.
Unut, 165a.
Unut-netchut, 167b.
Unut-Sethait, 167b.
unveil, 793b.
unveiling, 769b.
unwashed, 142a.
unweighable, 527a.
unwilling, 749b.
unwise, 528a.
unwittingly, 265a.
unwonted, 341a.
unwrapped, 598a.
unyoke, 613a.
up to, 30b, 414a b, 415a, 449a, 590a, 723a.
up to now, 100b.
Upȧst, 162a.
Upȧu, 162a.
Up-f-senui, 162b.
Up-hai, 162b.
Upi-sekhemti, 162b.
Upi-shāt-taui, 162b.
Upi-shet, 162b.
Upit, 162a.
Upi-taui, 163a.
Upit-taui, 163a.
Upi-Ṭuat, 163a.
Upi-ṭuui, 163a.
uplifted, 145a.
Up-Maāt, 162b.
upon, 264a, 266a, 339a, 414a, 492b, 828b, 901a.
upper, 494b, 579b.
upper chamber, 112a.
upper part, 498b.
upper region, 77b.
upright, 139a, 246a, 270b.
uprightness, 270b, 334a.
uproar, 381a.
upset, 232b, 247b, 522a, 695b ; of the stomach, 577b.
Upshit, 163b.
upside down, 618a, 694b, 897b.
Upsit, 163b.
upstream, 693b.
Upt-ent-Geb, 163a.
Upt-ent-khat, 163a.
Upt-ent-mu, 163a.
Upt-ent-Qaḥu, 163a.
Upti, 162a.
Upt Tenent, 163a.
Upu, god, 162a.
Upu (Set), 163b.
Upu Ȧqa, 162a.

Up Uatu, 162a, 242a ; day of, 450b ; of South and North, 162b.
Uqeṭneferu, 187a.
Ur-ā, 171a, 173a.
uraei (and see uraeus), 29a ; on royal crown, 23a.
uraei, the fiery, 23a.
uraei, the living, 130a.
Uraei, the Seven Great, 29b.
uraei, the two divine, 72a.
uraei, young, 388b.
Uraei-goddesses, 29a, 130a.
uraeus, 130a, 189a.
uraeus amulet, 105a.
uraeus diadem, 130a.
uraeus of Horus, 1a.
uraeus of Setesh, 29b.
Uraeus-god, 29b.
Uraeus-goddess, 21b, 125b.
uraeus guide, 699b.
Ur-ami-sheṭ, 172b.
Urȧres, 173a.
Ur-at, 172b.
Urȧtenti, 174b.
urban, 350b.
Urek, 175b.
Ur-em-Neṭȧt, 173a.
urge, 338a b, 443b, 707b.
urgency, 338a.
urgent, 292b.
Urgerti, 174a.
Urhāu, 171b.
Urḥeb, 171b, 173b.
Urḥebu, 171b.
Ur-ḥeka, 173b ; a tool, 171b.
Ur-ḥekau (Set), 173b.
Ur-henhenu, 173b.
Ur-henu, 173b.
urine, 184a b, 280a, 293a, 621a, 652b, 700b.
Urit, 172b, 174b.
Urit-ȧmit-Ṭuat, 172b.
Urit-em-ȧb-Rāit, 173a.
Urit-em-sekhemus, 173a.
Urit-en-kru, 173b.
Urit-ḥekait, 173b.
Urit-ḥekau, 173b ; an amulet and sceptre, 171b.
Urit-shefit, 174a.
Urkaf, 174a.
Ur-khert, 173b.
Ur-maati-f, 173a.
Ur-mentchf, 173a.
Ur-merti-ṭesher-sheniu, 173a.
Ur-metun-ḥer-ȧat-f, 173a.
Urm'r, 174b.
urn, 877b.
Ur-nekhtut, 171a.
Ur-nes, 47a, 173a.
Ur-peḥti, 173a.
Ur-peḥuif, 173a.
Urrtȧ, 172b, 341b.
Ur-saḥ-f, 173b.
Ursaur, 173b.
Ur-seket, 174a.
Ur-senṭ, 174a.
Ur-senu, 173b.
Ur-sheps-f, 174a.
Urshiu, 175b.
Urṭ, 175b.
Urṭ ḥat, 175b.
Urti, 171a, 172b.
Urti-ḥethati, 173b.
Urtt, 171a, 174b.
Urttbu, 171a.
Urui-ṭenṭen, 174a.
Uru-nef-ta, 173a.
Ur-urti, 173a.
us, 164a, 339a.
Usāau, 181b.
use, 609a, 694a ; use and wont, 723a.
used up, 570b.
useful, 458b, 724b ; to be, 22b.
Usekh-ḥer, 182b.
Usekh-nemmȧt, 182b.
Usekht-ȧst- etc., 182b.
Usekht-ḥett, 183a.
useless, 140b, 634b.
User, god, 182a.
User-ba, 182a.
User-baiu- etc., 182a.
User-en-Rā, 418a.
User-ḥat, 182a.
User-ḥati, a barge, 182a.
Userit, 182a.
User-ka-f, 418a.
User-Rā, 182a.
Usert, Lake, 182a.
Usert-Geb, 182a.
Userti, 182a.
Usertsen III, 696a.
Ushat, a Dekan, 185b.
Ushat-bakat, 185b.
Ushati, 185b.

Usheb, ġod, 186a.
Ushem-ḥat- etc., 186b.
Ushur-ḥat, 185b.
Usṭ, ġod, 184a.
Usten, ġod, 184a.
usual, 332a, 826a.
usurp, 112b.
usury, 55a, 324a.
Utȧnu, 188b.
Utau ġods, 189a.
Utau-Ȧsȧr, 189a.
Utau-ta, 189a.
Utcha, ġod, 193b.
Utchā, ġod, 195a.
Utchā-aābt, 195a.
Utchā-fent, 195a.
Utchā-ḥat, 193b.
Utchait, 194a.
Utchā-mestcher, 195a.
Utchat, Dekan and ġoddess, 193b.
Utchats, the two, 382a.
Utchat-Sekhmit, 194a.
Utchat-Shu, 194a.
Utch-ḥetep, 192b.
Utch-meṭu, 192a.
Utch-meṭu-Ȧsȧr, 192a.
Utch-meṭu-Kheperȧ, 192a.
Utch-meṭu-Rā, 192a.
Utch-meṭu-Tem, 192a.
Utch-nef, 192a.
Utch-nesr, 192a.
Utch-sekhit, 192a.
Uṭeb, ġod, 191a.
Uṭekh, 191b.
Uṭennu, 191b.
Utenu, 189b.
uterus, 12b, 13a, 102a, 481b, 847b ; the ġravid, 785b.
Utet-f-em-ḥer, 189a.
Utet-f-em-pet, 189a.
Utet-f-em-utcha, 188b.
Uteth, 189b.
Utet-ḥeḥ, 189a.
Utet-neferu-set, 189a.
Utetteff, 189a.
Uthes, 190a.
Uthesi-ḥeḥtt, 190a.
Uthesit, 190a.
Uthes-neferu, 190a.
Uthesu, 190a.
Uthes-ur, 190a.
utility, 722b.
Utit, 188b.
Utt, 188a.
utter cries, to, 29a, 73b, 92b, 440a, 472b, 705b.
utterance, 104b, 549a, 669b, 754a, 831a.
utterly, 415a.
uttermost, 414a.
Utu, ġod, 188a.
Uṭu, ġod, 190b.
Utu-Shu, 189a.
Uu, city and ġod, 144a.

V.

vacant, 622b.
vacillation, 352b.
vaġina, 758a, 769b, 785b.
vainly, 184b.
valiant, 402a, 738a, 839a.
valley, 56b, 58a, 111b, 252b, 574a, 896b ; festival of, 474b.
Valley of the cedar, 58a.
Valley of myrrh, 58a.
Valley of the Shadow, 58a.
Valley, the Dark, 58a.
Valley, the Great, 58a.
valley-reġion, 58a.
valour, 107b, 379a, 544a, 738a, 772a ; ġold of, 353a.
valuable, 93a.
valuables, 568b.
value, 134a, 283b.
value, to adjudġe, 41a.
value, to be of, 724b.
valueless, 802a.
vanish, 787b.
vanquish, 145a, 400a, 452b, 772a.
vanquished, 560b.
vanquisher, 378b, 379a.
vapour, 27a, 516b ; hot, 6a.
varieġated, 4a, 117b, 278b, 346a, 821b, 837a.
various, 736a.
various colours, 855b.
vary, 420b.
vase, 1b, 2a, 28b, 38a, 41b, 62b, 63a, 72b, 114a, 117a, 118a, 123b, 126b, 128a, 131a b, 134b, 137a, 186a, 191a b, 222b, 276b, 278a, 281b, 284a, 295a, 300a, 301b, 303a, 318b, 348a, 374b, 376a, 400b, 448b, 449a, 486b, 499b,

510a, 512a, 537b, 539b, 558b, 569b, 581b, 606a, 676a, 708b, 725a, 728a, 731a, 744a, 751b, 758a, 767b, 768b, 776b, 786b, 791b, 809a, 854a, 872b, 876a, 877a, 881b, 884a, 888a, 895b, 907b, 911b.
vase on censer, 2a.
vase, sacred, 737b.
vases, the four ceremonial, 376a.
vassal, 50a, 311a, 411a, 457b, 579b, 809b.
vassal-lord, 357b.
vassals of Osiris, 50a.
vassalage, 50a, 206b.
vat, 511b ; wine, 374b.
vault of heaven, 462b, 793a, 854b.
vegetable, 8a, 77b, 119b, 150a, 188b, 210b, 232b, 242b, 427a, 449b, 451b, 563a, 589a, 598b, 600b, 647b, 667a, 709b, 749a, 822b, 825a, 890b, 897a, 900a, 915a.
vegetable garden, 203b.
vegetable growth, 635b.
vegetables, dealer in, 707b ; young, 423b.
vegetation, 25a ; god of, 9a.
veil, to veil, 220a, 304b, 326a, 376a, 573a, 904b.
vein, 331b.
vendange (jeter la), 708b.
venerable, 737a, 881b.
vengeance, 807a ; to take, 768a.
venom, 300b, 332a, 348b.
Venus, 234b, 403b, 647a, 656b, 870b, 895a.
verandah, 701b.
verdict, 160b, 335a.
verdigris, 571a.
verdure, 77b, 709b.
verify, 673a.
verily, 265a, 602a, 670a, 782a.
veritable, 270b, 271a.
verity, 270b.
vertebrae, 249a, 250a, 859b.
very, 108a, 170b.
very great, 170b.
very many, 838a.
very much, 414a, 431b.
very very, 910a.
vessel, 1b, 19b, 28a b, 41b, 63a, 94b, 104a, 107a, 114a, 118a, 123b, 126b, 128a, 131a, 137a, 143a, 183a, 186a, 204a, 208b, 209a, 213b, 218a, 228b, 233a, 253a, 281b, 284a, 292b, 295a, 300a, 303a, 314a, 331a, 339a, 344b, 348a, 374b, 394a, 429b, 443a, 467a, 473a, 485a, 486b, 499b, 510a, 512a, 516b, 536b, 539b, 558b, 603a, 605b, 606a, 613a, 635b, 652a, 662a, 672b, 676a b, 689a, 708b, 713a, 716b, 725a, 731a, 744a, 751b, 754b, 758a, 763b, 776b, 790b, 791a b, 797a, 850b, 851b, 852a, 854a, 857a, 868b, 872b, 876a, 877a b, 878a, 881b, 888a, 892a, 895b, 900a, 907b, 911b.
vessel for altar, 196a, 426a, 438a, 870a.
vessel, circular, 838b.
vessel, cooking, 429a.
vessel for grain, 374b.
vessel, holy, 737b.
vessel, incense, 789b.
vessel, libation, 72b.
vessel, purification, 110b.
vessel, sacrificial, 704b.
vessel, sanctuary, 789a.
vessels of the body, 332a.
vestibule, 275a.
vestment, 419b, 652a, 864b, 868a, 874b.
vestment, sacred, 155b.
vestments, chamber of, 455a.
veteran, 17b.
vex, 27b, 768a.
vexation, 664b.
vexations, 2a.
vexed, 524b, 665a.
viaticum, 894b.
vicar, 98b, 103a.
viceroy, 392a.
vicinity, 638a.
vicissitudes, 246b.
victim, 561a, 669a.
victim, human, 846a, 862b.
victorious, 108a, 171a, 378b.
victory, 354b, 378b, 379a, 775b ; prize of, 772a.
victuals, 126a, 832a.
victuallers, the divine, 469b.

W.

walk with trees in it, 724a.
walker, 373b, 374a.
walking, place of, 80a.
walking stick, 726a, 822a.
wall, 60b, 380b, 457a, 587a, 595a, 605b, 633b, 637a, 650b, 660b, 661a, 707a, 823b, 858a, 896b, 910a b.
wall up, 750a, 873b.
wall, to build a, 769b.
wall, girdle, 676b.
wall, massive, 164a.
walled places, 902a.
wall paintings, 619b.
wallet, 803a ; sculptor's, 804a.
wallow, 842a.
wand, 825b, 900b.
wand-bearer, 849a.
wander, 568a, 640a, 839a.
wander away, 587b.
wander in mind, 841a.
wander round, 875a.
wander through, 881a.
wanderer, 883a.
wandering, 797b.
want, 12a, 19a, 25b, 64b, 127b, 226a, 397b, 514a, 580b, 618b, 726a, 732b, 800a, 897a.
want, to be in, 204b, 469b, 800a.
wanting, 395b, 732b, 754b.
wanton (act), 396b.
war, 241a, 315b, 320a, 459a, 461b, 549b.
War-god, 208a ; Syrian, 213a.
War-goddess, 112b, 127b.
war-ship, 132b, 330a, 592a.
ward off, 646b.
warden, 145a, 562a.
warder, 586b, 746b.
wardrobe, 70b, 613a.
warehouse, 180b, 193b, 286b, 549b, 723a, 900a.
warm, 611b, 623a, 676a, 681a, 700a.
warm-hearted, 681a.
warmth, 429a, 439b, 611b, 681a.
warped, 530a.
warrant, 848a.
warrior, 132a, 224b, 240b, 241a, 243a, 330a, 381b, 389a, 639b, 640a, 704a, 744b, 772a, 885a.
Warrior-god, 132b ; gods, 26a.
Warriors, the Two, 132b.
warts, 824a.
wash, 15a, 17a, 27b, 142a, 431a.
wash clean, 155a.
wash out, 726a.
wash over with something, 689a.
wash the heart, 28a.
washer, 136a, 170a, 431a.
washer of gold, 28a.
washerman, 318a.
washhouse, 155b.
washing, 117a ; gold, 317b.
washing place, 431a.
wasp, 539a.
waste, 114b, 168a, 311a, 348b, 440a, 459a, 594a, 628b, 711b.
waste ground, 532a.
waste lands, 16b, 815b.
wasted, 544b, 716a.
waster, 538b, 641b.
watch, 83a, 257b, 351b, 382a, 586b.
watch over, 506b.
watch, to keep, 175a, 432a, 903b.
watches, night, 432a.
watcher, 109a, 175a b, 266b, 382a, 468a, 716a.
Watcher (Rā), 432b.
watchers of Ārits, 432a.
Watchers of Nekhen and Pe, 175b.
Watchers, the divine, 175b, 267b, 382a.
Watchers, the Nine, 251a, 432b.
watchful, to make, 607b.
watch-house, 267a.
watchman, 432a, 586b, 862b.
watch-night of Isis, 811b.
watch tower, 254a, 273a, 274b, 275a, 432a.
water, 143a, 280a, 293a, 400a, 470a, 472b, 841b.
water, boiling, 293b, 400a.
water, celestial, 12a.
water, deep, 216a, 475b.
water, filthy, 31b.
water, holy, 156a.
water, mass of, 213a, 349b.
water of eyes, 223b.
water of fire, 293b.
water of well, 294a.
water, ornamental, 720a.

water, primeval, 349b, 469a.
water, pure, 77b.
water, running, 569a.
water, salt, 280b.
water, sweet, 294a.
water that turns round, 294a.
water, to, 368b, 589a, 621a, 902a.
water, to make, 181b, 184a b, 237a, 260b, 262b, 429b, 528b, 708b.
water, troubled, 293b.
water-bird, 547b.
water-carrier, 148a.
water-channel, 144b.
water-clock, 315b.
water-course, 56b, 144b, 145a, 499b, 576a, 707b, 758a.
water-flood, 12a, 160a, 213a, 317b, 467a, 637b, 681a.
water-fowl, 5b, 294b, 324a, 541b, 579a, 621b, 647a, 768b, 772b.
water-garden, 401a.
Water-god, 10b, 12a, 71b, 281a, 293b, 467b.
water-house, 407b.
water-jar, 911b.
water-melon, 227b, 725b.
water-onion, 288b.
water-plant, 8b, 22b, 637b, 803a, 808b.
water-pot, 680b, 775b ; of palette, 247b ; scribe's, 205a.
water-skin, 569b, 576a, 758a, 887a.
water-station, 576a.
water-supply, 593a.
watered, 708b.
watering place, 99b.
waterless, 340b.
watery mass, 293a.
wave, 145a, 440a, 441b, 448b, 813b, 839a, 843b.
wax, 303b ; figure of men, 436a.
way, 32a, 144b, 276b, 277b, 290a b, 291a b, 293a, 333b, 334b, 499a, 595a, 604a, 739b.
way, to find a, 807a.
way, to lose, 883a.
way, to make a, 445a b, 623b, 700b.
Wazîr, 848b.
weak, 398b, 472b, 506b, 520a.
we, 34a, 164a, 333a, 339a.
weak, 8a, 10b, 22a, 26b, 39a, 55b, 78a, 111a, 149a, 152b, 187b, 207b, 208b, 225b, 226a, 227a, 228a, 245a, 260b, 296b, 315a, 538b, 574a, 587a, 627b, 640a, 661a, 698a, 706a, 733b, 764a, 771b, 774b, 775b, 778a, 802a, 803a, 809a, 812b, 840a.
weak man, 809a.
weak things, 809a.
weak, to be, 634b, 891b ; to become, 11b ; to make, 520a, 644a.
weak-armed, 634b.
weak-hearted, 534b.
weaken, 594b, 635a, 640a.
weakness, 26b, 76b, 142b, 226a, 443a, 574a, 641a, 698a, 772b, 802a, 809a, 838b, 897a ; in judgment, 352b ; moral, 674b ; of old age, 152b.
wealth, 91b, 134b, 525a, 631b, 737a ; to get, 66b.
wealthy, 171a ; the, 663a, 736a, 737a.
wealthy woman, 182a.
weaned, 322a.
weapon, 2a, 11a, 21a, 72a, 132b, 138a, 232a, 275b, 278b, 290a, 300a, 305a, 321a, 327b, 334a b, 338b, 343a, 345b, 351a, 352b, 354b, 390a, 419a, 482b, 490b, 516b, 528b, 532a, 535b, 544a, 561b, 619a, 693b, 705a, 710a, 715a, 747a, 762a, 770a, 799a, 810b, 811b, 828a, 845a, 907a b.
weapon bag, 528b.
weapons, wooden, 640a.
wear, 189b, 860a.
wearer, 861a.
wearied, 32b, 262b, 802b.
weariness, 142a, 534a, 744b.
weary, 10b, 176b, 225b, 377a, 522a, 574a, 665a, 753a, 803b ; of heart, 260b.
weasel, 522a.
weather, bad, 608b.
weave, 66a, 116b, 131a, 291a, 323b, 325a, 399b, 532b, 624b, 627b, 695a, 709b, 859b.
weave words, 695a.
weaver, 372b, 532b, 773a.
Weavers, the two divine, 116b.

weaving, goddess of, 819a.
web, 623b, 806b.
weed, 902b.
week of 10 days, 331a.
weep, 12b, 26a, 33b, 49a, 94b, 424a, 425b, 537b, 605b, 763b, 771b, 772a, 786a, 808b, 821b, 826b, 857a, 858a ; to make, 611b, 642b, 681a.
weeper, 94b, 424a, 446a, 821b.
Weepers, the Two, 424a, 462a ; goddesses, 462a.
weeping, 40a, 225b, 419b, 424a.
weeping woman, 794b, 808b.
weevil, 798b, 845b.
weigh, 285a, 527a, 363a, 614b, 622a, 688a, 808a.
weigh out, 899b.
weigh words, 194b.
weigher, 258b, 669b, 842b.
weighings, 258b.
weighing room, 527a.
weight, 189b, 191b, 301b, 356a, 728b, 828a, 854a, 856b, 875b, 883b, 908a.
weight, just, 842b.
weight, measured, 295a, 329a, 411b, 527a, 757a.
weight of a net, 210b, 883b.
weight of balance, 887b.
weighted with care, 883b.
weights, to falsify, 647a.
weighty, 108a, 839b, 883b.
welcome, 345a, 348a b, 354b.
well, 110a, 123b, 148b, 187b, 203b, 490b, 491a, 563b, 574a, 576a, 579a, 593b, 724b, 733b ; to be, 128a, 716b.
well, western, 579a.
well in Great Oasis, 477a.
well of water, 121b, 144a, 159b, 202a.
well then, 548b.
well-being, 148b, 893b.
well-conducted, 304a.
well-disposed, 209b.
well-doing, 217b, 304a, 370b.
well-favoured, 550a.
well-fed, 773b.
well-founded, 811b.
well-known, 583a.
well-pleased, 766a.
well-seasoned, 334a.
well-to-do folk, 134b, 663a.
well-trained, 304a.
west, 45a, 53b, 274b, 298a ; Lion of the, 221b.
west bank of Nile, 53b.
west wind, 53b, 506b, 524a, 895a.
west wind, god of the, 474a.
wet, 31b, 39b, 843a ; to make, 212b, 451a.
wet lands, 104b.
wharf, 180b.
what ?, 36b, 77a, 92b, 235b, 253b, 279b.
what is, 146b, 399a.
what is it ?, 253b.
what is not, 37a.
what is this ?, 26b.
whatsoever, 158a.
wheat, 50b, 126a, 242b, 399b, 466a, 468a, 523b, 529a, 559b, 592a, 648b, 788b.
wheaten bread, 788b.
wheedle, 650b, 804a.
when, 64b, 266a, 815a, 908b.
whence, 837b, 838a.
where ?, 77a, 92b, 837b, 856a b, 882b.
whereby, 348a.
wherefore, 77a, 92b, 279b, 904b.
whet, 878a.
whey, 733b.
which, 37a, 398b.
which not, 348a.
while, 339a, 815a.
whilst, 815a, 908b.
whip, 89a, 90a, 139b, 387a b, 449b, 669b, 701b, 729b ; leather, 725a ; part of, 27a.
whirlwind, 180a, 465a.
whistling (of the wind), 560b.
white, 159a, 160a, 522b ; to be, 697b.
white, dead, 389a.
white apparel, 622b.
white (of bread, grain, etc.), 523b.
white-cake, 730b.
White Crown, 523a, 593b.
White Goddess, 522b.
white-haired, 704b.
who, 37a, 348b. 398b.
who is not, 37a.
who ?, 61b, 82b, 92b, 279b, 373a, 378a.

whole, 193a, 779b, 834a, 851a, 880a.
whole, the, 765a, 908b.
wholly, 681a, 834a.
why ?, 77a, 92b, 279b.
wick, 254b, 256b, 533b, 808a.
wicked, 3b, 141a, 211a, 216b, 260a, 343a, 434a, 469b, 534a.
wicked man, 636a, 657a, 824a, 860a.
wicked, the, 340a, 377a, 431a.
wickedness, 14b, 31b, 208a, 214a b, 216b, 226a, 352b, 356b, 388a, 467b, 488b, 540a, 572a, 582a, 594a, 649a, 726a, 868b, 869a.
wicker box, 835b.
wickerwork, 204a, 307b.
wicket gate, 723a.
wide, 2b, 180b, 182b, 183b, 260a, 635b.
wide, to be, 255b.
wide, to make, 652a.
wide-tailed (i.e., Isis), 2b.
widow, 532b, 808b.
widower, 532a.
Widows, the Two, 532b.
width, 182b, 615a, 685b.
wield a battle axe, 201a.
wife, 331b, 477a, 481a, 599b.
wife, King's, 312a ; the first, 392a.
wife of the god, 481b.
wig, 120a, 123b, 216a, 367a, 368a, 745b, 810b.
wild ass, 243b.
wilderness, 311a.
will, 37b, 45a, 107b, 155a, 192a, 270b, 351b, 460b, 508b, 521b, 865a.
will (testament), 45a, 106b.
will, to, 309b.
willing, 533a.
willingly, 309b.
willow, 825b.
willow stick, 825b.
willow tree, 840a, 857b.
wind, 13b, 82a, 89b, 96a, 98b, 130b, 141b, 174a, 198b, 273a, 280a, 342a, 344b, 346b, 356a, 369b, 377b, 593a, 605a, 648b, 651b, 683a b, 732a, 750a, 767b, 775a, 822b, 823b, 824a, 849b.
wind bandages, 188a.
wind, contrary, 343b.
wind, cool, 605b.
wind, dawn, 370a.
wind, fair, 836b.
wind, gentle, 354b.
wind, hot, 547a, 740a, 750b.
wind, moist, 902b.
wind, north, 318b.
wind of the belly, 732a.
wind round, 282a, 850b.
wind, south, 445b.
wind up, to, 827a.
wind, unfavourable or violent, 657b.
wind, warm, 451b.
wind, west, 467b, 506b, 524b, 895a ; god of, 474a.
Wind-god, 555a.
wind-goddess, 90b, 126a, 543a.
wind-pipe, 77a.
wind-plant, 370a.
wind-pole, 566b.
wind-storm, 903b, 814a.
winding sheet, 776a.
windings, 763a ; of lake, 763a.
window, 157b, 625a, 701b, 728b, 764b.
wine, 20b, 49a, 72a, 118b, 137a, 143a, 300a, 383a, 408a, 462b, 485a, 510b, 536b, 671b, 722a, 723a.
wine bowl, 462b.
wine, carob, 839a.
wine cellar, 72b, 106a, 238a, 868b.
wine cup, 72b, 842b.
wine, date, 217b.
wine, honey, 72a, 72b.
wine jar, 72a, 143a, 287a.
wine, medicated, 328a.
wine, new, 231b, 759b.
wine of Pelusium, 72b, 605b, 676a.
wine of Syene, 592b.
wines of various places, 72b.
wine, palm, 20b.
wine, place of, 213b.
wine plant, 72b.
wine pot, 801a.
wine press, 374b.
wine shop, 32a, 72b, 106a.
wine skin, 287a, 568b, 842b.

wing, 275a, 462b, 522a, 607b, 733a, 809b, 878b, 883a, 907b ; to spread the, 65b.
wing of army, 873b.
winged disk, 118b.
wings, pair of, 836b, 839a, 879a, 907a.
wings, variegated, 117b.
wink, to, 344a, 814b.
winnow, 121b, 527b, 724a.
winnowed, 751a.
winnower, 527a.
winnowing instrument, 527a, 531b.
wipe, 590a.
wipe out, 315b, 591a, 840a.
wisdom, 37b, 214a, 588a, 634a, 640b, 655b, 896a ; words of, 335b.
wisdom, ancient, 896a.
wise, 178b, 246a, 430a, 640b, 659b, 698a, 751b, 634a.
wise folk, 23a, 583a, 613a, 634a, 650b, 655b, 682b, 698a, 739a, 896a, 900a.
wise member, 751b.
wise speech, 896a.
wise, to be, 430a, 622a ; in speech, 430b.
wise woman, 751b.
wisely, 637a.
wish, 37b, 149b, 270b, 310a, 417b, 464a, 521b, 561b.
wish, dearest, 79b.
wish for, 4b, 19a, 309b, 464a.
wishing that, 310a.
witchcraft, 217a.
with, 37a, 60a, 73a, 116b, 264a b, 296a, 333a, 339b, 373a, 414a b, 415a, 466a, 467b, 486a, 489b, 492b, 506b, 545a, 560a, 573b.
with him, 342a.
with the exception of, 493a.
withdraw, 63b, 152a, 246b, 481a, 487b, 499a, 538b, 635b, 707b, 755a, 757b, 847b.
withdraw arrow, 9a.
withdraw from, 240a.
withdrawal, 57b, 594b, 670b.
withering, 696b.
withholding, 537a.
within, 44a, 265a, 266a, 573a, 575b, 763a.
without, 37a, 78a, 98a, 265a, 282a, 339b, 340a, 414b, 546a, 548a, 732b, 800a, 835a.
without, he who is, 12b.
without like, 177a.
without second, 341a.
without, to be, 296b.
withstand, 818b.
withy, 151a.
witness, 332b, 334a.
wittingly, 265a, 430a.
woe, 7b, 49a, 219b.
wolf, 40a, 169b, 588a, 868a.
Wolf-god, 588a.
wolf's bane, 169b.
wolf's foot, 823b.
wolf's paw, 850a.
woman, 18a, 230b, 466a, 481a, 583a, 613b, 753b, 785b ; married, 357b, 358a ; parturient, 321b ; singing, 111b ; suckling, 69a ; unmarried, 376a ; wailing, 26a ; wise, 430a ; with child, 663a ; young, 426b.
womb, 570a.
womb, disease of, 9a.
womb, opener of, 160b.
women, apartments of, 79a, 481b.
women, divorced, 194b, 329a.
women, Egyptian, 430a.
women, foreign dancing, 234b.
women, house of the, 239a.
women of the chambers, 237b.
Women, the Two, 429b.
wonder, 200a, 202b, 209b, 213b, 215a b, 292b, 544a ; to do a, 209b.
wonderful, 209b, 213b, 215a.
wont, 609a, 694a.
wood, 13a, 73b, 79a, 93b, 95b, 114b, 115b, 139b, 216b, 217a, 235a, 280b, 283b, 299a, 446a, 520b, 566a, 586a, 597a, 624a, 664a, 677a, 716b, 749a, 821a, 841a b.
wood, a medicine, 35b, 231b.
wood, black, 566b.
wood, costly, 697a.
wood for chariots, 202b.
wood, objects in, 351a.
wood of life, 126b.

wood packing, 89a.
wood, scented, 730a.
wood, white, 566b.
woodcutter, 770b.
woodwork, 206b, 905a.
wool, 610b, 680a, 726b.
woolly-headed, 809b.
word, 104b, 240b, 335a, 416a, 549a, 560a, 669a b, 717a, 860b, 862a, 913a b.
word, boastful, 335a.
word, evil, 136b, 202a, 335a.
word, last, of a book, 764a.
word, last year's, 335b.
word, magical, 22b.
word of hidden meaning, 63a.
word of ill omen, 185a.
word of power, 22b, 515a, 783a.
word of praise, 3b.
word of shame, 737b.
word of the sky, 335a.
word of Thoth, 335b, 402a.
word, rebellious or vile, 335b.
word, smooth, 335b.
word, strange, 541b.
Word, the divine, 886b, 913b.
Word, the Great, 913b.
work, 19b, 67a, 158a, 160b, 206b, 383b, 418b, 439a, 487a, 762a, 784a.
work, director of, 562b.
work about, 79a, 470b.
work a mine, 209b.
work a rope, 178b.
work at a trade, 65b, 66a.
work contentedly, 65b.
work, daily, 278b.
work in the field, 167a.
work in metal, 287a, 366b, 396a, 770a.
work in stone, 279a, 737b, 850b.
work in wood, 11a, 304b, 336b.
work out, 757b.
work skilfully, 447b.
work the bottle, 801a.
work the mouth, 351b.
work, to, 206a, 225a, 710a, 809b, 849b, 910a.
worked, 771a ; of metal, 711b, 849b.
worker, 67a, 111a, 160b, 771a.
worker, i.e., creator, 67a.
working, 419a ; of oars, 757b.
working folk, 860b.
workless, 341a.
workmen, 67a, 74b, 76b, 82a, 94a, 105b, 124a, 158a, 201a, 206b, 215a, 220a, 439a, 440b, 483a b, 532b, 547b, 558b, 747b, 784a, 786a, 805a ; King's, 392a.
workpeople, 579b.
workshop, 75a, 81b, 273b, 445b, 483b, 484b.
workshop of gods, 82a.
workshop of gold and silver, 239a.
workshop, sculptor's, 780a.
workwomen, 67a.
world, 525a, 815a ; Four quarters of, 766b, 815b.
World, Other, 36b.
worm, 62b, 124a, 155a, 237b, 259b, 260b, 261a, 262b, 346b, 374a, 471a, 497b, 499b, 596a, 791a, 878a, 882b, 913a, 914b.
worm at a tooth, 185b.
Worm, the, 6a ; Āapep, 878a, 882b ; of evil, 480a.
worm-eaten, 878a.
worms, intestinal, 252b, 499b.
Worms of Åmente, 261a.
Worms, the Nine, 480a.
worms, to become, 153a, 263a.
worship, 50a, 149b, 593a, 652b, 840b ; worthy of, 50a.
worshipped, 50a.
worshipper, 479b, 603b.
worth, 722b ; moral, 209b.
worthless, 165b, 339b, 340a, 546b.
would that ! 50b, 279b, 292b, 441b, 457a, 464a, 468a.
wound, 26b, 159b, 169b, 179a, 296b, 330a, 392b, 446a, 519b, 549b, 561a, 603b, 615a, 632b, 688b, 698a, 730a, 731b, 735b, 736a, 751a, 771b, 772a, 809b, 881a, 914b ; bloody, 715b.
wounded, 14a, 685b.
woven, 157b, 160a ; work, 110a.
wrangle, 744b, 852b.
wrangler, 744b.
wrap, 256b.
wrap round, 58a, 61a, 63a.
wrap up, 131b, 629b, 651b, 713a, 717a, 849a.

wrap up a body, i.e., bury, 775b, 776b, 778a.
wrap up in, 269a, 850b.
wrapped, 776a.
wrapped up, 208b, 810b.
wrapping, 301a, 904b.
wrath, 12b, 14a, 536b, 774b, 794b, 796a, 907b ; man of, 14a.
wrathful, 532a, 615b, 689b.
wreath, 148b, 275a, 383b, 511b, 595a ; funerary, 127a.
wreathe, 530a, 572a.
wreck, 219b.
wrecked, 32a.
wretch, 319a.
wretched, 93b, 94b, 114b, 139b, 202b, 207b, 315a, 472b, 476a, 574a, 604a, 652b, 675a, 733b, 802a, 899b ; man, 715a.
wretchedness, 211a, 214a, 270a, 524b, 815a, 906b.
wriggle, 131b, 262b ; away, 594b.
wriggler, 374a.
wring, 28b, 114a, 156a.
wrinkled, 517a.
write, 190b, 191b, 597a, 610b, 619a, 662b, 680a, 690a, 841a, 854b.
write a book, 65b.
writer, 619b, 688a.
writing, 106b, 131b, 337b, 346a, 440a, 619a, 661a, 688a, 694a, 722b, 725a, 730b, 738b, 739a, 784a, 836b, 848a, 849a, 855a b, 857b, 885a.
writing, a, 129a, 567b ; writings, 82a, 619a, 622b, 755a, 836a, 882a, 885a.
writing, demotic, 619b.
writing, goddess of, 665b.
writing, hieroglyphic, 619b.
writing, sacred, 619b.
writing, to do into, 56b, 619a, 866b.
writing box, 447b.
writing instrument, 314a.
writing reed, 129a.
writing tablet, 123a, 129b, 302a, 303a.
writings, ancient, 345b.
written, 291b, 723b.
wrong, 30b, 31b, 89b, 136b, 141b, 211a, 260a, 472b, 772b, 774b, 894a, 895b.
wrong order, in, 844a.
wrong, to, 101a ; to do, 165b, 647a.
wrongdoer, 373a.
wrongfully, 894a.
wroth, 774b, 809b ; to be, 744b.
wrought, 771a.

X.

Xerxes, 534a, 536b, 566a.

Y.

Yankhamu, 143a.
yarn, 773a.
yaw about, 657b.
ye, 164a, 333b, 400b, 408a, 822b, 855b.
ye two, 782a.
yea, 96a, 348a.
year, 422b, 427b, 857b ; empty, 732b ; first of King's reign, 460a.
year, ancestors of, 830b.
year, first season of, 22a.
year, last, 606a.
year, last day of, 131b.
year of famine, 514a.
year, the great and little, 427b.
year, the past, 677a.
year, the rolling, 247a.
Year-god and goddess, 427b.
yearly event, 561b.
years, ḥenti, 488a.
yeast, 348a, 548a, 611b, 743a, 758b.
yellow, 113a, 797b.
yellowish-green, 150a.
yes, 348a ; to say, 823a.
yesterday, 225a, 381a, 664b.
yesterday, day before, 664b.
yet, 321a, 342b.
yield, 356b, 528a, 587b, 889a.
yoke, 6a, 100a, 274a, 384a, 520b.
yoke of beasts, 27b, 100a, 435a.
yonder, 282b.

you, 164a, 400b, 822b, 824a, 826b, 837b.
young, 269a, 716b.
young, to be, 150a, 386b, 423a, 427a, 471a, 487b, 664b.
young (collective), 471b.
young folk, 739a.
young man, 17a; men and women, 141b, 811b, 898a.
young, of animals, 573b.
your, 229b, 342a, 818b, 824a, 837b, 855b.
youth, 17a, 27a, 76b, 269a, 303a, 347b, 372b, 471a, 525a, 532a, 898a.
youth, a, 487b, 749b; youths, 466a.
youth, water of, 427a.
youthful, 150a, 547b.

Z.

zarîbas, 60b.
zealous, 338b.
zenith, 163a.
zephyr, 354b.
zither, 902a.
zizyphus, spina Christi, 368a.
zodiacal light (?), 663b.

II.

INDEX

OF THE HORUS, NEBTI, HORUS-OF-GOLD, NESU-BÅT, AND SON-OF-RĀ NAMES OF THE PRINCIPAL KINGS OF EGYPT.

A.

Åā-åb, 925.
Āa-åb (Psammetichus I), 940.
Āa-åb-meri-taui (Hagr), 941.
Āa-ārq-Rā, 929.
Āa-baiu (Åmen-em-ḥat III), 923.
Āa-ḥetep-Rā, 922, 929.
Åāḥmes I, 932.
Åāḥmes II, 940.
Āa-khā-Rā, 922, 929.
Āa-kheper-en-Rā (Thothmes II), 932.
Āa-kheper-ka-Rā (Thothmes I), 937.
Āa-kheper-Rā (Pasebkhān III), 937.
Āa-kheper-Rā (Shashanq IV), 939.
Āa-kheper-Rā (Uasarkenå), 939.
Āa-kheperu-Rā (Åmen-ḥetep II), 932.
Āa - khepesh - ḥu - Satiu (Åmen - ḥetep III), 933.
Āa-khepesh-ḥu-Satiu (Meneph-thah I), 934.
Åakhu-en-Åmen (Rameses VIII), 935.
Åakhu-en-Åten (Åmen-ḥetep IV), 933.
Åakhu-en-Rā (Sa-Ptaḥ), 934.
Āa-mu, 929.
Āanatå, 928.
Āa-nekhtut-en-taiu-nebu (Seti I), 934.
Āa-neter-Rā, 929.
Āa-peḥ, 929.
Āa-peḥ-Rā, 929.
Āa-peḥti-Set (Nubti), 929.
Āa-peḥti-uaḥ-sepu (Psa-mut), 941.
Āa-qenu-Rā (Åpepå III), 929.
Āa-user-Rā (Åpepå I), 928.
Åb, 920.
Åb-meri-Rā (Khati I), 921.
Åḥtes, 919.
Åi I, 925.
Åi II, 933.
Åi-em-ḥetep, 921.
Åkåu-Ḥeru, 920.
Ἀχθώης, 921.
Ἄχωρις, 941.
Alexander I, the Great, the Macedonian, 942.
Alexander II, the Macedonian, 942.
Alexander I (Ptolemy XI), 943.
Åmen-em-ḥat I, 923.
Åmen-em-ḥat II, 923.
Åmen-em-ḥat III, 923.
Åmen-em-ḥat IV, 923.
Åmen-em-ḥat V, 923.
Åmen-em-ḥat VI, 924.
Åmen-em-ḥat VII, 924.
Åmen-em-ḥat VIII, 924.
Åmen-em-ḥat IX, 924.
Åmen-em-ḥeb, 934.
Ἀμενέμης, 923.
Åmen-ḥer-khepesh-f (Rameses X), 935.
Åmen-ḥetep I, 932.
Åmen-ḥetep II, 932.
Åmen-ḥetep III, 933.
Åmen-ḥetep IV, 933.
Åmeni Åntef VII (?), 924.

Ȧmen-mes, 936.
Ȧmen-meses, 934.
'Αμενοφθίς, 932.
'Αμένοφις, 933.
'Αμενωφαθ, 934.
Ȧmen-Rā-mes, 936.
Ȧmen-rut, 942.
'Αμενσίς, 932.
'Αμερής, 923.
'Αμμανέμης, 923.
'Αμμενέμης, 923.
'Αμώσις, I, 932.
'Αμώσις, 740.
Ȧn (En-user-Rā), 919.
Ȧn (Qa-ka-Rā II), 942.
Ān- . . . , 925.
Ȧn-ȧb- . . . , 930.
Ȧn-kau-Rā, 921.
Ānkh-ȧb-taui (Sebek-ḥetep IV), 925.
Ānkh-ka-Rā, 928.
Ānkh-ka-Rā (Psammetichus III), 940.
Ānkh-khāu, 920.
Ānkh-kheperu-Rā, 933.
Ānkh-mesut (Usertsen I), 923.
Ānnu, 921.
Ȧn-nub- . . . , 928.
Ānq-taui (Khian), 929.
Āntch-ȧb, 917.
Ȧntef I, the Erpā, 922.
Ȧntef II, the Erpā, 922.
Ȧntef III, 922.
Ȧntef IV, 922.
Ȧntef V, 922.
Ȧntef VI, 922.
Ȧntef VII, 924.
Ȧntef VIII Āa, 931.
Ȧntef IX Āa, 931.
Ȧntef X Āa, 931.
Ȧnt-ḥer, 929.
Antoninus Pius, 946.
Ȧntriusha (Darius I), 941.
Ȧntriusha (Darius II), 941.
Ȧpepȧ I, 928.
Ȧpepȧ II, 929.
Ȧpepȧ III, 929.
Aphobis ('Αφώβις) I, 928.
Aphobis II, 929.
Aphobis III, 929.
'Απρίης, 940.
Ȧ- . . . -Rā, 927.
Ȧri-maāt (Userkaf), 919.
Ȧri-maāt (Ȧi II), 933.
Ȧri-maāt-en-Rā (Tche-ḥer), 941.
Ȧri-maāt-Rā (Ptolemy VII, IX, X, XI, XIII), 943.
Ȧri-mes-neteru (Nectanebus II), 942.
Ȧrksȧnṭrs (Alexander), 942.
Ȧrksenṭrs (Alexander), 942.
Ȧrsenai (Arsinoë) I, 944.
Ȧrsenai II, 944.
Ȧrsenai III, 944.
Ȧrsu the Syrian, 934.
Artakhashassha (Artaxerxes), 941.
Ȧsȧ, 919.
Ȧst-ȧb-taui (Ȧn), 919.
Ȧta, 917.
Ȧtati, 917.
Ȧtet I, 917.
Ȧtet II, 917.
Ȧtet III, 917.
Ȧtet IV, 918.
Ȧtet V, 920.
'Αθωθις, 917.
Ȧtht-em-sekhem-f-em-taiu nebu (Ȧmen-ḥetep II), 932.
Ȧti I, 920.
Ȧti II, 921.
Ȧu- . . . - . . . , 930.
Au-ȧb-Rā I (Ḥer), 923.
Au-ȧb-Rā II, 924.
Ȧuapeth, 937.
Ȧuā-en-neter-menkh (Ptolemy X and Ptolemy XI), 943.
Ȧuā-en-netert-menkht (Ptolemy X), 943.
Ȧuā-en-netert-menkht-Rāt (Ptolemy XI), 943.
Ȧuā-en-neterui-menkhui (Ptolemy IV), 943.
Ȧuā-en-neterui-merui ȧtu (Ptolemy V), 943.
Ȧuā-en-neterui-perui (Ptolemy VII and Ptolemy IX), 943.
Ȧuā - en - neterui - senui (Ptolemy III), 942.
Ȧuā-en-p-neter-enti-neḥem (Ptolemy XIII), 943.
Ȧufni, 924.
Augustus, 945.
Aurelius, 946.
Aut-ȧb-Rā, 927.
Ȧuuapet, 937.

B.

Ba-en-neter, 918.
Ba-en-Rā (Menephthah I), 934.
Ba-en-Rā (Nepherites), 941.
Baiu-neter, 918.
Ba-ka-Rā (Tanut-Åmen), 940.
Bak-en-ren-f, 939.
Batchau, 918.
Bebenem, 928.
Bebi, 918.
Berenice I, II, III, IV, 944.
Βίνωθρις, 918.
Βοηθός, 918.

C.

Caesar, 944.
Caesarion, 944, 945.
Caligula, 945.
Cambyses, 940.
Caracalla, 946.
Cleopatra I, Syra, 944.
Cleopatra II, Soteira, 944.
Cleopatra III, Kokke, 944.
Cleopatra IV, Berenice, 944.
Cleopatra V, Tryphaena, 944.
Cleopatra VI, 945.
Commodus, 946.

D.

Darius (Δαρεῖος), the Great, 941.
Darius Ochus, 941.
Decius, 946.
Domitian, 946.

E.

En-ka-Rā I, 921.
En-ka-Rā II, 929.
En-maāt-Rā (Åmen-em-ḥat III), 923.
En-user-Rā (Ån), 919.
Epiphanes (Ptolemy V), 943.
Euergetes I (Ptolemy III), 942.
Euergetes II (Ptolemy IX), 943.
Eupator (Ptolemy VI), 943.

G.

Galba, 945.
Gerg-taui (Nefer-ḥetep I), 925.
Gerg-taui-f, 922.
Geta, 946.

H.

Ḥāā-åb-Rā I (Apries), 940.
Ḥāā-åb-Rā II (Alexander II), 942.
Hadrian, 946.
Ḥat-shepsut, 932.
Ḥeken-em-Maāt, 923.
Heker (Hagr), 941.
Ḥeq Ḥequ (Augustus, Caligula, Tiberius, Nero), 945.
Ḥeq-maāt-sekheper-taui (Åi II), 933.
Ḥeq-qennu (Alexander I), 942.
Ḥeq-semut (Philip), 942.
Ḥer (Au-åb-Rā I), 923.
Her-åb-Rā, 927.
Ḥer-Ḥeru, 936.
Ḥer-Ḥeru-sa-Åmen, 936.
Ḥeri-åb-Bat (?), 923.
Ḥeri-ḥer-maāt-sekheper-taui, 934.
Ḥeru- . . . . - . . . . , 930.
Ḥeruå, 925.
Ḥeru-Åkau, 920.
Ḥeru-Ipeq, 929.
Ḥeru-ka-nefer, 921.
Ḥeru-men khāu, 920.
Ḥeru-mer-en I, 921.
Ḥeru-mer-en II, 934.
Ḥeru-nefer-kau, 921.
Ḥeru-netch-tef, 931.
Ḥeru-sa-Åst, 938.
Ḥetch-kheper-Rā (Smendes), 937.
Ḥetch-kheper-Rā (Shashanq I, Thekreth II, and Ḥeru-sa-Åst), 938.
Ḥetep-åb-Rā, 931.
Ḥetep-åb-taui, 923.
Ḥetep-ḥer-maāt, 934.
Ḥetep-neteru (Sebekemsaf I), 931.
Ḥetep-sekhemiu, 918.
Ḥu, 917.
Ḥuni, 918.
Ḥunnu (Neos, Ptolemy VIII), 943.
Ḥunu-user-peḥti (Alexander II), 942.
Ḥutchfa, 918.

I.

Iābeq-her, 929.
Iāmu, 929.
'Ιάννας, 929.
Iāpeq-her, 929.
Ipeq Ḥeru, 929.
Iqebārhu (?), 929.
Iuȧa, 933.

K.

Ka, 917.
Ka-Ḥeru, 919.
Καίχως, 918.
Kakaȧ, 919.
Ka-kau, 918.
Ka-kha, 919.
Kambasuṭent, 940.
Kambȧthet, 940.
Ka-meri-Rā I (Khati I), 921.
Ka-meri-Rā II, 921.
Ka-nekht-āa-nekht-sānkh-taui (Rameses VI), 935.
Ka-nekht-āa-sutenit (Rameses II), 935.
Ka-nekht-ān-em-nesu (Rameses VII), 935.
Ka-nekht-ānkh-em-maāt (Rameses IV), 935.
Ka-nekht-Ȧten-meri (Ȧmen-ḥetep IV), 933.
Ka-nekht-ḥāi-em-maāt (Meneph-thah I), 934.
Ka-nekht-ḥen-nesiu (Rameses I), 934.
Ka-nekht-khā-em-maāt (Thoth-mes III and Ȧmen-ḥetep III), 932, 933.
Ka-nekht-khā-em-Uast (Rameses IX), 935.
Ka-nekht-khā-em-Uast-sānkh-taui (Seti I), 934.
Ka-nekht-meri-maāt (Thothmes I, and Rameses II and Philip Arrhidaeus), 932, 934, 942.
Ka-nekht-meri-Rā (Seti II and Rameses XI), 934, 935.
Ka-nekht-qa-shuti (Ȧmen-ḥetep IV), 933.
Ka-nekht-sa-Ȧmen, 936.
Ka-nekht-sekhā-Rā (Rameses X), 935.
Ka-nekht-sepṭ-sekheru (Ȧmen-em-ḥeb), 934.
Ka-nekht-tekhen-maāt (Rameses V), 935.
Ka-nekht-theḥen-khāu (Ȧi II), 933.
Ka-nekht-tut-khāu (Thothmes IV), 932.
Ka-nekht-tut-mesut (Tut-ānkh-Ȧmen), 733.
Ka-nekht-ur-peḥti (Ȧmen-ḥetep II and Set-nekht), 932, 934.
Ka-nekht-user-peḥti (Thothmes II), 932.
Ka- . . . . -Rā, 927.
Ka-Set-Rā, 925, 929.
Kashta, 939.
Ka-uāf-taui (Ȧmen-ḥetep I), 932.
Kenbutcha, 940.
Κενκένης, 917.
Κεφρήν, 919.
Khā-ānkh-Rā (Sebek-ḥetep V), 925.
Khaȧu, 917.
Khā-ba, 919.
Khabasha, 941.
Khā-em-Khebit (Sa-Ptaḥ), 934.
Khā-em-maāt (Rameses IX), 935.
Khā-em-maāt-seshem-taui (Tcheḥer), 941.
Khā-em-nesert-āa-peḥti (Thoth-mes I), 932.
Khā-em-Uast (Rameses XI), 935.
Khā-f-Rā, 919.
Khā-ḥetep-Rā (Sebek-ḥetep VI), 925.
Khā-ka-Rā, 925.
Khā-kau-Rā (Usertsen III), 923.
Khā-kheru-Rā, 926.
Khā-mȧ-Ptaḥ, 934.
Khā-mu-Rā, 929.
Khā-nefer-Rā (Sebek-ḥetep IV), 925.
Khā- . . . . -Rā, 927.
Khā-sekhem, 918.
Khā-sekhemui, 918.
Khā-seshesh-Rā (Nefer-ḥetep I), 925.
Khati I, II, III, 921.
Khāu-f-Rā, 919.
Khā-user-Rā I, 922.
Khā-user-Rā II, 929.
Khentcher, 928.

Khent-tȧ, 917.
Khenṭu, 920.
Χέοψ, 919.
Kheper-ka-Rā (Usertsen I and Nectanebus II), 923, 942.
Kheper-khā-Rā (Usertsen II, and Pasebkhān I and Pasebkhān II), 923, 936, 937.
Kheper-Kheperu-Rā (Ȧi II), 933.
Kheper-maāt-Rā (Rameses X), 935.
Kheper-Ptaḥ (Ptolemy VII), 943.
Kheperu (?) (Ȧmen-em-ḥat IV), 923.
Kheperu - neb - Rā (Tut - ānkh - Ȧmen), 933.
Khian, 929.
Khnem-ȧb-en-maāt (Arsinoë II), 944.
Khnem-ȧb-Rā (Ȧāḥmes II), 940.
Khnem-maāt-Rā (Hagr), 941.
Khshaiarsha, 941.
Khu-ȧqer, 928.
Khufu (Cheops), 919.
Khui-Beq-t-uāf-taiu (Tcheḥer), 941.
Khu-taui (Sebek-ḥetep III and Tirhakah), 925, 940.
Khu-taui-Rā (Ugaf), 924.
Khu-taui-sekhem-Rā, 930.
Kilgipa, 923.

L.

Λαχαρῆς, 923.
Lathyrus (Ptolemy X), 943.

M.

Maā- . . . . 920.
Maā-ȧb-Rā, 922.
Maā-kheru-Rā (Ȧmen-em-ḥat IV), 923.
Maāt-ka-Rā I (Ȧssȧ), 920.
Maāt-ka-Rā II Ḥatshepsut), 932.
Mak-Kamt-uāf-setu (Seti II), 934.
Mak - Kamt - uāfu - Petchtiu IX (Rameses IV), 935.
Mak-Kam-uāf-Khaskht (Rameses II), 934.
Masaherth, 936.
Meḥ-ȧb-taui, 924.
Meḥti-em-sa-f I, 920.
Meḥti-em-sa-f II, 920.
Mekha, 917.
Men, 917.
Menȧ, 917.
Menephthah I, 934.
Menephthah II, 934.
Μήνης, 917.
Men-ka-Rā, 920.
Men-kau-Ḥeru, 920.
Men-kau-Rā, 919.
Men-khāu (Men-kau-Ḥeru), 920.
Men-khāu-Rā, 928.
Men-kheper-Rā (Thothmes III, and the son of Painetchem I and Piānkhi), 932, 937, 940.
Men-kheperu-Rā (Thothmes IV), 932.
Μενχέρης, 919.
Men-khet (Psammetichus II), 940.
Men-maāt-Rā (Seti I and Rameses XI), 934, 935.
Men-mȧ-Rā (Ȧmenmeses), 934.
Men-peḥti-Rā (Rameses I), 934.
Menthu-ḥetep, I, II, III, IV, V, and VI, 922, 926.
Mentu-em-sa-f, 926.
Μήφρης, 932.
Mer-ānkh-Rā, 926.
Mer-en-Ḥeru I, 921.
Mer-en-Ḥeru II, 934.
Mer-en-Ptaḥ I, II and III, 934.
Mer-en-Rā I, 920.
Mer-en-Rā II, 920.
Mer-ḥetep-Rā I (Ȧnȧ), 925.
Mer-ḥetep-Rā II (Sebek-ḥetep VII), 925.
Meri-Ȧāḥ, 921.
Meri-Ȧmen, a title of Seti II, Set-nekht, Rameses II, V, VI, VII, VIII, IX, XI (Rameses XII ?), Painetchem I, Smendes, Pasebkhān II and III, Ȧmen-em-ȧpt, Sa-Ȧmen, Shashanq I, II, III and IV, Usarken I, II and III, Thekreth I, II and III, Ḥeru-sa-Ȧst, Peṭa-Bast, Pamai, Piānkhi, Nectanebus I, Ȧmen-ruṭ, Alexander the Great, Philip Arrhidaeus, and Ptolemy, 934–942.
Meri-Ȧmen-Rā (Uasarkenȧ), 939.

Meri-Åmen-Rā-neb Heb (Darius Ochus), 941.
Meri-Åst (Ptolemy IV), 943.
Meri - maāt - sekhut - pau - neteru (Tcheḥer), 941.
Meri-Ptaḥ, a title of Seti I (934), Ptolemy III (942) and Ptolemy V, VII, IX, X, XI and XIII, 943.
Meri-Ptaḥ Åst, a title of Tiberius, Caligula and Nero, 945.
Meri-Rā (Pepi I), 920.
Meri-senu (Philadelphus), 942.
Meri-taui (Pepi I), 920 (Nectanebus I), 941.
Meri-tef (Philopator), 943.
Mer-ka-Rā, Mer-kau-Rā, 926.
Mer-kheper-Rā, 926.
Mer-mashāu, 924.
Mer-nefer-Rā (Åi I), 925.
Mer-netchem-Rā, 925.
Mer-neteru, 934.
Merpeba, 917.
Mer-sekhem-Rā I, 925.
Mer-sekhem-Rā II, 926.
Mer-sekhem-Rā III, 928.
Mer-tchefau-Rā, 927.
Mer-user-Rā, 929.
Mes-ḥemut, 940.
Mesut-Rā (Cambyses), 940.
Metcha (Khufu), 919.
Μεθουσουφίς, 920.
Μιεβις, 917.
Μισάφρις, 932.
Μισφραγμουθωσίς, 932.

N.

Na-ap-khar-ri-ya, 933.
Na-ap-khu-ra-ri-ya, 933.
Na-ap-khu-ru-ri-a, 933.
Naifāaurut, 941.
Nār-mer, 917.
Neb-ā (Psammetichus I), 940.
Neb-åri-au-Rā I, II, 930.
Neb-f-au-Rā, 926.
Neb-ḥep-Rā, 922.
Nebi (Nefer-ka-Rā V), 920.
Neb-ka I, 918.
Neb-ka II, 918.
Neb-ka-Rā I, 918.
Neb-ka-Rā II, 918.
Neb-kau (Khati III), 921.
Neb-khāu (Saḥu-Rā), 919.
Neb-khepesh (Apries), 940.
Neb-khepesh-Rā (Åpepå II), 929.
Neb-maāt (Seneferu), 919.
Neb-maāt-Rā I, 926.
Neb-maāt-Rā II, 926.
Neb-maāt-Rā (Åmen-ḥetep III), 933.
Neb-maāt-Rā (Rameses VI), 935.
Neb-peḥti-Rā (Åāḥmes I), 932.
Neb-sen-Rā, 927.
Neb-seṭu-må-Tenen (Åmenmeses) 934.
Neb-taui (Menthu-ḥetep IV), 922.
Neb-taui-Rā (Menthu-ḥetep IV), 922.
Neb-ṭeṭ-Rā, 929.
Necho, 940.
Nefer-åb-Rā I, 927.
Nefer-åb-Rā II (Psammetichus II), 940.
Nefer-åri-ka-Rā I, 919.
Nefer-åri-ka-Rā II, 921.
Nefer-f-Rā, 919.
Nefer-hepu sgerḥ-taui, 933.
Nefer-ḥetep I, 925.
Nefer-ḥetep II, 926.
Nefer-ka, 920.
Nefer-ka-Ḥeru, 921.
Nefer-ka-Rā I, 918.
Nefer-ka-Rā II, 918.
Nefer-ka-Rā III (Pepi II), 920.
Nefer-ka-Rā IV, 920.
Nefer-ka-Rā V (Nebi), 920.
Nefer-ka-Rā VI (Khenṭu), 920.
Nefer-ka-Rā VII (Terrl), 921.
Nefer-ka-Rā VIII (Senb), 921.
Nefer-ka-Rā IX, 921.
Nefer-ka-Rā X, 921.
Nefer-ka-Rā XI (Rameses IX), 935.
Nefer-ka-Rā XII (Shabaka), 939.
Nefer-ka-Seker, 918.
Nefer-kau-Ḥeru, 921.
Nefer-kau-Rā, 921.
Nefer-khāu, 919.
Nefer-kheperu, 931.
Nefer-kheperu-Rā, 933.
Nefer-renput- etc., 932.
Nefer-Tem- . . . 927.
Nefer-Tem-khu-Rā, 950.
Nefres, 920.

Neheb, 917.
Neḥsi, 926.
Nekau, 940.
Νεχαώ, 940.
Nekht, 917.
Nekht-Ḥeru-ḥeb, 941.
Nekht-neb-f, 942.
Nekht-neb-tep-nefer, 922.
Νεκώς, 940.
Νεκτανέβης, 941.
Νεκτανεβός, 942.
Neos Dionysos (Ptolemy XIII), 943.
Neos Philopator (Ptolemy VIII), 943.
Νεφερίτης, 941.
Νεφερχέρης, 918.
Nero, 945.
Nerva, 946.
Nes-ba-neb-Ṭeṭ, 937.
Net-åqerti (Nitocris), 920.
Netch (Soter I), 942.
Netchem-åb-Rā, 924.
Neter-baiu, 921.
Neter-ḥetch, 922.
Neter-ka-Rā, 920.
Neter-khāu, 920.
Neter-kheper-Rā, 937.
Neter-kheperu, 923.
Neter-menkh, 943.
Neter-mert, 922.
Netert-khāu, 932.
Netert-nesi, 932.
Ni-ib-mu-a-ri-ya, 933.
Ni-ip-khu-ur-ri-ri-ya, 933.
Νίτωκρις, 920.
Nub-ka-Rā, 929.
Nub-kau-Rā, 923.
Nub-kheper-Rā, 931.
Nub- . . . -Rā, 929.
Nub-taui-Rā, 922.
Nubti, 929.

O.

Ὄννος, 918.
Ὀσόρθων, 938.
Otho (Marcus), 945.
Οὔαφρις, 940.
Οὐενέφης, 917.
Οὐσαφαίδος, 917.
Οὐσερχέρης, 919.

P.

Pa-ḥeq-qen (Kames), 932.
Pai-ānkh, 936.
Pai-netchem I, 936.
Pai-netchem II, 937.
Pamai, 939.
Pasebkhān I, II, III, 937.
Penen-set- . . . 930.
Pepi I, 920.
Pepi II, 920.
Pepi III, 921.
Per-åb-sen, 918.
Per-en-maāt, 918.
Peṭa-Bast, 938.
Peṭa-Bast sa Bast, 739.
Pharaoh, Great, 941.
Philadelpha I, 944.
Philadelphus I (Ptolemy II), 942.
Philadelphus II (Ptolemy XIII), 943.
Philip Arrhidaeus, 942.
Philip (Emperor), 946.
Philometor I (Ptolemy IV), 943.
Philometor II (Ptolemy X), 943.
Philometor III (Ptolemy XI), 943.
Philometor IV (Ptolemy XVI), 944.
Philopator I (Ptolemy IV), 943.
Philopator II (Ptolemy VIII), 943.
Philopator III (Ptolemy XIII), 943.
Philopator (Ptolemy XVI), 944.
Philotera, 944.
Phiriupus (Philiupus), 942.
Piānkhi the Great, 939.
Piānkhi-sa-Bast, 939.
Piānkhi, son of Shabataka, 940.
Pilatura, 944.
Pillppas or Pirrppas (Philip), 942.
P-neter-ḥunnu (Neos), 943.
P-neter-menkh (Euergetes), 942.
P-neter-mer-mut-f (Philometor), 943.
P-neter-peri (Epiphanes), 943.
Pripus or Plipus (Philip), 942.
Ψαμμήτιχος, 940.
Ψάμμουθις, 941.
Psa-mut, 941.
Psemthek (Psammetichus), I, II, III, 940.

Ptaḥ-Seti-sa-Ptaḥ-meri, 936.
Pṭlmis (Ptolemy I, the Satrap), 942.
Ptlmis (Ptolemy I), 942.
Ptlumis (Ptolemy), 942.
Ptolemy I-III, 942; IV-XIII, 943; XIV-XVI, 944.
Ptulmis, Pṭulmis (Ptolemy), 942.

Q.

Qa-ā, 917.
Qa-ka-Rā (Ȧntef V), 922.
Qa-ka-Rā II (Ȧn), 942.
Qa-khāu (Tirhakah), 940.
Qar, 930.
Qebḥu, 917.
Qennu (Haġr), 941.
Qennu (Psammetichus I), 940.

R.

Rā-ȧ- . . . 927.
Rā-āa-ārq, 929.
Rā-āa-ḥetep, 922.
Rā-āa-khā I, 922.
Rā-āa-khā II, 929.
Rā-āa-kheper I (Pasebkhān III), 937.
Rā-āa-kheper II (Shashanq IV), 939.
Rā-āa-kheper III (Uasarkenȧ), 939.
Rā-āa-kheper-en (Thothmes II), 932.
Rā-āa-kheper-ka (Thothmes I), 932.
Rā-āa-kheperu, 932.
Rā-ȧakhu-en (Sa-Ptaḥ), 934.
Rā-āa-neter, 929.
Rā-āa-peḥ, 929.
Rā-āa-qenu (Ȧpepȧ III), 929.
Rā-āa-user (Ȧpepȧ I), 728.
Rā- . . . -ȧb-khent, 922.
Rā-ȧn (?) kau, 921.
Rā-ānkh-ka I, 928.
Rā-ānkh-ka II (Psammetichus III), 940.
Rā-ānkh-kheperu, 933.
Rā-ȧri-maāt, title of Ptolemy VII, IX, X, XI and XIII, 943.
Rā-au-ȧb I (Ḥer), 923.
Rā-au-ȧb II, 924.
Rā-aut-ȧb III, 927.
Rā-ba-en I (Menephthah I), 934.
Rā-ba-en II (Nepherites), 941.
Rā-ba-ka (Tanut-Ȧmen), 940.
Rā-en-ka I, 921.
Rā-en-ka II, 929.
Rā-en-maāt (Ȧmen-em-ḥat III), 923.
Rā-en-user (Ȧn), 919.
Rā-ḥāā-ȧb (Apries), 940.
Rā-ḥāā-ȧb (Alexander II), 942.
Rā-her-ȧb, 927.
Rā-ḥetch-kheper I (Smendes), 937.
Rā-ḥetch-kheper II (Shashanq I), 938.
Rā-ḥetch-kheper III (Ḥeru-sa-Ȧst), 938.
Rā-ḥetch-kheper IV (Thekreth II), 938.
Rā-ḥetep, 931.
Rā-ḥetep-āa, 929.
Rā-ka- . . . , 927.
Rā-ka-meri (Khati I), 921.
Rā-ka-Set I, 925.
Rā-ka-Set II, 929.
Rā-khā- . . . , 927.
Rā-khā-ānkh, 925.
Rā-khā-f, Rā-khāu-f, 919.
Rā-khā-ḥetep, 925.
Rā-khā-ka, 925.
Rā-khā-kau, 923.
Rā-khā-kheper (Usertsen II), 923.
Rā-khā-kheru, 926.
Rā-khā-mu, 929.
Rā-khā-nefer, 925.
Rā-khā-Seshesh, 925.
Rā-khā-user I, 922.
Rā-khā-user II, 929.
Rā-kheper-ka I (Usertsen I), 923.
Rā-kheper-ka II (Nectanebus II), 942.
Rā-kheper-khā I (Pai-netchem I), 936.
Rā-kheper-khā II (Pasebkhān), 937.
Rā-kheper-kheperu (Ȧi II), 933.
Rā-kheper-maāt (Rameses X), 935.
Rā-khnem-ȧb (Ȧāḥmes II), 940.
Rā-khnem-maāt, 941.
Rā-khu-taui (Uġaf), 924.
Rā-khu-taui-sekhem, 920.
Rā-maā-ȧb, 922.

Rā-maā-kheru (Ȧmen-em-ḥat IV), 923.
Rā-maāt-ka I (Ȧssȧ), 920.
Rā-maāt-ka II (Ḥatshepsut), 932.
Rā-men-ka, 920.
Rā-men-kau, 919.
Rā-men-khāu (Seshȧb), 928.
Rā-men-kheper I (Thothmes III), 932.
Rā-men-kheper II (son of Pai-netchem), 937.
Rā-men-kheper III (Piānkhi), 940.
Rā-men-kheperu (Thothmes IV), 932.
Rā-men-mȧ (Ȧmen-meses), 934.
Rā-men-maāt (Seti I), 934.
Rā-men-maāt (Rameses XI), 935.
Rā-men-peḥti (Rameses I), 934.
Rā-mer-ānkh (Menthu-ḥetep VI), 926.
Rā-mer-en I (Meḥti-em-sa-f I), 920.
Rā-mer-en II (Meḥti-em-sa-f II), 920.
Rā-mer-ḥetep I (Ȧnȧ), 925.
Rā-mer-ḥetep II (Sebek-ḥetep VII), 925.
Rā-meri (Pepi I), 920.
Rā-mer-ka, Rā-mer-kau (Sebek-ḥetep VIII), 926.
Rā-mer-kheper, 926.
Rā-mer-nefer (Ȧi I), 925.
Rā-mer-netchem, 925.
Rā-mer-sekhem I (Ȧn- . . .), 925.
Rā-mer-sekhem II (Nefer-ḥetep II), 926.
Rā-mer-sekhem III, 928.
Rā-mert (Sebek-neferu-Rā), 923.
Rā-mer-tchefau, 927.
Rā-mer-user (Iābeqher), 929.
Rameses, Ramessu, I-XII, 934-935.
Rā-messes meri Ȧmen, 936.
Ῥαμέσσης I, 934.
Ῥαμέσσης Μιαμοῦν, 934.
Rā-mes-suser-taui I, 931.
Ῥαμψίνιτος, 935.
Rā-neb, 918.
Rā-neb-ȧri-au I and II, 930.
Rā-neb-f-au, 926.
Rā-neb-ḥep (Menthu-ḥetep III), 922.
Rā-neb-ka I, 918.
Rā-neb-ka II, 918.
Rā-neb-kheperu (Tutānkh-Ȧmen), 933.
Rā-neb-khepesh (Ȧpepȧ II), 929.
Rā-neb-maāt I, 926.
Rā-neb-maāt II, 926.
Rā-neb-maāt III (Ȧmen-ḥetep III), 933.
Rā-neb-maāt IV (Rameses VI), 935.
Rā-neb-peḥti (Ȧāḥmes I), 932.
Rā-neb-sen, 927.
Rā-neb-taui (Menthu-ḥetep IV), 922.
Rā-neb-tchefau I, 927.
Rā-neb-tchefau II, 927.
Rā-neb-ṭeṭ, 929.
Rā-nefer-ȧb I, 927.
Rā-nefer-ȧb II (Psammetichus II), 940.
Rā-nefer-ȧri-ka I, 919.
Rā-nefer-ȧri-ka II, 921.
Rā-nefer-f, 919.
Rā-nefer-ka I, 918.
Rā-nefer-ka II, 918.
Rā-nefer-ka III (Pepi II), 920.
Rā-nefer-ka IV, 920.
Rā-nefer-ka V (Nebi), 920.
Rā-nefer-ka VI (Khenṭu), 920.
Rā-nefer-ka VII (Terrl), 921.
Rā-nefer-ka VIJI (Pepi III Senb), 921.
Rā-nefer-ka IX, 921.
Rā-nefer-ka X, 921.
Rā-nefer-ka XI (Rameses IX), 935.
Rā-nefer-ka XII (Shabaka), 939.
Rā-nefer-kau, 921.
Rā-nefer-kheperu (Ȧmen-ḥetep IV), 933.
Rā-netchem-ȧb, 924.
Rā-neter-ka, 920.
Rā-neter-kheper (Sa-Ȧmen), 937.
Rā-nub- . . . , 929.
Rā-nub-ka, 929.
Rā-nub-kau (Ȧmen-em-ḥat II), 923.
Rā-nub-kheper (Ȧntef X), 931.
Rā-nub-taui, 922.
Rā-qa-ka I (Ȧntef V), 922.
Rā-qa-ka II (Ȧn), 942.
Rā-sāa-ka, 933.

Rā-saḥu, 919.
Rā-sānkh-ȧb (Ȧntef VIII), 924,
Rā-sānkh-en (Senb), 925.
Rā-sānkh-ka I (Menthu-ḥetep), 922.
Rā-sānkh-ka II, 927.
Rā-seba- . . . , 928.
Rā-Sebek-ka, 928.
Rā-Sebek-neferu, 923.
Rā-seḥeb, 927.
Rā-seher-ȧb (Peṭa-Bast sa Bast), 939.
Rā-seḥetep-ȧb I (Ȧmen-em-ḥat I), 923.
Rā-seḥetep-ȧb II, 924.
Rā-seḥetep-ȧb III, 924.
Rā-sekhā-en (Rameses XII), 935.
Rā-sekheper-en, 927.
Rā-sekhem- . . . I, 927.
Rā-sekhem- . . . II, 930.
Rā-sekhem- . . . III, 930.
Rā-sekhem- . . . IV, 930.
Rā-sekhem- . . . V, 930.
Rā-sekhem-ka I, 921.
Rā-sekhem-ka II, 924.
Rā-sekhem-kheper (Uasarken I), 938.
Rā-sekhem-khu-taui (Sebek-ḥetep II), 924.
Rā-sekhem-nefer-kau, 931.
Rā-sekhem-sheṭ-taui, 931.
Rā-sekhem-smen-taui, 931.
Rā-sekhem-suatch-taui (Sebek-ḥetep III), 925.
Rā-sekhem-uatch-kau, 931.
Rā-sekheper-en (Rameses V), 935.
Rā-senb-ka, 927.
Rā-senefer-ȧb I (Usertsen IV), 923.
Rā-senefer-ȧb II, 924.
Rā-senefer-f, 929.
Rā-senefer-ka I, 921.
Rā-senefer-ka II, 924.
Rā-senekht-en, 931.
Rā-senetchem-ȧb (Nekht-Ḥer-ḥeb), 941.
Rā-ses- . . . 930.
Rā-seshesh-kheper, 938.
Rā- . . . -Set, 929.
Rā-setchef-[Ra], 924.
Rā-shepses (Tafnekht I), 939.
Rā-shepses-ka, 919.
Rā-skhā-en, 922.
Rā-skhent-en, 931.
Rā-smen- . . . 928.
Rā-smen-ka, 924.
Rā-smenkh-ka, 924.
Rā-smen-taui, 930.
Rā-suaḥ-en, 926.
Rā-suatch-en I, 931.
Rā-suatch-en II, 931.
Rā-suatch-ka (Ḥeruȧ), 925.
Rā-suser- . . . 930.
Rā-suser-en (Khian), 929.
Rā-taȧ-kheperu, 937.
Rā-tcheser-ka (Ȧmen-ḥetep I), 932.
Rā-tcheṭ-f, 919.
Rā-ṭeṭ-ānkh, 926.
Rā-ṭeṭ-f, 919.
Rā-ṭeṭ-ḥetep, 926.
Rā-ṭeṭ-ka I (Ȧssȧ), 920.
Rā-ṭeṭ-ka II (Maā- . . . - . . .), 920.
Rā-ṭeṭ-kau (Shabataka), 940.
Rā-ṭeṭ-kheru, 927.
Rā-ṭeṭ-nefer, 926.
Rā-uaḥ-ȧb I (Ȧā-ȧb), 925.
Rā-uaḥ-ȧb II (Psammetichus I), 940.
Rā-uaḥ-ka I (Khati II), 921.
Rā-uaḥ-ka II (Bokchoris), 939.
Rā-uatch-ka I, 921.
Rā-uatch-ka II, 929.
Rā-uatch-kheper (Kames), 932.
Rā-uhem-ȧb (Necho), 940.
Rā-user-ka I (Ȧti I), 920.
Rā-user-[ka] II, 924.
Rā-user-ka III (Khentcher), 928.
Rā-user-ka IV (Ptolemy II), 942.
Rā-user-ka V (Ptolemy IV), 943.
Rā-user-ka VI (Ptolemy V), 943.
Rā-user-khāu, 934.
Rā-user-kheperu (Seti II), 934.
Rā-user-maāt I (Rameses II), 934.
Rā-user-maāt II (Rameses III), 935.
Rā-user-maāt III (Rameses IV), 935.
Rā-user-maāt IV (Rameses V), 935.
Rā-user-maāt V (Rameses VII), 935.
Rā-user-maāt VI (Rameses VIII), 935.
Rā-user-maāt VII (Ȧmen-em-ȧpt), 937.
Rā-user-maāt VIII (Thekreth I), 938.

Rā-user-maāt IX (Uasarken II), 938.
Rā-user-maāt X (Peṭa-Bast), 938.
Rā-user-maāt XI (Uasarken III), 938.
Rā-user-maāt XII (Thekreth III), 938.
Rā-user-maāt XIII (Shashanq III), 938.
Rā-user-maāt XIV (Pamȧi), 939.
Rā-user-maāt XV (Piānkhi), 939.
Rā-user-maāt XVI (Ȧmenruṭ), 942.
Ren-senb, 924.
Rhampsinitus, 935.

S.

Sāa-ka-Rā, 933.
Sa-Ȧmen (Ḥer-Ḥeru), 936.
Σαβάκων, 939.
Sa-Bast (Piānkhi), 939.
Sa-Hathor, 925.
Sa-Ḥet-Ḥer, 925.
Saḥu-Rā, 919.
Salitis, 928.
Sa-nekht (Neb-ka-Rā II), 918.
Sa Net (Amasis II), 940.
Sānkh-ȧb-Rā (Ȧntef VII ?), 924.
Sānkh-ȧb-taui (Menthu-ḥetep III), 922.
Sānkh-en-Rā (Senb), 925.
Sānkh-ka-Rā I (Menthu-ḥetep V), 922.
Sānkh-ka-Rā II, 927.
Sānkh-taui-f, 922.
Sa-Ptaḥ I, 934.
Sa-Ptaḥ II (Rameses XII ?), 935.
Sāsh-qennu (Piānkhi), 940.
Seba- . . . -Rā, 928.
Sebek-em-sa-f I, 931.
Sebek-em-sa-f II, 931.
Sebek-ḥetep I, 924.
Sebek-ḥetep II, 924.
Sebek-ḥetep III, 925.
Sebek-ḥetep IV, 925.
Sebek-ḥetep V, 925.
Sebek-ḥetep VI, 925.
Sebek-ḥetep VII, 925.
Sebek-ḥetep VIII, 926.
Sebek-ka-Rā I, 923.
Sebek-ka-Rā II, 928.
Sebek-neferu-Rā, 923.
Sebek-sheṭ (?)-neferu, 923.
Σεβιχώς, 940.
Sebkai, 928.
Seḥeb-Rā, 927.
Seher-ȧb-neteru (Nectanebus I), 941.
Seher-ȧb-Rā (Peṭa-Bast sa Bast), 939.
Seher-taui I, 921.
Seher-taui II, 924.
Seḥetep-ȧb-Rā I (Ȧmen-em-ḥat I), 923.
Seḥetep-ȧb-Rā II, 924.
Seḥetep-ȧb-Rā III, 924.
Seḥetep-ȧb-taui, 923.
Seḥetep-neteru (Hagr), 941.
Seḥetep-taui I (Ȧtet V), 920.
Seḥetep-taui II (Ȧpepȧ III), 929.
Seḥetep-taui-f (Piānkhi), 939.
Seket, 930.
Sekhā-en-Rā (Rameses XII ?), 935.
Sekhem-ȧb, 918.
Sekhem-ānkh-[en]-Ȧmen, a title of Ptolemies III, IV, V, IX, X, XI, XIII, 942, 943.
Sekhem-ka-Rā I, 921.
Sekhem-ka-Rā II, 924.
Sekhem-khāu (Ȧti I), 920.
Sekhem-kheper-Rā (Usertsen I), 938.
Sekhem-kheperu (Thothmes II), 932.
Sekhem-khu-taui-Rā (Sebek-ḥetep II), 924.
Sekhem-nefer-khāu-Rā, 931.
Sekhem-peḥti-khu-khāu (Thothmes III), 932.
Sekhem - peḥti - ṭer - Petchtiu IX (Seti I), 934.
Sekhem-peḥti-ṭer-Satt (Ȧi II), 933.
Sekhem- . . . -Rā I, 927.
Sekhem- . . . -Rā II, 930.
Sekhem- . . . -Rā III, 930.
Sekhem-Rā-ānkh-taui, 931.
Sekhem-Rā-sāa-taui, 931.
Sekhem-sheṭ-taui-Rā, 931.
Sekhem-smen-taui-Rā, 931.
Sekhem-suatch-taui-Rā, 925.
Sekhem-uaḥ-khā-Rā, 931.
Sekhem-uatch-khāu-Rā, 931.
Sekhenn . . . 929.
Sekheper-en-Rā I, 927.

Sekheper-en-Rā II (Rameses V), 935.
Σεμέμψης, 917.
Semqen, 929.
Semti, 917.
Senb I, 921.
Senb II, 925.
Senb-f, 924.
Senb-ka-Rā, 927.
Senb-mȧ-au, 926.
Senefer-ȧb-Rā I (Usertsen IV ?), 923.
Senefer-ȧb-Rā II, 924.
Senefer-f-Rā (Piānkhi), 939.
Senefer-ka I, 921.
Senefer-ka II (Ānnu), 921.
Senefer-ka-Rā I, 921.
Senefer-ka-Rā II, 924.
Senefer-taui (Psammetichus II), 940.
Senefer-taui-f I (Ȧntef V), 922.
Senefer-taui-f (Ȧn), 942.
Senefer-taui-Rā Sekhem, 926.
Seneferu, 919.
Senekht-en-Rā, 931.
Senen-ānkh-en-Ȧmen, title of Ptolemy XI, 943.
Senen-en-Ptaḥ, title of Khabbasha, 941.
Senetchem-ȧb-Rā, 941.
Sentȧ, 918.
Senusert I-IV, 923.
Sepṭ-taui (Amasis II), 940.
Seqeb-taui (Shabaka), 939.
Seqenen-Rā I Tau-āa, 931.
Seqenen-Rā II Tau-āa Āa, 931.
Seqenen-Rā III Tau-āa Qen, 931.
Sesh-ȧb, 928.
Seshesh-ka-Rā, 924.
Seshesh-kheper-Rā (Shashanq II), 938.
Seshesh-Rā-her-ḥer-maāt, 931.
Seshesh-Rā-upu-em-maāt, 931.
Σεσώγχις, 938.
Σεσόγχωσις, 923.
Σέσωστρις, 923.
Ses- . . . -Rā, 930.
Set- . . . - . . . 930.
Set-āa-peḥti (Nubti), 929.
Setchef-[ka]-Rā, 924.
Setchef-taui (Kames), 932.
Setches, 918.
Setep-en-Ȧmen, a title of Rameses IV (935), Painetchem I (936), Pasebkhān II, Pasebkhān III, Ȧmen-em-ȧpt, Sa-Ȧmen, Thekreth I, Thekreth II, Uasarken II, Shashanq II, Ḥeru-sa-Ast Peṭa-Bast, Uasarkenȧ, Ȧmen-ruṭ, Alexander II, Ptolemy I, 937-942.
Setep-en-Ȧnḥer, 941.
Setep-en-Ptaḥ, a title of Ptolemy IV, Ptolemy V, Ptolemy IX, Ptolemy X, Ptolemy XI, Ptolemy XIII (943), Augustus, Nero (945).
Setep-en-Rā, a title of Rameses II, Sa-Ptaḥ, Set-nekht (934), Rameses VII, Rameses IX, Rameses X (935), Rameses XI (935), Pasebkhān, Smendes (937), Shashanq I, Uasarken I, Thekreth II, Shishak III, Psamut (941), Alexander the Great, Philip, Ptolemy III (942).
Setep[en]Tenen, a title of Khabbasha, 941.
Setep-neteru (Amasis II), 940.
Σεθένης, 918.
Σέθως, Σέθωσις, 934.
Seti I Meri Ptaḥ, 934.
Seti II, 934.
Set-nekht, 934.
Setut-Rā (Darius the Great), 941.
Severus, 946.
Sha-ba-ku-u, 939.
Shabaka, 939.
Shabataka, 940.
Shashanq I-IV, 938, 939.
Shepses-ka-f, 919.
Shepses-ka-Rā, 919.
Shepses Rā (Tafnekht I), 939.
Sheshȧ, 930.
Shishak, 938.
Ska, 917.
Σκεμίοφρις, 923.
Skhā-en-Rā, 922.
Skhent-en-Rā, 931.
Sma-taui (Sebek-ḥetep V), 925.
Smai-taui I (Piānkhi), 940.
Smai-taui II (Cambyses), 940.
Smendes, Σμένδης, 937.
Smen-hepu I, Sgerḥ-taui (Ȧmen-ḥetep III), 933.

Smen-hepu II (Nectanebus I), 941.
Smen-ka-Rā, 924.
Smenkh-ka-Rā (Mer-Mashāu), 924.
Smenkh-taui (Nectanebus II), 942.
Smen-maāt (Amasis II), 940.
Smen-maāt-Rā (Åmenmer), 936.
Smen ... Rā, 928.
Smen-taui-Rā, 930.
Smerkha (Ḥu or Nekht), 917.
Soter I, 942.
Soter II, 943.
Stenḥ, 919.
Suaḥ-en-Rā, 926.
Suatch-en-Rā, I, 931.
Suatch-en-Rā II, 931.
Suatch-ka-Rā (Ḥeruȧ), 925.
Suatch-taui I (Sesh-ȧb), 928.
Suatch-taui II (Apries), 940.
Su-ḥetes, 919.
Sunu -..... 930.
Suser-en-Rā (Khian), 929.
Suser -....- Rā, 930.

T.

Taȧ-kheperu-Rā, 937.
Tafnekht I, 939.
Tafnekht II, 939.
Taharqa, 940.
Tan-da-ma-ni-e, 940.
Ταυχέρης, 920.
Tanuat-Åmen, 940.
Tariusha (Darius), 941.
Taruasha (Darius), 941.
Ṭaṭa-mesu, 926.
Ṭaṭau-mes, 926.
Tȧu, 917.
Tau-āa, 931.
Tau-āa Āa, 931.
Tau-āa Qen, 931.
Tchar, 917.
Tchatchai, 917.
Tche-ḥer, 941.
Tche-khensu-ȧuf-ānkh, 936.
Tcheser I, Sa, 918.
Tcheser II, 918.
Tcheser-ka-Rā (Åmen-ḥetep I), 932.
Tcheser-kheperu, 933.
Tcheser-kheperu-Rā, 934.
Tcheṭ Åt, 917.
Tcheṭ-f-Rā, 919.
Tef-f-meri I (Philopator I), 943.
Tef-f-meri II (Philopator II), 943.
Teḥuti, 931.
Teḥuti-mes I-IV (Thothmes I-IV), 932.
Te-i-i, 933.
Ṭema-ā, 942.
Ṭemt-ȧb-taui, 921.
Τέως, 941.
Ṭeriusha (Darius), 941.
Terrl, 921.
Tetȧ (Åtet V), 920.
Ṭeṭ-ānkh-Rā, 926.
Ṭeṭ-f-Rā, 919.
Ṭeṭ-ḥetep-Rā, 926.
Τέθμωσις, 932.
Ṭeṭ-ka-Rā I (Åssȧ), 920.
Ṭeṭ-ka-Rā II, 920.
Ṭeṭ-kau-Rā, 940.
Ṭeṭ-khāu (Åssȧ), 920.
Ṭeṭ-kheru-Rā, 927.
Ṭeṭ-nefer-Rā, 926.
Ṭeṭ-ṭeṭ-nesiu-mȧ-Tem (Thothmes IV), 932.
Thekreth (Thekleth) I-III, 938.
Thesh, 917.
Thes-khāu-em-Ånu-resu (Åmen-ḥetep IV), 933.
Thes-rer-en-Åten (Åmen-ḥetep IV), 933.
Thes-taui (Amasis I), 932.
Thothmes I-IV, 932.
Thuȧu, 933.
Ti, 933.
Tiberius, 945.
Titus, 945.
Τλᾶς, 918.
Τούθμωσις, 932.
Trajan, 946.
Tut-ānkh-Åmen, 933.
Tut-mesut (Åāḥmes I), 932.

U.

Uā-en-Rā (Åmen-ḥetep IV), 933.
Uaḥ-ȧb-Rā I (Åā-ȧb), 925.
Uaḥ-ȧb-Rā II (Tafnekht II), 939.
Uaḥ-ȧb-Rā III (Psammetichus I), 940.
Uaḥ-ȧb-Rā IV (Apries), 940.
Uaḥ-ānkh (Åntef III), 922, 931.
Uaḥ-ka-Rā I (Khati II), 921.

Uaḥ-ka-Rā II (Bokchoris), 939.
Uaḥ-sutenit-mȧ-Rā-em-pet, 932.
Uasarken (Usarken) I-III, 938.
Uasarkenȧ (Uasarkenȧ), 939.
Uatcheṭ, 929.
Uatchet-renput, 932.
Uatch-ka-Rā I, 921.
Uatch-ka-Rā II, 929.
Uatch-kheper-Rā (Kames), 932.
Uatch-kheperu (Amasis I), 932.
Uatch-nār (?), 917.
Uatchnes, 918.
Uatch-taui (Unȧs), 920.
Uben-Rā I, 926.
Uben-Rā II, 927.
Uben-Rā III, 927.
Uġaf (?), 924.
Uhem-ȧb-Rā (Necho), 940.
Uhem-khāu, etc. (Seti I), 934.
Uhem-mesut (Ȧmen-em-ḥat I), 923.
Unȧs, 920.
Up-uat-em-sa-f, 931.
Upu-em-maāt, 931.
Ur-bȧt-em-Ȧpt, 934.
Ur-bi-em-Ȧpt (Ȧmenmeses), 934.
Ur-seṭu-mȧ-Tenen, 935.
Ur-sutenit, etc., 933.
User-ā (Psammetichus II), 940.
User-ȧb (Khāfrā) I, 919.
User-f-au, etc., 932.
Userkaf, 919.
User-ka-Rā I (Ȧti I), 920.
User-ka-Rā II, 924.
User-ka-Rā III (Khentcher), 928.
User-ka-Rā IV (Ptolemy II, 942.
User-ka-Rā V (Ptolemy IV), 943.
User-ka-Rā VI (Ptolemy V), 943.
User-khāu, 919.
User-khāu-Rā, 934.
User-kheperu-Rā (Seti II), 934.
User-khepesh-heṭ-ḥefnu, 935.
User-khepesh-sānkh-taui, 935.
User-khepesh-ṭer-Petchtiu IX, 932.
User-maāt-Rā I (Rameses II), 934.
User-maāt-Rā II (Rameses III), 935.
User-maāt-Rā III (Rameses IV), 935.
User-maāt-Rā IV (Rameses V), 935.
User-maāt-Rā V (Rameses VII), 935.
User-maāt-Rā VI (Rameses VIII), 935.
User-maāt-Rā VII (Ȧmen-em-ȧpt), 937.
User-maāt-Rā VIII (Thekreth I), 938.
User-maāt-Rā IX (Uasarken II), 938.
User-maāt-Rā X (Peṭa-Bast), 938.
User-maāt-Rā XI (Uasarken III), 938.
User-maāt-Rā XII (Thekreth III), 938.
User-maāt-Rā XIII (Shashanq III), 938.
User-maāt-Rā XIV (Pamȧi), 939.
User-maāt-Rā XV (Piānkhi), 939.
User-maāt-Rā XVI (Ȧmen-ruṭ), 942.
User-Ptaḥ (Psamut), 941.
User-renput-āa-nekhtut, 934.
User-renput-mȧ-Temu, etc., 935.
User-renput-ur-nekhtut, etc., 935.
Usert-kau (Ḥatshepsut), 932.
Usertsen I–IV, 923.
Uthes-khāu-seḥetep-neteru, 933.

V.

Verus, 946.
Vespasian, 945.

X.

Xerxes (Ξερξες) the Great, 941.

III.

INDEX OF GEOGRAPHICAL NAMES.

A.

Aboccis, 956a.
Abram's Field, 983a.
Abûkîr, 1042b.
Abû Simbel, 956a, 957b, 968a, 988a.
Abûṣîr, 985b.
Abûṣîr al-Malik, 947b.
Abutig, 982a.
Abydos, 947b, 950a, 952b, 956a b, 984b, 993a, 994b, 1004b, 1006a, 1009a, 1013b, 1023b, 1049b, 1050b.
Abydos, Great Canal of, 1004a.
Abydos, Necropolis of, 976b, 1019b.
Abydos, sacred lake of, 1040b.
Abydos shrine, 996b.
Abydos, well of, 1029b.
Abydos of the North (in the Fayyûm), 947b.
Accho, 968b.
Achshaph, 965b.
Adamah, 967a.
Addâr, 967a.
Adoraim, 967a.
Ahnâs al-Madînah, 1022a.
Ajalon, 952b.
Akhmîm, 949b, 956a.
Akko, 971a.
Alabastronpolis, 985b, 1015a b, 1041a, 1044b.
Alashiya, 961a.
Al-Batnûn, 1057a.
Aleppo, 1025a b.
Alexandria, 967b, 1009b, 1035a ; suburb of, 949a.
Al-Hîbah, 951b, 1062a.
Al-Hîbu, 1014a.
Al-Kâb, 958b, 980b, 1024b.
Al-Lahûn, 1011a, 1050b.
'Alwah, 960a.
Ȧmen, temple estate of, 990a.
Amorite, land of the, 957a.
Andropolis, 997b.
Andropolis-Gynaecopolis, 952a.
Ānep, 1029a.
Antinopolites, 1060b.
Apamea, 956b.
Aphroditopolis, 985b, 989a, 1013b, 1056a.
Aphroditopolites, 973b, 994a, 999a, 1008b, 1061a.
Apis Bull House, 1016a.
Apis-city, 1004b, 1035b.
Apis tomb, 970b.
Apollinopolis Magna, 1061b.
Apollinopolis Parva, 1044b.
Apollinopolites, 966a, 976b, 1060a.
Arabia, 948a, 957b, 1062b.
Arabian Peninsula, 1051a.
Arad, 968a.
Aradus, 951a.
Armant, 958b, 988a.
Armenia, 948a.
Arsinoë, 949a.
Arsinoïtes, 992a, 1041b.
Arvad, 961a.
Ascalon, 965a.
Asfûn al-Matâ'nah, 990b.
Ashdod, 965a.
Asher, 964b.
Asia, 1037a ; Western, 968a.
Asklepeion, 985a.
Asnâ, 951b, 959a, 963a, 964a, 971a, 974b, 989b, 1002a, 1007a, 1031b, 1034b, 1050a b.
Asphynis, 990b, 1017b, 1018a, 1021a, 1023a, 1023b.
'Asqalân, 965a.
Assyria, 964b.
Aswân, 960b, 1017b, 1034a.
Asyûṭ, 964b, 1002b, 1011b, 1030b.
Atfîḥ, 992a, 1004b, 1061b.

Athach, 968b.
Athribis, 950b, 967b, 989a, 1006b, 1012b, 1013a, 1019a, 1045b, 1049a.
Athribites, 951a, 961b, 1047a.
Avaris, 992a, 1013b ; canal of, 984a.

B.

Ba-bi-i-lu, 980a.
Ba-bi-lu, 980a.
Babirush, 980a.
Babylon of Egypt, 958a, 974a, 987a, 1030a, 1056a.
Babylon the Great, 977b, 980a.
Babylonia, 1033a, 1035a.
Bactria, 978a.
Bagrawîr, 977b.
Baḥarîyah, 973a.
Baḥêrah, 1035b.
Bakchis, 986a.
Balbês, 962b.
Ballâs, 1005a.
Balyanâ, 1049b.
Barullus, Lake, 1030b.
Basti, 1041b.
Beeroth, 977a.
Behbit, 1021b.
Bekhten, 981a.
Belbes, 982a.
Benhâ, 989a.
Beni Ḥasan, 952b, 958b, 987a, 994a, 1016a, 1032b.
Berenice on the Red Sea, 1038b.
Bêrût, 978a.
Beth-anoth, 977a.
Beth-dagon, 977a.
Beth-horon, 978b.
Biggah, 1000a, 1031b.
Bileam, 977b.
Bi-ru-ta, 978a.
Bitter Lake, 1046a.
Boiling Lake, 999b.
Bubastis, 975a, 976a b, 978a, 981a, 987a.
Bubastis of the South (Denderah), 987a.
Bubastites, 958a, 968a, 1036a.
Bur-ku-na, 980a.
Busiris, 950a, 980b, 992b, 1005b, 1023b, 1062b, 1065b.
Busirites, 966a, 973b, 985b, 1010b, 1033b, 1038a, 1039a.
Buto, 973b, 981a, 983b, 986b, 1013b, 1061b.
Buto, Lakes of, 1012b.

C.

Cabasa, 1021b, 1023b.
Cabasites, 995a, 1023b, 1047a.
Cabul, 1045b.
Canaan, 1048a.
Canal of Thothmes III, 975a.
Canopus, 994b, 1049a b.
Cappadocia, 1050a.
Carchemish, 1046b, 1047a, 1049b.
Casius, 1025a.
Chemmis, 1027a.
Chenoboscion, 1005b.
Chun, 1046a.
Circle, the, 1045a.
City of Life, 969b.
Coptites, 984a, 1022b, 1044a.
Coptos, 966b, 1008b, 1010b, 1028b, 1032b, 1044a, 1048a.
Crocodilopolis, 958a, 984b, 992a, 1016a, 1034b, 1041b, 1051b.
Crocodilopolis (Gabalên), 948a.
Cusae, 1044b.
Cush, 965b, 1048b.
Cynopolis, 1016a, 1047a.
Cynopolites, 959b, 1029a, 1033b.
Cyprus, 950a, 964b, 1005b.

D.

Dabûd, 1053b.
Dâkhlah, Oasis of, 962b; 1065a.
Dakkah, 964a, 1046b.
Damanhûr, 1061b, 1062a.
Damascus, 1056b.
Daphnae, 1059a, 1062a.
Deadland, 986a.
Delta, the, 1050b, 1065b.
Delta, the Eastern, 1050a.
Denderah, 947a, 950a b, 951b, 952a, 953b, 958a, 960a, 962a b, 963a b, 964a b, 969b, 975b, 976a, 978a, 986a b, 987b, 988b, 989a b, 990a b, 991a b, 992b, 993a b,

994a, 1002a, 1004b, 1007b, 1009a, 1013a b, 1014b, 1015a b, 1016a, 1017b, 1018a b, 1019a, 1022b, 1023a b, 1024b, 1025b, 1026a, 1027a, 1029a, 1032a, 1037a, 1042a, 1044a, 1051a b, 1052a.
Denderah, sacred lake of, 1039a, 1040a.
Dendûr, 1008b, 1051a, 1060b.
Dêr al-Baḥarî, 1062a ; temple of, 1016a.
Desert, the, 1024b.
Desert, the Eastern, 1051a.
Dibon, 1053a.
Diospolis Magna, 973a.
Diospolis Parva, 948b, 963b, 973a, 1004b, 1013a, 1015b, 1018a, 1032a.
Diospolites, 950b, 973a, 1031a.
Door of the Circles (Abydos), 1034b.
Drangiana, 1033b.
Dûsh, 1048b.

E.

Edfû, 949a, 949b, 951a b, 953b, 962b, 963b, 964a b, 967b, 968a, 975a, 976a, 979a, 980b, 981a, 984a, 1000a, 1002a, 1007b, 1008a, 1009a, 1013a, 1014a, 1015b, 1016a b, 1017a, 1018b, 1023a b, 1026a, 1027a, 1036a, 1044a, 1045b, 1056a, 1060a, 1061b, 1062a.
Edfû, Lake of, 1041a.
Edfû, Necropolis of, 1061a.
Edfû, quarry of, 959b, 1053b.
Edom, 967a.
Egypt, 977a, 979a, 981a, 1043b, 1044a, 1045b, 1050b, 1063b.
Egypt, Lower, 976b, 1024b, 1043b.
Egypt, Middle, 1029b
Egypt, Upper, 1039b, 1043b, 1052a.
Egypt, Upper and Lower, 1036b, 1043b.
Egypts, the Two, 962a.
Eileithyiaspolis, 989a, 1007b, 1024a, 1057a.
Elam, 970b.
Elephantine, 952b, 954b, 955b, 971b, 976b, 1001b, 1009a, 1015a, 1017b, 1019b, 1020a, 1023b.
Elephantine of the South and North, 947b.
Elysian Fields, 1035b.
Equatorial Lakes, 1004a.
Etham, 1028b.
Euphrates, district of, 1050a.

F.

Faḳûs, 991a, 992b.
Farāfrah, 1050a.
Farshût, 987a.
Fayyûm, 967b, 974b, 991b, 992a, 1000a, 1027b, 1037b, 1039b, 1041a, 1052a.
Fayyûm Lake, 1010b.
Feshn, 1040a.
Field of God, 1036a.
Field of Reeds, 1035b.
Field of Salt, 1036a.
Field of Zoan, 1036a b.
Fire-city, 948a.
Fûm al-Khalîg, 1056a.
Fusṭâṭ, 1030a.

G.

Gap, the, at Abydos, 972b, 974a.
Gau al-Kabîr, 997a.
Gaza, 1043a, 1049a.
Gazelle Country, 1050a.
Gazîrat al-Malik, Island of, 1028a.
Geba, 1043b.
Gebal, 1047b, 1048a.
Gebel Aḥmar, 953b, 965b.
Gebel Barkal, 1005b, 1014b, 1050b, 1060b.
Gebel Silsilah, 1029a.
Gebelên (Jabalên), 948a, 949b, 958a b, 968b, 970a, 1031a, 1054b.
Gezer, 1043a.
Gibeon, 1043b.
Girgâ, 993b.
Gîzah, 951b.
Goshen, 1045a.
Grasshopper City, 1030b.

Great Bend, 994a.
Great Circle, 1040b.
Great Green Water, 973b.
Great House, 986a.
Greece, 972b.
Gynaecopolites, 1025a.

H.

Hamath, 1022a.
Ḥammâmât, 1041b.
Ḥebron, 1026b.
Heliopolis, 954a, 958a, 964a, 975b, 988b, 995a, 1004a, 1005a, 1014a, 1021b, 1034b.
Heliopolis, Lake of, 994b, 1041a.
Heliopolis, Necropolis of, 955b, 965b.
Heliopolis, sanctuary of, 962a.
Heliopolis near Tanis, 958b.
Heliopolites, 1023b.
Ḥenu-Boat, sanctuary of, 990b.
Ḥerakleopolis, 951a, 958b, 963a, 970b, 991a, 1004a, 1013b, 1022a, 1023a, 1040a.
Herakleopolis, sacred Lake of, 1039b.
Herakleopolites, 1029a, 1034b.
Herakleum, 966a.
Herat, 1013a.
Hermonthis, 958a b, 988a, 993a.
Hermopolis Magna, 951b, 955b, 956a, 974b, 975a, 976a, 991b, 992b, 993b, 1013a b, 1023b, 1027b, 1042a, 1056b.
Hermopolis Parva, 986a, 993b, 1011a, 1062a.
Hermopolites, 950b, 974b, 978a, 1037b.
Heroonpolis, 1023a.
Heroopolites, 958a, 959b, 969a, 993a, 1006a, 1040b.
Hibis, 1019b.
Hierakonpolis, 978a, 1007b, 1014a.
Hipponon, 1014a, 1031a.
Hippopotamus Land, 1024b.
Holy Land, i.e., the Necropolis, 1052a.
Horns of the Earth, 1061a.
House of Rā, 989b.
House of Shu and Tefnut, 990a.
House of Tem, 986a.
Hyksos Country, 1038b.
Hypsele, 988a, 1037b.
Hypselis, 991b, 1021a.
Hypselites, 1037a.

I.

Ibrîm, 989a, 996a, 998a.
Ijon, 967b.
India, 1012b.
Ionia, 960b, 972b.
Ionian Sea, 972a, 973b.
Ir-ka-da, 970b.

J.

Jarâbîs, 1046b.
Joppa, 971b.
Jordan, 971b, 972a.
Jupiter Ammon, 1035b.

K.

Kadesh, 1045a.
Kafr ‘Anâ(?), 954b.
Kalâbshah, 1052b, 1057a, 1058b.
Ḳanâ-Ḳusêr Road, stations on the, 953a, 966a, 967a, 968b, 973a, 976b.
Karbaniti, 1042b.
Karnak, 953b, 956b, 1026a b.
Khârgah, Oasis of, 973a, 976a, 1012b, 1048a b, 1060b.
Khi-ish-sha-ash-kha-pa, 1026b.
Kirjath Sepher, 1043a.
Kôm al-Aḥmar, 980b, 1007b.
Kôm Yasîn, 1050a.
Kummah, 1000a.
Kûsh, 1048b.

L.

Labyrinth, 949b, 975a, 992a, 1039b, 1056a, 1060b.
Lake Mareotis, 982a, 996a.
Lake Moeris, 964a, 971b, 983b, 986a, 1001a, 1039b, 1040a, 1040b, 1046a.
Lake Land, 1052a.

Lake of Fire, 1008a, 1040a b.
Lake Timsaḥ, 1025a, 1028a, 1041a.
Land of Life, 969b.
Land of the God, 1051a.
Land of the Spirits, 1050a.
Latopolis, 951b, 954a b, 955a, 992a, 1002a, 1014a, 1015a, 1017a, 1019a, 1022b, 1030b, 1033a, 1034b, 1035b, 1046a, 1050a.
Latopolites, 1058b.
Lebanon, 1010a.
Leontopolis, 948a, 951a, 962a, 1015b.
Letopolis, 949a, 957a b, 960b, 1002a, 1032a.
Letopolites, 1027b, 1029a.
Libya, 1060a, 1010a, 1057a.
Libya-Mareotis, 948b, 953a, 957b, 1013b, 1041b.
Libyan frontier town, 1025b.
Life of the Two Lands, 969b.
Li-ikh-zi-na, 1011a.
Lycopolis, 956a, 964b, 986b, 1013b, 1039a, 1082b.
Lykopolites, 948b, 1016a.
Luxor, 985a.
Luxor, Temple of, 956b.
Luz, 1012a.

M.

Macedonia, 999a.
Maḏînat Habû, 949a.
Maghârah, 1001b.
Mahallah, 1021b.
Mahanaim, 998a.
Maḥetch, 950b, 986a.
Manshîyah, 1008a.
Mareotis, 949b, 988a, 1001a, 1013b.
Matâʻanah, 971a.
Maxyes, 998a.
Meae, 1001b.
Mediterranean, 973b.
Mêdûm, 1001b.
Megiddo, 998b.
Memphis, 947a, 954b, 958a, 959a b, 972a b, 975a, 982a, 984a, 988a, 988b, 995a b, 996b, 1001a b, 1002a, 1006b, 1007a, 1009a, 1018b, 1019a, 1026a, 1029b, 1031b, 1034a, 1035b, 1040a, 1053b.
Memphis, irrigated land of, 1040a.
Memphis, Lake of Isis at, 1039b.
Memphis, Necropolis of, 1019b, 1022b, 1037a.
Memphis, suburb of, 948b.
Memphis, Ṭuat of, 1011b.
Mendes, 968b, 974a, 977a, 986b, 1017a, 1026a, 1051a, 1062b, 1065b.
Mendesians, 1020a.
Meroë, 977b, 980a, 997a, 1001a.
Meroë, Island of, 960a.
Metelis, 985b, 1003a.
Metelites, 981a, 1003a, 1006a, 1025b, 1027a, 1031b, 1036b.
Methen, 999a.
Metropolis, 1004b.
Migdol, 999a, 1002a.
Migdol behind Sai, 1002b.
Migdol of Baal Zephon, 1002b.
Mi-id-ta-an-ni (Mitani), 999a.
Minyâ, 988a, 1000a, 1001b.
Mitani, 999a.
Mît Ḳamr, 980b.
Mît Rahînah, 997a.
Moeris, City, 997b.
Moses' Wells, 1029b.
Muthi, 988a.
Mycia, 998b.

N.

Na-akh-ri-ma, 1007a.
Nahărayîm, 1007a.
Naharina, 1007a.
Nahrina, 1003b.
Napata, 956b, 986a, 992b, 1003b, 1005b, 1035a, 1046b, 1050b.
Natho, 960a, 967b.
Natron Island, 951b.
Natron Mountain, 958b.
Natron Valley, 958b ; Necropolis of, 1061a.
Naucratis, 979b, 988a, 1005a, 1028b, 1047a, 1061b.
Negro Land, 1007a, 1051a.
Neherna, 1007a.
Nekhen, 949a, 951a.

Ni, 1004a.
Nile, 1020b, 1021b.
Nile at the First Cataract, 1041a.
Nile, Canopic Arm of, 958b, 966a, 1035b.
Nile, sources of, 1044b.
Nile of Nubia, 972b.
Nilopolis, 990b.
Nitriotes, 1036a.
Noa, 1006b.
Nomus Arabicus, 1035a.
North, Land of the, 1050b.
Nubia, 952b, 1022a, 1032b, 1044b, 1047a, 1048a b, 1051b, 1052a.
Nubia, frontier of, 1027b.
Nubia, Lower, 1036b.

O.

Oases, region of, 975b.
Oasis, 975b.
Oasis, the Great, 973a, 1033a.
Oasis, the Northern, 973a.
Oasis of Jupiter Ammon, 1035b.
Oasis Parva, 973a.
Oasis, the Southern, 973a.
Ocean, the, 1040b.
Old Cairo, 1030a.
Ombites, 1005a.
Ombos, 992a, 1002a, 1005a, 1013b, 1014b, 1015a ; Kom Ombos, 1024a.
On, 958a, 964a.
Onuphites, 1010b.
Orchoë, 972b.
Orontes, 961a.
Osiris, death-place of, 1008b.
Osiris, tomb of, 949a, 950a.
Oxyrhynchites, 972b, 979b, 1031a.
Oxyrhynchus, 970b, 987b, 988a, 1044a.

P.

Palestine, Southern, 1008a.
Pampinis, 1005a.
Panopolis, 956a, 1013a, 1019a, 1027a b, 1035a.
Panopolites, 956a, 1000a.
Papa, 984a.
Parthia, 993b.
Pathyris, 983b, 1003a.
Pathyrites, 991a, 994a.
Pekhit, 987a.
Pekht, 987a.
Pelusium, 950a, 959a, 989b, 992a, 1009a, 1018a, 1028b, 1031a, 1056a, 1059a.
Persia, 982b, 992a.
Pe-Tep, 949b, 981a.
Pharbaetites, 949b, 952a, 1041b ; Pharbaethus, 991a.
Philae, 951a, 962b, 973b, 984a, 1017b.
Philae, Island of, 949a.
Philistines, 984a.
Phoenicia, 1064a.
Pithom, 964a, 1001a.
Pithom Succoth, 993b.
Pontyris, 995a.
Primis, 987b, 989a, 996a, 998a.
Prosopis, 985b.
Prosopites, 951b, 970a, 1034a.
Ptolemais, 968b, 1008a, 1031b.
Punt, 969a, 984a.

R.

Rakoti, 985b.
Rameses, town of, 985a, 1040a.
Red Mountain, 1061a.
Red Sea, 972a, 103b, 1038b.
Rehoboth, 1021a.
Rethen, Upper, 1012a.
Rome, 1010b, 1012b.
Ruwâd, 950b, 961b.

S.

Saba, 1038a.
Saïs, 981a, 989b, 1030b, 1032a, 1034a.
Saïs, Necropolis of, 989a.
Ṣaḳḳârah, 1009b, 1011b, 1018a, 1032b.
Ṣaḳḳârah, Necropolis of, 1047a.
Salt-Field, 1036a.
Sân, 1063a.
Sararîyah, 968b.
Scythia, 1037a.
Sebennytus, 970a, 985b, 990b, 1059a b, 1063a.

Semnah, 947b, 1023a.
Serbonian Bog, 1054a.
Sethroïs, 1037a.
Sethroïtes, 1009a, 1041a.
Shârûkhen, 1038b.
Shasu, Land of the, 1038b.
Shechem, 1033b.
Shimshon, 1038b.
Shinar, 1033a, 1035a.
Shunem, 1038b.
Sidon, 1064b, 1065b.
Sile, 1017b.
Silḥu, 956b.
Sin, 1059a.
Sinaitic Peninsula, 996a, 1011b.
Sinjâr, 1033a, 1035a.
Sîwah, 1035b.
Smataui, 987a.
Smen Ḥeru, 1040a.
Sogdiana, 1033b.
Sôkhôh, 1037b.
Somaliland, 1051a.
South Lake, 1041a.
South Land, 1052a.
Speos Artemidos, 987a, 994a, 1016a.
Succoth, 986a, 993b, 1017a.
Sûdân, the, 1051a.
Sûdân, the Southern, 1028a.
Ṣûlb, 1014b.
Ṣumra, 1063b.
Sunrise, Mount of, 1061a.
Sunset, Mount of, 1061a.
Sun-temples, 962b, 1009b, 1031a, 1036a, 1041a, 1053b.
Syene, 1017b, 1028a, 1030b, 1034a.
Syria, 965a, 1024b.

T.

Taanak, 1052b.
Tabenna, 1014a.
Tabor, 1050b, 1061b.
Tachompso, 1054b.
Tahpanhes, 1056a.
Tahtah, 1019a.
Takh-shi, 1057b.
Tall al-'Amârnah, 953b, 986a, 1000b.
Tall al-Kabîr, 1000a.
Tall al-Yahûdîyah, 1003a.
Tall Dafannah, 1056a.
Tanis, 965a, 975b, 980b, 1002a, 1004b, 1027b, 1028b, 1029a, 1036b, 1051a, 1052b, 1058a, 1064a.
Tanites, 974a, 1027b.
Ṭara, 985b.
Tasitia, 966b.
Taud, 1065b.
Tebtynis, 1056b.
Tentyra, 958a, 1051a, 1052a.
Tentyrites, 952a, 1051a.
Termes, 1057a.
Thebaïd, 1044a.
Thebes, 947a, 953b, 958a, 969b, 975b, 976a, 980a, 983b, 997a, 1004a b, 1005a, 1007b, 1013b, 1022b, 1026a, 1027a.
Thebes, foreshore of, 1027b.
Thebes, gate of, 1027a.
Thebes, Necropolis of, 957b, 964a, 1005b, 1032b, 1053a, 1058a.
Thebes, Sacred Lake of, 948b.
Thebes, Western, 952a, 966b, 1052a.
Thebes of the North, 973a, 1004b.
Thebes of the South, 973a.
Thinites, 947b.
This, 985b, 986a.
Thmuis, 969b.
Thufi, 1059a.
Tibhath, 1060b.
Ṭibkhath, 1061b.
Timnah, 1055a.
Tomb of Osiris, 991b, 1000b.
Ṭuat, 950a b.
Tunep, 1055a, 1059b.
Tunipa, 1055b.
Tunpa, 1055b.
Tuphium, 990b, 1017b, 1018a, 1065a.
Ṭûrah Quarry, 969b, 1009a.
Two Lands, 977a.
Tyre, 955b.

U.

Udfû, see Edfû, 980b.
Ullaza, 960a.
Uzzen, 967b.

W.

Wâdî an-Naṭrûn, 962b, 1036a.
Wâdî Ḥalfah, 957a, 979b, 982a, 986b, 988b, 1050b.
Wâdî Ḥammâmât, 1010b, 1061a.
Wâdî Naṭrûn, 951b, 958b, 1061a.
Wâdî Ṭumilât, 1040b.
Well between Egypt and Syria, 1029b.
Well near Ethâm, 1030a.
Well near Latopolis, 1029b.
Well of Abydos, 1029b.
Well of Ȧbsaqba, 1029b.
Well of Seti I., 1030a.
Well of Seti II., 1030a.
Well, the Great, 1029b.
Well, the Sweet-water, 1030a.
Well, the Upper, 1030a.
Well, the Western, 1029b.
White Wall, 959b.

X.

Xoïs, 1017b, 1025a.
Xoïtes, 1047a.

Z.

Zarepta, 1064a.
Zoan, Field of, 1036ab, 1064a.

COPTIC GEOGRAPHICAL NAMES.

Ⲁⲑⲣⲉⲃⲉ, 1019a.
Ⲁⲡⲟⲑⲩⲕⲏ, 982a
Ⲁⲣⲙⲁⲛⲑ, 988a.
Ⲁⲣⲙⲟⲛⲑ, 988a.
Ⲁⲧⲃⲱ, 1061b.
Ⲁⲫⲟⲃⲱⲥ, 994a.

Ⲃⲉⲥⲓⲁ, 978.

Ⲉⲃⲱⲧ, 947b.
Ⲉⲓⲟⲙ, 971b.
Ⲉⲕⲉⲡϯⲁ, 1018b.
Ⲉⲙⲃⲱ, 1005a.
Ⲉⲙϩⲓⲧ, 1001b.
Ⲉⲣⲙⲉⲛⲧ, 958b.
Ⲉⲣⲙⲟⲛⲧ, 958b.
Ⲉϭⲱϣ, 1048b.

Ⲕⲁⲓⲥ, 1033b, 1047a.
Ⲕⲁⲙⲉ, 1045b.
Ⲕⲃⲁϩⲥ, 1021b, 1023b.
Ⲕⲉϥⲧ, 1044a.
Ⲕⲏⲙⲉ, 1045b.
Ⲕⲏⲙⲓ, 1045b.
Ⲕⲟⲉⲓⲥ, 1047a.
Ⲕⲟⲥ, 1044b.
Ⲕⲱⲥ, 1044b.
Ⲕⲱⲧⲉ, 1045a.

Ⲗⲓⲟⲩⲓ, 1009a.

Ⲙⲁⲛⲕⲁⲡⲱⲧ, 1002b.
Ⲙⲉⲗⲉϫ, 1031b.
Ⲙⲉⲙⲃⲉ, 1000b.
Ⲙⲉⲙⲃⲓ, 1000b.
Ⲙⲉⲛϥⲓ, 1000a, b.
Ⲙⲉⲛⲫⲉⲱⲛ, 1000b.
Ⲙⲉϥⲓ, 1000b.
Ⲙⲉϭⲧⲟⲗ, 998b.
Ⲙϩⲓⲧ, 1001b.

ⲍⲉⲟⲥ, 1025a.

Ⲟⲩⲁϩⲉ, 973a, 975b.
Ⲟⲩⲉⲉⲓⲉⲛⲓⲛ, 960b.
Ⲟⲩⲉⲓⲛⲓⲛ, 960b.

Ⲡⲁⲑⲁⲛⲟⲛ, 951b, 1057a.
Ⲡⲁⲑⲩⲣⲓⲥ, 991a.
Ⲡⲁⲑⲩⲣⲓⲧⲏⲥ, 991a.
Ⲡⲁⲛⲁϩⲟ, 989a.
Ⲡⲁⲛⲟⲩϥϩⲏⲧ, 989a.
Ⲡⲁⲡⲏ, 984a.
Ⲡⲉⲑⲱⲙ, 986a.
Ⲡⲉⲙϫⲉ, Ⲡⲙ̅ϫⲏ, 987b, 988b.
Ⲡⲉⲥⲟⲕ, 994a.
Ⲡⲉⲧⲟⲃ, 983b.
Ⲡⲉⲧⲡⲓⲉϩ, 989a, 1056a.
Ⲡⲓⲗⲁⲕ, 951a, 984a.
Ⲡⲓⲛⲡⲟⲱⲣ, 981b, 984a.
Ⲡⲙⲟϣ, 984b.
Ⲡⲟⲩⲃⲁⲥϯ, 987a.
Ⲡⲟⲩⲥⲓⲣⲓ, 985b.
Ⲡⲟⲩⲧⲟ, 986b.
Ⲡⲟⲩϣⲓⲛ, 1040a.
Ⲡⲧⲉⲛⲉⲧⲱ, 983b.
Ⲡⲧⲟⲟⲩ ⲙ̅ ⲡⲓϩⲟⲥⲉⲙ, 958b.
Ⲡϫⲱϫ, 993b, 995b.

Ⲣⲁⲕⲟϯ, 985b, 1009b.

Ⲥⲓⲟⲟⲩⲧ, 1080b.
Ⲥⲟⲩⲁⲛ, 1030b.
Ⲥϧⲱⲟⲩ, 1025a.

Ⲧⲁⲃⲉⲛⲛⲏⲥⲉ, 1014a.
Ⲧⲁⲣⲕⲓⲥ, 1053a.
Ⲧⲃⲱ, 1061b.
Ⲧⲉⲛⲧⲱⲣⲉ, 1051a.
Ⲧⲉⲣⲱⲧ, 1059b.
Ⲧⲉϩⲛⲓ, 1062a.
Ⲧⲙⲟⲟⲛⲏ, 988a.
Ⲧⲟⲗⲕⲓⲥ, 1053a.
Ⲧⲡⲟⲩⲣⲁⲛⲏ, 1049b.

Ⲫⲁⲣⲃⲁⲓⲧ, 991a, 1022b.

Ⲭⲃⲁϩⲥ, 1021b, 1023b.
Ⲭⲙⲓⲙ, 1027a.

Ⲯⲉⲗⲭⲓⲥ, 994b.
Ⲯⲟⲓ, 1008a.
Ⲯⲱⲓ, 1008a.

Ⲱⲙⲃⲟⲛ, 1005a.
Ⲱⲛ, 958a.

Ϣⲗⲏⲙⲓ, 1018b.
Ϣⲙⲓⲛ, 949b, 956a, 1027a.
Ϣⲱⲧⲡ̅, 1037b.

Ϩⲁϭⲱⲣ, 1013a.
Ϩⲛⲏⲥ, 1016b, 1022a.
Ϩⲡ̅ⲧⲟⲩ, 1012b.
Ϩⲟⲩ, 1013a.
Ϩⲟⲩⲱϩ, 1022b.

Ϫⲁⲁⲛⲉ, 1063a.
Ϫⲁⲛⲉ, 1036a.
Ϫⲁⲡⲏ, 1064a.
Ϫⲉⲙⲉ, 1058a.
Ϫⲉⲙⲏ, 1058a.
Ϫⲉⲙⲛⲟⲙϯ, 1064b.
Ϫⲉⲙⲛⲟⲩϯ, 1059b, 1063a.
Ϫⲏⲙⲉ, 952a, 966b, 1058a, 1063b.
Ϫⲏⲙⲏ, 1058a.
Ϫⲟⲟⲩϥ, 1059a

Ϯⲙⲉⲛϩⲟⲩⲣ, 1062a.
Ϯⲙⲉⲛϩⲱⲣ, 1062a.
Ϯⲙⲓⲛϩⲱⲣ, 1051b.

GREEK GEOGRAPHICAL NAMES.

ΑΒΑΤΟΝ, 949a.
ΑΒΟΥΓΚΙΣ, 956a, 978a.
ΑΒΥΔΟΣ, 947b.
ΑΔΑΣΑ, 1021a.
ΑΔΡΑΑ, 955b.
ΑΚΗ, 968b.
ΑΚΙΝΗ, 971a.
ΑΛΑΒΑΣΤΡΗΝΟΝ ΟΡΟΣ, 1060b.
ΑΛΑΒΑΣΤΡΟΝ ΠΟΛΙΝ, 1044b.
ΑΛΑΒΑΣΤΡΩΝ ΠΟΛΙΣ, 1041a.
ΑΠΟΘΗΚΗ, 982a.
ΑΡΑΔΟΣ, 950b.
ΑΡΡΑΠΑΧΙΤΙΣ, 948a, 960b.
ΑΣΟΡ, 1021b.

ΒΗΡΥΤΟΣ, 978a.
ΒΟΜΠΑΗ, 979b.
ΒΟΥΒΑΣΤΙΣ, 978a.
ΒΟΥΤΩ, 986b.
ΒΟΩΝ, 979b, 980b.
ΒΥΒΛΟΣ, 1047b.

ΓΑΖΑ, 1049a.
ΓΕΡΡΟΝ, 959b.

ΔΑΜΑΣΚΟΣ, 1056b.
ΔΑΡΔΑΝΟΣ, 1062a.

ΕΣΒΕΝΔΗΤΙΣ, 1007b.
ΕΔΡΑΙΝ, 955b.

ΗΡΩΩΝΠΟΛΙΣ, 1023a.

ΘΙΝΙΣ, 1057a.
ΘΙΣ, 1057a.

ΙΔΟΥΜΑΙΑ, 967a.
ΙΕΡΑΚΩΝ ΠΟΛΙΣ, 1014a.
ΙΗΒ, 947b.
ΙΟΠΠΗ, 972a.

ΚΑΡΙΑΣΣΑΦΑΡ, 1043a.
ΚΟΥΣΑΙ, 1044b.
ΚΡΩΦΙ, 1000b.
ΚΥΠΡΟΣ, 955a, 964b.
ΚΥΣΙΣ, 1048b.
ΚΩΧΩΜΗ, 1047a.

ΛΕΥΚΟΝ ΤΕΙΧΟΣ, 959b.
ΛΕΩΝΤΩΝ, 1015b.

ΜΑΓΑΡΩΘ, 998b.
ΜΑΓΕΔΔΩ, 998b.
ΜΑΓΔΩΛΟΝ, 998b.
ΜΑΚΕΔΟΝΙΑ, 999a.
ΜΕΡΟΑΙΟΣ, 977b.
ΜΕΡΟΗ, 977b, 980a, 997a, 1001a.
ΜΩΦΙ, 1006b.

ΝΑΘΩ, 960a, 1004a.
ΝΕΙΛΟΣ, 1007a.
ΝΕΟΥΤ, 960a.
ΝΗΡΑΒΟΣ, 1004a.

ΟΘΟΜ, ΟΘΩΜ, 1028b.
ΟΡΘΩΣΙΑ, 950b, 961b.

ΠΑΤΟΥΜΟΣ ΑΡΑΒΙΑΣ, 986a.
ΠΝΟΥΨ, 982a, 984b, 988b.
ΠΤΕΜΥΘΙΣ, 995a.
ΠΤΙΜΥΡΙΣ, 1050b.

ΡΑΦΙΑ, 1010a.
ΡΩΜΗ, 1010b, 1012b.

ΣΑΙΝ, 1031a.
ΣΑΚΟΛΧΗ, 1032b.
ΣΑΡΕΠΤΑ, 1064a.
ΖΙΔΩΝ, 1064a.
ΣΜΕΝΔΗΣ, 1007b.
ΣΥΗΝΗ, 1030b.
ΣΥΧΕΜ, 1033b.

ΤΑΛΜΙΣ, 1057a.
ΤΑΝΙΣ, 1064a.
ΤΑΣΤΑΣ, 1060a.
ΤΑΦΟΣ ΟΣΙΡΙΔΟΣ, 1000b.
ΤΑΧΟΜΨΩ, 1054b.
ΤΙΑΒΩΝΙΣ, 1052a.
ΤΟΥΦΙΟΝ, 1021b.

ΦΑΚΚΟΥΣΑ, 1045a.

ΧΑΛΥΒΟΝ, 1025a, 1026b.
ΧΕΜΜΙΣ, 1027a.

HEBREW GEOGRAPHICAL NAMES.

אבוט (Abydos), 952b.
אָבֵל, 949b, 954b, 955b.
אֶבֶן, 956b.
אֱדוֹם, 967a.
אֲדוֹרַיִם, 967a.
אָדָם, 967a.
אֲדֻמִּים, 952a, 966b.
אַדָּר, 967a.
אֶדְרֶעִי, 955b.
אוֹן, 958a.
אוֹנוֹ, 954b.
אֶזֶן, 967b.
אַכְשָׁף, 965b, 971a.
איּוֹן, 967b.
אַיָּלוֹן, 952b.
אֶלְתְּקֹן, 961b.
אַמָּה, 957b.
אֱמֹרִי, 957a.
אֲנָחֲרָת, 959a.
אֲפֵק, 956b.
אֲפֵקָה, 956b.

אַרְוָד, 950b.
אַשְׁדּוֹד, 965a.
אֵתָם, 1028b.

בְּאֵרוֹת, 977a.
בָּבֶל, 977b, 980a.
בַּהַט, 978a.
בִּלְעָם, 977b.
בָּמוֹת, 980a.
בֵּית־דָּגוֹן, 977a.
בֵּית־חֹרֹן, 978b.
בֵּית־סֵפֶר, 978b.
בֵּית־עוֹלָם, 978b.
בֵּית־עֲנוֹת, 977a.
בֵּית־שְׁאָן, 978b.
בֵּית־שֶׁמֶשׁ, 989b.
בֵּית־תַּפּוּחַ, 978b.
בְּנֵי הַיְּוָנִים, 960b.

גְּבַל, 1047b.
גֶּבַע, 1043b.
גִּבְעוֹן, 1043b.
גֶּרְשׁוֹן, 1049a.
גֶּזֶר, 1043a.
גְּרָר, 1048b.
גֹּשֶׁן, 1145a.

דּוֹר, 1060b.
דִּיבוֹן, 1053a.
דַּמֶּשֶׂק, 1056b.

הָם, 1012b.
הַר, 1012a.
הַר־אֵל, 1012b.

חֶבְרוֹן, 1026b.
חֲדָשָׁה, 1021a.
חֶלֶץ, 1024b.
חֶלְקַת, 1025a.
חֲמָת, 1020a, 1022a.
חָנֵס, 1016a, 1022a.
חֹסָה, 1025b.
חֲפָרַיִם, 1020a.
חָצוֹר, 1021b.
חרב√, 1024b.
חָרְבָּה, 1024b.
חֶרֶס, 1026b.
חֵת, 1026b, 1028b.

טִבְחַת, 1060b.

יב, 971b.
יִבְלְעָם, 971b.
יָוָן, 960b.
יָם, 971b.
יַעֲקֹב־אֵל, 971a.
יָפוֹ, 972a.
יַרְדֵּן, 971b, 972a.
יְשָׁנָה, 972b.

כָּבוּל, 1045b.
כּוּן, 1046a.
כּוּשׁ, 965b, 1047a.
כְּנַעַן, 1046a.
כִּנֶּרֶת, 1048a.
כַּפְתּוֹר, 1048a.
כַּרְכְּמִישׁ, 1042b.
כְּרָן, 1046b.

לָבָן, 1009b.
לִבְנָה, 1009b.
לְבָנוֹן, 1010a.
לוּבִי, 1010a.
לוּז, 1012a.

מְגִדּוֹ, 998b.
מִגְדּוֹל, 998b, 1002b.
מַחֲנַיִם, 998a.
מַעֲרָת, 998b.
מָרוֹם, 996b, 998a.
מַקֵּדָה, 998b.
מִשְׁאָל, 998a.

נֹא אָמוֹן, 1004a.
נָבוֹת, 1005a.
נֶגֶב, 1008a.
נַחַל, 1007a.
נַחַל מִצְרַיִם, 1007a.
נַעֲמָן, 1004a.

סְוֵנֵה, 1030b.
סוּף, 1059a.
סִין, 1059a.
סֻכּוֹת, 1060a.

עֶדְרֶעִי, 969a.
עַזָּה, 1043a, 1049a.
עֵילָם, 970b.
עַי, 968b, 969b.
עַד, 968b.
עַכּוֹ, 968b.
עֵמֶק, 968a.

ASSYRIAN AND PERSIAN GEOGRAPHICAL NAMES.

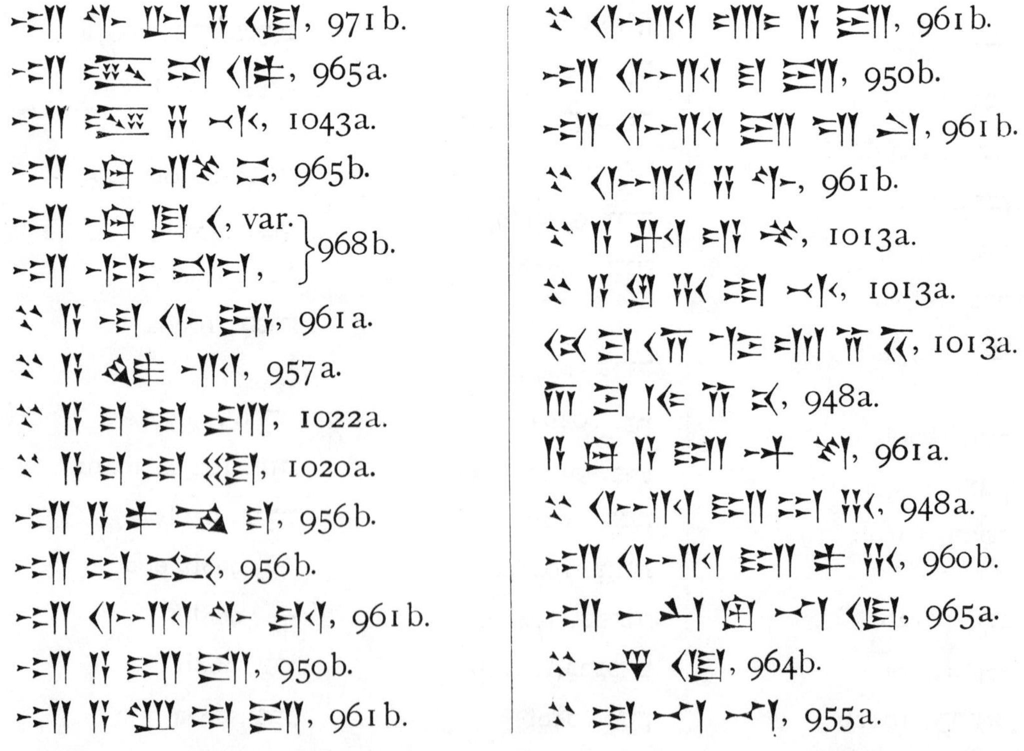

[illegible], 977b.
[illegible], 977b.
[illegible], 978a.
[illegible], 978a.
[illegible], 988 b.
[illegible], 986 b.
[illegible], 977b.
[illegible], 978a.
[illegible], 985b.
[illegible], 1047b.
[illegible], 1047b.
[illegible], 1049a.
[illegible], 1043a.
[illegible], 1043b.
[illegible], 1042b.
[illegible], 1056b.
[illegible], 1056b.
[illegible], 1055a.
[illegible], 1033b.

[illegible], 1013a.
[illegible], 955a.
[illegible], 965b.
[illegible], 967a.
[illegible], 955b.
[illegible], 958a.

Zi-ib-la-an-da, 1063a.
[illegible] 1060b.
[ilu]Za-kha-bu-na-ash, 1033b.
[illegible], 1035a, 1059a.

[illegible], 1063b.

[illegible], 1043a.
[illegible], 1025a, 1026b.
[illegible], 1024b.
[illegible], 1024b.
[illegible], 1027b.
[illegible], 1016a, 1022a.
[illegible], 1021b.
[illegible], 1024b.
[illegible], 1024b.
[illegible], 1019b.
[illegible], 1026b, 1028b.

[illegible], 972a.
[illegible], 952b.
[illegible], 960b.
[illegible], 960b.
[illegible], 972a.
[illegible], 955a.

[illegible], 1042b.
[illegible], 1045b.
[illegible], 1046a.
[illegible], 1050a.
[illegible], 965b, 1048b.
[illegible], 1048b.

[illegible], 1011b.

[illegible], 1000b.

ETHIOPIC GEOGRAPHICAL NAMES.

SYRIAC GEOGRAPHICAL NAMES.

ܐܝܪܐܘܪܘܐ, 950b.
ܐܟܘܪܐ, 964b.
ܪܙܘܝܬܡܘܡ, 1056b.
ܘܪܡܝ, 1021b.

ܣܘܦܡ, 972a.
ܣܠܡܐ, 1007a.
ܚܕܒ, 968b.

ARABIC GEOGRAPHICAL NAMES.

ابو صبير, 985b.

اخميم, 949b, 956a, 1027a.

اتريب, 1019a.

ادفو, 1051b.

ارواد, 950b, 961b.

اسوان, 1030b.

اصغون, 990b, 1017b, 1021a.

اطفيج, 1056a.

الغيم, 971b.

القبط, 1044a.

القوصيّة, 1044b.

القيس, 1047a.

اهناس, 1016b, 1022a.

بلاق, 951a.

بنها, 989a.

بيروت, 978a.

بهبيت, 990b, 1008a, 1021b.

تل بسطه, 987a.

تل دفنو, 1059a.

دمشق, 1056b.

سنجار, 1035a.

سكين القوم, 1039a.

سخا, 1025a.

سمنود, 1059b.

شنهور, 1041a.

صان, 1036b, 1064a.

عكه, 968b.

علوه, 960a.

غزه, 1043a.

فاقوس, 1045a.

قابيل, 1045b.

قراقره, 1049b.

قرطة, 1046b.

كوم امبو, 1005a.

منقباض, 1002b.

هور, 1022b.

واح, 973a.

وادى النطرون, 958b.

يافا, 972a.

LIST OF THE COPTIC WORDS AND NAMES QUOTED IN THE EGYPTIAN DICTIONARY.

Ⲁ

ⲁⲃⲥⲱⲛ, 39b.
ⲁⲃⲱ, 40a.
ⲁⲑⲣⲉⲩ, 27b, 520b.
ⲁⲑⲱⲣ, 455b.
ⲁⲓⲁⲓ, 107b.
ⲁⲕⲉ, 12a, 92b.
ⲁⲕⲗⲏ, 139b.
ⲁⲕⲟ, 10b, 92b.
ⲁⲕⲱ, 10b, 11b, 92b, 139a.
ⲁⲕⲱⲣⲓ, 11b.
ⲁⲕϩⲧⲏ, 766a.
ⲁⲗ, 112a.
ⲁⲗⲁⲕ, 451b.
ⲁⲗⲁϫ, 7b.
ⲁⲗⲉ, 28a, 29a, 112a, 129a.
ⲁⲗⲓϫⲓ, 7b.
ⲁⲗⲕⲉ, 131b.
ⲁⲗⲟⲗⲓ, 21b.
ⲁⲗⲟⲟⲩⲉ, 4a.
ⲁⲗⲟⲩ, 130b.
ⲁⲗⲟⲩⲗⲁ, 499b.
ⲁⲙⲁϩⲧⲉ, 54b, 317b.
ⲁⲙⲓⲥⲓ, 55a.
ⲁⲙⲟⲛⲓ, 54b.
ⲁⲙⲟⲩ, 48b, 266b, 292b.
ⲁⲙⲟⲩⲛ, 51b.
ⲁⲙⲣⲏϩⲉ, 315a.
ⲁⲛ, 34b.
ⲁⲛⲁⲩ, 60a.
ⲁⲛⲁϣ, 112a, 126a.
ⲁⲛⲉⲙⲣⲱ, 105a.
ⲁⲛⲍⲏⲃⲉ, 106b.
ⲁⲛⲑⲏⲣ, 407b.
ⲁⲛⲑⲟⲩⲥ, 472a, 492b.
ⲁⲛⲕⲟⲧ, 780b.
ⲁⲛⲟⲕ, 60b, 356a.
ⲁⲛⲟⲕ, ϩⲱ, 60b.
ⲁⲛⲟⲙ, 34a, 56a, 62a, 376b.
ⲁⲛⲟⲩⲛ, 61a.
ⲁⲛⲧⲉⲗⲉⲙ, 307b.
ⲁⲛⲧⲱⲟⲩ, 105b.
ⲁⲛϧⲃⲁ, 106a.
ⲁⲛϩⲟⲩⲣⲉ, 57a.
ⲁⲟⲩⲁⲛ, 34b, 58a.
ⲁⲟⲩⲉⲓⲛ, 34b.
ⲁⲟⲩⲱ, 32b.
ⲁ-ⲡⲁϩⲧⲉ, 245a.
ⲁⲣⲏϫ, 100a, 104b, 130b.
ⲁⲣⲟ, 29b.
ⲁⲣⲟⲟⲩⲉ, 29b.
ⲁⲣⲟⲩ, 130b.
ⲁⲣⲡⲟⲛⲟⲛ, 423b.
ⲁⲣⲱ, 35a, 69a.
ⲁⲣϣⲁⲛ, 112a.
ⲁⲣϣⲓⲛ, 112a.
ⲁⲥ, 9b.
ⲁⲥⲓⲁⲓ, 9b.
ⲁⲥⲓⲟⲩⲓ, 33b.
ⲁⲥⲟⲩ, 88b.
ⲁⲥⲫⲟⲩⲓ, 460a.
ⲁⲧ, 12b, 339b.
ⲁⲧϣⲁⲩ, 140b.
ⲁⲩⲉⲓⲛ, 34b.
ⲁⲩⲱ, 32b.
ⲁⲫⲟⲫⲓ, 111a.
ⲁⲫⲱⲫⲓ, 111a.
ⲁϫⲓ, 9a.
ⲁϣ, 77a.
ⲁϣⲁⲓ, 136a, 137a.
ⲁϣⲕⲁⲕ, 138a.
ⲁϥ, 34a, 119b.
ⲁϥⲟⲩⲓ, 34a.
ⲁϥⲧⲉ, 44a.
ⲁϧⲓ, 22b.
ⲁϧⲟ, 77a.
ⲁϧⲱⲙ, 135a.
ⲁϩⲉ, 7b, 22b, 133b.
ⲁϩⲟⲙ, 74a and b.
ⲁϩⲣⲟⲕ, 77a.
ⲁϭⲟⲗⲧⲉ, 112b.

B

ⲃⲁⲓⲣⲓ, 202b, 219b.
ⲃⲁⲕⲓ, 206b, 207a.
ⲃⲁⲗ, 68a, 203b, 219b, 313b.
ⲃⲁⲣⲓ, 202b, 204a.
ⲃⲁϩⲥⲉ, 205a.
ⲃⲉⲃⲉ, 212b.
ⲃⲉⲕⲉ, 206b.
ⲃⲉⲗⲗⲉ, 203b.
ⲃⲉⲛⲓⲡⲉ, 203b, 210a, 218a.
ⲃⲉⲣⲃⲉⲣ, 204a.
ⲃⲉⲣⲃⲱⲣ, 219b.
ⲃⲉⲣⲉϣⲉⲩ, 243b.
ⲃⲉⲣⲉϩⲉ, 204a.
ⲃⲉⲣⲉϭⲱⲟⲩⲧ, 283b.
ⲃⲉⲣϣⲉⲩ, 169b.
ⲃⲉⲣϣⲏⲟⲩ, 169b, 242b.
ⲃⲉⲧⲩⲕⲉ, 227b.
ⲃⲏⲃ, 201b, 216a.
ⲃⲏⲛⲉ, 217b, 299b.
ⲃⲏⲛⲓ, 217b.
ⲃⲏⲛⲛⲉ, 218b.

ⲃⲏⲥ, 223a.
ⲃⲏⲧ, 208a, 874a.
ⲃⲏϭ, 206a, 211b, 225a.
ⲃⲓⲣ, 202b, 219b.
ⲃⲓⲥⲉ, 181a, 648b.
ⲃⲓϫⲓ, 207a, 225b.
ⲃⲗ̄ⲃⲓⲗⲉ, 204a.
ⲃⲛ̄ⲛⲉ, 203a, 218b.
ⲃⲡ̄ⲧ, 237b.
ⲃⲟ, 202a.
ⲃⲟⲓⲛⲉ, 216b.
ⲃⲟⲓⲛⲏ, 211a.
ⲃⲟⲓⲛⲓ, 202b.
ⲃⲟⲕⲓ, 206a, 207a, 225a.
ⲃⲟⲗ, 214b, 218b, 219b.
ⲃⲟⲗⲃⲗ̄, 204a.
ⲃⲟⲥⲉⲣ, 182b.
ⲃⲟⲧⲉ, 208a, 228a.
ⲃⲟⲩⲃⲟⲩ, 212b.
ⲃⲟⲱⲛ, 502b.
ⲃⲟϯ, 208a.
ⲃⲣⲉϩⲓ, 315a.
ⲃⲣⲏⲩⲉ, 242b.
ⲃⲣⲏϫ, 215b.
ⲃⲣⲏϭⲉ, 215b.
ⲃⲱ, 202a.
ⲃⲱ ⲛ̄ ⲧⲱⲣⲉ, 840a.
ⲃⲱⲧⲉ, 208a and b, 215b, 227b.
ⲃⲱⲱⲛ, 211a, 217a.
ⲃⲱⲱⲛⲉ, 216b.
ⲃⲱϣ, 205b.
ⲃⲱϯ, 827b.

Ⲅ

ⲅⲱⲃϩ̄, 254b.

Ⲇ

ⲇⲓⲇⲓⲟⲩ, 844a.

Ⲉ

ⲉⲃ, 4a.
ⲉⲃⲏ, 209b.
ⲉⲃⲓⲏⲛ, 202b, 211a.
ⲉⲃⲓⲱ, 39a.
ⲉ ⲃⲟⲗ, 219b, 414a.
ⲉ ⲃⲟⲗ ϩⲛ̄ 422b.
ⲉⲃⲟⲧ, 40b.
ⲉⲃⲣⲏⲩⲉ, 242b.
ⲉ ⲑⲉ, 414a.
ⲉⲑⲟϣ, 790b.
ⲉⲑⲱϣ, 790b.
ⲉⲓ, 30a, 31a, 68a.
ⲉⲓⲁⲁⲃⲉ, 142a.
ⲉⲓⲁⲁⲩ, 110a and b, 155a.
ⲉⲓⲁⲗ, 143b.
ⲉⲓⲁⲧ, 68a.
ⲉⲓⲃⲉ, 38a, 642a.
ⲉⲓⲉ, 33b.
ⲉⲓⲉⲃⲧ̄, 19a.
ⲉⲓⲉⲟⲩⲗ, 2b.
ⲉⲓⲉⲣ ⲃⲟⲟⲛⲉ, 68a.
ⲉⲓⲉⲣⲟ, 69a, 142a, 356a.
ⲉⲓⲙⲉ, 120a, 121b.
ⲉⲓⲛⲉ, 56a and b.
ⲉⲓⲟⲙ, 143a.
ⲉⲓⲟⲟⲣ, 35b, 69a, 99b, 142a.
ⲉⲓⲟⲟϩⲉ, 8a.
ⲉⲓⲣⲉ, 65a.
ⲉⲓⲥ, 79b.
ⲉⲓⲧⲉⲛ, 27b, 30b.
ⲉⲓⲧⲛ̄, 13b, 37a, 99a, 838a.
ⲉⲓⲱ, 142a.
ⲉⲓⲱⲙ, 142b.
ⲉⲓⲱⲣϩ̄, 68a.
ⲉⲓⲱⲧ, 97a, 98a, 821b.
ⲉⲓⲱⲧⲉ, 27a, 97a, 101b, 142a, 143b.
ⲉⲓⲱϩⲉ, 1a, 8a, 75a, 453a, 457b.
ⲉⲓⲱ ϩⲏⲧ, 28a.
ⲉⲓϣⲉ, 2b.
ⲉⲕⲓⲃⲉ, 763a.
ⲉⲗⲉⲟⲟⲗⲉ, 21a.
ⲉⲗⲟⲟⲗⲉ, 7a, 21a, 72a.
ⲉⲗϩⲏⲙ, 385b.
ⲉⲗϩⲟⲃ, 131a.
ⲉⲗϩⲱⲃ, 131a, 429a.
ⲉⲙⲁⲧⲉ, 290a.
ⲉⲙⲁϣⲱ, 266a.
ⲉⲙⲓⲥⲓ, 55a.
ⲉⲙⲕⲏ, 279a.
ⲉⲙⲛⲁⲓ, 296a.
ⲉⲙⲛⲟⲩⲧ, 45a.
ⲉⲙⲛ̄ⲧ, 53b.
ⲉⲙⲛ̄ⲧϥ, 340a.
ⲉⲙⲟⲩ, 50b, 273b, 278a.
ⲉⲙⲣⲟ, 308a.
ⲉⲛ, 2a, 28b, 111b, 114a, 123b.
ⲉⲛⲁⲛⲟⲩ, 342b.
ⲉⲛⲁⲛⲟⲩⲥ, 342b.
ⲉⲛⲁϣⲉ, 342b.
ⲉⲛⲁϣⲱⲟⲩ, 342b.
ⲉⲛⲉ, 56a.
ⲉⲛⲉϩ, 383a.
ⲉⲛϩ̄, 63a.
ⲉⲟⲟⲩ, 3b, 17b, 129a.
ⲉⲡⲁϩⲟⲩ, 30b, 244a.
ⲉⲡⲏⲡ, 42a.
ⲉⲡⲓⲫⲓ, 41b.
ⲉⲡⲟϯ, 233a, 234a.
ⲉⲣⲃⲟⲕⲓ, 65b.
ⲉⲣⲉ, 417b.
ⲉⲣⲏⲩ, 69b.
ⲉⲣⲟ, 414a.
ⲉⲣⲟⲕ, 434a.
ⲉⲣⲟⲩ, 130b.
ⲉⲣⲡⲉ, 423b.
ⲉⲣⲥⲱ, 432a.

ⲉⲣⲧⲱⲃ, 73b.
ⲉⲣⲫⲉⲓ, 423b.
ⲉ ⲣⲱⲟⲩ, 415b.
ⲉⲣⲱⲧⲉ, 21b.
ⲉⲣⲱⲧⲓ, 21b.
ⲉⲣⲱϯ, 21b.
ⲉⲣϣⲁⲁⲣ, 723b.
ⲉⲥ, 36a.
ⲉⲥⲁⲩ, 583b, 649a.
ⲉⲥⲑⲏⲙ, 329a, 715b.
ⲉⲥⲟⲟⲩ, 583b, 642a, 649a.
ⲉⲥⲱⲟⲩ, 649a.
ⲉⲧ, 37a, 398b.
ⲉ ⲧⲃⲉ, 30b, 874a, 904a.
ⲉ ⲧⲃⲏⲏⲧⲟⲩ, 904b.
ⲉ ⲧⲃⲏⲏⲧϥ, 904b.
ⲉⲧ ⲙ̅ⲙⲁⲩ, 399a.
ⲉⲧⲟⲩⲛ, 882b.
ⲉⲧⲡⲱ, 13b.
ⲉⲧ ϩⲏ, 37a.
ⲉⲩⲟⲟⲣ, 21b.
ⲉⲩϣⲏ, 22b, 179b, 288a, 529b, 649a.
ⲉⲫⲱⲧ, 19b, 20a.
ⲉϣⲟⲟⲡ, 92a.
ⲉϣⲧ̅, 135a.
ⲉϣⲱ, 722a.
ⲉϣⲱⲡ, 542a.
ⲉϩⲉ, 74b, 114a, 132a.
ⲉϩⲡⲉ, 448a.
ⲉϩⲣⲉⲛ, 65a.
ⲉϭⲟⲟϣⲉ, 790b.
ⲉϭⲱϣ, 95b, 187a, 790b.

H

ⲏⲓ, 32a, 106a.
ⲏⲡⲓ, 42a.
ⲏⲥⲉ, 633a.
ⲏⲧⲏⲧ, 461a.
ⲏϫⲓ, 261a.
ⲏϭⲉ, 26a.

Θ

ⲑⲁⲡⲉⲛ, 832a.
ⲑⲁϧⲓ, 843a.
ⲑⲁϩⲑⲉϩ, 844a.
ⲑⲃⲓⲱ, 824b.
ⲑⲉⲃⲓ, 873b, 904b.
ⲑⲉⲛⲓⲱ, 838b.
ⲑⲏⲛⲟⲩ, 855b, 856b.
ⲑⲏⲟⲩ, 822b.
ⲑⲓϧⲓ, 842b.
ⲑⲙⲉⲥⲓⲟ, 602b, 671b, 855b.
ⲑⲟ, 815a, 818a.
ⲑⲟⲟⲩⲧ, 886a, 911a.
ⲑⲟⲩⲱⲧ, 826a.
ⲑⲟϭⲟⲗⲕ, 323b.
ⲑⲣⲓⲣ, 822a.
ⲑⲣⲓⲫⲓⲥ, 422b.
ⲑⲣⲟϣ, 889b.
ⲑⲱⲑ, 886a.
ⲑⲱⲕⲥ̅, 846a.
ⲑⲱⲙⲥ̅, 837a.
ⲑⲱⲟⲩⲓ, 823b.
ⲑⲱⲟⲩⲧ, 826b, 847a, 853a.
ⲑⲱⲣ, 840a.
ⲑⲱⲣϣ̅, 889b.
ⲑⲱϣ, 844b.
ⲑⲱϩ, 859a.
ⲑⲱϯ, 868a.

I

ⲓⲁⲃⲓ, 142b.
ⲓⲁⲗ, 142b.
ⲓⲁⲙ, 142b.
ⲓⲁⲩ, 110b, 155a.
ⲓⲁⲩⲱ, 142b.
ⲓⲁϩ, 1a, 8a, 453a.
ⲓⲁϩⲁⲗⲟⲗⲓ, 8a.
ⲓⲉⲗⲉⲗ, 142b.
ⲓⲏⲥ, 25a, 143b.
ⲓⲟⲓϩ, 29b.
ⲓⲟⲙ, 142b, 143a.
ⲓⲟⲟϩ, 29b.
ⲓⲟⲧ, 821b.
ⲓⲟϩ, 29b, 75b.
ⲓⲟϩⲉ, 1a, 8a.
ⲓⲟϩⲓ, 453a, 457b.
ⲓⲱ, 142a.
ⲓⲱⲃ, 38b.
ⲓⲱⲥ, 9b, 25a, 82b.
ⲓⲱϩⲉ, 1a, 8a, 453a, 457b.
ⲓϧ, 24a, 3a and b, 77b.

K

ⲕⲁⲉⲓⲉ, 760a.
ⲕⲁⲉⲓⲥⲉ, 777a
ⲕⲁⲑⲁⲡⲉⲣ, 779b.
ⲕⲁⲓⲉ, 761b, 767a.
ⲕⲁⲓⲥ, 766b.
ⲕⲁⲓⲥⲉ, 776a, 778b.
ⲕⲁⲕ (in ⲁϣⲕⲁⲕ), 804b.
ⲕⲁⲕⲉ, 778b, 779a, 791a, 798a.
ⲕⲁⲗⲁⲕⲁⲛⲑⲥ̅, 803a.
ⲕⲁⲗⲟⲩⲕⲓ, 784b.
ⲕⲁⲙⲉ, 787b.
ⲕⲁⲥ, 778a.
ⲕⲁⲥⲕⲉⲥ, 778b, 797b.
ⲕⲁϣ, 778b, 804a, 814b.
ⲕⲁϣ (in ⲕⲁϣⲁⲃⲏⲗ), 790b.
ⲕⲁϣⲟⲩⲗⲓ, 778a.
ⲕⲁϩ, 766b.
ⲕⲁϩⲕϩ̅, 777b.
ⲕⲁϫⲓ, 791a.
ⲕⲃⲁ, 769b, 807a.
ⲕⲩⲏⲣ, 784a.
ⲕⲉ, 792a, 799a.
ⲕⲉⲃⲓ, 768a.

ⲕⲉⲕ, 798b.
ⲕⲉⲗⲉⲩⲕⲉϩ, 766b.
ⲕⲉⲗⲉⲛⲕⲉϩ, 766b.
ⲕⲉⲗⲓ, 810a.
ⲕⲉⲗⲗⲓ, 763b.
ⲕⲉⲗⲱⲗ, 775b, 789b.
ⲕⲉⲙⲕⲉⲙ, 771b.
ⲕⲉⲛⲓ, 772b.
ⲕⲉⲛⲛⲉ, 772b.
ⲕⲉ ⲟⲩⲁ, 791b.
ⲕⲉⲭⲱⲟⲩⲛⲓ, 799a.
ⲕⲉϩ, 766b.
ⲕⲉ ϩⲕⲉ, 93b.
ⲕⲉϩⲕⲉϩ, 778b.
ⲕⲏⲃ, 767b.
ⲕⲏⲗ, 810a.
ⲕⲏⲗⲗⲓ, 775a.
ⲕⲏⲛ, 773a.
ⲕⲏⲡ, 787a.
ⲕⲏⲡⲉ, 793b.
ⲕⲓⲙ, 771a.
ⲕⲓⲧⲉ, 781a.
ⲕⲓⲱⲟⲩ, 801a, 804a, 805a.
ⲕⲓϥⲓ, 763a.
ⲕⲓϯ, 781a.
ⲕⲗⲁⲗ, 764a.
ⲕⲗ̅ⲗⲉ, 762a, 763b.
ⲕⲗⲟⲙ, 790a, 810b.
ⲕⲙⲉⲙ, 787b.
ⲕⲙⲟⲙ, 787b.
ⲕⲛⲁⲁⲩ, 795a.
ⲕⲛ̅ⲛⲉ, 772b.
ⲕⲛⲟⲟⲥ, 774b.
ⲕⲛ̅ϩⲉ, 789a.
ⲕⲛ̅ⲧⲉ, 792b.
ⲕⲛ̅ϩⲉ, 789a, 812b.
ⲕⲟⲃⲓ, 768a.
ⲕⲟⲓ, 761b.
ⲕⲟⲗⲗⲉ, 805a.
ⲕⲟⲙⲏ, 771a.
ⲕⲟⲟⲩⲉ, 792a.
ⲕⲟⲟϩ, 766b, 777b.
ⲕⲟⲧ, 779b, 780b.
ⲕⲟⲩⲓ, 767a, 798b.
ⲕⲟⲩⲕⲉ, 798b, 814b.
ⲕⲟⲩⲕⲟⲩⲛⲁⲣⲓⲁ, 793a.
ⲕⲟⲩⲛ, 773b.
ⲕⲣⲁⲙ, 810b.
ⲕⲣⲟⲩⲣ, 764a, 775b, 789a.
ⲕⲣⲟϥ, 776b, 790a.
ⲕⲥⲟⲩⲣ, 804a.
ⲕⲱ, 528a, 782b.
ⲕⲱⲃ, 762b, 768a,
ⲕⲱⲣϣ̅, 790a, 804a.
ⲕⲱⲧ, 779a, 780a.
ⲕⲱⲧⲉ, 780a.
ⲕⲱⲱⲃⲉ, 768a, 806a.
ⲕⲱⲱⲥ, 777a, 778a.
ⲕⲱⲱϥⲉ, 738a, 769b.
ⲕⲱϩ, 764b.
ⲕⲟϩⲧ̅, 764b, 765a.

ⲗ

ⲗⲁ, 419a.
ⲗⲁⲃⲟⲓ, 422b.
ⲗⲁⲃⲱ, 378a.
ⲗⲁⲉⲓⲛ, 417a.
ⲗⲁⲗⲱ, 129b.
ⲗⲁⲙϫⲁⲛⲧ̅, 428a.
ⲗⲁⲥ, 389b, 432b.
ⲗⲁϣⲁⲛⲉ, 313a.
ⲗⲁϫⲓ, 433b.
ⲗⲁϭ, 433b.
ⲗⲉⲓϥⲓ, 423b.
ⲗⲉⲙⲏⲏϣⲉ, 312a.
ⲗⲉⲟⲥ, 356a.
ⲗⲉⲧ, 435a.
ⲗⲉϥⲗⲓϥⲓ, 423b.
ⲗⲉϩ, 428b.
ⲗⲏⲗ, 428b.
ⲗⲓⲃⲉ, 419b.
ⲗⲟ, 429a, 435a.
ⲗⲟⲓϩⲉ, 421a.
ⲗⲟⲟⲗⲉ, 129b.
ⲗⲟⲩⲗⲁⲓ, 419a.
ⲗⲟϫⲗⲉϫ, 434a.
ⲗⲟϭ ⲗⲉϭ, 434a.
ⲗⲱⲃϣ̅, 419b.
ⲗⲱⲓⲗⲓ, 428b.

ⲙ

ⲙ̅, 266a.
ⲙⲁ, 213b, 278a.
ⲙⲁⲁⲃ, 281a.
ⲙⲁⲁⲩ, 294b.
ⲙⲁⲁϫⲉ, 329b.
ⲙⲁⲉⲓⲛ, 298a.
ⲙⲁⲉⲓⲛⲉ, 298a.
ⲙⲁⲕⲁⲧ, 290a.
ⲙⲁⲕϩ, 285b.
ⲙⲁⲡ̅ⲉⲣⲟⲩⲱⲓⲛⲓ, 157b.
ⲙⲁⲛⲟⲩ, 300b.
ⲙⲁⲡ̅ⲧⲱϭ, 334b.
ⲙⲁⲣⲉ, 292b.
ⲙⲁⲣⲓⲭⲟⲣⲉⲓ, 283a.
ⲙⲁⲥⲉ, 323a.
ⲙⲁⲧⲉ, 290a.
ⲙⲁⲧⲟⲉⲓ, 292a.
ⲙⲁⲧⲟⲓ, 292a, 333a.
ⲙⲁⲧⲟⲩ, 332a.
ⲙⲁϣ, 295b.
ⲙⲁϣⲉ, 287a, 320a, 330a.
ⲙⲁϣⲓ, 285b, 330a.
ⲙⲁϣϫ, 329b.
ⲙⲁϩⲃⲁⲗ, 319b.
ⲙⲁϩⲉ, 316a, 319a.
ⲙⲁϩⲓ, 284b, 319a.
ⲙⲁϩⲟⲩⲗ, 316b.
ⲙⲁϩⲧ, 286a, 320a.
ⲙⲁϫⲓ, 337b.
ⲙⲉ, 213b, 270b, 309b.
ⲙⲉⲩⲛⲓⲑⲓⲁⲥ, 862b.
ⲙⲉⲉⲣⲉ, 332a, 333b.
ⲙⲉⲉⲩⲉ, 274a.

ⲙⲉⲑⲣⲉ, 334a.
ⲙⲉⲗⲱⲧ, 310b.
ⲙⲉⲛⲉⲛⲥⲁ, 214b.
ⲙⲉⲣⲓⲧ, 310a.
ⲙⲉⲣⲥ̄, 213b.
ⲙⲉⲣϣ̄, 283b.
ⲙⲉⲥ, 279a.
ⲙⲉⲥⲓⲱ, 321a.
ⲙⲉⲥⲧⲉ, 329a.
ⲙⲉⲥⲧ ϩⲏⲧ, 55a.
ⲙⲉⲥⲱⲣⲏ, 500b.
ⲙⲉⲧⲁⲓⲟ, 268b.
ⲙⲉⲧⲧⲓⲟⲩ, 331a.
ⲙⲉⲩⲓ, 274a.
ⲙⲉⲭⲓⲣ, 286a, 434b.
ⲙⲉϣ, 295b, 330a.
ⲙⲉϣⲁⲕ, 328a.
ⲙⲉϣⲱⲧ, 288a.
ⲙⲉϩ, 316a.
ⲙⲉϩⲉ, 275a.
ⲙⲉϩⲙⲟⲩϩⲉ, 286a.
ⲙⲉϭⲧⲟⲗ, 289b, 330b.
ⲙⲏ, 293a.
ⲙⲏⲏϣⲉ, 278a.
ⲙⲏⲓ, 50b, 270b, 279b.
ⲙⲏⲛⲉ, 278b, 297a.
ⲙⲏⲣ, 282b, 308a.
ⲙⲏⲣⲉ, 279a, 292b, 307b.
ⲙⲏⲥⲉ, 55a, 324a.
ⲙⲏⲧ, 271a, 331a.
ⲙⲏⲧⲉ, 332a.
ⲙⲓⲉ, 268a.
ⲙⲓⲏ, 268a.
ⲙⲓⲛⲉ, 297b, 819b.
ⲙⲓϣⲉ, 285b, 320b.
ⲙⲓⲭⲧⲟⲗ, 289b.
ⲙ̄ⲕⲁϩ, 55b, 330b, 331a.
ⲙ̄ⲗⲁϩ, 315b.
ⲙ̄ⲙⲁⲧⲉ, 376b.
ⲙ̄ⲙⲁⲩ, 44a.
ⲙ̄ⲙⲁϩ, 205a, 264b, 265a, 316a.
ⲙ̄ⲙⲏⲏⲛⲉ, 297a.
ⲙ̄ⲙⲏⲛⲉ, 264b, 339a.
ⲙ̄ⲙⲏⲛⲓ, 264b.
ⲙ̄ⲙⲟⲕ, 279a.
ⲙ̄ⲙⲟⲛ, 34a, 51a, 282a.
ⲙ̄ⲙⲟϥ, 302b, 345a.
ⲙⲛ̄, 340a.
ⲙⲛ̄ⲛ̄ⲥⲁ, 265a, 305a.
ⲙⲛ̄ⲛ̄ⲥⲱⲥ, 305a.
ⲙ̄ⲛⲟϯ, 219b, 307a.
ⲙⲛ̄ⲧ, 335a.
ⲙⲛ̄ⲧⲉⲓ, 306a.
ⲙⲛ̄ⲧⲛⲁϣⲧⲉ, 306b.
ⲙⲛ̄ⲧⲣⲉ, 334a.
ⲙⲛ̄ⲧⲱⲗ, 306b.
ⲙⲟⲉⲓⲧ, 276b, 277b, 280b, 290b.
ⲙⲟⲉⲓϩⲉ, 292b.
ⲙⲟⲓ, 50b.
ⲙⲟⲓϩⲉ, 292b.
ⲙⲟⲕⲙⲉⲕ, 330b.
ⲙⲟⲛⲙⲉⲛ, 298a.
ⲙⲟⲟⲛⲉ, 300b, 301a, 302a.
ⲙⲟⲟⲩⲓ, 278a.
ⲙⲟⲟⲩⲧ, 295b.
ⲙⲟⲟϣⲉ, 289b, 330a, 741a.
ⲙⲟⲣϣ̄, 283b.
ⲙⲟⲥⲧⲉ, 328a and b, 329a and b.
ⲙⲟⲧⲉⲛ, 291a.
ⲙⲟⲧⲭϩ, 334b.
ⲙⲟⲩ, 295a.
ⲙⲟⲩⲉ, 270a, 274a, 375a.
ⲙⲟⲩⲓ, 268a, 269a, 273b.
ⲙⲟⲩⲕⲉ, 320b.
ⲙⲟⲩⲕⲓ, 276a, 288b.
ⲙⲟⲩⲗϩ̄, 303b.
ⲙⲟⲩⲙⲉ, 280a.
ⲙⲟⲩⲛ, 296b.
ⲙⲟⲩⲛⲕ, 304b, 305b, 306a.
ⲙⲟⲩⲛϩⲱⲟⲩ, 294a.
ⲙⲟⲩⲣ, 313b.
ⲙⲟⲩⲣⲉ, 306a.
ⲙⲟⲩⲣⲕ, 305b.
ⲙⲟⲩⲥ, 324a.
ⲙⲟⲩⲧ, 332a.
ⲙⲟⲩⲧⲉ, 295b, 335a.
ⲙⲟⲩϩ, 275b, 316b.
ⲙⲟⲩϩ ⲕⲁϯ, 317a.
ⲙⲟⲩⲭⲓ, 334b.
ⲙⲟⲩⲭⲧ, 330b.
ⲙⲟⲩⲭϩ̄, 338b.
ⲙⲟⲭϩ̄, 334b, 338b.
ⲙⲟϯ, 332b, 333a.
ⲙ̄ⲡⲁⲧⲉ, 213b, 296a.
ⲙ̄ⲡⲉ, 213b, 218a.
ⲙ̄ⲡⲣ̄, ⲙ̄ⲡⲉⲣ, 65a, 307b.
ⲙ̄ⲡⲱⲣ, 307b.
ⲙ̄ⲡϣⲁ, 50a, 394a.
ⲙ̄ ⲡϩⲟⲟⲩ, 438b.
ⲙ̄ⲥⲁϩ, 324a, 325b.
ⲙ̄ⲧⲟ, 332a, 333b.
ⲙ̄ⲧⲱ, 337a.
ⲙⲱⲓⲧ, 290a and b, 293a, 333b.
ⲙⲱⲛⲑ, 306b.
ⲙ̄ϣⲁ, 394a.
ⲙϣⲓⲣ, 286a, 330b.
ⲙ̄ϩⲁⲁⲩ, 278a, 285a.
ⲙ̄ϩⲓⲧ, 318a.

Ⲛ

ⲛ̄, ⲛ, 216b, 339a and b.
ⲛⲁ, 339a, 341b, 346b, 348a.
ⲛⲁⲁ, 341b, 342b.
ⲛⲁⲁⲁ, 342b.

ⲡⲁⲁϫϩⲉ, 413a.
ⲡⲁⲃⲓ, 342a.
ⲡⲁⲓ, 342b.
ⲡⲁⲓϥ, 342a.
ⲡⲁⲙ, 374b.
ⲡⲁⲙⲉ, 105a.
ⲡⲁⲡⲉ, 341b.
ⲡⲁⲡⲟⲩ, 342b.
ⲡⲁⲡⲣⲉ, 369a.
ⲡⲁⲥⲧⲟⲣ, 356a.
ⲡⲁⲩ, 344b, 348a, 351a.
ⲡⲁⲫⲣⲓ, 369a, 372b.
ⲡⲁϣⲉ, 341b, 342b.
ⲡⲁϣⲧ, 347b.
ⲡⲁϣⲧⲉ, 344a.
ⲡⲁϩⲃ̄, 355b.
ⲡⲁϩⲃⲉ, 384a.
ⲡⲁϩⲣⲁϥ, 342a.
ⲡⲁϩϯ, 382b.
ⲡⲁϫϩⲉ, 386b.
ⲡⲁϫϩⲓ, 413a.
ⲡⲉ, 341b, 342b, 348b.
ⲡⲉⲃⲑⲱ, 362b.
ⲡⲉⲃϯ, 368a.
ⲡⲉⲉⲃ, 370a.
ⲡⲉⲉⲃⲉ, 354a, 366b.
ⲡⲉⲉϥ, 370a.
ⲡⲉⲙ, 373a.
ⲡⲉⲡ, 342a.
ⲡⲉⲧ, 342a.
ⲡⲉⲧⲉⲡ, 342a.
ⲡⲉⲩ, 342a.
ⲡⲉϩ, 382b, 383a.
ⲡⲉϩ ⲉ ⲃⲟⲗ, 380b.
ⲡⲉϩⲡⲉ, 381b.
ⲡⲉϩⲥⲉ, 382a.
ⲡⲉϫⲓ, 346a.
ⲡⲏⲃ, 357a.
ⲡⲏⲣ, 347a.
ⲡⲏⲩ, 346a.
ⲡⲓⲙ, 61b, 348b, 357a, 373a, 375a.
ⲡⲓϥⲉ, 369b, 370a.
ⲡ̄ⲕⲁ, 395b, 396b, 398a.
ⲡ̄ⲕⲏ, 396b.
ⲡ̄ⲕⲟⲧ, 780b.
ⲡ̄ⲕⲟⲧⲕ̄, 344a, 396a.
ⲡⲙ̄, 73a, 414a.
ⲡⲙ̄ⲙⲁⲡ, 414a.
ⲡⲙ̄ⲙⲁϥ, 414a.
ⲡⲟⲃⲓ, 367a.
ⲡⲟⲉⲓⲕ, 395b, 396b.
ⲡⲟⲉⲓⲧ, 411a.
ⲡⲟⲉⲓϣ, 378a.
ⲡⲟⲕⲉⲣ, 396a.
ⲡⲟⲙϯ, 376b.
ⲡⲟⲧⲙ̄, 401a.
ⲡⲟⲩ, 342b, 346a.
ⲡⲟⲩⲃ, 353a.
ⲡⲟⲩⲃⲧ, 368a.
ⲡⲟⲩⲉϣ, 340a.
ⲡⲟⲩⲕⲉⲣ, 356a.
ⲡⲟⲩⲡ, 349b.
ⲡⲟⲩⲡⲓ, 351a.
ⲡⲟⲩⲣⲉ, 378b.
ⲡⲟⲩⲣⲓ, 354b.
ⲡⲟⲩⲧ, 356b, 411a.
ⲡⲟⲩⲧⲉ, 401a.
ⲡⲟⲩⲧⲙ̄, 412a.
ⲡⲟⲩⲧϥ̄, 401a.
ⲡⲟⲩϥⲣⲉ, 343b.
ⲡⲟⲩϩ, 355a.
ⲡⲟⲩϩⲉ, 380a and b.
ⲡⲟⲩϩⲙ̄, 385a.
ⲡⲟϣⲉⲣ, 395a.
ⲡⲟϩ, 355a.
ⲡⲟϩⲉⲃ, 355b.
ⲡⲟϩⲉⲙ, 608a.
ⲡⲟϫⲡⲉϫ, 410b.
ⲡⲟϭ, 344a.
ⲡⲟϭⲡⲉϭ, 410b.
ⲡ̄ⲥⲁ, 265b.
ⲡ̄ⲥⲁϥ, 324b.
ⲡ̄ⲥⲱⲟⲩ, 265b.
ⲡ̄ⲧ, 398b.
ⲡ̄ⲧⲁ, 333a, 336a.
ⲡ̄ⲧⲁϥ, 333a.
ⲡ̄ⲧⲉ, 333a, 336a, 399a.
ⲡ̄ⲧⲉⲡ, 333a.
ⲡ̄ⲧⲉⲧⲡ̄, 333b.
ⲡ̄ⲧⲏⲣ, 401a.
ⲡ̄ⲧⲟ, 55b, 408a.
ⲡ̄ⲧⲟⲕ, 409b.
ⲡ̄ⲧⲟⲟⲩⲡ, 336b.
ⲡ̄ⲧⲟⲥ, 408a, 409b.
ⲡ̄ⲧⲟϥ, 306a, 401a.
ⲡ̄ⲧⲱⲧⲡ̄, 408a.
ⲡ̄ϣⲟⲧ, 388b, 395b.
ⲡ̄ϩ, 63a.
ⲡ̄ϩⲟⲩⲟ, 384a, 469b.
ⲡ̄ϭⲟⲡⲥ̄, 397b.

Ⲟ

ⲟⲃϣ̄, 163b.
ⲟⲃϩⲉ, 5a, 39b, 220a.
ⲟⲉⲓⲕ, 12a, 138b.
ⲟⲉⲓϣ, 223b.
ⲟⲓⲡⲉ, 41b, 42b.
ⲟⲓⲫⲉ, 41b.
ⲟⲓⲫⲉⲓ, 41b.
ⲟⲕⲉ, 94a.
ⲟⲕⲉⲙ, 11a.
ⲟⲙⲉ, 49b, 122a.
ⲟⲙⲓ, 49b, 122a.
ⲟⲡ, 122b.
ⲟⲟⲧⲉ, 102a.
ⲟⲟⲩϣ, 36b.
ⲟⲣⲡⲟⲩⲱⲣϥ, 112a.
ⲟⲥⲉ, 9b, 90a.
ⲟⲥⲓ, 90a.
ⲟⲧ, 188a.
ⲟⲧⲓ, 12b, 13a, 102a, 481b.
ⲟⲩⲁ, 110a, 145b, 153a.
ⲟⲩⲁⲙ ⲥⲡⲟϥ, 168b.
ⲟⲩⲁⲓ, 153a.

ⲟⲩⲃⲁϣ, 159a, 160a.
ⲟⲩⲃⲉ, 146a, 158a.
ⲟⲩⲉ, 144a.
ⲟⲩⲉⲓ, 144a, 157b.
ⲟⲩⲉⲓⲛ, 124a.
ⲟⲩⲉⲓⲛⲉ, 166a.
ⲟⲩⲉⲓⲛⲓⲛ, 463b.
ⲟⲩⲉⲓⲥⲉ, 181a.
ⲟⲩⲉⲓⲧ, 151a.
ⲟⲩⲉⲗⲟⲩⲉⲗⲉ, 157a.
ⲟⲩⲉⲛⲁⲃⲉⲣ, 165b.
ⲟⲩⲉⲛⲛⲁⲃⲣⲉ, 165b.
ⲟⲩⲉⲛⲟϥⲣⲉ, 165b.
ⲟⲩⲉⲣⲏⲧⲉ, 156b.
ⲟⲩⲉⲣⲧ, 147a.
ⲟⲩⲉⲥⲑⲱⲛ, 181b.
ⲟⲩⲉⲥⲧⲱⲛ, 184a.
ⲟⲩⲉⲧ, 187b.
ⲟⲩⲉⲧⲉⲩⲟⲧ, 150a.
ⲟⲩⲉϣ, 184b.
ⲟⲩⲉϣⲟⲩⲱϣ, 185a.
ⲟⲩⲉϩⲥⲁϩⲛⲉ, 136b, 677b.
ⲟⲩⲏⲏⲃ, 155a.
ⲟⲩⲏⲣ, 158a, 170b.
ⲟⲩⲓⲥⲓ, 220a.
ⲟⲩⲗⲁⲓ, 174b.
ⲟⲩⲙⲟⲧ, 164a.
ⲟⲩⲛ, 164b.
ⲟⲩⲛⲁⲙ, 168a.
ⲟⲩⲛⲟⲩ, 169a.
ⲟⲩⲛⲟϥ, 168a.
ⲟⲩⲛϯ, 164b.
ⲟⲩⲟⲉⲓ, 32b.
ⲟⲩⲟⲉⲓⲉ, 157b.
ⲟⲩⲟⲉⲓⲛ, 157b, 167a.
ⲟⲩⲟⲉⲓⲧ, 192b.
ⲟⲩⲟⲓ, 499a.
ⲟⲩⲟⲙⲧⲉ, 164a.
ⲟⲩⲟⲛ, 164b.
ⲟⲩⲟⲟϩⲉ, 179a.
ⲟⲩⲟⲟϭⲉ, 187b.
ⲟⲩⲟⲡ, 155a.
ⲟⲩⲟⲥⲑⲉⲛ, 149a, 184a.
ⲟⲩⲟⲥⲣ̄, 182b.
ⲟⲩⲟⲧⲟⲩⲉⲧ, 113a, 188b.
ⲟⲩⲟϩ, 74b, 148b.
ⲟⲩⲟϩⲉ, 176a, 179a.
ⲟⲩⲟϩⲓ, 148b, 178b.
ⲟⲩⲟϫ, 193a.
ⲟⲩⲟϫⲓ, 187b.
ⲟⲩⲟϭⲉ, 187b, 206a.
ⲟⲩⲣⲁⲥ, 130a, 147a.
ⲟⲩⲣⲉϩ, 35b, 147a, 175a.
ⲟⲩⲣⲓⲥ, 175a.
ⲟⲩⲣⲟ, 171a.
ⲟⲩⲣⲟⲧ, 175b.
ⲟⲩⲣ̄ϣⲉ, 175a.
ⲟⲩⲧⲉ, 32b, 37a, 102a.
ⲟⲩⲱ, 145b.
ⲟⲩⲱⲓⲛⲓ, 157b, 211a.
ⲟⲩⲱⲗⲉ, 157a.
ⲟⲩⲱⲗⲥ̄, 175a.
ⲟⲩⲱⲙ, 48b, 49b, 168b.
ⲟⲩⲱⲙⲓ, 168b.
ⲟⲩⲱⲙⲟⲩⲏⲣ, 49a.
ⲟⲩⲱⲛ, 166a, 592b, 650a.
ⲟⲩⲱⲛϣ̄, 169b.
ⲟⲩⲱⲛϩ̄, 34b, 166b, 169a.
ⲟⲩⲱⲣⲡ̄, 147a.
ⲟⲩⲱⲥϥ̄, 181a and b.
ⲟⲩⲱⲧ, 150a.
ⲟⲩⲱⲧⲃ̄, 189a, 191a, 195a.
ⲟⲩⲱⲧⲉ, 190a.
ⲟⲩⲱⲧⲉⲃ, 97b.
ⲟⲩⲱⲧⲉⲛ, 189a.
ⲟⲩⲱⲧϩ̄, 189b, 191b, 195b.
ⲟⲩⲱϩⲱⲧⲉ, 194b.
ⲟⲩⲱϣ, 148b, 149b.
ⲟⲩⲱϣⲃ̄, 185b.
ⲟⲩⲱϣⲉ, 179b.
ⲟⲩⲱϣⲙ̄, 186b.
ⲟⲩⲱϣⲥ̄, 182b.
ⲟⲩⲱϣⲧ̄, 186b.
ⲟⲩⲱϣϥ̄, 91b.
ⲟⲩⲱϥ, 163b.
ⲟⲩⲱϩ, 148a.
ⲟⲩⲱϩⲙ̄, 176b, 177a.
ⲟⲩⲱϫⲡ̄, 187b.
ⲟⲩⲱϭⲡ̄, 187b.
ⲟⲩⲱϯ, 149b, 187b.
ⲟⲩϣⲏ, 184b, 529b.
ⲟⲩϩⲁⲣ, 177b.
ⲟⲩϩⲟⲣ, 147b, 177b, 179b.
ⲟⲩϫⲁⲓ, 193a.
ⲟϣ, 137b.
ⲟϩⲉ, 178a.
ⲟϫⲓ, 14b, 141b, 344a, 896a.
ⲟϭⲥ̄, 803b.

Ⲡ

ⲡⲁⲁⲡⲉ, 236b.
ⲡⲁⲓ, 229a.
ⲡⲁⲕ ⲉⲛ ϩⲏⲧ, 252b.
ⲡⲁⲛⲟⲩⲣ̄ϣⲉ, 230a.
ⲡⲁⲟⲡⲓ, 305a.
ⲡⲁⲡⲉ, 233b, 234b, 235a.
ⲡⲁⲡⲱⲓ, 230a.
ⲡⲁⲣⲉⲙϩⲁⲧⲡ, 236b.
ⲡⲁⲣⲙ̄ϩⲁⲧ, 236b.
ⲡⲁⲧ, 233a, 255b.
ⲡⲁⲱⲛⲉ, 41b, 236b, 504b.
ⲡⲁϣ, 245b.
ⲡⲁϣⲉ, 248b.
ⲡⲁϩ, 245b, 246a.
ⲡⲁϩⲟ ⲣⲟϥ, 234a.
ⲡⲁϩⲟⲩ, 244a.
ⲡⲁϩⲣⲉ, 247a.
ⲡⲁϩⲥ̄, 243b.
ⲡⲁϩⲧ̄, 247a and b.
ⲡⲁϩⲧⲉ, 245a.

ⲡⲁϭⲥⲉ, 249a, 252b, 253a.
ⲡⲉ, 229a, 234a.
ⲡⲉⲓⲣⲉ, 240a.
ⲡⲉⲓⲣⲉ ⲉ ⲃⲟⲗ, 242a.
ⲡⲉⲕ, 252b.
ⲡⲉⲕⲣⲟⲩⲣ, 233a.
ⲡⲉⲛⲧ, 231b.
ⲡⲉⲟⲡⲓ, 236b.
ⲡⲉⲣⲁ, 243a.
ⲡⲉⲣⲉⲙⲟⲩⲛ, 238a.
ⲡⲉⲧ, 233b.
ⲡⲉⲧⲉⲛ, 229b.
ⲡⲉⲧⲕⲱⲕ, 233a.
ⲡⲉⲩ, 229b.
ⲡⲉϩ, 245b, 246a.
ⲡⲉϩⲧ̄, 247a and b.
ⲡⲏ, 229a.
ⲡⲏⲓ, 230a, 234b, 236a.
ⲡⲓⲟⲟⲣ, 231b.
ⲡⲓⲣⲉ, 240a.
ⲡⲓⲥⲉ, 247b.
ⲡⲓⲧⲉ, 253b, 256a.
ⲡⲟⲟⲩ, 232a.
ⲡⲟⲥⲉ, 247b.
ⲡⲟⲧⲡⲧ̄, 253a.
ⲡⲣ̄ⲣ̄ⲉ, 661b.
ⲡⲣⲱ, 242b.
ⲡⲥ̄ⲧⲁⲓⲟⲩ, 250a.
ⲡⲱⲓ, 229b.
ⲡⲱⲕ, 229b.
ⲡⲱⲗϭ, 237b.
ⲡⲱⲛ, 229b.
ⲡⲱⲛⲅ̄, 237a.
ⲡⲱⲛⲧ (read ⲡⲱⲛⲅ), 237a.
ⲡⲱⲣϣ̄, 235a, 243b.
ⲡⲱⲣϫ̄, 243b.
ⲡⲱⲥ, 229b.
ⲡⲱⲧ, 253a, 255b.
ⲡⲱⲱⲛⲉ, 236a and b.
ⲡⲱϣ, 248b, 251a.
ⲡⲱϥ, 229b.
ⲡⲱϩ, 244a, 245b, 246a.
ⲡⲱϩⲧ̄, 247a and b.
ⲡⲱϭⲉ, 252b.
ⲡϩⲟⲟⲩ, 438b.

Ⲣ

ⲣⲁ, 419a.
ⲣⲁⲙⲓ, 424b.
ⲣⲁⲙⲡⲓⲧⲉ, 257a.
ⲣⲁⲛ, 379b, 426a.
ⲣⲁⲥⲟⲩ, 432b.
ⲣⲁⲥⲟⲩⲓ, 432b.
ⲣⲁⲥⲧⲉ, 432b.
ⲣⲁⲧ, 435a, 436a.
ⲣⲁⲩⲏ, 417b.
ⲣⲁϣⲉ, 433a.
ⲣⲁϣⲓ, 433a.
ⲣⲁϩⲧ, 431a.
ⲣⲁϩⲧⲉ, 429a.
ⲣⲉⲧ (in ⲣⲥⲧⲧⲉⲛϩ̄), 436b.
ⲣⲉϥⲙⲟⲟⲛⲉ, 435b.
ⲣⲉϥϯϯ, 866b.
ⲣⲏ, 418a.
ⲣⲏⲓ, 419a.
ⲣⲏⲥ, 431b.
ⲣⲓ, 419a.
ⲣⲓⲕⲉ, 434a, 435a.
ⲣⲓⲙⲉ, 419b, 424a, 428b, 611b.
ⲣⲓⲛ, 379b.
ⲣⲓⲣ, 428a.
ⲣ̄ⲙ̄ⲉⲓⲏ, 424a.
ⲣ̄ⲙ̄ⲙ̄ⲁⲟ, 423b, 436a.
ⲣ̄ⲙ̄ⲙ̄ⲙ̄ⲉ, 423b.
ⲣ̄ⲙ̄ⲣⲁϣ, 436a.
ⲣⲟ, 416a.
ⲣⲟⲉⲓⲥ, 432a.
ⲣⲟⲙⲡⲉ, 427a.
ⲣⲟⲟⲩϣ, 131a, 421a, 433b.
ⲣⲟⲧⲡⲉ, 436a.
ⲣⲟⲩϩⲉ, 421a, 429a.
ⲣⲟϯ, 344b, 429a and b, 448b.
ⲣ̄ⲡⲉ, 72b, 423a.
ⲣ̄ⲣⲟ, 238a.
ⲣ̄ⲥⲙⲟⲩ, 66b.
ⲣⲱⲕϩ̄, 434b.
ⲣⲱⲙⲉ, 423b, 425b, 435a and b.
ⲣⲱⲧ, 421a and b, 422a.
ⲣⲱϣⲉ, 433b.
ⲣⲱϩⲉ, 431a, 435a.
ⲣ̄ϣⲱⲣⲡ̄, 734b.

Ⲥ

ⲥⲁ, 583a.
ⲥⲁⲁⲛϣ, 645a.
ⲥⲁⲉⲓⲛ, 172a, 572b, 605b.
ⲥⲁⲕ, 647a.
ⲥⲁⲛⲛⲉϩ, 608a.
ⲥⲁⲣϩ̄, 689a, 700b.
ⲥⲁⲧ, 630b, 714a.
ⲥⲁⲧⲃⲉ, 715a.
ⲥⲁⲧⲉ, 628a, 630b, 708a, 714b, 716a.
ⲥⲁⲧⲉⲉⲣⲉ, 712a.
ⲥⲁⲫϯ, 597b.
ⲥⲁϣ, 614a, 685b, 688b, 698a.
ⲥⲁϣϥ̄, 665b, 690a.
ⲥⲁϥ, 664b.
ⲥⲁϧ, 646a.
ⲥⲁϧⲉⲙ, 688b.
ⲥⲁϩ, 646a.
ⲥⲁϩⲛⲉ, 613b, 683b, 689a.
ⲥⲁϩⲟⲩ, 652a, 683a.
ⲥⲁϩⲣ̄, 684a, 689a, 700b.
ⲥⲁϩⲧⲉ, 685a.
ⲥⲁϫⲓ, 717a.
ⲥⲁϯ, 652b.

ⲥⲉ, 592a, 593a, 635b.
ⲥⲉⲃⲉ, 696b.
ⲥⲉⲃⲓ, 645a, 654b.
ⲥⲉⲉⲡⲉ, 596a, 661a.
ⲥⲉⲓ, 634b.
ⲥⲉⲕ, ϩⲟ, 701b.
ⲥⲉⲗⲥⲱⲗ, 603b, 678a, 680a.
ⲥⲉⲗϩⲟ, 676a.
ⲥⲉⲙⲓ, 669b.
ⲥⲉⲙⲛⲓ, 602a, 670a.
ⲥⲉⲙⲥⲙⲏ, 740a.
ⲥⲉⲡ, 596a.
ⲥⲉⲡⲡⲓ, 596b, 661a.
ⲥⲉⲡⲥⲱⲡ, 596a.
ⲥⲉⲥⲃⲟϩ, 656b.
ⲥⲉⲧⲉⲓⲱϩⲉ, 585b.
ⲥⲉⲩ, 643b.
ⲥⲉϩ, 682b.
ⲥⲉϩⲥⲱϩ, 648a.
ⲥⲃ̄ⲃⲉ, 641b, 645a, 656b, 696b.
ⲥⲃⲉ, 594b, 655a.
ⲥⲃⲟ, 587b.
ⲥⲃⲟⲕ, 657a.
ⲥⲃⲟϩ, 658a.
ⲥⲃ̄ⲧⲉ, 663a.
ⲥⲃ̄ⲧⲱⲧ, 663a.
ⲥⲃⲱ, 594b, 655a and b.
ⲥⲃ̄ϣⲉ, 656b, 659a.
ⲥⲏⲃⲉ, 594a, 654a.
ⲥⲏⲃⲓ, 636a.
ⲥⲏⲛⲓ, 592b.
ⲥⲏⲧ, 10a, 83a, 627b.
ⲥⲏⲧⲉ, 652b.
ⲥⲏⲩ, 696a.
ⲥⲏϣⲉ, 685b.
ⲥⲏϥⲉ, 597b, 666b, 665a.
ⲥⲏϧ, 615b.
ⲥⲏϫ, 639b.
ⲥⲏϭ, 705a.
ⲥⲓⲃ, 594a.
ⲥⲓⲃⲉ, 654a.
ⲥⲓⲕⲉ, 702b.
ⲥⲓⲙ, 598b, 647b, 667a, 709b, 711a.
ⲥⲓⲙⲓⲁⲙ, 647b.
ⲥⲓⲛⲉ, 604a, 622a, 676a.
ⲥⲓⲟⲩ, 647a, 655b.
ⲥⲓⲟⲩⲣ, 822b.
ⲥⲓⲧ, 584b.
ⲥⲓⲧⲉ, 708a.
ⲥⲓϣⲉ, 686a, 689b.
ⲥⲓϩⲉ, 647b, 648a.
ⲥⲓϯ, 628a, 707a, 712a.
ⲥⲕⲁⲓ, 626a, 704a and b.
ⲥⲕⲓⲙ, 626b, 704b.
ⲥⲕⲟⲩⲣ, 822b.
ⲥⲗⲏ, 611a.
ⲥⲙⲁⲙⲁⲁⲧ, 668b.
ⲥⲙⲁⲧ, 672b.
ⲥⲙⲁⲩ, 600b.
ⲥⲙⲁϩ, 671b.
ⲥⲙⲓⲛⲉ, 602a, 670a.
ⲥⲙ̄ⲙⲉ, 669b.
ⲥⲙⲟⲧ, 666b, 672b, 673a.
ⲥⲙⲟⲩ, 598b, 666b, 668b.
ⲥⲙⲟⲩⲛⲉ, 602a, 670b.
ⲥⲛⲁⲉⲓⲛ, 604a.
ⲥⲛⲁⲧ, 609b, 678a and b, 679a.
ⲥⲛⲁⲩ, 673b.
ⲥⲛⲏⲓⲛⲓ, 604a.
ⲥⲛⲟϥ, 606a, 677a.
ⲥⲛⲟⲩϥ, 606a, 677a.
ⲥⲛ̄ⲧⲉ, 609a.
ⲥⲟⲃⲕ̄, 659b, 660b.
ⲥⲟⲃⲧ̄, 595a, 660b, 661a.
ⲥⲟⲃⲧⲉ, 660b, 661a.
ⲥⲟⲃϯ, 660b.
ⲥⲟⲓ, 79b, 583b, 633b.
ⲥⲟⲕ, 640a, 701b.
ⲥⲟⲗ, 589a, 637b.
ⲥⲟⲗⲥⲗ̄, 610b.
ⲥⲟⲙⲥ̄, 672a.
ⲥⲟⲛ, 674a.
ⲥⲟⲛⲓ, 674b.
ⲥⲟⲛⲧⲉ, 650b, 678b.
ⲥⲟⲟⲩ, 643b.
ⲥⲟⲟⲩⲛ, 643b, 650b.
ⲥⲟⲟⲩⲧⲛ̄, 653b.
ⲥⲟⲟⲩϩ ⲓϧ, 652a.
ⲥⲟⲟⲩϩⲉ, 593a, 646b, 649b, 651b.
ⲥⲟⲟϥ, 642b.
ⲥⲟⲡ, 596a.
ⲥⲟⲣⲉⲙ, 611b.
ⲥⲟⲡⲧ̄, 610b, 635b, 680a.
ⲥⲟⲧⲃⲉϥ, 710a.
ⲥⲟⲧⲉ, 709b.
ⲥⲟⲧϥ̄, 714b.
ⲥⲟⲩ-, 648b, 696a.
ⲥⲟⲩⲉⲛ, 649a.
ⲥⲟⲩⲉⲛⲧ, 642a.
ⲥⲟⲩⲛ̄, 642a, 650a.
ⲥⲟϭ ⲛ̄, 705b, 706a.
ⲥⲟⲩⲛⲧ̄, 650b.
ⲥⲟⲩⲟ, 592a, 648b.
ⲥⲟⲩⲣⲓ, 680a.
ⲥⲟⲩⲥⲟⲩ, 648b, 696a.
ⲥⲟϩⲉ, 646b, 648a.
ⲥⲟϫ, 716b.
ⲥⲟϫⲡ̄, 702b.
ⲥⲟϭ, 640a, 652b.
ⲥⲟϭⲛ̄, 705a.
ⲥⲟϭⲛⲓ, 717a.
ⲥⲡⲓⲣ, 662a.
ⲥⲡⲟⲧⲟⲩ, 662b.
ⲥⲣⲏⲧ, 637b, 681b.
ⲥⲣⲟϥⲧ, 611b.
ⲥⲣ̄ϥⲉ, 611b.
ⲥⲧⲏⲗ, 708a.
ⲥⲧⲏⲙ, 327a, 672b, 673b.

ⲥⲧⲱⲧ, 91a, 589a, 628a, 631a, 640a, 714b.
ⲥϫⲁⲓ, 704b.
ⲥϫⲓⲙ, 704b.
ⲥⲱ, 648b, 651a.
ⲥⲱⲃⲉ, 656b, 657b, 660b, 696b.
ⲥⲱⲃⲓ, 636a, 696b.
ⲥⲱⲃϩ, 658a.
ⲥⲱⲓⲥ, 640a.
ⲥⲱⲕ, 701b.
ⲥⲱⲛⲕ̄, 608b, 678a.
ⲥⲱⲛⲧ̄, 609a.
ⲥⲱⲛϩ, 607b.
ⲥⲱⲟⲩϩ, 613b, 683a.
ⲥⲱⲟⲩϩⲓ, 651b.
ⲥⲱⲣ, 610b, 679b.
ⲥⲱⲧⲉ, 647a.
ⲥⲱⲧⲙ̄, 629a, 715b.
ⲥⲱⲧⲡ̄, 628a, 710b.
ⲥⲱⲱϥ, 642b.
ⲥⲱϣ, 614a, 621a, 639a.
ⲥⲱϣⲉ, 614b, 686a.
ⲥⲱϣⲙ̄, 698a.
ⲥⲱϣⲧ̄, 646b.
ⲥⲱϣϥ̄, 564b.
ⲥⲱϧⲉⲙ, 688b.
ⲥⲱϩ, 614b, 615a, 682b, 688b.
ⲥⲱϩⲉ, 695a.
ⲥϣ̄ⲛⲉ, 265b.
ⲥϧⲓ, 688a.
ⲥϩⲁⲓ, 619a, 688a, 689b.
ⲥϩⲓⲙⲉ, 481a, 583a, 613b.
ⲥϩⲟⲩⲉⲣ, 613b, 689a.
ⲥϩⲟⲩⲣ, 613b, 652a, 689a.
ⲥϩⲟⲩⲱⲣ, 683a.
ⲥϭⲏⲣ, 702a and b.
ⲥϭⲣⲁϩⲧ̄, 706b.
ⲥϯ, 627b, 629b, 648a, 709b.
ⲥϯⲉⲗⲗⲓ, 708a.
ⲥϯⲟϩⲉ, 585b.

T

ⲧ, 864b.
ⲧⲁ, 818b.
ⲧⲁⲓ, 815a, 824b, 868a.
ⲧⲁⲓⲟ, 818b, 819a, 824a.
ⲧⲁⲓⲟⲩ, 819a.
ⲧⲁⲕⲟ, 10b, 824a, 865b.
ⲧⲁⲙⲙⲟ, 667b, 865b.
ⲧⲁⲛϩⲟ, 843b, 865b.
ⲧⲁⲟⲩⲟ, 865b.
ⲧⲁⲡ, 873b.
ⲧⲁⲡⲉⲛ, 832a.
ⲧⲁⲡⲡ̄, 832a.
ⲧⲁⲡⲣⲁ, 831a.
ⲧⲁⲡⲣⲟ, 831a.
ⲧⲁⲣ, 908b.
ⲧⲁⲥⲑⲉ, 707b.
ⲧⲁⲧϩⲟ, 101b, 915b.
ⲧⲁⲩ, 823b.
ⲧⲁϩⲧ̄, 842a, 887a, 911a.
ⲧⲁϩⲧϩ, 844a.
ⲧⲁϭⲥⲉ, 891b.
ⲧⲃⲁ, 905b.
ⲧⲃ̄ⲃⲉ, 865b, 904a, 906a.
ⲧⲃⲉⲟⲩ, 827b.
ⲧⲃ̄ⲛⲏ, 854a.
ⲧⲃ̄ⲛⲟⲟⲩⲉ, 868b.
ⲧⲉ, 818b.
ⲧⲉⲃⲗⲉ, 833b.
ⲧⲉⲕⲙ̄, 846a.
ⲧⲉⲗⲏⲗ, 820a.
ⲧⲉⲧ, 818b.
ⲧⲉϥ, 819a.
ⲧⲉϩ, 844a, 859a.
ⲧⲉϩⲉⲙ, 841b.
ⲧⲉϩⲛⲉ, 820a, 841b, 885b.
ⲧⲉϭ, 862b.
ⲧⲏ, 815a, 821a, 840b, 868a, 884b.
ⲧⲏⲃⲉ, 827b, 905b.
ⲧⲏⲏⲃⲉ, 905b.
ⲧⲏⲛⲉ, 881b, 882a.
ⲧⲏⲛⲟⲩ, 837b.
ⲧⲏⲟⲩ, 822b.
ⲧⲏⲣ, 908b.
ⲧⲏⲩ, 822b, 823b, 824a, 849b.
ⲧⲏⲩⲧⲡ̄, 826b.
ⲧⲓⲕ, 823a.
ⲧⲙⲏ, 835b, 836a and b, 855a.
ⲧⲙ̄ⲟ, 601a.
ⲧⲙ̄ⲧⲙ̄, 836a.
ⲧⲡ̄ⲛⲟ, 822b.
ⲧⲡ̄ⲟⲩⲧⲉ, 401b.
ⲧⲡ̄ϩ, 839a, 883a.
ⲧⲟ, 815a, 821b.
ⲧⲟⲃϩ, 254b.
ⲧⲟⲉ, 824a.
ⲧⲟⲉⲧⲟⲉ, 821b.
ⲧⲟⲓ, 821b, 824a.
ⲧⲟⲕⲙ̄, 845a, 846a.
ⲧⲟⲙⲓ, 836b.
ⲧⲟⲟⲙⲉ, 819b, 837a.
ⲧⲟⲟⲙⲥ̄, 879a.
ⲧⲟⲟⲧ, 908b.
ⲧⲟⲟⲩ, 823b, 869b, 904a.
ⲧⲟⲟⲩⲉ, 823b, 853b, 864a.
ⲧⲟⲟⲩⲓ, 819a, 824b, 870b.
ⲧⲟⲟⲩⲧ, 853a.
ⲧⲟⲡ, 832a, 877a.
ⲧⲟⲩ, 823b.
ⲧⲟⲩⲁ, 819a.
ⲧⲟⲩⲉⲓⲧ, 826b.

ⲧⲟⲩⲗⲧ̄, 825b.
ⲧⲟⲩⲱⲧ, 826a and b.
ⲧⲟϣ, 844b, 852a.
ⲧⲟϫ, 846a.
ⲧⲟϭ, 846a.
ⲧⲣⲉ, 909b, 910a and b.
ⲧⲣⲓⲣ, 822a.
ⲧⲣⲟϣ, 845a, 889b.
ⲧⲣ̄ⲣⲉ, 840a.
ⲧⲥⲃⲕⲟ, 659b.
ⲧⲥⲓⲟ, 696a, 866b.
ⲧⲥⲛ̄ⲕⲟ, 678a.
ⲧⲱ, 818b.
ⲧⲱⲃⲁϩ, 254b.
ⲧⲱⲃⲉ, 778b, 819b, 827b, 874a, 905a.
ⲧⲱⲃⲓ, 778b, 819b.
ⲧⲱⲃϩ̄, 876a.
ⲧⲱⲓ, 818b.
ⲧⲱⲕ, 818b.
ⲧⲱⲕⲥ̄, 845a, 846a and b.
ⲧⲱⲙ, 819b, 879a.
ⲧⲱⲙⲉ, 835b, 879a.
ⲧⲱⲙⲓ, 715b, 879a.
ⲧⲱⲙⲛ̄ⲧ, 880a and b.
ⲧⲱⲙ ⲛ̄ϩⲏⲧ, 835b.
ⲧⲱⲙⲥ̄, 599a, 837a.
ⲧⲱⲛ, 818b, 824b, 837b, 838b, 851a and b.
ⲧⲱⲟⲩ, 823b.
ⲧⲱⲟⲩⲛ, 824b, 873a.
ⲧⲱⲟⲩ ⲛ ϩⲱⲟⲩ, 825a.
ⲧⲱⲡ, 832a, 876b.
ⲧⲱⲣⲉ. 825b, 844a, 857b, 863b, 909b, 910b.
ⲧⲱⲣⲧ̄, 841a, 885a.
ⲧⲱⲥ, 820b, 867a.
ⲧⲱⲱⲃⲉ, 874a, 904a, 906a.
ⲧⲱⲱⲙⲉ, 879a.
ⲧⲱϣ, 844b, 889b.
ⲧⲱϥ, 818b, 819a.
ⲧⲱϩ, 841b, 842a, 844a, 859a, 886a.
ⲧⲱϩⲡ̄, 842a, 887a.
ⲧⲱϭⲉ, 846b, 867b, 891b.
ⲧⲱϭⲡ̄, 846a.
ⲧϣⲟⲩⲓⲟ, 732a.
ⲧϩⲉⲙⲥⲟ, 866a.

Ⲩ

ⲩⲉⲣⲓ ⲓⲟⲩ, 443b.

Ⲫ

ⲫⲁⲕⲓ, 205b, 252a.
ⲫⲁⲙⲉⲛⲱⲑ, 236b, 435a.
ⲫⲁⲣⲙⲟⲩⲑⲓ, 237a, 427a.
ⲫⲁⲣⲙⲟⲩⲧⲉ, 237a.
ⲫⲁⲣⲙϩⲟⲧⲓ, 237a.
ⲫⲁⲥ, 261b.
ⲫⲁⲫⲉ, 42a, 233b, 234b, 235a.
ⲫⲁϯⲧ, 247a and b.
ⲫⲉⲓ, 234b.
ⲫⲉⲥ, 261b.
ⲫⲓⲧ, 256a.
ⲫⲓⲥⲓ, 261b.
ⲫⲟⲛϩ̄, 219a.
ⲫⲟⲣϣⲓ, 243b.
ⲫⲟⲥⲓ, 261b.
ⲫⲟⲩⲟⲣ, 244b.
ⲫⲟⲩⲧⲏⲧ, 244b.
ⲫⲣⲏ, 230a.
ⲫⲱⲣϫ̄, 219b.
ⲫⲱϩ, 244b.
ⲫⲱϫⲓ, 245b.

Ϫ

ϫⲁϥ, 794a.
ϫⲃⲟⲃ, 767b.
ϫⲉⲣⲉⲃ, 532b.
ϫⲏⲛⲁⲅⲣⲓⲟϫ, 610b.
ϫⲛⲟⲩⲃⲓⲥ, 795a.
ϫⲛⲟⲩⲫⲓⲥ, 795a.
ϫⲟⲓⲁⲕ, 691b, 783b.
ϫⲟⲓⲁϩⲕ, 783b.
ϫⲣⲟⲃⲓ, 572a.
ϫⲱ, 528a.
ϫⲱⲗⲉⲙ, 562b.
ϫⲱⲛⲥ̄, 553a.

Ⲯ

ⲯⲓⲥ, 250a.
ⲯⲓⲧ, 249b, 250a.

Ⲱ

ⲱ̄, 642a.
ⲱⲃⲉⲛ, 5a, 39b.
ⲱⲃⲧ̄, 5b, 42b.
ⲱⲃϣ̄, 5a.
ⲱⲑ, 140a.
ⲱⲕⲉⲙ, 94b.
ⲱⲕⲙ̄, 26a, 139b.
ⲱⲗ, 7a, 129a.
ⲱⲛⲉ, 58a, 60a.
ⲱⲛⲓ, 58a.
ⲱⲛϣ, 131a.
ⲱⲛϯ, 112a, 124b.
ⲱⲟⲩ, 2b.
ⲱⲟⲩ ⲛ ϩⲏⲧ, 33b.
ⲱⲡ, 41a, 42b.
ⲱⲣⲃ, 7a, 72a.
ⲱⲣⲉⲃ, 112a.
ⲱⲣ ⲥⲓ ⲏⲥⲉ, 504b.
ⲱⲣϥ̄, 7a, 112a, 131a.
ⲱⲣϫ̄, 7b.
ⲱⲥⲕ̄, 9b, 10a, 90b.
ⲱⲥϯ, 10a, 614b, 685b.
ⲱⲥϩ, 90b, 614b.
ⲱⲧ, 13a, 128a, 140a and b.
ⲱⲧⲡ̄, 13a and b, 97b, 102b.

ⲱⲧϩ̄, 100a.
ⲱϣ, 17a, 25b, 30a, 136b, 137b, 592a, 649b, 722b.
ⲱϣⲙ̄, 135b.
ⲱⲱ, 35a, 642a.
ⲱϥⲉ, 113b, 114a, 119b, 156a.
ⲱϩⲉ, 133a.
ⲱϩⲥ̄, 10a.
ⲱϫⲡ̄, 141b.
ⲱϭⲃ̄, 12a, 96a, 207a.

Ϣ

ϣⲁ, 535a, 590a, 723a.
ϣⲁⲁⲛⲧ̄, 261a.
ϣⲁⲁⲣ, 532a.
ϣⲁⲃⲟⲗ, 723b.
ϣⲁⲑⲟⲩⲗ, 534b.
ϣⲁⲓ, 750a.
ϣⲁⲗ, 561b, 723b.
ϣⲁⲙⲉⲧ, 548b.
ϣⲁⲙⲓⲥⲉ, 723a.
ϣⲁⲛ, 548b.
ϣⲁⲛⲉϣ, 645a.
ϣⲁⲛⲧ̄, 554a.
ϣⲁⲛⲧⲉ, 260b.
ϣⲁⲛⲧⲉϥ, 559a, 723b.
ϣⲁⲡ, 736a.
ϣⲁⲣ, 532a, 560a.
ϣⲁⲣⲓ, 535b.
ϣⲁⲧⲉ, 723a.
ϣⲁⲩ, 535b, 722b.
ϣⲁϥⲉ, 726a, 738b.
ϣⲁϥⲧ̄, 545b, 726a.
ϣⲁϥⲧⲉ, 738b.
ϣⲁϥⲱⲟⲩ, 738b.
ϣⲁϫⲉ, 632b, 717a, 719b.
ϣⲁϣⲛⲓ, 617a, 693b.
ϣⲁϣⲟⲩ, 728a, 754b.
ϣⲃⲉ, 734a.
ϣⲃⲉⲣ, 636a.
ϣⲃⲏⲣ, 530b, 540a.
ϣⲃⲓⲛ, 736a.
ϣⲃⲱⲃⲉ, 735a.
ϣⲃⲱⲧ, 726a.
ϣⲉ, 79a, 525a, 566a, 583b, 721b, 739a.
ϣⲉⲃⲓⲟ, 735b.
ϣⲉⲓ, 739a.
ϣⲉⲙⲉⲓ, 723b.
ϣⲉⲙⲏⲣ, 548a.
ϣⲉⲙⲧ̄, 548b.
ϣⲉⲛⲛⲟϩ, 567a, 573a.
ϣⲉⲛⲥ̄, 653b, 751a, 754a.
ϣⲉⲛⲧⲱ, 749a.
ϣⲉⲣϣⲓ, 727b, 734b.
ϣⲉⲧ, 731b.
ϣⲉⲧϣⲱⲧ, 755a, 757b.
ϣⲉⲩⲛⲉ, 747a.
ϣⲏⲓ, 720a, 724b, 731b.
ϣⲏⲙ, 546a, 692b, 734a and b, 739a.
ϣⲏⲙ ϩⲣϣⲏⲣⲉ, 734b.
ϣⲏⲛ, 745b.
ϣⲏⲟⲩⲓ, 538a.
ϣⲏⲣⲉ, 749b.
ϣⲏⲧ, 721b, 756b.
ϣⲏⲩ, 526b.
ϣⲏⲩⲉ, 529b, 538a.
ϣⲑⲉⲙⲣⲱ, 757a.
ϣⲓ, 526b, 527a.
ϣⲓⲁⲓ, 526b.
ϣⲓⲃⲉ, 538b, 735a.
ϣⲓⲃⲓ, 538b.
ϣⲓⲃϯ, 538b.
ϣⲓⲛⲉ, 549a, 744b, 745a, 747a.
ϣⲓⲡⲉ, 541b, 731b, 736a.
ϣⲓⲣⲉ, 749b.
ϣⲓⲧⲉ, 757b, 758b.
ϣⲓϣ, 536b, 614b, 688a.
ϣⲕⲁⲛ, 705b.
ϣⲗⲉϩ, 750b.
ϣⲗⲏⲗ, 726b.
ϣⲗⲓⲗ, 775a.
ϣⲗⲟⲩⲗⲁⲓ, 727a.
ϣⲗⲟϥ, 727a.
ϣⲙⲁ, 547b.
ϣⲙ̄ⲙⲟ, 740b, 741a and b.
ϣⲙⲟⲩⲛ, 547b.
ϣⲙ̄ϣⲉ, 742a.
ϣⲛⲉ, 745b.
ϣⲛⲟϣ, 554a, 617b, 726b.
ϣⲛ̄ϥⲉ, 747b.
ϣⲟⲉⲓϣ, 536b, 538a, 723b, 731a.
ϣⲟⲓ, 526b.
ϣⲟⲗ, 561b.
ϣⲟⲗⲙⲥ̄, 552a.
ϣⲟⲙ, 739a.
ϣⲟⲙⲧ̄, 548b.
ϣⲟⲛⲃ̄, 577b, 736a.
ϣⲟⲛⲧⲉ, 749a.
ϣⲟⲛϥ, 736a.
ϣⲟⲟⲃⲉ, 725a, 753a.
ϣⲟⲟⲙⲉ, 547a.
ϣⲟⲟⲩ, 735a.
ϣⲟⲟⲩⲉ, 528a, 724b, 732a, 734a.
ϣⲟⲡ, 752b, 753a.
ϣⲟⲣⲡ, 562a.
ϣⲟⲣϣⲣ̄, 499b, 560b.
ϣⲟⲧϣⲉⲧ, 567b.
ϣⲟⲩ, 721b.
ϣⲟⲩⲃⲉⲛⲉ, 745b.
ϣⲟⲩⲉ, 734a.
ϣⲟⲩⲉⲓⲧ, 732b.
ϣⲟⲩⲓⲉ, 732a.
ϣⲟⲩⲱⲃⲉ, 735a.
ϣⲟⲩⲱⲟⲩ, 732a.
ϣⲟⲩϣⲟⲩ, 724a.
ϣⲟⲩϣⲧ̄, 625a, 701b, 728b.

ϣⲟⲩϩⲉ, 10b.
ϣⲟϣ, 752a, 754b.
ϣⲟϣⲟⲓ, 754b.
ϣⲟϣⲟⲩ, 752a.
ϣⲡⲉⲉⲣⲉ, 544a.
ϣⲡⲏⲣⲉ, 544a.
ϣⲡⲓⲧ, 737b.
ϣⲥ̄ⲡⲉ, 617a.
ϣⲥ̄ⲡⲏ, 617a.
ϣⲧⲁ, 755a.
ϣⲧⲁⲙ, 708a.
ϣⲧⲉⲕⲟ, 758b.
ϣⲧⲉⲙ, 708a, 757a.
ϣⲧⲏⲟⲩⲧ, 758b.
ϣⲧⲟⲃ, 729b.
ϣⲧⲟⲣ, 575a.
ϣⲫⲏⲣ, 636a.
ϣⲫⲏⲣⲓ, 544a.
ϣⲫⲱⲛⲓ, 736b.
ϣⲱ, 137b, 723a, 730a.
ϣⲱⲃ, 538b.
ϣⲱⲃⲉ, 725b.
ϣⲱⲉⲓϣ, 536b.
ϣⲱⲓ, 536a.
ϣⲱⲓϣ, 536b.
ϣⲱⲗ, 532a.
ϣⲱⲗ̄ⲙ̄, 551a, 747b.
ϣⲱⲙ, 740a and b, 770a.
ϣⲱⲙⲉ, 739a.
ϣⲱⲛ, 746a.
ϣⲱⲛⲃ̄, 725b.
ϣⲱⲛⲉ, 550a, 675a, 744b.
ϣⲱⲛϩ̄, 746a.
ϣⲱⲡ, 698b, 752a.
ϣⲱⲡⲉ, 541a, 736a, 753a.
ϣⲱⲡϣ̄, 544a, 726a, 737b.
ϣⲱⲣ, 734a.
ϣⲱⲣⲡ̄, 562a and b.
ϣⲱⲥ, 728a.
ϣⲱⲥϥ̄, 564b.
ϣⲱⲧ, 622a.
ϣⲱⲧⲉ, 758b.
ϣⲱⲧⲙ̄, 568a.
ϣⲱⲱⲧ, 731a.
ϣⲱϣ, 614a, 620b.
ϣⲱϣ ⲉ ⲃⲟⲗ, 724a.
ϣⲱϣⲉⲛ, 623b.
ϣⲱϣⲧ̄, 624b, 701a.
ϣⲱϥ, 538b, 544b, 726a.
ϣⲱϩⲉⲃ, 750b.
ϣⲱϯ, 758b.
ϣϣⲏⲛ, 745b.
ϣϣⲛⲟⲩ, 722a.
ϣϥⲉ, 665b.
ϣϥⲱ, 690a.
ϣϫⲟⲙ, 690b.
ϣϫⲟⲥ, 812b.
ϣϭⲁⲛ, 705b.
ϣϭⲏⲣ, 566a, 589a, 729a.
ϣϭⲛⲏⲛ, 729a and b.
ϣϭⲟⲩⲣ, 729a and b, 804a.

ϥ

ϥⲁⲓ ⲙⲟⲟⲩ, 258a.
ϥⲁϩ, 204b, 220a.
ϥⲉⲓ, 258a.
ϥⲓ, 260a.
ϥⲓ ⲙⲟⲟⲩ, 258a.
ϥⲓ ⲛ ϩⲟ, 260a.
ϥⲛ̄ⲧ̄, 237b, 261a.
ϥⲟⲩ, 44a.
ϥⲟϫ, 262a.
ϥⲟϯ, 44a.
ϥⲣⲉ, 242b.
ϥⲧⲟⲟⲩ, 44a, 263a.
ϥⲧⲟⲩ, 44a.
ϥⲧⲱⲟⲩ, 44a.
ϥⲱ, 260a.
ϥⲱⲓ, 260a.
ϥⲱⲧⲉ, 44a, 262b, 263a.
ϥⲱϭⲓ, 262a.
ϥⲱϯ, 44a, 262b.

ϧ

ϧⲁ, 579b.
ϧⲁⲉ, 527b, 579b.
ϧⲁⲙⲛⲉ, 548a.
ϧⲁⲣⲁⲃⲁⲓ, 571b.
ϧⲁϧ, 533a, 563a, 573b.
ϧⲁϯ, 575a and b.
ϧⲉⲗⲗⲓⲃϣ, 582a.
ϧⲉⲗⲗⲟ, 532a.
ϧⲉⲗϣⲏⲣⲓ, 532a, 582b.
ϧⲉⲗϧⲉⲗ, 532b.
ϧⲉⲙ, 531a.
ϧⲉⲙⲛⲉ, 485a.
ϧⲉⲙⲥ̄, 548a, 573a, 726b, 743a.
ϧⲉⲧϧⲉⲧ, 575a.
ϧⲉⲣϧⲱⲣ, 499b.
ϧⲏ, 570a.
ϧⲏⲃⲥ̄, 530b.
ϧⲏⲓⲃⲓ, 475b, 529a.
ϧⲓⲣ, 529b, 532a.
ϧⲓⲥⲓ, 574a.
ϧⲙⲟⲙ, 471a, 531a and b, 572b.
ϧⲟⲧϧⲉⲧ, 695a.
ϧⲟⲩⲛ, 575b.
ϧⲣⲉ, 528b, 532a, 580b.
ϧⲣⲏⲓ, 579b.
ϧⲣⲟϯ, 573b.
ϧⲱⲕ, 574b, 755a.
ϧⲱⲛⲧ̄, 558b.
ϧⲱⲧⲉⲃ, 534a, 575b.

ϩ

ϩⲁ, 579b.
ϩⲁⲃⲗⲉⲗⲉ, 43b.
ϩⲁⲉ, 527b, 579b.
ϩⲁⲉⲓⲧ, 443b, 529b.
ϩⲁⲑⲱⲣ, 455b.
ϩⲁⲓ, 439a, 443a, 444a.
ϩⲁⲓⲃⲉⲥ, 529a.

ϩⲁⲗⲁⲕ, 451b.
ϩⲁⲙⲛ̄ⲧⲱⲛ, 320a.
ϩⲁⲙϣⲉ, 483a and b.
ϩⲁⲙϣⲓ, 320a.
ϩⲁⲛ, 444a.
ϩⲁⲡ, 441a, 446a, 478a.
ϩⲁⲣⲉϩ, 473a, 506b.
ϩⲁⲣⲟⲥ, 582b.
ϩⲁⲥⲓⲉ, 443b, 509b.
ϩⲁⲧⲉ, 516b.
ϩⲁⲧⲣⲉ, 27b, 100a, 520a.
ϩⲁⲧⲣⲉⲩ, 520b.
ϩⲁⲧϩⲏ, 580a.
ϩⲁϥⲗⲉⲉⲗⲉ, 480a.
ϩⲁϩ, 507a.
ϩⲁϫ, 517a.
ϩⲃⲁ, 445a.
ϩⲃ̄ⲃⲉ, 445b.
ϩⲃⲟⲣⲃⲣ̄, 446a, 476a.
ϩⲃⲥ̄, 530b.
ϩⲃⲱ, 479b.
ϩⲉ, 439a.
ϩⲉⲃⲓ, 445b.
ϩⲉⲃⲥⲱ, 511b.
ϩⲉⲓ, 440a, 444a.
ϩⲉⲓⲣ, 532a.
ϩⲉⲗⲓ, 499b.
ϩⲉⲗϩⲱⲗ, 450a.
ϩⲉⲙⲉ, 446b.
ϩⲉⲙⲓ, 447b, 484b.
ϩⲉⲙⲥⲓ, 485a.
ϩⲉⲙϩⲱⲙ, 547a.
ϩⲉⲛ, 444a.
ϩⲉⲛϥ̄, 490b.
ϩⲉⲣⲓ, 449b.
ϩⲉⲣⲙⲁⲛ, 62b.
ϩⲏ, 460a, 570a.
ϩⲏⲃⲉ, 475b, 476a.
ϩⲏⲃⲉⲥ, 530b.
ϩⲏⲃⲥ̄, 530b.
ϩⲏⲕⲉ, 514a.
ϩⲏⲙⲓ, 547b.
ϩⲏⲗ, 498b.
ϩⲏⲧ, 460b, 516b, 570a, 571b.
ϩⲏⲩ (in ⲕⲁϩⲏⲩ), 443b, 453a, 458a, 459a, 470a.
ϩⲏϫ, 467b.
ϩⲓ, 468b, 492b.
ϩⲓⲃⲱⲓ, 440b, 445a.
ϩⲓⲉⲓⲧ, 444b, 465a.
ϩⲓⲏ, 499a.
ϩⲓⲕ, 468a.
ϩⲓⲛⲓⲙ, 559b.
ϩⲓⲛ, 448b.
ϩⲓⲛⲏⲃ, 559b.
ϩⲓⲟⲓ, 445a.
ϩⲓⲟⲩⲉ, 470a.
ϩⲓⲣ, 532a.
ϩⲓⲥⲉ, 533b, 574a.
ϩⲓⲥⲓ, 533b.
ϩⲓⲧⲉ, 444b, 523b.
ϩⲓⲱⲧϥ̄, 465a.
ϩⲓⲱⲓϣ, 468b, 632b.
ϩⲓϫⲛ̄, 901a.
ϩⲕⲟ, 473b, 514a and b.
ϩⲕⲟⲉⲓⲧ, 514b.
ϩⲗ̄ⲗⲟ, 532a.
ϩⲗⲟϭ, 464a and b.
ϩⲗ̄ⲡⲉ, 533a, 572b.
ϩⲙⲉ, 480b.
ϩⲙⲉⲛⲉ, 548a.
ϩⲙ̄ⲙⲉ, 447a and b, 482a, 572b.
ϩⲙⲟⲙ, 447a, 547a, 572b, 740a.
ϩⲙⲟⲟⲥ, 485a.
ϩⲙⲟⲩ, 484a.
ϩⲙⲥ̄, 548a, 573a, 726b, 743a.
ϩⲙ̄ⲯ, 573a.
ϩⲙ̄ϩⲁⲗ, 482b, 532a, 546b.
ϩⲙ̄ϩⲙ̄, 442b, 447a.
ϩⲙ̄ϫ̄, 471a.
ϩⲛ̄, 265a.
ϩⲛ̄ⲁⲁⲩ, 486b, 489b, 487b.
ϩⲛ̄ⲕⲉ, 491b.
ϩⲛⲟ, 449a.
ϩⲟ, 460a.
ϩⲟⲉⲓⲙ, 440a, 441b, 448b.
ϩⲟⲉⲓⲣⲉ, 467a.
ϩⲟⲉⲓⲛⲉ, 444b.
ϩⲟⲉⲓⲧⲉ, 458b, 521b.
ϩⲟⲓⲧⲉ, 516b.
ϩⲟⲕⲉⲣ, 464b, 473b, 614a, 684a.
ϩⲟⲗⲓ, 499b.
ϩⲟⲗϭ̄, 973a.
ϩⲟⲙⲛ̄ⲧ, 485b.
ϩⲟⲙⲧ̄, 485b.
ϩⲟⲛⲃⲉ, 579a.
ϩⲟⲛϩⲉⲛ, 449a.
ϩⲟⲟⲩ, 438b, 442a, 444b, 450a, 459b, 469b.
ϩⲟⲟⲩⲧ, 132a, 188b, 473b.
ϩⲟⲣⲉ, 473a.
ϩⲟⲣⲛ̄, 613a.
ϩⲟⲣⲧϥ̄, 473a.
ϩⲟⲣϣ̄, 451b, 507a.
ϩⲟⲥⲙ̄, 464b, 511b, 512a.
ϩⲟⲥⲉⲙ, ⲉϥⲧⲣⲟϣⲣⲉϣ, 512a.
ϩⲟⲧⲉ, 438b, 473b, 517a, 521a.
ϩⲟⲧⲣⲉ, 520b.
ϩⲟⲧϩⲉⲧ, 575a.
ϩⲟⲧϩⲧ̄, 695a.
ϩⲟⲩⲁ, 458b.

ϩⲟⲩ, 459b, 469a.
ϩⲟⲩⲛⲧ, 473b.
ϩⲟⲩⲛ, 575b.
ϩⲟⲩⲟ, 449a, 459a, 469b, 470a.
ϩⲟⲩⲣⲱ, 473a.
ϩⲟⲩϥ, 490b.
ϩⲟⲩϩⲉ, 178a.
ϩⲟϥ, 471a, 479b.
ϩⲟϯ, 445a, 452a.
ϩⲣⲁⲓ, 498b, 579b.
ϩⲣⲉ, 450a, 532a, 580b.
ϩⲣⲏⲣⲉ, 464a, 472b, 500a.
ϩⲣⲏϣⲉ, 473a.
ϩⲣⲟⲩⲙⲡⲉ, 560a.
ϩⲣⲟⲩⲣ, 174b, 499b.
ϩⲣⲟⲟⲩϣ, 473a.
ϩⲣⲟϣ, 507a.
ϩⲣ̄ⲣⲉ, 449b.
ϩⲣⲱⲟⲩ, 560a.
ϩⲣ̄ϣⲓⲣⲉ, 811b.
ϩⲧⲁⲣ, 575a.
ϩⲧⲟ, 517a, 521a.
ϩⲧⲟⲟⲩⲉ, 522b.
ϩⲧⲟⲣ, 521b.
ϩⲧⲟⲩⲉ, 870b.
ϩⲱ, 470b.
ϩⲱⲃ, 445a.
ϩⲱⲃⲕ̄, 441a, 446a.
ϩⲱⲃ ⲛⲓⲙ, 475b.
ϩⲱⲃⲥ̄, 470b, 476b.
ϩⲱⲕ, 515b, 516a.
ϩⲱⲗ, 449b, 450a, 472b, 532a.
ϩⲱⲗⲕ̄, 532b.
ϩⲱⲗϭ̄, 451b.
ϩⲱⲙⲓ, 482a.
ϩⲱⲛ, 486b, 487b, 576a.
ϩⲱⲛⲧ̄, 558a.
ϩⲱⲟⲩ, 459b, 467b, 469a.
ϩⲱⲡ, 463a, 477b.
ϩⲱⲣ, 500a.
ϩⲱⲣⲡ̄, 451a.
ϩⲱⲥ, 508a and b.
ϩⲱⲧ, 473b.
ϩⲱⲧⲃ̄, 534a, 575a and b.
ϩⲱⲧⲡ̄, 517b.
ϩⲱⲧⲣ̄, 520b.
ϩⲱⲱ, 466a.
ϩⲱⲱⲕⲉ, 574b, 731a, 754b, 755a.
ϩⲱⲱⲙⲉ, 481b.
ϩⲱⲱϥ, 470b.
ϩⲱϣ, 445a.
ϩⲱϥⲧ̄, 471a, 572b.
ϩⲱϫ, 464b, 474a.
ϩⲱϯ, 516b, 521a.
ϩϥⲱ, 479b.

Ϫ

ϫⲁⲓ, 895b.
ϫⲁⲓⲉ, 902a.
ϫⲁⲓⲱⲟⲩ, 895a.
ϫⲁⲗ, 898b, 903b.
ϫⲁⲗϫⲉⲗ, 840a.
ϫⲁⲗϫⲟⲩ, 891b.
ϫⲁⲙⲏ, 898b.
ϫⲁⲙⲟⲩⲗ, 788b.
ϫⲁⲛⲉ, 898b.
ϫⲁⲣⲃⲁⲗ, 899b.
ϫⲁⲥⲓ ϩⲏⲧ, 861b.
ϫⲁⲥϥⲉ, 900a.
ϫⲁⲧⲙⲉ, 814b.
ϫⲁⲧϥⲉ, 914b.
ϫⲁϩ, 900a.
ϫⲁϫⲓ, 895b.
ϫⲉ, 913a.
ϫⲉⲃⲉⲗ, 741b.
ϫⲉⲃⲓ, 802a.
ϫⲉⲃⲓⲱⲟⲩ, 802a.
ϫⲉⲕϫⲓⲕ, 900a.
ϫⲉⲗⲙⲓ, 857a.
ϫⲉⲗϫⲟⲩ, 885a.
ϫⲉⲙ, 807a.
ϫⲉⲛϫⲉⲛ, 803a.
ϫⲉⲛ, 906a.
ϫⲉⲛⲏϩ, 877b.
ϫⲉⲣ, 899a.
ϫⲉⲥ, 812b.
ϫⲉϩϫϩ̄, 778b.
ϫⲏ, 804b.
ϫⲏⲙⲉ, 850b, 898a.
ϫⲏⲛ, 803a, 809a, 898b.
ϫⲏⲟⲩ, 800a.
ϫⲏⲣ, 903b.
ϫⲏⲣⲉ, 899b.
ϫⲏⲥ, 767a.
ϫⲏⲩ, 849a.
ϫⲏϫ, 902a.
ϫⲓ. 100b, 849a.
ϫⲓⲙⲓ, 807a.
ϫⲓ ⲙⲟⲉⲓⲧ, 101a.
ϫⲓⲛ, 100b, 105b, 232a.
ϫⲓⲛⲉⲓⲙⲉ, 852b.
ϫⲓⲛⲓⲟⲟⲣ, 894b.
ϫⲓ ⲛ̄ ϭⲟⲛⲥ̄, 101a.
ϫⲓⲛⲓⲣⲓ, 763b.
ϫⲓⲛⲙⲉ, 271a, 332b.
ϫⲓⲟⲟⲣ, 850a.
ϫⲓⲟⲩⲉ, 849a, 895a.
ϫⲓⲥⲉ, 713b, 861a and b.
ϫⲓϥ, 906b.
ϫⲓϫⲓ, 892a.
ϫⲛⲁ, 291b.
ϫⲛⲁⲁⲩ, 898b.
ϫⲛⲟ, 882a.
ϫⲛⲟⲟⲩ, 907a.
ϫⲟ, 848a, 896b.
ϫⲟⲉⲓⲥ, 860a and b, 862a.
ϫⲟⲉⲓⲧ, 877a, 903b, 913b.
ϫⲟⲓ, 894b, 895a, 896b.
ϫⲟⲗϩ̄, 899b.
ϫⲟⲟⲗⲉ, ϩⲙⲥ, 899b.
ϫⲟⲟⲣ, 851a.
ϫⲟⲟⲣⲉ, 851a.

ϫⲟⲟⲩϥ, 853a, 854b, 897a.
ϫⲟⲣ, 851a.
ϫⲟⲥ, 812b.
ϫⲟⲥⲉ, 861a.
ϫⲟⲩⲱⲧ, 897a.
ϫⲟⲩϫ, 791a.
ϫⲟϥ, 897b.
ϫⲟϩ, 900a.
ϫⲡ̅, 753a.
ϫⲣⲟ, 883a, 899a.
ϫⲣⲟϫ, 777a.
ϫⲫⲟⲓ, 802a, 806a.
ϫⲱ, 895b.
ϫⲱⲃ, 802a, 906a.
ϫⲱⲓ, 895b.
ϫⲱⲕ, 900a.
ϫⲱⲕ ⲉ ⲃⲟⲗ, 900a.
ϫⲱⲗ, 899a, 909b.
ϫⲱⲙ, 898a.
ϫⲱⲛⲧ̅, 907b.
ϫⲱⲛϥ̅, 898b.
ϫⲱⲣ, 899a, 903b.
ϫⲱⲣⲉ, 899b.
ϫⲱⲣⲓ, 899b.
ϫⲱⲣⲙ̅, 899b.
ϫⲱⲣϩ̅, 776b, 803b.
ϫⲱⲱⲗⲉ, 714b, 903b.
ϫⲱⲱⲙⲉ, 337b, 896b.
ϫⲱⲱⲣⲉ, 810a, 839a, 899a and b.
ϫⲱⲧϩ̅, 915b.
ϫⲱϣ, 814a.
ϫⲱϥ, 906b.
ϫⲱϩ, 858b, 900a.
ϫⲱϫ, 901a.

ϭ

ϭⲁⲁϭⲉ, 139b.
ϭⲁⲉⲓⲟ, 895a.
ϭⲁⲓⲙⲉ, 792b, 802b.
ϭⲁⲗⲁϩⲧ̅, 764b, 776b.
ϭⲁⲙⲏ, 896b.
ϭⲁⲙⲟⲩⲗ, 788b, 808a.
ϭⲁⲡⲓϫⲏ, 544a.
ϭⲁⲣⲁⲧⲉ, 803b, 940b.
ϭⲁϩ, 514b.
ϭⲁϩⲟⲓ, 514b, 812b.
ϭⲁϫⲙⲏ, 814b.
ϭⲁϭⲉ, 862b.
ϭⲃ̅ⲃⲉ, 802a.
ϭⲃ̅ⲃⲥ, 806a.
ϭⲃⲟⲓ, 802a, 806a.
ϭⲉ, 809b.
ϭⲉⲛϭⲉⲗⲟ, 717b.
ϭⲉⲧϭⲱⲧ, 799b.
ϭⲉϫϭⲟϫ, 799b.
ϭⲏⲛ, 803a, 809a.
ϭⲏⲟⲩ, 805a.
ϭⲏⲡⲉ, 793b.
ϭⲏⲡⲓ, 96a.
ϭⲏⲩ, 800a.
ϭⲓ, 849a.
ϭⲓ (in ⲟⲩⲉⲙϭⲓ), 801b.
ϭⲓ ⲁⲟⲩⲱ, 32b, 101a.
ϭⲓⲃϭⲓⲃ, 768a, 806b.
ϭⲓⲉ, 762a.
ϭⲓ-ⲛ, 765b.
ϭⲓⲛ, 105b, 807a.
ϭⲓⲛⲉ, 770a, 807a.
ϭⲓⲛⲉⲓ, 804b.
ϭⲓⲛⲏⲣⲁ, 795a.
ϭⲓⲛⲟⲩⲱⲙ, 761b, 804b.
ϭⲓⲛⲣⲱⲧ, 761b.
ϭⲓⲛⲥⲱ, 761b, 804b.
ϭⲓⲛⲱⲗϩ̅, 804b.
ϭⲓⲛⲱⲛϩ̅, 766b, 804b.
ϭⲓⲛϭⲁⲗⲟ, 804b.
ϭⲓⲛϭⲱⲣ, 796b.
ϭⲓⲟⲩⲣ, 822b.
ϭⲓⲥ, 812b, 861b.
ϭⲓⲫⲉⲓ, 230a.
ϭⲓ ϩⲧⲟⲣ, 101a.
ϭⲓϫ, 805a.
ϭⲗ̅, 775a, 810a.
ϭⲗⲁϩ, 776a.
ϭⲗⲏⲙⲓ, 899b.
ϭⲗⲓⲗ, 764a, 775a and b, 796a, 810a.
ϭⲗⲟ, 896b.
ϭⲙⲥ̅, 788b.
ϭⲙ̅ϭ ⲟⲙ, 794b.
ϭⲛⲁϩ, 883a, 898b.
ϭⲛⲟ, 803a, 809a.
ϭⲛⲟⲛ, 803a, 809b.
ϭⲛⲟⲩ, 809a.
ϭⲛⲱⲟⲩ, 809a.
ϭⲛ̅ϭⲛ, 803a.
ϭⲟ, 848a.
ϭⲟⲓⲗⲉ, 810b.
ϭⲟⲗ, 330b, 776a, 803a.
ϭⲟⲗⲃⲓ, 776a.
ϭⲟⲙ, 807b.
ϭⲟⲛⲥ̅, 774b, 778a, 795b.
ϭⲟⲟⲃ, 802a.
ϭⲟⲟⲙⲉ, 650a, 741b, 808a.
ϭⲟⲟⲩⲛⲉ, 773a and b, 801b.
ϭⲟⲡ, 786b, 793a, 807a.
ϭⲟⲣⲧⲉ, 536a, 812b.
ϭⲟⲣϭ, 796b.
ϭⲟⲥ, 812b.
ϭⲟⲥⲉ, 861a.
ϭⲟⲥⲙ̅, 814a.
ϭⲟⲩϭ, 791a.
ϭⲟϩⲥⲉ, 514b.
ϭⲟϩⲥⲓ, 812b.
ϭⲟϫⲓ, 813a, 814a, 896b.
ϭⲣⲏϭⲉ, 811b.
ϭⲣⲟ, 775b.
ϭⲣⲟⲙⲡⲉ, 803b, 809b.
ϭⲣⲟⲙⲡⲓ, 810b.
ϭⲣⲟϭ, 777a.
ϭⲣⲱϩ, 899b.
ϭⲱ, 804b, 810a.

ϭⲱⲃ, 802a, 897a.
ϭⲱⲃⲥ̄, 802b, 806a, 897a.
ϭⲱⲗ, 561b, 811b, 899a.
ϭⲱⲗⲡ̄, 796a, 810b.
ϭⲱⲙ, 770a, 788b.
ϭⲱⲙⲉ, 770a.
ϭⲱⲛⲧ̄, 774b, 796a, 809b.
ϭⲱⲛϩ̄, 774a.
ϭⲱⲟⲩ, 782b, 800a, 805a.
ϭⲱⲡ, 793b.
ϭⲱⲣⲙ̄, 790a.
ϭⲱⲣϥ̄, 533a.
ϭⲱⲣϩ̄, 796a, 811a.
ϭⲱⲣϭ̄, 811b.
ϭⲱⲥ, 813b, 859b.
ϭⲱⲥⲙ̄, 797b, 814a.
ϭⲱⲧ, 814b.
ϭⲱϣ, 792b.
ϭⲱϩ, 858b.
ϭϣⲟⲩⲣ, 729b.
ϭϩⲟⲥ, 514b, 777b, 803b, 812b.
ϭϫⲟⲥ, 812b.

ϯ

ϯⲁⲕⲱ, 865b.
ϯ ⲉⲃⲟⲗ, 866a.
ϯ ⲑⲫⲁϩⲟⲩ, 865b.
ϯⲏ, 868b.
ϯⲕ, 845a and b.
ϯⲙⲉ, 836b, 879b.
ϯⲙⲟⲟϣⲉ, 866a.
ϯⲙⲟϩ, 866a.
ϯⲛⲉ, 348b.
ϯⲛⲉⲓ, 866a.
ϯⲟⲥⲉ, 865b.
ϯⲡⲉ, 876b, 877a.
ϯⲥⲉⲓ, 866b.
ϯⲥⲉⲥⲃⲟϩ, 658a.
ϯⲧⲟⲟⲧ, 865b.
ϯϣⲱⲡⲉ, 866b.
ϯϧⲓ, 842b.
ϯϩⲉ, 842b, 887b.
ϯϩⲟ, 436b.
ϯϩⲱⲡ, 866a.
ϯϩⲙⲟⲙ, 866a.
ϯϫⲓ, 865b.
ϯϯ, 866b.

LIST OF THE NON-EGYPTIAN WORDS AND NAMES QUOTED IN THE EGYPTIAN DICTIONARY.

I. HEBREW.

א

אָב, 5a.
√אבד, 39a.
אֶבֶד (read עֶבֶד), 111a.
√אבה, 4b.
אָבוֹת, 4b.
אֲבַטִּחִים, 227b.
אָבִיר, 39a.
אַבִּיר, 39a.
אַבְרֵךְ, 18b.
אַגָּן, 94b.
אֱדוֹם, 97b.
√אהב, 74b.
אֹהֶל, 7b, 22a, 74b.
√אור, 31a.
אוֹרִים, 172b.
אֹזֶן, 103a.
אֵזֶר, 141b.
אָחוּ, 8b, 22b, 75b.
אַחְלָמָה, 551b.
אֲחַשְׁדַּרְפְּנִים, 566a.
אֲחַשְׁוֵרוֹשׁ, 534a, 566a.
אִי, 16a.
אֵיזֶה, 26b.
אַיָּל, 2b, 17b, 129a.
אֵיפָה, 41b.
אִישׁוֹן, 471b.
אֵל, 449a.
אֶל־גָּבִישׁ, 73a.
אֱלָה, 129b.
אַלּוֹן, 62b.
אלי, 72a.
אֵם, 50b.
אָמוֹן, 51b.
אָנוֹכִי, 60b, 356a.
אָסִיר, 101b.
אָסְנַת, 389b.
√אפה, 20a.
אֶפְעֶה, 43b.
אֶצְבַּע, 905b.
אֶצְבָּעוֹת, 104b.
√אצל, 104a.
אֲרִי, 21b, 129a.
אֲרִיאֵל, 21b.
אֹרֶן, 62b.
אָשְׁיָה, 88b.
אֵשֶׁל, 90a.
אַשְׁפָּה, 89a.

ב

בְּאֵר, 203b.
בְּאֵרוֹת, 202a.
בַּהַט, 204b.
בָּחַל, 215b.
בַּיִת, 201a, 202b, 208a.
בֵּית־אֵל, 208a.
בָּכָה, 207a.
בָּמוֹת, 216b.
בנת־ענת, 203b.
בַּעַל, 202a, 203b, 213a.
(הַבַּעַל, 230a.)
בעל־מהר, 213a.
בַּעַל־צְפוֹן, 213a.
בַּעֲלַת, 213a.
בְּרוֹשׁ, 237a.
בַּרְזֶל, 232a.
בְּרִיר, 204b.
√ברך, 204a.
בָּרַךְ, 204b, 207a.
בְּרָכָה, 204b.
בְּרֵכָה, 204a and b.
בָּרַל, 204b, 215b.
√בקר, 225a.
בֹּקֶר, 225a.
√בקק, 224b.
בַּת־עַיִן, 471b.
בת־ענת, 208a.

ג

גַּל, 789b.
גַּלְגַּל, 789b.
גֹּמֶא, 770a.
גָּמָל, 788b.
גֵּר, 810b.
גַּרְזֶן, 11a, 764b.

ד

דְּבִיר, 874b.
דַּף, 877a.
דָּרְיָוֶשׁ, 408a, 984b.
דֶּשֶׁן, 890b.

ה

הָבְנִי, 441a, 445b.
הָבְנִים, 142b.
הֲדֹם, 443a, 452a and b.
הוּא, 633a.
הִיא, 633a.
הַיְאוֹר, 358b.
הִין, 442a, 448b.
הִן, 486b.
הַר, 442a.
הַרְאֵל, 449b.
הָרָה, 35a.

ז

זְאֵב, 588a, 641b, 868a.
זֵיבָה, 868a.
זַיִת, 850a, 903b, 913b.
זכר־בעל, 552a.

ח

חָבֵר, 530b, 539b, 540a.
חָבַשׁ, 476b.
חור, 500a.
חוֹתָם, 568b.
חָטַב, 534a.
חִטָּה, 559b.
חֹלֶד, 580a, 809b.
חֲלַקְלַקּוֹת, 536b.
חָמִיץ, 484a.
חָמַם, 572b, 740a.
חַמָּן, 485a.
חָמָס, 536b.
חֹמֶץ, 471a.
חֵן, 528a.
חנום, 578a.
חִנְטָא, 559b.
חֲנִית, 489b.
חֹסָה, 534b.
חִפֵּז, 471a.
חָפְרַע, 466b.
חֶרֶב, 473a.
חֹרִי, 532b.
חֹרִית, 532b.
חִשֵּׁב, 510b.
חשיארש, 566a.
חשישרש, 534a.
חַשְׁמַל, 512a.
חָתַם, 568b, 569b.

ט

טֶבַח, 876b.
טַבַּעַת, 906a.
טִיט, 822b.
טֶנֶא, 882a.

י

יְאֹר, 35b, 99b, 142a and b.
יָבָל, 142b.
יבש√, 143a.
יָהּ, 15a, 142a.
יוֹדֵעַ, 143b.
יָוָן, 157b, 463b.
יוֹצֵר, 143b.
יָם, 142b, 143a.
יָמִין, 53a.
ינחם, 143a.
יָנַק, 608b, 678a.
יָקָר, 93a.
יָרֵחַ, 29b, 75b.
ירעבעל (?), 143b.
יָשַׁב, 1b, 25b, 88b.
יִשְׂרָאֵל, 143b.

כ

כָּבַשׁ, 769a, 787a.
כֶּבֶשׂ, 786b.
כּוֹרֵשׁ, 784b.
כִּכָּר, 789b, 796b.
כֶּלֶא, 789b.
כְּלִי, 789b.
כָּלַף, 803a.
כְּמוֹ, 788b.
כָּמָן, 789a.
כַּמֹּן, 808a.
כִּנּוֹר, 795a.
כִּנְעָה, 792b.

כִּנֹּרוֹת, 795a.
כְּסוּת, 791b.
כַּעְכָּא, 139b.
כַּף, 752b, 786b, 793a.
כֶּפֶר, 787a.
כֹּר, 790a.
כְּרוּבִים, 562a.
כֶּרֶם, 788b, 789a.
כַּרְפַּס, 790a.
כָּשַׁף, 814b.
כֶּתֶם, 781b, 791a.

ל

לֹא, 339b.
לֵב, 37b.
לָבִיא, 422b.
לְבֹנָה, 348b, 377b, 378a.
לָבַשׁ, 422a.
לְבוּשׁ, 422a.
לָהַב, 429a.
לוּז, 411b.
לָשׁוֹן, 389b.

מ

מִגְדֹּל, 289b, 290a, 330b.
√מדד, 276b.
מָה, 279b.
מְהִיר, 286b.
מהר־בעל, 284a.
מוֹט, 274a.
מוּצָקָה, 282b.
מוּת, 295b.
מָוֶת, 295b.
מִי, 279b.
מַיִם, 280a.
√מכר, 289b.
√מלא, 314b.
מַלְקוֹחַ, 283b.
מָנֶה, 301b.
מְנוֹרָה, 274b.
מִנְחָה, 304a.
מְעָרָה, 225b, 290a.
מָצוֹר, 338b.
מִצְרַיִם, 338b.
מַקֵּל, 276a.
מָרִין, 315a.
מַרְכָּבָה, 283b.
מַשְׁאָב, 287a.
מַשְׁחִית, 287a.
מִשְׁתֶּה, 287a.

נ

נֹא, 342a.
נָבַח, 343a.
נָבָל, 373a.
נהר, 343a and b.
נוּם, 374b.
נַחַל, 387b.
נָחַשׁ, 386a.
נִמְרֹד, 343b.
נָעַם, 412a.
√נעס, 347a.
נַעַר, 342b, 347b.
נְעָרִים, 342b, 347b.
נָפַח, 369b.
נֶתֶר, 407b, 498b.

ס

סְגוֹר, 729a.
סוּלְתָּא, 851b.
סוּס, 618b, 695b.
סוּסִים, 618b, 696a and b.
סוּסַיִם, 667a, 696b.
סוּף, 853a, 854b.
סוֹפֵר, 853a.
סָלַח, 851a.
סֹלְלָה, 857a.
סָלְעָם, 588b, 608a.
סֹלֶת, 851b, 853a.
סִפְרָא, 853a.
סַקָּא, 647a.
סִרְפַּד, 611b, 637b.

ע

√עבד, 5a.
עֶבֶד, 39a.
עֲגָלָה, 112b.
עֲגָלוֹת, 12a.
עֶדֶשׁ, 113a.
עוֹבֵד, 111a.
עוּף, 111a.
עוֹר, 129a.
עֲטַלֵּף, 885a.
עַיִן, 123b.
עָלָה, 129a.
עֲלִיָּה, 112a.
עֵמֶק, 111b.

עֵנֶב, 124a.
עָנָה, 111b.
ענת, 127b.
עֶכֶס, 113a.
עֲפָאִים, 34a.
עָרְלָה, 764b.
עָשַׁק, 112b.
עַשְׁתֹּרֶת, 136b.
עַשְׁתָּרוֹת, 136b.
עָתַק, 803a.

פ

פֶּדֶר, 260a.
פּוֹטִיפְרַע, 256b.
פּוּל, 235a.
√פלג, 237b.
פֶּרֶא, 243b.
פָּרַח, 243b.
פְּרִי, 242b.
פַּרְעֹה, 238a.
פַּרְפַּר, 243a.
פָּרַר, 243a.
פָּרַשׁ, 235a.
פֵּשֶׁת, 252a.
פְּתִיל, 254b, 256b.

צ

צָב, 905a.
צְבָאִים, 897b.
צָבַע, 897b.
צִוָּה, 191b.
צִחָא, 911b.

צִיץ, 903b.
צִמָּאוֹן, 898a.
צָעַק, 896b.
צְעָקָה, 896b.
צִפּוֹר, 897b.
צָפִיר, 897b.
צְפִירָה, 897b.
צָפְנַת פַּעְנֵחַ, 914b.

ק

קִדָּה, 781a.
קוֹפִים, 792b, 802b, 804a, 807a.
קוֹץ, 765b.
קוֹר, 775a.
קִיא, 762a and b.
קִינָה, 773a.
קִיקָיוֹן, 791a.
קְטֹרֶת, 765a.
קַלַּחַת, 764b, 776b.
קָלַל, 764a, 774b.
קִלְשׁוֹן, 803b.
קָמַח, 771b.
קֶמַח, 788b, 789a.
קָנָא, 794b.
קִנְאָה, 794b.
קַנְבּוּזִי, 795a.
קָנֶה, 773a, 795a, 803a, 808b.
קֹפִים, 807a.
קְצִיעָה, 563b.
קָצַץ, 765b.
קָרָא, 790a.

קֶרֶב, 763a, 767b.
קִרְיָת, 765b.
קֶרֶת, 764b.
קְשִׁיטָה, 778b.

ר

רָאָה, 68a.
רֹאשׁ, 433b.
ראשׁ קדשׁ, 417b.
רוּחַ הַיּוֹם, 421a.
רוּם, 424b.
רָחַץ, 431a.
√רחק, 283b.
רֶכֶשׁ, 435a.
רִמּוֹן, 62b.
√רמה, 283a.
רֵעַ, 418a.
√רשף, 433b.

שׂ, שׁ

שֵׁבֶט, 726a.
שָׁבִיב, 725a.
שִׁבֹּלֶת, 636a.
שִׁבֹּלֶת, 89a, 725b.
שְׁבַע, 665b.
שְׂדֵרָה, 640b.
שֶׂה, 587a, 649a.
שׁוֹט, 729b.
שׁוּל, 649b.
שׁוּמִים, 822b.
שׁוֹק, 659b.
שׁוּשַׁן, 608b, 623b, 700b.
שׁוֹשָׁן, 608b, 623b, 700b.

שׁוּשַׁנְתָּא, 688b.
שַׁחֲרַיִם, 586a, 634a.
שִׁטָּה, 749a.
שָׂטַם, 757a.
שֶׁלֶג, 637b.
שָׁלוֹם, 676a, 727a.
שִׂלְמָה, 727a.
שְׂמֹאל, 671a.
שמבעל, 726a.
שָׁמִיר, 89b.
שְׁמֹנָה, 547b.
שַׁמֵּשׁ, 742a.
שְׂעִיר, 611a.
שֵׂעִיר, 635b.
שַׁעַר, 723b.
שַׂעֲרָה, 635b.
שֹׁפָר, 853a.
שְׂפַת־הַיְאֹר, 662b.
שְׂפָתַיִם, 662b.
שַׂק, 647a, 701b.
שִׁריוֹן, 851b, 853a.
שָׂרַף, 611b.
שֵׁשׁ, 695b, 751a, 754a.

ת

תְּאֵנָה, 825a.
תֵּבָה, 904b.
תּוֹב, 635b.
תַּחַשׁ, 859a.
תחְרָא, 822a.
תִּינְתָא, 825a.
תָּמַם, 834a.
תַּנּוּר, 840a.
תֹּף, 827a.
תַּפּוּח, 832b, 877b, 906a.
תְּרַע, 822a, 823a.

II. GREEK.

ΑΒΛΑΝΑΘΑΝΑΛΒΑ, 5a.
ΑΒΡΑΣΑΞ, 118a.
ΑΔΗΣ, 443a.
ΑΘΛΟΦΟΡΟΣ, 259a.
ΑΛΗΘΕΙΑ, 130a.
ΑΛΛΟΣ, 809b.
ΑΛΧΑΙ, 7b.
ΑΜΕΘΥΣΤΟΣ, 551b.
ΑΜΕΝΗΒΙΣ, 52b.
ΑΜΕΝΩΦΙΣ, 52a.
ΑΜΜΩΝ, 51b.
ΑΜΟΝΡΑΣΩΝΘΗΡ, 52b.
ΑΝΗΘΟΝ, 55a.
ΑΝΙΣΟΝ, 63b.
ΑΠΕΛΛΑΙΟΣ, 5a.
ΑΠΟΛΛΩΝΙΔΗΣ, 5b.
ΑΠΡΙΗΣ, 466b.
ΑΡΓΥΡΟΣ, 131b
ΑΡΕΝΔΩΤΗΣ, 502b.
ΑΡΟΝΤΩΤΗΣ, 502b.
ΑΡΟΥ, 130a and b.
ΑΡΟΥΗΡΙΣ, 501a.
ΑΡΟΥΡΑ, 585b.
ΑΡΠΟΚΡΑΤΗΣ, 501b.
ΑΡΣΙΗΣΙΣ, 504b.
ΑΡΤΑΒΗ, 73b.
ΑΡΤΑΒΗΣ, 28b.
ΑΡΧΙΚΥΝΗΓΟΣ, 562a.
ΑΡΩΗΡΙΣ, 501a.
ΑΣΕΝΕΘ, 389b.
ΑΣΚΛΗΠΙΕΙΟΝ, 30b.
ΑΣΜΑΧ, 602b, 671a and b.
ΑΣΤΗΡ, 10a.
ΑΤΤΕΛΑΒΟΣ, 885a.
ΑΥΤΟΓΕΝΗΣ, 543b.
ΑΦΟΣΟ, 42b.
ΑΧΑΙΜΕΝΗΣ, 25a.
ΑΧΑΝΗ, 94b.
ΑΧΕΣ, 22b.
ΑΨΕΥΣΤΩΣ, 119b.

ΒΑΙΗΘ, 211b.
ΒΑΚΙΣ, 221b.
ΒΑΡΙΣ, 202b.
ΒΑΤΑΝΗ, 208b.
ΒΕΒΩΝ, 200b.
ΒΕΒΩΝΑ, 200b.
ΒΗ, 200a.
ΒΗΣ, 205b.
ΒΙΚΩΤ, 200a.
ΒΙΟΥ, 200a.
ΒΙΤΗΣ, 203a, 211b.
ΒΛΕΜΜΥΕΣ, 204a.
ΒΟΩΝ, 502b.
ΓΥΝΑΙΚΕΙΟΝ, 79a.

ΔΑΡΕΙΟΣ, 408a, 820a.
ΔΙΚΑΙΟΣΥΝΗ, 385b.

ΕΙΔΩΛΟΝ, 782b.
ΕΞΑΤΡΑΠΗΣ, 566a.
ΕΟΡΤΗ, 449b.
ΕΠΕΙΔΗ, 414b.
ΕΠΙ ΠΛΕΟΝ, 571a.
ΕΡΩ, 130a.
ΕΣΕΓΧΗΒΙΣ, 81a.
ΕΥΛΟΓΙΣΤΗΣ, 790a.
ΕΦΗΜΕΡΙΔΕΣ, 450a.

ΘΑΛΕΙΑ, 841b.
ΘΕΣΟΛΚ, 860a.

ΙΑΟΝΕΣ, 463b.
ΙΜΟΥΘΗΣ, 30b.
ΙΣΕΙΟΝ, 117b.
ΙΣΡΩ, 585a.

ΚΑΘ ΟΛΟΝ, 765a.
ΚΑΙΣΑΡΟΣ, 801b.
ΚΑΚΕΙΣ, 139b.
ΚΑΜΒΥΣΗΣ, 763b, 793a.

ΚΑΜΗΦΙΣ, 785a.
ΚΑΝΗΦΟΡΟΣ, 259a.
ΚΑΝΘΑΡΟΣ, 295a.
ΚΑΡΑΒ, 804b.
ΚΑΡΑΒΟΣ, 804b.
ΚΑΣΑΝΤΡΑ, 804b.
ΚΑΣΣΙΑ, 563b.
ΚΑΤΑ ΛΟΓΟΝ, 277a.
ΚΑΤΚΟΥΑΤ, 780b.
ΚΕΙΠΟΣ, 802b.
ΚΕΝΤΕΧΘΑΙ, 556b.
ΚΗΒ, 805b.
ΚΗΒΟΣ. 802b.
ΚΗΠΟΣ, 802b.
ΚΙΚΗΛΛΙΑ, ΤΑ, 801a.
ΚΙΚΙ, 791a.
ΚΙΚΙΝΟΝ, 791a.
ΚΙΝΝΥΡΑ, 795a.
ΚΙΤΤΩ, 781a.
ΚΝΗΦ, 795a.
ΚΝΟΥΦΙΣ, 795a.
ΚΟΓΧΗ, 774b, 789a.
ΚΟΓΧΟΣ, 774b.
ΚΟΛΟΚΥΝΘΟΣ, 803a.
ΚΟΜΜΙ, 771a.
ΚΟΝΙΜΕ, 794b, 795b.
ΚΟΡΗ, 471b.
ΚΟΥΚΙΟΦΟΡΟΝ, 767a.
ΚΡΟΚΟΣ, 810b.
ΚΥΛΛΑΣΤΙΣ, 790a, 793a, 796a and b.
ΚΥΜΙΝΟΝ, 808a.
ΚΥΡΙΟΣ ΔΙΑΔΗΜΑΤΩΝ, 357a.
ΚΥΦΙ, 786b.

ΛΕΣΩΝΙΣ, 313a.
ΛΙΤΡΟΝ, 407b.
ΛΟΥΤΗΡΙΟΝ, 421a.

ΜΑΝΕΡΩΣ, 452a.
ΜΕΙΣΙ, 323b.
ΜΕΝΕΚΡΑΤΕΙΑ, 280b.
ΜΙΕΒΙΣ, 315a.
ΜΝΗΥΙΣ, 374a.
ΜΟΥΘ, 295a.
ΜΟΥΘΙΣ, 295a.

ΝΕΒΧΟΥΝΙΣ, 343a.
ΝΗΙΘ, 379b. 399b.
ΝΗΡΙΟΝ, 347a.
ΝΙΤΡΟΝ, 407b, 408b.

ΞΑΝΘΑ, 797b.
ΞΙΦΟΣ, 597b, 666a.

ΟΙΚΟΥΜΕΝΗ, 538a.
ΟΛΥΡΑ, 215b.
ΟΝΟΥΡΙΣ, 57a.
ΟΝΝΩΦΡΙΣ, 165b.
ΟΣΤΑΝΗΣ, 91a.
ΟΥΑΦΡΗ, 466b.
ΟΥΑΦΡΙΣ, 466b.
ΟΥΕΣΤΕ, 185b.
ΟΥΕΣΤΕ ΒΙΚΩΤΙ, 185b.
ΟΥΝ, 336b.

ΠΑΜΥΛΗΣ, 198b.
ΠΑΡΑΔΕΙΣΩΝ, 891b.
ΠΑΣΤΟΦΟΡΟΣ, 107b.
ΠΕΡΙΠΛΟΥΣ, 828a.
ΠΕΤΕΦΡΗ, 256b.
ΠΙΝΑΞ, 234b.
ΠΟΛΥΟΦΘΑΛΜΟΣ, 83a.
ΠΡΟΑΥΛΙΟΝ, 443b.
ΠΡΟΝΗΣΙΟΝ, 356a.
ΠΡΟΣΗΚΟΝ, ΤΟ, 804b.
ΠΤΙΜΥΡΙΣ, 315a.
ΠΥΡΑΜΙΣ, 243b.

ΡΕΜΕΝΑΙΡΕ, 425b.
ΡΕΜΕΝΧΑΡΕ, 425b.
ΡΩΜΑΙΟΣ, 442b, 445a.

ΣΑΙΝ, 605b, 676a.
ΣΑΚΚΟΣ, 701b.
ΣΑΞ, 591b.
ΣΑΡΙ, 637b, 645b.
ΣΑΡΙΣΑ, 635b.
ΣΑΤΡΑΠΗΣ, 566a.
ΣΑΩΣΙΣ, 834b.
ΣΕΙΡΑ, 647b.
ΣΕΣΜΕ, 557b, 585a, 753b.
ΣΕΣΟΩΣΙΣ, 696a.
ΣΙΑΞ, 627a.
ΣΙΚΕΤ, 585a.
ΣΙΣΕΣΜΕ, 585a.
ΣΙΣΡΩ, 585a.
ΣΙΤ, 755a.
ΣΜΑΤ, 603a.
ΣΜΥΡΙΣ 89b.
ΣΟΥΣΟΝ, 608b, 623b, 700b.
ΣΟΥΧΙΣ, 657b.
ΣΟΥΧΟΣ, 660a.
ΣΟΥΧΩΣ, 575a, 615a, 659a.
ΣΠΤΧΝΕ, 636b, 663a.
ΣΡΩ, 610a, 635a.
ΣΤΑΤΗΡ, 712a.
ΣΤΙΜΜΙΣ, 715b.
ΣΤΡΑΤΗΓΟΣ, 171a.
ΣΤΡΑΤΙΩΤΗΣ, 638a.
ΣΥΓΓΕΝΗΣ, 637a.
ΣΥΝΝΑΟΣ, 588b.
ΣΥΝΤΑΞΙΣ, 609b.
ΣΦΗΞ, 539a.
ΣΧΟΙΝΙΟΝ, 567a, 573a.
ΣΩΘΙΣ, 664a.
ΣΩΣΙΣ, 731b.
ΣΩΤΗΡ, 653b.

ΤΑΡΙΧΕΥΤΗΣ, 580b.
ΤΠΗΒΙΟΥ, 830b.
ΤΠΗΧΟΝΤΑ, 831a.
ΤΠΗΧΥ, 830b.
ΤΠΙΒΙΟΥ, 830b.
ΤΥΦΩΝ, 828a, 875b.
ΤΩΜ, 851a.

ΦΙΛΑΝΘΡΩΠΟΣ, 310a.
ΦΟΙΝΙΚΕΣ, 260b.
ΦΟΙΝΙΞ, 213b.

ΧΑΛΚΙΑ, 533a.
ΧΑΛΚΙΟΝ, 533a.
ΧΑΜΨΑΙ, 325b, 485b.
ΧΑΡΧΝΟΥΜΙΣ, 581b.
ΧΙΤΩΝ, 799b.
ΧΝΕΦ, 795a.
ΧΝΟΥΒΙΣ, 578a.
ΧΝΟΥΜΙΣ, 578a, 795a and b.
ΧΝΟΥΦΙΣ, 578a.
ΧΟΑΧΥΤΗΣ, 148a.
ΧΟΝΤΑΡ, 503b.
ΧΟΝΤΑΡΕ, 556b.
ΧΟΝΤΑΧΡΕ, 557a.
ΧΟΥΣ, 769a.
ΧΥ, 23a.
ΧΩΟΥ, 528a.

ΨΧΕΝΤ, 617a, 692b, 693b.

ΩΡΟΛΟΓΙΟΝ, 315b.

III. SUMERIAN, ASSYRIAN, PERSIAN, ETC.

, 17b.

, 95a.

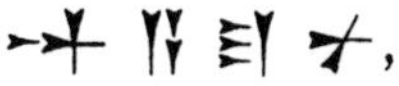, 51b.

, 53a.

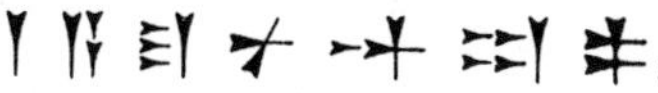, 52a.

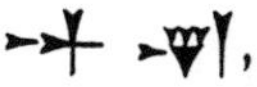, 136b.

, 792b.

, 822b.

, 867a.

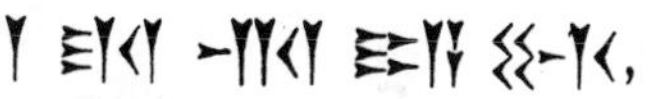, 64a, 408a, 820a.

, 137a.

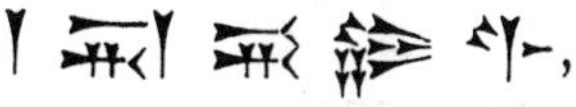, 185b.

, 868a.

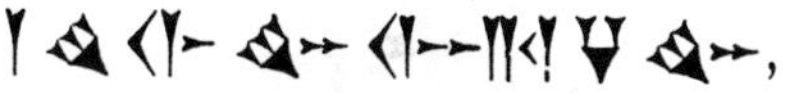, 534a.

, 463b.

, 463b.

, 463b.

, 143a.

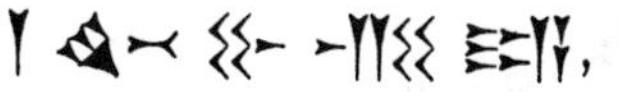, 763b, 793a.

, "hands" (only in plural, Ashurnaṣirpal I, l. 117), 752b.

, 787a.

, 336a.

, 286b.

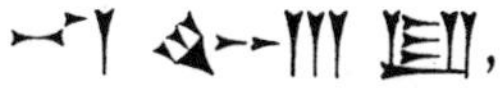, 387b.

, 325b.

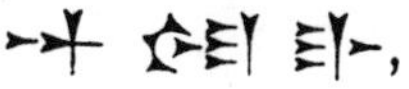, 60a.

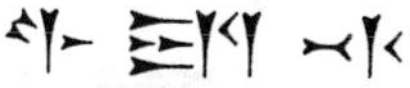 (Berlin tablet No. 102, ed. Winckler, p. 102b), 257a.

, pl. 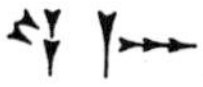, 897b.

, 897b.

, 765a.

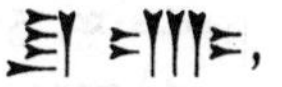, 587a.

, 822b.

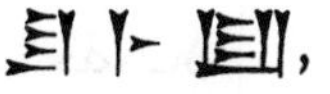, 671a.

, 89a.

𒑖𒑖, 647a.

𒑖𒑖𒑖𒑖 } 859a.

𒑖𒑖𒑖, 840a.

𒑖𒑖𒑖𒑖𒑖, 64a,
408a, 820a, 884b.

𒑖𒑖𒑖𒑖𒑖𒑖𒑖, 763b,
793a.

𒑖𒑖𒑖𒑖𒑖𒑖𒑖, 534a,
566a.

𒑖𒑖𒑖𒑖𒑖𒑖𒑖, 566a.

𒑖𒑖𒑖𒑖𒑖𒑖, 185b.

𒑖𒑖𒑖, 463b.

𒑖𒑖𒑖, 336a.

IV. SYRIAC.

, 94b.
, 129a.
, 88b.

, 457a.

, 788b.

, 588a, 868a.

, 903b.

, 740a.

, 876b.

, 139b.
, 789a.

, 139b.
, 795a, 902a.
, 786b.
, 787a.

, 283a.

, 374b.
, 407b.

, 597b, 642b, 666a.
, 671a.
, 853a.
, read , 647a.

, 34a.

, 255b.

, 897b.
, 905b.
, 897b.

, 771b.

, 62b.

, 716a.
, 608b, 623b.

, 825a.
, 635b.
, 822b.
, 637b.
, 834a.
, 846a.
, 822a, 823a.

V. ARABIC.

ابن آوى, 4a.
اردبّ, 73b.
إسبة, 88b.
اصبع, 905b.
افعى, 43b.
انكح, 345b.
إيل, إيّال, 2b, 129a.

بربة, 423a.
برق, 204b.
بطّيخ, 227b.
بلع, 203b.
بنت العين, 471b.
بيت, 457a.

تاب, 635b.
تفاح, 877b.
تلج, 637b.
تم, 834a.
تنّور, 840a.
تين, 825a.

ثوم, 822b.

جبس (الجبس), 73a.
جمل, 788b.

حبّس, 476b.
حجر, 464b.
حربة, 473a.
حريم, 79a.
حسب, 510b.
حطب, 534a.
حمض, 484a.
حمّ, 572b, 740a.
حنطة, 559b.

دقّة, 877a.

ذاب, 868a.
ذهبيّة, 11a, 762b.
ذيب, 588a.

رشاد, 899b.
رمّان, 62b.

زعفران, 141b.
زيت, 913b.
زيتون, 903b.
زير, 645b.

ساق, 659b.
سفة, 662a.
سلب, 851b.
سلمات, 727a.
سلوقى, 5a.
سمسم, 740a.
سمّ, 547a.
سنط, 749a.
سوس, 608b, 623b.
سوق, 549b.
سيف, 597b, 642b, 666a.

شاة, 587a, 649a.
شتم, 757a.
شرق, 723b.
شمال, 671a.

صبغ, 897b.
صعق, 896b.

طبخ, 876b.

ظمى, 898a.

عنقريب, 43b.

غنّى, 111b.

فجّا, 257b.
فض, 255b.

فَلّاح, 75a.
فول, 69a, 235a.
قاء, 762b.
قتة, 765b.
قُلَّة, 775b.
قَمْح, 771b, 789a.
قوس, 795b.
كَاك, 139b.
كبير, 768b, 806b.
كَعْك, 139b.
كَفْر, 787a.
كَفّ, 786a.
كَمّان, 808a.
كَمَن, 789a.
كنار, 795a.
لاب, 38a.
ناريون, 347a.
نام, 374b.
نجّار, 413a.
نَعِم, 412a.
نبخ, 343a.
نَفَح, 369b.
نَبْق, 368a.
وَرْد, 147a.

VI. ETHIOPIC AND AMHARIC.

ሀየል:, 129a.
መጽየ: ብሔር:, 522b.
ሠቅ:, 647a.
ሮሚና:, 62b.
ሰብእ:, 725b.
ሰው:, 583a, 729b.
ሴት:, 583a.
ሰይፍ:, 597b, 666a.
ሽፍታ:, 726a.
ቀምሕ:, 771b, 789a.
ቀይእ:, 762b.
በቀልተ:, 276a.
ብነት: ዐይኑ:, 471b.
ናመ:, 374b.
ነግሀ: ብሔር:, 522b.
ነፍኁ:, 369b.
እጽበዕት:, 905b.
እፍዖት:, 43b.
ዝእብ:, 868a.
ዘይት:, 903b.
ድንክ:, 867b.
ገመል:, 788b.
ጎሜዕ:, 770a.
ሒት:, 824b, 870b.
ጸምእ:, 898a.
ፀብእ:, 897b.